Musical Settings
of
Late Victorian and
Modern British Literature:
A Catalogue

Garland Reference Library of the Humanities (Vol. 31)

Musical Settings
of
Late Victorian and
Modern British Literature:
A Catalogue

Bryan N.S. Gooch
and
David S. Thatcher

Editorial Assistant:
Odean Long

Garland Publishing, Inc., New York & London

1976

Copyright © 1976

by Garland Publishing, Inc.

All Rights Reserved

Library of Congress Cataloging in Publication Data

Gooch, Bryan N   S
   Musical settings of late Victorian and modern
British literature.

   (Garland reference library of the humanities ;
v. 31)
·   1. Vocal music, English--Bibliography.
I. Thatcher, David S., joint author. II. Long,
Odean.   III. Title.
ML120.G7G66   016.784'094 1   75-24085
ISBN 0-8240-9981-8

Contents

This catalogue of musical settings is designed to meet the
diverse needs of literary scholars, musicologists, music
bibliographers, librarians, performers, planners of radio and
television features, and, indeed, all those with an interest in
the interrelationship of literature and music over the last
hundred years. As a work of reference it attempts to be thorough
(up to the cut-off date of July 1975), accurate, and detailed in
its documentation; it supplements existing indices, whether they
cover the field of song-literature generally (e.g., Sergius
Kagen's Music for the Voice: A Descriptive List of Concert and
Teaching Materials and J. Merrill Knapp's Selected List of Music
for Men's Voices) or deal with specific authors or composers
(e.g., Carl J. Weber's Hardy Music at Colby: A Check-List and
Graham Parlett's Arnold Bax: A Catalogue of His Music). It
provides information on such matters as vocal specifications and
instrumental accompaniment, and also information not always
readily available from alternative sources (e.g., publication
details for texts and settings).

We have catalogued published and unpublished settings of
texts by leading British authors who were born after 1840 and
lived to 1900 or later (for the purposes of this catalogue the
term "British author" refers to someone 1. born and mainly
resident in the British Isles or 2. naturalised British, e.g.,
Conrad, Eliot, James and Koestler or 3. born outside the U.K.
but sufficiently identified with the English literary tradition
to warrant inclusion, e.g., Roy Campbell and Katherine Mansfield). These guidelines, though they have afforded a welcome
measure of control over the material we have assembled, are
somewhat arbitrary, and we have transgressed them when we felt,
as in the cases of two writers who died before 1900, Gerard
Manley Hopkins (1844-1899) and Aubrey Beardsley (1872-1898),
that more was to be lost than gained by strict adherence to a
rule of practicality and convenience. Deciding who could be
accounted a "leading" British author presented a more difficult
test of conscience, and we can only hope that our choices, based
on actual or potential reputation of the authors concerned, will
not appear sadly and culpably wayward. We have, if anything,
erred on the side of leniency, especially in regard to contemporary authors: we have tended to favour younger writers who
are not fully established, casting a cold, unfriendly eye on
deceased authors whose names, though perhaps familiar in their
day, seem to be destined for oblivion. We have not included settings of texts by Welsh and Irish poets writing in their own
language (for such information see Robert Smith's A Complete
Catalogue of Welsh Music (No. 5) and Edgar M. Deale's A
Catalogue of Contemporary Irish Composers) or settings expres-

i

sly written for a composer by admirers with misplaced literary
ambitions. Nor have we listed settings of libretti in the
technical sense. However, settings of translations by the
authors we have chosen <u>are</u> included provided that these form
an acknowledged part of the author's literary achievement. A
number of prominent figures are conspicuously absent from this
catalogue simply because, as far as can be ascertained, no settings have been made of their work.

The format is largely self-evident, but perhaps the following
diagram, sample, and explanatory notes will be helpful.

Entry in diagram form:

    Author's names   Author's dates

        Title of literary work First line (substituted by an
           abbreviation of the literary form if other than a poem)
           Volume (underlined) and date of first publication (if
           preceded by "In", the first <u>verifiable</u> publication)

        Entry number Composer's name (name of collaborator).
                   Variant title of the setting (pub-
                   lication details of the single setting),
                   title of collection in which it appears
                   (underlined), place of publication, name
                   of publisher, date of publication. Form
                   of the musical composition: vocal
                   specifications, accompaniment required.
                   Additional information regarding the
                   setting.

Sample (hypothetical) entry:

JONES, Arthur Cecil   1898-1952

    Sleeper, The   "Once upon a midnight wind"   <u>Outlook</u>
    (Jan. 1946), rev. same year

      623 Barton, Charles G. "On a Midnight Wind", L: BH,
           1947. Song: 2 pt. chorus of male v., a cap.
           Setting of stanzas 1, 6 and 7.

      624* Jeffries, Anthony. "Once upon...", <u>Silence</u>, NY:
           GS, 1970. Cyc.: t solo, vln.

Two Solitudes (DR) In coll. with C.D. Chilton Outlook (Mar.-Apr. 1923), publ. sep. 1924

   625 Chambers, L.D. in coll. with Albert Fenton. "Six
        Who Came", MS 1956, avail. ACA. Opera: 2 ms,
        t, 3 bar, b soli, chorus of boys' v., ch.
        orch. Libr. by Michael P. Simpson.

   626 Fenton, Albert in coll. with L.D. Chambers. See
        entry immediately preceding.

   627 Lamoureux, Henri. P: OL, 1936. Incidental music
        for radio: str. orch. Fr. title: "Les Jeux
        Esprits", transl. by Jean-Claude Garnier.

"When they meet" Repose and Other Verses (1937)

   628 Lougheed, M. Colin. Tor.: FH, 1942, Six Songs,
        Tor.: FH, 1950. Song: high or med. v., pf.
        Also arr. for low v., pf.; arr. publ. Tor.:
        FH, 1953.

Wind of Sleep See: Sleeper, The

Miscellanea

   629 Barton, Charles G. "Tribute to A.C.J.", MS, perf.
        Birmingham, Dec. 1952. Orch. only.

Explanatory notes:

Periods are used to demark the various sections of each entry,
while square brackets indicate the interpolation of information
not congruent with the diagram form outlined above. With regard
to spelling and terminology, we have usually adopted the
practice of the authors and composers themselves. If the first
word of the title of a work happens to be a definite or in-
definite article, the second word is employed for alphabetical
listing. Revised titles are cross-indexed. First lines
(occasionally in edited form) are provided for poems, but not
for novels, short stories, plays, radio scripts, etc.; such
works are denoted by means of an abbreviation. Revision dates

denote text or title changes and apply to the date the work was
re-issued in revised form; in cases of frequent republication
(e.g., Hardy's Tess_of_the_d'Urbervilles), a revision date is
replaced by the date of the definitive edition ("def. edn.").
An asterisk appearing after the title of a work, or after an
entry number, refers the reader to footnote information which
will be found under the appropriate entry number at the end of
the catalogue. In some cases information is provided for compositions known to have been inspired by an author's works in
general rather than by any one of his writings in particular;
such information, together with details of settings which defied
complete verification, has been collected in the "Miscellanea"
at the end of the relevant author section. A key to all abbreviations is appended to this preface.
        Whenever a text has been set by more than one composer, the
various settings are listed alphabetically by composer's name.
If the composer has used the author's title, no indication of
composition title follows the composer's name, but if he has
changed it the new title is given in quotation marks. An abbreviated form of the author's first line indicates that the
composer has employed the first line as his title. In the case
of collections to which the composer has given the same title
(e.g., Three Songs) an opus number or a date is used to dis-
tinguish one collection from its namesake. Individual songs in a
musical (e.g., Cyril Ornadel's Ann_Veronica) or individual arias
in an opera (e.g., Werner Egk's Irische_Legende) are not listed
separately, as all relevant information is given under the main
title of the work. Note has sometimes been taken of copyright
renewal (a second date within brackets) and copyright re-
assignment. If a setting has been recorded, but not published,
details of the recording are substituted. Dates are ascribed to
unpublished manuscripts wherever possible, together with an indication, in abbreviated form, of where the MSS can be obtained
(e.g., MS 1949, avail. CMC). In a number of instances MS
material, as well as published (but possibly out-of-print)
scores, are available on request from the composer himself. Composers' addresses are readily available from their respective
national music centres or from such reference works as Arthur
Jacobs' British_Music_Yearbook.
        We have endeavoured to provide in as many entries as possible
some indication of the form of the setting (e.g., song cycle or
opera) and the resources needed to perform it, whether vocal
(e.g., high v. or satb) or instrumental (e.g., orch. or ch. orch.
with mrmb.). Whenever such general indications might tend to mis-
lead we have set out the accompaniment in greater detail. Additional information (e.g., alternative arrangements and indications as to which part of the text has been set) is sometimes given. Names of arrangers are not cross-referenced in

iv

section two of the catalogue except in cases where earlier music
(e.g., a traditional air) has been employed. This second section
lists alphabetically the names of all composers who appear in
the main author section: against each composer's name are listed
the names of the authors whose texts he has set to music, the
item numbers referring to the individual settings as previously
listed.

Complete indices, alphabetically arranged (and cross-
referenced to the authors in this catalogue), of the titles and
first lines of the literary works which have been listed are
available upon request from the Interlibrary Loan Services,
McPherson Library, University of Victoria, Victoria, B.C.

If this catalogue does answer a real need much of the credit
must go to those who gave us advice, encouragement, and support.
We gladly extend our thanks to Dr. Roy Daniells, University
Professor of English Language and Literature, University of
British Columbia, and to Helmut Kallmann, Chief of the Music
Division, National Library of Canada.

We are most grateful to the University of Victoria and to the
Canada Council for financial assistance in the form of research
grants, and to the staffs of the McPherson Library and Computing
Services of the University of Victoria for their kind co-
operation and assistance. To those institutions, literary and
musical societies, publishing firms, and individuals who have
given so much of their time and energy to respond to our
requests for information we would also like to tender our appreciation. They are so numerous that we regret we cannot
mention them all by name. We would, however, like to place on
record a special debt of gratitude to The Poetry Collection,
Lockwood Memorial Library, State University of New York at
Buffalo; to The Housman Society; to the Svaz českých Skladatelů
a Koncertních Umělců; to Roberton Publications; to Chappell &
Co. Ltd.; to Mr. Stewart R. Craggs; and to Professor David M.
Green.

Finally, we must single out our Research Assistant, Miss
Odean Long, for a special word of praise. She has given to the
compilation of this catalogue many hours of cheerful, unflagging
effort. We could not have asked for a more reliable or more
dedicated collaborator.

Victoria, B.C.   Bryan N.S. Gooch
                                                  David S. Thatcher

v

ABBREVIATIONS: MUSICAL AND OTHER TERMS

It should be noted that choral specifications frequently involve a combination of certain abbreviations, e.g., satb, ttbb, etc.

a	alto	dr(s).	drum(s)
a cap.	a cappella	DS	documentary script
acc.	accordion	e.g.	for example
adapt.	adapted, adaptation	ea.	each
ad lib.	ad libitum	ed.	editor, edited by
anon.	anonymous	edn(s).	edition(s)
Apr.	April	eds.	editors
arr.	arranger, arranged, arrangement	elect.	electric
		eng. hn.	english horn
Aug.	August	Engl.	English
autohp.	autoharp	et al.	et alii
avail.	available	euph.	euphonium
b	bass	Feb.	February
b. dr.	bass drum	fl.	flute
b-bar	bass-baritone	fl.-org.	flute-organ
bells	orchestral or tubular bells	flhn.	flugelhorn
		Fr.	French
br.	brass	gl.	glockenspiel
bsn(s).	bassoon(s)	gtr.	guitar
c-t	counter-tenor	harm.	harmonium
ca.	circa	harmonis.	harmonisation
cbsn.	contra bassoon	i.e.	id est
cel.	celesta	incl.	including, includes included
ch.	chamber		
chapt.	chapter	instr.	instruments
cl.	clarinet	Ital.	Italian
Co.	Company	Jan.	January
coll.	collaboration	libr.	libretto
cond.	conductor	Mar.	March
cs	coloratura soprano	mc	mezzo contralto
cta.	cantata	med.	medium
cyc.	cycle	mrmb.	marimba
cym.	cymbals	ms	mezzo soprano
Czech.	Czechoslovakian	MS(S)	manuscript(s)
db.	double bass	n.d.	no date
dbl.	double	n.p.	no publisher cited
Dec.	December	narr.	narrator
def.	definitive	Nov.	November
Dept.	Department	NV	novel
distr.	distributed	ob.	oboe
doubl.	doubling	obbl.	obbligato
DR	drama	Oct.	October

ABBREVIATIONS: MUSICAL AND OTHER TERMS

opt.	optional	sn. dr.	snare drum
orch.	orchestra	SP	screenplay
orchn.	orchestration	sp(s).	speaker(s)
org.	organ	SS	short story
p.	page	ste.	suite
perc.	percussion	stereoph.	stereophonic
perf.	performed, perfor-	stgs.	strings
	mance	str.	string
pf.	pianoforte	symph.	symphony, symphonic
pic.	piccolo	t	tenor
posth.	posthumous	t-bar	tenor-baritone
PR	prose	timp.	timpani
prep.	preparation	tpt(s).	trumpet(s)
priv.	private	trad.	traditional
prod.	produced, produc-	transl.	translated, trans-
	tion		lation
pseud.	pseudonym	trbn(s).	trombones
pt(s).	part(s)	trg.	triangle
publ.	published, pub-	TV	television
	lication	unacc.	unaccompanied
qnt.	quintet	unavail.	unavailable
qrt.	quartet	unf.	unfinished
rearr.	rearranged, rear-	unpubl.	unpublished
	rangement	unspecif.	unspecified
rec.	recorder	v.	voice
reprod.	reproduction	vcl(s)	violoncello(s)
RP	radio play	vers.	version
RS	radio script	vibra.	vibraphone
s	soprano	vln(s).	violin(s)
sax.	saxophone	vol(s).	volume(s)
sep.	separate,	ww.	woodwind
	separately	xyl.	xylophone
Sept.	September	z.	zither

ABBREVIATIONS: PLACES OF PUBLICATION

Amst.	Amsterdam	Mz.	Mainz
B	Boston	Nebr.	Nebraska
Chi.	Chicago	NY	New York
Cin.	Cincinnati	N.Z.	New Zealand
Cl.	Cleveland	Oxf.	Oxford
Croy.	Croydon	P	Paris
DWG	Delaware Water Gap	Ph.	Philadelphia
Grt. Y.	Great Yarmouth	R	Rome
L	London	S. Croy.	South Croydon
Lz.	Leipzig	Tor.	Toronto
Mass.	Massachusetts	Wi.	Wiesbaden
Mi.	Milan	Wisc.	Wisconsin
Minn.	Minneapolis		

ABBREVIATIONS: NAMES AND ADDRESSES OF PUBLISHERS

Every effort has been made to discover and list below the
current addresses of publishers in this Catalogue. Un-
fortunately, in certain instances addresses could neither
be obtained nor verified. The Catalogue entries provide the
name of the city in which a firm was located when it
published a specific work.

A	Augener. See: G.
ABC	American Book Co., Division of Litton Educational Publications Inc., 450 W. 33 St., New York, New York, 10001.
Acott	Acott, London. Present address unknown.
AD	Abingdon Press, 201 8th Ave. S., Nashville, Tennessee, 37303.
Affiliated Musicians	Affiliated Musicians, Los Angeles, California. Present address unknown.
Affl.	Affiliated Music Publishers Ltd., 138-140 Charing Cross Rd., London, WC2H OLD.
AH&C	Ascherberg, Hopwood, and Crew. See: C.
Alexander & Cable	Alexander & Cable. Present address unknown.
Alhambra	Alhambra Theatre, London. Present address un-known.
Allan	Allan & Co. Pty., Ltd., 276-278 Collins St., Melbourne, Australia.
AMP	Associated Music Publishers, 866 3rd Ave., New York, New York, 10022.
Arcadia	Arcadia Music Publishing Co. Ltd., 10 Sher-lock Mews, Baker St., London, W1.
Arrow	Arrow Music Press. See: AMP or BH (New York).
Ars Musica	Ars Musica, Paris. Present address unknown.
ASH	Edwin Ashdown Ltd., 275-281 Cricklewood Broadway, London, NW2 6QR.
Astoria	Astoria Verlag GmbH., Brandenburische Str. 22, 1000 Berlin 31, Germany.
Atlas	Atlas [Music Corp.], [488 Madison Ave., New York, New York].
A&U	Allen & Unwin Ltd., 40 Museum St., London, WC1A 1LU.
Augs	Augsburg Publishing House, 426 S. 5th St., Minneapolis, Minnesota, 55415.
Avison	Charles Avison Ltd. See: JWC.
Aviva	Aviva Music, c/o Shapiro, Bernstein & Co. Ltd., 246/248 Great Portland St., London, W1N 5HF.
AVV	Ars Viva Verlag GmbH., Weihergarten 5, 6500 Mainz, Germany.

ABBREVIATIONS: PUBLISHERS

Banks	Banks Music Publications, 139 Holgate Rd., York, Yorkshire, YO2 4DF.
Bärenreiter	Bärenreiter Ltd., Kassel. In Britain: 32-34 Titchfield St., London, W1.
B&B	Bote & Bock, Berlin 12, Hardenbergstrasse 9a, Germany.
BBC	British Broadcasting Corporation, Broadcasting House, London, W1A 1AA.
B&C	British & Continental Music Agencies Ltd., 64 Dean St., London, W1V 6AU.
Beaumont	Beaumont Press, 68 Bedford Court Mansions, Bedford Ave., London, WC1.
Beekman	Beekman. See: TP.
Belaieff	M.P. Belaieff (Belaieff Editions). See: H.
Benn	Ernest Benn Ltd., 154 Fleet St., London, EC4A 2DQ.
Berandol	Berandol Music Ltd., 11 St. Joseph St., Toronto, Ontario, M4Y 1J8.
Berben	Edizioni Berben, Via Redipuglia 65, 60100 Ancona, Italy.
B&F	Bayley & Ferguson Ltd., Sovereign House, 65 Berkeley St., Glasgow, C3, Scotland.
BH	Boosey & Hawkes (Boosey & Co.), 295 Regent St., London, W1A 1BR. In U.S.A.: 30 W. 57th St., New York, New York, 10019. In Canada: 279 Yorkland Blvd., Willowdale, Ontario, M2J 1S7.
B&H	Breitkopf & Härtel, Wiesbaden, Postfach 74, Walkmuhlstrasse 52, Germany. In Britain: Breitkopf & Härtel (London) Ltd., 8 Horse and Dolphin Yard, London, W1V 7LG.
Birchard	C.C. Birchard & Co. See: Summy-B.
Blake	Blake Music Publishers, New York. Present address unknown.
B-M	Belwin-Mills Publishing Corp., Melville, New York, 11746. In Britain: 230 Purley Way, Croydon, Surrey, CR9 4QD. York, 11746. In Britain: 230 Purley Way, Croy-
BMC	Boston Music Co., c/o Frank Distributing Corp., 116 Boylston St., Boston, Massachusetts, 02116.
BMI	BMI (Canada) Ltd. See: Berandol.
Bodnant	The Bodnant Press, Leicester, Leicestershire. Present address unknown.
Bourne	Bourne Co. See: LZ.
Bradley	Milton Bradley Co., 74 Park St., Springfield, Massachusetts (possibly no longer publishing from this address).

ABBREVIATIONS: PUBLISHERS

Brentano	Brentano Bros. (Brentano's), c/o Coward, McConn & Geoghegan Inc., 200 Madison Ave., New York, New York, 10016.
Brockhaus	Max Brockhaus, Oskar-Gretherstr. 13, Baden, Germany.
Bron	Sydney Bron Music, Bron Associated Publishers Ltd., 29-31 Oxford St., London, W1R 1RE.
Broude-A	Alexander Broude Inc., 225 W. 57th St., New York, New York, 10019.
Broude-B	Broude Bros. Ltd., 56 W. 45th St., New York, New York, 10036.
B&VP	Broekmans & Van Poppel, Van Baerlstr. 92, Amsterdam, The Netherlands.
BW	Bosworth & Co. Ltd., 14-18 Heddon St., London, W1R 8DP.
C	Chappell & Co. Ltd., 50 New Bond St., London, W1A 2BR.
Canyon	Canyon Press Inc., 1801 Gilbert St., Cincinnati, Ohio, 45201.
CAP	Composers' Autograph Publications, P.O. Box 671, Hamilton, Ohio, 45012.
Cary	L.J. Cary & Co. Ltd., 16 Mortimer St., London, W1.
CF	Carl Fischer Inc., 56-62 Cooper Square, New York, New York, 10003.
CFE	Composers Facsimile Edition. See: ACA.
CFP	C.F. Peters Corp., 373 Park Ave. S., New York, New York, 10016.
Channel, NEMO	Channel, NEMO Music Centre, High Woods, Chinnor Hill, Chinnor, Oxfordshire.
CHD	Charles H. Ditson Co., New York. Present address unknown.
ČHF	Český hudební fond. Ceased to exist in 1962.
Chrysalis	Chrysalis Music Ltd., 388-396 Oxford St., London, W1.
Church	John Church Co. See: TP.
Clarendon	Clarendon Press. See: OUP.
Clarke, Irwin	Clarke, Irwin & Co. Ltd., Clarke House, 791 St. Clair Ave. West, Toronto 347, Ontario.
Clowes	William Clowes & Sons Ltd., 15 Cavendish Square, London, W1M 0HT.
CMP	Contemporary Music Project Library Edition. Has ceased to exist; publications now handled by the composers concerned.
CMS	Canadian Music Sales Corp. Ltd., 58 Advance Rd., Toronto 570, Ontario.
Cocks	Robert Cocks & Co., London. Present address unknown.

ABBREVIATIONS: PUBLISHERS

Continuo	Continuo Music Press Inc. See: Broude-A.
Cos Cob	Cos Cob Press. See: AMP or BH (New York).
CPE	Composer Performer Edition, Davis, California.
CPH	Concordia Publishing House, 3558 S. Jefferson Ave., St. Louis, Missouri, 63118.
CPI	The Composers Press Inc. See: SMC.
CPMC	Composers Music Corporation. See: CF.
CR	J.B. Cramer & Co. Ltd., 99 St. Martin's Lane, London, WC2N 4AZ.
Cranz	Aug. Cranz GmbH., Musik Verlag, 6200 Wiesbaden, Adelheidstrasse 68, Postfach 1026, Germany. In Britain: Cranz & Co. Ltd., c/o United Music Publishers Ltd., 1 Montague St., London, WC1B 5BS.
Criador	Criador Press, 20 Foster Ave., Blackrock, Co. Dublin, Ireland.
Cuala	Cuala Press, 116 Lower Baggot St., Dublin 2, Ireland.
CUMP	Columbia University (Music) Press, 562 W. 113th St., New York, New York, 10025.
CUP	Cambridge University Press, Bentley House, P.O. Box 92, 200 Euston Rd., London, NW1 2DD.
Curwen	J. Curwen & Sons Ltd. See: RP.
Deanne	H.W.F. Deanne & Sons. See: C.
Dent	J.M. Dent & Sons Ltd., 10 Bedford St., London, WC2E 9HG.
Derry	Derry Music Co., 240 Stockton St., San Fran- cisco, California, 94108.
DeS	Edizioni De Santis, Rome. In Britain: c/o Hinrich- sen Edition Ltd., 10-12 Baches St., London, N1 6DN.
Dilia	Dilia, Vyšehradská 28, 128 24 Praha 2 - Nové Město, Czechoslovakia.
Dimit Edn.	Dimit Edition, New York. Present address un- known.
DM	Donemus, Amsterdam. In Britain: Donemus Foundation, c/o Alfred Lengnick & Co. Ltd., 421a Brighton Rd., South Croydon, Surrey, CR2 6YR.
Donovan	Donovan Music Ltd. See: SMP.
Doric	Doric Music Co., 50 St. Andrewgate, York, York- shire.
Doubleday	Doubleday & Co. Inc., 277 Park Ave., New York, New York, 10017.
Dow	Dow Publishers Inc., P.O. Box 176, Oyster Bay, New York.
DT	E.P. Dutton & Co. Inc., 201 Park Ave. S., New York, New York, 10003.
Duchess	Duchess Music Corp. See: MCA.

ABBREVIATIONS: PUBLISHERS

Duckworth	Gerald Duckworth Co. Ltd., The Old Piano Factory, 43 Gloucester Crescent, London, NW1 7DY.
Durand	Editions Durand & Cie., 4 place de la Madeleine, Paris, 8e.
E	Enoch & Sons (Enoch & Cie.). See: ASH.
EA	Edward Arnold (E.J. Arnold). See: N.
EBM	Edward B. Marks Music Corp., 1790 Broadway, New York, New York, 10019.
EC	E. Christian, London. Present address unknown.
ECK	E.C. Kerby Ltd., 198 Davenport Rd., Toronto, Ontario, M5R 1J2.
ECS	E.C. Schirmer Music Co., 112 South St., Boston, Massachusetts, 02111.
Editio Musica	Edicio Musica Budapest, Vörösmarty tér 1, Budapest 5, Hungary.
EFM	Editions Françaises de Musique, Siège Social, 12, rue Magellan, Paris, 8e.
EHM	Edwin H. Morris & Co. Inc., c/o Chappell & Co. Ltd., 810 7th Ave., New York, New York, 10019.
Elkin	Elkin & Co. See: N.
Empire	Empire Publishers, New York. Present address unknown.
Eschig	Max Eschig & Cie., 48 rue Rome, Paris, 8e.
EV	Elkan-Vogel Co. Inc. See TP.
F	Faber Music Ltd., 38 Russell Square, London, WC1B 5DA.
Famedram	Famedram Publishers Ltd., Gartocharn, Dunbartonshire, Scotland.
FB	František Borový, Praha, Czechoslovakia. Ceased to exist in 1950.
F&BG	F. & B. Goodwin. For F&BG (Curwen) publications, see: Curwen. For Goodwin & Tabb (G&T) publications, see: N.
FC	Franco Colombo Publications. See: B-M.
FD&H	Francis, Day & Hunter Ltd. See: Affl.
Feldman	B. Feldman & Co. Ltd., 64 Dean St., London, W1V 6AU.
FH	The Frederick Harris Music Co. Ltd., P.O. Box 670, Oakville, Ontario, L6J 5C2.
FMC	Frank Music Corp., c/o Frank Distributing Corp., 116 Boylston St., Boston, Massachusetts, 02116.
Forsyth	Forsyth Bros. Ltd., 190 Grays Inn Rd., London, WC1X 8EW.
FPH	F. Pitmen Hart & Co. Ltd. See: CR.

ABBREVIATIONS: PUBLISHERS

Freeman	E.H. Freeman Ltd., c/o H. Freeman & Co., c/o B. Feldman & Co. Ltd., c/o EMI Music Publishing Ltd., Educational Showroom, 21 Denmark St., London, WC2H 8NE.
Fürstner	Adolph Fürstner, Berlin, Germany. In Britain: c/o Boosey & Hawkes, 295 Regent St., London, W1A 1BR.
G	Galliard, 82 High Rd., E. Finchley, London, N2 9PW.
Gardner Darton	Gardner Darton & Co., London. Present address unknown.
G&C	G&C Music Crop., c/o Chappell & Co. Ltd., 810 7th Ave., New York, New York, 10019.
GenPS	General [Publishing] Society, London. Present address unknown.
GH	Gamble Hinged Music Co. See: CF.
Ginn	Ginn & Co., Xerox Education Group, 191 Spring St., Boston, Massachusetts, 02173.
Girl Scouts	Girl Scouts Inc., 830 3rd Ave., New York, New York, 10022.
GMP	General Music Publishing Co. Inc., P.O. Box 267, Hastings-on-Hudson, New York, 10706.
G&T	Goodwin & Tabb. See: N.
GVT	Gordon V. Thompson Ltd., 29 Birch Ave., Toronto, Ontario, M4V 1E2.
Gwynn	W.S. Gwynn Williams Publishing Co., Llangollen, Denbighs, Wales.
GX	Galaxy Music Corp., 2121 Broadway, New York, New York, 10023.
H	Hinrichsen Edition Ltd., 10-12 Baches St., London, N1 6DN.
Hale	E.M. Hale & Co., 1201 S. Hastings Way, Eau Claire, Wisconsin, 54701.
Hargail	Hargail [Press], 28 W. 38th St., New York, New York, 10018.
Harmonie	Harmonie Verlagsgesellschaft, Berlin (München), Germany. Present address unknown.
Harms	T.B. Harms Co. See: Affl.
HB	Harcourt Brace Jovanovich Inc., 757 3rd Ave., New York, New York, 10017.
H-C	Hill-Coleman. See: S-C.
HD	Herman Darewski, [Darewski Publishing Co. Ltd., c/o B. Feldman & Co. Ltd., 64 Dean St., London, W1V 6AU].
Heffelfinger	R.W. Heffelfinger, Los Angeles. Present address unknown.
Heugel	Heugel & Cie., 2 bis, Rue Vivienne, Paris.

ABBREVIATIONS: PUBLISHERS

HFD&H	T.B. Harms, Francis, Day & Hunter Ltd. See: Atfl.
HFL	Harold Flammer Inc., Delaware Water Gap, Pennsylvania, 18327.
HH&E	Hinds, Hayter & Eldridge, c/o Barnes & Noble Inc., 105 5th Ave., New York, New York, 10003.
H&McC	Hall & McCreary (Schmitt, Hall & McCreary Co.), 110 N. 5th St., Minneapolis, Minnesota, 55403.
HM	Houghton Mifflin, 1 Beacon St., Boston, Massachusetts, 02108.
HMUB	Hudební matice Umelěcké Besedy. Ceased to exist in 1962.
Ho	Charles W. Homeyer & Co. Inc. See: CF.
Horn Realm	The Horn Realm, Box 542, Far Hills, New Jersey, 07931.
Hours Press	Hours Press (Heures de France [Editions]), Docteur Jean Garnier, 30 rue des Saints-Pères, 74 Paris 07.
HP	Highgate Press. See: GX.
H&S	Hodder & Stoughton Ltd., St. Paul's House, 8-12 Warwick Lane, London, EC4.
Hu	Hughes, Marija Matich, 2116 F St., NW, Box 72, Washington, D.C., 20037.
HUP	Harvard University Press, 79 Garden St., Cambridge, Massachusetts, 02138.
HWG	H.W. Gray. See: B-M.
HZ	[P.L.] Huntzinger [Inc.], [Lawson Court, P.O. Box 854, Cincinnati, Ohio, 45201].
I	International Music Corp. See: K.
IMI	Israel Music Institute, 6 Sd Hen, Tel Aviv, Israel.
Impero	Impero Verlag, Wiesbaden, Germany. In Britain: c/o Hinrichsen Edition Ltd., 10-12 Baches St., London, N1 6DN.
Ione	Ione Press. See: ECS.
Jack	T.C. & E.C. Jack, London. Present address unknown.
Jennings	George B. Jennings Co., Cincinnati, Ohio. Present address unknown.
JF	J. Fischer & Bro. See: B-M.
JFL	Joseph Flammer, Milwaukee, Wisconsin. Present address unknown.
JM	Jack Mills, New York. Present address unknown.
JW	Joseph Williams. See: S&B.
JWC	J. & W. Chester Ltd., 7-9 Eagle Court, London, EC1M 5QD.
K	Alfred A. Kalmus, 2-3 Fareham St., London, W1V 4DU.

Kalmus   Edwin F. Kalmus Music Publishers, Miami-Dade
International Park, Box 1007, Opa-Locka, Florida,
33054.

Kaun   Richard Kaun Verlag KG., Kunigundestr. 56,
8000 München 23, Germany.

Kj   Neil A. Kjos Music Co., 525 Busse, Park Ridge,
Illinois, 60068.

Knopf   Alfred A. Knopf. See: Random.

KP   Keith Prowse Music Publishing Co., Ltd., KPM Music
Group, 21 Denmark St., London, WC2H 8NE.

L   Alfred Lengnick & Co. Ltd., 421a Brighton Rd.,
South Croydon, Surrey, CR2 6YR.

Labour Press   Labour Press, Manchester, Lancashire. Present
address unknown.

Laidlaw   Laidlaw Bros., Division of Doubleday & Co. Inc.,
Thatcher & Madison Streets, River Forest, Illinois, 60305.

Lance   Lance Productions, 353 W. 57th St., New York, New
York, 10019.

L&B   Luckhardt & Belder. See: HFL.

LD   Leeds Music Ltd., 138 Piccadilly Square, London,
W1V 9FH.

Lechte   Heinrich & J. Lechte KG, Schulstr. 16, 4407,
Emsdetlen, Germany.

Leduc   Alphonse Leduc & Cie., 175 Rue Saint-Honoré,
Paris, 1er.

Leechman   Leechman Co., San Francisco, California. Present
address unknown.

Leslie   Leslie Music Supply, Box 471, Oakville, Ontario,
L6J 5A8.

Leuckart   F.E.C. Leuckart, Leipzig, Germany. In Britain:
c/o Novello & Co. Ltd., Fairfield Rd., Borough
Green, Sevenoaks, Kent, TN15 8DT.

LG   Lawson-Gould Music Publishers Inc., 866 3rd Ave.,
New York, New York, 10022.

LG&B   Leonard, Gould & Bolttler, 99 St. Martin's Lane,
London, WC2N 4AZ.

L&H   Lyon & Healey, Chicago, Illinois. In Britain:
c/o Boosey & Hawkes, 295 Regent St., London, W1A
1BR.

LMC   Leeds Music Corp., New York. See: MCA.

Longmans,
Green   Longmans, Green & Co., Longman Group Ltd.,
74 Grosvenor St., London, W1X 0AS.

LW   Ludwig Music Publishing Co., 557-559 E. 140th
St., Cleveland, Ohio, 44110.

LZ   Lorenz Publishing Co., 501 E. 3rd St., Dayton,
Ohio, 45401.

M   Mercury Music Corp. See: TP.

MacM	Macmillan, 4 Little Essex St., London, WC2R 3LF.
Marko	Marko Press. See: MF.
Maxwell	The William Maxwell Music Co., New York. Present address unknown.
MCA	MCA Music, 543 W. 43rd St., New York, New York, 10036. In Canada: MCA Bldg., 2450 Victoria Park Ave., Willowdale, Ontario, M2J 4A2.
McK	McKinley Music Co., c/o Larry Spier Inc., Caytronis Bldg., 653 10th Ave., New York, New York, 10036.
Medici	The Medici Society Ltd., 34-42 Pentonville Rd., London, N1 9HG.
Merion	Merion Music Inc. See: TP.
Methuen	Methuen & Co. Ltd., 11 New Fetter Lane, London, EC4P 4EE.
MF	Mark Foster Music Co., P.O. Box 4012, Champaign, Illinois, 61820.
Milford	Humphrey Milford. See: OUP.
Mills	Mills Music. See: B-M.
MJQ	MJQ Music Inc., 200 W. 57th St., New York, New York, 10019.
MK	Michael Keane, [New York ?]. Present address unknown.
M.L. Reid	M.L. Reid, New York. Present address unknown.
MM	Murdoch, Murdoch & Co. See: C.
MML	Modern Music Library, London. Present address unknown.
MMP	Merrymount Music Press. See: TP.
Mor	Mor Press, Itchen Bank, Shawford, nr Winchester, Hampshire, England.
MPA	Musical [Publications] Association, London. Present address unknown.
MPH	Music Publishers Holding Corp., New York. No longer in existence.
MPI	Music Press Inc. See: TP.
MST	Editions Maurice Sénart, Paris. In Britain: c/o Novello & Co. Ltd., Fairfield Rd., Borough Green, Sevenoaks, Kent, TN15 8DT or c/o United Music Publishers Ltd., 1 Montague St., London, WC1B 5BS.
M&T	Miles & Thompson, Boston, Massachusetts. Present address unknown.
Musicus	Edition Musicus Inc., 333 W. 52nd St., New York, New York, 10019.
MV	Musica Viva, 558 Galleywood Rd., Chelmsford, Essex, CM2 8BX.
MZ	Metzler & Co. Ltd. See: CR.

N	Novello & Co. Ltd., Fairfield Rd., Borough Green, Sevenoaks, Kent, TN15 8DT.
NCA	National Concert Agency, London. Present address unknown.
NME	New Music Edition. See: TP. Enquiries might also be made to the American Music Center regarding items published by the New Music Edition Corporation Publisher.
NV	New Valley Music Press, Sage Hall, Smith College, Northampton, Massachusetts, 01060.
OD	Oliver Ditson Co., Bryn Mawr, Pennsylvania, 19010.
OL	Editions de l'Oiseau-Lyre, Les Remparts, Monaco. In Britain: c/o United Music Publishers, 1 Montague St., London, WC1B 5BS.
Omega	Omega Publishing Co., 170 W. 44th St., New York, New York, 10036.
OP	The Olivan Press. See: UE.
Ostara	Ostara Press Inc., c/o Western International Music Co., 2859 Holt Ave., Los Angeles, California, 90034.
OUP	Oxford University Press, Music Department, 44 Conduit St., London, W1R 0DE. In U.S.A.: 200 Madison Ave., New York, New York, 10016.
P	Peters Edition, 119-125 Wardour St., London, W1V 4DN.
Panton	Panton, Říční 12, 118 39 Prahal - Malá Strana, Czechoslovakia.
Paramount (Daniel & Wilson)	Paramount (Daniel & Wilson), San Francisco, California. Present address unknown.
Parks	J.A. Parks Co., York, Nebraska. Present address unknown.
Pass	James Pass & Co. Ltd., 216 Corporation St., Birmingham, Warwickshire.
Paull	E.T. Paull Music Co. See: SPI.
PDM	Piedmont Music Co. Inc., 1790 Broadway (6th floor), New York, New York, 10019.
Peer	Peer International. See: P-S.
Penguin	Penguin Books Ltd., Harmondsworth, Middlesex.
Pigott	McCullough-Pigott Ltd., 11/13 Suffolk St., Dublin 2, Ireland.
Pilgrim	The Pilgrim Press, 14 Beacon St., Boston, Massachusetts, 02108.
PM	Peter Maurice Music Co. Ltd., KPM Music Group, 21 Denmark St., London, WC2H 8NE.
Poetry Bookshop	The Poetry Bookshop, London. Present address unknown.

ABBREVIATIONS: PUBLISHERS

P&P	Phillips & Page, London. Present address unknown.
P&R	Price & Reynolds, London. Present address unknown.
Pro Art	Pro Art Publications Inc., 469 Union Ave., Westbury, New York, 11590.
P-S	Peer-Southern Organization, 1740 Broadway, New York, New York, 10019.
PT	Paterson's Publications Ltd., 36-40 Wigmore St., London, W1.
PWM	Polski Wydawnictwo Muzyczne, ul. Krasinskiejo 11a, Kraków, Poland.
PWP	Przedstawicielstwo Wydawnictw Polskich, Warsaw, Poland.
PX	W. Paxton & Co. Ltd. See: N.
QUP	Queen's University Press, University Rd., Belfast, N. Ireland, BT7 1NN.
R	G. Ricordi & Co., Milan. In Britain: G. Ricordi (London) Ltd., The Bury, Church St., Chesham, Buckinghamshire, HP5 1JG. In U.S.A.: c/o Belwin-Mills Publishing Corp., Melville, New York, 11746. In Australia: G. Ricordi & Co. (A'Sia) Pty. Ltd., 71 Chandos St., St. Leonards 2065, New South Wales.
Random	Random House Inc., 201 E. 50th St., New York, New York, 10022.
Reeves	Reeves, London. Present address unknown.
Reid	Reid Bros. Ltd. See: C.
RM	Remick Music Corp., c/o Warner Bros. Inc., 9200 Sunset Blvd., Los Angeles, California, 90069.
RMC	Robbins Music Corp. Ltd., 35 Soho Square, London, W1.
Rongwen	Rongwen Music. See: Broude-B.
Row	R.D. Row. See: CF.
RP	Roberton Publications, The Windmill, Wendover, Aylesbury, Buckinghamshire, England.
RSCM	Royal School of Church Music, Addington Palace, Croydon, Surrey, CR9 5AD.
RTE	Radio Telefís Éireann, Donnybrook 4, Dublin, Ireland.
RW	Ridgeway's Ltd., London. Present address unknown.
S	B. Schott's Söhne Musikverlag, 65 Mainz, Weihergarten, Postfach 3640, Germany. In Britain: Schott & Co. Ltd., Cobbs Wood Estate, Brunswick Rd., Ashford, Kent.
Salabert	Editions Salabert Inc., 575 Madison Ave., New York, New York, 10022.

Saunders	Saunders Publishing Ltd. See: FMC.
S&B	Stainer & Bell Ltd., 82 High Rd., E. Finchley, London, N2 9PW.
S-C	Sprague-Coleman Inc., c/o Mr. John McKellen, M.C.A. Inc., 445 Park Ave., New York, New York, 10022.
Schmidt	The Arthur P. Schmidt Co., 120 Boylston St., Boston 12, Massachusetts.
Scribner's	Charles Scribner's Sons, 597 5th Ave., New York, New York, 10017.
SFM	Sparta Florida Music Group Ltd., 155-157 Oxford St., London, W1R 1TB.
SH	Charles Sheard, London. Present address unknown.
SH&McC	Schmitt, Hall & McCreary Co., 110 N. 5th St., Minneapolis, Minnesota, 55403.
Silver	Silver, Burdett Co., Division of General Learning Corp., 250 James St., Morristown, New Jersey, 07960.
Skidmore	Skidmore Music Co. Inc., c/o Shapiro, Bernstein & Co. Inc., 10 E. 53rd St., New York, New York, 10022.
SMC	Seesaw Music Corp., 177 E. 87th St., New York, New York, 10028.
SMP	Southern Music Publishing Co. Inc. See: P-S.
Snell	Snell, Wales. Present address unknown.
SPI	Shawnee Press Inc., Delaware Water Gap, Pennsylvania, 18327.
Standard	Standard Music Publishing Inc., Turnersville, New Jersey.
STB	Skandinavisk Teater Bureau, Copenhagen, Denmark. In Britain: Skandinavisk Musikforlag, c/o J. & W. Chester Ltd., 7-9 Eagle Court, London, EC1M 5QD.
STV	H.B. Stevens Co., London. Present address unknown.
SUDM	Samfundet til Udgivelse af dansk Musik, Graabr∮dretorv 7, DK-1154 Copenhagen K, Denmark.
Summy	Clayton F. Summy Co. See: Summy-B.
Summy-B	Summy-Birchard Co., Evanston, Illinois, 60204.
Swan	Swan & Co. Music Publishers Ltd., c/o Arcadia Music Publishing Co. Ltd., 10 Sherlock Mews, Baker St., London, W1.
SZ	Edizioni Suvini Zerboni, 20122 Milano, Corso Europa 5/7, Italy.
Tetra	Tetra Music Corp. See: Broude-A.
Thames	Thames Publishing, 14 Barlby Rd., London, W10 6AP.

ABBREVIATIONS: PUBLISHERS

TP   Theodore Presser Co., Presser Place, Bryn Mawr,
              Pennsylvania, 19010.
Triton   Triton Press, Box 158, Southern Station, Hatties-
              burg, Massachusetts.
Turret   The Turret Bookshops, 5 Kensington Church Walk,
              London, W8 4NB.
UE   Universal Edition Ltd., Karlsplatz 6, Postfach
              3, A-1015 Wien, Austria. In Britain: Universal
              Edition (London) Ltd., 2-3 Fareham St., London,
              W1V 4DU.
UMP   United Music Publishers Ltd., 1 Montague St.,
              London, WC1B 5BS.
UWP   University of Wales Press, University College,
              P.O. Box 78, Cardiff, Wales, CF1 1XL.
Veronica   Veronica Music Ltd., 246-8 Great Portland St.,
              London, W1.
Vincent   Vincent Music Co., London. Present address un-
              known.
Viterbo   Viterbo College, Lacrosse, Wisconsin.
  College
VMP   Valley Music Press. See: NV.
Warne   Frederick Warne & Co. Ltd., Chandos House, 40
              Bedford Square, London, WC1B 3HE.
Warren   Warren & Son Ltd. (Wykeham Press), 85 High St.
              and Staple Gardens, Winchester, Hampshire.
Waterloo   Waterloo Music Co. Ltd., 913 Carling Ave.,
              Ottawa 613, Ontario.
Wa-Wan   Wa-Wan Press. See: GS.
Weinberger   Josef Weinberger Ltd., 10-16 Rathbone St.,
              London, W1P 2BJ.
Weintraub   Weintraub Music Co., 33 W. 60th St., New York,
              New York, 10023.
West   West & Co. [West Ltd.?], London. Present ad-
              dress unknown.
Western   Western Music. See: Leslie.
Westwood   Westwood Press Inc., 2145 Central Parkway, Cin-
              cinnati, Ohio, 45214.
WH   Wilhelm Hansen, Musik-Forlag, Gothersgade
              9-11, DK 1123 Copenhagen K, Denmark.
Willis   Willis Publishing Co., 124E 4th St., Cincinnati,
              Ohio.
Witmark   M. Witmark & Sons, c/o Warner Bros. Inc., 9200
              Sunset Blvd., Los Angeles, California, 90069.
WK   A. Weekes & Co. Ltd. See: G.
WLP   World Library Publications Inc., 2145 Central
              Parkway, Cincinnati, Ohio, 45214.
WMA   Workers' Music Association, London. Present
              address unknown.

ABBREVIATIONS: PUBLISHERS

WmS	William Sloane Associates, New York. No longer in existence.
WR	Winthrop Rogers Ltd. See: BH.
WRC	Whaley, Royce & Co., 310 Yonge St., Toronto, Ontario.
Wright	Lawrence Wright Music Co. Ltd., c/o ATV-Kirshner Music Ltd., 12 Bruton St., London, W1X 7AH.
W-S	White-Smith Music Publishing Co., c/o Chappell and Co. Inc., 810 7th Ave., New York, New York, 10019.
W&T	Whitcombe & Tombs Ltd., P.O. Box 1465, Christchurch 1, New Zealand.
WTA	Wai-te-ata Press, Wellington, New Zealand.
WUP	Washington University Press, Publications Dept., Box 1070, St. Louis, Missouri, 63130.
YBP	Year Book Press. See: C.
YL	Ylioppilaskunnan Laulajat, Helsinki, Finland.

ABBREVIATIONS: OTHER SOURCES

The following list is not comprised of publishers, but, rather, national agencies, institutions, and other such bodies which are repositories of certain works included in this Catalogue. Please note that addresses of university libraries are not provided, as the editors assume that readers can locate these easily.

ACA   American Composers Alliance, 170 W. 74th St., New York, New York, 10023.

AMC   American Music Center Inc., Ste. 15-79, 2109 Broadway, New York, New York, 10023.

BMIC   British Music Information Centre, 10 Stratford Place, London, W1N 9AE.

British   British [Museum] Library, Music Section
Museum   Great Russell St., London, WC1B 3DG.

CMC   Canadian Music Centre, 1263 Bay St., Toronto, Ontario, M5R 2C1; Centre de musique canadienne, 250 est, boulevard Saint-Joseph, bureau 501, Montréal, Québec, H2T 1H7.

FMIC   Finnish Music Information Centre, Runeberginkatu 15 A, SF-00100 Helsinki 10, Finland.

Julliard   Julliard Repertory Library, c/o Canyon Press Inc., 1801 Gilbert St., Cincinnati, Ohio, 45201.

MZS   Magyar Zeneművészek Szövetsége, Budapest, V., Vörösmarty-tér 1, Hungary.

NYPL   Music Division, Library & Museum of the Performing Arts, The New York Public Library at Lincoln Center, 111 Amsterdam Avenue, New York, New York, 10023.

PMC   Polish Music Centre, Warszawa, Rynek Starego Miasta 27, Poland.

RCM   Royal College of Music, Prince Consort Rd., London, SW7 2BS.

RTE   Radio Telefís Éireann, Donnybrook 4, Dublin, Ireland.

SČSKU   Svaz Českých Skladatelů a Koncertnícn Umělců, Praha 1, Valdštejnské Nám. 1, Czechoslovakia.

SMA   Scottish Music Archive, c/o University of Glasgow, 7 Lilybank Gardens, Glasgow, W2, Scotland.

SUNYAB   The Poetry Collection, Lockwood Memorial Library, State University of New York at Buffalo, Buffalo, New York, 14214.

University   University Microfilms, 300 Zeeb Rd., Ann Arbor,
Microfilms   Michigan, 48104.

INDEX OF AUTHORS

Abercrombie, Lascelles

ABERCROMBIE, Lascelles   1881-1938

   Elizabeth's Song   "Shining white clouds in the cherry trees
      tangled"   In Twelve_Idyls_and_Other_Poems (1928)

      1 Head, Michael. L: BH, 1970. Song: s solo, pf.

   Epitaph   "Sir, you should notice me: I am the Man"   In
      Twelve_Idyls_and_Other_Poems (1928)

      2 Orton, Richard. MS 1962. Song: bar solo, ob., hn.,
         vcl.

   Stream's Song, The   "Make way, make way"   In Twelve_Idyls
      and_Other_Poems (1928)

      3 Garlick, Antony. Eleven_Canzonets, Cin.: Westwood,
         1967. Canzonet: chorus of 2 equal v., a cap.
         Setting of stanzas 1 and 4.

ACTON, Harold Mario Mitchell   1904-

   Miscellanea

      4 Crowder, Henry. "From Tiresias", Henry-Music, P:
         Hours Press, 1930. Song: v., pf.

AE   1867-1935

   Affinity   "You and I have found the secret way"   In
      Collected_Poems (1913)

1

5 Hart, Fritz. Seven Sets of Seven Songs, Set IV, MS 1918, avail. State Library of Victoria, Melbourne. Song: v., pf.

Alien "Dark glowed the vales of amethyst" In The Earth Breath and Other Poems (1897)

6 Hart, Fritz. Seven Songs, L: S&B, 1923. Song: v., pf.

Awakening "Lights shone down the street, The" In Collected Poems (1913)

7 Hart, Fritz. Seven Sets of Seven Songs, Set V, MS 1918, avail. State Library of Victoria, Melbourne. Song: v., pf.

Carrowmore "It's a lonely road through bogland" In The Divine Vision and Other Poems (1903)

8 Bantock, Granville. L: Swan, 1926. Song: v., pf.

Creation "As one by one the veils took flight" In Collected Poems (1913)

9 Hart, Fritz. Seven Sets of Seven Songs, Set VI, MS 1918, avail. State Library of Victoria, Melbourne. Song: v., pf.

Dawn "Still as the holy of holies" In Homeward: Songs by the Way (1894)

10 Hart, Fritz. Seven Sets of Seven Songs, Set V, MS 1918, avail. State Library of Victoria, Melbourne. Song: v., pf.

Desire "With Thee a moment! Then what dreams have play!" In Homeward: Songs by the Way (1894)

11 Hart, Fritz. Seven Sets of Seven Songs, Set VII, MS 1918, avail. State Library of Victoria, Melbourne. Song: v., pf.

2

AE continued

Destiny   "Like winds or waters were her ways"   In Homeward:
Songs by the Way (1894)

   12 Hart, Fritz. Seven Sets of Seven Songs, Set IV, MS
       1918, avail. State Library of Victoria, Mel-
       bourne. Song: v., pf.

Dream Love   "I did not deem it half so sweet"   In The Earth
Breath and Other Poems (1897)

   13 Hart, Fritz. Seven Sets of Seven Songs, Set V, MS
       1918, avail. State Library of Victoria, Mel-
       bourne. Song: v., pf.

Dream, The   "I woke to find my pillow wet"   In Collected
Poems (1913)

   14 Hart, Fritz. Seven Sets of Seven Songs, Set V, MS
       1918, avail. State Library of Victoria, Mel-
       bourne. Song: v., pf.

Dusk   "Dusk wraps the village in its dim caress"   In Homeward: Songs by the Way (1894)

   15 Hart, Fritz. Seven Sets of Seven Songs, Set VII, MS
       1918, avail. State Library of Victoria, Mel-
       bourne. Song: v., pf.

Dust   "I heard them in their sadness say"   In Homeward:
Songs by the Way (1894)

   16 Hart, Fritz. Seven Songs, L: S&B, 1923. Song: v.,
       pf.

Echoes   "Might that shaped itself through storm and stress,
The"   In Homeward: Songs by the Way (1894)

   17 Hart, Fritz. Seven Sets of Seven Songs, Set VII, MS
       1918, avail. State Library of Victoria, Mel-
       bourne. Song: v., pf.

Fountain of Shadowy Beauty, The   "I would I could weave in"
   In The Earth Breath and Other Poems (1897)

    18 Hart, Fritz. "A Dream", Seven Sets of Seven Songs,
          Set IV, MS 1918, avail. State Library of Vic-
          toria, Melbourne. Song: v., pf. Setting of begin-
          ning stanzas only.

    19 Hart, Fritz. "The Awakening", Seven Sets of Seven
          Songs, Set IV, MS 1918, avail. State Library of
          Victoria, Melbourne. Song: v., pf. Setting of
          lines beginning: "Well it is gone now".

Freedom   "I will not follow you, my bird"   In The Divine
   Vision and Other Poems (1903)

    20 Hart, Fritz. Seven Sets of Seven Songs, Set II, MS
          1918, avail. State Library of Victoria, Mel-
          bourne. Song: v., pf.

Frolic   "Children were shouting together, The"   In The
   Divine Vision and Other Poems (1903)

    21 Bainton, Edgar L. L: Curwen, 1920. Song: solo v.,
          pf.

    22 Coulthard, Jean. Five Irish Songs for Maureen, MS
          1958-1964, avail. CMC. Song: ms solo, pf.

    23 Glanville-Hicks, Peggy. P: OL, 1938. Song: v., pf.

    24 Hart, Fritz. Seven Sets of Seven Songs, Set II, MS
          1918, avail. State Library of Victoria, Mel-
          bourne. Song: v., pf.

Gift, The   "I thought, beloved, to have brought to you"   In
   The Earth Breath and Other Poems (1897)

    25 Hart, Fritz. Seven Sets of Seven Songs, Set III, MS
          1918, avail. State Library of Victoria, Mel-
          bourne. Song: v., pf.

Great Breath, The   "Its edges foamed with amethyst and rose"
   In Homeward: Songs by the Way (1894)

26 Dillon, Shaun. <u>Cantata in Memoriam</u>, MS, perf. Nov.
    1974. Song (in cta.): s solo, fl., gtr., pf.

27 Hart, Fritz. <u>Seven Sets of Seven Songs</u>, Set VII, MS
    1918, avail. State Library of Victoria, Mel-
    bourne. Song: v., pf.

Heroic Love   See: Love

Holy Hill, A   "Be still: be still: nor dare"   In <u>Voices of
the Stones</u> (1925)

28 Lora, Antonio. MS, avail. ACA. Song: med. v., pf.

Illusion   "What is the love of shadowy lips"   In <u>The Earth
Breath and Other Poems</u> (1897)

29 Hart, Fritz. <u>Seven Sets of Seven Songs</u>, Set IV, MS
    1918, avail. State Library of Victoria, Mel-
    bourne. Song: v., pf.

Inspiration   "Lightest of dancers"   In <u>Collected Poems</u>
(1913)

30 Hart, Fritz. <u>Seven Sets of Seven Songs</u>, Set VII, MS
    1918, avail. State Library of Victoria, Mel-
    bourne. Song: v., pf.

Janus   "Image of beauty, when I gaze on thee"   In <u>The Earth
Breath and Other Poems</u> (1897)

31 Hart, Fritz. <u>Seven Sets of Seven Songs</u>, Set VII, MS
    1918, avail. State Library of Victoria, Mel-
    bourne. Song: v., pf.

Leader, A   "Though your eyes with tears were blind"   In
<u>The Earth Breath and Other Poems</u> (1897)

32 Bax, Arnold. MS 1916. Song: v., pf.

33 Hart, Fritz. _Seven Sets of Seven Songs_, Set VI, MS
1918, avail. State Library of Victoria, Melbourne. Song: v., pf.

Light and Dark   "Not the soul that's whitest"   In _The
Divine Vision and Other Poems_ (1903)

34 Hart, Fritz. _Seven Sets of Seven Songs_, Set V, MS
1918, avail. State Library of Victoria, Melbourne. Song: v., pf.

Lonely, The   "Lone and forgotten"   In _Voices of the Stones_
(1925)

35 Edmunds, John. NY: CF, 1948. Song: med. v., pf.

Love   "When our glowing dreams were dead"   In _The Earth
Breath and Other Poems_ (1897), rev. 1913

36 Hart, Fritz. "Heroic Love", _Seven Sets of Seven
Songs_, Set IV, MS 1918, avail. State Library of
Victoria, Melbourne. Song: v., pf.

Michael   "Wind blew by from icy hills, A"   (1919)

37 Boydell, Brian. _A Terrible Beauty is Born_, MS 1965.
Cta.: a, bar soli, chorus, orch. Incl. setting of
lines beginning: "Was it because the Easter
Time".

Mid-World, The   "This is the red, red region"   In _The Earth
Breath and Other Poems_ (1897)

38 Hart, Fritz. _Seven Sets of Seven Songs_, Set III, MS
1918, avail. State Library of Victoria, Melbourne. Song: v., pf.

Mistrust   "You look at me with wan, bright eyes"   In
Collected Poems (1913)

AE continued

39 Hart, Fritz. Seven Sets of Seven Songs, Set II, MS 1918, avail. State Library of Victoria, Melbourne. Song: v., pf.

Momentary "Sweetest song ever sung, The" In Collected Poems (1913)

40 Hart, Fritz. Seven Sets of Seven Songs, Set II, MS 1918, avail. State Library of Victoria, Melbourne. Song: v., pf.

Mountaineer, The "Oh, at the eagle's height" In The Earth Breath and Other Poems (1897)

41 Hart, Fritz. Seven Songs, L: S&B, 1923. Song: v., pf.

Natural Magic "We are tired who follow after" In Homeward: Songs by the Way (1894)

42 Hart, Fritz. MS 1925. Song: female chorus, pf.

New Being, A "I know myself no more" In The Divine Vision and Other Poems (1903)

43 Bax, Arnold. "I know...", MS ca. 1916. Song: v., pf.

44 Hart, Fritz. Seven Songs, L: S&B, 1923. Song: v., pf.

Night "Heart-hidden from the outer things I rose" In Homeward: Songs by the Way (1894)

45 Hart, Fritz. Seven Sets of Seven Songs, Set VII, MS 1918, avail. State Library of Victoria, Melbourne. Song: v., pf.

Our Thrones Decay "I said my pleasure shall not move" In Homeward: Songs by the Way (1894)

7

AE continued

    46 Hart, Fritz. <u>Seven Sets of Seven Songs</u>, Set VI, MS
        1918, avail. State Library of Victoria, Mel-
        bourne. Song: v., pf.

Pain   "Men have made them gods of love" In <u>Homeward: Songs
by the Way</u> (1894))

    47 Hart, Fritz. <u>Seven Sets of Seven Songs</u>, Set II, MS
        1918, avail. State Library of Victoria, Mel-
        bourne. Song: v., pf.

Pain of Earth, The "Does the earth grow grey with grief"
In <u>Homeward: Songs by the Way</u> (1894)

    48 Hart, Fritz. <u>Seven Songs</u>, L: S&B, 1923. Song: v.,
        pf.

Parting "As from our dream" In <u>Homeward: Songs by the Way</u>
(1894)

    49 Bax, Arnold. L: MM, 1917, copyright assigned L: C,
        1943. Song: v., pf.

    50 Hart, Fritz. <u>Seven Songs</u>, L: S&B, 1923. Song: v.,
        pf.

Recall "What call may draw thee back again" In <u>The Divine
Vision and Other Poems</u> (1903)

    51 Hart, Fritz. <u>Seven Sets of Seven Songs</u>, Set III, MS
        1918, avail. State Library of Victoria, Mel-
        bourne. Song: v., pf.

Reconciliation "I begin through the grass once again" In
<u>Collected Poems</u> (1913)

    52 Treharne, Bryceson. B: BMC, 1917. Song: v., pf.

Reflections "How shallow is this mere that gleams!" <u>Dana</u>
(Mar. 1905)

8

AE continued

53 Hart, Fritz. Seven Sets of Seven Songs, Set VI, MS
    1918, avail. State Library of Victoria, Mel-
    bourne. Song: v., pf.

Refuge "Twilight, a timid fawn, when glimmering by" In
The Divine Vision and Other Poems (1903)

54 Hart, Fritz. L: Curwen, 1946. Song: v., pf.

Rest "On me to rest, my bird, by bird" In The Divine
Vision and Other Poems (1903)

55 Busch, William. L: OUP, 1944. Song: v., pf.

56 Glanville-Hicks, Peggy. P: OL, 1938. Song: v., pf.

57 Hart, Fritz. Seven Sets of Seven Songs, Set III, MS
    1918, avail. State Library of Victoria, Mel-
    bourne. Song: v., pf.

Sacrifice "Those delicate wanderers" In Homeward: Songs
by the Way (1894)

58 Hart, Fritz. Seven Sets of Seven Songs, Set II, MS
    1918, avail. State Library of Victoria, Mel-
    bourne. Song: v., pf.

Truth "Hero first thought it, The" In Homeward: Songs by
the Way (1894)

59 Hart, Fritz. Seven Sets of Seven Songs, Set VI, MS
    1918, avail. State Library of Victoria, Mel-
    bourne. Song: v., pf.

Unconscious "Winds, the stars, and the skies though
wrought, The" In Complete Poems (1913)

60 Hart, Fritz. Seven Songs, L: S&B, 1923. Song: v.,
    pf.

Unknown God, The "Far up the dim twilight fluttered" In
Homeward: Songs by the Way (1894)

9

61 Hart, Fritz. Seven Sets of Seven Songs, Set V, MS
    1918, avail. State Library of Victoria, Mel-
    bourne. Song: v., pf.

62 Read, Gardner. NY: AMP, 1946, Four Nocturnes (MS
    1934). Song: ms solo, pf. Also publ. for ssa (or
    unchanged voices), pf. Avail. from the composer
    (hire) for ms solo, orch.

Veils of Maya, The   "Mother, with whom our lives should be"
  In Homeward: Songs by the Way (1894)

    63 Hart, Fritz. Seven Sets of Seven Songs, Set IV, MS
        1918, avail. State Library of Victoria, Mel-
        bourne. Song: v., pf.

Vesture of the Soul, The   "I pitied one whose tattered
  dress" In Homeward: Songs by the Way (1894)

    64 Hart, Fritz. Seven Sets of Seven Songs, Set V, MS
        1918, avail. State Library of Victoria, Mel-
        bourne. Song: v., pf.

Voice of the Sea, The   "Sea was hoary, hoary, The"   In The
  Earth Breath and Other Poems (1897)

    65 Hart, Fritz. Seven Sets of Seven Songs, Set III, MS
        1918, avail. State Library of Victoria, Mel-
        bourne. Song: v., pf.

Waiting   "When the dawn comes forth I wonder"   In Homeward:
  Songs by the Way (1894)

    66 Hart, Fritz. Seven Sets of Seven Songs, Set VI, MS
        1918, avail. State Library of Victoria, Mel-
        bourne. Song: v., pf.

When   "When mine hour is come"   In Collected Poems (1913)

    67 Dillon, Shaun. Cantata in Memoriam, MS, perf. Nov.
        1974. Song (in cta.): s, bar soli, fl., gtr., pf.

10

AE continued

    68   Hart, Fritz. _Seven Sets of Seven Songs_, Set II, MS
            1918, avail. State Library of Victoria, Mel-
            bourne. Song: v., pf.

Winter   "Diamond glow of winter o'er the world, A"   In _The
Earth Breath and Other Poems_ (1897)

    69   Hart, Fritz. _Seven Sets of Seven Songs_, Set III, MS
            1918, avail. State Library of Victoria, Mel-
            bourne. Song: v., pf.

Miscellanea

    70   Bax, Arnold. "A Patriot". Song: v., pf. Presumably
            a missing MS, known only from a list of songs
            given at the end of the 1924 MS of Bax's "I
            Heard a Soldier". Words attributed to AE.

    71   Deale, Edgar M. "Breathe a gay good-night", L:
            Elkin, 1963. Song: satb, a cap.

    72   Walters, Leslie. The reader is referred to Robert
            Smith's _A Complete Catalogue of Contemporary
            Welsh Music (No. 5)_ for details regarding a MS
            setting by Walters of a text by AE.

ALDINGTON, Richard Edward Godfree   1892-1962

After Two Years   "She is all so slight"   In _Images (1910-
1915)_ (1915)

    73   Andrews, Mark. "As a May Morning", MS pre-1939, NY:
            GS. Song: [v., pf.].

    74* Goode, Herbert. NY: Witmark, pre-1940. Song: [v.,
            pf.].

    75   Poston, Elizabeth. "She...", L: BH, 1942. Song: v.,
            pf.

Aldington, Richard continued

76   Warlock, Peter. L: OUP, 1931. Song: bar solo, pf.

Madrigal   "Oh, by what right shall I upbraid"   In Exile and
Other Poems (1923)

77   Crowder, Henry. Henry Music, P: Hours Press, 1930.
Song: v., pf.

To a Greek Marble   "Potnia, Potnia"   In Images (1910-1915)
(1915) Originally, the poem's 1st line was printed in
Greek

78   ApIvor, Denis. Songs Opus 6, MS 1940-46. Song: t
solo, pf.

Wine Cup, The   "Life was to us an amphora of war"   In
Images of War, enlarged edn. (1919)

79   Harris, George. MS 1927, NY: GS. Song: [v., pf.?].

ARDEN, John   1930-

Island of the Mighty   (DR)   In coll. with Margaretta D'Arcy
(1974)

80   Davis, Carl. MS, perf. Aldwych, Dec. 1972. Incidental music.

Ashton, Winifred

ASHTON, Winifred   See: DANE, Clemence

AUDEN, Wystan Hugh   1907-1973

Academic Graffiti   "Henry Adams"   Homage to Clio (1960)
Portions appeared in New Yorker (Apr. 1953)

    81* Bialosky, Marshall. Seven Academic Graffiti, MS
        1972-74. Songs: ssa, a cap.

    82 Smit, Leo. MS 1962, NY: CF (hire). Songs: s or high
        bar solo, cl., vcl., pf., perc.

Age of Anxiety, The: A Baroque Eclogue   (1947)

    83 Bernstein, Leonard. Symphony No. 2 for Piano and
        Orchestra, NY: GS, 1960, rev. 1965. Symph.: pf.,
        orch.

    84 Symonds, Norman. MS 1959. Ste. for radio prod.: v.,
        10 member jazz ensemble.

Anthem for St. Cecilia's Day   See: Three Songs For St.
Cecilia's Day

Ascent of F6, The   (DR)   In coll. with Christopher
Isherwood (1936)

    85 Britten, Benjamin. See: "Stop all the clocks...".

    86 Britten, Benjamin. MS, prod. BBC 1937. Incidental
        music.

    87* Duncan, Chester. MS 1945-50. Incidental music: s, a,
        t, bar soli, chorus, pf.

    88 Rorem, Ned. See: "Stop all the clocks...".

Auden, W.H. continued

89 Southam, T. Wallace. See: "Stop all the clocks...".

"As it is, plenty" Look, Stranger! (1936), rev. 1945

90 Britten, Benjamin. On This Island, L: WR, 1938.
    Cyc.: high v., pf. Score contains Fr. transl. by
    Maurice Pourchet.

"Babies in their mothers' arms" See: Infants in their
    mothers' arms"

Ballad "O what is that sound" New Verse (Dec. 1934),
    rev. 1945, rev. 1958

91 Bennett, William D. "The Quarry", L: BH, 1967. Song:
    v., pf.

92 Kreuger, Randall. "O what...", MS 1968. Song: [v.,
    pf.?].

Ballad of Barnaby, The "Listen good people" New York
    Review of Books (Dec. 1969) Based on the medieval legend
    of "The Juggler of Notre Dame"

93* Beard, Vivian, et al. NY: GS, 1970. Opera: male and
    treble voices, actors, dancers, pf. or org. with
    occasional use of fl., cl., vln., vcl., gtr.,
    perc. Additional words by Helen Emmit. Score
    prepared for publ. by Charles Turner.

Bassarids, The Libr. in coll. with Chester Kallman, after
    The Bacchae of Euripides. German title: Die Bassariden.
    Not publ. sep.

94 Henze, Hans Werner. Mz.: S, 1966. Opera: s, ms, a,
    2 t, 2 bar, b soli, chorus, actors, orch.

"Before this loved one" Poems (1930), rev. 1945, rev. 1966

95 Duncan, Chester. "The One", MS 1947, Five Songs (MS
    1940-72). Song: s solo, pf. The complete col-
    lection also requires ms, a, bar soli.

14

Auden, W.H. continued

Calypso   "Driver, drive faster"   Another Time (1940)

       96 Britten, Penjamin. Four Cabaret Songs for Helli
           Anderson, MS 1938. Song: [v., pf.?].

"Carry her over the water"   The Collected Poetry of W.H.
Auden (1945) An excerpt from Auden's libr. entitled "Paul
Bunyan".

       97 Berkeley, Lennox. Five Poems, L: JWC, 1960. Song:
           med. v., pf.

       98 Britten, Benjamin. See: Paul Bunyan.

       99 Cohn, James M. Three Phases of Love, MS 1969. Set-
           ting for satb, a cap.

      100 Dickinson, Peter. Four W.H. Auden Songs, MS 1956.
           Cyc.: high female v., pf.

      101 Gibbs, Geoffrey D. MS. Song: med. v., pf.

      102 Hyde, Lewis. MS 1951. Song: solo v., pf.

      103 Pinkham, Daniel. "Sing Agreeably of Love", B: Row,
           1949, Three Lyric Scenes, B: Row, 1949. Song:
           med. v., str. qrt. or med. v., orch.

      104 Swift, Richard. "Epithalamium", MS. Song: s solo,
           bsn., vln. or s solo, pf.

"Clocks cannot tell our time of day"   The Double Man (1941)

      105 Foss, Lukas. "We're Late", Time Cycle, NY: CF, 1960,
           1962. Song: s solo, orch. Arr. for s solo, ca.
           orch. publ. NY: CF, 1964.

Coal Face   (DS)   (Unpubl.; written 1935)

      106 Britten, Benjamin. MS, prod. G.P.O. Film Unit. In-
           cidental music.

Composer, The   "All the others translate"   New Writing
(Spring 1939)

15

Auden, W.H. continued

107 Hyde, Lewis. MS 1953-54. Song: solo v., pf.

Dance of Death, The   (DR)   (1933)

108 Clair, Leonard. "Cunarder Waltz", MS 1943. Setting
     of lines beginning: "You were a great Cunarder,
     I".

109 Duncan, Chester. MS 1972, Five Songs, MS 1940-72.
     Song: a solo, pf. The complete collection also
     requires s, ms, bar soli.

110 Murrill, Herbert. MS pre-1952. Incidental music.

Danse Macabre   See: Song for the New Year

Dark Valley, The   (RS)   Best Broadcasts of 1939-1940 (1940)

111 Britten, Benjamin. MS, prod. CBS. Incidental music.

"Dear, though the night is gone"   See: Dream, The

Decoys, The   "There are some birds"   The Oratorio: An
     English Study (1932)

112 Rimmer, John F. Three Songs by W.H. Auden, MS 1964,
     avail. University of Auckland. Song: solo v., pf.

Dog Beneath the Skin, The   (DR)   In coll. with Christopher
     Isherwood (1935)

113 Britten, Benjamin. See: "Now through night's cares-
     sing grip".

114 Hyde, Lewis. See: "Seen when night is silent".

115 Murrill, Herbert. MS pre-1952. Incidental music.

Dream, The   "Dear, though the night is gone"   New Verse
     (Apr.-May 1936), rev. same year

16

Auden, W.H. continued

116 Hyde, Lewis. "Dear...", MS 1951. Song: solo v., pf.

Duchess of Malfi, The   (DR)   Adapt. from John Webster
(Unpubl.)

117 Britten, Benjamin. MS, prod. NY 1946. Incidental
     music.

Elegy for J.F.K.   "Why then, why there"   Sunday Times
(Nov. 1964)

118 Stravinsky, Igor. L: BH, 1964. Elegy: ms or bar
     solo, 3 cl. Sets lines beginning: "When a man
     just dies".

Elegy For Young Lovers   Libr. in coll. with Chester Kallman.
German title: Elegie für junge Liebende. Not publ. sep.

119 Henze, Hans Werner. Mz.: S, 1961. Opera: cs, s, a,
     t, bar soli, sp., actors, orch.

Entertainment of the Senses, The*   (Libr.)   In coll. with
Chester Kallman   Thank You Fog (1974)

120 Gardner, John L. MS 1974. Masque: 5 soli, 6 instr.

Epitaph on a Tyrant   "Perfection, of a kind"   New Statesman
and Nation (Jan. 1939)

121 Smith, Russell. MS. Song: high or med. v., pf.

"Eyes look into the well"   Best Broadcasts 1939-40 (1940)

122 Berkeley, Lennox. Five Poems, L: JWC, 1960. Song:
     med. v., pf.

123 Dickinson, Peter. Four W.H. Auden Songs, MS 1956.
     Cyc.: high female v., pf.

124 Hyde, Lewis. MS 1951. Song: solo v., pf.

17

Auden, W.H. continued

125   Senator, Ronald. <u>Summer Soon is Past</u>, in prep. for
       publ. Song: s solo, satb, a cap.

"Fish in the unruffled lakes"   <u>Listener</u> (Apr. 1936)

126   Britten, Benjamin. L: BH, 1937. Song: high v., pf.

127   Hyde, Lewis. MS 1951. Song: solo v., pf.

<u>For the Time Being: A Christmas Oratorio</u>   (1945), rev. same
year

128   Bliss, Arthur. "He is the Way", Cambridge: CUP,
       1967 in <u>The Cambridge Hymnal</u>; publ. sep. L: N,
       1968. Hymn: unison v., org. (or pf.). Employs the
       tune "Santa Barbara". Sets lines beginning: "He
       is the Way".

129*   Britten, Benjamin. "Chorale", in <u>Score</u> (Jan. 1961).
       Carol: ssaattbb, a cap. After an old Fr. carol.
       Sets lines beginning: "Our Father, whose creative
       Will".

130*   Duncan, Chester. MS 1946-65. Settings for s, ms, a,
       t, b soli, pf.

131   Fulton, Norman. "Canon", Cambridge: CUP, 1967 in <u>The
       Cambridge Hymnal</u>. Canon: 2 equal v., org. (or
       pf.). Sets lines beginning: "Released by love".

132   Fulton, Norman. "Round", Cambridge: CUP, 1967 in <u>The
       Cambridge Hymnal</u>. Round: voices, org. (or pf.).
       Second setting of liens beginning: "Released by
       love".

133   Gardner, John L. See: "My Dear One is mine...".

134   James, Philip. MS (not publ. in entirety). Oratorio.
       An excerpt entitled "Chorus of Shepherds and
       Angels" was publ. L: R, 1959 for ssa. This ex-
       cerpt is a setting of lines beginning: "Let us
       run to learn".

Auden, W.H. continued

135 Levy, Marvin D. L: R, 1959. Oratorio: 2 s, a, t,
    bar, b soli, narr., satb, orch. Also publ. NY:
    BH, 1967 for cs, s, ms, t, bar, b soli, narr.,
    satb, orch.; this publication incl. a German
    transl. by Suzanne Szekely.

136 Persichetti, Vincent. "Our Father, whose creative
    Will", Hymns and Responses for the Church Year,
    Ph.: FV, 1965. Hymn: unison v. (or satb), pf.
    (or org.) or unison v. (or satb), a cap.

137 Rimmer, John F. See: "Sing, Ariel, sing".

Funeral Blues   See: "Stop all the clocks..."

God's Chillun   (DS)   (Unpubl.; written 1939)

138 Britten, Benjamin. MS, prod. G.P.O. Film unit.
    Commentary set as recitative.

Hadrian's Wall: An Historical Survey   (RS)   (Unpubl. in
    entirety; written 1937; script avail. BBC)

139 Britten, Benjamin. MS, prod. BBC, Nov. 1937. In-
    cidental music.

Happy Ending   See: "Silly fool, the silly fool, The"

His Excellency   See: "As it is, plenty"

Hymn to the United Nations   "Eagerly, Musician"   In New
    York Times (Oct. 1971), rev. 1972

140 Casals, Pablo. NY: Tetra, 1972. Hymn: satb, opt.
    orch.; orch. score on hire only.

In Father's Footsteps   See: Poem "Our hunting fathers told
    the story"

Auden, W.H. continued

"Infants in their mothers' arms" The Double Man (1941),
    rev. 1966

    141 Drakeford, Richard. "Babies in their mothers' arms",
         Four Songs, MS. Song: bar solo, pf.

Invocation to Ariel See: "Sing, Ariel, sing"

Johnny "O the valley in the summer" Another Time (1940)

    142 Britten, Benjamin. Four Cabaret Songs for Hedli
         Anderson, MS 1938. Song: [v., pf.?].

    143 Hyde, Lewis. "O the valley...", MS 1951. Song: solo
         v., pf.

Lauds* "Among the leaves" The Shield of Achilles (1955)

    144 Berkeley, Lennox. Five Poems, L: JWC, 1960. Song:
         med. v., pf.

    145 Mellers, Wilfrid H. Ex Nihilo and Lauds, L: Mills,
         1961. Song: satb, a cap.

Leap Before You Look "Sense of danger, The" Decision
    (Apr. 1941), rev. 1950

    146 Talma, Louise. MS 1945. Song: s solo, pf.

"Lights are moving" The Age of Anxiety: A Baroque Eclogue
    (1947) Incl. as one of "Three Dreams" in W.H. Auden: A
    Selection by the author (1958)

    147 Yannay, Yehuda. "Incantations", Tel Aviv: IMI, 1975.
         Setting for s solo, pf. (keyboard and interior
         pt. using perc. mallets).

Like a Dream See: "This lunar beauty"

"Look, stranger, at this island now" See: Seaside

Auden, W.H. continued

Lullaby "Hush-a-bye, Baby" Delos (1968) as part of "Songs
from Mutter Courage" transl. from Berthold Brecht, rev.
1969

148 Routh, Francis. Three Short Songs, MS 1973. Song:
ms solo, pf.

Lullaby "Lay your sleeping head" See: Poem "Lay your
sleeping head"

Madrigal "O lurcher-loving collier" New Verse (Summer
1938), rev. 1945. Originally a portion of Auden's
documentary script entitled "Coal Face"

149 Berkeley, Lennox. "O lurcher-loving...", Five Poems,
L: JWC, 1960. Song: med. v., pf.

150 Hyde, Lewis. "O lurcher-loving...", MS 1951. Song:
solo v., pf.

151 Orton, Richard. Four Partsongs, Grt. Y.: G, 1970.
Song: satb, a cap.

152 Senator, Ronald. "O lurcher-loving...", Summer Soon
is Past, in prep. for publ. Song: satb, a cap.

Markings (PR) (1964) Transl. (in coll. with Leif Sjöberg)
of Dag Hammarskjöld's Vägmärken

153 Strilko, Anthony. Songs from "Markings", NY: M,
1966. Song: [v., pf.?].

Miranda's Song See: "My Dear One is mine..."

Monk and His Cat, The "Pangur, white Pangur" Transl. of
anon Irish text. Not publ. sep.

154 Barber, Samuel. Hermit Songs, NY: GS, 1954. Song:
solo v., pf. Also avail. for satb, pf.

Moralities (Libr.) London Magazine (Feb. 1968)

Auden, W.H. continued

155　Henze, Hans Werner. Mz.: S, 1969. "3 scenic plays":
a, bar soli, vocal qrt. (s, a, t, b), sp., satb,
small orch. (or 2 pf.). Also avail. with accompaniment of 2 pf., hp. German transl. by Maria
Bass-Sporleder.

"My Dear One is mine as mirrors are lonely" For_the_Time
Being (1947) Incl. under the title "Miranda's Song" in
W.H._Auden:_A_Selection_by_the_author (1958)

156　Gardner, John L. "Miranda's Song", The_Noble_Heart,
L: OUP, 1966. Cta.: s solo, satb, orch.

"My second thoughts condemn" The_Collected_Poetry_of_W.H.
Auden (1945)

157　Dickinson, Peter. "My Second Thoughts", Three_Comic
Songs, MS 1960. Cyc.: high male v., pf.

158　Drakeford, Richard. Four_Songs, MS. Song: bar solo,
pf.

New Year Letter　"Under the familiar weight" Atlantic
(Jan. & Feb. 1941)

159　Young, Douglas. "Canticle", L: F, 1972. Setting for
6 pt. chorus, a cap. Setting of lines beginning:
"O Unicorn among the cedars". An arr. for satb,
a cap. was publ. as a musical supplement to the
Aug. 1973 issue of Musical_Times.

"Night covers up the rigid land" Look,_Stranger! (1936)

160　Berkeley, Lennox. L: WR, 1939. Song: med. v., pf.

161　Duncan, Chester. MS 1940, Five_Songs (MS 1940-72).
Song: bar solo, pf. The complete collection also
requires s, ms, a soli.

Night Mail　(DS)　(Unpubl. in entirety; written 1936; a poem
[entitled "Night Mail"] from the script was publ. in GPO
Film_Library:_Notes_and_Synopses_1936)

22

Auden, W.H. continued

162 Britten, Benjamin. MS, prod. G.P.O. Film Unit. In-
     cidental music.

Nocturne II   "Make this night lovable"   The Shield of
Achilles (1955)

163 Maw, Nicholas. "Nocturne", Nocturne, L: JWC, 1960.
     Cyc.: ms solo, ch. orch.

Nones   "What we know"   Nones (1951)

     164* Berio, Luciano. Mi.: SZ, 1955. Orch. only.

No Time   See: "clocks cannot tell our time of day"

"Now the leaves are falling fast"   See: Poem "Now the
leaves"

"Now through night's caressing grip"   The Dog Beneath the
Skin (1935)

     165 Britten, Benjamin. "Nocturne", On This Island, L:
          WR, 1938. Cyc.: high v., pf. Score contains Fr.
          transl. by Maurice Pourchet. "Nocturne" was publ.
          sep. L: BH [1949?].

"O lift your little pinkie"   Musical Times (Oct. 1952) Not
publ. sep.

     166 Britten, Benjamin. "Shepherd's Carol", L: N, 1962
          in Musical Times (Oct. 1962 supplement). Carol:
          s, a, t, b soli, satb, a cap.

"O lurcher-loving collier, black as night"   See: Madrigal

O Tell Me the Truth About Love   "Some say that Love's"
Another Time (1940), rev. 1966

     167 Britten, Benjamin. Four Cabaret Songs for Hedli
          Anderson, MS 1938. Song: [v., pf.?].

23

Auden, W.H. continued

168 Cohn, James M. <u>Three Phases of Love</u>, MS 1969. Setting for satb, a cap.

O What is that Sound   See: Ballad

<u>On the Frontier</u>   (DR)   In coll. with Christopher Isherwood (1938)

169 Britten, Benjamin. MS, prod. 1939. Incidental music.

170 Britten, Benjamin. <u>Ballad of Heroes</u>, L: WR, 1939. Ballad: t or s solo, chorus (largely unison), orch. Sets lines beginning: "Europe lies in the dark".

On This Island   See: Seaside

One Circumlocution   "Sometimes we see"   <u>Third Hour</u> (1951)

171 Segerstam, Leif. <u>Six Songs of Experience</u>, MS 1970-71, avail. FMIC. Cyc.: s solo, stereoph. placed orch. without cond. Can also be perf. as ballet or theatre music.

One Evening   See: Song "As I walked out one evening"

Orpheus   "What does the song"   <u>London Mercury</u> (June 1937)

172 Hyde, Lewis. MS 1954. Song: solo v., pf.

173 Segerstam, Leif. <u>Six Songs of Experience</u>, MS 1970-71, avail. FMIC. Cyc.: s solo, stereoph. placed orch. without cond. Can also be perf. as ballet or theatre music.

Our Hunting Fathers   See: Poem "Our hunting fathers told the story"

"Over the heather the wet winds blow"   See: Roman Wall Blues

Auden, W.H. continued

Paid on Both Sides: A Charade   (DR)   Criterion (Jan. 1930)
   Portions were 1st publ. in Poems (1928)

   174 Lutyens, Elisabeth. MS, prod. BBC 1972. Incidental
        music.

Paul Bunyan   (Libr.)   (Unpubl. in entirety; written 1941;
   MS avail. Columbia University)

   175 Britten, Benjamin. MS, prod. Columbia University
        1941. Opera. Withdrawn by the composer, but later
        employed as quarry for other works.

Petition   See: "Sir, no man's enemy, forgiving all"

Play of Daniel, The   (DR)   Narration after 13th cent.
   musical drama   (1959)

   176 Greenberg, Noah, ed. NY: OUP, 1959. Musical drama:
        2 s, 3 t, 2 s or t, 6 bar, 2 b soli, choir (8 s,
        4 t, 4 bar, 4 b), 4 actors, ob., s. rec., tpt.,
        vla., z. (or autohp.), gtr., chimes, hb., perc.
        Anon score ed. by Greenberg.

Poem   "For what as easy"   New Signatures (1932), rev. 1945.

   177 Duncan, Chester. "To You Simply", MS 1943, Five
        Songs (MS 1940-72). Song: ms solo, pf. The
        complete collection also requires s, a, bar soli.

Poem   "Lay your sleeping head, my love"   New Writing
   (Spring 1937), rev. 1958

   178 Drakeford, Richard. "Lullaby," Four Songs, MS.
        Song: bar solo, pf.

   179 Hyde, Lewis. "Lay your...", MS 1951. Song: solo v.,
        pf.

Poem   "Now the leaves are falling fast"   New Statesman and
   Nation (Mar. 1936); incl. as "Autumn Song" in W.H. Auden:
   A Selection by the author (1958); rev. 1968

Auden, W.H. continued

180 Britten, Benjamin. <u>On This Island</u>, L: WR, 1938.
Cyc.: high v., pf. Score contains Fr. transl. by
Maurice Pourchet.

181 Hyde, Lewis. "Now the leaves...", MS 1951. Song:
solo v., pf.

Poem "Our hunting fathers told the story" <u>Listener</u> (May
1934)

182 Britten, Benjamin. <u>Our Hunting Fathers</u>, L: BH, 1936.
Symph. cyc.: s solo, orch. Epilogue sets lines
beginning: "Our hunting fathers". The text for
the complete cyc. was devised by Auden employing
various sources.

<u>Praises of God, The</u> "How foolish the man" Transl. of anon.
Irish text. Not publ. sep.

183 Barber, Samuel. <u>Hermit Songs</u>, NY: GS, 1954. Song:
solo v., pf. Also avail. for satb, pf.

Pur See: "This lunar beauty"

Quarry, The See: Ballad

<u>Rake's Progress, The</u> Libr. in coll. with Chester Kallman,
after Hogarth. Not publ. sep.

184 Stravinsky, Igor. L: BH, 1949. Opera: s, 2 ms, 2 t,
bar, 2 b soli, chorus, orch. Vocal score by
Leopold Spinner. Score contains German transl. by
Fritz Schröder.

Refugee Blues "Say this city has" <u>New Yorker</u> (Apr. 1939)

185 Lutyens, Elisabeth. L: OP, 1942. Song: bar solo, pf.

Rocking-Horse Winner, The (RS) In coll. with James Stern,
after D.H. Lawrence (Unpubl.; written 1940)

26

Auden, W.H. continued

186 Britten, Benjamin. MS, prod. CBS 1941. Incidental
     music.

Roman Wall Blues   "Over the heather"   Another Time (1940)
Originally a part of Auden's radio script entitled "Hadrian's Wall: An Historial Survey"

187 Dickinson, Peter. "Over the...", Three Comic Songs,
     MS 1960. Cyc.: high male v., pf.

188 Harvey, Alex. MS ca. 1969. Song: [v., pf.?]. Issued
     on Fontana recordings #TR 1063 and #STL 5334.

189 Hyde, Lewis. "Over the...", MS 1951. Song: solo v.,
     pf.

"Say this city has ten million souls"   See: Refugee Blues

Seascape   See: Seaside

Seaside   "Look, stranger"   Listener (Dec. 1935), rev. 1936,
rev. 1958, rev. 1966

     190* Britten, Benjamin. "Seascape," On This Island, L:
          WR, 1938. Cyc.: high v., pf. Score contains Fr.
          transl. by Maurice Pourchet.

     191 Burtch, Mervyn. "Seascape", MS. Song: ttbb, pf. or
          sab, pf.

     192 Dickinson, Peter. "Look Stranger", Four W.H. Auden
          Songs, MS 1956. Cyc.: high female v., pf.

     193 Pinkham, Daniel. "Look, stranger...", Three Lyric
          Scenes, B: Row, 1949. Song: med. v., str. qrt.,
          or med. v., str. orch.

     194 Small, N.C.C. "Look, stranger...", MS 1954, avail.
          Victoria University of Wellington. Song: chorus,
          orch.

     195 Stevens, James. "Look Stranger at this Island now",
          MS 1949. Song: solo v., pf.

27

Auden, W.H. continued

"Seen when night is silent"   The Dog Beneath the Skin
    (1935), rev. same year, rev. 1966

    196   Hyde, Lewis. MS 1951. Song: solo v., pf.

    197   Murrill, Herbert. See: Dog Beneath the Skin, The.

Shield of Achilles, The   "She looked over his shoulder"
    Poetry (Oct. 1952)

    198   Bargielski, Zbigniew. MS 1971, avail. PMC. Song:
          a solo, b. cl. Polish title: "Tarcza Achillesa",
          transl. by Paweł Mayewski.

    199   Kelly, Bryan. L: N, 1967. Song: t solo, stgs.,
          timp., 3 perc.

"Silly fool, the silly fool, The"   Poems (1930), rev. 1945

    200   Dickinson, Peter. "Happy Ending", Three Comic Songs,
          MS 1960. Song: high male v., pf.

    201   Duncan, Chester. "Happy Ending", MS 1947, Five
          Songs (MS 1940-72). Song: s or to solo, pf. The
          complete collection also requires ms, a, bar
          soli.

"Sing, Ariel, sing"   For the Time Being (1947) Incl. under
    the title "Invocation to Ariel" in W.H. Auden: A Selection
    by the author (1958)

    202   Rimmer, John F. "Invocation to Ariel", Three Songs
          by W.H. Auden, MS 1964, avail. University of
          Auckland. Song: solo v., pf.

"Sir, no man's enemy, forgiving all"   Poems (1930)

    203   Saffle, Michael B. "Petition", MS 1969. Song: [v.,
          pf.?].

"Some say that love's a little boy"   See: O Tell Me the
    Truth About Love

Auden, W.H. continued

Song "As I walked out one evening"   New Statesman and
   Nation (Jan. 1938)

   204 Bennett, Richard R. "One Evening", MS ca. 1968.
         Song: t solo, gtr. Issued on Jupiter recording
         #JUR OA10 entitled The Jupiter Book of Contempor-
         ary Ballads.

   205 Gibbs, Geoffrey D. "As I walked...", MS. Song: low
         v., pf.

   206 Lutyens, Elisabeth. "As I walked...", L: OP, 1942.
         Song: solo v., pf.

Song "Let the florid music praise"   Look, Stranger!
   (1936), rev. 1966

   207 Britten, Benjamin. "Let the florid...", On This
         Island, L: WR, 1938. Cyc.: high v., pf. Score
         contains Fr. transl. by Maurice Pourchet.

   208 Pinkham, Daniel. "Let the florid...", Three Lyric
         Scenes, B: Row, 1949. Song: med. v., str. qrt.
         or med. v., str. orch.

Song "Seen when night is silent"   See: "Seen when night
   is silent"

Song "Warm are the still and lucky miles"   Another Time
   (1940)

   209 Senator, Ronald. "Warm are...", Summer Soon is Past,
         in prep. for publ. Song: satb, a cap.

Song for St. Cecilia's Day   See: Three Songs for St.
   Cecilia's Day

Song for the New Year   "It's farewell to the drawing-room's"
   Listener (Feb. 1937), rev. 1945, rev. 1966

   210 Britten, Benjamin. Ballad of Heroes, L: WR, 1939.
         Ballad: t or s solo, chorus (largely unison),
         orch.

Song of the Ogres   "Little fellow, you're amusing"   Two Songs (1968)

   211   Routh, Francis. Three Short Songs, MS 1973. Song: ms solo, pf.

Song of the Soldier Before the Inn   "Drink man, quick!, A" Delos (1968) as part of "Songs from Mutter Courage", transl. from Berthold Brecht, rev. 1969

   212   Routh, Francis. Three Short Songs, MS 1973. Song: ms solo, pf.

"Stop all the clocks, cut off the telephone"   The Ascent of F6 (1936), rev. 1940

   213   Britten, Benjamin. See: Ascent of F6, The.

   214   Britten, Benjamin. "Funeral Blues", Four Cabaret Songs for Hedli Anderson, MS 1938. Song: [v., pf.?].

   215   Duncan, Chester. See: Ascent of F6, The.

   216* Rorem, Ned. Poems of Love and the Rain, NY: BH, 1965. Cyc.: ms solo, pf. 2 settings of "Stop all the clocks...".

   217   Southam, T. Wallace. Poetry Set in Jazz, L: RMC, 1966. Song: v., pf.

Summer Night   "Out on the lawn"   Listener (Mar. 1934), rev. 1936, rev. 1945, rev. 1966

   218   Britten, Benjamin. "Out on the Lawn", Spring Symphony, L: BH, 1949. Choral symph.: s, a, t soli, satb, boys' choir, orch.

Summer Night, A   See: Summer Night

Summer Night 1933, A   See: Summer Night

Auden, W.H. continued

"That night when joy began"   Twentieth Century (Nov. 1933)
    as one of "Two Poems"

    219 Hyde, Lewis. MS 1951. Song: solo v., pf.

This Loved One   See: "Before this loved one"

"This lunar beauty"   Poems (1930), rev. 1945, rev. 1950,
    rev. 1958

    220 Hyde, Lewis. "Like a Dream", MS 1959. Song: solo v.,
         pf.

    221 Rimmer, John F. Three Songs by W.H. Auden, MS 1964,
         avail. University of Auckland. Song: solo v., pf.

This One   See: "Before this loved one"

Three Songs for St. Cecilia's Day   "In a garden shady"
    Harper's Bazaar (Dec. 1941), rev. 1945, rev. 1966

    222 Britten, Benjamin. "Hymn to St. Cecilia", L: WR,
         1942; new edn. publ. L: BH, 1967. Hymn: soli,
         ssatb, a cap.

    223 Gibbs, Geoffrey D. "I Cannot Grow," MS. Song: med.
         to low v., pf. Setting of poem's 2nd section.

    224 Graves, William. "Song for St. Cecilia's Day", NY:
         CF (hire). Song: solo v., str. qrt., cl., pf.

    225 Hyde, Lewis. "I cannot grow", MS 1951. Song: solo
         v., pf. Setting of poem's 2nd section.

    226 Warren, Raymond. "A Song for St. Cecilia's Day",
         Belfast: QUP, 1967. Cta.: t solo, fl., vla., gtr.

To You Simply   See: Poem "For what as easy"

Traveller, The   "Holding the distance up before his face"
    New Statesman and Nation (Aug. 1938)

31

227 Hyde, Lewis. MS 1952. Song: solo v., pf.

Twelve, The "Without arms or charms of culture" 1st publ.
with Walton's music; publ. sep. in Christian_Century (Oct.
1969)

228 Walton, William. L: OUP, 1966. Anthem: satb, orᴊ.
Also avail. for satb, orch.

"Underneath the [an] abject willow" Look,_Stranᴊer! (1936),
rev. 1945

229 Britten, Penjamin. "Underneath the...", Two_Ballads,
L: BH, 1937. Ballad: s duet, pf.

230 Cohn, James M. "Underneath an...", Three_Phases_of
Love, MS 1969. Setting for satb, a cap.

231 Drakeford, Richard. "Underneath an...," Four_Songs,
MS. Song: bar solo, pf.

232 Southam, T. Wallace. "Underneath the...", Poetry_Set
in_Jazz, L: RMC, 1966. Song: v., pf.

United Nations Hymn See: Hymn to the United Nations

Unknown Citizen, The "He was found by the Bureau of
Statistics to be" Listener (Aug. 1939), rev. 1940

233 Cohen, David. MS. Setting for satb, a cap.

US (DS) (Unpubl.; written 1968)

234 Amram, David. MS, prod. U.S. Dept. of Commerce. Incidental music.

"Warm are the still and lucky miles" See: Song "Warm are
the still and lucky miles"

Way To The Sea, The (DS) (Unpubl.; written 1937)

Auden, W.H. continued

235 Britten, Benjamin. MS, prod. for Strand Film Co.
     Incidental music.

We're Late   See: "Clocks cannot Tell our Time of day"

"What's in your mind, my dove, my coney"   Twentieth Century
(Nov. 1933) as one of "Two Poems"

   236 Berkeley, Lennox. Five Poems, L: JWC, 1960. Song:
        med. v., pf.

   237 Dickinson, Peter. Four W.H. Auden Songs, MS 1955.
        Cyc.: high female v., pf.

Miscellanea

   238 Greenberg, Noah and William Smoldon, eds. "The Play
        of Herod", MS, perf. NY 1963, NY: OUP. Musical
        drama. Text by Auden, after a Medieval Christmas
        play. Music adapt. by Greenberg and Smoldon.

   239 Nabokov, Nicolas. "Love's Labor's Lost", Berlin:
        B&B, 1972. Opera: 3 s, s or c-t, ms, t, 3 bar, b
        soli, orch. Libr. by Auden and Chester Kallman,
        after Shakespeare. German title: "Verlor'ne
        Liebesmüh", transl. by Claus H. Henneberg.

   240 Smoldon, William and Noah Greenberg, eds. See entry
        #238.

AUSTIN, Altred   1835-1913

Flodden Field   (DR)   (1903)

   241 Pitt, Percy. MS pre-1932. Incidental music.

Love's Blindness   "How do I know that Love is blind"   In
Soliloquies in Song (1882)

                         33

242   Hart, Fritz. Three Sonnets for Voice and Pianoforte,
      MS 1935, avail. State Library of Victoria, Mel-
      bourne. Song: v., pf.

Love's Wisdom   "Now on the summit of Love's topmost peak"
In Soliloquies in Song (1882)

243   Hart, Fritz. Three Sonnets for Voice and Pianoforte,
      MS 1935, avail. State Library of Victoria, Mel-
      bourne. Song: v., pf.

Sleepless Night, A   "Within the hollow silence of the night"
In Soliloquies in Song (1882)

244   Hart, Fritz. Three Sonnets for Voice and Pianoforte,
      MS 1935, avail. State Library of Victoria, Mel-
      bourne. Song: v., pf.

Wild Rose, A   "First wild rose in wayside hedge, The"   In
English Lyrics, 4th edn. (1896)

245   Mallinson, Albert. Oakville: FH, 1904. Song: v., pf.

BALDWIN, Michael   1930-

Housewife, The   "My love could come home early"   In Buried
God (1973)

246   Southam, T. Wallace. Poetry Set in Jazz, L: RMC,
      1966. Song: v., pf.

Baring, Maurice

BARING, Maurice   1874-1945

Blue Harlequin, The   (DR)   In Diminutive Dramas (1919)

   247 Edmunds, Christopher. MS. Opera: s, t, b soli,
        actor, orch.

Catherine Parr   (DR)   In Diminutive Dramas (1919)

   248 Collins, Anthony. MS pre-1954. Opera.

Clown, The   "There was once a poor clown all dressed in
   white"   In Collected Poems (1925)

   249 Smyth, Ethel. Three Songs, MS 1913. Song: v., orch.

Dusk   (DR)   In Collected Poems (1925)

   250 Edmunds, Christopher. MS. Opera. Withdrawn by the
        composer for revision.

Fatal Rubber, The   (DR)   In Diminutive Dramas (1919)

   251 Edmunds, Christopher. MS. Opera: s, a, t, bar soli,
        orch.

Miscellanea

   252 Fox, J. Bertram. "A Ballad", MS 1921. Song: [v.,
        pf.?].

   253 Smyth, Ethel. "Fête Galante", Wien: UE, 1923. Opera.
        Poetic version by Edward Shanks.

35

Barker, George

BARKER, George Granville   1913-

Ballad of Wild Children, The   "Down the long hall or night"
    In A_Vision_of_Beasts_and_Gods (1954) as one of "Justice
    at Midnight"

        254 Williamson, Malcolm. A_Vision_of_Beasts_and_Gods, L:
             BH, 1969. Cyc.: high v., pf.

Dedication   "Lean down, O loving hydra"   In A_Vision_of
    Beasts_and_Gods (1954)

        255 Williamson, Malcolm. A_Vision_of_Beasts_and_Gods, L:
             BH, 1969. Cyc.: high v., pf.

Epitaph for Many Young Men   "In that ordinary year of
    anxieties and rain"   In A_Vision_of_Beasts_and_Gods
    (1954)

        256 Williamson, Malcolm. A_Vision_of_Beasts_and_Gods, L:
             BH, 1969. Cyc.: high v., pf.

Love Letter   "I write this to you, my dear love"   In A
    Vision_of_Beasts_and_Gods (1954)

        257 Williamson, Malcolm. A_Vision_of_Beasts_and_Gods, L:
             BH, 1969. Cyc.: high v., pf.

Ode Against St. Cecilia's Day   "Rise, underground sleepers"
    In News_of_the_World (1950)

        258 Finzi, Gerald. "Ode on the rejection of St.
             Cecilia", To_a_Poet, L: BH, 1965. Song:
             low v., pf.

On the Death of Manolete   "You, king, die"   In A_Vision_of
    Beasts_and_Gods (1954)

        259 Williamson, Malcolm. A_Vision_of_Beasts_and_Gods, L:
             BH, 1969. Cyc.: high v., pf.

Barker, George continued

To a Child   "By the mad dead Moon"   In A Vision of Beasts
    and Gods (1954)

    260 Williamson, Malcolm. A Vision of Beasts and Gods, L:
         BH, 1969. Cyc.: high v., pf.

Miscellanea

    261 Demuth, Norman. "The Degradation of Guatemozin", MS
         ca. 1947. Incidental music.

    262 Duncan, Chester. "Saturday and Sunday", MS. Song:
         high v., pf. Also avail. for med. v., pf. Text
         begins: "I sat by the Shanandoah River".

BARRIE, James Matthew   1860-1937

Admirable Crichton, The   (DR)   (1914)

    263 Lee, David. "Our man Crichton", L: H&S, 1965.
         Musical. Lyrics by H. Kretzmer.

    264 Read, Gardner. MS 1955. Incidental music: ww. qnt.,
         pf.

Boy David, The   (DR)   (1938)

    265 Walton, William. MS, perf. Edinburgh, Nov. 1936.
         Incidental music.

Jane Annie   (Libr.) In coll. with Arthur Conan Doyle. 1st
    publ. 1893 with Ford's music.

    266 Ford, Ernest. L: C, 1893. Opera: soli, duets,
         chorus, orch.

Kiss for Cinderella, A   (DR)   (1920)

Barrie, J.M. continued

267 Engel, Lehman. MS pre-1954. Incidental music.

268 O'Neill, Norman. L: CR, 1925. Incidental music: pf.
     solo.

Little Minister, The   (NV)   (1891)

269 Tunbridge, Joseph in coll. with Jack Waller. "Wild
     Grows the Heather", L: C, 1957. Musical. Lyrics
     by Ralph Reader, adapt. by Hugh Ross Williamson.

270 Waller, Jack. See entry immediately preceding.

Little Minister, The   (DR)   (Priv. publ. 1898)

271 Mackenzie, Alexander. MS, prod. 1897. Incidental
     music [to accompany the 1st prod. of the play?].

Mary Rose   (DR)   (1924)

272 O'Neill, Norman. MS 1920. Incidental music [to the
     1st prod. of the play?]. Portions publ. L: S for
     orch. and for pf.

Pantaloon   (DR)   Half Hours (1914)

273 Willan, Healey. MS, perf. Tor. 1921. Incidental
     music: 2 pf.

Peter Pan   (DR)   (1928)

274 Beeler, Walter, arr. 'Peter Pan' Medley. NY: EHM,
     1956. Arr. for band only.

275 Bernstein, Leonard. NY: GS, 1950. [Musical]. Lyrics
     by the composer. Songs [for various vocal com-
     binations] also publ. sep.

276 Brydson, John. S. Croydon: L, 1947. Album of works
     for pf. solo.

Barrie, J.M. continued

277 Charlap, Mark in coll. with Jule Styne. MS, prod.
     NY, Oct. 1954. Musical. Lyrics by Carolyn Leigh;
     additional lyrics by Betty Comden and Adolph
     Green. Portions publ. NY: EHM, 1954 for soli,
     unsion v., pf.

278 Crook, John. L: P&R, 1905. Incidental music (with
     song settings). Productions (Coliseum, London)
     since 1972 have employed a new version by Grant
     Foster (see below).

279 Davies, H. Walford. 'Peter Pan' Suite, MS ca. 1909.
     Str. qrt. only.

280 Foster, Grant. MS 1972. Incidental music: soli,
     unison v., orch. (subsequently reduced). This
     new version replaced John Crook's incidental
     music (see above) employed for productions at the
     Coliseum, London.

281 George, Graham. MS 1948. Ballet music.

282 Henriques, Fini. MS 1930. Opera. Danish libr. by
     Aage Barfoed.

283 Shauer, Mel. NY: Empire, 1924. Song (in film score,
     prod. Paramount under the direction of Herbert
     Brenon): v., pf.

284 Styne, Jule in coll. with Mark Charlap. See entry
     #277.

285 Toch, Ernest. Mz.: S, 1954. Orch. only.

286 Trevalsa, Joan. Peter Pan Song Cycle, L: BH, 1910.
     Cyc.: [v., pf.]. Words by Marry Farrah, based on
     Barrie's work.

Quality Street   (DP)   (1913)

287 O'Neill, Norman. MS 1921. Incidental music. Portions
     arr. for pf.; arr. publ. L: S.

Rosy Rapture   (DP)   (MS, prod. 1915; unpubl.)

39

Barrie, J.M. continued

288* Crook, John in coll. with Herman Darewski and Jerome
    Kern. "Rosy Rapture, The Pride of the Beauty
    Chorus", MS, prod. Mar. 1915. "Burlesque". Lyrics
    by F.W. Mark.

289 Darewski, Herman. See entry immediately preceding.

290 Kern, Jerome. See entry #288.

Truth about the Russian Dancers, The   (DR)   (MS, prod.
    1920; unpubl.)

291 Bax, Arnold. MS 1920. Incidental music [to the 1st
    prod. of the play?]. Score rev. 1926. Advertised
    to be publ. L: MM [1920's], but remains unpubl.

What Every Woman Knows   (DR)   (1918)

292 Roy, William. "Maggie", MS, prod. NY, Feb. 1953.
    [Musical]. Lyrics by the composer, based on
    Barrie's play.

Miscellanea

293 Poulenc, Francis. "La Nuit de la Saint-Jean", MS
    ca. 1944. Incidental music.

BAX, Clifford*   1886-1962

Hymn*   "Turn back, O man, forswear thy foolish ways"   In
    Farewell My Muse (1932)

294 Gilbert, Norman. "Turn back, O man", L: OUP, 1959.
    Hymn: satb, org.

295 Holst, Gustav. "Turn back O Man", L: S&B, 1919;
     [Three] Festival Choruses, L: S&B, 1919, 1924.
     Setting for mixed v., orch. Arr. by Holst for
     accompaniment of military band; arr. avail. L:
     S&B (hire). Arr. for male voices by Channing
     Lefebure; arr. publ. NY: GX, 1953. Arr. for con-
     cert band by Samuel Hall; this arr. publ. NY: GX,
     1961. The melody of the work is based on the "old
     124th Psalm" from the Genevan Psalter.

296 Ward, Robert. Earth Shall Be Fair, NY: HP, 1960.
     Cta.: s solo, satb, youth choir (satb), org. (or
     orch.).

Midsummer Madness   (DR)   (MS 1923; portions publ. in
Farewell My Muse [1932])

     297 Gibbs, C. Armstrong. L: Curwen, 1924. Musical play:
          mixed v. (soli, duets, trios), orch.

Mr. Pepys   (DR)   (MS 1924; portions publ. in Farewell My
Muse [1932])

     298 Shaw, Martin. L: CR, 1926. [Ballad] opera: satb, pf.
          Also avail. for satb, orch.

Old Song   "Blow, northern wind"   In Farewell My Muse (1932)
Adapt. from early Engl.

     299 Bax, Arnold. "Blow...", MS [1926?]. Song: v., pf.

Waterloo Leave   (DR)   (MS 1923; portions publ. in Farewell
My Muse [1932])

     300 Shaw, Martin. MS 1925. [Ballad] opera.

Youth   "Within a primrose wood I lay content"   In Poems
Dramatic & Lyrical (1911)

     301 Bax, Arnold. L: MM, 1920, copyright assigned L: C,
          1943. Song: v., pf.

Bax, Clifford continued

Miscellanea

302 Bax, Arnold. "Aspiration", L: MM, 1921. Song: v., pf. Also arr. for v., pf. trio. Text (adapt. by Clifford Bax from Richard Dehmel) begins: "Give me just your hand.

303 Bax, Arnold. "Golden Eagle", MS 1945. Incidental music: bar solo, orch.

304 Bax, Arnold. "I will dream, I will dream, in my Boat", MS 1900. Song: v., pf.

305 Bax, Arnold. "Midsummer", MS 1918. Song: v., pf.

306 Bax, Arnold. "What is it like to be young and fair?", L: C, 1953. Setting for ssaat, a cap. Bax's contribution to A Garland for the Queen.

307 Bridgewater, Leslie. "The Highwayman's Song", L: Arcadia, pre-1951 in The Beaux' Stratagem. Song: [in musical]: [v., pf.?]. Text by Bax and John Clements.

308 Holst, Gustav. "A Festival Chime", L: S&B, 1919; [Three] Festival Choruses, L: S&B, 1919, 1924. Setting for mixed v., orch. Arr. by Holst for accompaniment of military band; arr. avail. L: S&B (hire). Arr. for concert band by Samuel Hall; this arr. publ. NY: GX, 1961. The melody of the work is based on the Welsh hymn tune "St. Denio".

309 Holst, Gustav, arr. Old Airs and Glees, L: S&B, 1916. Songs: ssa, a cap. Original music by Arne, Baildon, Martini, et al. Texts by Bax entitled: "A measure to pleasure your leisure", "Beside a lake", "Cherry-Stones", "Nothing fairer have I seen", "Once in England's age of old". Four additional arrangements [with texts by Bax] are still in MS; these are entitled: "Come forth you ladies", "Fallen Summer", "In the Bay", "The Picnic".

310 Holst, Gustav. "The Sneezing Charm", MS 1918. Incidental music: orch. (with ms solo). The music was later used as a foundation for Holst's "The Perfect Fool".

Bax, Clifford continued

311   Holst, Gustav. "The Wandering Scholar" [originally
       entitled "The Tale of the Wandering Scholar"],
       ed. by Benjamin Britten and Imogen Holst, L: F,
       1968. Ch. opera: s, t, bar, b soli, fl., pic.,
       ob., eng. hn., 2 cl., 2 bsn., 2 hn., stgs. Libr.
       by Bax, founded on an incident in Helen Waddell's
       The Wandering Scholars.

312   Naylor, Bernard. "The Cloak (A Modern Mystery)", MS
       1967. Opera: s, ms soli, sp., str. qrt. Opera
       from Bax's one-act play entitled "The Cloak".

313   Reynolds, Alfred. Five Centuries of Love, L: Elkin,
       1946. Cyc.: bar solo, pf. Songs entitled: "1570-
       The Yeoman", "1660-The Courtier", "1770-The
       Cynic", "1860-The Emigrant", "1910-The Motorist".

314   Shaw, Martin. "The Melodies You Sing", L: CR, 1933.
       Song: v., pf.

315   Shaw, Martin. "The Wind and the Sea", MS 1933, L:
       CR. Song: v., pf.

316   Woodgate, Leslie, arr. "Bernice", L: OUP, pre-1946
       in Oxford Choral Songs from the Old Masters.
       Song: unison v., opt. ww., stgs. Arr. for ssa.
       Text begins: "Come, see where Golden-hearted
       Spring". Text adapt. to a melody by George
       Frideric Handel.

BEARDSLEY, Aubrey Vincent   1872-1898

Catullus: Carmen CI   "By ways remote and distant waters
    sped"   In Under the Hill (1904) Transl. from Catullus

    317   Rorem, Ned. "Catullus: On the Burial of His
           Brother", NY: BH, 1969. Song: med. v., pf.

43

Beckett, Samuel

BECKETT, Samuel Barclay*   1906-

Acte sans Paroles   (DR)   Fin de partie, suivi de Acte sans
   Paroles (1957)

   318* Beckett, John. MS pre-1957. Play with music.

   319 Charpentier, Gabriel. MS 1962. Incidental music.

Cascando   (RP)   (1963)

   320* Mihalovici, Marcel. P: Heugel, 1963 (hire). Radio
       play for music and voice.

Comédie   (DR)   Lettres Nouvelles (June-Aug. 1964)

   321 Haubenstock-Ramati, Roman. MS 1967, L: UE. Play with
       music: 2 female sp., 1 male sp., chorus ad lib.,
       3 perc. players.

Dernière Bande, La   (DR)   Lettres Nouvelles (Mar. 1959)

   322 Kopelent, Marek. See: Krapp's Last Tape.

   323 Mihalovici, Marcel. "Krapp" or "La Dernière Bande",
       P: Heugel, 1961. Opera: bar solo, pf. Score
       contains Engl. transl. by Beckett, and German
       transl. by Elmar Tophoven.

Dieppe   "Again the last ebb"   In Poems in English (1961)

   324 Christiansen, Henning. See: Dieppe "Encore le der-
       nier reflux".

   325 Douglas, James. Dieppe Poems, MS 1971, avail. SMA.
       Song: s or t solo, pf.

   326 Hopkins, Bill. See: Dieppe "Encore le dernier re-
       flux".

   327 Rands, Bernard. Serena, MS 1972, L: UE. Settings for
       singing actress, 2 mimes, 1 melody wind instr.,
       vcl., perc., elec. org.

Beckett, Samuel continued

Dieppe   "Encore le dernier reflux"   Temps Modernes (Nov.
1946)

    328 Christiansen, Henning. 3 Beckett-sange, Copenhagen:
        SUDM, 1967. Song: bar solo, cel., vln., hp.,
        vibra., perc. Fr. text.

    329 Douglas, James. See: Dieppe "Again the last ebb".

    330 Hopkins, Bill. "Encore...", Sensation, MS 1965. Song
        sequence: s solo, tpt., t. sax., hp., vla.

    331 Rands, Bernard. See: Dieppe "Again the last ebb".

"Elles viennent"   Temps Modernes (Nov. 1946)

    332 Christiansen, Henning. 3 Beckett-sange, Copenhagen:
        SUDM, 1967. Song: bar solo, cel., vln., hp.,
        vibra., perc. Fr. text.

    333 Hopkins, Bill. Sensation, MS 1965. Song sequence:
        s solo, tpt., t. sax., hp., vla.

Embers   (RP)   Evergreen Review (Nov.-Dec. 1959)

    334 Kopelent, Marek. "Krapp's Last Tape" and "Embers",
        MS 1966, avail. SČSKU. Incidental music for radio
        productions. Czech. title: "Krappova poslední
        nahrávka", transl. by Josef Kaušitz.

Endgame   (DR)   Endgame, Followed by Act Without Words
(1958)

    335 Winslow, Richard. MS, perf. Kingston, Rhode Island,
        Nov. 1974. [Opera].

From the Only Poet to a Shining Whore   "Rahab of the holy
battlements"   Whoroscope (1930)

    336 Crowder, Henry. Henry-Music, P: Hours Press, 1930.
        Song: v., pf.

How It Is   (NV)   (1964)

Beckett, Samuel continued

337 Linjama, Jouko. MS 1964-68. Oratorio: bar solo, male
     sextet, orch., 3 tapes. Employs fragments from
     the novel. Finnish title: "Millaista on", transl.
     by Juha Mannerkorpi.

"I would like my love to die"   In Poems in English (1961)

338 Christiansen, Henning. See: "Je voudrais que mon
     amour meure".

339 Douglas, James. Dieppe Poems, MS 1971, avail. SMA.
     Song: s or t solo, pf.

340 Hopkins, Bill. See: "Je voudrais que mon amour
     meure".

341 Rands, Bernard. Serena, MS 1972, L: UE. Settings for
     singing actress, 2 mimes, 1 melody wind instr.,
     vcl., perc., elec. org.

"Je suis ce cours de sable qui glisse"   Transition Forty-
Eight (June 1948)

342 Douglas, James. See: "My way is in the sand flow-
     ing".

343 Hopkins, Bill. Sensation, MS 1965. Song sequence:
     s solo, tpt., t. sax., hp., vla.

344 Rands, Bernard. See: "My way is in the sand flow-
     ing".

"Je voudrais que mon amour meure"   Transition Forty-Eight
(June 1948)

345 Christiansen, Henning. 3 Beckett-sange, Copenhagen:
     SUDM, 1967. Song: bar solo, cel., vln., hp.,
     vibra., perc. Fr. text.

346 Douglas, James. See: "I would like my love to die".

347 Hopkins, Bill. Sensation, MS 1965. Song sequence:
     s solo, tpt., t. sax., hp., vla.

348 Rands, Bernard. See: "I would like my love to die".

Beckett, Samuel continued

Krapp's Last Tape   (DR)   Evergreen Review (Summer 1958)

    349 Kopelent, Marek. "Krapp's Last Tape" and "Embers",
        MS 1966, avail. SČSKU. Incidental music for radio
        productions. Czech. title: "Krappova poslední
        nahrávka", transl. by Josef Kaušitz.

    350 Mihalovici, Marcel. See: Dernière Bande, La.

Lessness   (NV)   (1967)

    351* Hoyland, D. Victor. "Piaf", L: UE (hire). "Tab-
        leaux": ms solo, 2 perc. players. Composition
        influenced by the novel.

"My way is in the sand flowing"   In Poems in English (1961)

    352 Douglas, James. Dieppe Poems, MS 1971, avail. SMA.
        Song: s or t solo, pf.

    353 Hopkins, Bill. See: "Je suis ce cours de sable qui
        glisse".

    354 Rands, Bernard. Serena, MS 1972, L: UE. Settings for
        singing actress, 2 mimes, 1 melody wind instr.,
        vcl., perc., elec. org.

Unnamable, The   (NV)   (1958)

    355 Rands, Bernard. Wildtrack 2, MS 1972, L: UE. Work
        for fl., a. fl., cl., b. cl., t. sax., bsn., 2
        hrn., 2 tpt., 2 trbn., elec. org., vibra., mrmb.,
        3 perc., stgs. Makes use of passages beginning:
        "...none will ever know what I am...", "...to
        hell with silence...", "the trouble is I forget
        how it goes on", "That's why there are all these
        little silences...", "When they go, when they go
        silent...", "I'll go silent, for want of air...",
        "I want it to go silent...".

Waiting for Godot   (DR)   (1953)

47

Beckett, Samuel continued

356 Blatný, Pavel. MS 1970, avail. SČSKU. Incidental
     music. Czech. title: "Čekání na Godota", transl.
     by Jaromír Vavroš.

357 Haubenstock-Ramati, Roman. "Credentials" or "Think,
     Think Lucky", MS 1960, L: UE. Setting for v.,
     cl., trbn., vln., pf., cel., vibra., bells, 2
     perc. players.

358 Wilkinson, Marc. "Voices", L: UE, 1960. Setting for
     a solo, 2 cl., vcl. Text from 2nd act of the
     play.

"What would I do without this world faceless incurious"   In
Poems in English (1961)

359 Douglas, James. Dieppe Poems, MS 1971, avail. SMA.
     Song: s or t solo, pf.

360 Rands, Bernard. Serena, MS 1972, L: UE. Settings for
     singing actress, 2 mimes, 1 melody wind instr.,
     vcl., perc., elec. org.

Words and Music   (RP)   Evergreen Review (Nov.-Dec. 1962)

361* Beckett, John. MS, prod. BBC, 13 Nov. 1962. Play
     with music.

362 Patten, James. Songs of Farewell, MS. Cyc.: a solo,
     3 fl., 2 ob., 3 cl., 2 tpt., euph. (or bsn.),
     hp., pf., perc., stgs. Incl. setting of passage
     beginning: "Then down a little way".

Miscellanea

363 Patten, James. Songs of Farewell, MS. Cyc.: a solo,
     3 fl., 2 ob., 3 cl., 2 tpt., euph. (or bsn.),
     hp., pf., perc., stgs. Incl. texts by Beckett
     beginning: "It's a winter's night, where I was,
     where I'm going", "That's all I remember this
     evening".

Beerbohm, Max

BEERBOHM, Max   1872-1956

Happy Hypocrite, The   (NV)   Yellow Book (Oct. 1896)

364 Addinsell, Richard. MS pre-1954, L: KP. Incidental
     music for play. Text adapt. by Clemence Dane.

365 Elwell, Herbert. MS 1925. Ballet music. Arr. as
     orch. ste.; arr. publ. B: Birchard, 1925.

366 Ghedini, Giorgio. Mi.: R, 1956. Opera. Ital. title:
     "L'Ipocrita felice". Libr. by Franco Antonicelli.

367 Rawsthorne, Alan. MS 1940. Incidental music for
     radio play.

Zuleika Dobson   (NV)   (1911)

368 Tranchell, Peter. "Zuleika", MS pre-1962. Musical
     play, based on Beerbohm's work.

BEHAN, Brendan   1923-1964

Richard's Cork Leg   (DR)   (1973)

369* Dubliners, The, arr. MS, prod. Dublin, Sept. 1972.
     Incidental music arr. and scored by the Dub-
     liners.

Belloc, Hilaire

BELLOC, (Joseph) Hilaire Pierre   1870-1953

Auvergnat   "There was a man was half a crown"   In Verses
and Sonnets (1896)

   370   Abady, H. Temple. "He broke his heart in Clermont
       town", L: Curwen, 1926. Song: solo v., pf.

   371   Bliss, Arthur. L: N, 1944. Song: solo v., pf.

   372   Fleming, Robert. MS 1948, avail. CMC. Song: v., pf.

   373   Goodhart, A.M. "The Bells of Clermont Town", L: BH,
       pre-1957. Song: v., pf.

   374   Potter, A.J. Three Songs of Hilaire Belloc, Dublin:
       RTE, 1952. Song: satb, a cap.

Ballade to Our Lady of Czestochowa   "Lady and Queen and
   Mystery manifold"   In Sonnets and Verse (1923)

   375   Milner, Anthony. "Dusk", Our Lady's Hours, L: N,
       1959. Cyc.: s or t solo, pf.

   376   Taylor, M.L. "Hymn to Our Lady", L: PX, 1966. Song:
       s solo, chorus, pf. or s solo, chorus, org.

Big Baboon, The   "Big Baboon is found upon, The"   The Bad
   Child's Book of Beasts (1896)

   377   Kraft, William. "Four Beasts", Three Humorous Songs,
       MS, NY: MCA (hire). Song: s or ms solo, pf.

   378   Mannes, Leopold. NY: HB, 1928 in New Songs for New
       Voices. Song: v., pf.

   379   Peel, Graham. The Bad Child's Songs about Beasts, L:
       BH, 1908. Song: v., pf.

   380   Scherman, Thomas. NY: HB, 1928 in New Songs for New
       Voices. Song: v., pf.

Birds, The   "When Jesus Christ was four years old"   In
   Verses (1910)

Belloc, Hilaire continued

381 Britten, Benjamin. L: BH (WR edn.), 1935. Song:
     [med.] solo v., pf.

382 Buck, Vera. L: Elkin, 1932. Song: solo v., pf.

383 Buczynski, Walter. Cycle_of_Three_Songs, priv. publ.
     1954. Cyc.: high v., pf.

384 Bush, Geoffrey. A_Christmas_Cantata, L: N, 1948.
     Carol (in cta.): satb, a cap. Complete cta. also
     requires stgs., ob. obbl. Also publ. as sep.
     carol.

385 Davies, H. Walford. Twenty-One_Songs, L: N, 1931.
     Song: high v., pf.

386 Duarte, John. Five_Quiet_Songs, Ancona: Bèrben,
     1971. Cyc.: high v., classical gtr.

387 Fagge, Arthur. L: BH, pre-1940. Song: v., pf.

388 Fearing, John. "When Jesus...", Vancouver: Western,
     1966. Song: med. v., pf. or med. v., org.

389 Gilbert, Norman. L: N, 1964. Song: unison v., solo
     descant rec., pf. or unison v., solo ob., pf.

390 Gurney, Ivor. MS n.d. Song: [solo v., pf.].

391 Gwyther, Geoffrey. L: Poetry Bookshop, n.d. Song:
     v., pf.

392 James, Phyllis M. L: A, pre-1940. Song: [v., pf.?].

393 Murray, Dom Gregory. L: OUP, 1939. Song: satb, a
     cap.

394 Pasfield, W.R. L: C, 1962. Carol: unison v. with
     opt. descant, [pf.].

395 Persichetti, Vincent. "Thou Child So Wise", Hilaire
     Belloc_Songs, Ph.: EV, 1965. Song: med. v., pf.

396 Rathbone, George. "When Christ was Four Years Old",
     L: N, 1924. Song: sss, a cap.

397 Roff, Joseph. "Toys of Gold", NY: CF, 1959. Song:
     sa, pf. or unison v., pf.

51

Belloc, Hilaire continued

398 Simpson, H. Haley. L: Curwen, 1922. Song: solo v.,
     pf.

399 Sweetman, Paul. Waterloo: Waterloo, 1961. Song: ssa,
     pf.

400 Thiman, Eric. L: N, pre-1940. Song: [v., pf.].

401 Walters, Leslie. L: WK, 1935 (avail. only from the
     composer). Song: med. v., pf.

402 Warlock, Peter. L: JW, 1927. Song: unison boys' v.,
     pf. Also publ. for solo v., pf.

Bison, The "Bison is vain, and (I write it with pain), The"
More Beasts for Worse Children (1897)

403 Skolnik, Walter. Three Zoological Studies, Bryn
     Mawr: EV, 1970. Song: satb, pf., opt. db.

Californy Song, The   See: "I am sailing for America"

Charles Augustus Fortescue who always did what was right, and
so accumulated an immense fortune "Nicest child I ever
knew, The" Cautionary Tales for Children (1907)

404 Bullard, Alan. "Charles Augustus Fortescue", Seven-
     oaks: N, 1972. Song: unison v., pf. or sa, pf.

405 Lehmann, Liza. "Charles Augustus Fortescue", Four
     Cautionary Tales and a Moral, L: C, 1909. Song:
     ms, bar duet, pf. Portions of the collection
     require ms solo and bar solo.

Courtesy "Of Courtesy, it is much less" In Verses (1910)

406 Teed, Roy. So Blest a Day, MS ca. 1960. Song (in
     cta.): bar solo, orch. or bar solo, pf. Trans-
     posed vers. for t solo, pf. is also avail.
     Complete cta. requires soli, chorus, orch.

Cuckoo! "In woods so long time bare" In Verses and Sonnets (1896)

Belloc, Hilaire continued

407 James, Phyllis M. L: A, 1947. Song: v., pf.

Dedicatory Ode   "I mean to write with all my strength"   In
Verses (1910)

    408 Field, Robin. "In the Western Wolds", Two Songs, MS
         1965. Song: high v., pf. Setting of lines beginn-
         ing: "The quiet evening kept her tryst".

Dodo, The "Dodo used to walk around, The"   The Bad Child's
Book of Beasts (1896)

    409 Peel, Graham. The Bad Child's Songs about Beasts, L:
         BH, 1908. Song: v., pf.

    410 Skolnik, Walter. Three Zoological Studies, Bryn
         Mawr: EV, 1970. Song: satb, pf., opt. db.

Down Channel   "Channel pours out on the Ebb in a river
gigantic, The"   In Sonnets and Verse (1938)

    411 Duncan, Chester. MS 1973. Song: v., pf.

Drinking Song On the Excellence of Burgundy Wine   "My jolly
fat host"   In Verses (1910)

    412 Teed, Roy. MS ca. 1958. Song: bar solo, pf.

Dromedary, The   "Dromedary is a cheerful bird, The"   The
Bad Child's Book of Beasts (1896)

    413 Berger, Jean. A Child's Book of Beasts, Glen Rock:
         JF, pre-1968. Song: sa, pf.

Early Morning, The   "Moon on the one hand, the dawn on the
other, The"   In Verses and Sonnets (1896)

    414 Garlick, Antony. Eleven Canzonets, Cin.: Westwood,
         1967. Canzonet: 2 pt. chorus of equal v., a cap.

    415 Peel, Graham. The Country Lover, L: C, 1910. Song:
         [solo v., pf.].

53

Elephant, The   "When people call this beast to mind"   The Bad Child's Book of Beasts (1896)

    416   Faulkner, David. Two Songs for Children, L: C, 1963. Song: unison v., pf.

    417   Gehrkens, Karl. NY: HH&E, 1933 in New Universal School Music Series: My First Song Book. Song: v., unacc.

False Heart, The   "I said to Heart"   In Verses (1910)

    418   Fontrier, Gabriel. Three Choruses to Texts by Hilaire Belloc, NY: M, 1965. Song: satb, a cap.

Farewell to Juliet   "How shall I round the ending of a story"   The Verse of Hilaire Belloc (1954)

    419   Duncan, Chester. MS 1973. Song: v., pf.

Fatigue   "I'm tired of Love"   In Sonnets and Verse (1923)

    420   Potter, A.J. "On Fatigue", Ten Epigrams by Hilaire Belloc, Dublin: NIRC, 1972. Cta.: satb, a cap.

February   "Winter Moon has such a quiet car, The"   In Verses and Sonnets (1896) as one of "Sonnets of the Twelve Months"

    421   Dodgson, Stephen. Three Winter Songs, L: C, 1974. Cyc.: s or t solo, ob. obbl., pf.

    422   Rose, Michael. Winter Music, L: N, 1967. Cta.: satb, pf. duet, perc. ad lib.

First Drinking Song, The   See: "On Sussex hills where I was bred"

Frog, The   "Be kind and tender to the Frog"   The Bad Child's Book of Beasts (1896)

Belloc, Hilaire continued

423 Berger, Jean. A_Child's_Book_of_Beasts, Glen Rock:
     JF, pre-1968. Song: sa, pf.

Ha'nacker Mill   "Sally is gone that was so kindly"   In
Sonnets_and_Verse (1923)

424 Brown, Hubert. L: Curwen, 1932. Song: solo v., pf.

425 Fontrier, Gabriel. Three_Choruses_to_Texts_by
     Hilaire_Belloc, NY: M, 1965. Song: satb, a cap.

426 Gurney, Ivor. A_First_Volume_of_Ten_Songs, L: OUP,
     1938. Song: solo v., pf.

427 Le Fleming, Christopher. Valley_of_Arun, L: N, 1962.
     Choral ste.: bar solo, satb, orch.

428 Noble, Harold. L: AH&C, 1947. Song: ttbb, [pf.?].

429 Pasfield, W.R. L: Elkin, 1964. Song: ttbb, a cap.

430 Warlock, Peter. Three_Belloc_Songs, L: OUP, 1927.
     Song: bar solo, pf.

"'He does not die' (I wrote) 'that can bequeath'"   The_Four
Men (1912), rev. 1954

431 Moule-Evans, David. "Duncton Hill", L: JW, ca. 1948.
     Song: satb, a cap.

"He does not die that can bequeath"   See: "'He does not die'
(I wrote) 'that can bequeath'"

Henry King who chewed bits of string, and was early cut off
in dreadful agonies   "Chief Defect of Henry King, The"
Cautionary_Tales_for_Children (1907)

432 Gilbert, Norman. "Henry King", L: N, 1964. Canon:
     equal v., pf.

433 Lehmann, Liza. "Henry King", Four_Cautionary_Tales
     and_a_Moral, L: C, 1909. Song: bar solo, pf.
     Portions of the collection require ms solo and
     ms, bar duet.

55

Belloc, Hilaire continued

Hippopotamus, The   "I shoot the Hippopotamus"   The Bad
    Child's Book of Beasts (1896)

    434   Berger, Jean. A Child's Book of Beasts, Glen Rock:
          JF, pre-1968. Song: sa, pf.

His Own Country   See: "I shall go without companions"

"I am sailing for America"   The Four Men (1912), rev. 1954

    435   Raynor, John. "The Californy Song", L: OUP, 1947.
          Song: bar solo, pf.

"I shall go without companions"   The Four Men (1912), rev.
    1954

    436   Moule-Evans, David. "My Own Country", Three Songs,
          L: JW, ca. 1951. Song: med. v., pf.

    437   Raynor, John. "My Own Country", L: OUP, 1950. Song:
          t or bar solo, pf.

    438   Warlock, Peter. "My Own Country", Three Belloc
          Songs, L: OUP, 1927. Song: bar solo, pt.

Introduction   "I call you bad, my little child"   The Bad
    Child's Book of Beasts (1896)

    439   Peel, Graham. The Bad Child's Songs about Beasts, L:
          BH, 1908. Song: v., pf.

January   "It freezes: all across a soundless sky"   In Ver-
    ses and Sonnets (1896) as one of "Sonnets of the Twelve
    Months"

    440   Rose, Michael. Winter Music, L: N, 1967. Cta.: satb,
          pf. duet, perc. ad lib.

Jim who ran away from his nurse, and was eaten by a lion
    "There was a Boy whose name was Jim"   Cautionary Tales
    for Children (1907)

Belloc, Hilaire continued

441 Lehmann, Liza. "Jim", Four_Cautionary_Tales_and_a
     Moral, L: C, 1909. Song: ms solo, pf. Portions
     of the collection require bar solo and ms, bar
     duet.

"Lift up your hearts in Gumber, laugh the Weald"   In Sonnets
and_Verse (1923)

442 Le Fleming, Christopher. Valley_of_Arun, L: N, 1962.
     Choral ste.: bar solo, satb, orch.

Little Serving Maid, The   "There was a Queen of England"
In Verses (1910)

443 Fleming, Robert. MS 1948, avail. CMC. Song: v., pf.

Matilda who told lies, and was burned to death   "Matilda
told such Dreadful Lies"   Cautionary_Tales_for_Children
(1907)

444 Bergmann, Walter. "Matilda, A Cautionary Tale for
     Children", L: S, 1967. Song: voices, descant
     rec., t. rec., gl., xyl., vcl., perc., pf.

445 Lehmann, Liza. "Matilda", Four_Cautionary_Tales_and
     a_Moral, L: C, 1909. Song: ms, bar duet, pf.
     Portions of the collection require ms solo and
     bar solo.

Microbe, The   "Microbe is so very small, The"   More_Beasts
for_Worse_Children (1897)

446 Persichetti, Vincent. Hilaire_Belloc_Songs, Ph.: EV,
     1965. Song: med. v., pf.

Moon's Funeral, The   "Moon is dead, The. I saw her die"
In Verses_and_Sonnets (1896)

447 Wilson, Thomas. Night_Songs, Glasgow: B&F, 1968 (L:
     AH&C). Song: satb, a cap.

Belloc, Hilaire continued

Moral Alphabet, A   "A stands for Archibald who told no lies"
    (1899)

    448   Josephs, Wilfred. "Twelve Letters: A Moral
            Alphabet", MS (Opus 16). Setting for sp., orch.

Mrs. Rhys   "I love to roam from mere caprice"   (1919)

    449   Belloc, Hilaire. Dublin: Cuala, 1937 in Broadside,
            No. 2. Song: v., unacc. Words and music by Bel-
            loc.

Night, The   "Most holy Night, that still dost keep"   In
    Verses and Sonnets (1896)

    450   Barlow, David. MS. Song: a solo, pf.

    451   Fleming, Robert. MS 1940, avail. CMC. Song: v., pf.

    452   Gill, Harry. L: OUP, 1943. Song: a or bar solo, pf.

    453   Gurney, Ivor. "Most Holy Night", A Fourth Volume of
            Ten Songs, L: OUP, 1959. Song: solo v., pf.

    454   Herbert, Muriel. "Most Holy Night", L: A, pre-1949.
            Song: v., pf.

    455   Hind, John. "Most Holy Night", L: N, 1955. Song:
            satb, a cap.

    456   Potter, A.J. Three Songs of Hilaire Belloc, Dublin:
            RTE, 1952. Song: satb, a cap.

    457   Rubbra, Edmund. Two Songs, L: OUP, 1926. Song: v.,
            pf. Also publ. sep.

    458   Treharne, Bryceson. B: BMC, 1917. Song: high or med.
            v., pf.

    459   Warlock, Peter. Three Belloc Songs, L: OUP, 1927.
            Song: bar solo, pf.

Noël   "On a winter's night long time ago"   In Verses and
    Sonnets (1896)

Belloc, Hilaire continued

460   Bower, Neville. "Carillon, carilla", L: BH, 1965.
      [Carol]: ssa, pf.

461   Fraser, Shena. "On...", Carillon, L: Curwen, 1958.
      Song (in cta.): ssa, pf., stgs. or ssa, pf.

462   O'Neill, Norman. MS 1914, L: S&B. Carol: satb, bells
      ad lib.

463   Warlock, Peter. "Carillon, Carilla", L: N, 1930.
      Carol: satb, org. Also avail. for unison v., org.

"Noël! Noël! Noël! Noël!"   The Four Men (1912), rev. 1954

464   Harvey, Trevor. "A Sailor's Carol", L: OUP, 1933.
      Carol: t solo, pf.

465   Willan, Healey. "Noel, Noel, Noel, a Catholic Tale",
      MS. Carol: bar solo, ttbb, a cap.

"O my companion, O my sister Sleep"   In Sonnets and Verse
(1923)

466   Le Fleming, Christopher. Valley of Arun, L: N, 1962.
      Choral ste.: bar solo, satb, orch.

On a Dead Hostess   "Of this bad world"   In Sonnets and
Verse (1923)

467   Duncan, Chester. MS 1974. Song: v., pf.

On a General Election   "Accursed power which stands on
Privilege, The"   In Sonnets and Verse (1923)

468   Potter, A.J. Ten Epigrams by Hilaire Belloc, Dublin:
      NIRC, 1972. Cta.: satb, a cap.

On a Puritan   "He served his God so faithfully"   In Sonnets
and Verse (1938)

469   Potter, A.J. Ten Epigrams by Hilaire Belloc, Dublin:
      NIRC, 1972. Cta.: satb, a cap.

59

Belloc, Hilaire continued

On a Sleeping Friend "Lady, when your lovely head" In
Sonnets and Verse (1923)

   470 Besly, Maurice. "Dawn Shall Over Lethe Break", L:
       BH, pre-1940. Song: [v., pf.?].

   471 Campbell, Colin MacLeod. "Dawn Shall Over Lethe
       Break", L: BH, 1925. Song: solo v., pf.

   472 Duncan, Chester. MS 1974. Song: v., pf.

   473 Hageman, Richard. "Dawn Shall Over Lethe Break", L:
       BH, 1934. Song: v., pf.

   474 Potter, A.J. "Epigram on a Sleeping Friend", Three
       Songs of Hilaire Belloc, Dublin: RTE, 1952. Song:
       satb, a cap.

On a Sundial "In soft deluding lies" In Sonnets and
Verse (1938)

   475 Duncan, Chester. "On a Sundial I", MS 1974. Song:
       v., pf.

On Another "How slow the Shadow creeps" In Sonnets and
Verse (1938)

   476 Duncan, Chester. "On a Sundial II", MS 1974. Song:
       v., pf.

On His Books "When I am dead, I hope it may be said" In
Sonnets and Verse (1923)

   477 Potter, A.J. Ten Epigrams by Hilaire Belloc, Dublin:
       NIRC, 1972. Cta.: satb, a cap.

On Lady Poltrague: A Public Peril "Devil, having nothing
else to do, The" In Sonnets and Verse (1923)

   478 Potter, A.J. "On Lady Poltrague", Ten Epigrams by
       Hilaire Belloc, Dublin: NIRC, 1972. Cta.: satb,
       a cap.

479 Stevens, Halsey. "Epigram: On Lady Poltrague, a
     Public Peril", MS 1941. Song: solo v., pf.

On Mundane Acquaintances "Good morning, Algernon" In
Sonnets and Verse (1923)

     480 Potter, A.J. Ten Epigrams by Hilaire Belloc, Dublin:
          NIRC, 1972. Cta.: satb, a cap.

On Noman: a Guest "Dear Mr Noman" In Sonnets and Verse
(1923)

     481 Potter, A.J. Ten Epigrams by Hilaire Belloc, Dublin:
          NIRC, 1972. Cta.: satb, a cap.

"On Sussex hills where I was bred" The Four Men (1912)
Incl. in collected edns. of Belloc's verse under the title
"The First Drinking Song"

     482 Gurney, Ivor. "On Sussex Hills", MS n.d. Song: [solo
          v., pf.].

On Torture: A Public Singer "Torture will give a dozen
pence" In Verses and Sonnets (1896)

     483 Potter, A.J. Ten Epigrams by Hilaire Belloc, Dublin:
          NIRC, 1972. Cta.: satb, a cap.

On Vital Statistics "Ill fares the land" In Sonnets and
Verse (1938)

     484 Potter, A.J. Ten Epigrams by Hilaire Belloc, Dublin:
          NIRC, 1972. Cta.: satb, a cap.

Our Lord and Our Lady "They warned Our Lady for the Child"
In Verses (1910)

     485 Bower, Neville. L: BH, 1961. Song: sa, [pf.].

     486 Gover, Gerald. L: BH, [?]. Song: v., pf.

Belloc, Hilaire continued

487 Murray, Dom Gregory. L: OUP, 1939. Song: unison v.,
pf. or unison v., org.

Polar Bear, The   "Polar bear is unaware, The"   The Bad
Child's Book of Beasts (1896)

488 Berger, Jean. A Child's Book of Beasts, Glen Rock:
JF, pre-1968. Song: sa, pf.

Python, The   "Python I should not advise, A"   More Beasts
for Worse Children (1897)

489 Couper, Mildred. NY: HB, 1928 in New Songs for New
Voices. Song: v., pf.

490 Frackenpohl, Arthur. Three Cautionary Tales, NY:
EBM, 1961. Song: sa, pf. Also avail. for ssa, pf.
or sab, pf. or satb, pf.

Rebecca who slammed doors for fun and perished miserably
"Trick that everyone abhors, A"   Cautionary Tales for
Children (1907)

491 Lehmann, Liza. "Rebecca", Four Cautionary Tales and
a Moral, L: C, 1909. Song: ms, bar duet, pf.
Portions of the collection require ms solo and
bar solo.

492 Patterson, Paul. "Rebecca", L: Weinberger, 1971-72.
Setting for narr., any ww., trbn., vln(s).,
vcl(s)., pf., perc.

Rhinoceros, The   "Rhinoceros, your hide looks all undone"
The Bad Child's Book of Beasts (1896)

493 Berger, Jean. A Child's Book of Beasts, Glen Rock:
JF, pre-1968. Song: sa, pf.

Rose   "Rose, little Rose, the youngest of the Roses"
'Memorial' to the Daughter of Laura, Lady Lovat (1942)

494 Raynor, John. L: C, 1950. Song: [v., pf.].

elloc, Hilaire continued

Sailor's Carol, The   See: "Noël! Noël! Noël! Noël!"

Tarantella   "Do you remember an Inn"   In Sonnets and Verse
(1923)

495 ApIvor, Denis. Songs Opus 3, MS 1935-40. Song: med.
     v., pf.

496 Burtch, Mervyn. MS. Song: satb, [a cap.?].

497 Coulthard, Jean. Two Night Songs, MS 1960, avail.
     CMC. Song: bar solo, str. qrt., pf.

498 Elgar, Edward. Unf. MS 1932-33. Song: bar solo,
     orch.

499 Fontrier, Gabriel. Three Choruses to Texts by
     Hilaire Belloc, NY: M, 1965. Song: satb, a cap.

500 Gurney, Ivor. MS 1925. Song: [solo v., pf.].

501 Hageman, Richard. "Miranda", NY: GX (L: Elkin,
     1940). Song: high v., pf. Also avail. for med.
     v., pf.

502 Le Fleming, Christopher. Valley of Arun, L: N, 1962.
     Choral ste.: bar solo, satb, orch.

503 Noble, Harold. "Do you...", L: AH&C, 1965. Song:
     ttbb, pf.

504 Rawlinson, Bertha. L: C, 1963. Song: solo v., pf.

505 Thompson, Randall. B: ECS, 1937. Song: ttbb, orch.
     or ttbb, pf.

506 Toye, Francis. "The Inn", L: Curwen, 1925. Song:
     [bar] solo v., pf.

507 Williams, Grace. The Dancers, L: OUP, 1953. Choral
     ste.: s solo, ssa, stgs., hp. Also avail. for
     s solo, ssa, pf.

To Dives   "Dives, when you and I go down to Hell"   In
Verses (1910)

508   Potter, A.J. "Ode to Dives", Dublin: Criador, 1958.
Song: b-bar solo, pf.

Twelfth Night   "As I was lifting over Down"   In Sonnets and
Verse (1938)

509   Copley, I.A. L: Curwen, 1962. Song: unison v., pf.
Publ. Wendover: Curwen, 1974 for (treble) solo
v., pf.

510   Le Fleming, Christopher. Valley of Arun, L: N, 1962.
Choral ste.: bar solo, satb, orch.

511   Moule-Evans, David. Three Songs, L: JW, ca. 1951.
Song: med. v., pf.

West Sussex Drinking Song   "They sell good Beer at Hasle-
mere"   In Verses (1910)

512   Cook, A. Melville. L: Curwen, 1957. Song: ttbb, a
cap.

513   Cork, Peter. "A Sussex Drinking Song", L: OUP, 1966.
Song: sab, pf. or atb, pf. or satb, pf.

514   Gow, David. "A West Sussex Drinking Song", L: BH,
1966. Song: v., pf.

515   Gurney, Ivor. L: C, 1921. Song: solo v., pf.

516   Kittleson, Carl. MS. Song: bar solo, satb, pf.

517   Raynor, John. Eleven Songs, L: G, 1971. Song: [v.,
pf.].

518   Wilkinson, Philip G. L: Freeman, 1959. Song: tbb, a
cap.

Vulture, The   "Vulture eats between his meals, The"   More
Beasts for Worse Children (1897)

519   Chasins, Abram. NY: JF, 1928. Song: med. v., pf.

Belloc, Hilaire continued

520 Frackenpohl, Arthur. Three Cautionary Tales, NY:
     EBM, 1961. Song: sa, pf. Also avail. for ssa, pf.
     or sab, pf. or satb, pf.

521 Scherman, Thomas. NY: HB, 1928 in New Songs for New
     Voices. Song: v., pf.

522 Skolnik, Walter. Three Zoological Studies, Bryn
     Mawr: EV, 1970. Song: satb, pf., opt. db.

Yak, The   "As a friend to the children"   The Bad Child's
Book of Beasts (1896)

    523 Berger, Jean. A Child's Book of Beasts, Glen Rock:
         JF, pre-1968. Song: sa, pf.

    524 Frackenpohl, Arthur. Three Cautionary Tales, NY:
         EBM, 1961. Song: sa, pf. Also avail. for ssa,
         pf. or sab, pf. or satb, pf.

    525 Peel, Graham. The Bad Child's Songs about Beasts, L:
         BH, 1908. Song: v., pf.

Miscellanea

    526 Belloc, Hilaire. Documentation regarding melodies
         the author composed for his own texts can be
         found in I.A. Copley's "Hilaire Belloc: A Folk-
         Song Composer", Music Review (Feb. 1975).

    527 Glass, Dudley. Songs from "The Bad Child's Book of
         Beasts", L: Duckworth, 1932. Songs: [v., pf.?].

    528 Goodhart, A.M. "When Jesus Christ was Four", L: S&B,
         pre-1967. Carol: unison v., pf. [Text by Belloc?]

    529 Hely-Hutchinson, Victor. The May 1944 issue of
         Musical Times makes passing reference to Hely-
         Hutchinson's having set words by Belloc.

    530 Peel, Graham. "A Song of Four Beasts", The Bad
         Child's Songs about Beasts, L: BH, 1908. Song:
         v., pf.

Belloc, Hilaire continued

531 Potter, A.J. "On the Death of a Politician", Ten
Epigrams of Hilaire Belloc, Dublin: NIBC, 1972.
Cta.: satb, a cap. [Setting of "Another on the
Same" ("This, the last ornament among the
peers")?]

BENNETT, (Enoch) Arnold   1867-1931

Don Juan de Manara   (DR)   (1923)

532 Enna, August. "Don Juan Manara", Copenhagen: STB,
1925. Opera.

533 Goossens, Eugene. L: JWC, 1935. Opera: 3 s, 3 ms,
6 t, 2 bar, b-bar, 2 b soli, sp., chorus, orch.
Libr. by Bennett, after his play of the same
title.

Judith   (DR)   (1919)

534 Bantock, Granville. MS, prod. 1919. Incidental
music.

535 Goossens, Eugene. L: JWC, 1929. Opera: s, ms, t,
bar, b-bar soli, chorus, orch.

Miscellanea

536 Fox, Fred. "It Pays", NY: GX, 1968. Song: satb, a
cap.

66

Benson, E.F.

BENSON, Edward Frederic   1867-1940

Miscellanea

537 Miles, Philip. "Westward Ho!", MS pre-1936. Opera.
Text by Benson, after the novel by Charles
Kingsley.

BETJEMAN, John   1906-

Bristol "Green upon the flooded Avon"   In New Bats in Old
Belfries (1945)

538 Warren, Raymond. A Star Shone over Bristol, MS 1973.
Cta.: s solo, satb, orch.

Calvinistic Evensong "Six bells stopped, and in the dark I
heard, The"   In Continual Dew (1937)

539* Beeson, Jack. NY: Mills, 1962 (in prep. for 1975
re-issue NY: BH). Song: bar solo, pf.

Caprice "I sat only two tables off from the one I was sacked at"   In High and Low (1966)

540 Horder, Mervyn. Six Betjeman Songs, L: Duckworth,
1967. Song: v., pf. or v., gtr. Portions of the
collection are set with descant and opt. 2nd v.

How to Get On in Society "Phone for the fish-knives, Norman"   In A Few Late Chrysanthemums (1954)

541 Horder, Mervyn. Six Betjeman Songs, L: Duckworth,
1967. Song: v., pf. or v., gtr. Portions of the
collection are set with descant and opt. 2nd v.

Hymn "Church's Restoration, The"   In Mount Zion (1931)

67

Betjeman, John continued

542* Horder, Mervyn. "The Church's Restoration", Six Betjeman Songs, L: Duckworth, 1967. Song: unison
v. with descant, pf. or unison v. with descant,
gtr. Portions of the collection are set without
descant.

In Westminster Abbey   "Let me take this glove off"   In Old
Lights for New Chancels (1940)

543 Horder, Mervyn. Six Betjeman Songs, L: Duckworth,
1967. Song: v. (with opt. 2nd v.), pf. or v.
(with opt. 2nd v.), gtr. Portions of the collection are set without opt. 2nd v.

Licorice Field of Pontefract, The   "In the licorice fields
of Pontefract"   In A Few Late Chrysanthemums (1954)

544 Swann, Donald. A Collection of Songs, L: C, 1963.
Song: v., pf.

Margate, 1940   "From out the Queen's Highcliffe"   In New
Bats in Old Belfries (1945)

545 Swann, Donald. A Collection of Songs, L: C, 1963.
Song: v., pf.

Senex   "Oh would I could subdue the flesh"   In Old Lights
for New Chancels (1940)

546* Beeson, Jack. NY: BH, in prep. for 1975 publ. Song:
bar solo, pf.

547 Swann, Donald. A Collection of Songs, L: C, 1963.
Song: v., pf.

Subaltern's Love-song, A   "Miss J. Hunter Dunn, Miss J. Hunter Dunn"   In New Bats in Old Belfries (1945)

548 Horder, Mervyn. Six Betjeman Songs, L: Duckworth,
1967. Song: v., pf. or v., gtr. Portions of the
collection are set with descant and opt. 2nd v.

Betjeman, John continued

549 Swann, Donald. A Collection of Songs, L: C, 1963.
     Song: v., pf.

Westgate-on-Sea   "Hark, I hear the bells of Westgate"   In
Mount Zion (1931)
     550 Horder, Mervyn. Six Betjeman Songs, L: Duckworth,
          1967. Song: v., pf. or v., gtr. Portions of the
          collection are set with descant and opt. 2nd v.

BINYON, Laurence   1869-1943

Authur (DR)   (1923)
     551 Elgar, Edward. "King Arthur", MS 1922-23, perf. Lon-
          don, Mar. 1923. Incidental music.

Attila (DR)   (1907)
     552 Stanford, C.V. "Attila the Hun", MS (Opus 102),
          perf. 1907. Incidental music.

Bab-Lock-Hythe   "In the time of wild roses"   In England and
Other Poems (1909)
     553 Shaw, Martin. L: Curwen, 1919. Song: solo v., pf.

Ferry Hinksey   "Beyond the ferry water"   In Auguries (1913)
     554 Elkus, Albert. NY: GS, 1939. Song: solo v., pf.

For the Fallen   "With proud thanksgiving, a mother for her
children"   In The Winnowing-Fan (1914)
     555 Elgar, Edward. L: N, 1916, The Spirit of England,
          L: N, 1916-17. Setting for s or t solo, chorus,
          orch.

69

Binyon, Laurence continued

556 Rootham, C.B. L: N, 1915. Setting for semi-chorus
     (or s, a, b soli), satb (with a final ssaattbb
     portion), orch. Also avail. with pf. accompani-
     ment.

557 Walter, Arnold. MS 1949. Setting for choir, orch.

Fourth of August, The   "Now in thy splendour go before us"
    In The Winnowing-Fan (1914)

558 Elgar, Edward. L: N, 1917, The Spirit of England,
     L: N, 1916-17. Setting for s or t solo, chorus,
     orch.

Little Dancers, The   "Lonely, save for a few faint stars"
    In Poems (1895)

559 Hageman, Richard. L: BH, [1935?]. Song: [v., pf.].

560 Rosser, Mervyn. MS 1952, avail. University of Auck-
     land. Song: satb, a cap.

Mother of Exiles   "What far-off trouble steals"   In London
    Visions (1898)

561 Bennett, Richard R. London Pastoral, MS, perf.
     July 1962, L: Mills (hire). Setting for t solo,
     ch. ensemble.

Nothing is Enough   "Nothing is enough!"   In The Augustan
    Books of Poetry: Laurence Binyon (1926)

562 Adler, Samuel. Five Choral Poems, NY: AMP, 1957.
     Song: satb, a cap.

Sursum Cor!   "Lament no more my heart"   In The Death of
    Adam (1904)

563 Shaw, Martin. "Sursum Corda", L: N, 1933. Cta.: t
     solo, satb, orch.

70

Binyon, Laurence continued

To Women   "Your hearts are lifted up"   In The Winnowing-
Fan (1914)

    564 Elgar, Edward. L: N, 1916, The Spirit of England,
         L: N, 1916-17. Setting for s or t solo, chorus,
         orch.

Unreturning Spring, The   "Leaf on the gray sand-path, A"
In The Augustan Books of Poetry: Laurence Binyon (1926)

    565 Cooper, Walter Gaze. Symphony No. 6 (A Symphony of
         War), MS (Opus 59). Symph.: sp., orch.

Miscellanea

    566* Elgar, Edward. "Carillon", L: Elkin, 1942. Setting
         for reciter, orch. Text begins: "Over all this
         home-land of our fathers".

    567 Quilter, Roger. "At Close of Day", L: BH, 1904.
         Song: v., pf.

    568 Quilter, Roger. "The Answer", L: BH, 1904. Song:
         [v., pf.].

    569 Robbins, Reginald. "Invocation to Youth", P: MST,
         ca. 1922. Song: b solo, [pf.]. Also suitable for
         bar (or a) solo, [pf.].

    570 Shaw, Martin, arr. "The Shepherd", L: OUP, 1928 in
         The Oxford Book of Carols. Song: 4 pt. chorus,
         pf. Arr. of an anon. Austrian tune. Text begins:
         "Down in the valley where summer's laughing
         beam".

Blackburn, Thomas

BLACKBURN, Thomas   1916-

Judas Tree, The   "Listen! The hounds of the judge and the
    priest"   In The Fourth Man (1971)

    571 Dickinson, Peter. L: N, 1967. Musical drama: 2 t
        soli, incidental soli for s and b, 5 actors,
        satb, orch.

Mark   "Fallen city rides from the dark, The"   In A Breath-
    ing Space (1964)

    572 Dickinson, Peter. L: N, 1965. Motet: atb, a cap.

Martin of Tours   "You start with a question. It dips be-
    neath"   In The Fourth Man (1971)

    573 Dickinson, Peter. L: N, 1967. Cta.: t, bar soli,
        satb, ch. org. (or pf. duet).

Miscellanea

    574 Dickinson, Peter. "John", L: N, 1963. Motet: atb,
        a cap. Text begins: "John, the martyr, that we
        may utter".

BLAIR, Eric Arthur   See: ORWELL, George

72

Blunden, Edmund

BLUNDEN, Edmund Charles   1896-

Harvest   "So there's my year, the twelvemonth duly told"
    In English Poems (1925)

    575 Finzi, Gerald. Oh Fair to See, L: BH, 1966. Song:
        high v., pf.

Idlers, The   "Gipsies lit their fuels by the chalk-pit gate
    anew, The"   In The Shepherd (1922)

    576 Gurney, Ivor. MS 1925. Song: [solo v., pf.].

Midnight Skaters, The   "Hop-poles stand in cones, The"   In
    English Poems (1925)

    577 Rose, Michael. Winter Music, L: N, 1967. Cta.: satb,
        pf. duet, perc. ad lib.

Ode for St. Cecilia's Day, An   "Delightful Goddess, in white
    fashionings"   In A Hong Kong House (1962)

    578* Finzi, Gerald. "For St. Cecilia", L: BH, 1948. Set-
        ting for t solo, satb, orch.

One Among the Rose   "While by the rosebud gay you stood"
    In Shells by a Stream (1944)

    579 Klein, Ivy. "Among the Roses", L: A, 1949. Song:
        [v., pf.].

Sunlit Vale, The   "I saw the sunlit vale"   In Poems 1914-
    30 (1930)

    580 Holloway, Robin. Georgian Songs, MS 1972, L: OUP.
        Song: bar solo, pf.

To Joy   "Is this not enough for moan"   In To Nature (1923)

    581 Finzi, Gerald. Oh Fair to See, L: BH, 1966. Song:
        high v., pf.

73

Blunden, Edmund continued

Miscellanea

582 Finzi, Gerald. "White Flowering Days", MS 1952-53,
     L: OUP. The composer's contribution to A Garland
     for the Queen.

583 Young, Percy, arr. "Life, be kind", L: C, [?]. Song:
     unison v., pf. Arr. of a work by Daniel Purcell.

BLUNT, Wilfrid Scawen   1840-1922

Nocturne, A   "Moon has gone to her rest, The"   In The Love
     Lyrics of Proteus (1880)

584 Brown, James. MS. Song: solo v. (best suited for
     ms, a, t or bar solo), pf.

BOTTOMLEY, Gordon   1874-1948

"Between April and May"   In Chambers of Imagery, 2nd series
     (1912) as one of "Night and Morning Songs"

585 Hart, Fritz. Five Songs for Voice and Pianoforte,
     MS 1938 (Opus 128), avail. State Library of Vic-
     toria, Melbourne. Song: v., pf.

Dawn   "Thrush is tapping a stone, A"   In Chambers of
     Imagery, 2nd series (1912) as one of "Night and Morning
     Songs"

586 Bainton, Edgar L. L: WR, 1924. Song: med. v., pf.

587 Hart, Fritz. Five Songs for Voice and Pianoforte,
     MS 1938 (Opus 128), avail. State Library of Vic-
     toria, Melbourne. Song: v., pf.

74

Bottomley, Gordon continued

"I am tired of the wind" In Chambers_of_Imagery, 2nd series
(1912) as one of "Night and Morning Songs"

    588 Garlick, Antony. Twelve_Madrigals, Cin.: WLP, 1967.
        Madrigal: ssa, a cap.

    589 Hart, Fritz. Five_Songs_for_Voice_and_Pianoforte,
        MS 1938 (Opus 128), avail. State Library of Vic-
        toria, Melbourne. Song: v., pf.

Mad Maid's Song, A   "Day had a sunless dawning, The"   In
Poems_of_Thirty_Years (1925)

    590 Hart, Fritz. Five_Songs_for_Voice_and_Pianoforte,
        MS 1938 (Opus 128), avail. State Library of Vic-
        toria, Melbourne. Song: v., pf.

New Year's Eve, 1913   "O, Cartmell bells ring soft to-night"
In Poems_of_Thirty_Years (1925)

    591 Somers-Cocks, John P. L: A, 1933. Song: s solo, pf.

"Out of the high skies birds are falling" In Chambers_of
Imagery, 2nd series (1912) as one of "Night and Morning
Songs"

    592 Hart, Fritz. "Out of the High Skies", Five_Songs_for
        Voice_and_Pianoforte, MS 1938 (Opus 128), avail.
        State Library of Victoria, Melbourne. Song: v.,
        pf.

Pride of Westmoreland, The   "I met a man of ninety-three"
In Poems_of_Thirty_Years (1925)

    593 Liebich, Frank. Dublin: Cuala, 1937 in Broadside,
        No. 5. Song: v., unacc.

Sanctuaries   "There is a chamber in the dawn"   In Chambers
of_Imagery, 2nd series (1912) as one of "Night and Morning
Songs"

    594 Bainton, Edgar L. L: WR, 1924. Song: high v., pf.

Bottomley, Gordon continued

Song of Apple-Gathering, A   "Harvest is over in mist and
    moist moonlight"   In The Gate of Smaragdus (1904)

    595 Bishop, Franklin H. NY: GS, pre-1940. Song: [v.,
         pf.?].

Miscellanea

    596 Bainton, Edgar L. "Spring Comes", L: WR, 1924. Song:
         med. v., pf. Text from Chambers of Imagery.

    597 Gibbs, C. Armstrong. "Before Daybreak", L: BH, 1941.
         Cta.: a solo, ssa, str. qrt., str. orch., pf.
         Text begins: "Listen to us. Who threatens our
         purpose?".

    598 Johnson, William S. "Beneath Her Window", B: BMC,
         pre-1940. Song: [v., pf.?].

BRIDGES, Robert Seymour*   1844-1930

Achilles in Scyros   (DR)   (1890)

    599 Edmonds, Paul. "The Earth Loveth the Spring", L: CR,
         1928. Song: ssa, pf. Sets lines beginning: "The
         earth loveth the spring".

    600 Rootham, C.B. The Choruses from "Achilles in
         Scyros", L: S&B, 1912. Songs: s, a soli, sa, a
         cap. Originally composed with accompaniment of
         stgs., hp. (not publ.). Settings of lines begin-
         ning: "The earth loveth the spring", "O daughter
         of Nereus old", "Now the glorious sun", "We live
         well-ruled by an honoured king" and "Go not, go
         not, Achilles".

"Angel spirits of sleep"   The Shorter Poems of Robert
    Bridges (1890)

    601 Bainton, Edgar L. L: OUP, pre-1940. Song: [v., pf.].

602 Gayfer, James M. Three Songs, Willowdale: BH, 1970.
     Song: med. v., pf.

603 Hart, Fritz. Five Part-Songs for Women's Choir, Set
     I, MS 1935. Song: chorus of female v., a cap.

604 Holst, Gustav. L: N, 1926, Seven Partsongs, L: N,
     1974. Song: ssa, stgs. Complete work also re-
     quires s solo.

605 MacCunn, Hamish. Six Songs, L: JW, pre-1940. Song:
     [v., pf.].

606 Rootham, C.B. In Highland and Meadow, L: S&B, 1910.
     Song: satb, orch. or satb, pf.

607 Willan, Healey. L: OUP, 1927. Song: ssa, pf.

April, 1885 "Wanton with long delay" The Shorter Poems of
Robert Bridges (1890)

608 May, Frederick. "April", MS. Song: solo v., pf.

609 Milford, Robin. Autumn and Spring, L: OUP, 1946.
     Cyc.: satb, a cap.

"Awake my heart to be loved, awake, awake" Poems (1884)

610 Harris, William H. "Awake, my heart, to be loved",
     L: N, 1946. Song: satb, a cap.

611* Holst, Gustav. "Awake, my heart", B: Schmidt, 1908
     as one of Two Songs. Song: med. v., pf.

612 Wordsworth, William. "Awake My Heart", Four Songs,
     L: L, 1947. Song: high v., pf.

"Birds that sing on autumn eyes, The" The Shorter Poems
of Robert Bridges (1890)

613 Milford, Robin. L: OUP, 1936. Song: satb, a cap.

Child's Hymn, A (The First Spring Morning) "Look! Look! the
spring is come" Shorter Poems, Book V (1893)

614 Blower, Maurice. "First Spring Morning", L: Curwen, 1967. Song: sa, pf.

615 Brook, Harry. "First Spring Morning", L: OUP, 1939. Song: unison v., pf.

616 Eagles, Moneta. "First Spring Morning", Melbourne: Allan, 1962. Song: sa, a cap.

617* Milford, Robin. "First Spring Morning", Joy_and Memory, L: OUP, ca. 1944. Cyc.: unison children's v., [pf.?]. Complete cyc. also requires 2 pt. and 3 pt. children's v.

618 Schlotel, Brian. "First Spring Morning", Cl.: LW, 1960. Madrigal: satb, a cap.

Chivalry of the Sea, The   "Over the warring waters"   The Times (Aug. 1916)

619 Parry, C.H.H. L: N, 1916. Setting for ssatb, orch.

Christmas Poem, A   "Frosty Christmas Eve, A"   The_Times (Dec. 1913), rev. 1914, rev. 1925

620 Finzi, Gerald. In_Terra_Pax, L: BH, 1958. Settings for s, bar soli, satb, stgs., hp. (or pf.), cym. or s, bar soli, satb, orch.

621 Milford, Robin. "A Frosty...", L: OUP, pre-1958. Song: unison v., pf.

"Clouds have left the sky, The"   The_Shorter_Poems_of_Robert Bridges (1890)

622* Swain, Freda. "The Twilight Shore", MS ca. 1925, avail. Chinnor: Channel, NEMO. Setting for ms (or high bar) and pf. (or org.) ensemble.

"Crown Winter with green"   The_Shorter_Poems_of_Robert Bridges (1890)

623 Hart, Fritz. Five_Part-Songs_for_Women's_Choir, Set II, MS 1935. Song: chorus of female v., a cap

Bridges, Robert continued

624   MacCunn, Hamish. Six Songs, L: JW, pre-1940. Song:
      [v., pf.].

625   Tomlins, Greta. "This good Yuletide", Times and
      Seasons, L: AH&C, 1967. Cyc.: ssa, pf.

"Dear lady, when thou frownest"   Poems (1873)

626   Gurney, Ivor. "Dear Lady", MS ca. 1914. Song: solo
      v., pf.].

Dejection   "Wherefore to-night so full of care"   Poems
(1879)

627   Finzi, Gerald. "Wherefore...", Seven Unaccompanied
      Partsongs, L: OUP, 1934-37. Song: satb, a cap.
      Complete work requires various choral
      combinations (e.g., sat, ssatb).

Demeter   (DR)   (1905)

628   Hadow, W.H. Oxf.: Clarendon, 1905. Incidental music.

Eclogue I: The Months   "Man hath with man on earth no holier
bond"   Poetical Works of Robert Bridges, Vol. II (1899)

629   Tomlins, Greta. "On Frosty Morns", Times and
      Seasons, L: AH&C, 1967. Cyc.: ssa, pf. Sets
      lines beginning: "On frosty morns with the woods
      aflame, down, down".

Eden   (Oratorio)   (1891)

630   Stanford, C.V. L: N, 1891. Oratorio: 2 s, a, t, bar,
      b soli, satb, orch.

Elegy   "Assemble, all ye maidens, at the door"   Poems
(1873)

Bridges, Robert continued

631   Holst, Gustav. "Assemble all ye maidens", L: N,
       1927, Seven Partsongs, L: N, 1974. Song: s solo,
       ssa, stgs. Portions of the collection are set
       without s solo.

Elegy   "Clear and gentle stream"   Poems (1873)

632   Finzi, Gerald. "Clear...", Seven Unaccompanied Part-
       songs, L: OUP, 1934-37. Song: satb, a cap.
       Complete work requires various choral
       combinations (e.g., sat, ssatb).

"Eternal Father, Who didst all create"   The Growth of Love
(1876)

633   Holst, Gustav. "Eternal Father", L: Curwen, 1928.
       Anthem: s solo, chorus, org., bells ad lib.

634   Stanford, C.V. "Eternal Father", Three Motets, L:
       S&B, 1913. Motet: 6 v., a cap. Complete work
       requires 6, 4 and 8 v., a cap.

Eton Memorial Ode   "Resound! Resound! To jubilant music
ring!" 1st publ. (as text to Parry's music) 1908; incl.
under the title "In Memory of the Old-Etonians" in
Poetical Works of Robert Bridges (1912)

635   Parry, C.H.H. L: N, 1908. Setting for satb, orch.

"Fire of heaven, whose starry arrow"   The Shorter Poems of
Robert Bridges (1890)

636   MacCunn, Hamish. Six Songs, L: JW, pre-1940. Song:
       [v., pf.].

First Spring Morning, The   See: Child's Hymn, A (The First
Spring Morning)

"Gay Marigold is frolic" See: Spring's Children

ridges, Robert continued

"Gáy Róbin is seen no more"   The Shorter Poems of Robert
Bridges (1890)

637 Raphael, Mark. L: Curwen, 1932. Song: sa, [pf.?].

638 Ritchie, John. Then Laugheth the Year, MS 1948,
     avail. University of Canterbury. Cta.: combined
     satb choirs, 2 pf.

639 Schlotel, Brian. Cl.: LW, 1959. Madrigal: satb, a
     cap.

"Haste on, my joys! your treasure lies"   See: Song "Haste
on..."

"Hill pines were sighing, The"   The Shorter Poems of Robert
Bridges (1890)

640 Gurney, Ivor. MS 1925. Song: [solo v., pf.].

641 Jacobson, Maurice. MS ca. 1923. Song: [solo v.,
     pf.?].

Hymn of Nature, A   "Power eternal, power unknown, uncreate"
Cornhill Magazine (Sept. 1898)

642 Blower, Maurice. "Gird on thy sword, O man", L: N,
     1937. Song: unison v., pf. Sets lines beginning:
     "Gird on thy sword, O man, thy strength endue".

643 Bullock, Ernest. "Gird on Thy Sword", L: OUP, 1928.
     Song: unison v., pf. Sets lines beginning: "Gird
     on thy sword, O man, thy strength endue".

644 Christopher, Cyril. MS ca. 1940. Setting for s,
     bar soli, chorus, orch.

645 Holst, Gustav. "Man Born to Toil", L: Curwen, 1927.
     Anthem: satb, org., bells ad lib. Sets lines
     beginning: "Man, born to toil, in his labour
     rejoiceth". Final hymn from the anthem publ.
     sep. (L: Curwen, 1927) under the title: "Gird
     on thy sword". Hymn: qrt. (s, a, t, b), org.,
     bells ad lib.

Bridges, Robert continued

646   Parry, C.H.H. "A Song of Darkness and Light", L: N,
       1898. Setting for s solo, satb, orch.

"I found to-day out walking"   Poems (1873)

647   Gurney, Ivor. "The Heart's Prevention", MS 1925.
       Song: [solo v., pf.].

"I have loved flowers that fade"   Poems (1879)

648   Boyd, Malcolm. L: JW, 1961. Song: satb, a cap.

649   Dorward, David. Three Songs for High Voice and
       Piano, MS, avail. SMA. Cyc.: s or t solo, pf.

650   Finzi, Gerald. Seven Unaccompanied Partsongs, L:
       OUP, 1934-37. Song: sat, a cap. Complete work
       requires various choral combinations (e.g., satb,
       ssatb).

651   Gurney, Ivor. MS 1920. Song: [solo v., pf.].

652   Ratcliffe, Desmond. Sevenoaks: N, 1950. Song: satb,
       a cap.

"I heard a linnet courting"   Poems (1873)

653   Brook, Harry. "I Heard a Linnet", L: OUP, 1949.
       Song: unison v., pf.

654   Dale, Benjamin. "I Heard a Linnet", MS ca. 1939.
       Song: [solo v., pf.?].

655   Edge, Dorothea. L: Curwen, 1958. Song: 2 pt. chorus
       of equal v., pf.

656   Galway, Victor. Wellington: W&T, n.d. in Dominion
       Song Book, No. 13. Song: 2 pt. chorus of treble
       v., pf.

657   Herbert, Ivy. "The Linnet", L: OUP, 1947. Song:
       solo v., pf.

658   Noble, Harold. L: R, 1969. Song: satb, a cap.

82

ridges, Robert continued

659   Parrott, Ian. L: L, 1948. Song: med. v., pf.

660   Stone, David. "The Linnet", L: Elkin, 1948. Song:
      ms or t solo, pf.

661   Turner, James O. "The Linnet", L: AH&C, 1959. Song:
      satb, [pf.].

"I love all beauteous things"   The Shorter Poems of Robert
Bridges (1890)

662   Chandler, Mary. L: N, 1960. Song: unison v. with
      descant, pf.

663   Clements, John H. York: Banks, 1938. Song: ssatb,
      pf.

664   Davies, H. Walford. Twenty-One Songs, L: N, 1931.
      Song: med. v., pf.

665   Eagles, Moneta. L: C, 1951. Song: ms solo, pf.

666   Gurney, Ivor. MS ca. 1911. Song: [solo v., pf.].

667   Hart, Fritz. Five Part-Songs for Women's Choir, Set
      II, MS 1935. Song: chorus of female v., a cap.

668   Le Fleming, Christopher. L: CR, 1943. Song: unison
      v. with descant, pf. or unison v. with descant,
      pf., stgs.

669   Russell, Leslie. Two Robert Bridges Songs, L: OUP,
      1953. Song: unison v., pf.

"I praise the tender flower"   Poems (1884)

670   Bridge, Frank. MS 1905-06. Song: bar solo, orch.

671   Finzi, Gerald. Seven Unaccompanied Partsongs, L:
      OUP, 1934-37. Song: satb, a cap. Complete work
      requires various choral combinations (e.g., sat,
      ssatb).

672   Lehmann, Liza. MS pre-1918, L: JW. Song: [solo v.,
      pf.?].

Bridges, Robert continued

673 Parry, W.H. L: Elkin, 1954. Song: ssa, a cap.

674 Stanford, C.V. Three Songs, L: A, 1897. Song: solo
     v., pf.

675 Stewart, C. Hylton. L: S&B, pre-1940. Song: [v.,
     pf.].

"I will not let thee go" Poems (1873)

676* Holst, Gustav. MS 1903. Song: bar solo, pf.

677 Milford, Robin. A Book of Songs, L: OUP, 1939. Song:
     b solo, pf.

"Idle life I lead, The" The Shorter Poems of Robert Bridges
(1890)

678 Hart, Fritz. Five Part-Songs for Women's Choir, Set
     II, MS 1935. Song: chorus of female v., a cap.

679 MacCunn, Hamish. Six Songs, L: JW, pre-1940. Song:
     [v., pf.].

680 Osmond, Clara. L: Curwen, 1927. Song: ssa, [a cap.].

Invocation to Music "Myriad-voiced Queen, Enchantress of
the air" 1st publ. (as text to Parry's music) 1895;
portions 1st appeared in The Growth of Love (1876) & in
Pelican Record (June 1895); rev. 1896

681 Holst, Gustav. "Choral Fantasia", L: Curwen, 1931.
     Setting for s solo (or semichorus), satb, 3 tpt.,
     2 t. trbn., b. trbn., tuba, org., stgs. Stanza
     order rearr. by Holst.

682 Parry, C.H.H. L: N, 1895. Setting for s, t, b soli,
     satb, orch.

Larks "What voice of gladness, hark!" Shorter Poems, Book
V (1893)

683 Marshall, Patricia A. MS 1955, avail. University of
     Auckland. Song: solo v., pf.

Bridges, Robert continued

684 Parry, C.H.H. "What voice of gladness", Six Modern
      Lyrics, L: N, 1897. Song: satb, a cap.

685 Rootham, C.B. L: Curwen, 1914. Song: equal treble
      voices: unison, 2 pt., 3 pt., pf.

Last Week of February, 1890 "Hark to the merry birds" The
Shorter Poems of Robert Bridges (1890)

686 Eagles, Moneta. "Hark...", L: C, 1956. Song: saa,
      a cap.

687 Ritchie, John. "Hark...", Then Laugheth the Year,
      MS 1948, avail. University of Canterbury. Cta.:
      combined satb choirs, 2 pf.

Laus Deo "Let praise devote thy work" The Shorter Poems
of Robert Bridges (1890)

688 Milford, Robin. L: N, 1933. Setting for unison v.,
      pf.

689 Peach, Clare. "Let praise...", NY: CF, 1954. Setting
      for satb, pf.

690 Ritchie, John. Then Laugheth the Year, MS 1948,
      avail. University of Canterbury. Cta.: combined
      satb choirs, 2 pf.

691 Whitfield, J.B.R. "Let praise...", L: AH&C, 1956.
      Setting for unison v., [pf.?].

Love Lyric, A "Why art thou sad, my dearest" Poetical
Works of Robert Bridges, Vol. II (1899)

692 Gurney, Ivor. MS 1925. Song: [solo v., pf.].

"Love on my heart from heaven fell" The Shorter Poems of
Robert Bridges (1890)

693 Carey, Clive. L: BH, pre-1957 in Fifty Modern
      English Songs. Song: [v., pf.].

694 Hart, Fritz. Five Part-Songs for Women's Choir, Set
     I, MS 1935. Song: chorus of female v., a cap.

695 Holst, Gustav. L: N, 1926, Seven Partsongs, L: N,
     1974. Song: s solo, ssa, stgs. Portions of the
     collection are set without s solo.

696 Raphael, Mark. L: Elkin, 1936. Song: med. v., pf.

"My bed and pillow are cold"   The Shorter Poems of Robert
Bridges (1890)

     697 MacCunn, Hamish. Six Songs, L: JW, pre-1940. Song:
          [v., pf.].

"My delight and thy delight"   Poetical Works of Robert
Bridges, Vol. II (1899)

     698 Parry, C.H.H. Six Partsongs, L: N, 1909. Song: satb,
          a cap.

     699 Whiting, Arthur. NY: GS, 1903. Song: s, t duet, pf.

"My eyes for beauty pine"   The Shorter Poems of Robert
Bridges (1890)

     700 Howells, Herbert. L: OUP, 1928. Song: unison v. with
          several bars of 4 pt. writing, org.

"My spirit kisseth thine"   The Shorter Poems of Robert
Bridges (1890)

     701 Gurney, Ivor. MS 1925. Song: [solo v., pf.].

"My spirit sang all day"   The Shorter Poems of Robert
Bridges (1890)

     702 Finzi, Gerald. Seven Unaccompanied Partsongs, L:
          OUP, 1934-37. Song: satb, a cap. Complete work
          requires various choral combinations (e.g., sat,
          ssatb).

703 Ritchie, John. <u>Then Laugheth the Year</u>, MS 1948, avail. University of Canterbury. Cta.: combined satb choirs, 2 pf.

Nightingales "Beautiful must be the mountains whence ye come" <u>Shorter Poems, Book V</u> (1893)

704 Cone, Edward T. <u>Philomela, Three Nightingale Songs</u>, MS. Cyc.: s solo, fl., vla., pf.

705 Dorward, David. "Beautiful...", <u>Three Songs for High Voice and Piano</u>, MS, avail. SMA. Cyc.: s or t solo, pf.

706 Finzi, Gerald. <u>Seven Unaccompanied Partsongs</u>, L: OUP, 1934-37. Cyc.: ssatb, a cap. Complete work requires various choral combinations (e.g., sat, satb).

707 Hart, Fritz. MS 1917. Song: trio of female v., [a cap.?].

708 Jones, Kenneth V. MS. Song: ssa, pf. or ssa, hpd. or ssa, hp.

709 Mattila, Edward. MS. Song: satb, a cap.

710 Robbins, Reginald. P: MST, ca. 1922. Song: b solo, [pf.]. Also suitable for bar (or a) solo, [pf.].

711 Saar, Louis. "The Nightingales", B: ECS, 1932. Song: t solo, ssa, pf. with obbl. for ob. or fl. or vln.

712 Sacco, P. Peter. Los Angeles: Ostara, 1974. Song: satb, ww., pf.

713 Swanson, Howard. "The Nightingales", NY: Weintraub, 1952. Song: ttbb, a cap.

Noel   See: Christmas Poem, A

Noel: Christmas Eve, 1913   See: Christmas Poem, A

Bridges, Robert continued

"O Love, I complain"   Poetical Works of Robert Bridges, Vol.
II (1899)

714   Hart, Fritz. Five Part-Songs for Women's Choir, Set
      I, MS 1935. Song: chorus of female v., a cap.

715   Holst, Gustav. L: N, 1926, Seven Partsongs, L: N,
      1974. Song: s solo, ssa, stgs. Portions of the
      collection are set without s solo.

"O youth whose hope is high"   Poems (1884)

716   Ritchie, John. Then Laugheth the Year, MS 1948,
      avail. University of Canterbury. Cta.: combined
      satb choirs, 2 pf.

Ode to Music   See: Invocation to Music

Passer By, A   "Whither, O splendid ship"   Poems (1879)

717   Robbins, Reginald. P: MST, ca. 1922. Song: b solo,
      [pf.]. Also suitable for bar (or a) solo, [pf.].

718   Rootham, C.B. MS 1910, avail. Pendlebury Library,
      Cambridge. Rhapsody for orch.

"Poppy grows upon the shore, A"   Poems (1873)

719   Gurney, Ivor. "The Sea Poppy", MS 1925. Song: [solo
      v., pf.].

"Say who is this with silvered hair"   The Shorter Poems of
Robert Bridges (1890)

720   Hart, Fritz. "Say who is this?", Five Part-Songs for
      Women's Choir, Set I, MS 1935. Song: chorus of
      female v., a cap.

721   Holst, Gustav. "Say who is this?", L: N, 1926,
      Seven Partsongs, L: N, 1974. Song: ssa, stgs.
      Complete work also requires s solo.

"Since thou, O fondest and truest" The Shorter Poems of
Robert Bridges (1890)

722 Carey, Clive. L: WR, 1926. Song: solo v., pf.

723 Gurney, Ivor. L: BH, 1921. Song: solo v., pf.

724 Liddle, Samuel. "Since Thou, O Fondest", L: BH,
     1901. Song: solo v., pf.

725 Naylor, Bernard. L: S&B, 1930. Song: ssaa, pf.

726 Orr, C.W. Album of Four Songs, L: OUP, 1960. Song:
     t solo, pf.

727 Parry, C.H.H. Six Modern Lyrics, L: N, 1897. Song:
     satb, a cap.

728 Stanford, C.V. Three Songs, L: A, 1897. Song: solo
     v., pf.

729 Willan, Healey. Healey Willan Song Albums No. 1,
     Oakville: FH, 1925 (B: BMC, 1929). Song: [med.]
     solo v., pf.

"Since to be loved endures" Shorter Poems, Book V (1893)

730 Gurney, Ivor. MS n.d. Song: [solo v., pf.].

"Since we loved, --(the earth that shook" Poetical Works
of Robert Bridges, Vol. II (1899)

731 Finzi, Gerald. "Since we loved", Oh Fair to See, L:
     BH, 1966. Cyc.: high v., pf.

"So sweet love seemed that April morn" Shorter Poems, Book
V (1893)

732 Piggott, David. L: A, pre-1940. Song: [v., pf.?].

Song "Haste on, my joys! your treasure lies" The Shorter
Poems of Robert Bridges (1890), rev. 1899

733 Dorward, David. "Haste on, my joys", Three_Songs_for
High_Voice_and_Piano, MS, avail. SMA. Cyc.: s or
t solo, pf.

734 Finzi, Gerald. "Haste on, my joys!", Seven
Unaccompanied_Partsongs, L: OUP, 1934-37. Song:
ssatb, a cap. Complete work requires various
choral combinations (e.g., sat, satb).

Song "I love my lady's eyes" The_Shorter_Poems_of_Robert
Bridges (1890)

735 Bullard, Frederic. "I love...", MS pre-1904, B: BMC.
Song: [solo v., pf.?].

736 Stanford, C.V. "Say, O say!", Three_Songs, L: A,
1897. Song: solo v., pf.

"Sorrow and joy, two sisters coy" New_Verse (1925)

737 Hart, Fritz. "Sorrow and joy", Five_Part-Songs_for
Women's_Choir, Set I, MS 1935. Song: chorus of
female v., a cap.

738 Holst, Gustav. "Sorrow and Joy", L: N, 1926, Seven
Partsongs, L: N, 1974. Song: ssa, stgs. Complete
work also requires s solo.

"Spring goeth all in white" The_Shorter_Poems_of_Robert
Bridges (1890)

739 Berkeley, Lennox. Three_Songs_for_Four_Male_Voices,
L: JWC, 1966. Song: ttbb, a cap.

740 Bissell, Keith. Three_Songs_in_Praise_of_Spring,
Tor.: ECK, 1972. Song: ssaa, pf., perc.

741 Clements, John H. L: AH&C, 1957. Song: ss, pf. or
sa, pf.

742 Elkin, Robert. L: Elkin, 1925. Song: solo v., pf.

743 Hart, Fritz. Five_Part-Songs_for_Women's_Choir,
Set II, MS 1935. Song: chorus of female v., a
cap.

Bridges, Robert continued

744   Jacob, Gordon. L: EA, pre-1951. Song: 2 pt. chorus,
       pf.

745   Loots, Joyce. MS. Song: s or t solo, pf.

746   Milford, Robin. Autumn_and_Spring, L: OUP, 1946.
       Cyc.: satb, a cap.

747   Moeran, E.J. L: Curwen, 1924. Song: med. v., pf.

748   Osborne, Reginald. L: BH, 1969. Song: solo v., pf.

749   Ritchie, John. Then_Laugheth_the_Year, MS 1948,
       avail. University of Canterbury. Cta.: combined
       satb choirs, 2 pf.

750   Rosser, Mervyn. "White Spring", MS 1952, avail.
       University of Auckland. Song: high v., pf.

751   Russell, Leslie. "Spring", Two_Robert_Bridges_Songs,
       L: OUP, 1953. Song: unison v., pf.

752   Thiman, Eric. A_Spring_Garland, L: N, 1948. Cyc.:
       satb, fl., stgs., pf.

753   Tomlins, Greta. Times_and_Seasons, L: AHSC, 1967.
       Cyc.: ssa, pf.

754   Whittaker, W.G. "Spring", Two_Songs, L: OUP, pre-
       1927. Song: unison chorus of female v., [pf.?].

Spring's Children   "Gay Marigold is frolic"   Country_Life
(July 1906), rev. 1912

755   Bullock, Ernest. "Gay...", L: EA, ca. 1954. Song:
       [v., pf.?].

756   Rootham, C.B. "Gay Marigold", L: Curwen, 1914. Song:
       equal treble voices: unison, 2 pt., 3 pt., pf.

"Storm is over, the land hushes to rest, The"   The_Shorter
Poems_of_Robert_Bridges (1890)

757   Maves, David. "The Storm is Over", NY: CMP, copy-
       right by composer 1968. Song: satb, orch. or
       satb, pf.

91

Bridges, Robert continued

758 Milford, Robin. "The Storm is Over", Autumn and
Spring, L: OUP, 1946. Cyc.: satb, a cap.

"Thou didst delight my eyes" Poems (1880)

759 Bridge, Frank. MS ca. 1905. Song: bar solo, orch.

760 Duncan, Chester. MS 1938. Song: bar solo, pf.

761 Finzi, Gerald. L: BH (WR), 1952. Song: ttb, a cap.

762 Holst, Gustav. "Thou didst delight mine eyes", L: N,
1904. Song: satb, a cap.

Triolet "All women born are so perverse" Poems (1873)

763 Bridge, Frank. "So Perverse", L: WR, 1916. Song:
solo v., pf.

Triolet "When first we met we did not guess" Poems (1873)

764 Holst, Gustav. "When first we met", L: N, 1926,
Seven Partsongs, L: N, 1974. Song: s solo, ssa,
stgs. Portions of the collection are set without
s solo.

"Upper skies are palest blue, The" The Shorter Poems of
Robert Bridges (1890)

765 Hart, Fritz. Five Part-Songs for Women's Choir, Set
II, MS 1935. Song: chouus of female v., a cap.

Vignette, A "Among the meadows" Through Human Eyes (1901)

766 Rootham, C.B. L: N, 1914. Song: [a] solo v., pf.
Arr. 1918 (not publ.) for [a] solo v., orch. Also
arr. 1918 (not publ.) for [a] solo v., str. qrt.

Vivamus "When thou didst give thy love to me" Saturday
Review (Jan. 1903)

767 Busch, William. "When thou...", MS ca. 1937. Song:
[solo v., pf.?].

"When Death to either shall come"   Poetical_Works_of_Robert
Bridges, Vol. II (1899)

768 Gurney, Ivor. A_First_Volume_of_Ten_Songs, L: OUP,
1938. Song: solo v., pf.

769 Herbert, Muriel. L: A, pre-1940. Song: [v., pf.].

770 Homer, Sidney. Four_Modern_Poems, MS (Opus 34), NY:
GS. Song: [solo v., pf.?].

771 Young, Monroe. Publ. by composer, pre-1940. Song:
[v., pf.?].

"When June is come, then all the day"   The_Shorter_Poems_of
Robert_Bridges (1890)

772 Cockshott, Gerald. "Summer", MS 1944. Song: solo v.,
pf.

773 Drever, Rose. "When June is Come", L: S&B, pre-1940.
Song: [v., pf.].

774 Gurney, Ivor. "When June is Come", MS 1910. Song:
[solo v., pf.].

775 Hart, Fritz. "When June is Come", Book_of_Five
Songs, MS 1938, avail. State Library of Victoria,
Melbourne. Song: solo v., pf.

776 Hazlehurst, Cecil. "When June is Come", Three_Songs,
L: E, 1920. Song: high or med. v., pf.

777 Moeran, E.J. "When June is Come", L: Curwen, 1924.
Song: bar solo, pf.

778 Osborne, Reginald. "When June is Come", L: BH, 1967.
Song: solo v., pf.

779 Tomlins, Greta. Times_and_Seasons, L: AH&C, 1967.
Cyc.: ssa, pf.

Bridges, Robert continued

"When my love was away"   The Shorter Poems of Robert Bridges
(1890)

780 Gurney, Ivor. MS 1925. Song: [solo v., pf.].

Windmill, The   "Green corn waving in the dale, The"   The
Shorter Poems of Robert Bridges (1890)

781 Whittaker, W.G. L: OUP, 1936. Song: unison v., pf.

"Ye thrilled me once, ye mournful strains"   The Shorter
Poems of Robert Bridges (1890)

782 Parry, C.H.H. "Ye thrilled me", Eight Fourpart
Songs, MS. Song: 4 pt. chorus, a cap.

Miscellanea

783 Allitsen, Frances. "Love's Victory", Moods and Ten-
ses, MS pre-1912, L: BH. Cyc.: [v., pf.?].

BROOKE, Jocelyn   1908-

Epitaph   "War eats our days"   In December Spring (1946)

784 Searle, Humphrey. Three Songs of Jocelyn Brooke, L:
F (hire). Cyc.: high v., ensemble. Publ. L: F,
1969 for high v., pf.

Song for Christmas   "Cold winter, catalytic, now"   In
December Spring (1946)

785 Searle, Humphrey. Three Songs of Jocelyn Brooke, L:
F (hire). Cyc.: high v., ensemble. Publ. L: F,
1969 for high v., pf.

ooke, Jocelyn continued

White Hellebarine, The   "In the copse behind the village"
    in December Spring (1946)

    786 Searle, Humphrey. Three Songs of Jocelyn Brooke, L:
        F (hire). Cyc.: high v., ensemble. Publ. L: F,
        1969 for high v., pf.

BROOKE, Rupert Chawner   1887-1915

Beauty and Beauty   "When Beauty and Beauty meet"   Poetry
Review (Nov. 1912)

    787 Dunhill, Thomas F. L: S&B, pre-1940. Song: [v.,
        pf.?].

Clouds   "Down the blue night"   Poetry and Drama (Dec. 1913)

    788* Gurney, Ivor. Five Songs, MS. Song: v., pf.

    789 Wordsworth, William. Three Songs, L: L, 1946. Song:
        low v., pf.

Dance, The   "As the Wind"   The Collected Poems of Rupert
Brooke: With a Memoir (1918)

    790 Gipps, Ruth. Four Songs of Youth, MS. Song: s or t
        solo, pf.

Day That I Have Loved   "Tenderly, day that I have loved"
Westminster Gazette (June 1910)

    791 Le Fleming, Christopher. L: JWC, 1946. Song: ssa,
        2 pf. or ssa, pf., stgs.

    792 Rowton, S.J. L: A, pre-1940. Song: [v., pf.?].

    793 Sibson, Arthur. MS, avail. BMIC. Song: ms solo,
        3 fl., vla., 2 vcl. or ms solo, pf.

95

Brooke, Rupert continued

Dead, The   "Blow out, you bugles"   New Numbers (Dec. 1914)
    from "1914"

    794 Bridge, Frank. "Blow out...", L: WR, 1919. Song:
         high v., orch. Also arr. for high v., pf.

    795 Gray, Alan. 1914, L: S&B, pre-1967. Cyc.: satb, org.

    796 Ireland, John. "Blow out...", L: WR, 1918, Two
         Songs, L: WR, 1917-18. Song: solo v., pf.

Dead, The   "These hearts were woven"   New Numbers (Dec.
    1914) from "1914"

    797 Gray, Alan. 1914, L: S&B, pre-1967. Cyc.: satb, org.

Failure   "Because God put His adamantine fate"   Cambridge
    Review (May 1908)

    798 Gipps, Ruth. Four Songs of Youth, MS. Song: s or t
         solo, pf.

Granchester   See: Old Vicarage, Granchester, The

Heaven   "Fish (fly-replete, in depth of June...)"   1914 and
    Other Poems (1915)

    799 Gipps, Ruth. MS. Song: s solo, pf.

Jealousy   "When I see you, who were so wise"   Poems (1911)

    800 Maganini, Quinto. NY: Musicus, pre-1940. Song: [solo
         v., pf.?].

Love Poem, A   "Safe in the magic of my woods"   Saturday
    Westminster (Apr. 1909), rev. 1911

    801 Rowton, S.J. "Night and the Woods and You", L: A,
         pre-1940. Song: [solo v., pf.?].

96

Brooke, Rupert continued

Old Vicarage, Granchester, The   "Just now the lilac"
    Poetry Review (Nov. 1912) Fragments appeared in Basileon H
    (June 1912)

    802 Ives, Charles. "Granchester", 114 Songs, NY: GS,
         1921, copyright 1922. Song: med. v., pf. Contains
         "a quotation from Debussy".

One Day   "Today I have been happy"   New Numbers (Feb. 1914)

    803* Gurney, Ivor. Five Songs, MS. Song: v., pf.

Peace   "Now, God be thanked"   New Numbers (Dec. 1914) from
    "1914"

    804 Gipps, Ruth. "Peace 1914", Four Songs of Youth, MS.
         Song: s or t solo, pf.

    805 Gray, Alan. 1914, L: S&B, pre-1967. Cyc.: satb, org.

Safety   "Dear! of all happy in the hour"   New Numbers
    (Dec. 1914) from "1914"

    806 Cripps, A. Redgrave. Two Sonnets, L: A, ca. 1939.
         Song: v., pf.

    807 Gray, Alan. 1914, L: S&B, pre-1967. Cyc.: satb, org.

Soldier, The   "If I should die, think only this of me"
    New Numbers (Dec. 1914) from "1914"

    808 Cripps, A. Redgrave. Two Sonnets, L: A, ca. 1939.
         Song: v., pf.

    809 Foote, Arthur. Three Songs, MS (Opus 79). Song: [v.,
         pf.].

    810 Gover, Gerald. L: BH, 1962. Song: sab, pf. or sb,
         pf.

    811 Gray, Alan. 1914, L: S&B, pre-1967. Cyc.: satb, org.

    812 Ireland, John. L: WR, 1917, Two Songs, L: WR, 1917-
         18. Song: solo v., pf.

97

813   Sumsion, Corbett. Two Songs, MS pre-1936, L: N.
Song: [v., pf.?].

814   Vermeulen, Matthijs. MS 1916. Song: ms solo, pf.

Song   "All suddenly the wind comes soft"   Poetry Review
(Nov. 1912)

815   Anderson, Dwight. "The Hawthorn Hedge", Cin.: Willis, pre-1940. Song: [v., pf.?].

816* Gurney, Ivor. "All suddenly...", Five Songs, MS.
Song: v., pf.

817   Gurney, Ivor. "Heart's Pain", MS 1920. Song: v., pf.

818   Ireland, John. "Spring Sorrow", L: WR, 1918. Song:
solo v., pf.

819   Le Lacheur, Rex. "All suddenly...", Tor.: CMS, 1941.
Song: v., pf.

820   Peterkin, Norman. "All suddenly...", L: OUP, pre-
1940. Song: med. v., pf.

821   Rowton, S.J. "Spring Song", L: A, pre-1940. Song:
[v., pf.?].

822* Swain, Freda. "Spring Sorrow", MS 1942, Chinnor:
Channel, NEMO. Setting for ms (or bar) and pf.
ensemble.

823   Thomas, Muriel. "The Buds in Spring", L: BH, 1961.
Song: v., pf.

Song of the Pilgrims, The   "What light of unremembered
skies"   Westminster Gazette (Mar. 1908)

824   Shepherd, Arthur. B: Birchard, 1937. Cta.: t solo,
ssaattbb, orch. or pf.

Sonnet   "Oh! Death will find me"   Cambridge Review (Nov.
1909)

Brooke, Rupert continued

825 Boehle, William. "Sonnet for Voice and Piano", MS.
Song: ms or high bar solo, pf.

There's Wisdom in Women   "Oh love is fair"   New Statesman
(Oct. 1913)

826 Brown, James. "Oh love...", MS. Song: t or bar solo,
pf.

827* Gurney, Ivor. Five Songs, MS. Song: v., pf.

Treasure, The   "When colour goes home"   New Numbers (Dec.
1914) from "1914"

828 Gray, Alan. 1914, L: S&B, pre-1967. Cyc.: satb, org.

829* Gurney, Ivor. Five Songs, MS. Song: v., pf.

Unfortunate   "Heart, you are restless"   Poetry Review
(Nov. 1912)

830 Gipps, Ruth. Four Songs of Youth, MS. Song: s or t
solo, pf.

Voice, The   See: Love Poem, A

Waikiki   "Warm perfumes like a breath"   New Numbers (Aug.
1914)

831 Griffes, Charles T. Three Poems, NY: GS, 1918.
Song: high v., pf.

Way That Lovers Use, The   "Way that lovers use, The"
Poetry and Drama (Dec. 1913)

832 Crist, Bainbridge. NY: CF, pre-1940. Song: [v.,
pf.?].

833 Ganz, Rudolph. NY: CF, pre-1940. Song: [v., pf.?].

834 Rowley, Alec. L: WR, pre-1940. Song: [v., pf.?].

Brooke, Rupert continued

835   Rowton, S.J. L: A, pre-1940. Song: [v., pf.?].

836   Sumsion, Corbett. _Two Songs_, MS pre-1936, L: N.
      Song: [v., pf.?].

Miscellanea

837   Hughes, Gervase. The 1962 edn. (rev. by Sir Jack
      Westrup) of Eric Blom's _Everyman's Dictionary of
      Music_ (L: Dent) indicates that Hughes' work incl.
      settings of texts by Brooke.

BUCHAN, John   1875-1940

Eternal Feminine, The   "When I was a freckled bit bairn"
In _Poems: Scots and English_, rev. edn. (1936)

838   Dorward, David. _Three Scotch Songs_, MS, avail. SMA.
      Cyc.: b solo, pf.

South Countrie, The   "I never likit the Kingdom o' Fife"
In _Poems: Scots and English_, rev. edn. (1936)

839   Dorward, David. _Three Scotch Songs_, MS, avail. SMA.
      Cyc.: b solo, pf.

Wood Magic   "I will walk warily in the wise woods"   In
Poems: Scots and English (1917)

840   Shaw, Martin. L: CR, 1924. Song: solo v., pf.

Buchanan, Robert

BUCHANAN, Robert Williams   1841-1901

Ballad of Judas Iscariot, The   "'Twas the body of Judas Iscariot"   In The Complete Poetical Works of Robert Buchanan, Vol. I (1901)

    841 Purvis, Richard. Ph.: EV, 1949. Cta.: solo v., male
         chorus, org. (or pf.).

Book of the Visions seen by Orm the Celt, The   "There is a
mortal, and his name is Orm"   In The Complete Poetical
Works of Robert Buchanan, Vol. I (1901) as part of "The
Book of Orm"

    842 Cowen, Frederic H. "The Veil", L: N, 1910. Setting
         for s, a, t, bar soli, satb, orch. Sets lines
         beginning: "O brother, hold me by the hand and
         hearken".

Dreamer of Dreams, The   "'We are men in a world of men, not
gods!'"   In The Complete Poetical Works of Robert Buchanan, Vol. II (1901)

    843 Boughton, Rutland. "The Dreamers", MS 1924. Song:
         chorus, a cap.

Meg Blane   "'Lord, hearken to me!...'"   In North Coast and
Other Poems (1868)

    844 Coleridge-Taylor, Samuel. L: N, 1902. Setting for
         ms solo, chorus, orch.

O'Connor's Wake   "To the wake of O'Connor"   In The Complete
Poetical Works of Robert Buchanan, Vol. I (1901)

    845 Bath, Hubert. "The Wake of O'Connor", L: N, 1912.
         Setting for satb, orch.

Wedding of Shon Maclean, The   "To the wedding of Shon
Maclean"   In The Complete Poetical Works of Robert
Buchanan, Vol. I (1901)

101

Buchanan, Robert continued

846 Bath, Hubert. L: C, 1909. Rhapsody: s, bar soli,
     chorus, orch.

Miscellanea

847 Bower, Neville. "The Coming of Spring", L: BH, 1962.
     Song: sa, pf.

848 Mackenzie, Alexander. "Marmion", MS, prod. 1891. In-
     cidental music. Text by Buchanan, based on a text
     by Sir Walter Scott.

849 Mackenzie, Alexander. "The New Covenant", L: N,
     1888. Setting for satb, orch.

850 Mackenzie, Alexander. Two Choral Odes from "The
     Bridge of Love", MS ca. 1891. Settings entitled:
     "Rejoice for love is lord", "O thou divine".

CAINE, Thomas Henry Hall   1853-1931

Eternal City, The   (DR)   (1901)

851 Mascagni, Pietro. MS, prod. 1902. Incidental music.

CAMPBELL, (Ignatius) Roy Dunnachie   1902-1957

Autumn "I love to see, when leaves depart"   In Adamastor
(1930)

852 Brown, James. MS. Song: s (or t) or ms (or bar)
     solo, pf.

Campbell, (I.) Roy continued

En Una Noche Oscura   "Upon a gloomy night"   In Talking
   Bronco (1946) Transl. from St. John of the Cross. Incl.
   in The Collected Poems of Roy Campbell, Vol. 3 (1960)
   under the title "Upon a Gloomy Night".

   853 Routh, Francis. "Elegy", MS 1964. Song: s solo,
        vln., pf.

Upon a Gloomy Night   See: En Una Noche Oscura

Miscellanea

   854 Barnes, Fairbairn. The Feb. 1938 issue of Musical
        Times incl. a score supplement of Barnes' "Ye
        choirs of New Jerusalem" (L: N, 1937). This
        Easter anthem for satb, org. is a setting of a
        transl. by "R. [Roy?] Campbell".

   855 Ridout, Alan. "O Flame of Love so Living", L: S&B,
        ca. 1962. Anthem: sab, a cap. The text is a
        transl. by Campbell from St. John of the Cross.

   856 Ridout, Alan. "Sequence", L: S&B, ca. 1962. Setting
        for unison male chorus, org. The text is a
        transl. by Campbell from St. John of the Cross.

   857 Rubbra, Edmund. "A Song of the Soul", MS (Opus 78),
        L: L. Setting for ssatbb, hp., timp., stgs. The
        text is a transl. by Campbell from St. John of
        the Cross.

CAMPBELL, Joseph   1879-1944

As I Came over the Grey, Grey Hills   "As I came over the
   grey, grey hills"   In The Gilly of Christ (1907)

   858 Bax, Arnold. Five Irish Songs, L: MM, 1922, assigned
        L: C, 1943. Song: solo v., pf.

103

Campbell, Joseph continued

859   Hart, Fritz. "The Gilly of Christ", The Gilly of
      Christ, MS 1922, avail. State Library of Vic-
      toria, Melbourne. Song: v., pf.

At Morning Tide   "At morning tide"   In The Gilly of Christ
(1907)

   860   Hart, Fritz. The Gilly of Christ, MS 1922, avail.
         State Library of Victoria, Melbourne. Song: v.,
         pf.

Black Sile of the Silver Eye   "As I rode down to Gartan
   fair"   In The Mountainy Singer (1909)

   861   Harty, Hamilton. "Black Sheela of the Silver Eye",
         Three Traditional Ulster Airs, L: BH, pre-1940.
         Song: v., pf.

By a Wondrous Mystery   "By a wondrous mystery"   In The
   Gilly of Christ (1907)

   862   Hart, Fritz. The Gilly of Christ, MS 1922, avail.
         State Library of Victoria, Melbourne. Song: v.,
         pf.

Cherry Valley   "In Cherry Valley the cherries blow"   In
   The Mountainy Singer (1909)

   863   Quilter, Roger. Three Pastoral Songs, L: Elkin,
         1921. Cyc.: low v., pf. or low v., vln., vcl.,
         pf.

Christ, Wandering with the Twelve   "Christ, wandering with
   the Twelve"   In The Gilly of Christ (1907)

   864   Hart, Fritz. The Gilly of Christ, MS 1922, avail.
         State Library of Victoria, Melbourne. Song: v.,
         pf.

Cradle-Song, A   "Sleep, white love, sleep"   In The
   Mountainy Singer (1909)

Campbell, Joseph continued

865   Peterkin, Norman. "Sleep, White Love", L: OUP, 1940.
       Song: ms solo, pf.

Dark is Magical, The   "Dark is magical, the air, The"   In
The Gilly of Christ (1907)

    866   Hart, Fritz. The Gilly of Christ, MS 1922, avail.
           State Library of Victoria, Melbourne. Song: v.,
           pf.

Every Shuiler is Christ   "Every shuiler is Chist"   In
The Gilly of Christ (1907)

    867   Scott, Annie D. "The Shuiler", Four Irish Songs, L:
           BH, pre-1940. Song: [v., pf.].

Go, Ploughman, Plough   "Go, ploughman, plough"   In The
Mountainy Singer (1909)

    868   Haufrecht, Herbert. MS, avail. ACA. Song: high or
           low v., pf.

He Staggered Thro' the Burning Street   "He staggered thro'
the burning street"   In The Gilly of Christ (1907)

    869   Hart, Fritz. The Gilly of Christ, MS 1922, avail.
           State Library of Victoria, Melbourne. Song: v.,
           pf.

I am the Gilly of Christ   "I am the gilly of Christ"   In
The Gilly of Christ (1907)

    870   Hart, Fritz. The Gilly of Christ, MS 1922, avail.
           State Library of Victoria, Melbourne. Song: v.,
           pf.

I am the Mountainy Singer   "I am the mountainy singer"   In
The Gilly of Christ (1907)

    871   Hart, Fritz. The Gilly of Christ, MS 1922, avail.
           State Library of Victoria, Melbourne. Song: v.,
           pf.

Campbell, Joseph continued

I Follow a Star   "I follow a star"   In The Gilly of Christ
(1907)

  872 Hart, Fritz. The Gilly of Christ, MS 1922, avail.
       State Library of Victoria, Melbourne. Song: v.,
       pf.

I Heard a Piper Piping   "I heard a piper piping"   In The
Mountainy Singer (1909)

  873 Bax, Arnold. Five Irish Songs, L: MM, 1922, assigned
       L: C, 1943. Song: solo v., pf.

  874 Peterkin, Norman. L: OUP, 1924. Song: ms solo, un-
       acc.

I Love the Din of Beating Drums   "I love the din of beating
drums"   In The Mountainy Singer (1909)

  875 Peterkin, Norman. L: OUP, 1924. Song: bar solo, pf.

I will Go with My Father A-Ploughing   "I will go with my
father a-ploughing"   In The Mountainy Singer (1909)

  876 Gurney, Ivor. MS pre-1937, L: BH. Song: solo v.,
       pf.

  877 Mulliner, Michael. L: OUP, 1951. Song: t solo, pf.

  878 Quilter, Roger. Three Pastoral Songs, L: Elkin,
       1921. Cyc.: low v., pf. or low v., vln., vcl.,
       pf.

I Wish and I Wish   "I wish and I wish"   In The Mountainy
Singer (1909)

  879 Peterkin, Norman. L: OUP, 1925. Song: ms solo, pf.

  880 Quilter, Roger. Three Pastoral Songs, L: Elkin,
       1921. Cyc.: low v., pf. or low v., vln., vcl.,
       pf.

Journeyman Weaver, The   "Beam and shuttle seem to know"   In
Irishry (1913)

    881 Peterkin, Norman. L: OUP, pre-1940. Song: [v., pf.].

Moon is in the Marshes, The   "Moon is in the marshes, The"
In The Gilly of Christ (1907)

    882 Hart, Fritz. "The Moon in the Marshes", The Gilly of
    Christ, MS 1922, avail. State Library of Vic-
    toria, Melbourne. Song: v., pf.

My Fidil is Singing   "My fidil is singing"   In The
Mountainy Singer (1909)

    883 Peterkin, Norman. L: OUP, pre-1940. Song: [solo v.,
    pf.].

Night-Piece   "Fill me, O stars"   In The Mountainy Singer
(1909)

    884 Newman, Roy. "Fill Me, O Stars, with a Golden Tune",
    NY: GS, pre-1940. Song: [solo v., pf.].

Night Prayer, A   "Pray for me, Seachnal"   In The Mountainy
Singer (1909)

    885 Scott, Annie D. Four Irish Songs, L: BH, pre-1940.
    Song: [v., pf.].

Ninepenny Fidil, The   "My father and mother were Irish"   In
The Mountainy Singer (1909)

    886 Hughes, Herbert, arr. L: C, 1904. Song: v., pf.
    Text adapt. to an old Irish tune.

Old Woman, The   "As a white candle"   In Irishry (1913)

    887 Dillon, Shaun. Cantata in Memoriam, MS, perf. Nov.
    1974. Song (in cta.): s solo, fl., gtr., pf.

Campbell, Joseph continued

888　Hart, Fritz. _Five Songs for Voice and Pianoforte_,
　　　MS 1938, avail. State Library of Victoria, Mel-
　　　bourne. Song: v., pf.

889　Haufrecht, Herbert. MS, avail. ACA. Song: med. v.,
　　　pf.

890　Parke, Dorothy. "As...", MS 1966. Song: v., pf.

891*　Roberton, Hugh. L: PT, 1927. Song: ttbb, a cap.

Twilight Fallen White and Cold　"Twilight fallen white and
　cold"　In _The Gilly of Christ_ (1907)

892　Hart, Fritz. _The Gilly of Christ_, MS 1922, avail.
　　　State Library of Victoria, Melbourne. Song: v.,
　　　pf.

893　Scott, Annie D. _Four Irish Songs_, L: BH, pre-1940.
　　　Song: [v., pf.].

When Rooks Fly Homeward　"When rooks fly homeward"　In _The
Gilly of Christ_ (1907)

894　Gurney, Ivor. MS n.d. Song: [solo v., pf.].

895　Hart, Fritz. _The Gilly of Christ_, MS 1922, avail.
　　　State Library of Victoria, Melbourne. Song: v.,
　　　pf.

896　Rowley, Alec. L: Swan, pre-1940. Song: [v., pf.].

897　Shepherd, Arthur. MS, avail. University of Utah.
　　　Song: v., pf.

Women Bore their Children, The　"Women bore their children,
　The"　In _The Gilly of Christ_ (1907)

898　Hart, Fritz. _The Gilly of Christ_, MS 1922, avail.
　　　State Library of Victoria, Melbourne. Song: v.,
　　　pf.

Miscellanea

Campbell, Joseph continued

899 Deale, Edgar M. "The Blue Hills of Antrim", L:
Elkin, 1950. Song: ssa, a cap.

900 Deale, Edgar M. "Kitty, my love, will you marry
me?", L: OUP, 1945. Song: satb, a cap. Publ. L:
OUP, 1953 for ssa, a cap. and for ttbb, pf.

901* Edmonds, Paul. "The Old Woman", L: Elkin, ca. 1922.
[Text by Joseph Campbell?]

902 Harty, Hamilton. "The Blue Hills of Antrim", L: BH,
1905. Song: med. v., pf.

903 Harty, Hamilton. "My Lagan Love", L: BH, 1905. Song:
med. v., pf.

904 Hughes, Herbert. "The Gartan Mother's Lullaby", L:
BH, 1909 in Irish Country Songs, Vol. I. Song:
solo v., pf. Text begins: "Sleep, O babe, for the
red bee hums".

905 Maconchy, Elizabeth. Three Songs, L: C. Song: t
solo, hp. Incl. words by [Joseph?] Campbell.

906 May, Frederick. "The Traveller", MS pre-1968. Song:
v., pf.

907 Mulliner, Michael. "Harvest Song", L: OUP, 1951.
Song: unison v., pf.

908 Newman, Roy. "Fill me, O stars, with a golden tune",
NY: GS, pre-1940. Song: [v., pf.].

909 Parke, Dorothy. "The Blue Hills of Antrim", L: BH,
1959. Song: ssa, a cap.

910 Parke, Dorothy. "The Gartan Mother's Lullaby", L:
Elkin, 1955. Song: ssa, pf.

911 Persichetti, Vincent. "Now in the Tomb is Laid",
Hymns and Responses for the Church Year, Ph.: EV,
1965. Hymn: chorus of unison v. (or satb), pf.
(or org.) or chorus of unison v. (or satb), a
cap.

912 Scott, Annie D. "The Shrine", Four Irish Songs, L:
BH, pre-1940. Song: [v., pf.].

Carpenter, Edward

CARPENTER, Edward   1844-1929

April   "O April, month of Nymphs and Fauns and Cupids"   In
Towards Democracy (1883)

   913 Gardiner, H. Balfour. MS pre-1950, L: S&B. Cta.:
        chorus, orch.

Child of the Lonely Heart   "Child of the lonely heart"   In
Towards Democracy (1883)

   914 Boughton, Rutland. Three Songs, L: Curwen, 1919.
        Song: solo v., pf.

Dead Christ, The   "Once more the dead Christ lies"   In Towards Decocracy (1883)

   915 Boughton, Rutland. Four Songs, L: N, 1909. Song:
        solo v., pf.

England, Arise!   "England, arise! The long long night is
over"   In Sketches from Life in Town and Country And some
Verses (1908)

   916 Carpenter, Edward. Three Songs, Manchester: Labour
        Press, 1896. Song: [v., pf.]. "England, Arise!"
        was arr. by John Curwen for ttbb; arr. publ. L:
        Curwen, 1906.

   917 Day, Edgar F. L: Curwen, 1932. Song: unison v., pf.

   918 Thiman, Eric. L: N, 1934. Song: unison v., pf.

   919 Vaughan Williams, Ralph. "Guildford ('England
        Arise')", L: OUP, 1925. Song: unison v., org.

   920 Warrell, Arthur. L: OUP, 1929. Song: unison v.,
        orch. or unison v., pf.

"Fly messenger! through the streets of the cities ancle-
plumed Mercury fly!"   In Towards Democracy (1883)

Carpenter, Edward continued

921 Boughton, Rutland. "Fly Messenger", Four Songs, L:
     N, 1909. Song: solo v., pf.

High in My Chamber   "High in my chamber I hear the deep
bells chime"   In Towards Democracy (1883)

     922 Boughton, Rutland. "Midnight", L: N, 1909. Setting
          for satb, orch.

Lake of Beauty, The   "Let your mind be quiet"   In Towards
Democracy (1883)

     923 Boughton, Rutland. Three Songs, L: Curwen, 1919.
          Song: solo v., pf.

"O Freedom, beautiful beyond compare"   In Towards Democracy
(1883)

     924 Boughton, Rutland. "To Freedom", Four Songs, L: N,
          1909. Song: solo v., pf.

"Standing beyond Time"   In Towards Democracy (1883)

     925 Boughton, Rutland. Four Songs, L: N, 1909. Song:
          solo v., pf.

Triumph of Civilisation, The   "On the outskirts of a great
city"   In Towards Democracy (1883)

     926 Boughton, Rutland. Three Songs, L: Curwen, 1919.
          Song: solo v., pf.

Miscellanea

     927 Boughton, Rutland. "The Wind", MS 1909. Partsong.
          [Possibly a setting of "The Wind of May" from
          Towards Democracy (1883)?]

     928 Carpenter, Edward. "The City of the Sun", Man-
          chester: Labour Press, 1908. Song with words and
          music by Carpenter.

Carpenter, Edward continued

929   Carpenter, Edward. "The People to their Land", Three
      Songs, Manchester: Labour Press, 1896. Song with
      words and music by Carpenter.

930   Herbert, Victor. "Out of his heart he builds a
      home", Cinderella Man, NY: Witmark, 1916. Song:
      v., pf. Text begins: "The world is blind".

931   Romberg, Sigmund. "Melody", NY: Harms, 1933.
      Musical. Lyrics by Irving Caesar.

CAUSLEY, Charles Stanley   1917-

Able Seaman Hodge Remembers Ceylon   "O the blackthorn and
   the wild cherry"   In Farewell, Aggie Weston (1951)

      932   Hurd, Michael. Shore Leave, L: N, 1968. Cyc.: bar
            solo, str. orch.

At the British War Cemetary, Bayeux   "I walked where in
   their talking graves"   In Union Street (1957)

      933   Fulton, Norman. "At Bayeux", A Norman Diary, MS.
            Cyc.: med. v., pf.

At the Statue of William the Conqueror, Falaise   "See him
   ride the roaring air"   In Union Street (1957)

      934   Fulton, Norman. "At Falaise", A Norman Diary, MS.
            Cyc.: med. v., pf.

Convoy   "Draw the blanket of ocean"   In Farewell, Aggie
   Weston (1951)

      935   .Hurd, Michael. Shore Leave, L: N, 1968. Cyc.: bar
            solo, str. orch.

112

Causley, Charles continued

Elizabethan Sailor's Song   "My love my love is a green box-
    tree"   In Farewell, Aggie Weston (1951)

    936 Hurd, Michael. Shore Leave, L: N, 1968. Cyc.: bar
         solo, str. orch.

I Am the Great Sun   "I am the great sun, but you do not see
    me"   In Union Street (1957)

    937 Fulton, Norman. "At Lisieux", A Norman Diary, MS.
         Cyc.: med. v., pf.

Sailor's Carol   "Lord, the snowful sky"   In Survivor's
    Leave (1953)

    938 Hurd, Michael. Shore Leave, L: N, 1968. Cyc.: bar
         solo, str. orch.

Shore Leave   "See the moon her yellow landau"   In Sur-
    vivor's Leave (1953)

    939 Hurd, Michael. Shore Leave, L: N, 1968. Cyc.: bar
         solo, str. orch.

Timothy Winters   "Timothy Winters comes to school"   In
    Union Street (1957)

    940 Southam, T. Wallace. L: Turret, 1970 in Contemporary
         Poetry Set to Music. Song: v., pf. Text arr. by
         Pat Smythe.

CHESTERTON, Gilbert Keith   1874-1936

Ballad of the White Horse, The   "Before the gods that made
    the gods"   (1911) Portions 1st publ. under the title
    "Ballad of Alfred" in A Chesterton Calendar (1911)

113

941 Gardner, John L. L: S&B, 1960. Cta.: opt. bar solo,
     satb, orch. Settings of extracts from Books 1,
     2, 3, 7 and 8.

Child of the Snows, A   See: Feast of the Snow, The

Christmas Carol, A   "Christ-child lay on Mary's lap, The"
The Wild Knight and Other Poems (1900)

942 Anon. "The World's Desire", L: OUP as "Oxford Carol
     Leaf #143". Carol: [v., pf.].

943 Barlow, David. "The World's Desire", L: N, 1958.
     Carol-anthem: satb, a cap.

944 Black, Charles. "The Stars Looked Down", Glen Rock:
     JF, 1961. [Carol]: s solo obbl., satb, a cap.

945 Cashmore, Donald J. "The Worlds's Desire", L: N,
     1962. Carol: satb, a cap.

946 Chapman, Marion C. "The World's Desire", NY: Row,
     1941. Carol: satb, pf.

947 Conant, J. Willis. "The Christ-child...", NY: GX,
     1956. Song: high or med. v., pf.

948 Daniels, Mabel W. "The Christ-Child", B: Schmidt,
     1931. Carol: satb, a cap.

949 Dello Joio, Norman. NY: EBM, 1962. Carol: satb, pf.
     or ssa, pf.

950 Gayfer, James M. "The World's Desire", MS 1965,
     avail. CMC. Song: med. v., pf.

951 Heys, Sidney. "The Christ-child...", Two Carols,
     Croy.: RSCM, 1970. Carol. Melody arr. by G.H.
     Knight.

952 Johnstone, Margaret. "The Christ-Child", L: OUP,
     1951. [Carol]: satb, pf.

953 Noble, T.T., arr. "The World's Desire", Round of
     Carols, L: OUP, 1935. Carol. Trad. air arr. by
     Noble.

954 Pitfield, Thomas B. "The Christ Child", L: A, avail.
   only from composer. Carol: unison v., pf. or
   unison v., org. Also arr. for satb, pf. or satb,
   org.

955 Rathbone, George. "The Christ-Child", L: N, 1924.
   [Carol]: solo v., pf. Publ. L: N, 1926 for satb,
   pf.

956 Shaw, Martin, arr. "The World's Desire", L: OUP,
   1928 in The Oxford Book of Carols. Carol: mixed
   v., pf.

957 Tatton, J. Meredith. "The Christ-Child", L: Deanne
   (YBP), 1939. Carol: unison v., pf.

958 Teed, Roy. "The Christ-child", So Blest a Day, MS
   ca. 1960. Song (in cta.): s (or ms), bar duet,
   orch. or s (or ms), bar duet, pf. Complete cta.
   requires soli, chorus, orch.

959 Weigl, Vally. NY: M, 1962. Carol: ms solo, opt. sa,
   a cap.

960 Williamson, Malcolm. L: Weinberger, 1965. Carol:
   low v., pf.

961 Wills, Arthur. "The Christ-child...", L: N, 1966.
   Carol: unison v., pf.

Cider Song, A   "Wine they drink in Paradise, The"   Odd
Volume (1912)

962 Boughton, Rutland. "Song of Cyder", MS 1930. Song:
   solo v., pf.

963 Vaughan Williams, Ralph. "In Praise of Wine". An
   incomplete composition found in the composer's
   late sketchbooks.

Donkey, The   "When fishes flew and forests walked"   The
Wild Knight and Other Poems (1900)

964 Baas, Alexius. NY: HWG, pre-1940. Song: [v., pf.].

965 Besly, Maurice. L: BH, pre-1940. Song: [v., pf.].

Chesterton, G.K. continued

966   Boughton, Rutland. Three Partsongs, L: JW, 1929.
      Song: chorus, a cap.

967   Bright, Dora. L: Elkin, 1936. Song: med. v., pf.

968   Buck, Vera. L: Cary, 1935. Song: [v., pf.].

969   Buczynski, Walter. Cycle of Three Songs, priv.
      publ., 1954, avail. CMC. Cyc.: high v., pf.

970   Cowell, Henry. NY: MPI, 1947. Song: [high] solo v.,
      pf.

971   Hageman, Richard. L: BH, ca. 1934. Song: high v.,
      pf.

972   Purdie, Hunter. NY: GS, 1962. Song: satb, a cap.

973   Roberton, Hugh. L: Curwen, 1936. Song: ttbb, a cap.

974   Roff, Joseph. MS 1948. Song: [solo v., choir, a
      cap.].

975   Searle, Humphrey. Wendover: RP, 1974. Song: med.
      male v., pf.

976   Smit, Leo. MS n.d., avail. CMC. Song: med. v., pf.

977   Tomlins, Greta. S. Croy.: L, 1968. Song: unison v.
      (last verse ssa), pf.

978   Treharne, Bryceson. B: BMC, pre-1940. Song: [v.,
      pf.].

Elegy in a Country Churchyard   "Men that worked for England,
  The"   The Ballad of St. Barbara and Other Verses (1922)

979   Boughton, Rutland. "Song of Graves", L: Curwen,
      1926. Song: chorus, a cap.

Feast of the Snow, The   "There is heard a hymn when the
  panes are dim"   Parents' Review (Dec. 1900), rev. 191?

980   Treharne, Bryceson. "A Child of the Snows", B: BMC,
      1917. Song: high v., pf.

981 Turner, Robert. "A Child of the Snows", The House of Christmas, MS 1963, avail. CMC. Carol: ssa, a cap. Complete set of four carols requires ssa, ttbb, and satb.

House of Christmas, The   "There fared a mother driven forth"
Poems (1915)

982 Griffiths, T. Vernon. "There fared...", priv. printed for a Christmas card. Round: 4 ms, a cap. Setting of first four lines only.

983 Turner, Robert. The House of Christmas, MS 1963, avail. CMC. Carol: satb, a cap. Complete set of four carols requires satb, ssa, and ttbb.

Hymn, A   See: "O God of earth and altar"

"I come from Castlepatrick, and me heart is on me sleeve"
The Flying Inn (1914), rev. 1915

984 Foss, Hubert J. "Castlepatrick", L: OUP, 1929. Song: bar solo, pf.

985 Hely-Hutchinson, Victor. "Castlepatrick", L: Elkin, 1933. Song: med. v., pf. or med. v., orch.

986 Meredith, Evan. "The Folks that Live in Liverpool", Twelve Drinking Songs, L: MML. Song: [v., pf.]. Setting of poem's 2nd stanza.

"In the city set upon slime and loam"   The Flying Inn
(1914), rev. 1915

987 Hely-Hutchinson, Victor. "Who Goes Home?", L: Elkin, 1933. Song: med. v., pf. or med. v., orch.

Man Who Was Thursday, The   (NV)   (1908) Dramatised vers. in coll. with Mrs. Cecil Chesterton and Ralph Neale was publ. 1926

988 Ježek, Jaroslav. MS 1927. Incidental music. Polish title: "Kamarád Čtvrtek".

117

Chesterton, G.K. continued

Me Heart   See: "I come from Castlepatrick, and me heart is
     on me sleeve"

Nativity, The   "Thatch on the roof was as golden, The"
     Parents' Review (Dec. 1897), rev. 1915.

     989 Turner, Robert. The House of Christmas, MS 1963,
          avail. CMC. Carol: satb, a cap. Complete set of
          four carols requires satb, ssa, and ttbb.

"O God of earth and altar"*   The English Hymnal (1906), rev.
     1915

     990 Barrell, Bernard. MS 1948. Hymn: satb, str. orch.,
          opt. org. Also arr. for unison v., str. orch.,
          opt. org. Accompaniment also reduced for org. or
          pf.

     991 Blake, Leonard. L: EA, pre-1951. [Hymn]: unison v.,
          pf.

     992 Ridout, Godfrey. See footnote to the poem.

     993 Wordsworth, William. "Hymn of Dedication", L: L,
          1947. Hymn: satb, orch. or satb, str. orch. Also
          arr. for satb, org.

Rolling English Road, A   See: Song of Temperance Reform, A

"Saracen's Head, The"   See: Song of the Temperance Hotel

Song of Quoodle, The   See: Song of the Dog Named Quoodle,
     The

Song of Temperance Reform, A   "Before the Roman came to
     Rye"   New Witness (Sept. 1913), rev. 1914

     994 Besly, Maurice. "The Rolling English Road", L: WR,
          pre-1940. Song: [v., pf.].

     995 Bourgeois, Derek. "The Rolling English Road", Six
          Songs of Wandering, MS 1962. Cyc.: bar solo, pf.

118

996 Cohen, Dudley. "The Rolling English Road", L: Bron, 1970. Song: unison v., pf.

997 Gilbert, Norman. "The Rolling English Road", L: L, 1961. Song: ssa, a cap. Also avail. for ssb, a cap. or ttb, a cap.

998 Griffiths, T. Vernon. "The Rolling English Road", MS. Song: satb, pf.

999 Hely-Hutchinson, Victor. "The Rolling English Road", L: Elkin, 1933. Song: med. v., pf. or med. v., orch.

Song of the Dog Named Quoodle, The   "They haven't got no noses"   New Witness (Nov. 1913), rev. 1915.

1000 Hart, Fritz. "Quoodles", Five Part Songs for Women's Unaccompanied Three-Part Choir, MS 1935 (Opus 112). Song: 3 pt. female choir, a cap.

Song of the Second Deluge, The   "Old Noah he had an ostrich farm"   New Witness (Feb. 1913), rev. 1914

1001 Batton, Joseph. "Old Noah", L: BH, 1954. Song: [v., pf.].

1002 Brown, Hubert. "Wine and Water", L: C, 1932. Song: solo v., pf.

1003 Gilbert, Norman. "Wine and Water", L: L, 1961. Song: ssa, pf. or ssb, pf. or ttb, pf.

1004 Mulliner, Michael. "Wine and Water", L: C, 1959. Song: solo v., pf.

1005 Parry, W.H. "Wine and Water", L: OUP, 1963. Song: sab, pf.

Song of the Temperance Hotel   "'Saracen's Head, The'"   New Witness (Feb. 1913), rev. 1914

1006 Meredith, Evan. "The Saracen's Head", Twelve Drinking Songs, L: MML. Song: [v., pf.].

119

Chesterton, G.K. continued

Who Goes Home?   See: "In the city set upon slime and loam"

Wine and Water   See: Song of the Second Deluge, The

Wise Men, The   "Step softly, under snow or rain"   Daily
   News (Dec. 1905), rev. 1915

   1007 Daunton, Frank. L: S, 1967. Cta.: satb, pf.

   1008 Turner, Robert. The House of Christmas, MS 1963,
      avail. CMC. Carol: ttbb, a cap. Complete set of
      four carols requires ttbb, ssa, and satb.

Miscellanea

   1009 Buck, Vera. "The Donkey", L: C, pre-1966. Song: [v.,
      pf.]. [Text by Chesterton?]

   1010 Butterley, Nigel. "The World's Desire", MS 1953.
      Setting for choir. [Text by Chesterton?]

   1011 Clarke, F.R.C. Two Songs, MS 1952-57. Song: low v.,
      pf. Incl. one song employing words by Chesterton.

   1012 Halski, Czeslaw. Four English Songs, MS pre-1954.
      Incl. one song employing words by Chesterton.

CHURCH, Richard Thomas   1893-1972

Hay's Wharf   "Who hasn't heard of London Bridge?"   In The
   Inheritors (1957)

   1013 Parfrey, Raymond. Fair Thames, MS 1974. Choral ste.:
      satb, pf.

Windless Day   "Almost I hear the dying leaf"   In The Collected Poems of Richard Church (1948)

hurch, Richard continued

1014 Klein, Ivy. L: CR, 1946. Song: solo v., pf.

HURCHILL, Winston Spencer   1874-1965

History of the English-Speaking Peoples, A   (PR)   (1956-58)

1015 Walton, William. "March: A History of the English-
     Speaking Peoples", MS (recorded Mar. 1959),
     avail. L: OUP. Incidental music for TV prod.:
     orch.

1016 Williamson, Malcolm. "Churchill's People", MS, prod.
     BBC 1974-75. Incidental music for TV.

Miscellanea

1017 Bliss, Arthur. "March: Homage to a Great Man". MS
     1964, broadcast Jan. 1965. Orch. only. Arr. for
     military band by W.J. Duthoit; arr. publ. L: C.

CLARKE, Arthur Charles   1917-

Transcience   (SS)   In The Other Side of the Sky (1958)

1018 Bedford, David. "The Tentacles of the Dark Nebula",
     L: UE, 1970. Setting for t solo, 8 solo stgs.
     (3 vln., 2 vla., 2 vcl., db.).

Clarke, Austin

CLARKE, Austin   1896-

Blessing   "O Woman of the House, no sorrow come"   In The Cattledrive in Connaught and Other Poems (1925) as one of "Three Sentences"

    1019* Swain, Freda. L: Curwen, 1950 (avail. Chinnor: Channel, NEMO). Song: bar and pf. ensemble.

Lost Heifer, The   "When the black herds of the rain were grazing"   In The Cattledrive in Connaught and Other Poems (1925)

    1020* Swain, Freda. MS 1939-40, avail. Chinnor: Channel, NEMO. Song: bar and pf. ensemble.

COLERIDGE, Mary Elizabeth   1861-1907

"Arm thee! Arm thee! Forth upon the road!"   In Poems (1907)

    1021 Davies, H. Walford. "Arm thee! Arm Thee!", L: N, 1914. Song: 3 pt. chorus (t, bar, b), a cap.

Armida's Garden   "I have been there before thee"   In Poems (1907)

    1022 Parry, C.H.H. English Lyrics, 9th Set, L: N, 1909. Song: v., pf.

Chillingham I   "Through the sunny garden"   In Poems (1907)

    1023 Quilter, Roger. "Through...", Two September Songs, L: Elkin, 1916. Song: low v., pf. Also avail. for high v., pf.

Chillingham II   "O the high valley, the little low hill" In Poems (1907)

oleridge, Mary continued

1024 Quilter, Roger. "The Valley and the Hill", Two
      September Songs, L: Elkin, 1916. Song: low v.,
      pf. Also avail for high v., pf.

Contents of an Ink-bottle, The   "Well of blackness"   In
      Poems (1907)

      1025 Stanford, C.V. "The Inkbottle", Eight Part Songs, MS
            (Opus 119), L: S&B, 1910. Song: ssaa, a cap.

Deserted House, The   "There's no smoke in the chimney"   In
      Poems (1907)

      1026 Sykes, Harold. L: N, 1968. Song: ss, pf.

"Egypt's might is tumbled down"   In Poems (1907)

      1027 Le Fleming, Christopher. L: JWC, 1949. Song: ms or
            bar solo, pf.

Gibberish   "Many a flower have I seen blossom"   In Poems
      (1907)

      1028 Thomson, Bothwell. "The Flower-Bird", L: C, 1911.
            Song: solo v., pf.

Guy's Cliffe at Night   "Heavily plumed the stately elm-tree
      hung"   In Poems (1907)

      1029 Rootham, C.B. L: OUP, 1935. Song: sa, pf.

Hail and Farewell   "Farewell, my joy!"   In Poems (1907)

      1030 Stanford, C.V. "Farewell, My Joy", Eight Part Songs,
            MS (Opus 119), L: S&B, 1910. Song: ssaa, a cap.

Haven, The   "Where the gray bushes by the gray sea grow"
      In Poems (1907)

      1031 Stanford, C.V. Eight Part Songs, L: S&B, 1912. Song:
            satb, a cap.

Coleridge, Mary continued

Hush   "She sleeps so lightly"   In Poems (1907)

   1032 Bridge, Frank. "Where she lies asleep", L: WR, 1916.
      Song: v., pf.

Imagination   "I called you, fiery spirits"   In Poems (1907)

   1033 Rootham, C.B. Four Dramatic Songs (ea. publ. sep.),
      L: N, 1913. Song: v., pf.

In London Town   "It was a bird of Paradise"   In Poems
(1907)

   1034 Rootham, C.B. L: OUP, 1935. Song: ssa, pf.

In Spring   "Love went a-riding over the earth"   In Poems
(1907)

   1035 Bridge, Frank. "Love went a-riding", L: WR, 1916.
      Song: v., pf.

Larghetto   "Grant me but a day, love"   In Poems (1907)

   1036 Stanford, C.V. Eight Part Songs, L: S&B, 1912. Song:
      satb, a cap.

"Low-flying swallow, tho' the sky be fair"   In Poems (1907)

   1037 Stanford, C.V. "The Swallow", Eight Part Songs, MS
      (Opus 119), L: S&B, 1910. Song: ssaa, a cap.

Maiden, The   "Who was this that came by the way"   In Poems
(1907)

   1038 Parry, C.H.H. English Lyrics, 9th Set, L: N, 1909.
      Song: v., pf.

Master and Guest   "There came a man across the moor"   In
Poems (1907)

oleridge, Mary continued

1039 Stanford, C.V. "The Guest", Eight Part Songs, L: S&B, 1912. Song: satb, a cap.

"Night is fallen within, without" In Poems (1907)

1040 Garlick, Antony. "Night Is Fallen", Eleven Canzonets, Cin.: Westwood, 1967. Canzonet: 2 pt. chorus of equal v., a cap.

Oiseau Bleu, L' "Lake lay blue below the hill, The" In Poems (1907)

1041 Busch, William. MS ca. 1944. Song: [v., pf.].

1042 Stanford, C.V. "The Blue Bird", Eight Part Songs, MS (Opus 119), L: S&B, 1910. Song: ssaa, a cap.

On Such a Day "Some hang above the tombs" In Poems (1907)

1043 Ireland, John. "Remember", L: WR, 1918 (copyright held by the John Ireland Estate). Song: solo v., pf.

Our Lady "Mother of God! no lady thou" In Poems (1907)

1044 Hart, Fritz. "The Song of Mary", L: S&B, 1926. Song: 6 pt. chorus (2 s, 2 ms, 2 a), vln., pf.

"Over the Hills and Far Away" "All around was dumb and still" In Poems (1907)

1045 Rootham, C.B. "Over the Hills", Four Dramatic Songs (ea. publ. sep.), L: N, 1913. Song: v., pf.

Song "Thy hand in mine, thy hand in mine" In Poems (1907)

1046 Bridge, Frank. "Thy Hand in Mine", L: WR, 1917. Song: v., pf.

1047 Ireland, John. "The Sacred Flame", L: WR, 1918. Song: solo v., pf.

125

Coleridge, Mary continued

St. Andrew's   "While the sun was going down"   In _Poems_
(1907)

   1048 Parry, C.H.H. "A Fairy Town", _English Lyrics_, 9th
         Set, L: N, 1909. Song: v., pf.

   1049 Rootham, C.B. _Four Dramatic Songs_ (ea. publ. sep.),
         L: N, 1913. Song: v., pf.

Street Lanterns   "Country roads are yellow and brown"   In
Poems (1907)

   1050 Greenhill, Harold. L: EA, pre-1951. Song: 2 pt.
         chorus, [pf.?].

There   "There, in that other world"   In _Poems_ (1907)

   1051 Parry, C.H.H. _English Lyrics_, 9th Set, L: N, 1909.
         Song: v., pf.

Three Aspects   "Some showed me Life as 'twere a royal game"
In _Poems_ (1907)

   1052 Parry, C.H.H. _English Lyrics_, 9th Set, L: N, 1909.
         Song: v., pf.

Train, The   "Green eye--and a red--in the dark, A"   In
Poems (1907)

   1053 Stanford, C.V. _Eight Part Songs_, MS (Opus 119), L:
         S&B, 1910. Song: ssaa, a cap.

Unwelcome   "We were young, we were merry"   In _Poems_ (1907)

   1054 Rootham, C.B. _Four Dramatic Songs_ (ea. publ. sep.),
         L: N, 1913. Song: v., pf.

Veneta   "Wind and waters ring the bells"   In _Poems_ (1907)

   1055 Stanford, C.V. _Eight Part Songs_, L: S&B, 1912. Song:
         satb, a cap.

ɔleridge, Mary continued

When Mary Thro' the Garden Went   "When Mary thro' the garden
went" In Poems (1907)

   1056 Judd, Percy. L: OUP, 1925. Song: ssa, pf. Also
      publ. L: OUP for unison v., pf.

   1057 Stanford, C.V. Eight Part Songs, L: S&B, 1912. Song:
      satb, a cap.

"Whether I live, or whether I die"   In Poems (1907)

   1058 Parry, C.H.H. English Lyrics, 9th Set, L: N, 1909.
      Song: v., pf.

Wilderspin   "In the little red house by the river"   In
Poems (1907)

   1059 Stanford, C.V. Eight Part Songs, L: S&B, 1912. Song:
      satb, a cap.

Witch, The   "I have walked a great while"   In Poems (1907)

   1060 Stanford, C.V. Eight Part Songs, MS (Opus 119), L:
      S&B, 1910. Song: ssaa, a cap.

Witches' Wood, The   "There was a wood, a witches' wood"   In
Poems (1907)

   1061 Parry, C.H.H. English Lyrics, 9th Set, L: N, 1909.
      Song: v., pf.

Miscellanea

   1062 Stanford, C.V. "Chillingham", Eight Part Songs, MS
      (Opus 119), L: S&B, 1910. Song: ssaa, a cap.

   1063 Stanford, C.V. "My heart is thine", Eight Part
      Songs, MS (Opus 119), L: S&B, 1910. Song: ssaa,
      a cap.

   1064 Stanford, C.V. "Plighted", Eight Part Songs, L: S&B,
      1912. Song: satb, a cap.

Coleridge, Mary continued

1065 Stanford, C.V. "To a Tree", Eight Part Songs, L:
S&B, 1912. Song: satb, a cap. [Possibly a setting
of "Lines to a Tree"?]

COLUM, Padraic 1881-1972

Across the Door "Fiddles were playing and playing, The"
In Wild Earth (1907)

1066 Bax, Arnold. Five Irish Songs, L: MM, 1922, copyright assigned L: C, 1943. Song: solo v., pf.

At the Fore of the Year "At the fore of the year, and on
Candlemas Day" In Old Pastures (1930) Incl. (untitled)
as part of "Reminiscence" in Poems (1932)

1067 Herreshoff, Constance. "In the Fore of the Year",
NY: JF, pre-1940. Song: [v., pf.?].

"At the fore of the year, and on Candlemas Day" See: At the
Fore of the Year

Ballad Maker, A "Once I loved a maiden fair" In Wild
Earth (1907)

1068 Deale, Edgar M. Padraic Colum: Four Facets, MS 1968.
Choral ste.: satb, pic.

Ballad of Downal Baun, The "Moon cradle's rocking and rocking, The" In Wild Earth and Other Poems (1916), rev.
1960

1069 Hughes, Herbert. "The Moon Cradle", Songs from
Connacht, MS pre-1937, L: BH. Song: [v., pf.].

1070 Tatton, J. Meredith. "The Moon Cradle's Rocking",
Tor.: Clarke, Irwin, 1959 in The Classroom
Chorister. Song: v., pf.

128

Colum, Padraic continued

Beggar's Child, The   "Mavourneen we'll go far away"   In
Wild Earth and Other Poems (1916)

1071 Dillon, Shaun. Cantata in Memoriam, MS, perf. Nov.
      1974. Song (in cta.): s solo, fl., gtr.

Black Tassels   "Black tassels, black tassels"   In The
Poet's Circuits (1960)

1072 Fleischmann, Aloys. The Poet's Circuits, MS 1972.
      Cyc.: s or t solo, Irish hp.

City Clocks, The   "City clocks point out the hours"   In
Wild Earth (1907)

1073 Hughes, Herbert. Songs from Connacht, MS pre-1937,
      L: BH. Song: [v., pf.].

Cradle Song, A   "O, men from the fields!"   In Wild Earth
(1907)

1074 Angel, James. L: OUP, 1949. Song: 2 pt. chorus, pf.

1075 Bax, Arnold. "Cradle Song", Three Irish Songs, L:
      MM, 1922, copyright assigned L: C, 1943. Song:
      ms solo, pf.

1076 Brand, Margaret. "O, men...", MS pre-1943. Song: ms
      solo, pf.

1077 Bridge, Frank. "Mantle of Blue", L: WR, 1919. Song:
      v., pf.

1078 Cadoret, Charlotte. "Cradle Song", NY: GS, pre-1940.
      Song: [v., pf.?].

1079 Cooke, Arnold A. "O, men...", L: OUP, 1961. Song:
      solo v. (or unison v.), pf. (or org.).

1080 Coulthard, Jean. MS 1927, avail. CMC. Song: s or
      ms solo, pf. Arr. 1928 for sa (or s, a duet),
      pf.; arr. publ. Tor.: BMI, 1960.

1081 Deale, Edgar M. "O, men...", MS 1967. Song: solo v.,
      pf.

129

Colum, Padraic continued

1082   Deale, Edgar M. "O, men...", Padraic Colum: Four Facets, MS 1968. Choral ste.: satb, pic.

1083   Deale, Edgar M. "O, men...", L: OUP, 1973. Song: satb, a cap.

1084   Dear, James R. "Tread Softly", Two Songs, L: S&B, pre-1940. Song: [v., pf.].

1085   Duarte, John. In New York Guitar Review, No. 12 (1951). Song: high v., classical gtr.

1086   Edmonds, Paul. "Cradle Song", L: Curwen, 1920. Song: solo v., pf.

1087   Fleming, Robert. "Cradle Song", MS 1937, avail. CMC. Song: v., pf.

1088   Ganz, Rudolph. "Cradle Song", NY: HWG, pre-1940. Song: [v., pf.?].

1089   Hart, Fritz. Book of Five Songs, MS 1938, avail. State Library of Victoria, Melbourne. Song: solo v., pf.

1090   Harty, Hamilton. "Cradle Song", L: N, pre-1940. Song: [v., pf.].

1091   Hind, John. L: N, 1951. Song: med. v., pf.

1092   Hughes, Herbert. "O, men...", MS pre-1937, L: BH. Song: [v., pf.].

1093   Lodge, Ernest. "The Mantle of Blue", L: OUP, pre-1940. Song: [v., pf.?].

1094   Loughborough, Raymond. "O, men...", L: S&B, pre-1940. Song: [v., pf.?].

1095   McIntyre, Paul. "Cradle Song", MS 1945. Song: v., pf.

1096   Parke, Dorothy. L: BH, 1963. Song: ssa, pf.

1097   Pentland, Barbara. MS 1938. Song: 4 pt. chorus, a cap.

1098 Rubbra, Edmund. "Cradle Song", MS 1923. Song: v.,
pf.

1099 Sheldon, Mary. "Cradle Song", L: Swan, pre-1940.
Song: [v., pf.?].

1100 Stout, Alan. "Cradle Song", MS, avail. ACA. Song:
high v., pf.

1101 Sweetman, Paul. "Lullaby", Waterloo: Waterloo, 1962.
Song: ssa, a cap.

1102 Thomas, Christopher. "O, men...", NY: GX, pre-1940.
Song: [v., pf.?].

1103 Tod, Kenneth. "Cradle Song", NY: GS, pre-1940. Song:
[v., pf.?].

1104 Treharne, Bryceson. "O, men...", NY: JF, pre-1940.
Song: [v., pf.?].

1105 Weaver, Mary W. "Cradle Song", NY: GS, pre-1940.
Song: [v., pf.?].

1106 Weigl, Karl. MS copyright by composer 1946, avail.
ACA. Song: [med.] solo v., pf.

1107 Wilkinson, Philip G. L: EA, 1957. Song: 2 pt.
chorus, pf.

Crane "I know you, Crane" In Creatures (1927), rev. 1960

1108 Fleischmann, Aloys. "The Crane", The Poet's Circuits, MS 1972. Cyc.: s or t solo, Irish hp.

Crane, The See: Crane

Dermott Donn MacMorna "One day you'll come to my husband's
door" In Wild Earth (1907)

1109 Bax, Arnold. MS 1922. Song: v., pf.

Glen Nevin "Once I went over the ocean" In Wild Earth
(1907)

Colum, Padraic continued

    1110   Hughes, Herbert. Songs from Connacht, MS pre-1937,
           L: BH. Song: [v., pf.].

Good Men of Eirinn, The   "Are they not the good men of
   Eirinn" In Wild Earth (1907)

    1111   Hughes, Herbert. Songs from Connacht, MS pre-1937,
           L: BH. Song: [v., pf.].

Island Spinning Song, An   "One came before her" In Wild
   Earth (1909)

    1112   Hughes, Herbert, arr. L: BH, 1909 in Irish County
           Songs, Vol. I. Song: solo v., pf. Arr. of an old
           Irish air.

Mogu, The Wanderer or The Desert   (DR)   (1917)

    1113   May, Frederick. "Mogu", MS pre-1968. Incidental
           music.

Monkeys   See: Monkeys, The

Monkeys, The   "Two little creatures" In Dramatic Legends
   and Other Poems (1922), rev. 1927

    1114   Wyner, Yehudi. "Monkeys", MS copyright by composer
           1957, avail. ACA. Song: [med.] solo v., pf.

"Moon-cradle's rocking and rocking, The" See: Ballad of
   Downal Baun, The

Moytura: A Play for Dancers   (DR)   (1963)

    1115   Victory, Gerard. "Moytura", MS. Incidental music.

No Child   "I heard in the night the pigeons" In Wild Earth
   (1907)

Colum, Padraic continued

1116 Hughes, Herbert. "I heard...", Songs from Connacht,
      MS pre-1937, L: BH. Song: [v., pf.].

"Nor right, nor left, nor any road I see a comrade's face"
See: Rann of Exile, A

"Now, coming on Spring, the days will be growing"   See:
Wandering and Sojourning

"Oh I wish the sun was bright in the sky"   See: Terrible
Robber Men, The

Old Woman of the Roads, An   "Oh, to have a little house!"
In Wild Earth (1907)

     1117* Burnett, R. "Oh, to have...", NY: CF. Song: satb, a
           cap.

     1118 Souther, Louise. NY: Ho, pre-1940. Song: [v., pf.?].

     1119 Victory, Gerard. MS 1954. Song: a or bar solo, pf.

Pidgeons   See: Pidgeons, The

Pidgeons, The   "Odalisques, odalisques"   In Dramatic
Legends and Other Poems (1922), rev. 1927

     1120 Bax, Arnold. Five Irish Songs, L: MM, 1922, copy-
           right assigned L: C, 1943. Song: solo v., pf.

Rann of Exile, A   "Nor right, nor left, nor any road"   In
Wild Earth (1907), rev. 1960

     1121 Bax, Arnold. "Rann of Exile", Three Irish Songs, L:
           MM, 1922, copyright assigned L: C, 1943. Song:
           ms solo, pf.

     1122 Fleischmann, Aloys. "Caoine", The Poet's Circuits,
           MS 1972. Cyc.: s or t solo, Irish hp.

133

1123   Hughes, Herbert. "Rann of Exile", Songs from Connacht, MS pre-1937, L: BH. Song: [v., pf.].

Rann of Wandering, A   "On Saint Bride's Day"   In Wild
Earth (1907)

1124   Bax, Arnold. "Rann of Wandering", Three Irish Songs,
L: MM, 1922, copyright assigned L: C, 1943. Song:
ms solo, pf.

1125   Harty, Hamilton. "Rann of Wandering", L: N, pre-
1940. Song: [v., pf.].

She Moved Through the Fair   "My young love said to me"   In
Wild Earth and Other Poems (1916)

1126   Hughes, Herbert, arr. L: BH, 1909 in Irish County
Songs, Vol. I. Song: solo v., pf. Arr. of an old
Irish air.

Terrible Robber Men, The   "O! I wish the sun was bright"
In Wild Earth (1907), rev. 1960

1127   Hughes, Herbert. Songs from Connacht, MS pre-1937,
L: BH. Song: [v., pf.].

1128   O'Murnaghan, Art, arr. Dublin: Cuala, 1937 in Broadside, No. 11. Song: v., unacc.

1129   Treharne, Bryceson. B: BMC, pre-1940. Song: [v.,
pf.].

Tin-whistle Player, The   "'Tis long since, long since"   In
Old Pastures (1930)

1130   Deale, Edgar M. Padraic Colum: Four Facets, MS 1968.
Choral Ste.: satb, pic.

Singing Bird   "O Forest Bird, forget your songs!"   In
Creatures (1927)

1131   May, Frederick. "O Forest Bird", MS pre-1968. Song:
v., pf.

olum, Padraic continued

Wandering and Sojourning   "Now, coming on Spring"   In
Dramatic_Legends_and_Other_Poems (1922), rev. 1960

   1132 Fleischmann, Aloys. "Spring", The_Poet's_Circuits,
         MS 1972. Cyc.: s or t solo, Irish hp. Setting of
         the portion of "Wandering and Sojourning" sub-
         titled "Spring".

Miscellanea

   1133 Deale, Edgar M. "Séan O'Dwyer a Gleanna", Pairaic
         Colum:_Four_Facets, MS 1968. Choral ste.: satb,
         pic.

   1134 Hughes, Herbert. "A Day's End", Songs_from_Connacht,
         MS pre-1937, L: BH. Song: [v., pf.].

   1135 Nevin, Arthur. "When the Swans Fly", NY: GS, pre-
         1940. Song: [v., pf.?].

   1136 Walters, Leslie. The reader is referred to Robert
         Smith's A_Complete_Catalogue_of_Contemporary
         Welsh_Music_(No._5) for details regarding a MS
         setting by Walters of a text by Colum.

CONRAD, Joseph   1857-1924

Heart_of_Darkness (SS)   Blackwood's_Magazine (Feb.-Apr.
   1899) under the title "The Heart of Darkness", rev. 1902

   1137 Powell, John. "Rhapsodie Nègre", MS, perf. 1918.
         Rhapsody: orch., pf.

Lord_Jim (NV)   Blackwood's_Magazine (Oct. 1899-Nov. 1900),
   publ. sep. 1900

   1138 Kaper, Bronislaw. MS, issued 1965 on Colpix record-
         ing #CP-521. Film music.

135

Conrad, Joseph continued

1139 Twardowski, Romauld. MS 1970-73, avail. PMC. Opera.
      Libr. by the composer. Polish text.

Romance (NV) In coll. with Ford Madox Hueffer (1903)

1140 Arundell, Dennis. MS pre-1954. Incidental music.

To-Morrow (SS) Pall Mall Magazine (Aug. 1902)

1141 Baird, Tadeusz. MS 1964-66, avail. PMC. Opera. Libr.
      by Jerzy S. Sito. Polish title: "Jutro".

Under Western Eyes (NV) English Review (Dec. 1910-Oct.
      1911), publ. sep. 1911

1142 Joubert, John. Borough Green: N, 1968. Opera: 13
      soli, 5 actors, girls' chorus, orch. Libr. by
      Cedric Cliffe.

Victory (NV) Munsey's Magazine (Feb. 1915), pub. sep.
      same year

1143 Bennett, Richard R. MS 1968-69, L: UE (hire). Opera:
      3 s, ms, 4 t, 2 bar, 2 b-bar, b soli, 3 sp.,
      actors, 2 choirs, hp., pf., timp., perc., vcl.,
      stgs., stage orch. (fl., vlns., vcls., mandolin,
      gtr., acc.). Also avail. with pf. accompaniment
      only. Libr. by B. Cross.

Miscellanea

1144 Hollander, Frederick. "Typhoon", MS ca. 1940, prod.
      by Paramount Pictures. Film music. Scored by
      Sigmund Korngold. Orchn. and additional music
      by Milan Roder and Leo Shuken. [Film music for
      Conrad's Typhoon?]

1145 Lutyens, Elisabeth. "Vision of Youth", MS 1970, L:
      OP. Setting for s solo, 3 cl. (doubl. b. cl.),
      pf. (doubl. cel.), perc. (1 player).

1146 Roder, Milan. See entry #1144.

Conrad, Joseph continued

1147   Schuman, William. "Epitaph for Joseph Conrad", Four
        Canonic Choruses for Mixed Voices, MS 1933, NY:
        GS. Canon: mixed v., a cap. Text of "Epitaph for
        Joseph Conrad" written by Countee Cullen.

1148   Shuken, Leo. See entry #1144.

1149   Whithorne, Emerson. "Typhoon", MS, prod. London,
        pre-1949. Incidental music [to a stage version
        of Conrad's Typhoon?]

COPPARD, Alfred Edgar   1878-1957

Andante   "Now dusk, now sleep"   In The Collected Poems of
    A.E. Coppard (1928)

    1150* Swain, Freda. MS 1934, Night Pieces (MS 1933-38),
        avail. Chinnor: Channel, NEMO. Cyc.: ms and pf.
        ensemble.

Apostate, The   "I'll go, said I, to the woods and hills"
    In The Collected Poems of A.E. Coppard (1928)

    1151 Brown, James. MS. Song: s or t solo, pf.

April   "Now rejoicing plights each bird"   In The Collected
    Poems of A.E. Coppard (1928)

    1152* Swain, Freda. MS 1933, avail. Chinnor: Channel,
        NEMO. Song: s (or t) and pf. ensemble.

Bride, The   "I could not look into those eyes"   In The Col-
    lected Poems of A.E. Coppard (1928)

    1153* Swain, Freda. MS ca. 1937-38, Rare Fancy (MS 1933-
        38), avail. Chinnor: Channel, NEMO. Cyc.: bar and
        pf. ensemble.

Coppard, A.E. continued

Invisible Rain, The   "Alone with thoughts that chill me"
In The Collected Poems of A.E. Coppard (1928)

1154* Swain, Freda. MS 1933, Rare Fancy (MS 1933-38),
avail. Chinnor: Channel, NEMO. Cyc.: bar and pf.
ensemble.

Lock, The   "Easy is unhappiness, difficult is joy"   In The
Collected Poems of A.E. Coppard (1928)

1155* Swain, Freda. MS 1934, avail. Chinnor: Channel,
NEMO. Song: ms (or high bar) and pf. ensemble.

Night Piece   "Pole, the Bear, and Cassiopeia, The"   In The
Collected Poems of A.E. Coppard (1928)

1156* Swain, Freda. MS 1936-38, Night Pieces (MS 1933-38),
avail. Chinnor: Channel, NEMO. Cyc.: ms and pf.
ensemble.

Nocturne: New Moon   "Moon unfolds to-night, The"   In The
Collected Poems of A.E. Coppard (1928)

1157* Swain, Freda. "Nocturne", MS 1933, Night Pieces (MS
1933-38), avail. Chinnor: Channel, NEMO. Cyc.:
ms and pf. ensemble.

Oracle, The   "Night has come truly now"   In The Collected
Poems of A.E. Coppard (1928)

1158* Swain, Freda. MS 1933, avail. Chinnor: Channel,
NEMO. Song: t, bar (duet) and pf. ensemble. Also
suitable for s, ms (duet) and pf. ensemble.

Prodigal Son, The   "When I forsook my homely town"   In The
Collected Poems of A.E. Coppard (1928)

1159* Swain, Freda. MS ca. 1937, avail. Chinnor: Channel,
NEMO. Song: bar and pf. ensemble.

Return, The   "Road lies white before me, The"   In The Collected Poems of A.E. Coppard (1928)

oppard, A.E. continued

1160 Swain, Freda. MS 1936, avail. Chinnor: Channel,
NEMO. Song: bar solo, pf.

Stay, O Stay   "Of love designèd joys"   In The Collected
Poems of A.E. Coppard (1928)

1161* Swain, Freda. MS 1934, avail. Chinnor: Channel,
NEMO. Song: t and pf. ensemble.

Threshold, The   "Bright is the morning"   In The Collected
Poems of A.E. Coppard (1928)

1162* Swain, Freda. MS 1938   avail. Chinnor: Channel,
NEMO. Rhapsody: s and pf. ensemble.

To One Unknown and Gone   "You were like this loop of pine
trees"   In The Collected Poems of A.E. Coppard (1928)

1163* Swain, Freda. MS 1934, Rare Fancy (MS 1933-38),
avail. Chinnor: Channel, NEMO. Cyc.: bar and pf.
ensemble.

Winter Field   "Sorrow on the acres"   In The Collected Poems
of A.E. Coppard (1928)

1164* Swain, Freda. L: A, avail. Chinnor: Channel, NEMO.
Song: bar and pf. ensemble.

CORNFORD, Frances Crofts   1886-1960

Cornish April   "Come out and climb the cliffs"   In Different Days (1928)

1165 Brown, James. Four Poems by Frances Cornford, MS.
Song: s or t solo, pf.

Cornford, Frances continued

Dandelion, The   "Dandelion is brave and gay, The"   In Poems
(1910)

1166 Bliss, Arthur. Two Nursery Rhymes, L: JWC, 1922.
Song: s solo, cl. Other song in the collection
also requires pf. Arr. 1923 by Lionel Tertis for
v., vla.

Fragment of Empedocles, A   "I heard a thrush sing in the
flowering may"   In Different Days (1928)

1167 Brown, James. Four Poems by Frances Cornford, MS.
Song: s or t solo, pf.

Garden Near the Sea, The   "Wild fell the rain from the soak-
ed apple branches"   In Different Days (1928)

1168 Brown, James. Four Poems by Frances Cornford, MS.
Song: s or t solo, pf.

In Dorset   "From muddy road to muddy lane"   In Spring Morning (1915)

1169 Toye, Francis. L: Curwen, 1920. Song: solo v., pf.

Ragwort, The   "Thistles on the sandy flats, The"   In Poems
(1910)

1170 Bliss, Arthur. Two Nursery Rhymes, L: JWC, 1922.
Song: s solo, cl., pf. Other song in the collection is a setting for s solo, cl. Arr. 1923
by Lionel Tertis for v., vla.

Unbeseechable, The   See: Words for Music

Words for Music   "'Time stands still...'"   In Different
Days (1928) The poem was originally entitled "The Unbeseechable"

1171 Brown, James. "The Unbeseechable", Four Poems by
Frances Cornford, MS. Song: s or t solo, pf.

Cornford, Frances continued

Miscellanea

1172 Holloway, Robin. Georgian Songs, MS 1972, L: OUP.
      Songs: bar solo, pf. Incl. words by Cornford.

1173 Jackson, Stanley. "On a Summer Shore", MS 1961,
      avail. Victoria University of Wellington. Song:
      solo v., pf.

1174 Toye, Francis. "A Hans Andersen Song", L: Curwen,
      1920. Song: solo v., pf. Text attributed to Corn-
      ford.

COUSINS, James Henry   1873-1956

To Eire   "To Thee, Beloved, of old there came"   In The
Quest (1908)

1175 Bax, Arnold. Album of Seven Songs, L: JWC, 1919.
      Song: v., pf.

COWARD, Noël Pierce*   1899-1973

Blithe Spirit   (DR)   (1941)

1176 Addinsell, Richard. MS, perf. London, Apr. 1945.
      Incidental music to Coward's screen adapt. of
      the play for the film (by the same title) direct-
      ed by David Lean.

1177 Addinsell, Richard. "Blithe Spirit Ballet", MS,
      perf. Manchester, July 1945. Ballet music. The
      work, adapt. from the film vers. of the play,
      was incl. in Coward's revue entitled "Sigh No
      More".

141

Coward, Noel continued

Nude_with_Violin   (DR)   Plays_and_Players (Dec. 1956-Jan.
1957), publ. sep. 1957

    1178 Smetana, Josef. MS 1962, avail. SČSKU. Incidental
          music. Czech. title: "Akt s houslemi", transl. by
          Jiří Mucha.

Miscellanea

    1179 Bennett, Robert R. Etudes, MS, perf. 1942. Ea. etude
          is sub-titled to indicate a personality, e.g.,
          Walter Damrosch, Aldous Huxley, Noël Coward.

    1180 Pech, Josef. "High Spirit", MS 1966, avail. SČSKU.
          Incidental music. Czech. title: "Neposedný duch",
          transl. by Lexa Kozák. [Incidental music for
          Blithe_Spirit?]

CROSSLEY-HOLLAND, Kevin John William   1941-

Beowulf   (Transl.)   (1968)

    1181 Douglas, James. "Scenes from Beowulf", MS 1971-72,
          avail. SMA. Orch. only.

Bookworm   "Moth devoured words, A. When I heard"   In The
    Battle_of_Maldon_and_Other_Old_English_Poems (1965), rev.
    1970. Transl. from Old Engl.

    1182 Bliss, Arthur. "A Bookworm", A_Knot_of_Riddles, L:
          N, 1964. Song: bar solo, 11 instr.

Confessional   "I come once more to this terrible place"   In
    Norfolk_Poems (1970)

    1183 Douglas, James. Five_Songs, MS 1971-72, avail. SMA.
          Song: high v., str. orch.

Crossley-Holland, Kevin continued

1184 Douglas, James. "Betrübniss", MS 1966, avail. SMA.
      Str. orch. only.

"Deep sea suckled me, the waves sounded over me, The" See:
Oyster

Dog-Days   "Dog-days within the brain" In The Rain-Giver
(1972)

1185 Douglas, James. Five Songs, MS 1971-72, avail. SMA.
      Song: high v., str. orch.

Dream of the Rood, The   "Listen! I will describe the best of
dreams" In The Battle of Maldon and Other Old English
Poems (1965) Transl. from Old Engl.

1186 Douglas, James. MS 1969, avail. SMA. Setting for t
      solo, hn., stgs., pf., perc.

Fish and River   "My abode's by no means silent" In The
Battle of Maldon and Other Old English Poems (1965), rev.
1970. Transl. from Old Engl.

1187 Bliss, Arthur. "Fish in River", A Knot of Riddles,
      L: N, 1964. Song: bar solo, 11 instr.

Geese   "At the skim of evening" In Norfolk Poems (1970)

1188 Douglas, James. Five Songs, MS 1971-72, avail. SMA.
      Song: high v., str. orch.

"I am supple of body and sport with the wind" In Storm and
other Old English Riddles (1970) Transl. from Old Engl.

1189 Bliss, Arthur. "A Cross of Wood", A Knot of Riddles,
      L: N, 1964. Song: bar solo, 11 instr.

"I saw a strange creature" See: Sun and Moon

143

Crossley-Holland, Kevin continued

Marshland   "This green land is almost inviolate"   In Norfolk Poems (1970)

    1190 Douglas, James. Five Songs, MS 1971-72, avail. SMA.
          Song: high v., str. orch.

"Moth devoured words, A. When I heard"   See: Bookworm

"My abode's by no means silent"   See: Fish and River

"My breast is puffed up and my neck is swollen"   See:
Weathercock

Oyster   "Deep sea suckled me, the waves sounded over me,
    The"   In The Battle of Maldon and Other Old English Poems
    (1965), rev. 1970. Transl. from Old Engl.

    1191 Bliss, Arthur. "An Oyster", A Knot of Riddles, L: N,
          1964. Song: bar solo, 11 instr.

Recovering   "I am recovering: the quickening sun"   In The
Rain-Giver (1972)

    1192 Douglas, James. Five Songs, MS 1971-72, avail. SMA.
          Song: high v., str. orch.

Suggestions   "Convoluted exercise begins, The"   In The
Rain-Giver (1972)

    1193 Douglas, James. "Juxtapositions", MS 1972-73, avail.
          SMA. Pf. solo.

Sun and Moon   "I saw a strange creature"   In The Battle of
Maldon and Other Old English Poems (1965), rev. 1970.
Transl. from Old Engl.

    1194 Bliss, Arthur. A Knot of Riddles, L: N, 1964. Song:
          bar solo, 11 instr.

Swallows   "This wind wafts little creatures"   In The Battle
    of Maldon and Other Old English Poems (1965), rev. 1970.
    Transl. from Old Fngl.

    1195 Bliss, Arthur. A Knot of Riddles, L: N, 1964. Song:
        bar solo, 11 instr.

"This wind watts little creatures"   See: Swallows

Weathercock   "My breast is puffed up and my neck is swollen"
    In The Battle of Maldon and Other Old English Poems
    (1965), rev. 1970. Transl. from Old Engl.

    1196 Bliss, Arthur. "A Weather Cock", A Knot of Riddles,
        L: N, 1964. Song: bar solo, 11 instr.

Miscellanea

    1197 Douglas, James. "The Fates of Men", MS 1972, avail.
        SMA. Setting for s, bar soli, satb, stgs., pf.,
        org., perc. Text [Crossley-Holland's transl. from
        Old English] begins: "Often and again, through
        God's grace, man and woman usher a child into the
        world".

DANE, Clemence   1888-1965

Adam's Opera   (DR)   (1928)

    1198 Addinsell, Richard. MS, perf. London, Dec. 1928.

Come of Age   (DR)   (1938)

    1199 Addinsell, Richard. MS ca. 1938. Incidental music.

England's Darling   (DR)   (1940) Incl. as one of The
    Saviours (1942)

Dane, Clemence continued

    1200 Addinsell, Richard. MS [ca. 1940?]. Incidental
          music for radio.

Granite   (DR)   (1926)

    1201 Shaw, Martin. MS. Incidental music.

Hope of Britain, The   (DR)   The Saviours (1942)

    1202 Addinsell, Richard. MS pre-1942. Incidental music
          for radio.

L'Aiglon   (DR)   (1934) Adapt. from Rostand

    1203 Addinsell, Richard. MS [ca. 1934?]. Incidental
          music.

Light of Britain, The   (DR)   The Saviours (1942)

    1204 Addinsell, Richard. MS pre-1942. Incidental music
          for radio.

May King, The   (DR)   The Saviours (1942)

    1205 Addinsell, Richard. MS pre-1942. Incidental music
          for radio.

Merlin   (DR)   The Saviours (1942)

    1206 Addinsell, Richard. MS pre-1942. Incidental music
          for radio.

Moonlight is Silver   (DR)   (1934)

    1207 Addinsell, Richard. L: C, 1934. Incidental music.

Remember Nelson   (DR)   The Saviours (1942)

1208 Addinsell, Richard. MS pre-1942. Incidental music for radio.

Unknown Soldier, The   (DR)   The Saviours (1942)

1209 Addinsell, Richard. MS pre-1942. Incidental music for radio.

Will Shakespeare   (DR)   (1927)

1210 Duncan, Chester. MS 1949. Incidental music: pf. solo, also 3 songs for v., pf.

Miscellanea

1211 Addinsell, Richard. "Did We Meet or Was It a Dream", L: C, 1936, The Amateur Gentleman, MS pre-1936. Song [from incidental music to film entitled "The Amateur Gentleman"].

1212 Addinsell, Richard. Fire Over England, L: C, 1937. Incidental music.

1213 Addinsell, Richard. The Happy Hypocrite, MS pre-1954. Incidental music to Dane's adapt. of Max Beerbohm's work.

1214 Anon. The eds. have seen references to the fact that the Tonbridge School song is a setting of the last verse of Dane's "Old Boys All", beginning: "When I'm a hundred, if I've been good".

1215 Stevens, Halsey. "If Luck and I Should Meet", MS 1950. Madrigal: satb, a cap.

Davidson, John

DAVIDSON, John   1857-1909

Ballad ot a Runnable Stag, A   "When the pods went pop on the
    broom"   Pall Mall Magazine (July-Dec. 1905), rev. 1906

    1216 Young, Douglas. Of Birds and Beasts, L: F (hire).
          Cta.: sa, orch. Portions of the cta. require
          satb.

'Boat is Chafing, The'   "Boat is chafing at our long delay,
    The"   Plays (1889) as part of "Scaramouch in Naxos"

    1217 Gurney, Ivor. A Second Volume of Ten Songs, L: OUP,
          1938. Song: solo v., pf.

    1218 Scott, Anthony. MS 1961. Song: ttb, pf.

    1219 Stevenson, Ronald. Songs of Quest, MS 1974. Cyc.:
          bar solo, pf.

Runnable Stag, A   See: Ballad of a Runnable Stag, A·

Testament of John Davidson, The   "I waken at dawn and your
    head"   (1908)

    1220 Stevenson, Ronald. "The Last Journey", Songs of
          Quest, MS 1974. Cyc.: bar solo, pf. Setting of
          "Epilogue--The Last Journey".

To the Generation Knocking at the Door   "Break--break it
    open"   Glasgow Evening News (Mar. 1905)

    1221 Stevenson, Ronald. Songs of Quest, MS 1974. Cyc.:
          bar solo, pf.

Vive la Mort   "In the thick of battle we"   Diabolus Amans
    (1885)

    1222 Stevenson, Ronald. Songs of Quest, MS 1974. Cyc.:
          bar solo, pf.

avidson, John continued

Vive la Vie   "Spring, begin to wake the dene"   Diabolus
Amans (1885)

1223 Stevenson, Ronald. Songs of Quest, MS 1974. Cyc.:
      bar solo, pf.

Miscellanea

1224 Baynon, Arthur. "A Harvest Song", L: OUP, 1939.
      Song: unison v., pf. [Possibly a setting of
      "Autumn" ("All the waysides now are flower-
      less")?]

1225 Foss, Hubert J. "Unrest", L: OUP, 1926. Song: t
      solo, pf.

DAVIES, William Henry   1871-1940

Armed for War   "Is life on Earth a viler thing"   In The
Loneliest Mountain and Other Poems (1939)

1226 Roderick-Jones, Richard. The Weeping Child, MS 1966.
      Cyc.: s or t solo, pf.

Beggar's Song   "Good people keep their holy day"   In True
Travellers (1923)

1227 Webber, W.S. Lloyd. Four Bibulous Songs, L: Elkin,
      1951. Cyc.: bar solo, pf.

Bird's Anger, A   "Summer's morning that has but one voice,
A"   In The Song of Life and Other Poems (1920)

1228 Gurney, Ivor. MS 1924. Song: [solo v., pf.].

Clouds   "My Fancy loves to play with Clouds"   In Farewell
to Poesy And Other Pieces (1910)

149

Davies, W.H. continued

1229 Boughton, Rutland. _Two Duets for Soprano and Con-_
      tralto, L: Curwen, 1929. Song: s, a duet, pf.

Days that have Been   "Can I forget those sweet days"   In
      Songs of Joy And Others (1911)

1230 Roderick-Jones, Richard. _Visions and Remembrances_,
      MS 1973. Song: chorus of treble v., ssa, orch.

Days too Short   "When primroses are out in Spring"   In
      Songs of Joy And Others (1911)

1231 Garlick, Antony. _Twelve Madrigals_, Cin.: WLP, 1967.
      Madrigal: ssa, a cap.

1232 Partrey, Raymond. MS. Song: s solo, pf.

Dreams of the Sea   "I know not why I yearn for thee"   In
      Foliage (1913)

1233 Gurney, Ivor. "Dreams by the Sea", MS 1914. Song:
      [solo v., pf.].

1234 Hewitt-Jones, Tony. _Seven Sea Poems_, L: N, 1958.
      Choral ste.: a or bar or b solo, satb, stgs, ob.
      obbl. The complete ste. also requires enj. hn.
      obbl.

1235 Naylor, Bernard. Vancouver: Western, 1950. Song:
      med. v., pf.

1236 Robbins, Reginald. P: MST, ca. 1922. Song: b solo,
      [pf.]. Also suitable for bar (or a) solo, [pf.].

Early Morn   "When I did wake this morn"   In _Nature Poems_
      And Others (1908)

1237 Boughton, Rutland. _Five Partsongs_, L: Curwen, 1914.
      Song: satb, a cap.

1238 Gurney, Ivor. MS n.d. Song: [solo v., pf.].

150

avies, W.H. continued

Evening Star, The   "See how her body pants"   In A_Poet's
    Calendar (1927)

    1239 Roderick-Jones, Richard. The_Weeping_Child, MS 1966.
          Cyc.: s or t solo, pf.

Example, The   "Here's an example from"   In Songs_of_Joy_And
    Others (1911)

    1240 Garlick, Antony. Eleven_Canzonets, Cin.: Westwood,
          1967. Canzonet: 2 pt. chorus of equal v., a cap.

Flirt, The   "Pretty game, my girl, A"   In The_Song_of_Life
    and_Other_Poems (1920)

    1241 Kunz, Alfred. Three_Works_for_Male_Chorus, Waterloo:
          Waterloo, 1972. Song: ttbb, pf.

Great Time, A   "Sweet Chance, that led my steps abroad"   In
    The_Bird_of_Paradise_and_other_Poems (1914)

    1242 Head, Michael. "Sweet...", L: BH, 1929, Songs_of_the
          Countryside (ea. publ. sep.). Cyc.: high v., pf.
          Also avail. for low v., pf. This song is also
          avail. for high (or low) v., orch.

    1243 Hunt, Wynn. W.H._Davies_Song_Cycle, MS. Cyc.: b-bar
          solo, pf.

    1244 Wallbank, Newell. S. Croy.: L, 1948. Song: high v.,
          pf.

Green Tent, The   "Summer has spread a cool, green tent"   In
    Farewell_to_Poesy_And_Other_Pieces (1910)

    1245 Boughton, Rutland. Two_Duets_for_Soprano_and_Con-
          tralto, L: Curwen, 1929. Song: s, a duet, pf.

Greeting, A   "Good morning, Life--and all"   In Foliage
    (1913)

    1246 Benson, Warren. NY: CF, in prep. for publ. Song: t
          solo, tpt., pf.

151

Davies, W.H. continued

1247 Webber, W.S. Lloyd. L: EA, pre-1951. Song: unison
      v., pf.

Happy Child, The   "I saw this day sweet flowers grow thick"
In Songs of Joy And Others (1911)

    1248 Garlick, Antony. Twelve Madrigals, Cin.: WLP, 1967.
          Madrigal: ssa, a cap.

    1249 Lydiate, Frederick. MS. Song: t solo, pf.

    1250 Premru, Raymond. "I saw...", Triptych for Voices and
          Brass, MS copyright by composer 1969. Song: satb,
          2 t. trbn., 3 tpt., b. trbn.

Happy Wind   "Oh, happy wind, how sweet"   In Farewell to
Poesy And Other Pieces (1910)

    1251 Gurney, Ivor. "O Happy Wind", MS 1918. Song: [solo
          v., pf.].

    1252 Hunt, Wynn. W.H. Davies Song Cycle, MS. Cyc.: b-bar
          solo, pf.

    1253 Kunz, Alfred. MS 1953, English and German Songs (MS
          ca. 1953-62), avail. CMC. Song: solo v., pf.

How Kind is Sleep   "How kind is sleep, how merciful"   In
The Song of Life and Other Poems (1920)

    1254 Roderick-Jones, Richard. The Weeping Child, MS 1966.
          Cyc.: s or t solo, pf.

In the Snow   "Hear how my friend the robin sings!"   In
Forty New Poems (1918)

    1255 Garlick, Antony. Eleven Canzonets, Cin.: Westwood,
          1967. Canzonet: 2 pt. chorus of equal v., a cap.

Kingfisher, The   "It was the Rainbow gave thee birth"   In
Farewell to Poesy And Other Pieces (1910)

avies, W.H. continued

1256   Hart, Fritz. Five Part Songs for Women's Unac-
       companied Three-Part Choir, MS 1935. Song: 3 pt.
       female choir, a cap.

1257   Naylor, Peter. Bird Songs, MS. Cyc.: t or bar solo,
       pf.

Laughing Rose   "If I were gusty April now"   In Foliage
(1913)

    1258   Bainton, Edgar L. L: Curwen, pre-1940. Song: solo
           v., pf.

Leisure   "What is this life if, full of care"   In Songs of
Joy And Others (1911)

    1259   Bliss, Arthur. Three Songs, NY: CPMC, 1923. Song:
           solo v., pf. Rev. for re-issue L: N, 1972.

    1260   Kunz, Alfred. Three Works for Male Chorus, Waterloo:
           Waterloo, 1972. Song: ttbb, pf.

    1261   Leigh, Eric. L: N, 1960. Canon: 2 pt. chorus of
           equal v., pf.

    1262   Milford, Robin. Rain, Wind, and Sunshine, L: OUP,
           1930. Song (in children's cta.): 2 pt. chorus of
           children's v., pf.

    1263   Pentland, Barbara. MS 1938. Song: 3 pt. chorus, a
           cap.

Likeness, The   "When I came forth this morn"   In New Poems
(1907)

    1264   Head, Michael. "When...", L: BH, 1929, Songs of the
           Countryside (ea. publ. sep.). Cyc.: high v., pf.
           Also avail. for low v., pf. Portions of the cyc.
           are also avail. for high (or low) v., orch.

Love, Like a Drop of Dew   "When I pass down the street"   In
Secrets (1924)

Davies, W.H. continued

1265 Fleming, Robert. Secrets, L: OUP, 1945. Song: [med.]
      solo v., pf.

Love's Caution   "Tell them, when you are home again"   In
The Song of Life and Other Poems (1920)

1266 Fox, George. Tor.: BMI, 1961. Song: solo v., pf.

Margery "Butterfly loves Mignonette, The"   In New Poems
(1907)

1267 Webber, W.S. Lloyd. L: N, 1960. Song: satb, a cap.

Mask, The   "When I complained of April's day"   In A Poet's
Calendar (1927)

1268 Pentland, Barbara. MS 1938, avail. CMC. Song: s
      solo, pf.

Money   "When I had money, money, O!"   In Nature Poems And
Others (1908)

1269 Head, Michael. "Money, O!", L: BH, 1929, Songs of
      the Countryside (ea. publ. sep.). Cyc.: high v.,
      pf. Also avail. for low v., pf. This song is also
      avail. for high (or low) v., orch.

Moon, The   "Thy beauty haunts me heart and soul"   In The
Bird of Paradise and other Poems (1914)

1270 Farley, Roland. NY: NME, pre-1940. Song: [solo v.,
      pf.?].

1271 Garlick, Antony. Eleven Canzonets, Cin.: Westwood,
      1967. Canzonet: 2 pt. chorus of equal v., a cap.

1272* Garlick, Antony. Twelve Madrigals, Cin.: WLP, 1967.
      Madrigal: ssa, a cap.

1273 Gurney, Ivor. MS n.d. Song: [solo v., pf.].

154

avies, W.H. continued

1274 Read, Gardner. NY: AMP, 1946, Four Nocturnes (MS
      1934). Song: ms solo, pf. Also publ. for ssa, pf.
      Avail. from the composer for ms solo, orch.

1275 Smith, Robert Yale. "Thy Beauty Haunts Me", NY: GS,
      pre-1940. Song: [solo v., pf.?].

1276 Ticciati, Francesco. L: Curwen, 1926. Song: solo v.,
      pf.

1277 Webber, W.S. Lloyd. L: N, 1960. Song: satb, a cap.

Nature's Friend "Say what you like" In Nature Poems And
Others (1908)

1278 Head, Michael. L: BH, 1929, Songs of the Country-
      side (ea. publ. sep.). Cyc.: high v., pf. Also
      avail. for low v., pf. Portions of the cyc. are
      avail. for high (or low) v., orch.

No Careless Mind "Granted joy can make a careless mind, A"
In Poems 1930-31 (1932)

1279 Naylor, Bernard. Four Poems by W.H. Davies, MS 1935.
      Cyc.: high v., ch. orch.

No Place or Time "This curly childhood of the year" In
Poems 1930-31 (1932)

1280 Naylor, Bernard. Four Poems by W.H. Davies, MS 1935.
      Cyc.: high v., ch. orch.

Old Autumn "Is this old Autumn standing here" In Poems
1930-31 (1932)

1281 Naylor, Bernard. Four Poems by W.H. Davies, MS 1935.
      Cyc.: high v., ch. orch.

P for Pool "I know a deep and lonely pool" In A Poet's
Alphabet (1925), subsequently rev.

1282 Holland, Theodore. "P is for Pool", MS pre-1947.
      Setting for sp., pf.

155

Davies, W.H. continued

P is for Pool   See: P for Pool

Rain, The   "I hear leaves drinking rain"   In Nature_Poems
And_Others (1908)

    1283 Garlick, Antony. Eleven_Canzonets, Cin.: Westwood,
          1967. Canzonet: 2 pt. chorus of equal v., a cap.

Raptures   "Sing for the sun your lyric, lark"   In Forty_New
Poems (1918)

    1284 Housman, Rosalie. MS 1931, avail. NYPL. Song: [v.,
          pf.].

Rich Days   "Welcome to you rich Autumn days"   In The_Bird
of_Paradise_and_other_Poems (1914)

    1285 Berkeley, Lennox. "Welcome...", Autumn's_Legacy,
          L: JWC, 1963. Cyc.: s or t solo, pf.

Rich or Poor   "With thy true love I have more wealth"   In
Songs_of_Joy_And_Others (1911)

    1286 Bliss, Arthur. L: Curwen, 1927. Song: solo v., pf.

Rivals, The   "Pleasure is not the one I love"   In Secrets
(1924)

    1287 Fleming, Robert. "Pleasure and Joy", Secrets, L:
          OUP, 1945. Song: [med.] solo v., pf.

Robin Redbreast   "Robin on a leafless bough"   In Nature
Poems_And_Others (1908)

    1288 Head, Michael. L: BH, 1929, Songs_of_the_Country-
          side (ea. publ. sep.). Cyc.: high v., pf. Also
          avail. for low v., pf. Portions of the cyc. are
          also avail. for high (or low) v., orch.

    1289 Rubbra, Edmund. Three_Bird_Songs, L: OUP, 1938.
          Song: unison children's v., pf.

School's Out   "Girls scream"   In Nature Poems And Others
     (1908)

1290 Garlick, Antony. Eleven Canzonets, Cin.: Westwood,
     1967. Canzonet: 2 pt. chorus of equal v., a cap.

1291 Webber, W.S. Lloyd. L: N, 1961. Song: unison v., pf.

See Where Young Love   "See where Young Love sits all alone"
     In Secrets (1924)

1292 Fleming, Robert. Secrets, L: OUP, 1945. Song: [med.]
     solo v., pf.

Seeking Joy   "Joy, how I sought thee!"   In Foliage (1913)

1293 Roderick-Jones, Richard. Visions and Remembrances,
     MS 1973. Song: chorus of treble v., ssa, orch.

Silver Hours   "Come, lovely Morning, rich in frost"   In
     Poems 1930-31 (1932)

1294 Naylor, Bernard. Four Poems by W.H. Davies, MS 1935.
     Cyc.: high v., ch. orch.

Sleepers, The   "As I walked down the waterside"   In Songs
     of Joy And Others (1911)

1295 Austin, Frederic. L: N, pre-1940. Song: solo v., pf.

Strange Meeting, A   "Moon is full, and so am I, The"   In
     Forty New Poems (1918)

1296 Webber, W.S. Lloyd. Four Bibulous Songs, L: Elkin,
     1951. Cyc.: bar solo, pf.

Temper of a Maid, The   "Swallow dives in yonder air, The"
     In Songs of Joy And Others (1911)

157

Davies, W.H. continued

1297   Head, Michael. L: BH, 1929, Songs_of_the_Country-
       side (ea. publ. sep.). Cyc.: high v., pf. Also
       avail. for low v., pf. Portions of the cyc. are
       also avail. for high (or low) v., orch.

They're Taxing Ale again   "Ale's no false liar"   In Forty
New Poems (1918)

1298   Webber, W.S. Lloyd. Four_Bibulous_Songs, L: Elkin,
       1951. Cyc.: bar solo, pf.

This Night   "This night, as I sit here alone"   In Child
Lovers And other Poems (1916)

1299   Bliss, Arthur. Three Songs, NY: CPMC, 1923. Song:
       solo v., pf. Rev. for re-issue L: N, 1972.

1300   Hunt, Wynn. W.H. Davies Song Cycle, MS. Cyc.: b-bar
       solo, pf.

Thou Comest, May   "Thou comest, May, with leaves"   In Child
Lovers And other Poems (1916)

1301   Hunt, Wynn. W.H. Davies Song Cycle, MS. Cyc.: b-bar
       solo, pf.

Thunderstorms   "My mind has thunderstorms"   In Foliage
(1913)

1302   Bliss, Arthur. Three Songs, NY: CPMC, 1923. Song:
       solo v., pf. Rev. for re-issue L: N, 1972.

Time of Dreams, The   "What sweet, what happy days had I"
In A Poet's Calendar (1927)

1303   Smith, Robert. MS. Song: ttbb, pf.

Two Flocks, The   "Where are you going to now"   In Songs of
Joy And Others (1911)

1304   Vale, Charles. Green Meadow and Lane, L: BH, 1947.
       Song: children's v., pf.

vies, W.H. continued

Ways of Time, The*   "As butterflies are but winged flowers"
   In New Poems (1907), rev. 1923

   1305 Roderick-Jones, Richard. The Weeping Child, MS 1966.
         Cyc.: s or t solo, pf.

Weeping Child, The   "What makes thee weep so"   In The Bird
of Paradise and other Poems (1914)

   1306 Roderick-Jones, Richard. The Weeping Child, MS 1966.
         Cyc.: s or t solo, pf.

When on a Summer's Morn   "When on a summer's morn I wake"
   In The Bird of Paradise and other Poems (1914)

   1307 Gurney, Ivor. "When on a Summer Morning", MS ca.
         1919. Song: [solo v., pf.].

White Cascade, The   "What happy mortal sees that mountain
now"   In Child Lovers And other Poems (1916)

   1308 Gurney, Ivor. MS 1918. Song: [solo v., pf.].

   1309 Hunt, Wynn. W.H. Davies Song Cycle, MS. Cyc.: b-bar
         solo, pf.

You Interfering Ladies   "You interfering ladies, you"   In
The Song of Life and Other Poems (1920)

   1310 Webber, W.S. Lloyd. Four Bibulous Songs, L: Elkin,
         1951. Cyc.: bar solo, pf.

Miscellanea

   1311 Elliott, Michael. Three Songs of Gwent, MS pre-1968.
         Songs: s solo, pf. Texts by Davies.

   1312 Greenhill, [Harold?]. "Leisure", NY: BH. Song: uni-
         son chorus, [pf.]. [Text by Davies?]

   1313 Montgomery, Merle. "Leisure", NY: HWG, 1951. Mad-
         rigal: ssatbb, a cap. [Text by Davies?]

159

Davies, W.H. continued

    1314 Musgrave, Thea. Four Portraits, MS 1956. Songs: bar
           solo, cl., pf. Text by [W.H.?] Davies.

    1315 Tate, Phyllis. A setting publ. L: OUP, 1942 and
           cited in the Nov. 1944 issue of Monthly Musical
           Record has been withdrawn by the composer.

DAY LEWIS, Cecil   1904-1972

"Beauty's end is in sight" In From Feathers to Iron (1931)

    1316 Naylor, Bernard. Suite for High Voice and Piano,
           Wendover: RP, 1973. Song: high v., pf.

Christmas Rose, The "What is the flower that blooms each
    year" In The Gate and Other Poems (1962)

    1317* Ridout, Alan. L: S&B, 1961. "Sequence": satb, org.

Christmas Tree, The "Put out the lights now!" In Poems
    1943-1947 (1948) 1st publ. priv. [1945?]

    1318 Effinger, Cecil. MS. Song: s solo, pf.

"Come out in the sun, for a man is born today!" In From
    Feather to Iron (1931)

    1319 Lewis, Anthony. "Come Out in the Sun", MS 1944.
           Song: choir, a cap.

Ecstatic, The "Lark, skylark, spilling your rubbed and
    round" In A Time to Dance and Other Poems (1935)

    1320 Lindsay, Neil A. MS 1962, avail. Victoria University
           of Wellington. Song: high v., pf.

    1321 Naylor, Bernard. Vancouver: Western, 1949. Song:
           high v., pf.

Day Lewis, C. continued

1322 Naylor, Peter. "The Lark", Bird Songs, MS. Cyc.: t
      or bar solo, pf.

1323 Stark, Fleurette. MS 1955, avail. University of
      Auckland. Song: satb, a cap.

Elegiac Sonnet   "Fountain plays no more: those pure cas-
      cades, A"   In Pegasus and Other Poems (1957)

1324 Bliss, Arthur. L: N, 1955. Song: t solo, str. qrt.,
      pf.

Hornpipe   "Now the peak of summer's past"   In Poems in War-
      time (1940)

1325 Scott, Francis G. MS 1949, avail. SMA. Song: med.
      v., pf.

"In these our winter days"   In The Magnetic Mountain (1933)

1326 Farquhar, David. Two Songs of C. Day Lewis, MS 1951.
      Song: male chorus, 2 perc.

Jig   "That winter love spoke"   In Poems in Wartime (1940)

1327* Maw, Nicholas. Five Irish Songs, L: BH, 1974. Song:
      satb, a cap.

Love and Pity   "Love without pity is a child's hand reach-
      ing"   In Pegasus and Other Poems (1957)

1328 Orland, Henry. NY: SMC, 1969. Song: s solo, cl.,
      vla.

"Now she is like the white tree-rose"   In From Feathers to
      Iron (1931)

1329 Naylor, Bernard. Suite for High Voice and Piano,
      Wendover: RP, 1973. Song: high v., pf.

1330 Nisbet, Peter C. MS 1952, avail. University of Auck-
      land. Song: satb, a cap.

Day Lewis, C. continued

"Now to be with you, elate, unshared"   In The Magic Mountain
(1933)

  1331 LeFanu, Nicola. But Stars Remaining, Sevenoaks: N,
        1973. Setting for female v., a cap. Text adapt.
        from the 1st stanza of "Now to be..." and from
        the 1st and 3rd stanzas of Day Lewis' "Rest from
        living and be loving".

Poem for an Anniversary   "Admit then and be glad"   In A
Time to Dance and Other Poems (1935)

  1332 Bush, Alan. "Earth Has Grain To Grow", L: N, 1972.
        Song: satb, a cap.

Requiem for the Living   "Grant us untroubled rest"   In
The Gate and Other Poems (1962)

  1333* Swann, Donald. L: Curwen, 1971. Cta.: ms solo, male
        sp. (or bar solo, female sp.), satb, perc., cim-
        balon, pf.

"Rest from loving and be living"   In From Feathers to Iron
(1931)

  1334 Farquhar, David. Two Songs of C. Day Lewis, MS 1951.
        Song: male chorus, 2 perc.

  1335 LeFanu, Nicola. But Stars Remaining, Sevenoaks: N,
        1973. Setting for female v., a cap. Text adapt.
        from the 1st and 3rd stanzas of "Rest from..."
        and from the 1st stanza of Day Lewis' "Now to be
        with you, elate, unshared".

  1336 Naylor, Bernard. Suite for High Voice and Piano,
        Wendover: RP, 1973. Song: high v., pf.

"Twenty weeks near past"   In From Feathers to Iron (1931)

  1337 Naylor, Bernard. Suite for High Voice and Piano,
        Wendover: RP, 1973. Song: high v., pf.

Miscellanea

162

Day Lewis, C. continued

1338 Bliss, Arthur. "Birthday Song for a Royal Child", L:
     N, 1960. Song: satb, a cap.

1339 Bliss, Arthur. "River Music 1967", L: N, 1967. Set-
     ting for satb, a cap.

1340 Bliss, Arthur. "Song of Welcome", L: N, 1954. Cta.:
     s, bar soli, chorus, orch.

1341 Dyson, George. "Song for a Festival", L: N, 1951.
     Song: unison v., opt. descant, pf. (or orj.).
     Also publ. with accompaniment of pf. (or org.),
     stgs. and with orch. accompaniment. Also publ.
     for opt. b solo, satb.

1342 Rawsthorne, Alan. "The Enemy Speak", MS ca. 1936.
     Settings for [v., pf.?]. [Employs texts from
     Part Three of The Magnetic Mountain (1933)?]

DE LA MARE, Walter John   1873-1956

A--Apple Pie   "Little Pollie Pillikins"   In Bells and
Grass: A Book of Rhymes (1941)

     1343 Gibbs, C. Armstrong. L: Curwen, 1949. Song: unison
          v., pf.

A-Tishoo   "Sneeze, Pretty, sneeze, Dainty"   In Songs of
Childhood (1916)

     1344 Gibbs, C. Armstrong. L: Curwen, 1922. Song: sa, pf.

Absalom   "Vain, proud, rebellious Prince"   In Memory and
Other Poems (1938)

     1345 Wickens, Dennis. The Everlasting Voices, MS. Cyc.:
          high v., pf.

163

de la Mare, Walter continued

Alas, Alack!   "Ann, Ann!"   In _Peacock_Pie:_A_Book_of_Rhymes_
    (1913)

    1346   Crist, Bainbridge. _Queer_Yarns_, NY: CF, 1925. Song:
           v., pf.

    1347   Emeleus, John. _The_Huntsmen_, L: Weinberger, 1960.
           Song: girls' v., pf.

    1348   Greaves, Terence. _Follow_My_Leader_, L: OUP, 1965.
           Canon: 2 pt. chorus, pf.

    1349   Greene, R.G.H. _Three_Songs_, L: S&B, pre-1940. Song:
           [v., pf.?].

    1350   Howells, Herbert. _Peacock_Pie_, L: F&BG, 1923. Song:
           v., pf.

Alexander   "It was the Great Alexander"   In _The_Sunken_
    _Garden_and_Other_Poems_ (1917)

    1351   Gurney, Ivor. MS n.d. Song: [solo v., pf.].

Alice Hew   See: "Sleep sound, Mistress Hew!"

Alice Rodd   See: "Here lyeth our infant, Alice Rodd"

All that's Past   "Very old are the woods"   _Thrush_ (Jan.
    1910)

    1352   Berkeley, Lennox. _Songs_of_the_Half-Light_, L: JWC,
           1966. Song: high v., gtr. Gtr. pt. ed. by Julian
           Bream.

    1353   Bontoft, Frederic. L: Curwen, 1950. Song: solo v.,
           pf.

    1354   Elwyn-Edwards, Dilys. L: N, 1956. Song: satb, a cap.

    1355   Garrett, Gaynor. _Three_Poems_of_Walter_de_la_Mare_,
           MS 1954, avail. University of Otago. Song: s or
           t solo, pf.

    1356   Gurney, Ivor. MS n.d. Song: [solo v., pf.].

1357 Roper, Antony. L: N, 1963. Song: chorus of 2 equal
     v., pf.

Alone "Abode of the nightingale is bare, The"   In Motley
and Other Poems (1918)

   1358 White, James G. MS 1964, avail. Victoria University
        of Wellington. Song: med. v., pf.

Alone "Very old woman, A"   In The Listeners and Other
Poems (1912)

   1359 McIntyre, Paul. Four Poems of Walter de la Mare, MS
        1950, avail. CMC. Song: s solo, pf.

   1360 Smith, David S. Portraits, MS 1919, B: OD. Cyc.:
        [v., pf.].

Andy Battle   See: "Once and there was a young sailor, yeo
ho!"

Andy Battle and Nod's Song   See: "Once and there was a young
sailor, yeo ho!"

Andy's Love Song   See: "Me who have sailèd"

Ann Poverty   See: "Stranger, here lies"

Arabia "Far are the shades of Arabia"   In The Listeners
and Other Poems (1912)

   1361 Browne, W. Denis. In Monthly Chapbook (Dec. 1919);
        publ. sep. L: OUP, 1927. Song: [v., pf.?].

Araby   See: "Dark-browed Sailor, tell me now"

As Lucy Went a-Walking   "As Lucy went a-walking one morning"
In Songs of Childhood (1902), rev. 1916

de la Mare, Walter continued

1362 Gibbs, C. Armstrong. L: Curwen, 1949. Song: 2 pt.
      chorus of equal v., orch.

Autumn   "There is a wind where the rose was"   In Poems
(1906)

1363 Britten, Benjamin. Tit for Tat, L: F, 1969. Song:
      [med.] solo v., pf. "Autumn" was originally set
      for solo v., str. qrt.

1364 Herbert, Muriel. L: A, pre-1940. Song: [v., pf.?].

1365 Langley, James. L: AH&C, 1960. Song: satb, a cap.

1366 Milford, Robin. Days and Moments, L: H, 1959. Cta.:
      s solo, ssa, str. orch. or s solo, ssa, pf.

Away   "There is no sorrow"   In Memory and Other Poems
(1938)

1367 Fleming, Robert. MS 1943. Song: v., pf.

Ballad of Christmas, A   "It was about the deep of night"
(1924)

1368 Shaw, Martin, arr. "The Three Traitors", L: OUP,
      1928 in The Oxford Book of Carols. Carol: voices,
      accompanied. Arr. of tune "from Gilbert, 1823,
      'The Three Knights'".

Bandog, The   "Has anybody seen my Mopser?"   In Peacock Pie:
A Book of Rhymes (1913)

1369 Emeleus, John. The Huntsmen, L: Weinberger, 1960.
      Song: girls' v., pf.

1370 Greaves, Terence. Three Children's Songs, L: OUP,
      1964. Song: unison v., pf.

Barber's, The   "Gold locks, and black locks"   In Peacock
Pie: A Book of Rhymes (1913)

e la Mare, Walter continued

1371 Gibbs, C. Armstrong. Five_Children's_Songs_from
      "Peacock_Pie", L: BH, 1933. Song: unison v., pf.

"Be very quiet now" Ding_Dong_Bell (1924)

1372 Chanler, Theodore. Eight_Epitaphs, NY: Arrow, 1939.
      Song: solo v., pf.

Bees' Song, The "Thouzanz of thornz there be" In Peacock
Pie:_A_Book_of_Rhymes (1913)

1373 Gibbs, C. Armstrong. L: Curwen, 1938. Song: ssa, pf.

1374 Greene, R.G.H. Three_Songs, L: S&B, pre-1940. Song:
      [v., pf.?].

1375 Hely-Hutchinson, Victor. L: Elkin, 1927. Song: med.
      v., pf.

1376 Liddle, Samuel. Three_Songs, L: BH, 1923. Song: high
      or med. v., pf.

1377 Milner, Anthony. Peacock_Pie, L: UE, 1959. Song:
      ssa, a cap. Portions of the collection are set
      for unison v., pf. Score contains German transl.

1378 Peterkin, Norman. L: OUP, 1940. Song: ms or bar
      solo, pf.

Before_Dawn "Dim-berried is the mistletoe" The_Veil_and
Other_Poems (1921), publ. sep. 1924

1379 Benjamin, Arthur. L: Curwen, 1924. Song: solo v.,
      pf.

Bells, The "Shadow and light both strove to be" In The
Listeners_and_Other_Poems (1912)

1380 Gibbs, C. Armstrong. Five_Songs, L: S&B, 1920. Song:
      solo v., pf.

Beware! "Ominous bird sang from its branch, An" In The
Listeners_and_Other_Poems (1912)

de la Mare, Walter continued

1381 Gurney, Ivor. MS 1921. Song: [solo v., pf.].

Birthnight, The   "Dearest, it was a night"   In Poems
(1906), subsequently rev.

   1382 Finzi, Gerald. To a Poet, L: BH, 1965. Song: low v.,
        pf.

Birthnight: To F, The   See: Birthnight, The

Blackbirds   "In April, when these orchards blow"   In Bells
and Grass: A Book of Rhymes (1941)

   1383 Bruce, Margaret C. L: Curwen, 1958. Song: ssa, pf.

Blindman's In*   "Applecumjockaby, blindfold eye!"   In Bells
and Grass: A Book of Rhymes (1941)

   1384* Harrison, Pamela. Eight Poems of Walter de la Mare,
         L: OUP, 1956. Song: s or t solo, pf.

Bluebells   "Where the bluebells and the wind are"   In Songs
of Childhood (1902)

   1385 Dent, Edward. MS 1918. Song: [v., pf.?].

Bonum Omen   "As we sailed out of London River"   In Bells
and Grass: A Book of Rhymes (1941)

   1386 Hurd, Michael. "Sailor's Song", L: N, 1963; incl.
        under the title "London River" in Sea and Shore
        Songs, L: N, 1968. Song: unison v., pf.

   1387 Sykes, Harold. "As we...", L: Curwen, 1970. Song:
        unison v., pf. Arr. for ttbb, pf. by Trevor
        Widdicombe; arr. publ. Wendover: RP, 1972.

Boy, The   See: "Finger on lip I ever stand"

Bread and Cherries   "'Cherries, ripe cherries!'"   In Peacock Pie: A Book of Rhymes (1913)

   1388 Gurney, Ivor. A Second Volume of Ten Songs, L: OUP,
         1938. Song: solo v., pf.

   1389 Rogers, J.H. NY: Silver, 1929 in The Music Hour in
         the Kindergarten and First Grade. Song: v., pf.

"Bubble, bubble"   The Three Mulla-Mulgars (1910), rev. 1935

   1390 Peterkin, Norman. "Song of the Water Maiden", L:
         OUP, 1925. Song: [solo v., pf.].

Buckle, The   "I had a silver buckle"   In Songs of Childhood
(1902)

   1391 Bliss, Arthur. Three Romantic Songs, L: Curwen,
         1923. Song: v., pf.

   1392 Leigh, Eric. L: CR, 1962. Song: unison v., pf.

   1393 Piggott, H.E. Vancouver: Western, 1960, copyright
         assigned Oakville: Leslie, 1971. Song: unison v.,
         pf.

Bunches of Grapes   "'Bunches of grapes,' says Timothy"   In
Songs of Childhood (1902)

   1394 Armitage, Irène. L: Mills, 1960. Song: sa, pf.

   1395 Bullock, Ernest. L: EA, pre-1951. Song: unison v.,
         pf.

   1396 Forsyth, Cecil. "Says Jane", NY: GS, pre-1940. Song:
         ssaa, pf.

   1397 Gibbs, C. Armstrong. L: S&B, 1921. Song: s solo, pf.

   1398 Howells, Herbert. L: EA, pre-1951. Song: unison v.,
         pf.

   1399 Keel, Frederick. Four "Songs of Childhood", L: BH,
         1920. Cyc.: solo v., pf.

de la Mare, Walter continued

1400 Pitcher, Doland. L: BH, 1954. Song: unison v., pf.

1401 Wilkinson, Philip G. L: Curwen, 1957. Song: unison
      v., pf.

Cake and Sack   "Old King Caraway"   In Peacock Pie: A Book
of Rhymes (1913)

   1402 Chanler, Theodore. Four Rhymes from "Peacock Pie",
         NY: AMP, 1948. Song: med. v., pf.

   1403 Milner, Anthony. "Old...", Peacock Pie, L: UE, 1959.
         Song: unison v., pf. Portions of the collection
         are set for ssa, a cap. Score contains German
         transl.

   1404* Swain, Freda. "King Caraway", From "Peacock Pie",
         MS ca. 1949-50, avail. Chinnor: Channel, NEMO.
         Cyc.: bar and pf. ensemble. Also arr. for bar and
         str. qrt. ensemble.

   1405 Whittaker, W.G. "Old...", L: EA, 1919. Song: 2 pt.
         treble chorus, pf.

Captain Lean   "Out of the East a hurricane"   In Songs of
Childhood (1902)

   1406 Gibbs, C. Armstrong. Songs of Childhood, L: BH,
         1933. Song: vocal qrt. (s, a, t, b), pf.

Changeling, The   "'Ahoy, and ahoy!'"   In Peacock Pie: A
Book of Rhymes (1913)

   1407 Gibbs, C. Armstrong. In a Dream's Beguiling, L: BH,
         1951. Ste: ms solo (or semichorus), ssa, str.
         orch., pf.

Come--Gone   "Gone the snowdrop--comes the crocus"   In Bells
and Grass: A Book of Rhymes (1941)

   1408 Greaves, Terence. Follow My Leader, L: OUP, 1965.
         Canon: 2 pt. chorus, pf.

Comfort   "As I mused by the hearthside"   In The Fleeting
and Other Poems (1933)

1409   Allam, Edward. Leeds: EA, pre-1956. Song: [v., pf.].

Courage   "O heart, hold thee secure"   In Memory and Other
Poems (1938)

1410   Fleming, Robert. MS 1943. Song: v., pf.

Crazed   "I know a pool where nightshade preens"   In Flora:
A Book of Drawings (1919)

1411   Greene, R.G.H. Three Songs, L: S&B, pre-1940. Song:
       [v., pf.?].

Crossings: A Fairy Play   (DR)   (1921)

1412   Gibbs, C. Armstrong. MS 1919. Orch. ste.: fl., 3
       vln., vla., vcl., pf. The ste. was composed as
       incidental music for the 1st perf. of the play
       (June 1919).

1413   Gibbs, C. Armstrong. See: "Dark-browed Sailor, tell
       me how", "Fol, dol, do, and a south wind a-
       blowing O", "Listen, I who love thee well", "Now
       all the roads to London town", "Now silent falls
       the clacking mill".

1414   Hurd, Michael. See: "Dark-browed Sailor, tell me
       how".

Cupboard, The   "I know a little cupboard"   In Peacock Pie:
A Book of Rhymes (1913)

1415   Conn, Dwight. NY: HFL, pre-1940. Song: [v., pf.].

1416   Harris, Victor. NY: JF, ca. 1922. Song: [v., pf.].

1417   Hely-Hutchinson, Victor. Three Songs from "Peacock
       Pie", L: Elkin, 1927. Song: ms or bar solo, pf.

1418   Leigh, Eric. L: N, 1960. Song: unison v., pf.

de la Mare, Walter continued

1419   McKinney, Howard. Four Crumbs from "Peacock Pie",
       NY: JF, pre-1940. Song: [v., pf.?].

1420   Miessner, William. NY: Silver, 1929 in The Music
       Hour in the Kindergarten and First Grade. Song:
       v., pf.

1421   Milner, Anthony. Peacock Pie, L: UE, 1959. Song:
       unison v., pf. Portions of the collection are
       set for ssa, a cap. Score contains German transl.

1422   Moore, Douglas. NY: HB, 1928 in New Songs for New
       Voices. Song: v., pf.

1423   Parke, Dorothy. Tor.: GVT, 1962. Song: unison v.,
       pf.

1424   Strong, May A. NY: HB, 1928 in New Songs for New
       Voices. Song: v., pf.

Dame Hickory   "Dame Hickory, Dame Hickory"   In Songs of
Childhood (1902)

1425   Gibbs, C. Armstrong. L: Curwen, 1922. Song: sa, pf.

"Dark-browed Sailor, tell me how"   Crossings: A Fairy Play
(1921), incl. in collected edns. under the title "Araby"

1426   Gibbs, C. Armstrong. "Araby", L: Beaumont, 1921 in
       Crossings: A Fairy Play; publ. sep. L: Curwen,
       1924. Song: solo v., pf. Score accompanied the
       1st edn. of the play.

1427   Hurd, Michael. "Araby", L: N, 1963, Sea and Shore
       Songs, L: N, 1968. Song: unison v., pf.

Dear Delight   "Youngling fair, and dear delight"   Flora:
A Book of Drawings (1919)

1428   Head, Michael. L: BH, 1965. Song: s solo, pf. Also
       avail. for s solo, orch.

Done For   "Old Ben Bailey"   In Bells and Grass: A Book of
Rhymes (1941)

172

1429   Fiske, Roger. L: OUP, 1951. Song: med. v., pf.

Dove, The   "How often, these hours"   In Memory and Other
     Poems (1938)

1430   Brown, James. MS. Song: ms or bar solo, pf. Also
       suitable for s or t solo, pf.

Down-Adown-Derry   "Down-adown-derry"   In Songs of Childhood
     (1902), rev. 1916

1431   Gibbs, C. Armstrong. Songs of Childhood, L: BH,
       1933. Song: vocal qrt. (s, a, t, b), pf.

Dream-Song   "Sunlight, moonlight"   In Peacock Pie: A Book
     of Rhymes (1913)

1432   Carty, Doreen. MS 1956, avail. Victoria University
       of Wellington. Song: high v., pf.

1433   Hely-Hutchinson, Victor. L: OUP, 1927. Song: [ms or
       bar] solo v., pf.

1434   Miessner, William. NY: Silver, 1928-30 in The Music
       Hour, Vol. 5. Song: v., pf.

1435   Milner, Anthony. Peacock Pie, L: UE, 1959. Song:
       unison v., pf. Portions of the collection are set
       for ssa, a cap. Score contains German transl.

1436   Roberton, Hugh. Peacock Pie, L: AH&C, 1943. Choral
       ste.: satb, a cap. Portions of the ste. are set
       for ssa.

1437   Stringham, Edwin. NY: Witmark, 1935. Song: ssa, pf.

1438   Whittaker, W.G. L: Curwen, 1919. Song: solo v., pf.

Dreamland   "Annie has run to the mill dam"   In Bells and
     Grass: A Book of Rhymes (1941)

1439   Brown, James. Songs for Children, Set I, MS. Song:
       v., pf.

173

de la Mare, Walter continued

1440* Harrison, Pamela. Eight Poems of Walter de la Mare,
      L: OUP, 1956. Song: s or t solo, pf.

Dreams   "Be gentle, O hands of a child"   In The Listeners
and Other Poems (1912)

  1441 Buczynski, Walter. Four Poems of Walter de la Mare,
        MS 1955, avail. CMC. Song: [a] solo v., pf.

  1442 Galway, Victor. "Be gentle...", L: OUP, 1948. Song:
        satb, a cap.

  1443 Garrett, Gaynor. Three Poems of Walter de la Mare,
        MS 1954, avail. University of Otago. Song: s or
        t solo, pf.

Dunce, The   "Why does he still keep ticking?"   In Peacock
Pie: A Book of Rhymes (1913)

  1444 Belchamber, Eileen. Two Unison Songs, L: OUP, 1945.
        Song: unison v., pf.

  1445 Howells, Herbert. Peacock Pie, L: F&BG, 1923. Song:
        v., pf.

Earth Folk   "Cat she walks on padded claws, The"   In
Peacock Pie: A Book of Rhymes (1913)

  1446 Greene, R.G.H. L: S&B, pre-1940. Song: [v., pf.?].

Echo   "Seven sweet notes"   In Bells and Grass: A Book of
Rhymes (1941)

  1447 Brown, James. Songs for Children, Set I, MS. Song:
        v., pf.

  1448 Harrison, Pamela. Eight Songs for Voice and
        Recorder, MS. Song: solo v., rec., pf.

Echo   "'Who called?' I said"   In Poems (1906)

  1449 Wickens, Dennis. The Everlasting Voices, MS. Cyc.:
        high v., pf.

de la Mare, Walter continued

Echoes   "Sea laments, The" In Poems for Children (1930)

    1450 Housman, Rosalie. MS, avail. NYPL. Song: solo v.,
          pf.

Eeka, Neeka   "Eeka, Neeka, Leeka, Lea" In Bells and Grass:
    A Book of Rhymes (1941)

    1451 Gibbs, C. Armstrong. L: EA, 1953. Song: unison v.,
          pf.

    1452 Harrison, Pamela. Eight Songs for Voice and
          Recorder, MS. Song: solo v., rec., pf.

Enchanted Hill, The   "From height of noon"   Down-Adown-
    Derry: A Book of Fairy Poems (1922)

    1453 Weinzweig, John. MS pre-1973. Song: [v., pf.?].

England   "No lovelier hills than thine" In Poems (1906)

    1454 Mase, Owen. L: Curwen. Song: unison v., pf.

    1455 Rodewald, Bernice. MS 1949, avail. University of
          Auckland. Song: satb, pf.

Epitaph, An   "Here lies a most beautiful lady" In The
    Listeners and Other Poems (1912)

    1456 Barlow, David. MS. Song: a solo, pf.

    1457 Besly, Maurice. L: Curwen, 1922. Song: [med.-low]
          solo v., pf.

    1458 Cockshott, Gerald. "Here lies...", MS 1943. Song:
          solo v., pf.

    1459 Deale, Edgar M. "The Lady of the West Country", Five
          Poets--Seven Songs, MS 1961. Choral ste.: satb,
          cl., pf.

    1460 Duarte, John. Five Quiet Songs, Ancona: Berben,
          1971. Cyc.: high v., classical gtr.

175

de la Mare, Walter continued

1461 Gurney, Ivor. A Second Volume of Ten Songs, L: OUP,
1938. Song: solo v., pf.

1462 Hoggett, Alan. NY: HB, 1928 in New Songs for New
Voices. Song: v., pf.

1463 Housman, Rosalie. "Epitaph", MS, avail. NYPL. Song:
v., pf.

1464 Koch, John. Hastings-on-Hudson: GMP, 1965. Song: s
solo, pf.

1465 Mulliner, Michael. L: OUP, 1956. Song: bar solo, pf.

1466 Sheldon, Mary. L: Swan, pre-1940. Song: [v., pf.?].

1467 Stone, David. L: BH, 1961. Song: ttbb, a cap.

Ever   See: Why?

Exile   "Had the gods loved me"   In The Listeners and Other
Poems (1912)

1468 Gibbs, C. Armstrong. "The Exile", L: F&BG, 1923.
Song: solo v., pf.

Familiar, The   "Are you far away?'"   In The Veil and Other
Poems (1921)

1469 Deale, Edgar M. Walter de la Mare Suite, MS 1945,
avail. RTE. Choral ste.: ssatb, orch.

Fare Well   "When I lie where shades of darkness"   In The
Sunken Garden and Other Poems (1917)

1470 Baber, Joseph. Songs from English Poets, MS (Opus
12). Cyc.: high v., pf.

1471 Cone, Edward T. Around the Year, MS. Cyc.: satb,
str. qrt.

1472 Gurney, Ivor. MS n.d. Song: [solo v., pf.].

e la Mare, Walter continued

1473 Holloway, Robin. Georgian Songs, MS 1972, L: OUP.
      Song: bar solo, pf.

Feather, The "Feather, a feather!, A" In Bells and Grass:
A Book of Rhymes (1941)

1474 Parry, W.H. L: OUP, 1959. Song: sa, pf.

Feckless Dinner-Party, The "'Who are we waiting for?'"
In The Fleeting and Other Poems (1933)

1475 Holloway, Robin. Georgian Songs, MS 1972, L: OUP.
      Song: bar solo, pf.

Fiddlers, The "Nine feat fiddlers had good Queen Bess"
In Songs of Childhood (1902)

1476 Shepherd, Arthur. South Hadley: VMP, 1948. Song: s
      solo, pf.

"Finger on lip I ever stand" Ding Dong Bell (1924), incl.
in collected edns. under the title "The Boy"

1477 Le Fleming, Christopher. "A Boy", A Quiet Company,
      L: CR, 1953. Cyc.: ms or bar solo, pf.

Five Eyes "In Hans' old Mill his three black cats" In
Peacock Pie: A Book of Rhymes (1913)

1478 Crist, Bainbridge. Queer Yarns, NY: CF, 1925. Song:
      v., pf.

1479 Gibbs, C. Armstrong. L: Curwen, 1921. Song: sa, pf.
      Publ. L: WR, 1948 for ttbb, a cap. Arr. for
      satb, pf. by Tim H. Slessor; arr. publ. L: BH,
      1966.

1480 Kent, Ada. Waterloo: Waterloo, 1953. Song: med. v.,
      pf.

1481 Roberton, Hugh. Peacock Pie, L: AH&C, 1943. Choral
      ste.: satb, a cap. Portions of the ste. are set
      for ssa.

177

de la Mare, Walter continued

Fleeting, The   "Late wind failed, The"   In Poems for
Children (1930)

   1482   Berkeley, Lennox. Songs of the Half-Light, L: JWC,
      1966. Song: high v., gtr. Gtr. pt. ed. by Julian
      Bream.

   1483   Wordsworth, William. Three Songs, MS 1938. Song:
      med. v., pf.

Flight, The   "How do the days press on"   In The Sunken
Garden (1917)

   1484   Richards, Kathleen. L: OUP, pre-1958. Song: 2 pt.
      chorus [a cap.?].

Flower, The   "Horizon to horizon"   In The Veil and Other
Poems (1921)

   1485   Coulthard, Jean. "Horizon to Horizon", Two Visionary
      Songs, MS 1968, avail. CMC. Song: s solo, fl.,
      str. orch. or s solo, fl., str. ensemble.

Flower, The ("Listen, I who love...")   See: "Listen, I who
love thee well"

Fly, The   "How large unto the tiny fly"   In Songs of Childhood (1902)

   1486   Belchamber, Eileen. Two Unison Songs, L: OUP, 1945.
      Song: unison v., pf.

Fol Dol Do   See: "Fol, dol, do, and a south wind a-blowing
O"

"Fol, dol, do, and a south wind a-blowing O"   Crossings: A
Fairy Play (1921), incl. in collected edns. under the
title "Fol Dol Do"

   1487   Gibbs, C. Armstrong. "Fol Dol Do", L: Curwen, 1924.
      Song: male chorus, a cap.

Four Brothers, The   "Hithery, hethery--I love best"   In
    Poems for Children (1930)

    1488 Parry, W.H. L: N, 1957. Song: sa, pf.

Full Moon   "One night as Dick lay half asleep"   In Peacock
    Pie: A Book of Rhymes (1913)

    1489 Allam, Edward. Leeds: EA, pre-1956. Song: [v., pf.].

    1490 Berkeley, Lennox. Songs of the Half-Light, L: JWC,
          1966. Song: high v., gtr. Gtr. pt. ed. by Julian
          Bream.

    1491 Howells, Herbert. Peacock Pie, L: F&BG, 1923. Song:
          v., pf.

    1492 Wordsworth, William. Four Songs, L: L, 1947. Song:
          high v., pf.

Galliass, The   "'Tell me, tell me...'"   In The Veil and
    Other Poems (1921)

    1493 Gibbs, C. Armstrong. L: Curwen, 1924. Song: solo v.,
          pf.

    1494 Peterkin, Norman. L: OUP, pre-1940. Song: [solo v.,
          pf.].

Garden, The   "That wooden hive between the trees"   In This
    Year: Next Year (1937)

    1495* Milford, Robin. This Year: Next Year, L: OUP, 1948.
          Cyc.: 2 pt. chorus of high v., pf.

Ghost, The   "Peace in thy hands"   In The Listeners and
    Other Poems (1912)

    1496 Auerbach, Norman. Three Choral Songs, Bryn Mawr: TP,
          1968. Song: ssaa, a cap.

Ghost, The   "'Who knocks?''I, who was beautiful...'"   In
    Motley and Other Poems (1918)

de la Mare, Walter continued

1497 Tauber, Patricia. MS 1963, avail. Victoria Univer-
         sity of Wellington. Song: satb, str. orch.

Gnomies, The   "As I lay awake in the white moon light"   In
     Songs of Childhood (1902), rev. 1916

   1498 Keel, Frederick. "Sleepy Head", Four "Songs of
         Childhood", L: BH, 1920. Cyc.: solo v., pf.

Goldfinch, A   "This feather-soft creature"   In Bells and
     Grass: A Book of Rhymes (1941)

   1499* Harrison, Pamela. Eight Poems of Walter de la Mare,
         L: OUP, 1956. Song: s or t solo, pf.

Gone   "Where's the Queen of Sheba?"   In Bells and Grass:
     A Book of Rhymes (1941)

   1500 Cockshott, Gerald. "Where's...", MS 1941. Song: solo
         v., pf.

Grace   "For every sip the Hen says grace"   In Bells and
     Grass: A Book of Rhymes (1941)

   1501 Gibbs, C. Armstrong. L: Curwen, 1949. Song: unison
         v., pf.

Hare, The   "In the black furrow of a field"   In Songs of
     Childhood (1902)

   1502 Bliss, Arthur. Three Romantic Songs, L: Curwen,
         1923. Song: v., pf.

'Hawthorn Hath a Deathly Smell, The'   "Flowers of the field,
     The"   In The Listeners and Other Poems (1912)

   1503 Garrett, Gaynor. Three Poems of Walter de la Mare,
         MS 1954, avail. University of Otago. Song: s or
         t solo, pf.

e la Mare, Walter continued

"Here be the ashes of Jacob Todd" Ding_Dong_Bell (1924),
incl. in collected edns. under the title "Jacob Todd"

  1504 Le Fleming, Christopher. "Jacob Todd", A_Quiet
          Company, L: CR, 1953. Cyc.: ms or bar solo, pf.

"Here lies my husbands; One, Two, Three" Ding_Dong_Bell
(1924)

  1505* Chanler, Theodore. "Three Husbands (Epitaph No. 9)",
          NY: BH, 1962. Song: s solo, pf.

"Here lies Thomas Logge--A Rascally Dogge" Ding_Dong_Bell
(1924), incl. in collected edns. under the title "Thomas
Logge"

  1506 Chanler, Theodore. "Thomas Logge", Eight_Epitaphs,
          NY: Arrow, 1939. Song: solo v., pf.

"Here lieth a poor Natural" Ding_Dong_Bell (1924), incl.
in collected edns. under the title "A Poor Natural"

  1507 Le Fleming, Christopher. "Magpie Corner", A_Quiet
          Company, L: CR, 1953. Cyc.: ms or bar solo, pf.

"Here lyeth our infant, Alice Rodd" Ding_Dong_Bell (1924),
incl. in collected edns. under the title "Alice Rodd"

  1508 Chanler, Theodore. "Alice Rodd", Eight_Epitaphs, NY:
          Arrow, 1939. Song: solo v., pf.

"Here sleep I" Ding_Dong_Bell (1924), incl. in collected
edns. under the title "Susannah Fry"

  1509 Chanler, Theodore. "Susannah Fry", Eight_Epitaphs,
          NY: Arrow, 1939. Song: solo v., pf.

Hide and Seek "Hide and seek, says the Wind" In Peacock
Pie: A Book of Rhymes (1913)

  1510 Brown, James. Songs for Children, Set I, MS. Song:
          v., pf.

181

de la Mare, Walter continued

1511 Emeleus, John. The Huntsmen, L: Weinberger, 1960.
Song: girls' v., pf.

1512 Gibbs, C. Armstrong. Five Children's Songs from
"Peacock Pie", L: BH, 1933. Song: unison v., pf.

1513 McKinney, Howard. Four Crumbs from "Peacock Pie",
NY: JF, pre-1940. Song: [v., pf.?].

1514 Milner, Anthony. Peacock Pie, L: UE, 1959. Song:
ssa, a cap. Portions of the collection are set
for unison v., pf. Score contains German transl.

1515 Rose, Edwin. L: L, 1962. Song: unison female v., pf.
or unison children's v., pf.

Horn, The "Hark, is that a horn I hear" In Songs of
Childhood (1902)

1516 Butterworth, Arthur. "Hark...", Ancient Sorceries,
MS (Opus 49). Cyc.: c-t solo, rec. (treble and
tenor alternating), hpd.

1517 Gibbs, C. Armstrong. In a Dream's Beguiling, L: BH,
1951. Ste.: ms solo (or semichorus), ssa, str.
orch., pf.

1518 Richards, Kathleen. L: OUP, pre-1958. Song: 2 pt.
chorus, [pf.?].

Horseman, The "I heard a horseman" In Peacock Pie: A
Book of Rhymes (1913)

1519 Berkeley, Lennox. Five Songs, L: JWC, 1948. Song:
med. v., pf.

1520 Fischer, Irwin. MS. Song: solo v., pf.

1521 Howe, Mary. MS pre-1946. Song: ss, a cap. or ss, pf.

Horseman, The "There was a Horseman rode so fast" In
Peacock Pie: A Book of Rhymes (1913)

1522* Harrison, Pamela. Eight Poems of Walter de la Mare,
L: OUP, 1956. Song: s or t solo, pf.

House of Dream, The   "Candle, candle, burning clear"   In
    Bells and Grass: A Book of Rhymes (1941)

    1523 Pitfield, Thomas B. House of Song, L: JW, ca. 1944.
          Children's cta.: voices, 2 pf. Composition with-
          drawn by the composer.

Huntsmen, The   "Three jolly gentlemen"   In Peacock Pie: A
    Book of Rhymes (1913)

    1524 Bartholomew, Marshall. NY: Silver, 1928-30 in The
          Music Hour, Vol. 2 Song: v., unacc.

    1525 Bliss, Arthur. "Three...", NY: CPMC, 1923. Song:
          high v., pf.

    1526 Brown, James. Songs for Children, Set II, MS. Song:
          v., pf.

    1527 Butterworth, Neil. "Three...", L: Mills, 1960. Song:
          unison v., pf.

    1528 Emeleus, John. The Huntsmen, L: Weinberger, 1960.
          Song: girls' v., pf.

    1529 Gibbs, C. Armstrong. Peacock Pie, L: BH, 1933. Ch.
          ste.: 2 vln., vla., vcl., pf. or 3 vln., vcl.,
          pf.

    1530 Hely-Hutchinson, Victor. L: OUP, 1927. Song: t solo,
          pf.

    1531 O'Murnaghan, Art. Dublin: Cuala, 1937 in Broadside,
          No. 11. Song: v., unacc.

    1532 Roberton, Hugh. "Three...", Peacock Pie, L: AH&C,
          1943. Choral ste.: ssa, a cap. Portions of the
          ste. are set for satb.

    1533 Teed, Roy. "Three...", L: JWC, 1957. Song: med. v.,
          pf.

I Can't Abear   "I can't abear a Butcher"   In Peacock Pie:
    A Book of Rhymes (1913)

de la Mare, Walter continued

1534 Crist, Bainbridge. B: BMC, pre-1940. Song: [solo v., pf.?].

I Met at Eve "I met at eve the Prince of Sleep" In Songs of Childhood (1902)

1535 Dushkin, Dorothy. "The Prince of Sleep", Three Songs for Women's Voices and Woodwind Trio or Piano, NY: CF, 1955 (ww. pts. on hire only). Song: ssa, ww. trio or ssa, pf.

1536 Elgar, Edward. "The Prince of Sleep", L: Elkin, 1925. Song: satb, a cap.

"I rang yon bells a score of years" Ding Dong Bell (1924), incl. in collected edns. under the title "Tom Head"

1537 Le Fleming, Christopher. "Tom Head", A Quiet Company, L: CR, 1953. Cyc.: ms or bar solo, pf.

"In Munza a Mulgar once lived alone" The Three Mulla-Mulgars (1910), rev. 1935

1538 Peterkin, Norman. "Dubbuldideery: A Monkey's Journey Song", L: OUP, 1925. Song: solo v., pf.

Invocation "Burning fire shakes in the night, The" In Motley and Other Poems (1918)

1539 Osborne, Reginald. L: BH, 1968. Song: solo v., pf.

Jacob Todd See: "Here be the ashes of Jacob Todd"

Jim Jay "Do diddle di do" In Peacock Pie: A Book of Rhymes (1913)

1540 Crist, Bainbridge. Queer Yarns, NY: CF, 1925. Song: v., pf.

John Mouldy "I spied John Mouldy in his cellar" In Songs of Childhood (1902)

e la Mare, Walter continued

1541 Gibbs, C. Armstrong. L: WR, 1922. Song: med. v., pf.

1542 Keel, Frederick. Four "Songs of Childhood", L: BH,
1920. Cyc.: solo v., pf.

1543 Pitfield, Thomas B. L: OUP, 1937. Song: unison v.,
pf.

1544 Stevens, Halsey. MS 1955. Song: solo v., pf.

1545 Veitch, William. L: Curwen, 1940. Song: unison
children's v., pf. or unison female v., pt.

1546 Winn, Cyril. L: EA, 1927. Song: unison v., pf.

"Just a span and half a span" Ding Dong Bell (1924), incl.
in collected edns. under the title "The Midget"

1547 Chanler, Theodore. "A Midget", Eight Epitaphs, NY:
Arrow, 1939. Song: solo v., pf.

1548 Le Fleming, Christopher. "A Midget", A Quiet
Company, L: CR, 1953. Cyc.: ms or bar solo, pf.

King David "King David was a sorrowful man" In Peacock
Pie: A Book of Rhymes (1913)

1549 Gibbs, C. Armstrong. In a Dream's Beguiling, L: BH,
1951. Ste.: ms solo (or semichorus), ssa, str.
orch., pf.

1550 Howells, Herbert. L: BH, 1923. Song: v., pf.

1551 Hurd, Michael. Sea and Shore Songs, L: N, 1968.
Song: unison v., pf.

1552 Proctor, Charles. Four Various Songs, L: L, 1945.
Song: high v., pf. Also arr. for high v., str.
orch.

1553* Swain, Freda. From "Peacock Pie", MS ca. 1949-50,
avail. Chinnor: Channel, NEMO. Cyc.: bar and pf.
ensemble. Also arr. for bar and str. qrt. ensemble.

de la Mare, Walter continued

Last Night*   "Last night, as I sat here alone"   On the Edge
     (1930)

     1554 Field, Robin. Hearth-Songs, MS 1971. Cyc.: a solo,
           vcl.

Linnet, The   "Upon this leafy bush"   In Motley and Other
     Poems (1918)

     1555 Gibbs, C. Armstrong. Five Songs, L: S&B, 1920. Song:
           solo v., pf.

     1556 Leigh, Eric. L: CR, 1962. Song: unison v., pf.

     1557 Leighton, Kenneth. The Birds, L: N, 1957. Choral
           ste.: s or t solo, chorus, stgs., pf., timp. ad
           lib, cym. ad lib.

     1558 Naylor, Peter. Bird Songs, MS. Cyc.: t or bar solo,
           pf.

"Listen, I who love thee well"   Crossings: A Fairy Play
     (1921), incl. under the title "The Flower" in Poems for
     Children (1930) and under the title "Tidings" in Poems
     1919-1934 (1935)

     1559 Gibbs, C. Armstrong. "Candlestickmaker's Song", L:
           Beaumont, 1921 in Crossings: A Fairy Play; publ.
           sep. L: Curwen, 1924. Song: solo v., pf. Score
           accompanied the 1st edn. of the play.

Listeners, The   "'Is there anybody there?' said the Travel-
     ler"   In The Listeners and Other Poems (1912)

     1560 Dello Joio, Norman. NY: CF, 1960. Song: med. v., pf.

     1561 Gibbs, C. Armstrong. L: BH, 1951. Song: ttbb, pf.

     1562 Lander, Cyril. Flores de mi primavera, MS n.d.,
           avail. National Library of New Zealand. Song:
           high v., pf.

     1563 Stephenson, Robin. L: C, 1967. Song: voices, rec.,
           perc., pf.

186

e la Mare, Walter continued

1564 White, L.J. L: OUP, 1951. Song: satb, a cap.

1565 Young, Douglas. The Listeners, MS 1967, rev. 1969,
      L: F, 1973. Cta.: s solo, s chorus, male sp.,
      ch. orch. Choreographed for ballet 1969 by
      Geoffrey Cawley.

Little Bird, The "My dear Daddie bought a mansion" In
Peacock Pie: A Book of Rhymes (1913)

1566 Crist, Bainbridge. MS ca. 1916, B: BMC. Song: [solo
      v., pf.?].

Little Creature, The "Twinkum, twankum" Down-Adown-Derry:
A Book of Fairy Poems (1922)

1567 Hand, Colin. L: Curwen, 1958. Song: sa, pf.

Little Green Orchard, The "Some one is always sitting
there" In Peacock Pie: A Book of Rhymes (1913)

1568 Farjeon, Harry. The Little Green Orchard, L: S&B,
      pre-1940. Song: [v., pf.?].

1569 Gibbs, C. Armstrong. L: WR, 1932. Song: solo v.,
      ssaa, pf.

1570 Keel, Frederick. L: EA, pre-1951. Song: unison v.,
      pf.

Little Old Cupid, The "'Twas a very small garden" In
Peacock Pie: A Book of Rhymes (1913)

1571 Crist, Bainbridge. B: BMC, 1917. Song: solo v., pf.

1572 Hely-Hutchinson, Victor. Three Songs from "Peacock
      Pie", L: Elkin, 1927. Song: ms or bar solo, pf.

1573 McKinney, Howard. Four Crumbs from "Peacock Pie",
      NY: JF, pre-1940. Song: [v., pf.?].

Little Salamander, The "When I go free" In The Sunken
Garden and Other Poems (1917)

de la Mare, Walter continued

    1574   Deale, Edgar M. _Walter de la Mare Suite_, MS 1945,
           avail. RTE. Choral ste.: ssatb, orch.

    1575   Gibbs, C. Armstrong. L: Curwen, 1924. Song: solo v.,
           pf.

Lost Shoe, The   "Poor Little Lucy"   In _Peacock Pie: A Book
of Rhymes_ (1913)

    1576   Milner, Anthony. _Peacock Pie_, L: UE, 1959. Song:
           ssa, a cap. Portions of the collection are set
           for unison v., pf. Score contains German transl.

    1577   Turner, James O. L: AH&C, 1959. Song: satb, a cap.

Lovelocks   "I watched the Lady Caroline"   In _Songs of
Childhood_ (1902)

    1578   Bliss, Arthur. _Three Romantic Songs_, L: Curwen,
           1923. Song: v., pf.

    1579   Duke, John. "I watched...", NY: GS, pre-1969. Song:
           [med.-low] solo v., pf.

Mary   "Mary! Mary! Mary!"   In _Bells and Grass: A Book of
of Rhymes_ (1941)

    1580   Leigh, Eric. L: C, 1962. Song: unison v., pf.

"Me who have sailèd"   _The Three Mulla-Mulgars_ (1910), rev.
1935

    1581   Peterkin, Norman. "She's Me Forgot", L: OUP, 1924.
           Song: bar solo, pf.

Melmillo   "Three and thirty birds there stood"   In _Peacock
Pie: A Book of Rhymes_ (1913)

    1582   Carey, Clive. In _Monthly Chapbook_ (Dec. 1919); publ.
           sep. L: WR. Song: high v., pf.

    1583   Farjeon, Harry. _The Little Green Orchard_, L: S&B,
           pre-1940. Song: [v., pf.?].

1584 Gibbs, C. Armstrong. In a Dream's Beguiling, L: BH,
1951. Ste.: ms solo (or semichorus), ssa, str.
orch., pf.

1585 Liddle, Samuel. Three Songs, L: BH, 1923. Song: high
or med. v., pf.

Midget, The   See: "Just a span and half a span"

Mima   "Jemima is my name"   In Peacock Pie: A Book of Rhymes
(1913)

1586 Emeleus, John. The Huntsmen, L: Weinberger, 1960.
Song: girls' v., pf.

1587 McKinney, Howard. "An Introduction", Four Crumbs
from "Peacock Pie", NY: JF, pre-1940. Song: [v.,
pf.?].

Miss Cherry   "Once--once I loved"   In Bells and Grass: A
Book of Rhymes (1941)

1588 Fiske, Roger. L: OUP, 1951. Song: t or bar solo, pf.

Miss T.   "It's a very odd thing"   In Peacock Pie: A Book of
Rhymes (1913)

1589 Gibbs, C. Armstrong. Five Children's Songs from
"Peacock Pie", L: BH, 1933. Song: unison v., pf.

1590 Howells, Herbert. Peacock Pie, L: F&BG, 1923. Song:
v., pf.

1591 Kagen, Sergius. NY: Weintraub, 1950. Song: any solo
v. except b, pf.

Mistletoe   "Sitting under the mistletoe"   In Peacock Pie:
A Book of Rhymes (1913)

1592 Berkeley, Lennox. Five Songs, L: JWC, 1948. Song:
med. v., pf.

1593 Crist, Bainbridge. B: BMC, 1916. Song: solo v., pf.

de la Mare, Walter continued

1594   Gibbs, C. Armstrong. L: Curwen, 1922. Song: solo v.,
       pf. Also avail. for solo v., orch.

1595   Lodge, Ernest. L: OUP, pre-1940. Song: [v., pf.?].

1596   Pattison, Lee. NY: LG, 1958. Madrigal: satb, a cap.

Mistress Fell   "'Whom seek you here, sweet Mistress Fell?'"
In The Sunken Garden and Other Poems (1917)

1597   Burrows, Benjamin. Leicester: Bodnant, ca. 1952.
       Song: [v., pf.?].

Mocking Fairy, The   "'Won't you look out of your window,
Mrs. Gill?'"   In Peacock Pie: A Book of Rhymes (1913)

1598   Besly, Maurice. L: S&B, pre-1940. Song: [v., pf.?].

1599   Dyson, George. "Won't you look out of your window?",
       MS ca. 1920. Orch. ste.: orch. only.

Moonlight   "Far moon maketh lovers wise, The"   In Motley
and Other Poems (1918)

1600   Brinkworth, Francis. L: S&B, pre-1940. Song: [solo
       v., pf.?].

Moth, The   "Isled in the midnight air"   In Flora: A Book of
Drawings (1919)

1601   Berkeley, Lennox. Songs of the Half-Light, L: JWC,
       1966. Song: high v., gtr. Gtr. pt. ed. by Julian
       Bream.

1602   McIntyre, Paul. Four Poems of Walter de la Mare, MS
       1950, avail. CMC. Song: s solo, pf.

Mountains, The   "Still and blanched and cold and lone"
In The Listeners and Other Poems (1912)

1603   Gibbs, C. Armstrong. Five Songs, L: S&B, 1920. Song:
       solo v., pf.

la Mare, Walter continued

Mr. Punch "Screech across the sands, A" This_Year:_Next
Year (1937)

   1604 Hurd, Michael. Sea_and_Shore_Songs, L: N, 1968.
         Song: unison v., pf.

Mrs. MacQueen "With glass like a bull's eye" In Peacock
Pie: A Book_of_Rhymes (1913)

   1605 Hand, Colin. L: N, 1958. Song: unison v., pf., opt.
         descant rec.

   1606 Howells, Herbert. Peacock_Pie, L: F&BG, 1923. Song:
         v., pf.

Mulgar's Journey Song, The See: "In Munza a Mulgar once
lived alone"

Music "When music sounds, gone is the earth I know"
   In The_Sunken_Garden_and_Other_Poems (1917)

   1607 Cartwright, Patricia. "When Music Sounds", L: N,
         1958. Song: sa, pf.

   1608 Evans, T. Hopkins. "When Music Sounds", L: Curwen,
         1936. Song: solo v., pf.

   1609 Gover, Gerald. "When Music Sounds", L: BH, 1952.
         Song: high v., pf.

   1610 Murray, Dom Gregory. L: OUP, 1938. Song: satb, a
         cap.

   1611* Read, Gardner. MS 1947. Song: ssa, pf.

   1612 Smith, Edwin. L: N, 1951. Song: ssaa, a cap.

Music Unheard "Sweet sounds, begone" In The_Listeners_and
Other_Poems (1912)

   1613 Gibbs, C. Armstrong. "Sweet...", L: WR, 1932. Song:
         v., pf.

191

de la Mare, Walter continued

1614 Wickens, Dennis. <u>The Everlasting Voices</u>, MS. Cyc.:
high v., pf.

Ned Vaughan See: "Shepherd, Ned Vaughan, A"

Never More, Sailor "Never more, Sailor" In <u>The Listeners
and Other Poems</u> (1912)

1615 Peterkin, Norman. L: OUP, pre-1940. Song: [v., pf.].

Nicholas Nye "Thistle and darnel and dock grew there" In
<u>Peacock Pie: A Book of Rhymes</u> (1913)

1616 Dorward, David. L: G, 1967. Song: unison v., pf.

1617 Hughes-Jones, Llifon. L: Curwen, 1962. Song: unison
v., pf.

Nicoletta "Oh, my pretty Nicoletta" In <u>Bells and Grass: A
Book of Rhymes</u> (1941)

1618 Allam, Edward. Leeds: EA, pre-1956. Song: [v., pf.].

1619* Harrison, Pamela. <u>Eight Poems of Walter de la Mare</u>,
L: OUP, 1956. Song: s or t solo, pf.

Night "That shining moon" In <u>Memory and Other Poems</u>
(1938)

1620 Wordsworth, William. <u>Four Songs</u>, L: L, 1947. Song:
high v., pf.

Night-Swans, The "'Tis silence on the enchanted lake" In
<u>Songs of Childhood</u> (1902)

1621 Gibbs, C. Armstrong. "The Night Song", <u>In a Dream's
Beguiling</u>, L: BH, 1951. Ste.: ms solo (or semi-
chorus), ssa, str. orch., pf.

No Jewel "No jewel from the rock" In <u>Bells and Grass: A
Book of Rhymes</u> (1941)

192

e la Mare, Walter continued

1622 Harrison, Pamela. *Eight Songs for Voice and Recorder*, MS. Song: solo v., rec., pf.

"No Voice to scold"   *Ding Dong Bell* (1924)

1623 Chanler, Theodore. *Eight Epitaphs*, NY: Arrow, 1939. Song: solo v., pf.

Nod   "Softly along the road of evening"   In *The Listeners and Other Poems* (1912)

1624 Davies, H. Walford. "Softly...", *Twenty-One Songs*, L: N, 1931. Song: med. v., pf.

1625 Ford, Donald. L: MM, 1927, assigned L: C, 1943. Song: [solo v., pf.].

1626 Gibbs, C. Armstrong. In *Monthly Chapbook* (Dec. 1919); publ. sep. L: Curwen, 1922. Song: solo v., pf.

1627 Harmati, Sandor. NY: HB, 1928 in *New Songs for New Voices*. Song: v., pf.

1628 Harris, Victor. MS 1921, NY: JF, ca. 1922. Song: [v., pf.].

1629 Housman, Rosalie. MS 1930, avail. NYPL. Song: [solo v., pf.].

1630 Lekberg, Sven. "Softly...", NY: GS, 1964. Song: satb, a cap.

1631 Shepherd, Arthur. "Softly...", *Seven Songs*, Northampton, Mass.: NVMP, 1961. Song: [high] solo v., pf.

1632 Smith, David S. *Portraits*, MS 1919, B: OD. Cyc.: [v., pf.].

1633 Tobin, John. L: Elkin, 1946. Song: med. v., pf.

"Now all the roads to London town"   *Crossings: A Fairy Play* (1921)

de la Mare, Walter continued

    1634 Gibbs, C. Armstrong. "Beggar's Song", L: Beaumont,
        1921 in Crossings: A Fairy Play; publ. sep. L:
        Curwen, 1924. Song: solo v., pf. Score ac-
        companied the 1st edn. of the play.

"Now silent falls the clacking mill"   Crossings: A Fairy
Play (1921), incl. under the title "Wild Time" in Selected
Poems (1927)

    1635 Gibbs, C. Armstrong. "Lullaby", L: Beaumont, 1921 in
        Crossings: A Fairy Play; publ. sep. under the
        title "Ann's Cradle Song" L: Curwen, 1924. Song:
        solo v., pf. Score accompanied the 1st edn. of
        the play.

Off the Ground   "Three jolly Farmers"   In Peacock Pie: A
Book of Rhymes (1913)

    1636 Flay, Alfred. L: C, 1965. Cta.: 2 s soli, sss, s
        semichorus, rec., perc., (incl. tuned instru-
        ments), stgs., pf.

    1637 Gibbs, C. Armstrong. In a Dream's Beguiling, L: BH,
        1951. Ste.: ms solo (or semichorus), ssa, str.
        orch., pf.

Old Sailor, The   "There came an old sailor"   In Bells and
Grass: A Book of Rhymes (1941)

    1638 Hurd, Michael. Sea and Shore Songs, L: N, 1968.
        Song: unison v., pf.

Old Shellover   "'Come!' said Old Shellover"   In Peacock
Pie: A Book of Rhymes (1913)

    1639 Chanler, Theodore. Four Rhymes from "Peacock Pie",
        NY: AMP, 1948. Song: med. v., pf.

    1640 Gibbs, C. Armstrong. Five Children's Songs from
        "Peacock Pie", L: BH, 1933. Song: unison v., pf.

Old Soldier, The   "There came an Old Soldier to my door"
In Peacock Pie: A Book of Rhymes (1913)

1641 Crist, Bainbridge. MS ca. 1919. Song: [solo v.,
      pf.?].

1642 Dushkin, Dorothy. Three Songs for Women's Voices and
      Woodwind Trio or Piano, NY: CF, 1955 (ww. pts.
      on hire only). Song: ssa, ww. trio or ssa, pf.

1643 Gibbs, C. Armstrong. L: Curwen, 1925. Song: ttbb,
      a cap.

1644 Hely-Hutchinson, Victor. L: OUP, 1927. Song: bar
      solo, pf.

1645* Swain, Freda. From "Peacock Pie", MS ca. 1949-50,
      avail. Chinnor: Channel, NEMO. Cyc.: bar and pf.
      ensemble. Portions of the cyc. also arr. for
      bar and str. qrt. ensemble.

Old Stone House, The   "Nothing on the grey roof"   In
   Peacock Pie: A Book of Rhymes (1913)

1646 Milner, Anthony. Peacock Pie, L: UE, 1959. Song:
      ssa, a cap. Portions of the collection are set
      for unison v., pf. Score contains German transl.

1647 Roberton, Hugh. Peacock Pie, L: AH&C, 1943. Choral
      ste.: ssa, a cap. Portions of the ste. are set
      for satb.

Old Susan   "When Susan's work was done"   In The Listeners
   and Other Poems (1912)

1648 Smith, David S. Portraits, MS 1919, B: OD. Cyc.:
      [v., pf.].

Old Tailor, The   "There once was an old Tailor"   In Bells
   and Grass: A Book of Rhymes (1941)

1649 Greaves, Terence. Three Children's Songs, L: OUP,
      1964. Song: unison v., pf.

"Once and there was a young sailor, yeo ho!"   The Three
   Mulla-Mulgars (1910), rev. 1913, rev. 1947

195

de la Mare, Walter continued

1650   Gibbs, C. Armstrong. "Andy Battle", L: WR, 1933.
        Song: mixed v., a cap.

1651   Peterkin, Norman. "Once and there was a young
        sailor", L: OUP, 1927. Song: bar solo, unacc.

Peak and Puke   "From his cradle in the glamourie"   In
    Peacock Pie: A Book of Rhymes (1913)

1652   Young, Percy. Three Songs from "Peacock Pie", L:
        OUP, 1951. Song: ssa, pf. One song in the col-
        lection requires s duet.

Picture, The   "Here is a sea-legged sailor"   In Peacock
    Pie: A Book of Rhymes (1913)

1653   Hurd, Michael. Sea and Shore Songs, L: N, 1968.
        Song: unison v., pf.

Pigs and the Charcoal-burner, The   "Old Pig said to the
    little pigs, The"   In Peacock Pie: A Book of Rhymes
    (1913)

1654   Emeleus, John. The Huntsmen, L: Weinberger, 1960.
        Song: girls' v., pf.

'Please to Remember'   "Here am I"   This Year: Next Year
    (1937)

1655   Greaves, Terence. Three Children's Songs, L: OUP,
        1964. Song: unison v., pf.

1656   Hurd, Michael. L: N, 1963; incl. under the title
        "The Guy" in Sea and Shore Songs, L: N, 1968.
        Song: unison v., pf.

Poor Henry   "Thick in its glass"   In Peacock Pie: A Book of
    Rhymes (1913)

1657   Berkeley, Lennox. Five Songs, L: JWC, 1948. Song:
        med. v., pf.

196

de la Mare, Walter continued

Poor Natural, A   See: "Here lieth a poor Natural"

Portrait of a Warrior, The   "His brow is seamed"   In Songs
    of Childhood (1902)

    1658 Buczynski, Walter. "A Portrait of a Warrior", Four
          Poems of Walter de la Mare, MS 1955, avail. CMC.
          Song: [a] solo v., pf.

Quack   "What said the drake to his lady-love"   In Poems
    1919-1934 (1935)

    1659 Fleming, Robert. MS 1943. Song: v., pf.

Quartette, The   "Tom sang for joy"   In Peacock Pie: A Book
    of Rhymes (1913)

    1660 Grant-Schaefer, G.A. "The Quartet", NY: Silver,
          1932 in Music of Many Lands and Peoples. Song:
          v., pf.

    1661 Symons, Dom Thomas. Two de la Mare Songs, L: OUP,
          1937. Song: v., pf.

Queen Djenira   "When Queen Djenira slumbers through"   In
    The Listeners and Other Poems (1912)

    1662 Burrows, Benjamin. Leicester: Bodnant, ca. 1952.
          Song: [v., pf.?].

"Queen of Arabia, Uanjinee, The"   A Child's Day: A Book of
    Rhymes (1912)

    1663 Bartholomew, Marshall. "The Queen of Arabia", NY:
          Silver, 1928-30 in The Music Hour, Vol. 2. Song:
          v., unacc.

Rachel   "Rachel sings sweet"   In The Listeners and Other
    Poems (1912)

197

de la Mare, Walter continued

1664   Berkeley, Lennox. Songs of the Half-Light, L: JWC,
        1966. Song: high v., gtr. Gtr. pt. ed. by Julian
        Bream.

1665   Burrows, Benjamin. Leicester: Bodnant, ca. 1952.
        Song: [v., pf.?].

1666   McIntyre, Paul. Four Poems of Walter de la Mare, MS
        1950, avail. CMC. Song: s solo, pf.

1667   Smith, David S. Portraits, MS 1919, B: OD. Cyc.:
        [v., pf.].

Rainbow, The   "I saw the lovely arch"   In Songs of Childhood (1916)

1668   Britten, Benjamin. Three Two-Part Songs, L: OUP,
        1969. Song: boys' v., pf. or sa, pf.

Reverie   "When slim Sophia mounts her horse"   In Songs of
Childhood (1902)

1669   Duke, John. "When slim Sophia...", NY: M, 1965.
        Song: [med.] solo v., pf.

1670   Gibbs, C. Armstrong. Songs of Childhood, L: BH,
        1933. Song: vocal qrt. (s, a, t, b), pf.

1671   Keel, Frederick. Four "Songs of Childhood", L: BH,
        1920. Cyc.: solo v., pf.

1672   Shepherd, Arthur. Seven Songs, Northampton, Mass.:
        NVMP, 1961. Song: high v., pf.

Ride-by-nights, The   "Up on their brooms the Witches stream"
In Peacock Pie: A Book of Rhymes (1913)

1673   Britten, Benjamin. Three Two-Part Songs, L: OUP,
        1932. Song: boys' v., pf. or sa, pf.

1674   Gibbs, C. Armstrong. Peacock Pie, L: BH, 1933. Ch.
        ste.: 2 vln., vla., vcl., pf. or 3 vln., vcl.,
        pf.

1675   Hand, Colin. L: OUP, 1961. Song: ss, pf.

1676   Roberton, Hugh. Peacock Pie, L: AH&C, 1943. Choral
      ste.: ssa, a cap. Portions of the ste. are set
      for satb.

1677   Young, Percy. Three Songs from "Peacock Pie", L:
      OUP, 1951. Song: s duet, pf. Other songs in the
      collection require ssa.

Books in October   "They sweep up, crying"   In Memory and
Other Poems (1938)

1678   Cone, Edward T. Around the Year, MS. Cyc.: satb,
      str. qrt.

Sallie   "When Sallie with her pitcher goes"   In Bells and
Grass: A Book of Rhymes (1941)

1679   Harrison, Pamela. Eight Songs for Voice and
      Recorder, MS. Song: solo v., rec., pf.

1680   Waters, Rosemary. MS 1955, avail. University of
      Auckland. Song: high v., pf.

Sambo   "Nigger-boy Sambo who scours the pots"   In Bells and
Grass: A Book of Rhymes (1941)

1681   Harrison, Pamela. Eight Songs for Voice and
      Recorder, MS. Song: solo v., rec., pf.

Scarecrow, The   "All winter through"   In The Listeners and
Other Poems (1912)

1682   Gibbs, C. Armstrong. L: Curwen, 1931. Song: solo v.,
      orch. Also arr. for solo v., str. qrt. or solo
      v., pf.

1683   Smith, David S. Portraits, MS 1919, B: OD. Cyc.:
      [v., pf.].

Scribe, The   "What lovely things"   In Motley and Other
Poems (1918)

de la Mare, Walter continued

1684   Gurney, Ivor. A Second Volume of Ten Songs, L: JUP,
        1938. Song: solo v., pf.

Shadows   "Horse in the field, The"   In Bells and Grass: A
Book of Rhymes (1941)

1685   Stoker, Richard. L: LD, 1969. Song: unison choir,
        pf.

"Shepherd, Ned Vaughan, A"   Ding Dong Bell (1924), incl. in
collected edns. under the title "Ned Vaughan"

1686   Chanler, Theodore. "A Shepherd", Three Epitaphs, MS
        1940. Song: solo v., pf.

Ship of Rio, The   "There was a ship of Rio"   In Peacock
Pie: A Book of Rhymes (1913)

1687   Allam, Edward. Leeds: EA; pre-1956. Song: [v., pf.].

1688   Andrews, Mark. NY: Silver, 1932 in Music of Many
        Lands and Peoples. Song: v., pf.

1689   Archer, Violet. MS pre-1952. Song: [v., pf.?].

1690   Britten, Benjamin. Three Two-Part Songs, L: JUP,
        1932. Song: 2 pt. boys' v., pf. or sa, pf. Publ.
        sep. L: OUP, 1964 for [med.] solo v., pf.

1691   Campbell, Vance. "Nine and Ninety Monkeys", NY: GS,
        pre-1940. Song: [v., pf.].

1692   Chanler, Theodore. Four Rhymes from "Peacock Pie",
        NY: AMP, 1948. Song: med. v., pf.

1693   Crist, Bainbridge. NY: GS, pre-1940. Song: [v.,
        pf.].

1694   Daubney, Brian. L: EA, 1958. Song: unsion v., pf.

1695   Dushkin, Dorothy. Three Songs for Women's Voices
        and Woodwind Trio or Piano, NY: CF, 1955 (ww.
        pts. on hire only). Song: ssa, ww. trio or ssa,
        pf.

1696 Gibbs, C. Armstrong. L: WR, 1933. Song: solo v., pf.

1697 Greaves, Terence. Follow_My_Leader, L: OUP, 1965.
      Canon: 2 pt. chorus, pf.

1698 Jacob, Archibald. L: S&B, pre-1940. Song: [v.,
      pf.?].

1699 Milner, Anthony. Peacock_Pie, L: UE, 1959. Song:
      ssa, a cap. Portions of the collection are set
      for unison v., pf. Score contains German transl.

1700 Peterkin, Norman. "Nine and Ninety Monkeys", L: OUP,
      pre-1940. Song: [v., pf.].

1701 Rose, Michael. Reigate: S&B, 1967. Song: unison
      female v., pf. or unison children's v., pf.

1702 Smith, Edwin. L: N, 1936. Song: unison female v.,
      pf. or unison boys' v., pf.

"Sighs have no skill" Henry_Brocken (1904)

1703 Fricker, Peter Racine. Two_Madrigals, MS 1947.
      Madrigal: satb, a cap.

Silence "With changeful sound" In The_Listeners_and_Other
Poems (1912)

1704 Goossens, Eugene. L: JWC, 1922. Setting for chorus,
      orch.

Silver "Slowly, silently, now the moon" In Peacock_Pie:
A_Book_of_Rhymes (1913)

1705 Archer, Violet. MS pre-1952. Song: [v., pf.?].

1706 Berkeley, Lennox. Five_Songs, L: JWC, 1948. Song:
      med. v., pf.

1707 Britten, Benjamin. Tit_for_Tat, L: F, 1969. Song:
      [med.] solo v., pf.

1708 Buczynski, Walter. Four_Poems_of_Walter_de_La_Mare,
      MS 1955, avail. CMC. Song: [a] solo v., pf.

de la Mare, Walter continued

1709   Butterworth, Arthur. Four Nocturnal Songs, MS 1948.
       Song: s solo, pf.

1710   Duke, John. NY: GS, 1961. Song: solo v., pf.

1711   Emeleus, John. L: L, 1962. Song: unison v., pf.

1712   Farjeon, Harry. The Little Green Orchard, L: S&B,
       pre-1940. Song: [v., pf.?].

1713   Gibbs, C. Armstrong. L: WR, 1922; re-issued 1949.
       Song: low v., pf. Also arr. for high v., pf.

1714   Greenhill, Harold. L: Curwen, 1934. Song: 2 pt.
       children's v., pf. or 2 pt. female v., pf.

1715   Hand, Colin. L: N, 1955. Song: unison v., pf.

1716   Harris, Victor. NY: JF, 1922. Song: [v., pf.].

1717   Hely-Hutchinson, Victor. L: OUP, 1928. Song: ms or
       bar solo, pf.

1718   Koch, John. Hastings-on-Hudson: GMP, 1965. Song: s
       solo, pf.

1719   Milner, Anthony. Peacock Pie, L: UE, 1959. Song:
       ssa, a cap. Portions of the collection are set
       for unison v., pf. Score contains German transl.

1720   Redman, Reginald. L: Curwen, 1967. Song: solo v.,
       pf.

1721   Saunders, Neil. L: N, 1963. Song: satb, a cap.

1722   Shepherd, Arthur. "Slowly...", MS, avail. University
       of Utah. Song: ssa, pf.

1723   Smith, Edwin. L: N, 1951. Song: ssa, pf.

1724   Vosper, William. MS 1955, avail. University of
       Auckland. Song: med. v., pf.

1725   Weigl, Vally. MS, avail. ACA. Song: med. v., rec.,
       pf.

1726 Young, Douglas. The Listeners, MS 1967, rev. 1969,
L: F, 1973. Cta.: s solo, s chorus, male sp.,
ch. orch. Choreographed for ballet 1969 by
Geoffrey Cawley.

1727 Zanders, Douglas. MS 1952, avail. University of
Canterbury. Song: satb, a cap.

Silver Penny, The   "Sailorman, I'll give to you"   In Songs
of Childhood (1902)

1728 Gibbs, C. Armstrong. L: Curwen, 1925. Song: ttbb, a
cap.

1729 Hurd, Michael. L: N, 1963, Sea and Shore Songs, L:
N, 1968. Song: unison v., pf.

1730 Stoll, David. L: OUP, 1966. Song: unison v., pf.

"Sleep sound, Mistress Hew!"   Ding Dong Bell (1924), incl.
in collected edns. under the title "Alice Hew"

1731 Le Fleming, Christopher. "Alice Hew", A Quiet
Company, L: CR, 1953. Cyc.: ms or bar solo, pf.

Sleeping Beauty, The   "Scent of brambles fills the air, The"
In Songs of Childhood (1902)

1732 Gibbs, C. Armstrong. L: Curwen, 1924. Song: solo v.,
pf.

1733 Gibbs, C. Armstrong. Songs of Childhood, L: BH,
1933. Song: vocal qrt. (s, a, t, b), pf.

Sleepyhead   See: Gnomies, The

Snow   "No breath of wind"   In Peacock Pie: A Book of Rhymes
(1924)

1734 Bruce, Margaret C. "The Snow", L: Curwen, 1951.
Song: solo v., pf.

1735 Parfrey, Raymond. MS. Song: s solo, pf.

de la Mare, Walter continued

Snowflake, The   "See, now, this filigree"   In Flora: A Book
   of Drawings (1919)

   1736 Auerbach, Norman. Three Choral Songs, Bryn Mawr: TP,
         1968. Song: ssaa, a cap.

   1737 Wordsworth, William. Four Songs, L: L, 1947. Song:
         high v., pf.

Some One   "Some one came knocking"   In Peacock Pie: A Book
   of Rhymes (1913)

   1738 Adler, Samuel. Five Choral Poems, NY: AMP, 1957.
         Song: satb, a cap.

   1739 Archer, Violet. MS, avail. CMC. Song: v., pf.

   1740 Besly, Maurice. L: BH, 1923. Song: v., pf.

   1741 Crist, Bainbridge. B: BMC, pre-1940. Song: [v.,
         pf.].

   1742 Swift, Newton. NY: HB, 1928 in New Songs for New
         Voices. Song: v., pf.

   1743 Thompson, Randall. NY: HB, 1928 in New Songs for
         New Voices. Song: v., pf.

Song of Enchantment, A   "Song of Enchantment I sang me
   there, A"   In Peacock Pie: A Book of Rhymes (1913)

   1744 Boyle, Ina. L: S&B, pre-1940. Song: [solo v.,
         pf.?].

   1745 Britten, Benjamin. Tit for Tat, L: F, 1969. Song:
         [med.] solo v., pf.

   1746 Galway, Victor. L: OUP, 1939. Song: 2 pt. chorus,
         pf.

Song of Shadows, The   "Sweep thy faint strings, Musician"
   In Peacock Pie: A Book of Rhymes (1913)

   1747 Bennett, Joan. "A Song of Shadows", L: Curwen, 1934.
         Song: solo v., pf.

1748   Boyle, Ina. "A Song of Shadows", L: S&B, pre-1940.
Song: [v., pf.?].

1749   Fischer, Irwin. "Song of Shadows", MS. Song: solo
v., pf.

1750   Gibbs, C. Armstrong. L: G&T, 1921, copyright assigned L: BH, 1930. Song: ssa, pf. Also publ. L: G&T,
1921 for 3 pt. chorus of trebles and altos, pf.
Arr. for solo v., pf.; arr. publ. L: WR, 1922.

1751   Gwyther, Geoffrey. "A Song of Shadows", L: Curwen,
1920. Song: solo v., pf.

1752   Keel, Frederick. L: C, 1935. Song: v. duet, pf.

1753   Liddle, Samuel. "A Song of Shadows", Three Songs,
L: BH, 1923. Song: high or med. v., pf.

1754   Pedley, David. L: OUP, 1966. Song: satb, a cap.

1755   Whittaker, W.G. L: OUP, pre-1946. Song: sa, pf.

1756   Wordsworth, William. Three Songs, MS 1938. Song:
med. v., pf.

1757   Young, Percy. "The Song of the Shadows", Three Songs
from "Peacock Pie", L: OUP, 1951. Song: ssa, pf.
One song in the collection requires s duet.

Song of Soldiers, The   "As I sat musing by the frozen dyke"
In Peacock Pie: A Book of Rhymes (1913)

1758   Austin, Frederic. "A Song of Soldiers", L: Curwen,
1924. Song: solo v., unacc.

1759   Berkeley, Lennox. "The Song of the Soldiers", Five
Songs, L: JWC, 1948. Song: med. v., pf.

1760   Gibbs, C. Armstrong. "A Song of Soldiers", L: Curwen, 1927. Song: s or t solo, chorus of male v.,
a cap.

1761   Hely-Hutchinson, Victor. L: Elkin, 1933. Song: high
or med. v., pf.

1762   Holman, Derek. L: N, 1961. Song: unison v., pf.

de la Mare, Walter continued

    1763   McIntyre, Paul. Four Poems of Walter de la Mare, MS 1950, avail. CMC. Song: s solo, pf.

    1764* Swain, Freda. "Song of the Soldiers", From "Peacock Pie", MS 1949-50, avail. Chinnor: Channel, NEMO. Cyc.: bar and pf. ensemble. Portions of the cyc. also arr. for bar and str. qrt. ensemble.

    1765   Webber, W.S. Lloyd. L: N, 1963. Song: unison v., pf.

Song of the Mad Prince, The   "Who said, 'Peacock Pie'?"
In Peacock Pie: A Book of Rhymes (1913)

    1766   Anhalt, Istvan. Three Songs of Love, MS 1951, avail. CMC. Song: ssa, a cap.

    1767   Emeleus, John. L: L, 1961. Song: 2 pt. chorus, pf.

    1768   Gibbs, C. Armstrong. "The Mad Prince", L: Curwen, 1922. Song: solo v., pf. Also avail. for solo v., stgs.

Song of the Secret, The   "Where is beauty?"   In Peacock Pie: A Book of Rhymes (1913)

    1769   Peterkin, Norman. "The Song of Secret", L: OUP, 1935. Song: [v., pf.].

    1770   Roberton, Hugh. "Where...", Peacock Pie, L: AH&C, 1943. Choral ste.: satb, a cap. Portions of the ste. are set for ssa.

Song of the Water-Midden   See: "Bubble, bubble"

Sorcery   "'What voice is that I hear...'"   In Poems (1906)

    1771   Butterworth, Arthur. "What voice...", Ancient Sorceries, MS (Opus 49). Cyc.: c-t solo, rec. (treble and tenor alternating), hpd.

"Stranger, here lies"   Ding Dong Bell (1924), incl. in collected edns. under the title "Ann Poverty"

de la Mare, Walter continued

    1772 Chanler, Theodore. "Ann Poverty", _Eight_Epitaphs_,
          NY: Arrow, 1939. Song: solo v., pf.

Stranger, The   "In the woods as I did walk"   In _The_Sunken_
   Garden_and_Other_Poems_ (1917)

    1773 Gibbs, C. Armstrong. _Five_Songs_, L: S&B, 1920. Song:
          solo v., pf. Publ. sep. L: WR, 1948 for ssatbb,
          a cap.

Sunken Garden, The   "Speak not--whisper not"   In _The_Sunken_
   Garden_and_Other_Poems_ (1917)

    1774 Gibbs, C. Armstrong. L: BH, 1933. Song: 3 pt. chorus
          (s, ms, a), a cap.

    1775 Gibbs, C. Armstrong. _Peacock_Pie_, L: BH, 1933. Ch.
          ste.: 2 vln., vla., vcl., pf. or 3 vln., vcl.,
          pf.

Supper   "I supped where bloomed the red red rose"   In _Bells_
   and_Grass:_A_Book_of_Rhymes_ (1941)

    1776 Brown, James. _Songs_for_Children_, Set I, MS. Song:
          v., pf.

    1777 Harrison, Pamela. _Eight_Songs_for_Voice_and_
          Recorder_, MS. Song: solo v., rec., pf.

Susannah Fry   See: "Here sleep I"

Tartary   "If I were Lord of Tartary"   In _Songs_of_Childhood_
   (1902)

    1778 Allam, Edward. Leeds: EA, pre-1956. Song: [v., pf.].

    1779 Bantock, Granville. "If I...", L: C, 1942. Song:
          [v., pf.].

    1780 Stevens, Halsey. "Lord of Tartary", MS 1955. Song:
          solo v., pf.

de la Mare, Walter continued

Then   "Twenty, forty, sixty, eighty"   In Peacock Pie: A
Book of Rhymes (1913)

    1781 Gibbs, C. Armstrong. Five Children's Songs from
          "Peacock Pie", L: BH, 1933. Song: unison v., pf.

Thomas Logge   See: "Here lies Thomas Logge--A Rascally
Dogge"

Three Cherry Trees, The   "There were three cherry trees
once"   In The Listeners and Other Poems (1912)

    1782 Dent, Edward. MS 1918. Song: [v., pf.].

    1783* Johnson, Horace. NY: R, 1929. Song: v., pf.

Three Sisters   See: "Three sisters rest beneath"

"Three sisters rest beneath"   Ding Dong Bell (1924), incl.
in collected edns. under the title "Three Sisters"

    1784 Chanler, Theodore. "Three Sisters", Eight Epitaphs,
          NY: Arrow, 1939. Song: solo v., pf.

    1785 Le Fleming, Christopher. "Three Sisters", A Quiet
          Company, L: CR, 1953. Cyc.: ms or bar solo, pf.

Tidings   See: "Listen, I who love thee well"

Tillie   "Old Tillie Turveycombe"   In Peacock Pie: A Book of
Rhymes (1913)

    1786 Chanler, Theodore. Four Rhymes from "Peacock Pie",
          NY: AMP, 1948. Song: med. v., pf.

    1787 Hurd, Michael. L: N, 1963, Sea and Shore Songs, L:
          N, 1968. Song: unison v., pf.

    1788 Leigh, Eric. L: N, 1960. Song: unison v., pf.

e la Mare, Walter continued

Tired Tim   "Poor tired Tim! It's sad for him"   In Peacock
Pie: A Book of Rhymes (1913)

    1789 Belchamber, Eileen. L: EA, pre-1951. Song: unison
          v., pf.

    1790 Crist, Bainbridge. Queer Yarns, NY: CF, 1925. Song:
          v., pf.

    1791 Faulkner, David. Two Songs for Children, L: C, 1963.
          Song: unison v., pf.

    1792 Howells, Herbert. Peacock Pie, L: F&BG, 1923. Song:
          v., pf.

Tit for Tat   "Have you been catching of fish, Tom Noddy?"
In Peacock Pie: A Book of Rhymes (1913)

    1793 Britten, Benjamin. Tit for Tat, L: F, 1969. Song:
          [med.] solo v., pf.

    1794* Swain, Freda. From "Peacock Pie", MS ca. 1949-50,
          avail. Chinnor, Channel, NEMO. Cyc.: bar and pf.
          ensemble. Also arr. for bar and str. qrt. en-
          semble.

Tom Head   See: "I rang yon bells a score of years"

Tom's Angel   "No one was in the fields"   In The Fleeting
and Other Poems (1933)

    1795 Deale, Edgar M. Walter de la Mare Suite, MS 1945,
          avail. RTE. Choral ste.: ssatb, orch.

Trees   "Of all the trees in England"   In Peacock Pie: A
Book of Rhymes (1913)

    1796 Hely-Hutchinson, Victor. L: Elkin, 1927. Song: low
          v., pf.

    1797 Roberton, Hugh. "Of all...", Peacock Pie, L: AH&C,
          1943. Choral ste.: satb, a cap. Portions of the
          ste. are set for ssa.

de la Mare, Walter continued

1798   Wood, Charles. "The Trees in England", L: AHSC
        (YBP), 1927. Song: unison v., [pf.]. Arr. by
        Denis Wright for 2 pt. chorus, accompaniment
        unspecif.; arr. publ. L: AH&C, 1961.

Truants, The   "Ere my heart beats too coldly"   In Peacock
        Pie: A Book of Rhymes (1913)

1799   Shepherd, Arthur. "Truants", MS, avail. University
        of Utah. Song: solo v., pf.

Twilight   "When to the inward darkness of my mind"   In
        The Fleeting and Other Poems (1933)

1800   Buczynski, Walter. Four Poems of Walter de la Mare,
        MS 1955, avail. CMC. Song: [a] solo v., pf.

Unchanging, The   "After the songless rose of evening"   In
        Motley and Other Poems (1918)

1801   Mase, Owen. L: Curwen, 1926. Song: solo v., pf.

Up and Down   "Down the Hill of Ludgate"   In Peacock Pie:
        A Book of Rhymes (1913)

1802   Brown, James. Songs for Children, Set II, MS. Song:
        v., pf.

Vigil   "Dark is the night"   In Motley and Other Poems
        (1918)

1803   Britten, Benjamin. Tit for Tat, L: F, 1969. Song:
        [med.] solo v., pf.

Vision, The   "O starry face"   In The Burning-Glass and
        Other Poems (1945)

1804   Auerbach, Norman. Three Choral Songs, Bryn Mawr: TP,
        1968. Song: ssaa, a cap.

e la Mare, Walter continued

Voices   "Who is it calling by the darkened river"   In Poems
(1906)

    1805 Butterworth, Arthur. "Who is it...", Ancient
        Sorceries, MS (Opus 49). Cyc.: c-t solo, rec.
        (treble and tenor alternating), hpd.

Wanderers   "Wide are the meadows of night"   In Peacock Pie:
A Book of Rhymes (1913)

    1806 Austin, Frederic. L: Curwen, 1924. Song: solo v.,
        unacc.

    1807 Farjeon, Harry. The Little Green Orchard, L: S&B,
        pre-1940. Song: [v., pf.?].

Warbler, A   "In the sedge a tiny song"   In Bells and Grass:
A Book of Rhymes (1941)

    1808 Harrison, Pamela. Eight Songs for Voice and
        Recorder, MS. Song: solo v., rec., pf.

Water Midden's Song, The   See: "Bubble, bubble"

Where   "Monkeys in a forest"   In Bells and Grass: A Book of
Rhymes (1941)

    1809 Brown, James. Songs for Children, Set I, MS. Song:
        v., pf.

    1810 Gibbs, C. Armstrong. L: EA, 1953. Song: unison v.,
        pf.

    1811* Harrison, Pamela. Eight Poems of Walter de la Mare,
        L: OUP, 1956. Song: s or t solo, pf.

White   "Once was a Miller"   In Bells and Grass: A Book of
Rhymes (1941)

    1812* Gibbs, C. Armstrong. L: Curwen, 1949. Song: unison
        v., pf.

de la Mare, Walter continued

1813* Harrison, Pamela. L: OUP, 1954, Eight Poems of
Walter de la Mare, L: OUP, 1956. Song: s or t
solo, pf.

Why? "Ever, ever" In Bells and Grass: A Book of Rhymes
(1941), subsequently rev.

1814* Gibbs, C. Armstrong. L: Curwen, 1949. Song: unison
v., pf.

1815* Harrison, Pamela. Eight Poems of Walter de la Mare,
L: OUP, 1956. Song: s or t solo, pf.

'Why, then comes in...' "Long-idling Spring may come"
In O Lovely England and Other Poems (1953)

1816 Cone, Edward T. Around the Year, MS. Cyc.: satb,
str. qrt.

Wild Time See: "Now silent falls the clacking mill"

Will Ever? "Will he ever be weary of wandering" In
Peacock Pie: A Book of Rhymes (1913)

1817 Crist, Bainbridge. "Into a Ship, Dreaming", NY: CF,
1918. Song: solo v., pf.

1818 Gibbs, C. Armstrong. "The Wanderer", L: Curwen,
1926. Song: solo v., pf.

Will-o'-the-Wisp "Will-o'-the-Wisp" In Bells and Grass: A
Book of Rhymes (1941)

1819 Bruce, Margaret C. L: Curwen, 1961. Song: ssa, pf.

1820 Harrison, Pamela. Eight Songs for Voice and
Recorder, MS. Song: solo v., rec., pf.

Willow, The "Leans now the fair willow" In The Veil and
Other Poems (1921)

1821 Cone, Edward T. Around the Year, MS. Cyc.: satb,
str. qrt.

1822 Schmidt, Joye. MS 1952, avail. University of Auckland. Song: low v., pf.

Window, The   "Behind the blinds I sit and watch"   In
Peacock Pie: A Book of Rhymes (1913)

1823 Hely-Hutchinson, Victor. Three Songs from "Peacock
Pie", L: Elkin, 1927. Song: ms or bar solo, pf.

Winter   "Clouded with snow"   In The Listeners and Other
Poems (1912)

1824 Cone, Edward T. Around the Year, MS. Cyc.: satb,
str. qrt.

1825 Stone, David. Winter, L: BH, 1960. Song: ssa, pf.

Winter Evening   "Over the wintry fields"   In Inward
Companion (1950)

1826 Cone, Edward T. Around the Year, MS. Cyc.: satb,
str. qrt.

Yeo Ho!   See: "Once and there was a young sailor, yeo ho!"

"You take my heart with tears"   Henry Brocken (1904)

1827 Fricker, Peter Racine. Two Madrigals, MS 1947.
Madrigal: satb, a cap.

Miscellanea

1828 Allam, Edward. "The Window", Leeds: EA, pre-1956.
Song: [v., pf.].

1829 Belchamber, Eileen. "The Night Watch", L: EA, pre-
1951. Song: unison v., pf. [Possibly a setting
of "Lullaby" ("Sleep, sleep, thou lovely one!")?]

1830   Belchamber, Eileen. "The Window", L: EA, pre-1951.
       Song: unison v., pf.

1831   Branson, David. Two Songs, MS ca. 1941. Texts by
       de la Mare.

1832   Britten, Benjamin. Grove's indicates that Britten's
       Friday Afternoons (MS 1933-35, L: BH) is made up
       of "words by Walter de la Mare and others". Al-
       though the texts were chosen from de la Mare's
       Tom Tiddler's Ground, the author merely edited
       and wrote the introduction to Tom Tiddler's
       Ground--none of the poems incl. in this work are
       de la Mare's, and no de la Mare text, therefore,
       appears in Friday Afternoons.

1833   Brown, James. "Alone", MS. Song: s or t solo, pf.

1834   Brown, James. "The Horseman", Songs for Children,
       Set II, MS. Song: v., pf.

1835   Burtch, Mervyn. Three Witch Songs, L: S&B. Song:
       unison v., pf. Incl. one text by de la Mare.

1836   Chanler, Theodore. "A One-Eyed Tailor", Three
       Epitaphs, MS 1940. Song: solo v., pf. [Possibly
       a setting of "The Tailor" ("Few footsteps
       stray...")?]

1837   Durrant, F.T. "Cake and Sack", L: S&B, pre-1967.
       Song: unison v., pf. [Text by de la Mare?]

1838   Durrant, F.T. "Tired Tim", L: S&B, pre-1967. Song:
       unison v., pf. [Text by de la Mare?]

1839   Fleming, Robert. "The Voice", MS 1943. Song: v., pf.

1840   Gibbs, C. Armstrong. "Love in the Almond Bough",
       Five Songs, L: S&B, 1920. Song: solo v., pf.
       Text begins: "Love in the Almond Bough buildeth
       his nest".

1841   Gibbs, C. Armstrong. "Mother Carey", L: WR, 1948.
       Song: satb, a cap. Text begins: "Sing a lo lay".

1842 Gibbs, C. Armstrong. "Take heed, young heart", L:
      Curwen, 1926. Song: solo v., pf. Text (employed
      "By Permission" of de la Mare) begins: "Take
      heed, young heart, to Time/How soft his footfall
      is".

1843 Gurney, Ivor. "The Ghost", MS n.d. Song: [solo v.,
      pf.].

1844 Harrison, Pamela. "A Present for Paul", L: OUP,
      1956. Song: s or t solo, pf. Text taken from
      de la Mare's collection entitled Bells_and_Grass:
      A_Book_of_Rhymes (1941).

1845 Howells, Herbert. "Inheritance", MS 1952-53, L: OUP.
      The composer's contribution to A_Garland_for_the
      Queen.

1846 Howells, Herbert. "The Key of the Kingdom", L: EA,
      pre-1951. Song: 2 pt. chorus, [a cap.?].

1847 Howells, Herbert. Grove's makes reference to a
      collection entitled Peacock_Pie, 2nd set.

1848 Miessner, William. "Ann's Teeth", NY: Silver, 1929
      in The_Music_Hour_in_the_Kindergarten_and_First
      Grade. Song: v., pf.

1849 Milford, Robin. Days_and_Moments, L: H, 1959. Cta.:
      s solo, ssa, str. orch. (or pf.). Sections are
      entitled: "Summer", "Autumn", "Winter", "Spring".
      Texts by de la Mare.

1850* Milford, Robin. This_Year:_Next_Year, L: OUP, 1948.
      Cyc.: 2 pt. chorus of high v., pf. A cyc. of 8
      songs, settings of texts from de la Mare's
      This_Year:_Next_Year (1937).

1851 Richards, Kathleen, arr. "The Window", L: OUP. Song:
      arr. for 2 pt. chorus.

1852 Richards, Kathleen, arr. "Winter", L: OUP. Song:
      arr. for 2 pt. chorus.

1853 Richardson, A. "The Silver Buckle", L: S&B, pre-
      1967. Song: unison v., pf. [Text by de la Mare?]

de la Mare, Walter continued

1854   Rose, Edwin. "The Watchman", L: L, 1962. Song: uni-
       son v., pf.

1855   Stewart, D.M. "The Stranger", L: A, pre-1940. Song:
       [v., pf.?].

1856   Stoll, David. "The Silver Penny", L: OUP, pre-1971.
       Song: unison v., pf. [Text by de la Mare?]

1857   Symons, Dom Thomas. "Winter", Two de la Mare Songs,
       L: OUP, 1937. Song: v., pf.

1858   Taylor, Gladys. "Bunches of Grapes", L: S&B, pre-
       1967. Song: unison v., pf. [Text by de la Mare?]

1859   Thomas, Mansel. Songs of Enchantment, MS pre-1972.
       Songs: ssa, pf. Texts by de la Mare.

1860   Weisgall, Hugo. Five Night Songs, MS 1933 (withdrawn
       by the composer). Songs: high v., pf. Incl. words
       by de la Mare.

1861   Wilson, Ray R. "Poplars", MS 1946, avail. University
       of Auckland. Song: s solo, pf. Text begins: "The
       poplar is a lonely tree".

DICKINSON, Patric Thomas   1914-

Bluebells   "Like smoke held down by frost"   In The World I
   See (1960)

   1862   Short, Michael. The World I See, MS. Cyc.: high v.,
          pf.

Comet, The   "Then there it was one night"   In The World I
   See (1960)

   1863   Short, Michael. The World I See, MS. Cyc.: high v.,
          pf.

216

ckinson, Patric continued

Invocation to Love   "Then come by Jodrell Bank"   In The
    World I See (1960)

    1864 Short, Michael. The World I See, MS. Cyc.: high v.,
          pf.

Jodrell Bank   "Who were they, what lonely men"   In The
    World I See (1960)

    1865 Short, Michael. The World I See, MS. Cyc.: high v.,
          pf.

Lullaby, A   "There was that ancient wind"   In The World I
    See (1960)

    1866 Short, Michael. "Lullaby", The World I See, MS.
          Cyc.: high v., pf.

On Dow Crag   "Shepherd on the fell, The"   In The World I
    See (1960)

    1867 Short, Michael. The World I See, MS. Cyc.: high v.,
          pf.

Theseus and the Minotaur   (DR)   Theseus and the Minotaur
    and Other Poems (1946)

    1868 Lucas, Leighton. MS, prod. BBC, July 1945. In-
          cidental music for radio.

OBSON, (Henry) Austin   1840-1921

April Pastoral, An   "Whither away, fair neat-herdess?"
    Belgravia (Apr. 1881)

    1869 Freer, Eleanor. Five Songs to Spring, Berlin: Kaun,
          1905. Song: ms or bar solo, pf.

Dobson, Austin continued

Dying of Tanneguy du Bois, The   "Yea, I am passed away"
    Under the Crown (June 1869)

    1870 Lutyens, Elisabeth. MS 1934. Song: t solo, [pf.].

Fancy from Fontenelle, A   "Rose in the garden slipped her
    bud, The"   Century Magazine (July 1885)

    1871 Foote, Arthur. "The Rose and the Gardener", MS pre-
          1937, B: Schmidt. Song: [v., pf.].

    1872 Johnson, Horace. "The Rose and the Gardener", NY:
          GS, [1930?]. Song: [v., pf.].

Garden Song, A   "Here in this sequested close"   At the Sign
    of Lyre (1885)

    1873 Noble, Harold. L: A, ca. 1923. Song: ssa, [a cap.?].

"Good-night Babette!"   "Once at the Angelus"   Evening Hours
    (June 1876)

    1874 Hart, Fritz. "Babette Sings", MS 1917, avail. State
          Library of Victoria, Melbourne. Song: solo v.,
          fl., cl., bsn.

Kiss, A   "Rose kissed me to-day"   Graphic (May 1874) as one
    of "Rose-Leaves"

    1875 Adler, Samuel. Five Choral Poems, NY: AMP, 1957.
          Song: satb, a cap.

    1876 Franke-Harling, W. "Rose...", B: OD, pre-1940. Song:
          [solo v., pf.].

Ladies of St. James's, The   "Ladies of St. James's, The"
    Harper's Monthly Magazine (Jan. 1883)

    1877 Clarke, Reginald. L: Elkin, pre-1940. Song: [v.,
          pf.].

    1878 del Riego, Teresa. "To Phyllida", L: C, 1906. Song
          [v., pf.].

1879 Dukelsky, Vladimir. *Five Victorian Songs*, NY: S-C, 1942. Song: v., pf.

1880 Olmstead, Clarence. NY: GS, pre-1940. Song: [v., pf.].

Love Song, A, A.D. 16-- "When I go" *Harper's Monthly Magazine* (Aug. 1885), subsequently rev.

1881 Horrocks, Amy. "A 17th Century Love Song", L: JW, pre-1940. Song: [solo v., pf.].

Madrigal, A   See: Who Can Dwell with Greatness

Milkmaid, The   "Across the grass I see her pass"   *Harper's Monthly Magazine* (Dec. 1883)

1882 Francillon, Rosamond. "Dolly", *Six Songs*, L: JW, pre-1940. Song: [v., pf.].

1883 Sousa, John P. MS pre-1932, NY: Church. Song: [v., pf.?].

1884 Webber, W.S. Lloyd. L: Elkin, 1957. Song: satb, a cap.

Secrets of the Heart, The   "This way"   *Proverbs in Porcelain and Other Verses* (1877)

1885 Lehmann, Liza. MS pre-1918, L: JW. Song: [v., pf.?].

Song of the Four Seasons, A   "When Spring comes laughing" *Good Words* (Apr. 1877)

1886 Allitsen, Frances. "A Song of Four Seasons", MS pre-1912, L: JW. Song: [v., pf.].

1887 Anderson, Rose. "When Spring...", L: BH, 1917. Song: v., pf.

1888 Creighton, J. "A Song of Four Seasons", *Four Songs*, L: JW, pre-1940. Song: [v., pf.].

Dobson, Austin continued

    1889 Foote, Arthur. "A Song of Four Seasons", MS pre-
            1937, B: OD in Album of Selected Songs. Song:
            [v., pf.].

    1890* Galloway, Tod. "When Spring...", Memory Songs, Ph.:
            TP, 1904. Song: [v., pf.].

    1891 Smith, David S. NY: GS, pre-1940. Song: [v., pf.].

    1892 Willeby, Charles. "When Spring...", L: BH, 1894.
            Song: [v., pf.].

Wanderer, The   "Love comes back to his vacant dwelling"
Vignettes in Rhyme and Other Verses (1880)

    1893* Galloway, Tod. "Love Comes Back", Memory Songs, Ph.:
            TP, 1904. Song: [v., pf.].

Who can Dwell with Greatness "Who can dwell greatness!
Greatness is too high" 1st publ. with Parry's music;
incl. in collected edn. of Dobson's works under the title
"A Madrigal"

    1894 Howells, Herbert. "A Madrigal", Four Songs, MS (Opus
            22), L: WR. Song: v., pf.

    1895* Parry, C.H.H. In Album of Choral Songs (1899), L:
            MacM, 1900. Song: 5 pt. chorus, [a cap.].

"With Pipe and Flute" "With pipe and flute the rustic Pan"
Proverbs in Porcelain and Other Verses, 2nd edn. (1877)

    1896 Rowley, Alec. L: Elkin, 1952. Song: ms solo, pf.

Miscellanea

    1897 Halski, Czeslaw. Four English Songs, MS pre-1954.
            Incl. one text by Dobson.

ouglas, Lord Alfred

OUGLAS, Alfred Bruce   1870-1945

Green River, The   "I know a green grass path"   In Sonnets
    by Lord Alfred Douglas (1909)

    1898 Carpenter, John A. NY: GS, 1912. Song: v., pf.

    1899 Pasfield, W.R. L: JW, 1960. Song: solo v., pf.

Night Coming Into a Garden   "Roses red and white"   In The
    City of the Soul (1899)

    1900 Hale, Alfred M. L: S&B, ca. 1934. Song: solo v.,
        orch., pf.

Travelling Companion, The   "Into the silence of the empty
    night"   In The City of the Soul (1899)

    1901* Swain, Freda. MS 1934, avail. Chinnor: Channel,
        NEMO. Song: bar and pf. ensemble.

Wine of Summer   "Sun holds all the earth and all the sky,
    The"   In The City of the Soul (1899)

    1902 Brian, Havergal. "Symphony No. 5: 'Wine of Summer'",
        Chelmsford: MV, 1971. Symph.: ms or bar solo,
        orch.

DOWSON, Ernest Christopher   1867-1900

Ad Domnulam Suam   "Little lady of my heart!"   Book of the
    Rhymers' Club (1892)

    1903 Treharne, Bryceson. "Little...", B: BMC, pre-1940.
        Song: [solo v., pf.].

Dowson, Ernest continued

After Paul Verlaine, I   "Tears fall within mine heart"
    Decorations (1899)

    1904   Hageman, Richard. "Grief", NY: CF, pre-1940. Song:
           solo v., pf.

After Paul Verlaine, III   "Around were all the roses red"
    Decorations (1899)

    1905   Ireland, John. "Spleen (after Paul Verlaine)",
           Marigold, York: Doric, 1917. Setting for solo v.,
           pf.

Amor Umbratilis   "Gift of Silence, sweet!, A"   Century
    Guild Hobby Horse (Oct. 1891) as one of "In Praise of
    Solitude"

    1906   Scott, Cyril. "A Gift of Silence", L: Elkin, 1905.
           Song: high v., pf. Also avail. for low v., pf.

April Love   "We have walked in Love's land"   Verses (1896)

    1907   Ronald, Landon. Songs of Springtime, L: E, 1918.
           Song: high v., pf. Also avail. for med. v., pf.
           or low v., pf.

Autumnal   "Pale amber sunlight falls across"   Verses (1896)

    1908   Delius, Frederick. Songs of Sunset, Lz.: L&B, 1911.
           Song: ms, bar soli, chorus, orch. Score contains
           German transl. by Jelka Rosen [Delius].

Beata Solitudo   "What land of Silence"   Verses (1896)

    1909   Harrison, Pamela. Five Poems of Ernest Dowson, MS.
           Cyc.: t solo, str. orch.

    1910   Peterkin, Norman. B: BMC, pre-1940. Song: [v., pf.].

    1911   Quilter, Roger. "A Land of Silence", Songs of Sor-
           row, L: BH, 1908. Song: solo v., pf.

222

wson, Ernest continued

1912 Scott, Cyril. "The Valley of Silence", L: Elkin,
      1911. Song: solo v., pf.

Beyond See: Roundel, A

Carmellite Nuns of the Perpetual Adoration, The "Calm, sad,
secure" Century Guild Hobby Horse (Oct. 1891) as one of
"In Praise of Solitude", rev. 1896

1913 Hill, Edward B. "Nuns of the Perpetual Adoration",
      MS (Opus 15), B: BMC. Song: ssaa, orch. or ssaa,
      pf.

"Cease smiling, Dear! a little while be sad" Verses (1896)

1914 Delius, Frederick. "Cease smiling, Dear!", Songs of
      Sunset, Lz.: L&B, 1911. Song: ms, bar soli,
      chorus, orch. Score contains German transl. by
      Jelka Rosen [Delius].

Coronal, A "Violets and leaves of vine" Verses (1896)

1915 Quilter, Roger. Songs of Sorrow, L: BH, 1908. Song:
      solo v., pf.

Dregs "Fire is out, and spent the warmth thereof, The"
Decorations (1899)

1916 Bedford, David. "The Golden Wine is Drunk", MS ca.
      1974. Setting for 16 soli.

Exchanges "All that I had I brought" Decorations (1899)

1917 Duncan, Chester. MS 1975. Song: solo v., pf.

Exile "By the sad waters of separation" Verses (1896)

1918 Delius, Frederick. Songs of Sunset, Lz.: L&B, 1911.
      Song: ms, bar soli, chorus, orch. Score contains
      German transl. by Jelka Rosen [Delius].

Dowson, Ernest continued

Fleur de la Lune   "I would not alter thy cold eyes"
    Century Guild Hobby Horse (Oct. 1891) as one of "In Praise
    of Solitude", rev. 1896

    1919 ApIvor, Denis. "Flos Lunae", Songs Opus 6, MS 1940-
          46. Song: t solo, pf.

Flos Lunae   See: Fleur de la Lune

Garden of Shadows, The   "Love heeds no more the sighing of
    the winds"   Book of the Rhymers' Club (1894)

    1920 Forsyth, Cecil. NY: GS, pre-1940. Song: [v., pf.].

In Spring   "See how the trees and the osiers lithe"
    Decorations (1899)

    1921 Delius, Frederick. Songs of Sunset, Lz.: L&B, 1911.
          Song: ms, bar soli, chorus, orch. Score contains
          German transl. by Jelka Rosen [Delius].

    1922 Quilter, Roger. Songs of Sorrow, L: BH, 1908. Song:
          solo v., pf.

Jadis   "Erewhile, before the world was old"   Decorations
    (1899)

    1923 Warlock, Peter. MS 1911-12. Song: v., pf.

Moritura   "Song of the setting sun!, A"   London Society
    (Mar. 1887)

    1924 Delius, Frederick. Songs of Sunset, Lz.: L&B, 1911.
          Song: ms, bar soli, chorus, orch. Score contains
          German transl. by Jelka Rosen [Delius].

Non suma qualis eram bonae sub regno Cynarae   "Last night,
    ah, yesternight, betwixt her lips and mine"   Century
    Guild Hobby Horse (Apr. 1891)

    1925* Delius, Frederick. "Cynara", L: WR, 1931. Song: bar
          solo, orch.

1926 Harrison, Pamela. Five Poems of Ernest Dowson, MS.
     Cyc.: t solo, str. orch.

1927 Jones, Robert W. "Cynara", Two Songs, MS. Song: high
     v. (preferably t solo), pf.

1928 Maganini, Quinto. "Cynara", NY: Musicus, pre-1940.
     Song: [solo v., pf.].

1929 Towsey, C.P. "Last...", MS 1951, avail. Victoria
     University of Wellington. Song: high v., pf.

Nuns of the Perpetual Adoration, The   See: Carmellite Nuns
   of the Perpetual Adoration, The

O Mors! Quam amara est memoria tua homini pacem habenti in
   substantiis suis   "Exceeding sorrow"   Book of the
   Rhymers' Club (1892)

1930 Delius, Frederick. "O Mors!", Songs of Sunset, Lz.:
     L&B, 1911. Song: ms, bar soli, chorus, orch.
     Score contains German transl. by Jelka Rosen
     [Delius].

Of His Lady's Treasures   "I took her dainty eyes"   Temple
   Bar (Aug. 1893), rev. 1896

1931 Lekberg, Sven. "A Villanelle", NY: GX, 1963. Song:
     satb, a cap.

1932 Roder, Milan. "Villanelle", NY: GS, pre-1940. Song:
     [solo v., pf.].

1933 Scott, Cyril. "And so I made a villanelle", L:
     Elkin, 1908. Song: high v., pf. Also avail. for
     low v., pf.

Of Marguerites   "Little, passionately, not at all?, A"
   Temple Bar (May 1894), rev. 1896

1934 Harrison, Pamela. "Villanelle of Marguerites", Five
     Poems of Ernest Dowson, MS. Cyc.: t solo, str.
     orch.

Dowson, Ernest continued

Pierrot of the Minute, The   (DR)   (1897)

    1935   Bantock, Granville. "Comedy Overture", Lz.: B&H,
           1909. Overture: orch. only.

    1936   Bantock, Granville. "Moon Maiden's Song", L: Swan,
           1921. Song: solo v., pf. Setting of lines begin-
           ning: "Sleep! Cast thy canopy".

    1937   Scott, Cyril. "Pierrot and the Moon Maiden", L:
           Elkin, 1912. Song: high v., pf. Also avail. for
           med. v., pf. Setting of lines beginning: "What is
           Love?".

Roundel, A   "Love's aftermath! I think the time is now"
Temple Bar (Sept. 1893), rev. 1899

    1938   Scott, Cyril. "Love's Aftermath", L: Elkin, 1911.
           Song: high v., pf. Also avail. for low v., pf.

Seraphita   "Come not before me now, O visionary face!"
Verses (1896)

    1939   Schoenberg, Arnold. Four Songs, Wien: UE, 1917.
           Song: v., pf. German transl. by Stefan George.

Soli cantare periti Arcades   "Oh, I would live in a dairy"
Verses (1896)

    1940   Collingwood, Lawrance A. "Oh, I...", L: Curwen,
           1921. Song: solo v., pf.

    1941   Harrison, Pamela. Five Poems of Ernest Dowson, MS.
           Cyc.: t solo, str. orch.

    1942   Scott, Cyril. "A Song of Arcady", L: Elkin, 1914.
           Song: high v., pf. Also avail. for med. v., pf.

Spleen   "I was not sorrowful, I could not weep"   Verses
    (1896)

    1943   Delius, Frederick. Songs of Sunset, Lz.: L&B, 1911.
           Song: ms, bar soli, chorus, orch. Score contains
           German transl. by Jelka Rosen [Delius].

226

1944 Ireland, John. "I was not sorrowful", Songs of a
 Wayfarer, L: BH, 1912. Cyc.: solo v., pf. Also
 publ. sep.

Terre Promise "Even now the fragrant darkness of her hair"
 Verses (1896)

 1945 Austin, Frederic. Love's Pilgrimage, L: E, 1920.
 Song: med. v., pf.

 1946 Forsyth, Cecil. B: OD, pre-1940. Song: [v., pf.].

Valediction, A "If we must part" Verses (1896)

 1947 Ireland, John. "If...", MS 1929. Song: [t] solo v.,
 pf.

 1948 Scott, Cyril. L: Elkin, 1904. Song: high v., pf.
 Also avail. for med. v., pf.

Villanelle of His Lady's Treasures See: Of His Lady's
 Treasures

Villanelle of Marguerites See: Of Marguerites

Villanelle of Sunset "Come hither, Child! and rest" Book
 of the Rhymers' Club (1892)

 1949 Gerstle, Henry. NY: GX, pre-1940. Song: [v., pf.?].

 1950 Lekberg, Sven. "Come...", NY: GX, 1963. Song: satb,
 a cap.

Villanelle of the Poet's Road "Wine and woman and song"
 Decorations (1899)

 1951 Scott, Cyril. L: BH, 1911. Song: v., pf.

Vitae summa brevis spem nos vetat incohare longam "They are
 not long, the weeping and the laughter" Verses (1896)

Dowson, Ernest continued

1952 Delius, Frederick. "Vitae summa", Songs of Sunset,
     Lz.: L&B, 1911. Song: ms, bar soli, chorus, orch.
     Score contains German transl. by Jelka Rosen
     [Delius].

1953 Forsyth, Cecil. "Within a Dream", B: OD, pre-1940.
     Song: [v., pf.].

1954 Harrison, Pamela. Five Poems of Ernest Dowson, MS.
     Cyc.: t solo, str. orch.

1955 Hill, Edward B. "They Are Not Long", B: BMC, pre-
     1940. Song: [v., pf.].

1956 Jones, Robert W. "Envoy", Two Songs, MS. Song: high
     v. (preferably t solo), pf.

1957 Pentland, Barbara. "They Are Not Long", MS 1935,
     avail. CMC. Song: solo v., pf.

1958 Quilter, Roger. "Passing Dreams", Songs of Sorrow,
     L: BH, 1908. Song: solo v., pf.

1959 Scott, Cyril. "Meditation", L: Elkin, pre-1940.
     Song: v., pf.

1960 Wells, Howard. "They Are Not Long", NY: GS, 1960.
     Song: v., pf.

Yvonne of Brittany   "In your mother's apple-orchard"
Verses (1896)

1961 Scott, Cyril. MS ca. 1903. Song: v., pf.

Miscellanea

1962 Scott, Cyril. "Evening", L: Elkin, 1910. Song: med.
     v., pf. Also publ. for low v., pf.

1963 Scott, Cyril. "Retrospect", L: Elkin, 1913. Song:
     high v., pf. Also publ. for low v., pf.

Dowson, Ernest continued

1964   Whittaker, George. <u>Seven Songs</u>, MS pre-1939. The
        Oct. 1939 issue of <u>Monthly Musical Record</u> com-
        ments that "...the words..., ranging from John
        Lydgate to the Japanese, via Dowson, Housman,
        Synge..., reveal wide literary interests".

DOYLE, Arthur Conan   1859-1930

<u>Adventures of Sherlock Holmes, The</u>   (SS)   (1892)

1965   Arnell, Richard. "The Great Detective", MS ca. 1953.
        Ballet music.

1966   McBride, Robert G. "Sherlock Holmes", MS ca. 1945.
        Ste.: military band.

1967   Raksin, David. MS, prod. 1939 by 20th Century-Fox.
        Film music.

1968   Rózsa, Miklós. "The Private Life of Sherlock
        Holmes", MS ca. 1971. Film music.

1969   Salter, Hans. "Sherlock Holmes and the Spider
        Woman", MS, prod. 1944 by Universal Pictures.
        Film music.

1970   Salter, Hans. "Sherlock Holmes Faces Death", MS,
        prod. 1943 by Universal Pictures. Film music.

1971   Skinner, Frank. "Sherlock Holmes and the Secret
        Weapon", MS, prod. 1943 by Universal Pictures.
        Film music.

1972   Skinner, Frank. "Sherlock Holmes and the Voice of
        Terror", MS, prod. 1942 by Universal Pictures.

1973   Skinner, Frank. "Sherlock Holmes in Washington", MS,
        prod. 1943 by Universal Pictures. Film music.

Ballad of the Ranks, A   "Who carries the gun?"   In <u>Songs of
Action</u> (1898)

229

Doyle, Arthur Conan continued

    1974 Stanford, C.V. L: Curwen, 1893. Song: 2 pt. chorus
        of female v., a cap.

Captain Sharkey   (SS)   In <u>The Works of Sir Arthur Conan
Doyle</u>, Crowborough edn., Vol. 21 (1930)

    1975 Grainger, Percy. "Sailor's Chanty", MS 1901. Song:
        male chorus, a cap. Setting of lines beginning:
        "A trader sailed from Stepney Town".

Frontier Line, The   "What makes the frontier line?"   In
<u>Songs of Action</u> (1898)

    1976 Stanford, C.V. L: Curwen, 1893. Song: 2 pt. chorus
        of female v., a cap.

Irish Colonel, The   "Said the king to the colonel"   In
<u>Songs of Action</u> (1898)

    1977 Nelson, Herbert H. L: C, 1913. Song: [v., pf.].

    1978 White, Maude V. L: C, 1901. Song: [v., pf.].

Jane Annie   (Libr.) In coll. with James Barrie. 1st publ.
1893 with Ford's music.

    1979 Ford, Ernest. L: C, 1893. Opera: soli, duets,
        chorus, orch.

Old Gray Fox, The   "We started from the Valley Pride"   In
<u>Songs of Action</u> (1898)

    1980 White, Maude V. L: C, 1899. Song: [v., pf.].

Ring of Thoth, The   (SS)   In <u>The Captain of the Polestar
and Other Tales</u> (1890)

    1981* Eluchen, Alexander. "The Ring of Death", Berlin:
        Russian Publishing House "Culture", 1921. Opera.
        Text adapt. by Heinrich Noeren. Russian title:
        "Kol'tso smerti", transl. by Victor Kolomitsov.

Doyle, Arthur Conan continued

Song of the Bow, The   "What of the bow?"   In Songs of
Action (1898)

 1982 Aylward, Florence. "Song of the Bow", L: C, 1898.
       Song: chorus, [a cap.?].

 1983 Thayer, Arthur W. "Archer's Marching Song", B:
       Schmidt, 1904. Song: ttbb, orch. or ttbb, pf.

DOYLE, John   See: GRAVES, Robert Ranke

DRINKWATER, John   1882-1937

Anthony Crundle   "Anthony Crundle of Dorrington Wood"   In
Olton Pools (1916)

 1984 Read, John. "Anthony Crundle R.I.P.", L: Elkin,
       1950. Song: low v., pf.

At Grafton   "God laughed when he made Grafton"   In Poems of
Love and Earth (1912)

 1985 Boughton, Rutland. Two Songs, L: BH, 1919. Song: v.,
       pf.

Cotswold Love   "Blue skies are over Cotswold"   In Tides
(1917)

 1986 Anderson, Ronald K. L: A, 1957. Song: solo v., pf.

 1987 Head, Michael. L: BH, 1938. Song: solo v., pf.

 1988 Rowley, Alec. L: WR, 1922; Five Songs, L: BH (WR
       edn.), n.d. Song: med. v., pf. Five Songs can
       also be perf. as a cyc.

Drinkwater, John continued

Cottage Song   "Morning and night I bring"   In Tides (1917)

    1989 Holford, Franz. Three Songs, L: C, 1950. Song: v.,
        pf. solo, orch.

Derbyshire Song   "Come loving me to Darley Dale"   In Olton
    Pools (1916)

    1990 Rowley, Alec. L: WR, 1925; Five Songs, L: BH (WR
        edn.), n.d. Song: med. v., pf. Five Songs can
        also be perf. as a cyc.

English Medley, An   (DR)   In The Collected Plays of John
    Drinkwater, Vol. I (1925)

    1991 Boughton, Rutland. MS pre-1925. Incidental music.

Feckenham Men, The   "Jolly men at Feckenham, The"   In Poems
    of Love and Earth (1912)

    1992 Boughton, Rutland. Two Songs, L: BH, 1919. Song: v.,
        pf.

Graduation Song for the University of London, A   "We are no
    knights of Lyonesse"   In Summer Harvest: Poems 1924-1933
    (1933)

    1993 Ireland, John. "Graduation Song", L: Curwen, 1926.
        Song: unison v., pf.

Holiness   "If all the carts were painted gay"   In Olton
    Pools (1916)

    1994 Boughton, Rutland. L: Curwen, 1928. Song: solo v.,
        pf. or unison v., pf.

January Dusk   "Austere and clad in sombre robes of grey"
    In Poems of Men and Hours (1911)

    1995 Belchamber, Eileen. L: OUP, 1966. Song: satb, a cap.

Drinkwater, John continued

1996   Marshall, Nicholas. Five Winter Songs, MS. Song:
        med. v., pf.

Mad Tom Tatterman   "'Old man, grey man, good man scavenger...'" In Swords and Ploughshares (1915)

1997   Rowley, Alec. L: WR, 1925; Five Songs, L: BH (WR
        edn.), n.d. Song: med. v., pf. Five Songs can
        also be perf. as a cyc.

Mamble   "I never went to Mamble" In Swords and Ploughshares
(1915)

1998   Head, Michael. L: BH, 1938. Song: solo v., pf.

1999   Jacobson, Maurice. L: Curwen, 1921. Song: solo v.,
        pf. Also avail. for solo v., orch.

Mary Stuart   (DR)   (1921)

2000   Drinkwater, George. MS pre-1925. Music to accompany
        the songs incl. in the play.

May   "Love brought me life in the glory of May" In Poems
of Men and Hours (1911)

2001   Prosser, Edward. MS pre-1911. Song: [v., pf.?].

Moonlit Apples   "At the top of the house the apples are laid
in rows" In Tides (1917)

2002   Teed, Roy. Such Were The Joys, MS 1954. Ste.: bar
        solo, str. orch. Also avail. for bar solo, pf.

Old Oliver   "Old Oliver, my uncle, went" In Olton Pools
(1916)

2003   Rowley, Alec. L: WR, 1922; Five Songs, L: BH (WR
        edn.), n.d. Song: med. v., pf. Five Songs can
        also be perf. as a cyc.

Drinkwater, John continued

Oliver Cromwell (DR) (1921)

    2004 Drinkwater, George. MS pre-1925. Music to accompany
         the songs incl. in the play.

Only Legend, The (DR) In The Collected Plays of John
Drinkwater, Vol. I (1925)

    2005 Brier, James. MS 1913, printed for priv. circulation
         only. Incidental music.

Pied Piper, The (DR) In The Collected Poems of John
Drinkwater, Vol. I (1925)

    2006 Sylvester, S.W. MS pre-1925. Incidental music.

Plough "Snows are come in early state, The" In Tides
(1917)

    2007 Holford, Franz. Three Songs, L: C, 1950. Song: v.,
         pf. solo, orch.

Prayer, A "Lord, not for light in darkness do we pray"
In Poems of Men and Hours (1911)

    2008 Boughton, Rutland. Six Spiritual Songs, L: Reeves,
         1911. Song: [chorus, a cap.].

    2009 Weaver, Mary D. NY: CF, 1955. Song: med. v., pf. (or
         org.).

Robert Burns (DR) (1925)

    2010* Austin, Frederic. MS pre-1925. Incidental music.

Robert E. Lee (DR) (1923)

    2011 de Filippi, Amadeo. MS ca. 1925. Incidental music.

Robin Hood and the Pedlar (DR) In The Collected Plays of
John Drinkwater, Vol. I (1925)

Drinkwater, John continued

2012 Brier, James. MS pre-1925. Incidental music.

Song for the City of Oxford School   "Mother of learning, let
    us be" In Summer Harvest: Poems 1924-1933 (1933)

    2013 Austin, Frederic. MS pre-1933. Song: [unison v.,
            pf.?].

Toll-Gate House, The   "Toll-gate's gone, but still stands
    lone, The" In Seeds of Time (1921)

    2014 Rowley, Alec. L: WR, 1923; Five Songs, L: BH (WR
            edn.), n.d. Song: med. v., pf. Five Songs can
            also be perf. as a cyc.

Town Window, A   "Beyond my window in the night"   In Swords
    and Ploughshares (1915)

    2015 Gurney, Ivor. MS n.d. Song: [solo v., pf.].

Vagabond, The   "I know the pools where the grayling rise"
    In Poems of Love and Earth (1912)

    2016 Head, Michael. "A Vagabond Song", L: BH, 1938. Song:
            solo v., pf.

    2017 Manners, Brian F. L: C, 1962. Song: unison v., pf.
            Also avail. L: C (hire) for unison v., str.
            orch., pf.

    2018 Meachen, Margaret. L: A, ca. 1938. Song: solo v.,
            pf.

    2019 Mulliner, Michael. "The Vagrant", L: C, 1920. Song:
            [solo v., pf.].

Wooden Pig, The   "Barcelle of Barcellona"   In More About Me
    (1929)

    2020 Parry, W.H. L: Curwen, 1960. Song: ss, pf.

Drinkwater, John continued

X=o: A Night of the Trojan War   (DR)   In Pawns: Three
Poetic Plays (1917)

    2021 Bush, Geoffrey. "The Equation (X=o)", L: Elkin,
           1967. Opera: 2 s, 2 t, bar, b-bar, b soli, female
           chorus, small orch., org.

Miscellanea

    2022 Boughton, Rutland. Grove's lists Four Festival
           Choruses (MS ca. 1910) employing texts by Drink-
           water.

    2023 Holford, Franz. "The Poet's Song", Three Songs, L:
           C, 1950. Song: v., pf. solo, orch.

DU MAURIER, Daphne   1907-

Miscellanea

    2024 Young, Victor. "Frenchman's Creek", MS ca. 1944,
           released by Paramount Pictures. Film music.
           Orchn. by George Parrish and Leo Shuken. [Film
           music for du Maurier's Frenchman's Creek
           (1942)?].

DUNSANY, Edward John Moreton Drax Plunkett   1878-1957

Glittering Gate, The   (DR)   In Five Plays (1914)

    2025 Glanville-Hicks, Peggy. NY: B-M (hire). Opera.

Gods of the Mountain, The   (DR)   In Five Plays (1914)

unsany, Lord continued

2026 O'Neill, Norman. MS 1911. Incidental music. Two
      dances (entitled "Dance of Wine" and "Sacrificial
      Dance") were publ. (L: S) for pf. solo.

Golden Doom, The   (DR)   In Five Plays (1914)

2027 O'Neill, Norman. MS 1912. Incidental music.

I see His Blood upon the Rose   "I see his blood upon the
rose"   In The Poems of Joseph Mary Plunkett (n.d.)

2028 Benjamin, Arthur. L: BH, 1958. Setting for s solo,
      ssatb, [a cap.].

2029 Gover, Gerald. NY: BH. Song: [v., pf.].

2030 Hageman, Richard. NY: GX, 1954. Song: solo v., pf.

2031 Lekberg, Sven. Lord of the Earth and Sky, NY: GS,
      pre-1971. Cta.: s, a soli, satb, pf. or s, bar
      soli, satb, pf.

2032 Nelson, Havelock. L: L, 1964. Song: ssa, pf.

2033 Werlé, Frederick. Bryn Mawr: Church, 1954. Song:
      med. v., pf.

Laughter of the Gods, The   (DR)   (1917)

2034 Butt, James. MS. Opera: 2 s, a, 2 bar, b soli, pf.
      (or orch.).

Night at the Inn, A   (DR)   (1916)

2035* Dello Joio, Norman. "The Ruby", NY: R, 1955. "Lyric
      drama": s, 2 t, bar, b soli, orch. Text by Wil-
      liam Mass [pseud.], based on Dunsany's play.

Miscellanea

2036 Bove, J. Henry. "The Glow-Worm and the Star", [NY?]:
      H-C, pre-1940.

237

Durrell, Lawrence

DURRELL, Lawrence George   1912-

    Ballad of the Good Lord Nelson, A   "Good Lord Nelson had a
        swollen gland, The"   A Treasury of Modern Poetry (1946)

        2037 Cumming, Richard. We Happy Few, NY: BH, 1969. Cyc.:
              med. v., pf.

    Echo   "Nothing is lost, sweet self"   The Batsford Book of
        Children's Verse (1958)

        2038 Routh, Francis. Songs of Lawrence Durrell, MS 1966-
              68. Song: high v., pf.

        2039 Southam, T. Wallace. "Nothing is lost...", L: Tur-
              ret, 1967 in Contemporary Poetry Set to Music.
              Song: solo v., pf.

    In Arcadia   "By divination came the Dorians"   Kingdom Come
        (1940)

        2040 Southam, T. Wallace. L: Turret, 1968 in Contemporary
              Poetry Set to Music. Song: solo v., pf.

    Lesbos   "Pleiades are sinking calm as paint, The"
        Spectator (Apr. 1953)

        2041 Berkeley, Lennox. Autumn's Legacy, L: JWC, 1963.
              Cyc.: s or t solo, pf.

        2042 Routh, Francis. Songs of Lawrence Durrell, MS 1966-
              68. Song: high v., pf.

        2043 Southam, T. Wallace. L: OUP, 1967. Song: solo v.,
              pf.

    Nemea   "Song in the valley of Nemea, A"   A Private Country
        (1943)

        2044 Routh, Francis. Songs of Lawrence Durrell, MS 1966-
              68. Song: high v., pf.

2045   Southam, T. Wallace. Two Songs for Voice and Piano,
       L: A, 1950. Song: solo v., pf.

Night Express   "Night falls. The dark expresses"   The
   Poetry of Railways (1966)

   2046   Butterworth, Arthur. Trains in the Distance, MS
          (Opus 41). Symph.: orator, chorus, semichorus,
          orch., tape.

Sappho   (DR)   (1950)

   2047   Ogdon, Wilbur L. MS 1975. Opera.

This unimportant morning   "This unimportant morning"   New
   Poetry (1944)

   2048   Routh, Francis. Songs of Lawrence Durrell, MS 1966-
          68. Song: high v., pf.

Water Music   "Wrap your sulky beauty up"   In Collected
   Poems (1968)

   2049   Routh, Francis. Songs of Lawrence Durrell, MS 1966-
          68. Song: high v., pf.

Miscellanea

   2050   Goldsmith, Jerry. "Justine", MS, released 1969 on
          Monument recording #18123. Film music. [Based
          on Durrell's Justine?]

239

Eastaway, Edward

EASTAWAY, Edward   See: THOMAS, (Philip) Edward

ELIOT, Thomas Stearns   1888-1965

  Ash-Wednesday   "Because I do not hope to turn"   (1930)
    Sections publ. as sep. poems 1927-29

    2051 Crawford, John C. NY: OUP, 1971. Oratorio: s, bar
          soli, narr., satb, orch.

  Burnt Norton   "Time present and time past"   Collected
    Poems 1909-1935 (1936)   Incl. as 1st of Four Quartets
    (1944)

    2052 Bargielski, Zbigniew. "Rose Garden", MS 1971, avail.
          PMC. Song: a or bar solo, b. cl. Polish title:
          "Różany Ogród", transl. by Czesław Miłosz.

    2053 Gruen, John. "Time and The Bell", Two Eliot Poems
          For Voice, photostatic reprod. of MS distr.
          [NY 1959?]. Song: v., [pf.?].

    2054 Polin, Claire. Infinito, NY: SMC, 1973. Requiem: s
          solo, narr., satb, a sax. All quotations from
          Four Quartets.

    2055 Whear, Paul W. Cl.: LW (hire). Setting for sp., ch.
          ensemble (fl., ob., 2 cl., 2 hn., vln., db.,
          timp., perc.).

  Bustopher Jones: The Cat about Town   "Bustopher Jones is not
    skin and bones"   Old Possum's Book of Practical Cats
    (1939)

    2056 Rawsthorne, Alan. Practical Cats, L: OUP, (hire).
          Setting for sp., orch. Issued on Angel recording
          #3002. New version (unpubl.) perf. London, May
          1971.

liot, T.S. continued

Cape Ann   "O quick quick quick"   Two Poems (1935)   Incl.
   as one of "Landscapes" in Collected Poetry 1909-1935
   (1936)

   2057 ApIvor, Denis. Landscapes, MS 1950. Cyc.: t solo,
         fl., cl., hn., str. trio.

   2058 Archer, Violet. Landscapes, Waterloo: Waterloo,
         1973. Song: satb, a cap.

   2059 Burritt, Lloyd. Landscapes, MS 1966. Cyc: s, a soli,
         tape.

   2060 Paynter, John. Landscapes, L: OUP, 1972. Choral ste:
         satb, a cap. or satb, ob.

   2061 Purser, J.W.R. Five Landscapes, MS 1963. Song: s, t
         soli, pf.

   2062* Smith, Gregg. Landscapes, NY: GS, 1962. Song: satb,
         a cap.

   2063 Thomas, Alan. Five Landscapes, Bryn Mawr: TP, 1957.
         Cyc.: high v., pf.

   2064 Young, Douglas. Landscapes and Absences, L: F
         (hire). Cyc.: t solo, eng. hn., with interludes
         for eng. hn., str. trio.

Dry Salvages, The   "I do not know much about gods"   New
   English Weekly (Feb. 1941), publ. sep. same year.   Incl.
   as 3rd of Four Quartets (1944)

   2065 Polin, Claire. Infinito, NY: SMC, 1973. Requiem:
         s solo, narr., satb, a sax. All quotations from
         Four Quartets.

East Coker   "In my beginning is my end"   New English
   Weekly (Mar. 1940)   Incl. as 2nd of Four Quartets
   (1944)

   2066 Bourgeois, Derek. Six Songs of Wandering, MS 1962.
         Cyc.: bar solo, pf. Incl. setting of lines begin-
         ning: "...In order to arrive there".

241

Eliot, T.S. continued

2067   Polin, Claire. <u>Infinito</u>, NY: SMC, 1973. Requiem: s
       solo, narr., satb, a sax. All quotations from
       <u>Four Quartets</u>.

2068* Whettam, Graham. "The Wounded Surgeon Plies the
       Steel", L: BH, 1960. Anthem: satb, a cap. Distr.
       delayed until 1962 printing.

Eyes that last I saw in tears   "Eyes that last"   <u>Chapbook</u>
(Nov. 1924) as one of "Doris' Dream Songs"

2069   Christou, Jani. <u>Symphony No. 1</u>, R: DeS, [1953?].
       Song (in symph.). Arr. 1955 as a sep. song for
       v., pf. (not publ.). Arr. 1957 as a sep. song for
       ms, orch.; this arr. publ. in <u>Six Songs for
       Mezzo-soprano and Orchestra</u>, Wi.: Impero,
       [1959?]. Text in Engl. and German.

2070   Gruen, John. <u>Two Eliot Poems for Voice</u>, photostatic
       reprod. of MS distr. [NY 1959?]. Song: v.,
       [pf.?].

2071* McCabe, John. <u>Five Elegies</u>, L: OUP, 1963. Cyc.: s
       solo, ch. orch.

<u>Family Reunion, The</u>   (DR)   (1939)

2072   Stevens, James. MS 1969. Incidental music for TV
       prod.: ste. for ch. orch.

Five-Finger Exercises   "Songsters of the air repair, The"
<u>Criterion</u> (Jan. 1933)

2073* Reif, Paul. NY: GMP, 1957. Cyc.: bar solo, pf.

Growltiger's Last Stand   "Growltiger was a Bravo Cat"   <u>Old
Possum's Book of Practical Cats</u> (1939)

2074   Searle, Humphrey. <u>Two Practical Cats</u>, L: OUP, 1956.
       Setting for sp., fl. (or pic.), vcl., gtr.

Gus: The Theatre Cat   "Gus is the Cat"   <u>Old Possum's Book
of Practical Cats</u> (1939)

2075 Rawsthorne, Alan. Practical Cats, L: OUP (hire).
Setting for sp., orch. Issued on Angel recording
#3002. New version (unpubl.) perf. London, May
1971.

Hippopotamus, The   "Broad-backed hippopotamus, The"   Poems
(1919)

2076 Beeson, Jack. Two Concert Arias, MS 1951. Concert
aria: high v., pf. or high v., orch.

Hollow Men, The   "We are the hollow men"   Poems 1909-1925
(1925)   Sections publ. sep. 1924-25

2077 ApIvor, Denis. L:OUP, 1951. Cta.: bar solo, ttbb,
orch.

2078 Beecroft, Norma. MS 1956, avail. CMC. Choral ste.:
s, t soli, satb, a cap.

2079 Burkinshaw, Sydney. MS. Setting for t, c-t, bar
soli, satb, sax., cl., vla., db., perc., mrmb.

2080 Burritt, Lloyd. MS 1968. Cta.: satb, orch., tape.
Incl. in Acid Mass, MS 1970. Work for theatre:
12 v. (satb), dancers, tapes, slides, films.

2081 Clarke, F.R.C. Two Songs from "The Hollow Men", MS
1950-51. Songs: high v., pf.

2082 Cone, Edward T. MS. Cta.: t solo, ttbb, ww. ensemble.

2083 Matuszczak, Bernadetta. A Chamber Drama, Warsaw:
PWP, 1968. Ch. drama: bar solo, voice (reciting),
b. cl., vcl., db., perc., tape. Polish title:
"Dramat Kameralny".

2084 Parris, Robert. MS. Setting for ttbb, ch. ensemble
(10 players).

2085 Persichetti, Vincent. "The Hollow Men" for Trumpet
and String Orchestra, Ph.: EV, 1948. Symph. poem:
tpt., str. orch. Also avail. for tpt., pf.

2086 van Baaren, Kees. MS 1948. Cta.: chorus, orch.

Eliot, T.S. continued

Journey of the Magi   "Cold coming we had of it, A"   (1927)

 2087 Anhalt, Istvan. MS 1952, avail. CMC. Song: bar
   solo, pf.

 2088* Britten, Benjamin. L: F, 1972. Cta.: trio (c-t, t,
   bar), pf.

La Figlia che Piange   "Stand on the highest pavement"
Poetry (Sept. 1916)

 2089 Cone, Edward T. NY: EBM (hire). Song: t solo, ch.
   ensemble.

Lines for an Old Man   See: Words for an Old Man

Little Gidding   "Midwinter spring is its own season"   New
English Weekly (Oct. 1942)   Incl. as 4th of Four Quartets
(1944)

 2090 Harvey, Jonathan. "The Dove Descending", L: N, 1975.
   Anthem: satb, org. Sets lines beginning: "The
   dove descending".

 2091 Lourié, Arthur. "The Dove", in Third Hour (NY), IV
   (1949). Song: v., pf.

 2092 Polin, Claire. Infinito, NY: SMC, 1973. Requiem: s
   solo, narr., satb, a sax. All quotations from
   Four Quartets.

 2093 Stravinsky, Igor. "Anthem", L: BH, 1962. Anthem:
   satb, a cap. Sets lines beginning: "The dove
   descending".

Macavity: The Mystery Cat   "Macavity's a Mystery Cat"   Old
Possum's Book of Practical Cats (1939)

 2094 Searle, Humphrey. Two Practical Cats, L: OUP, 1956.
   Setting for sp., fl. (or pic.), vcl., gtr.

Mélange Adultère de Tout   "En Amérique, professeur"   Poems
(1919)

2095 Christou, Jani. MS 1955 for v., pf. (not publ.).
Arr. 1957 for ms solo, orch.; this arr. publ. in
Six Songs for Mezzo-soprano and Orchestra, Wi.:
Impero, [1959?]. Text in Engl. and German.

Morning at the Window   "They are rattling breakfast plates"
Poetry (Sept. 1916)

2096 Healey, Derek. Six American Songs, MS 1961, avail.
CMC. Song: s or t solo, pf.

Murder in the Cathedral   (DR)   (1935)

2097 Buck, Percy. "Dead Upon the Tree, My Saviour", Oxf.:
Clarendon, 1936 in Hymn Book. Hymn: v., org.
Employs the tune "Judicum". Setting of lines
beginning: "Dead upon the tree, my Saviour".

2098 Dickinson, Peter. "Meditation on Murder in the
Cathedral", MS 1958. Org. solo.

2099 Elkus, Jonathan. Three Medieval Pieces, Bryn Mawr:
Beekman, 1966. Incidental music: org. solo.

2100 Engel, Lehman. MS pre-1954. Incidental music.

2101 Fortner, Wolfgang. "Aria", Mz.: S, 1951. Aria: ms
or a solo, fl., vla., ch. orch. [Complete] German
title: "Arie für Mezzosopran und Sol B. und
Kammerchor aus Eliot's Mord im Dom".

2102 Kellam, Ian. MS, prod. 1972. Incidental music.

2103 Lajtha, László. MS. Incidental music.

2104 Milhaud, Darius. MS 1939. Incidental music.

2105 Pizzetti, Ildebrando. Mi.: R, 1958. Opera: s, a, 2
t, 2 b soli, orch. Verse libr. by the composer,
after Alberto Castelli's prose transl. Ital.
title: "Assassinio nella cattedrale".

2106* Tippett, Michael. A Child of Our Time, L: S, 1944.
Oratorio: s, a, t, b soli, satb, orch.

Eliot, T.S. continued

2107   Togni, Camillo. Mi.: SZ, 1962. Setting for 5 pt.
       chorus (s, ms, a, t, b), a cap. Ital. title:
       "Assasinio nella cattedrale", transl. by Alberto
       Castelli. A portion entitled "Coro di T.S.
       Eliot" (setting lines beginning: "Torpido la
       mano") was publ. sep. (Mi.: SZ, 1962) for 5 pt.
       chorus (s, ms, a, t, b), orch.

2108   Tremain, Ronald. MS. Incidental music for radio:
       male v., a cap.

2109   Ware, John M. "Essay for Orchestra on T.S. Eliot's
       Murder in the Cathedral", MS 1966. Orch. only.

2110   Willan, Healey. MS ca. 1936. Incidental music adapt.
       from plainsong sources and the composer's publ.
       works.

Naming of Cats, The   "Naming of Cats, The"   Old Possum's
Book of Practical Cats (1939)

2111   Keats, Donald. NY: BH, 1962. Song: satb, pf.

2112   Rawsthorne, Alan. Practical Cats, L: OUP (hire).
       Setting for sp., orch. New version (unpubl.)
       perf. London, May 1971.

New Hampshire   "Children's voices in the orchard"   Virginia
Quarterly Review (Apr. 1934) as one of "Words for Music"
Incl. as one of "Landscapes" in Collected Poetry 1909-1935
(1936)

2113   ApIvor, Denis. Landscapes, MS 1950. Cyc.: t solo,
       fl., cl., hn., str. trio.

2114   Archer, Violet. Landscapes, Waterloo: Waterloo,
       1973. Song: satb, a cap.

2115   Burritt, Lloyd. Landscapes, MS 1966. Cyc.: s, a
       soli, tape.

2116   Burt, George. NY: Continuo, 1967. Song: dbl. chorus
       of female v., a cap.

2117   Christou, Jani. MS 1955 for v., pf. (not publ.).
        Arr. 1957 for ms solo, orch.; this arr. publ.
        in Six Songs for Mezzo-soprano and Orchestra,
        Wi.: Impero, [1959?]. Text in Engl. and German.

2118   Healey, Derek. Six American Songs, MS 1961, avail.
        CMC. Song: s or t solo, pf.

2119   Paynter, John. Landscapes, L: OUP, 1972. Choral
        ste.: satb, a cap. or satb, ob.

2120   Purser, J.W.R. Five Landscapes, MS 1963. Song: s, t
        soli, pf.

2121   Smith, Gregg. Landscapes, NY: GS, 1962. Song: satb,
        a cap.

2122   Thomas, Alan. Five Landscapes, Bryn Mawr: TP, 1957.
        Cyc.: high v., pf.

2123   Young, Douglas. Landscapes and Absences, L: F
        (hire). Cyc.: t solo, eng. hn., with interludes
        for eng. hn., str. trio.

Old Deuteronomy   "Old Deuteronomy's lived a long time"   Old
    Possum's Book of Practical Cats (1939)

2124   Rawsthorne, Alan. Practical Cats, L: OUP (hire).
        Setting for sp., orch. Issued on Angel recording
        #3002. New version (unpubl.) perf. London, May
        1971.

Old Gumbie Cat, The   "I have a Gumbie Cat"   Old Possum's
    Book of Practical Cats (1939)

2125   Rawsthorne, Alan. Practical Cats, L: OUP (hire).
        Setting for sp., orch. Issued on Angel recording
        #3002. New version (unpubl.) perf. London, May
        1971.

Preludes   "Winter evening settles down, The"   Blast (July
    1915)

2126   Peterson, Wayne. "Prelude I", in untitled col-
        lection, MS 1954. Cyc.: s or t solo, pf.

Eliot, T.S. continued

2127 Rautavaara, Einojuhani. _Two Preludes_, Helsinki: YL,
      No. 152, 1967. Songs: ttbb, a cap. with some
      tttbbb sections. Settings of lines beginning:
      "The winter evening settles down", "The morning
      comes to consciousness".

2128* Swanson, Howard. _4 Preludes_, NY: Weintraub, 1952.
      Cyc.: med. v., pf.

Rannoch, by Glencoe   "Here the crow starves"   _New English
Weekly_ (Oct. 1935)   Incl. as one of "Landscapes" in
Collected Poetry 1909-1935 (1936)

2129 ApIvor, Denis. _Landscapes_, MS 1950. Cyc.: t solo,
      fl., cl., hn., str. trio.

2130 Burritt, Lloyd. _Landscapes_, MS 1966. Cyc.: s, a
      soli, tape.

2131 Paynter, John. _Landscapes_, L: OUP, 1972. Choral
      ste.: satb, a cap. or satb, ob.

2132 Purser, J.W.R. _Five Landscapes_, MS 1963. Song: s, t
      soli, pf.

2133 Smith, Gregg. _Landscapes_, NY: GS, 1962. Song: satb,
      a cap.

2134 Thomas, Alan. _Five Landscapes_, Bryn Mawr: TP, 1957.
      Cyc.: high v., pf.

2135 Young, Douglas. _Landscapes and Absences_, L: F
      (hire). Cyc.: t solo, eng. hn., with interludes
      for eng. hn., str. trio.

Rock, The   (DR)   (1934)   "Choruses from _The Rock_" were
publ. in _Collected Poems 1909-1935_ (1936)

2136 Beversdorf, Thomas. MS 1957. Oratorio: b solo, sa,
      tb, combining to form satb, br. oct., str. orch.
      Text adapt. by composer. Sets lines beginning:
      "No man has hired us".

2137   Jones, Kenneth V. "O Light Invisible", L: JWC
       (hire). Cta.: s solo, mixed chorus, ch. orch.
       Setting of lines beginning: "You have seen the
       house built, you have seen it adorned".

2138   Leighton, Kenneth. The Light Invisible, L: N, 1958.
       Sinfonia sacra: t solo, satb, orch. Incl. setting
       of lines beginning: "The eagle soars in the sum-
       mit".

2139   Shaw, Martin. L: CR (for priv. circulation only).
       Incidental music.

2140   Shaw, Martin. "The Builders", L: CR, 1934. Song:
       unison v., pf. Also avail. (hire) for unison v.,
       orch. Also arr. as a pt. song.

2141   Shaw, Martin. "The Greater Light", L: Curwen, 1966.
       Anthem: t solo, dbl. choir, org. Sets lines
       beginning: "O light invisible".

Song for Simeon, A   "Lord, the Roman hyacinths"   (1928)

2142   Burkinshaw, Sydney. "A Song of Simeon", MS. Song:
       ms solo, fl., pf., perc.

2143   Persichetti, Vincent. "Dust in Sunlight and Memory
       in Corners", Poems for Piano, Vol. II, Ph.: EV,
       1947. Pf. solo.

Song of the Jellicles, The   "Jellicle Cats come out tonight"
Old Possum's Book of Practical Cats (1939)

2144   ApIvor, Denis. Lavenders Blue, MS 1946. Song: med.
       v., pf.

2145   Howell, Dorothy. L: EA, 1953. Song: ss, pf.

2146   Price, Beryl. A Cycle of Cats, L: OUP, 1972. Cyc.:
       ssa, pf.

2147   Rawsthorne, Alan. Practical Cats, L: OUP (hire).
       Setting for sp., orch. Issued on Angel recording
       #3002. New version (unpubl.) perf. London, May
       1971.

Eliot, T.S. continued

Sweeney Agonistes (DR) (1937) "Fragment of a Prologue"
1st appeared in Criterion (Oct. 1926), "Fragment of an
Agon" in Criterion (Jan. 1927)

2148 Dankworth, John. L: F (hire). Melodrama: 2 female
v. (med. to low), 5 male v. (med. to high), jazz
band of cl. (doubl. b. cl.), tpt., db., pf., drs.

2149 Elston, Arnold. MS. Opera: s, bar soli, satb, ch.
orch. (or pf.).

2150 Fortner, Wolfgang. MS, perf. Nov. 1973, avail. Mz.:
S (hire). Opera. German title: "Versuch Eines
Agon".

2151 Holloway, Robin. MS 1964. Incidental music: speak-
ers, 6 musicians.

2152 Porter, Quincy. MS pre-1954. Incidental music.

Usk "Do not suddenly break the branch" Two Poems (1935)
Incl. as one of "Landscapes" in Collected Poetry 1909-1935
(1936)

2153 ApIvor, Denis. Landscapes, MS 1950. Cyc.: t solo,
fl., cl., hn., str. trio.

2154 Burritt, Lloyd. Landscapes, MS 1966. Cyc.: s, a
soli, tape.

2155 Paynter, John. Landscapes, L: OUP, 1972. Choral
ste.: satb, a cap. or satb, ob.

2156 Purser, J.W.R. Five Landscapes, MS 1963. Song: s, t
soli, pf.

2157 Smith, Gregg. Landscapes, NY: GS, 1962. Song: satb,
a cap.

2158 Thomas, Alan. Five Landscapes, Bryn Mawr: TP, 1957.
Cyc.: high v., pf.

2159 Young, Douglas. Landscapes and Absences, L: F
(hire). Cyc. t solo, eng. hn., with interludes
for eng. hn., str. trio.

Virginia   "Red river, red river"   Virginia Quarterly Review
    (Apr. 1934) as one of "Words for Music"   Incl. as one of
    "Landscapes" in Collected Poetry 1909-1935 (1936)

    2160 ApIvor, Denis. Landscapes, MS 1950. Cyc.: t solo,
          fl., cl., hn., str. trio.

    2161 Archer, Violet. Landscapes, Waterloo: Waterloo,
          1973. Song: satb, a cap.

    2162 Burritt, Lloyd. Landscapes, MS 19669 Cyc.: s, a
          soli, tape.

    2163 Christou, Jani. MS 1955 for v., pf. (not publ.).
          Arr. 1957 for ms solo, orch.; this arr. publ. in
          Six Songs for Mezzo-soprano and Orchestra, Wi.:
          Impero, [1959?]. Text in Engl. and German.

    2164 Paynter, John. Landscapes, L: OUP, 1972. Choral
          ste.: satb, a cap. or satb, ob.

    2165 Purser, J.W.R. Five Landscapes, MS 1963. Song: s, t
          soli, pf.

    2166 Rathaus, Karol. Three Songs, Bryn Mawr: TP, 1959.
          Song: satb, a cap.

    2167 Smith, Gregg. Landscapes, NY: GS, 1962. Song: satb,
          a cap.

    2168 Thomas, Alan. Five Landscapes, Bryn Mawr: TP, 1957.
          Cyc.: solo v., pf.

    2169 Young, Douglas. Landscapes and Absences, L: F
          (hire). Cyc.: t solo, eng. hn., with interludes
          for eng. hn., str. trio.

Waste Land, The   "April is the cruellest month"   Criterion
    (Oct. 1922)

    2170 Burkinshaw, Sydney. "Phlebas", MS. Song: bar solo,
          pf. Setting of Part IV of the poem.

    2171 Dalby, Martin. "Whisper Music", L: N (hire). Ch.
          work for fl. (doubl. pic.), b. cl., tpt., hp.,
          perc., vcl. Inspired by lines beginning: "A woman
          drew her long black hair out tight".

251

Eliot, T.S. continued

2172   Christou, Jani. "Death by Water", MS 1955 for v.,
       pf. (not publ.). Arr. 1957 for ms solo, orch.;
       this arr. publ. in Six Songs for Mezzo-soprano
       and Orchestra, Wi.: Impero, [1959?]. Text in
       Engl. and German.

2173   MacInnis, Donald. MS 1957. Setting [for v., pf.?]
       of Part IV.

Wind sprang up at four o'clock, The   "Wind sprang up, The"
Chapbook (Nov. 1924) as one of "Doris' Dream Songs"

2174   Christou, Jani. MS 1955 for v., pf. (not publ.).
       Arr. 1957 for ms solo, orch.; this arr. publ. in
       Six Songs for Mezzo-soprano and Orchestra, Wi.:
       Impero, [1959?]. Text in Engl. and German.

Words for an Old Man   "Tiger in the tiger-pit, The"   New
English Weekly (Nov. 1935)

2175   Diamond, David. "For an Old Man", NY: SMP, 1951.
       Song: solo v., pf.

Miscellanea

2176   ApIvor, Denis. Francis Routh, in Contemporary
       British Music: the twenty-five years from 1945 to
       1970 (L: Macdonald, 1972), p. 116, suggests that
       Variation 12 (entitled "The Hanged Man") of
       ApIvor's Tarot (MS 1968) was perhaps in part in-
       spired by the hanged man in Eliot's "The Waste
       Land". This suggestion, according to the com-
       poser, is incorrect.

2177   Bliss, Arthur. Shield of Faith, L: N, 1975. Cta.:
       s, bar soli, satb, org. Incl. words by Eliot.

2178   Bujarski, Zbigniew. El Hombre, MS 1969-72, avail.
       PMC. Settings for s, ms, bar soli, satb, orch.
       Incl. words (in Engl.) by Eliot.

2179   Clements, Peter. The Cloud of Unknowing, MS 1967,
       avail. CMC. Settings (of selections from Eliot's
       works) for narr., chorus, orch., tape.

2180 Crosse, Gordon. The title-page of Crosse's _Changes, A Nocturnal Cycle_ (L: OUP, 1967) bears the following inscription from _Four Quartets_: "Time and the bell have buried the day, the black cloud carries the sun away". The composer has indicated to the eds. that Eliot's work was not the inspiration for the cyc., but that the inscription was added after the completion of the composition.

2181 Holloway, Robin. _Five Madrigals_, MS 1973. Madrigals: mixed v., [a cap.]. Incl. texts by Eliot.

2182 Holloway, Robin. _The Death of God_, MS 1972-73, L: OUP. Cta. Incl. words by Eliot.

2183 Joyce, Mary Ann. _The Passion, Death and Resurrection of Jesus Christ_, St. Louis: WUP, 1970. A passion for satb, orch. Incl. words by Eliot.

2184 Souster, Tim. The eds. have seen references to the composer's work entitled _Waste Land Music_. [Inspired by Eliot's "The Waste Land"?]

2185 Stravinsky, Igor. "Introitus. T.S. Eliot in memoriam", L: BH, 1965. Anthem: male chorus, ch. ensemble.

2186 Tavener, John. [Early] MSS incl. settings of Eliot's _Four Quartets_.

2187 Williams, Bryn. "The Hollow Men", MS pre-1972. Composition for chorus, ch. orch. [Text by Eliot?]

FLECKER, James Elroy   1884-1915

Ballad ot Hampstead Heath, The   "From Heaven's gate to Hampstead Heath"   In _The Bridge of Fire_ (1907)

2188 Wood, Thomas. MS pre-1929, L: S&B. Setting for chorus, orch.

Flecker, James Elroy continued

Ballad of the Londoner   "Evening falls on the smoky walls"
In Forty-Two Poems (1911)

  2189   Wald, Max. "Beyond the Thames", NY: GX, pre-1940.
         Song: [solo v., pf.?].

Don Juan   (DR)   (1925)

  2190   Alwyn, William. The Libertine, MS. Opera: 2 s, ms,
         t, bar, 2 b-bar, b soli, chorus, orch. Libr. by
         the composer, based in part on Flecker's play.

  2191   Arundell, Dennis. MS 1926. Incidental music.

  2192   Arundell, Dennis. "Tisbea's Song", L: Curwen, 1927.
         Song: solo v, pf. Setting of lines beginning: "I
         dreamt my sweetheart came".

Dying Patriot, The   "Day breaks in England"   In The Golden
Journey to Samarkand (1913)

  2193   Gurney, Ivor. MS n.d. Song: [solo v., pf.].

Fountains   "Soft is the collied night, and cool"   In Forty-
Two Poems (1911)

  2194   Persichetti, Vincent. Poems for Piano, Vol. I, Ph:
         EV, 1947. Pf. solo.

Golden Journey to Samarkand, The   "We who with songs beguile
your pilgrimage"   In The Golden Journey to Samarkand
(1913)

  2195   Bantock, Granville. MS 1922. Setting for mixed v.,
         a cap.

  2196   Godfrey, Graham. L: Curwen, 1922. Setting for mixed
         v., a cap.

  2197   Read, Gardner. MS 1939. Setting for s, a, t, bar, b
         soli, satb, orch.

<u>Hassan</u>   (DR)   <u>The Collected Poems of James Elroy Flecker</u>
   (1916), publ. sep. 1922

   2198   Delius, Frederick. "Hassan; or the Golden Journey to
          Samarkand", Wien: UE, 1923. Incidental music. The
          2nd edn. (also publ. Wien: UE, 1923) bears the
          title "Hassan".

   2199   Duncan, Chester. MS 1944. Incidental music: voices,
          pf.

In Phœacia   "Had I that haze of streaming blue"   In <u>The</u>
   <u>Golden Journey to Samarkand</u> (1913)

   2200   Parrott, Ian. L: L, 1948. Song: high v., pf.

November Eves   "November Evenings! Damp and still"   In <u>The</u>
   <u>Old Ships</u> (1915)

   2201* Holland, Theodore. <u>Three Songs</u>, L: WR, 1938. Song:
          v., pf.

Piper, The   "Lad went piping through the Earth, A"   <u>The</u>
   <u>Collected Poems of James Elroy Flecker</u> (1935)

   2202   Dent, Edward. In <u>Sackbut</u> (May 1920). Song: [v.,
          pf.].

   2203* Holland, Theodore. <u>Three Songs</u>, L: WR, 1938. Song:
          v., pf.

   2204   Steel, N. McLeod. L: C. Song: solo v., pf.

Rioupéroux   "High and solemn mountains"   In <u>The Bridge of</u>
   <u>Fire</u> (1907)

   2205   Foss, Hubert J. L: OUP, pre-1940. Song: [v., pf.?].

   2206   Tatton, J. Meredith. NY: HWG, pre-1940. Song: [v.,
          pf.?].

Saadabad   "Let us deal kindly with a heart of old"   In <u>The</u>
   <u>Golden Journey to Samarkand</u> (1913)

Flecker, James Elroy continued

2207   Anson, Hugo. MS pre-1954. Song: bar solo, chorus,
          orch.

Ship, an Isle, a Sickle Moon, A   "Ship, an isle, a sickle
   moon, A"   In The Golden Journey to Samarkand (1913)

   2208   Noble, Harold. "Crescent Moon", L: BH, 1968. Song:
             sa, pf.

Stillness   "When the words rustle no more"   In The Old
   Ships (1915)

   2209   Gurney, Ivor. MS. Song: [solo v., pf.].

Tenebris Interlucentem*   "Linnet who had lost her way, A"
   In Forty-Two Poems (1911)

   2210* Holland, Theodore. "A linnet who had lost her way",
             Three Songs, L: WR, 1938. Song: v., pf.

   2211   Rettich, Wilhelm. Eleven Songs for Voice and Piano,
             Berlin: Astoria, 1973. Song: high v., pf. or low
             v., pf.

To a Poet a thousand years hence   "I who am dead a thousand
   years"   In Forty-Two Poems (1911)

   2212   Carey, Clive. L: OUP, pre-1940. Song: [v., pf.?].

   2213   Finzi, Gerald. To a Poet, L: BH (WR edn.), 1965.
             Song: low v., pf.

Yasmin   "How splendid in the morning glows the lily"   In
   The Golden Journey to Samarkand (1913)

   2214   Dobson, Tom. NY: GS, pre-1940. Song: [v., pf.?].

Miscellanea

   2215   Gurney, Ivor. "Aspatia's Song", MS 1920. Song: [solo
             v., pf.].

lint, F.S.

LINT, Frank Stewart   1885-

Miscellanea

    2216   Taylor, Clifford. "Beggar", Collected Songs 1950-
           1954, MS 1950-54, avail. ACA. Song: s or t solo,
           pf.

ORD, Ford Madox   1873-1939

Consider   "Now green comes springing o'er the heath"   In
    Songs from London (1910)

    2217   Warlock, Peter. L: OUP, 1924. Song: solo v., pf.

End Piece, An   "Close the book and say good-bye to every-
    thing"   In The Face of the Night (1904)

    2218   Andrews, Herbert K. L: OUP, 1942. Song: t solo, pf.

Romance   (NV)   In coll. with Joseph Conrad (1903)

    2219   Arundell, Dennis. MS pre-1954. Incidental music.

Song of the Women, The   "When ye've got a child'ats whist
    for want of food"   In Poems for Pictures (1897)

    2220   Britten, Benjamin. "A Wealden Trio", MS 1929, ed.
           by the composer 1968, publ. L: F, 1968. Carol:
           ssa, a cap.

Miscellanea

    2221   Nordoff, Paul. "There shall be more joy", NY: S,
           pre-1940. Song: med. v., pf.

257

Ford, Ford Madox continued

    2222   Tweedy, Donald. "The Little Angels of Heaven", MS
            1923, NY: GS. Song: [v., pf.?].

FORSTER, Edward Morgan   1879-1970

  Miscellanea

    2223   Britten, Benjamin. "Billy Bud", L: BH, 1951 (rev.
            version publ. L: BH, 1961). Opera. Libr. by
            Forster and Eric Crozier, based on the work of
            Herman Melville.

    2224   Vaughan Williams, Ralph. In The Works of Ralph
            Vaughan Williams (L: OUP, 1964) Michael Kennedy
            comments on pageants written by Forster (with
            music composed and arr. by Vaughan Williams) for
            such occasions as the Pageant of Abinger held
            July 1934.

FOWLES, John   1926-

  Miscellanea

    2225   Jarre, Maurice. Steven Smolian's A Handbook of Film,
            Theatre, and Television Music on Record, 1948-
            1969 (NY: The Record Undertaker, 1970) incl.
            a listing of the 1965 sound track of Jarre's
            incidental music for "The Collector". [Film music
            for Fowles' The Collector (1963)?].

reeman, John

REEMAN, John   1880-1929

English Hills   "O that I were"   In Stone_Trees (1916)

    2226 Jarvis, Joyce E.K. MS 1956, avail. Victoria Univer-
            sity of Wellington. Song: med. v., pf.

It was the Lovely Moon   "It was the lovely moon"   In Stone
Trees (1916)

    2227 Gurney, Ivor. MS 1921. Song: [solo v., pf.].

Last Hours   "Gray day and quiet, A"   In Poems_New_and_Old
(1920)

    2228 Jacobson, Maurice. L: Curwen, 1922. Song: solo v.,
            pf.

Music Comes   "Music comes"   In Stone_Trees (1916)

    2229 Miles, Philip. L: BH, 1921. Setting for chorus,
            orch.

RY, Christopher   1907-

Boy_with_a_Cart,_The   (DR)   (1939)

    2230 Mayer, Lutz L. MS. Incidental music.

Lady's_Not_for_Burning,_The   (DR)   (1949), rev. 1950

    2231 Ponc, Miroslav. MS 1969, avail. SČSKU. Incidental
            music. Czech. title: "Dáme není k pálení",
            transl. by Břetislav Hodek.

Thursday's_Child   (Pageant)   (1939)

Fry, Christopher continued

2232   Shaw, Martin. L: CR, 1939. Songs: [v., pf.]. Songs
       entitled: "A Song of Life", "Leaving School",
       "What is a house", "Cooking", "Housework", "Rub-
       a-dub-dub", "Ploughing", "Sowing", "Reaping".
       Prod. (London 1939) as a pageant.

Miscellanea

2233   Bliss, Arthur. "Let us take the road", The Beggar's
       Opera, L: N, 1968. Song: ttb, orch. or ttb, pf.
       The complete collection requires various voices.

2234   Penderecki, Krzysztof. "Paradise Lost", MS, to be
       perf. Chicago, Dec. 1976. Opera. Libr. by Fry,
       after Milton's Paradise Lost. Details avail.
       Mz.: S.

2235   Tippett, Michael. Crown of the Year, L: S, 1958.
       Cta.: s duet, a solo, ssa, instruments. The 9
       movements of the work may be perf. (and are also
       publ.) sep.

2236   Tippett, Michael. "Dance, Clarion Air", MS 1952, L:
       S. Madrigal: ssatb, a cap. Tippett's contribution
       to A Garland for the Queen.

2237   Tippett, Michael. "Robert of Sicily", MS 1938. Opera
       for children. Text by Fry, adapt. from Robert
       Browning.

2238   Tippett, Michael. "Seven at One Stroke", MS 1939.
       Opera for children.

GALSWORTHY, John   1867-1933

Acceptation   "Blue sky, grey stones, and the far sea"
       Moods, Songs, & Doggerels (1912)

2239   Bryan, Gordon. L: C, 1922. Song: solo v., pf.

Autumn   "When every leaf has different hue"   Moods, Songs, & Doggerels (1912)

    2240 Burkinshaw, Sydney. MS. Song: ttbb, a cap.

Dedication   "Thine is the solitude that rare flowers know" In Verses New and Old (1926)

    2241 Rettich, Wilhelm. Eleven Songs for Voice and Piano, Berlin: Astoria, 1973. Song: t or bar solo, pf.

Downs, The   "O the Downs high to the cool sky"   English Review (June 1909)

    2242 Taylor, Colin. L: Curwen, 1919. Song: solo v., pf. Also avail. for solo v., str. qrt.

Flowers   See: Flowers, The

Flowers, The   "O my flowers!"   Moods, Songs, & Doggerels (1912), rev. 1934

    2243 Bryan, Gordon. "Flower Children", L: C, 1922. Song: solo v., pf.

Mood, A   "Love's a flower, 'tis born and broken"   Moods, Songs, & Doggerels (1912), rev. 1934

    2244 Bryan, Gordon. "Love's...", L: F&BG (Curwen), 1923. Song: solo v., pf.

Moor Grave, The   "I lie out here under a heather sod" Nation (Aug. 1908)

    2245 Burkinshaw, Sydney. MS. Song: ttbb, a cap.

Prayer for Gentleness to All Creatures   "To all the humble beasts there be"   In The Collected Poems of John Galsworthy (1934)

    2246 Ford, Donald. L: G, 1964. Song: unison v., pf.

Galsworthy, John continued

2247 Woodgate, Leslie. L: AH&C, 1958. Song: ttbb, a cap.

Promenade   "All sweet and startled gravity"   <u>English Review</u>
    (Feb. 1909)

    2248 Braine, Robert. MS 1934, B: OD. Song: [v., pf.].

Serenity   "Smiling sea, The"   <u>Moods, Songs, & Doggerels</u>
    (1926)

    2249 Bryan, Gordon. L: F&BG (Curwen), 1923. Song: solo
        v., pf.

Silver Point   "Sharp against a sky of gray"   In <u>Verses New</u>
    <u>and Old</u> (1926)

    2250 Bryan, Gordon. L: F&BG (Curwen), 1923. Song: solo
        v., pf.

Time   "Beneath this vast serene of sky"   <u>Scribner's</u>
    <u>Magazine</u> (Feb. 1912)

    2251 Burkinshaw, Sydney. MS. Song: chorus, a cap.

Tittle-Tattle   "Tittle-Tattle! Scandal and japes"   <u>Mool,</u>
    <u>Songs, & Doggerels</u> (1912)

    2252 Bryan, Gordon. L: Curwen, 1922. Song: solo v., pf.

"Voice in the night crying, down in the old sleeping"   <u>To</u>
    <u>Let</u> (1921), rev. & incl. in <u>The Collected Poems of John</u>
    <u>Galsworthy</u> (1934) under the title "Voice in the Night"

    2253 Crafton, Cyril. "Voice in the Night", L: A, pre-
        1940. Song: [v., pf.].

Wind   "Wind, wind--heather gipsy"   <u>Scribner's Magazine</u>
    (Feb. 1912)

    2254 Braine, Robert. NY: GS, pre-1940. Song: [v., pf.].

2255   Burkinshaw, Sydney. MS. Song: ssaa, a cap.

GASCOYNE, David Emery   1916-

De Profundis   "Out of these depths"   In Poems 1937-1942
   (1943) as one of "Miserere"

   2256   Naylor, Bernard. Six Poems from "Miserere", Wen-
            dover: RP, 1972. Ste.: 2 s soli, dbl. choir of
            mixed v., a cap.

Epode   "Then/The great Face turned"   In Poems 1937-1942
   (1943)

   2257   Naylor, Bernard. "'The Three Stars' and 'Epode'",
            MS 1972-73. Setting for s, t (or bar), b soli,
            ssaattbb, a cap.

Ex Nihilo   "Here am I now cast down"   In Poems 1937-1942
   (1943) as one of "Miserere"

   2258   Naylor, Bernard. Six Poems from "Miserere", Wen-
            dover: RP, 1972. Ste.: 2 s soli, dbl. choir of
            mixed v., a cap.

Fragments toward a Religio Poetae   "Son of Man is in revolt,
   The"   In A Vagrant and other poems (1950)

   2259   Douglas, James. "Fragments", MS 1970, avail. SMA.
            Setting for med. v., pf.

Kyrie   "Is man's destructive lust insatiable?"   In Poems
   1937-1942 (1943) as one of "Miserere"

   2260   Naylor, Bernard. Sis Poems from "Miserere", Wen-
            dover: RP, 1972. Ste.: 2 s soli, dbl. choir of
            mixed v., a cap.

Gascoyne, David continued

Lachrymae   "Slow are the years of light"   In Poems 1937-
1942 (1943) as one of "Miserere"

    2261   Naylor, Bernard. Six Poems from "Miserere", Wen-
dover: RP, 1972. Ste.: 2 s soli, dbl. choir of
mixed v., a cap.

Night Thoughts   (DR)   (1956)

    2262   Searle, Humphrey. MS, broadcast BBC, 7 Dec. 1955.
Incidental music.

Pieta   "Stark in the pasture"   In Poems 1937-1942 (1943) as
one of "Miserere"

    2263   Naylor, Bernard. Six Poems from "Miserere", Wen-
dover: RP, 1972. Ste.: 2 s soli, dbl. choir of
mixed v., a cap.

Requiem   "O hidden Face!"   Collected Poems (1965)

    2264* Rainier, Priaulx. MS 1956. Setting for t solo, satb,
a cap.

Rex Mundi   "I heard a hearld's note"   In A Vagrant and
other poems (1950)

    2265   Douglas, James. MS 1968, avail. SMA. Setting for
satb, org.

Sacred Hearth, The   "You must have been still sleeping"
In A Vagrant and other poems (1950)

    2266   Field, Robin. "Aubade", MS 1969. Setting for s solo,
a. fl., cl., vln., vcl., hp. Sets lines begin-
ning: "How slow the intimate Spring night swelled
through those depths".

Tenebrae   "'It is finished'"   In Poems 1937-1942 (1943) as
one of "Miserere"

2267　Naylor, Bernard. Six Poems from "Miserere", Wen-
　　　　dover: RP, 1972. Ste.: 2 s soli, dbl. choir of
　　　　mixed v., a cap.

Three Stars, The: A Prophecy　"Night was Time, The"　In
Poems 1937-1942 (1943)

2268　Naylor, Bernard. "'The Three Stars' and 'Epode'",
　　　　MS 1972-73. Setting for s, t (or bar), b soli,
　　　　ssaattbb, a cap.

GIBBON, Monk　1896-

Children　"These wayfarers"　In For Daws to Peck At (1929)

2269　Le Fleming, Christopher. Echoing Green, L: JWC,
　　　　1934. Song: solo v., pf. (or pf., stgs.) or
　　　　unison v., pf. (or pf., stgs.).

Innocence　"Now to praise Innocence"　In For Daws to Peck
At (1929)

2270　Coulthard, Jean. Five Irish Songs for Maureen, MS
　　　　1964, avail. CMC. Song: a solo, pf.

2271　Hart, Fritz. Five Songs, MS 1931, avail. State
　　　　Library of Victoria, Melbourne. Song: v., pf.

Little Field, The　"Within a little field"　In For Daws to
Peck At (1929)

2272　Hart, Fritz. Five Songs, MS 1931, avail. State
　　　　Library of Victoria, Melbourne. Song: v., pf.

Of a Child　"Earth, this child"　In For Daws to Peck At
(1929)

Gibbon, Monk continued

    2273 Hart, Fritz. _Five Songs_, MS 1931, avail. State
          Library of Victoria, Melbourne. Song: v., pf.

Singers, The   "Sing, crickets, in the dusk"   In _For Daws_
to Peck At (1929)

    2274 Hart, Fritz. _Five Songs_, MS 1931, avail. State
          Library of Victoria, Melbourne. Song: v., pf.

Wayfarers   "Bees are gone from the clover, The"   In _For_
Daws to Peck At (1929)

    2275 Hart, Fritz. MS 1931, avail. State Library of Vic-
          toria, Melbourne. Song: [v., pf.].

Wise Lover, The   "He who loves beauty wisely"   In _For Daws_
to Peck At (1929)

    2276 Coulthard, Jean. _Five Irish Songs for Maureen_, MS
          1964, avail. CMC. Song: a solo, pf.

Miscellanea

    2277 Hart, Fritz. "Kneel, Little Child to God", _Five_
          Songs, MS 1931, avail. State Library of Victoria,
          Melbourne. Song: v., pf.

GIBSON, Wilfrid Wilson   1878-1962

Audrey   "On the sea's edge she dances"   In _I Heard a Sailor_
(1925)

    2278 Hart, Fritz. _Two Sets of Five Songs Each_, Set II, MS
          1931, avail. State Library of Victoria, Mel-
          bourne. Song: solo v., pf.

Black Stitchel   "As I was lying on Black Stitchel"   In <u>Whin</u>
    (1918)

    2279 Gurney, Ivor. <u>A First Volume of Ten Songs</u>, L: OUP,
            1938. Song: solo v., pf.

Blaweary   "As I came by Blaweary"   In <u>Whin</u> (1918)

    2280 Gurney, Ivor. <u>A Second Volume of Ten Songs</u>, L: OUP,
            1938. Song: solo v., pf.

    2281 Whittaker, W.G. L: OUP, 1929. Song: unison v., stgs.

Bloom   "Laburnum, lilac, honeysuckle, broom"   In <u>Collected
    Poems 1905-1925</u> (1925)

    2282 Treharne, Bryceson. "My Dream Garden", NY: CPMC,
            pre-1940. Song: [solo v., pf.].

Cakewalk, The   "In smoky lamplight of a Smyrna cafe"   In
    <u>Neighbours</u> (1920)

    2283 Fulton, Norman. L: OUP, 1943. Song: b-bar solo, pf.

Chestnum-Blossom, The   "Chestnum-blossom fell, The"   In <u>I
    Heard a Sailor</u> (1925)

    2284 Peterkin, Norman. L: OUP, pre-1940. Song: [v., pf.].

Crowder, The   "'Twixt Coldmouth Hill and Butterstone Shank"
    In <u>Whin</u> (1918)

    2285 Gurney, Ivor. MS 1920. Song: [solo v., pf.].

    2286 Whittaker, W.G. L: OUP, pre-1940. Song: t solo, pf.

Cruel and Bright   "Cruel and bright as the whin"   In <u>Whin</u>
    (1918)

    2287 Thompson, E. Roy. L: Curwen, 1921. Song: solo v.,
            pf.

Gibson, W.W. continued

Dancers, The   "All day beneath the hurtling shells"   In
   Battle (1916)

   2288 Miles, Philip. Battle Songs, L: Curwen, [?]. Song:
         solo v., pf.

Dancing Seal, The   "When we were building Skua Light"   In
   Fires (1912)

   2289 Bainton, Edgar L. L: OUP, 1925. Song: chorus, orch.

Empty Purse, The   "One song leads on to another"   In
   Collected Poems 1905-1925 (1925)

   2290 Whittaker, W.G. L: OUP, pre-1940. Song: t solo, pf.

For G.   "All night under the moon"   In Friends (1916)

   2291 Bainton, Edgar L. "All Night Under the Moon", L: WR,
         1921. Song: solo v., pf.

   2292 Gurney, Ivor. "All Night Under the Moon", A First
         Volume of Ten Songs, L: OUP, 1938. Song: solo v.,
         pf.

   2293 Scott, Francis G. "All Night Under the Moon", Three
         Short Songs for Medium or High Voice, MS 1920,
         avail. SMA. Song: high or med. v., pf.

Fowler, The   "Wild bird filled the morning air, A"   In I
   Heard a Sailor (1925)

   2294 Hart, Fritz. Two Sets of Five Songs Each, Set I, MS
         1931, avail. State Library of Victoria, Mel-
         bourne. Song: solo v., pf.

Girl's Song   "I saw three black pigs riding"   In Friends
   (1916)

   2295 Howells, Herbert. Four Songs, L: WR, 1919. Song:
         solo v., pf.

He is tender with the Beasts...   "He is tender with the beasts"   In The Golden Room and other poems (1923)

    2296 Ford, Donald. L: C, [?]. Song: [v., pf.].

Hit   "Out of the sparkling sea"   In Battle (1916)

    2297 Miles, Philip. Battle Songs, L: Curwen, [?]. Song: solo v., pf.

Lament   "We who are left"   In Whin (1918)

    2298 Frankel, Benjamin. MS (Opus 15). Setting for t solo, female chorus, a cap.

    2299 Miles, Philip. "Epilogue-Lament", Battle Songs, L: Curwen, [?]. Song: solo v., pf.

    2300 Pentland, Barbara. MS 1934. Song: med. v., str. qrt.

Lark, The   "Lull in the racket and brattle, A"   In Battle (1916)

    2301 Miles, Philip. Battle Songs, L: Curwen, [?]. Song: solo v., pf.

Little Red Calf, The   "Little red calf, The"   In I Heard a Sailor (1925)

    2302 Taylor, Colin. L: EA, pre-1951. Song: unison v., pf.

Lonely Tree, The   "Twisted ash, a ragged fir, A"   In Whin (1918)

    2303 Hart, Fritz. Two Sets of Five Songs Each, Set II, MS 1931, avail. State Library of Victoria, Melbourne. Song: solo v., pf.

    2304 Housman, Rosalie. "A Lonely Tree", MS, avail. NYPL. Song: [v., pf.].

2305   Wordsworth, William. Three Songs, MS 1938. Song:
        med. v., pf. "The Lonely Tree" was issued on
        Jupiter recording #JUR OA11.

Mugger's Song, The   "Driving up the Mallerstang"   In Whin
    (1918)

    2306   Gurney, Ivor. MS 1920. Song: [solo v., pf.].

Old Meg   "There's never the taste of a cherry"   In Whin
    (1918)

    2307   Howells, Herbert. L: OUP, 1928. Song: a solo, pf.

Old Skinflint   "'Twixt Carrowbrough Edge and Settlingstones"
    In Whin (1918)

    2308   Howells, Herbert. L: Curwen, 1920. Song: solo v.,
            pf.

    2309   Rafter, Leonard. Three Songs, L: S, 1940. Song: med.
            v., pf.

Pedlar jack   "I came by Raw from Hungary Law"   In Whin
    (1918)

    2310   Gurney, Ivor. MS n.d. Song: [solo v., pf.].

Pity Me   "As I came down by Pity Me"   In Whin (1918)

    2311   Gurney, Ivor. MS n.d. Song: [solo v., pf.].

    2312   Hart, Fritz. Two Sets of Five Songs Each, Set II, MS
            1931, avail. State Library of Victoria, Mel-
            bourne. Song: solo v., pf.

Pool, The   "Her mind's a shallow bowl"   In I Heard a Sailor
    (1925)

    2313   Hart, Fritz. Two Sets of Five Songs Each, Set I, MS
            1931, avail. State Library of Victoria, Mel-
            bourne. Song: solo v., pf.

Quiet, The   "I could not understand the sudden quiet"   In
    Battle (1916)

    2314   Miles, Philip. Battle Songs, L: Curwen, [?]. Song:
               solo v., pf.

Retreat   "Broken, bewildered by the long retreat"   In
    Friends (1916)

    2315   Miles, Philip. Battle Songs, L: Curwen, [?]. Song:
               solo v., pf.

Return   "Rust-red the bracken"   In Neighbours (1920)

    2316   Hart, Fritz. Two Sets of Five Songs Each, Set II, MS
               1931, avail. State Library of Victoria, Mel-
               bourne. Song: solo v., pf.

Rocket, The   "Into the night"   In I Heard a Sailor (1925)

    2317   Housman, Rosalie. MS, avail. NYPL. Song: [v., pf.].

Roses   "Red roses floating in a crystal bowl"   In Friends
    (1916)

    2318   Blake, Anita M. "The Crystal Bowl", L: C, 1926.
               Song: [v., pf.].

    2319   Gurney, Ivor. "Red Roses", MS 1918. Song: [solo v.,
               pf.].

Sabbath   "Lowing of cattle as the twilight falls"   In
    Collected Poems 1905-1925 (1925)

    2320   Hart, Fritz. "Evening", Two Sets of Five Songs Each,
               Set I, MS 1931, avail. State Library of Victoria,
               Melbourne. Song: solo v., pf.

Sam Spraggon   "From Walsingham to Frosterly"   In Whin
    (1918)

    2321   Gurney, Ivor. MS 1920. Song: [solo v., pf.].

271

Gibson, W.W. continued

Scatterpenny   "You'd take me for a lucky lad"   In <u>Whin</u>
    (1918)

    2322 Thompson, E. Roy. L: Curwen, 1921. Song: solo v.,
              pf.

    2323 Whittaker, W.G. L: OUP, pre-1940. Song: t solo, pf.

Skirlnaked   "O came you by Skirlnaked"   In <u>Whin</u> (1918)

    2324 Hart, Fritz. <u>Two Sets of Five Songs Each</u>, Set II, MS
              1931, avail. State Library of Victoria, Mel-
              bourne. Song: solo v., pf.

Song of a Lass, O   "'Twixt Ridlees Cairn and Corby Pike"
    In <u>Whin</u> (1918)

    2325 Whittaker, W.G. L: OUP, pre-1940. Song: t solo, pf.

Stars   "Who travelling through a midnight wood"   In
    <u>Collected Poems 1905-1925</u> (1925)

    2326 Hart, Fritz. <u>Two Sets of Five Songs Each</u>, Set I, MS
              1931, avail. State Library of Victoria, Mel-
              bourne. Song: solo v., pf.

Wind, The   "To the lean, clean land"   In <u>Thoroughfares</u>
    (1914)

    2327 Wordsworth, William. <u>Three Songs</u>, L: L, 1946. Song:
              low v., pf.

Yeavering Bell   "Just to see the rain"   In <u>Whin</u> (1918)

    2328 Hart, Fritz. <u>Two Sets of Five Songs Each</u>, Set I, MS
              1931, avail. State Library of Victoria, Mel-
              bourne. Song: solo v., pf.

Miscellanea

    2329 Bainton, Edgar L. "A Casualty", L: A, pre-1940.
              Song: [v., pf.?].

272

2330   Bainton, Edgar L. "Honeymoon", L: S&B, pre-1940.
       Song: [v., pf.?].

2331   Busch, William. There Have Been Happy Days, MS ca.
       1944. Cyc. Texts by Gibson.

2332   Lohr, Hermann. "The Tavern", L: C, 1911. Song: [v.,
       pf.].

GILBERT, William Schwenck*   1836-1911

To the Terrestrial Globe   "Roll on, thou ball, roll on!"
Fun (Sept. 1865), rev. 1869

2333   Newsome, Eliot. MS. Motet: satb, a cap.

GOGARTY, Oliver St. John   1878-1957

Death May Be Very Gently   "Death may be very gentle after
   all"   In Selected Poems (1933)

2334   Healey, Derek. "Death May Be", Six Irish Songs, MS
       1962, avail. CMC. Song: solo v., pf.

Golden Stockings   "Golden stockings you had on"   In An Of-
   fering of Swans (1923)

2335   Shepherd, Arthur. Seven Songs, Northampton, Mass.:
       NVMP, 1961. Song: high v., pf.

Virgil   "From Mantua's meadows to imperial Rome"   In An Of-
   fering of Swans (1923)

Gogarty, Oliver St. John continued

2336 Shepherd, Arthur. <u>Seven Songs</u>, Northampton, Mass.:
      NVMP, 1961. Song: high v., pf.

Miscellanea

2337 Duff, Arthur. "Non Dolet", Dublin: Cuala, 1937 in
      <u>Broadside</u>, No. 2. Song: v., unacc. Text begins:
      "Our friends go with us as we go".

2338 Shepherd, Arthur. "To a Trout", <u>Seven Songs</u>,
      Northampton, Mass.: NVMP, 1961. Song: high v.,
      pf.

GOLDING, William   1911-

<u>Lord of the Flies</u>   (NV)   (1954)

2339 Leppard, Raymond. MS, pre-1963. Film music. The
      theme (beginning: "Kyrie, kyrie, kyrie eleison")
      was publ. B: Saunders, 1963 for solo v.

GOSSE, Edmund William   1849-1928

Miscellanea

2340 Elgar, Edward. "After many a Dusty Mile", <u>Five Part-
      songs from the Greek Anthology</u>, L: N, 1903. Song:
      ttbb, a cap. Text transl. from the Greek by
      Gosse.

GOULD, Gerald   1885-1936

"Give me one hour--the years are young"   In Lyrics (1906)

    2341   Massey, Gwen W. "Give Me One Hour", L: C. Song: [v., pf.].

Green Leaves   See: "'Tis but a week since down the glen"

Happy Tree, The   "There was a bright and happy tree" (1919)

    2342   Gurney, Ivor. A Third Volume of Ten Songs, L: OUP, 1952. Song: solo v., pf.

    2343   Hamerton, Ann. L: A, 1955. Song: v., pf.

"'Tis but a week since down the glen"   In Lyrics (1906), rev. 1920

    2344   Bridge, Frank. "'Tis but a week", L: WR, 1919. Song: v., pf.

Wander-Thirst   "Beyond the East the sunrise, beyond the West the sea"   In Lyrics (1906)

    2345   Baynon, Arthur. L: Curwen, 1935. Song: unison children's v., pf. or unison female v., pf.

    2346*   Davies, H. Walford. Four Songs, L: N, 1915. Song: med. v., pf.

    2347   Peel, Graham. The Country Lover, L: C, 1910. Song: [solo v., pf.].

    2348   Ronald, Landon. Song Fancies, L: E, 1923. Song: v., pf.

Miscellanea

Gould, Gerald continued

2349   Ihrke, Walter. "I walk the noisy streets", MS 1956,
       avail. University of Canterbury. Song: s or t
       solo, pf.

GRAHAME, Kenneth   1859-1932

Wind in the Willows, The   (NV)   (1908)

2350   Bailey, Judith M. "Animals' Carol from Wind in the
       Willows", Three Songs for Unison Voices, Win-
       chester: Mor, 1974. Song: female unison v., pf.
       Setting of lines beginning: "Villagers all, this
       frosty tide".

2351   Blake, Donna. "Villagers All", NY: Girl Scouts, 1930
       in Old Songs and Balladry for Girl Scouts. Song:
       v., pf. Setting of lines beginning: "Villagers
       all, this frosty tide".

2352   Fraser-Simson, Harold. Toad of Toad Hall, L: C,
       1930. Musical play. Employs A.A. Milne's adapt.
       entitled Toad of Toad Hall (1929).

2353   Gilbert, Norman. "The Ducks", L: OUP, 1956. Song:
       unison v., pf. Setting of lines beginning: "All
       along the backwater".

2354   Hand, Colin. "Ducks' Ditty", L: Elkin, 1963. Canon:
       chorus of equal v., pf. Setting of lines begin-
       ning: "All along the backwater".

2355   Head, Michael. "The Carol of the Field Mice", L: BH,
       1971. Song: med. v., pf. Setting of lines begin-
       ning: "Villagers all, this frosty tide".

2356   Hicks, Mary. "Ducks Ditty", L: Curwen, 1958. Song:
       unison v., pf. Setting of lines beginning: "All
       along the backwater".

276

ahame, Kenneth continued

2357 Jarrett, Jack M. "Joy Shall Be Yours", Three Christmas Songs, Turnersville: Standard, 1972. Song:
satb, a cap. Setting of lines beginning: "Villagers all, this frosty tide".

2358 Strilko, Anthony. "Carol of the Animals", NY: LG,
1965. Song: satb, a cap. Setting of lines beginning: "Villagers all, this frosty tide".

2359 Thompson, Randall. MS ca. 1924. Str. qrt. only.

GRAVES, Alfred Perceval*   1846-1931

Battle Hymn   "Above the thunder crashes"   In The Irish
Poems of Alfred Perceval Graves: Countryside Songs [and]
Songs and Ballads (1908)

2360 Gaul, Harvey B. "Irish Battle Hymn", MS pre-1945,
NY: GS. Song: ttbb, pf.

Cradle of Gold, The   See: Irish Lullaby

Irish Lullaby   "I'd rock my own sweet childie to rest"   In
Father O'Flynn And other Irish Lyrics (1889), rev. 1908

2361 Page, Nathaniel C. "An Irish Lullaby", B: Birchard,
1916 in Junior Laurel Songs. Song: v., pf.

Little Red Lark, The   "Oh, swan of slenderness"   In Irish
Songs and Ballads (1880)

2362 Willan, Healey, arr. Songs of the British Isles,
Vol. 2, Oakville: FH, 1928. Song: v. (best suited
for female v.), pf.

Lullaby, A   "I've found my bonny babe a nest"   In The Irish
Poems of Alfred Perceval Graves: Songs of the Gael [and]
A Gaelic Story-Telling (1908)

Graves, A.P. continued

2363   Holmes, Horace R., arr. "I've found...", L: CR,
       1962. Arr. for ss, pf.

Remember the Poor   "Oh! remember the poor when your future
    is sure"   In The Irish Poems of Alfred Perceval Graves:
    Songs of the Gael [and] A Gaelic Story-Telling (1908)

    2364   Deale, Edgar M. "O, remember the poor", L: OUP,
           1961. Song: 2 pt. chorus, org. (or pf.). Employs
           an Irish air.

She is My Love   "She is my love beyond all thought"   In The
    Irish Poems of Alfred Perceval Graves: Songs of the Gael
    [and] A Gaelic Story-Telling (1908)

    2365   Parry, C.H.H. "She is...", English Lyrics, Eleventh
           Set, L: N (publ. posth.). Song: v., pf.

    2366* Swain, Freda. "She is...", MS ca. 1922, avail. Chin-
           nor: Channel, NEMO. Setting for t and pf. en-
           semble.

Shuile Agra   "His hair was black, his eye was blue"   In
    Irish Songs and Ballads (1880), rev. 1908

    2367   Willan, Healey, arr. "Shule Agra", NY: OUP, 1929.
           Song: bar solo, ttbb, pf. Arr. of a trad. tune.

Shule Agra!   See: Shuile Agra

Trottin' to the Fair   "Trottin' to the fair"   In The Irish
    Poems of Alfred Perceval Graves: Countryside Songs [and]
    Songs and Ballads (1908)

    2368   Johnston, Tom. L: BH, 1960. Song: satb, a cap.

Miscellanea

    2369   Arundell, Dennis. "The Sailor", L: Curwen, 1924.
           Song: solo v., pf.

2370 Cripps, A. Redgrave. "Christmas Lullaby", MS pre-
     1942, L: A. Song: [v., pf.?].

2371 Lehmann, Liza. Songs of Spring, MS pre-1918, L: BH.

2372 Mackenzie, Alexander. Spring Songs and Others, MS
     pre-1935, L: N.

2373 Parry, C.H.H. The composer's English Lyrics, Sixth
     Set (L: N, 1902) incl. a setting of Graves'
     "A Lover's Garland" (transl. from the Greek), and
     of his "At the hour the long day ends". English
     Lyrics, Eleventh Set (L: N, publ. posth.) incl.
     settings of Graves' texts entitled: "The spirit
     of the Spring", "The Blackbird", "The Faithful
     Lover".

2374 Shaw, Martin. "Orange and Green", L: Curwen, 1917.
     Song: solo v., pf.

2375 Stanford, C.V. "Shamus O'Brien", MS, prod. Paris,
     Mar. 1896. Opera.

GRAVES, Robert Ranke   1895-

Allie   "Allie, call the birds in"   Country Sentiment (1920)

   2376 Crosse, Gordon. Four Songs, MS 1974, L: OUP, publ.
        forthcoming. Song: high v., pf.

   2377* Swain, Freda. Settings of Four Poems by Robert
        Graves, MS 1966, avail. Chinnor: Channel, NEMO.
        Cyc.: bar and pf. ensemble.

Apples and Water   "Dust in a cloud, blinding weather"
   Country Sentiment (1920)

   2378* Addison, John. MS 1965. Song: ms or bar solo, gtr.

Graves, Robert continued

Bedpost, The   "Sleepy Betsy from her pillow"   London
    Mercury (Sept. 1921)

    2379   Wishart, Peter. Half Way to Sleep, L: H, 1961. Cyc.:
           high v., pf. This setting also suitable for med.
           v.

Bird of Paradise   "At sunset, only to his true love"   Man
    Does, Woman Is (1964)

    2380   Wishart, Peter. A Book of Beasts, MS 1969. Cyc.:
           med. v., pf.

Blodeuwedd of Gwion ap Gwreang, The   "Not of father nor of
    mother"   Wales (Dec. 1945), rev. 1948

    2381   Mather, Bruce. "The Song of Blodeuwedd", The White
           Goddess, MS 1960-62, avail. CMC. Cta.: s, bar
           soli, satb, pf., orch. Complete work also
           requires pf. solo.

Brittle Bones   "Though I am an old man"   Country Sentiment
    (1920)

    2382   Gurney, Ivor. MS 1920. Song: [solo v., pf.].

Cat-Goddesses   "Perverse habit of cat-goddesses, A"   New
    Yorker (Mar. 1953)

    2383   Wishart, Peter. A Book of Beasts, MS 1969. Cyc.:
           med. v., pf.

Cool Web, The   "Children are dumb to say how hot the day
    is"   London Mercury (Dec. 1926)

    2384   Crosse, Gordon. Four Songs, MS 1974, L: OUP, publ.
           forthcoming. Song: high v., pf.

Counting the Beats   "You, love, and I"   Good Housekeeping
    (Apr. 1950)

aves, Robert continued

2385 Berkeley, Lennox. L: Thames, 1972. Song: high v.,
     pf.

2386 Mather, Bruce. <u>Three Songs to Poems of Robert
     Graves</u>, MS 1957-58, avail. CMC. Cyc.: s solo,
     str. orch.

2387 Maw, Nicholas. MS, avail. British Museum. Song: t
     solo, pf.

2388 Searle, Humphrey. L: F, 1966. Song: s or t solo, pf.

Cradle, The "He smiles within his cradle" <u>The Oxford
Book of Carols</u> (1928) Transl. of "Ein Kindlein in der
Wiegen" from D.G. Corner's <u>Geistliche Nachtigal</u>. Not publ.
sep.

2389 Bielawa, Herbert. NY: LG, 1969. [Carol]: 4 pt.
     chorus of treble v., a cap.

2390 Kelly, Bryan. L: OUP, 1964. [Carol]: satb, a cap.

2391 Shaw, Martin, arr. L: OUP, 1928 in <u>The Oxford Book
     of Carols</u>. Carol: v., pf. Melody from D.G. Cor-
     ner's <u>Geistliche Nachtigal</u>, 1649.

Cupboard, The "What's in that cupboard, Mary?" <u>Poetry</u>
(Aug. 1919)

2392 Finzi, Gerald. L: Curwen, 1923. Song: solo v., pf.

Despite and Still "Have you not read" <u>Poems 1938-1945</u>
(1945)

2393 Barber, Samuel. <u>Despite and Still</u>, NY: GS, 1969.
     Cyc.: high v., pf.

Door, The "When she came suddenly in" <u>Wales</u> (Jan. 1944)

2394 Wood, Hugh. MS (Opus 18). Cyc.: high v., pf.

Graves, Robert continued

Finding of Love, The   "Pale at first and cold"   London
   Mercury (Jan. 1921)

   2395 Mather, Bruce. Three Songs to Poems of Robert
             Graves, MS 1957-58, avail. CMC. Cyc.: s solo,
             str. orch.

Flying Crooked   "Butterfly, a cabbage-white, The"   Poems
   1926-1930 (1931)

   2396 Wishart, Peter. A Book of Beasts, MS 1969. Cyc.:
             med. v., pf.

Foreboding, The   "Looking by chance in at the open window"
   Poetry (Dec. 1951)

   2397 Wood, Hugh. MS (Opus 18). Cyc.: high v., pf.

Green Loving   "Grass green and aspen green"   Collected
   Poems (1938), rev. 1961

   2398 Hattey, Philip. "Variables of Green", Seven Poems of
             Robert Graves, L: BH, 1969. Song: solo v., pf.

Hawk and Buckle   "Where is the landlord"   Poetry (Aug. 1919)

   2399* Gurney, Ivor. A Second Volume of Ten Song, L: OUP,
             1938. Song: [bar] solo v., pf. Text attributed to
             "John Doyle".

Henry and Mary   "Henry was a young king"   Whipperginny
   (1923) Portions 1st publ. as "The Gifts" and "The Fiddle"
   in Treasure Box (1919)

   2400 Wishart, Peter. Half Way to Sleep, L: H, 1961. Cyc.:
             high v., pf. This setting also suitable for med.
             v.

Homer's Daughter   (NV)   (1955)

   2401 Glanville-Hicks, Peggy. "Nausicaa", MS 1961. Opera
             based on the novel. Libr. by Graves.

Horizon   "On a clear day how thin the horizon"   Saturday
    Evening Post (Nov. 1911)

    2402 Hattey, Philip. Seven Poems of Robert Graves, L: BH,
          1969. Song: solo v., pf.

I'd Love to Be a Fairy's Child   "Children born of fairy
    stock" Fairies and Fusiliers (1917)

    2403 Swift, Newton. NY: HB, 1935 in Songs to Sing to
          Children. Song: v., pf.

In Procession   "Often, half-way to sleep"   On English
    Poetry (1922)

    2404 Wishart, Peter. Half Way to Sleep, L: H, 1961. Cyc.:
          high v., pf. Portions of cyc. also suitable for
          med. v.

In the Wilderness*   "Christ of his gentleness"   Over the
    Brazier (1916)

    2405 Bainton, Edgar L. L: OUP, 1928. Song: satb, a cap.

    2406 Barber, Samuel. Despite and Still, NY: GS, 1969.
          Cyc.: high v., pf.

Is Now the Time?   "If he asks 'Is now the time?', it is not
    the time" In Poems 1965-68 (1968)

    2407 Hattey, Philip. Seven Poems of Robert Graves, L: BH,
          1969. Song: solo v., pf.

Lady Visitor in the Pauper Ward, The   "Why do you break upon
    this old, cool peace" Goliath and David (1916)

    2408 Berners, Gerald. Three Songs, L: JWC, 1920. Song:
          med. v., pf.

Lament for Pasiphae   "Dying sun, shine warm a little longer!"
    The Golden Fleece (1944)

Graves, Robert continued

2409 Mather, Bruce. The White Goddess, MS 1960-62, avail.
      CMC. Cta.: s, bar soli, satb, pf., orch. Complete
      work also requires pf. solo.

Last Poem, A   "Last poem, and a very last, and yet another
     A" Man Does, Woman Is (1964)

  2410 Barber, Samuel. "A Last Song", Despite and Still,
        NY: GS, 1969. Cyc.: high v., pf.

Leap, The   "Forget the rest: my heart is true"   Kenyon
Review (Winter 1964)

  2411* Swain, Freda. Settings of Four Poems by Robert
        Graves, MS 1966, avail. Chinnor: Channel, NEMO.
        Cyc.: bar and pf. ensemble.

Legs, The   "There was this road"   To Whom Else? (1931)

  2412 Blank, Allan. MS, avail. ACA. Song: med. v., pf.

Leveller, The   "Near Martinpuisch that night of hell"   New
Statesman (Jan. 1919)

  2413 Weisgall, Hugo. Soldier Songs, NY: MMP, 1953. Song:
        bar solo, pf. Score rev. 1965.

Litt-Boy   See: Tail Piece: A Song to Make You and Me Laugh

Like Snow   "She, then, like snow in a dark night"   Epilogue
1 (1935) as one of "A Poem Sequence: To the Sovereign
Muse"

  2414 Mather, Bruce. The White Goddess, MS 1960-62, avail.
        CMC. Pf. solo. Complete cta. also requires s, bar
        soli, satb, orch.

Lost Love   "His eyes are quickened so with grief"
Treasure Box (1919)

284

2415 Mather, Bruce. <u>Three Songs to Poems of Robert Graves</u>, MS 1957-58, avail. CMC. Cyc.: s solo, str. orch.

Loving Henry   "Henry, Henry, do you love me?"   <u>Land and Water</u> (May 1919)

2416 Gurney, Ivor. MS 1920. Song: [solo v., pf.].

Neglectful Edward   "Edward back from the Indian Sea"   <u>Land and Water</u> (Jan. 1919)

2417 Thackray, Rupert. L: OUP, 1952. Song: ms or bar solo, pf.

New Legends   "Content in you"   <u>Collected Poems</u> (1938)

2418 Wishart, Peter. <u>Half Way to Sleep</u>, L: H, 1961. Cyc.: high v., pf. Portions of cyc. also suitable for med. v.

Nine o'Clock   "Nine of the clock, oh!"   <u>Country Sentiment</u> (1920)

2419 Gurney, Ivor. "Goodnight to the Meadow", <u>A Third Volume of Ten Songs</u>, L: OUP, 1952. Song: [ms or bar] solo v., pf. Sets Part II of "Nine o'Clock".

2420* Gurney, Ivor. "Nine of the Clock", <u>A First Volume of Ten Songs</u>, L: OUP, 1938. Song: [ms or bar] solo v., pf. Text attributed to "John Doyle".

O Love in Me   "O Love, be fed with apples"   <u>Poems 1926-1930</u> (1931), rev. 1938

2421 Mather, Bruce. "Sick Love", <u>The White Goddess</u>, MS 1960-62, avail. CMC. Cta.: s, bar soli, satb, pf., orch. Complete work also requires pf. solo.

Philatelist Royal   "Philatelist Royal, The"   <u>Poems (1914-1927)</u> (1927)

Graves, Robert continued

2422 Wishart, Peter. Songs and Satires, L: S&B, 1961.
      Madrigal ste.: satb, a cap. Portions of ste.
      require ssatbb.

Sharp Ridge, The   "Since now I dare not ask"   Observer
    (Jan. 1961)

2423 Hattey, Philip. Seven Poems of Robert Graves, L: BH,
      1969. Song: solo v., pf.

She Tells Her Love While Half Asleep   "She tells her love
    while half asleep"   The Golden Fleece (1944)

2424 Hattey, Philip. Seven Poems of Robert Graves, L: BH,
      1969. Song: solo v., pf.

2425 Wishart, Peter. "She Tells Her Love", Half Way to
      Sleep, L: H, 1961. Cyc.: high v., pf. Portions
      of cyc. also suitable for med. v.

Sick Love   See: O Love in Me

Song: A Phoenix Flame   "In my heart a phoenix flame"   Man
    Does, Woman Is (1964)

2426* Swain, Freda. "A Phoenix Flame", Settings of Four
      Poems by Robert Graves, MS 1966, avail. Chinnor:
      Channel, NEMO. Cyc.: bar and pf. ensemble.

Song: Litt-Boy   See: Tail Piece: A Song to Make You and Me
    Laugh

Song of Blodeuwedd, The   See: Blodeuwedd of Gwion ap
    Gwreang, The

Song: Sword and Rose   "King of Hearts a broadsword bears,
    The"   New Republic (Apr. 1964)

2427* Swain, Freda. "Sword and Rose", Settings of Four
      Poems by Robert Graves, MS 1966, avail. Chinnor:
      Channel, NEMO. Cyc.: bar and pf. ensemble.

286

Star-Talk "'Are you awake, Gemelli...?'" Over the Brazier
    (1916)

    2428 Gurney, Ivor. L: S&B, 1927. Song: [solo v., pf.].

    2429 Vaughan Williams, Ralph. An incomplete composition
          found in the composer's late sketchbooks.

Succubus, The "Thus will despair" Poems 1930-1933 (1933)

    2430 Bevan, Clifford. MS. Song: t solo, orch.

Symptoms of Love "Love is a universal migraine" Observer
    (Jan. 1961)

    2431 Adler, Samuel. Two Views of Love, Bryn Mawr: TP,
          1973. Song: ttbb, a cap.

Tail Piece: A Song to Make You and Me Laugh "Let me tell
    you the story" Tens Poems More (1930), rev. 1931, rev.
    1948

    2432 Britten, Benjamin. "Lift Boy", Two Part Songs, L:
          BH, 1934. Song: satb, pf.

    2433 Hattey, Philip. "Lift-Boy", Seven Poems of Robert
          Graves, L: BH, 1969. Song: solo v., pf.

Three Kings "Three Kings are here, both wealthy and wise"
    The Oxford Book of Carols (1928) Transl. from the Flemish.
    Not publ. sep.

    2434 La Montaine, John. "The Magi and King Herod", Wonder
          Tidings, NY: HWG, pre-1969. Carol cyc.: s, a, t,
          b soli, narr., pf. (or hp.), timp., gong (or
          cym.). One carol of the cyc. may be perf. with
          opt. org.

    2435 Shaw, Martin, arr. L: OUP, 1928 in The Oxford Book
          of Carols. Carol: v., pf.

Two Witches, The "O sixteen hundred and ninety one" More
    Poems 1961 (1961)

Graves, Robert continued

   2436   Blank, Allan. MS, avail. ACA. Song: sa, pf.

   2437   Hattey, Philip. Seven Poems of Robert Graves, L: BH,
          1969. Song: solo v., pf.

Vanity   "Be assured, the Dragon is not dead"   Collected
   Poems (1938)

   2438   Crosse, Gordon. Four Songs, MS 1974, L: OUP, publ.
          forthcoming. Song: high v., pf.

Variables of Green   See: Green Loving

Miscellanea

   2439   Meredith, Evan. "Labour in Vain", Twelve Drinking
          Songs, L: MML, pre-1940. Song: [v., pf.?].

GREENE, (Henry) Graham   1904-

Complaisant Lover, The   (DR)   (1959)

   2440   Blatný, Pavel. MS 1964, avail. SČSKU. Incidental
          music to radio script by Josef Henke. Czech.
          title: "Uznalý milenec", transl. by Vladimír
          Pražák.

   2441   Kopelent, Marek. MS 1964, avail. SČSKU. Incidental
          music to radio script by Josef Henke. Czech.
          title: "Uznalý milenec", transl. by Vladimír
          Pražák.

Heart of the Matter, The   (NV)   (1948)

   2442   Pospíšil, Miloš. MS 1968, avail. SČSKU. Incidental
          music to TV script by Vladimír Goldman. Czech.
          title: "Jádro věci", transl. by Břetislav Hodek.

Lieutenant Died Last, The   (SS)   Collier's_Magazine (June
    1940)

    2443 Walton, William. "Went the Day Well?", MS, prod. by
          Ealing Studios 1942. Film music. Released in the
          U.S.A. under the title "Forty-Eight Hours".

Ministry of Fear, The   (NV)   (1943)

    2444 Jirko, Ivan. "The Strange Adventure of Arthur Rowe",
          Prague: Dilia, 1969. Opera. Czech. title:
          "Podivné dobrodružství Arthura Rowa". Libr. by
          the composer, employing portions of the TV script
          by B. Zelenková.

Our Man in Havana   (NV)   (1958)

    2445 Williamson, Malcolm. L: Weinberger, 1963. Opera:
          5 s, 4 ms, 2 a, 10 t, 7 bar, 3 b soli, chorus,
          orch. Libr. by Sidney Gilliat.

Miscellanea

    2446 Waxman, Franz. "Confidential Agent", MS, released by
          Warner Bros. 1945. Film music. Orchn. by Leonid
          Raab. [Film based on Greene's text?]

GREGORY, Isabella Augusta   1852-1932

Spreading the News   (DR)   Samhain (Dec. 1904)

    2447 Bath, Hubert. "Bubbles", MS, prod. 1923. Opera.

Story Brought by Brigit, The   (DR)   (1924)

    2448 May, Frederick. MS pre-1968. Incidental music.

Gregory, Lady Augusta continued

Travelling Man, The   (DR)   <u>Seven Short Plays</u> (1909)

2449 Hart, Fritz. MS 1920. Opera: soli, chorus, orch.
      Also arr. 1920 for pf. accompaniment.

Unicorn from the Stars, The   (DR)   In coll. with W.B. Yeats
    <u>The Unicorn from the Stars and Other Plays</u> (1908)

2450* Anon. L: MacM, 1922 in <u>Plays in Prose and Verse</u>.
      Spoken songs: v., unacc. Settings of
      lines beginning: "Oh come, all ye airy
      bachelors", "Oh, Johnny Gibbons, my five hundred
      healths to you", "When the lion will lose his
      strength". Scores (trad. Irish airs) accompanied
      the 1922 edn. of the play.

Miscellanea

2451 Davies, Filuned. "Will you be as hard?", Cardiff:
      UMP, 1964. Song: bar solo, pf. Welsh title:
      "Fyddi di mor gas?", transl. by T.H. Parry-
      Williams.

2452 Maddison, Adela. "The Heart of the Woods", L:
      Curwen, 1924. Song: solo v., pf.

2453 Maddison, Adela. "The Poet Complains", L: Curwen,
      1924. Song: solo v., pf.

2454 May, Frederick. "Irish Love Song", MS ca. 1930, Dub-
      lin: Pigott. Song: v., pf. Text employs Lady
      Gregory's transl. of a poem by Douglas Hyde.

GRIEVE, Christopher Murray   See: MACDIARMID, Hugh

aggard, Rider

AGGARD, Henry Rider   1856-1925

Cleopatra   (NV)   (1889)

    2455 Enna, August. Lz.: B&H, 1893. Opera.

Stella Fregelius   (NV)   (1904)

    2456 Holoubek, Ladislav. "Stella", MS (Opus 18), prod.
           1939; new version prod. 1948. Opera. Libr. by the
           composer.

Miscellanea

    2457 Chadwick, George W. "Sorais' Song", MS pre-1931.
           Song: [v., pf.?].

ARDY, Thomas   1840-1928

After Reading Psalms xxxix, xl., etc.   "Simple was I and
was young"   Late Lyrics and Earlier (1922)

    2458 Finzi, Gerald. "So I haved fared", Earth and Air
           and Rain, L: BH (WR edn.), 1936. Cyc.: bar solo,
           pf.

After the Club-Dance   "Black'on frowns east on Maidon"
   Time's Laughingstocks and Other Verses (1909) as one of
   "At Casterbridge Fair"

    2459 Goossen, Frederic. At Casterbridge Fair, MS. Cyc.:
           ms, bar soli, pf.

After the Fair   "Singers are gone from the Cornmarket-place,
The"   Time's Laughingstocks and Other Verses (1909) as
one of "At Casterbridge Fair"

2460 Goossen, Frederic. At Casterbridge Fair, MS. Cyc.:
      ms, bar soli, pf.

2461 Hale, Alfred M. At Casterbridge Fair, MS (Opus 27).
      Cyc.: solo v., pf.

Afterwards   "When the Present has latched its postern"
Moments of Vision and Miscellaneous Verses (1917)

2462 Finzi, Gerald. Unf. MS ca. 1930.

2463 Le Fleming, Christopher. Six Country Songs, L: N,
      1963. Cyc.: s, t soli, satb, orch.

Amabel   "I marked her ruined hues"   Wessex Poems (1898)

2464 Finzi, Gerald. Before and After Summer, L: BH, 1949.
      Cyc.: bar solo, pf.

At a Lunar Eclipse   "Thy shadow, Earth"   Poems of the Past
and the Present (1902)

2465 Finzi, Gerald. Till Earth Outwears, ed. by Howard
      Ferguson, Joyce Finzi, Christopher Finzi, L: BH
      (WR edn.), 1958. Cyc.: high v. (best suited for
      t or bar solo), pf.

At Casterbridge Fair   "Sing, Ballad-singer"   Cornhill
Magazine (Apr. 1902), rev. 1909

2466 Cooke, Arnold A. "The Ballad-singer", Country Songs
      MS. Cyc.: b solo, pf.

2467 Goossen, Frederic. "The Ballad-Singer", At
      Casterbridge Fair, MS. Cyc.: ms, bar soli, pf.

2468 Hale, Alfred M. "The Ballad-Singer" At Caster-
      bridge Fair, MS (Opus 27). Cyc.: solo v., pf.

2469 Waxman, Donald. "The Ballad Singer", NY: GX, 1962.
      Song: satb, pf.

At Day-Close in November   "Ten hours' light is abating,
The"   Satires_of_Circumstance (1914)

   2470   Britten, Benjamin. Winter_Words, L: BH, 1954. Cyc.:
       high v., pf.

   2471   Cooke, Arnold A. Country_Songs, MS. Cyc.: b solo,
       pf.

At Middle-Field Gate in February   "Bars are thick with
drops that show, The"   Moments_of_Vision_and
Miscellaneous_Verses (1917)

   2472   Finzi, Gerald. I_Said_to_Love, ed. by Howard
       Ferguson, Joyce Finzi, Christopher Finzi, L: BH
       (WR edn.), 1958. Cyc.: low v., pf.

At News of a Woman's Death   See: Thoughts of Phena

At Tea   "Kettle descants in a cozy drone, The"   Fortnightly
Review (Apr. 1911) as one of "Satires of Circumstance"

   2473   Maw, Nicholas. Six_Interiors, MS. Cyc.: t solo,
       gtr.

   2474   Perry, Zenobia. Choral_Suite_No._1, MS. Choral ste.:
       choir of young v. (satb), pf.

At the Railway Station, Upway   "'There is not much that I
can do...'"   Late_Lyrics_and_Earlier (1922)

   2475   Britten, Benjamin. Winter_Words, L: BH, 1954. Cyc.:
       high v., pf.

Background and the Figure, The   "I think of the slope"
Moments_of_Vision_and_Miscellaneous_Verses (1917)

   2476   Naylor, Bernard. Two_Lyrics, L: S&B, 1930. Song:
       ssaa, pf.

Ballad Singer, The   See: At Casterbridge Fair

Hardy, Thomas continued

Before and After Summer   "Looking forward to the spring"
    New Weekly (Apr. 1914)

    2477 Finzi, Gerald. Before and After Summer, L: BH, 1949.
          Cyc.: bar solo, pf.

Before Life and After   "Time there was--as one may guess,
    A"   Time's Laughingstocks and Other Verses (1909)

    2478 Britten, Benjamin. Winter Words, L: BH, 1954. Cyc.:
          high v., pf.

Bereft   "In the black winter morning"   Time's Laughing-
    stocks and Other Verses (1909)

    2479 Gurney, Ivor. "In the black...", MS 1924. Song:
          [solo v., pf.].

Best she Could, The   "Nine leaves a minute"   Human Shows,
    Far Phantasies, Songs, and Trifles (1925)

    2480 Finzi, Gerald. "The too short time", Before and
          After Summer, L: BH, 1949. Cyc.: bar solo, pf.

"Between us Now"   "Between us now and here"   Poems of the
    Past and the Present (1902)

    2481* Holst, Gustav. MS 1903. Song: bar solo, pf.

Birds at Winter Nightfall   "Around the house the flakes fly
    faster"   Poems of the Past and the Present (1902)

    2482 Finzi, Gerald. Unf. MS ca. 1940.

Blinded Bird, The   "So zestfully canst thou sing?"   Moments
    of Vision and Miscellaneous Verses (1917)

    2483 Dickinson, Peter. Outcry, L: N, 1969. Cyc.: ms solo,
          satb, orch.

294

Boys Then and Now   "'More than one cuckoo?'"   Winter_Words
in_Various_Moods_and_Metres (1928)

   2484 Healey, Derek. "More...", Five_Thomas_Hardy_Songs,
         MS 1961, avail. CMC. Song: s or t solo, pf.

Bullfinches, The   "Brother Bulleys, let us sing"   Poems_of
the_Past_and_the_Present (1902)

   2485 Serrell, Alys F. L: West, 1914. Song: v., pf.

By her Aunt's Grave   "'Sixpence a week,' says the girl"
Fortnightly_Review (Apr. 1911) as one of "Satires of
Circumstance", rev. 1914

   2486 Perry, Zenobia. Choral_Suite_No._1, MS. Choral ste.:
         choir of young v. (satb), pf.

By the Century's Deathbed   "I leant upon a coppice gate"
Graphic (Dec. 1900), rev. 1902

   2487 Caviani, Ronald. "The Darkling Thrush", MS. Song:
         satb, pf.

   2488 Milford, Robin. "The Darkling Thrush", L: OUP, 1930.
         Composition for vln. solo, orch.

By the Earth's Corpse   "'O Lord, why grievest Thou?...'"
Poems_of_the_Past_and_the_Present (1902)

   2489 Finzi, Gerald. Unf. MS ca. 1940.

Bygone Occasion, A   "That night, that night"   Late_Lyrics
and_Earlier (1922)

   2490 Binkerd, Gordon. Shut_Out_that_Moon, NY: BH, 1968.
         Cyc.: high v., pf.

Channel Firing   "That night your great guns, unawares"
Fortnightly_Review (May 1914)

Hardy, Thomas continued

2491 Finzi, Gerald. <u>Before and After Summer</u>, L: BH, 1949.
Cyc.: bar solo, pf.

2492 Heilner, Irwin. MS copyright by composer 1966,
avail. ACA. Song: [med.] solo v., pf.

2493 Smit, Leo. MS 1970. Song: bar solo, pf.

Childhood among the Ferns   "I sat one sprinkling day"
<u>Daily Telegraph</u> (Mar. 1928)

2494 Finzi, Gerald. <u>Before and After Summer</u>, L: BH, 1949.
Cyc.: bar solo, pf.

Choirmaster's Burial, The   "He often would ask us"   <u>Moments</u>
<u>of Vision and Miscellaneous Verses</u> (1917)

2495 Britten, Benjamin. <u>Winter Words</u>, L: BH, 1954. Cyc.:
high v., pf.

Church Romance, A   "She turned in the high pew"   <u>Saturday</u>
<u>Review</u> (Sept. 1906)

2496 Field, Robin. <u>Hearth-Songs</u>, MS 1971. Cyc.: a solo,
vcl.

Clock of the Years, The   "And the Spirit said"   <u>Moments of</u>
<u>Vision and Miscellaneous Verses</u> (1917)

2497 Finzi, Gerald. <u>Earth and Air and Rain</u>, L: BH (WR
edn.), 1936. Cyc.: bar solo, pf.

Colour, The   "'What shall I bring you?...'"   <u>Late Lyrics</u>
<u>and Earlier</u> (1922)

2498 Le Fleming, Christopher. <u>The Echoing Green</u>, L: JWC,
1934. Cta.: solo v. or unison v., pf. Also avail.
for solo v. or unison v., pf., stgs.

2499 Milford, Robin. <u>Four Hardy Songs</u>, L: OUP, 1939.
Song: s or t solo, pf.

2500 Sheldon, Mary. L: Swan, 1924. Song: v., pf.

Hardy, Thomas continued

Come not; yet Come! "In my sage moments" _Human Shows, Far Phantasies, Songs, and Trifles_ (1925)

2501 Ireland, John. "In my...", _Five Poems by Thomas Hardy_, L: OUP, 1927. Cyc.: bar solo, pf.

Comet at Yalbury or Yell'ham, The "It bends far over Yell'ham Plain" _Poems of the Past and the Present_ (1902), subsequently rev.

2502 Finzi, Gerald. _A Young Man's Exhortation_, L: OUP, 1933, copyright assigned L: BH, 1957. Cyc.: t solo, pf.

Comet at Yell'ham, The See: Comet at Yalbury or Yell'ham, The

Convergence of the Twain, The "In a solitude of the sea" _Fortnightly Review_ (June 1912), publ. sep. same year

2503 Shifrin, Seymour. _Satires of Circumstance_, NY: CFP, 1974. Song: ms solo, fl., pic., cl., vln., vcl., db., pf.

Dark-eyed Gentleman, The "I pitched my day's leazings" _Time's Laughingstocks and Other Verses_ (1909)

2504 Bliss, Arthur. [Early] MS. Song: [v., pf.?].

2505 Foss, Hubert J. _Seven Poems by Thomas Hardy_, L: OUP, 1925. Song: t, bar soli, tbar, pf.

Darkling Thrush, The See: By the Century's Deathbed

De Profundis I "Wintertime nighs" _Poems of the Past and the Present_ (1902), subsequently rev.

2506 Douglas, James. _In Tenebris_, MS copyright 1970 by composer, avail. SMA. Song: med. v., vla., pf.

2507 Maw, Nicholas. "In Tenebris", _Six Interiors_, MS. Cyc.: t solo, gtr.

297

Hardy, Thomas continued

De Profundis II   "When the clouds' swoln bosoms echo"
Poems of the Past and the Present (1902), subsequently
rev.

   2508   Douglas, James. In Tenebris, MS copyright 1970 by
          composer, avail. SMA. Song: med. v., vla., pf.

Dead Drummer, The   "They throw in Drummer Hodge"
Literature (Nov. 1899), subsequently rev.

   2509   Edmunds, John. "The Drummer", NY: Mills, pre-1969.
          Song: med. v., pf.

   2510   Hale, Alfred M. "Drummer Hodge", Five War Poems,
          MS (Opus 39), avail. Colby College. Cyc.: female
          solo v., orch.

Ditty   "Beneath a knap where flown"   Wessex Poems (1898),
subsequently rev.

   2511   Finzi, Gerald. A Young Man's Exhortation, L: OUP,
          1933, copyright assigned L: BH, 1957. Cyc.: t
          solo, pf.

Drummer Hodge   See: Dead Drummer, The

During Wind and Rain   "They sing their dearest songs"
Moments of Vision and Miscellaneous Verses (1917)

   2512   Finzi, Gerald. Unf. MS ca. 1950.

Dynasts, The   (DR)   (Vol. 1: 1903, rev. 1904; Vol. 2: 1906;
   Vol. 3: 1908)

   2513   Copley, I.A. "The King's Men", L: L, 1962. Song:
          unison (treble) v. with opt. 2nd part, pf. Sets
          lines beginning: "We be the King's men, hale and
          hearty".

   2514   Dunhill, Thomas F. "Song of the King's Men", L:
          Curwen, 1938. Song: ttbb, pf. Setting of lines
          beginning: "We be the King's men, hale and
          hearty".

2515   Finzi, Gerald. "Budmouth Dears", A_Young_Man's
       Exhortation, L: OUP 1933, copyright assigned L:
       L: BH, 1957. Cyc.: t solo, pf. Setting of lines
       beginning: "When we lay where Budmouth beach is".

2516   Gibbs, C. Armstrong. "The King's Men", L: BH, 1933.
       Song: ttbb, a cap. Sets lines beginning: "We be
       the King's men, hale and hearty".

2517   Gurney, Ivor. "The Night of Trafalgar", MS 1924.
       Song: [v., pf.]. Setting of lines beginning: "In
       the wild October night-time, when the wind raved
       round the land".

2518   Lane, Edgar A. "Sounds of Joyance", in The_Dorset
       Year-book, London (1935). Song: mixed chorus, pf.
       Text from After Scene, Part Third.

2519   Sarson, May. "The King's Men", L: N, 1934. Song:
       unison v., pf. Setting of lines beginning: "We be
       the King's men, hale and hearty".

2520   Scott, Cyril. "Trafalgar", L: BH, 1904. Song: v.,
       pf. Sets lines beginning: "In the wild October
       night-time, when the wind raved round the land".

2521   Sharp, Cecil. MS, perf. London 1914. Incidental
       music.

2522   Shaw, Martin. "Budmouth Dears", L: Curwen, 1927.
       Song: satb, a cap. Setting of lines beginning:
       "When we lay where Budmouth Beach is".

2523   Smith, Boyton. "Budmouth Dears", MS, incl. in the
       programme of The_Trumpet-Major held 5 Dec. 1912.
       Song: [v., pf.]. Setting of lines beginning:
       "When we lay where Budmouth Beach is".

2524   Smith, Boyton. "In the Wild October Night-time", MS,
       incl. in the programme of The_Trumpet-Major held
       5 Dec. 1912. Song: [v., pf.]. Setting of lines
       beginning: "In the wild October night-time, when
       the wind raved round the land".

2525   Smith, Boyton. "My Love's gone a-fighting", MS.
       Song: [v., pf.]. Setting of lines beginning: "My
       Love's gone a-fighting".

2526   Speyer, Charles A. "My love's gone a-fighting", L:
       S, 1921. Song: v., pf. Setting of lines begin-
       ning: "My Love's gone a-fighting".

2527   Vaughan Williams, Ralph. "Buonaparty", L: BH, 1909.
       Song: v., pf. Setting of lines beginning: "We be
       the King's men, hale and hearty".

2528   Wilkinson, Philip G. "The King's Men", L: N, 1956.
       Song: ttbb, a cap. Sets lines beginning: "We be
       the King's men, hale and hearty".

End of the Episode, The   "Indulge no more may we"   Time's
Laughingstocks and Other Verses (1909)

2529   Finzi, Gerald. Unf. MS ca. 1930.

Epeisodia   "Past the hills that peep"   Late Lyrics and
Earlier (1922)

2530   Finzi, Gerald. Before and After Summer, L: BH, 1949.
       Cyc.: bar solo, pf.

Exeunt Omnes   "Everybody else, then, going"   Satires of
Circumstance (1914)

2531   Finzi, Gerald. By Footpath and Stile, L: Curwen,
       1925. Cyc.: bar solo, str. qrt. Composition
       withdrawn by composer.

Face in the Mind's Eye, The   See: Phantom, The

Faithful Swallow, The   "When summer shone"   Human Shows,
Far Phantasies, Songs, and Trifles (1925)

2532   Finzi, Gerald. Unf. MS ca. 1940.

2533   Kittleson, Carl. Three Poems of Thomas Hardy, MS.
       Song: satb, a cap.

Fallow Deer at the Lonely House, The   "One without looks in
to-night"   Late Lyrics and Earlier (1922)

2534 Bliss, Arthur. L: Curwen, 1925. Song: solo v., pf.
      Also avail. for solo v., str. qrt.

Famous Tragedy of the Queen of Cornwall, The   (DR)   (1923),
rev. 1924

    2535* Boughton, Rutland. "The Queen of Cornwall", L: JW,
           1926. Music drama: 3 s, a, 2 t, 2 b soli, satb,
           orch.

Fiddler, The   "Fiddler knows what's brewing, The"   Time's
Laughingstocks and Other Verses (1909)

    2536 Austin, Frederic. Three Wessex Songs, L: BH, 1927.
          Song: bar solo, pf.

    2537 Cooke, Arnold A. Country Songs, MS. Cyc.: b solo,
          pf.

First or Last   "If grief come early"   Late Lyrics and
Earlier (1922)

    2538 Sheldon, Mary. MS 1925, avail. Colby College. Song:
          v., pf.

"For Life I have never Cared Greatly"   "For life I have
never cared greatly"   Moments of Vision and Miscellaneous
Verses (1917)

    2539 Finzi, Gerald. I Said To Love, ed. by Howard
          Ferguson, Joyce Finzi, Christopher Finzi, L: BH
          (WR edn.), 1958. Cyc.: low v., pf.

Former Beauties   "These market-dames, mid-aged"   Time's
Laughingstocks and Other Verses (1909) as one of "At
Casterbridge Fair"

    2540 Finzi, Gerald. A Young Man's Exhortation, L: OUP,
          1933, copyright assigned L: BH, 1957. Cyc.: t
          solo, pf.

    2541 Goossen, Frederic. At Casterbridge Fair, MS. Cyc.:
          ms, bar soli, pf.

Hardy, Thomas continued

2542 Hale, Alfred M. At Casterbridge Fair, MS (Opus 27). Cyc.: solo v., pf.

Friends Beyond   "William Dewy, Tranten Reuben"   Wessex Poems (1898)

2543 Foss, Hubert J. Seven Poems by Thomas Hardy, L: OUP, 1925. Song: t, bar soli, tbar, pf.

Gallant's Song   "When the maiden leaves off teasing" Winter Wards in Various Moods and Metres (1928)

2544 Adeney, Marcus. "The Gallant's Song", MS 1932, avail. CMC. Song: s solo, pf.

Garden Seat, The   "Its former green is blue"   Late Lyrics and Earlier (1922)

2545 Head, Michael. More Songs of the Countryside, L: BH, 1933. Song: low v., pf.

God-Forgotten   "I towered far, and lo! I stood within" Poems of the Past and the Present (1902)

2546 Finzi, Gerald. Unf. MS ca. 1950.

God's Education   See: His Education

Going of the Battery, The   "O it was sad enough"   Graphic (Nov. 1899)

2547 Hale, Alfred M. Five War Poems, MS (Opus 39), avail. Colby College. Cyc.: female solo v., pf.

Great Things   "Sweet cyder is a great thing"   Moments of Vision and Miscellaneous Verses (1917)

2548 Finzi, Gerald. Unf. MS ca. 1920.

2549 Ireland, John. L: A, 1935. Song: solo v., pf.

302

Hap   "If but some vengeful god would call"   Wessex_Poems
   (1898)

   2550 Foss, Hubert J. Seven_Poems_by_Thomas_Hardy, L: OUP,
         1925. Song: t, bar soli, tbar, pf.

He Abjures Love   "At last I put off love"   Time's_Laughing-
stocks_and_Other_Verses (1909)

   2551 Finzi, Gerald. Before_and_After_Summer, L: BH, 1949.
         Cyc.: bar solo, pf.

He Fears his Good Fortune   "There was a glorious time"
Moments_of_Vision_and_Miscellaneous_Verses (1917)

   2552 Finzi, Gerald. Unf. MS ca. 1950.

Her Definition   "I lingered through the night"   Time's
Laughingstocks_and_Other_Verses (1909)

   2553 Binkerd, Gordon. NY: BH, 1968. Song: low v., pf.

Her Song   "I sang that song on Sunday"   Late_Lyrics_and
Earlier (1922)

   2554 Ireland, John. Songs_to_Poems_by_Thomas_Hardy, L:
         CR, 1925. Song: solo v. (best suited for a solo),
         pf.

   2555 Le Fleming, Christopher. Six_Country_Songs, L: N,
         1963. Cyc.: s, t soli, satb, orch.

Her Temple   "Dear, think not that they will forget you"
Late_Lyrics_and_Earlier (1922)

   2556 Finzi, Gerald. A_Young_Man's_Exhortation, L: OUP,
         1933, copyright assigned L: BH, 1957. Cyc.:
         t solo, pf.

   2557 Ireland, John. "Dear...", Five_Poems_by_Thomas
         Hardy, L: OUP, 1927. Cyc.: bar solo, pf.

Hardy, Thomas continued

His Education   "I saw him steal the light away"   Time's
Laughingstocks and Other Verses (1909), subsequently rev.

    2558 Heilner, Irwin. "God's Education", MS copyright by
          composer 1966, avail. ACA. Song: [med.] solo v.,
          pf.

Homecoming, The   "Gruffly growled the wind"   Graphic
(Christmas Number 1903), rev. 1909

    2559 Holst, Gustav. L: S&B, 1913. Song: ttbb, a cap.

Horses Abroad   "Horses in horsecloths stand in a row"
Human Shows, Far Phantasies, Songs, and Trifles (1925)

    2560 Dickinson, Peter. Outcry, L: N, 1969. Cyc.: ms solo,
          satb, orch.

"I Am the One"   "I am the one whom ringdoves see"   Daily
Telegraph (Apr. 1928)

    2561 Finzi, Gerald. Unf. MS ca. 1930.

"I Found Her out There"   "I found her out there"   Satires
of Circumstance (1914)

    2562 Finzi, Gerald. Unf. MS ca. 1920.

"I Look into My Glass"   "I look into my glass"   Wessex
Poems (1898)

    2563 Maw, Nicholas. Six Interiors, MS. Cyc.: t solo,
          gtr.

"I Need not Go"   "I need not go"   Poems of the Past and
the Present (1902)

    2564 Finzi, Gerald. I Said to Love, ed. by Howard
          Ferguson, Joyce Finzi, Christopher Finzi, L: BH
          (WR edn.), 1958. Cyc.: low v., pf.

"I Rose up as My Custom is" "I rose up as my custom is"
Satires of Circumstance (1914)

    2565 Heilner, Irwin. MS copyright by composer 1966,
        avail. ACA. Song: [med.] solo v., pf.

"I Said To Love" "I said to love" Poems of the Past and
the Present (1902), subsequently rev.

    2566 Finzi, Gerald. I Said to Love, ed. by Howard
        Ferguson, Joyce Finzi, Christopher Finzi, L: BH
        (WR edn.), 1958. Cyc.: low v., pf.

"I Say I'll Seek Her" "I say, 'I'll seek her side...'"
Time's Laughingstocks and Other Verses (1909)

    2567 Finzi, Gerald. Oh Fair to See, L: BH, 1966. Cyc.:
        high v., pf.

"I Travel as a Phantom now" "I travel as a phantom now"
Moments of Vision and Miscellaneous Verses (1917)

    2568 Bourgeois, Derek. Six Songs of Wandering, MS 1962.
        Cyc.: bar solo, pf.

"If it's ever Spring again" "If it's ever spring again"
Late Lyrics and Earlier (1922)

    2569* Boughton, Rutland. "Foreboding", Three Hardy Songs,
        L: JW, 1924. Song: solo v., orch. or solo v., pf.

    2570 Le Fleming, Christopher. L: JWC, 1943. Song: ms or
        bar solo, pf.

    2571 Milford, Robin. Four Hardy Songs, L: OUP, 1939.
        Song: t solo, pf.

In a Whispering Gallery "That whisper takes the voice"
Moments of Vision and Miscellaneous Verses (1917)

    2572 Binkerd, Gordon. NY: BH, 1969. Song: satb, a cap.

Hardy, Thomas continued

In a Wood   "Pale beech and pine so blue"   In Wessex Poems
(1898)

2573* Holst, Gustav. MS 1903. Song: bar solo, pf.

In Tenebris I   See: De Profundis I

In Tenebris II   See: De Profundis II

In the Mind's Eye   See: Phantom, The

In Time of "The Breaking of Nations"   "Only a man harrowing
clods"   Saturday Review (Jan. 1916), rev. & publ. sep.
same year, rev. 1917

    2574 Austin, Frederic. "Though Dynasties Pass", Three
          Wessex Songs, L: BH, 1927. Song: bar solo, pf.

    2575 Baber, Joseph. Songs from English Poets, MS (Opus
          12). Cyc.: high v., pf.

    2576 Burritt, Lloyd. MS 1963. Madrigal: satb, a cap.

    2577 Finzi, Gerald. "Only...", MS 1923. Song: bar solo,
          orch. Rev. 1924 and incl. in Requiem in Camera.
          Composition for satb, orch.

    2578 Healey, Derek. Five Thomas Hardy Songs, MS 1961,
          avail. CMC. Song: s or t solo, pf.

    2579 Slater, Gordon. L: OUP, 1926. Song: bar solo, pf.

    2580 Zupko, Ramon. "The Breaking of Nations", NY: CF,
          1964. Song: satb, a cap.

Inquiry, The   "And are ye one of Hermitage"   Time's
Laughingstocks and Other Verses (1909) as one of "At
Casterbridge Fair"

    2581 Goossen, Frederic. At Casterbridge Fair, MS. Cyc.:
          ms, bar soli, pf.

2582 Hale, Alfred M. At Casterbridge Fair, MS (Opus 27).
      Cyc.: solo v., pf.

Inscriptions for a Peal of Eight Bells   "Thomas Tremble new-
      made me" Human Shows, Far Phantasies, Songs, and Trifles
      (1925)

2583 Marshall, Nicholas. L: G, 1965. Song: satb, a cap.

2584 Maw, Nicholas. Six Interiors, MS. Cyc.: t solo,
      gtr.

"It Never Looks like Summer"   "It never looks like summer
      here" Moments of Vision and Miscellaneous Verses (1917)

2585 Finzi, Gerald. Till Earth Outwears, ed. by Howard
      Ferguson, Joyce Finzi, Christopher Finzi, L: BH
      (WR edn.), 1958. Cyc.: high v. (best suited for
      t or bar solo), pf.

Julie-Jane   "Sing; how 'a would sing!"   Time's Laughing-
      stocks and Other Verses (1909)

2586 Cooke, Arnold A. Country Songs, MS. Cyc.: b solo,
      pf.

June Leaves and Autumn   "Lush summer lit the trees to green"
      Daily Telegraph (June 1928)

2587 Finzi, Gerald. Unf. MS ca. 1920.

Last Performance, The   "'I am playing my oldest tunes'"
      Moments of Vision and Miscellaneous Verses (1917)

2588 Rawling, Barbara. "The Old Tunes", L: Curwen, 1965.
      Song: [solo v., pf.].

Let Me Enjoy   "Let me enjoy the earth no less"   Cornhill
      Magazine (Apr. 1909) & Putnam's Magazine (Apr. 1909)

2589 Cooke, Arnold A. Country Songs, MS. Cyc.: b solo,
      of.

Hardy, Thomas continued

2590 Finzi, Gerald. "Let me...", <u>Till Earth Outwears</u>,
      ed. by Howard Ferguson, Joyce Finzi, Christopher
      Finzi, L: BH (WR edn.), 1958. Cyc.: high v. (best
      suited for t or bar solo), pf.

2591 Foster, Ivor. <u>Three Songs</u>, S. Croy.: L, 1947. Song:
      high v., pf.

Life Laughs Onward   "Rambling I looked for an old abode"
<u>Moments of Vision and Miscellaneous Verses</u> (1917)

2592 Finzi, Gerald. <u>Till Earth Outwears</u>, ed. by Howard
      Ferguson, Joyce Finzi, Christopher Finzi, L: BH
      (WR edn.), 1958. Cyc.: high v. (best suited for
      t or bar solo), pf.

Lines to a Movement in Mozart's E-Flat Symphony   "Show me
again the time"   <u>Moments of Vision and Miscellaneous
Verses</u> (1917)

2593 Naylor, Bernard. "Love Lures Life On", <u>Two Lyrics</u>,
      L: S&B, 1930. Song: ssaa, pf.

Little Old Table, The   "Creak, little wood thing, creak"
<u>Late Lyrics and Earlier</u> (1922)

2594 Britten, Benjamin. <u>Winter Words</u>, L: BH, 1954. Cyc.:
      high v., pf.

Looking Across   "It is dark in the sky"   <u>Moments of Vision
and Miscellaneous Verses</u> (1917)

2595 Grant, Parks. NY: AMP, 1949. Song: s or t solo, pf.

Lover to Mistress   "Beckon to me to come"   <u>Human Shows, Far
Phantasies, Songs, and Trifles</u> (1925)

2596 Ireland, John. "Beckon...", <u>Five Poems by Thomas
      Hardy</u>, L: OUP, 1927. Cyc.: bar solo, pf.

Market-Girl, The   "Nobody took any notice of her"   <u>The
Venture</u> (1903), rev. 1909

ardy, Thomas continued

2597 Bax, Arnold. L: MM, 1922, copyright assigned L: C,
1943. Song: solo v., pf.

2598 Finzi, Gerald. Till Earth Outwears, ed. by Howard
Ferguson, Joyce Finzi, Christopher Finzi, L: BH
(WR edn.), 1958. Cyc.: high v. (best suited for
t or bar solo), pf.

2599 Goossen, Frederic. At Casterbridge Fair, MS. Cyc.:
ms, bar soli, pf.

2600 Hale, Alfred M. At Casterbridge Fair, MS (Opus 27).
Cyc.: solo v., pf.

Master and the Leaves, The   "We are budding, Master"   Owl
(May 1919), rev. 1922

2601 Finzi, Gerald. By Footpath and Stile, L: Curwen,
1925. Cyc.: bar solo, str. qrt. Composition
withdrawn by composer.

Mayor of Casterbridge, The   (NV)   Graphic (Jan.-May 1886),
rev. & publ. sep. same year

2602 Tranchell, Peter. MS ca. 1951. Opera. Libr. by the
composer and Peter Scott Bentley.

2603* Vaughan Williams, Ralph. MS 1951, avail. British
Museum. Incidental music for radio.

Men who March Away   See: Song of the Soldiers, The

Merrymaking in Question, A   "'I will get a new string for
my fiddle...'"   Sphere (May 1916)

2604 Finzi, Gerald. Unf. MS ca. 1930.

Middle-Age Enthusiasms   "We passed where flag and flower"
Wessex Poems (1898)

2605 Finzi, Gerald. Unf. MS ca. 1930.

Hardy, Thomas continued

Midnight on the Great Western   "In the third-class seat"
Moments_of_Vision_and_Miscellaneous_Verses (1917)

    2606 Britten, Benjamin. Winter_Words, L: BH, 1954. Cyc.:
          high v., pf.

Mound, The   "For a moment pause"   Winter_Words_in_Various
Moods_and_Metres (1928)

    2607 Finzi, Gerald. MS 1921. Incl. in an incomplete cyc.
          for v., str. qrt.

"My Spirit Will Not Haunt the Mound"   "My spirit will not
haunt the mound"   Poetry_and_Drama (Dec. 1913)

    2608 Diamond, David. NY: SMP, 1952. Song: [med.] solo v.,
          pf.

Neutral Tones   "We stood by a pond"   Wessex_Poems (1898)

    2609 Maw, Nicholas. Six_Interiors, MS. Cyc.: t solo,
          gtr.

News for her Mother   "One mile more is"   Time's_Laughing-
stocks_and_Other_Verses (1909)

    2610 Finzi, Gerald. Unf. MS ca. 1950.

Night in the Old Home   "When the wasting embers redden"
Time's_Laughingstocks_and_Other_Verses (1909)

    2611 Foss, Hubert J. Seven_Poems_by_Thomas_Hardy, L: OUP,
          1925. Song: t, bar soli, tbar, pf.

Night of the Dance, The   "Cold moon hangs to the sky by its
horn, The"   Time's_Laughingstocks_and_Other_Verses (1909)

    2612 Finzi, Gerald. MS 1921. Incl. in an incomplete cyc.
          for v., str. qrt.

rdy, Thomas continued

1967 "In five-score summers!" Time's Laughingstocks and
    Other Verses (1909)

    2613 Finzi, Gerald. "In five-score...", I Said To Love,
         ed. by Howard Ferguson, Joyce Finzi, Christopher
         Finzi, L: BH (WR edn.), 1958. Cyc.: low v., pf.

On a Discovered Curl of Hair "When your soft welcomings
were said" Late Lyrics and Earlier (1922)

    2614 Finzi, Gerald. "On a Discarded Curl of Hair", unf.
         MS ca. 1920.

On a Midsummer Eve "I idly cut a parsley stalk" Selected
Poems of Thomas Hardy (1916)

    2615 Butterworth, Arthur. Four Nocturnal Songs, MS 1948.
         Song: s solo, pf.

Outside the Window "'My stick!' he says" Fortnightly
Review (Apr. 1911) as one of "Satires of Circumstance"

    2616 Perry, Zenobia. Choral Suite No. 1, MS. Choral ste.:
         choir of young v. (satb), pf.

Overlooking the River Stour "Swallows flew in the curves
of an eight, The" Moments of Vision and Miscellaneous
Verses (1917)

    2617 Finzi, Gerald. "Overlooking the River", Before and
         After Summer, L: BH, 1949. Cyc.: bar solo, pf.

Oxen, The "Christmas Eve, and twelve of the clock" The
Times (Dec. 1915), publ. sep. same year

    2618 Britten, Benjamin. L: F, 1968. Carol: sa, pf.

    2619 Cochran, Leslie. L: A, 1927. Carol: [v., pf.].

    2620 Dent, Edward. In Sackbut (Dec. 1920). Song: v., pf.

    2621 Elkus, Jonathan. MS. Song: high v., pf.

311

2622 Finzi, Gerald. By Footpath and Stile, L: Curwen, 1925. Cyc.: bar solo, str. qrt. Composition withdrawn by composer.

2623 Fleming, Robert. L: OUP, 1945. Song: med. v., pf.

2624 Gibbs, C. Armstrong. L: BH, 1952. Song: solo v., pf.

2625 Pasfield, W.R. L: G, 1963. Song: unison v., pf.

2626 Peel, Graham. L: C, 1919. Song: solo v., pf.

2627 Rawsthorne, Alan. L: OUP, pre-1967 in Carols of Today. Carol: mixed v., a cap.

2628* Vaughan Williams, Ralph. This Day (Hodie), L: OUP, 1954. Cta.: s, t, b soli, satb, orch., org.

2629 Williams, Robert. L: N, 1954. Song: unison v., pf.

2630 Winslow, Richard. Phi.: EV, 1958. Song: satb, pf. or satb, org.

Paying Calls "I went by footpath and by stile" Selected Poems of Thomas Hardy (1916)

2631 Finzi, Gerald. By Footpath and Stile, L: Curwen, 1925. Cyc.: bar solo, str. qrt. Composition withdrawn by composer.

Peasant's Confession, The "Good Father!---It was eve in middle June" Wessex Poems (1898)

2632 Gurney, Ivor. MS 1924. Song: [solo v., pf.].

Phantom, The "That was once her casement" Time's Laughingstocks and Other Verses (1909), rev. 1916, rev. subsequently

2633 Finzi, Gerald. "In the Mind's Eye", Before and After Summer, L: BH, 1949. Cyc.: bar solo, pf.

2634 Gurney, Ivor. MS n.d. Song: [solo v., pf.].

Phantom Horsewoman, The   "Queer are the ways of a man I
    know"   Satires_of_Circumstance (1914)

    2635 Finzi, Gerald. "The Phantom", Earth_and_Air_and
          Rain, L: BH (WR edn.), 1936. Cyc.: bar solo, pf.

Pink Frock, The   "O my pretty pink frock"   Moments_of
    Vision_and_Miscellaneous_Verses (1917)

    2636 Milford, Robin. A_Book_of_Songs, L: OUP, 1940. Song:
          Song: ms solo, pf.

Protean Maiden, The   "This single girl is two girls"   Human
    Shows,_Far_Phantasies,_Songs,_and_Trifles (1925)

    2637 Healey, Derek. "This single...", Five_Thomas_Hardy
          Songs, MS 1961, avail. CMC. Song: s or t solo,
          pf.

Proud Songsters   "Thrushes sing as the sun is going, The"
    Daily_Telegraph (Apr. 1928)

    2638 Britten, Benjamin. Winter_Words, L: BH, 1954. Cyc.:
          high v., pf.

    2639 Finzi, Gerald. Earth_and_Air_and_Rain, L: BH (WR
          edn.), 1936. Cyc.: bar solo, pf.

"Regret Not Me"   "Regret not me"   Satires_of_Circumstance
    (1914)

    2640 Finzi, Gerald. "The Dance Continued", A_Young_Man's
          Exhortation, L: OUP, 1933, copyright assigned L:
          BH, 1957. Cyc.: t solo, pf.

Return_of_the_Native,_The   (NV)   Belgravia (Jan.-Dec.
    1878), publ. sep. same year

    2641 Holst, Gustav. "Egdon Heath", L: N, 1928. Orch.
          only. The work was founded on a passage from the
          novel beginning: "...a place perfectly accordant
          with man's nature--neither ghastly, hateful, nor
          ugly...".

Hardy, Thomas continued

Riddle, The   "Stretching eyes west"   Moments of Vision
    and Miscellaneous Verses (1917)

    2642 Binkerd, Gordon. Shut Out that Moon, NY: BH, 1968.
          Cyc.: high v., pf.

Robin, The   "When up aloft"   Moments of Vision and
    Miscellaneous Verses (1917)

    2643 Leighton, Kenneth. The Birds, L: N, 1957. Choral
          ste.: s or t solo, satb, stgs., pf., timp.,
          cym. ad lib.

Rose-Ann   "Why didn't you say you was promised"   Time's
    Laughingstocks and Other Verses (1909)

    2644 Foster, Ivor. Three Songs, S. Croy.: L, 1947. Song:
          high v., pf.

    2645 Hale, Alfred M. L: G&T, 1926. Song: v., pf.

    2646 Sheldon, Mary. MS 1925, avail. Colby College. Song:
          v., pf.

Seasons of her Year, The   "Winter is white on turf and
    tree"   Poems of the Past and the Present (1902)

    2647 Boughton, Rutland. "Alone", Five Songs, MS 1944.
          Song: solo v., vln., pf.

    2648 Kittleson, Carl. Three Poems of Thomas Hardy, MS.
          Song: satb, a cap.

Self-Unseeing, The   "Here is the ancient floor"   Poems of
    the Past and the Present (1902)

    2649 Finzi, Gerald. Before and After Summer, L: BH, 1949.
          Cyc.: bar solo, pf.

    2650 Stewart, D.M. L: A, 1921. Song: solo v., pf., vln.
          obbl. or solo v., pf., vcl. obbl.

Sergeant's Song, The   "When Lawyers strive to heal a breach"
   Wessex Poems (1898) Portions 1st publ. as part of The
   Trumpet-Major in Good Words (Jan.-Dec. 1880)

   2651   Boughton, Rutland. "Quick March", Four Partsongs, L:
          Curwen, 1924. Song: chorus, a cap.

   2652   Finzi, Gerald. "Rollicum-Rorum", Earth and Air and
          Rain, L: BH (WR edn.), 1936. Cyc.: bar solo, pf.

   2653   Foss, Hubert J. Seven Poems by Thomas Hardy, L:
          OUP, 1925. Song: t, bar soli, tbar, pf.

   2654* Holst, Gustav. L: ASH, 1923. Song: bar solo, pf.

   2655   Keel, Frederick. MS pre-1954, L: CR. Song: v., pf.

   2656   Smith, Poyton. "Rollicum-rorum", MS, incl. in the
          programme of The Trumpet-Major held 5 Dec. 1912.
          Song: [v., pf.]. Harmonisation of an air by Harry
          Pouncy.

She, To Him I   "When you shall see me"   Wessex Poems (1898)

   2657   Binkerd, Gordon. Shut Out that Moon, NY: BH, 1968.
          Cyc.: high v., pf.

Sheep Fair, A   "Day arrives of the autumn fair, The"   Human
   Shows, Far Phantasies, Songs, and Trifles (1925)

   2658   Marshall, Nicholas. Five Winter Songs, MS. Song:
          med. v., pf.

Shortening Days at the Homestead   "First fire since the
   summer is lit, The"   Human Shows, Far Phantasies, Songs,
   and Trifles (1925)

   2659   Finzi, Gerald. "Shortening Days", A Young Man's
          Exhortation, L: OUP, 1933, copyright assigned
          L: BH, 1957. Cyc.: t solo, pf.

Shut Out that Moon   "Close up the casement"   Time's
   Laughingstocks and Other Verses (1909)

Hardy, Thomas continued

    2660 Binkerd, Gordon. Shut Out that Moon, NY: BH, 1968.
          Cyc.: high v., pf.

Sigh, The   "Little head against my shoulder"   Time's
Laughingstocks and Other Verses (1909)

    2661 Finzi, Gerald. A Young Man's Exhortation, L: OUP,
          1933, copyright assigned L: BH, 1957. Cyc.: t
          solo, pf.

Sitting on the Bridge   "Sitting on the bridge"   Moments
of Vision and Miscellaneous Verses (1917)

    2662 Bax, Arnold. "On the Bridge", L: MM, 1926, copyright
          assigned L: C, 1943. Song: solo v., pf.

Sleep-Worker, The   "When wilt thou wake"   Poems of the Past
and the Present (1902)

    2663 Foss, Hubert J. Seven Poems by Thomas Hardy, L: OUP,
          1925. Song: t, bar soli, tbar, pf.

So Various   "You may have met a man"   Daily Telegraph
(Mar. 1928)

    2664 Finzi, Gerald. Unf. MS ca. 1920.

Song of the Soldiers, The   "What of the faith and fire
within us"   The Times (Sept. 1914), rev. & publ. sep.
same year

    2665 Lane, Edgar A. "Men Who March Away", L: ASH, 1914.
          Song: solo v., pf.

    2666 Parish, F. Wilson. NY: HWG, 1916. Song: v., pf.

Song of the Soldiers' Wives   "At last! In sight of home
again"   Morning Post (Nov. 1900), rev. 1915

    2667 Hale, Alfred M. "Song of the Soldiers' Wives and
          Sweethearts", Five War Poems, MS (Opus 39),
          avail. Colby College. Cyc.: female solo v., orch.

                              316

Song of the Soldiers' Wives and Sweethearts   See: Song of
     the Soldiers' Wives

Spot, A   "In years defaced and lost"   Poems_of_the_Past_and
     the_Present_ (1902)

     2668 Finzi, Gerald. "In years defaced", Till_Earth
           Outwears, ed. by Howard Ferguson. Joyce Finzi,
           Christopher Finzi, L: BH (WR edn.), 1958. Cyc.:
           high v. (best suited for t or bar solo), pf.

Starlings on the Roof   "No smoke spreads out"   Nation (Oct.
     1913), rev. 1914

     2669 Heilner, Irwin. MS copyright by composer 1966,
           avail. ACA. Song: [med.] solo v., pf.

Stranger's Song, The   See: Three Strangers, The

Subalterns, The   "'Poor wanderer', said the leaden sky"
     Current_Literature (Feb. 1902)

     2670 Finzi, Gerald. MS 1921. Incl. in an incomplete cyc.
           for v., str. qrt.

Summer Schemes   "When friendly summer calls again"   Late
     Lyrics_and_Earlier (1922)

     2671 Cooke, Arnold A. Country_Songs, MS. Cyc.: b solo,
           pf.

     2672 Finzi, Gerald. Earth_and_Air_and_Rain, L: BH (WR
           edn.), 1936. Cyc.: bar solo, pf.

     2673 Ireland, John. Songs_to_Poems_by_Thomas_Hardy, L:
           CR, 1925. Song: solo v. (best suited for a solo),
           pf.

Temporary the All, The   "Change and chancefulness"   Wessex
     Poems (1898)

     2674 Finzi, Gerald. Unf. MS ca. 1950.

Hardy, Thomas continued

Tess_of_the_d'Urbervilles   (NV)   Graphic (July-Dec. 1891),
    subsequently rev. (def. edn. 1912)

2675 d'Erlanger, Frederic. "Tess", Mi.: R, 1909. Opera.
      Engl. libr. by C. Aveling; Ital. libr. by L.
      Illica.

Tess's Lament   "I would that folk forgot me"   Poems_of_the
    Past_and_the_Present (1902)

2676 Douglas, James. "Tess", MS 1973, avail. SMA. Song:
      a solo, vla., pf.

That Moment   "Tragedy of that moment, The"   Human_Snows,
    Far_Phantasies,_Songs,_and_Trifles (1925)

2677 Ireland, John. "The tragedy...", Five_Poems_by
      Thomas_Hardy, L: OUP, 1927. Cyc.: bar solo, pf.

Thoughts of Phena   "Not a line of her writing have I"
    Wessex_Poems (1898), rev. 1916

2678 Finzi, Gerald. "At News of a Woman's Death", unf.
      MS ca. 1920.

Three Strangers, The   (SS)   Longman's_Magazine (Mar. 1883)
    Dramatised version publ. sep. under the title The_Three
    Wayfarers (1893), rev. 1926

2679 Bath, Hubert. MS ca. 1924. Opera.

2680 Gardiner, H. Balfour. "Shepherd Fennel's Dance",
      L: Forsyth, 1911. Pf. only. Orch. score publ.
      1912.

2681* Gardiner, H. Balfour. "The Stranger's Song", L: BH,
      1903. Song: solo v., pf. Setting of lines begin-
      ning: "Oh, my trade it is the rarest one". Score
      based on opening bars composed by Hardy.

2682 Gardiner, Julian. MS, perf. RCM 1936. Opera.

2683 Grant, Parks. "Hangman's Song", MS (Opus 12), avail.
ACA. Song: med. v. (preferably male solo), pf.
Setting of lines beginning: "Oh, my trade it is
the rarest one".

2684 Maconchy, Elizabeth. MS, perf. Hertfordshire 1968.
Opera for children.

Three Wayfarers, The   See: Three Strangers, The

Timing Her   "Lalage's coming"   Moments of Vision and
Miscellaneous Verses (1917)

2685 Finzi, Gerald. Unf. MS ca. 1930.

To an Unborn Pauper Child   "Breathe not, his Heart"   Poems
of the Past and the Present (1902)

2686 Brings, Allen. MS. Song: tb, ww. qnt. or tb, pf.
duet.

To Carrey Clavel   "You turn your back"   Time's Laughingstocks and Other Verses (1909)

2687 Bax, Arnold. "Carrey Clavel", L: MM, 1926, copyright
assigned L: C, 1943. Song: solo v., pf.

2688 Sheldon, Mary. "Carrey Clavel", MS 1924, avail.
Colby College. Song: v., pf.

To Life   "O Life with the sad seared face"   Poems of the
Past and the Present (1902)

2689 Foss, Hubert J. Seven Poems by Thomas Hardy, L: OUP,
1925. Song: t, bar soli, tbar, pf.

2690 Maw, Nicholas. Six Interiors, MS. Cyc.: t solo,
gtr.

To Lizbie Brown   "Dear Lizbie Brown"   Poems of the Past
and the Present (1902)

Hardy, Thomas continued

2691 Finzi, Gerald. Earth and Air and Rain, L: BH (WR edn.), 1936. Cyc.: bar solo, pf.

To Meet, or Otherwise   "Whether to sally and see thee" Sphere (Dec. 1913)

2692 Finzi, Gerald. Unf. MS ca. 1920.

To Sincerity   "O sweet sincerity!"   Time's Laughingstocks and Other Verses (1909)

2693 Milford, Robin. Four Hardy Songs, L: OUP, 1939. Song: s or t solo, pf.

To the Moon   "'What have you looked at, Moon...'"   Moments of Vision and Miscellaneous Verses (1917)

2694 Fulton, Norman. Three Songs, L: A, 1953. Song: high v., pf.

Tolerance   "'It is a foolish thing,' said I"   Satires of Circumstance (1914), subsequently rev.

2695 Milford, Robin. Four Hardy Songs, L: OUP, 1939. Song: s or t solo, pf.

Transformations   "Portion of this yew"   Moments of Vision and Miscellaneous Verses (1917)

2696 Finzi, Gerald. A Young Man's Exhortation, L: OUP, 1933, copyright assigned L: BH, 1957. Cyc.: t solo, pf.

Trumpet-Major, The   See: Sergeant's Song, The

Two Lips   "I kissed them in fancy as I came"   Human Shows, Far Phantasies, Songs, and Trifles (1925)

2697 Finzi, Gerald. I Said To Love, ed. by Howard Ferguson, Joyce Finzi, Christopher Finzi, L: BH (WR edn.), 1958. Cyc.: low v., pf.

320

ardy, Thomas continued

Valenciennes   "We trenched, we trumpeted"   Wessex Poems
   (1898)

   2698 Smith, Boyton. MS, incl. in the programme of The
         Trumpet-Major held 5 Dec. 1912. Song: [v., pf.].

Voice of the Thorn, The   "When the thorn on the down"
   Time's Laughingstocks and Other Verses (1909)

   2699 Foster, Ivor. Three Songs, S. Croy.: L, 1947. Song:
         high v., pf.

Voices from Things Growing   "These flowers are I"   London
   Mercury (Dec. 1921), rev. 1922

   2700 Finzi, Gerald. "Voices from Things Growing in a
         Churchyard", By Footpath and Stile, L: Curwen,
         1925. Cyc.: bar solo, str. qrt. Composition
         withdrawn by composer.

Voices from Things Growing in a Churchyard   See: Voices from
   Things Growing

Wagtail and Baby   "Baby watched a ford, whereto, A"   Albany
   Review (Apr. 1907)

   2701 Britten, Benjamin. Winter Words, L: BH, 1954. Cyc.:
         high v., pf.

Waiting Both   "Star looks down at me, A"   London Mercury
   (Nov. 1924)

   2702 Finzi, Gerald. Earth and Air and Rain, L: BH (WR
         edn.), 1936. Cyc.: bar solo, pf.

   2703 Le Fleming, Christopher. Six Country Songs, L: N,
         1963. Cyc.: s, t soli, satb, orch.

   2704 Shifrin, Seymour. Satires of Circumstance, NY: CFP,
         1974. Song: ms solo, fl., pic., cl., vln., vcl.,
         db., pf.

321

Weathers   "This is the weather the cuckoo likes"   Good
Housekeeping, London (May 1922)

2705   Besly, Maurice. L: [?], 1926. Song: [v., pf.?].

2706   Brown, James. MS. Song: a, bar soli, pf. or a, b
       soli, pf.

2707   Butt, James. L: N, 1965. Song: unison v., pf. or
       high v., pf.

2708   Crossley-Holland, Peter. "The Weather the Cuckoo
       Likes", L: L, 1956. Song: high v., pf.

2709   Finzi, Gerald. Unf. MS ca. 1920.

2710   Fiske, Roger. L: OUP, 1951. Song: ms or bar solo,
       pf.

2711   Gilbert, Norman. L: N, 1957. Song: unison v., pf.

2712   Greenhill, Harold. "A Song of Weathers", L: C,
       1929. Song: solo v., pf.

2713   Head, Michael. More Songs of the Countryside, L:
       BH, 1933. Song: s solo, pf.

2714   Healey, Derek. "This is the weather...", Five
       Thomas Hardy Songs, MS 1961, avail. CMC. Song:
       s or t solo, pf.

2715   Holmes, Rae. MS 1962, avail. University of Auckland.
       Song: satb, a cap.

2716   Ireland, John. Songs to Poems by Thomas Hardy, L:
       CR, 1925. Song: solo v. (best suited for a solo),
       pf.

2717   Kittleson, Carl. Three Poems of Thomas Hardy, MS.
       Song: satb, a cap.

2718   Le Fleming, Christopher. Six Country Songs, L: N,
       1963. Cyc.: s, t soli, satb, orch.

2719   Lovelock, William. L: C, 1958. Song: 2 pt. chorus,
       [pf.?].

2720 Milford, Robin. Rain, Wind and Sunshine, L: OUP,
      1930. Song (in children's cta.): unison v., pf.
      Also publ. sep.

2721 Parry, W.H. Birmingham: Pass, pre-1972. Song: s
      solo, pf.

2722 Pritchard, Arthur J. S. Croy.: L, 1968. Song: satb,
      a cap.

2723 Stone, David. L: OUP, 1951. Song: sa, pf.

2724 Thiman, Fric. L: Elkin, ca. 1950. Song: ssa, a cap.

2725 Thompson, Alan D. Tor.: BMI (Berandol), 1949. Song:
      med. v., pf.

2726 Westrup, Jack. L: BH, 1941. Song: satb, a cap.

2727 Zupko, Ramon. MS. Song: satb, a cap.

"What's there to Tell?"   "What's there to tell of the world"
   Human Shows, Far Phantasies, Songs, and Trifles (1925)

2728 Shifrin, Seymour. Satires of Circumstance, NY: CFP,
      1974. Song: ms solo, fl., pic., cl., vln., vcl.,
      db., pf.

"When I Set Out for Lyonnesse"   "When I set out for
   Lyonnesse"   Satires of Circumstance (1914), subsequently
   rev.

2729 Austin, Frederic. Three Wessex Songs, L: BH, 1927.
      Song: bar solo, pf.

2730* Boughton, Rutland. "A Song of Lyonnesse", Three
      Hardy Songs, L: JW, 1924. Song: solo v., orch. or
      solo v., pf.

2731 Duke, John. NY: CF, 1953. Song: low or high v., pf.

2732 Finzi, Gerald. Earth and Air and Rain, L: BH (WR
      edn.), 1936. Cyc.: bar solo, pf.

2733 Gibbs, C. Armstrong. "Lyonnesse", L: BH, 1921.
      Song: solo v., pf.

2734 Harrison, Sidney. L: A, 1929. Song: [solo v., pf.?].

2735 Hart, Fritz. _Five Songs for Voice and Pianoforte_
      (Opus 120), MS 1938. Song: solo v., pf.

2736 Heilner, Irwin. MS copyright 1966 by composer,
      avail. ACA. Song: med. v., pf. Also avail. for
      low v., pf.

2737 Le Fleming, Christopher. _Six Country Songs_, L: N,
      1963. Cyc.: s, t soli, satb, orch.

2738 McCourt, Tom M. York: Banks, 1937. Song: 2 pt.
      chorus of treble v., pf.

2739 O'Brien, Katharine E. Chi.: H&McC, 1947. Song: ssa,
      s vsp.

2740 Speyer, Charles A. _Six Selected Lyrics_, L: S, 1920.
      Song: solo v., pf.

2741 Walters, Leslie. L: CR, 1957. Song: female or male
      high v., pf. or female or male low v., pf.

Where the Picnic Was   "Where we made the fire"   _Satires of
Circumstance_ (1914)

2742 Finzi, Gerald. _By Footpath and Stile_, L: Curwen,
      1925. Cyc.: bar solo, str. qtr. Composition
      withdrawn by composer.

While Drawing in a Churchyard   "'It is sad that so many of
worth...'"   _Moments of Vision and Miscellaneous Verses_
(1917)

2743 Finzi, Gerald. "In a Churchyard", _Earth and Air and
      Rain_, L: BH (WR edn.), 1936. Cyc.: bar solo, pf.

Wife Waits, A   "Will's at the dance in the Club-room"
Time's Laughingstocks and Other Verses (1909) as one of
"At Casterbridge Fair"

2744 Goossen, Frederic. _At Casterbridge Fair_, MS. Cyc.:
      ms, bar soli, pf.

ardy, Thomas continued

2745 Hale, Alfred M. At Casterbridge Fair, MS (Opus 27). Cyc.: solo v., pf.

2746 Spector, Irwin. MS. Song: ms solo, pf.

Winsome Woman, A "There's no winsome woman" Winter Words in Various Moods and Metres (1928)

2747 Healey, Derek. "There's...", Five Thomas Hardy Songs, MS 1961, avail. CMC. Song: s or t solo, pf.

Without, not Within Her "It was what you bore with you" Late Lyrics and Earlier (1922)

2748 Ireland, John. "It was...", Five Poems by Thomas Hardy, L: OUP, 1927. Cyc.: bar solo, pf.

Woodlanders, The (NV) Macmillan's Magazine (May 1886-Apr. 1887) & Harper's Bazaar (May 1886-Apr. 1887), publ. sep. 1887

2749 Hadley, Patrick. "Scene from The Woodlanders", L: OUP, 1926. Setting for s solo, ch. ensemble (fl., vln., vla., pf.). Text adapt. from the final passage of the novel (Marty South's lament over Giles Winterbourne's grave).

Yell'ham-Wood's Story "Coomb-Firtrees says that Life is a moan" Time's Laughingstocks and Other Verses (1909)

2750 Finzi, Gerald. Unf. MS ca. 1920.

Young Man's Exhortation, A "Call off your eyes from care" Late Lyrics and Earlier (1922)

2751 Finzi, Gerald. A Young Man's Exhortation, L: OUP, 1933, copyright assigned L: BH, 1957. Cyc.: t solo, pf.

Miscellanea

325

2752 Boyer, [?]. "When I Set Out for Lyonnesse". Mention is made of such a setting in Vere H. Collins' Talks with Thomas Hardy at Max Gate (NY: Doubleday, Doran, 1928).

2753 Branson, David. Grove's indicates that Branson's work incl. settings of texts by Hardy.

2754 Byfield, J. Allen. "John and Jane". Further details have not been found. The reader is referred to p. 22 of Carl J. Weber's Hardy Music at Colby: A Check-List (Waterville: Colby College Library, 1945).

2755 Franchi, Dorothy. "The Oxen", MS, perf. Westminster Abbey 1950. Carol. [Text by Hardy?]

2756 Gillis, Ivan M. "When I set out for Lyonesse" [sic], MS pre-1946. Song: [v., pf.?]. [Text by Hardy?]

2757 Holloway, Robin. The Death of God, MS 1972-73, L: OUP. Cta. Incl. verses by Hardy.

2758 May, Frederick. Four Romantic Songs, MS pre-1968. Incl. text by Hardy.

2759 Milford, Robin. Grove's makes reference to 3 songs (dated 1940 & 1944) for b-bar, incl. texts by Hardy.

2760 Pfautsch, Lloyd. "The Oxen", DWG: SPI. Song: satb, a cap. This song is now out of print. [Text by Hardy?]

2761 Smith, Boyton, arr. Carols Sung by the Mellstock Choir, MS 1910. Harmonisation of trad. carols for use in The Mellstock Quire (a dramatisation of Hardy's novel entitled Under the Greenwood Tree).

2762 Tate, Phyllis. A setting publ. L: OUP, 1935 and cited in Carl J. Weber's The First Hundred Years of Thomas Hardy 1840-1940: A Centenary Bibliography of Hardiana (NY: Russell & Russell, 1941) has been withdrawn by the composer.

2763 Warren, Elinor R. "Things We Wished", NY: CF, pre-1940. Song: [v., pf.?].

Hawkins, Anthony Hope

HAWKINS, Anthony Hope   See: HOPE, Anthony

HEATH-STUBBS, John Francis Alexander   1918-

    Canticle of the Sun   "I am the great Sun. This hour begins"
        In Selected Poems (1965)

        2764 Douglas, James. "Sky Canticles", MS 1972, avail.
              SMA. Orch. only.

    For the Nativity   "Shepherds, I sing you, this winter's
        night" In Selected Poems (1965)

        2765 Dickinson, Peter. L: N, 1967. Carol: satb, a cap.

    Hill, The   "All night long in the garden of the cypresses"
        In Selected Poems (1965)

        2766 Douglas, James. MS 1972-73, avail. SMA. Song: med.
              v., pf.

    History of the Flood, The   "Bang Bang Bang"   In The Blue-
        Fly in His Head (1959)

        2767 Crosse, Gordon. L: OUP, 1971. Setting for 2 pt.
              chorus of children's v., hp.

        2768 Lord, David. L: OUP, 1971. Setting for narr.,
              chorus, pf. duet, perc.

    Miscellanea

        2769 Duke, John. Three Gothic Ballads, NY: SMP, 1959.
              Songs: solo v., pf. Songs entitled: "The Old
              King", "The Mad Knight's Song", "The Coward's
              Lament". Score indicates that texts were taken
              from Heath-Stubbs' 1949 publ. entitled Charity
              of the Stars.

Henley, W.E.

HENLEY, William Ernest   1849-1903

"After the grim daylight"   In <u>Hawthorn and Lavender With</u>
      <u>Other Verses</u> (1901)

      2770 Willeby, Charles. <u>Hawthorne and Lavender</u>, L: BH,
            pre-1940. Song: [v., pf.?].

"All in a garden green"   In <u>Hawthorn and Lavender With Other</u>
      <u>Verses</u> (1901)

      2771 Lidgey, Charles A. <u>A Song of Life</u>, L: BH, 1909.
            Cyc.: solo v., pf.

      2772 Whelply, Benjamin. B: BMC, pre-1940. Song: [v.,
            pf.?].

      2773 Willeby, Charles. <u>Hawthorn and Lavender</u>, L: BH, pre-
            1940. Song: [v., pf.?].

"Bring her again, O western wind"   In <u>A Book of Verses</u>
      (1888)

      2774 Beach, Mrs. H.H.A. "Western Wind", MS pre-1914.
            Song: [v., pf.].

      2775 Forsyth, Cecil. NY: HWG, pre-1940. Song: [v., pf.?].

      2776 Hart, Fritz. "Western Wind", <u>Seven Songs</u>, MS 1912
            (Opus 11), avail. State Library of Victoria, Mel-
            bourne. Song: v., pf.

      2777 Hastings, Frank S. "Bring Her Again To Me", NY: GS,
            pre-1940. Song: [v., pf.?].

      2778 Hathaway, J.W.G. "Bring Her Again", L: S&B, ca.
            1926. Song: solo v., pf.

      2779 Johnson, Noel. "Wind of the Western Sea", L: C,
            1904. Song: solo v., pf.

      2780 Korbay, Francis. "Bring Her Again", <u>Album of Five</u>
            <u>Songs</u>, MS pre-1913, L: BH. Song: [v., pf.].

enley, W.E. continued

2781 Mallinson, Albert. "Over the Western Sea", Oakville:
      FH, 1907. Song: a solo, pf.

2782 Parker, Horatio. "Bring Her Again", NY: Silver, 1920
      in The Progressive Music Series, Book 4. Song:
      v., pf.

2783 Ronald, Landon. Echoes, L: E, 1908. Song: high v.,
      pf. Also avail. for med. v., pf. or low v., pf.

2784 Wald, Max. "The Western Sea", B: BMC, pre-1940.
      Song: [v., pf.?].

2785 Watts, Wintter. "Bring Her Again To Me", NY: GS,
      pre-1929. Song: med. v., pf.

"Come where my Lady lies"   In Hawthorn and Lavender With
Other Verses (1901)

2786 Walker, Ernest. "Bluebells from the Clearings", L:
      Elkin, 1904. Song: low v., pf.

"Dear hands, so many times so much"   In Hawthorn and
Lavender With Other Verses (1901)

2787 Lambert, Frank. "Dear Hands", L: C, 1906. Song:
      [solo v., pf.].

"Dearest, when I am dead"   In Hawthorn and Lavender With
Other Verses (1901)

2788 Gurney, Ivor. MS 1908. Song: [solo v., pf.].

2789 Homer, Sidney. "Dearest", NY: GS, 1910. Song: v.,
      pf.

2790 Lambert, Frank. L: C, 1904. Song: [solo v., pf.].

2791 Lidgey, Charles A. A Song of Life, L: BH, 1909.
      Cyc.: solo v., pf.

"Fill a glass with golden wine"   In A Book of Verses (1888)

329

Henley, W.E. continued

2792* Butterworth, George. <u>Love Blows as the Wind Blows</u>,
   MS 1911-12, L: N, n.d. Cyc.: [bar] solo v., str.
   qrt.

2793 Hadley, Henry. NY: GS, 1910. Song: v., pf.

2794 Quilter, Roger. L: BH, 1905. Song: solo v., pf.

Finale "Sigh sent wrong, A" In <u>Hawthorn and Lavender With
Other Verses</u> (1901)

2795 Lidgey, Charles A. "A sigh...", <u>A Song of Life</u>, L:
   BH, 1909. Cyc.: solo v., pf.

"From the brake the Nightingale" In <u>A Book of Verses</u> (1888)

2796 Homer, Sidney. MS (Opus 17), NY: GS. Song: [v.,
   pf.?].

2797 Quilter, Roger. "A Last Year's Rose", <u>Four Songs</u>,
   L: BH, 1910. Song: high v., pf.

2798 Watts, Wintter. "The Nightingale and the Rose", MS
   1922, NY: GS. Song: [v., pf.?].

"Full sea rolls and thunders, The" In <u>A Book of Verses</u>
(1888)

2799 Brinkworth, Francis. L: S&B, pre-1940. Song: [v.,
   pf.?].

2800 Gurney, Ivor. MS 1908. Song: [solo v., pf.].

2801 Korbay, Francis. <u>Album of Five Songs</u>, MS pre-1913,
   L: BH. Song: [v., pf.].

Gray hills, gray skies, gray lights" In <u>Hawthorn and
Lavender With Other Verses</u> (1901)

2802 Lidgey, Charles A. "Gray Hills", <u>A Song of Life</u>, L:
   BH, 1909. Cyc.: solo v., pf.

"Gulls in an aery morrice"   In The Song of Swords And Other Verses (1892)

2803   Gurney, Ivor. MS 1908. Song: [solo v., pf.].

2804   Rogers, Milton A. "Gulls", Five Songs, B: BMC, pre-1940. Song: [v., pf.?].

"I am the Reaper"   In A Book of Verses (1888)

2805*   Elkus, Albert. NY: HWG, 1922. Song: ttbb, pf.

2806   Hart, Fritz. Seven Songs, MS 1917 (Opus 26), avail. State Library of Victoria, Melbourne. Song: v., pf.

"I gave my heart to a woman"   In Poems (1898)

2807*   Hart, Fritz. Seven Songs, MS 1913 (Opus 16). Song: v., pf.

"I send you roses--red, like love"   In Hawthorn and Lavender With Other Verses (1901)

2808   Willeby, Charles. "I Send You Roses", Cin.: Church pre-1940. Song: [solo v., pf.?].

"In the red April dawn"   In Hawthorn and Lavender With Other Verses (1901)

2809   Raybould, Clarence. Four Songs, L: L, 1948. Song: med. v., pf.

2810   Willeby, Charles. Hawthorn and Lavender, L: BH, pre-1940. Song: [v., pf.?].

"In the year that's come and gone, love, his flying feather" In A Book of Verses (1888)

2811   Butterworth, George. Love Blows as the Wind Blows, MS 1911-12, L: N, n.d. Cyc.: [bar] solo v., str. qrt. Arr. (MS 1914), avail. L: N (hire) for [bar] solo v., orch.

2812 Hart, Fritz. "In the Year that's Come and Gone", Seven Songs, MS 1917 (Opus 26), avail. State Library of Victoria, Melbourne. Song: v., pf.

"It was a bowl of roses" In Hawthorn and Lavender With Other Verses (1901)

2813 Clarke, Robert C. "A Bowl of Roses", MS pre-1934, L: C. Song: solo v., pf.

2814 Scott, Francis G. "A Bowl of Roses", MS 1914, avail. SMA. Song: med. v., pf.

"June, and a warm, sweet rain" In Hawthorn and Lavender With Other Verses (1901)

2815 de Zulueta, Pedro. "Oh to be heart on heart", L: C, 1919. Song: solo v., pf.

2816 White, Maude V. "God with Us", L: C, 1902. Song: [v., pf.].

"Kate-a-Whimsies, John-a-Dreams" In A Book of Verses (1888)

2817 Hart, Fritz. "Kate-A-Whimsies", Seven Songs, MS 1912 (Opus 11), avail. State Library of Victoria, Melbourne. Song: v., pf.

Last Post, The "Day's high work is over and done, The" In For England's Sake (1900)

2818 Stanford, C.V. L: BH, 1900. Setting for mixed choir, orch.

"Late lark twitters from the quiet skies, A" In A Book of Verses (1888)

2819 Blower, Maurice. "Evensong", L: N, 1934. Song: satbb, a cap.

2820 Delius, Frederick. "A Late Lark", L: WR, 1931. Song: t solo, orch.

2821   Horne, Jonathan T. "A Late Lark", L: S&B, 1959.
       Song: satb, a cap.

2822   Shepherd, Arthur. "Sundown", MS, avail. University
       of Utah. Song: v., pf.

2823   Sweeting, E.T. "Evening", L: N, 1924. Song: 6 pt.
       choir (2 s, a, t, bar, b), a cap.

"Life in her creaking shoes"   In A Book of Verses (1888)

2824   Butterworth, George. Love Blows as the Wind Blows,
       MS 1911-12, L: N, n.d. Cyc.: [bar] solo v., str.
       qrt. Arr. (MS 1914) avail. L: N (hire) for [bar]
       solo v., orch.

"Life is bitter. All the faces of the years"   In A Book of
Verses (1888)

2825   Hart, Fritz. "Let Me Sleep", Seven Songs, MS 1917
       (Opus 26), avail. State Library of Victoria, Mel-
       bourne. Song: v., pf.

"Look down, dear eyes, look down"   In Hawthorn and Lavender
With Other Verses (1901)

2826   Lambert, Frank. "Look Down, Dear Eyes", L: C, 1904.
       Song: solo v., pf.

2827   Willeby, Charles. "Look Down, Dear Eyes", Hawthorn
       and Lavender, L: BH, pre-1940. Song: [v., pf.?].

"Madam Life's a piece in bloom"   In Poems (1898)

2828   Hart, Fritz. Seven Songs, MS 1913 (Opus 16), avail.
       State Library of Victoria, Melbourne. Song: v.,
       pf.

"Nightingale has a lyre of gold, The"   In A Book of Verses
(1888)

2829   Allitsen, Frances. Spring Contrasts, MS pre-1912,
       L: BH. Song: [v., pf.?].

333

2830* Beach, Mrs. H.H.A. "The Blackbird", MS pre-1914.
      Song: [v., pf.].

2831 Brainard, H.L. "The Blackbird", B: BMC, pre-1940.
      Song: [v., pf.?].

2832 Delius, Frederick. Fünf Gesänge, Köln: T&J, 1915.
      Song: s or t solo, pf.

2833 Densmore, John. "The Nightingale", B: OD, pre-1940.
      Song: [v., pf.?].

2834 Harris, Victor. "The Blackbird", B: Schmidt, 1895.
      Song: high v., pf. Publ. B: Schmidt, 1896 for low
      v., pf.

2835* Hart, Fritz. "The Blackbird", L: Curwen, 1920, Seven
      Songs (Opus 11). Song: v., pf.

2836 Lambert, Agnes H. L: BH, pre-1940. Song: [v., pf.?].

2837 McKinley, Carl. MS 1927, NY: GS. Song: [v., pf.?].

2838 Parker, Horatio. "The Blackbird", Four Songs, NY:
      GS, 1904. Song: med. v., pf.

2839 Quilter, Roger. "Song of the Blackbird", Four Songs,
      L: BH, 1910. Song: high v., pf. Also publ. sep.

2840 Rogers, Milton A. Five Songs, B: BMC, pre-1940.
      Song: [v., pf.?].

2841 Ronald, Landon. Echoes, L: E, 1908. Song: high v.,
      pf. Also avail. for med. v., pf. or low v., pf.

2842 Scollard, W.F. "The Blackbird", B: Birchard, 1925 in
      Folk Songs & Art Songs for Intermediate Grades,
      Vol. I. Canon: voices, pf.

2843 Whelply, Benjamin. B: BMC, pre-1940. Song: [v.,
      pf.?].

"O Falmouth is a fine town with ships in the bay"   In A Book
of Verses (1888)

2844   Duckworth, Arthur. "O Falmouth is a Fine Town",
        L: Elkin, 1959. Song: ttb, pf. Publ. L: Elkin,
        1968 for satb, pf.

2845   Francillon, Rosamond. "Falmouth is a Fine Town", L:
        [JW?], pre-1940. Song: [v., pf.?].

2846   Shaw, Martin. "O, Falmouth is a Fine Town", L: Cur-
        wen, 1920. Song: solo v., pf.

2847   Watts, Wintter. "Falmouth Town", NY: GS, pre-1940.
        Song: [v., pf.?].

"O Gather me the rose, the rose"   In A Book of Verses (1888)

2848   Hart, Fritz. Seven Songs, MS 1917 (Opus 26), avail.
        State Library of Victoria, Melbourne. Song: v.,
        pf.

Of Rain   "Sombre, sagging sky, A"   In A Book of Verses
        (1888)

2849   Willeby, Charles. "Summer Rain", Cin.: Church, pre-
        1940. Song: [v., pf.?].

"On the way to Kew"   In A Book of Verses (1888)

2850   Butterworth, George. Love Blows as the Wind Blows,
        MS 1911-12, L: N, n.d. Cyc.: [bar] solo v., str.
        qrt. Arr. (MS 1914) avail. L: N (hire) for [bar]
        solo, orch.

2851   Clarke, Robert C. L: C, 1921. Song: solo v., pf.

2852   Mallinson, Albert. Oakville: FH, 1907. Song: s or t
        solo, pf.

2853   Foote, Arthur. MS pre-1937, B: Schmidt. Song: [v.,
        pf.?].

"Or ever the knightly years were gone"   In A Book of Verses
        (1888)

335

Henley, W.E. continued

2854   Forsyth, Cecil. "I was a King in Babylon", NY: CF,
        1926. Song: med. v., orch.

"Out of the night that covers me"   In A_Book_of_Verses
   (1888)

2855   Beach, Mrs. H.H.A. "Dark is the Night", MS pre-1914.
        Song: [v., pf.].

2856   Huhn, Bruno. "Invictus", B: Schmidt, 1910. Song: ms
        or bar solo, pf. Also avail. for high v., pf. or
        low v., pf.

2857   Kernochan, Marshall. "Unconquered", NY: GX, 1911.
        Song: solo v., pf.

2858   Korbay, Francis. "Out of the Night", Album_of_Five
        Songs, MS pre-1913, L: BH. Song: [v., pf.].

2859   Lidgey, Charles A. "Out of the Night", A_Song_of
        Life, L: BH, 1909. Cyc.: solo v., pf.

2860   Mueller, Carl F. "Invictus", NY: CF, 1950. Song:
        satb, a cap.

2861   Shaw, Martin. "Invictus", L: Curwen, 1920. Song:
        solo v., pf.

"Praise the generous gods for giving"   In A_Book_of_Verses
   (1888)

2862   Hart, Fritz. "Praise the Generous Gods", Seven
        Songs, MS 1917 (Opus 26), avail. State Library of
        Victoria, Melbourne. Song: v., pf.

"Pretty washermaiden, The"   In A_Book_of_Verses (1888)

2863   Webber, W.S. Lloyd. L: C, 1950. Song: solo v., pf.

Pro Rege Nostro   See: "What have I done for you"

"Sea is full of wandering foam, The"   In A_Book_of_Verses
   (1888)

2864   Gurney, Ivor. MS 1911. Song: [solo v., pf.].

2865   Hart, Fritz. Seven Songs, MS 1917 (Opus 26), avail.
       State Library of Victoria, Melbourne. Song: v.,
       pf.

2866   Hart, Fritz. "The Night is Dark and Loud", Seven
       Songs, MS 1912 (Opus 11), avail. State Library of
       Victoria, Melbourne. Song: v., pf.

"She sauntered by the swinging seas"   In A Book of Verses
    (1888)

2867   Foss, Hubert J. L: OUP, 1927. Song: t solo, pf.

2868   Hart, Fritz. Seven Songs, MS 1917 (Opus 11), avail.
       State Library of Victoria, Melbourne. Song: v.,
       pf.

2869   Hill, Edward B. B: BMC, pre-1940. Song: [v., pf.?].

2870   Issacs, Lewis M. B: Schmidt, pre-1940. Song: [v.,
       pf.?].

"Sing to me, sing, and sing again"   In Hawthorn and Lavender
    With Other Verses (1901)

2871   Homer, Sidney. "Sing To Me, Sing", MS (Opus 28), NY:
       GS. Song: [solo v., pf.?].

2872   Johns, Clayton. "Sing To Me, Sing", MS pre-1932, B:
       BMC. Song: [solo v., pf.?].

2873   Lidgey, Charles A. "Sing To Me", A Song of Life, L:
       BH, 1909. Cyc.: solo v., pf.

"Skies are strown with stars, The"   In A Book of Verses
    (1888)

2874   Hart, Fritz. Seven Songs, MS 1913 (Opus 16), avail.
       State Library of Victoria, Melbourne. Song: v.,
       pf.

"Spirit of wine, The"   In A Book of Verses (1888)

2875   Waller, H. Newton Center: Wa-Wan, 1902 in _Two Songs_.
       Song: v., pf.

"Spring, my dear, The"   In _A Book of Verses_ (1888)

2876   Allitsen, Frances. _Spring Contrasts_, MS pre-1912, L:
       BH. Song: [v., pf.?].

2877   Hart, Fritz. "The Spring, My Dear, is No Longer
       Spring", _Seven Songs_, MS 1917 (Opus 26), avail.
       State Library of Victoria, Melbourne. Song: v.,
       pf.

2878   Palmer, Courtlandt. "Last Year", MS ca. 1920, avail.
       NYPL. Song:.solo v., pf.

2879   Ronald, Landon. _Echoes_, L: E, 1908. Song: high v.,
       pf. Also avail. for med. v., pf. or low v., pf.

"Surges gushed and sounded, The"   In _A Book of Verses_ (1888)

2880   Hart, Fritz. "The Blessing", _Seven Songs_, MS 1912
       (Opus 11), avail. State Library of Victoria, Mel-
       bourne. Song: v., pf.

"There is a wheel inside my head"   In _A Book of Verses_
(1888)

2881   Coppola, Piero. L: Curwen, 1923. Song: solo v., pf.

"Thick is the darkness"   In _A Book of Verses_ (1888)

2882   Hart, Fritz. _Seven Songs_, MS 1913 (Opus 16), avail.
       State Library of Victoria, Melbourne. Song: v.,
       pf.

2883   Johnson, William S. NY: CPMC, pre-1940. Song: [v.,
       pf.?].

2884   Korbay, Francis. _Album of Five Songs_, MS pre-1913,
       L: BH. Song: [v., pf.].

2885   Liddle, Samuel. "Onward", L: C, 1918. Song: solo v.,
       pf.

"This is the moon of roses"   In <u>Hawthorn and Lavender With Other Verses</u> (1901)

    2886   Bassett, Karolyn W. "The Moon of Roses", MS pre-
           1931, NY: GS. Song: [v., pf.?].

    2887   Crist, Bainbridge. NY: CF, 1918. Song: solo v., pf.

    2888   Johns, Clayton. "The Moon of Roses", MS pre-1932,
           B: BMC. Song: [v., pf.?].

"To me at my fifth-floor window"   In <u>A Book of Verses</u> (1888)

    2889   Mallinson, Albert. Oakville: FH, 1907. Song: s or t
           solo, pf.

To My Mother   "Chiming a dream by the way"   In <u>A Book of Verses</u> (1888)

    2890   Allen, Elizabeth Y. "Echoes", <u>Echoes</u>, B: OD, pre-
           1940. Song: [v., pf.?].

To My Wife   "Take, my dear, my little sheaf of songs"   In <u>A Book of Verses</u> (1888)

    2891   Riesenfeld, Hugo. "Dedication", MS pre-1939, NY: GS.
           Song: [solo v., pf.?].

    2892   Ronald, Landon. "Dedication", <u>Echoes</u>, L: E, 1908.
           Song: high v., pf. Also avail. for med. v., pf.
           or low v., pf.

"'Twas in a world of living leaves"   In <u>Hawthorn and Lavender With Other Verses</u> (1901)

    2893   Beach, John. Newton Center: Wa-Wan, pre-1940. Song:
           [v., pf.?].

Vigil   "Lived on one's back"   In <u>A Book of Verses</u> (1888)

    2894   Chanler, Theodore. "The Patient Sleeps", NY: GS,
           1949. Song: solo v., pf.

"Ways are green with the gladdening sheen, The"   In A Book
     of Verses (1888)

     2895   White, Maude V. "The Fifes of June", L: C, 1900.
            Song: solo v., pf.

"We flash across the level"   In A Book of Verses (1888)

     2896   Mallinson, Albert. "We Sway Along", Oakville: FH,
            1907. Song: a or bar solo, pf.

"We shall surely die"   In A Book of Verses (1888)

     2897   Hart, Fritz. Seven Songs, MS 1913 (Opus 16), avail.
            State Library of Victoria, Melbourne. Song: v.,
            pf.

"We'll go no more a-roving by the light of the moon"   In A
     Book of Verses (1888)

     2898   Ronald, Landon. "We'll go no more a-roving", Echoes,
            L: E, 1908. Song: high v., pf. Also avail. for
            med. v., pf. or low v., pf.

"We'll to the woods and gather may"   In A Book of Verses
     (1888)

     2899   Fletcher, H. Grant. "We'll to the Woods", MS. Song:
            ssa, pf. Incl. as a song for a solo, pf. in Three
            Songs for Low Voice and Piano, and as a song for
            s solo, pf. in Three Songs for High Voice and
            Piano.

     2900   Griffes, Charles T. Tone-Images, NY: GS, 1915. Song:
            v., pf. Arr. by Gwynn S. Bement for women's
            chorus; arr. publ. NY: GS, [1940?].

"What have I done for you"   In The Song of the Sword And
     Other Verses (1892), rev. 1900

     2901   Shaw, Martin. "England, my England", L: BH, pre-
            1914. Song: solo v., pf.

2902 Vaughan Williams, Ralph. "England, my England", L:
      OUP, 1941. Song: bar solo, dbl. choir, unison v.,
      orch. Also arr. for satb.

2903 Willan, Healey. "England My England", MS 1911. Cta.:
      unison v., pf. Rev. and arr. for satb, orch. (MS
      1914); arr. publ. NY: HWG, 1914 (re-issued Oak-
      ville: FH, 1941).

"Where forlorn sunsets flare and fade"   In A Song of Swords
And Other Verses (1892)

2904 Blosdale, Don L. "Over the Hills", NY: CPI, 1955.
      Song: satb, a cap.

"While the west is paling"   In A Book of Verses (1888)

2905 Gaul, Harvey B. MS 1926, B: OD. Song: [v., pt.?].

2906 Korbay, Francis. Album of Five Songs, MS pre-1913,
      L: BH. Song: [v., pf.].

2907 Watts, Wintter. "Only and Forever", MS 1923, NY: GS.
      Song: med. v., pf.

"Why, my heart, do we love her so?"   In The Song of the Sword
And Other Verses (1892)

2908 Clarke, Robert C. "Geraldine", L: C, 1921. Song:
      [solo v., pf.].

"Wind on the wold, The"   In Hawthorn and Lavender With Other
Verses (1901)

2909 Lidgey, Charles A. A Song of Life, L: BH, 1909.
      Cyc.: solo v., pf.

2910 Walker, Ernest. L: N, 1951. Song: high v., pf.

2911 Willan, Healey. MS 1914. Song: [v., pf.].

"Wink from Hesper, falling, A"   In A Book of Verses (1888)

341

Henley, W.E. continued

    2912   Hart, Fritz. <u>Seven Songs</u>, MS 1913 (Opus 16), avail.
           State Library of Victoria, Melbourne. Song: v.,
           pf.

"With strawberries we filled a tray"   In <u>A Book of Verses</u>
(1888)

    2913   O'Neill, Norman. "With Strawberries", <u>Five Rondels</u>,
           MS 1907, L: Cary (Avison edn.). Song: med. v.,
           pf.

    2914   Sowerby, Leo. B: BMC, pre-1940. Song: [v., pf.?].

"World of leafage murmurous and a-twinkle, A"   In <u>Hawthorn
and Lavender With Other Verses</u> (1901)

    2915   Willeby, Charles. "A World of Leafage", <u>Hawthorn and
           Lavender</u>, L: BH, pre-1940. Song: [v., pf.?].

"Your feet as glad"   In <u>Hawthorn and Lavender With Other
Verses</u> (1901)

    2916   Willeby, Charles. "Your Feet as Glad and Light",
           <u>Hawthorn and Lavender</u>, L: BH, pre-1940. Song:
           v., pf.?].

"Your heart has trembled to my tongue"   In <u>A Book of Verses</u>
(1888)

    2917   Hart, Fritz. NY: GS, 1920, <u>Seven Songs</u>, MS 1913
           (Opus 16). Song: v., pf.

    2918   Ronald, Landon. "Your Heart has trembled", <u>Echoes</u>,
           L: E, 1908. Song: high v., pf. Also avail. for
           med. v., pf. or low v., pf.

Miscellanea

    2919   Boughton, Rutland. "Sea Grave", <u>Six Songs of Man-
           hood</u>, MS 1903. Song: v., pf.

2920 Clough-Leighter, Henry. "Dearest, when I am dead",
Love_Sorrow, MS (Opus 44), NY: GS, pre-1929.
Cyc.: high v., pf., obbl. vln., obbl. vcl. [This
song a setting of Henley's text?]

2921 Hart, Fritz. "Flown", Seven_Songs, MS 1912 (Opus
11), avail. State Library of Victoria, Melbourne.
Song: v., pf.

2922 Lambert, Agnes H. "Philomel", Ten_Songs_from_a_Gar-
den, L: B, pre-1940. Song: [v., pf.?].

2923 McDonald, Harl. "Evening", MS 1940, Ph.: EV. Song:
ssaa, pf. [Possibly a setting of "A late lark
twitters from the quiet skies"?]

2924 O'Neill, Norman. "Rondeau", Five_Rondels, MS 1907,
L: Cary (Avison edn.). Song: med. v., pf.

2925 Spalding, Walter R. "Sea Song", NY: GS, pre-1940.
Song: [v., pf.?].

2926 Spalding, Walter R. "Sorrow and Joy", NY: GS, pre-
1940. Song: [v., pf.?].

2927 White, Maude V. "Last Year", L: C [ca. 1900?]. Song:
solo v., pf. [Possibly a setting of "From the
brake the Nightingale"?]

2928 Willeby, Charles. "A Garden Song", B: BMC, pre-1940.
Song: [v., pf.?].

HENRI, Adrian Maurice   1932-

Adrian Henri's Talking After Christmas Blues   "Well I woke
this mornin' it was Christmas Day"   In The_Mersey_Sound,
Penguin Modern Poets 10 (1967)

2929 Southam, T. Wallace. L: Turret, 1969 in Contemporary
Poetry_Set_to_Music. Song: v., pf.

Henri, Adrian continued

In the Midnight Hour   "When we meet in the midnight hour"
   In The Mersey Sound, Penguin Modern Poets 10 (1967)

2930   McCabe, John. "When we...", This Town's a Cor-
       poration full of Crooked Streets, L: N, 1969
       (hire). "An entertainment" for t solo, sp., mixed
       chorus, children's choir, stgs., tpt., perc.,
       keyboards.

Miscellanea

2931   McCabe, John. This Town's a Corporation full of
       Crooked Streets, L: N, 1969 (hire). "An enter-
       tainment" for t solo, sp., mixed chorus, child-
       ren's choir, stgs., tpt., perc., keyboards. Incl.
       a setting of Henri's "Liverpool 8" ("Liverpool
       8...A district of beautiful, fading, decaying
       Georgian terrace houses...").

HERBERT, Alan Patrick*   1890-1971

Bacon and Eggs   "Now blest be the Briton"   In Laughing Ann
   and Other Poems (1925)

2932   Blyton, Carey. Three Food Songs, L: S&B, copyright
       assigned Wendover: RP, 1973. Song: solo v., pf.
       or unsion v., pf. Setting of lines beginning:
       "What wonder the Frenchman, blown out with new
       bread".

Big Ben   (Libr.)   (1946)

2933   Ellis, Vivian. MS, perf. London, July 1946; publ.
       L: Elkin. Musical.

Bless the Bride   (Libr.)   (1948)

2934   Ellis, Vivian. MS, perf. London, Apr. 1947; publ.
       L: C. [Light] opera.

rbert, A.P. continued

Derby Day   (Libr.)   (1931) Portions were 1st publ. in Punch

    2935 Reynolds, Alfred. MS ca. 1931, L: Elkin. Opera.

Four Negro Commercials   "Dere ain't no wimmin in Hebb'n"
In Ballads_for_Broadbrows (1930) 1st publ. in Punch

    2936 Reynolds, Alfred. MS pre-1930. Song: [v., pf.?].

Helen   (Libr.)   (1932) Based on La_Belle_Helene by Henri
Meilhac & Ludovic Halevy.

    2937 Korngold, Erich, arr. L: C, 1932. Opera. Music arr.
         from the original score by Jacques Offenbach.

King of the Castle   (DR)   Unpubl. in entirety. A portion
was publ. in Laughing_Ann_and_Other_Poems (1925) under the
title "Bacon and Eggs".

    2938 Arundell, Dennis. MS, perf. Liverpool 1924. In-
         cidental music.

    2939 Blyton, Carey. See: "Bacon and Eggs".

Riverside_Nights   (DR)   In coll. with Nigel Playfair
(1926)

    2940 Austin, Frederic in coll. with Alfred Reynolds and
         Harold Scott. MS, perf. London, Apr. 1926.
         "Musical entertainment".

    2941 Reynolds, Alfred. "The Policeman's Serenade", MS,
         perf. London, Apr. 1926. [See entry above.]
         This selection was subsequently publ. L: C.

    2942 Scott, Harold in coll. with Frederic Austin and Al-
         fred Reynolds. MS, perf. London, Apr. 1926.
         "Musical entertainment".

    2943 Tate, Phyllis. "The Policeman's Serenade", MS ca.
         1932. Operetta.

Herbert, A.P. continued

Tantivy Towers (Libr.) (1931) Portions 1st publ. in
Ballads for Broadbrows (1930)

2944 Dunhill, Thomas F. L: CR, 1930. [Light] opera.

Water Gipsies, The (NV) (1930)

2945 Ellis, Vivian. L: C, 1957. Play with music. Lyrics
by Herbert, adapt. from his novel.

Miscellanea

2946 Austin, Richard. "Plain Jane", MS 1929. Opera.
Herbert's libr. was publ. L: Samuel French.

2947 Lidgey, Charles A. "The Likes Of They", L: C. Song:
solo v., pf.

2948 Sargent, Malcolm, arr. The 1959 issue of the British
Catalogue of Music lists a song entitled "Star in
the south" (words by Herbert) incl. in Two Folk
Carols (L: OUP, 1958). The song (for satb, a
cap.) is based on a Polish folk tune.

2949 Toye, Francis. Grove's lists an opera (prod. 1927)
entitled "The Red Pen". Libr. by Herbert.

HEWLETT, Maurice Henry 1861-1923

Ippolita in the Hills (NV) In Little Novels of Italy
(1899)

2950 Křička, Jaroslav. "Ippolita", Prague: FB, 1917.
Opera. Czech. title: "Hipolyta". Libr. by the
composer and Petr Křička.

Masque of Dead Florentines, A (DR) (1895)

wlett, Maurice continued

    2951 Kroeger, Ernest R. B: OD, 1917. Setting for reciter,
           unison chorus, pf.

LL, Geoffrey   1932-

  In Piam Memoriam "Created purely from glass the saint
  stands" In For_the_Unfallen (1959)

    2952 Orton, Richard. MS 1962. Song: 4 soli (s, a, t, b),
           unacc.

NKSON, Katharine   See: TYNAN, Katharine

ODGSON, Ralph   1871-1962

  Gipsy Girl, The "'Come, try your skill, kind gentlemen...'"
  Saturday_Review (June 1911), rev. 1917

    2953 Milford, Robin. L: OUP, 1924. Song: unison v., pf.

  Hammers, The "Noise of hammers once I heard" Saturday
  Review (Mar. 1907)

    2954 Baber, Joseph. Songs_from_English_Poets, MS (Opus
           12). Cyc.: high v., pf.

    2955 Taylor, Clifford. Collected_Songs_(1950-54), MS
           1950-54, avail. ACA. Song: s or t solo, pf.

Hodgson, Ralph continued

Moor, The   "World's gone forward to its latest fair, The"
     In Poems (1917)

     2956   Milford, Robin. L: OUP, [1924?]. Song: bar solo, pf.

Mystery, The   "He came and took me by the hand"   In The
     Mystery and Other Poems (1913)

     2957   Benjamin, Arthur. L: BH, 1958. Song: satb, a cap.

     2958   Rubbra, Edmund. Two Songs, MS 1922 (Opus 4). Song:
             v., unacc.

Time   "Time, you old gipsy man"   Saturday Review (Nov.
     1911), rev. 1917

     2959   Gurney, Ivor. "Time, you old Gipsy Man", MS 1920.
             Song: [solo v., pf.].

     2960   Warren, Elinor R. "Time, You Old Gipsy Man, NY: BH,
             avail. only from composer. Song: solo v., pf.

Time, you Old Gipsy Man   See: Time

HOLBROOK, David Kenneth   1923-

   Miscellanea

     2961   Joubert, John. "The Quarry", L: N, 1967. Opera [for
             young players]: s, 2 t, bar, b soli, speakers,
             chorus ad lib., orch. Libr. by Holbrook.

     2962   Mellers, Wilfrid H. Early Light, L: N, 1966. Songs
             (for young people): satb, pf. Texts entitled:
             "First Flames", "The Flowers Shake Themselves
             Free".

pe, Anthony

English Nell   See: Simon_Dale

Heart_of_Princess_Osra,_The   (NV)   (1896)

    2963 Bunning, Herbert. "Princess Osra", L: E, 1902.
          Opera.

Nell Gwyn   See: Simon_Dale

Simon_Dell   (NV)   (1898)

    2964 German, Edward. "Nell Gwyn", MS, prod. London 1900.
          Incidental music (overture and dances) to Hope's
          dramatic version (entitled "Nell Gwyn" or
          "English Nell") of his novel.

OPKINS, Gerard Manley   1844-1889

"As kingfishers catch fire, dragonflies draw fláme"   Poems
   of_Gerard_Manley_Hopkins (1918)

    2965 Hold, Trevor. Four_Sonnets_of_Gerard_Manley_Hopkins,
          MS 1965-67. Setting for satb, a cap.

Blessed Virgin compared to the Air we Breathe, The   See:
   Mother Mary of Divine Grace Compared to the Air We
   Breathe

Caged Skylark, The   "As a dare-gale skylark scanted in a
   dull cage"   Poems_of_Gerard_Manley_Hopkins (1918)

    2966 Campbell, Arthur. God's_Grandeur, MS. Cyc.: high v.,
          pf.

(Carrion Comfort)   "Not, I'll not, carrion comfort, Despair"
Poems of Gerard Manley Hopkins (1918)

2967   Langley, Bernard P. Three Dark Sonnets, MS. Setting
        for t solo, orch. or t solo, pf.

2968   Morgan, Diane. The Seeker, MS, avail. CMC. Cyc.: bar
        solo, pf.

2969   Talma, Louise. "Not, I'll Not...", MS 1950, Two
        Sonnets (MS 1946, 1950). Song: bar solo, pf.

2970   Wilson, James. "Not, I'll not...", Carrion Comfort,
        MS 1966. Cyc.: high bar solo, pf.

Easter   "Break the box and shed the nard"   Poems of Gerard
Manley Hopkins (1930)

2971   Gow, David. Two Choral Songs, L: Elkin, 1965. Song:
        ssaa, a cap. Other song in the collection
        requires ssa.

God's Grandeur   "World is charged with the grandeur of God,
The"   Lyra Sacra: A Book of Religious Verse (1895)

2972   Bliss, Arthur. The World is Charged with the
        Grandeur of God, L: N, 1970. Cta.: satb, 2 fl.,
        3 tpt., 4 trbn.

2973   Brown, Newel K. Hopkins Set, MS. Song: bar solo,
        t trbn.

2974   Campbell, Arthur. God's Grandeur, MS. Cyc.: high v.,
        pf.

2975   Dickinson, Peter. Four Gerard Manley Hopkins Poems,
        MS 1960-64. Cyc.: s, bar soli, satb, org.

2976   Douglas, James. Light Shining Out of Darkness, MS
        1966, avail. SMA. Song: med. v., vcl.

2977   Leighton, Kenneth. L: N, 1959. Motet: satb, a cap.

2978   Maves, David. NY: CMP, copyright by composer 1968.
        Setting for satb, orch. or satb, pf.

2979   Pellegrini, Ernesto. MS 1967. Song: satb, a cap.

2980   Perry, Malcolm. L: Curwen, 1964. Setting for equal
       v. (ss), pf.

2981   Robertson, Donna N. Five Odes to God in Nature on
       Poems by Gerard M. Hopkins, MS 1969. Choral ste.:
       satb, a cap.

2982   Rubbra, Edmund. Inscape, S. Croy.: L, 1965. Ste.:
       satb, stgs., hp. or satb, pf.

2983   Shaw, Martin. L: OUP, 1948. Anthem: satb, stgs.,
       drums, org.

2984   Unsworth, Arthur. "Never Spent", MS. Setting for
       satb, pf.

2985   Ward, Robert. Sacred Songs for Pantheists, NY: HP,
       1966. Song: s solo, orch. or s solo, pf.

2986   Whear, Paul W. Cl.: LW, 1975. Song: ms solo, pf.

Habit of Perfection, The   "Elected Silence, sing to me"
The Poets and the Poetry of the XIXth Century, Vol. VIII
(1893)

2987   Krenek, Ernst. Instant Remembered, MS 1967-68,
       avail. Kassel: Bärenreiter. Cta.: s solo, ch.
       orch.

Heaven-Haven   "I have desired to go"   Lyra Sacra: A Book
of Religious Verse (1895)

2988   Barber, Samuel. "A Nun takes the Veil", NY: GS,
       1961. Setting for satb, a cap. Also avail. for
       ssaa, a cap. or ttbb, a cap.

2989   Barlow, David. MS. Song: a solo, pf.

2990   Bliss, Arthur. "I have...", The World is Charged
       with the Grandeur of God, L: N, 1970. Cta.: satb,
       2 fl., 3 tpt., 4 trbn.

2991   Cruft, Adrian. Two Songs of Quiet, L: JW, 1961.
       Song: s solo, vln.

2992   Dickinson, Peter. Four Gerard Manley Hopkins Poems,
        MS 1960-64. Cyc.: s, bar soli, satb, org.

2993   Dougherty, Celius. NY: CF, 1956. Song: med. v., pf.

2994   Flanagan, William. NY: Peer, 1952. Song: [med.] solo
        v., pf.

2995   Freed, Arthur. NY: Dow, 1957. Song: satb, a cap.

2996   Pinkham, Daniel. Eight Poems of Gerard Manley
        Hopkins, B: Ione, 1970. Song: t-bar or bar solo,
        vla.

2997   Ward, Robert. Sacred Songs for Pantheists, NY: HP,
        1966. Song: s solo, orch. or s solo, pf.

"How looks the night? There does not miss a star"   Poems of
Gerard Manley Hopkins (1948)

2998   Orton, Richard. "Four Fragments", MS 1963. Song: ms
        solo, pf. One song only comprised of four Hopkins
        fragments.

Hurrahing in Harvest   "Summer ends now; now, barbarous in
    beauty, the stooks arise"   Poems of Gerard Manley Hopkins
    (1918)

2999   Berkeley, Lennox. "Summer ends...", Autumn's Legacy,
        L: JWC, 1963. Cyc.: high v., pf.

3000   Langley, Bernard P. MS 1970-72. Song: t solo, orch.
        or t solo, pf.

3001   Robertson, Donna N. Five Odes to God in Nature on
        Poems by Gerard M. Hopkins, MS 1969. Choral ste.:
        satb, a cap.

3002   Williams, Grace. Six Poems by Gerard Manley Hopkins,
        MS 1958, avail. BBC. Cyc.: a solo, str. sextet.

"I wake and feel the fell of dark, not day"   Poems of Gerard
Manley Hopkins (1918)

3003 Druckman, Jacob. "Antiphonies II", NY: BH, in prep.
for publ. Setting for 2 satb choruses, a cap.

3004 Kunz, Alfred. "I wake and feel the fell of dark",
MS 1960, English and German Songs (MS ca. 1953-
62), avail. CMC. Song: solo v., pf.

3005 Langley, Bernard P. "Most Dark Decree", Three Dark
Sonnets, MS. Setting for t solo, orch. or t solo,
pf.

3006 Souster, Tim. Two Choruses, L: I, 1968. Setting for
2 s, a, 2 t, 2 b septet, unacc. or ssattbb, a cap.

3007 Talma, Louise. MS 1946, Two Sonnets (MS 1946, 1950).
Song: bar solo, pf.

3008 Wilson, James. Carrion Comfort, MS 1966. Cyc.: high
bar solo, pf.

Inversnaid   "This darksome burn, horseback brown"   The
Poets and the Poetry of the XIXth Century, Vol. VIII
(1893)

3009 Langley, Bernard P. MS 1963-67. Song: s solo, fl.,
cl., str. qrt.

3010 Peterson, Wayne. MS 1954. Song: s or t solo, pf.
This setting is incl. in an untitled cyc.

Jesu, Dulcis Memoria   "Jesus to cast one thought upon"
America (Sept. 1947) Transl. of a Latin hymn

3011 Davies, Hubert. MS. Setting for satb, pf. or satb,
pf., stgs. or satb, stgs.

3012 Pinkham, Daniel. "Jesus to cast...", Eight Poems of
Gerard Manley Hopkins, B: Ione, 1970. Song: t-bar
or bar solo, vla.

3013 Woollen, Russell. Suite for High Voice, MS copyright
by composer 1959, avail. ACA. Ste.: high v., pf.

Lantern out of Doors, The   "Sometimes a lantern moves along
the night"   Poems of Gerard Manley Hopkins (1918)

3014 Rubbra, Edmund. Inscape, S. Croy.: L, 1965. Ste.:
      satb, stgs., hp. or satb, pf.

Leaden Echo and the Golden Echo, The   "How to keep--is
   there any any, is there none such, nowhere"   Poems of
   Gerard Manley Hopkins (1918)

   3015 Farquhar, David. MS. Song: s solo, satb, orch.

   3016 Klimko, Ronald. Echoes, MS reprod. (1968), avail.
         Ann Arbor: University Microfilms. Dance cta.:
         satb, orch., elec. sounds.

   3017* Maconchy, Elizabeth. MS. Setting for satb, ch. orch.

   3018 Nowak, Lionel. "Maidens' Song from St. Winefred's
         Well", MS, avail. ACA. Song: s solo, cl., vln.,
         pf.

   3019 Parris, Robert. MS 1960, avail. ACA. Song: bar solo,
         orch. or bar solo, pf.

   3020 Talma, Louise. MS 1950-51. Song: s solo, mixed dbl.
         chorus, pf.

   3021 Wellesz, Egon. L: S, 1942. Cta.: s solo, cl., vln.,
         vcl., pf.

Mary Mother of Divine Grace Compared to the Air We Breathe
   "Wild air, world-mothering air"   A Book of Christmas
   Verse (1895), rev. 1918

   3022 Milner, Anthony. "Noon", Our Lady's Hours, L: N,
         1959. Cyc.: s or t solo, pf.

May Magnificat, The   "May is Mary's month"   Poems of Gerard
   Manley Hopkins (1918)

   3023 Mellers, Wilfrid H. "A May Magnificat", MS 1966, L:
         N (hire). Setting for ms solo, orch.

"Moonless darkness stands between"   Poems of Gerard Manley
   Hopkins (1948)

opkins, Gerard Manley continued

3024 La Montaine, John. "Now begin on Christmas day",
Songs of the Nativity, NY: HWG, pre-1969. Cyc.:
v., pf.

3025 Pinkham, Daniel. "Christmas Day", Eight Poems of
Gerard Manley Hopkins, B: Ione, 1970. Song: t-bar
or bar solo, vla.

Moonrise   "I awake in Midsummer not-to-call night"   Poems
of Gerard Manley Hopkins (1918)

3026 Krenek, Ernst. Four Songs, Kassel: Bärenreiter,
1970. Song: high v., pf.

3027 Robertson, Donna N. Five Odes to God in Nature on
Poems by Gerard M. Hopkins, MS 1969. Choral ste.:
satb, a cap.

3028 Woollen, Russell. Suite for High Voice, MS copyright
by composer 1959, avail. ACA. Ste.: high v., pf.

Morning, Midday, and Evening Sacrifice   "Dappled die-away,
The" Lyra Sacra: A Book of Religious Verse (1895) 1st
stanza was publ. under the title "First Fruits" in Bible
Birthday Book (1887)

3029 Langley, Bernard P. MS 1963-67. Song: s solo, fl.,
cl., str. qrt.

"My own heart let me more have pity on; let"   Poems of
Gerard Manley Hopkins (1918)

3030 Wilson, James. Carrion Comfort, MS 1966. Cyc.: high
bar solo, pf.

New Readings   "Although the letter said"   Criterion (Oct.
1935)

3031 Langley, Bernard P. MS 1963-67. Song: s solo, fl.,
cl., str. qrt.

"No worst, there is none. Pitched past pitch of grief"
Poems of Gerard Manley Hopkins (1918)

Hopkins, Gerard Manley continued

3032   Brown, Harold. "Choral Setting No. 1", NY: Arrow.
       Setting for ssaa, a cap.

3033   Williams, Grace. "No worst, there is none", Six
       Poems by Gerard Manley Hopkins, MS 1958, avail.
       BBC. Cyc.: a solo, str. sextet.

3034   Wilson, James. Carrion Comfort, MS 1966. Cyc.: high
       bar solo, pf.

O Deus, ego amo te   "O God, I love thee"   Poems of Gerard
Manley Hopkins (1930)

3035   Rorem, Ned. "O God...", Three Motets, NY: BH, 1974.
       Motet: satb, org.

(On a Piece of Music)   "How's all to one thing wrought!"
Month (Feb. 1936)

3036   Krenek, Ernst. Four Songs, Kassel: Bärenreiter,
       1970. Song: high v., pf.

Oratrio Patris Condren: O Jesu vivens in Maria   "Jesu that
dost in Mary dwell"   Poems of Gerard Manley Hopkins
(1930)

3037   Pinkham, Daniel. "Jesu that dost...", Eight Poems of
       Gerard Manley Hopkins, B: Ione, 1970. Song: t-bar
       or bar solo, vla.

3038   Rorem, Ned. "Jesu that dost...", Three Motets, NY:
       BH, 1974. Motet: satb, org.

"Patience, hard thing! the hard thing but to pray"   Poems of
Gerard Manley Hopkins (1918)

3039   Krenek, Ernst. Four Songs, Kassel: Bärenreiter,
       1970. Song: high v., pf.

3040   Wilson, James. Carrion Comfort, MS 1966. Cyc.: high
       bar solo, pf.

Peace   "When will you ever, Peace, wild wooddove, shy wings
    shut"   Poems of Gerard Manley Hopkins (1918)

    3041 Gow, David. L: Elkin, 1966. Song: satb, a cap.

    3042 Hold, Trevor. Four Sonnets of Gerard Manley Hopkins,
          MS 1965-67. Setting for satb, a cap.

    3043 Krenek, Ernst. Four Songs, Kassel: Bärenreiter,
          1970. Song: high v., pf.

    3044* Maconchy, Elizabeth. MS 1964. Song: s solo, ch.
          orch.

    3045 Morgan, Diane. The Seeker, MS, avail. CMC. Cyc.: bar
          solo, pf.

    3046 Talma, Louise. "When will you...", Voices of Peace,
          MS 1973. Setting for satb, stgs.

    3047 Williams, Grace. Six Poems by Gerard Manley Hopkins,
          MS 1958, avail. BBC. Cyc.: a solo, str. sextet.

    3048 Woollen, Russell. MS (Opus 28), priv. publ. 1956.
          Setting for ttbb, pf. duet. Later rev. and incl.
          in Suite for High Voice, MS copyright by
          composer 1959, avail. ACA. Ste.: high v., pf.

Pied Beauty   "Glory be to God for dappled things"   Poems of
    Gerard Manley Hopkins (1918)

    3049 Brown, Newel K. Hopkins Set, MS. Song: bar solo,
          t trbn.

    3050 Campbell, Arthur. God's Grandeur, MS. Cyc.: high v.,
          pf.

    3051 Chandler, Mary. "Glory...", L: N, 1960. Song: ss,
          pf.

    3052 Dickinson, Peter. Four Gerard Manley Hopkins Poems,
          MS 1960-64. Cyc.: s, bar soli, satb, org.

    3053 Druckman, Jacob. "Antiphonies III", NY: BH, in prep.
          for publ. Setting for 2 satb choruses, a cap.

3054   George, Graham. "Glory...", MS 1973. Setting for
        choir [a cap.?].

3055   Hold, Trevor. Four_Sonnets_of_Gerard_Manley_Hopkins,
        MS 1965-67. Setting for satb, a cap.

3056   Morgan, Diane. The_Seeker, MS, avail. CMC. Cyc.:
        bar solo, pf.

3057   Pinkham, Daniel. Eight_Poems_of_Gerard_Manley
        Hopkins, B: Ione, 1970. Song: t-bar or bar solo,
        vla.

3058   Plumstead, Mary. L: Elkin, 1963. Song: ssa, a cap.

3059   Rubbra, Edmund. Inscape, S. Croy.: L, 1965. Ste.:
        satb, stgs., hp. or satb, pf.

3060   Talma, Louise. MS 1946. Song: s solo, pf.

3061   Ward, Robert. Sacred_Songs_for_Pantheists, NY: HP,
        1966. Song: s solo, orch. or s solo, pf.

3062   Widdoes, Lawrence. NY: CMP, copyright by composer
        1968. Song: satb, pf.

3063   Williams, Grace. Six_Poems_by_Gerard_Manley_Hopkins,
        MS 1958, avail. BBC. Cyc.: a solo, str. sextet.

3064   Woollen, Russell. Suite_for_High_Voice, MS copyright
        by composer 1959, avail. ACA. Ste.: high v., pf.

3065   Zupko, Ramon. MS. Song: satb, a cap.

"Repeat that, repeat"   Poems_of_Gerard_Manley_Hopkins (1918)

3066   Druckman, Jacob. "Antiphonies I", NY: BH, in prep.
        for publ. Setting for 2 satb choruses, a cap.

3067   Epstein, David. "Cuckoo", Four_Songs, NY: M, 1964.
        Cyc.: s solo, hn. solo, str. orch.

3068   Füssl, Karl. "Concerto Rapsodico", Wien: UE, 1964.
        Setting for ms [or a] solo, ch. orch. Engl. text.

Hopkins, Gerard Manley continued

3069   Orton, Richard. "Four Fragments", MS 1963. Song: ms
        solo, pf. One song only comprised of four Hopkins
        fragments.

Ribblesdale   "Earth, sweet Earth, sweet landscape"   Poems
   of Gerard Manley Hopkins (1918)

3070   Peterson, Wayne. "Earth, Sweet Earth", NY: LG, 1956.
        Song: satb, a cap.

S. Thomae Aquinatis Rhythmus   "Godhead here in hiding, whom
   I adore"   Poems of Gerard Manley Hopkins (1930)

3071   Poston, Elizabeth. "Godhead...", Cambridge: CUP,
        1967 in The Cambridge Hymnal. Hymn: v., [pf. or
        org.]. Tune: "Adoro Te". Accompaniment by Poston.

"Sea took pity: it interposed with doom, The"   Poems of
   Gerard Manley Hopkins (1918)

3072   Orton, Richard. "Four Fragments", MS 1963. Song: ms
        solo, pf. One song only comprised of four Hopkins
        fragments.

"Shepherd's brow, fronting forked lightning, owns, The"
   Poems of Gerard Manley Hopkins (1918)

3073   Wilson, James. Carrion Comfort, MS 1966. Cyc.: high
        bar solo, pf.

Spelt from Sibyl's Leaves   "Earnest, earthless, equal, at-
   tuneable"   Poems of Gerard Manley Hopkins (1918)

3074   Allen, Harold. MS 1971. Setting for s solo, satb,
        instr. ensemble.

3075   Babbitt, Milton. Two Sonnets, MS reprod. (1956),
        avail. NY: CFP. Song: bar solo, cl., vla., vcl.

Spring   "Nothing is so beautiful as Spring"   The Poets and
   the Poetry of the XIXth Century, Vol. VIII (1893)

3076 Campbell, Arthur. God's Granleur, MS. Cyc.: high v.,
      pf.

3077 Morgan, Diane. The Seeker, MS, avail. CMC. Cyc.:
      bar solo, pf.

3078 Pellegrini, Ernesto. MS 1969. Song: satb, fl., cl.,
      tpt., vln., vcl., pf.

3079 Pinkham, Daniel. Eight Poems of Gerard Manley
      Hopkins, B: Ione, 1970. Song: t-bar or bar solo,
      vla.

3080 Rorem, Ned. NY: BH, 1953. Song: high v., [pf.].

3081 Rubbra, Edmund. Inscape, S. Croy.: L, 1965. Ste.:
      satb, stgs., hp. or satb, pf.

3082 Stoker, Richard. Songs of Spring, L: LD, 1969.
      Song: ssa, a cap.

Spring and Fall "Márgarét, áre you gríeving" The Poets
and the Poetry of the XIXth Century, Vol. VIII (1893)

3083 Epstein, David. Four Songs, NY: M, 1964. Cyc.: s
      solo, hn. solo, str. orch.

3084 Farquhar, David. Six Songs of Women, Wellington:
      WTA, 1969. Song: s solo, pf.

3085 George, Graham. "Márgarét...", MS 1949. Song: solo
      v., pf.

3086 Gow, David. Two Choral Songs, L: Elkin, 1965. Song:
      ssa, a cap. Other song in the collection requires
      ssaa.

3087 Gruber, Albion. MS. Song: s, a duet, pf. Also avail.
      for s solo, 2 pt. chorus, orch.

3088 Morgan, Diane. "Margaret", Tor.: BMI, 1957. Song:
      high v., pf.

3089 Nisbet, Peter C. MS 1952, avail. University of
      Auckland. Song: med. v., pf.

Hopkins, Gerard Manley continued

3090   Pinkham, Daniel. Eight Poems of Gerard Manley
       Hopkins, B: Ione, 1970. Song: t-bar or bar solo,
       vla.

3091   Rorem, Ned. MS 1946, NY: M. Song: med. v., pf.

3092   Shifrin, Seymour. MS. Song: s solo, pf.

3093   Talma, Louise. MS 1946. Song: s solo, pf.

3094   Uszler, Marienne. MS. Song: s solo, pf.

3095   Westergaard, Peter. MS 1960. Song: s solo, pf.
       Rev. 1964 as cta. ("Cantata IV") for s solo,
       fl., b. cl., vln., vcl., hp.

3096   Williams, Grace. Six Poems by Gerard Manley Hopkins,
       MS 1958, avail. BBC. Cyc.: a solo, str. sextet.

Starlight Night, The   "Look at the stars!"   The Poets and
the Poetry of the XIXth Century, Vol. VIII (1893)

3097   Bliss, Arthur. "Look...", The World is Charged with
       the Grandeur of God, L: N, 1970. Cta.: satb, 2
       fl., 3 tpt., 4 trbn.

3098* Maconchy, Elizabeth. MS 1964. Song: s solo, ch.
       orch.

3099   Robertson, Donna N. Five Odes to God in Nature on
       Poems by Gerard M. Hopkins, MS 1969. Choral ste.:
       satb, a cap.

3100   Wilson, James. "The Starry Night", Three Canticles,
       MS 1966. Choral cyc.: s, a soli, sa, str. orch.

3101   Woollen, Russell. Suite for High Voice, MS copyright
       by composer 1959, avail. ACA. Ste.: high v., pf.

"Strike, churl; hurl, cheerless wind, then; heltering hail"
Poems of Gerard Manley Hopkins (1918)

3102   Epstein, David. "Strike, churl", Four Songs, NY: M,
       1964. Cyc.: s solo, hn. solo, str. orch.

361

Hopkins, Gerard Manley continued

    3103   Orton, Richard. "Four Fragments", MS 1963. Song: ms
            solo, pf. One song only comprised of four Hopkins
            fragments.

    3104   Pinkham, Daniel. Eight Poems of Gerard Manley
            Hopkins, B: Ione, 1970. Song: t-bar or bar solo,
            vla.

Summa   "Best ideal is the true, The"   Poems of Gerard
Manley Hopkins (1918)

    3105 Wordsworth, William. Cambridge: CUP, 1967 in The
           Cambridge Hymnal. Round.

That Nature is a Heraclitean Fire and of the comfort of the
Resurrection   "Cloud-puffball, torn tufts"   Poems of
Gerard Manley Hopkins (1918)

    3106 Babbitt, Milton. Two Sonnets, MS reprod. (1956),
           avail. NY: CFP. Song: bar solo, cl., vla., vcl.

    3107 Mellers, Wilfrid H. Canticum Ressurectionis,
           Grt. Y.: G, 1972. Setting for dbl. choir (16
           v.), a cap.

"Thee, God, I come from, to thee go"   Lyra Sacra: A Book of
Religious Verse (1895)

    3108 Ridout, Alan. "Thee, God, I come from", Reigate:
           S&B, 1969. [Anthem]: s voices, a cap.

    3109 Rorem, Ned. Three Motets, NY: BH, 1974. Motet: satb,
           org.

"Thou art indeed just, Lord, if I contend"   Poems of Gerard
Manley Hopkins (1918)

    3110 Briccetti, Thomas. "Thou art indeed just, Lord", NY:
           CMP, copyright by composer 1968. Setting for
           satb, orch. or satb, pf.

    3111 Dickinson, Peter. "Thou Art indeed Just, Lord", Four
           Gerard Manley Hopkins Poems, MS 1960-64. Cyc.:
           s, bar soli, satb, org.

3112   Hold, Trevor. "Thou art indeed just, Lord", Four
       Sonnets of Gerard Manley Hopkins, MS 1965-67.
       Setting for satb, a cap.

3113   Langley, Bernard P. "Justus Quidem tu es, Domine",
       Three Dark Sonnets, MS. Setting for t solo, orch.
       or t solo, pf.

3114   Robertson, Donna N. "Thou Art Indeed Just", Five
       Odes to God in Nature on Poems by Gerard M.
       Hopkins, MS 1969. Choral ste.: satb, a cap.

3115   Wilson, James. Carrion Comfort, MS 1966. Cyc.: high
       bar solo, pf.

"Times are nightfall, look, their light grows less, The"
   Poems of Gerard Manley Hopkins (1918)

3116   Kirchner, Leon. "The Times are Nightfall", MS 1943.
       Song: s solo, pf.

To his Watch   "Mortal, my mate, bearing my rock-a-heart"
   Poems of Gerard Manley Hopkins (1918)

3117   McDermott, Vincent. Swift Wind, MS 1974. Cta.: high
       v., db. Incl. setting of excerpt beginning: "The
       time our task is; time's some part".

Windhover, The   "I caught this morning morning's minion"
   Poems of Gerard Manley Hopkins (1918)

3118   Berkeley, Lennox. L: N, 1968. Song: satb, a cap.

3119   Brindle, Reginald S. L: N, 1971. Song: s, t soli,
       satb, a cap.

3120   Brown, Newel K. Hopkins Set, MS. Song: bar solo,
       t trbn.

3121   Campbell, Arthur. God's Grandeur, MS. Cyc.: high v.,
       pf.

3122   Paynter, John. L: OUP, 1972. Song: satb, a cap.

3123   Tippett, Michael. L: S, 1942. Madrigal: satb, a cap.

Hopkins, Gerard Manley continued

    3124 Williams, Grace. <u>Six Songs by Gerard Manley Hopkins</u>,
          MS 1958, avail. BBC. Cyc.: a solo, str. sextet.

    3125 Woollen, Russell. MS (Opus 28), priv. publ. 1955.
          Setting for ttbb, pf. duet.

Winter with the Gulf Stream "Boughs, the boughs are bare
  enough, The" <u>Once a Week</u> (Feb. 1863)

    3126 Langley, Bernard P. MS 1963-67. Song: s solo, fl.,
          cl., str. qrt.

Wreck of the Deutschland, The "Thou mastering me" <u>Poems
of Gerard Manley Hopkins</u> (1918) 1st stanza only publ. in
<u>The Spirit of Man</u> (1916)

    3127 Morgan, Diane. "Master of the Sea", MS 1971, avail.
          CMC. Cta.: s, t soli, chorus, orch. Text adapt.
          from the poem.

    3128 Oliver, Stephen. "Music for 'The Wreck of the
          Deutschland'", L: N, 1974. Str. qrt, pf. only.
          Chamber music to accompany a reading of the poem.

    3129 Pellegrini, Ernesto. MS 1966. Song: satb, a cap.
          Setting of 1st stanza.

    3130 Wilson, James. "Fourth Canticle", MS 1967. Cta.: a
          solo, sp., vcl. solo, orch. Setting of one half
          of the poem.

Miscellanea

    3131 Britten, Benjamin. Settings (MS 1939) for chorus,
          a cap. have been withdrawn by the composer.

    3132 Gellman, Steven. <u>Quartets: Poems of Gerard Manley
          Hopkins</u>, MS 1966-67. Songs: v., fl., vcl., hp.

3133 Gilbert, Anthony. Inscapes, MS (in prep. for publ.),
perf. June 1975. Songs: s solo, sp., 2 cl. (1
doubl. s sax.), perc. The composer has indicated
to the eds. that the text consists of passages
from Hopkins' Journals ("observations on the
formation of rocks, glaciers, waterfalls, waves,
plants and trees, sky and light"). The work was
composed to be perf. at previews of a travelling
exhibition (1975) of Hopkins' graphic work.

3134 Graves, William. "The Grandeur of God", NY: CF,
1959. Song: low v., pf. Text made up of various
lines from Hopkins' sonnets.

3135 Harries, David. Noctuary, MS (Opus 14). Songs: s
solo (or semi-chorus), chorus, stgs. Employs 5
of Hopkins' sonnets.

3136 Joyce, Mary Ann. The Passion, Death and Resurrection
of Jesus Christ, St. Louis: WUP, 1970. A passion
for satb, orch. Incl. words by Hopkins.

3137 Paynter, John. May Magnificat, L: OUP, 1973. Three
choruses for mixed v.

3138 Posamanick, Beatrice. "Praise", MS ca. 1936.

HOUSMAN, Alfred Edward   1859-1936

"Along the field as we came by"   A Shropshire Lad (1896)

3139 Gurney, Ivor. "The Aspens", The Western Playland,
L: S&B, 1926. Cyc.: bar solo, str. qrt., pf.

3140 Keeney, Wendell. "The Aspen", NY: GS, 1940. Song:
high or med. v., pf.

3141 Orr, C.W. "Along the field", Seven Songs from "A
Shropshire Lad", L: JWC, 1934. Song: bar solo,
pf.

Housman, A.E. continued

3142   Vaughan Williams, Ralph. "Along the field", Along
       the Field, L: OUP, 1954. Song: [high] solo v.,
       vln.

Alta Quies   See: Parta Quies

"Amelia mixed the mustard"   Edwardian (Sept. 1936)

   3143   Mopper, Irving. "Amelia", NY: CF, 1955. Song: high
          v., pf.

Amphisbaena, The   "In the back back garden, Thomasina"
Union Magazine (June 1906), rev. 1937

   3144   Stevens, Halsey. Champaign: Marko, 1972. Madrigal:
          satb, pf.

"Be still, my soul, be still; the arms you bear are brittle"
A Shropshire Lad (1896)

   3145   Leichtling, Alan. "Be Still, My Soul", Eleven Songs
          from "A Shropshire Lad", NY: SMC, 1971. Cyc.:
          bar solo, orch.

"Bells in the tower at evening toll"   More Poems (1936)

   3146   Cone, Edward T. MS. Song: s solo, pf.

Bredon Hill   "In summertime on Bredon"   A Shropshire Lad
(1896)

   3147   Butterworth, George. "Bredon Hill" and Other Songs,
          L: A, 1912. Song: [med.] solo v., pf.

   3148   Duke, John. NY: GS, 1934. Song: [v., pf.].

   3149   Gray, Alan. L: OUP, 1936. Song: bar solo, [pf.].

   3150   Hamilton, Janet. "In summertime...", L: WR, 1919.
          Song: high v., pf.

3151   Harrison, Julius. L: BH, 1942. Rhapsody: vln., orch.
        Avail. for vln., pf.

3152   Johnson, Reginald. "In summertime...", L: Elkin,
        1939. Song: satb, a cap.

3153   Peel, Graham. "In summertime...", L: C, 1911. Song:
        [solo v., pf.].

3154   Raynor, John. Eleven Songs, L: G, 1971. Song: [v.,
        pf.?].

3155   Roberton, Hugh. "In summertime...", L: RP, 1931.
        Song: male choir, a cap. Publ. L: RP, 1942 for
        satb, a cap.

3156   Somervell, Arthur. A Shropshire Lad, L: BH, 1904.
        Cyc.: solo v., pf.

3157   Twigg, Douglas. York: Banks, 1936. Song: satb, pf.

3158   Vaughan Williams, Ralph. On Wenlock Edge, L: BH,
        1911; rev. edn. publ. L: BH, 1946. Cyc.: t solo,
        pf., str. qrt. ad lib.

3159*   Ward-Casey, S[amuel?]. York: Banks, 1936. Song:
        [solo v., pf.?].

3160   Young, Dalhousie. L: C, 1905. Song: [solo v., pf.].

"Bring, in this timeless grave to throw"   A Shropshire Lad
    (1896)

3161   Leichtling, Alan. Eleven Songs from "A Shropshire
        Lad", NY: SMC, 1971. Cyc.: bar solo, orch.

Carpenter's Son, The   "Here the hangman stops his cart"
    A Shropshire Lad (1896)

3162   Orr, C.W. L: JWC, 1923. Song: t solo, pf.

"Chestnut casts his flambeaux, and the flowers, The"   Last
    Poems (1922)

367

Housman, A.E. continued

3163 Heilner, Irwin. "The Chestnut Casts His Flambeaux",
MS copyright by composer 1965, avail. ACA. Song:
med. v., pf.

"Could man be drunk forever" Last Poems (1922)

3164 Heilner, Irwin. MS copyright by composer 1965,
avail. ACA. Song: med. v., pf.

Deserter, The "What sound awakened me, I wonder" Last
Poems (1922)

3165 Lutyens, Elisabeth. Six Songs, MS 1934-36. Song:
[solo v., pf.?].

3166 Mason, Daniel G. Songs of the Countryside, NY: R,
1927 (hire). Cyc.: soli, chorus, orch.

Eight O'Clock "He stood, and heard the steeple" Last
Poems (1922)

3167 Clarke, Rebecca. "He stood...", L: WR, 1928. Song:
solo v., pf.

Elephant, or the Force of Habit, The See: Force of Habit,
The

Epitaph, An "Stay, if you list, O passer by the way"
A.E.H. (1937)

3168 Cone, Edward T. MS. Song: b-bar solo, pf.

Epitaph on an Army of Mercenaries "These, in the day when
heaven was falling" The Times (Oct. 1917)

3169 Gurney, Ivor. MS 1918. Song: [solo v., pf.].

Fancy's Knell "When lads were home from labour" Last
Poems (1922)

ousman, A.E. continued

3170   Mason, Daniel G. Songs of the Countryside, NY: R,
        1927 (hire). Cyc.: soli, chorus, orch.

3171   Symons, Dom Thomas. L: Curwen, 1928. Song: solo v.,
        pf.

3172   Vaughan Williams, Ralph. Along the Field, L: OUP,
        1954. Song: [high] solo v., vln.

"Far in a western brookland"   A Shropshire Lad (1896), rev.
    1922

3173   Bax, Arnold. Three Songs, L: E, 1919. Song: med. v.,
        pf.

3174   Cripps, A. Redgrave. Nine "Shropshire Lad" Songs,
        L: A, pre-1940. Song: [solo v., pf.].

3175*   Field, Robin. MS 1973. Diptych for orch. Two move-
        ments entitled: "The Starlit Fences", "The Glim-
        mering Weirs".

3176   Field, Robin. When I was One and Twenty, MS 1960.
        Cyc.: med. v., pf.

3177   Gurney, Ivor. Ludlow and Teme, L: S&B, 1923. Cyc.:
        t solo, str. qrt., pf.

3178   Ley, Henry G. L: S&B, pre-1940. Song: [v., pf.?].

3179   Moeran, E.J. L: WR, 1926. Song: bar solo, pf.

3180   Sumsion, Corbett. L: S&B, ca. 1936. Song: ttbb, [a
        cap.].

3181*   Swain, Freda. MS 1926, rev. 1973, The Lost Heart
        (MS 1925-26), avail. Chinnor: Channel, NEMO. Set-
        ting for t and pf. ensemble.

3182   Van Vactor, David. NY: GX, 1968. Song: satb, a cap.

3183   Wilson, Stanley. Four Songs from "A Shropshire Lad",
        L: S&B, pre-1967. Song: ttbb, [a cap.].

"Farewell to barn and stack and tree"   A Shropshire Lad
    (1896)

Housman, A.E. continued

3184 Moeran, E.J. Ludlow_Town, L: OUP, 1924. Song: bar
solo, pf.

3185 Orr, C.W. "Farewell to barn", Seven_Songs_from_"A
Shropshire_Lad", L: JWC, 1934. Song: bar solo,
pf.

"Farms of home lie lost in even, The"   More_Poems (1936)

3186 Meyerowitz, Jan. "The Farms of Home", Two_Choruses,
NY: Rongwen, 1957. Setting for ttbb, hn.

First of May, The   "Orchards half the way, The"   Cambridge
Review (Apr. 1914), rev. 1922

3187 Head, Michael. "Ludlow Town", L: BH, 1931. Song:
t or bar solo, pf.

3188 Stewart, D.M. L: Elkin, 1923. Song: high v. or low
v., pf.

3189 Symons, Dom Thomas. L: OUP, 1936. Song: bar solo,

3190 Wilson, Stanley. "Ludlow Fair", Four_Songs_from_"A
Shropshire_Lad", L: S&B, pre-1967. Song: ttbb,
[a cap.].

Force of Habit, The   "Tail behind, a trunk in front, A"
Edwardian (Dec. 1936), rev. 1937

3191 Franco, Johan. "Elephants, or The Force of Habit",
NY: WmS, 1946 (reassigned NY: Hargail, 1959) in
Rounds_and_Rounds. Round: 4 v. (best suited for
satb), a cap.

"From far, from eve and morning"   A_Shropshire_Lad (1896)

3192 Priestley-Smith, Hugh. From_the_West_Country, L:
JW, pre-1943. Cyc.: v., pf.

3193 Vaughan Williams, Ralph. On_Wenlock_Edge, L: BH,
1911; rev. edn. publ. L: BH, 1946. Cyc.: t solo,
pf., str. qrt. ad lib.

370

ousman, A.E. continued

"From the wash the laundress sends"   More Poems (1936)

  3194 Glanville-Hicks, Peggy. "Homespun Collars", Five
        Songs, NY: Weintraub, 1952. Song: med. v., pf.

Grenadier "Queen she sent to look for me, The"   Last
Poems (1922)

  3195 Addison, John. L: JW, 1951. Song: ttbb, a cap.

  3196 Morawetz, Oskar. MS 1950, priv. publ. 1962. Song:
        med. v., pf.

"Half-moon westers low, my love"   Last Poems (1922)

  3197 Calvin, Susan. "The Half-moon Westers Low", NY: AMP,
        1965. Song: satb, a cap.

  3198 Russell, Leslie. The Ludlow Cycle, MS 1973. Cyc.:
        s or t solo, pf.

  3199 Wilding-White, Raymond. "The Halfmoon Westers Low",
        Three Housman Poems, NY: HP, 1969 in Contemporary
        Art Song Album, Vol. I. Song: high v., pf.

"He would not stay for me; and who can wonder?"   A.E.H.
(1937)

  3200 Glanville-Hicks, Peggy. "He would not stay", Five
        Songs, NY: Weintraub, 1952. Song: med. v., pf.

"Here are the skies, the planets seven"   A.E.H. (1937)

  3201 Glanville-Hicks, Peggy. "Mimic Heaven", Five Songs,
        NY: Weintraub, 1952. Song: med. v., pf.

"Here dead lie we because we did not choose"   More Poems
(1936)

  3202 Cumming, Richard. We Happy Few, NY: BH, 1969. Cyc.:
        med. v., pf.

371

Housman, A.E. continued

Hughley Steeple   "Vane on Hughley Steeple, The"   A
Shropshire Lad (1896)

   3203 Orr, C.W. Seven Songs from "A Shropshire Lad", L:
         JWC, 1934. Song: bar solo, pf.

"I hoed and trenched and weeded" A Shropshire Lad (1896)

   3204 Merriman, Margarita. MS. Song: a or bar solo, pf.

"I promise nothing: friends will part" More Poems (1936)

   3205 Avshalomov, Jacob. "I Promise Nothing", Bryn Mawr:
         M, pre-1969. Song: satb, a cap.

   3206 Glanville-Hicks, Peggy. "Unlucky Love", Five Songs,
         NY: Weintraub, 1952. Song: med. v., pf.

"I wake from dreams and turning" More Poems (1936)

   3207 Babin, Victor. "I Wake from Dreams", L: A, 1951.
         Song: bar solo, pf.

"If it chance your eye offend you" A Shropshire Lad (1896)

   3208 Cone, Edward T. MS. Song: s solo, pf.

   3209 Grant, Parks. A Shropshire Lad, MS (Opus 7). Cyc.:
         high v. (preferably t solo), pf.

"If truth in hearts that perish" A Shropshire Lad (1896)

   3210 Ireland, John. "The Vain Desire", The Land of Lost
         Content, L: A, 1921. Song: solo v., pf.

"In the back back garden, Thomasina"   See: Amphisbaena

"In the morning, in the morning" Last Poems (1922)

   3211 Bax, Arnold. "In the Morning", L: MM, 1926, copy-
         right assigned L: C, 1943. Song: solo v., pf.

372

3212 Cone, Edward T. "In the Morning", MS. Song: s solo,
      pf.

3213 Stewart, D.M. "In the Morning", L: Elkin, 1923.
      Song: high v. or low v., pf.

3214 Vaughan Williams, Ralph. Along_the_Field, L: OUP,
      1954. Song: [high] solo v., vln.

3215 Wilding-White, Raymond. "In the Morning", Three
      Housman_Poems, NY: HP, 1969 in Contemporary_Art
      Song_Album, Vol. I. Song: high v., pf.

"In valleys green and still" Last_Poems (1922)

3216 Mason, Daniel G. Songs_of_the_Countryside, NY: R,
      1927 (hire). Cyc.: soli, chorus, orch.

3217 Orr, C.W. Oakville: Leslie, 1954. Song: t solo, pf.

3218 Russell, Leslie. The_Ludlow_Cycle, MS 1973. Cyc.:
      s or t solo, pf.

"In valleys of springs of rivers" A_Shropshire_Lad (1896)

3219 Vaughan Williams, Ralph. "Clun", On_Wenlock_Edge,
      L: BH, 1911; rev. edn. publ. L: BH, 1946. Cyc.:
      t solo, pf., str. qrt. ad lib.

"Into my heart an air that kills" A_Shropshire_Lad (1896)

3220 Armstrong, Thomas H.W. Five_Short_Songs, MS ca.
      1920. Song: [solo v., pf.?].

3221 Avril, Edwin. A Shropshire_Lad, MS. Song: t solo, pf.

3222 Cone, Edward T. "Into My Heart", MS. Song: s solo,
      pf.

3223 Cripps, A. Redgrave. "Into My Heart", Nine_"Shrop-
      shire_Lad"_Songs, L: A, pre-1940. Song: [solo v.,
      pf.].

3224   Duke, Vernon. "Into my heart", Six Songs from "A
      Shropshire Lad", NY: Broude-B, 1955. Song: med.
      v., pf.

3225   Duncan, Chester. "The Land of Lost Content", MS
      1939, Four Songs (MS 1937-63). Song: med. v., pf.

3226   Field, Robin. "The Land of Lost Content", When I
      Was One and Twenty, MS 1960. Cyc.: med. v., pf.

3227   Gurney, Ivor. "The Far Country", The Western Play-
      land, L: S&B, 1926. Cyc.: bar solo, str. qrt.,
      pf.

3228* Hoskins, William. The Lost Lands, MS 1940-45, rev.
      1946-47, NY: CFE. Cyc.: ms solo, str. orch. (24-
      36 vln., 9 vla., 8 vcl., 4-6 db.).

3229   Kilby, Muriel L. "No. 40 from A Shropshire Lad",
      MS 1949. Song: [solo v., pf.?].

3230   Lang, Margaret R. "Into My Heart", B: Schmidt, pre-
      1940. Song: [solo v., pf.?].

3231   Leichtling, Alan. Eleven Songs from "A Shropshire
      Lad", NY: SMC, 1971. Cyc.: bar solo, orch.

3232   Manney, Charles F. "Home-Longing", A Shropshire Lad,
      B:OD, 1914. Cyc.: [solo v., pf.?].

3233   Orr, C.W. "Into my heart", Three Songs from "A
      Shropshire Lad", L: JWC, 1940. Song: t solo, pf.

3234   Priestley-Smith, Hugh. From the West Country, L: JW,
      pre-1943. Cyc.: v., pf.

3235   Proctor-Gregg, Humphrey. "The Land of Lost Content",
      L: S&B, ca. 1935. Song: [solo v., pf.?].

3236   Rose, Edwin. "The Far Country", Two Songs, L:
      Curwen, 1926. Song: solo v., pf.

3237   Russell, Leslie. MS 1970-74. Song: solo v., pf.

3238   Somervell, Arthur. A Shropshire Lad, L: BH, 1904.
      Cyc.: solo v., pf.

usman, A.E. continued

Introductory Lecture   (1937) Priv. publ. 1892, 1933

    3239 Gibbs, Geoffrey D. Symposium, MS. Oratorio: soli,
          chorus, symph. band. Incl. setting of passage:
          "Knowledge...is not merely a means of procuring
          good, but is good in itself simply".

"Is my team ploughing"   A Shropshire Lad (1896)

    3240* Butterworth, George. Six Songs from "A Shropshire
          Lad", L: A, 1911. Song: med.-high v., pf.

    3241 Cripps, A. Redgrave. Nine "Shropshire Lad" Songs,
          L: A, pre-1940. Song: [solo v., pf.].

    3242 Gurney, Ivor. The Western Playland, L: S&B, 1926.
          Cyc.: bar solo, str. qrt., pf.

    3243 Orr, C.W. Five Songs from "A Shropshire Lad", L:
          OUP, 1925-27 (1960). Song: t solo, pf.

    3244 Vaughan Williams, Ralph. MS 1908. Song: solo v.,
          pf. Unpubl. in this form. Revised for On Wenlock
          Edge, L: BH, 1911. Cyc.: t solo, pf., str. qrt.
          ad lib. Rev. edn. of cyc. publ. L: BH, 1946.

Isle of Portland, The   "Star-filled seas are smooth
    to-night, The"   A Shropshire Lad (1896)

    3245* Dunhill, Thomas F. L: BH, pre-1946. Song: any v.
          except high, light s, pf.

    3246 Edmunds, John. L: BH, 1950. Song: bar solo, pf.

    3247 Orr, C.W. L: JWC, 1940. Song: bar solo, pf.

"It nods and curtseys and recovers"   A Shropshire Lad (1896)

    3248 Cripps, A. Redgrave. Nine "Shropshire Lad" Songs, L:
          A, pre-1940. Song: [solo v., pf.].

    3249 Field, Robin. "The Nettle", Then I was One and
          Twenty, MS 1960. Cyc.: med. v., pf.

375

"Lads in their hundreds to Ludlow come in for the fair, The"
A Shropshire Lad (1896)

3250* Butterworth, George. "The Lads in Their Hundreds",
Six Songs from "A Shropshire Lad", L: A, 1911.
Cyc.: med.-high v., pf.

3251 Cripps, A. Redgrave. Nine "Shropshire Lad" Songs,
L: A, pre-1940. Song: [solo v., pf.].

3252 Gurney, Ivor. "Ludlow Fair", Ludlow and Teme, L:
S&B, 1923. Cyc.: t solo, str. qrt., pf.

3253 Moeran, E.J. Ludlow Town, L: OUP, 1924. Song: bar
solo, pf.

3254 Orr, C.W. "The lads in their hundreds", L: S&B,
1937. Song: t solo, pf.

3255 Somervell, Arthur. A Shropshire Lad, L: BH, 1904.
Cyc.: solo v., pf.

"Laws of God, the laws of man, The"   Last Poems (1922)

3256 Barrell, Joyce. MS. Song: solo v., unacc.

Lent Lily, The   "'Tis spring; come out to ramble"   A
Shropshire Lad (1896)

3257 Champion, Constance. "The Flowers of Easter", NY:
GS, 1964. Song: 4 pt. chorus, pf.

3258 Cripps, A. Redgrave. Five "Shropshire Lad" Songs,
L: S&B, pre-1944. Song: [solo v., pf.].

3259 Gurney, Ivor. Ludlow and Teme, L: S&B, 1923. Cyc.:
t solo, str. qrt., pf.

3260 Ireland, John. The Land of Lost Content, L: A, 1921.
Song: solo v., pf.

3261 Milvain, Hilda. "The Lenten Lily", L: BH, 1925.
Song: solo v., pf.

3262 Orr, C.W. Seven Songs from "A Shropshire Lad", L:
JWC, 1934. Song: bar solo, pf.

3263   Russell, Leslie. MS 1970-74. Song: solo v., pf.

3264   Wilson, Stanley. Four Songs from "A Shropshire Lad",
       L: S&B, pre-1967. Song: ttbb, [a cap.].

"Look not in my eyes, for fear"   A Shropshire Lad (1896)

3265   Branson, David. L: OUP, 1939. Song: ms or bar solo,
       pf.

3266* Butterworth, George. Six Songs from "A Shropshire
       Lad", L: A, 1911. Cyc.: med.-high v., pf.

3267   Cripps, A. Redgrave. Five "Shropshire Lad" Songs, L:
       S&B, pre-1944. Song: [solo v., pf.].

3268* Gorecki, Thaddeus. MS ca. 1933. Song.

3269   Ireland, John. "Ladslove", The Land of Lost Content,
       L: A, 1921. Song: solo v., pf.

3270* Ireland, John. "A Grecian Lad", Three Pastels, L:
       A, 1941. Pf. solo.

3271* Sumsion, Corbett. "Look Not In My Eyes", L: S&B, ca.
       1936. Song: ttbb, a cap.

"Loveliest of trees, the cherry now"   A Shropshire Lad
(1896)

3272   Abramson, Robert. "Loveliest of Trees", NY: CF,
       1960. Song: satb, a cap.

3273   Bissell, Keith. "Loveliest of Trees", Three Songs in
       Praise of Spring, Tor.: ECK, 1972. Song: ssaa,
       pf., perc.

3274* Butterworth, George. "The Cherry Tree", L: N, 1917.
       Prelude for orch. Work later entitled: "A Shrop-
       shire Lad (Rhapsody for Orchestra)".

3275* Butterworth, George. "Loveliest of Trees", Six Songs
       from "A Shropshire Lad", L: A, 1911. Cyc.: med.-
       high v., pf.

Housman, A.E. continued

3276 Cockshott, Gerald. "The Cherry Tree", MS 1939. Song: solo v., pf.

3277 Colson, William. "Loveliest of Trees", Three Songs from "A Shropshire Lad", MS. Song: high v., pf.

3278 Cone, Edward T. "Loveliest of Trees", MS. Song: s solo, of.

3279 Dougherty, Celius. "Loveliest of Trees", NY: BH, 1948. Song: solo v., pf.

3280 Duke, John. "Loveliest of Trees", NY: GS, 1934. Song: any v. except high, light s, pf.

3281 Duke, Vernon. "Loveliest of Trees", Six Songs from "A Shropshire Lad", NY: Broude-B, 1955. Song: med. v., pf.

3282 Field, Robin. "Loveliest of Trees", When I was One and Twenty, MS 1960. Cyc.: med. v., pf.

3283* Gorecki, Thaddeus. MS ca. 1933. Song.

3284 Grant, Parks. "Loveliest of Trees", A Shropshire Lad, MS (Opus 7). Cyc.: high v. (preferably t solo), pf.

3285 Gurney, Ivor. "The Cherry Tree", MS 1918. Song: [solo v., pf.].

3286 Gurney, Ivor. "Loveliest of Trees", The Western Playland, L: S&B, 1926. Cyc.: bar solo, str. qrt., pf.

3287 Hamilton, Janet. "The Cherry Tree", L: WR, 1919. Song: med. v., pf.

3288 Herbert, Muriel. "Loveliest of Trees", L: A, pre-1940. Song: [solo v., pf.].

3289 Herreshoff, Constance. "Loveliest of Trees", NY: JF, pre-1940. Song: [solo v., pf.].

3290 Leichtling, Alan. "Loveliest of Trees", Eleven Songs from "A Shropshire Lad", NY: SMC, 1971. Cyc.: bar solo, orch.

378

3291 Mann, Leslie. "The Cherry Tree", Green Buds, MS
      1954, avail. CMC. Song: high v., pf.

3292 Manney, Charles F. "Youth", A Shropshire Lad, B: OD,
      1914. Cyc.: [solo v., pf.?].

3293 Manson, Willie B. Three Poems from "A Shropshire
      Lad", L: BH, 1920. Song: solo v., pf.

3294 Marillier, Christabel. "Loveliest of Trees", L: BH,
      1923; copyright returned to composer 1949. Song:
      solo v., pf.

3295* Mechem, Kirke. "Loveliest of Trees", Five Centuries
      of Spring, publ. in USA pre-1969. Madrigal cyc.:
      ssa, a cap.

3296 Moeran, E.J. "Loveliest of Trees", L: Curwen, 1932.
      Song: bar solo, pf.

3297 Orr, C.W. "Loveliest of Trees", Two Songs from "A
      Shropshire Lad", L: JWC, 1923. Song: t solo, pf.

3298 Peel, Graham. "Loveliest of Trees", Songs of a
      Shropshire Lad, L: C, 1911. Song: [solo v., pf.].

3299 Priestley-Smith, Hugh. "Loveliest of Trees", From
      the West Country, L: JW, pre-1943. Cyc.: v., pf.

3300 Proctor-Gregg, Humphrey. "Loveliest of Trees", L:
      JW, pre-1943. Song: [solo v., pf.?].

3301 Raynor, John. "Loveliest of Trees", Eleven Songs,
      L: G, 1971. Song: [v., pf.?].

3302 Roberton, Hugh. "Loveliest of Trees", L: PX, 1943
      (reassigned Wendover: RP). Song: satb, a cap.

3303 Ross, Colin. "The cherry hung with snow", L: Curwen,
      1963. Song: solo v., pf.

3304 Somervell, Arthur. A Shropshire Lad, L: BH, 1904.
      Cyc.: solo v., pf.

3305 Wilson, Stanley. "The Cherry Tree", Four Songs from
      "A Shropshire Lad", L: S&B, pre-1967. Song: ttbb,
      [a cap.].

Housman, A.E. continued

  3306   Woolley, C. "Loveliest of Trees", L: N, 1934. Song:
         solo v., pf.

March   "Sun at noon to higher air, The"   A Shropshire Lad
  (1896)

  3307   Gurney, Ivor. The Western Playland, L: SSB, 1926.
         Cyc.: bar solo, str. qrt., pf.

  3308* Ireland, John. "The Heart's Desire", L: WR, ca.
         1918. Song: solo v., pf. Also avail. (hire) for
         solo v., orch. Sets lines beginning: "The boys
         are up the woods with day".

"Mill-stream, now that noises cease, The"   More Poems
  (1936)

  3309   Mann, Leslie. "The Mill Stream", Green Buds, MS
         1954, avail. CMC. Song: high v., pf.

New Mistress, The   "Oh, sick I am to see you"   A Shropshire
  Lad (1896)

  3310   Foss, Hubert J. L: OUP, 1925. Song: bar solo,

  3311   Marillier, Christabel. "A Farewell", L: Curwen,
         1920. Song: solo v., pf.

"Night is freezing fast, The"   Last Poems (1922)

  3312   Andrews, Herbert K. Two Songs, L: OUP, 1945. Song:
         s or t solo, pf.

  3313   Garlick, Antony. Eleven Canzonets, Cin.: Westwood,
         1967. Canzonet: 2 pt. chorus of equal v., a cap.

  3314   Hollister, David. Winter Madrigals, MS. Madrigal:
         satb, a cap.

  3315   Merriman, Margarita. MS. Song: a or bar solo, pf.

  3316   Russell, Leslie. The Ludlow Cycle, MS 1973. Cyc.:
         s or t solo, pf.

380

ousman, A.E. continued

"Now dreary dawns the eastern light"   Last_Poems (1922)

   3317 Heilner, Irwin. MS copyright by composer 1955,
      avail. ACA. Song: med. v., pf.

   3318 Russell, Leslie. The Ludlow_Cycle, MS 1973. Cyc.:
      s or t solo, pf.

"Now hollow fires burn to black"   A Shropshire_Lad (1896)

   3319 Duke, Vernon. "Now hollow fires", Six_Songs_from
      "A_Shropshire_Lad", NY: Broude-B, 1955. Song:
      med. v., pf.

"Oh fair enough are sky and plain"   A_Shropshire_Lad (1896)

   3320 Butterworth, George. "Bredon_Hill"_and_Other_Songs,
      L: A, 1912. Song: [med.] solo v., pf.

   3321 Crerar, Louis. MS 1954, Housman_Songs (MS 1954-56),
      avail. CMC. Song: high v., pf.

   3322* Gorecki, Thaddeus. MS ca. 1933. Song.

   3323 Moeran, E.J. L: JW, 1957. Song: bar solo, pf.

   3324 Orr, C.W. Seven Songs_from_"A_Shropshire_Lad", L:
      JWC, 1934. Song: bar solo, pf.

   3325* Sumsion, Corbett. L: S&B, ca. 1936. Song: ttbb, a
      cap.

   3326* Swain, Freda. MS 1925, rev. 1947, The_Lost_Heart
      (MS 1925-26), avail. Chinnor: Channel, NEMO.
      Setting for t and pf. ensemble.

"Oh see how thick the goldcup flowers"   A_Shropshire_Lad
(1896)

   3327 Cripps, A. Redgrave. Nine_"Shropshire_Lad"_Songs,
      L: A, pre-1940. Song: [solo v., pf.].

   3328 Orr, C.W. Three Songs_from_"A_Shropshire_Lad", L:
      JWC, 1940. Song: t solo, pf.

Housman, A.E. continued

3329 Tauber, Patricia. "The Shropshire Lad", MS 1963,
       avail. Victoria University of Wellington. Song:
       high v., pf.

3330 Vaughan Williams, Ralph. "Good-bye", Along_the
       Field, L: OUP, 1954. Song: [high] solo v., vln.

"Oh stay at home, my lad, and plough" Last_Poems (1922)

3331 Russell, Leslie. The_Ludlow_Cycle, MS 1973. Cyc.:
       s or t solo, pf.

"Oh, when I was in love with you" A_Shropshire_Lad (1896)

3332 Duke, Vernon. "Oh, when I was in love", Six_Songs
       from_"A_Shropshire_Lad", NY: Broude-B, 1955.
       Song: med. v., pf.

3333 Duncan, Chester. MS 1938, Four_Songs (MS 1937-63).
       Song: med. v., pf.

3334 Heussenstamm, George. "When I was...", Cin.: WLP,
       1970. Song: ttbb, a cap.

3335 Leichtling, Alan. Eleven_Songs_from_"A_Shropshire
       Lad", NY: SMC, 1971. Cyc.: bar solo, orch.
       Lines from the poem are incorporated into the
       setting of "When I was one-and-twenty".

3336 Nunlist, Juli. NY: GX, 1972 in Contemporary_Art_Song
       Album, Vol. II. Song: med. v., pf.

3337 Orr, C.W. Five_Songs_from_"A_Shropshire_Lad", L:
       OUP, 1925-27 (1960). Song: t solo, pf.

3338 Vaughan Williams, Ralph. On_Wenlock_Edge, L: BH,
       1911; rev. edn. publ. L: BH, 1946. Cyc.: t solo,
       pf., str. qrt. ad lib.

3339 Whitcomb, Mervin. "When I was in Love", Two_Housman
       Poems, NY: Bourne, 1953. Song: satb, pf.

"On moonlit heath and lonesome bank" A_Shropshire_Lad
(1896)

3340   Leichtling, Alan. Eleven Songs from "A Shropshire Lad", NY: SMC, 1971. Cyc.: bar solo, orch.

"On the idle hill of summer"   A Shropshire Lad (1896)

3341   Ainsworth, Robert. L: BH, 1939. Song: [solo v., pf.].

3342   Baber, Joseph. Songs from the English Poets, MS (Opus 12). Cyc.: high v., pf.

3343   Butterworth, George. "Bredon Hill" and Other Songs, L: A, 1912. Song: solo v., pf.

3344   Cripps, A. Redgrave. Nine "Shropshire Lad" Songs, L: A, pre-1940. Song: [solo v., pf.].

3345   Gurney, Ivor. Ludlow and Teme, L: S&B, 1923. Cyc.: t solo, str. qrt., pf.

3346   Searle, Humphrey. "March Past", Two Songs, L: JW, 1948. Song: med. male v., pf.

3347   Somervell, Arthur. A Shropshire Lad, L: BH, 1904. Cyc.: solo v., pf.

"On Wenlock Edge the wood's in trouble"   A Shropshire Lad (1896)

3348   Gurney, Ivor. "On Wenlock Edge", MS 1917. Song: [solo v., pf.].

3349   Vaughan Williams, Ralph. "On Wenlock Edge", On Wenlock Edge, L: BH, 1911; rev. edn. publ. L: BH, 1946. Cyc.: t solo, pf., str. qrt. ad lib.

"On your midnight pallet lying"   A Shropshire Lad (1896)

3350* Gorecki, Thaddeus. MS ca. 1933. Song.

3351   Gurney, Ivor. "On Your Midnight Pallet", MS 1907. Song: [solo v., pf.].

3352   Orr, C.W. Five Songs from "A Shropshire Lad", L: OUP, 1925-27 (1960). Song: t solo, pf.

Housman, A.E. continued

"Others, I am not the first"   A Shropshire Lad (1896)

    3353 Leichtling, Alan. Eleven Songs from "A Shropshire Lad", NY: SMC, 1971. Cyc.: bar solo, orch.

Parta Quies   "Good-night. Ensured release"   Waifs and Strays (Mar. 1881), rev. 1936

    3354 Cone, Edward T. MS. Song: s solo, pf.

    3355 Edmunds, John. "Have These For Yours", NY: SMP, 1957. Song: solo v., pf.

    3356 Kalmanoff, Martin. "Alta Quies", MS 1949. Song: solo v., pf.

R.L.S.   "Home is the sailor, home from sea"   Academy (Dec. 1894)

    3357 Whear, Paul W. "Requiem", Cl.: LW, 1964. Song: bar solo, pf.

Recruit, The   "Leave your home behind, lad"   A Shropshire Lad (1896)

    3358 Ainsworth, Robert. L: BH, 1932. Song: [solo v., pf.].

    3359 Gardiner, H. Balfour. "Leave your home...", L: G&T (Curwen), 1906. Song: solo v., pf. or solo v., orch.

    3360 Parker, Horatio. NY: Silver, 1920 in The Progressive Music Series, Book 4. Song: v., pf.

Reveille   "Wake: the silver dusk returning"   A Shropshire Lad (1896)

    3361 Dyson, George. Three Songs of Courage, L: N, 1935. Song: satb, stgs. with opt. tpt., trbn., timp. or satb, stgs. with opt. pf. or org. Also publ. L: FA, 1935 for unison v., stgs. with opt. tpt., trbn., timp. or unison v., stgs. with opt. pf. or org.

3362 Gurney, Ivor. The Western Playland, L: S&B, 1926.
Cyc.: bar solo, str. qrt., pf.

3363 Leichtling, Alan. Eleven Songs from "A Shropshire
Lad", NY: SMC, 1971. Cyc.: bar solo, orch.

3364 Peel, Graham. Songs of a Shropshire Lad, L: C, 1911.
Song: [solo v., pf.].

"Say, lad, have you things to do?"   A Shropshire Lad (1896)

3365 Field, Robin. When I was One and Twenty, MS 1960.
Cyc.: med. v., pf.

3366 Moeran, E.J. Ludlow Town, L: OUP, 1924. Song: bar
solo, pf.

3367 Peel, Graham. Songs of a Shropshire Lad, L: C, 1911.
Song:

3368 Van Vactor, David. NY: GX, 1968. Song: satb, a cap.

"Sigh that heaves the grasses, The"   Last Poems (1922)

3369 Stewart, D.M. L: Elkin, 1923. Song: high v., pf. or
low v., pf.

3370 Vaughan Williams, Ralph. Along the Field, L: OUP,
1954. Song: [high] solo v., vln.

"Sloe was lost in flower, The"   Last Poems (1922)

3371 Wilding-White, Raymond. Three Housman Poems, NY:
HP, 1969 in Contemporary Art Song Album, Vol. I.
Song: high v., pf.

"Soldier from the wars returning"   Last Poems (1922)

3372 Orr, C.W. L: S&B, 1937. Song: bar or b-bar solo,
pf.

"Stars have not dealt me the worst they could do, The"
A.E.H. (1937)

3373 Heilner, Irwin. MS copyright by composer 1965, avail. ACA. Song: med. v., pf.

"Stars, I have seen them fall" More Poems (1936)

3374 Bacon, Ernst. "Stars", Quiet Airs, NY: M, 1952. Song: med. v., pf.

3375 Glanville-Hicks, Peggy. "Stars", Five Songs, NY: Weintraub, 1952. Song: med. v., pf.

"Stone, steel, dominions pass" More Poems (1936)

3376 Meyerowitz, Jan. Two Choruses, NY: Rongwen, 1957. Setting for ttbb, hn.

"Street sounds to the soldiers' tread, The" A Shropshire Lad (1896)

3377 Boughton, Rutland. "The Street", MS 1940. Song: solo v., pf.

3378 Cone, Edward T. MS. Song: b-bar solo, pf.

3379 Crerar, Louis. MS 1956, Housman Songs (MS 1954-56), avail. CMC. Song: high v., pf.

3380 Cripps, A. Redgrave. Five "Shropshire Lad" Songs, L: S&B, pre-1944. Song: [solo v., pf.].

3381 Ireland, John. "The Encounter", The Land of Lost Content, L: A, 1921. Song: solo v., pf.

3382 Lambert, Frank. L: S&B, pre-1940. Song: [solo v., pf.].

3383 Peel, Graham. "Soldier, I wish you well", L: C, 1911. Song: [solo v., pf.].

3384 Somervell, Arthur. A Shropshire Lad, L: BH, 1904. Cyc.: solo v., pf.

"There pass the careless people" A Shropshire Lad (1896)

ousman, A.E. continued

    3385   Somervell, Arthur. <u>A Shropshire Lad</u>, L: BH, 1904.
           Cyc.: solo v., pf.

"Think no more, lad; laugh, be jolly"   <u>A Shropshire Lad</u>
    (1896)

    3386   Baksa, Robert. "Think no more, lad", NY: BH, 1967.
           Song: [med.] solo v., pf.

    3387   Barrell, Joyce. "Think no more, Lad", MS. Song: ssa,
           a cap.

    3388* Butterworth, George. "Think No More, Lad", <u>Six Songs</u>
           <u>from "A Shropshire Lad"</u>, L: A, 1911. Cyc.: med.-
           high v., pf.

    3389   Cripps, A. Redgrave. <u>Nine "Shropshire Lad" Songs</u>,
           L: A, pre-1940. Song: [solo v., pf.].

    3390   Manney, Charles F. "Disillusion", <u>A Shropshire Lad</u>,
           B:OD, 1914. Cyc.: [solo v., pf.?].

    3391   Manson, Willie B. <u>Three Poems from "A Shropshire</u>
           <u>Lad"</u>, L: BH, 1920. Song: solo v., pf.

    3392   Priestley-Smith, Hugh. <u>From the West Country</u>, L: JW,
           pre-1943. Cyc.: v., pf.

    3393   Somervell, Arthur. <u>A Shropshire Lad</u>, L: BH, 1904.
           Cyc.: solo v., pf.

"This time of year a twelvemonth past"   <u>A Shropshire Lad</u>
    (1896)

    3394   Orr, C.W. "This time of year", <u>Five Songs from "A</u>
           <u>Shropshire Lad"</u>, L: OUP, 1925-27 (1960). Song:
           t solo, pf.

"'Tis time, I think, by Wenlock town"   <u>A Shropshire Lad</u>
    (1896)

    3395   Armstrong, Thomas H.W. L: Curwen, 1934. Song: 3 pt.
           chorus of children's v., pf. or 3 pt. chorus of
           female v., pf.

3396   Branson, David. "The Unseen Spring", L: OUP, 1939.
        Song: solo v., pf.

3397   Grant, Parks. "'Tis Time, I Think", A_Shropshire
        Lad, MS (Opus 7). Cyc.: high v. (preferably t
        solo), pf.

3398   Gurney, Ivor. "'Tis time, I think", Ludlow_and_Teme,
        L: S&B, 1923. Cyc.: t solo, str. qrt., pf.

3399   Hamilton, Janet. L: WR, 1919. Song: high v., pf.

3400   Ireland, John. "Hawthorn Time", L: WR, 1920. Song:
        solo v., pf.

3401   Ireland, John. "Spring will not wait", We'll_to_the
        Woods_no_more, L: OUP, 1928. Pf. only. Complete
        cyc. also requires solo v.

3402   Moeran, E.J. L: WR, 1926. Song: bar solo, pf.

3403   Orr, C.W. Two_Songs_from_"A_Shropshire_Lad", L: JWC,
        1923. Song: t solo, pf.

3404*   Swain, Freda. MS 1925, rev. 1973, The_Lost_Heart
        (MS 1925-26), avail. Chinnor: Channel, NEMO.
        Setting for t and pf. ensemble.

"Twice a week the winter thorough"   A_Shropshire_Lad (1896)

3405*   Gorecki, Thaddeus. MS ca. 1933. Song.

3406   Gurney, Ivor. "Twice a Week", The_Western_Playland,
        L: S&B, 1926. Cyc.: bar solo, str. qrt., pf.

3407   Ireland, John. "Goal and Wicket", The_Land_of_Lost
        Content, L: A, 1921. Song: solo v., pf.

3408   Turner, Charles. "In Youth and May", NY: GS, pre-
        1969. Song: med. v., pf.

"We'll to the woods no more"   Last_Poems (1922)

3409   Chanwai, Mayme. MS 1962, avail. Victoria University
        of Wellington. Song: a solo, pf.

3410 Crerar, Louis. MS 1954, Housman Songs MS 1954-56, avail. CMC. Song: high v., pf.

3411 Duncan, Chester. "The End", MS 1963, Four Songs (MS 1937-63). Song: med. v., pf.

3412 Ireland, John. We'll to the Woods no more, L: OUP, 1928. Cyc.: solo v., pf. Complete work also requires pf. solo.

3413 Stewart, D.M. L: Elkin, 1923. Song: high v. or low v., pf.

3414 Thomas, Harold F. L: OUP, 1930. Song: [v., pf.?].

3415 Vaughan Williams, Ralph. Along the Field, L: OUP, 1954. Song: [high] solo v., vln.

"Westward on the high-hilled plain"   A Shropshire Lad (1896)

3416 Orr, C.W. Three Songs from "A Shropshire Lad", L: JWC, 1940. Song: t solo, pf.

"When first my way to fair I took"   Last Poems (1922)

3417* Burrows, Benjamin. "The Fair", MS pre-1928, L: A. Song: [solo v., pf.?].

3418 Lydiate, Frederick. MS. Song: t solo, pf.

3419 Mason, Daniel G. NY: Witmark, 1936. Song: solo v., pf.

3420 Russell, Leslie. The Ludlow Cycle, MS 1973. Cyc.: s or t solo, pf.

"When green buds hang in the elm like dust"   More Poems (1936)

3421 Mann, Leslie. "Green Buds", Green Buds, MS 1954, avail. CMC. Song: high v., pf.

"When I came last to Ludlow"   A Shropshire Lad (1896)

3422 Manson, Willie B. Three Poems from "A Shropshire Lad", L: BH, 1920. Song: solo v., pf.

3423 Owen, Morfydd L. MS pre-1968. Song: [solo v., pf.?].

"When I was one-and-twenty"   A Shropshire Lad (1896)

3424 Adams, Stephen. L: BH, 1904. Song: solo v., pf.

3425 Avril, Edwin. A Shropshire Lad, MS. Song: t solo, pf.

3426 Baksa, Robert. NY: BH, 1967. Song: [med.] solo v., pf.

3427 Bax, Arnold. Three Songs, L: E, 1919. Song: med. v., pf.

3428 Bilger, H.L. Bryn Mawr: TP, pre-1940. Song: solo v., pf.

3429 Blank, Allan. MS. Song: med. v., pf.

3430* Bliss, Arthur. NY: R, pre-1940. Song: [solo v., pf.].

3431 Burns, Lorraine J. MS 1962, avail. Victoria University of Wellington. Song: satb, pf.

3432* Butterworth, George. Six Songs from "A Shropshire Lad", L: A, 1911. Song: med.-high v., pf.

3433 Crerar, Louis. MS 1956, Housman Songs (MS 1954-56), avail. CMC. Song: high v., pf.

3434 Cripps, A. Redgrave. Five "Shropshire Lad" Songs, L: S&B, pre-1944. Song: [solo v., pf.].

3435 DeBeer, Alan. L: JWC, 1936. Song: solo v., pf.

3436 Dobson, Tom. NY: GS, 1916. Song: high or med. v., pf.

3437 Duke, John. NY: GS, 1972. Song: solo v., pf.

3438 Fast, Willard. NY: GS, 1972. Song: satb, a cap.

3439 Field, Robin. When I was One and Twenty, MS 1960.
      Cyc.: med. v., pf.

3440 Freed, Isadore. NY: SMP, 1960. Song: solo v., pf.

3441 Gardiner, H. Balfour. Two Lyrics, L: G&T (Curwen),
      1908. Song: solo v., pf.

3442 Gibbs, C. Armstrong. L: Curwen, 1924. Song: solo v.,
      pf. Also avail. for v., stgs.

3443 Godwin, Joscelyn. Carmina Amoris, MS. Cta.: ssaa,
      2 trbn., 2 perc., 4 vcl., 2 db., pf., hpd.

3444 Grant, Parks. A Shropshire Lad, MS (Opus 7). Cyc.:
      high v. (preferably t solo), pf.

3445 Gurney, Ivor. Ludlow and Teme, L: S&B, 1923. Cyc.:
      t solo, str. qrt., pf.

3446 Johnson, Ora. Los Angeles: Heffelfinger, 1915.
      Song: [solo v., pf.?].

3447 Kalmanoff, Martin. NY: Skidmore, 1959. Song: satb,
      pf. Also arr. for satb, str. qrt.

3448 Leichtling, Alan. Eleven Songs from "A Shropshire
      Lad", NY: SMC, 1971. Cyc.: bar solo, orch. Lines
      from "When I was in love with you" are in-
      corporated into this setting.

3449 Manney, Charles F. "Heart Wounds", A Shropshire Lad,
      B: OD, 1914. Cyc.: [solo v., pf.?].

3450 Orr, C.W. L: JWC, 1925. Song: t solo, pf.

3451 Robinson, Clarence. NY: GS, 1950. Song: [solo v.,
      pf.].

3452 Somervell, Arthur. A Shropshire Lad, L: BH, 1904.
      Cyc.: solo v., pf.

3453* Sumsion, Corbett. L: S&B, ca. 1936. Song: ttbb, a
      cap.

3454 Van Vactor, David. NY: GX, 1968. Song: satb, a cap.

Housman, A.E. continued

3455 Wedberg, Conrad. Chi.: Summy, 1946. Song: [solo v.,
       pf.?].

3456 Whitcomb, Mervin. *Two Housman Poems*, NY: Bourne,
       1953. Song: satb, pf.

3457 Wilson, Stanley. L: S&B, pre-1967. Song: sab, [a
       cap.].

3458 Woolley, C. L: N, 1938. Song: solo v., pf.

"When I watch the living meet"   *A Shropshire Lad* (1896)

3459 Duke, Vernon. *Six Songs from "A Shropshire Lad"*, NY:
       Broude-B, 1955. Song: med. v., pf.

3460 Orr, C.W. *Seven Songs from "A Shropshire Lad"*, L:
       JWC, 1934. Song: bar solo, pf.

"When I would muse in boyhood"   *Last Poems* (1922)

3461 Ireland, John. "In Boyhood", *We'll to the Woods no
       more*, L: OUP, 1928. Cyc.: solo v., pf. Complete
       work also requires pf. solo.

3462 Russell, Leslie. *The Ludlow Cycle*, MS 1973. Cyc.:
       s or t solo, pf.

"When smoke stood up from Ludlow"   *A Shropshire Lad* (1896)

3463 Colson, William. MS. Song: high v., pf.

3464 Gurney, Ivor. *Ludlow and Teme*, L: S&B, 1923. Cyc.:
       t solo, str. qrt., pf.

3465 Moeran, E.J. *Ludlow Town*, L: OUP, 1924. Song: bar
       solo, pf.

3466 Orr, C.W. *Seven Songs from "A Shropshire Lad"*, L:
       JWC, 1934. Song: bar solo, pf.

3467 Russell, Leslie. "Ludlow Town", MS 1970-74. Song:
       solo v., pf.

Housman, A.E. continued

"When the bells justle in the tower"   A.E.H. (1937)

3468 Foss, Lukas. "When the Bells Justle", Time Cycle,
NY: CF, 1960 (1962). Cyc.: s solo, orch.

"When the lad for longing sighs"   A Shropshire Lad (1896)

3469 Baksa, Robert. NY: BH, 1967. Song: [med.] solo v.,
pf.

3470 Butterworth, George. "Bredon Hill" and Other Songs,
L: A, 1912. Song: [med.] solo v., pf.

3471 Leichtling, Alan. Eleven Songs from "A Shropshire
Lad", NY: SMC, 1971. Cyc.: bar solo, orch.

3472 Orr, C.W. L: JWC, 1925. Song: t solo, pf.

3473 Peel, Graham. Songs of a Shropshire Lad, L: C, 1911.
Song: [solo v., pf.].

"White in the moon the long road lies"   A Shropshire Lad
(1896)

3474 Brown, James. "White in the Moon", MS. Song: ms or
bar solo, pf. Also avail. for s or t solo, pf.

3475 Duke, John. "White in the Moon", Two Songs, Northampton, Mass.: VMP, 1948. Song: med. v., pf.

3476 Fox, Oscar J. NY: CF, 1932. Song: ssa, pf. or ttbb,
pf.

3477 Grant, Parks. A Shropshire Lad, MS (Opus 7). Cyc.:
high v. (preferably t solo), pf.

3478 Ley, Henry G. "White in the Moon", L: S&B, pre-1940.
Song: [v., pf.?].

3479 Manney, Charles F. "Exile", A Shropshire Lad, B: OD,
1914. Cyc.: [solo v., pf.?].

3480 Priestley-Smith, Hugh. From the West Country, L: JW,
pre-1943. Cyc.: v., pf.

Housman, A.E. continued

3481　Somervell, Arthur. A_Shropshire_Lad, L: BH, 1904.
　　　Cyc.: solo v., pf.

3482*　Swain, Freda. MS 1925, rev. 1973, The_Lost_Heart
　　　(MS 1925-26), avail. Chinnor: Channel, NEMO.
　　　Setting for t and pf. ensemble.

3483　Taylor, E. Kendal. "White in the Moon", L: OUP,
　　　1925. Song: [v., pf.].

"With rue my heart is laden"　A_Shropshire_Lad (1896)

3484　Atherton, Percy. B: BMC, pre-1940. Song: [solo v.,
　　　pf.].

3485　Barber, Samuel. MS 1928, NY: GS. Song: solo v., pf.

3486　Branscombe, Gena. NY: GS, pre-1940. Song: [solo v.,
　　　pf.].

3487　Butterworth, George. "Bredon_Hill"_and_Other_Songs,
　　　L: A, 1912. Song: solo v., pf.

3488　Chanwai, Mayme. MS 1962, avail. Victoria University
　　　of Wellington. Song: a solo, pf.

3489　Colson, William. Three_Songs_from_"A_Shropshire
　　　Lad", MS. Song: high v., pf.

3490　Cone, Edward T. MS. Song: a solo, pf.

3491　Cripps, A. Redgrave. Nine_"Shropshire_Lad"_Songs, L:
　　　A, pre-1940. Song: [solo v., pf.].

3492　Duke, Vernon. Six_Songs_from_"A_Shropshire_Lad",
　　　NY: Broude-B, 1955. Song: med. v., pf.

3493　Duncan, Chester. MS 1937, Four_Songs (MS 1937-63).
　　　Song: med. v., pf.

3494　Gurney, Ivor. The_Western_Playland, L: S&B, 1926.
　　　Cyc.: bar solo, str. qrt., pf.

3495　Hamilton, Janet. L: WR, 1919. Song: high v., pf.

3496　Heussenstamm, George. Bryn Mawr: EV, 1971. Song: 2
　　　pt. chorus (satb), a cap.

3497 Leichtling, Alan. Eleven Songs from "A Shropshire
      Lad", NY: SMC, 1971. Cyc.: bar solo, orch.

3498 Mann, Leslie. Green Buds, MS 1954, avail. CMC. Song:
      high v., pf.

3499 Manney, Charles F. "Grief", A Shropshire Lad, B: OD,
      1914. Cyc.: [solo v., pf.?].

3500 Orr, C.W. Five Songs from "A Shropshire Lad", L:
      OUP, 1925-27 (1960). Song: t solo, pf.

3501 Russell, Leslie. "With grief my heart is laden", MS
      1970-74. Song: solo v., pf.

3502 Van Vactor, David. NY: GX, 1968. Song: satb, a cap.

3503 Vaughan Williams, Ralph. Along the Field, L: OUP,
      1954. Song: [high] solo v., vln.

3504 Walker, George. Hastings-on-Hudson: GMP, 1972. Song:
      high v., pf.

3505 Ward, Robert. NY: MMP, 1949. Song: satb, a cap.

"With seeds the sowers scatter"   More Poems (1936)

3506 Searle, Humphrey. "The Stinging Nettle", Two Songs,
      L: JW, 1948. Song: med. male v., pf.

"Yonder see the morning blink"   Last Poems (1922)

3507* Burrows, Benjamin. "Yonder See", MS pre-1928, L: A.
      Song: [solo v., pf.?].

3508 Douglas, Keith. MS pre-1943. Song: [v., pf.?].

3509 Kagen, Sergius. A Song Cycle, MS pre-1964, NY: M.
      Cyc.: v., pf.

3510 Russell, Leslie. The Ludlow Cycle, MS 1973. Cyc.:
      s or t solo, pf.

3511* Swain, Freda. MS 1929. avail. Chinnor: Channel,
      NEMO. Setting for bar and pf. ensemble.

Housman, A.E. continued

"You smile upon your friend to-day"   A Shropshire Lad (1896)

    3512 Cripps, A. Redgrave. Five "Shropshire Lad" Songs,
          L: S&B, pre-1944. Song: [solo v., pf.].

    3513 Ireland, John. "Epilogue", The Land of Lost Content,
          L: A, 1921. Song: solo v., pf.

Miscellanea

    3514 Armstrong, Thomas H.W. Five Short Songs, MS ca.
          1920. Songs: [solo v., pf.?]. One song is a set-
          ting of "Into my heart an air that kills"; the
          other four songs are also settings of poems by
          Housman.

    3515 Bate, Stanley. Four Songs, MS pre-1954. Texts by
          Housman.

    3516 Baynon, Arthur. A Shropshire Lad, L: A, ca. 1922.
          Ste. for pf. solo, after verses by Housman.

    3517 Branson, David. Three Songs, MS ca. 1939. Texts by
          Housman.

    3518 Edmunds, John. "Loveliest of Trees", MS pre-1943.
          Song. [Text by Housman?]

    3519 Flanagan, William. The Weeping Pleiades, MS 1953.
          Cyc.: [v., pf.?]. Texts by Housman.

    3520 France, William E. "With rue my heart is laden", MS.
          Song. [Text by Housman?]

    3521 Holloway, Robin. Four Housman Fragments, MS 1966.
          Settings for med. v., instr. ensemble.

    3522 Holloway, Robin. Georgian Songs, MS 1972, L: OUP.
          Song: bar solo, pf. Incl. words by Housman.

3523   Nicholls, Dr. A letter dated 22 Aug. 1935 (not incl.
       in Henry Maas' The Letters of A.E. Housman) from
       Housman to his publisher is cited as follows on
       p. 15 of the Summer-Fall 1941 issue of Mark Twain
       Quarterly:
              Dr. Nicholls is at liberty to publish
              his settings of the poems which he has
              selected from "A Shropshire Lad" except
              LXII ["The Merry Guide"], which would
              be absurd as a song: I do not object to
              his combining LVIII ["When I came last
              to Ludlow"] with LIX ["The Isle of Port-
              land"]. Perhaps he had better be told
              that many of them have been set by other
              composers, and XIII ["When I was one-
              and-twenty"] by a considerable number.

3524   Scholl, Barbara. [Six Songs from "A Shropshire
       Lad"], MS 1952. Songs: v., pf.

3525   Whittaker, George. Seven Songs, MS pre-1939. The
       Oct. 1939 issue of Monthly Musical Record com-
       ments that "...the words..., ranging from John
       Lydgate to the Japanese, via Dowson, Housman,
       Synge..., reveal wide literary interests".

HOUSMAN, Laurence   1865-1959

Bethlehem   (DR)   (1902)

    3526 Moorat, Joseph. MS. Incidental music.

Chinese Lantern, The   (DR)   (1908)

    3527 Moorat, Joseph. MS, prod. 1908. Incidental music.

Christmas Songs   "Maker of the sun and moon, The"   In
    Bethlehem, The Pageant of Our Lady and Other Poems (1902)

    3528* Moorat, Joseph. MS. Songs: [v., pf.?].

Housman, Laurence continued

3529 Willan, Healey. "The Three Kings", L: OUP, 1928.
Carol: ssatbb, a cap. Arr. by J. Running for 2 t,
bar soli, ttbb, a cap; arr. publ. L: OUP, 1966.
Also arr. by J. Running for 2 s, a soli, ssaa, a
cap; arr. publ. L: OUP, 1968. Setting of lines
beginning: "Who knocks to-night so late".

Little Plays of St. Francis   (DR)   (1922)

3530 Boughton, Rutland. MS 1924-25. Incidental music:
voices, instruments.

Pageant of Our Lady, The   (DR)   In Bethlehem, The Pageant
of Our Lady and Other Poems (1902)

3531 Moorat, Joseph. MS. Incidental music.

3532 Willan, Healey. Unf. MS ca. 1936. Incidental music:
4 soli (s, b), chorus, [orch. accompaniment in-
tended].

Prunella   (DR)   In coll. with Harley Granville Barker
(1906)

3533 Moorat, Joseph. MS, prod. 1906; L: Elkin, 1923.
Incidental music.

Song   "Down to death, my dear, together"   In The Heart of
Peace and Other Poems (1919)

3534 Lander, Cyril. Flores de mi primavera, MS n.d.,
avail. National Library of N.Z. Song: high v.,
pf.

Miscellanea

3535 Holst, Gustav, arr. "The Pageant of St. Martin-in-
the-Fields", MS 1921. Incidental music: satb,
orch. Arr. of Engl. march tunes, ancient Irish
and Latin hymns, etc.

3536   Lehmann, Liza. The Vicar of Wakefield, L: BH, 1907.
        Opera. Based on the novel by Oliver Goldsmith.
        Incl. lyrics by Housman.

3537   Paget, Michael. "Carol of the Innocents", L: Curwen,
        1963. Carol: satb, a cap.

3538   Shaw, Geoffrey. "Father Eternal, Ruler of Creation",
        Cambridge, Mass.: HUP, 1964 in The Harvard Univ-
        ersity Hymn Book. Hymn: v., org. Employs the tune
        "Langham".

3539   Willan, Healey. "Schola Cantorum", MS 1961. Hymn for
        choir. Text begins: "Lord God of Hosts, within
        whose hand".

HUDSON, William Henry   1841-1922

Far Away and Long Ago   (NV)   (1918)

3540   Tippett, Michael. "Boyhood's End", L: S, 1945. Cta.:
        t solo, pf. Sets passage beginning: "What, then,
        did I want?".

Green Mansions   (NV)   (1904)

3541   Gruenberg, Louis. MS 1937, perf. CBS. Opera for
        radio. Libr. by composer.

3542   Kalmanoff, Martin. MS 1967. Musical: 3 female roles,
        5 male roles, pf. Lyrics by Gerald Lebowitz after
        Marlene Brenner's adapt. of the novel.

3543   Scott, Cyril. "Rima's Call to the Birds", L: Elkin,
        1933. Song: s solo, orch.

Huetter, Ford Hermann Madox

HUEFFER, Ford Hermann Madox   See: FORD, Ford Madox

HUGHES, Ted   1930-

  Esther's Tomcat   See: Tomcat

  Grandma   "My grandmother's a peaceful person"   In Meet My
    Folks! (1961)

      3544 Crosse, Gordon. "My Grandma", Meet My Folks, L: OUP,
            1964. Song: children's v., perc., instr. en-
            semble.

  Hawk in the Rain, The   "I drown in the drumming ploughland"
    In The Hawk in the Rain (1957)

      3545 Wood, Hugh. Three Choruses, L: UE, 1967. Song: satb,
            a cap.

  Horses, The   "I climbed through woods in the hour-before-
    dawn dark"   In The Hawk in the Rain (1957)

      3546 Wood, Hugh. The Horses, MS 1967-68. Cyc.: high v.,
            pf. Issued on Argo recording #ZRG 750.

  "I've heard so much about other folks' folks"   In Meet my
    Folks! (1961)

      3547 Crosse, Gordon. "Dedication", Meet My Folks, L: OUP,
            1964. Song: children's v., perc., instr. en-
            semble.

  My Aunt   "You've heard how a green thumb"   In Meet My
    Folks! (1961)

      3548 Crosse, Gordon. Meet My Folks, L: OUP, 1964. Song:
            children's v., perc., instr. ensemble.

My Brother Bert   "Pets are the Hobby of my brother Bert"
In Meet My Folks! (1961)

   3549 Crosse, Gordon. "Brother Bert", Meet My Folks, L:
         OUP, 1964. Song: children's v., perc., instr.
         ensemble.

My Father   "Some fathers work at the office"   In Meet My
Folks! (1961)

   3550 Crosse, Gordon. Meet My Folks, L: OUP, 1964. Song:
         children's v., perc., instr. ensemble.

My Grandpa   "Truth of the matter, the truth of the matter--,
The"   Meet My Folks! (1961)

   3551 Crosse, Gordon. Meet My Folks, L: OUP, 1964. Song:
         children's v., perc., instr. ensemble.

My Sister Jane   "And I say nothing--no, not a word"   In
Meet My Folks! (1961)

   3552 Crosse, Gordon. "Sister Jane", Meet My Folks, L:
         OUP, 1964. Song: children's v., perc., instr. en-
         semble.

Pennines in April   "If this country were a sea"   In Lupercal (1960)

   3553 Wood, Hugh. The Horses, MS 1967-68. Cyc.: high v.,
         pf. Issued on Argo recording #ZRG 750.

September   "We sit late, watching the dark slowly unfold"
In The Hawk and the Rain (1957)

   3554 Wood, Hugh. The Horses, MS 1967-68. Cyc.: high v.,
         pf. Issued on Argo recording #ZRG 750.

Tomcat   "Daylong this tomcat lies stretched flat"
Originally publ. in New Yorker; subsequently incl. in
Lupercal (1960) under the title "Esther's Tomcat"

3555   Young, Douglas. "Esther's Tomcat", Of Birds and
       Beasts, L: F (hire). Cyc.: satb, orch.

Miscellanea

3556   Cole, Hugo. "The Story of Vasco", MS, prod. Mar.
       1974, L: OUP. Opera. Libr. by Hughes, after
       a work by Georges Schehade.

3557   Crosse, Gordon. "The Demon of Adachigahara", L: OUP,
       1969. Cta.: sp., children's choir (unison and
       ad lib. satb), jr. orch., pf. A version with
       accompaniment of (full) youth orch., jr. orch.
       exists in MS.

3558   Crosse, Gordon. The New World, L: OUP, 1974. Cyc.:
       solo, v., pf. The cyc. consists mainly of unpubl.
       texts specifically written by Hughes for the
       composition. The composer has indicated to the
       eds. that the cyc. is suitable for s (or t) or
       ms solo. The publisher's advertisement in the
       June 1975 issue of Musical Times indicates that
       the texts are set for med. v.

HUXLEY, Aldous Leonard   1894-1963

Devils of Loudun, The   (NV)   (1952)

3559   Davies, Peter Maxwell. The Devils, MS, perf. London,
       Dec. 1971. Music for film based on John Whiting's
       adapt. of the novel.

3560   Penderecki, Krzysztof. MS 1968-69, Mz.: S. Opera:
       3 s, ms, 2 a, 3 t, 3 bar, b-bar, 3 b soli, 3 sp.,
       actors, orch. Libr. by the composer. Transl. into
       German by Erich Fried.

Leda   "Brown and bright as an agate"   In Leda (1920)

3561   Beeson, Jack. MS 1957. Setting for reciter, pf.

uxley, Aldous continued

Miscellanea

3562   Bennett, Robert R. Etudes, MS, perf. 1942. Ea. etude
       is sub-titled to indicate a personality, e.g.,
       Walter Damrosch, Aldous Huxley, Noel Coward.

3563   Ireland, John. "The Trellis", Two Songs, L: A, 1920.
       Song: solo v., pf.

3564   Stravinsky, Igor. The Apr. 1967 issue of Musical
       Times cites the composer's Variations in Memory
       of Aldous Huxley.

HYDE, Douglas   1860-1949

I am Raftery   "I am Raftery the poet"   In Poems from the
Irish (1963) Transl. from the Irish

   3565   Burrows, Benjamin. "Raftery", L: A, pre-1928. Song:
          [solo v., pf.?].

   3566   Dillon, Shaun. Cantata in Memoriam, MS, perf. Nov.
          1974. Song (in cta.): s solo, pf.

I shall not die for thee   "For then I shall not die"   In
The Love Songs of Connacht (1904) Transl. from the Irish

   3567   Maw, Nicholas. Five Irish Songs, L: BH, 1973. Song:
          satb, a cap.

My Grief on the Sea   "My grief on the sea"   In The Love
Songs of Connacht (1904) Transl. from the Irish

   3568   Trimble, Joan. L: BH, 1938. Song: low v., pf.

Ringleted Youth of My Love   "Ringleted youth of my love"
In The Love Songs of Connacht (1904) Transl. from the
Irish

403

Hyde, Douglas continued

    3569 Maw, Nicholas. _Five Irish Songs_, L: BH, 1973. Song:
           satb, a cap.

  Miscellanea

    3570 Esposito, Michele. "The Tinker and the Fairy", MS
           1910. Incidental music.

    3571 May, Frederick. "Irish Love Song", MS ca. 1930,
           Dublin: Pigott. Song: v., pf. Text employs Lady
           Gregory's transl. of Hyde's poem.

ISHERWOOD, Christopher William Bradshaw   1904-

  Ascent of F6, The   (DR)   In coll. with W.H. Auden (1936)

    3572 Britten, Benjamin. MS, prod. BBC 1937. Incidental
           music.

    3573 Britten, Benjamin. See: "Stop all the clocks...".

    3574* Duncan, Chester. MS 1945-50. Incidental music: s, a,
           t, bar soli, chorus, pf.

    3575 Rorem, Ned. See: "Stop all the clocks...".

    3576 Southam, T. Wallace. See: "Stop all the clocks...".

  Dog Beneath the Skin, The   (DR)   In coll. with W.H. Auden
    (1935)

    3577 Britten, Benjamin. See: "Now through night's cares-
           sing grip".

    3578 Hyde, Lewis. See: "Seen when night is silent".

    3579 Murrill, Herbert. MS pre-1952. Incidental music.

"Now through night's caressing grip"   In coll. with W.H.
Auden   The_Dog_Beneath_the_Skin (1935) Incl. as a sep.
poem in collections of Auden's verse

    3580   Britten, Benjamin. "Nocturne", On_this_Island, L:
        WR, 1938. Cyc.: high v., pf. Score contains Fr.
        transl. by Maurice Pourchet. "Nocturne" was publ.
        sep. L: BH [1949?].

On_the_Frontier   (DR)   In coll. with W.H. Auden (1938)

    3581   Britten, Benjamin. MS, prod. 1939. Incidental music.

    3582   Britten, Benjamin. Ballad_of_Heroes, L: WR, 1939.
        Ballad: t or s solo, chorus (largely unison),
        orch. Sets lines beginning: "Europe lies in the
        dark".

"Seen when night is silent"   In coll. with W.H. Auden   The
Dog_Beneath_the_Skin (1935) Incl. as a sep. poem in collections of Auden's verse

    3583   Hyde, Lewis. MS 1951. Song: solo v., pf.

    3584   Murrill, Herbert. See: Dog_Beaneath_the_Skin,_The.

"Stop all the clocks, cut off the telephone"   In coll. with
W.H. Auden   The_Ascent_of_F6 (1936) Incl. as a sep. poem
in collections of Auden's verse.

    3585   Britten, Benjamin. See: Ascent_of_F6,_The.

    3586   Britten, Benjamin. "Funeral Blues", Four_Cabaret
        Songs_for_Hedli_Anderson, MS 1938. Song: [v.,
        pf.?].

    3587   Duncan, Chester. See: Ascent_of_F6,_The.

    3588* Rorem, Ned. Poems_of_Love_and_the_Rain, NY: BH,
        1965. Cyc.: ms solo, pf. 2 settings of "Stop all
        the clocks...".

    3589   Southam, T. Wallace. Poetry_Set_in_Jazz, L: RMC,
        1966. Song: v., pf.

Jacobs, W.W.

JACOBS, William Wymark   1863-1943

Boatswain's Mate, The   (SS)   In <u>Captains All</u> (1905)

   3590   Smyth, Ethel. L: Forsyth, 1913. Opera.

Miscellanea

   3591   Brent-Smith, Alexander. "The Captain's Parrot", L:
          N, 1950. Opera: 12 soli, satb, orch.

   3592   Smyth, Ethel. Smyth set (as an opera)"The Boat-
          swain's Mate" from Jacobs' collection of short
          stories entitled <u>Captains All</u>, and <u>Grove's</u> lists
          an opera entitled "Captains All". However, the
          eds. believe that the entry in <u>Grove's</u> is either
          incomplete or inaccurate because 1) Christopher
          St. John's <u>Ethel Smyth: A Biography</u> (L: Long-
          man's, Green, 1959) lists only "The Boatswain's
          Mate" and 2) the eds. have no evidence that Smyth
          also set the story "Captains' All" which was
          publ. in Jacobs' collection of the same title.

JAMES, Henry   1843-1916

Last of the Valerii, The   (SS)   <u>Atlantic Monthly</u> (Jan.
   1874)

   3593   Musgrave, Thea. "The Voice of Ariadne", L: N, 1974.
          Ch. opera. Libr. by Amalia Elguera.

Owen Wingrave   (SS)   <u>Graphic</u> (Nov. 1892)

   3594   Britten, Benjamin. L: F, 1973. Opera: 3 s, ms, 2 or
          3 t, bar, b-bar soli, chorus of treble v., orch.
          Libr. by Myfanwy Piper. German transl. by Claus
          Henneberg and Karl Marz.

Turn of the Screw, The   (SS)   Collier's Weekly (Jan.-Apr.
     1898)

     3595 Britten, Benjamin. L: BH, 1955. Ch. opera. Libr. by
           Myfanwy Piper; vocal score by Imogen Holst;
           German transl. by Ludwig Landgraf.

Washington Square   (NV)   Cornhill Magazine (June-Nov.
     1880), publ. sep. 1881

     3596 Copland, Aaron. "The Heiress", MS, prod. NY, Oct.
           1949. Film music to screenplay by Ruth and
           Augustus Goetz.

     3597 Damase, Jean-Michel. "The Heiress", MS, to be perf.
           Nancy, Mar. 1975. Opera. Libr. by Louis Ducreaux.
           Fr. title: "L'Héritière".

Wings of the Dove, The   (NV)   (1902)

     3598 Moore, Douglas. NY: GS, 1963. Opera: 2 s, ms, a, 2
           t, 4 bar soli, orch. Libr. by Ethan Ayer.

JHNSON, Lionel Pigot   1867-1902

Autumn Song   See: Comfort

Comfort   "Winter is at the door"   Wykehamist (Apr. 1888)
     The poem was originally entitled "Autumn Song"

     3599 Braine, Robert. "Winter at the Door", B: Schmidt,
           pre-1940. Song: [v., pf.?].

In Memory   "Under the clear December sun"   In The Complete
     Poems of Lionel Johnson (1953)

     3600 Jervis-Read, Harold. L: MM, pre-1940. Song: [v.,
           pf.].

Johnson, Lionel continued

    3601   McCabe, John. "Ah! fair face gone from sight", Time
          Remembered, L: N, 1973. Cyc.: s solo, fl., cl.,
          hn., tpt., vln., vcl., pf. Incl. a setting of
          lines beginning: "Ah! fair face gone from sight".

To Morfydd   "Voice on the winds, A"   The Second Book of the
Rhymers Club (1894)

    3602   Clarke, Robert C. "Mine are your eyes", L: C.
          Song: [v., pf.]. Also publ. in the composer's
          "Portrait Series" album.

    3603   Ryder, Arthur H. "A voice...", B: BMC, pre-1940.
          Song: [v., pf.?].

JOYCE, James Augustine Aloysius   1882-1941

"All day I hear the noise of waters"   Chamber Music (1907)

    3604   Allen, Creighton. "Lay of Solitude", NY: GS, 1929.
          Song: [v., pf.?].

    3605   Berio, Luciano. "Monotone", Chamber Music, Mi.: SZ,
          1954. Song: s or a solo, cl., vcl., hp.

    3606   Betts, Lorne. Six Songs to Poems of James Joyce,
          MS 1951, avail. CMC. Song: high v., pf.

    3607   Calabro, Louis. Three Songs for Medium Voice, MS
          1952, avail. NYPL. Song: med. v., pf.

    3608   Coulthard, Jean. Three Songs, MS 1946, avail. CMC.
          Song: med. v., pf.

    3609   Del Tredici, David. "Monotone", Four Songs on Texts
          of James Joyce, NY: BH, 1974. Song: solo v., pf.

    3610   Ferris, Joan. Six Songs, NY: CF, 1967. Song: satb,
          a cap.

3611 Fetler, Paul. "All Day I Hear", NY: LG, 1957 (1962).
      Song: satb, a cap.

3612 Goossens, Eugene. Chamber Music, L: Curwen, 1930.
      Song: med. v., pf.

3613 Kagen, Sergius. "All Day I Hear", NY: Weintraub,
      1950. Song: med. v., pf.

3614 Kauder, Hugo. "All Day I Hear", Ten Poems, NY: BH,
      1955. Song: s, a, t soli, str. qrt.

3615 Persichetti, Vincent. "Noise of Waters", James
      Joyce Songs, Ph.: EV, 1959. Song: solo v., pf.

3616 Read, Gardner. "All Day I Hear", Songs for a Rainy
      Night, NY: BH, 1950. Song: ms solo, pf.

3617 Serly, Tibor. MS 1926, Four Songs from "Chamber
      Music". Song: ms solo, ch. orch. Issued on
      Keyboard recording #K 101 entitled The Music of
      Tibor Serly.

Alone "Moon's greygolden meshes make, The" Poetry,
      Chicago (Nov. 1917)

3618 Boydell, Brian. MS 1941. Song: bar solo, pf.

3619 Carducci, Edgardo. L: OUP, 1933 in The Joyce Book.
      Song: [solo v., pf.].

3620 Field, Robin. "The moon's...", The Sly Reeds
      Whisper, MS 1967. Cyc.: t solo, ob., str. qrt.

3621 Gruen, John. MS. Song: [s] solo v., pf. Issued on
      Lyrichord recording #LL 83 entitled Songs To
      Texts by James Joyce.

3622 Jarrett, Jack M. The Unquiet Heart, MS 1964. Song:
      s or t solo, pf.

3623 Martino, Donald. Three Songs, B: ECS (Ione), 1970.
      Song: s or t solo, pf. or b solo, pf.

"At that hour when all things have repose" Chamber Music
      (1907)

Joyce, James continued

    3624 Billingsley, William. James Joyce Songs, MS. Song:
           t solo, pf.

    3625 Kauder, Hugo. "At That Hour", Ten Poems, NY: BH,
           1955. Song: s, a, t soli, str. qrt.

    3626 Ritchie, Tom. Serenade, MS. Song: solo v., str.
           qrt. or solo v., pf.

    3627 Spector, Irwin. Songs of Love and Music, MS. Cyc.:
           med. v., ob., vla., pf.

    3628 White, John D. Three Joyce Songs, MS. Song: a or
           bar solo, pf.

Bahnhofstrasse   "Eyes that mock me sign the way, The"
Anglo-French Review (Aug. 1919)

    3629 Bate, Stanley. Five Songs, L: R, 1951. Song: low
           v., pf.

    3630 Field, Robin. "Eyes...", The Sly Reeds Whisper,
           MS 1967. Cyc.: t solo, ob., str. qrt.

    3631 Gruen, John. MS. Song: [s] solo v., pf. Issued on
           Lyrichord recording #LL 83 entitled Songs to
           Texts by James Joyce.

    3632 Orr, C.W. L: OUP, 1933 in The Joyce Book; re-issued
           L: OUP, 1960 in Album of Four Songs. Song: t
           solo, pf.

"Be not sad because all men"   Chamber Music (1907)

    3633 Pisk, Paul. Songs from "Chamber Music" by James
           Joyce, MS (Opus 101). Song: t solo, pf. Issued
           on Washington University recording #T4RM-5570.

"Because your voice was at my side"   Chamber Music (1907)

    3634 Avshalomov, Jacob. "Because Your Voice", NY: HP,
           1957. Song: satb, a cap.

    3635 Boydell, Brian. MS 1948. Song: high v., ob., str.
           trio or high v., pf.

yce, James continued

3636 Lombardo, Robert M. Three Madrigals, MS 1960.
       Madrigal: s, 2 a soli, unacc. or ssa, a cap.

3637* Lombardo, Robert M. Two Lyric Poems, NY: CMP,
       copyright 1968 by composer. Song: satb, cl.

3638 Mengelberg, Rudolf. Chamber Music, Amst.: B&VP,
       n.d. (NY: CFP, 1960). Cyc.: med. v., pf.

"Bid adieu, adieu, adieu"   Chamber Music (1907)

3639 Citkowitz, Israel. "Bid Adieu", Five Songs for
       Voice and Piano, NY: Cos Cob, 1930. Cyc.: solo
       v., pf.

3640 Diamond, David. Three Madrigals, NY: Kalmus, 1938.
       Madrigal: 4 pt. chorus, a cap. Rev. edn. publ.
       NY: SMP, 1965.

3641 Pendleton, Edmund in coll. with James Joyce. "Bid
       Adieu", P: Ars Musica, 1949. Song: solo v., pf.
       "Air by Joyce".

"Bright cap and streamers"   Chamber Music (1907)

3642 Betts, Lorne. Six Songs to Poems of James Joyce,
       MS 1951, avail. CMC. Song: high v., pf.

3643 Ferris, Joan. Six Songs, NY: CF, 1967. Song: satb,
       a cap.

3644 Jarrett, Jack M. NY: LG, 1964. Song: satb, pf.

3645 Klotzman, Dorothy H. Three Songs from "Chamber
       Music", NY: M, 1963. Song: ssa, a cap.

3646 Moeran, E.J. "Bright Cap", Seven Poems by James
       Joyce, L: OUP, 1930. Song: ms or bar solo, pf.

3647 Spencer, Williametta. Champaign: MF, 1972. Song:
       satb, a cap.

3648 Treacher, Graham. L: S, 1963. Song: 2 pt. children's
       choir, pf.

411

Joyce, James continued

3649   Victory, Gerard. <u>Five Songs by James Joyce</u>, MS 1954,
        Song: t solo, satb, 2 fl., 10 br., 2 cl., 2 hn.

Dead, The   (SS)   <u>Dubliners</u> (1914)

3650   Wood, Ralph W. MS. Originally composed as a radio
        narration for speaking voices, orch. Adapt. as
        opera: 2 s, ms, 2 t soli, mimed roles, orch.
        Text adapt. by K. Greenwood.

"Dear heart, why will you use me so?"   <u>Chamber Music</u> (1907)

3651   Goossens, Eugene. <u>Chamber Music</u>, L: Curwen, 1930.
        Song: med. v., pf.

3652   Jarrett, Jack M. <u>Songs about the End of Love</u>, MS
        1962. Song: satb, pf.

3653   Sterne, Colin. "Dear Heart", NY: Peer, 1953. Song:
        solo v., pf.

Ecce Puer   "Of the dark past"   <u>New Republic</u> (Nov. 1932)

3654*   Del Tredici, David. <u>Syzygy</u>, NY: BH, 1974. Song: s
        solo, ww. oct., hn., 2 tpt., str. sextet, bells.

3655   Naylor, Bernard. L: N, 1963 in <u>Sing Nowell</u>. Carol:
        satb, a cap.

3656   Schickele, Peter. "Of the Dark Past", MS. Setting
        for s solo, orch. Issued on Vanguard recordings
        #VRS 9275 and VSD 79275 entitled <u>Baptism: A
        Journey through Our Time</u>.

<u>Finnegan's Wake</u>*   (NV)   (1939)   Portions 1st publ. in
    <u>Transatlantic Review</u> (Apr. 1924) and in various other
    journals later

3657   Barber, Samuel. "Nuvoletta", NY: GS, 1952. Song:
        high v., pf. Sets extracts from pp. 157-9.

3658   Buller, John. <u>Two Night Pieces from "Finnegan's
        Wake"</u>, MS. Songs: s solo, ch. ensemble.

3659 Buller, John. "Scribenrey", MS. Vcl. solo. Programme
of concert by Miss Ward Clarke held March 1973
incl. sequence of phrases from the novel.

3660 Cage, John. "The Wonderful Widow of Eighteen
Springs", NY: CFP, 1961. Song: solo v., closed
pf. Text adapt. from p. 556.

3661 Erickson, Robert. "The End of the Mime of Mick,
Nick and the Maggies", NY: Okra, n.d. Song: satb,
pf. Text from p. 219 ff.

3662 Felman, Hazel. "Anna Livia Plurabelle", Chi.: Argus
Book Shop, 1935. Song: solo v., pf. Sets passage
beginning: "Wait till the honeying of the lune,
love!" (pp. 215-16). Text (which predates publ.
of the novel) taken from _Anna Livia Plurabelle_
(1928).

3663 Hodeir, André. "Anna Livia Plurabelle", NY: MJQ,
1967. Jazz cta.: ms, a soli, 9 sax. (doubl. 1
cl.), 3 tpt. (doubl. 1 flhn.), 3 trbn., 2 vibra.,
drums, gtr., vln., clapping section (can be
played by members of the orchestra). Setting
of passage beginning: "O tell me all about Anna
Livia!" (p. 196).

3664 Ito, Teiji. "Coach with the Six Insides", MS.
Musical play adapt. from the novel. Issued on
ESP recording #1019.

3665 Jarrett, Jack M. ....riverrun, MS 1964. Settings
for bar solo, orch. Settings entitled "The
rivering waters of", "A leaptear", "Annah: the
Bringer of Plurabilities", "Renew". Texts adapt.
from pp. 216, 159, 104, [?].

3666 Lerdahl, Alfred. "Wake", MS. Setting for s solo, ch.
orch. Text from p. 196 ff. Issued on Deutsche
Grammophone recording #0654 083.

3667 Lutyens, Elisabeth. "Notturno 4° ", _The Tears of
Night_, L: OP, 1971. Setting for 6 s, c-t soli,
2 tpt., 2 trbn., db. Complete work requires
various instr. ensembles. Sets passage beginning:
"Oh, how it was duusk" (p. 158).

3668 Rands, Bernard. Wildtrack 2, MS 1972, L: UE. Work
for fl., a. fl., cl., b. cl., t. sax., bsn., 2
hrn., 2 tpt., 2 trbn., elec. org., vibra., mrmb.,
3 perc., stgs. Makes use of passage beginning:
"Soft morning, city!" (p. 619 f.).

3669 Searle, Humphrey. The Riverrun, MS 1951, L: S
(hire). Setting for Irish female sp., orch. Sets
passage beginning: "Soft morning, city!" (p. 619
f.).

Flood   "Goldbrown upon the sated flood"   Poetry, Chicago
(May 1917)

3670 Betts, Lorne. "Goldbrown...", Five Songs, MS 1952,
avail. CMC. Song: [med.-high] solo v., pf.

3671 Howells, Herbert. L: OUP, 1933 in The Joyce Book.
Song: [solo v., pf.].

Flower Given to My Daughter, A   "Frail the white rose"
Poetry, Chicago (May 1917)

3672 Betts, Lorne. "Frail...", Five Songs, MS 1952,
avail. CMC. Song: [med.-high] solo v., pf.

3673 Dallapiccola, Luigi. Tre poemi, Mz.: AVV, 1960.
Song: s solo, ch. orch. Ital. title: "Per un
fiore data alla mia bambina", transl. by Eugenio
Montale.

3674 Del Tredici, David. Four Songs on Texts of James
Joyce, NY: BH, 1974. Song: solo v., pf.

3675 Diamond, David. NY: Arrow, 1942. Song: [v., pf.].

3676 Moeran, E.J. "Rosefrail", L: A, 1931. Song: med. v.,
pf. Also arr. for high v., pf.

3677 Roussel, Albert. L: OUP, 1933 in The Joyce Book;
publ. sep. P: Durand, 1948. Song: solo v., pf.
Durand edn. incl. Fr. transl. by Rollo H. Myers.

3678 Stevenson, Ronald. MS 1971. Song: med. v., pf.

3679 Strickland, William. NY: GX, 1961. Song: med. high
      v., pf.

"From dewy dreams, my soul, arise"   Chamber Music (1907)

3680 Bonner, Eugene. "From Dewy Dreams", L: JWC, 1924.
      Song: [v., pf.?].

3681 Victory, Gerard. Five Songs by James Joyce, MS 1954.
      Song: t solo, satb, 2 fl., 10 br., 2 cl., 2 hn.

"Gentle Lady, do not sing"   Chamber Music (1907)

3682 Boydell, Brian. "Gentle Lady", Five Joyce Songs,
      MS 1946. Cyc.: bar solo, pf. Arr. 1948 for bar
      solo, ch. orch., avail. Cultural Relations Dept.,
      Dublin.

3683 Citkowitz, Israel. NY: Cos Cob, 1935 in Cos Cob
      Song Volume. Song: [v., pf.].

3684 Clarke, Laurence. "Chamber Music": Five Poems by
      James Joyce, MS. Song: s solo, pf. Issued on
      Fantasy recording #5010.

3685 Coulthard, Jean. MS 1947, avail. CMC. Song: bar
      solo, pf.

3686 Diamond, David. Three Madrigals, NY: Kalmus, 1938.
      Madrigal: 4 pt. chorus, a cap. Rev. edn. publ.
      NY: SMP, 1965.

3687 Goossens, Eugene. Chamber Music, L: Curwen, 1930.
      Song: med. v., pf.

3688 Jarrett, Jack M. Songs about the End of Love, MS
      1962. Song: satb, pf.

3689 Serly, Tibor. MS 1926, Four Songs from "Chamber
      Music". Song: ms solo, ch. orch. Issued on
      Keyboard recording #K 101 entitled The Music of
      Tibor Serly.

3690 Sterne, Colin. "Gentle Lady", NY: Peer, 1953. Song:
      solo v., pf.

Joyce, James continued

       3691   Szymanowski, Karol. 4 Songs, Cracow: PWM, 1949.
              Song: [solo v., pf.]. Polish title: 4 Pieśni,
              transl. by J. Iwaszkiewicz. Texts in Engl. and
              Polish.

   "Go seek her out all courteously"   Chamber Music (1907)

     3692   Billingsley, William. James Joyce Songs, MS. Song:
            t solo, pf.

     3693   Brown, James. MS. Song: t or bar solo, pf.

     3694   Jarrett, Jack M. Love's Counsel, MS 1965, NY: CMP.
            Song: satb, pf.

   "He who hath glory lost, nor hath"   Chamber Music (1907)

       3695   Diamond, David. Three Madrigals, NY: Kalmus, 1938.
              Madrigal: 4 pt. chorus, a cap. Rev. edn. publ.
              NY: SMP, 1965.

       3696   Mihály, András. Chamber Music, MS 1958, avail. MZS.
              Song: ms solo, pf. Hungarian transl. by Agnes
              Gergely.

       3697   Susa, Conrad. Chamber Music, B: ECS, 1973. Song:
              satb, pf.

   "I hear an army charging upon the land"   Chamber Music
       (1907)

       3698   Barber, Samuel. "I Hear an Army", Three Songs, NY:
              GS, 1939. Song: med. or low v., pf. Also publ.
              for high v., pf.

       3699   Betts, Lorne. Three Songs to Poems of James Joyce,
              MS 1949. Song: high v., pf.

       3700   Boydell, Brian. "I Hear an Army", Five Joyce Songs,
              MS 1946. Cyc.: bar solo, pf. Arr. 1948 for bar
              solo, ch. orch., avail. Cultural Relations Dept.,
              Dublin.

       3701   Del Tredici, David. "I Hear an Army", NY: BH, 1974.
              Song: s solo, str. qrt.

                              416

oyce, James continued

3702 Genzmer, Harald. "Ich höre eine Heerschaar", Irische
      Harpe, Frankfurt: P, 1965. Song: satb, a cap.
      Text in German only.

3703 Goossens, Eugene. Chamber Music, L: Curwen, 1930.
      Song: med. v., pf.

3704 Harrison, Sidney. "I Hear an Army", L: CR, 1927.
      Song: solo v., pf.

3705 Healey, Derek. "I Hear an Army Charging", Six Irish
      Songs, MS 1962, avail. CMC. Song: solo v., pf.

3706 Jarrett, Jack M. "I Hear an Army", The Unquiet
      Heart, MS 1964. Song: s or t solo, pf.

3707 Kunz, Alfred. Will You Come?, Waterloo: Waterloo,
      1966. Song: satb, pf.

3708 Mengelberg, Rudolf. Chamber Music, Amst.: BVP,
      n.d. (NY: CFP, 1960). Cyc.: med. v., pf.

3709 Read, Gardner. "I Hear an Army", Songs for a Rainy
      Night, MS 1940. Song: bar solo, orch. or bar
      solo, pf.

3710 Susa, Conrad. Chamber Music, B: ECS, 1973. Song:
      satb, pf.

"I would in that sweet bosom be"   See: Wish, A

"In the dark pine-wood"   Chamber Music (1907)

3711 Betts, Lorne. Five Songs, MS 1950, avail. CMC. Song:
      high v., pf.

3712 Kittleson, Carl. Three Songs for Soprano and Wood-
      winds, MS. Cyc.: s solo, fl., ob., hn., cl., bsn.

3713 Spencer, Williametta. Champaign: MF, 1972. Song:
      satb, a cap.

"Lean out of the window"   Chamber Music (1907)

Joyce, James continued

3714   Betts, Lorne. <u>Three Songs to Poems of James Joyce</u>,
       MS 1949, avail. CMC. Song: high v., pf.

3715   Billingsley, William. <u>James Joyce Songs</u>, MS. Song:
       t solo, pf.

3716   Bridge, Frank. "Goldenhair", L: C, 1925. Song: solo
       v., [pf.].

3717   Coulthard, Jean. MS 1946, avail. CMC. Song: bar
       solo, pf.

3718   Griffis, Elliot. "Goldenhair", NY: CPMC, 1922
       (1949). Song: solo v., pf.

3719   Hart, Fritz. <u>Five Songs for Voice and Pianoforte</u>,
       MS 1938. Song: solo v., pf.

3720   Head, Michael. L: BH, 1961. Song: bar solo, pf.

3721   Jarrett, Jack M. NY: LG, 1964. Song: satb, pf.

3722   Kauder, Hugo. <u>Ten Poems</u>, NY: BH, 1955. Song: s, a,
       t soli, str. qrt.

3723   Klotzman, Dorothy H. <u>Three Songs from "Chamber
       Music"</u>, NY: M, 1963. Song: ssa, a cap.

3724   Lydiate, Frederick. "Goldenhair", MS. Song: t solo,
       pf.

3725   Mengelberg, Rudolf. <u>Chamber Music</u>, Amst.: B&VP,
       n.d. (NY: CFP, 1960). Cyc.: med. v., pf.

3726   Pisk, Paul. <u>Songs from "Chamber Music" by James
       Joyce</u>, MS (Opus 101). Song: t solo, pf. Issued
       on Washington University recording #T4RM-5570.

3727   Ritchie, Tom. "Goldenhair", MS. Song: solo v., pf.

3728   Reutter, Hermann. <u>Chamber Music</u>, MS 1972, Mz.: S.
       Song: low male v., pf.

3729   Spector, Irwin. <u>Songs of Love and Music</u>, MS. Cyc.:
       med. v., ob., vla., pf.

3730   Spencer, Williametta. Champaign: MF, 1970. Madrigal:
       satb, a cap.

3731 Steiner, Gitta. Three Songs for Medium Voice and Piano, NY: SMC, 1970. Song: ms or bar solo, pf.

3732 Szymanowski, Karol. 4 Songs, Cracow: PWM, 1949. Song: [solo v., pf.]. Polish title: 4 Pieśni, transl. by J. Iwaszkiewicz. Texts in Engl. and Polish.

3733 Victory, Gerard. "Goldenhair", Five Songs by James Joyce, MS 1954. Song: t solo, satb, 2 fl., 10 br., 2 cl., 2 hn.

"Lightly come or lightly go"   Chamber Music (1907)

3734 Betts, Lorne. Six Songs to Poems of James Joyce, MS 1951, avail. CMC. Song: high v., pf.

3735 Clarke, Laurence. "Chamber Music": Five Poems by James Joyce. MS. Song: s solo, pf. Issued on Fantasy recording #5010.

3736 Jarrett, Jack M. Love's Counsel, MS 1965, NY: CMP. Song: satb, pf.

3737 Pisk, Paul. Songs from "Chamber Music" by James Joyce, MS (Opus 101). Song: t solo, pf. Issued on Washington University recording #T4RM-5570.

3738 Susa, Conrad. Chamber Music, B: ECS, 1973. Song: satb, pf.

"Love came to us in time gone by"   Chamber Music (1907)

3739 Jarrett, Jack M. Songs about the End of Love, MS 1962. Song: satb, pf.

Memory of the Players in a Mirror at Midnight, A   "They mouth love's language"   Poesia (Apr. 1920)

3740 Del Tredici, David. Night Conjure-Verse, MS. Song: s, ms (or c-t) soli, ww. sextet, str. qrt. Issued on Composers Recording Inc. #CRI SD 243.

3741 Goossens, Eugene. "A Memory", L: OUP, 1933 in The Joyce Book. Song: solo v., pf.

Joyce, James continued

3742   Martino, Donald. Three Songs, B: ECS (Ione), 1970.
        Song: s or t solo, pf. or b solo, pf.

"My dove, my beautiful one"   Chamber Music (1907)

   3743   Brown, James. MS. Song: t or bar solo, pf.

   3744   Del Tredici, David. "Dove Song", Songs on Texts of
           James Joyce, NY: BH, 1974. Song: solo v., pf.

   3745   Jarrett, Jack M. Love's Counsel, MS 1965, NY: CMP.
           Song: satb, pf.

   3746   Kauder, Hugo. Ten Poems, NY: BH, 1955. Song: s, a,
           t soli, str. qrt.

   3747   Mengelberg, Rudolf. Chamber Music, Amst.: B&VP, n.d.
           (NY: CFP, 1960). Cyc.: med. v., pf.

   3748   Pisk, Paul. Songs from "Chamber Music" by James
           Joyce, MS (Opus 101). Song: t solo, pf. Issued
           on Washington University rcording #T4RM-5570.

   3749   Reutter, Hermann. Chamber Music, MS 1972, Mz.: S.
           Song: low male v., pf.

   3750   Spector, Irwin. Songs of Love and Music, MS. Cyc.:
           med. v., ob., vla., pf.

   3751   Susa, Conrad. Chamber Music, B: ECS, 1973. Song:
           satb, pf.

   3752   Szymanowski, Karol. 4 Songs, Cracow: PWM, 1949.
           Song: [solo v., pf.]. Polish title: 4 Pieśni,
           transl. by J. Iwaszkiewicz. Texts in Engl. and
           Polish.

   3753   Treacher, Graham. "The Dove", L: S, 1963. Song: 3
           soli, 2 pt. chorus of children's v., a cap.

"My love is in a light attire"   See: Song "My love is in a
   light attire"

Nightpiece   "Gaunt in gloom"   Poetry, Chicago (May 1917)

420

Joyce, James continued

3754   Antheil, George. L: OUP, 1933 in The Joyce Book.
       Song: [solo v., pf.].

3755* Del Tredici, David. Syzygy, NY: BH, 1974. Song: s
       solo, ww. oct., hn., 2 tpt., str. sextet, bells.

"Now, O now, in this brown land"   Chamber Music (1907)

3756   Goossens, Eugene. Chamber Music, L: Curwen, 1930.
       Song: med. v., pf.

3757   Jarrett, Jack M. Songs about the End of Love, MS
       1962. Song: satb, pf.

3758   Moeran, E.J. Seven Poems by James Joyce, L: OUP,
       1930. Song: ms or bar solo, pf.

3759   Spector, Irwin. Songs of Love and Music, MS. Cyc.:
       med. v., ob., vla., pf.

3760   White, John D. Three Joyce Songs, MS. Song: a or
       bar solo, pf.

"O cool is the valley now"   Chamber Music (1907)

3761   Betts, Lorne. Five Songs, MS 1950, avail. CMC.
       Song: high v., pf.

3762   Beveridge, Thomas. B: ECS, pre-1964. Song: ssa, pf.

3763   Calabro, Louis. Three Songs for Medium Voice, MS
       1952, avail. NYPL. Song: med. v., pf.

3764   Ferris, Joan. Six Songs, NY: CF, 1967. Song: satb,
       a cap.

3765   Freed, Arnold. MS pre-1964, Oyster Bay: Dow. Song:
       high v., pf.

3766   Goossens, Eugene. Chamber Music, L: Curwen, 1930.
       Song: med. v., pf.

3767   Kagen, Sergius. MS pre-1953. Song: [v., pf.].

Joyce, James continued

3768   Karlins, M. William. Four Inventions and a Fugue,
        MS 1962, avail. ACA. Song: opt. s or opt. a solo,
        bsn., pf.

3769   Kauder, Hugo. Ten Poems, NY: BH, 1955. Song: s, a,
        t soli, str. qrt.

3770   Kittleson, Carl. Three Songs for Soprano and Wood-
        winds, MS. Song: s solo, fl., ob., hn., cl., bsn.

3771   Koemmenich, Louis. NY: JF, 1919. Song: [v., pf.].

3772   Kunz, Alfred. Three Works for Male Chorus, Waterloo,
        Waterloo, 1972. Song: ttbb, pf.

3773   Moeran, E.J. "The Pleasant Valley", Seven Poems by
        James Joyce, L: OUP, 1930. Song: ms or bar solo,
        pf.

3774   Persichetti, Vincent. Ph.: EV, 1972. Band only.

3775   Spencer, Williametta. Champaign: MF, 1970. Madrigal:
        satb, a cap.

3776   Susa, Conrad. Chamber Music, B: ECS, 1973. Song:
        satb, pf.

"O, it was out by Donnycarney"   Chamber Music (1907)

3777   Betts, Lorne. Five Songs, MS 1950, avail. CMC.
        Song: high v., pf.

3778   Boydell, Brian. "It was out by Donnycarney", Five
        Joyce Songs, MS 1946. Cyc.: bar solo, pf. Arr.
        1948 for bar solo, ch. orch., avail. Cultural
        Relations Dept., Dublin.

3779*   Citkowitz, Israel. Five Songs for Voice and Piano,
        NY: Cos Cob, 1930. Cyc.: solo v., pf.

3780   Mann, Adolph. "Out by Donnycarney", Cin.: Church,
        1910. Song: [v., pf.].

3781   Mengelberg, Rudolf. Chamber Music, Amst.: B&VP,
        n.d. (NY: CFP, 1960). Cyc.: med. v., pf.

422

Joyce, James continued

3782 Moeran, E.J. "Donnycarney", <u>Seven Poems by James Joyce</u>, L: OUP, 1930. Song: bar solo, pf.

3783 Smith, Russell. "Donneycarney" [<u>sic</u>], MS. Song: satb, a cap.

"O Sweetheart, hear you" <u>Speaker</u> (July 1904)

3784 Mihály, Andras. <u>Chamber Music</u>, MS 1958, avail. MZS. Song: ms solo, pf. Hungarian transl. by Agnes Gergely.

On the Beach at Fontana "Wind whines and whines the shingle" <u>Poetry</u>, Chicago (Nov. 1917)

3785 Betts, Lorne. <u>Five Songs</u>, MS 1952, avail. CMC. Song: [med.-high] solo v., pf.

3786 Hopkins, Bill. <u>Two Pomes</u>, L: UE, 1967. Song: s solo, b. cl., tpt., vla., hp.

3787 Jarrett, Jack M. <u>The Unquiet Heart</u>, MS 1964. Song: s or t solo, pf.

3788 Sessions, Roger. L: OUP, 1933 in <u>The Joyce Book</u>; publ. sep. NY: EBM, ca. 1950 (also L: B&C, 1964). Song: high v., pf.

Portrait of the Artist as a Young Man, A* (NV) <u>Egoist</u> (Feb. 1914-Sept. 1915), rev. & publ. sep. 1916.

3789 Berio, Luciano. <u>Epifanie</u>, L: UE, 1969. Cyc.: ms solo, orch. Text arr. by Umbreto Eco. Incl. setting of passage beginning: "A girl stood before him in midstream..." (E 199).

3790 Dallapiccola, Luigi. <u>Requiescant</u>, Mi.: SZ, 1960. Settings for satb, children's chorus, orch. Incl. setting of passage beginning: "Dingdong! The castle bell!" (E 22).

3791 Diamond, David. "Brigid's Song", NY: M, 1947. Song: high v., pf. Sets passage beginning: "Dingdong! The castle bell!" (E 22).

423

Joyce, James continued

    3792 Persichetti, Vincent. "Brigid's Song", James_Joyce
          Songs, Ph.: EV, 1959. Song: any v. except high,
          light s, pf. Sets passage beginning: "Dingdong!
          The castle bell!" (E 22).

    3793 Schickele, Peter. "From Portrait_of_the_Artist_as
          a_Young_Man", MS. Incidental music for sp., orch.
          to a reading of opening pages of the novel.
          Issued on Vanguard recordings #VRS 9275 and #VSD
          79275 entitled Baptism:_A_Journey_through_Our
          Time.

    3794 Seiber, Mátyás. Three_Fragments_from_"A_Portrait_of
          the_Artist_as_a_Young_Man", L: S, 1958. Ch. cta.:
          sp., satb (wordless), fl., cl., b. cl., vln.,
          vcl., pf., perc. Sp. fragments: "A veiled sun-
          light lit up taintly the grey sheet of water..."
          (F 194), "The last day had come..." (E 128), "He
          closed his eyes in the langour of sleep..."
          (E 200).

Prayer, A   "Again!/Come, give, yield"   Pomes_Penyeach
 (1927)

    3795 van Dieren, Bernard. L: OUP, 1933 in The_Joyce
          Book. Song: [solo v., pf.].

"Rain has fallen all the day"   Chamber_Music (1907)

    3796 Barber, Samuel. "Rain Has Fallen", Three_Songs, NY:
          GS, 1939. Song: med. or low v., pf. Also publ.
          for high v., pf.

    3797 Betts, Lorne. Three_Songs_to_Poems_of_James_Joyce,
          MS 1949, avail. CMC. Song: high v., pf.

    3798 Boydell, Brian. Five_Joyce_Songs, MS 1946. Cyc.:
          bar solo, pf. Arr. 1948 for bar solo, ch. orch.,
          avail. Cultural Relations Dept., Dublin.

    3799 Coulthard, Jean. Three_Songs, MS 1946, avail. CMC.
          Song: med. v., pf.

    3800 Jarrett, Jack M. Songs_about_the_End_of_Love, MS
          1962. Song: satb, pf.

3801 Kagen, Sergius. MS pre-1953. Song: [v., pf.].

3802 Kauder, Hugo. Ten Poems, NY: BH, 1955. Song: s, a,
t soli, str. qrt.

3803 Mengelberg, Rudolf. Chamber Music, Amst.: B&VP,
n.d. (NY: CFP, 1960). Cyc.: med. v., pf.

3804 Moeran, E.J. "Rain Has Fallen", Seven Poems by James
Joyce, L: OUP, 1930. Song: ms or bar solo, pf.

3805 Pisk, Paul. Songs from "Chamber Music" by James
Joyce, MS (Opus 101). Song: t solo, pf. Issued on
Washington University recording #T4RM-5570.

3806 Richards, Howard. "Rain", NY: LG, 1960. Song: satb,
a cap.

3807* Smith, William R. Ph.: EV, 1948. Song: ssa.

3808 Spencer, Williametta. Champaign: MF, 1970. Madrigal:
satb, a cap.

3809 Ward, Robert. NY: Peer, 1951. Song: [high] solo v.,
pf.

She Weeps Over Rahoon   "Rain on Rahoon falls softly"
Poetry, Chicago (Nov. 1917), rev. 1927

3810 Betts, Lorne. "Rain...", Five Songs, MS 1952, avail.
CMC. Song: [med.-high] solo v., pf.

3811 Del Tredici, David. Four Songs on Texts of James
Joyce, NY: BH, 1974. Song: solo v., pf.

3812 Boydell, Brian. MS 1936. Song: low v., pf.

3813 Fine, Vivian. Four Songs, Bryn Mawr: NME, 1933.
Song: ms solo, 2 vln., vla., vcl.

3814 Hopkins, Bill. Two Pomes, L: UE, 1967. Song: s solo,
b. cl., tpt., vla., hp.

3815 Hughes, Herbert. L: OUP, 1933 in The Joyce Book.
Song: [solo v., pf.].

3816 Jarrett, Jack M. The Unquiet Heart, MS 1964. Song:
s or t solo, pf.

3817 Kagen, Sergius. MS pre-1953. Song: [v., pf.].

3818 Moeran, E.J. "Rahoon", L: OUP, 1947. Song: a solo,
pf.

3819 Patrick, Laughton. MS 1959, avail. Victoria
University of Wellington. Song: med. v., pf.

3820 Reed, Alfred. "Rahoon", NY: PDM, 1965. Rhapsody:
cl. solo, band or wind ensemble. Also avail. for
cl. solo, pf.

3821 Strickland, William. NY: GX, 1961. Song: med. high
v., pf.

3822 Triggs, Harold. NY: GX, 1935. Song: solo v., pf.

"Silently she's combing"   See: Song "Silently she's combing"

Simples   "Of cool sweet dew and radiance mild"   Poetry,
Chicago (May 1917)

3823 Bate, Stanley. Five Songs, L: R, 1951. Song: low v.,
pf.

3824 Bliss, Arthur. L: OUP, 1933 in The Joyce Book; publ.
sep. L: OUP, 1971. Song: solo v., pf.

3825 Del Tredici, David. Night Conjure-Verse, MS. Song:
s, ms (or c-t) soli, ww. sextet, str. qrt. Issued
on Composers Recording Inc. #CRI SD 243.

3826 Field, Robin. "Of cool...", The Sly Reeds Whisper,
MS 1967. Cyc.: t solo, ob., str. qrt.

3827 Patrick, Laughton. MS 1959, avail. Victoria
University of Wellington. Song: med. v., vln.,
pf.

3828 White, John D. Three Joyce Songs, MS. Song: low v.,
pf.

Joyce, James continued

"Sleep now, O sleep now"   Chamber_Music (1907)

3829 Barber, Samuel. Three Songs, NY: GS, 1939. Song:
      med. v., pf. Also publ. for high v., pf.

3830 Betts, Lorne. Six_Songs_to_Poems_of_James_Joyce,
      MS 1951, avail. CMC. Song: high v., pf.

3831 Boydell, Brian. MS 1944. Song: s solo, ob. solo,
      orch. or s solo, vln. solo, orch.

3832 Jarrett, Jack M. The_Unquiet_Heart, MS 1964. Song:
      s or t solo, pf.

3833 Kagen, Sergius. "Sleep Now", NY: LMC, 1951. Song:
      low v., [pf.].

3834 Kauder, Hugo. Ten_Poems, NY: BH, 1955. Song: s, a,
      t soli, str. qrt.

3835 Mengelberg, Rudolf. Chamber_Music, Amst.: B&VP,
      n.d. (NY: CFP, 1960). Cyc.: med. v., pf.

3836 Pattison, Lee. "Sleep Now", NY: GS, 1926. Song: [v.,
      pf.].

3837 Persichetti, Vincent. "Sleep to Dreamier Sleep be
      Wed", Night_Dances, Ph.: EV, 1972. Orch. only.

3838* Persichetti, Vincent. "Unquiet Heart", James_Joyce
      Songs, Ph.: EV, 1959. Song: high or med. v., pf.
      Complete work requires various voices.

3839 Reutter, Hermann. Chamber_Music, MS 1972, Mz.: S.
      Song: low male v., pf.

3840 Serly, Tibor. MS 1926, Four_Songs_from_"Chamber
      Music". Song: ms solo, ch. orch. Issued on
      Keyboard recording #K 101 entitled The_Music_of
      Tibor_Serly.

3841 Steiner, Gitta. Three_Songs_for_Medium_Voice_and
      Piano, NY: SMC, 1970. Song: ms or bar solo, pf.

3842 Szymanowski, Karol. 4_Songs, Cracow: PWM, 1949.
      Song: [solo v., pf.]. Polish title: 4_Pieśni,
      transl. by J. Iwaszkiewicz . Text in Engl. and
      Polish.

Joyce, James continued

3843 Victory, Gerard. <u>Five Songs by James Joyce</u>, MS
      1954. Song: t solo, satb, 2 fl., 10 br., 2 cl.,
      2 hn.

Song   "My love is in a light attire"   <u>Dana</u> (Aug. 1904),
   rev. 1907

3844 Betts, Lorne. "My love...", <u>Five Songs</u>, MS 1950,
      avail. CMC. Song: high v., pf.

3845 Billingsley, William. "My love...", <u>James Joyce
      Songs</u>, MS. Song: t solo, pf.

3846 Calabro, Louis. <u>Three Songs for Medium Voice</u>, MS
      1952, avail. NYPL. Song: med. v., pf.

3847 Citkowitz, Israel. "My love...", <u>Five Songs for
      Voice and Piano</u>, NY: Cos Cob, 1930. Song: solo
      v., pf.

3848 Mihály, András. <u>Chamber Music</u>, MS 1958, avail. MZS.
      Song: ms solo, pf. Hungarian transl. by Agnes
      Gergely.

3849 Sterne, Colin. "My love...", NY: Peer, 1953. Song:
      [med.] v., pf.

Song   "Silently she's combing"   <u>Saturday Review</u> (May 1904),
   rev. 1907

3850 Serly, Tibor. MS 1927, <u>Four Songs from "Chamber
      Music"</u>. Song: ms solo, ch. orch. Issued on
      Keyboard recording #K 101 entitled <u>The Music of
      Tibor Serly</u>.

3851 Victory, Gerard. "Silently...", <u>Five Songs by James
      Joyce</u>, MS 1954. Song: t solo, satb, 2 fl., 10
      br., 2 cl., 2 hn.

"Strings in the earth and air"   <u>Chamber Music</u> (1907)

3852 Adler, Samuel. "Strings in the Earth", <u>Five Choral
      Poems</u>, NY: AMP, 1957. Song: satb, a cap.

3853   Berio, Luciano. Chamber Music, Mi.: SZ, 1954. Song:
        s or a solo, cl., vcl., hp.

3854   Betts, Lorne. Six Songs to Poems of James Joyce,
        MS 1951, avail. CMC. Song: high v., pf.

3855   Boydell, Brian. Five Joyce Songs, MS 1946. Cyc.:
        bar solo, pf. Arr. 1948 for bar solo, ch. orch.,
        avail. Cultural Relations Dept., Dublin.

3856   Citkowitz, Israel. Five Songs for Voice and Piano,
        NY: Cos Cob, 1930. Song: solo v., pf.

3857   Clarke, Laurence. "Chamber Music": Five Poems by
        James Joyce, MS. Song: s solo, pf. Issued on
        Fantasy recording #5010.

3858   Coulthard, Jean. Three Songs, MS 1946, avail. CMC.
        Song: med. v., pf.

3859   Ferris, Joan. Six Songs, NY: CF, 1967. Song: satb,
        a cap.

3860   Fox, J. Bertram. "Strings in the Earth", NY: JF,
        1926.

3861   Healey, Derek. "Strings in the Earth", Six Irish
        Songs, MS 1962, avail. CMC. Song: solo v., pf.

3862   Jarrett, Jack M. "Strings in the Earth", NY: LG,
        1964. Song: satb, pf.

3863   Kagen, Sergius. MS pre-1953. Song: [v., pf.].

3864   Karlins, M. William. "Quartet for Strings", MS,
        avail. ACA. Setting for s solo, stgs.

3865   Kauder, Hugo. "Strings in the Earth", Ten Poems,
        NY: BH, 1955. Song: s, a, t soli, str. qrt.

3866   Le Fleming, Christopher. L: Elkin, 1955. Song: sa,
        pf. or sa, opt. pf., stgs.

3867   Mengelberg, Rudolf. Chamber Music, Amst.: B&VP,
        n.d. (NY: CFP, 1960). Cyc.: med. v., pf.

Joyce, James continued

3868   Mihály, András. Chamber Music, MS 1958, avail. MZS.
        Song: ms solo, pf. Hungarian transl. by Agnes
        Gergely.

3869   Moeran, E.J. Seven Poems by James Joyce, L: OUP,
        1930. Song: ms or bar solo, pf.

3870   Pawle, Ivan. MS. Orch. only. Issued on Island
        recording #LPIS 9106 entitled Kip of the Serenes.

3871   Pellegrini, Ernesto. Chamber Music, I, MS 1966.
        Song: s solo, pf.

3872   Rettich, Wilhelm. "Strings in the Earth", Eleven
        Songs for Voice and Piano, Berlin: Astoria, 1973.
        Song: high or low v., pf.

3873   Reutter, Hermann. Chamber Music, MS 1972, Mz.: S.
        Song: low male v., pf.

3874   Spector, Irwin. Songs of Love and Music, MS. Cyc.:
        med. v., ob., vla., pf.

3875   Susa, Conrad. Chamber Music, B: ECS, 1973. Song:
        satb, pf.

"This heart that flutters near my heart"   Chamber Music
    (1907)

3876   Ferris, Joan. Six Songs, NY: CF, 1967. Song: satb,
        a cap.

Tilly   "He travels after a winter sun"   Pomes Penyeach
    (1927)

3877   Bate, Stanley. Five Songs, L: R, 1951. Song: low
        v., pf.

3878   Fine, Vivian. Four Songs, Bryn Mawr: NME, 1933.
        Song: ms solo, 2 vln., vcl. Complete work also
        requires vla.

3879   Moeran, E.J. L: OUP, 1933 in The Joyce Book. Song:
        high v., pf.

Joyce, James continued

Tutto E Sciolto   "Birdless heaven, seadusk, one lone star,
   A"   Poetry, Chicago (May 1917), rev. 1927

   3880 Bate, Stanley. Five Songs, L: R, 1951. Song: low v.,
         pf.

   3881 Betts, Lorne. "A birdless...", Five Songs, MS 1952,
         avail. CMC. Song: [med.-high] solo v., pf.

   3882 Ireland, John. L: OUP, 1933 in The Joyce Book. Song:
         solo v., pf.

   3883 Jarrett, Jack M. The Unquiet Heart, MS 1964. Song:
         s or t solo, pf.

   3884 Martino, Donald. Three Songs, B: ECS (Ione), 1970.
         Song: s or t solo, pf. or b solo, pf.

"Twilight turns from amethyst, The"   Chamber Music (1907)

   3885 Ritchie, Tom. Serenade, MS. Song: solo v., str.
         qrt. or solo v., pf.

Ulysses*   (NV)   (1922) Portions 1st publ. in Little Review
   (Mar. 1918-Dec. 1920) & in Egoist (Jan.-Dec. 1919)

   3886 Antheil, George. In "Antheil Musical Supplement",
         This Quarter (Autumn-Winter 1925-26). Extract
         ("Mr. Bloom and the Cyclops") from composer's
         unfinished opera based on the novel. Setting of
         RH 287. 1-3.

   3887 Barber, Samuel. "Solitary Hotel", Despite and Still,
         NY: GS, 1969. Cyc.: high v., pf. Setting of RH
         668. 27-36.

   3888* Berio, Luciano. Epifanie as issued on RCA Victor
         recordings #LSC-3189 and #SB6850. Cyc.: ms solo,
         orch. Incl. a passage from the novel.

Joyce, James continued

3889   Berio, Luciano. Thema (Omaggio a Joyce), Mi.: SZ
       (hire). Setting for elec. tape superimposing on
       each other the original English together with
       Fr. and Ital. transl. of one paragraph from "The
       Sirens" chapt. (RH 252 ff.). Issued on various
       recordings, incl. Turnabout-Vox #TV 34177
       entitled Electronic Music III.

3890   Chaun, František. MS 1970, avail. SČSKU. Str. qrt.
       only.

3891* de Hartmann, Thomas. Six Commentaires pour "Ulysses"
       de James Joyce, P: Belaieff, 1948. Settings for
       solo v., pf. Settings entitled: "Introduction"
       (RH 252), "Complainte du Testament" (RH 200-1),
       "Valse des heures" (RH 561), "Eglogue" (RH 340),
       "Cou-cou" (RH 375-6), "Nuit a Gibraltar" (RH
       767-8). Texts from the Fr. transl. by A. Monnier.

3892   Godwin, Joscelyn. Carmina Amoris, MS. Cta.: ssaa,
       2 trbn., 2 perc., 4 vcl., 2 db., pf., hpd. Incl.
       setting of lines beginning: "I suppose theyre
       just getting up in China now" (RH 766).

3893   Herlinger, Jan. "The Ormond Bar", MS, n.d., avail.
       SUNYAB. Setting for s, a, t, bar soli, fl.
       (doubl. a. fl., sleigh bells), cl. (doubl. b.
       cl., sleigh bells), gtr. (doubl. three coins),
       timp., perc. Setting from "The Sirens" chapt.
       (RH 252 ff.).

3894   Myers, Stanley. MS ca. 1967. Film music: orch.
       Issued on RCA Victor recordings #LOC 1138 and
       #LSO 1138.

3895   Seiber, Mátyás. L: S, 1948. Cta.: t solo, satb,
       orch. Settings entitled:"The heaventree" (RH 682-
       3), "Meditations of evolution increasingly vast-
       er" (RH 683), "Observe meditations of involution"
       (RH 683), "Nocturne-Intermezzo" (RH 685),
       "Epilogue" (RH 686). The 4th section of the cta.
       quotes from the last of Arnold Schoenberg's Six
       Little Piano Pieces (Opus 19).

3896   Wood, Hugh. "Sirens", Three Choruses, L: UE, 1967.
       Song: satb, a cap. Text arr. by composer from
       RH 252-4, 260, 269, 276.

oyce, James continued

Watching the Needleboats at San Sabba   "I heard their young
    hearts crying"   Saturday Review (Sept. 1913)

    3897 Bate, Stanley. Five Songs, L: R, 1951. Song: low v.,
          pf.

    3898 Bax, Arnold. L: OUP, 1933 in The Joyce Book. Song:
          solo v., pf.

    3899 Boydell, Brian. MS 1936, rev. 1937. Song: low v.,
          pf.

    3900 Field, Robin. "I heard...", The Sly Reeds Whisper,
          MS 1967. Cyc.: t solo, ob., str. qrt.

    3901 Gruen, John. MS. Song: [s] solo v., pf. Issued on
          Lyrichord recording #LL83 entitled Songs to
          Texts by James Joyce.

"What counsel has the hooded moon"   Chamber Music (1907)

    3902 Jarrett, Jack M. Love's Counsel, MS 1965, NY: CMP.
          Song: satb, pf.

"When the shy-star goes forth in heaven"   Chamber Music
    (1907)

    3903 Billingsley, William. James Joyce Songs, MS. Song:
          t solo, pf.

    3904 Citkowitz, Israel. Five Songs for Voice and Piano,
          NY: Cos Cob, 1930. Song: solo v., pf.

    3905 Ritchie, Tom. Serenade, MS. Song: solo v., str.
          qrt. or solo v., pf.

"Who goes amid the green wood"   Chamber Music (1907)

    3906 Betts, Lorne. Six Songs to Poems of James Joyce,
          MS 1951, avail. CMC. Song: high v., pf.

    3907 Brown, James. MS. Song: t or bar solo, pf.

Joyce, James continued

3908   Clarke, Laurence. "Chamber Music": Five Poems by
        James Joyce, MS. Song: s solo, pf. Issued on
        Fantasy recording #5010.

3909   Kauder, Hugo. Ten Poems, NY: BH, 1955. Song: s, a,
        t soli, str. qrt.

3910   Kittleson, Carl. Three Songs for Soprano and Wood-
        winds, MS. Cyc.: s solo, fl., ob., hn., cl., bsn.

3911   Mihály, András. Chamber Music, MS 1958, avail. MZS.
        Song: ms solo, pf. Hungarian transl. by Agnes
        Gergely.

3912   Moeran, E.J. "The Merry Green Wood", Seven Poems by
        James Joyce, L: OUP, 1930. Song: bar solo, pf.

3913   Richards, Howard. NY: LG, 1960. Song: satb, a cap.

3914   Spencer, Williametta. Champaign: MF, 1970. Madrigal:
        satb, a cap.

"Winds of May, that dance on the sea"   Chamber Music (1907)

3915   Berio, Luciano. "Winds of May", Chamber Music, Mi.:
        SZ, 1954. Song: s or a solo, cl., vcl., hp.

3916   Betts, Lorne. Five Songs, MS 1950, avail. CMC.
        Song: high v., pf.

3917   Billingsley, William. James Joyce Songs, MS. Song:
        t solo, pf.

3918   Ferris, Joan. Six Songs, NY: CF, 1967. Song: satb,
        a cap.

3919   Kittleson, Carl. "Winds of May", MS. Song: solo v.,
        pf.

3920   Kauder, Hugo. "Winds of May", Ten Poems, NY: BH,
        1955. Song: s, a, t soli, str. qrt.

3921   Klotzman, Dorothy H. Three Songs from "Chamber
        Music", NY: M, 1963. Song: ssa, a cap.

3922   Mengelberg, Rudolf. Chamber Music, Amst.: B&VP,
        n.d. (NY: CFP, 1960). Cyc.: med. v., pf.

434

3923 Spencer, Williametta. Champaign: MF, 1972. Song:
satb, a cap.

3924 Treacher, Graham. "Winds of May", L: S, 1963.
Song: 2 pt. children's choir, pf.

Wish, A   "I would in that sweet bosom be"   Speaker (Oct.
1904), rev. 1907

3925 Billingsley, William. "I would...", James Joyce
Songs, MS. Song: t solo, pf.

3926 Clarke, Laurence. "I would...", "Chamber Music":
Five Poems by James Joyce, MS. Song: s solo, pf.
Issued on Fantasy recording #5010.

Miscellanea

3927 Anderson, Barry. Songs Penyeach, MS, perf. London,
21 Mar. 1971. [Texts by Joyce?]

3928 Bate, Stanley. Pomes Penyeach, MS pre-1954. [Texts
by Joyce?]

3929 Bate, Stanley. Three Songs, MS pre-1954. Incl. words
by Joyce.

3930 Claman, Dolores O. Three Songs, MS 1948-50. Texts by
Joyce.

3931 Fenton, Howard. In Vocal and Instrumental Music in
Print (NY: Scarecrow Press, 1965), Jed H. Taylor
makes reference to an out of print (L: BH) vocal
publ. entitled "Finnigan's Wake" [sic]. [Text by
Joyce?]

3932 Finney, Ross Lee. The Jan. 1967 issue of Musical
Quarterly states incorrectly that Finney's Still
Are New Worlds (MS 1962, NY: CFP) includes set-
tings of texts by Joyce.

3933 Greenberg, David L. Chamber Music, copyright by
composer 1956. Ste.: chorus of mixed v., a cap.
Texts from Joyce's Chamber Music.

435

3934   Holloway, Robin. Five Madrigals, MS 1973. Madrigals: mixed v., [a cap.]. Incl. texts by Joyce.

3935   Hubers, Klaus. "James Joyce's Chamber Music", MS pre-1970. Ch. orch. only.

3936   Kocsár, Miklós. "Glide away, Love", Budapest: Editio Musica, 1961. Song: satb, [a cap.]. Hungarian transl. (by Agnes Gergely) of a Joyce text.

3937   Linn, Robert T. Three Madrigals, Los Angeles: Affiliated Musicians, 1953. Madrigals: chorus, pf. Texts from Chamber Music.

3938   Lockwood, Normand. Four Songs from James Joyce's "Chamber Music", MS 1948. Songs: med. v., str. qrt.

3939   Palmer, Geoffrey M. The reader is referred to p. 163 of John J. Slocum and Herbert Cahoon's A Bibliography of James Joyce (1882-1941) (New Haven: Yale University Press, 1953) for references concerning Palmer's settings of poems from Chamber Music.

3940   Reynolds, W.B. References concerning Reynolds' settings of poems from Chamber Music can be found in the vol. cited above (viz., Slocum and Cahoon).

3941   Shaw, Christopher. Four Poems by James Joyce, MS, perf. Nov. 1956. Songs: high v., fl., hp., str. qrt.

3942   van Dieren, Bernard. Grove's makes reference to 3 settings of texts by Joyce.

yes, Sidney

YES, Sidney Arthur Kilworth   1922-1943

Nocturne for Four Voices   "Night again, look at the sky"
   In The Collected Poems of Sidney Keyes (1945)

      3943 Tate, Phyllis. L: OUP, 1949. Ch. cta.: s, t, bar, b
            soli, b. cl., str. qrt., db., cel.

Remember Your Lovers   "Young men walking the open streets"
   In The Collected Poems of Sidney Keyes (1945)

      3944 Tippett, Michael. The Heart's Assurance, L: S, 1951.
            Cyc.: [t] solo v., pf.

Song: The Heart's Assurance   "O never trust the heart's
   assurance"   In The Collected Poems of Sidney Keyes (1945)

      3945 Tippett, Michael. "The Heart's Assurance", The
            Heart's Assurance, L: S, 1951. Cyc.: [t] solo v.,
            pf.

Spring Night   "Spring night, the owls crying"   In The Collected Poems of Sidney Keyes (1945) as one of "Against a
   Second Coming"

      3946 Routh, Francis. MS 1971, perf. London 1974. Concert
            aria: ms solo, orch.

Snow, The   "They said, It will be like snow falling"   In
   The Collected Poems of Sidney Keyes (1945)

      3947 Clark, Harold. L: Elkin, 1963. Song: ms solo, pf.

Kipling, Rudyard

KIPLING, (Joseph) Rudyard* 1865-1936

Absent-Minded Beggar, The   "When you've shouted 'Rule
    Britannia'"   Daily Mail (Oct. 1899), publ. sep. same year

    3948 Sullivan, Arthur. L: E, 1899. Song: [v., pf.]. Publ.
          NY: BH, 1899 (also NY: N, 1899) for chorus.

"All the world over, nursing their scars"   With Number Three
    (1900)

    3949 Shaw, Martin. "Pity Poor Fighting Men", L: Curwen,
          1919. Song: bar solo, pf.

Anchor Song   See: Envoy

Astrologer's Song, An   "To the Heavens above us"   Rewards
    and Fairies (1910)

    3950 Bellamy, Peter. "The Heavens Above Us", Merlin's
          Isle of Gramarye, L: RMC, 1972. Song: male solo
          v. with c-t, b accompaniment, fl.-org., vln.
          Portions of the collection are unacc. Issued on
          Argo recording #ZFB 81.

"At the hole where he went in"   The Jungle Book (1894)

    3951 Hatch, Homer. "The Challenge of Rikki-Tikki-Tavi"
          NY: GS, 1915. Song: 4 pt. male chorus, a cap.

"Back to the Army Again"   "I'm 'ere in a ticky ulster"
    Pall Mall Magazine (Aug. 1894)

    3952 Cobb, Gerard F. "For to Admire", Glasgow: B&F, 1897
          in The Scottish Students' Song Book. Song: v.,
          pf. Publ. sep. L: CR, 1898 under the title: "Back
          to the Army Again".

Ballad of Fisher's Boarding-House, The   "'Twas Fultah Fish-
    er's boarding-house"   Week's News (Mar. 1888)

pling, Rudyard continued

3953 Grainger, Percy. "Fisher's Boarding House", MS 1899.
      Orch. only.

Ballad of Minepit Shaw, The   "About the time that taverns
shut" Rewards and Fairies (1910)

3954 Bellamy, Peter. Oak, Ash and Thorn, L: RMC, 1970.
      Song: male solo v., acoustic gtr. Portions of the
      collection are unacc. Issued on Argo recording
      #ZFB 11.

Ballad of the 'Bolivar', The   "We put out from Sunderland"
St. James's Gazette (Jan. 1892)

3955 Grainger, Percy. MS 1901, avail. British Museum.
      Song: chorus of tenors and basses, orch. (2
      scorings).

Ballad of the "Clampherdown", The   "It was our war-ship
Clampherdown" St. James's Gazette (Mar. 1890)

3956 Bridge, Frederick. "The Ballad of the Clampherdown",
      L: N, 1899. Song: [v., pf.?].

3957 Grainger, Percy. Unf. MS 1899, avail. British
      Museum. Song: v., pf. Also unf. MS for v., ww.,
      br., stgs.

Banjo Song, A   See: Lost Legion, A

"Be well assured that on our side"   Daily Telegraph (Nov.
1915), rev. 1919

3958 Elgar, Edward. "Submarines", The Fringes of the
      Fleet, L: E, 1917. Cyc.: bar grt., orch. Arr.
      as a setting for choir by R.D. Metcalfe.

3959 German, Edward. "Be Well Assured", L: C, 1916. Song:
      [v., pf.].

Bee Boy's Song, The   "Maiden in glory, A"   Puck of Pook's
Hill (1906)

3960   Bellamy, Peter. Merlin's Isle of Gramarye, L: RMC,
       1972. Song: male solo v., vln. Portions of the
       collection are unacc. Issued on Argo recording
       #ZFB 81.

Belts   "There was a row in Silver Street"   Barrack-Room
Ballads And Other Verses (1892)

3961   Cobb, Gerard F. Barrack-Room Ballads, Third Series,
       L: SH, 1897. Song: [v., pf.].

Big Steamers   "Oh, where are you going to, all you Big
Steamers"   A History of England (1911)

3962* Elgar, Edward. L: MZ, 1918. Song: v., pf.

Bill 'Awkins   "''As anybody seen Bill 'Awkins?'"   The Seven
Seas (1896)

3963   Ward-Higgs, W. L: SH, 1906. Song: [v., pf.].

'Birds of Prey' March   "March! The mud is cakin' good"
Pall Mall Gazette (May 1895)

3964* Dampier, L. L: P&P, 1900. Song: [v., pf.].

Blue Roses   See: Misunderstood

Boots   "We're foot--slog--slog--slog--sloggin' over Africa!"
The Five Nations (1903)

3965   Felman, Hazel. Chi.: GH, 1916. Song: [v., pf.].

3966   Flagler, Robert F. NY: HFL, 1936. Song: chorus,
       [a cap.?].

3967   McCall, J.P. L: Swan, 1928. Song: [v., pf.].

3968   Sousa, John P. NY: HFD&H, 1916, Song: [v., pf.].

Brookland Road   "I was very pleased with what I knowed"
   Rewards_and_Fairies (1910)

   3969 Bellamy, Peter. Oak,_Ash_and_Thorn, L: RMC, 1970.
            Song: male solo v., unacc. Portions of the col-
            lection require accompaniment. Issued on Argo
            recording #ZFB 11.

   3970 Shaw, Martin. "The Brookland Road", L: Curwen, 1919.
            Song: bar solo, pf.

Butterfly that Stamped, The   (SS)   Ladies_Home_Journal (Oct.
   1902)

   3971 Flosman, Oldřich. MS 1967, avail. SČSKU. Incidental
            music for radio. Czech. title: "Motýl, který dup-
            al", transl. by Oldřich Hobzík.

   3972 Martinů, Bohuslav. MS 1926. Ballet music. Czech.
            title: "Motýl, který dupal"; story adapt. by the
            composer. An orch. ste. from the ballet was publ.
            Prague: ČHF, 1965.

   3973 Thompson, Randall. "Solomon and Balkis", B: ECS,
            1942. Opera: 2 s, ms, t, bar soli, sp., chorus,
            orch. Libr. by the composer.

"By the hoof of the Wild Goat up-tossed"   Plain_Tales_from
   the_Hills (1888)

   3974 Grainger, Percy. "The Fall of the Stone", L: S,
            1924. Song: mixed chorus, 10 instr.

"Camel's hump is an ugly lump, The"   Just_So_Stories (1902)

   3975 Berger, Jean. "The Camel's Hump", Just_So, NY:
            Tetra, 1971. Song: satb, a cap.

   3976 German, Edward. "The Camel's Hump", The_Just_So_Song
            Book, L: MacM, 1903. Song: v., pf. Also publ.
            sep. Publ. NY: HWG, 1911 for 2 pt. chorus and NY:
            HWG, 1926 for 4 pt. chorus. Arr. by Gordon Jacob
            as ste. for satb, orch.; arr. publ. L: N.

Carol, A   "Our Lord Who did the Ox command"   Everybody's
    Magazine (Oct. 1900)

    3977 Bellamy, Peter. "Who Shall Judge The Lord?", Mer-
              lin's Isle of Gramarye, L: RMC, 1972. Song: male
              solo v., unacc. Portions of the collection re-
              quire accompaniment. Issued on Argo recording
              #ZFB 81.

Cells "I've a head like a concertina"   Barrack-Room Bal-
    lads And Other Verses (1892)

    3978 Bellamy, Peter. MS. Song.

    3979 Cobb, Gerard F. L: SH, 1893. Song: [v., pf.]. Also
              publ. L: SH, 1893 in Barrack-Room Ballads, Second
              Series.

    3980 McCall, J.P. L: Swan, 1930. Song: solo v., pf.

Children's Song, The*   "Land of our Birth, we pledge to
    thee"   Puck of Pook's Hill (1906)

    3981 Agassiz, Edward. L: WK, 1915. Hymn: [v., pf.].

    3982 Ames, Phillip. L: Milford, 1929 in Church Hymnary.
              Hymn: [v., org.]. Set to the tune "Jubilee".

    3983 Armitage, Marie T., arr. "Invocation", B: Birchard,
              1916 in Junior Laurel Songs. Song: v., pf. Words
              adapt. to a score by John Liptrot Hatton.

    3984 Balmires, B. L: [?], 1898 in National Chorister.
              Anthem: chorus, [pf.].

    3985 Chanter, R.J.C. L: Curwen, 1910. Song: unison v.,
              pf.

    3986 Crompton, G. L: [?], pre-1932 in Children's News-
              paper. Hymn: [v., pf.].

    3987 Davison, Archibald T., Thomas W. Surette, Augustus
              D. Zanzig, arr. "Land of our birth", NY: ECS,
              1924 in A Book of Songs. Hymn: unison children's
              v., pf. Also suitable for pt. singing. Arr. of a
              melody by J.S. Bach.

442

3988   Diack, J. Michael. "Land of Our Birth", NY: CF, pre-
       1932. Hymn: unison v., pf. Melody adapt. from
       Brahms' 4th Symphony.

3989   Gaccon, J.A. B: GS, 1913. Song: [v., pf.].

3990   Gartlan, George. NY: HH&E, 1935 in New Universal
       School Music Series: Art Songs and Part Songs.
       Song: v., unacc.

3991   Gore, W.C. L: N, pre-1932. Song: unison v., pf. or
       satb, pf.

3992   Harris, G. Percy. L: N, 1909. Song: 2 pt. chorus,
       [pf.].

3993   Lawrence, C.H., arr. B: Ginn, n.d. in The American
       Song Book. Song: [v., pf.].

3994   Mainzer, Joseph. L: Curwen, 1908. Hymn: [v., pf.].

3995   Miles, J.B. L: Curwen, 1916 in 101 Union Songs.
       Song: [v., pf.].

3996   Owen, Morfydd L. L: Milford, 1918 in Songs of
       Praise. Hymn: [v., pf.]. Employs the tune
       "Richard".

3997   Parker, Horatio. NY: Silver, 1920 in The Progressive
       Music Series, Book 4. Song: v., pf.

3998   Riley, L.G. Winter. L: N, 1914. Song: 4 pt. chorus,
       [a cap.?].

3999* Statham, F.B. "Land of Our Birth", L: N, ca. 1910.
       Hymn.

4000   Vaughan Williams, Ralph. "Land of Our Birth",
       Thanksgiving for Victory (later renamed A Song of
       Thanksgiving), L: OUP, 1945. Settings for s solo,
       sp., satb, orch. Adapt. as a sep. song for unison
       v. with opt. descant, stgs., pf.; adapt. publ. L:
       OUP, 1946. Arr. for ssa, pf. or ssa, orch.; arr.
       publ. L: OUP, 1950.

4001   Whittaker, W.G. L: OUP, 1925. Song: unison v., pf.

Kipling, Rudyard continued

"China-going P. and O.'s"   Just So Stories (1902)

    4002 German, Edward. "The Riddle", The Just So Song Book,
          L: MacM, 1903. Song: v., pf. Also publ. sep.
          Arr. by Gordon Jacob as ste. for satb, orch.;
          arr. publ. L: N.

"Cities and Thrones and Powers"   Puck of Pook's Hill (1906)

    4003 Hely-Hutchinson, Victor. L: Elkin, 1937. Song: [v.,
          pf.].

City of Sleep, The   See: "Over the edge of the purple down"

Coastwise Lights, The   "Our brows are bound with spindrift"
    English Illustrated Magazine (May 1893) as one of "A Song
    of the English"

    4004 Bantock, Granville. L: Curwen, 1919. Song: chorus,
          [a cap.?].

    4005 Bennett, J.S.L.D. MS pre-1932. Song: [v., pf.].

    4006 Boughton, Rutland. Songs of the English, MS 1901.
          Song: bar solo, orch., pf.

Cold Iron   "Gold is for the Mistress"   Rewards and Fairies
    (1910)

    4007 Bellamy, Peter. Oak, Ash and Thorn, L: RMC, 1970.
          Song: male solo v., unacc. Portions of the col-
          lection require accompaniment. Issued on Argo
          recording # ZFB 11.

Cuckoo Song   "Tell it to the locked-up trees"   (1909)

    4008 Bellamy, Peter. "Heffle Cuckoo Fair", MS. Song.

    4009 Finlayson, Barbara. MS 1958, avail. Victoria Univer-
          sity of Wellington. Song: solo v., pf.

    4010 Hely-Hutchinson, Victor. L: Elkin, 1937. Song: [v.,
          pf.].

...pling, Rudyard continued

4011   Shaw, Martin. "Heffle Cuckoo Fair", L: Curwen, 1919.
       Song: bar solo, pf.

Dane-Geld   See: What 'Dane-geld' Means

Danny Deever   "'What are the bugles blowin' for?' said
   Files-on-Parade"   Scots Observer (Feb. 1890)

   4012   Bellamy, Peter. MS. Song.

   4013   Cobb, Gerard F. L: SH, 1893. Song: [v., pf.]. Also
          publ. L: SH, 1893 in Barrack-Room Ballads, Second
          Series.

   4014   Damrosch, Walter. Cin.: Church, 1897, re-issued
          Ph.: TP, 1930. Song: chorus, [pf.?].

   4015   Dixon, Harold. NY: Mills, 1927. Song: [v., pf.].

   4016   Grainger, Percy. L: S, 1924. Song: opt. bar solo,
          ttbb, pf. or opt. bar solo, ttbb, orch.

   4017   Nevin, Ethelbert. MS pre-1901. Song: [v., pf.].

   4018   Ward-Higgs, W. L: SH, 1906. Song: chorus, [pf.?].

   4019   Whiting, Arthur. Barrack-Room Ballads, NY: GS, 1900.
          Song: [v., pf.]. Also publ. sep.

"Dawn off the Foreland--the young flood making"   Daily
   Telegraph (Nov. 1915), rev. 1919

   4020   Elgar, Edward. "The Sweepers", The Fringes of the
          Fleet, L: E, 1917. Cyc.: bar. qrt., orch. Arr.
          as a setting for choir by R.D. Metcalfe.

Dawn Wind, The   "At two o'clock in the morning"   A History
   of England (1911), rev. same year

   4021   Finlayson, Barbara. MS 1958, avail. Victoria Univer-
          sity of Wellington. Song: s solo, pf.

   4022   Green, Charles. Three Kipling Songs, L: S, 1923.
          Song: [v., pf.].

Kipling, Rudyard continued

Deep-Sea Cables, The   "Wrecks dissolve above us, The"
    English Illustrated Magazine (May 1893) as one of "A Song
    of the English"

    4023 Boughton, Rutland. Songs of the English, MS 1901.
          Song: bar solo, orch., pf.

Drums of the Fore and Aft, The   (SS)   Wee Willie Winkie and
    Other Child Stories (1888), publ. sep. 1899

    4024 Molloy, [?]. L: BH, 1897. Song: [v., pf.]. Text
          adapt. by Clement Scott.

Eddi's Service   "Eddi, priest of St. Wilfrid"   Rewards and
    Fairies (1910)

    4025 Bellamy, Peter. Merlin's Isle of Gramarye, L: RMC,
          1972. Song: male solo v., unacc. Portions of the
          collection require accompaniment. Issued on Argo
          recording #ZFB 81.

Egg-Shell, The   See: "Wing went down with the sunset, The"

England's Answer   "Truly ye come of The Blood"   English Il-
    lustrated Magazine (May 1893) as one of "A Song of the
    English"

    4026 Bridge, Frederick. L: N, 1911. Cta.: bar solo,
          chorus, orch.

    4027 Hunt, Raymond. L: BH, 1897. Song: [v., pf.].

English Flag, The   See: Flag of England, The

Envoy   "Heh! Walk her round!"   Many Inventions (1893), rev.
    1896

    4028 Bennett, J.S.L.D. "The Anchor Song", MS pre-1932.
          Song: chorus, [a cap.?].

    4029 Edmonds, Paul. "The Anchor Song", L: Curwen, 1920.
          Song: [v., pf.].

446

4030 Grainger, Percy. "The Anchor Song", L: S, 1923.
      Song: bar solo, ttbb, pf.

4031 Whitehorne, Annie. "The Anchor Song", L: BH, 1897.
      Song: [v., pf.].

"Fair is our lot--O goodly is our heritage!" English Illustrated Magazine (May 1893) as one of "A Song of the
English"

4032 Boughton, Rutland. "Fair is our lot", Songs of the
      English, MS 1901. Song: bar solo, orch., pf.

Feet of the Young Men, The "Now the Four-way Lodge is opened" Scribner's Magazine (Dec. 1897), publ. sep. 1920

4033 Bingham, Seth. "The Four-Way Lodge", NY: GS, 1909.
      Song: [v., pf.].

Fires, The "Men make them fires on the hearth" Collected
Verse of Rudyard Kipling (1907)

4034* Ives, Charles. "Tolerance", 114 Songs, NY: GS, 1921
      [1922]. Song: v., pf. Setting of lines begin-
      ning: "How can I turn from any fire".

First Chantey, The "Mine was the woman to me" The Seven
Seas (1896)

4035 Grainger, Percy. MS 1899. Song: [bar] solo v., pf.

Flag of England, The "Wind of the World, give answer!"
National Observer (Apr. 1891) & St. James's Gazette (May
1891), rev. 1892

4036 Bridge, Frederick. L: N, 1897. Cta.: s solo, chorus,
      orch.

'Follow Me 'Ome' "There was no one like 'im" Pall Mall
Magazine (June 1894)

4037   Bell, Maurice. "Barrack Ballad", L: BH, 1897. Song:
       [v., pf.].

4038   Ward-Higgs, W. L: SH, 1906. Song: [v., pf.].

'For All We Have and Are'   "For all we have and are"
   (1914) 1st publ. in various newspapers (Sept. 1914)

4039   Parry, C.H.H. MS pre-1927. Song: [v., pf.?].

"For out white and our excellent nights--for the nights of
   swift running"   Pall Mall Gazette (July 1895)

4040   Grainger, Percy. "Red Dog", L: S, 1958, Kipling
       "Jungle Book" Cycle, L: S. Song: ttbb, a cap.

Ford o' Kabul River   "Kabul town's by Kabul river"
   National Observer (Nov. 1890)

4041   Cobb, Gerard F. L: SH, 1893. Song: [v., pf.]. Also
       publ. L: SH, 1893 in Barrack-Room Ballads, Second
       Series.

Frankie's Trade   "Old Horn to All Atlantic said"   Rewards
   and Fairies (1910)

4042   Bellamy, Peter. Oak, Ash and Thorn, L: RMC, 1970.
       Song: male solo v., choral accompaniment. Por-
       tions of the collection require instr. accompani-
       ment. Issued on Argo recording #ZFB 11.

'Fuzzy-Wuzzy'   "We've fought with many men"   Scots Observer
   (Mar. 1890)

4043   Cobb, Gerard F. L: SH, 1892. Song: [v., pf.]. Also
       publ. L: SH, 1892 in Barrack-Room Ballads, First
       Series.

4044   Speaks, Oley. NY: Church, 1924. Song: [v., pf.].

4045   Whiting, Arthur. Barrack-Room Ballads, NY: GS, 1900.
       Song: [v., pf.]. Also publ. sep.

Galley-Slave, The   "Oh gallant was our galley"   Depart-
mental_Ditties_And_Other_Verses (1890)

    4046 Hoiby, Lee. "Song of the Galley Slaves", NY: GS,
           1958. Song: 4 pt. male chorus, timp.

Gipsy Trail, The   "White moth to the closing bine, The"
Century_Magazine (Dec. 1890)

    4047* Galloway, Tod. "The Gypsy Trail", Memory_Songs,
           Ph.: TP, 1904. Song: [v., pf.]. Publ. Ph.: TP,
           1917 for solo v., pf. Also publ. Ph.: TP, 1922
           for mixed chorus.

    4048 Mácha, Otmar. The_Songs_of_Men, MS 1947, avail.
           SČSKU. Cyc.: low v., pf. Czech. title: "Tuláci",
           transl. by Otokar Fischer.

Gunga Din   "You may talk o' gin and beer"   Scots_Observer
(June 1890)

    4049 Bellamy, Peter. MS. Song.

    4050 Cobb, Gerard F. Barrack-Room_Ballads, Third Series,
           L: SH, 1897. Song: [v., pf.].

    4051 Dixon, Harold. NY: Mills, 1927. Song: [v., pf.].

    4052* Flagler, Robert F. NY: HFL, 1927. Song: solo v., 4
           pt. chorus, [a cap.?].

    4053 Spross, Charles G. NY: Church, 1925. Song: [v.,
           pf.].

    4054 Tag, Ralph W. NY: L&B, 1923. Song: [v., pf.].

    4055 Wood, Erskine. A_Book_of_Songs_by_Erskine_Wood, NY:
           GS, 1922 (priv. publ.). Song: v., pf. Pf. pt. by
           Randall Thompson.

Harp Song of the Dane Women   "What is a Woman that you for-
sake her"   Puck_of_Pook's_Hill (1906)

4056   Bellamy, Peter. Merlin's Isle of Gramarye, L: RMC,
       1972. Song: female or male solo v., modal-tuned
       gtr., bodhran. Portions of the collection are un-
       acc. Issued on Argo recording #ZFB 81.

4057   Burtch, Mervyn. MS. Song: ssa, [a cap.?].

"'Have you any news of my boy Jack?'"   Destroyers at Jut-
land, I (1916), rev. same year

4058   German, Edward. "Have You News Of My Boy Jack?",
       L: GenPS, 1917. Song: [v., pf.].

Hour of the Angel, The   "Sooner or late--in earnest or in
jest"   Land and Sea Tales (1923)

4059   Tranchell, Peter. MS ca. 1951. Song: male chorus,
       a cap.

Hunting-Song of the Seeonee Pack   "As the dawn was breaking
the Sambhur belled"   The Jungle Book (1904)

4060   Fogg, C.W. Eric. L: Elkin, 1925. Song: [v., pf.].

4061   Grainger, Percy. L: S, 1922, Kipling "Jungle Book"
       Cycle, L: S. Song: ttbb, a cap.

Hymn Before Action   "Earth is full of anger, The"   (1896)
1st publ. in The Echo (1896) under the title "A Little
Sermon"

4062   Baldwin, Ralph L. B: W-S, 1918. Song: 4 pt. chorus,
       [a cap.?].

4063   Campbell, E.M. L: West, 1915. Song: [v., pf.].

4064   Davies, H. Walford. L: N, 1897. Song: chorus, [a
       cap.?]. Also publ. L: N, 1897 for male chorus.

Hymn to Physical Pain   "Dread Mother of Forgetfulness"
London Magazine (Dec. 1929)

4065 Mácha, Otmar. The Songs of Men, MS 1947, avail.
SČSKU. Cyc.: low v., pf. Czech. title: "Chvaloz-
pěv na tělesnou bolest", transl. by Otokar Fischer.

"I am the [a] Most Wise Baviaan, saying in most wise tones"
Just So Stories (1902)

4066 German, Edward. "I Am the Most Wise Baviaan", The
Just So Song Book, L: MacM, 1903. Song: v., pf.
Also publ. sep. Arr. by Gordon Jacob as ste. for
satb, orch.; arr. publ. L: N.

"I have slipped my cable, messmates, I'm drifting down the
tide" The Light that Failed (1890)

4067 Grainger, Percy. "Ganges Pilot", MS 1899. Song: med.
v., pf.

"I keep six honest serving-men" Just So Stories (1902)

4068 German, Edward. The Just So Song Book, L: MacM,
1903. Song: v., pf. Also publ. sep. Arr. by Gordon Jacob as ste. for satb, orch.; arr. publ. L:
N.

"I will remember what I was, I am sick of rope and chain"
The Jungle Book (1894)

4069* Bright, Dora. "Toomai's Mother's Song", Six Songs
from "The Jungle Book", L: Elkin, 1903. Song:
[v., pf.].

"I've never sailed the Amazon" Just So Stories (1902)

4070 German, Edward. "Rolling Down to Rio", The Just So
Song Book, L: MacM, 1903. Song: v., pf. Also
publ. sep. Publ. L: N, 1916 for ttbb, pf.; NY:
HWG, 1918 as pt. song; NY: HWG, 1919 for mixed
v. Arr. by Gordon Jacob as ste. for satb, orch.;
arr. publ. L: N.

Kipling, Rudyard continued

If   "If you can keep your head when all about you"
      American Magazine (Oct. 1910), publ. sep. same year

      4071 Mácha, Otmar. The Songs of Men, MS 1947, avail.
            SČSKU. Cyc.: low v., pf. Czech. title: "Když",
            transl. by Otokar Fischer.

"In Lowestoft a boat was laid"   Daily Telegraph (Nov. 1915),
      rev. 1919

      4072 Elgar, Edward. "The Lowestoft Boat", The Fringes of
            the Fleet, L: E, 1917. Cyc.: bar qrt., orch. Arr.
            as a setting for choir by R.D. Metcalfe.

Irish Guards, The   "We're not so old in the Army List"
      The Times (Mar. 1918), publ. sep. same year

      4073 German, Edward. L: C, 1917. Song: [v., pf.].

Juggler's Song, The   "When the drums begin to beat"   Songs
      from Books (1912) A portion was 1st publ. in Kim (1901)

      4074 Adams, A. Davies. L: BH, 1921. Song: [v., pf.].

Jungle Book, The   (SS)   (1894) Portions were 1st publ. in
      various journals 1893-94

      4075 Gilkyson, Terry in coll. with Richard M. Sherman
            and Robert B. Sherman. MS ca. 1967. Film music.
            Issued 1968 on Disney recording #ST-3948.

      4076 Koechlin, Charles. "La Loi de la Jungle", MS 1939.
            Symph. poem: orch.

      4077 Koechlin, Charles. "Les Bandar-Log", P: Eschig,
            1967. Symph. poem: orch.

      4078 Kučerová-Herbstová, Marie. "Mowgli", MS 1947, avail.
            SČSKU. Incidental and ballet music. Czech. title:
            "Maugli", transl. by Vladimír Volkenstein.

452

Kipling, Rudyard continued

4079* Rózsa, Miklós. The Jungle Book, NY: Broude-B, 1972
(hire). Ste.: a solo, narr., orch. The solo pt.
is avail. in an arr. (entitled "Lullaby") for
satb. Text for narr. tells the story of Mowgli.
Score incl. German transl. of the narration.

4080 Schaefer, Theodor. "Mowgli", MS 1932, avail. SČSKU.
Incidental music for play: chorus, orch. Czech.
title: "Maugli", transl. by Vladimír Volkenstein.

4081 Scott, Cyril. Impressions from "The Jungle Book",
MS pre-1932, L: S. Ste.: pf. solo. Impressions
entitled: "Jungle", "Dawn", "Rikki-Tikki-Tavi",
"Morning Song", "Elephants' Dance".

4082 Sherman, Richard M. See entry #4075.

4083 Sherman, Robert B. See entry #4075.

King Henry VII and the Shipwrights   "Harry our King in
England" Rewards and Fairies (1910)

4084 Bellamy, Peter. Oak, Ash and Thorn, L: RMC, 1970.
Song: male solo v., vln. Portions of the collection are unacc. Issued on Argo recording
#ZFB 11.

Last Chantey, The   "Thus said the Lord in the Vault" Pall
Mall Magazine (June 1893)

4085 Cook, Theodore. Cin.: Church, pre-1932. Song: [v.,
pf.].

4086 McEwen, John B. MS ca. 1894. Song: chorus, orch.

[Last] Rhyme of True Thomas, The   "King has called for
priest and cup, The" To-day (Mar. 1894), publ. sep same
year under the title The Rhyme of True Thomas

4087 Bellamy, Peter. "The Last Rhyme of True Thomas", MS.
Song.

Law of the Jungle, The   "Now this is the Law of the Jungle"
The Second Jungle Book (1895)

Kipling, Rudyard continued

4088   Koechlin, Charles. See: Jungle_Book,_The.

"Law whereby my lady moves, The"   In coll. with Wolcott
    Balestier   The_Naulahka (1892), rev. 1912

    4089   Bellamy, Peter. "My Lady's Law", MS. Song.

L'Envoi   "When Earth's last picture is painted"   Sun, NY
    (May 1892)

    4090   Agassiz, Edward. L: WK, pre-1932. Song: [v., pf.].

    4091   Bornschein, Franz C. "When Earth's Last Picture is
           Painted", NY: JF, 1925. Song: male chorus, [a
           cap.?].

    4092   Dale, Frederic. "When Earth's Last Picture is Paint-
           ed", Oakville: FH, 1910. Song: [v., pf.].

    4093   Kalmanoff, Martin. MS 1949. Song: solo v., pf.

    4094   Mácha, Otmar. "When Earth's...", The_Songs_of_Men,
           MS 1947, avail. SČSKU. Cyc.: low v., pf. Czech.
           title: "Až stvoří se poslední obraz...", transl.
           by Otokar Fischer.

"'Let us now praise famous men'"   Harper's_Weekly (Sept.
    1899), rev. 1912

    4095   Gibbs, Geoffrey D. Symposium, MS. Oratorio: soli,
           chorus, symph. band.

Lichtenberg   "Smells are surer than sounds"   The_Five
    Nations (1903)

    4096   Cobb, Gerard F. L: SH, 1904. Song: [v., pf.].

Looking-Glass, The   "Queen was in her chamber, The"
    Rewards_and_Fairies (1910)

Kipling, Rudyard continued

4097 Bellamy, Peter. Oak, Ash and Thorn, L: RMC, 1970.
      Song: solo v., unacc. Portions of the collection
      require male solo v., accompaniment. Issued on
      Argo recording #ZFB 11.

4098 Damrosch, Walter. B: GS, 1916. Song: [v., pf.].

Loot   "If you've ever stole a pheasant-egg"   Scots Observer
(Mar. 1890)

4099 Bellamy, Peter. MS. Song.

Lost Legion, The   "There's a Legion that never was 'listed"
Sun, NY (May 1893), rev. same year

4100 Ward-Higgs, W. L: SH, 1906. Song: [v., pf.].

Love Song of Har Dyal, The   "Alone upon the housetops to the
North"   Plain Tales from the Hills (1888)

4101 Adams, A. Davies. L: BH, 1921. Song: [v., pf.].

4102 Batten, Mrs. George. L: NZ, 1892. Song: [v., pf.].

4103* Foote, Arthur. "Bisesa's Song", B: Schmidt, 1902.
      Song: [v., pf.].

4104* Galloway, Tod. "Alone upon...", Memory Songs, Ph.:
      TP, 1904. Song: [v., pf.].

4105 Grainger, Percy. L: S, 1923. Song: s solo, pf. Arr.
      (MS 1957-58) for unison female chorus, vln.,
      vcl., harm.

4106* Hunt, Thomas. B: BMC, 1923. Song: [v., pf.].

4107 Ives, Charles. "Alone upon...", MS ca. 1898. Song:
      v., pf.

4108 Kernochan, Marshall. B: OD, 1917. Song: [v., pf.].

4109 Scott, Anthony. L: N, 1966. Song: ss, pf.

455

Kipling, Rudyard continued

Lovers' Litany, The   "Eyes of grey--a sodden quay"
   Departmental Ditties and Other Verses (1886)

   4110   Atkinson, Holway. Seven Songs from Tilfredshaden,
            [NY?]: McK, pre-1940. Song: [v., pf.].

   4111   Gower, E. Leveson. L: SH, 1894. Song: [v., pf.].

Lowestoft Boat, The   See: "In Lowestoft a boat was laid"

Lukannon   "I met my mates in the morning"   The Jungle Book
   (1894)

   4112   Grainger, Percy. "The Beaches of Lukannon", L: S,
            1958, Kipling "Jungle Book" Cycle, L: S. Song:
            satb, 9 stgs., harm. ad lib.

M.I.   "I wish my mother could see me now"   McClure's
   Magazine (Oct. 1901) & Windsor Magazine (Oct. 1901), publ.
   sep. same year

   4113   Cobb, Gerard F. L: SH, 1904. Song: [v., pf.].

Mandalay   "By the old Moulmein Pagoda"   Scots Observer
   (June 1890)

   4114   Ayres, Frederic. NY: GS, 1924. Song: [v., pf.].

   4115* Beverley, Bewicka. "Mandalay Waltz", L: SH, 1893.
            Song: [v., pf.?]. Also publ. L: SH, 1893 in Bar-
            rack-Room Ballads, Second Series.

   4116   Damrosch, Walter. Cin.: Church, 1898. Song: solo v.,
            chorus, [a cap.?].

   4117   Dixon, Harold. "On the Road to Mandalay", NY: Mills,
            1927. Song: [v., pf.].

   4118   Foote, Arthur. B: Schmidt, 1915. Song: [v., pf.].

   4119   Genzmer, Harald. Lieder der Welt, MS ca. 1963, Mz.:
            S. Song: 4-8 v., [pf.?].

Kipling, Rudyard continued

4120 Hedgcock, Walter. "On the Road to Mandalay", L: SH, 1899. Song: [v., pf.].

4121 Prince, Dyneley. "On the Road to Mandalay", B: GS, 1903. Song: [v., pf.].

4122 Speaks, Oley. "On the Road to Mandalay", Cin.: Church, 1907. Song: [v., pf.]. Publ. Ph.: TP, 1930 for mixed chorus.

4123 Thayer, Arthur W. Ph.: TP, 1892. Song: [v., pf.].

4124* Travannion, H. "On the Road to Mandalay", Milwaukee: JFL, 1898. Song: [v., pf.].

4125 Whiting, Arthur. Barrack-Room Ballads, NY: GS, 1900. Song: [v., pf.]. Also publ. sep.

4126 Willeby, Charles. Cin.: Church, 1911. Song: [v., pf.].

Married Man, The "Bachelor 'e fights for one, The" The Five Nations (1903)

4127 Cobb, Gerard F. L: SH, 1904. Song: [v., pf.].

4128 Gro, Josephine. NY: OD, 1900. Song: [v., pf.].

4129 Ward-Higgs, W. L: SH, 1915. Song: [v., pf.].

Men that Fought at Minden, The "Men that fought at Minden, they was rookies in their time, The" Pall Mall Gazette (May 1895) & Pall Ball Budget (May 1895)

4130 Bennett, J.S.L.D. MS pre-1932. Song: [v., pf.].

Merchantmen, The "King Solomon drew merchantmen" Pall Mall Budget (May 1893)

4131* Dampier, L. L: P&P, 1903. Song: [v., pf.].

4132 Grainger, Percy. MS 1902-03, rev. 1909-11. Song: ttbbbb, whistlers, hns., bsns., stgs.

Kipling, Rudyard continued

Merrow Down   "There runs a road by Merrow Down"   Just So
    Stories (1902)

    4133 German, Edward. The Just So Song Book, L: MacM,
          1903. Song: v., pf. Setting of part I of the
          poem. Also publ. sep. Arr. by Gordon Jacob as
          ste. for satb, orch.; arr. publ. L: N.

    4134 German, Edward. "Of All the Tribe of Tegumai", The
          Just So Song Book, L: MacM, 1903. Song: [v.,
          pf.]. Setting of part II of the poem. Also publ.
          sep. Arr. by Gordon Jacob as ste. for satb,
          orch.; arr. publ. L: N.

Mine-Sweepers   See: "Dawn off the Foreland--the young flood
    making"

Miracle of Purun Bhagat, The   (SS)   World (Oct. 1895)

    4135 Koechlin, Charles. "Méditation de Purun Baghât", MS
          1936. Symph. poem: orch.

Misunderstood   "Roses red and roses white"   Civil and
    Military Gazette (Aug. 1887), rev. 1902

    4136 Bellamy, Peter. "Blue Roses", MS. Song.

Morning Song in the Jungle   "One moment past our bodies
    cast"   The Second Jungle Book (1895)

    4137 Grainger, Percy. L: S, 1912, Kipling "Jungle Book"
          Cycle, L: S. Song: satbb, a cap.

    4138 Scott, Cyril. See: Jungle Book, The.

Mother O' Mine   "If I were hanged on the highest hill"   The
    Light That Failed (1891)

    4139 Aitken, G. L: R, 1926. Song: [v., pf.].

    4140 Burleigh, Henry. NY: R, 1914. Song: male chorus,
          [a cap.?].

4141 Claassen, Arthur. Cin.: Church, 1914. Song: [v., pf.].

4142 Grainger, Percy. "Dedication", L: S, 1912. Song: t solo, pf.

4143 Kellogg, Arthur. Ph.: TP, 1937. Song: [v., pf.].

4144 Kramer, A. Walter. NY: CF, 1915. Song: [v., pf.].

4145 Liddle, Samuel. L: BH, 1926. Song: [v., pf.].

4146 Maude, Mrs. Raymond. L: KP, pre-1932. Song: [v., pf.].

4147* Norris, Homer. Ph.: TP, 1900. Song: [v., pf.].

4148 Ornstein, Leo. NY: CF, 1915. Song: [v., pf.].

4149 Petrželka, Vilém. Solitude of Sole, Prague: HMUB, 1923. Cyc.: high v., pf. Czech. title: "Matko má!".

4150 Piggot, Robert S. Tor.: WRC, 1909. Song: 3 pt. chorus of male v., [a cap.?] or 4 pt. chorus of male v., [a cap.?].

4151 Protheroe, Daniel. L: BH, 1926. Song: male chorus, [a cap.?].

4152 Remick, Bertha. Ph.: TP, 1907. Song: [v., pf.].

4153 Roma, Caro. NY: Witmark, 1914. Song: [v., pf.].

4154 Sington, Louie. In To-day Magazine (July 1904). Song: [v., pf.]. Publ. sep. L: Medici, 1922.

4155 Tours, Frank E. L: C, 1903. Song: solo v., pf.

4156* Weyman, B. Maxwell. Ph.: TP, 1909. Song: [v., pf.].

Mother-Lodge, The "There was Rundle, Station Master" Pall Mall Gazette (May 1895) & Pall Mall Budget (May 1895)

4157* Dampier, L. L: P&P, 1903. Song: [v., pf.].

Mowgli's Song Against People   "I will let loose against you"
The_Second_Jungle_Book (1895)

    4158   Grainger, Percy. L: S, 1924, Kipling_"Jungle_Book"
          Cycle, L: S. Song: satbb, 10 or more instr.

    4159   Scott, Anthony. MS. Song: ss, pf.

My Boy Jack   See: "'Have you any news of my boy Jack?'"

My Father's Chair   "There are four good legs to my Father's
Chair"   A_History_of_England (1911)

    4160   Green, Charles. Three_Kipling_Songs, L: S, 1923.
          Song: [v., pf.].

My Lady's Law   See: "Law whereby my lady moves, The"

Neighbours   "Man that is open of heart to his neighbour"
Order_of_Proceedings_at_Royal_Albert_Hall (Jan. 1932) &
The_Times (Jan. 1932)

    4161   Davies, H. Walford. L: BH, 1933. Song: [v., pf.].

"Non Nobis, Domine!"   "Non nobis Domine!"   Three_Poems
(1934)

    4162   Quilter, Roger. L: BH, 1938. Song: [v., pf.].

"Now Chil, the Kite, brings home the night"   The_Jungle_Book
(1894)

    4163   Bright, Dora. "Night Song in the Jungle", Six_Songs
          from_"The_Jungle_Book", L: Elkin, 1903. Song:
          [v., pf.].

    4164   Delage, Maurice. "Chil le Vanteur", Trois_Chants_de
          la_Jungle, P: MST, 1935. Song: [v., pf.].

    4165   Grainger, Percy. "Night Song in the Jungle", L: S,
          1925, Kipling_"Jungle_Book"_Cycle, L: S. Song:
          ttbb, a cap.

4166 Koechlin, Charles. Trois Poèmes du Livre de la Jungle, MS 1899-1910. Song: a, b soli, female chorus, [a cap.?]. Other songs in the collection require various voices. Fr. title: "Chanson de nuit dans la jungle".

"Oh! hush thee, my baby, the night is behind us" The Jungle Book (1894)

4167 Atkinson, Robert. "The Seal's Lullaby", B: GS, 1909. Song: [v., pf.].

4168* Bright, Dora. "Mother Seal's Lullaby", L: Elkin, 1903. Song: [v., pf.].

4169 Davies, H. Walford. "The Seal's Lullaby", L: N, 1942. Song: unison v., pf.

4170 Delage, Maurice. "Maktah, Berceuse phoque", Trois Chants de la Jungle, P: MST, 1935. Song: [v., pf.].

4171 Johns, Clayton. "The Seal's Lullaby", MS pre-1932, avail. NYPL. Song: solo v., pf.

4172 Koechlin, Charles. Trois Poèmes du Livre de la Jungle, MS 1899-1910. Song: ms solo, female chorus, [a cap.?]. Other songs in the collection require various voices. Fr. title: "Berceuse phoque".

4173 Lehmann, Liza. "Mother Seal's Lullaby", Two Seal Songs, L: C, 1908. Song: [solo v., pf.].

4174 Leich, Roland. "Seal Lullaby", NY: GS, pre-1940. Song: [solo v., pf.?].

4175 Spalding, Walter R. "Seal Lullaby", NY: GS, pre-1940. Song: [solo v., pf.?].

4176 Wood, Erskine. "The White Seal's Lullaby", A Book of Songs by Erskine Wood, NY: GS, 1922 (priv. publ.). Song: v., pf. Pf. pt. by Randall Thompson.

Kipling, Rudyard continued

Old Mother Laidinwool   "Old Mother Laidinwool had nigh
   twelve months been dead"   Puck of Pook's Hill (1906)

   4177 Shaw, Martin. L: Curwen, 1919. Song: bar solo, pf.

Only Son, The   "She dropped the bar, she shot the bolt"
   Songs from Books (1913) A portion was 1st publ. in Many
   Inventions (1893)

   4178 Grainger, Percy. L: S, 1958, Kipling "Jungle Book"
         Cycle, L: S. Song: s, t soli, satbb ad lib., 8-23
         instr.

   4179* Ives, Charles. MS.

Oonts   "Wot makes the soldier's 'eart to penk"   Scots
   Observer (Mar. 1890)

   4180 Baas, Alexius. NY: JF, 1927. Song: male chorus,
         [a cap.?].

   4181 Cobb, Gerard F. Barrack-Room Ballads, Third Series,
         L: SH, 1897. Song: [v., pf.].

'Our Fathers of Old'   "Excellent herbs had our fathers of
   old"   Rewards and Fairies (1910)

   4182 Bellamy, Peter. Oak, Ash and Thorn, L: RMC, 1970.
         Song: male solo v., unacc. Portions of the col-
         lection require accompaniment. Issued on Argo
         recording #ZFB 11.

Our Lady of the Snows   "Nation spoke to a Nation, A"   The
   Times (Apr. 1897)

   4183 Davies, H. Walford. L: N, 1897. Song: [v., pf.].

"Over the edge of the purple down"   Century Magazine (Dec.
   1895), rev. 1912

   4184 Bradford, H.N. "The City of Sleep", L: Forsyth,
         1902. Song: [v., pf.].

4185 Elliott, Muriel. L: JW, 1902. Song: [v., pf.].

4186* Grainger, Percy. "Merciful Town", MS 1899? Song:
med. v., unison chorus, pf.

4187 Kernochan, Marshall. "The City of Sleep", B: GS,
1908. Song: [v., pf.].

4188 Little, A.R. "The City of Sleep", NY: GS (Wa-Wan),
pre-1940. Song: [v., pf.?].

4189 Rogers, Milton A. Five Songs, B: BMC, pre-1940.
Song: [v., pf.].

"People of the Eastern Ice, they are melting like the snow,
The" Pall Mall Gazette (Oct. 1895)

4190 Grainger, Percy. "The Inuit", L: S, 1912, Kipling
"Jungle Book" Cycle, L: S. Song: satbbb, a cap.

Philadelphia "If you're off to Philadelphia in the morning"
Rewards and Fairies (1910)

4191 Bellamy, Peter. Oak, Ash and Thorn, L: RMC, 1970.
Song: male solo v., concertina. Portions of the
collection are unacc. Issued on Argo recording
#ZFB 11.

Piet "I do not love my Empire's foes" The Five Nations
(1903)

4192* R-W., A.C. L: BH, 1908. Song: [v., pf.].

Pink Dominoes "Jenny and Me were engaged" Civil and
Military Gazette (Mar. 1886)

4193 Elkin, W.A. L: SH, 1894. Song: [v., pf.].

"Pit where the buffalo cooled his hide" Plain Tales from
the Hills (1888)

Kipling, Rudyard continued

    4194   Grainger, Percy. "The Peora Hunt", L: S, 1924, Kip-
           ling "Jungle Book" Cycle, L: S. Song: satbb,
           instr. ad lib.

  'Poor Honest Men'   "Your jar of Virginny"   Rewards and
    Fairies (1910)

    4195   Bellamy, Peter. Oak, Ash and Thorn, L: RMC, 1970.
           Song: male solo v., vln. Portions of the col-
           lection are unacc. Issued on Argo recording
           #ZFB 11.

  Prophets at Home   See: "Prophets have honour all over the
    Earth"

  "Prophets have honour all over the Earth"   Puck of Pook's
    Hill (1906), rev. 1912

    4196   Bellamy, Peter. "Prophets at Home", Merlin's Isle of
           Gramarye, L: RMC, 1972. Song: male solo v., vln.,
           Portions of the collection are unacc. Issued on
           Argo recording #ZFB 81.

  Puck's Song   "See you the ferny ride that steals"   Puck of
    Pook's Hill (1906), rev. 1912

    4197   Bellamy, Peter. Merlin's Isle of Gramarye, L: RMC,
           1972. Song: male solo v., vln. Portions of the
           collection are unacc. Issued on Argo recording
           #ZFB 81.

  "Pussy can sit by the fire and sing"   Just So Stories (1902)

    4198   German, Edward. "The First Friend", The Just So Song
           Book, L: MacM, 1903. Song: v., pf. Also publ.
           sep. Arr. by Gordon Jacob as ste. for satb,
           orch.; arr. publ. L: N.

  Queen's Men, The   See: Two Cousins, The

  Queen's Uniform, The   See: Tommy

ipling, Rudyard continued

<u>Recessional</u>* "God of our fathers, known of old" <u>The Times</u>
    (July 1897), publ. sep. same year

4199 Bennett, J.S.L.D. "God of Our Fathers", MS pre-1932.
      Anthem (for Durham Cathedral): chorus, org.

4200* Berridge, A. In <u>Garrett Horder's Worship Song</u>.

4201 Blanchard, G.F. "God of Our Fathers", B: Birchard,
      1920 in <u>Boy Scout Song Book</u>. Song: v., pf. Publ-
      sep. L: Reid, 1920.

4202 Bouverie, H.M.P. "God of Our Fathers", L: N, 1918.
      Hymn: [v., org.].

4203 Bunning, Herbert. "Lest We Forget", L: BH, 1911.
      Song: [v., pf.].

4204 Clark, S. L: Curwen, 1907. Song: chorus, [pr.?].

4205 Clough-Leighter, Henry. B: BMC, 1915. "Ode": chorus,
      [a cap.?].

4206 Coulter, A.J. Humphrey. L: N, 1910. Song: unison v.,
      org., perc.

4207 de Koven, Reginald. Cin.: Church, 1898. Song publ.
      in the following arr.: high v., pf.; low v., pf.;
      2 pt. female chorus; 3 pt. female chorus; 4 pt.
      male chorus; 4 pt. mixed chorus. Arr. by J.L.
      Frank for pf. solo; arr. publ. Cin.: Church,
      1916.

4208 Elliott, D. Morgan. L: N, 1912. Cta.: chorus,
      [orch.?].

4209 Fogg, D. St. C. L: JW, 1919. Hymn: [v., org.].

4210 Foote, Arthur. B: Schmidt, 1915. Song: chorus, [a
      cap.?].

4211 Foster, G. L: West, 1918. Setting for chorus, [a
      cap.?].

4212 Gentry, A.J. L: N, 1918. Hymn: [v., org.].

465

Kipling, Rudyard continued

4213 Gibb, Robert W. "God of Our Fathers", MS pre-1964,
NY: CF. Setting for s or t solo, satb, pf. (or
org.). Also publ. NY: CF for ttbb, pf. (or org.).

4214 Gilchrist, William W. NY: GS, 1902. Anthem: [chorus,
org.].

4215 Grainger, Percy. L: S, 1930. Hymn: satbb, org. ad
lib.

4216 Hadley, Henry. B: Schmidt, 1904. Song: [v., pf.].

4217 Holt, G.E. L: N, 1914. Hymn: [v., org.].

4218* Hopkins, E.G. San Francisco: Leechman, 1906. Song:
[v., pf.].

4219 Huss, Henry H. "God of Our Fathers", B: Birchard,
1901 in Laurel Song Book. Song: [v., pf.].

4220 Lawrence, C.H., arr. B: Ginn, n.d. in The American
Song Book. Song: [v., pf.].

4221 Manney, Charles F. B: Schmidt, 1907. Song: solo v.,
pf.

4222 Martin, George C. L: N, 1908. Anthem: chorus,
[org.].

4223 Matthews, H. Alexander. B: GS, 1918. Anthem: mixed
chorus, orch.

4224 Naylor, Edward W. L: N, 1909. Hymn: [v., org.].

4225 Nevin, George B. "God of Our Fathers", in The Church
Choir (copyright by George F. Rosche 1900). Hymn:
male qrt., [pf.].

4226 Parks, J.A. "Lest We Forget", York, Nebr.: Parks,
1922. Setting for 2 pt. chorus, [a cap.?].

4227 Parmor, Arthur A. In Kipling Journal (Apr. 1931).
Setting for v., pf.

4228 Penn, Arthur A. "Lest We Forget", NY: Witmark, 1925.
Song: [v., pf.]. Also publ. NY: Witmark, 1925 for
ssa (or tbb) or 4 pt. mixed chorus.

466

ipling, Rudyard continued

4229 Shelley, Harry R. B: GS, 1917. Song: [v., pf.].

4230 Sterns, C.C. "God of Our Fathers", B: W-S, 1906.
      Song: [v., pf.].

4231 Straker, J.A. "Lest We Forget", L: West, 1915. Hymn:
      [v., org.].

4232 Sweeting, E.T. "Lest We Forget", L: Deanne, 1924.
      Song: chorus, [a cap.?].

4233 Walker, A.F. "Lest We Forget", copyright by the
      composer, Altrinsham 1914. Hymn: [v., org.].

4234 Warren, George W. "God of Our Fathers", NY: CF
      (hire). Setting arr. by Carl F. Mueller for satb,
      band.

4235 Willan, Healey. Oakville: FH, 1928. Hymn: unison
      v., pf. (or org.) or satb, pf. (or org.).

4236 Wood, Charles. "God of Our Fathers", L: Milford,
      1927 in Church Hymnary. Hymn: [v., org.]. Set to
      the tune "Fokkingham".

4237* Woodman, H.H. B: GS, 1900. Setting for male chorus,
      [a cap.?].

Reeds of Runnymede, The "At Runnymede, at Runnymede" A
History of England (1911)

    4238 Green, Charles. Three Kipling Songs, L: S, 1923.
          Song: [v., pf.].

Rhyme of the Three Sealers, The "Now this is the Law of the
Muscovite" Pall Mall Budget (Dec. 1893), publ. sep. same
year

    4239* Grainger, Percy. MS 1900-01. Song: sattbbb.

Rhyme of True Thomas, The See: [Last] Rhyme of True Thomas,
The

Kipling, Rudyard continued

"Ride with an idle whip, ride with an unused heel"   _Civil and Military Gazette_ (Apr. 1887)

   4240 Grainger, Percy. "Ride with an Idle Whip", MS 1399, avail. British Museum. Song: v., pf.

'Rikki-Tikki-Tavi' (SS) _St. Nicholas Magazine_ (Nov. 1893) & _Pall Mall Magazine_ (Nov. 1893)

   4241 Scott, Cyril. See: _Jungle Book, The_.

'Rimini'   See: "When I left Rome for Lalage's sake"

Ripple Song, A   "Once a ripple came to land"   _The Second Jungle Book_ (1895)

   4242* Dampier, L. "The Ripple", MS pre-1932. Song: [v., pf.].

Road-Song of the Bandar-Log   "Here we go in a flung festoon"   _The Jungle Book_ (1894)

   4243 Bright, Dora. _Six Songs from "The Jungle Book"_, L: Elkin, 1903. Song: [v., pf.].

   4244* Eppert, Carl. MS pre-1930. Song: male chorus, pf. or male chorus, orch.

   4245 Koechlin, Charles. See: _Jungle Book, The_.

Route Marchin'   "We're marchin' on relief over Injia's sunny plains"   _Barrack-Room Ballads And Other Verses_ (1892)

   4246 Bellamy, Peter. MS. Song.

   4247 Cobb, Gerard F. L: SH, 1892. Song: [v., pf.]. Also publ. L: SH, 1892 in _Barrack-Room Ballads, First Series_.

   4248 McCall, J.P. L: Swan, 1930. Song: [v., pf.].

   4249 Stock, George C. NY: Church, 1915. Song: [v., pf.].

Run of the Downs, The   "Weald is good, the Downs are best,
    The"   Rewards_and_Fairies (1910)

    4250 Bellamy, Peter. Merlin's_Isle_of_Gramarye, L: RMC,
          1972. Song: male solo v., vln. Portions of the
          collection are unacc. Issued on Argo recording
          #ZFB 81.

School Song, A   See: "'Let us now praise famous men'"

Screw-Guns   "Smokin' my pipe on the mountings"   Scots_Ob-
    server (July 1890)

    4251 Cobb, Gerard F. Barrack-Room_Ballads, Third Series,
          L: SH, 1897. Song: [v., pf.].

Sea-Wife, The   See: "There dwells a wife by the Northern
    Gate"

Shillin' a Day   "My name is O'Kelly"   Barrack-Room_Ballads
    And_Other_Verses (1892)

    4252 Bellamy, Peter. MS. Song.

    4253 Cobb, Gerard F. L: SH, 1893. Song: [v., pf.]. Also
          publ. L: SH, 1893 in Barrack-Room_Ballads, Second
          Series.

"Ships await us above, The"   Daily_Telegraph (Nov. 1915)

    4254 Elgar, Edward. "Submarines", The_Fringes_of_the
          Fleet, L: E, 1917. Cyc.: bar qrt., orch. Arr.
          as a setting for choir by R.D. Metcalfe.

Shiv and the Grasshopper   "Shiv, who poured the harvest"
    The_Jungle_Book (1894)

    4255 Hunt, Raymond. L: BH, 1896. Song: [v., pf.].

4256 Koechlin, Charles. "Song of Kala Nag", Trois Poèmes du Livre de la Jungle, MS 1899-1910. Song: t solo, t chorus, [a cap.?]. Fr. title: "Chant de Kala Nag".

4257 Whitehead, Percy. L: G&T, 1912. Song: [v., pf.].

Shut-Eye Sentry, The   "'Sez the Junior Orderly Sergeant" The Seven Seas (1896)

4258 Crimp, H.E. L: KP, 1900. Song: [v., pf.].

Sir Richard's Song   "I followed my Duke ere I was a lover" Puck of Pook's Hill (1906)

4259 Bellamy, Peter. Oak, Ash and Thorn, L: RMC, 1970. Song: male solo v., acoustic gtr. Portions of the collection are unacc. Issued on Argo recording #ZFB 11.

4260 Fitzgerald, Augustine. Four Songs, L: Curwen, pre-1940. Song: [v., pf.].

Smuggler's Song, A   "If you wake at midnight, and hear a horse's feet"   Puck of Pook's Hill (1906)

4261 Bellamy, Peter. Merlin's Isle of Gramarye, L: RMC, 1972. Song: "trad. 3 pt. harmony", unacc. Portions of the collection require accompaniment. Issued on Argo recording #ZFB 81.

4262 Boult, Adrian. L: B&H, 1912. Song: [v., pf.].

4263 Kernochan, Marshall. B: GS, 1911. Song: [v., pf.].

4264 Le Fleming, Christopher. L: OUP, ca. 1960. Song: unison v., pf. or 2 pt. chorus, pf.

4265 Mortimer, C.G. L: Swan, 1914. Song: [v., pf.].

4266 Müller, Max. L: NCA, 1907. Song: [v., pf.].

4267 Mulliner, Michael. L: C, 1918 (1960). Song: unison v., pf.

ɔling, Rudyard continued

'Snarleyow' "This 'appened in a battle" National Observer
   (Nov. 1890)

   4268 Cobb, Gerard F. Barrack-Room Ballads, Third Series,
           L: SH, 1897. Song: [v., pf.].

"Soldier an' Sailor Too" "As I was spittin' into the Ditch"
   McClure's Magazine (Apr. 1896) & Pearson's Magazine (Apr.
   1896)

   4269 Ward-Higgs, W. L: SH, 1906. Song: [v., pf.].

Soldier, Soldier "Soldier, soldier come from the wars"
   Scots Observer (Apr. 1890)

   4270 Bellamy, Peter. MS. Song.

   4271 Cobb, Gerard F. L: SH, 1892. Song: [v., pf.]. Also
           publ. L: SH, 1892 in Barrack-Room Ballads, First
           Series.

   4272 Grainger, Percy. L: S, 1925. Song: a, 3 t, 2 b soli,
           satbb, harm. ad lib.

   4273 Whiting, Arthur. Barrack-Room Ballads, NY: GS, 1900.
           Song: [v., pf.]. Also publ. sep.

Song in Storm, A   See: "Be well assured that on our side"

Song of the Dead, The "Hear now the Song of the Dead"
   English Illustrated Magazine (May 1893) as one of "A Song
   of the English"

   4274 Bantock, Granville. "We Have Fed Our Seas", L: Cur-
           wen, 1919. Song: [v., pf.?]. Setting of part II
           of the poem.

   4275 Boughton, Rutland. Songs of the English, MS 1901.
           Song: bar solo, orch., pf. Part II of the poem is
           incl. in the collection as a sep. song entitled
           "The Price of the Admiralty".

4276 Grainger, Percy. "We Have Fed Our Seas", L: S, 1912. Song: mixed chorus, br. choir, stgs. ad lib. Setting of part II of the poem.

4277 Grainger, Percy. "We Were Dreamers", MS pre-1899. Setting for satb of part I of the poem.

4278 Grainger, Percy. "We Were Dreamers", MS 1899. Orch. only.

Song of the Men's Side   "Once we feared the Beast"   Rewards and Fairies (1910)

4279 Bellamy, Peter. Merlin's Isle of Gramarye, L: RMC, 1972. Song: male solo v., male chorus, flints. Portions of the collection are unacc. Issued on Argo recording #ZFB 81.

Song of the Red War-Boat   "Shove off from the wharf-edge! Steady!"   Rewards and Fairies (1910)

4280 Bellamy, Peter. Merlin's Isle of Gramarye, L: RMC, 1972. Song: male solo v., with male choral accompaniment. Portions of the collection require instr. accompaniment. Issued on Argo recording #ZFB 81.

Song of the Sons, The   "One from the ends of the earth" English Illustrated Magazine (May 1893) as one of "A Song of the English"

4281 Boughton, Rutland. Songs of the English, MS 1901. Song: bar solo, orch., pf.

Sons of the Widow, The   "'Ave you 'eard o' the Widow at Windsor"   Scots Observer (Apr. 1890), rev. 1892

4282 Bellamy, Peter. "The Widow at Windsor", MS. Song.

4283* Sutherland, Gordon. "The Widow at Windsor", L: SH, 1893. Song: [v., pf.]. Also publ. L: SH, 1893 in Barrack-Room Ballads, Second Series.

Spring Running, The   (SS)   Pall Mall Gazette (Sept. 1895)

   4284   Koechlin, Charles. MS 1925-27. Symph. poem: orch.
          Fr. title: "La Course de printemps".

St. Helena Lullaby, A   "How far is St. Helena"   Rewards and
   Parlers (1910)

   4285   Bellamy, Peter. "St. Helena", Merlin's Isle of
          Gramarye, L: RMC, 1972. Song. male solo v., vln.
          Portions of the collection are unacc. Issued on
          Argo recording #ZFB 81.

Tarrant Moss   "I closed and drew for my love's sake"   Songs
   from Books (1912) Portions were 1st publ. in Plain Tales
   from the Hills (1888)

   4286* Ives, Charles. 114 Songs, NY: GS, 1921 [1922]. Song:
          [v., pf.].

"There dwells a wife by the Northern Gate"   Steve Brown's
   Bunyip and Other Stories (1893), rev. 1896

   4287   Grainger, Percy. "The Sea Wife", L: S, 1948. Song:
          satb, pf. duet or satb, br. and/or stgs.

"There is pleasure in the wet, wet clay"   In coll. with Wolcott Balestier   The Naulahka (1892)

   4288   Edmonds, Paul. "The Lie", L: Curwen, 1919. Song:
          chorus, [a cap.?].

"There never was a Queen like Balkis"   Just So Stories
   (1902)

   4289   Berger, Jean. "Butterflies", Just So, NY: Tetra,
          1971. Song: satb, a cap.

   4290   German, Edward. The Just So Song Book, L: MacM,
          1903. Song: v., pf. Also publ. sep. Arr. by Gor-
          don Jacob as ste. for satb, orch.; arr. publ. L:
          N.

Kipling, Rudyard continued

"There were three friends that buried the fourth"   <u>The Light</u>
<u>that Failed</u> (1890)

    4291 Grainger, Percy. "A Northern Balled", MS 1898-99.
          Song: med. v., pf.

    4292* Grainger, Percy. "There Were Three Friends", MS
          1899. Orch. only.

"There's a convict more in the Central Jail"   <u>Macmillan's</u>
<u>Magazine</u> (Jan. 1890)

    4293 Grainger, Percy. "The Running of Shindland", L: S,
          1922. Song: tttbbb, a cap.

"This is the mouth-filling song"   <u>Just So Stories</u> (1902)

    4294 Berger, Jean. "The Race", <u>Just So</u>, NY: Tetra, 1971.
          Song: satb, a cap.

    4295* German, Edward. "Kangaroo and Dingo", <u>The Just So</u>
          <u>Song Book</u>, L: MacM, 1903. Song: [v., pf.]. Also
          publ. sep. Arr. by Gordon Jacob as ste. for satb,
          orch.; arr. publ. L: N.

"This Uninhabited Island"   <u>Just So Stories</u> (1902)

    4296 German, Edward. <u>The Just So Song Book</u>, L: MacM,
          1903. Song: v., pf. Also publ. sep. Arr. by Gor-
          don Jacob as ste. for satb, orch.; arr. publ. L:
          N.

Thousandth Man, The   "One man in a thousand, Solomon says"
<u>Rewards and Fairies</u> (1910)

    4297 Behrend, Arthur H. B: OD, 1926. Song: [v., pf.].

    4298 Wood, Ralph W. MS. Song: ttbb, a cap.

Three-Part Song, A   "I'm just in love with all these three"
<u>Puck of Pock's Hill</u> (1906)

*ling, Rudyard continued

4299* Bellamy, Peter. Oak, Ash and Thorn, L: RMC, 1970.
    Song: "3 pt. trad.-style harmony", unacc. Por-
    tions of the collection require solo v. and ac-
    companiment. Issued on Argo recording #ZFB 11.

To T.A.   "I have made for you a song"   Barrack-Room Ballads
And Other Verses (1892)

4300 Cobb, Gerard F. L: SH, 1890. Song: [v., pf.]. Also
    publ. L: SH, 1893 in Barrack-Room Ballads, Second
    Series.

To the True Romance   "Thy face is far from this our war"
Many Inventions (1893)

4301* Dennis, Terrence P. MS pre-1932. Song: [v., pf.?].

To Wolcott Balestier*   "Beyond the path of the outmost sun"
Barrack-Room Ballads And Other Verses (1892)

4302 Grainger, Percy. Unf. MS 1901. Orch. only.

Tommy   "I went into a public-'ouse"   Scots Observer (Mar.
1890), rev. same year

4303 Bellamy, Peter. MS. Song.

4304 Carmichael, Mary. L: SH, 1892. Song: [v., pf.]. Also
    publ. L: SH, 1892 in Barrack-Room Ballads, First
    Series.

4305 Cobb, Gerard F. L: SH, 1906. Song: [v., pf.].

Tree Song, A   "Of all the trees that grow so fair"   Puck of
Pook's Hill (1906)

4306 Aylward, Florence. L: C, 1910. Song: solo v., pf.

4307 Bellamy, Peter. "Oak, Ash and Thorn", Oak, Ash and
    Thorn, L: RMC, 1970. Song: male solo v. with
    choral harmony, unacc. Portions of the collection
    require accompaniment. Issued on Argo recording
    #ZFB 11.

475

Kipling, Rudyard continued

4308   Fitzgerald, Augustine. Four Songs, L: Curwen, pre-
       1940. Song: [v., pf.].

Troopin'   "Troopin', troopin', troopin' to the sea"   Scots
   Observer (May 1890)

   4309   Bellamy, Peter. MS. Song.

   4310   Cobb, Gerard F. L: SH, 1893. Song: [v., pf.]. Also
          publ. L: SH, 1893 in Barrack-Room Ballads, Second
          Series.

   4311   Strickland, Lily. NY: CF, 1933. Song: male chorus,
          [a cap.?].

   4312   Ward-Higgs, W. L: SH, 1906. Song: [v., pf.].

Truthful Song, A   "I tell this tale, which is strictly true"
   Rewards and Fairies (1910)

   4313   Bellamy, Peter. "The Bricklayer and the Shipwright",
          Merlin's Isle of Gramarye, L: RMC, 1972. Song:
          male solo v., vln. Portions of the collection are
          unacc. Issued on Argo recording #ZFB 81.

Two Cousins, The   "Valour and Innocence"   Rewards and
   Fairies (1910)

   4314   Bellamy, Peter. Merlin's Isle of Gramarye, L: RMC,
          1972. Song: c-t solo, lute, fl.-org. Portions of
          the collection are unacc. Issued on Argo record-
          ing #ZFB 81.

   4315   Hely-Hutchinson, Victor. "The Queen's Men", L:
          Elkin, 1937. Song: [v., pf.].

Vampire, The   "Fool there was and he made his prayer, A"
   (1897)

   4316   O'Neill, Florence. Cin.: Jennings, 1901. Song: [v.,
          pf.].

Way through the Woods, The   "They shut the road through the
    woods"   Rewards_and_Fairies (1910)

    4317 Bellamy, Peter. Merlin's_Isle_of_Gramarye, L: RMC,
          1972. Song: male solo v., concertina. Portions of
          the collection are unacc. Issued on Argo record-
          ing #ZFB 81.

What 'Dane-geld' Means   "It is always a temptation to an
    armed and agile nation"   A_History_of_England (1911),
    rev. 1919

    4318 German, Edward. L: MZ, 1909. Song: [v., pf.].

"What of the hunting, hunter bold?"   The_Jungle_Book (1894)

    4319 Bright, Dora. "Tiger, Tiger", Six_Songs_from_"The
          Jungle_Book", L: Elkin, 1903. Song: [v., pf.].

    4320 Delage, Maurice. "Themmangu, Chant et danse du
          tigre", Trois_Chants_de_la_Jungle, P: MST, 1935.
          Song: [v., pf.].

    4321 Grainger, Percy. "Tiger, Tiger", L: S, 1912, Kipling
          "Jungle_Book"_Cycle, L: S. Song: t solo ad lib.,
          ttbbb, a cap.

    4322 Hatch, Homer. "Tiger, Tiger", B: GS, 1915. Song:
          4 pt. male chorus, [a cap?].

"When I left Rome for Lalage's sake"   Puck_of_Pook's_Hill
    (1906), rev. 1912. A portion was 1st publ. in Strand
    (July 1906) & McClure's_Magazine (July 1906)

    4323 Edmonds, Paul. "Rimini", L: E, 1919. Song: [v.,
          pf.].

    4324 Troubridge, Amy. "Rimini", L: Elkin, 1908. Song:
          [v., pf.]. Setting of 1st stanza only.

"When 'Omer smote 'is bloomin' lyre"   The_Seven_Seas (1896)

    4325 Scott, Anthony. MS. Song: ss, pf.

Kipling, Rudyard continued

"When the cabin port-holes are dark and green"   Just So
    Stories (1902)

    4326   German, Edward. "When the Cabin Portholes", The Just
           So Song Book, L: MacM, 1903. Song: [v., pf.].
           Also publ. sep. Arr. by Gordon Jacob as ste. for
           satb, orch.; arr. publ. L: N.

Widow at Windsor, The   See: Sons of the Widow, The

Widow's Party, The   "'Where have you been this while away?'"
    Barrack-Room Ballads And Other Verses (1892)

    4327   Bellamy, Peter. MS. Song.

    4328   Cobb, Gerard F. Barrack-Room Ballads, Third Series,
           L: SH, 1897. Song: [v., pf.].

    4329   Grainger, Percy. L: S, 1923. Song: unison male
           chorus, pf. duet or unison male chorus, orch.
           (or ch. orch.).

    4330   Ward-Higgs, W. L: SH, 1906. Song: [v., pf.].

"Wind went down with the sunset, The"*   Traffics and Dis-
    coveries (1904), rev. 1912

    4331   Shaw, Martin. "The Egg-Shell", L: Curwen, 1919.
           Song: bar solo, pf.

Wishing Caps, The   "Life's all getting and giving"   Songs
    from Books (1912) Portions were 1st publ. in Kim (1901)

    4332* Binkerd, Gordon. Oceanside: BH, 1971. Song: low v.,
           pf.

"Ye that bore us, O restore us!"   The Light that Failed
    (1890)

    4333   Grainger, Percy. "The Men of the Sea", L: S, 1923.
           Song: med. or low v., pf.

"You mustn't swim till you're six weeks old" The Jungle Book (1894)

    4334 Bright, Dora. "Mother Seal's Song", Six Songs from "The Jungle Book", L: Elkin, 1903. Song: [v., pf.].

    4335 Lehmann, Liza. "You Mustn't Swim", Two Seal Songs, L: C, 1908. Song: [solo v., pf.].

Young British Soldier, The "When the 'arf-made recruity goes out to the East" Scots Observer (June 1890)

    4336 Bellamy, Peter. MS. Song.

    4337 Cobb, Gerard F. L: SH, 1892. Song: [v., pf.]. Also publ. L: SH, 1892 in Barrack-Room Ballads, First Series.

    4338 Grainger, Percy. MS 1899. Song: [bar] solo v., pf.

Miscellanea

    4339 Alain, Jehan. "Chanson", MS ca. 1936. Song: [v., pf.?].

    4340 Atkins, Norton. "Oh! Mr. Kipling (The Blood-red tape)", L: SH, 1900. Song: [v., pf.].

    4341 Ayres, Frederic. "The Song of the Panthan Girl", MS pre-1926. Song: [v., pf.?].

    4342 Delage, Maurice. Grove's cites ballet music by Delage entitled "Les Batisseurs de ponts" (MS 1914) of which only the overture is extant. The work is based on Kipling.

    4343 Foote, Arthur. "The Eden Rose", B: Schmidt, 1892. Song: [v., pf.].

    4344 Haydon, Claude. "Lullaby", MS n.d., avail. National Library of N.Z. Song: solo v., pf.

Kipling, Rudyard continued

4345   Ives, Charles. In The Songs of Charles Ives (1874-
       1954) (Ann Arbor: University Microfilms, 1967),
       P.E. Newman claims there is a missing MS of one
       other Ives setting of words by Kipling.

4346   Jordon, Jules. "Triumphant Love", B: Schmidt, 1892.
       Song: [v., pf.].

4347   Monico, L.J. Rudyard Kipling Waltzes, NY: Paull,
       1898.

4348   Newman, Alfred. "Gunga Din", MS ca. 1939, released
       RKO Radio. Film music. [Based on Kipling's
       poem?]

4349   Sachs, Henry. "Tommy", NY: HFL, pre-1929. Song: high
       or med. v., pf. [Text by Kipling?]

4350   Sanders, Robert L. "Recessional", NY: HWG, pre-1964.
       Setting for satb, org. [Text by Kipling?]

4351   Weill, Kurt. Zaubernacht. A pantomime prod. 1922,
       incl. several of Kipling's ballads.

KIRKUP, James   1923-

   Coming of the Fool, The   "He will not come"   In The Submerged Village (1951)

      4352   Cole, Hugo. A Company of Fools, MS, perf. Oxf., Nov.
             1954. Cyc.: satb, stgs.

   Fool and His Shadow, The   "Kitten will kiss his hand, A"
   In The Submerged Village (1951)

      4353   Cole, Hugo. A Company of Fools, MS, perf. Oxf., Nov.
             1954. Cyc.: satb, stgs.

   Fool in the Dark, The   "Look! he holds his own bright torch"
   In The Submerged Village (1951)

Kirkup, James continued

4354 Cole, Hugo. A Company of Fools, MS, perf. Oxf., Nov.
1954. Cyc.: satb, stgs.

Fool Making Music, A "Out of his heart" In The Submerged
Village (1951)

4355 Cole, Hugo. A Company of Fools, MS, perf. Oxf., Nov.
1954. Cyc.: satb, stgs.

Fool with a Harp, A "In the harp's golden cage" In The
Submerged Village (1951)

4356 Cole, Hugo. A Company of Fools, MS, perf. Oxf., Nov.
1954. Cyc.: satb, stgs.

Ghost, Fire, Water "Those are the ghosts of the unwilling
dead" In The Descent into the Cave (1957)

4357 Mews, Douglas. MS pre-1974, L: OUP. Song: a solo,
chorus of mixed v., a cap.

"How calm, how constant are the hills!" In A Spring Journey
(1954)

4358 Ireland, John. "The Hills", L: S&B, 1953 in A Garland for the Queen. Song: satb, a cap.

Local Fool, A "He from the furnace" In The Submerged
Village (1951)

4359 Cole, Hugo. A Company of Fools, MS, perf. Oxf., Nov.
1954. Cyc.: satb, stgs.

Nativity at Night, The "He who is our day" In A Spring
Journey (1954)

4360 Teed, Roy. L: JWC, 1954. Song: satb, a cap.

Miscellanea

Kirkup, James continued

    4361   Teed, Roy. "The Dripping Tap" and "Cosy Cat Nap",
           publ. together L: Curwen, 1962 (avail. only
           from the composer). Songs: ssa, a cap. Texts
           begin: "Drip drop goes the dripping tap", "Pussy-
           kitten, pussy-cat".

    4362   Teed, Roy. Five Funny Songs, MS, L: JWC (hire).
           Cyc.: v., cl., pf. Also arr. for v., orch. Texts
           by Kirkup.

    4363   Teed, Roy. "Song for Sunrise", L: JWC, 1955. Song:
           med. v., pf. Text begins: "Leap from your bed,
           the dawn is breaking".

KOESTLER, Arthur   1905-

  Twilight Bar   (DR)   (1945)

    4364 Bowles, Paul. MS ca. 1946. Incidental music.

KORZENIOWSKI, Jozef Teodor Konrad Nalecz   See: CONRAD, Joseph

LANG, Andrew   1844-1912

  Changeful Beauty   "Whether I find thee bright with fair"
    In The Poetical Works of Andrew Lang, Vol. II (1923)

    4365 Elgar, Edward. "Whether I find Thee", Five Part-
          songs from the Greek Anthology, L: N, 1903. Song:
          ttbb, a cap. Text transl. from the Greek by Lang.

Lang, Andrew continued

Romance   "My Love dwelt in a northern land"   In The
   Poetical Works of Andrew Lang, Vol. III (1923)

   4366   Elgar, Edward. "My Love...", L: N, 1890. Song: satb,
          a cap.

Miscellanea

   4367   Stanford, C.V. "Sweeter than the violet", Six Songs,
          L: BH, 1882. Song: v., pf.

LAWRENCE, David Herbert   1885-1930

Aware   "Slowly the moon is rising"   Love Poems and Others
   (1913)

   4368   Rieti, Vittorio. Four D.H. Lawrence Songs, Hastings-
          on-Hudson: GMP, 1964. Song: ms solo, pf.

Body of God, The   "God is the great urge"   Last Poems
   (1932)

   4369   Douglas, James. God is Born, MS 1971, avail. SMA.
          Song: satb, a cap.

Bride, The   "My love looks like a girl to-night"   Amores
   (1916), rev. 1932

   4370* Ronsheim, John. MS. Song: female solo v., pf.

Cherry Robbers   "Under the long dark boughs"   Love Poems
   and Others (1913)

   4371   Raphael, Mark. Three D.H. Lawrence Love Poems, L:
          Thames, 1973. Cyc.: t solo, pf.

   4372   Taylor, Clifford. Five Songs on English Texts, NY:
          AMP, 1954. Song: s or t solo, pf.

483

Lawrence, D.H. continued

David   (DR)   (1926)

    4373 Dello Joio, Norman. "Lamentation of Saul", NY: CF,
          1970. Song: bar solo, orch. or bar solo, ch.
          ensemble. Text adapt. from the play.

Dead Mother, The   See: Bride, The

December Night   "Take off your cloak and your hat"   Look!
We Have Come Through! (1917)

    4374 Rieti, Vittorio. Four D.H. Lawrence Songs, Hastings-
          on-Hudson: GMP, 1970. Song: ms solo, pf.

    4375* Ronsheim, John. MS. Song: female solo v., pf.

Demiurge   "They say that reality exists only in the spirit"
Last Poems (1932)

    4376 Douglas, James. God is Born, MS 1971, avail. SMA.
          Song: satb, a cap.

Desire goes down into the Sea   "I have no desire any more"
Pansies (1929)

    4377 Sculthorpe, Peter. Sun, MS. Cyc.: med. v., pf.

Dog-Tired   "If she would come to me here"   Love Poems and
Others (1913)

    4378 Raphael, Mark. Three D.H. Lawrence Love Poems, L:
          Thames, 1973. Cyc.: t solo, pf.

    4379 Wood, Hugh. MS 1966. Song: high v., pf.

Elephant is Slow to Mate, The   "Elephant, the huge old
beast, The"   Pansies (1929)

    4380 Beeson, Jack. "The Elephant", Two Concert Arias, MS.
          Concert aria: high v., pf. or high v., orch.

Elephants in the Circus   "Elephants in the circus"   Pansies
    (1929)

    4381 Knight, Morris. Pansies, Hattiesburg: Triton, 1962.
          Cyc.: bar solo, cl., hn., vln., vcl., db.

End, The Beginning, The   "If there were not an utter"   Last
    Poems (1932)

    4382 Riley, Dennis. Cantata I, NY: CFP, 1972. Cta.: ms
          solo, t. sax., vcl., vibra., pf.

Fidelity   "Fidelity and love are two different things"
    Pansies (1929)

    4383 Douglas, James. MS 1972, avail. SMA. Song: s or t
          solo, orch.

Flapper   See: Song "Love has crept out of her sealed heart"

Giorno dei Morti   See: Service of All the Dead

Gloire de Dijon   "When she rises in the morning"   Poetry
    (Jan. 1914) as one of "All of Roses"

    4384* Ronsheim, John. MS. Song: female solo v., pf.

    4385 Wood, Hugh. MS 1966. Song: high v., pf.

Glory   "Glory is of the sun, too"   Pansies (1929)

    4386 Knight, Morris. Pansies, Hattiesburg: Triton, 1962.
          Cyc.: bar solo, cl., hn., vln., vcl., db.

God is Born   "History of the cosmos, The"   Last Poems
    (1932)

    4387 Douglas, James. God is Born, MS 1971, avail. SMA.
          Song: satb, a cap.

Lawrence, D.H. continued

Green   "Dawn was apple-green, The"   Poetry (Jan. 1914)

   4388 Kramer, A. Walter. MS 1916, NY: JF. Song: [v., pf.].

Houseless Dead, The   "Oh pity the dead that are dead"   Last
Poems (1932)

   4389 Wordsworth, William. MS 1939. Choral work for bar
      solo, satb, orch.

Humming-Bird   "I can imagine, in some otherworld"   New
Republic (May 1921)

   4390 Young, Douglas. Of Birds and Beasts, L: F (hire).
      Cta.: satb, orch.

I Heard a Little Chicken Chirp   "I heard a little chicken
chirp"   Last Poems (1932), rev. 1947

   4391 Rieti, Vittorio. "Thomas Earp", Four D.H. Lawrence
      Songs, Hastings-on-Hudson: GMP, 1964. Song: ms
      solo, pf.

I Wish I Knew a Woman   "I wish I knew a woman"   Pansies
(1929)

   4392* Ronsheim, John. MS. Song: female solo v., pf.

Invocation to the Moon   "You beauty, O you beauty"   Last
Poems (1932)

   4393 Ronsheim, John. MS 1962, Two Prayers (MS 1957,
      1962). Song: s solo, pf. Sets selected lines
      only. Complete work also requires s solo, unacc.

Kangaroo   (NV)   (1923)

4394 Sculthorpe, Peter. "The Fifth Continent", L: F,
      1963. Setting for narr., orch. Text employs
      passage beginning: "The world revolved and re-
      volved and disappeared. Like a stone that has
      fallen into the sea, his old life, the old mean-
      ing fell, and rippled, and there was vacancy,
      with the sea and the Australian shore in it".

Kisses in the Train   "I saw the midlands"   Love Poems and
    Others (1913)

    4395 Wood, Hugh. MS 1966. Song: high v., pf.

Little Fish   "Tiny fish enjoy themselves, The"   Pansies
    (1929)

    4396 Knight, Morris. Pansies, Hattiesburg: Triton, 1962.
          Cyc.: bar solo, cl., hn., vln., vcl., db.

Lizard   "Lizard ran out on a rock, A"   Dial (July 1929)

    4397 Knight, Morris. Pansies, Hattiesburg: Triton, 1962.
          Cyc.: bar solo, cl., hn., vln., vcl., db.

New Moon   "New moon, of no importance, The"   Pansies (1929)

    4398 Knight, Morris. Pansies, Hattiesburg: Triton, 1962.
          Cyc.: bar solo, cl., hn., vln., vcl., db.

November by the Sea   "Now in November nearer comes the sun"
    Dial (July 1929)

    4399 Sculthorpe, Peter. Sun, MS. Cyc.: med. v., pf.

Old Song   "Day is ending, the night descending, The"
    Pansies (1929)

    4400 Knight, Morris. Pansies, Hattiesburg: Triton, 1962.
          Cyc.: bar solo, cl., hn., vln., vcl., db.

Lawrence, D.H. continued

Pax   "All that matters is to be at one with the living God"
     Last Poems (1932)

     4401 Douglas, James. God is Born, MS 1971, avail. SMA.
           Song: satb, a cap.

Piano   "Softly, in the dusk, a woman is singing to me"
     New Poems (1918)

     4402 Warren, Elinor R. NY: GS, pre-1940. Song: [v., pf.].

Prayer   "Give me the moon at my feet"   Last Poems (1932)

     4403 Ronsheim, John. MS 1957, Two Prayers (MS 1957,
           1962). Song: s solo, unacc. Complete work also
           requires pf.

Quite Forsaken   "What pain, to wake and miss you!"   Look!
     We Have Come Through! (1917)

     4404 Rieti, Vittorio. Four D.H. Lawrence Songs, Hastings-
           on-Hudson: GMP, 1964. Song: ms solo, pf.

River Roses   "By the Isar, in the twilight"   Poetry (Jan.
     1914) as one of "All of Roses"

     4405 Cooke, Arnold A. Nocturnes, L: OUP, 1963. Cyc.: s
           or t solo, hn., pf.

Rocking-Horse Winner, The   (SS)   The Ghost-Book (1926)

     4406 Britten, Benjamin. MS, prod. CBS, 1941. Incidental
           music to radio adaptation (by W.H. Auden and
           James Stern) of the story.

Search for Love, The   "Those that go searching for love"
     Last Poems (1932)

     4407 Riley, Dennis. Cantata I, NY: CFP, 1972. Cta.: ms
           solo, t. sax., vcl., vibra., pf.

Lawrence, D.H. continued

Sea-Weed   "Sea-weed sways and sways"   _Dial_ (July 1929)

   4408 Knight, Morris. _Pansies_, Hattiesburg: Triton, 1962.
         Cyc.: bar solo, cl., hn., vln., vcl., db.

Service of All the Dead   "Along the avenue of cypresses"
   New Statesman (Nov. 1913), rev. 1917

   4409 Williams, Grace. MS 1929. Song: s or t solo, pf.

Shadows   "And if tonight my soul may find her peace"   _Last_
   Poems (1932)

   4410 Douglas, James. "Noctium Phantasmata", MS 1973,
         avail. SMA. Work for cl., hn., vcl. pf. only.

Ship of Death, The   "Now it is autumn"   _Last Poems_ (1932)

   4411 Douglas, James. MS 1970, avail. SMA. Settings for
         bar solo, pf.

   4412 Mellers, Wilfrid H. MS 1966, L: N (hire). Cta.: s, t
         soli, cl., b. cl., str. qrt.

Silence   "Since I lost you"   _Amores_ (1916)

   4413 Starer, Robert. NY: LMC, 1951. Song: solo v. (best
         suited for bar solo), pf.

Song   "Love has crept out of her sealed heart"   _Egoist_
   (Apr. 1914), rev. 1918

   4414 Raphael, Mark. "Flapper", _Three D.H. Lawrence Love_
         Poems, L: Thames, 1973. Cyc.: t solo, pf.

Song of Huitzilopochtli   "I am Huitzilopochtli"   _Selected_
   Poems (1947)

   4415 Blank, Allan. MS copyright by composer 1967, avail.
         ACA. Song: t or bar solo, pf.

Lawrence, D.H. continued

Spray   "It is a wonder foam is so beautiful"   _Pansies_
   (1929)

   4416 Knight, Morris. _Pansies_, Hattiesburg: Triton, 1962.
         Cyc.: bar solo, cl., hn., vln., vcl., db.

There is Rain in Me   "There is rain in me"   _Pansies_ (1929)

   4417 Knight, Morris. _Pansies_, Hattiesburg: Triton, 1962.
         Cyc.: bar solo, cl., hn., vln., vcl., db.

Thomas Earp   See: I Heard a Little Chicken Chirp

To Be Superior   "How nice it is to be superior!"   _Pansies_
   (1929)

   4418 Starer, Robert. NY: LMC, 1951. Song: solo v. (best
         suited for bar solo), pf.

Tropic   "Sun, dark sun"   _Birds, Beasts and Flowers_ (1923)

   4419 Sculthorpe, Peter. _Sun_, MS. Cyc.: med. v., pf.

Willy Wet-Leg   "I can't stand Willy wet-leg"   _Pansies_
   (1929)

   4420* Ronsheim, John. MS. Song: female solo v., pf.

You   "You, you don't know me"   _Pansies_ (1929)

   4421* Ronsheim, John. MS. Song: female solo v., pf.

Miscellanea

   4422 Cohn, Arthur. _Quotations in Percussion_, NY: Mills,
         1961. Composition for 103 perc. The composer has
         indicated to the eds. that "a one-line quotation
         [from Lawrence was part of] the generating im-
         pulse for the composition".

Lawrence, D.H. continued

    4423 Easdale, Brian. Grove's makes reference to a cyc.
           employing texts by Lawrence.

    4424 May, Frederick. Four Romantic Songs, MS pre-1968.
           Incl. text by Lawrence.

    4425 Rafter, Leonard. "Twilight", Three Songs, L: S,
           1940. Song: med. v., pf.

    4426 Smalley, Roger. Two Poems of D.H. Lawrence, MS 1965.
           Songs: bar solo, cl., trbn., pf.

LEDWIDGE, Francis   1891-1971

Desire in Spring   "I love the cradle songs the mothers sing"
   In Songs of the Fields (1916)

    4427 Gurney, Ivor. L: OUP, 1928. Song: t solo, pf. Also
           avail. for bar solo, pf.

Had I a Golden Pound   "Had I a golden pound to spend"   In
   The Complete Poems of Francis Ledwidge (1919)

    4428 Ardayne, Paul. Three Songs, NY: GS, pre-1929. Song:
           high v., pf.

    4429 Head, Michael. L: BH, 1966. Song: bar solo, pf.

Homecoming of the Sheep, The   "Sheep are coming home in
   Greece, The" In Songs of Peace (1917)

    4430 Head, Michael. L:BH, 1966. Song: v., pf.

In September   "Still are the meadowlands"   In Songs of
   Peace (1917)

    4431 Garlick, Antony. Twelve Madrigals, Cin.: WLP, 1967.
           Madrigal: ssa, a cap.

Ledwidge, Francis continued

Mother's Song, A   "Little ships of whitest pearl"   In The
   Complete Poems of Francis Ledwidge (1919)

   4432 Cockshott, Gerald. "Little Ships", MS 1935. Song:
         v., pf.

Nocturne   "Rim of the moon, The"   In Songs of Peace (1917)

   4433 Coulthard, Jean. Five Irish Poems for Maureen, MS
         1958-64, avail. CMC. Song: ms solo, pf.

   4434 Head, Michael. Over the Rim of the Moon, L: BH,
         1919. Cyc.: high v., pf. or low v., pf.

Ships of Arcady, The   "Thro' the faintest filigree"   In
   Songs of Peace (1917)

   4435 Head, Michael. Over the Rim of the Moon, L: BH,
         1919. Cyc.: high v., pf. or low v., pf.

Song   "Nothing but sweet music wakes"   In Songs of Peace
   (1917)

   4436 Head, Michael. "Beloved", Over the Rim of the Moon,
         L: BH, 1919. Cyc.: high v., pf. or low v., pf.

Thomas McDonagh   "He shall not hear the bittern cry"   In
   Songs of Peace (1917)

   4437 Boydell, Brian. "In Memoriam Thomas McDonagh", A
         Terrible Beauty is Born, MS 1965. Cta.: a solo,
         orch. Portions of the cta. require various soli.
         "In Memoriam Thomas McDonagh" was arr. 1966 for
         a solo, pf.; arr. avail. RTE.

To One Dead   "Blackbird singing, A"   In Songs of Peace
   (1917)

   4438 Head, Michael. "A blackbird...", Over the Rim of the
         Moon, L: BH, 1919. Cyc.: high v., pf. or low v.,
         pf.

492

Lee, Laurie

LEE, Laurie   1914-

April Rise   "If ever I saw blessing in the air"   In _The Bloom of Candles_ (1947)

    4439   Premru, Raymond. MS 1973. Song: ssa, pf.

    4440   Teed, Roy. MS ca. 1969. Song: a solo, pf.

    4441   Wood, Hugh. _Laurie Lee Songs_, MS 1956-58. Cyc.: ms solo, pf.

Boy in Ice   "O river, green and still"   In _My Many-coated Man_ (1955)

    4442   Wood, Hugh. _Laurie Lee Songs_, MS 1956-58. Cyc.: ms solo, pf.

Day of These Days   "Such a morning it is when love"   In _The Bloom of Candles_ (1947)

    4443   Berkeley, Lennox. _Signs in the Dark_, L: JWC, 1968. Song: satb, str. orch.

East Green, The   "Not dross, but dressed with good"   In _My Many-coated Man_ (1955)

    4444   Wood, Hugh. _Laurie Lee Songs_, MS 1956-58. Cyc.: ms solo, pf.

Edge of Day, The   "Dawn's precise pronouncement waits, The" In _My Many-coated Man_ (1955)

    4445   Wood, Hugh. _Laurie Lee Songs_, MS 1956-58. Cyc.: ms solo, pf.

Poem for Easter   "Wrapped in his shroud of wax"   In _The Bloom of Candles_ (1947)

    4446   Berkeley, Lennox. _Signs in the Dark_, L: JWC, 1968. Song: satb, str. orch.

Lee, Laurie continued

Three Winds, The   "Hard blue winds of March, The"   In The
    Sun My Monument (1944)

    4447 Berkeley, Lennox. Signs in the Dark, L: JWC, 1968.
          Song: satb, str. orch.

Town Owl   "On eves of cold, when slow coal fires"   In My
    Many-coated Man (1955)

    4448 Wood, Hugh. Laurie Lee Songs, MS 1956-58. Cyc.: ms
          solo, pf.

Twelfth Night   "No night could be darker than this night"
    In My Many-coated Man (1955)

    4449 Berkeley, Lennox. Signs in the Dark, L: JWC, 1968
          Song: satb, str. orch.

LE GALLIENNE, Richard   1866-1947

    At Midsummer   "Do you remember how we used to go"   In The
        Junk-Man and Other Poems (1920)

        4450 Worth, Amy. "Midsummer", NY: GS, pre-1940. Song:
              [v., pf.?].

    Autumn Treasure   "Who will gather with me the fallen year"
        In The Lonely Dancer and Other Poems (1914)

        4451 Wald, Max. L: A, pre-1940. Song: [v., pf.?].

    Caravan from China Comes, A   "Caravan from China comes, A"
        In New Poems (1910)

        4452 Barnett, Alice. NY: GS, pre-1940. Song: [v., pf.?].

        4453 Griffis, Elliot. NY: CF, pre-1940. Song: [v., pf.?].

494

Le Gallienne, Richard continued

4454 Storey-Smith, Warren. B: BMC, pre-1940. Song: [v.,
      pf.?].

4455 Uterhart, Josephine. NY: R, pre-1940. Song: [v.,
      pf.?].

"For lack and love of you, love" In New Poems (1910)

4456 Lohr, Hermann. "For Lack and Love of You", Two Lit-
      tle Love Songs, L: C, 1905. Song: solo v., pf.

Homeward Bound "Across the scarce-awakened sea" In The
Junk-Man and Other Poems (1920)

4457 Glen, Katherine A. B: BMC, pre-1940. Song: [v.,
      pf.?].

"I Meant to Do My Work To-day" "I meant to do my work to-
day" In The Lonely Dancer and Other Poems (1914)

4458 Mowrey, Dent. NY: CF, pre-1940. Song: [solo v.,
      pf.?].

Love's Wisdom "Sometimes my idle heart would roam" In
Robert Louis Stevenson and Other Poems (1895)

4459 Creighton, J. Four Songs, L: JW, pre-1940. Song:
      [v., pf.].

Moon-Marketing "Let's go to market in the moon" In A
Jongleur Strayed (1922)

4460 Corbett, Horton. NY: TP, pre-1940. Song: [v., pf.?].

4461 Weaver, Powell. NY: GS, pre-1940. Song: [v., pf.?].

October Moonlight "This year, I said" In New Poems (1910)

4462 Rummel, Walter. "Moonlight", NY: GS, pre-1940.
      Song: [v., pf.?].

495

Le Gallienne, Richard continued

Orbits   "Two stars once in their lonely way"   In English
   Poems (1892)

   4463   Marriott, I.N. Two Songs, L: JW, pre-1940. Song:
          [v., pf.].

Primrose and Violet   "Primrose and Violet"   In English
   Poems (1892)

   4464   Bradford, H.N. L: JW, pre-1940. Song: [v., pf.?].

Song   "She's somewhere in the sunlight strong"   In Robert
   Louis Stevenson and Other Poems (1895)

   4465   Bennett, Charles. "A Song", NY: R, pre-1940. Song:
          [v., pf.?].

   4466   Cain, Noble. "She's...", NY: GS, pre-1940. Song:
          [v., pf.?].

   4467   Hammond, Richard. "She's...", NY: CPMC, pre-1940.
          Song: [v., pf.?].

   4468   Lander, Cyril. Flores de mi primavera, MS n.d.,
          avail. National Library of N.Z. Song: high v.,
          pf.

   4469   Osborne, Reginald. "She's...", L: BH, 1969. Song:
          v., pf.

   4470   Versel, Louis. "She's...", NY: GS, pre-1940. Song:
          [v., pf.?].

Spring   "This is the spring"   In New Poems (1910)

   4471   Wyman, Frances. "Song of Spring", NY: GS, pre-1940.
          Song: [v., pf.?].

Miscellanea

   4472   Bassett, Karolyn W. "Called Away", MS pre-1931, NY:
          GS. Song: [v., pf.?].

4473* Brian, Havergal. "Little Sleeper", Chelmsford: MV,
1974. Song: s or t solo, pf. Text from Le Gallienne's Odes_from_the_Divan_of_Hafiz (L: Duckworth, 1905).

4474 Eyre, Laurence. "Song", NY: HZ, pre-1940. Song: [v.,
pf.?].

4475 Franke-Harling, W. The_Divan_of_Hafiz, B: BMC, pre-
1940. Songs: [v., pf.?]. Songs entitled: "Heart!
Have you heard the News?", "Love, it for Nothing
Else", "Love, the Beauty of the Moon is Thine",
"Wind of the East". [Texts from Odes_from_the_
Divan_of_Hafiz?]

4476 Hawley, Charles. "All the leaves were calling me",
MS pre-1915, NY: Church. Song: [solo v., pf.?].

4477 Lohr, Hermann. "World that once was a garden", Two
Little_Love_Songs, L: C, 1905. Song: solo v., pf.

4478 MacFadyen, Alexander. "Take the Laughter", NY: GS,
pre-1940. Song: [v., pf.?]. [Possibly a setting
of "Song" ("Take it, love!...Take the laughter
first of all") from Le Gallienne's New_Poems
(1910)?]

4479 Mana-Zucca. "Persian Song", B: BMC, pre-1940. Song:
[v., pf.?].

4480 Remick, Bertha. "Little Flower", NY: GS, pre-1940.
Song: [v., pf.?].

4481 Ridge, Kirk. "Blue Flower", NY: GS, pre-1940. Song:
[v., pf.?].

4482 Ryan, Margaret. "She Calls Me", NY: GS, pre-1940.
Song: [v., pf.?].

4483 Van Nuys Fogel, Clyde. "The Nightingale and the
Rose", NY: GS, pre-1940. Song: [v., pf.?]. Text
by Le Gallienne, after Hafiz.

4484 Wald, Max. "The Return", NY: GS, pre-1940. Song:
[v., pf.?].

4485 Watts, Wintter. "The Poet Sings", B: OD, pre-1940.
Song: [v., pf.?].

Le Gallienne, Richard continued

4486   Young, Monroe. "An Idyl", [NY?]: Atlas, pre-1940.
       Song: [v., pf.?].

LEVI, Peter   1931-

In Midwinter   "In midwinter a wood was"   In The Gravel
Ponds (1960)

   4487   Cockshott, Gerald. "In midwinter a wood...", NY:
          Broude-B, in prep. for publ. Song: satb, a cap.

LEWIS, Alun   1915-1944

Compassion   "She in the hurling night"   In Ha! Ha! Among
the Trumpets (1945)

   4488   Maw, Nicholas. Nocturne, L: JWC, 1960. Cyc.: ms
          solo, ch. orch.

   4489   Tippett, Michael. The Heart's Assurance, L: S, 1951.
          Cyc.: [t] solo v., pf.

Dancer, The   "He's in his grave and on his head"   In Raid-
ers' Dawn (1942)

   4490   Tippett, Michael. The Heart's Assurance, L: S, 1951.
          Cyc.: [t] solo v., pf.

Madman, The   "Shattered crystal of his mind, The"   In Raid-
ers' Dawn (1942)

   4491   Burtch, Mervyn. MS pre-1972. Song: high v., pf.

498

Miscellanea

> 4492 Burtch, Mervyn. Five Poems of Alun Lewis, MS pre-
> 1972. Songs: high v., pf.

> 4493 Tippett, Michael. "Song", The Heart's Assurance, L:
> S, 1951. Cyc.: [t] solo v., pf. Text begins: "Oh
> journeyman, Oh journeyman".

EWIS, Clive Staples   1898-1963

Lion, the Witch, and the Wardrobe, The   (NV)   (1950)

> 4494 McCabe, John. L: N, 1971. Opera: 13 soli (s, 3 s or
> 3 trebles, 2 trebles, 2 a, a or bar, 3 bar,
> b-bar), orch. Libr. by Gerald Larner.

Perelandra   (NV)   (1943)

> 4495 Swann, Donald. MS, assigned NY: GX, 1970. Opera:
> s, t, bar, b soli, mimed acting pts., chorus,
> pf. (or orch.). Libr. by David Marsh.

INDSAY, (John) Maurice   1918-

Miscellanea

> 4496 Davie, Cedric Thorpe. "Ode for St. Andrew's Night",
> MS pre-1954. Setting for t solo, satb, orch.

> 4497 Musgrave, Thea. Cantata for a Summer's Day, L: JWC,
> 1964, subsequently assigned L: PX (hire). Cta.:
> sp., vocal qrt., fl., cl., str. qrt., db. Incl.
> text by Lindsay.

Lindsay, Maurice continued

4498   Musgrave, Thea. "The Decision", MS 1964-65. Opera.

4499   Musgrave, Thea. A Suite of Bairnsangs, L: JWC, 1962.
       Texts by Lindsay.

4500   Scott, Francis G. "Love of Alba", Thirty-Five Scot-
       tish Lyrics and Other Poems, Glasgow: B&F, 1939.
       Song: med. v., pf. Text begins: "Her face it was
       that fankl't me".

LOGUE, Christopher   1926-

Ass' Song, The   "In a nearby town"   In Songs (1959)

    4501   Kinsey, Tony in coll. with Stanley Myers. "The Ass's
           Song", Seven Songs from the Establishment, L:
           Bron, 1962. Song: v., pf.

    4502   Myers, Stanley in coll. with Tony Kinsey. See entry
           above.

"Bargain my love; say 'bright you'"   In Wand and Quadrant
(1953) as one of "Thirteen Love Poems"

    4503   Wood, Hugh. Four Songs to Poems by Christopher
           Logue, MS 1959-61, rev. 1963. Song: ms solo, cl.,
           vln., vcl.

"Image of love grows, The"   In Wand and Quadrant (1953) as
one of "Thirteen Love Poems"

    4504   Wood, Hugh. Four Songs to Poems by Christopher
           Logue, MS 1959-61, rev. 1963. Song: ms solo, cl.,
           vln., vcl.

"In the beloved's face"   In Wand and Quadrant (1953) as one
of "Thirteen Love Poems"

4505   Wood, Hugh. Four Songs to Poems by Christopher
       Logue, MS 1959-61, rev. 1963. Song: ms solo, cl.,
       vln., vcl.

Sonnet   "Love, do not believe, if you forget you"   In Wand
and Quadrant (1953) as one of "Thirteen Love Poems"

4506   Wood, Hugh. Four Songs to Poems by Christopher
       Logue, MS 1959-61, rev. 1963. Song: ms solo, cl.,
       vln., vcl.

Miscellanea

4507   Barber, Samuel. The Lovers, NY: GS, 1972. Settings
       (of poems by Pablo Neruda, transl. by Logue and
       W.S. Merwin) for bar solo, chorus, orch.

4508   Birtwistle, Harrison. "Ring a Dumb Carillon", L: UE,
       1969. Setting for v., cl., perc. (5 suspended
       cym., 4 timbales, 4 wood blocks, 4 temple blocks,
       5 cow bells, 1 miraca, 1 pair of claves, 1 pair
       of bongos).

4509   Kinsey, Tony in coll. with Stanley Myers. Seven
       Songs from the Establishment, L: Bron, 1962.
       Songs: v., pf. Incl. songs entitled: "Bellini",
       "Duet for One Voice", "Go to the Wall", "He",
       "The Liberal Man", "Things".

4510   Myers, Stanley in coll. with Tony Kinsey. See entry
       above.

4511   Southam, T. Wallace. "Gone Ladies", L: Turret, 1968
       in Contemporary Poetry Set to Music. Song: v.,
       pf.

4512   Wood, Hugh. Song Cycle to Poems of Neruda in the
       English Translation of Christopher Logue, MS
       (Opus 19). Cyc. (of 7 songs) for high v., ch.
       orch.

Lucie-Smith, Edward

LUCIE-SMITH, Edward   1933-

   Silence   "Silence: one would willingly"   In Towards Silence
      (1968)

      4513   Southam, T. Wallace. L: Turret, 1967 in Contemporary
               Poetry Set to Music. Song: v., pf.

   To Max Ernst   "Nightingale, A/As big as a house"   In To-
      wards Silence (1968) as one of "Three Songs for Sur-
      realists"

      4514   Tavener, John. Three Surrealist Songs, L: JWC,
               1971. Song: ms solo, tape, pf. (doubl. bongos).

   To René Magritte   "Eye is watching, An"   In Towards Silence
      (1968) as one of "Three Songs for Surrealists"

      4515* Tavener, John. Three Surrealist Songs, L: JWC,
               1971. Song: ms solo, tape, pf. (doubl. bongos).

   To Salvador Dali   "We sleep. The earth"   In Towards Silence
      (1968) as one of "Three Songs for Surrealists"

      4516   Tavener, John. Three Surrealist Songs, L: JWC,
               1971. Song: ms solo, tape, pf. (doubl. bongos).

MACBETH, George Mann   1932-

   Bats   "have no accident. They loop"   In The Colour of Blood
      (1967)

      4517   ApIvor, Denis. MS 1969. Song: t solo, pic., vln.,
               pf.-hp.

   Miscellanea

4518 Gilbert, Anthony. "The Scene-Machine", L: S, 1971 (performing pts. on hire only). Opera: ms, t, bar soli, satb, orch.

ACCATHMHAOIL, Seosamh   See: CAMPBELL, Joseph

ACDIARMID, Hugh   1892-

Aerial City, The   "At the peep o day in the lift forgether" In Poetry Scotland, No. 4 (1949)

4519 Stevenson, Ronald. The Infernal City, MS 1971. Cyc.: t solo, pf.

Apprentice Angel, An   "Try on your wings"   In Scots Unbound and Other Poems (1932)

4520 Scott, Francis G. Scottish Lyrics, Book 3, Glasgow: B&F, 1934. Song: v., pf. Setting of section II of the poem.

At my Father's Grave   "Sunlicht still on me, you row'd in clood, The"   In First Hymn to Lenin and Other Poems (1931)

4521 Stevenson, Ronald. Nineteen Songs to Poems by Hugh MacDiarmid, MS 1961-69. Song: t solo, pf. The complete collection requires various voices.

Barren Fig, The   "O Scotland is"   In A Drunk Man Looks at the Thistle (1926)

MacDiarmid, Hugh continued

4522   Stevenson, Ronald. Nineteen Songs to Poems by Hugh
       MacDiarmid, MS 1961-69. Song: med. v., pf. The
       complete collection requires various voices.

Better One Golden Lyric   "Better a'e gowden lyric"   In To
Circumjack Cencrastus (1930)

4523   Stevenson, Ronald. "A'e Gowden Lyric", Nineteen
       Songs to Poems by Hugh MacDiarmid, MS 1961-69.
       Song: high v., pf. The complete collection re-
       quires various voices.

Bobbin-Winder, The   "Not even the fine threads in a lace
factory"   In Collected Poems (1967)

4524   Stevenson, Ronald. Nineteen Songs to Poems by Hugh
       MacDiarmid, MS 1961-69. Song: high v., pf. The
       complete collection requires various voices.

Bonnie Broukit Bairn, The   "Mars is braw in crammasy"   In
Sangschaw (1925)

4525   Stevenson, Ronald. Nineteen Songs to Poems by Hugh
       MacDiarmid, MS 1961-69. Song: high v., pf. The
       complete collection requires various voices.

Bubblyjock   "It's hauf like a bird"   In Penny Wheep (1926)
as one of "From 'Songs for Christine'"

4526   Stevenson, Ronald. Nineteen Songs to Poems by Hugh
       MacDiarmid, MS 1961-69. Song: high v., pf. The
       complete collection requires various voices.

Cophetua   "OH! The King's gane gyte"   In Sangschaw (1925)

4527   Stevenson, Ronald. Nineteen Songs to Poems by Hugh
       MacDiarmid, MS 1961-69. Song: high v., pf. The
       complete collection requires various voices.

Coronach for the End of the World   "Mony a piper has played
himsel"   Poetry Scotland, No. 4 (1949)

4528 Stevenson, Ronald. *Nineteen Songs to Poems by Hugh MacDiarmid*, MS 1961-69. Song: bar solo, pf. The complete collection requires various voices.

Country Life   "OOTSIDE!...Ootside!" In *Sangschaw* (1925)

4529 Scott, Francis G. *Songs*, Glasgow: B&F, 1949. Song: [high] v., pf.

Crowdieknowe   "Oh to be at Crowdieknowe" In *Sangschaw* (1925)

4530 Scott, Francis G. *Scottish Lyrics*, Book 3, Glasgow: B&F, 1934. Song: v., pf.

Eemis-Stane, The   "I' the how-dumb-deid o the cauld hairst nicht" In *Sangschaw* (1925)

4531 Scott, Francis G. *Scottish Lyrics*, Book 3, Glasgow: B&F, 1934. Song: v., pf.

Empty Vessel   "I met ayont the cairney" In *Penny Wheep* (1926)

4532 Scott, Francis G. *Scottish Lyrics*, Book V, Glasgow: B&F, 1936. Song: low v., pf.

Fairy Tales   "Ither folks' fairy tales" In *Penny Wheep* (1926) as one of "From 'Songs for Christine'"

4533 Stevenson, Ronald. *Nineteen Songs to Poems by Hugh MacDiarmid*, MS 1961-69. Song: s solo, pf. The complete collection requires various voices.

First Love   "I have been in this garden of unripe fruit" In *Stony Limits and Other Poems* (1934)

4534 Scott, Francis G. *Songs*, Glasgow: B&F, 1949. Song: [med.] v., pf.

MacDiarmid, Hugh continued

Fool, The   "He said that he was God"   In Annals_of_the_Five
    Senses (1923)

    4535 Stevenson, Ronald. Nineteen_Songs_to_Poems_by_Hugh
          MacDiarmid, MS 1961-69. Song: bar solo, pf. The
          complete collection requires various voices.

Gaelic Muse, The   "At last, at last, I see her again"   In
    Lucky_Poet (1943)

    4536 Stevenson, Ronald. Nineteen_Songs_to_Poems_by_Hugh
          MacDiarmid, MS 1961-69. Song: high v., pf. The
          complete collection requires various voices.

Glasgow   "Wagner might call Berlin a city"   In Lucky_Poet
    (1943)

    4537 Stevenson, Ronald. The_Infernal_City, MS 1971. Cyc.:
          t solo, pf.

Glasgow 1960   "Returning to Glasgow after long exile"   In
    Collected_Poems (1967)

    4538 Stevenson, Ronald. The_Infernal_City, MS 1971. Cyc.:
          t solo, pf.

Hungry Waters   "Auld men o' the sea, The"   In Penny_Wheep
    (1926)

    4539 Scott, Francis G. MS 1925, L: Curwen; incl. in
          Songs, Glasgow: B&F, 1949. Song: v., pf.

I Who Once in Heaven's Height   "I wha aince in Heaven's
    heicht"   In To_Circumjack_Cencrastus (1930)

    4540 Scott, Francis G. "I wha...", Songs, Glasgow: B&F,
          1949. Song: [med.] v., pf.

In Mysie's Bed   "They ha'e laid the black ram i' Mysie's
    bed"   In Penny_Wheep (1926)

    4541 Scott, Francis G. MS 1951. Song: med. v., pf.

In the Fall   "Let the only consistency"   In In Memoriam
James Joyce (1955)

   4542 Stevenson, Ronald. Nineteen Songs to Poems by Hugh
         MacDiarmid, MS 1961-69. Song: high v., pf. The
         complete collection requires various voices.

Innumerable Christ, The   "Wha kens on whatna Bethlehems"
   In Sangschaw (1925)

   4543 Scott, Francis G. Songs, Glasgow: B&F, 1949. Song:
         v., pf.

Last Trump, The   "Owre the haill warl' there's a whirrin'"
   In Sangschaw (1925)

   4544 Stevenson, Ronald. Nineteen Songs to Poems by Hugh
         MacDiarmid, MS 1961-69. Song: bar solo, pf. The
         complete collection requires various voices.

Little White Rose, The   "Rose of all the world is not for
   me, The"   In Stony Limits and Other Poems (1934)

   4545 Stevenson, Ronald. "The Rose of All the World",
         Nineteen Songs to Poems by Hugh MacDiarmid, MS
         1961-69. Song: high v., pf. The complete col-
         lection requires various voices.

Lourd on my hert   "Lourd on my hert as winter lies"   In
   To Circumjack Cencrastus (1930)

   4546 Scott, Francis G. Songs, Glasgow: B&F, 1949. Song:
         [med.] v., pf.

Love   "As white's the blossom on the rise"   In Penny Wheep
   (1926)

   4547 Scott, Francis G. Scottish Lyrics, Book 3, Glasgow:
         B&F, 1934. Song: v., pf.

Love-sick Lass, The   "Luvin' wumman is a licht, A"   In
   Penny Wheep (1926)

MacDiarmid, Hugh continued

    4548   Scott, Francis G. Scottish Lyrics, Book V, Glasgow:
           B&F, 1936. Song: low v., pf.

Man in the Moon, The   "Moonbeams kelter i' the lift"   In
   Sangschaw (1925)

    4549   Scott, Francis G. Songs, Glasgow: B&F, 1949. Song:
           [med.] v., pf.

Milk-wort and Bag-cotton   "Cwa een like milk-wort"   In
   Scots Unbound and Other Poems (1932)

    4550   Scott, Francis G. "Milkwort and Bag-cotton", Scot-
           tish Lyrics, Book 3, Glasgow: B&F, 1934. Song:
           v., pf.

Munestruck   "When the warl's couped roun'"   In Sangschaw
   (1925)

    4551   Scott, Francis G. "Moonstruck", Scottish Lyrics,
           Book 3, Glasgow: B&F, 1934. Song: v., pf.

O Jesu Parvule   "His mither sings to the bairnie Christ"
   In Sangschaw (1925)

    4552   Dalby, Martin. L: N (hire). Carol: satb, a cap.

    4553   Scott, Francis G. Glasgow: B&F. Song: satb, a cap.

O Wha's the Bride?   "O wha's the bride that carries the
   bunch"   In A Drunk Man Looks at the Thistle (1926)

    4554   Stevenson, Ronald. Nineteen Songs to Poems by Hugh
           MacDiarmid, MS 1961-69. Song: s solo, pf. The
           complete collection requires various voices.

Old Wife in High Spirits   "Auld wumman cam' in, An"   In
   Collected Poems (1967)

    4555   Stevenson, Ronald. "Auld Wife in High Spirits", The
           Infernal City, MS 1971. Cyc.: t solo, pf.

Reid-E'en   "Ilka hert an' hind are met"   In Sangschaw
    (1925)

    4556 Scott, Francis G. Seven Songs for Baritone Voice,
          Glasgow: B&F, 1946. Song: bar solo, pf.

Robber, The   "Robber cam' to my hoose, A"   In Penny Wheep
    (1926)

    4557 Stevenson, Ronald. Nineteen Songs to Poems by Hugh
          MacDiarmid MS 1961-69. Song: s solo, pf. The
          complete collection requires various voices.

Sabine   "Lass cam' to oor gairden-yett, A"   In Penny Wheep
    (1926)

    4558 Scott, Francis G. MS pre-1954. Song: v., pf.

Sauchs in the Reuch Heuch Haugh, The   "There's teuch sauchs
    growin' i' the Reuch Heuch"   In Sangschaw (1925)

    4559 Scott, Francis G. Songs, Glasgow: B&F, 1949. Song:
          [high] v., pf.

Skeleton of the Future, The   "Red granite and black diorite"
    In Stony Limits and Other Poems (1934)

    4560 Stevenson, Ronald. Nineteen Songs to Poems by Hugh
          MacDiarmid, MS 1961-69. Song: bar solo, pf. The
          complete collection requires various voices.

Sunny Gale   "Trees were like bubblyjocks"   In Penny Wheep
    (1926)

    4561 Scott, Francis G. Songs, Glasgow: B&F, 1949. Song:
          [low] v., pf.

Three Fishes, The   "I am a fisher lad and nane"   In Penny
    Wheep (1926)

    4562 Scott, Francis G. Glasgow: B&F. Song: ttbb, a cap.

509

MacDiarmid, Hugh continued

Trompe l'oeil   "As I gaed doon the hedgeback"   In Penny
   Wheep (1926)

   4563   Stevenson, Ronald. Nineteen Songs to Poems by Hugh
          MacDiarmid, MS 1961-69. Song: high v., pf. The
          complete collection requires various voices.

Watergaw, The   "Ae weet forenicht i the yow-trummle"   In
   Sangschaw (1925)

   4564   Scott, Francis G. Scottish Lyrics, Book V, Glasgow:
          B&F, 1936. Song: low v., pf.

Wheesht, Wheesht   "Wheesht, wheesht, my foolish hert"   In
   Penny Wheep (1926)

   4565   Scott, Francis G. Scottish Lyrics, Book 3, Glasgow:
          B&F, 1934. Song: v., pf.

Miscellanea

   4566   Campsie, Alistair K. "Moladh MhicDhiarmid (In Praise
          of MacDiarmid)", Hugh MacDiarmid Poems and a Pib-
          roch on his 80th birthday, Gartocharn: Famedram
          [1972]. Pibroch: bagpipe only.

   4567   Scott, Francis G. "At the Window", MS 1950, avail.
          SMA. Song: med. v., pf.

   4568   Stevenson, Ronald. Border Boyhood, MS 1970. Cyc.:
          t solo, pf. Songs entitled: "The Joys I Knew",
          "Memories", "A Celebration of Colour", "The Nut
          Trees", "Fighting Spirit", "The Nook of the Night
          Paths".

   4569   Stevenson, Ronald. The Infernal City, MS 1971. Cyc.:
          t solo, pf. Incl. song entitled "Calvary".

   4570   Stevenson, Ronald. "The Song of the Nightingale",
          Nineteen Songs to Poems by Hugh MacDiarmid, MS
          1961-69. Song: s solo, pf. The complete col-
          lection requires various voices.

cleod, Fiona

CLEOD, Fiona   1855-1905

Al far della Notte   "Hark!"   In <u>Sospiri di Roma</u> (1891)

    4571 Griffes, Charles T. "Nightfall", <u>Roman Sketches</u>, NY:
        GS, 1917. Pf. solo. The score of "Nightfall"
        incl. a quotation of the last 4 lines of "Al far
        della Notte". [The composer's original title for
        the work was "Al far della Notte".]

At the Last   "She cometh no more"   In <u>From the Hills of
Dream</u> (1896)

    4572 Bax, Arnold. <u>A Celtic Song Cycle</u>, L: JWC (Avison
        edn.), 1906. Cyc.: [bar] solo v., pf.

    4573 Hart, Fritz. <u>Six Sets of Five Songs</u>, Set II, MS
        1927, avail. State Library of Victoria, Mel-
        bourne. Song: v., pf.

    4574 Hawes, Jack. MS. Song: med. v., pf.

At the Rising of the Moon   (PR)   <u>From the Hills of Dream</u>
(1896) as part of "The Silence of Amor"

    4575 Bantock, Granville. <u>Celtic Songs</u>, MS 1921, L: Swan.
        Song: [v., pf.].

Autumnal Evening, An   "Deep against the dying glow"   In
<u>Poems</u> (1912)

    4576 Hart, Fritz. <u>Twenty-Five Songs</u>, Set II, MS 1926,
        avail. State Library of Victoria, Melbourne.
        Song: v., pf.

Bandruidh, The   "My robe is of green"   In <u>From the Hills
of Dream</u> (1896)

    4577 Hopekirk, Helen. <u>Five Songs</u>, NY: GS, 1904. Song:
        [v., pf.].

    4578 Taylor, Colin. "The Green Lady", L: S&B, pre-1940.
        Song: [solo v., pf.?].

Macleod, Fiona continued

4579 Wood, Nora F. L: A, pre-1940. Song: [solo v., pf.?].

Bell-Bird, The   "Stillness of the Austral noon, The"   In
Poems (1912)

4580 Hart, Fritz. Twenty-Five Songs, Set III, MS 1927,
       avail. State Library of Victoria, Melbourne.
       Song: v., pf.

Bells of Youth, The   "Bells of Youth are ringing in the
gateways of the South, The"   In The Hour of Beauty (1907)

4581 Bantock, Granville. L: PX, pre-1940. Song: [v.,
       pf.].

4582 Bath, Hubert. L: C, 1907. Song: v., pf.

4583 Clough-Leighter, Henry. B: BMC, pre-1940. Song: [v.,
       pf.?].

4584 Fletcher, Percy E. L: C, 1925. Song: v., pf.

4585 Fulton, Norman. L: Curwen, 1962. Song: satb, a cap.

4586 Hawes, Jack. The Bells of Youth, MS. Choral ste.:
       satb, pf. The complete ste. also requires s solo.

4587 Speaks, Oley. NY: GS, pre-1940. Song: [v., pf.?].

Bird of Christ, The   "Holy, Holy, Holy"   In From the Hills
of Dream (1896)

4588 Boughton, Rutland. Six Spiritual Songs, L: Reeves,
       1911. Song: v., pf.

4589 Hopekirk, Helen. Six Poems by Fiona Macleod, NY: GS,
       pre-1929. Song: med. v., pf.

Black Swans on the Murray Lagoons   "Long lagoons lie still
and white, The"   In Poems (1912)

4590 Hart, Fritz. Twenty-Five Songs, Set III, MS 1927,
       avail. State Library of Victoria, Melbourne.
       Song: v., pf.

Blossom of Snow   "'Sing a song of blossom'"   In Poems
    (1912)

    4591   Besly, Maurice. Four More Poems, L: BH, pre-1940.
              Song: [v., pf.].

Breaking Billows at Sorrento   "Sky of whirling flakes of
    foam, A"   In Poems (1912)

    4592   Hart, Fritz. Twenty-Five Songs, Set III, MS 1927,
              avail. State Library of Victoria, Melbourne.
              Song: v., pf.

Bugles of Dreamland, The   "Swiftly the dews of the gloaming
    are falling"   In From the Hills of Dream (1896)

    4593   Bath, Hubert. L: C, 1909. Song: v., pf.

Burthen of the Tide, The   "Tide was dark an' heavy with the
    burden that it bore, The"   In From the Hills of Dream
    (1896)

    4594   Peterkin, Norman. "Rune of the Burden of the Tide",
              L: OUP, pre-1940. Song: [v., pf.?].

Closing Doors   "O sands of my heart"   In From the Hills of
    Dream (1896)

    4595   Bax, Arnold. A Celtic Song Cycle, L: JWC (Avison
              edn.), 1906. Cyc.: [bar] solo v., pf.

Clouds   "As though the dead cities"   In Sospiri di Roma
    (1891)

    4596   Griffes, Charles T. Roman Sketches, NY: GS, 1917.
              Pf. solo. The score of "Clouds" incl. a quotation
              from the poem.

Crystal Forest, A   "Air is blue and keen and cold, The"   In
    Poems (1912)

Macleod, Fiona continued

   4597   Hart, Fritz. Twenty-Five Songs, Set II, MS 1926,
          avail. State Library of Victoria, Melbourne.
          Song: v., pf.

Dalua   "I have heard you calling, Dalua"   In From the Hills
of Dream (1901)

   4598   Boughton, Rutland. Six Celtic Choruses, L: SJB,
          1924. [Setting for chorus, a cap.].

   4599   Fulton, Norman. Prelude, Recitative and Aria, L:
          JWC, 1956. Song: high v., str. orch.

Day and Night   "From grey of dusk, the veils unfold"   In
From the Hills of Dream (1896)

   4600   Hart, Fritz. Five Songs, MS 1919 (Opus 36), avail.
          State Library of Victoria, Melbourne. Song: v.,
          pf.

De Profundis   "Whence hast thou gone"   In Sospiri di Roma
(1891)

   4601* Griffes, Charles T. MS 1915. Pf. solo.

Dead Calm and Mist, A   "Slow heave of the sleeping sea, The"
In Earth's Voices (1884)

   4602   Benjamin, Arthur. "Calm Sea and Mist", Three Impres-
          sions, L: Curwen, 1925. Song: med. v., pf. Also
          publ. for med. v., str. qrt. Also publ. sep.

   4603   Hart, Fritz. Twenty-Five Songs, Set II, MS 1926,
          avail. State Library of Victoria, Melbourne.
          Song: v., pf.

Dead Love   "It is the grey rock I am"   In From the Hills
of Dream (1896)

   4604   Hart, Fritz. Six Sets of Five Songs, Set II, MS
          1927, avail. State Library of Victoria, Mel-
          bourne. Song: v., pf.

514

Desire   "Desire of love, Joy, The"   In From the Hills of
    Dream (1896)

    4605 Hart, Fritz. Six Sets of Five Songs, Set II, MS
          1927, avail. State Library of Victoria, Mel-
          bourne. Song: v., pf.

Dream Fantasy   "There is a land of Dream"   In From the
    Hills of Dream (1896)

    4606 Hawes, Jack. MS. Song: med. v., pf.

Dream-Wind, The   "When, like a sleeping child"   In Poems
    (1912)

    4607 Bath, Hubert. "Dream-Wind", Voices of the Air, L: C,
          1911. Song: ssaatbb, [a cap.?].

    4608 Hart, Fritz. Twenty-Five Songs, Set V, MS 1927,
          avail. State Library of Victoria, Melbourne.
          Song: v., pf.

Easter   "Stars wailed when the reed was born, The"   In The
    Hour of Beauty (1907)

    4609 Boughton, Rutland. "Song of Easter", Six Spiritual
          Songs, L: Reeves, 1911. Song: v., pf.

    4610 Hart, Fritz. Six Sets of Five Songs, Set IV, MS
          1927, avail. State Library of Victoria, Mel-
          bourne. Song: v., pf.

    4611 Hawes, Jack. The Bells of Youth, MS. Choral ste.:
          satb, pf. The complete ste. also requires s solo.

Eilidh my Fawn   "Far away upon the hills"   In From the
    Hills of Dream (1896)

    4612 Bax, Arnold. A Celtic Song Cycle, L: JWC (Avison
          edn.), 1906. Cyc.: [bar] solo v., pf.

    4613 Hopekirk, Helen. Five Songs, NY: GS, 1904. Song:
          [v., pf.].

Empire (Persepolis)   "Yellow waste of yellow sands, The"
In Poems (1912)

    4614   Hart, Fritz. "Persepolis", Twenty-Five Songs, Set
        II, MS 1926, avail. State Library of Victoria,
        Melbourne. Song: v., pf.

Evoë   (PR)   From the Hills of Dream (1896) as part of "The
Silence of Amor"

    4615   Bath, Hubert. MS pre-1945, L: C. Song: v., pf.

    4616   Foulds, John H. L: PX, 1925, Mood-Pictures, Chelms-
        ford: MV, 1975. Cyc.: solo v., pf.

Falias   "In the frost-grown city of Falais"   In The Hour of
Beauty (1907)

    4617   Barnes, Marshall. A Dirge of Four Cities, MS. Set-
        ting for mixed chorus, orch.

Finias   "In the torch-lit city of Finias"   In The Hour of
Beauty (1907)

    4618   Barnes, Marshall. A Dirge of Four Cities, MS. Set-
        ting for mixed chorus, orch.

Fireflies   "Softly sailing emerald lights"   In Poems (1912)

    4619   Hart, Fritz. Twenty-Five Songs, Set I, MS 1926,
        avail. State Library of Victoria, Melbourne.
        Song: v., pf.

Fountain of the Acqua Paolo, The   "Not where thy turbid
wave"   In Sospiri di Roma (1891)

    4620   Griffes, Charles T. Roman Sketches, NY: GS, 1917.
        Pf. solo. The score of "The Fountain of the Acqua
        Paola" incl. a quotation from the poem.

From Oversea   "From oversea"   In Poems (1912)

Macleod, Fiona continued

4621 Hart, Fritz. Twenty-Five Songs, Set V, MS 1927,
avail. State Library of Victoria, Melbourne.
Song: v., pf.

From the Hills of Dream   "Across the silent stream"   In
From the Hills of Dream (1896)

4622 Allen, Creighton. NY: M.L. Reid, 1948. Song: v., pf.

4623 Bax, Arnold. MS 1907. Song: v., pf.

4624 Eichheim, Henry. "Across...", B: BMC, pre-1940.
Song: [v., pf.?].

4625 Forsyth, Cecil. B: OD, pre-1940. Song: [v., pf.?].

4626 Hopekirk, Helen. Six Poems by Fiona Macleod, NY: GS,
pre-1929. Song: med. v., pf.

4627 Redman, Reginald. S. Croy.: L, 1948. Song: t solo,
satb, timp., stgs.

Gorias   "In Gorias are gems"   In The Hour of Beauty (1907)

4628 Barnes, Marshall. A Dirge of Four Cities, MS. Setting for mixed chorus, orch.

Green Branches   "Wave, wave, green branches"   In From the
Hills of Dream (1896)

4629 Bax, Arnold. MS 1905. Song: v., pf.

4630 Boughton, Rutland. Five Celtic Songs, L: S&B, 1923.
Song: v., pf. or v., stgs.

4631 Hart, Fritz. Six Sets of Five Songs, Set VI, MS
1927, avail. State Library of Victoria, Melbourne. Song: v., pf.

4632 Watts, Wintter. B: OD, pre-1940. Song: [v., pf.?].

Grey Pastures   "In the grey gloaming"   In From the Hills of
Dream (1901)

Macleod, Fiona continued

4633 Hart, Fritz. Six Sets of Five Songs, Set IV, MS
1927, avail. State Library of Victoria, Melbourne. Song: v., pf.

Heart o' Beauty   "O where are thy white hands"   In From the
Hills of Dream (1901)

4634 Bax, Arnold. MS 1907. Song: v., pf.

Hushing Song   "Eilidh, Eilidh"   In From the Hills of Dream
(1896)

4635 Anderson, A. L: S&B, pre-1940. Song: [v., pf.].

4636 Bath, Hubert. L: C, 1909. Song: v., pf.

4637 Bax, Arnold. MS 1906. Song: v., pf.

4638 Buzzi-Peccia, Arturo. "Brown Birdeen", NY: GS, pre-
1940. Song: [v., pf.].

4639 Cox, Ralph. "Brown Birdeen", B: Schmidt, pre-1940.
Song: [v., pf.].

4640 Hopekirk, Helen. Five Songs, NY: GS, 1904. Song:
[v., pf.].

4641 Rummel, Walter. L: A, pre-1940. Song: [v., pf.].

4642 Thornley, Barbara. L: S&B, pre-1940. Song: [v.,
pf.].

4643 Watts, Wintter. B: OD, pre-1940. Song: [v., pf.].

I-Brasîl   "There's sorrow on the wind, my grief"   In The
Hour of Beauty (1907)

4644 Delius, Frederick. Fünf Gesänge, Köln: T&J, 1915.
Song: [med.] v., pf.

4645 Moule-Evans, David. Two Celtic Songs, L: JW, ca.
1946. Song: s solo, pf.

Immortal Hour, The   (DR)   (1907)

Macleod, Fiona continued

4646 Boughton, Rutland. L: S&B, 1920. Opera: 2 s, a, t, bar, 3 b soli, satb, orch.

In Memoriam   "He laughed at Life's Sunset Gates"   In Poems (1912)

4647 Hart, Fritz. Twenty-Five Songs, Set V, MS 1927, avail. State Library of Victoria, Melbourne. Song: v., pf.

In the Fern   "Feathery fern-trees make a screen, The"   In Poems (1912)

4648 Hart, Fritz. Twenty-Five Songs, Set III, MS 1927, avail. State Library of Victoria, Melbourne. Song: v., pf.

"In the hollows of quiet places we may meet..."   (PR)   From the Hills of Dream (1896) as part of "The Silence of Amor"

4649 Bantock, Granville. "In the Hollow of Quiet Places", L: Swan, 1930. Song: [v., pf.].

In the Night   "O wind, why break in idle pain"   In From the Hills of Dream (1901)

4650 Hart, Fritz. Six Sets of Five Songs, Set III, MS 1927, avail. State Library of Victoria, Melbourne. Song: v., pf.

In the Silences of the Woods   "In the silences of the woods"   In From the Hills of Dream (1901)

4651 Bax, Arnold. MS 1905. Song: v., pf.

4652 Hart, Fritz. "In the Silences of the Wood", Five Songs, MS 1919 (Opus 36), avail. State Library of Victoria, Melbourne. Song: v., pf.

Isla   "Isla, Isla, heart of my heart"   In From the Hills of Dream (1896)

519

Macleod, Fiona continued

4653   Bax, Arnold. MS 1908. Song: v., pf.

4654   Stephens, Ward. NY: GS, pre-1940. Song: [v., pf.?].

Isle of Lost Dreams, The   "There is an isle beyond our ken"
In Romantic Ballads (1888)

4655   Hart, Fritz. Twenty-Five Songs, Set V, MS 1927,
       avail. State Library of Victoria, Melbourne.
       Song: v., pf.

Kye-Song of St. Bride, The   "O sweet St. Bride"   In From
the Hills of Dream (1896)

4656   Edmunds, Christopher. S. Croy.: L, 1951. Song: s
       solo, satb, orch.

Lament of Ian the Proud, The   "What is this crying that I
hear in the wind?"   In From the Hills of Dream (1901)

4657   Eichheim, Henry. B: BMC, pre-1940. Song: [v., pf.?].

4658   Griffes, Charles T. Three Poems of Fiona Macleod,
       NY: GS, 1918. Song: high v., pf. Arr. 1918 for
       high v., orch.; arr. avail. NY: GS (hire).

Lances of Gold   (PR)   From the Hills of Dream (1896) as
part of "The Silence of Amor"

4659   Foulds, John H. L: Curwen, 1921, Mood-Pictures,
       Chelmsford: MV, 1975. Cyc.: solo v., pf.

4660   Wood-Hill, Mabel. Reactions to Fiona McLeod (Four
       Moods), NY: Dimit Edn., 1943. Composition for 5
       wind instr., hp. (or pf.), stgs.

Leaves, Shadows, and Dreams   "I have seen all things pass"
In From the Hills of Dream (1901)

4661   Bax, Arnold. MS 1905. Song: v., pf.

Little Children of the Wind   "I hear the little children of the wind"   In From the Hills of Dream (1901)

 4662 Hart, Fritz. Six Sets of Five Songs, Set III, MS 1927, avail. State Library of Victoria, Melbourne. Song: v., pf.

Lonely Hunter, The   "Green branches, green branches, I see you beckon"   In From the Hills of Dream (1896)

 4663 Hopekirk, Helen. Six Poems by Fiona Macleod, NY: GS, pre-1929. Song: med. v., pf.

Longing   "O would I were the cool wind"   In From the Hills of Dream (1901)

 4664 Bantock, Granville. L: Elkin, 1929. Song: [v., pf.].

 4665 Bax, Arnold. MS 1907. Song: v., pf.

 4666 Buzzi-Peccia, Arturo. NY: GS, pre-1940. Song: [solo v., pf.?].

 4667 Clough-Leighter, Henry. "Would I were the Cold Wind", B: BMC, pre-1940. Song: [solo v., pf.?].

 4668 Ferrari, Gustave. B: BMC, pre-1940. Song: [solo v., pf.?].

 4669 Hart, Fritz. Six Sets of Five Songs, Set III, MS 1927, avail. State Library of Victoria, Melbourne. Song: v., pf.

 4670 Lucke, Katharine E. A setting [for solo v., pf.?] was publ. (pre-1940) by the publisher Fred Kranz [?].

 4671 Rummel, Walter. L: A, pre-1940. Song: [v., pf.?].

 4672 Thompson, E. Roy. L: S&B, pre-1940. Song: [solo v., pf.?].

Lost Star, The   "Star was loosed from heaven, A"   In From the Hills of Dream (1896)

4673   Hart, Fritz. *Six Sets of Five Songs*, Set VI, MS
       1927, avail. State Library of Victoria, Mel-
       bourne. Song: v., pf.

4674   Hawes, Jack. *The Bells of Youth*, MS. Choral ste.:
       satb, pf. The complete ste. also requires s solo.

Lullaby   "Lennavan-mo"   In *From the Hills of Dream* (1896)

4675   Whitehead, Percy. "Lennavan-Mo", L: C, 1912. Song:
       [v., pf.].

Milking Sian   "Give up thy milk to her who calls"   In *From
the Hills of Dream* (1896)

4676   Bax, Arnold. *Album of Seven Songs*, L: JWC, 1919.
       Song: JWC, 1919. Song: v., pf.

4677   Boughton, Rutland. "St. Bride's Milking Song", *Six
       Spiritual Songs*, L: Reeves, 1911. Song: v., pf.

4678   Read, John. L: Elkin, 1950. Song: low v., pf.

4679   Thompson, E. Roy. L: S&B, pre-1940. Song: [v., pf.].

Mo Bròn!   "O come across the grey wild seas"   In *The Hour
of Beauty* (1907)

4680   Hart, Fritz. *Six Sets of Five Songs*, Set IV, MS
       1927, avail. State Library of Victoria, Mel-
       bourne. Song: v., pf.

4681   Lucke, Katharine E. A setting [for v., pf.?] was
       publ. (pre-1940) by the publisher Fred Kranz [?].

Mo-Lennav-a-Chree   "Eilidh, Eilidh, Eilidh, dear to me, dear
and sweet"   In *From the Hills of Dream* (1896)

4682   Hopekirk, Helen. *Five Songs*, NY: GS, 1904. Song:
       [v., pf.].

4683   Pearson, T.E. L: OUP, 1932. Song: satb, [a cap.].

Moonrise   "First snows of the green lie white, The"   In
   Poems (1912)

   4684   Hart, Fritz. Twenty-Five Songs, Set I, MS 1926,
          avail. State Library of Victoria, Melbourne.
          Song: v., pf.

Motherland   "Beneath the awful full-orb'd moon"   In The
   Human Inheritance (1882)

   4685   Griffes, Charles T. "Barcarolle", Fantasy Pieces,
          NY: GS, 1915. Pf. solo. The score of the "Bar-
          carolle" incl. a quotation from verses 16, 17 and
          18 of Part III of the poem.

Murias*   "In the sunken city of Murias"   In The Hour of
   Beauty (1907)

   4686   Barnes, Marshall. A Dirge of Four Cities, MS. Set-
          ting for mixed chorus, orch.

Mystic's Prayer, The   "Lay me to sleep in sheltering flame"
   In The Hour of Beauty (1907)

   4687   Hart, Fritz. Five Songs, MS 1919 (Opus 36), avail.
          State Library of Victoria, Melbourne. Song: v.,
          pf.

My Birdeen   "On bonnie birdeen"   In From the Hills of Dream
   (1896)

   4688   Black, Jennie P. NY: GS, pre-1940. Song: [v., pf.?].

   4689* Hopekirk, Helen. "On...", Six Poems by Fiona Mac-
          leod, NY: GS, pre-1929. Song: med. v., pf.

Nightingale Lane   "Down through the thicket"   In Poems
   (1912)

   4690   Barnett, Alice. NY: GS, pre-1940. Song: [v., pf.?].

   4691   Benjamin, Arthur. MS ca. 1937. Song: 2 voices, pf.

523

Macleod, Fiona continued

4692 Hart, Fritz. _Twenty-Five Songs_, Set IV, MS 1927,
avail. State Library of Victoria, Melbourne.
Song: v., pf.

Nocturne   (PR)   _From the Hills of Dream_ (1896) as part of
"The Silence of Amor"

4693 Bantock, Granville. _Celtic Songs_, MS 1921, L: Swan.
Song: [v., pf.].

4694 Wood-Hill, Mabel. _Reactions to Fiona McLeod (Four
Moods)_, NY: Dimit Edn., 1943. Composition for 5
wind instr., hp. (or pf.), stgs.

Orchil   (PR)   _From the Hills of Dream_ (1896) as part of
"The Silence of Amor"

4695 Foulds, John H. L: PX, 1925, _Mood-Pictures_, Chelmsford: MV, 1975. Cyc.: solo v., pf.

Phospherescent Sea   "Sea scarce heaves in its calm sleep,
The" In _Poems_ (1912)

4696 Hart, Fritz. _Twenty-Five Songs_, Set II, MS 1926,
avail. State Library of Victoria, Melbourne.
Song: v., pf.

Record, A   "I hear the dark tempestuous sea"   In _Earth's
Voices_ (1884)

4697 Griffes, Charles T. "Barcarolle", _Fantasy Pieces_,
NY: GS, 1917. Pf. solo. The score of the "Barcarolle" incl. a quotation from verse 39 of the
poem.

Red Poppies   "Through the seeding corn"   In _Sospiri di Roma_
(1891)

4698 Fraser, Shena. L: OUP, 1954. Song: ssa, pf.

Reed Player, The   (PR)   _From the Hills of Dream_ (1896) as
part of "The Silence of Amor"

4699   Bantock, Granville. Celtic Songs, MS 1921, L: Swan.
          Song: [v., pf.].

4700   Foulds, John H. L: Curwen, 1921, Mood-Pictures,
          Chelmsford: MV, 1975. Cyc.: solo v., pf.

4701   Wood-Hill, Mabel. Reactions to Fiona McLeod (Four
          Moods), NY: Dimit Edn., 1943. Composition for 5
          wind instr., hp. (or pf.), stgs.

Remembrance   "No more: let there be no more said"   In From
   the Hills of Dream (1901)

4702   Hart, Fritz. Six Sets of Five Songs, Set V, MS 1927,
          avail. State Library of Victoria, Melbourne.
          Song: v., pf.

Rose of the Night, The   "Dark rose of thy mouth, The"   In
   The Hour of Beauty (1907)

4703   Griffes, Charles T. Three Poems of Fiona Macleod,
          NY: GS, 1918. Song: high v., pf. Arr. 1918 for
          high v., orch.; arr. avail. NY: GS (hire).

Roseen-Dhu   "Little wild-rose of my heart"   In The Hour of
   Beauty (1907)

4704   Bainton, Edgar L. L: S&B, pre-1940. Song: [solo v.,
          pf.?].

4705   Clough-Leighter, Henry. B: BMC, pre-1940. Song:
          [solo v., pf.?].

Rune of Age, The   "O thou that on the hills and wastes of
   Night"   In From the Hills of Dream (1896)

4706   Bax, Arnold. MS 1905. Song: v., orch.

Secret Dews, The   "Poor little songs"   In From the Hills of
   Dream (1901)

Macleod, Fiona continued

4707   Hart, Fritz. <u>Six Sets of Five Songs</u>, Set VI, MS
        1927, avail. State Library of Victoria, Mel-
        bourne. Song: v., pf.

Shadowy Woodlands, The   (PR)   <u>From the Hills of Dream</u>
(1896) as part of "The Silence of Amor"

4708   Bantock, Granville. <u>Celtic Songs</u>, MS 1921, L: Swan.
        Song: [v., pf.].

4709   Foulds, John H. L: Curwen, 1921, <u>Mood-Pictures</u>,
        Chelmsford: MV, 1975. Cyc.: solo v., pf.

Shea-Oak Trees on a Stormy Day   "O'er sandy tracts"   In
<u>Poems</u> (1912)

4710   Hart, Fritz. <u>Twenty-Five Songs</u>, Set III, MS 1927,
        avail. State Library of Victoria, Melbourne.
        Song: v., pf.

Sheiling Song   "I go where the sheep go"   In <u>From the Hills
of Dream</u> (1896)

4711   Bax, Arnold. <u>Album of Seven Songs</u>, L: JWC, 1919.
        Song: v., pf.

4712   Hart, Fritz. <u>Six Sets of Five Songs</u>, Set V, MS 1927,
        avail. State Library of Victora, Melbourne.
        Song: v., pf.

4713   Hawes, Jack. <u>The Bells of Youth</u>, MS. Choral ste: s
        solo, satb, pf. Other selections in the ste. are
        set for satb, pf.

4714   Titherington, Frederick. L: Curwen, 1920. Song: s
        (or ms) or t solo, pf.

Shrewmouse, The   "Creatures with shining eyes, The"   In <u>The
Hour of Beauty</u> (1907)

4715   Hart, Fritz. <u>Six Sets of Five Songs</u>, Set IV, MS
        1927, avail. State Library of Victoria, Mel-
        bourne. Song: v., pf.

Macleod, Fiona continued

Shule, Shule, Shule, Agrah!   "His face was glad as dawn to
    me"   In From_the_Hills_of_Dream (1896)

    4716 Boughton, Rutland. "Shule Agrah", Five_Celtic_Songs,
          L: S&B, 1923. Song: v., pf. or v., stgs.

    4717 Lemont, Cedric. B: OD, pre-1940. Song: [v., pf.].

    4718 Rawlinson, Bertha. "Shule Agrah", L: C, 1963. Song:
          solo v., pf.

    4719 Thompson, E. Roy. "Shule, Shule, Agrah", L: S&B,
          pre-1940. Song: [v., pf.].

Singer in the Woods, The   "Where moongrey-thistled dunes
    divide"   In From_the_Hills_of_Dream (1901)

    4720 Bantock, Granville. L: CR, 1930. Song for children.

Song of Apple-Trees   "Song of Apple-trees, honeysweet and
    murmurous"   In The_Hour_of_Beauty (1907)

    4721 Boughton, Rutland. "Avalon", Six_Celtic_Choruses, L:
          S&B, 1924. [Setting for chorus, a cap.].

    4722 Fletcher, Percy E. "Song of Apple Trees", L: N,
          1924. Song: satb, a cap.

Song of Fionula, The   "Sleep, sleep, brothers dear, sleep
    and dream"   In From_the_Hills_of_Dream (1901)

    4723 Peterkin, Norman. L: OUP, 1935. Song: ms or a solo,
          pf.

Song of the Sea-Wind, The   "King of the winds"   In Poems
    (1912)

    4724 Shepherd, Arthur. "Song of the Sea Wind", B:
          Schmidt, 1915. Song: ssa, pf.

St. Bride's Lullaby   "Oh, Baby Christ, so dear to me"   In
    From_the_Hills_of_Dream (1896)

527

Macleod, Fiona continued

4725   Boughton, Rutland. "St. Bride's Cradle Song", <u>Six</u>
        <u>Spiritual Songs</u>, L: Reeves, 1911. Song: v., pf.

4726   Hopekirk, Helen. <u>Six Poems by Fiona Macleod</u>, NY: GS,
        pre-1929. Song: med. v., pf.

Summer Wind, The   "Bugling of the summer wind, The"   In
    <u>Poems</u> (1912)

4727   Hart, Fritz. <u>Twenty-Five Songs</u>, Set IV, MS 1927,
        avail. State Library of Victoria, Melbourne.
        Song: v., pf.

Sun Lord, The   "Low laughing, blithely scorning"   In <u>Poems</u>
    (1912)

4728   Hart, Fritz. <u>Twenty-Five Songs</u>, Set IV, MS 1927,
        avail. State Library of Victoria, Melbourne.
        Song: v., pf.

Sunrise above broad Wheatfields   "Pale tints of the twilight
    fields, The"   In <u>Poems</u> (1912)

4729   Hart, Fritz. <u>Twenty-Five Songs</u>, Set I, MS 1926,
        avail. State Library of Victoria, Melbourne.
        Song: v., pf.

Thy Dark Eyes to Mine   "Thy dark eyes to mine, Eilidh"   In
    <u>From the Hills of Dream</u> (1901)

4730   Bax, Arnold. <u>A Celtic Song Cycle</u>, L: JWC (Avison
        edn.), 1906. Cyc.: [bar] solo v., pf.

4731   Fletcher, H. Grant. MS. Song: t solo, pf.

4732   Griffes, Charles T. <u>Three Poems of Fiona Macleod</u>,
        NY: GS, 1919. Song: high v., pf. Also arr. for
        high v., orch.; arr. avail. NY: GS (hire).

4733   Hart, Fritz. <u>Six Sets of Five Songs</u>, Set VI, MS
        1927, avail. State Library of Victoria, Mel-
        bourne. Song: v., pf.

528

4734 Hopekirk, Helen. <u>Five Songs</u>, NY: GS, 1904. Song:
[v., pf.].

Time "I saw a happy Spirit" In <u>The Hour of Beauty</u> (1907)

4735 Hart, Fritz. <u>Five Songs</u>, MS 1919 (Opus 36), avail.
State Library of Victoria, Melbourne. Song: v.,
pf.

Triad "From the Silence of Time" In <u>Poems</u> (1912)

4736 Hart, Fritz. <u>Twenty-Five Songs</u>, Set IV, MS 1927,
avail. State Library of Victoria, Melbourne.
Song: v., pf.

Under the Evening Star "Poor little songs" In <u>From the
Hills of Dream</u> (1901)

4737 Rummel, Walter. L: A, pre-1940. Song: [v., pf.?].

Undersong, The "I hear the sea-song of the blood in my
heart" In <u>From the Hills of Dream</u> (1896)

4738 Eichheim, Henry. B: BMC, pre-1940. Song: [solo v.,
pf.?].

4739 Hart, Fritz. "Under Song", <u>Six Sets of Five Songs</u>,
Set VI, MS 1927, avail. State Library of Vic-
toria, Melbourne. Song: v., pf.

Unknown Wind, The "When the day darkens" In <u>From the
Hills of Dream</u> (1901)

4740 Genzmer, Harald. "Es ist ein Wind, der keinen Namen
hat", <u>Irische Harfe</u>, MS ca. 1965, L: P. Setting for
4-8 mixed v.

4741 Hart, Fritz. <u>Six Sets of Five Songs</u>, Set III, MS
1927, avail. State Library of Victoria, Melbourne. Song: v., pf.

Macleod, Fiona continued

Vale, Amor!   "We do not know this thing"   In The Hour of
    Beauty (1907)

    4742   Hart, Fritz. Six Sets of Five Songs, Set V, MS 1927,
              avail. State Library of Victoria, Melbourne.
              Song: v., pf.

Valley of Silence, The   "In the secret Valley of Silence"
    In From the Hills of Dream (1901)

    4743   Bantock, Granville. L: CR, 1929. Song: [v., pf.].

    4744   Hart, Fritz. Six Sets of Five Songs, Set III, MS
              1927, avail. State Library of Victoria, Mel-
              bourne. Song: v., pf.

    4745   Rummel, Walter. L: A, pre-1940. Song: [v., pf.?].

Vision, The   "In a fair place"   In From the Hills of Dream
    (1896)

    4746   Hart, Fritz. Six Sets of Five Songs, Set V, MS 1927,
              avail. State Library of Victoria, Melbourne.
              Song: v., pf.

Voice Among the Dunes, The   "I have heard the sea-wind
    sighing"   In From the Hills of Dream (1896)

    4747   Hart, Fritz. Five Songs, MS 1919 (Opus 36), avail.
              State Library of Victoria, Melbourne. Song: v.,
              pf.

War Song of the Vikings, The   "Let loose the hounds of war"
    In From the Hills of Dream (1896)

    4748   Bax, Arnold. "Viking-Battle-Song", MS 1905. Song:
              v., pf. Originally set for v., orch. (MS no long-
              er extant).

    4749   Griffes, Charles T. MS 1914. Song: [male] v., pf.

Washer of the Ford, The   "There is a lonely stream"   In
    From the Hills of Dream (1896)

4750   Bantock, Granville. L: CR, 1929. Song for children.

Wasp, The   "Where the ripe pears droop heavily"   In Poems
   (1912)

   4751   Benjamin, Arthur. Three Impressions, L: Curwen,
          1925. Song: med. v., pf. Also publ. for med. v.,
          str. qrt. Also publ. sep.

   4752   Hawes, Jack. MS. Song: med. v., pf.

When the Dew is Falling   "When the dew is falling"   In From
   the Hills of Dream (1896)

   4753   Eichheim, Henry. B: BMC, pre-1940. Song: [v., pf.?].

   4754   Hart, Fritz. Six Sets of Five Songs, Set II, MS
          1927, avail. State Library of Victoria, Mel-
          bourne. Song: v., pf.

   4755   Hopekirk, Helen. Six Poems by Fiona Macleod, NY: GS,
          pre-1929. Song: med. v., pf.

   4756   Johnson, William S. NY: CPMC, pre-1940. Song: [v.,
          pf.?].

   4757   Moule-Evans, David. Two Celtic Songs, L: JW, ca.
          1946. Song: s solo, pf.

   4758   Schneider, Edwin. L: BH, pre-1940. Song: [v., pf.?].

When the Greeness is come again   "West wind lifts the plumes
   of the fir, The"   In Poems (1912)

   4759   Hart, Fritz. Twenty-Five Songs, Set V, MS 1927,
          avail. State Library of Victoria, Melbourne.
          Song: v., pf.

When There is Peace   "There is peace on the sea to-night"
   In The Hour of Beauty (1907)

   4760   Hart, Fritz. Six Sets of Five Songs, Set IV, MS
          1927, avail. State Library of Victoria, Mel-
          bourne. Song: v., pf.

Macleod, Fiona continued

White Merle, The   (PR)   From the Hills of Dream (1896) as
    part of "The Silence of Amor"

    4761   Wood-Hill, Mabel. "White Merle", Reactions to Fiona
           McLeod (Four Moods), NY: Dimit Edn., 1943.
           Composition for 5 wind instr., hp. (or pf.),
           stgs.

White Peace, The   "It lies not on the sunlit hill"   In From
    the Hills of Dream (1896)

    4762   Bax, Arnold. Album of Seven Songs, L: JWC, 1919.
           Song: v., pf.

    4763   Hart, Fritz. Six Sets of Five Songs, Set II, MS
           1927, avail. State Library of Victoria, Mel-
           bourne. Song: v., pf.

White Peacock, The   "Here where the sunlight"   In Sospiri
    di Roma (1891)

    4764   Griffes, Charles T. Roman Sketches, NY: GS, 1917.
           Pf. solo. The score of "The White Peacock" incl.
           a quotation from the beginning of Sharp's poem.

White Rose   "Far in the inland valleys"   In Poems (1912)

    4765   Hart, Fritz. Twenty-Five Songs, Set IV, MS 1927,
           avail. State Library of Victoria, Melbourne.
           Song: v., pf.

White Star of Time   "Each love-thought in thy mind"   In
    From the Hills of Dream (1896)

    4766   Hart, Fritz. Six Sets of Five Songs, Set V, MS 1927,
           avail. State Library of Victoria, Melbourne.
           Song: v., pf.

Wild Roses   "Against the dim hot summer blue"   In Poems
    (1912)

4767 Hart, Fritz. Twenty-Five Songs, Set I, MS 1926,
avail. State Library of Victoria, Melbourne.
Song: v., pf.

Winter Hedgerow, A   "Wintery wolds are white, The"   In
Poems (1912)

4768 Benjamin, Arthur. "Hedgerow", Three Impressions, L:
Curwen, 1925. Song: med. v., pf. Also publ. for
med. v., str. qrt. Also publ. sep.

4769 Hart, Fritz. Twenty-Five Songs, Set I, MS 1926,
avail. State Library of Victoria, Melbourne.
Song: v., pf.

Miscellanea

4770 Bantock, Granville. "Prelude", Celtic Songs, MS
1921, L: Swan. Song: [v., pf.].

4771 Bath, Hubert. "Eily", L: C, 1908. Song: [v., pf.].

4772 Bath, Hubert. "Love in a Cottage", L: C. Song: [v.,
pf.].

4773 Bath, Hubert. Grove's states that Bath composed 30
songs to texts by Macleod.

4774 Bax, Arnold. "A Celtic Lullaby", A Celtic Song
Cycle, L: JWC (Avison edn.), 1906. Cyc.: [bar]
solo v., pf. [Possibly a setting of Macleod's
poem entitled "Lullaby"?].

4775 Boughton, Rutland. Five Celtic Songs, L: S&B, 1923.
Songs: v., pf. or v., stgs. Incl. songs entitled:
"Daughter of the Sun", "My Grief" [possibly a
setting of Macleod's "Mo Bròn"?], "Tragic Lullaby".

4776 Boughton, Rutland. Six Celtic Choruses, L: S&B,
1924. [Settings for chorus, a cap.]. Incl.
choruses entitled: "A Celtic Lullaby" [possibly
a setting of Macleod's "Lullaby"?], "A Sea Rune".

4777 Buzzi-Peccia, Arturo. "Fate", NY: GS, pre-1940.
Song: [v., pf.?].

533

4778   de Koven, Reginald. "Love Came One Day", B: BMC,
       pre-1940. Song: [v., pf.?].

4779   Edwyn, Richard E. "Love came in at the door one
       day", NY: GS, pre-1940. Song: [v., pf.?].

4780   Forsyth, Cecil. NY: JF, pre-1940. Song: [v., pf.?].

4781   Hart, Fritz. Six Sets of Five Songs, Set I, MS
       1927. Songs to texts by Macleod. Unlike the MSS
       of sets II-VI, the MS of this set cannot be
       located.

4782   Loomis, Harvey. "Coming of the Prince", MS pre-1914.
       Song: v., pf., vln.

4783   McKay, George F. "The Prayer of Fiona Macleod",
       Glen Rock: JF, pre-1969. Song: ssaa, a cap.

4784   Nelson, Herbert H. "A Cavalry Catch", L: C, 1913.
       Song: [v., pf.].

4785* Parker, Horatio, et al., arr. "A Cavalry Catch", NY:
       Silver, 1920 in The Progressive Music Series,
       Book 4. Song: v., pf. Text adapt. to a melody by
       Jean Sibelius.

4786   Warford, Claude. "Phantom Pirate", NY: R, pre-1940.
       Song: [v., pf.?].

MACNEICE, Louis   1907-1963

Agamemnon of Aeschylus, The   (DR)   (1936) Transl. from
   Aeschylus

   4787   Britten, Benjamin. MS, prod. 1936. Incidental music.

April Fool   "Here come I, old April Fool"   Visitations
   (1957)

acNeice, Louis continued

4788 Dodgson, Stephen. <u>The Distances Between</u>, MS. Cyc.:
      s, bar duet, pf.

Autobiography   "In my childhood trees were green"   <u>Harper's
   Bazaar</u> (Sept. 1941)

   4789 Duncan, Chester. MS 1943. Song: solo v., pf.

   4790 Warren, Raymond. "In My Childhood", L: N, 1965.
         Song: satb, a cap.

Bagpipe music   "It's no go the merrygoround"   <u>Poems 1937</u>
   (1937)

   4791 Farquhar, David. MS. Song: v., pf.

Canzonetta   "Thousand years and none the same, A"   <u>Observer</u>
   (May 1953)

   4792 Rawsthorne, Alan. "Canzonet", L: OUP, 1953 in <u>A
         Garland for the Queen</u>. Setting for s solo, satb,
         a cap.

Christina   "It all began so easy"   <u>New Republic</u> (Apr. 1940)
   Incl. as one of "Novelettes" in <u>Poems 1925-1940</u> (1941)

   4793 Stevens, James. <u>Three Dramatic Songs</u>, MS 1953. Song:
         ms solo, pf.

<u>Christopher Columbus</u>   (RP)   (1944)

   4794 Walton, William. MS 1942, prod. BBC same year.
         Incidental music. "Beatriz's Song" adapt. for
         v., gtr. by Hector Quine; adapt. publ. L: OUP,
         1974.

County Sligo   See: "In Sligo the country was soft"

Creditor, The   "Quietude of a soft wind, The"   <u>Mosaic</u>
   (Spring 1935)

535

MacNeice, Louis continued

    4795   Spedding, Frank. MS ca. 1958, avail. SMA. Song: b
           solo, pf.

  Cushenden   "Fuschia and ragweed"   Horizon (Jan. 1940) Incl.
    as one of "The Coming of War" in Poems 1925-1940 (1941)
    and as one of "The Closing Album" in Collected Poems
    1925-1948 (1949)

    4796   Lawson, Peter. Sitting in Farmyard Mud, L: C, 1974.
           Cyc.: high v., pf. Sets various passages from
           "The Closing Album".

  Dark Tower, The   (RS)   The Dark Tower and Other Radio
    Scripts (1947), publ. sep. 1964

    4797   Britten, Benjamin. MS, prod. 1946. Incidental music.

  Dreams in middle age   "Sooner let nightmares whinny"
    Visitations (1957)

    4798   Dodgson, Stephen. The Distances Between, MS. Cyc.:
           s, bar duet, pf.

  Dublin   "Grey brick upon brick"   Horizon (Feb. 1940) Incl.
    as one of "The Coming of War" in Poems 1925-1940 (1941)
    and as one of "The Closing Album" in Collected Poems
    1925-1948 (1949)

    4799   Lawson, Peter. Sitting in Farmyard Mud, L: C, 1974.
           Cyc.: high v., pf. Sets various passages from
           "The Closing Album".

  East of the Sun and West of the Moon   (RP)   Persons from
    Porlock and Other Plays for Radio (1969)

    4800   Cary, Tristram. MS, prod. BBC 1959. Incidental
           music.

  Enter Caesar   (RP)   Persons from Parlock and Other Plays
    for Radio (1969)

cNeice, Louis continued

4801   Lutyens, Elisabeth. MS, prod. BBC 1946. Incidental
        music.

Flight of the heart   "Heart, my heart, what will you do?"
    New Republic (Nov. 1940)

    4802   Stevens, James. Three Dramatic Songs, MS 1953. Song:
            ms solo, pf.

Galway   "O the crossbones of Galway"   The Last Ditch (1940)
    Incl. as one of "The Coming of War" in Poems 1925-1940
    (1941) and as one of "The Closing Album" in Collected
    Poems 1925-1948 (1949)

    4803   Lawson, Peter. Sitting in Farmyard Mud, L: C, 1974.
            Cyc.: high v., pf. Sets various passages from
            "A Closing Album".

Goethe's "Faust"   (DR)   (1951) Abridged and transl. by
    MacNeice

    4804   Seiber, Mátyás. "Invocation", "Epilogue", To Poetry,
            L: S, 1954. Cyc.: high v., pf. Cyc. begins and
            ends with identical settings of lines beginning:
            "Oh, heavenly Poesy".

    4805   Seiber, Mátyás. Two Songs from "Goethe's 'Faust'",
            L: A, 1951. Songs: solo v., pf. Settings of lines
            beginning: "There was a King in Thule" and "My
            peace is gone".

"In Sligo the country was soft"   The Last Ditch (1940), rev.
    and incl. as one of "The Coming of War" in Poems 1925-1940
    (1941); rev. and incl. as one of "The Closing Album" in
    Collected Poems 1925-1948 (1949)

    4806   Lawson, Peter. Sitting in Farmyard Mud, L: C, 1974.
            Cyc.: high v., pf. Sets various passages from "The
            Closing Album".

Intimations of Mortality   "Shadows of the banisters march
    march, The"   Poems (1935)

537

MacNeice, Louis continued

    4807 Spedding, Frank. MS ca. 1958, avail. SMA. Song: b
          solo, pf.

Invocation   "Dolphin plunge, fountain play"   Solstices
    (1961)

    4808 Dodgson, Stephen. The Distances Between, MS. Cyc.:
          s, bar duet, pf.

Merman, The   See: "Merman under the Plough, The"

"Merman under the Plough, The"   London Magazine (Nov. 1955)
    as one of "Visitations", rev. 1955

    4809 Dodgson, Stephen. "Visitation", The Distances
          Between, MS. Cyc.: s, bar duet, pf.

Now It Has Happened   See: "Why, now it has happened"

Out of the Picture   (DR)   (1937) Portions 1st publ. as
    "Lyrics from a play" in New Verse (Christmas 1936)

    4810 Britten, Benjamin. MS, prod. 1937. Incidental music.

    4811 Dalby, Martin. See: Pindar is dead.

Pindar is dead   "There are hikers on all the roads"   New
    Verse (Christmas 1936) as one of "Lyrics from a play"

    4812* Dalby, Martin. L: N (hire). Ch. music: cl., pf.
          only.

Prayer before birth   "I am not yet born; O hear me"
    Penguin New Writing (Jan. 1944)

    4813 Farquhar, David. MS. Song: narr., ssa, org.

    4814 Field, Robin. "A Prayer Before Birth", MS 1971.
          Setting for sp., pf.

                        538

Sligo and Mayo   See: "In Sligo the country was soft"

Slum song   "O the slums of Dublin fermenting with children"
   Penguin New Writing (Apr. 1946)

   4815* Alwyn, William. L: OUP, 1948. Song: bar solo, unacc.

Song   "Sunlight on the garden, The"   Listener (Jan. 1937),
   rev. 1938

   4816 Farquhar, David. "The Sunlight on the Garden", MS.
         Song: v., pf.

Sunlight on the garden, The   See: Song "Sunlight on the
   garden, The"

They Met on Good Friday   (RP)   Persons from Porlock and
   Other Plays for Radio (1969)

   4817 Cary, Tristram. MS, prod. BBC 1959. Incidental
         music.

This way out   "You're not going yet?"   Springboard (1944)

   4818 Stevens, James. Three Dramatic Songs, MS 1953. Song:
         ms solo, pf.

To Hedli   "Days running into each other, but oh the distance
   between!, The"   Visitations (1957)

   4819 Dodgson, Stephen. "Prologue", The Distances Between,
         MS. Cyc.: s, bar duet, pf.

"Why, now it has happened"   The Last Ditch (1940), rev. and
   incl. as one of "The Coming of War" in Poems 1925-1940
   (1941); incl. as one of "The Closing Album" in Collected
   Poems 1925-1948 (1949)

   4820 Lawson, Peter. Sitting in Farmyard Mud, L: C, 1974.
         Cyc.: high v., pf. Sets various passages from
         "The Closing Album".

Mansfield, Katherine

MANSFIELD, Katherine   1888-1923

  In the Rangitaki Valley   "O valley of waving broom"   In
    Poems (1924)

    4821 Coulthard, Jean. "O valley...", Songs for the
          Distaff Muse, MS 1972, avail. CMC. Song: s, a
          soli, vcl.

  Sea-Child, The   "In the world you sent her, mother"   In
    Poems (1924)

    4822 Freed, Dorothy. MS 1957, avail. N.Z. Broadcasting
          Corp. Song: solo v., pf.

  Winter Song   "Rain and wind, and wind and rain"   In Poems
    (1924)

    4823 Pitfield, Thomas B. Two Seasonal Songs, L: OUP,
          1953. Song: ss, a cap.

MASEFIELD, John Edward   1878-1967

  Ballad of Cape St. Vincent, A   "Now, Bill, ain't it prime
    to be a-sailing'"   Salt-Water Ballads (1902)

    4824 Lohr, Hermann. L: C, 1923. Song: [v., pf.].

  Beauty   "I have seen dawn and sunset on moors"   Speaker
    (July 1903)

    4825 Barratt, Edgar. L: Elkin, 1928. Song: high v., pf.
          Also avail. for med. v., pf.

    4826 Bartley, Ewart A. MS 1949. Song: [v., pf.?].

    4827 Cope, Cecil. L: BH, 1966. Song: ttbb, a cap.

asefield, John continued

4828   Davidson, Malcolm. L: Curwen, 1921. Song: solo v.,
       pf. Also avail. for solo v., stgs.

4829   Gilbert, Norman. L: OUP, 1951. Song: ssa, [a cap.?].

4830   Hageman, Richard. NY: GX, pre-1940. Song: [solo v.,
       pf.?].

4831   Kramer, A. Walter. "I Have Seen Dawn", MS 1922, NY:
       GS. Song: [v., pf.].

4832   Lewis, Samuel R. B: Birchard, pre-1940. Song: [solo
       v., pf.?].

4833   Lohr, Hermann. L: C, 1922. Song: [v., pf.].

4834   Martin, Easthope. Five Poems by John Masefield, L:
       E, 1919. Song: med. v., pf.

4835   Posamanick, Beatrice. [NY?]: MK, pre-1940. Song:
       [solo v., pf.?].

4836   Warren, Elinor R. "I Have Seen Dawn", B: BMC, pre-
       1940. Song: [solo v., pf.?].

Cape Horn Gospel I   "'I was in a hooker once,' said Karls-
    sen"   Salt-Water Ballads (1902)

4837   Boyd, Jeanne M. NY: GX, 1945. Song: v., pf.

4838   Keel, Frederick. Four "Salt-Water Ballads", 2nd set,
       L: BH. Cyc.: v., pf.

4839   Lewis, Samuel R. B: Birchard, pre-1940. Song: [v.,
       pf.?].

Captain Stratton's Fancy   "Oh some are fond of red wine"
    Speaker (May 1903)

4840   Bristol, Esmond. "The Old, Bold Mate", L: N, 1922.
       Song: bar solo, pf.

4841   Gurney, Ivor. MS 1914, L: S&B. Song: solo v., pf.

4842   Taylor, Deems. NY: JF, 1952. Song: ttbb, [a cap.].

Masefield, John continued

4843 Warlock, Peter. L: A, 1922. Song: bar solo, pf. Also
     publ. for t solo, pf. and for b solo, pf.

Cargoes   "Quinquireme of Nineveh from distant Ophir"   Broad
Sheet (May 1903)

4844 Burkinshaw, Sydney. MS. Song: unison boys' v., pf.

4845 Clarke, Robert C. Three Sailor Songs, L: C, 1920.
     Song: [solo v., pf.].

4846 Dobson, Tom. NY: GS, 1920. Song: any v. except high,
     light s, pf.

4847 Grant, Parks. MS (Opus 12). Song: med. v., pf.

4848 Lewis, Samuel R. B: Birchard, pre-1940. Song: [v.,
     pf.?].

4849 Martin, Easthope. Five Poems by John Masefield, L:
     E, 1919. Song: med. v., pf.

4850 Shaw, Martin. L: CR, 1924. Song: unison v., pf.
     Publ. L: CR, 1935 for satb, pf.

4851 Tomblings, Philip. York: Banks, 1936. Song: unison
     v., pf.

Cavalier   "All the merry kettle-drums are thudding"   Salt-
Water Ballads (1902)

4852 Gardiner, H. Balfour. L: EA, pre-1951. Song: unsion
     v., pf.

4853 Hickey, Vivian. L: C, 1924. Song: [solo v., pf.].

4854 Lewis, Samuel R. MS pre-1928, NY: GS. Song: [v.,
     pf.?].

4855 Turnbull, Percy. L: OUP, 1927. Song: solo v., pf.

Chief Centurions, The   See: Tragedy of Pompey the Great, The

sefield, John continued

Christmas Eve at Sea   "Wind is rustling 'south and south',
    A"   Salt-Water Ballads (1902)

    4856 Ayres, Frederic. MS pre-1926, NY: GS. Song: [v.,
            pf.?].

    4857 Davidson, Malcolm. "A Christmas Carol", in Chapbook
            (Dec. 1920); publ. sep. L: WR. Carol: [v., pf.].
            Setting of 3 verses only.

Coming into Salcombe   "Twilight. Red in the west"   Broad
    Sheet (Dec. 1903), rev. 1910

    4858 Forsyth, Cecil. "The Wild Duck", NY: JF, pre-1940.
            Song: [v., pf.?].

Coming of Christ, The   (DR)   (1928)

    4859 Holst, Gustav. L: Curwen, 1928. Incidental music:
            s, t, bar, b soli, satb, tpt., pf., org. (or str.
            orch.). Re-issued L: F as a choral ste. for satb,
            org. and for unison male chorus, pf. Settings en-
            titled: "As, after thunder", "Man was dark", "The
            days are past", "Prometheus", "O sing, as thrush-
            es", "Glory to God", "By weary stages". "As,
            after thunder" was publ. sep. (L: Curwen, 1928)
            for bar, b soli, ttbb, a cap.

Cry to Music, A   See: Music 1939-40

D'Avalos' Prayer   See: Last Prayer, A

Easter   (DR)   (1929)

    4860 Shaw, Martin. L: Curwen, 1929. Incidental music:
            satb, orch.

Emigrant, The   "Going by Daly's shanty I heard the boys
    within"   Ballads (1903)

    4861 Boughton, Rutland. Five Songs, MS 1944. Song: solo
            v., pf., vln.

Masefield, John continued

4862 Fothergill, Helen. L: A, pre-1940. Song: [v., pf.?].

4863 Russell, Lionel. L: S&B, pre-1940. Song: [v., pf.?].

4864 Scott, Francis G. "Going Westward", MS 1922, avail.
      SMA. Song: med. v., pf.

4865 Smith, Breville. L: Elkin, 1922. Song: med. v., pf.
      Also avail. for low v., pf.

Everlasting Mercy, The   "From '41 to '51"   English Review
(Oct. 1911), subsequently publ. sep.

4866 Homer, Sidney. MS (Opus 42), NY: GS. Song: [v.,
      pf.?].

Galley-Bowers, The   "Staggering over the running combers"
Salt-Water Ballads (1902)

4867 Walters, Leslie. Wendover: RP, 1974. Song: ttbb, pf.
      Also avail. for ttbb, orch.

Gentle Lady, The   "So beautiful, so dainty-sweet"   Ballads
(1903)

4868 Shepherd, Arthur. MS, avail. University of Utah.
      Song: solo v., pf.

4869* Swain, Freda. MS ca. 1923, avail. Chinnor: Channel,
      NEMO. Setting for light bar (or t) and pf. en-
      semble.

Golden City of St. Mary, The   "Out beyond the sunset"
Salt-Water Ballads (1902)

4870 Clarke, Robert C. Songs of a Rover, L: C, 1919.
      Song: solo v., pf.

4871 Copley, I.A. L: Elkin, 1957. Song: unison v., pf. or
      solo treble v., pf.

4872 Wood, Thomas. L: S&B, pre-1940. Song: [v., pf.?].

Good Friday   (DR)   Fortnightly Review (Dec. 1915), publ.
   sep. 1916

   4873 Jacobson, Maurice. MS ca. 1948. Incidental music for
         radio.

   4874 Miles, Philip. L: OUP, 1933. Music drama: s, 2 t,
         bar, 4 b soli, chorus, orch.

Halt of the Legion, The   See: "Here the legion halted, here
   the ranks were broken"

Hell's Pavement   "'When I'm discharged in Liverpool...'"
   Speaker (Sept. 1902), rev. same year

   4875 Keel, Frederick. Four "Salt-Water Ballads", 2nd set,
         L: BH. Cyc.: v., pf.

"Here the legion halted, here the ranks were broken"   In
   Lillingdon Downs and Other Poems (1917), subsequently rev.

   4876 Gurney, Ivor. "The Halt of the Legion", MS 1919.
         Song: [solo v., pf.].

June Twilight   "Twilight comes; the sun, The"   Speaker
   (June 1904)

   4877 Agnew, Roy E. B: Schmidt, pre-1940. Song: [v.,
         pf.?].

   4878 Clarke, Rebecca. MS pre-1927, L: WR. Song: [v.,
         pf.?].

   4879 Martin, Easthope. Five Poems by John Masefield, L:
         E, 1919. Song: med. v., pf.

   4880 Wishart, Peter. L: H, 1960. Song: med. v., pf.

Last Prayer, A   "When the last sea is sailed"   Broad Sheet
   (Oct. 1902), rev. same year, rev. 1910

   4881 Forsyth, Cecil. "When the last...", NY: JF, pre-
         1940. Song: [v., pf.?].

Masefield, John continued

   4882   Gibbs, Geoffrey D. "Be Good to Me, O Lord", MS.
          Anthem: satb, org. or satb, pf.

   4883   Keel, Frederick. "A Sailor's Prayer", Four "Salt-
          Water Ballads", 2nd set, L: BH. Cyc.: v., pf.

Laugh and be Merry   "Laugh and be merry, remember, better
   the world with a song"   Ballads (1903)

   4884   Boughton, Rutland. Five Songs, MS 1944. Song: solo
          v., pf., vln.

   4885   Griffiths, T. Vernon. MS. Song: ttbb, pf.

   4886   Holbrooke, Joseph. "Choral: Laugh and be Merry", L:
          MML, 1934. Song: satb, pf.

Lemmings, The   "Once in a hundred years the Lemmings come"
   Enslaved and Other Poems (1920)

   4887   Durkó, Zsolt. "Dartmouth Concerto", Budapest: Editio
          Musica, 1966. Setting for ms solo, orch.

"Let that which is to come be as it may"   Good Friday and
   Other Poems (1916)

   4888   Pimsleur, Solomon. "Let that which is to come", MS
          (Opus 21), avail. NYPL. Setting for satb, a cap.

London Town   "Oh London Town's a fine town"   Pall Mall
   Magazine (May 1903)

   4889   Ashbee, C.R. in coll. with Janet E. Ashbee. L: [?],
          1903-05 in The Essex House Song Book. Song: [v.,
          pf.].

   4890   Ashbee, Janet E. See entry immediately preceding.

   4891   Clarke, Robert C. L: C, 1904. Song: [solo v., pf.].

   4892   German, Edward. L: N, 1921. Song: ttbb, a cap.

   4893   Shaw, Martin. L: CR, 1923. Song: solo v., pf.

Mother Carey   "Mother Carey? She's the mother o' the
    witches"   Speaker (1902)

    4894 Barnes, Marshall. Salt Water Ballads, MS. Song:
          satb, orch. or satb, ensemble of 13 players (ww.,
          br., perc.).

    4895 Keel, Frederick. Three "Salt-Water Ballads", 1st
          set, L: BH, 1919. Song: v., pf. Also publ. sep.

Music 1939-40   "Speak to us, Music"   In Poems (1951), rev.
    1961

    4896 Diamond, David. "Invocation to Music", To Music, NY:
          SMP, 1969. Choral symph.: t, b-bar soli, satb,
          orch.

New Bedford Whaler, The   "There was a Bedford Whaler"
    Salt-Water Poems and Ballads (1916)

    4897 Ritchie, Tom. MS. Song: solo v., pf.

News from Whydah   "Oh did you come by Whydah Roads"
    Ballads (1903)

    4898 Gardiner, H. Balfour. L: N, 1912. Setting for
          chorus, orch. Arr. for orch. by Gustav Holst
          also publ. L: N, 1912. Arr. for 2 pf. by Geoffrey
          Bush publ. L: N, 1966.

Night at Dago Tom's, A   "Oh yesterday, I t'ink it was"
    Speaker (Oct. 1902)

    4899 Lewis, Samuel R. B: Birchard, pre-1940. Song: [solo
          v., pf.?].

Odtaa   (NV)   (1926)

    4900 Carwithen, Doreen. MS. Overture [for orch.].

Old Song re-sung, An   "I saw a ship a-sailing"   Ballads and
    Poems (1910)

Masefield, John continued

    4901 Dobson, Tom. _Three Songs_, NY: GS, 1916. Song: high
           or med. v., pf.

    4902 Gardiner, H. Balfour. L: N, 1920. Song: satb, a cap.

    4903 Griffes, Charles T. _Two Poems by John Masefield_,
           NY: GS, 1920. Song: solo v., pf. Arr. by Harvey
           Enders for 4 pt. male chorus, pf.; arr. publ. NY:
           GS.

    4904 Martin, Easthope. _Five Poems by John Masefield_, L:
           E, 1919. Song: med. v., pf.

    4905 Pennicuick, Ramsay. "I Saw a Ship a-Sailing", L:
           Curwen, 1921. Song: solo v., pf.

 On Eastnor Knoll   "Silent are the woods"   _Salt-Water_
 Ballads (1902)

    4906 Gurney, Ivor. MS 1926. Song: [solo v., pf.].

    4907 Redman, Reginald. "A Land of Shadows", L: A, pre-
           1957. Song: satb, [a cap.].

    4908 Vercoe, Barry. MS, avail. University of Auckland.
           Song: satb, a cap.

 Philip the King   (DR)   _Philip the King and other Poems_
   (1914)

    4909 Arundell, Dennis. MS pre-1954. Incidental music for
           radio.

    4910 Holst, Gustav. MS, perf. London, Nov. 1914. In-
           cidental music.

 Pier-Head Chorus, A   "Oh I'll be chewing salted horse"
 Salt-Water Ballads (1902)

    4911 Wood, Thomas. "Pier Head Chorus", L: S&B, pre-1940.
           Song: [v., pf.?].

 Play of St. George, A   (DR)   (1948)

Masefield, John continued

4912 Bax, Arnold. "The Pageant of St. George", unf.
      (late) MS. Incidental music originally intended
      for bar solo, chorus, orch. (only pf. score is
      extant).

'Port o' Many Ships'   "It's a sunny pleasant anchorage"
Speaker (Aug. 1902), subsequently rev.

4913 Keel, Frederick. "Port of Many Ships", Three "Salt-
      Water Ballads", 1st set, L: BH, 1919. Song: v.,
      pf. Also publ. sep.

Port of Holy Peter   "Blue laguna rocks and quivers, The"
Broad Sheet (Dec. 1902)

4914 Hewitt-Jones, Tony. Seven Sea Poems, L: N, 1958.
      Choral ste.: a or bar or b solo, satb, stgs. The
      complete ste. also requires obbl. for ob., eng.
      hn.

Port of Many Ships   See: 'Port o' Many Ships'

Prayer   See: Last Prayer, A

"Rest Her Soul, She's Dead"   "She has done with the sea's
sorrow"   Salt-Water Ballads (1902)

4915 Barnes, Marshall. Salt Water Ballads, MS. Song:
      satb, orch. or satb, ensemble of 13 players (ww.,
      br., perc.).

Roadways   "One road leads to London"   Speaker (May 1903),
rev. same year

4916 Densmore, John. B: OD, pre-1940. Song: [v., pf.?].

4917 Edeson, Donald. L: MM, 1933, copyright assigned L:
      C, 1943. Song: [solo v., pf.].

4918 Finch, Harold N. NY: CF, 1947. Song: satb, a cap.

4919 Hickey, Vivian. L: A, pre-1940. Song: [v., pf.?].

4920   Holst, Gustav. L: YBP, 1932. Song: unison v., pf.

4921   Lewis, Samuel R. B: Birchard, pre-1940. Song: [v., pf.?].

4922   Lohr, Hermann. L: C, 1921. Song: v., orch.

4923   Mulliner, Michael. L: OUP, 1934. Song: unison v., pf.

4924   Pasfield, W.R. L: KP, 1957. Song: unison v., pf.

4925*   Rose, Edith. Chi.: GH, pre-1940. Song: high or med. v., pf.

4926   Thorp, L. Gordon. York: Banks, 1937. Song: unison v., pf.

Sea-Fever   "I must go down to the seas again"   Speaker
(Feb. 1902)

4927   Andrews, Mark. NY: GS, pre-1940. Song: [solo v., pf.?].

4928   Barnes, Marshall. "I must...", Salt Water Ballads, MS. Song: satb, orch. or satb, ensemble of 13 players (ww., br., perc.).

4929   Bratt, C. Griffith. MS. Song: bar solo, pf.

4930   Bullock, Flora. York, Nebr.: Parks, pre-1940. Song: [solo v., pf.?].

4931   Clarke, Robert C. Songs of a Rover, L: C, 1919. Song: solo v., pf.

4932   Crawford, Dawn. MS 1942. Song: bar solo, pf.

4933   Densmore, John. "I Must Down to the Seas Again", B: BMC, pre-1940. Song: [solo v., pf.?].

4934   Enos, Joseph. NY: BH, pre-1957. Song: t solo, pf.

4935   Gest, Elizabeth. "Down to the Sea", Ph.: TP, 1927. Song: solo v., pf.

550

4936 Ireland, John. L: A, 1915. Song: med. v. or unison
      v., pf.

4937 Loud, John A. NY: CF, 1924. Song: solo v., pf.

4938 Mitchell, Raymond E. "I must...", Chi.: GH, pre-
      1940. Song: [solo v., pf.?].

4939 Ritchie, Tom. MS. Song: solo v., pf.

4940 Rogers, J.H. NY: GS, pre-1940. Song: [solo v., pf.?].

4941 Sabin, Wallace. NY: GS, pre-1929. Song: med. v., pf.

4942 Treharne, Bryceson. NY: CPMC, pre-1940. Song: [solo
      v., pf.?].

Seal Man, The* Manchester Guardian (Apr. 1907), rev. 1913

4943 Clarke, Rebecca. MS pre-1927, L: WR. Song: [v.,
      pf.?].

Seekers, The "Friends and loves we have none" Ballads
(1903)

4944 Dyson, George. Three Songs of Courage, L: N, 1935.
      Song: satb, stgs. with opt. tpt., trbn., timp.
      or satb, stgs. with opt. pf. or org. Also publ.
      L: EA, 1935 for unison v., stgs. with opt. tpt.,
      trbn., timp. or unison v., stgs. with opt. pf.
      or org.

4945 Slater, Gordon. L: OUP, 1929. Song: b solo, [pf.].

Sorrow o' Mydath "Weary the cry of the wind is" Speaker
(Feb. 1902)

4946 Alison-Crompton, C. L: BH, pre-1940. Song: [solo v.,
      pf.].

4947 Davidson, Malcolm. L: WR, pre-1940. Song: [v.,
      pf.?].

4948 Griffes, Charles T. Two Poems by John Masefield,
      NY: GS, 1920. Song: solo v., pf.

Masefield, John continued

4949 Miles, Philip. MS pre-1935. Song: [v., pf.?].

4950 Ward, Robert. NY: Peer, 1952. Song: [high] solo v.,
       pf.

St. Mary's Bells   "It's pleasant in Holy Mary"   <u>Ballads</u>
 (1903)

4951 Ireland, John. "The Bells of San Marie", L: A, 1919.
       Song: med. v., pf.

4952 Jackson, Francis A. L: OUP, 1950. Song: ssa,
       [a cap.].

4953 Martin, Easthope. <u>Five Poems by John Masefield</u>, L:
       E, 1919. Song: med. v., pf.

4954 Roberton, Hugh. L: RP, 1942. Setting for mixed
       choir, a cap. Also avail. for male choir, a cap.

4955 Sykes, Harold. L: EA, pre-1951. Song: unison v., pf.

Tewkesbury Road   "It is good to be out on the road"
 <u>Salt-Water Ballads</u> (1902)

4956 Brown, James. MS. Song: s or t solo, pf.

4957 Hand, Colin. L: Elkin, 1963. Song: unison v., pf.

4958 Head, Michael. L: BH, 1924. Song: bar solo, pf.

4959 Thiman, Eric. <u>Songs of England</u>, L: N, 1944. Song:
       satb, dbl. ww., 2 hn., 2 tpt., 2 trbn., timp.,
       perc., stgs. Arr. for ssa publ. L: N, 1961.

Theodore   "They sacked the ships of London town"   <u>Broad
 Sheet</u> (July 1905)

4960 Berners, Gerald. "Theodore, or The Pirate King",
       <u>Three Songs</u>, L: JWC, 1922. Song: med. v., pf.

There's a Wind a-Blowing   "It's a warm wind, the west wind"
 <u>Speaker</u> (June 1902), rev. same year

Masefield, John continued

4961 Alison-Crompton, C. "The West Wind", L: BH, 1918.
Song: solo v., pf.

4962 Cooper, Walter Gaze. "Symphony No. 4:'The West
Wind'", MS (Opus 41). Symph.: s solo, satb (hum-
ming), orch.

4963 Cundick, Robert. "The West Wind", L: BH, 1964. Song:
ttbb, pf.

4964 Mitchell, Raymond E. "The White Road Westward", NY:
HZ, pre-1940. Song: [solo v., pf.?].

4965 Redman, Reginald. "The West Wind", L: OUP, 1937.
Song: ssa, a cap.

4966 Rootham, C.B. "The West Wind", L: Curwen, 1923.
Song: solo v., pf. Also avail. for solo v.,

4967 Stewart, D.M. "The West Wind", L: A, pre-1940. Song:
solo v., pf.

Third Mate   "All the sheets are clacking"   Ballads and
Poems (1910)

4968 Hickey, Vivian. L: A, pre-1940. Song: [v., pf.?].

To an Old Tune   "Twilight it is, and the far woods are dim"
Speaker (Dec. 1905), rev. 1910

4969 Alison-Crompton, C. "Twilight", L: BH, 1919. Song:
solo v., pf.

4970 Dobson, Tom. "Twilight", NY: GS, 1920. Song: high
v., pf.

4971 Marples, Ann. "Twilight", L: C, 1931. Song: [solo
v., pf.].

4972 Moeran, E.J. "Twilight", L: PX, 1936. Song: s or t
solo, pf. Also arr. for med. v., pf.

4973 Moule-Evans, David. "Twilight", Three Songs, L: JW,
ca. 1951. Song: med. v., pf.

Masefield, John continued

To-Morrow   "Oh, yesterday the cutting edge drank thirstily"
    Salt-Water Ballads (1902)

    4974 Keel, Frederick. L: C, 1918. Song: solo v., pf.

Trade Winds   "In the harbour, in the island"   Outlook
    (Oct. 1901)

    4975 Keel, Frederick. Three "Salt-Water Ballads", 1st
              set, L: BH, 1919. Song: v., pf. Also publ. sep.

    4976 Lewis, Samuel R. NY: GS, pre-1940. Song: [v., pf.?].

    4977 Ritchie, Tom. MS. Song: solo v., pf.

Tragedy of Pompey the Great, The   (DR)   (1910) Portions
    were publ. in collected edns. under individual titles

    4978 Whittaker, W.G. "The Chief Centurion", L: OUP, pre-
              1940. Song: [v., pf.?]. [Setting of lines begin-
              ning: "Man is a sacred city, built of marvelous
              earth"?].

Twilight   See: To an Old Tune

Vagabond   "Dunno a heap about the what an' why"   Outlook
    (Feb. 1902)

    4979 Clarke, Robert C. Songs of a Rover, L: C, 1919.
              Song: solo v., pf.

    4980 Ireland, John. L: A, 1922. Song: med. v., pf.

Valediction, A   "We're bound for blue water"   Salt-Water
    Ballads (1902)

    4981 Barnes, Marshall. Salt Water Ballads, MS. Song:
              satb, orch. or satb, ensemble of 13 players (ww.,
              br., perc.).

Wanderer's Song, A   See: Wind's in the Heart o' Me, A

Masefield, John continued

West Wind, The   See: There's a Wind a-Blowing

Widow in the Bye Street, The   "Down Bye street, in a little
    Shropshire town" English Review (Feb. 1912), publ. sep.
    same year

    4982 Homer, Sidney. MS (Opus 39), NY: GS. Songs: med. v.,
                pf. Settings of 3 excerpts from Masefield's work.

Wild Duck, The   See: Coming into Salcombe

Wind's in the Heart o'Me, A   "Wind's in the heart of me, a
    fire's in my heels, A" Speaker (July 1902), rev. same
    year

    4983 Hewitt-Jones, Tony. "A Wanderer's Song", Seven Sea
                Poems, L: N, 1958. Choral ste.: a or bar or b
                solo, stgs. The complete ste. also requires obbl.
                for ob., eng. hn.

    4984 Keel, Frederick. "A Wanderer's Song", Four "Salt-
                Water Ballads", 2nd set, L: BH. Cyc.: v., pf.

    4985 Rasbach, Oscar. "A Wanderer's Song", NY: GS, 1927.
                Song: high or med. v., pf.

Miscellanea

    4986 Bax, Arnold. "To Russia", MS 1944. Setting for bar
                solo, chorus, orch.

    4987 Branson, David. Grove's cites five settings of works
                by Masefield composed 1947-48.

    4988 Davies, H. Walford. "A Prayer for King and Country",
                L: BH. Setting for unison v., chorus of male v.
                ad lib.

    4989 Elgar, Edward. "So many true princesses who have
                gone", MS 1932. Ode for chorus, perf. June 1932
                for the unveiling of the memorial to Queen Alex-
                andra, Marlborough House.

Masefield, John continued

4990   Elliott, Zo. "British Eighth March", NY: CF, 1944.
        Setting for v., pf. The work also requires pf.
        solo. Text begins: "When the cruel war is done".

4991   Fordham, Corysande. "I Saw a Star Tonight", L: C.
        Song: solo v., pf.

4992   Gibbs, C. Armstrong. "By a Bier-side (This is a
        sacred city)", L: Curwen, 1924.

4993   Greaves, Ralph. "I will go look for death", L: OUP,
        pre-1940. Song: [v., pf.].

4994   Greaves, Ralph. "Once, very long ago", L: OUP, 1925.
        Song: v., pf.

4995   Greaves, Ralph. "Song of Ronin", L: OUP, pre-1940.
        Song: [v., pf.].

4996   Greaves, Ralph. "Yellow Wine", MS ca. 1926. [Song:
        v., pf.].

4997   Gurney, Ivor. "By a Bierside", MS 1916. Song: [solo
        v., pf.].

4998   Kodály, Zoltán. "I will go look for death", L: BH,
        1959. Song: satb, a cap. Text transl. by Melinda
        Kistétényi.

4999   May, Frederick. Four Romantic Songs, MS pre-1968.
        Song: v., instruments. Incl. text by Masefield.

5000   Scull, [?]. "Sea Fever", Glasgow: PT. Song: unison
        v., pf. [Text by Masefield?]

5001   Shaw, Martin. "Arise in Us", L: N, 1931. Anthem:
        satb, org.

5002   Shaw, Martin. "O Christ who holds the open gate", L:
        N, 1934. Song: [v., pf.].

5003   Shaw, Martin. The Seaport and her Sailors, L: CR,
        1931. Cta.: satb, org.

Masefield, John continued

    5004   Walton, William. "Where does the uttered music go?",
            L: OUP, 1947. Setting for satb, a cap. of Mase-
            field's poem entitled "Sir Henry Wood"
            (specifically written for the Apr. 1946 unveiling
            of the Memorial Window in St. Sepulchre's Church,
            Holborn, London).

    5005   Warren, Elinor R. "Lonely Roads", NY: GX, ca. 1937.
            Song: [v., pf.?].

    5006   Weigl, Karl. "Hymne", Two Religious Choruses, NY:
            AMP, 1953; copyright subsequently reassigned to
            Mrs. Vally Weigl. Setting for satb, a cap.

    5007   Wilson, Stanley. "Tewkesbury Road", L: S&B, pre-
            1967. Song: ttbb, a cap. [Text by Masefield?]

MAUGHAM, William Somerset   1874-1965

Cakes and Ale (NV)   Harper's Bazaar (Mar.-July 1930),
   publ. sep. same year

    5008   Kubik, Gail. "Like a clear, deep pole", Songs about
            Women, NY: SMP, 1951. Song: [med.] solo v., pf.
            Setting of lines beginning: "You see, she wasn't
            a woman, who ever inspired love".

East of Suez (DR) (1922)

    5009   Goossens, Eugene. MS (Opus 33), prod. London, Sept.
            1922. Incidental music. "Suite from the Inciden-
            tal Music to East of Suez" publ. L: JWC, 1922.

Miss Thompson   See: Rain

Moon and Sixpence, The (NV) (1919)

5010* Gardner, John L. MS 1953-57. Opera: soli, chorus, orch. Libr. by Patrick Terry. An aria (for b solo, orch.) entitled "It's this island" is avail. L: OUP (hire).

Of Human Bondage   (NV)   (1915)

5011 Goodwin, Ron. MS ca. 1964. Film music. Issued 1964 on MGM recording #E-4261.

5012 Korngold, Erich. MS, prod. Warner Bros. 1946. Film music. Orchn. arr. by Hugo Friedhofer.

5013 Steiner, Max. MS, prod. RKO-Radio 1934. Film music.

Rain   (SS)   The Trembling of a Leaf (1921), rev. 1938. Adapt. for stage by John Colton and Clemence Randolf; publ. sep. in this form 1923

5014 Arapov, Boris. "The Rains", prod. Leningrad 1968. Opera. Based on the short story.

5015 Duke, Vernon. "Sadie Thompson", MS, avail. NYPL; prod. NY, Nov. 1944. Musical. Text (by Howard Dietz and Rouben Mamoulian) based on the adapt. by John Colton and Clemence Randolf.

Razor's Edge, The   (NV)   Redbook (Dec. 1943-May 1944), publ. sep. 1944

5016 Newman, Alfred. MS, prod. 20th Century-Fox 1948. Film music.

Sadie Thompson   See: Rain

Miscellanea

Maugham, Somerset continued

5017   Jones, Robert W. "Love, Pure and Simple", MS. Set-
            ting for satb, a cap. Text begins: "...and these
            two young things, she was sixteen and he was
            twenty". The composer has indicated to the eds.
            that the form of this work is a "scena mad-
            rigal (a madrigal with interpolated spoken nar-
            rative and recitative)".

MCGOUGH, Roger   1937-

Aren't We All   "Look quite pretty lying there"   In The Mer-
      sey Sound, Penguin Modern Poets 10 (1967)

      5018   McCabe, John. This Town's a Corporation full of
               Crooked Streets, L: N, 1969 (hire). "An enter-
               tainment" for t solo, sp., mixed chorus, child-
               ren's choir, stgs., tpt., perc., keyboards.

Comeclose and Sleepnow   "it is afterwards"   In The Mersey
      Sound, Penguin Modern Poets 10 (1967)

      5019   McCabe, John. This Town's a Corporation full of
               Crooked Streets, L: N, 1969 (hire). "An enter-
               tainment" for t solo, sp., mixed chorus, child-
               ren's choir, stgs., tpt., perc., keyboards.

Square Dance, A   "In Flanders field in Northern France"   In
      The Mersey Sound, Penguin Modern Poets 10 (1967)

      5020   McCabe, John. This Town's a Corporation full of
               Crooked Streets, L: N, 1969 (hire). "An enter-
               tainment" for t solo, sp., mixed chorus, child-
               ren's choir, stgs., tpt., perc., keyboards.

Miscellanea

5021 McCabe, John. <u>This Town's a Corporation full of Crooked Streets</u>, L: N, 1969 (hire). "An entertainment" for t solo, sp., mixed chorus, children's choir, stgs., tpt., perc., keyboards. Incl. settings of McGough's poems beginning: "It all started yesterday evening", "Monika, the tea things are taking over", "ten milk bottles standing in the hall".

5022 McGear, Mike. <u>Grimms</u>, L: Chrysalis, 1972. Songs: [v., pf.]. Incl. 2 settings of poems by McGough: "Nuclear Band" ("I've got my three star general's helmet"), "Bored as Butterscotch" ("You're as bored as butterscotch").

MEREDITH, George   1828-1909

By Morning Twilight   "Night, like a dying mother"   <u>Modern Love</u> (1862)

5023 Roberts, Mervyn. L: N, 1949. Song: satb, a cap.

Dirge in Woods   "Wind sways the pines, A"   <u>Fortnightly Review</u> (Aug. 1870)

5024 Boyle, Ina. MS 1952-54. Song: ms solo, pf.

5025 Copland, Aaron. MS 1954, NY: BH. Song: v., pf.

5026 Duarte, John. <u>Five Quiet Songs</u>, Ancona: Bèrben, 1971. Cyc.: high v., classical gtr.

5027 Heussenstamm, George. NY: SMC, 1971. Song: ttbb, a cap.

5028 Jones, Robert W. MS. Song: high v., pf.

5029 Mayer, Max. L: C. Song: solo v., pf. German title: "Grablied Im Walde".

5030 Parry, C.H.H. English Lyrics, 8th Set, L: N, ca.
      1902-09. Song: v., pf.

5031 Roberts, Mervyn. MS pre-1972. Song: satb, a cap.

5032 Vaughan Thomas, David. L: Swan, ca. 1924. Song: [v.,
      pf.].

5033 Walker, Ernest. L: OUP, 1939 (L: N, 1952). Song:
      satb, a cap.

Lark Ascending, The "He rises and begins to round" Fortnightly Review (May 1881)

5034 McKay, George F. NY: LG, 1968. Song: satb, fl. or
      satb, pf. Setting of lines beginning: "For sing-
      ing till his heaven fills".

5035 Vaughan Williams, Ralph. MS 1914. Composition for
      vln., orch.

Love in the Valley "Under yonder beech-tree" Macmillan's
Magazine (Oct. 1878)

5036 Kernochan, Marshall. "Portrait", NY: GX, 1931. Song:
      low v., pf. Setting of stanza beginning: "Heart-
      less she is as the shadow in the meadows".

5037 Mack, Albert A. "Shy as the Squirrel", NY: GS, pre-
      1940. Song: [v., pf.]. [Setting of 2nd stanza
      only?]

5038 Parker, Kitty. L: A, 1921. Song: solo v., pf.

Lucifer in Starlight "On a starred night Prince Lucifer up-
rose" Poems and Lyrics of the Joy of Earth (1883)

5039 Bantock, Granville. L: N, 1911. Song: male chorus,
      a cap.

5040 Radcliffe, Philip. L: S&B, ca. 1957. Song: [v.,
      pf.?].

Marian "She can be as wise as we" Modern Love (1862)

Meredith, George continued

    5041   Parry, C.H.H. English Lyrics, 8th Set, L: N, ca.
            1902-09. Song: v., pf.

    5042   Schindler, Kurt. NY: GS, pre-1940. Song: [v., pf.].

Men and Man   "Men the Angels eyed"   Ballads and Poems of
    Tragic Life (1887)

    5043   Boughton, Rutland. "Man and Men", Six Songs of Man-
            hood, MS 1903. Song: v., pf.

Night of Frost in May   "With splendour of a silver day"
    The Empty Purse (1892)

    5044   Ives, Charles. NY: GS, 1921 (1922). Song: v., pf.
            Setting of last stanza only.

"Roar through the tall twin elm-trees, A"   Modern Love
    (1862)

    5045   Vaughan Thomas, David. "The Winter Rose", Five
            Meredith Songs, MS 1922. Song: [v., pf.].

Song   "Come to me in any shape!"   Poems (1851)

    5046   Kostelanetz, Andre. "Come to Me!", NY: CF, pre-1940.
            Song: [v., pf.].

Song   "I cannot lose thee for a day"   Poems (1851)

    5047   Herbert, Muriel. "I cannot...", L: Elkin, pre-1940.
            Song: [solo v., pf.].

Song   "Love within the lover's breast"   Poems (1851)

    5048   Converse, Frederick. "Love within...", L: Elkin,
            pre-1940. Song: [v., pf.].

Song   "Thou to me art such a spring"   Poems (1851)

562

5049   Maconchy, Elizabeth. "The Arab", MS ca. 1935. Song:
       [solo v., pf.].

5050   Roberts, Mervyn. "Thou...", L: N, 1951. Song: satb,
       a cap.

5051   Vaughan Thomas, David. "Thou...", Five Meredith
       Songs, MS 1922. Song: [v., pf.].

Song in the Songless   "They have no song, the sedges dry"
A Reading of Life (1901)

5052   Clark, Harold. L: Elkin, 1963. Song: high v., pf.

5053   Plumstead, Mary. Two Songs, L: JWC, 1953. Song: med.
       v., pf.

5054   Talma, Louise. MS 1928. Song: s solo, pf.

5055   Vaughan Thomas, David. Five Meredith Songs, MS 1922.
       Song: [v., pf.].

Stave of Roving Tim, A   "Wind is East, the Wind is West,
The"   Reflector (Feb. 1888)

5056   Shaw, Martin. L: Curwen, 1919. Song: solo v., pf.

5057   Vaughan Thomas, David. "A Stave of Roving Tim", Five
       Meredith Songs, MS 1922. Song: [v., pf.].

Sweet o' the Year, The   "Now the frog, all lean and weak"
Fraser's Magazine (June 1852)

5058   Shaw, Martin. L: OUP, 1954. Song: sa, a cap. or tb,
       a cap.

To a Skylark   "O Skylark! I see thee and call thee joy!"
Poems (1851)

5059   Roberts, Mervyn. L: N, 1950. Song: ttbb, a cap.

Violets   "Violets, shy violets!"   Poems (1851)

Meredith, George continued

5060 Herbert, Muriel. L: Elkin, pre-1940. Song: [v., pf.].

5061 Roberts, Mervyn. L: N, 1950. Song: satb, a cap.

When I would Image   "When I would image her features"
Modern Love (1862)

5062 Vaughan Thomas, David. "When...", Five Meredith Songs, MS 1922. Song: [v., pf.].

Wind on the Lyre   "That was the chirp of Ariel"   Anti-Jacobin (Dec. 1891)

5063 Roberts, Mervyn. "The Wind on the Lyre", MS pre-1972. Song: s solo, satb, a cap.

Woods of Westermain, The   "Enter these enchanted woods"
Poems and Lyrics of the Joy of Earth (1883)

5064 Elwyn-Edwards, Dilys. "Enter...", MS pre-1972. Song: st, pf.

5065 Vaughan Thomas, David. "Enter...", L: Swan, ca. 1923. Song: [v., pf.].

Miscellanea

5066 Allitsen, Frances. "Whether We Die or Live", MS pre-1912, NY: GS.

5067 Holst, Gustav. The Nov. 1950 issue of Monthly Musical Record incl. an article by Robin Gregory entitled "The Uncompleted". Gregory indicates that in Holst's library "there existed a well-marked copy of Meredith's poems, and that apparently these were to form the basis of his 'Second Choral Symphony'".

5068 Mayer, Max. "Song of Cuchulain's Enchantment", L: C. Song: [v., pf.].

5069 Moir, F.L. "Blue is the Sky, Blue is Thine Eye", L: JW, pre-1940. Song: [solo v., pf.?].

eredith, George continued

5070 O'Neill, Norman. "The Rossetti Scene", MS, perf.
      London ca. 1914-18. Incidental music to a script
      by Monckton Hoffe. In Norman O'Neill: A Life of
      Music (L: Quality Press, 1945), Derek Hudson
      indicates that the work "...was a short sketch...
      in which the ghosts of Rossetti, Meredith, Mor-
      ris, Carlyle and others, met at midnight in a
      Chelsea garden".

5071 Parker, Kitty. "Love in the Valley", L: A, pre-1940.
      Song: [v., pf.].

5072 Scott, Cyril. "Love's Quarrel", L: Elkin, pre-1940.
      Song: [v., pf.?].

5073 Thomson, Bothwell. "The First Farewell", L: C. Song:
      solo v., pf.

EYNELL, Alice Christina   1847-1922

Advent Meditation   See: Meditation

At Night   "Home, home from the horizon"   In Other Poems
(1896)

5074 Bairstow, Edward. Two Songs, L: S&B, pre-1940. Song:
      [v., pf.?].

5075 Brown, Gwyneth L. MS 1962, avail. Victoria Univer-
      sity of Wellington. Song: med. v., pf.

5076 Hart, Fritz. Book of Five Songs, MS 1938, avail.
      State Library of Victoria, Melbourne. Song: solo
      v., pf.

5077 Hickey, Vivian. L: A, pre-1940. Song: [v., pf.?].

5078 Johnstone, Maurice. Two Songs, L: OUP, 1944. Song:
      v., pf.

Meynell, Alice continued

5079   Lovering, Mabel. L: OUP, 1931. Canon: 2 pt. chorus,
        [pf.].

5080   Treharne, Bryceson. NY: GS, pre-1940. Song: [v.,
        pf.?].

Chimes   "Brief, on a flying night"   In Later Poems (1902)

5081   Hand, Colin. Carillons, L: N, 1970. Setting for
        treble v. choir, speakers, recs., pf., perc.,
        stgs.

5082   Hart, Fritz. Book of Five Songs, MS 1938, avail.
        State Library of Victoria, Melbourne. Song: solo
        v., pf.

5083   Meachen, Margaret. L: OUP, pre-1940. Song: [v.,
        pf.?].

5084   Rawlinson, Bertha. L: C, 1963. Song: solo v., pf.

5085   Sykes, Harold. L: Curwen, 1967. Canon: ss, pf.

Christ in the Universe   "With this ambiguous earth"   In
    Collected Poems of Alice Meynell (1913)

5086   Davies, H. Walford. MS ca. 1929. Setting for s, t
        soli, chorus, orch.

5087   Douglas, James. Light Shining Out of Darkness, MS
        1966, avail. SMA. Song: med. v., vcl.

Garden, The   See: Sonnet "My heart shall be..."

Joyous Wanderer, The   "I go by road, I go by street"   In
    Collected Poems of Alice Meynell (1913) Transl. from M.
    Catulle Mendès

5088   Horsman, Edward. NY: GS, pre-1940. Song: [solo v.,
        pf.?].

Lover Urges the Better Thrift, The   See: Song

eynell, Alice continued

Meditation "No sudden thing of glory and fear" In
Preludes (1875 [publ. under her maiden name of A.C. Thomp-
son]), rev. 1913

    5089 Ireland, John. "The Advent", Songs Sacred and Pro-
fane, L: S, 1934. Cyc.: solo v., pf.

October Redbreast, The "Autumn is weary, halt, and old"
In The Last Poems of Alice Meynell (1923)

    5090 Hart, Fritz. Five Part Songs for Women's Unac-
companied Three-Part Choir, MS 1935. Song: 3 pt.
choir of female v., a cap.

Renouncement "I must not think of thee" In Poems (1893)

    5091 Elwell, Herbert. NY: GS, pre-1940. Song: med. v.,
pf.

    5092 Herbert, Muriel. L: A, pre-1940. Song: [solo v.,
pf.].

    5093 Lohr, Hermann. Two Sonnets, L: C, 1917. Song: [solo
v., pf.].

    5094 Treharne, Bryceson. NY: JF, pre-1940. Song: [solo
v., pf.?].

Roaring Frost, The "Flock of winds came winging from the
North, A" In Later Poems (1902)

    5095 Milhaud, Darius. Trois Poèmes, MS ca. 1916. Song:
[v., pf.?].

Shepherdess, The "She walks--the lady of my delight" In
Later Poems (1902)

    5096 Atkins, Ivor. L: A, ca. 1922. Song: [solo v., pf.].

    5097 Avery, Stanley. NY: GS, pre-1929. Song: [high] solo
v., pf.

    5098 Bleadon, Alice. Two Songs, L: S&B, pre-1940. Song:
[solo v., pf.?].

Meynell, Alice continued

5099   Cook, Greville. L: S&B, pre-1940. Song: [solo v.,
        pf.?].

5100   Galway, Victor. "The Shepherdess of Sheep", L: OUP,
        1937. Song: satb, a cap.

5101   Horsman, Edward. NY: GS, pre-1929. Song: high v.,
        pf. Also avail. for low v., pf.

5102   Hunt, Wynn. MS. Song: satb, pf.

5103   MacMurrough, Dermot. L: E, 1924. Song: v., pf.

5104   Robbins, Reginald. P: MST, ca. 1922. Song: b solo,
        [pf.]. Also suitable for a (or bar) solo, [pf.].

5105   Roberton, Hugh. L: Curwen, 1917. Song: ssa, a cap.

5106   Salter, Lionel. L: OUP, 1947. Song: t solo, pf. Also
        avail. for t solo, orch.

5107   Smith, David S. "The Lady of the Lambs", NY: GX,
        pre-1940. Song: [solo v., pf.?].

5108   Treharne, Bryceson. "The Lady of My Delight", NY:
        GS, pre-1940. Song: [solo v., pf.?].

5109   Watts, Harold E. York: Banks, 1938. Song: ss, pf. or
        sa, pf.

Song   "My Fair, no beauty of thine will last"   In Preludes
        (1875 [publ. under her maiden name of A.C. Thompson]),
        rev. 1913

5110   Ireland, John. "My Fair", Songs Sacred and Profane,
        L: S, 1934. Cyc.: solo v., pf.

Sonnet   "My heart shall be thy garden. Come, my own"   In
        Preludes (1875 [publ. under her maiden name of A.C. Thomp-
        son]), rev. 1913

5111   Lohr, Hermann. "My Heart Shall Be Thy Garden", Two
        Sonnets, L: C, 1917. Song: [solo v., pf.].

568

Sonnet "Who knows what days I answer for to-day?" In
Preludes (1875 [publ. under her maiden name of A.C. Thomp-
son]), rev. 1913

5112 White, Felix. "The Neophyte", L: G&T, 1921. Song:
solo v., pf.

Unto Us a Son is Given   "Given, not lent"   In Later Poems
(1902)

5113 George, Graham. L: OUP, 1945. Song: satb, a cap.

5114 Taylor, Albert. York: Banks, 1958. Carol: satb, pf.
or satb, org.

Wind is Blind, The   "Wind is blind, The"   In The Last Poems
of Alice Meynell (1923)

5115 Galloway, The Countess of. L: MM, 1927, assigned L:
C, 1943. Song: solo v., pf.

Young Neophyte, The   See: Sonnet "Who knows what days..."

Miscellanea

5116 Bruce, Margaret C. "The Shepherdess", L: N, 1952.
Song: t solo, pf. Also publ. for unison v., pf.
[Text by Meynell?]

5117 Elwell, Herbert. Three Songs for Orchestra, 1st
perf. (employing texts) ca. Dec. 1944. Songs: v.,
orch. Also arr. for v., pf. One song employs a
text by Meynell.

5118 Gover, Gerald. The Feb. 1956 issue of Musical Times
reports a concert of 3 songs for a solo, incl.
words by Meynell.

569

Middleton, Christopher

MIDDLETON, Christopher   1926-

Pointed Boots   "At three in the morning"   In _Torse 3_ (1962)

   5119 Orton, Richard. _Four Partsongs_, Grt. Y.: G, 1970.
      Song: satb, a cap.

Miscellanea

   5120 Britten, Benjamin. "Blurt, Master Constable", _Noc-_
      turne, L: BH, 1959. Cyc.: t solo, str. orch., hn.
      obbl. Complete work also requires fl., cl., bsn.,
      eng. hn., hp., timp. (all obbl.).

MILNE, Alan Alexander   1882-1956

Alchemist, The   "There lives an old man at the top of the
   street"   _When We Were Very Young_ (1924)

   5121 Fraser-Simson, Harold. _Teddy Bear and Other Songs_,
      NY: DT, 1926. Song: v., pf.

At the Zoo   "There are lions and roaring tigers"   _When We_
   Were Very Young (1924)

   5122 Fraser-Simson, Harold. _Teddy Bear and Other Songs_,
      NY: DT, 1926. Song: v., pf.

Bad Sir Brian Botany   "Sir Brian had a battleaxe"   _When We_
   Were Very Young (1924)

   5123 Davies, H. Walford. _Bad Sir Brian Botany, and Other_
      Rhymes, L: N, 1939. Song: satb, pf.

   5124 Fraser-Simson, Harold. _Teddy Bear and Other Songs_,
      NY: DT, 1926. Song: v., pf.

Before Tea   "Emmeline"   When_We_Were_Very_Young (1924)

    5125 Fraser-Simson, Harold. Teddy_Bear_and_Other_Songs,
          NY: DT, 1926. Song: v., pf.

Binker   "Binker--what I call him--is a secret of my own"
    Now_We_Are_Six (1927)

    5126 Fraser-Simson, Harold. More_"Very_Young"_Songs, NY:
          DT, 1929. Song: v., pf.

Brownie   "In a corner of the bedroom is a great big cur-
    tain"   When_We_Were_Very_Young (1924)

    5127 Fraser-Simson, Harold. Fourteen_Songs_from_"When_We
          Were_Very_Young", NY: DT, 1925. Song: v., pf.

Buckingham Palace   "They're changing guard at Buckingham
    Palace"   When_We_Were_Very_Young (1924)

    5128 Fraser-Simson, Harold. Fourteen_Songs_from_"When_We
          Were_Very_Young", NY: DT, 1925. Song: v., pf.

Cherry Stones   "Tinker, Tailor,/Soldier, Sailor"   Now_We
    Are_Six (1927)

    5129 Fraser-Simson, Harold. Songs_from_"Now_We_Are_Six",
          NY: DT, 1927. Song: v., pf.

Christening, The   "What shall I call"   When_We_Were_Very
    Young (1924)

    5130 Davies, H. Walford. Bad_Sir_Brian_Botany,_and_Other
          Rhymes, L: N, 1939. Song: satb, pf.

    5131 Fraser-Simson, Harold. Fourteen_Songs_from_"When_We
          Were_Very_Young", NY: DT, 1925. Song: v., pf.

Cradle Song   "O Timothy Tim"   Now_We_Are_Six (1927)

    5132 Fraser-Simson, Harold. Songs_from_"Now_We_Are_Six",
          NY: DT, 1927. Song: v., pf.

Milne, A.A. continued

Daffodowndilly   "She wore her yellow sun-bonnet"   When We
   Were Very Young (1924)

   5133   Clarke, Garry E. When We Were Very Young, MS. Cyc.:
          high v., pf.

   5134   Fraser-Simson, Harold. Teddy Bear and Other Songs,
          NY: DT, 1926. Song: v., pf.

Disobedience   "James James/Morrison Morrison"   When We Were
   Very Young (1924)

   5135   Davies, H. Walford. Bad Sir Brian Botany, and Other
          Rhymes, L: N, 1939. Song: satb, pf.

   5136   Fraser-Simson, Harold. Teddy Bear and Other Songs,
          NY: DT, 1926. Song: v., pf.

Down by the Pond   "I'm fishing"   Now We Are Six (1927)

   5137   Fraser-Simson, Harold. Songs from "Now We Are Six",
          NY: DT, 1927. Song: v., pf.

Emperor's Rhyme, The   "The King of Peru"   Now We Are Six
   (1927)

   5138   Fraser-Simson, Harold. Songs from "Now We Are Six",
          NY: DT, 1927. Song: v., pf.

End, The   "When I was One"   Now We Are Six (1927)

   5139   Fraser-Simson, Harold. More "Very Young" Songs, NY:
          DT, 1929. Song: v., pf.

Engineer, The   "Let it rain!"   Now We Are Six (1927)

   5140   Fraser-Simson, Harold. Songs from "Now We Are Six",
          NY: DT, 1927. Song: v., pf.

Forgiven   "I found a little beetle, so that Beetle was his
   name"   Now We Are Six (1927)

5141   Fraser-Simson, Harold. More "Very Young" Songs, NY:
       DT, 1929. Song: v., pf.

Four Friends, The   "Ernest was an elephant"   When We Were
Very Young (1924)

5142   Fraser-Simson, Harold. Teddy Bear and Other Songs,
       NY: DT, 1926. Song: v., pf.

Friend, The   "There are lots and lots of people who are
always asking things"   Now We Are Six (1927)

5143   Fraser-Simson, Harold. Songs from "Now We Are Six",
       NY: DT, 1927. Song: v., pf.

Furry Bear   "If I were a bear"   Now We Are Six (1927)

5144   Fraser-Simson, Harold. Songs from "Now We Are Six",
       NY: DT, 1927. Song: v., pf.

Growing Up   "I've got shoes with grown up laces"   When We
Were Very Young (1924)

5145   Fraser-Simson, Harold. Fourteen Songs from "When We
       Were Very Young", NY: DT, 1925. Song: v., pf.

Halfway Down   "Halfway down the stairs"   When We Were Very
Young (1924)

5146   Clarke, Garry E. When We Were Very Young, MS. Cyc.:
       high v., pf.

5147   Fraser-Simson, Harold. Fourteen Songs from "When We
       Were Very Young", NY: DT, 1925. Song: v., pf.

Happiness   "John had/Great Big Waterproof/Boots on"   When
We Were Very Young (1924)

5148   Fraser-Simson, Harold. Fourteen Songs from "When We
       Were Very Young", NY: DT, 1925. Song: v., pf.

573

Milne, A.A. continued

Hoppity   "Christopher Robin goes/Hoppity, hoppity"   When We
    Were Very Young (1924)

    5149   Fraser-Simson, Harold. Fourteen Songs from "When We
           Were Very Young", NY: DT, 1925. Song: v., pf.

    5150   Scherman, Thomas. NY: HB, 1928 in New Songs for New
           Voices. Song: v., pf.

House at Pooh Corner, The   (NV)   (1928)

    5151   Fraser-Simson, Harold. Hums of Pooh, NY: DT, 1930.
           Song: v., pf. Settings (from The House at Pooh
           Corner) entitled: "Christopher Robin is going",
           "Here lies a tree", "I could spend a happy morn-
           ing", "I lay on my chest", "If Rabbit was big-
           ger", "The more it snows", "Oh, the butterflies
           are flying", "This warm and sunny Spot", "What
           shall we do about poor little Tigger".

If I Were King   "I often wish I were a King"   When We Were
    Very Young (1924)

    5152   Clarke, Garry E. When We Were Very Young, MS. Cyc.:
           high v., pf.

    5153   Fraser-Simson, Harold. Teddy Bear and Other Songs,
           NY: DT, 1926. Song: v., pf.

In the Dark   "I've had my supper"   Now We Are Six (1927)

    5154   Fraser-Simson, Harold. More "Very Young" Songs, NY:
           DT, 1929. Song: v., pf.

In the Fashion   "Lion has a tail and a very fine tail, A"
    When We Were Very Young (1924)

    5155   Fraser-Simson, Harold. Fourteen Songs from "When We
           Were Very Young", NY: DT, 1925. Song: v., pf.

Independence   "I never did, I never did"   When We Were Very
    Young (1924)

ilne, A.A. continued

5156 Fraser-Simson, Harold. Teddy Bear and Other Songs, NY: DT, 1926. Song: v., pf.

Invaders, The   "In careless patches through the wood"   When We Were Very Young (1924)

5157 Clarke, Garry E. When We Were Very Young, MS. Cyc.: high v., pf.

Ivory Door, The   (DR)   (1929)

5158 O'Neill, Norman. MS 1929. Incidental music.

Jonathan Jo   "Jonathan Jo"   When We Were Very Young (1924)

5159 Fraser-Simson, Harold. Teddy Bear and Other Songs, NY: DT, 1926. Song: v., pf.

King's Breakfast, The   "King asked, The"   When We Were Very Young (1924)

5160 Fraser-Simson, Harold. NY: DT, 1925. Song: v., pf.

Knights and Ladies   "There is in my old picture-book"   When We Were Very Young (1924)

5161 Fraser-Simson, Harold. More "Very Young" Songs, NY: DT, 1929. Song: v., pf.

Lines and Squares   "Whenever I walk in a London street"   When We Were Very Young (1924)

5162 Fraser-Simson, Harold. Fourteen Songs from "When We Were Very Young", NY: DT, 1925. Song: v., pf.

Market Square   "I had a penny"   When We Were Very Young (1924)

5163 Fraser-Simson, Harold. Fourteen Songs from "When We Were Very Young", NY: DT, 1925. Song: v., pf.

575

Milne, A.A. continued

Mirror, The   "Between the woods the afternoon"   When We
    Were Very Young (1924)

    5164 Clarke, Garry E. When We Were Very Young, MS. Cyc.:
          high v., pf.

    5165 Davies, H. Walford. Bad Sir Brian Botany, and Other
          Rhymes, L: N, 1939. Song: satb, pf.

    5166 Mason, Daniel G. MS pre-1946, priv. publ. Song:
          ss, pf.

Missing   "Has anybody seen my mouse?"   When We Were Very
    Young (1924)

    5167 Fraser-Simson, Harold. Fourteen Songs from "When We
          Were Very Young", NY: DT, 1925. Songs v., pf.

Nursery Chairs   "One of the chairs is South America"   When
    We Were Very Young (1924)

    5168 Fraser-Simson, Harold. More "Very Young" Songs, NY:
          DT, 1929. Song: v., pf.

Politeness   "If people ask me"   When We Were Very Young
    (1924)

    5169 Fraser-Simson, Harold. Fourteen Songs from "When We
          Were Very Young", NY: DT, 1925. Song: v., pf.

Puppy and I   "I met a man as I went walking"   When We Were
    Very Young (1924)

    5170 Fraser-Simson, Harold. Teddy Bear and Other Songs,
          NY: DT, 1926. Song: v., pf.

Rice Pudding   "What is the matter with Mary Jane?"   When We
    Were Very Young (1924)

    5171 Fraser-Simson, Harold. Teddy Bear and Other Songs,
          NY: DT, 1926. Song: v., pf.

Sand-Between-the-Toes   "I went down to the shouting sea"
    When We Were Very Young (1924)

    5172 Fraser-Simson, Harold. Teddy Bear and Other Songs,
          NY: DT, 1926. Song: v., pf.

Shoes and Stockings   "There's a cavern in the mountain where
    the old men meet"   When We Were Young (1924)

    5173 Fraser-Simson, Harold. More "Very Young" Songs, NY:
          DT, 1929. Song: v., pf.

Sneezles   "Christopher Robin/Had wheezles and sneezles"
    Now We Are Six (1927)

    5174 Fraser-Simson, Harold. Songs from "Now We Are Six",
          NY: DT, 1927. Song: v., pf.

Spring Morning   "Where am I going? I don't quite know"
    When We Were Very Young (1924)

    5175 Fraser-Simson, Harold. More "Very Young" Songs, NY:
          DT, 1929. Song: v., pf.

Success   (DR)   Four Plays (1926)

    5176 O'Neill, Norman. MS 1923. Incidental music.

Summer Afternoon   "Six brown cows walk down to drink"   When
    We Were Very Young (1924)

    5177 Worth, Amy. NY: GS, pre-1940. Song: [v., pf.].

Teddy Bear   "Bear, however hard he tries, A"   When We Were
    Very Young (1924)

    5178 Fraser-Simson, Harold. Teddy Bear and Other Songs,
          NY: DT, 1926. Song: v., pf.

Three Foxes, The   "Once upon a time there were three little
    foxes"   When We Were Very Young (1924)

Milne, A.A. continued

5179   Fraser-Simson, Harold. <u>Fourteen Songs from "When We Were Very Young"</u>, NY: DT, 1925. Song: v., pf.

<u>Toad of Toad Hall</u>   (DR)   (1929) Adapt. of Kenneth Grahame's <u>The Wind in the Willows</u>

5180   Fraser-Simson, Harold. L: C, 1930. Musical play.

Twice Times   "There were Two little Bears who lived in a Wood"   <u>Now We Are Six</u> (1927)

5181   Fraser-Simson, Harold. <u>Songs from "Now We Are Six"</u>, NY: DT, 1927. Song: v., pf.

Us Two   "Wherever I am"   <u>Now We Are Six</u> (1927)

5182   Fraser-Simson, Harold. <u>More "Very Young" Songs</u>, NY: DT, 1929. Song: v., pf.

Vespers   <u>"Little Boy kneels at the foot of the bed"</u>   <u>When We Were Very Young</u> (1924)

5183   Fraser-Simson, Harold. <u>Fourteen Songs from "When We Were Very Young"</u>, NY: DT, 1925. Song: v., pf.

Waiting at the Window   "These are my two drops of rain" <u>Now We Are Six</u> (1927)

5184   Fraser-Simson, Harold. <u>More "Very Young" Songs</u>, NY: DT, 1929. Song: v., pf.

Water-Lilies   "Where the water-lilies go"   <u>When We Were Very Young</u> (1924)

5185   Clarke, Garry E. <u>When We Were Very Young</u>, MS. Cyc.: high v., pf.

Wind on the Hill   "No one can tell me"   <u>Now We Are Six</u> (1927)

5186   Fraser-Simson, Harold. Songs from "Now We Are Six",
        NY: DT, 1927. Song: v., pf.

5187   Stoker, Richard. The World's Way, L: LD, 1969. Song:
        choir of unison v., pf.

Winnie-the-Pooh   (NV)   (1926)

5188   Fraser-Simson, Harold. MS, perf. London, Dec. 1971.
        Musical play. Text adapt. by Julian Slade.

5189   Fraser-Simson, Harold. Hums of Pooh, NY: DT, 1930.
        Song: v., pf. Settings (from Winnie-the-Pooh)
        entitled: "Cottleston Pie", "How sweet to be a
        cloud", "Isn't it funny", "Sing ho! for the life
        of a Bear", "They all went off to discover the
        Pole", "3 cheers for Pooh", "Lines written by a
        bear of very little brain", "It's very, very
        funny".

5190   Sherman, Richard M. in coll. with Robert B. Sherman.
        MS ca. 1965-68, released by Disneyland. Film
        music.

5191   Sherman, Robert B. in coll. with Richard M. Sherman.
        MS ca. 1965-68, released by Disneyland. Film
        music.

Miscellanea

5192   Fraser-Simson, Harold. "Feed-My-Cow", NY: DT, 1925.
        Song: v., pf.

5193   Fraser-Simson, Harold. Three Christopher Robin
        Songs, L: A. Songs: [v., pf.]. Settings entitled:
        "Christopher Robin Alone in the Dark",
        "Christopher Robin at Buckingham Palace",
        "Christopher Robin is Saying his Prayers".

5194   Mansfield, Purcell J. "Morag", L: PX, 1957. Song:
        unison v., pf.

Mitchell, Adrian

MITCHELL, Adrian   1932-

    Fifteen Million Plastic Bags   "I was walking in a government
        warehouse"   In Poems (1964)

        5195 Gardner, John L. MS 1965. Setting for t solo, gtr.

    Miscellanea

        5196 Bennett, Richard R. "The Ledge", L: Mills, 1963.
                Opera: s, t, bar soli, orch. Libr. by Mitchell.

MITCHISON, Naomi Margaret   1897-

    Corn King and his Spring Queen, The   (NV)   (1931)

        5197 Easdale, Brian. "The Corn King", MS ca. 1935. Opera.

MONRO, Harold   1879-1932

    Cat's Meat   "Ho, all you cats in all the street"   In
        Strange Meetings (1917)

        5198 Hand, Colin. L: Curwen, 1956. Canon: chorus of equal
                v., pf.

    Nightingale near the House, The   "Here is the soundless
        cypress"   In Real Property (1922)

        5199 Bainton, Edgar L. L: Curwen, 1920. Song: solo v.,
                pf.

5200 Coulthard, Jean. "The Nightingale", Two Night Songs, MS 1960, avail. CMC. Song: bar solo, str. qrt., pf.

Overheard on a Saltmarsh "Nymph, nymph, what are your beads?" In Children of Love (1914)

5201 Bissell, Keith. Tor.: ECK, 1970. Song: ms solo, fl., pf.

5202 Bruce, Margaret C. L: N, 1951. Song: satb, a cap.

5203 Hand, Colin. L: N, 1958. Song: ss, pf.

5204 Miles, Philip. MS pre-1935. Song: [v., pf.?].

5205 Oliver, Stephen. MS 1972, L: N. [Song: v., pf.?]

Silent Pool, The "I have discovered finally to-day" In Real Property (1922)

5206 Coulthard, Jean. Two Visionary Songs, MS 1963, avail. CMC. Song: s solo, fl., str. orch. Setting of pt. V only.

Solitude "When you have tidied all things for the night" In Strange Meetings (1917)

5207 Shepherd, Arthur. MS, avail. University of Utah. Song: v., pf.

Week-End "Train! The twelve o'clock for paradise, The" In Strange Meetings (1917)

5208 Wood, Ralph W. Two Sonnets, MS ca. 1945. Song: s solo, fl., ob., vln., vla., vcl.

Miscellanea

5209 Bush, Alan. Two Songs for Soprano Voice and Chamber Orchestra, MS 1925. Texts by Monro.

Monro, Harold continued

5210   Ireland, John. "Earth's Call", L: WR, 1918. Song: a
        solo, pf. [Setting of Monro's poem entitled
        "Earthliness"?]

MOORE, George   1852-1933

Diarmuid and Grania   (DR)   In coll. with W.B. Yeats   Dublin Magazine (Apr.-June 1951), publ. sep. same year
A portion was 1st publ. under the title "Spinning Song" in
Broad Sheet (Jan. 1920), although this song was not incl.
in the 1951 edn. of the play.

5211   Elgar, Edward. "Grania and Diarmid", MS 1901, L: N,
        1902. Incidental music, incl. a setting of "There
        are Seven that pull the Thread" ["Spinning
        Song"].

Esther Waters   (NV)   (1894)

5212   Jacob, Gordon. MS ca. 1948. Film music.

"Lilacs are in bloom, The"   Mayfair Magazine (May 1884)

5213   O'Neill, Norman. Five Rondels, MS 1907, L: Cary
        (Avison edn.). Song: med. v., pf.

5214   Tyson, Mildred L. NY: GS, 1934. Song: v., pf. Also
        publ. for 3 pt. chorus of female v.

Miscellanea

5215   Fothergill, Helen. "When faded are the chaplets
        woven of May", L: A, pre-1927. Song: [v., pf.].

5216   Mellers, Wilfrid H. A masque cited in Grove's has
        been withdrawn by the composer.

Moore, T. Sturge

MOORE, Thomas Sturge   1870-1944

Lullaby   "Laugh, laugh"   In Selected Poems (1934)

    5217 Moore, Timothy. "Night Song", L: Curwen, 1969. Song:
           sa, pf.

That Land   "Oh, would that I might live for ever"   in Medea
    and Lyrics (1904)

    5218 Jervis-Read, Harold. L: ASH, 1913. Song: satb, orch.

Wind's Work   "Kate rose up early as fresh as a lark"   In
    The Sea is Kind (1914)

    5219 Benjamin, Arthur. L: WR, 1936. Song: solo v., pf.

Miscellanea

    5220 Hindemith, Paul. "Echo", Nine English Songs, L: AMP,
           1944. Song: high or med. v., pf. Text by Thomas
           [Sturge?] Moore.

    5221 Miles, Philip. "Demeter", MS pre-1936. Opera.

    5222 Rubbra, Edmund. "Bee-Bee-Bei", MS 1933. Opera. Libr.
           by Moore, based on a story from the Arabian
           Nights.

MUIR, Edwin   1887-1959

All We   "All we who make"   The Voyage and Other Poems
    (1946)

    5223 Wood, Hugh. Three Choruses, L: UE, 1967. Song: satb,
           a cap.

Muir, Edwin continued

Annunciation, The   "Angel and the girl are met, The"   See:
From a Roman Bas-Relief

Bird, The   "Adventurous bird walking upon the air"   The
Narrow Place (1943)

    5224 Wood, Hugh. The Rider Victory, MS. Cyc.: high v.,
          pf. Issued on Argo recording #ZRG 750.

Christmas, The   See: Year's Christmas, The

Confirmation, The   "Yes, yours, my love"   The Narrow Place
(1943)

    5225 Wood, Hugh. The Rider Victory, MS. Cyc.: high v.,
          pf. Issued on Argo recording #ZRG 750.

Debtor, The   "I am debtor to all"   The Labyrinth (1949)

    5226 Hedges, Anthony. "I am debtor...", L: N, 1969.
          Anthem: unison v., org. or satb, org.

From a Roman Bas-Relief   "Angel and the girl are met, The"
Botteghe Oscure, VI (1950), rev. 1952

    5227 Harvey, Jonathan. "The Annunciation", L: S, 1967.
          Anthem: satb, org.

Grave of Prometheus, The   "No one comes here now"   Listener
(Jan. 1955)

    5228 Orr, Robin. Journeys and Places, MS 1970, avail.
          SMA. Cyc.: ms solo, 2 vln., vla., vcl., db. or
          ms solo, str. orch.

Late Wasp, The   "You that through all the dying summer"
Botteghe Oscure, V (1950)

    5229 Orr, Robin. Journeys and Places, MS 1970, avail.
          SMA. Cyc.: ms solo, 2 vln., vla., vcl., db. or
          ms solo, str. orch.

Muir, Edwin continued

Loss and Gain   "One foot in Eden still, I stand"   <u>Listener</u>
(May 1950), rev. 1956

    5230 Binkerd, Gordon. "One Foot in Eden", NY: BH, 1974.
Song: low v., pf.

Merlin   "O Merlin in your crystal cave"   <u>Spectator</u> (Sept.
1935)

    5231 Lewis, Anthony. MS 1944. Song: s solo, pf.

    5232 Scott, Francis G. MS 1940. Song: med v., pf.

One Foot in Eden   See: Loss and Gain

Rider Victory, The   "Rider Victory reins his horse, The"
<u>Horizon</u> (Dec. 1944)

    5233 Wood, Hugh. <u>The Rider Victory</u>, MS. Cyc.: high v.,
pf. Issued on Argo recording #ZRG 750.

Road, The   "There is a road that turning always"   <u>Journeys
and Places</u> (1937)

    5234 Orr, Robin. <u>Journeys and Places</u>, MS 1970, avail.
SMA. Cyc.: ms solo, 2 vln., vla., vcl., ib. or
ms solo, str. orch.

Song of Sorrow   "I do not want it so"   <u>Poetry Scotland</u>
(July 1946), rev. same year

    5235 Wood, Hugh. "Sorrow", <u>The Rider Victory</u>, MS. Cyc.:
high v., pf. Issued on Argo recording #ZRG 750.

Sorrow   See: Song of Sorrow

Threefold Place, The   See: Transmutation

Transmutation   "This is the place"   <u>Bookman</u> (Nov. 1929),
rev. 1937

Muir, Edwin continued

5236   Orr, Robin. "The Threefold Place", <u>Journeys and</u>
        <u>Places</u>, MS 1970, avail. SMA. Cyc.: ms solo, 2
        vln., vla., vcl., db. or ms solo, str. orch.

Year's Christmas, The   "Now Christmas comes"   <u>Observer</u>
   (Dec. 1952), rev. 1956

5237   Shaw, Christopher. MS, perf. Oct. 1962. Song: [v.,
        pf.?].

MUNRO, Hector Hugh   1870-1916

Background, The   (SS)   <u>The Chronicles of Clovis</u> (1911)

5238   Maw, Nicholas. "One-Man Show", L: BH, 1968. Opera.
        Libr. by Arthur Jacobs, based on an idea from
        the story.

Open Window, The   (SS)   <u>Beasts and Super-Beasts</u> (1914)

5239   Jones, Robert W. MS. Opera: s, a, t, b soli, pf.
        duet. Also avail. for s, a, t, b soli, ch. orch.
        (wind qnt., str. qrt., pf.).

NEWBOLT, Henry John   1862-1938

Admiral Death   "Boys, are ye calling a toast to-night?"
   In <u>The Island Race</u> (1898)

5240   Bantock, Granville. <u>Three Sea Songs</u>, L: JW, 1927.
        Song: ttbb, a cap. Arr. for t solo, pf. Arr.
        publ. sep. under the title "Admirals All", L: JW,
        1940.

5241 Gray, Alan. L: JW, pre-1940. Song: [v., pf.?].

5242 Pascal, Florian. "Hear What the Sea-Wind Saith",
      Eight Songs for Male Voice, L: JW, pre-1940.
      Song: male v., [pf.?].

Admirals All "Effingham, Grenville, Raleigh, Drake" In
Admirals All and Other Verses (1897)

5243 Lee, E. Markham. L: Curwen, n.d. Song: sa, [pf.].

Against Oblivion "Cities drowned in olden time" In Songs
of Memory and Hope (1909)

5244 Western, Joan. L: OUP, 1939. Song: satb, a cap.

Death of Admiral Blake, The "Laden with spoil of the
South" In The Island Race (1898)

5245 Phillips, Montague. L: C, 1913. Cta.: bar solo,
      chorus, orch.

Drake's Drum "Drake he's in his hammock an' a thousand mile
away" In Admirals All and Other Verses (1897)

5246 Bantock, Granville. Three Sea Songs, L: JW, 1927.
      Song: ttbb, a cap. Arr. for t solo, pf. Arr.
      publ. sep. L: JW, 1940.

5247 Chadwick, George W. MS pre-1931, B: OD. Song: [v.,
      pf.?].

5248 Coleridge-Taylor, Samuel. L: Curwen, 1906. Song: sa,
      [pf.].

5249 Farwell, Arthur. Newton Center: Wa-Wan, pre-1940.
      Song: [v., pf.?].

5250 Hedgcock, Walter. L: CR, 1891. Song: solo v., pf.
      Setting of lines beginning: "Drake he was a
      Devon man, an' ruled the Devon seas".

5251 Leonard, Lady Barrett. "Plymouth Hoe", L: N, pre-
      1940. Song: [v., pf.?].

587

Newbolt, Henry continued

5252 Stanford, C.V. <u>Songs of the Sea</u>, L: BH, 1904. Song:
      bar solo, ttbb, orch.

5253 Wheeler, J.R. L: LG&B, 1939. Song: solo v., pf.

5254 Wrightson, Herbert. NY: CF, 1924. Song: [med.] v.,
      pf.

Farewell "Mother, with unbowed head" In <u>Poems: New and
Old</u> (1912) as one of "Songs of the Fleet"

5255 Stanford, C.V. "Fare Well", <u>Songs of the Fleet</u>, L:
      S&B, 1910. Song: bar solo, mixed chorus, orch.

Fighting Téméraire, The "It was eight bells ringing" In
<u>Admirals All and Other Verses</u> (1897)

5256* Bantock, Granville. <u>Three Sea Songs</u>, L: JW, 1927.
      Song: ttbb, a cap. Arr. for t solo, pf. Arr.
      publ. sep. L: JW, 1940.

5257 Pascal, Florian. L: JW, pre-1940. Song: [v., pf.?].

Gavotte "Memories long in music sleeping" In <u>The Island
Race</u> (1898)

5258 Howells, Herbert. L: OUP, 1927. Song: s or t solo,
      pf.

Gay Gordons, The "Who's for the Gathering" In <u>The Island
Race</u> (1898)

5259 Lee, E. Markham. L: Curwen, 1909. Song: sa, [pf.].

Hawke "In seventeen hundred and fifty-nine" In <u>Admirals
All and Other Verses</u> (1897)

5260 Lloyd, Charles H. L: JW, pre-1940. Song: [v., pf.?].

He fell among thieves "'Ye have robbed,' said he" In <u>The
Island Race</u> (1898)

Newbolt, Henry continued

5261   Jones, John Owen. MS pre-1962, L: S&B. Song: chorus, orch.

Homeward Bound   "After the long labouring in the windy ways"
   In The Island Race (1908)

5262   Stanford, C.V. Songs of the Sea, L. BH, 1904. Song:
      bar solo, ttbb, orch.

Hope the Hornblower   "Hark ye, hark to the winding horn"
   In The Sailing of the Long-Ships and Other Poems (1902)

5263   Ireland, John. L: A, 1911. Song: solo v., pf.

King's Highway, The   "When moonlight flecks the cruiser's
   deck"   In Poems: New and Old (1919)

5264   Stanford, C.V. L: S&B, 1914. Song: v., pf.

Little Admiral, The   "Stand by to reckon up your battle-
   ships"   In Poems: New and Old (1912) as one of "Songs of
   the Fleet"

5265   Stanford, C.V. Songs of the Fleet, L: S&B, 1910.
      Song: bar solo, mixed chorus, orch.

Messmates   "He gave us all a good-bye cheerily"   In The
   Island Race (1898)

5266   Dear, James R. Songs of the Open Air, L: S&B, pre-
      1940. Song: [v., pf.?].

5267   Lohr, Hermann. L: C, pre-1940. Song: [v., pf.?].

5268   Squire, Hope. L: S&B, pre-1940. Song: [v., pf.?].

5269   Wier, Lilias. L: N, pre-1940. Song: [v., pf.?].

Middle Watch, The   "In a blue dusk the ship astern"   In
   Poems: New and Old (1912) as one of "Songs of the Fleet"

589

Newbolt, Henry continued

5270   Stanford, C.V. <u>Songs of the Fleet</u>, L: S&B, 1910.
       Song: bar solo, mixed chorus, orch.

Old Superb, The   "Wind was rising easterly, The"   In <u>The</u>
<u>Island Race</u> (1908)

   5271   Stanford, C.V. <u>Songs of the Sea</u>, L: BH, 1904. Song:
          bar solo, ttbb, orch.

Outward Bound   "Dear Earth, near Earth"   In <u>The Sailing of</u>
<u>the Long-Ships and Other Poems</u> (1902)

   5272   Stanford, C.V. <u>Songs of the Sea</u>, L: BH, 1904. Song:
          bar solo, ttbb, orch.

Rilloby-Rill   "Grasshoppers four a-fiddling went"   In
<u>Poems: New and Old</u> (1912)

   5273   Marillier, Christabel. L: Curwen, 1920. Song: solo
          v., pf.

   5274   Mitchell, Cyril J. L: OUP, 1947. Song: unison v.,
          pf.

Sailing at Dawn   "One by one the pale stars die before the
   day now"   In <u>Poems: New and Old</u> (1912) as one of "Songs
   of the Fleet"

   5275   Stanford, C.V. <u>Songs of the Fleet</u>, L: S&B, 1910.
          Song: bar solo, mixed chorus, orch.

Sailing of the Long-Ships, The   "They saw the cables
   loosened"   In <u>The Sailing of the Long-Ships and Other</u>
   <u>Poems</u> (1902)

   5276   Aylward, Florence. L: C, 1900. Song: solo v., pf.

Song of Exmoor, A   "Forest above and the Combe below, The"
   In <u>The Island Race</u> (1898)

   5277   Lloyd, Charles H. "Song of Exmoor", L: JW, pre-1940.
          Song: [v., pf.?].

Newbolt, Henry continued

Song of the Children in Paladore   "To Aladore, to Aladore"
    In Poems: New and Old (1919)

    5278 Bantock, Granville. L: Curwen, 1929. Song: ss,
          [pf.].

Song of the Sou'Wester, The   "Sun was lost in a leaden sky,
    The" In Poems: New and Old (1912) as one of "Songs of
    the Fleet"

    5279 Stanford, C.V. Songs of the Fleet, L: S&B, 1910.
          Song: bar solo, mixed chorus, orch.

Toy Band, The   "Dreary lay the long road" In Poems: New
    and Old (1919)

    5280 Paget, Richard. L: Curwen, 1925. Song: solo v., pf.

Victoria Regina   "Thousand years by sea and land, A"   In
    Collected Poems 1897-1907 (1910)

    5281* Lloyd, Charles H. MS ca. 1897. Song: [v., pf.?].

Vigil, The   "England! where the sacred flame" In The
    Island Race (1898)

    5282 Lloyd, Charles H. "Vigil", L: JW, pre-1940. Song:
          [v., pf.?].

Vitaï Lampada   "There's a breathless hush in the Close
    to-night" In Admirals All and Other Verses (1897)

    5283 Aylward, Florence. "Play the Game", L: C, ca. 1900.
          Song: solo v., pf.

Waggon Hill   "Drake in the North Sea grimly prowling"   In
    The Sailing of the Long-Ships and Other Poems (1902)

    5284 Stanford, C.V. "Devon, O Devon", Songs of the Sea,
          L: BH, 1904. Song: bar solo, ttbb, orch.

Newbolt, Henry continued

Miscellanea

5285   Anon. An anon. composition entitled "Brightly, with
       two swings per measure" is avail. SUNYAB (copy-
       righted 1973). The text is attributed to Newbolt.

5286   Davies, H. Walford. "Song of the Road", Twenty-One
       Songs, L: N, 1931. Song: v., pf.

5287   Larson, Earl R. "Homeward Bound", NY: JF, 1954.
       Song: ttbb, a cap. [Text by Newbolt?]

5288   Stanford, C.V. "The Travelling Companion", L: S&B,
       1919. Opera. Libr. by Newbolt, after a tale by
       Hans Andersen.

5289   Swift, Newton. "Finis", NY: HB, 1928 in New Songs
       for New Voices. Song: v., pf. Text begins: "Night
       is come". The score indicates that the poem was
       taken from Newbolt's The Flying Carpet. The poem
       has been publ. under such titles as "The End" and
       "Day's End".

NICHOLS, Robert Malise Bowyer   1893-1944

"Alas, poor rhapsodist, how sad art thou"   In Aurelia &
Other Poems (1920) as one of "Swansong"

5290   Darnton, Christian. Swan Song, MS 1935. Song: s
       solo, orch.

Alone   "Grey wind and the grey sea, The"   In Ardours and
Endurances, also A Faun's Holiday and Poems and Phantasies
(1917) as one of "The Aftermath"

5291   Frankel, Benjamin. The Aftermath, L: A, 1949. Cyc.:
       t solo, str. orch., tpt., timp.

5292   Norén, Helmer. L: Curwen, 1925. Song: ms or bar
       solo, pf.

Annihilated   "Upon the sweltering sea's enormous round"   In
Ardours_and_Endurances,_also_A_Faun's_Holiday_and_Poems
and_Phantasies (1917) as one of "The Aftermath"

    5293 Frankel, Benjamin. The_Aftermath, L: A, 1949. Cyc.:
        t solo, str. orch., tpt., timp.

At the Ebb   "Alone upon the monotonous ocean's verge"   In
Ardours_and_Endurances,_also_A_Faun's_Holiday_and_Poems
and_Phantasies (1917) as one of "The Aftermath"

    5294 Frankel, Benjamin. The_Aftermath, L: A, 1949. Cyc.:
        t solo, str. orch., tpt., timp.

Catch for Spring   See: "Now has the blue-eyed Spring"

"Come, ye sorrowful, and steep"   In Ardours_and_Endurances,
also_A_Faun's_Holiday_and_Poems_and_Phantasies (1917) as
part of "A Faun's Holiday", rev. 1942

    5295 Bliss, Arthur. "The Naiads' Music", Pastoral:_Lie
        Strewn_the_White_Flocks, L: N, 1953. Song: ms
        solo, chorus, solo fl., str. orch., drums. "The
        Naiads' Music" was also publ. (L: N, 1949) as a
        sep. song for satb.

Dawn on the Somme   "Last night rain fell over the scarred
plateau"   In Aurelia_&_Other_Poems (1920) as one of
"Yesterday"

    5296 Bliss, Arthur. Morning_Heroes, L: N, 1930. Symph.:
        orator, chorus, orch.

Deliverance   "Out of the Night!"   In Ardours_and
Endurances,_also_A_Faun's_Holiday_and_Poems_and_Phantasies
(1917) as one of "The Aftermath"

    5297 Frankel, Benjamin. The_Aftermath, L: A, 1949. Cyc.:
        t solo, str. orch., tpt., timp.

Nichols, Robert continued

Don Juan's Address to the Sunset   "Exquisite stillness! What
   serenities"   In Such Was My Singing (1942) Incl. in section
   headed "Extracts from Works in Progress"

   5298   Moeran, E.J. "Nocturne", L: N, 1935. Setting for bar
          solo, satb, orch. Also avail. for bar solo, satb,
          pf.

Full Heart, The   "Alone on the shore in the pause"   In
   Ardours and Endurances, also A Faun's Holiday and Poems
   and Phantasies (1917) as one of "The Aftermath"

   5299   Frankel, Benjamin. "Night Song", The Aftermath, L:
          A, 1949. Cyc.: t solo, str. orch., tpt., timp.

   5300   Warlock, Peter. L: OUP, 1921. Song: satb, a cap.

"It is still under the pines"   In Aurelia & Other Poems
   (1920) as one of "Swansong"

   5301   Darnton, Christian. Swan Song, MS 1935. Song: s
          solo, orch.

"Little pidgeon, grave and fleet"   In Ardours and
   Endurances, also A Faun's Holiday and Poems and Phantasies
   (1917) as part of "A Faun's Holiday", rev. 1942

   5302   Bliss, Arthur. "The Pidgeon Song", Pastoral: Lie
          Strewn the White Flocks, L: N, 1953. Song: ms
          solo, chorus, solo fl., str. orch., drums.

Naiad Music   See: "Come, ye sorrowful, and steep"

"Now arched [dark] boughs hang dim and still"   In Ardours
   and Endurances, also A Faun's Holiday and Poems and
   Phantasies (1917) as part of "A Faun's Holiday", rev. 1942

   5303   Bliss, Arthur. "The Shepherd's Night Song",
          Pastoral: Lie Strewn the White Flocks, L: N,
          1953. Song: ms solo, chorus, solo fl., str.
          orch., drums.

594

ichols, Robert continued

"Now has the blue-eyed Spring" In Ardours_and_Endurances,
also_A_Faun's_Holiday_and_Poems_and_Phantasies (1917) as
part of "A Faun's Holiday", rev. 1942

 5304 Moeran, E.J. "Blue-eyed Spring", L: Curwen, 1932.
       Setting for male solo v. (or semichorus), satb,
       a cap. Arr. as a song for high v., pf.; arr.
       publ. L: Curwen, 1934.

"O Nightingale, my heart" In Aurelia_&_Other_Poems (1920)
as one of "Swansong"

 5305 Darnton, Christian. Swan_Song, MS 1935. Song: s
       solo, orch.

Pidgeon Song See: "Little pidgeon, grave and fleet"

"Put by the sun my joyful soul" In Aurelia_&_Other_Poems
(1920) as one of "Swansong"

 5306 Darnton, Christian. Swan_Song, MS 1935. Song: s
       solo, orch.

Shepherd's Night Song See: "Now arched [dark] boughs hang
dim and still"

Shut of Night "Sea darkens, The. Waves roar and rush" In
Ardours_and_Endurances,_also_A_Faun's_Holiday_and_Poems
and_Phantasies (1917) as one of "The Aftermath"

 5307 Frankel, Benjamin. The_Aftermath, L: A, 1949. Cyc.:
       t solo, str. orch., tpt., timp.

Tailor, The Libr. in coll. with van Dieren. Unpubl. in
entirety; "Girl's Song from 'The Tailor'" was publ. in
Ardours_and_Endurances,_also_A_Faun's_Holiday_and_Poems
and_Phantasies (1917)

 5308 van Dieren, Bernard. MS (Opus 10). Ch. opera.

595

Nichols, Robert continued

To--   "Asleep within the deadest hour of night"   In Ardours
and Endurances, also A Faun's Holiday and Poems and
Phantasies (1917) as one of "The Summons"

    5309   Rettich, Wilhelm. Eleven Songs for Voice and Piano,
          Berlin: Astoria, 1973. Song: t or bar solo, pf.

"Wood is still, The. I do not here"   In Aurelia & Other
Poems (1920) as one of "Swansong"

    5310   Darnton, Christian. Swan Song, MS 1935. Song: s
          solo, orch.

Miscellanea

    5311   Coleman, Ellen. Five Songs, L: A, pre-1936. Texts by
          Nichols.

NICHOLSON, Norman Corntheaite   1914-

Carol   "Mary laid her Child among"   In Selected Poems
(1966)

    5312   McCabe, John. "Mary laid her child", L: N, 1965.
          Carol: satb, a cap.

NOYES, Alfred   1880-1958

Alzuna   "Forest of Alzuna hides a pool, The"   In Shadows
on the Down and other poems (n.d.)

    5313   Gipps, Ruth. Three Incantations for Voice and Harp,
          MS. Song: s solo, hp.

Barrel-Organ, The   "There's a barrel-organ carolling"   In
    Poems (1904)

    5314 Deis, Carl. "Cown Down to Kew", NY: GS, pre-1940.
          Song: [v., pf.].

    5315 Foote, Arthur. "Lilac-Time", MS 1917, B: Schmidt.
          Song: [v., pf.?].

    5316 Steere, William C. "Lilac-Time", B: OD, pre-1940.
          Song: [v., pf.?].

    5317 Willeby, Charles. "Lilac-Time", NY: Church, pre-
          1940. Song: [v., pf.?].

Call of the Spring, The   "Come, choose your road and away,
    my lad"   In The Enchanted Island And Other Poems (1909)

    5318 Kern, Mary R. "The Call of Spring", B: Ginn, 1925 in
          Three-Part Music. Song: 3 pt. chorus, pf.

    5319 Parfrey, Raymond. MS. Song: s solo, pf.

    5320 West, John E. NY: ABC, 1925 in Junior Songs. Song:
          v., pf.

"For in the warm blue summer weather"   In Forty Singing Sea-
    men And Other Poems (1907) as one of "Slumber-Songs of the
    Madonna"

    5321 Taylor, Colin. "In the warm blue summer weather", L:
          N, 1910. Song: ssaa, a cap.

Forest of Wild Thyme, The   "One more hour to wander free"
    (1911)

    5322 Griswold, Ruth R. "The Heart of a Rose", Chi.:
          Summy, pre-1940. Song: [v., pf.?]. Setting of
          lines beginning: "What is there hid in the heart
          of a rose".

    5323 Protheroe, Daniel. "What is there hid in the heart
          of a rose?", B: OD, pre-1940. Song: [v., pf.?].
          Setting of lines beginning: "What is there hid in
          the heart of a rose".

Noyes, Alfred continued

5324 Warren, Elinor R. "The Heart of a Rose", NY: HFL,
      pre-1940. Song: [v., pf.?]. Setting of lines
      beginning: "What is there hid in the heart of a
      rose".

Forty Singing Seamen   "Across the seas of Wonderland"   In
Forty Singing Seamen And Other Poems (1907)

5325 Wood, Thomas. L: S&B, ca. 1934. Cyc.: bar solo,
      chorus, orch.

Golden Hynde, The   "With the fruit of Aladdin's garden"   In
Forty Singing Seamen And Other Poems (1907)

5326 Silver, Alfred J. L: Curwen, 1912. Song: unison v.,
      pf.

Haunted in Old Japan   "Music of the star-shine"   The Loom
of Years (1902)

5327 Blair, William. Haunted in Old Japan, NY: Church,
      pre-1940. Songs: [v., pf.?]. Songs entitled:
      "Music of the Star-Shine" (setting of pt. I),
      "Lonely, Starry Faces" (setting of pt. VI), "We,
      the Songs of Reason" (setting of pt. VIII).

Highwayman, The   "Wind was a torrent of darkness among the
gusty trees, The"   In Forty Singing Seamen And Other
Poems (1907)

5328 Andrews, Mark. NY: HWG, 1922. Cta.: s solo, ttbb,
      orch. (or pf.).

5329 Gibbs, C. Armstrong. L: BH, 1934. Setting for satb,
      orch.

5330 Taylor, Deems. B: OD, 1914. Cta.: bar solo, male
      chorus, orch. Also arr. for mixed or female
      chorus, orch.

In the Cool of the Evening   "In the cool of the evening,
when the low sweet whispers waken"   In Forty Singing Seamen And Other Poems (1907)

oyes, Alfred continued

5331 Shepherd, Arthur. MS, avail. University of Utah.
      Setting for ttbb, a cap.

Lights of Home, The   "Pilot, how far from home?"   In The
      Enchanted_Island_And_Other_Poems (1909)

   5332 Seiler, C. Linn. L: BH, pre-1940. Song: [v., pf.].

May-tree, The   "May-tree on the hill, The"   In A_Salute
      from_the_Fleet_and_Other_Poems (1915)

   5333 Besly, Maurice. Four_More_Poems, L: BH, 1928. Song:
         solo v., pf.

   5334 Coulthard, Jean. Three_Songs, MS 1962, avail. CMC.
         Song: s solo, pf.

   5335 Garlick, Antony. Eleven_Canzonets, Cin.: Westwood,
         1967. Canzonet: 2 pt. chorus of equal v., a cap.

New Carol, A   "Sing you in the dark sky"   In Dick_Turpin's
      Ride_And_Other_Poems (1927)

   5336 Fordham, Corysande. L: MM, 1931, copyright assigned
         L: C, 1943. Song: chorus of mixed v., [a cap.?].

New Duckling, The   "'I want to be new,' said the duckling"
      In The_Elfin_Artist_And_Other_Poems (1920)

   5337 Palmer, Florence M.S. L: CR, 1970. Song: solo v.,
         pf.

Night Journey   "Thou who never canst err"   In A_Letter_to
      Lucian (1956)

   5338 Rettich, Wilhelm. "Journey by Night (A Blind Man's
         Prayer)", Berlin: Astoria, 1973. Song: t solo,
         str. orch.

On a Railway Platform   "Drizzle of drifting rain, A"   In
      Forty_Singing_Seamen_And_Other_Poems (1907)

599

Noyes, Alfred continued

    5339   Butterworth, Arthur. Trains in the Distance, MS
           (Opus 41). Symph.: orator, chorus, semichorus,
           orch., tape.

On Rembrandt's Portrait of a Rabbi   "He has thought and suf-
fered" In Songs of Shadow-of-a-Leaf and Other Poems
(1924)

    5340   Rettich, Wilhelm. Two Jewish Portraits for Voice and
           Piano, Berlin: Astoria, 1973. Song: s or t solo,
           pf. or a (or b-bar solo), pf.

Orpheus and Eurydice   "Cloud upon cloud, the purple pine-
woods clung" In Forty Singing Seamen And Other Poems
(1907)

    5341   Boardman, Herbert R. MS (Opus 12), avail. NYPL.
           Overture: orch. only.

Red of the Dawn   "Dawn peered in with blood-shot eyes, The"
In The Enchanted Island And Other Poems (1909)

    5342   Coleridge-Taylor, Samuel. "Red o' the Dawn", MS pre-
           1912, avail. NYPL. Setting for v., orch. Also
           arr. for v., pf.

River of Stars, The   "She watched from the Huron tents"
In A Salute from the Fleet and Other Poems (1915)

    5343   Bawden, Clarence. NY: GS, 1917. Song: s solo, 4 pt.
           female chorus, pf.

"See, what a wonderful smile! Does it mean" In Forty Singing Seamen And Other Poems (1907) as one of "Slumber-Songs
of the Madonna"

    5344   Coolidge, Elizabeth. "See, What a Wonderful Smile",
           NY: GS, pre-1940. Song: [v., pf.?].

    5345   Taylor, Colin. "See see what a wonderful smile", L:
           N, 1910. Song: ssaa, a cap.

Sherwood   "Sherwood in the twilight, is Robin Hood awake?"
    In Poems (1904); incl. in Collected Poems (1950) under the
    title "A Song of Sherwood"

    5346 Dear, James R. L: S&B, pre-1940. Song: [v., pf.?].

    5347 de Zulueta, Pedro. L: C, 1911. Song: solo v., pf.

    5348 Rogers, J.H. "A Song of Sherwood", NY: Silver, 1932
             in Music of Many Lands and Peoples. Song: v., pf.

    5349 Webber, W.S. Lloyd. L: Elkin, 1951. Song: bar solo,
             pf.

Sherwood   (DR)   (1911)

    5350 De Rego, Iris. "The Forest Shall Conquer", L: C,
             1959. Song: ssa, [a cap.?]. Setting of the
             fairies' song beginning: "The Forest shall con-
             quer! The Forest shall conquer!".

    5351 Edmunds, Christopher. L: JW. Cta.: children's v.,
             orch.

"Sleep, little baby, I love thee"   In Forty Singing Seamen
    And Other Poems (1907) as one of "Slumber-Songs of the
    Madonna"

    5352 Head, Michael. "A Slumber Song of the Madonna", L:
             BH, 1921. Song: ms or a solo, pf.

    5353 Taylor, Colin. "Sleep little Baby", L: N, 1910.
             Song: s solo, ssaa, a cap.

Song   "Good luck befall you, mariners all"   Drake: An
    English Epic (1906)

    5354 Johns, E.W. "The Mariners", NY: ABC, 1925 in Junior
             Songs. Song: v., pf.

Song   "I know a land called 'home'"   In Shadows on the
    Down and other poems (n.d.)

Noyes, Alfred continued

5355   Davies, H. Walford. "I know a Land", L: N, 1935.
          Song: solo v., pf. or unison v., pf.

Song   "Maidens of Miyako, The"   In The Flower of Old Japan
(1903)

5356   Palm, Augustus O. "The Maidens...", NY: CF, 1926.
          Song: med. v., pf.

Song   "Moon is up: the stars are bright, The"   Drake: An
English Epic (1906)

5357   Hand, Colin. "The moon is up", L: JW, 1963. Song:
          unison v., pf.

5358   Johns, F.W. "Beyond the Spanish Main", NY: ABC, 1925
          in Junior Songs. Song: v., pf.

5359   Roff, Joseph. "The moon is up", NY: CF, 1958. Song:
          ttbb, pf.

Song   "When that I loved a maiden"   In Forty Singing Seamen And Other Poems (1907)

5360   Bartholomew, Marshall. "When that I...", NY: GS,
          pre-1940. Song: [solo v., pf.?].

Song of Sherwood, A   See: Sherwood

Song of the Wooden-Legged Fiddler   "I lived in a cottage
adown in the West"   In Poems (1904)

5361   Peel, Graham. L: C, 1910. Song: solo v., pf.

Sussex Sailor, The   "O, once, by Cuckmere Haven"   In The
Elfin Artist And Other Poems (1920)

5362 Charles, Ernest. NY: GS, pre-1940. Song: [v., pf.?].

Trumpet-Call, The   "Trumpeter, sound the great recall!"
In A Salute from the Fleet and Other Poems (1915)

602

5363   Willan, Healey. MS 1941. Setting for satb, orch.
       Arr. for satb, pf.; arr. publ. Tor.: OUP, 1941.

Two Painters, The   "Yoichi Tenko, the painter"   In The Enchanted Island And Other Poems (1909)

   5364   Coleridge-Taylor, Samuel. "A Tale of Old Japan", L:
          N, 1911. Cta.: s, a, t, b soli, chorus, orch.

Victory Ball, The   See: Victory Dance, A

Victory Dance, A   "Cymbals crash, The"   In Ballads and
Poems (1929) Incl. in Collected Poems, 2nd edn. (1963)
under the title "The Victory Ball"

   5365   Schelling, Ernest. "A Victory Ball", Lz.: Leuckart,
          1925. Orch. only.

Wizardry   "There's many a proud wizard in Araby and Egypt"
In Collected Poems (1950)

   5366   Rosser, Mervyn. "Wizards", MS 1952, avail. Univer-
          sity of Auckland. Song: unison v., pf.

World's May-Queen, The   "Whither away is the Spring to-day?"
In Poems (1904)

   5367* Davies, H. Walford. "When Spring comes back to Eng-
          land", L: Girls' Friendly Society. Song: solo v.,
          pf. or unison v., pf. Setting of pt. II or the
          poem.

Miscellanea

603

5368   Elgar, Edward. [A] Pageant of Empire, L: E, 1924.
Settings entitled: "Shakespeare's Kingdom" ([bar]
solo v., pf.), "The Islands" ([bar] solo v.,
pf.), "The Blue Mountains" ([bar] solo v., pf.),
"The Heart of Canada" ([bar] solo v., pf.),
"Sailing Westward" ([bar] solo v., pf.; also arr.
for satb), "Merchant Adventurers" ([bar] solo v.
with opt. harmonised refrain, pf.), "The Immortal
Legions" ([bar] solo v., pf.; also arr. for
satb), "A Song of Union" (satb, pf.).

5369   Harris, William H. "Slumber Song", L: A, ca. 1956.
Song: unison v. with opt. 2nd and 3rd pts., pf.

5370   Hickey, F.G. "The Very Best Ship", L: BW, 1957.
Song: t solo, ttbb, pf.

5371   Keel, Frederick. "Lullaby", L: S&B, pre-1940. Song:
[v., pf.?].

5372   Owen, Morfydd L. "Slumber Song to the Madonna", L:
Cary, pre-1940. Song: [v., pf.?].

5373   Protheroe, Daniel. "The Pilot", B: OD, pre-1940.
Song: [v., pf.?].

5374   Thornley, Barbara. "Silk O' the Kine", L: S&B, pre-
1940. Song: [v., pf.?].

O'CASEY, Sean   1880-1964

Juno and the Paycock   (DR)   Two Plays (1925)

5375 Blitzstein, Marc. MS, prod. NY, Mar. 1959. Musical.

Plough and the Stars, The   (DR)   (1926)

5376 Siegmeister, Elie. MS, perf. Louisiana State University, Mar. 1969. Opera. Libr. by Edward Mabley.

Silver Tassie, The   (DR)   (1928)

    5377 Binkerd, Gordon. Songs from "The Silver Tassie", NY:
             BH, 1972. Song: tbb, pf. Settings of lines begin-
             ning: "Would God I smok'd an' walk'd an' watch'd
             th'", "Oh, bear it gently, carry it softly".

    5378 Shaw, Martin. MS. Incidental music.

Star Turns Red, The   (DR)   (1940)

    5379 Bush, Alan. MS 1940. Incidental music.

Within the Gates   (DR)   (1933)

    5380* Hughes, Herbert. L: MacM, 1950 in Collected
             Plays [of Sean O'Casey], Vol. 2. Songs: v.,
             unacc. Settings of lines beginning: "Our mother
             the Earth is a maiden again...", "A fig for th'
             blossoms th' biggest vase can hold", "Ye who are
             haggard and giddy with care...", "Life has pass'd
             us by to the loud roll of her drum", "Her legs
             are as pliant and slim", "Sing and dance, dance
             and sing", "There were ninety and nine that
             safely lay", "When souls are lin'd out on th'
             cold Judgment Day", "Way for the strong and the
             swift and the fearless". Settings accompanied the
             1950 edn. of the play.

Miscellanea

    5381 Charpentier, Gabriel. "L'ombre d'un franc tireur",
             MS 1963. Incidental music to accompany a play by
             O'Casey [possibly his Behind the Green Curtains
             (1961)?].

O'Connor, Frank

O'CONNOR, Frank   1903-1966

Autumn   "Autumn's good, a cosy season"   in <u>Kings, Lords, &</u>
    <u>Commons</u> (1959) Transl. from the Irish

    5382 Fleischmann, Aloys. <u>The Fountain of Magic</u>, MS 1946.
          Cyc.: s or t solo, pf. Also avail. for s or t
          solo, orch.

Journeyman, The   "Ah never never more will I go to Cashel"
    In <u>Lords and Commons</u> (1938) Transl. from the Irish

    5383 O'Murnaghan, Art, arr. Dublin: Cuala, 1937 in <u>Broad-</u>
          <u>side</u>, No. 12. Song: v., unacc.

Kilcash   "What shall we do for timber?"   In <u>The Wild Bird's</u>
    (1932) Transl. from the Irish

    5384 Duff, Arthur, arr. Dublin: Cuala, 1937 in <u>Broad-</u>
          <u>side</u>, No. 5. Song: v., unacc.

<u>Midnight Court, The</u>   "I liked to walk in the river meadows"
    <u>Bell</u> (May 1941), publ. sep. 1945. Transl. from the Irish
    of Bryan Merriman

    5385 Victory, Gerard. MS 1959. Orch. only. Irish title:
          "Cúirt an Mheán-oíche".

She Is My Dear   "She is my dear"   In <u>Kings, Lords, & Com-</u>
    <u>mons</u> (1959) Transl. from the Irish

    5386 Fleischmann, Aloys. "The Lover", <u>The Fountain of</u>
          <u>Magic</u>, MS 1946. Cyc.: s or t solo, pf. Also
          avail. for s or t solo, orch.

Student, The   "Student's life is pleasant, The"   In <u>The</u>
    <u>Wild Bird's Nest</u> (1932) Transl. from the Irish

    5387 Brown, James. MS. Song: s or t solo, pf.

*Connor, Frank continued

5388   Fleischmann, Aloys. The Fountain of Magic, MS 1946.
       Cyc.: s or t solo, pf. Also avail. for s or t
       solo, orch.

Winter   "Winter is a dreary season"   In Kings, Lords, &
Commons (1959) Transl. from the Irish

5389   Fleischmann, Aloys. The Fountain of Magic, MS 1946.
       Cyc.: s or t solo, pf. Also avail. for s or t
       solo, orch.

'DONOVAN, Michael Francis   See: O'CONNOR, Frank

RWELL, George   1903-1950

Animal Farm   (NV)   (1945)

5390   Wesley-Smith, Martin. Beasts of England, MS 1966.
       Setting [of passages from the novel] for choir,
       ww., perc.

Miscellanea

5391   Seiber, Mátyás. "Animal Farm", MS pre-1955. Film
       music [based on Orwell's novel?].

O'Sullivan, Seumas

O'SULLIVAN, Seumas   1897-1958

Ballad of the Fiddler, The   "He had played by the cottage
    fire"   In Poems (1912)

    5392 Johnston, Richard. The Irish Book, Waterloo: Water-
          loo, 1971. Song: high v., pf.

Cottager, A   "Rafters blacken year by year, The"   In The
    Earth-Lover and Other Verses (1909)

    5393 Moeran, E.J. Six Poems by Seumas O'Sullivan, L: JW,
          1946. Song: high or med. v., pf.

Dustman, The   "At night when everyone's asleep"   In The
    Rosses and Other Poems (1918)

    5394 Moeran, E.J. Six Poems by Seumas O'Sullivan, L: JW,
          1946. Song: high or med. v., pf.

Evening   "I will go out and meet the evening hours"   In
    The Earth-Lover and Other Verses (1909)

    5395 Moeran, E.J. Six Poems by Seumas O'Sullivan, L: JW,
          1946. Song: high or med. v., pf.

Herdsman, The   "O herdsman, driving your slow twilight
    flock"   In The Twilight People (1905)

    5396 Fletcher, H. Grant. "The Shadows", NY: MPH, 1942.
          Song: satb, a cap.

    5397 May, Frederick. MS. Song: v., pf.

    5398 Moeran, E.J. Six Poems by Seumas O'Sullivan, L: JW,
          1946. Song: high or med. v., pf.

"Love-Gift of Sorrow, The"   "For all my sorrow I have been
    more glad"   In Poems (1912)

    5399 Howells, Herbert. "The Sorrows of Love", Five Songs
          for Low Voice, MS pre-1954. Song: low v., pf.

O'Sullivan, Seumas continued

5400 Johnston, Richard. The Irish Book, Waterloo: Water-
      loo, 1971. Song: high v., pf.

Lullaby "Husheen the herons are crying" In An Epilogue To
the Praise of Angus and Other Poems (1914)

5401 Moeran, E.J. Six Poems by Seumas O'Sullivan, L: JW,
      1946. Song: high or med. v., pf.

Monk, The "I go with silent feet and slow" In The Poems
of Seumas O'Sullivan (1923)

5402 Dillon, Shaun. Cantata in Memoriam, MS, perf. Nov.
      1974. Song (in cta.): s, bar soli, fl., jtr., pf.

Nelson Street "There is hardly a mouthful of air" In The
Poems of Seumas O'Sullivan (1923)

5403 Dillon, Shaun. Cantata in Memoriam, MS, perf. Nov.
      1974. Song (in cta.): s solo, pf.

Path, The "Tremulous grey of dusk" In The Twilight People
(1905)

5404 Scott, Francis G. "Tremulous...", Three Short Songs
      for Medium or High Voice, MS 1920, avail. SMA.
      Song: high or med. v., pf.

Piper, A "Piper in the streets today, A" In Verses Sacred
and Profane (1908)

5405 Benjamin, Arthur. "The Piper", L: Elkin, 1924. Song:
      ms solo, pf.

5406 Brown, Gwyneth L. MS 1962, avail. Victoria Univer-
      sity of Wellington. Song: med. v., pf.

5407 Crossley-Holland, Peter. "The Piper", S. Croy.: L,
      1956. Song: high v., pf.

5408 Duke, John. NY: GS, pre-1940. Song: high v., pf.

609

5409 Greenhill, Harold. York: Banks, 1936. Song: ss, pf.
      or sa, pf.

5410 Gurney, Ivor. A Fourth Volume of Ten Songs, L: OUP,
      1959. Song: solo v., pf.

5411 Hand, Colin. L: N, 1957. Song: unison v., pf.

5412 Head, Michael. L: BH, 1923. Song: v., pf. with fl.
      obbl.

5413 Peterkin, Norman. L: OUP, pre-1940. Song: [v., pf.].

5414 Vaughan Williams, Ralph. Two Poems by Seumas O'Sul-
      livan, L: OUP, 1925. Song: [med.] solo v., opt.
      pf.

5415 Webber, W.S. Lloyd. L: EA, pre-1951. Song: 3 pt.
      female chorus, pf.

Poplars, The   "As I went dreaming"   In The Twilight People
(1905)

5416 Moeran, E.J. Six Poems by Seumas O'Sullivan, L: JW,
      1946. Song: high or med. v., pf.

Rosses, The   "My sorrow that I am not by the little dun"
In The Rosses and Other Poems (1918)

5417 Shepherd, Arthur. "The Starling Lake", Northampton,
      Mass.: NVMP, 1948. Song: solo v., pf.

Sheep, The   "Slowly they pass"   In The Twilight People
(1905)

5418 Hadley, Patrick. L: OUP, 1928. Song: ms or bar solo,
      pf.

5419 Johnston, Richard. The Irish Book, Waterloo: Water-
      loo, 1971. Song: high v., pf.

Twilight People, The   "It is a whisper among the hazel bushes"   In The Twilight People (1905)

O'Sullivan, Seumas continued

5420   Glass, Dudley. L: S&B, pre-1940. Song: [v., pf.].

5421   Howells, Herbert. Five Songs for Low Voice, MS pre-
       1954. Song: low v., pf.

5422   Vaughan Williams, Ralph. Two Poems by Seumas O'Sul-
       livan, L: OUP, 1925. Song: [a or bar] solo v.,
       opt. pf. Publ. sep. L: OUP, 1932.

Miscellanea

5423   Moeran, E.J. "Invitation in Autumn", L: N, 1946.
       Song: t solo, pf.

5424   Repper, Charles. "Dusk", B: OD, pre-1940. Song: [v.,
       pf.]. Text attributed to O'Sullivan.

OWEN, Wilfred Edward Slater   1893-1918

Anthem for Doomed Youth   "What passing-bells for these who
    die"   Poems (1920)

5425   Britten, Penjamin. "Requiem aeternam", War Requiem,
       L: BH, 1961. Requiem: s, t, bar soli, satb, boys'
       choir, orch., ch. orch., org., with ch. org. or
       harm. to accompany boys' choir.

5426   Cooper, Walter Gaze. Symphony No. 6 (A Symphony of
       War), MS (Opus 59). Symph.: sp., orch.

Arms and the Boy   "Let the boy try along this bayonet-blade"
    Arts and Letters (Spring 1920)

5427   Cousins, John E. Dulce et Decorum est Pro Patria
       Mori, MS 1971. Cyc.: bar solo, fl. (doubl. pic.),
       cl., b. cl., trbn., pf., 3 perc.

At a Calvary Near the Ancre   "One ever hangs where shelled
    roads part"   Poems (1931)

611

Owen, Wilfred continued

5428   Britten, Benjamin. "Agnus Dei", War Requiem, L: BH,
       1961. Requiem: s, t, bar soli, satb, boys' choir,
       orch., ch. orch., org., with ch. org. or harm. to
       accompany boys' choir.

Dulce et Decorum Est   "Bent double, like old beggars"
  Poems (1920)

5429   Ashton, John H. Hamilton, Ohio: CAP, 1972. Song: bar
       solo, 3 tpt., 3 hn., 3 trbn., bar hn., tuba.

End, The   "After the blast of lightning from the East"
  Saturday Westminster Gazette (Nov. 1919)

5430   Britten, Benjamin. "Sanctus", War Requiem, L: BH,
       1961. Requiem: s, t, bar soli, satb, boys' choir,
       orch., ch. orch., org., with ch. org. or harm. to
       accompany boys' choir.

Fragment: A Farewell   "I saw his round mouth's crimson
  deepen as it fell"   Poems (1931)

5431   Cousins, John E. Dulce et Decorum est Pro Patria
       Mori, MS 1971. Cyc.: bar solo, fl. (doubl. pic.),
       cl., b. cl., trbn., pf., 3 perc.

Futility   "Move him into the sun"   Nation (June 1918)

5432   Britten, Benjamin. "Dies irae", War Requiem, L: BH,
       1961. Requiem: s, t, bar soli, satb, boys' choir,
       orch., ch. orch., org., with ch. org. or harm. to
       accompany boys' choir.

5433   Cousins, John E. Dulce et Decorum est Pro Patria
       Mori, MS 1971. Cyc.: bar solo, fl. (doubl. pic.),
       cl., b. cl., trbn., pf., 3 perc.

5434   Myers, Emerson. "In Memoriam", MS, issued on
       Westminster recording #WGS 9126 entitled
       Provocative Electronics. Song: lyric s solo,
       pre-recorded tape avail. from the composer.

5435   Weisgall, Hugo. Soldier Songs, NY: MMP, 1953. Song:
       bar solo, pf. Score rev. 1965.

Owen, Wilfred continued

Inspection   "'You! What d'you mean by this?'"   Poems (1931)

5436 Cousins, John E. Dulce et Decorum est Pro Patria
      Mori, MS 1971. Cyc.: bar solo, fl. (doubl. pic.),
      cl., b. cl., trbn., pf., 3 perc.

Kind Ghosts, The   "She sleeps on soft, last breaths"   Poems
(1931)

5437 Britten, Benjamin. Nocturne, L: BH, 1959. Cyc.: t
      solo, str. orch., eng. hn. obbl. Complete work
      also requires fl., cl., bsn., hn., hp., timp.
      (all obbl.). Score contains German transl. by
      Ludwig Landgraf.

Music   "I have been urged by earnest violins"   Poems (1931)

5438 Smith, Robert. MS. Song: satb, a cap.

My Shy Hand   "My shy hand shades a hermitage apart"   Poems
(1931)

5439 Langley, Bernard P. MS 1970-72. Song: t solo, orch.
      or t solo, pf.

Next War, The   "Out there, we've walked quite friendly up
to Death"   Arts and Letters (Spring 1920)

5440 Britten, Benjamin. "Dies irae", War Requiem, L: BH,
      1961. Requiem: s, t, bar soli, satb, boys' choir,
      orch., ch. orch., org., with ch. org. or harm. to
      accompany boys' choir.

Parable of the Old Man and the Young, The*   "So Abram rose"
Poems (1920)

5441 Britten, Benjamin. "Offertorium", War Requiem, L:
      BH, 1961. Requiem: s, t, bar soli, satb, boys'
      choir, orch., ch. orch., org., with ch. org. or
      harm. to accompany boys' choir.

613

Owen, Wilfred continued

5442   Tepper, Albert. <u>Cantata 1969</u>, MS 1969. Cta.:
      ssattbb, 2 hn., 2 tpt., 2 trbn., tuba, 2 perc.
      Complete work also requires t, bar soli.

Shadwell Stair   "I am the ghost of Shadwell Stair"   <u>Poems</u>
(1931)

5443 Roe, Betty. L: Thames, 1970. Song: satb, fl.

Song of Songs   "Sing me at morn"   <u>Hydra</u> (Sept. 1917)

5444 Hellerman, William. "Poem for Soprano and Four
      Instruments", MS, avail. ACA. Song: s solo, fl.,
      cl., trbn., vcl. Score does not attribute the
      words to Owen.

5445 Langley, Bernard P. MS 1970-72. Song: t solo, orch.
      or t solo, pf.

Sonnet: On Seeing a Piece of Our Artillery Brought into
   Action   "Be slowly lifted up" <u>Poems</u> (1931)

5446 Britten, Benjamin. "Dies irae", <u>War Requiem</u>, L: BH,
      1961. Requiem: s, t, bar soli, satb, boys' choir,
      orch., ch. orch., org., with ch. org. or harm. to
      accompany boys' choir.

5447 Cousins, John E. <u>Dulce et Decorum est Pro Patria
      Mori</u>, MS 1971. Cyc.: bar solo, fl. (doubl. pic.),
      cl., b. cl., trbn., pf., 3 perc.

Sonnet: To a Child   "Sweet is your antique body"   <u>Poems</u>
(1931)

5448 Langley, Bernard P. MS 1970-72. Song: t solo, orch.
      or t solo, pf.

Spring Offensive   "Halted against the shade of a last hill"
   <u>Poems</u> (1920)

5449 Bliss, Arthur. <u>Morning Heroes</u>, L: N, 1930. Symph.:
      orator, chorus, orch.

Owen, Wilfred continued

Strange Meeting   "It seemed that out of battle I escaped"
    Wheels, 1919: Fourth Cycle (1919) A variant from the
    original was publ. in Athenaeum (Aug. 1920) under the
    title "Fragment"

    5450   Britten, Benjamin. "Libera Me", War Requiem, L: BH,
           1961. Requiem: s, t, bar soli, satb, boys' choir,
           orch., ch. orch., org., with ch. org. or harm. to
           accompany boys' choir.

Voices   "Bugles sang, sadd'ning the evening air"   Poems
    (1931)

    5451   Britten, Benjamin. "Dies irae", War Requiem, L: BH,
           1961. Requiem: s, t, bar soli, satb, boys' choir,
           orch., ch. orch., org., with ch. org. or harm. to
           accompany boys' choir. Setting of stanzas 1, 2
           and 3 only.

Miscellanea

    5452   Burtch, Mervyn. Threnody, MS pre-1972. Cyc.: med.
           v., pf. Incl. words by Owen.

    5453   Smith, Leland. "Diary Fragments", Three Pacifist
           Songs, MS 1951, avail. ACA. Song: [med.] solo v.,
           pf. The composer's text begins: "Already I have
           comprehended a light which never will filter into
           the dogma..."; he has indicated to the eds. that
           the words were chosen from pp. 10-11 of Virginia
           Woolf's Three Guineas (NY: HB, 1938). Woolf's
           notes credit the words to p. 25 and p. 41 of the
           Blunden edn. of The Poems of Wilfred Owen.

PATTEN, Brian   1946-

Sleep Now   "Sleep now/Your blood moving in the quiet wind"
    In The Mersey Sound, Penguin Modern Poets 10 (1967)

Patten, Brian continued

    5454   McCabe, John. <u>This Town's a Corporation full of</u>
              <u>Crooked Streets</u>, L: N, 1969 (hire). "An enter-
              tainment" for t solo, sp., mixed chorus, child-
              ren's choir, stgs., tpt., perc., keyboards.

PHILLIPS, Stephen   1868-1915

  <u>Faust</u>   (DR)   (1908)

    5455 Coleridge-Taylor, Samuel. MS 1908. Incidental music.

  <u>Herod</u>   (DR)   (1901)

    5456 Coleridge-Taylor, Samuel. MS 1900. Incidental music.

  <u>King, The</u>   (DR)   (1912)

    5457 Hart, Fritz. MS 1921. Opera.

  <u>Nero</u>   (DR)   (1906)

    5458 Coleridge-Taylor, Samuel. MS 1906. Incidental music.

  <u>Paolo and Francesca</u>   (DR)   (1900)

    5459 Nápravník, Edward. "Francesca da Rimini", MS 1902,
          avail. SČSKU. Opera. Libr. by Josef Paleček and
          E.P. Ponomarev.

    5460 Pitt, Percy. MS 1902. Incidental music. Portions of
          the work were publ. L: R.

  <u>Ulysses</u>   (DR)   (1902)

    5461 Coleridge-Taylor, Samuel. L: N, 1902. Incidental
          music.

Phillips, Stephen continued

Miscellanea

    5462 O'Neill, Norman. "The Bride of Lammermoor ('The Last
           Heir')", MS 1908. Incidental music to play by
           Phillips (after Walter Scott).

    5463 Wordsworth, William. "Red Skies", Three_Songs, L: L,
           1946. Song: solo v., pf.

PINERO, Arthur Wing   1855-1934

Beauty_Stone,_The   (DR)   In coll. with J. Comyns Carr
   (1898)

    5464 Sullivan, Arthur. L: C, 1898. Musical drama.

Miscellanea

    5465 Wilkinson, Marc. The eds. have seen references to
           Wilkinson's incidental music for a prod.
           [National Theatre?] of Pinero's Trelawny_of_the
           "Wells" (1897).

PITTER, Ruth   1897-

Comet, The   "O still withold thyself, be not possessed"   In
   A Trophy_of_Arms (1936)

    5466 Head, Michael. L: BH, 1945, Six_Poems_of_Ruth_Pit-
           ter. Song: bar solo, pf. Other songs in the col-
           lection require various soli.

Estuary, The   "Light, stillness and peace"   In The_Bridge
   (1945)

Pitter, Ruth continued

    5467   Head, Michael. L: BH, 1945, <u>Six Poems by Ruth Pit-</u>
           <u>ter</u>. Song: ms or bar solo, pf. or ms or bar solo,
           orch. Other songs in the collection require
           various soli.

Fair is the Water   "Fair is the water when the land is
fainting"   In <u>A Trophy of Arms</u> (1936)

    5468   Chandler, Mary. <u>Recollections</u>, MS. Cyc.: s solo,
           vln., vla., vcl., hp.

For Sleep, or Death   "Cure me with quietness"   In <u>A Trophy</u>
<u>of Arms</u> (1936)

    5469   Pitfield, Thomas B. "Little Litany", <u>Two Little</u>
           <u>Litanies</u>, L: FPH, 1968. Song: satb, a cap.

Joy and Grief   "What of my Joy?"   In <u>A Trophy of Arms</u>
(1936)

    5470   Chandler, Mary. <u>Recollections</u>, MS. Cyc.: s solo,
           vln., vla., vcl., hp.

"Last vermilion, The"   In <u>Still By Choice</u> (1966) as one of
"Three Feminine Things"

    5471   Naylor, Bernard. <u>Three Feminine Things</u>, MS 1974.
           Song: high v., pf.

Last Hermitage, The   "I'll none of time"   In <u>A Trophy of</u>
<u>Arms</u> (1936)

    5472   Chandler, Mary. <u>Recollections</u>, MS. Cyc.: s solo,
           vln., vla., vcl., hp.

Matron-Cat's Song, The   "So once again the trouble's o'er"
In <u>A Mad Lady's Garland</u> (1934)

    5473   Head, Michael. L: BH, 1936, <u>Six Poems of Ruth Pit-</u>
           <u>ter</u>. Song: a solo, pf. Other songs in the col-
           lection require various soli.

Pitter, Ruth continued

    5474   Price, Beryl. A Cycle of Cats, L: OUP, 1972. Cyc.:
          ssa, pf.

"See how my yew-tree"   In Still By Choice (1966) as one of
"Three Feminine Things"

    5475   Naylor, Bernard. Three Feminine Things, MS 1974.
          Song: high v., pf.

Simile   "Like a song that shall be heard"   In A Trophy of
Arms (1936)

    5476   Head, Michael. "Constancy", L: BH, 1945, Six Poems
          of Ruth Pitter. Song: ms solo, pf. Other songs in
          the collection require various soli.

"Sorrow and weakness"   In Still By Choice (1966) as one of
"Three Feminine Things"

    5477   Naylor, Bernard. Three Feminine Things, MS 1974.
          Song: high v., pf.

Viper, The   "Barefoot I went and made no sound"   In A
Trophy of Arms (1936)

    5478   Head, Michael. L: BH, 1945, Six Poems of Ruth Pit-
          ter. Song: ms or bar solo, pf. Other songs in the
          collection require various soli.

What Old Nelly Really Meant   "When wheat is green"   In
Still By Choice (1966)

    5479   Chandler, Mary. Recollections, MS. Cyc.: s solo,
          vln., vla., vcl., hp.

Miscellanea

    5480   Head, Michael. "Holiday in Heaven", Six Poems of
          Ruth Pitter, L: BH, 1945. Song: s solo, pf. Text
          begins: "I saw the people dance by the water".

Plunkett, Joseph Mary

PLUNKETT, Joseph Mary   See: DUNSANY, Edward J.M.D. Plunkett

POTTER, Beatrix   1866-1943

   Tale of Benjamin Bunny, The   (SS)   (1904)

      5481 Glass, Dudley. Peter Rabbit, MS. Operetta. Libr. by
            the composer. A song album entitled The Songs of
            Peter Rabbit was publ. L: Warne, 1962.

   Tale of Peter Rabbit, The   (SS)   (1902)

      5482 Glass, Dudley. Peter Rabbit, MS. Operetta. Libr. by
            the composer. A song album entitled The Songs of
            Peter Rabbit was publ. L: Warne, 1962.

   Tale of Squirrel Nutkin, The   (SS)   (1903)

      5483 Le Fleming, Christopher. "Squirrel Nutkin", L:
            Warne, 1967. Musical play: children's unison v.,
            pf.

   Miscellanea

      5484 Lanchbery, John. Tales of Beatrix Potter, MS ca.
            1971. Film music.

      5485 Le Fleming, Christopher. Homage to Beatrix Potter,
            L: JWC, 1971. Composition for fl., ob., 2 cl.,
            bsn. Pieces entitled: "The Flopsy Bunnies", "The
            Puddle-ducks take a walk", "Two Bad Mice", "Mr.
            Jackson calls on Mrs. Tittlemouse", "Samuel
            Whiskers and Anna Maria".

Powys, John Cowper

POWYS, John Cowper   1872-1963

Miscellanea

    5486   Field, Robin. "The Tune", MS 1968. Song: ssatb, a
           cap. Text begins: "I played a crazy tune".

    5487   Field, Robin. "They say the sky is azure fair", Two
           Songs, MS 1965. Song: high v., pf.

PRIESTLEY, John Boynton   1894-

Dangerous Corner   (DR)   (1932)

    5488   Blatný, Pavel. MS 1964, avail. SČSKU. Incidental
           music. Czech. title: "Nebezpečná křižovatka",
           transl. by Marie Horská and Jan Makarius.

Ever Since Paradise   (DR)   (1949)

    5489   Arundell, Dennis. MS 1947. Incidental music.

Good Companions, The   (DR)   (1929)

    5490   Addinsell, Richard. MS, perf. London, May 1931.
           "Play with music". Lyrics by Harry Graham and
           Frank Fyton.

Johnson Over Jordan   (DR)   (1939)

    5491   Britten, Benjamin. MS, prod. 1939. Incidental music.

    5492   Tranchell, Peter. MS ca. 1947. [Incidental music].

Music at Night   (DR)   (1947)

    5493   Murrill, Herbert. MS pre-1952. [Incidental music].

Priestley, J.B. continued

Rose and Crown, The   (DR)   (1947)

   5494   Fišer, Loboš. MS 1964, avail. SČSKU. Incidental
         music for TV prod. Czech. title: "Růže a koruna",
         transl. by Josef Najman.

Miscellanea

   5495   Bliss, Arthur. "The Olympians", L: N, 1949. Opera.
         Libr. by Priestley.

PUDNEY, John Sleigh   1909-

Miscellanea

   5496   Stevens, Halsey. Stevens' works incl. two songs
         (MS 1945) for solo v., pf. employing texts from
         Pudney's Flight Above Cloud (1944).

Q   See: QUILLER-COUCH, Arthur Thomas

QUILLER-COUCH, Arthur Thomas   1863-1944

Carol, A   "Fling out, fling out your windows wide"   In
  Poems and Ballads by Q (1896)

   5497   Stanford, C.V. L: Dent, 1948 in Q Anthology. Carol:
         v., pf.

Raine, Kathleen

RAINE, Kathleen Jessie   1908-

"At the day's end I found"   In The Year One (1952) as one of
"Three Poems of Incarnation"

   5498   Mellers, Wilfrid H. Canticum Incarnationis, MS 1960,
          L: F (hire). Cta.: 2 s, a, 2 t, b soli, unacc. or
          ssattb, a cap.

End of Love, The   "Now he is dead"   In The Pythoness (1949)

   5499   Bush, Geoffrey. The End of Love, MS. Cyc.: bar solo,
          pf.

Ex Nihilo   "Out of nothing we are made"   In The Pythoness
(1949)

   5500   Mellers, Wilfrid H. Ex Nihilo and Lauds, L: Mills,
          1961. Song: satb, a cap.

Far-darting Apollo   "I saw the sun step like a gentleman"
In Stone and Flower (1943)

   5501   Bush, Geoffrey. The End of Love, MS. Cyc.: bar solo,
          pf.

Goddess, The   "She goes by many names"   In Living in Time
(1946)

   5502   Kasemets, Udo. Poetic Suite, MS 1954, avail. CMC.
          Song: s solo, stgs., pf.

Harvest   "Day is the hero's shield"   In Stone and Flower
(1943)

   5503   Bliss, Arthur. Angels of the Mind, L: N, 1969. Cyc.:
          s solo, pf.

"Him I praise with my mute mouth of night"   In The Year One
(1952) as one of "Northumbrian Sequence"

Raine, Kathleen continued

5504 Aston, Peter. <u>Northumbrian Sequence</u>, MS. Cyc.: ms
      solo, pf.

In the Beck   "There is a fish, that quivers in the pool"
In <u>Stone and Flower</u> (1943)

5505 Bliss, Arthur. <u>Angels of the Mind</u>, L: N, 1969. Cyc.:
      s solo, pf.

Introspection   "If you go deep"   In <u>The Year One</u> (1952)

5506 Bush, Geoffrey. <u>The End of Love</u>, MS. Cyc.: bar solo,
      pf.

Invocation   "Child in the little boat"   In <u>The Year One</u>
(1952) as one of "Three Poems of Incarnation"

5507 Mellers, Wilfrid H. <u>Canticum Incarnationis</u>, MS 1960,
      L: F (hire). Cta.: 2 s, a, 2 t, b soli, unacc. or
      ssattb, a cap.

Lament   "Where are those dazzling hills touched by the sun"
In <u>The Year One</u> (1952)

5508 Bush, Geoffrey. <u>The End of Love</u>, MS. Cyc.: bar solo,
      pf.

Lenten Flowers   "Primrose, anemone, bluebell, moss"   In <u>The</u>
<u>Pythoness</u> (1949)

5509 Bliss, Arthur. <u>Angels of the Mind</u>, L: N, 1969. Cyc.:
      s solo, pf.

"Let in the wind"   In <u>The Year One</u> (1952) as one of "Northumbrian Sequence"

5510 Aston, Peter. <u>Northumbrian Sequence</u>, MS. Cyc.: ms
      solo, pf.

Moment, The   "Never, never again"   In <u>The Year One</u> (1952)

aine, Kathleen continued

5511* Gallaher, Christopher S. Three Fragments, MS 1971.
"Chamber music": a solo, 2 cl., b. cl., fl. Incl.
setting of 1st and last stanzas only.

Nocturne   "Night comes, an angel stands"   In Stone and
Flower (1943)

5512 Bliss, Arthur. Angels of the Mind, L: N, 1969. Cyc.:
s solo, pf.

Out of Nothing   "Within the centre of the rose"   In The
Pythoness (1949)

5513 Aston, Peter. "Love Song", L: N, 1967. Song: satb,
a cap.

Passion   "Full of desire I lay"   In Stone and Flower (1943)

5514 Kasemets, Udo. Poetic Suite, MS 1954, avail. CMC.
Song: s solo, stgs., pf.

"Pure I was before the world began"   In The Year One (1952)
as one of "Northumbrian Sequence"

5515 Aston, Peter. Northumbrian Sequence, MS. Cyc.: ms
solo, pf.

Seal-woman, The   "Out of the sea the actress came"   In
Stone and Flower (1943)

5516 Flothuis, Marius. Four Trifles, Amst.: DM, 1949.
Song: high v., pf.

"See, the clear sky is threaded with a thousand rays"   In
The Year One (1952) as one of "Northumbrian Sequence"

5517 Aston, Peter. Northumbrian Sequence, MS. Cyc.: ms
solo, pf.

Seed   "From star to star, from sun and spring and leaf"
In Stone and Flower (1943)

5518   Bliss, Arthur. <u>Angels of the Mind</u>, L: N, 1969. Cyc.:
       s solo, pf.

Spring, The   "Out of hope's eternal spring"   In <u>Living in</u>
   <u>Time</u> (1946)

5519   Routh, Francis. <u>Songs of Farewell</u>, MS 1965. Song:
       s solo, pf.

Storm   "God in me is the fury on the bare heath"   In <u>The</u>
   <u>Pythoness</u> (1949)

5520   Bliss, Arthur. <u>Angels of the Mind</u>, L: N, 1969. Cyc.:
       s solo, pf.

"Who stands at the door in the storm and rain"   In <u>The Year</u>
   <u>One</u> (1952) as one of "Three Poems of Incarnation"

5521   Mellers, Wilfrid H. <u>Canticum Incarnationis</u>, MS 1960,
       L: F (hire). Cta.: 2 s, a, 2 t, b soli, unacc. or
       ssattb, a cap.

World, The   "It burns in the void"   In <u>The Pythoness</u> (1949)

5522* Gallaher, Christopher S. <u>Three Fragments</u>, MS 1971.
       "Chamber music": a solo, 2 cl., b. cl., fl.

5523   Kasemets, Udo. <u>Poetic Suite</u>, MS 1954, avail. CMC.
       Song: s solo, stgs., pf.

Worry about Money   "Wearing worry about money like a hair
   shirt"   In <u>The Pythoness</u> (1949)

5524   Bliss, Arthur. <u>Angels of the Mind</u>, L: N, 1969. Cyc.:
       s solo, pf.

Miscellanea

5525   Bliss, Arthur. <u>The Golden Cantata</u> <u>("Music is the</u>
       <u>Golden Form")</u>, L: N, 1964. Cyc.: t solo, mixed
       chorus, orch. Cyc. of 8 poems by Raine.

5526 Mellers, Wilfrid H. <u>Spells</u>, MS 1960, L: Mills
(hire). Settings for s solo, fl., ob., vla.,
perc. Words by Raine.

5527 Williams, Grace. "To the Wild Hills", <u>The Dancers</u>,
L: OUP, 1953. Choral ste.: s solo, ssa, stgs.,
hp. or s solo, ssa, pf.

RATTIGAN, Terence Marvyn   1911-

<u>Adventure Story</u>   (DR)   (1949)

5528 Klusák, Jan. MS 1963, avail. SČSKU. Incidental
music. Czech. title: "O jednom dobrodružství",
transl. by Jiří Zdeněk Novák.

<u>Winslow Boy, The</u>   (DR)   (1946)

5529 Carr, Howard. MS 1948. Film music.

READ, Herbert Edward   1893-1968

Beata l'Alma   "Time ends when vision sees it lapse in liber-
ty"   In <u>Mutations of the Phoenix</u> (1923)

5530 Blake, David. L: N, in prep. for 1975 publ. Cta.: s
solo, pf.

Carol   "Until I wander'd through the world"   In <u>Moon's Farm</u>
(1955)

5531 Brook, Harry. "Until I...", L: Elkin, 1957. Carol:
unison v., pf.

627

Read, Herbert continued

5532　Ridout, Alan. "Until I wander'd", L: N, 1963 in <u>Sing</u>
　　　<u>Nowell</u>. Carol: satb, a cap.

Legend　"This X"　In <u>Poems 1914-1934</u> (1935)

5533　Bax, Arnold. MS 1929, L: MM. Composition for vla.,
　　　pf.

Night's Negation　"Trees"　In <u>Poems 1914-1934</u> (1935)

5534　Maw, Nicholas. <u>Nocturne</u>, L: JWC, 1960. Cyc.: ms
　　　solo, ch. orch.

REED, Henry　1914-

Judging Distances　"Not only how far away, but the way that
you say it"　In <u>A Map of Verona</u> (1946) as one of "Lessons
of the War"

5535　Tepper, Albert. <u>Cantata 1969</u>, MS 1969. Cta.: t, bar
　　　soli, ssattbb, 2 hn., 2 tpt., 2 trbn., tuba, 2
　　　perc. A portion of the cta. is set without soli.

Naming of Parts　"To-day we have naming of parts"　In <u>A Map</u>
<u>of Verona</u> (1946) as one of "Lessons of the War"

5536　Tepper, Albert. <u>Cantata 1969</u>, MS 1969. Cta.:
　　　ssattbb, 2 hn., 2 tpt., 2 trbn., tuba, 2 perc.
　　　Complete work also requires t, bar soli.

Miscellanea

5537　Bliss, Arthur. "Aubade for Coronation Morning", L:
　　　S&B, 1953 in <u>A Garland for the Queen</u>. Setting for
　　　2 s soli, satb, a cap. Publ. sep. L: N, 1954.
　　　Text begins: "Then the first bird".

eeves, James

EEVES, James   1909-

At the Window   "Then more-than-morning quiet"   In The
Natural Need (1936)

   5538 Shackford, Charles. MS. Song: s solo, vln.

Bottom's Dream   "His hands move absently across the threads"
In The Talking Scull (1958)

   5539 Gardner, John L. The Noble Heart, L: OUP, 1966.
         Cta.: mixed chorus, orch.

Miscellanea

   5540 Clements, John H. "Run a little", L: AH&C, 1959.
         Song: solo v., (or unison v.), accompaniment
         unspecif.

   5541 Cope, Cecil. Two Songs, L: BH, 1959. Song: chorus,
         accompaniment unspecif. Texts entitled: "Fire",
         "Shiny".

   5542 Gill, Harry. The eds. understand that Gill has com-
         posed settings of poems by Reeves.

   5543 Hedges, Anthony. "Brand the Blacksmith", MS 1966.
         Song: unison v., pf. Text begins: "Brand the
         Blacksmith with his hard hammer".

   5544 Hedges, Anthony. "Father Un", L: N, 1965. Song: uni-
         son v., pf. Text begins: "Uncut is your corn,
         Father Un".

   5545 Hedges, Anthony. Tarlingwell", L: N, 1965. Song: ss,
         pf. Text begins: "A town of ten towers is Tar-
         lingwell".

   5546 Hedges, Anthony. "The Song of D", L: N, 1965. Song:
         ss, pf. Text begins: "Who will sing me the Song
         of D?".

   5547 Hedges, Anthony. "Yonder", MS 1966. Song: unison v.,
         pf. Text begins: "Through yonder park there runs
         a stream".

629

5548   Hold, Trevor. <u>Sevens</u>, MS 1967. Songs: high v., pf.
        or unison v., pf. The collection incl. the fol-
        lowing songs employing texts by Reeves: "A Pig
        Tale", "The Snail", "Mrs. Button", "Time To Go
        Home".

5549   Parfrey, Raymond. "Boating", <u>Fair Thames</u>, MS.
        Choral ste.: satb, pf.

5550   Plumstead, Mary. "Slowly", L: BH, 1974. Setting for
        3 pt. chorus of female v., pf.

5551   Rose, Michael. "What Kind of Music?", Reigate: S&B,
        1967. Song: female (or children's) unison v.,
        pf.

5552   Rowley, Alec. "Cows", L: N, 1958. Song: satb, a cap.
        Text begins: "Half the time they munched the
        grass".

5553   Veal, Arthur. "The Ceremonial Band", L: C, 1967.
        Song: soli, 2 pt. chorus, pf.

REEVES, John Morris   See: REEVES, James

RHYS, Ernest   1859-1946

Flower Maiden, The   "They could not find a mortal wife"
   In <u>Lays of the Round Table and Other Lyric Romances</u> (1905)

   5554   Williams, W.S. Gwynn. <u>Two Celtic Love Songs</u>, L: CR,
           1930. Song: solo v., hp. or solo v., pf.

Morning Light   "Light is woven about you, The"   In <u>Lays of</u>
   <u>the Round Table and Other Lyric Romances</u> (1905)

5555 Williams, W.S. Gwynn. Two Celtic Love Songs, L: CR, 1930. Song: solo v., hp. or solo v., pf.

Miscellanea

5556 Williams, W.S. Gwynn. "Night Song", L: CR, 1924. Song: solo v., hp. or solo v., pf. Text begins: "I have waited long in the night for you".

IDLER, Anne Barbara   1912-

Departure, The   (Libr.)   Some Time After and Other Poems (1972)

5557 Maconchy, Elizabeth. MS 1960-61. Opera.

Jesse Tree, The   (DR)   (1972)

5558 Maconchy, Elizabeth. MS, perf. 1970. Masque: 4 soli, chorus, 4 dancers, actors (mimed pts.), 12 instrumentalists. A copy of the reduced score was publ. with the 1st edn. of the play (L: Lyrebird Press, 1972).

Miscellanea

5559 Maconchy, Elizabeth. "Witnesses", MS 1966. Incidental music: 2 s soli, fl., ob., cl., hn., vcl., perc., ukelele (or banjo).

Rodgers, W.R.

RODGERS, William Robert   1909-1969

   Carol   "Deep in the fading leaves of night"   In _Europa and_
   the Bull (1952)

      5560   Baker, Michael. MS, avail. CMC. Setting for ssatb,
              a cap.

      5561   Rawsthorne, Alan. L: OUP, 1948. Song: med. v., pf.

   Song for War   "Put away the flutes"   In _Europa and the Bull_
   (1952)

      5562   Searle, Humphrey. "Put away...", L: L, 1948. Setting
              for high v., fl., ob., str. qrt.

   Miscellanea

      5563   Lutyens, Elisabeth. "Nativity", MS 1951, L: N.
              Carol: s solo, str. orch. or s solo, org. Publ.
              L: N, 1953 in _Sing Nowell_ for s solo (or semi-
              chorus), a (or bar) solo, s and t duet, org.
              Text begins: "And hark! the Herod angels sing
              tonight!".

      5564   Lutyens, Elisabeth. "The Pit", MS 1947, L: Mills
              (hire). "Dramatic scene": t, b soli, female
              chorus, orch.

      5565   Rawsthorne, Alan. "Circle on Circle", MS 1947.
              Incidental music for radio play.

RUSSELL, Bertrand Russell   1872-1970

   Miscellanea

      5566   Jones, Robert W. "Through the long years", MS. Song:
              med. v., hpd. Text begins: "Through the long
              years, I sought peace".

632

5567   Whettam, Graham. "Sinfonia Contra Timore", MS, perf.
       Birmingham, Feb. 1965, avail. Meriden Music.
       Symph. The composition of "Sinfonia Contra
       Timore" (originally entitled "Fourth Symphony")
       was influenced by Russell and his writings; the
       work is dedicated to him.

USSELL, George William   See: AE

ACKVILLE-WEST, Edward Charles   1901-1965

Rescue, The   (RP)   (1945) Based on Homer's Odyssey

   5568   Britten, Benjamin. MS, prod. BBC 1943. Incidental
          music.

ACKVILLE-WEST, Victoria Mary   1892-1962

Full Moon   "She was wearing the coral taffeta trousers"   In
Orchard and Vineyard (1921)

   5569   Anson, Hugo. L: Curwen, 1924. Song: solo v., pf.

King's Daughter   "If I might meet her in the lane"   (1929)

   5570   Greville, Ursula. "Goosey, Goosey, Gander", L: Cur-
          wen, 1930. Song: solo v., pf. Setting of lines
          beginning: "Goosey, goosey, gander".

Sackville-West, Victoria continued

Land, The   "I sing the cycle of my country's year"   (1926)

  5571 Maconchy, Elizabeth. MS, perf. London 1930. Orch.
        ste.

Phantom   "I saw a ship sailing"   In Orchard and Vineyard
(1921)

  5572 Bryan, Gordon. L: Curwen, 1924. Song: solo v., pf.

Saxon Song, A   "Tools with the comely names"   In Orchard
and Vineyard (1921)

  5573 Gill, Harry. L: OUP, 1943. Song: bar solo, pf.

Song: My Spirit Like a Shepherd Boy   "My spirit like a
shepherd boy"   In Poems of West and East (1917)

  5574 Russell, Sydney K. "My Spirit Like a Shepherd Boy",
        B: BMC, pre-1940. Song: [solo v., pf.?].

Miscellanea

  5575 Bryan, Gordon. "The Persian Coat", L: Curwen, 1924.
        Song: solo v., pf.

  5576 Burney, Angela. "The Pedlar", L: BH, pre-1939. Song:
        [v., pf.].

SAKI   See: MUNRO, Hector Hugh

ASSOON, Siegfried Lorraine   1886-1967

"Across the land a faint blue film of mist"   Sonnets and
Verses (1909), rev. same year, rev. 1911

   5577   Morgan, Howard. "October", Five Lyric Poems, L:
          Forsyth, 1968. Cyc.: s or t solo pf.

Aftermath   "Have you forgotten yet?..."   Picture Show
(1919)

   5578   Kalmanoff, Martin. Kaddish for a Warring World, MS
          1972. Cta.: t, bar soli, satb, orch.

Alone   "I've listened: and all the sounds I heard"
Discoveries (1915)

   5579   Beaumont, Adrian. The Heart's Journey, MS, perf.
          Mar. 1972. Cyc.: s solo, pf.

Alone   ("'When I'm alone'...")   See: Prelude: Alone

At Daybreak   "I listen for him through the rain"   Poems
(1911)

   5580   Beaumont, Adrian. The Heart's Journey, MS, perf.
          Mar. 1972. Cyc.: s solo, pf.

Autumn   See: "Across the land a faint blue film of mist"

Autumn   "October's bellowing anger"   Counter-Attack (1918)

   5581   Blumenfeld, Harold. Songs of War, NY: SMC, 1971.
          Song: satb, a cap.

Before the Battle   "Music of whispering trees"   The Old
Huntsman And other Poems (1917)

   5582   Blumenfeld, Harold. Songs of War, NY: SMC, 1971.
          Song: satb, a cap.

Sassoon, Siegfried continued

Brothers   "Give me your hand, my brother, search my face"
   Saturday Review (Feb. 1916), subsequently rev.

   5583   Kalmanoff, Martin. "To My Brother", Kaddish for a
          Warring World, MS 1972. Cta.: t, bar soli, satb,
          orch.

Butterflies   "Frail Travellers, deftly flickering"   New
   Statesman (Jan. 1919)

   5584   Rootham, C.B. Three Song-Pictures, L: West, 1920.
          Cyc.: high v., pf.

Child's Prayer, A   "For Morn, my dome of blue"   Morning-
   Glory (1916)

   5585   Bliss, Arthur. L: Curwen, 1927. Song: solo v., pf.

   5586   Rootham, C.B. L: Curwen, 1921. Song: solo v., pf.
          Also publ. for solo v., cl., stgs.

Death-Bed, The   "He drowsed and was aware of silence heaped"
   The Old Huntsman And other Poems (1917)

   5587   Blumenfeld, Harold. Songs of War, NY: SMC, 1971.
          Song: satb, a cap.

Dream-Forest   "Where sunshine flecks the green"   Morning-
   Glory (1916)

   5588   Beaumont, Adrian. The Heart's Journey, MS, perf.
          Mar. 1972. Cyc.: s solo, pf.

Dug-out, The   "Why do you lie with your legs ungainly hud-
   dled"   Nation (Aug. 1918)

   5589   Flanagan, William. NY: Peer, 1953. Song: high v.,
          pf.

   5590   Taylor, Clifford. Collected Songs (1950-54), MS
          1950-54, avail. ACA. Song: s or t solo, pf.

assoon, Siegfried continued

Everyone Sang   "Everyone suddenly burst out singing"
Picture Show (1919), rev. same year

5591 Edwards, Clara. NY: GS, pre-1940. Song: [v., pf.?].

5592 Gurney, Ivor. MS, n.d. Song: solo v., pf.

5593 Harris, William H. L: N, 1938. Song: t solo, sa,
      orch.

5594 Horrocks, Herbert. L: OUP, 1955. Song: satb, a cap.

5595 Lang, C.S. "Everyone suddenly...", L: N, 1936. Song:
      satb, a cap.

5596 Rafter, Leonard. L: S, ca. 1940. Song: [v., pf.].

5597 Rooper, Jasper. Bird Songs and Lovers, MS. Cta.:
      satb, str. qrt. with db., fl. (doubl. pic.).

5598 Rootham, C.B. Three Song-Pictures, L: West, 1920.
      Cyc.: high v., pf.

5599 Tomlins, Greta. Songs of Happiness, L: JW, 1959.
      Song: satb, pf. or satb, a cap.

5600 Walker, May S. L: A, ca. 1939. Song: solo v., pf.

5601 Wells, Howard. NY: GS, 1967. Song: solo v., pf.

5602 Williams, Dorothy I. MS 1963, avail. Victoria
      University of Wellington. Song: solo v., pf.

Ex-Service   "Derision from the dead"   Spectator (Nov. 1934)

5603 Smith, Leland. Three Pacifist Songs, MS 1951, avail.
      ACA. Song: [med.] solo v., pf.

"Flower has opened in my heart, A"   See: Nativity

Goblin Revel   "In gold and gray, with fleering looks of sin"
Academy (Apr. 1910)

5604 Morgan, Howard. Five Lyric Poems, L: Forsyth, 1968.
      Cyc.: s or t solo, pf.

637

Sassoon, Siegfried continued

5605 Wickens, Dennis. Five Songs for Tenor and Orchestra,
      MS. Song: t solo, orch.

Idyll "In the grey summer garden" New Statesman (June
       1918)

   5606 Beaumont, Adrian. The Heart's Journey, MS, perf.
         Mar. 1972. Cyc.: s solo, pf.

   5607 Rootham, C.B. Three Song-Pictures, L: West, 1920.
         Cyc.: high v., pf.

Limitations: Everyone Sang   See: Everyone Sang

Lovers "You were glad to-night" Oxford Outlook (May 1919)

   5608 Fischer, Irwin. "You were glad...", MS. Song: solo
         v., pf.

   5609 Rowley, Alec. "You were glad...", The Heart's
         Journey, L: WR, 1934. Song: high v., pf.

Memory "When I was young my heart and head were light"
Today (Mar. 1918)

   5610 DeGolier, Palph [?] J. "Now My Heart is Heavy-
         Laden", NY: GS, pre-1940. Song: [solo v., pf.].

Message, The "Toward sunset this November day" Common
Chords (1950)

   5611 Pinkham, Daniel. B: Ione, 1973. Song: satb, jtr. or
         satb, pf.

Morning Express "Along the wind-swept platform" The Old
Huntsman And other Poems (1917)

   5612 Butterworth, Arthur. Trains in the Distance, MS
         (Opus 41). Symph.: orator, chorus, semichorus,
         orch., pf., tape.

638

assoon, Siegfried continued

Morning-Glory   "In this meadow starred with spring"
Morning-Glory (1916)

   5613 Rootham, C.B. L: Curwen, 1921. Song: solo v., pf.
          Also publ. for solo v., cl., stgs.

   5614 Shepherd, Arthur. Seven Songs, Northampton, Mass.:
          NVMP, 1961. Song: high v., pf.

Mystery of You, The   See: Song "What you are I cannot say"

Nativity   "Flower has opened in my heart, A"   (1927), rev.
1928

   5615 Rowley, Alec. "A flower...", The Heart's Journey,
          L: WR, 1934. Song: high v., pf.

   5616 Taylor, James. "The Heart's Journey", MS 1955,
          avail. University of Auckland. Song: satb, pf.

Night-Piece   See: "Ye hooded witches, baleful shapes that
moan"

Noah   "When old Noah stared across the floods"   Discoveries
(1915)

   5617 Morgan, Howard. Five Lyric Poems, L: Forsyth, 1968.
          Cyc.: s or t solo, pf.

October   See: "Across the land a faint blue film of mist"

Old French Poet, An   "When in your sober mood"   Academy
(June 1910)

   5618 Morgan, Howard. Five Lyric Poems, L: Forsyth, 1968.
          Cyc.: s or t solo, pf.

Poplar and the Moon, A   "There stood a Poplar"   Morning-
Glory (1916)

   5619 Greaves, Ralph. L: OUP, pre-1940. Song: [v., pf.].

Sassoon, Siegfried continued

5620　Morgan, Howard. _Five Lyric Poems_, L: Forsyth, 1968.
　　　Cyc.: s or t solo, pf.

5621　Rootham, C.B. L: Curwen, 1921. Song: solo v., pf.

Prelude: Alone　"'When I'm alone'--the words tripped off his
tongue"　_Lingual Exercises_ (1925), rev. 1926

　　5622　Newsome, Fliot. "Alone", MS. Song: s solo, pf.

Slumber-Song　"Sleep; and my song shall build"　_Picture_
Show (1919)

　　5623　Carpenter, John A. NY: GS, 1921. Song: solo v., pf.
　　　　　or solo v., orch.

　　5624　Isherwood, Cherry. "Sleep", L: OUP, 1943. Song: a or
　　　　　bar solo, pf.

Song　"What you are I cannot say"　_London Mercury_ (Mar.
1924), rev. 1927, rev. 1928

　　5625　Fischer, Irwin. "What you are...", MS. Song: solo
　　　　　v., pf.

　　5626　Rowley, Alec. "What you are...", _The Heart's_
　　　　　Journey, L: WR, 1934. Song: high v., pf.

"Song, be my soul; set forth the fairest part"　_The Heart's_
Journey (1927)

　　5627　Beaumont, Adrian. "Song Be My Soul", _The Heart's_
　　　　　Journey, MS, perf. Mar. 1972. Cyc.: s solo, pf.

　　5628　Rowley, Alec. _The Heart's Journey_, L: WR, 1934.
　　　　　Song: high v., pf.

　　5629　Shepherd, Arthur. "Heart's Journey", MS, avail.
　　　　　University of Utah. Song: high v., pf.

South Wind　"Where have you been, South Wind"　_Discoveries_
　　　(1915)

Sassoon, Siegfried continued

5630   Rootham, C.B. L: Curwen, 1921. Song: solo v., pf.

Suicide in the Trenches   "I knew a simple soldier boy"
       Cambridge Magazine (Feb. 1918), rev. 1919

5631   Blumenfeld, Harold. Songs of War, NY: SMC, 1971.
       Song: satb, a cap.

5632   Weisgall, Hugo. Soldier Songs, NY: MMP, 1953. Song:
       bar solo, pf. Score rev. 1965.

Suicide in Trenches   See: Suicide in the Trenches

To My Brother   See: Brothers

Vigils   "Lone heart, learning"   Spectator (Apr. 1934)

5633   Beaumont, Adrian. The Heart's Journey, MS, perf.
       Mar. 1972. Cyc.: s solo, pf.

"What you are I cannot say"   See: Song "What you are I can-
       not say"

"Ye hooded witches, baleful shapes that moan"   Melodies
       (1912), rev. 1917

5634   Wickens, Dennis. Five Songs for Tenor and Orchestra,
       MS. Song: t solo, orch.

Miscellanea

5635   Carpenter, John A. "Serenade", NY: GS, 1921. Song:
       v., pf.

5636   Laufer, Beatrice. "Everyone Sang", NY: M, 1925.
       Song: satb, [a cap.?]. [Text by Sassoon?]

Sayers, Dorothy L.

SAYERS, Dorothy Leigh   1893-1957

Just Vengeance, The   (DR)   (1946)

   5637 Hopkins, Antony. MS 1946, avail. L: JWC. Incidental
         music: chorus, stgs., org.

Zeal of thy House, The   (DR)   (1937)

   5638 Knight, Gerald H. MS, prod. 1937. Incidental music.

Miscellanea

   5639 Moeran, E.J. "The Bean Flower", Two Songs, L: JWC,
         1924. Song: high v., pf.

SHANKS, Edward Buxton   1892-1953

Boats at Night   "How lovely is the sound of oars at night"
In The Island of Youth (1921)

   5640 Perks, Robert E. MS 1941, avail. University of
         Otago. Song: satb, a cap.

Dover's Hill   "From this hill where the air's so clear"   In
The Island of Youth (1921)

   5641 Gurney, Ivor. MS 1920. Song: [solo v., pf.].

Fairy's Child, The   "I have known love"   In The Shadowgraph
(1925)

   5642 Rettich, Wilhelm. Eleven Songs for Voice and Piano,
         Berlin: Astoria, 1973. Song: t or bar solo, pf.

Shanks, Edward continued

Fields are Full, The   "Fields are full of summer still, The"
   In The Queen of China and Other Poems (1919)

   5643 Gibbs, C. Armstrong. L: WR, 1920. Song: med. v., pf.

   5644 Gurney, Ivor. L: OUP, 1952. Song: bar solo, pf.

   5645 Warlock, Peter. "Late Summer", L: A, 1925. Song: v.,
         pf.

Meadow and Orchard   "My heart is like a meadow"   In Poems
   (1916)

   5646 Gurney, Ivor. MS 1920. Song: [solo v., pf.].

Singer, The   "In the dim light of the golden lamp"   In The
   Queen of China and Other Poems (1919)

   5647 Gurney, Ivor. A First Volume of Ten Songs, L: OUP,
         1938. Song: solo v., pf.

   5648 Warlock, Peter. L: A, 1925. Song: v., pf.

Song   "As I lay in the early sun"   In The Queen of China
   and Other Poems (1919)

   5649 Finzi, Gerald. "As I...", Oh Fair to See, L: BH,
         1966. Song: high v., pf.

   5650 Gibbs, C. Armstrong. "As I...", L: BH, 1920. Song:
         solo v., pf.

   5651 Gurney, Ivor. "As I...", MS 1920. Song: [solo v.,
         pf.].

Woman's Song   "No more upon my bosom rest thee"   In The
   Shadowgraph (1925)

   5652 Rettich, Wilhelm. Eleven Songs for Voice and Piano,
         Berlin: Astoria, 1973. Song: s or a solo, pf.

Miscellanea

643

Shanks, Edward continued

    5653   Gurney, Ivor. "The Latmian Shepherd", <u>A First Volume</u>
               <u>of Ten Songs</u>, L: OUP, 1938. Song: solo v., pr.
               Text begins: "The moon's a drowsy fool tonight".

    5654   Smyth, Ethel. "Fête Galante", Wien: UE, 1923. Opera.
               Poetic version by Shanks, after the text by
               Maurice Baring.

SHARP, William   See: MACLEOD, Fiona

SHAW, George Bernard   1856-1950

 <u>Androcles and the Lion</u>   (DR)   (1916)

    5655   Blitzstein, Marc. MS ca. 1947. Incidental music.

    5656   Fischer, Jan F. MS 1946, avail. SČSKU. Incidental
               music. Czech. title: "Androkles a lev", transl.
               by Karel Mušek.

    5657   Flosman, Oldřich. MS 1956, avail. SČSKU. Incidental
               music. Czech. title: "Androkles a lev", transl.
               by Břetislav Hodek.

    5658   Karel, Jaromír. MS 1968, avail. SČSKU. Incidental
               music. Czech. title: "Androkles a lev", transl.
               by Břetislav Hodek.

 <u>Arms and the Man</u>   (DR)   <u>Plays Pleasant and Unpleasant</u>
 (1898), subsequently publ. sep.

    5659   Straus, Oscar. "The Chocolate Soldier", NY: RM,
               1909. Opera. Libr. by Rudolph Bernauer and Leo-
               pold Jacobson. German title: "Der Tapfere Sol-
               dat". Engl. version by Stanislaus Stange.

Shaw, George Bernard continued

Back to Methuselah   (DR)   (1921)

5660 Hopkins, Antony. Four Dances, L: S, 1949. Incidental
      music to play: rec., hpd. or rec., spinet.

5661 Ponc, Miroslav. MS 1932, avail. SČSKU. Incidental
      music. Czech. title: "Zpět k Methuselah", transl.
      by Alfred Pflanzer and Karel Mušek.

Caesar and Cleopatra   (DR)   Three Plays for Puritans
(1901), subsequently publ. sep.

5662 Andriessen, Jurriaan. Amst.: DM, 1956. Ch. music:
      sextet (fl., ob., cl., bsn., hn., pf.). Based on
      themes composed as incidental music to the play.

5663 Auric, Georges. MS 1945. Film music.

5664 Ponc, Miroslav. MS 1936, avail. SČSKU. Incidental
      music. Czech. title: "Caesar a Kleopatra",
      transl. by Karel Mušek.

5665 Vorlová, Sláva. MS 1956-57, avail. SČSKU. Incidental
      music. Czech. title: "Caesar a Kleopatra",
      transl. by Zdeněk Vančura.

Devil's Disciple, The   (DR)   Three Plays for Puritans
(1901), subsequently publ. sep.

5666 Bennett, Richard R. MS 1959. Film music.

5667 Brubeck, Howard. "Overture to 'The Devil's Dis-
      ciple'", MS 1954. Overture: orch.

5668 Fischer, Jan F. MS 1946, avail. SČSKU. Incidental
      music. Czech. title: "Pekelník", transl. by Karel
      Mušek.

5669 Vaughan Williams, Ralph. MS 1913. Incidental music.

Great Catherine   (DR)   (1919)

5670 Lilien, Ignace. Wien: UE, 1932. Opera. German title:
      "Die grosse Katharina". Libr. by Konrad Maril.

645

5671 Srnka, Jiří. MS 1966, avail. SČSKU. Czech. title: "Kateřina Veliká", transl. by Břetislav Hodek.

Heartbreak House (DR) (1919)

5672 Chagrin, Francis. MS pre-1954. Incidental music.

Major Barbara (DR) (1907)

5673 Walton, William. MS, perf. London 1941. Film music.

Pygmalion (DR) (1916)

5674 Axt, William. See entry following.

5675 Honegger, Arthur. MS 1938, prod. MGM 1939. Film music. Additional composition provided by William Axt.

5676 Kadlec, Jaroslav. MS 1951, avail. SČSKU. Incidental music. Czech. title: "Pygmalion", transl. by Frank Tetauer.

5677 Loewe, Frederick. "My Fair Lady", NY: C, 1956. Musical. Lyrics by Alan Jay Lerner.

5678 Simon, Ladislav. MS 1968, avail. SČSKU. Incidental music. Czech. title: "Pygmalion", transl. by Milan Lukeš.

Saint Joan (DR) (1924)

5679 Arundell, Dennis. MS 1934. Incidental music.

5680 Fischer, Jan F. MS 1948, avail. SČSKU. Incidental music. Czech. title: "Svatá Jana", transl. by Frank Tetauer.

5681 Foulds, John H. L: PX, 1925. Ste. (from the incidental music for the play): orch.

5682 Jíra, Milan. MS 1967, avail. SČSKU. Incidental music. Czech. title: "Svatá Jana", transl. by Frank Tetauer.

Shaw, George Bernard continued

5683 Kupka, Karel. MS 1965, avail. SČSKU. Incidental
music. Czech. title: "Svatá Jana", transl. by
Frank Tetauer.

Six of Calais, The (DR) (1936) Priv. printing 1934

5684 Berg, Josef. MS 1956, avail. SČSKU. Incidental
music. Czech. title: "Měšťane calaiští", transl.
Frank Tetauer.

Widowers' Houses (DR) (1893)

5685 Bělohlávek, Jiří. MS 1972, avail. SČSKU. Incidental
music. Czech. title: "Domy pana Sartoria",
transl. by Jaroslav Bílý.

Miscellanea

5686 Eisler, Hanns. Grove's indicates that Eisler composed incidental music to Shaw's plays.

5687 Freed, Isadore. "Pygmalion", MS 1926. Symph. rhapsody [inspired by Shaw's play?].

SITWELL, Edith 1887-1964

Ass-Face "Ass-Face drank" Bucolic Comedies (1923)

5688 Walton, William. Façade, MS, perf. 12 June 1923.
Setting for reciter, ch. ensemble.

Aubade "Jane, Jane" Saturday Westminster Gazette (Oct.
1920)

5689 Walton, William. Façade, MS, perf. 24 Jan. 1922.
Setting for reciter, ch. ensemble.

Sitwell, Edith continued

Bank Holiday, I & II   "Houses on a see-saw rush"   Oxford and Cambridge Miscellany (June 1920), rev. same year

    5690 Walton, William. Façade, MS, perf. 24 Jan. 1922.
          Setting for reciter, ch. ensemble.

Bee-Keeper, The   "In the plain of the world's dust"
Penguin New Writing, 32 (1947)

    5691 Rainier, Priaulx. "The Bee Oracles", L: S, 1969.
          Song: t or high bar solo, fl., ob., vln., vcl.,
          hpd. Sets lines beginning: "...the Priestesses of
          the Gold Comb".

Bells of Grey Crystal   "Bells of grey crystal"   Troy Park
(1925)

    5692 Bennett, Richard R. Time's Whiter Series, L: N, in
          prep. for publ. Song: c-t solo, lute.

Black Mrs. Bemoth   "In a room of the palace"   Troy Park
(1925)

    5693 Walton, William. Façade (perf. 14 Sept. 1928), L:
          OUP, 1951 (hire). Setting for reciter, fl.
          (doubl. pic.), cl. (doubl. b. cl.), tpt., a sax.,
          vcl(s)., perc.

By the Lake   "Across the thick and the pastel snow"   Chapbook (May 1923)

    5694 Walton, William. Façade (perf. 27 Apr. 1926 [pos-
          sibly 12 June 1923]), L: OUP, 1951 (hire). Set-
          ting for reciter, fl. (doubl. pic.), cl. (doubl.
          b. cl.), tpt., a sax., vcl(s)., perc.

Came the Great Popinjay   See: Herodiade's Plea

Canticle of the Rose, The   "Rose upon the wall, The"   The
Canticle of the Rose (1949)

    5695 Searle, Humphrey. L: F, 1966. Cta.: ssaattbb, a cap.

Centaurs and Centauresses (Yodelling Song)   "We bear velvet
   cream"   Rustic Elegies (1927) as part of "Prelude to a
   Fairy Tale", rev. 1949

   5696* Walton, William. "Jodelling Song", Façade (perf.
            27 Apr. 1926 [possibly 12 June 1923]), L: OUP,
            1951 (hire). Setting for reciter, fl. (doubl.
            pic.), cl. (doubl. b. cl.), tpt., a sax.,
            vcl(s)., perc. Incl. in "Façade" First Suite for
            Orchestra, L: OUP. Ste.: orch. (incl. dbl. ww.).
            Arr. by Roy Douglas as one of "Façade" Suite for
            Harmonica and Orchestra, L: OUP. Ste.: harmonica,
            orch. Also avail. for harmonica, pf. Arr. by
            Robert O'Brien for concert band; L: OUP. Arr. by
            Constant Lambert for pf. duet; L: OUP.

Cherry Tree, The   "Why has the Shepherdess black with the
   Sun"   Time and Tide (Jan. 1929)

   5697* Cole, Hugo. Six Sitwell Songs, L: N, 1968. Cyc.:
            high v., pf.

"Come, my Arabia"   Five Variations on a Theme (1933) as one
   of "Two Songs"

   5698 Beckwith, John. Four Songs to Poems by Edith Sit-
            well, MS 1949. Cyc.: s or t solo, pf.

Country Dance   "That hobnailed goblin, the bob-tailed Hob"
   Bucolic Comedies (1923)

   5699 Walton, William. Façade (perf. 27 Apr. 1926), L:
            OUP, 1951 (hire). Setting for reciter, fl.
            (doubl. pic.), cl. (doubl. b. cl.), tpt., a
            sax., vcl(s)., perc. Incl. in "Façade" Second
            Suite for Orchestra, L: OUP. Ste.: orch. (incl.
            dbl. ww., eng. hn. and/or a sax.).

Dame Souris Trotte   "Madame Mouse trots"   Façade (programme
   notes of perf. held Jan. 1922), rev. same year

   5700 Dawney, Michael. "Madam Mouse Trots", MS. Song: high
            v., pf.

Sitwell, Edith continued

5701   Walton, William. _Façade_, MS, perf. 24 Jan. 1922.
       Setting for reciter, ch. ensemble.

Daphne   "When green as a river was the barley"   _Spectator_
  (May 1923), rev. 1940

5702   Walton, William. _Façade_, MS, perf. 27 Apr. 1926
       [possibly 12 June 1923]. Setting for reciter, ch.
       ensemble.

5703* Walton, William. _Three Songs_, L: OUP, 1932. Song:
       s solo, pf.

Dirge for the New Sunrise   "Bound to my heart as Ixion to
  the wheel"   _Orion_, IV (1949)

5704   Kelly, Bryan. "Dirge for a New Sunrise", MS pre-
       1960. Song: t solo, str. orch.

En Famille   "In the early springtime, after their tea"
  Chapbook (July 1920)

5705   Walton, William. _Façade_ (perf. 24 Jan. 1922), L:
       OUP, 1951 (hire). Setting for reciter, fl.
       (doubl. pic.), cl. (doubl. b. cl.), tpt., a sax.,
       vcl(s)., perc.

English Eccentrics, The   (PR)   (1933)

5706   Williamson, Malcolm. MS ca. 1964. Opera. Libr. by
       Geoffrey Dunn.

Eurydice   "Fires on the hearth! Fires in the heavens!"
  Horizon (Aug. 1945)

5707   Fussell, Charles. MS 1974. Cta.: ms solo, fl., cl.
       vln., vcl., pf., with obbl. for hn., tpt., trbn.
       b. dr.

Sitwell, Edith continued

Façade
    The reader is referred to the individual poems by Sitwell
    for which William Walton's Façade music was composed.
    With the most helpful assistance of Mr. Stewart R.
    Craggs, the eds. have reconstructed what they be-
    lieve to be an accurate account of the six Façade
    concerts (given on 24 Jan. 1922, 12 June 1923, 27 Apr.
    1926, 29 June 1926, 14 Sept. 1928, and 29 May 1942).
    Reconstruction of the various programmes was rendered
    difficult by the fact that the programme notes of the
    concert held 12 June 1923 have not been located, so
    that certain entries will read "perf. 27 Apr. 1926
    [possibly 12 June 1923]". The last concert is consider-
    ed Walton's "definitive version". No new poems were
    incl. in this concert, all having appeared in one or
    more of the previous ones. It is from this 1942 con-
    cert that Walton drew his material for the 1951 publ.
    of Façade (OUP holds some of the musical MS, much re-
    mains unlocated). The reader should also be aware that
    incidental--or "interlude"--music was also composed for
    the various concerts at which Sitwell and Walton per-
    formed; this incidental music was not accompanied by
    Sitwell's reading.
    Certain of the poems which were read to Walton's music had
    been publ. earlier by Sitwell, but certain others re-
    ceived their 1st publ. in the programme notes for con-
    cert performances of Façade and were subsequently re-
    printed in edns. of Sitwell's verse. In two instances
    poems were recited to music but were only publ. in the
    programme notes.
    Finally, it should be noted that "Façade (programme notes
    of perf. held Jan. 1922)" is distinct from "Façade
    (1922)", the latter publ. being Sitwell's own 1st edn.
    of a Façade collection.

Four in the Morning   "Cried the navy-blue ghost"   Vogue,
London (Dec. 1924), rev. 1950

    5708* Walton, William. Façade (perf. 27 Apr. 1926), L:
        OUP, 1951 (hire). Setting for reciter, fl.
        (doubl. pic.), cl. (doubl. b. cl.), tpt., a sax.,
        vcl(s)., perc.

Fox Trot   "Old Sir Faulk"   Bucolic_Comedies (1923)

651

Sitwell, Edith continued

    5709 Walton, William. "Old Sir Faulk", _Façade_ (perf. 27
          Apr. 1926 [possibly 12 June 1923]), L: OUP, 1951
          (hire). Setting for reciter, fl. (doubl. pic.),
          cl. (doubl. b. cl.), tpt., a sax., vcl(s).,
          perc. Incl. in _"Façade" Second Suite for
          Orchestra_, L: OUP. Ste.: orch. (incl. dbl. ww.,
          eng. hn. and/or a sax.). Arr. by Robert O'Brien
          for concert band; L: OUP. Arr. by Constant Lam-
          bert for pf. duet. L: OUP.

    5710* Walton, William. "Old Sir Faulk", _Three Songs_, L:
          OUP, 1932. Song: s solo, pf.

Gardener Janus Catches a Naiad   "Baskets of ripe fruit in
    air"   _Bucolic Comedies_ (1923)

    5711 Walton, William. _Façade_, MS, perf. 12 June 1923.
          Setting for reciter, ch. ensemble.

Gold Coast Customs   "One fantee wave"   _Gold Coast Customs_
    (1929), rev. 1930

    5712 Searle, Humphrey. S. Croy.: L, 1950. Melodrama: fe-
          male narr., male narr., ttbb, orch.

Greengage Tree, The   "From gold-mosaic'd wave"   _Five Poems_
    (1928)

    5713* Cole, Hugo. _Six Sitwell Songs_, L: N, 1968. Cyc.:
          high v., pf.

Herodiade's Flea   "Came the great Popinjay"   _Bucolic
    Comedies_ (1923), rev. 1930

    5714 Walton, William. _Façade_, MS, perf. 12 June 1923.
          Setting for reciter, ch. ensemble.

Hornpipe   See: Introduction, and Hornpipe

'I Do Like to be Beside the Seaside'   "When/Don/Pasquito
    arrived at the seaside"   _Troy Park_ (1925)

Sitwell, Edith continued

5715* Walton, William. Façade (perf. 27 Apr. 1926 [pos-
sibly 12 June 1923]); "Tango Pasodoble", Façade,
L: OUP, 1951 (hire). Setting for reciter, fl.
(doubl. pic.), cl. (doubl b. cl.), tpt., a sax.,
vcl(s)., perc. Incl. in "Façade" First Suite for
Orchestra, L: OUP. Ste.: orch. (incl. dbl. ww.).
Arr. by Walter Goehr as one of Four Dances from
"Façade", L: OUP. Setting for small orch. (with
additional opt. pts.). Arr. by Roy Douglas as one
of "Façade" Suite for Harmonica and Orchestra, L:
OUP. Ste.: harmonica, orch. Also avail. for
harmonica, pf. Arr. by Constant Lambert for pf.
duet; L: OUP.

Introduction, and Hornpipe   "Sailors came"   Façade
(programme notes of perf. held Jan. 1922), rev. same year

5716 Walton, William. Façade (perf. 24 Jan. 1922); "Hornpipe", Façade, L: OUP, 1951 (hire). Setting for
reciter, fl. (doubl. pic.), cl. (doubl. b. cl.),
tpt., a sax., vcl(s)., perc.

Jodelling Song   See: Centaurs and Centauresses (Yodelling
Song)

Jumbo Asleep   See: Jumbo's Lullaby

Jumbo's Lullaby   "Jumbo asleep!"   Façade (programme notes
of perf. held Jan. 1922), rev. same year, rev. 1930

5717 Walton, William. Façade (perf. 24 Jan. 1922); "Lullaby for Jumbo", Façade, L: OUP, 1951 (hire).
Setting for reciter, fl. (doubl. pic.), cl.
(doubl. b. cl.), tpt., a sax., vcl(s)., perc.

King of China's Daughter, The   "King of China's daughter,
The"   Wheels: An Anthology of Verse (1916), rev. 1920

5718 Daniels, Mabel W. NY: Silver, 1930 in The Music
Hour, Book 5. Song: v., pf.

5719 Duff, Arthur. Dublin: Cuala, 1937 in Broadside, No.
4. Song: v., unacc.

653

Sitwell, Edith continued

> 5720 Head, Michael. _Five Songs_, L: BH, 1938. Song: bar solo, pf.

> 5721* Kramer, A. Walter. NY: HB, 1928 in _New Songs for New Voices_. Song: v., pf.

> 5722 Latham, Richard. L: EA, pre-1951. Song: 2 pt. chorus, [pf.?].

> 5723 Rootham, C.B. L: S, 1923. Song: high v., pf. Also avail. for low v., pf.

> 5724 Swift, Newton. NY: HB, 1928 in _New Songs for New Voices_. Song: v., pf.

> 5725 van Someren-Godfery, Masters. L: A, pre-1940. Song: v., pf.

> 5726 Veal, Arthur. MS ca. 1965. Song: [v., pf.?].

Long Steel Grass "Long steel grass" _Saturday Westminster Gazette_ (Sept. 1921), rev. 1926

> 5727 Walton, William. _Façade_ (perf. 24 Jan. 1922), L: OUP, 1951 (hire). Setting for reciter, fl. (doubl. pic.), cl. (doubl b. cl.), tpt., a sax., vcl(s)., perc.

Lullaby for Jumbo See: Jumbo's Lullaby

Madam Mouse Trots See: Dame Souris Trotte

Mandoline "Down in Hell's gilded street" _Arts and Letters_ (Autumn 1919), rev. 1920.

> 5728 Carr, Edwin. _An Edith Sitwell Song-Cycle_, L: R, 1966. Cyc.: ms solo, ob., pf.

Mariner Man See: Mariner-Men

Mariner-Men "What are you staring at" _Clowns' Houses_ (1918), rev. 1950

Sitwell, Edith continued

5729 Walton, William. Façade (perf. 24 Jan. 1922);
"Mariner Man", Façade, L: OUP, 1951 (hire). Setting for reciter, fl. (doubl. pic.), cl. (doubl.
b. cl.), tpt., a sax., vcl(s)., perc.

Mazurka   See: Pluto (Mazurka)

"My desert has a noble sun for heart"   Five Variations on
a Theme (1933) as one of "Two Songs"

5730 Beckwith, John. Four Songs to Poems by Edith Sitwell, MS 1949. Cyc.: s or t solo, pf.

Nectarine Tree, The   "This rich and swanskin tree has
grown"   Gold Coast Customs (1929)

5731* Cole, Hugo. Six Sitwell Songs, L: N, 1968. Cyc.:
high v., pf.

Neptune (Polka)   See: Polka

Nursery Rhyme   See: Said King Pompey

O Yet Forgive   "O yet forgive my heart in your long night!"
Green Song and Other Poems (1944)

5732 Carr, Edwin. A Edith Sitwell Song-Cycle, L: R,
1966. Cyc.: ms solo, ob., pf.

5733 Lutyens, Elisabeth. MS pre-1954. Song: [solo v.,
pf.?].

Octogenarian, The   "Octogenarian, The"   Façade (programme
notes of perf. held Jan. 1922)

5734 Walton, William. Façade, MS, perf. 24 Jan. 1922.
Setting for reciter, ch. ensemble.

Old Nurse's Song, The   "Ptolemy, poor Ptolemy"   Clowns'
House (1918)

655

Sitwell, Edith continued

5735   van Someren-Godfery, Masters. L: A, pre-1940. Song:
       v., pf.

Owl, The   "Currants moonlit as Mother Bunch, The"   Bucolic
Comedies (1923), rev. 1957

   5736   Walton, William. Façade, MS, perf. 12 June 1923.
          Setting for reciter, ch. ensemble.

Peach Tree, The   "Between the amber portals of the sea"
Saturday Review of Literature (Apr. 1928)

   5737* Cole, Hugo. Six Sitwell Songs, L: N, 1968. Cyc.:
          high v., pf.

Pluto (Mazurka)   "God Pluto is a kindly man"   Rustic
Elegies (1927) as part of "Prelude to a Fairy Tale", rev.
1950

   5738   Walton, William. "Mazurka", Façade, MS, perf. 29
          June 1926. Setting for reciter, ch. ensemble.

Polka   "Tra la la la la la"   Façade (programme notes of
perf. held June 1926), rev. 1927

   5739   Walton, William. Façade (perf. 27 Apr. 1926 [pos-
          sibly 12 June 1923]), L: OUP, 1951 (hire). Set-
          ting for reciter, fl. (doubl. pic.), cl. (doubl.
          b. cl.), tpt., a sax., vcl(s)., perc. Incl. as
          one of "Façade" First Suite for Orchestra, L:
          OUP. Ste.: orch. (incl. dbl. ww.). Arr. by Roy
          Douglas as one of "Façade" Suite for Harmonica
          and Orchestra, L: OUP. Ste.: harmonica, orch.
          Arr. by Walter Goehr as one of Four Dances from
          "Façade", L: OUP. Setting for small orch. (with
          additional opt. pts.). Arr. by Robert O'Brien for
          concert band; L: OUP.

Popular Song   "Lily O'Grady"   (1928)

5740 Walton, William. Façade (perf. 27 Apr. 1926 [pos-
sibly 12 June 1923]), L: OUP, 1951 (hire). Setting for reciter, fl. (doubl. pic.), cl. (doubl.
b. cl.), tpt., a sax., vcl(s)., perc. Incl. as
one of "Façade" First Suite for Orchestra, L:
OUP. Ste.: orch. (incl. dbl. ww.). Arr. by Roy
Douglas as one of "Façade" Suite for Harmonica
and Orchestra, L: OUP. Ste.: harmonica, orch.
Also avail. for harmonica, pf. Arr. by Walter
Goehr as one of Four Dances from "Façade", L:
OUP. Setting for small orch. (with additional
opt. pts.). Arr. by Robert O'Brien for concert
band; L: OUP. Arr. by Constant Lambert for pf.
duet; L: OUP. Also publ. L: OUP for pf. solo and
for 2 pf.

Rose Castles* ["?"] Façade (programme notes of perf. held
Jan. 1922)

5741 Walton, William. Façade, MS, perf. 24 Jan. 1922.
Setting for reciter, ch. ensemble.

Said King Pompey "Said King Pompey, the emperor's ape"
Façade (programme notes of perf. held Jan. 1922), rev.
1949

5742 Walton, William. Façade, MS, perf. 24 Jan. 1922.
Setting for reciter, ch. ensemble.

Scotch Rhapsody "Do not take a bath in Jordon, Gordon"
The Legion Book (1929)

5743 Walton, William. Façade (perf. 27 Apr. 1926), L:
OUP, 1951 (hire). Setting for reciter, fl.
(doubl. pic.), cl. (doubl. b. cl.), tpt., a
sax., vcl(s)., perc. Incl. in "Façade" Second
Suite for Orchestra, L: OUP. Ste.: orch. (incl.
dbl. ww., eng. hn. and/or a sax.). Arr. by
Robert O'Brien for concert band; L: OUP.

Second Sylph See: Valse Maigre, 1843

Shadow of Cain, The "Under great yellow flags" (1947)

Sitwell, Edith continued

5744   Searle, Humphrey. L: S, 1953 (hire). Melodrama:
        female narr., male narr., male chorus, orch.

Sir Beelzebub   See: When Sir Beelzebub

Sleeping Beauty, The   "When we came to that dark house"
    (1924) Portions 1st publ. in various journals 1923-24

    5745   Lucas, Leighton. MS ca. 1936. Masque.

Small Talk, I & II   "Upon the noon Cassandra died"   Arts
    and Letters (Spring 1920)

    5746   Walton, William. Façade, MS, perf. 24 Jan. 1922.
            Setting for reciter, ch. ensemble.

Soldan's Song   See: Daphne

Something Lies Beyond the Scene   "Something lies beyond the
    scene"   Troy Park (1925) as 2nd part of "'I Do Like to be
    Beside the Seaside'", rev. 1950

    5747   Walton, William. Façade (perf. 27 Apr. 1926 [pos-
            sibly 12 June 1923]), L: OUP, 1951 (hire). Set-
            ting for reciter, fl. (doubl. pic.), cl. (doubl.
            b. cl.), tpt., a sax., vcl(s)., perc.

Song   "O Dionysus of the tree"   Green Song and Other Poems
    (1944), rev. 1945

    5748   Carr, Edwin. "Dionysus of the Tree", An Edith Sit-
            well Song-Cycle, L: R, 1966. Cyc.: ms solo, ob.,
            pf.

Song   "Queen Bee sighed, 'How heavy is my sweet gold', The"
    Green Song and Other Poems (1944)

    5749   Beckwith, John. "The Queen Bee...", Four Songs to
            Poems of Edith Sitwell, MS 1949. Cyc.: s or t
            solo, pf.

5750   Carr, Edwin. "The Queen Bee Sighed", An Edith Sit-
           well Song-Cycle, L: R, 1966. Cyc.: ms solo, ob.,
           pf.

Song for Two Voices   See: Song "O Dionysus of the Tree"

Song of the Man from a Far Country   "Rose and Alice"   The
Sleeping Beauty (1924), rev. 1945, rev. 1948

    5751   Walton, William. "A Man from the Far Countree",
           Façade (perf. 27 Apr. 1926 [possibly 12 June
           1923]); "A Man from a Far Countree", Façade, L:
           OUP, 1951 (hire). Setting for reciter, fl.
           (doubl. pic.), cl. (doubl. b. cl.), tpt., a sax.,
           vcl(s)., perc.

Song of the Man from the Far Countree, The   See: Song of the
Man from a Far Country

Song of the Man from the Far Country, The   See: Song of the
Man from a Far Country

Spinning Song   "Miller's daughter, The"   Bucolic Comedies
(1923)

    5752   Shepherd, Arthur. MS, avail. University of Utah.
           Song: solo v., vla., pf.

Springing Jack   "Green wooden leaves clap light away"
Coterie (Dec. 1919), rev. 1920, rev. 1930

    5753   Walton, William. Façade, MS, perf. 24 Jan. 1922.
           Setting for reciter, ch. ensemble.

Still Falls the Rain   "Still falls the Rain"   Times Literary Supplement (Sept. 1941)

    5754   Britten, Benjamin. "Canticle III", L: BH, 1956.
           Song: t solo, hn., pf.

Sitwell, Edith continued

Strawberry, The   "Beneath my dog-furred leaves"   Five Poems
    (1928)

    5755* Cole, Hugo. Six Sitwell Songs, L: N, 1968. Cyc.:
        high v., pf.

Switchback   "By the blue wooden sea"   Wheels: A Third Cycle
    (1919)

    5756 Walton, William. Façade, MS, perf. 24 Jan. 1922.
        Setting for reciter, ch. ensemble.

Sylph, The   "Cornucopia of Ceres, The"   Rustic Elegies
    (1927) as part of "Prelude to a Fairy Tale", rev. 1930

    5757* Cole, Hugo. "A Sylph's Song", Six Sitwell Songs, L:
        N, 1968. Cyc.: high v., pf.

Sylph's Song   See: Valse Maigre, 1843

Sylph's Song, The   See: Sylph, The

Tarantella*   "Where the satyrs are chattering, nymphs with
    their flattering"   Façade (programme notes of perf. held
    June 1926)

    5758 Walton, William. Façade (perf. 29 June 1926), L:
        OUP, 1951 (hire). Setting for reciter, fl.
        (doubl. pic.), cl. (doubl. b. cl.), tpt., a
        sax., vcl(s)., perc. Incl. in "Façade" First
        Suite for Orchestra, L: OUP. Ste.: orch. (incl.
        dbl. ww.). Arr. by Walter Goehr as one of Four
        Dances from "Façade", L: OUP. Setting for small
        orch. (with additional opt. pts.). Also publ.
        L: OUP (hire) for 2 pf.

Through Gilded Trellises   "Through gilded trellises like the
    sun"   Façade (1922)

    5759 Meale, Richard. "Through...", MS 1949. Song: s solo,
        pf.

660

itwell, Edith continued

5760 Walton, William. Façade (perf. 2(Apr. 1926 [pos-
      sibly 12 June 1923]), L: OUP, 1951 (hire). Set-
      ting for reciter, fl. (doubl. pic.), cl. (doubl.
      b. cl.), tpt., a sax., vcl(s)., perc.

5761* Walton, William. Three Songs, L: OUP, 1932. Song:
      s solo, pf.

Trams "Castles of crystal" Twentieth Century Harlequin
       and Other Poems (1916), rev. 1920

5762 Walton, William. Façade, MS, perf. 27 Apr. 1926.
      Setting for reciter, ch. ensemble.

Trio for Two Cats and a Trombone   See: Long Steel Grass

Valse Maigre, 1843   "Daisy and Lily"   Vogue, London (Dec.
      1925), rev. 1926, rev. 1927, rev. 1936

5763 Walton, William. "Valse", Façade (perf. 27 Apr.
      1926 [possibly 12 June 1923]), L: OUP, 1951
      (hire). Setting for reciter, fl. (doubl. pic.),
      cl. (doubl. b. cl.), tpt., a sax., vcl(s).,
      perc. Incl. in "Façade" First Suite for
      Orchestra, L: OUP. Ste.: orch. (incl. dbl. ww.).
      Also publ. L: OUP for 2 pf.

Waltz   See: Valse Maigre, 1843

Weeping Babe, The   "Snow is near gone, The"   In coll. with
      Tippett (1945) Not publ. sep.

5764 Tippett, Michael. L: S, 1945. Motet: s solo, satb,
      a cap.

When Sir Beelzebub   "When/Sir/Beelzebub called for his syl-
      labub" Façade (programme notes of perf. held Jan. 1922),
      rev. 1923

661

Sitwell, Edith continued

    5765 Walton, William. Façade (perf. 24 Jan. 1922), L:
          OUP, 1951 (hire). Setting for reciter, fl.
          (doubl. pic.), cl. (doubl. b. cl.), tpt., a
          sax., vcl(s)., perc.

White Owl, The   See: Owl, The

Wind's Bastinado, The   "Wind's bastinado, The"   Façade
    (programme notes of concert held Jan. 1922)

    5766 Walton, William. Façade, MS, perf. 24 Jan. 1922.
          Setting for reciter, ch. ensemble.

Young Girl, A   "Is it the light of the snow"   Green Song
    and Other Poems (1944)

    5767 Williamson, Malcolm. L: Weinberger, 1964. Song:
          satb, a cap.

Youth with the Red-Gold Hair, The   "Gold-armoured ghost from
    the Roman road, The"   Life and Letters To-day (Jan. 1941)

    5768 Beckwith, John. Four Songs to Poems by Edith Sit-
          well, MS 1949. Cyc.: s or t solo, pf.

Miscellanea

    5769 Hoddinott, Alun. A setting cited in Musical Times
          (Oct. 1955) has been withdrawn by the composer.

    5770 Williamson, Malcolm. Epitaphs for Edith Sitwell, L:
          Weinberger, 1967. Org. only. Also arr. for str.
          orch.

662

itwell, Osbert

SITWELL, Osbert   1892-1969

Dusk   "Night like a hawk"   Argonaut_and_Juggernaut (1919)
    5771 Williams, Gerrard. L: Curwen, 1921. Song: solo v.,
          pf.

Winter the Huntsman   "Through his iron glades rides"   Poor
Young_People (1925)
    5772 Dodgson, Stephen. Three_Winter_Songs, L: C, 1974.
          Cyc.: s or t solo, ob. obbl., pf.
    5773 Hand, Colin. L: BH, 1956. Song: ss, pf.
    5774 Lutyens, Elisabeth. MS ca. 1934. Ch. cta.: chorus,
          tpt., vcl., pf.
    5775 McCracken, Colleen. "The Huntsman", MS 1953, avail.
          University of Auckland. Song: med. v., pf.
    5776 Pedley, David. L: OUP, 1966. Song: satb, a cap.

Miscellanea
    5777 Walton, William. Belshazzar's_Feast, L: OUP, 1931.
          Oratorio: bar solo, satb, orch. Text selected
          (from the Bible) and arr. by Sitwell. German
          transl. by Beryl de Zoete and Baronin Imma Doern-
          berg.

SITWELL, Sacheverell   1897-

Pindar   "Pindar asleep beneath the planes"   The_People's
Palace (1918)
    5778 Bailey, Judith M. "Legende of Pindar", MS. Song: ms
          or a solo, cl., pf.

663

Sitwell, Sacheverell continued

Rio Grande, The   "By the Rio Grande"   The Thirteenth Caesar
and Other Poems (1924)

  5779 Lambert, Constant. L: OUP, 1930 (1974). Setting for
      satb, orch., pf. solo.

Serenade I   "Sigh soft, sigh softly"   Selected Poems of
Sacheverell Sitwell (1948) as one of "Serenades"

  5780 Shepherd, Arthur. Seven Songs, Northampton, Mass.:
      NVMP, 1961. Song: high v., pf., vla. obbl.

Miscellanea

  5781 Berners, Gerald. "The Triumph of Neptune", L: JWC,
      1927. Music drama. Text by Sitwell.

  5782 Walton, William. "The First Shoot", MS, prod. Man-
      chester, Dec. 1935. Ballet music: orch. Scenario
      by Sitwell.

SMITH, Florence Margaret   See: SMITH, Stevie

SMITH, Stevie   1902-1971

Actress, The   "I cant say I enjoyed it"   In Mother, What is
Man? (1942)

  5783 Lutyens, Elisabeth. Nine Songs, L: OP, 1948. Song:
      v., pf.

Avondale   "How sweet the birds of Avondale"   In The Frog
Prince (1966)

nith, Stevie continued

5784 Hedges, Anthony. MS 1967. Song: ss, pf.

Away, Melancholy   "Away, melancholy"   In Not Waving but Drowning (1957)

5785 Parker, Alice. B: ECS, 1973. Song: sa, sa semi-chorus, tambourine.

Be Off!   "I'm sorry to say my dear wife is a dreamer"   In Mother, What is Man? (1942)

5786 Lutyens, Elisabeth. L: OP, n.d. Song: [solo] v., pf.

Bereaved Swan, The   "Wan"   In a good time was had by all (1937)

5787 Young, Douglas. Not Waving but Drowning, MS 1970, L: F (hire). Cyc.: ms solo, pf.

Ceux qui luttent   "Ceux qui luttent ce sont ceux qui vivent" In Tender Only to One (1938)

5788 Lutyens, Elisabeth. Nine Songs, L: OP, 1948. Song: v., pf.

'Come on, Come Back'   "Left by the ebbing tide of battle" In Not Waving but Drowning (1957)

5789 Young, Douglas. Not Waving but Drowning, MS 1970, L: F (hire). Cyc.: ms solo, pf.

Fafnir and the Knights   "In the quiet waters"   In Not Waving but Drowning (1957)

5790 Young, Douglas. "Fafnir", Of Birds and Beasts, L: F (hire). Cta.: satb, orch.

Father for a Fool, A   "Little Master Home-from-School"   In Tender Only to One (1938)

5791 Young, Douglas. Not Waving but Drowning, MS 1970, L: F (hire). Cyc.: ms solo, pf.

Film Star, The   "Donnez à manger aux affamées"   In Mother, What is Man? (1942)

5792 Lutyens, Elisabeth. Nine Songs, L: OP, 1948. Song: v., pf.

Frog Prince, The   "I am a frog"   In The Frog Prince (1966)

5793 Crosse, Gordon. Four Songs, L: OUP, publ. forth-coming. Song: high v., pf.

Lady 'Rogue' Singleton   "Come, wed me, Lady Singleton"   In Mother, What is Man? (1942)

5794 Lutyens, Elisabeth. Nine Songs, L: OP, 1948. Song: v., pf.

Magic Morning, The   "Boating party, The"   In Mother, What is Man? (1942)

5795 Young, Douglas. Not Waving but Drowning, MS 1970, L: F (hire). Cyc.: ms solo, pf.

Night-Time in the Cemetery   "Funeral paths are hung with snow, The"   In a good time was had by all (1937)

5796 Young, Douglas. Not Waving but Drowning, MS 1970, L: F (hire). Cyc.: ms solo, pf.

Not Waving but Drowning   "Nobody heard him, the dead man"   In Not Waving but Drowning (1957)

5797 Young, Douglas. Not Waving but Drowning, MS 1970, L: F (hire). Cyc.: ms solo, pf.

Pad, Pad   "I always remember your beautiful flowers"   In Harold's Leap (1950)

5798 Lutyens, Elisabeth. Nine Songs, L: OP, 1948. Song:
       v., pf.

Poor Soul, poor Girl! (A Debutante)   "I cannot imagine any-
    thing nicer"   In Selected Poems (1962)

    5799 Cousins, John E. MS. Song: s solo, pf.

Progression   "I fell in love with Major Spruce"   In a good
    time was had by all (1937)

    5800 Lutyens, Elisabeth. Nine Songs, L: OP, 1948. Song:
           v., pf.

Repentance of Lady T, The   "I look in the glass"   In
    Mother, What is Man? (1942)

    5801 Lutyens, Elisabeth. Nine Songs, L: OP, 1948. Song:
           v., pf.

Songster, The   "Miss Pauncefort sang at the top of her
    voice"   In a good time was had by all (1937)

    5802 Lutyens, Elisabeth. Nine Songs, L: OP, 1948. Song:
           v., pf.

Up and Down   "Up and down the streets they go"   In a good
    time was had by all (1937)

    5803 Lutyens, Elisabeth. Nine Songs, L: OP, 1948. Song:
           v., pf.

When the Sparrow flies   "When the sparrow flies to the
    delicate branch"   In Mother, What is Man? (1942)

    5804 Orton, Richard. Grt. Y.: G, 1970. Song: satb, a cap.

Miscellanea

    5805 Holloway, Robin. The Death of God, MS 1972-73, L:
           OUP. Cta. Incl. verses by Stevie Smith.

667

Smith, Stevie continued

    5806   Holloway, Robin. Five Little Songs about Death, MS
           1972-73. Songs: s solo, [pf.?]. Texts by Stevie
           Smith.

    5807   Holloway, Robin. Four Poems of Stevie Smith, MS
           1968-69. Songs: s solo, [pf.?].

SNOW, Percy Charles   1905-

  Miscellanea

    5808   Wordsworth, William. "The Young and Ancient Men",
           MS 1951. Incidental music [to dramatic
           production].

SOUTAR, William   1898-1943

  Ae Simmers Day   "Up by the caller fountain"   In Seeds in
  the Wind (1933)

    5809   Dalby, Martin. The Fiddler, L: N (hire). Cyc.: s or
           t solo, vln.

  Auld Aik, The   "Auld aik's doun, The"   In Collected Poems
  (1948)

    5810   Britten, Benjamin. Who are these children?, L: F,
           1972. Cyc.: t solo, pf.

  Bairn-Time   "Fa'owre, fa'owre, wi' the auld sang"   In Collected Poems (1948)

    5811   Dalby, Martin. "Cradle Sang", The Fiddler, L: N
           (hire). Cyc.: s or t solo, vln.

Ballad "O! shairly ye hae seen my love" In <u>Collected</u>
<u>Poems</u> (1948)

 5812 Cheslock, Louis. MS, avail. NYPL. Song: ms or a
       solo, pf.

Bawsy Broon "Dinna gang out the nicht" In <u>Poems in Scots</u>
<u>and English</u> (1961)

 5813 Stevenson, Ronald. "Hallowe'en Sang", <u>Eleven Soutar</u>
       <u>Songs</u>, MS 1966-73. Song: med. v., pf.

Bed-time "Cuddle-down, my bairnie" In <u>Collected Poems</u>
(1948)

 5814 Britten, Benjamin. <u>Who are these children?</u>, L: F,
       1972. Cyc.: t solo, pf.

Black Day "Skelp frae his teacher, A" In <u>Collected Poems</u>
(1948)

 5815 Britten, Benjamin. <u>Who are these children?</u>, L: F,
       1972. Cyc.: t solo, pf.

Buckie Braes, The "It isna far frae our toun" In <u>Collect-</u>
<u>ed Poems</u> (1948)

 5816 Stevenson, Ronald. <u>Eleven Soutar Songs</u>, MS 1966-73.
       Song: med. v., pf.

Child You Were, The See: "It was your faither and mither"

Corbie Sang "Merle in the hauch sings sweet, The" In
<u>Poems in Scots and English</u> (1961)

 5817 Scott, Francis G. MS 1943, avail. SMA. Song: med.
       v., pf.

Daft Tree, The "Tree's a leerie kind o' loon, A" In <u>Seeds</u>
<u>in the Wind</u> (1933)

Soutar, William continued

5818 Dalby, Martin. Bairn-rhymes, L: N, 1964. Song: high
v., pf. or children's v., pf.

Day is Düne   "Lully, lylly, my ain wee dearie"   In Collected Poems (1948)

5819 Stevenson, Ronald. In Child Education (Spring 1968).
Song: high or med. v., pf.

Dreepin Weather   "Out stapp't the ae duck"   In Collected
Poems (1948)

5820 Stevenson, Ronald. Eleven Soutar Songs, MS 1966-73.
Song: med. v., pf.

Droll Wee Man, The   "There was a wee bit mannie"   In
Collected Poems (1948)

5821 Stevenson, Ronald. Eleven Soutar Songs, MS 1966-73.
Song: med. v., pf.

Earth, The   See: "There's pairt o' it young"

Fiddler, The   "Fiddler gaed fiddlin' thru oor toun, A"   In
Seeds in the Wind (1933)

5822 Dalby, Martin. The Fiddler, L: N (hire). Cyc.: s or
t solo, vln.

Gowk, The   "Half doun the hill, whaur fa's the linn"   In
Seeds in the Wind (1933)

5823 Scott, Francis G. MS 1934, avail. SMA. Song: med.
v., pf.

Hill Sang   "Liggan on a mossy knowe"   In Collected Poems
(1948)

5824 Stevenson, Ronald. Eleven Soutar Songs, MS 1966-73.
Song: med. v., pf.

outar, William continued

In Time of Tumult   "Thunder and the dark, The"   In In the
Time of Tyrants (1939)

5825 Scott, Francis G. Seven Songs for Baritone Voice,
      Glasgow: B&F, 1946. Song: bar solo, pf.

"It was your faither and mither"   In Collected Poems (1948)

5826 Britten, Benjamin. "A Riddle (The Child You Were)",
      Who are these children?, L: F, 1972. Cyc.: t
      solo, pf.

Laddie's Sang, A   "O! it's owre the braes abüne our toun"
In Collected Poems (1948)

5827 Britten, Benjamin. Who are these children?, L: F,
      1972. Cyc.: t solo, pf.

Lanely Müne, The   "Saftly, saftly through the mirk"   In
Seeds in the Wind (1933)

5828 Dalby, Martin. Bairn-rhymes, L: N, 1964. Song: high
      v., pf. or children's v., pf.

Larky Lad, The   "Larky lad frae the pantry, The"   In
Collected Poems (1948)

5829 Britten, Benjamin. Who are these children?, L: F,
      1972. Cyc.: t solo, pf.

Lea, The   "I think no heaven shall ever be"   In The
Solitary Way (1934)

5830 Stevenson, Ronald. Eleven Soutar Songs, MS 1966-73.
      Song: med. v., pf.

Lucky Chap, A   "Wee cock-robin he bobbit east and west"   In
Collected Poems (1948)

5831 Stevenson, Ronald. Eleven Soutar Songs, MS 1966-73.
      Song: med. v., pf.

671

Soutar, William continued

Nightmare   "Tree stood flowering in a dream, The"   In In
    the Time of Tyrants (1939)

    5832 Britten, Benjamin. Who are these children?, L: F,
          1972. Cyc.: t solo, pf.

Plum-Tree, The   "Come oot, come oot"   In Seeds in the Wind
    (1933)

    5833 Stevenson, Ronald. Eleven Soutar Songs, MS 1966-73.
          Song: med. v., pf.

Quiet Comes In, The   "Whan the rage is by"   In Collected
    Poems (1948)

    5834 Stevenson, Ronald. Eleven Soutar Songs, MS 1966-73.
          Song: med. v., pf.

Samson   "Man comes, at last, to his necessitous hour"   In
    In the Time of Tyrants (1939)

    5835* Scott, Francis G. MS 1940. Song: med. v., pf.

Sang   "Hairst the licht o' the müne"   In Poems in Scots and
    English (1961)

    5836 Dalby, Martin. Bairn-rhymes, L: N, 1964. Song: high
          v., pf. or children's v., pf.

Slaughter   "Within the violence of the storm"   In But the
    Earth Abideth (1943)

    5837 Britten, Benjamin. Who are these children?, L: F,
          1972. Cyc.: t solo, pf.

Supper   "Steepies for the bairnie"   In Collected Poems
    (1948)

    5838 Britten, Benjamin. Who are these children?, L: F,
          1972. Cyc.: t solo, pf.

672

Soutar, William continued

"There's pairt o' it young" In Collected_Poems (1948)

5839 Britten, Benjamin. "A Riddle (The Earth)", Who_are
      these_children?, L: F, 1972. Cyc.: t solo, pf.

Thistle, The   "Blaw, wind, blaw"   In Seeds_in_the_Wind
(1933)

  5840 Dalby, Martin. The_Fiddler, L: N (hire). Cyc.: s or
        t solo, vln.

To the Future*   "We [He], the unborn, shall bring"   In In
the_Time_of_Tyrants (1939), rev. 1943

  5841 Stevenson, Ronald. Eleven_Soutar_Songs, MS 1966-73.
        Song: med. v., pf.

Tryst, The   "O luely, luely, cam she in"   In Poems_in_Scots
(1935)

  5842 Scott, Francis G. Songs, Glasgow: B&F, 1949. Song:
        t solo, pf.

Waggletail   "Out rins Waggletail"   In Collected_Poems
(1948)

  5843 Stevenson, Ronald. Eleven_Soutar_Songs, MS 1966-73.
        Song: med. v., pf.

Who Are These Children?   "With easy hands upon the rein"
In Collected_Poems (1948)

  5844 Britten, Benjamin. Who_are_these_children?, L: F,
        1972. Cyc.: t solo, pf.

Miscellanea

  5845 Britten, Benjamin. "The Children", Who_are_these
        children?, L: F, 1972. Cyc.: t solo, pf.

673

Soutar, William continued

    5846 Dalby, Martin. "The Bubbly Jock", *The Fiddler*, L: N
           (hire). Cyc.: s or t solo, vln. Text begins: "The
           bubbly jock's been at the barm".

    5847 Dunlop, Isobel. "Such is the Beauty", MS pre-1954.
           Song: chorus, a cap.

    5848 Dunlop, Isobel. *Seven Songs*, MS pre-1954. Songs: v.,
           pf. Texts by Soutar.

SPENDER, Stephen Harold   1909-

Cries of Evening, The   See: "I hear the cries of evening,
    while the paw"

Express, The   "After the first powerful plain manifesto"
  New Signatures (1932), rev. 1955

    5849 Finney, Ross Lee. MS, perf. NY 1958. Song: s solo,
           pf.

"I am the witness through whom the whole" In *Poems of
Dedication* (1947) as one of "Spiritual Explorations", rev.
1955

    5850 Brown, Newel K. "I am that witness", *On the Third
           Summer Day*, MS. Cyc.: s solo, orch.

"I hear the cries of evening, while the paw" *Twenty Poems*
(1930), rev. 1955

    5851 Maw, Nicholas. "I Hear the Cries of Evening",
           Nocturne, L: JWC, 1960. Cyc.: ms solo, ch. orch.

I think continually   See: I Think of Those

Spender, Stephen continued

"I think continually of those who were truly great"   See: I
Think of Those

I Think of Those   "I think of those who were truly great"
Listener (Nov. 1931), rev. 1932, rev. 1933, rev. 1955

5852 Joubert, John. The Choir Invisible, L: N, 1968.
Choral symph.: bar solo, orch. Complete work also
requires satb.

5853 Lawson, Richard A. "I think continually of those who
were truly great", MS 1966, avail. Hamilton
Teachers' College. Song: satb, pf.

Ice   "She came in from the snowing air"   Horizon (Mar.
1949), rev. 1955

5854 Wood, Hugh. MS. Song: high v., pf.

Man-made World, A   "What a wild room"   In The Edge of Being
(1949), rev. 1955

5855 Brown, Newel K. Spender Cycle, MS. Cyc.: s solo,
pf., str. qrt. or s solo, pf.

My Parents   "My parents kept me from children who were
rough"   New Signatures (1932), rev. 1933, rev. 1955

5856 Brown, Newel K. "My parents kept...", On the Third
Day, MS. Cyc.: s solo, orch.

"My parents kept me from children who were rough"   See: My
Parents

On the Third Day   "On the first summer day"   In The Edge of
Being (1949)

5857 Brown, Newel K. On the Third Summer Day, MS. Cyc.:
s solo, orch.

675

Spender, Stephen continued

"One is the witness through whom the whole"   See: "I am the
witness through whom the whole"

"Rolled over on Europe: the sharp dew frozen to stars"
Poems (1933)

5858 Brown, Newel K. "Rolled Over On Europe", Spender
Cycle, MS. Cyc.: s solo, pf., str. qrt. or s
solo, pf.

Stopwatch and an Ordnance Map, A   "Stopwatch and an ordnance map, A"   In The Still Centre (1939), rev. 1955

5859* Barber, Samuel. NY: GS, 1942. Song: male v. chorus,
3 timp. Rev. for male v. chorus, 3 timp., 4 hn.,
3 trbn., tuba ad lib.

Two Kisses   "I wear your kiss like a feather"   In The Still
Centre (1939), rev. 1955

5860 Brown, Newel K. Spender Cycle, MS. Cyc.: s solo,
pf., str. qrt. or s solo, pf.

Weep, Girl, Weep   "Weep, girl, weep"   In The Edge of Being
(1949)

5861 Brown, Newel K. Spender Cycle, MS. Cyc.: s solo,
pf., str. qrt. or s solo, pf.

What I Expected   See: "What I expected, was"

"What I expected, was"   New Statesman (Feb. 1931), rev.
1933, rev. 1955, rev. 1964

5862 Corigliano, John. NY: GS, 1966. Song: satb, pf. or
satb, br. choir, perc.

Miscellanea

Spender, Stephen continued

5863 Finney, Ross Lee. The Jan. 1967 issue of **Musical**
    Quarterly states incorrectly that Finney's **Still**
    Are New Worlds (MS 1962, NY: CFP) includes set-
    tings of texts by Spender.

5864 Meale, Richard. **This I**, MS 1955. Three songs for
    s solo, pf. to words by Spender.

SQUIRE, John Collings   1884-1958

Epitaph in Old Mode   "Leaves fall gently on the grass, The"
  In **Poems**, Second Series (1922)

5865 Gurney, Ivor. **A Second Volume of Ten Songs**, L: OUP,
    1938. Song: solo v., pf.

March, The   "I heard a voice that cried, 'Make way for those
who died!'"   In **Twelve Poems** (1916)

5866 Bantock, Granville. L: JWC, 1919. Song: male v., pf.

Meditation in Lamplight   "What deaths men have died, not
fighting but impotent"   In **Poems**, Second Series (1922)

5867 Tranchell, Peter. "What Deaths Men have Died", MS
    ca. 1942. Song: t solo, [pf.].

Mr. H. Belloc   "At Martinmas, when I was born"   In **Tricks**
of the Trade (1917)

5868 Warlock, Peter. "Mr. Belloc's Fancy", L: A, 1922.
    Song: t solo, pf. Also publ. for bar solo, pf.
    Rev. 1930; rev. version publ. L: A, 1930.

Mr. W.H. Davies   "I'm sure that you would never guess"   In
Tricks of the Trade (1917)

Squire, J.C. continued

5869 Malotte, Albert. "The Poor Old Man", NY: GS, 1939.
        Song: med. v., pf.

Ship, The "There was no song nor shout of joy" In Twelve
    Poems (1916)

    5870 Gurney, Ivor. A Third Volume of Ten Songs, L: OUP,
            1952. Song: solo v., pf.

    5871 Parfrey, Raymond. MS. Song: bar solo, pf.

    5872 Sang, Henry. MS ca. 1936. Song: [v., pf.?].

Sir Henry Newbolt "It was eight bells in the forenoon" In
    Tricks of the Trade (1917)

    5873 Rootham, C.B. "Eight Bells", L: Curwen, 1926. Song:
            ttbb, a cap.

Song "You are my sky; beneath your circling kindness" In
    Poems, Second Series (1922)

    5874 Gurney, Ivor. "You Are My Sky", A First Volume of
            Ten Songs, L: OUP, 1938. Song: solo v., pf.

STARKEY, James Sullivan See: O'SULLIVAN, Seumas

STEPHENS, James 1882-1950

An Evening Falls See: As Evening Falls

And it was Windy Weather "Now the winds are riding by" In
    Songs from the Clay (1915)

678

Stephens, James continued

5875 Adler, Samuel. "And it was stormy weather", Four
Poems of James Stephens, NY: OUP, 1963. Song:
high v., pf.

5876 Parke, Dorothy. "As it was windy weather", MS 1962.
Song: chorus, [a cap.?].

Anthony O'Daly   "Since your limbs were laid out"   In
Reincarnations (1918)

5877 Barber, Samuel. Reincarnations, NY: GS, 1942. Song:
satb, a cap.

5878 Mourant, Walter. MS, avail. ACA. Song: med. v., pf.

Arpeggio   "He wills to be"   In Collected Poems (1926)

5879 Mourant, Walter. MS, avail. ACA. Song: med. v., pf.

As Evening Falls   "At eve the horse is freed of plough"   In
Songs from the Clay (1915), rev. 1926

5880 Mourant, Walter. "An Evening Falls", MS, avail. ACA.
Song: med. v., pf.

At the Edge of the Sea   "There was a river that rose"   In
Songs from the Clay (1915)

5881 Dobson, Tom. NY: GS, pre-1940. Song: [v., pf.?].

Barbarians   "I pause beside the stream"   In Songs from the
Clay (1915)

5882 Mourant, Walter. MS copyright by composer 1963,
avail. ACA. Song: med. v., pf.

Bessie Bobtail   "As down the road she wambled slow"   In The
Hill of Vision (1912)

5883* Barber, Samuel. NY: GS, 1955, Three Songs (Opus 2).
Song: v., pf.

679

Stephens, James continued

5884   Mourant, Walter. MS, avail. ACA. Song: a solo, pf.

Bird sings now, A   See: Ora Pro Nobis

Breakfast Time   "Sun is always in the sky, The"   In The
Adventures of Seumas Beg [and] The Rocky Road to Dublin
(1915) as one of "The Adventures..."

    5885   Dobson, Tom. The Rocky Road to Dublin, B: OD, pre-
            1940. Cyc.: [v., pf.?].

    5886   Mourant, Walter. MS, avail. ACA. Song: med. v., pf.

Buds, The*   "Now I can see"   In Songs from the Clay (1915),
rev. 1926

    5887   Mourant, Walter. MS copyright by composer 1953,
            avail. ACA. Song: med. v., pf.

Canal Bank, The   "I know a girl"   In The Adventures of
Seumas Beg [and] The Rocky Road to Dublin (1915) as one of
"The Rocky..."

    5888   Bowles, M. Five Songs on Poems by James Stephens,
            NY: AMP, pre-1959. Song: med.-high v., pf.

    5889   Lapp, Horace. "I know...", MS 1964, avail. CMC.
            Song: med. v., pf.

    5890   Parke, Dorothy. A Honeycombe, MS 1951. Song: v., pf.

    5891   Strilko, Anthony. Bryn Mawr: M, pre-1969. Song: med.
            v., pf.

Centaurs, The   "Playing upon the hill three centaurs were!"
In Songs from the Clay (1915)

    5892   Busch, William. L: JWC, 1944. Song: v., pf.

Check   "Night was creeping on the ground"   In The Adventures of Seumas Beg [and] The Rocky Road to Dublin
(1915) as one of "The Adventures..."; subsequently rev.

Stephens, James continued

5893 Butterworth, Arthur. Four Nocturnal Songs, MS 1948.
       Song: s solo, pf.

5894 Mourant, Walter. MS copyright by composer 1963,
       avail. ACA. Song: med. v., pf.

Chill ot the Eve   "Long, green swell, A"   In Insurrections
(1909)

5895 Adler, Samuel. Four Poems of James Stephens, NY:
       OUP, 1963. Song: high v., pf.

5896 Mourant, Walter. MS, avail. ACA. Song: med. v., pf.

Christmas at Freelands   "Red-Bud, the Kentucky Tree, The"
In Collected Poems (1926)

5897 Parke, Dorothy. "A Snowy Field", L: Curwen, 1951.
       Song: solo v., satb, a cap. Setting ot lines
       beginning: "A snowy field! A stable piled".

Coolin, The   See: Coolun, The

Coolun, The   "Come with me, under my coat"   In Reincarnations (1918), rev. 1926

5898 Barber, Samuel. "The Coolin", Reincarnations, NY:
       GS, 1942. Song: satb, a cap.

5899 Lapp, Horace. "The Coolin'", MS 1964, avail. CMC.
       Song: med. v., pf.

5900 Mourant, Walter. "The Coolin", MS, avail. ACA. Song:
       med. v., pf.

5901 Parke, Dorothy. "The Coolin", A Honeycombe, MS 1951.
       Song: v., pf.

County Mayo, The   "Now with the coming in of the spring"
In Reincarnations (1918) Transl. from Raftery

5902 Trimble, Joan. The County Mayo, MS. Cyc.: bar solo,
       2 pf.

Daisies, The   "In the scented bud of the morning-O"   In
Here are Ladies (1913)

5903* Barber, Samuel. NY: GS, 1936 (1942), Three Songs
(Opus 2). Song: v., pf.

5904 Bowles, M. Five Songs on Poems by James Stephens,
NY: AMP, pre-1959. Song: med.-high v., pf.

5905 Farley, Roland. NY: NME, pre-1940. Song: [v., pf.?].

5906 Mann, Leslie. Three Songs, MS 1955, avail. CMC.
Song: [t] solo v., pf.

5907 Mourant, Walter. MS, avail. ACA. Song: med. v., pf.

5908 Mulliner, Michael. L: OUP, 1950. Song: t solo, pf.

5909 Parke, Dorothy. A Honeycombe, MS 1951. Song: v., pf.

5910 Quilter, Roger. "In the...", L: BH, 1927. Song: v.,
pf.

5911 Shepherd, Arthur. "In the...", MS, avail. University
of Utah. Song: v., pf.

5912 Wyrill, Marion. L: MM, 1931, assigned L: C, 1943.
Song: [v., pf.].

Egan O'Rahilly   "Here in a distant place"   In Reincarnations (1918)

5913 Mourant, Walter. MS, avail. ACA. Song: med. v., pf.

"Everything that I can spy"   In The Hill of Vision (1912)

5914 Mourant, Walter. MS, avail. ACA. Song: med. v., pf.

Fifteen Acres, The   "I cling and swing"   In The Adventures
of Seumas Beg [and] The Rocky Road to Dublin (1915) as one
of "The Rocky..."

5915* Bridge, Frank. "So Early in the Morning, O", L: WR,
1918. Song: solo v., pf.

Stephens, James continued

5916 Gwyther, Geoffrey. "So Early in the Morning, O", L:
      C, 1921. Song: [solo v., pf.].

Follow, Follow, Follow   See: Prelude and a Song, A

Four Old Men, The   "In the Café where I sit"   In Songs from
the Clay (1915)

   5917* Swain, Freda. MS 1958, avail. Chinnor: Channel,
         NEMO. Setting for s and pf. ensemble.

Glass of Beer, A   See: Righteous Anger

Goat Paths, The   "Crooked paths, The"   In Songs from the
Clay (1915)

   5918 Howells, Herbert. In Green Ways, L: OUP, 1929. Cyc.:
         high v., pf.

   5919 Mourant, Walter. MS, avail. ACA. Song: med. v., pf.

Grafton Street   "At four o'clock, in dainty talk"   In The
Adventures of Seumas Meg [and] The Rocky Road to Dublin
(1915) as one of "The Rocky..."

   5920 Dobson, Tom. The Rocky Road to Dublin, B: OD, pre-
         1940. Cyc.: [v., pf.?].

Hesperus*   "Upon the sky"   In Songs from the Clay (1915),
rev. 1926

   5921 May, Frederick. MS. Song: v., pf.

In the Night   "There always is a noise"   In Songs from the
Clay (1915)

   5922 Cone, Edward T. Three Miniatures, MS. Choral ste.:
         ttbb, a cap.

683

In the Poppy Field   "Mad Patsy said, he said to me"   In <u>The Hill of Vision</u> (1912)

    5923 Clark, Joyce McGowan. L: Curwen, 1924. Song: solo
        v., pf.

    5924 Treharne, Bryceson. "Mad Patsy", B: BMC, pre-1940.
        Song: [solo v., pf.?].

    5925 Trimble, Joan. <u>The County Mayo</u>, MS. Cyc.: bar solo,
        2 pf.

Inis Fál   "Now may we turn aside"   In <u>Reincarnations</u> (1918)

    5926 Trimble, Joan. <u>The County Mayo</u>, MS. Cyc.: bar solo,
        2 pf.

Katty Gollagher   "Hill is bare, The"   In <u>The Adventures of Seumas Beg [and] The Rocky Road to Dublin</u> (1915) as one of "The Rocky..."

    5927 Cone, Edward T. <u>Three Miniatures</u>, MS. Choral ste.:
        ttbb, a cap.

    5928 Dobson, Tom. "Pastoral", <u>The Rocky Road to Dublin</u>,
        B: OD, pre-1940. Cyc.: [v., pf.?].

    5929 Mourant, Walter. MS, avail. ACA. Song: med. v., pf.

King of the Fairy Men, The   "I know the man without a soul" In <u>Songs from the Clay</u> (1915)

    5930 Homer, Sidney. NY: GS, pre-1940, <u>Four Modern Poems</u>,
        MS (Opus 34). Song: [v., pf.?].

    5931* Swain, Freda. MS 1934, avail. Chinnor: Channel,
        NEMO. Setting for s (or t) and pf. ensemble.

Lesbia*   "Sweet/And delicate"   In <u>Little Things</u> (1924),
rev. 1926

    5932 Parke, Dorothy. <u>A Honeycombe</u>, MS 1951. Song: v., pf.

Stephens, James continued

Little Things   "Little things that run and quail"   In
    Little Things (1924), rev. 1926

    5933 Duckworth, Arthur. "Little Creatures Everywhere", L:
          Curwen, 1966. Song: sa, pf.

    5934 Mourant, Walter. MS, avail. ACA. Song: med. v., pf.

    5935 Ward, Robert. Sacred Songs for Pantheists, NY: HP,
          1966. Song: s solo, orch. or s solo, pf.

Main Deep, The   "Long-rólling, The"   In A Poetry Recital
    (1925)

    5936 Duff, Arthur. Dublin: Cuala, 1937 in Broadside, No.
          4. Song: v., unacc.

Market, The   "Man came to me at the fair, A"   In Songs from
    the Clay (1915)

    5937 Gibbs, C. Armstrong. L: Curwen, 1926. Song: solo v.,
          pf.

Mary Hynes   "She is the sky of the sun"   In Reincarnations
    (1918)

    5938 Barber, Samuel. Reincarnations, NY: GS, 1942. Song:
          satb, a cap.

    5939 Mourant, Walter. MS, avail. ACA. Song: med. v., pf.

Mary Ruane   "Sky-like girl whom we knew!, The"   In Re-
    incarnations (1918)

    5940 Mourant, Walter. MS, avail. ACA. Song: med. v., pf.

Messenger, The   "Bee! tell me whence do you come?"   In
    Songs from the Clay (1915), rev. 1926

    5941 Parke, Dorothy. "Queen of the Bees", A Honeycombe,
          MS 1951. Song: v., pf.

Stephens, James continued

5942 Taylor, Deems. <u>Three Songs</u>, MS 1920, NY: JF. Song:
[v., pf.].

Midnight* "And suddenly I wakened in a fright" In <u>The</u>
<u>Adventures of Seumas Beg [and] The Rocky Road to Dublin</u>
(1915) as one of "The Adventures...", rev. 1926

5943 Lapp, Horace. MS 1964, avail. CMC. Song: med. v.,
pf.

Nancy Walsh "It is not on her gown" In <u>Reincarnations</u>
(1918)

5944 Mourant, Walter. MS, avail. ACA. Song: med. v., pf.

Nothing at All "There was a man was very old" In <u>The Hill</u>
<u>of Vision</u> (1912)

5945 Mourant, Walter. MS, avail. ACA. Song: med. v., pf.

Nucleolus "I look from Mount Derision" In <u>The Hill of</u>
<u>Vision</u> (1912)

5946* Swain, Freda. MS 1924, avail. Chinnor: Channel,
NEMO. Setting for s (or t) and pf. ensemble.

Ora Pro Nobis* "Bird is singing now, A" In <u>The Hill of</u>
<u>Vision</u> (1912), rev. 1926

5947 Mourant, Walter. "A Bird Sings Now", MS, avail. ACA.
Song: med. v., pf.

Out and Away "Silvery-black, and silvery-blue" In <u>A</u>
<u>Poetry Recital</u> (1925)

5948 Bax, Arnold. L: MM, 1926, assigned L: C, 1943. Song:
v., pf.

Paps of Dana, The "Mountains stand and stare around, The"
In <u>The Adventures of Seumas Beg [and] The Rocky Road to</u>
<u>Dublin</u> (1915) as one of "The Rocky..."

686

Stephens, James continued

5949   Mourant, Walter. MS, avail. ACA. Song: med. v., pf.

Peggy Mitchell   "As lily grows up easily"   In Re-incarnations (1918)

5950   Duke, John. NY: GS, 1965. Song: solo v., pf.

5951   Mourant, Walter. MS, avail. ACA. Song: med. v., pf.

5952   Parke, Dorothy. A Honeycombe, MS 1951. Song: v., pf.

5953   Trimble, Joan. The County Mayo, MS. Cyc.: bar solo,
       2 pf.

Piper, The   "Shepherd! while the lambs do feed"   In The
Adventures of Seumas Beg [and] The Rocky Road to Dublin
(1915) as one of "The Rocky..."

5954   Adler, Samuel. Four Poems of James Stephens, NY:
       OUP, 1963. Song: high v., pf.

5955   Stickles, William. "Shepherd, Play a Little Air",
       NY: HFL, pre-1940. Song: [v., pf.?].

5956   Taylor, Phyllis. L: Curwen, 1926. Song: unison v.,
       pf.

Prelude and a Song, A   "Song! glad indeed I am that we nave
met"   In The Hill of Vision (1912) A rev. portion was
incl. in Collected Poems (1926) under the title "Follow,
Follow, Follow"

5957   Hageman, Richard. "Me Company Along", NY: CF, 1925.
       Song: solo v., pf. Setting of lines beginning:
       "O follow, follow, follow!".

Reply, A   "You have sent your verse to me"   In Songs from
the Clay (1915)

5958* Swain, Freda. MS, avail. Chinnor: Channel, NEMO.
       Setting for bar and pf. ensemble. Setting of
       lines beginning: "Still lift up my heart and
       sing".

687

Stephens, James continued

Righteous Anger   "Lanky hank of a she in the inn over there,
   The" In Reincarnations (1918), rev. 1926

   5959 Andrews, Herbert K. "A Glass of Beer", L: OUP, 1949.
         Song: t solo, pf.

   5960 Wilson, James. "A Glass of Beer", Irish Songs, MS
         (Opus 40). Song: s solo, pf. or s solo, orch.

Rivals, The   "I heard a bird at dawn"   In Songs from the
   Clay (1915)

   5961 Bowles, M. Five Songs on Poems by James Stephens,
         NY: AMP, pre-1959. Song: med.-high v., pf.

   5962 Duff, Arthur. Dublin: Cuala, 1937 in Broadside, No.
         6. Song: v., unacc.

   5963 Mourant, Walter. MS, avail. ACA. Song: med. v., pf.

   5964 Taylor, Deems. Three Songs, MS 1920, NY: JF. Song:
         [v., pf.].

   5965 Teed, Roy. MS ca. 1963. Song: high v., pf.

   5966 White, L.J. L: OUP, 1952. Song: ss, [pf.].

Rose in the Wind, The   "Dip and swing"   In A Poetry Recital
   (1925)

   5967 Mourant, Walter. MS, avail. ACA. Song: med. v., pf.

Sarasvati   "As bird to nest, when, moodily"   In Strict Joy
   (1930)

   5968 Shepherd, Arthur. MS, avail. University of Utah.
         Song: v., pf.

Secret, The   "I was frightened, for a wind"   In The Adventures of Suemas Beg [and] The Rocky Road to Dublin
   (1915) as one of "The Adventures..."

   5969 Mourant, Walter. MS, aviil. ACA. Song: a solo, pf.

688

Stephens, James continued

Seumas Beg   "Man was sitting underneath a tree, A"   In
Insurrections (1909)

    5970 Dobson, Tom. The Rocky Road to Dublin, B: OD, pre-
        1940. Cyc.: [v., pf.?].

Shell, The   "And then I pressed the shell"   In Insurrections (1909)

    5971 Mourant, Walter. MS, avail. ACA. Song: med. v., pf.

Song for Lovers, A   "Moon is shining on the sea, The"   In
Songs from the Clay (1915)

    5972 Taylor, Deems. Three Songs, MS 1920, NY: JF. Song:
        [v., pf.].

Stephen's Green   "Wind stood up, and gave a shout, The"   In
The Adventures of Seumas Beg [and] The Rocky Road to Dublin (1915) as one of "The Rocky...", rev. 1926

    5973 Adler, Samuel. "The Wind", Four Poems of James
        Stephens, NY: OUP, 1963. Song: high v., pf.

    5974 Cone, Edward T. "The Wind", Three Miniatures, MS.
        Choral ste.: ttbb, a cap.

    5975 Lucas, Mary. "The Wind", L: Curwen, 1931. Song: solo
        v., pf.

Sweet Apple   "At the end of the bough"   In Here are Ladies
(1913)

    5976 Spier, Harry. NY: GS, pre-1940. Song: [v., pf.?].

Tale of Mad Brigid, The   "And then"   In Insurrections
(1909)

    5977 Mourant, Walter. MS, avail. ACA. Song: med. v., pf.

Tanist   "Remember the spider"   In Kings and the Moon (1938)
as one of "Kings and Tanists"

5978 Lapp, Horace. "Sermon", MS, avail. CMC. Song: v.,
pf.

This Way to Winter   "Day by day"   In Songs from the Clay
(1915)

5979 Mann, Leslie. Three Songs, MS 1955, avail. CMC.
Song: [t] solo v., pf.

To the Queen of the Bees   See: Messenger, The

Voice of God, The   "I bent again unto the ground"   In Songs
from the Clay (1915)

5980 Mourant, Walter. MS, avail. ACA. Song: med. v., pf.

Washed in Silver   "Gleaming in silver are the hills"   In
Songs from the Clay (1915)

5981 Mourant, Walter. MS, avail. ACA. Song: med. v., pf.

Watcher, The   "Rose for a young head, A"   In Insurrections
(1909)

5982 Forsyth, Cecil. NY: JF, pre-1940. Song: [v., pf.?].

5983 Treharne, Bryceson. NY: CPMC, pre-1940. Song: [v.,
pf.?].

Westland Row   "Every Sunday there's a throng"   In The
Adventures of Seumas Beg [and] The Rocky Road to Dublin
(1915) as one of "The Rocky..."

5984 Dobson, Tom. The Rocky Road to Dublin, B: OD, pre-
1940. Cyc.: [v., pf.?].

White Fields   "In the winter children go"   In The Adventures of Seumas Beg [and] The Rocky Road to Dublin
(1915) as one of "The Rocky..."

5985 Mourant, Walter. MS, avail. ACA. Song: med. v., pf.

Stephens, James continued

White Swan, The   "Could you but see her"   In Strict Joy
    (1930)

    5986 Bowles, M. Five Songs on Poems by James Stephens,
         NY: AMP, pre-1959. Song: med.-high v., pf.

White Window, The   "Moon comes every night to peep, The"
    In The Adventures of Seumas Beg [and] The Rocky Road to
    Dublin (1915) as one of "The Adventures..."

    5987 Heath, John. The Enchanted Hour, L: E, 1920. Cyc.:
         solo v., pf.

    5988 Mourant, Walter. MS, avail. ACA. Song: a solo, pf.

Wind, The   See: Stephen's Green

Wind and Tree   "Woman is a branchy tree, A"   In The Hill of
    Vision (1912), rev. 1926

    5989 Mann, Leslie. "A woman...", Three Songs, MS 1955.
         Song: [t] solo v., pf.

    5990 Mourant, Walter. "A woman...", MS, avail. ACA. Song:
         med. v., pf.

Woman is a Branchy Tree, A   See: Wind and Tree

Wood of Flowers, The   "I went to the Wood of Flowers"   In
    The Adventures of Seuman Beg [and] The Rocky Road to Dub-
    lin (1915) as one of "The Adventures..."

    5991 Klein, Ivy. L: CR, 1958. Song: solo v., pf.

Miscellanea

    5992 Besly, Maurice. "The Cat", Four Songs, L: BH, pre-
         1940. Song: [v., pf.].

    5993 Bowles, M. "Solitude", Five Songs on Poems by James
         Stephens, NY: AMP, pre-1959. Song: med.-high v.,
         pf.

Stephens, James continued

5994   Bruce, Robert. Four Part-Songs, MS pre-1972. Songs:
        satb, a cap. Incl. words by Stephens.

5995* Castleman, Henry. "If the Moon", NY: GS, pre-1940.
        Song: [v., pf.].

5996   Dobson, Tom. "The Cat", The Rocky Road to Dublin,
        B:OD, pre-1940. Song: [v., pf.?].

5997   Dunhill, Thomas F. "A Visit from the Moon", L: CR,
        pre-1940. Song: [v., pf.?].

5998   Farley, Roland. "Spring is Singing", NY: NME, pre-
        1940. Song: [v., pf.?].

5999   Holloway, Robin. Georgian Songs, MS 1972, L: OUP.
        Songs: bar solo, pf. Incl. words by Stephens.

6000   Lucas, Leighton. Grove's makes reference to 22 songs
        (MS 1944) for v., fl., vla., hp. to texts by
        Stephens.

6001   Mourant, Walter. "Lovers", MS, avail. ACA. Song: s
        solo, pf.

6002   Mourant, Walter. "When You Walk", MS, avail. ACA.
        Song: med. v., pf.

6003   Taylor, Colin. "The Hill", L: OUP, pre-1940. Song:
        [v., pf.?].

STEVENSON, Robert Louis   1850-1894

Alcaics to H.F. Brown   "Brave lads in olden musical
   centuries"   Letters of Robert Louis Stevenson to his
   Family and Friends (1899)

   6004   Wishart, Peter. "Old Songs", Songs and Satires, L:
           S&B, 1961. Madrigal ste.: satb, a cap.

"All this on earth and sea"   Three Short Poems (1898)

692

tevenson, Robert Louis continued

6005 Moore, Francis. "This Love of Ours", MS pre-1946,
      NY: HZ. Song: [v., pf.].

Armies in the Fire   "Lamps now glitter down the street"   A
Child's Garden of Verses (1885)

6006 Hill, Edward B. Stevensonia Suite #2 for Orchestra,
      NY: GS, 1925. Ste.: orch. only.

6007 Richards, Kathleen. L: OUP, 1950. Song: unison v.,
      pf.

At the Sea-Side   "When I was down beside the sea"   A
Child's Garden of Verses (1885)

6008 Curtis, Natalie. "At the Seashore", Songs from "A
      Child's Garden of Verses", Newton Center: Wa-Wan,
      1902. Song: med. v., pf.

6009 Falk, Edward. A Child's Garden of Verses, NY: GS,
      pre-1940. Song: [v., pf.].

6010 Gambogi, F. Elvira. Child-Land, L: BH, 1902. Cyc.:
      solo v., pf.

6011 Gehrkens, Karl. NY: HH&E, 1933 in New Universal
      School Music Series: My First Song Book. Song:
      v., unacc.

6012 Miessner, William. NY: Silver, 1929 in The Music
      Hour in the Kindergarten and First Grade. Song:
      v., pf.

6013 Warner, Lorraine, arr. B: ECS, 1923 in A Kinder-
      garten Book of Folk-Songs. Song: v., pf. Text
      adapt. to a Belgian folk air.

Auntie's Skirt   "Whenever Auntie moves around"   A Child's
Garden of Verses (1885)

6014 Drozdoff, Vladimir. Stevensonia, NY: Omega, 1951.
      Song: pf. solo or v., pf.

6015 Falk, Edward. A Child's Garden of Verses, NY: GS,
      pre-1940. Song: [v., pf.].

693

Stevenson, Robert Louis continued

    6016 Warner, Lorraine, arr. B: ECS, 1923 in A_Kinder-
          garten_Book_of_Folk-Songs. Song: v., pf. Text
          adapt. to an Hungarian folk air.

Autumn Fires   "In the other gardens"   A_Child's_Garden_of
    Verses (1885)

    6017 Bright, Houston. From_"A_Child's_Garden_of_Verses",
          DWG: SPI, 1967. Cyc.: satb, a cap.

    6018 Dorr, T.A. "Sing a song of seasons, something bright
          in all", B: Pilgrim, 1925 in Song_and_Play_for
          Children. Song: v., pf.

    6019 McLauglin, Marian. NY: LG, 1963. Song: ssa, pf.

    6020 Radnor, Marvin. Songs_for_Little_Children, Book 1,
          Buffalo: the composer, 1923. Song: v., pf.

    6021 Rossiter, Aleta. "Song of the Seasons", Chi.: Laid-
          law, 1907 in Song_Primer. Song: v., pf.

    6022 Smith, Eleanor. Song_Pictures, Chi.: Summy, pre-
          1940. Song: [v., pf.].

Beach_of_Falesá,_The   (SS)   Illustrated_London_News (July-
    Aug. 1892) under the title "Uma", rev. & publ. sep. same
    year

    6023 Hoddinott, Alun. L: OUP, 1974. Opera: ms, a, 4 t,
          2 bar, b soli, chorus, orch. Libr. by Glyn Jones.

Bed in Summer   "In winter I get up at night"   A_Child's
    Garden_of_Verses (1885)

    6024 Andrews, Mark. "Does It Not Seem Hard", Nine_Songs
          from_"A_Child's_Garden_of_Verse", NY: HWG, 1911.
          Song: [v., pf.].

    6025 Bell, Florence E.E., arr. L: Longmans, Green, 1911
          in Singing_Circle. Song: v., pf. Text adapt. to
          an "old air".

    6026 Blaney, Norah. L: C, 1918. Song: solo v., pf.

6027   Brook, Harry. L: OUP, 1930. Song: unison v., pf.

6028   Crawford, Thomas. Songs_with_Music_from_"A_Child's
       Garden_of_Verses", L: Jack, 1915. Song: v., pf.

6029   Crowninshield, Ethel. Robert_Louis_Stevenson_Songs,
       Springfield: Bradley, 1910. Song: v., pf.

6030   Falk, Edward. A_Child's_Garden_of_Verses, NY: GS,
       pre-1940. Song: [v., pf.].

6031   Ireland, John. L: Curwen, 1916. Song: solo v., pf.
       or unison v., pf.

6032   Mallinson, Albert. Oakville: FH, 1907. Song: a or
       bar solo, pf.

6033   Moule-Evans, David. L: EA, pre-1951. Song: unison
       v., pf.

6034   Nevin, Ethelbert. "In winter...", Three_Songs, MS
       pre-1901, B: BMC. Song: [v., pf.].

6035* Parker, Horatio, et al., arr. NY: Silver, 1920 in
       The_Progressive_Music_Series. Song: v., unacc.
       Text adapt. to an Engl. folk air.

6036* Parry, W.H. L: FD&H, ca. 1952. Song: s solo, pf.

6037   Radnor, Marvin. Songs_for_Little_Children, Book 1,
       Buffalo: the composer, 1923. Song: v., pf.

6038* Rowley, Alec. L: Curwen, 1963. Song: unison v., pf.

6039   Shaw, Geoffrey. L: Curwen, 1915. Song: unison v.,
       pf.

6040   Stanford, C.V. A_Child's_Garland_of_Songs, L: Long-
       mans, Green, 1892 (L: Curwen, 1914). Song: unison
       v., pf.

6041   Wardale, Joseph. L: Elkin, 1958. Song: unison v.
       (with canon), pf.

6042   Wilkinson, Philip G. L: N, 1955. Song: unison v.,
       pf.

Stevenson, Robert Louis continued

  6043 Zaninelli, Luigi. The World Is So Full, DWG: SPI,
        1962. Song: ssa, fl., ob., cl., bsn., pf. or ssa,
        pf.

Block City   "What are you able to build with your blocks?"
  A Child's Garden of Verses (1885)

  6044 Crowninshield, Ethel. Robert Louis Stevenson Songs,
        Springfield: Bradley, 1910. Song: v., pf.

  6045 Lekberg, Sven. Park Ridge: Kj, 1960. Song: satb, a
        cap.

  6046 Radnor, Marvin. Songs for Little Children, Book 1,
        Buffalo: the composer, 1923. Song: v., pf.

Bottle Imp, The   (SS)   Black and White (Mar.-Apr. 1891)

  6047 Liviabella, Lino. "The Shell", MS pre-1961. Opera.
        Ital. title: "La Conchiglia".

"Bright is the ring of words"   Songs of Travel and other
  Verses (1896)

  6048 Carey, Clive. Two "Songs of Travel", L: S&B, pre-
        1940. Song: [v., pf.].

  6049 Farley, Roland. MS pre-1932, Bryn Mawr: NME. Song:
        [v., pf.].

  6050 Gurney, Ivor. "Song and Singer", MS 1911. Song:
        [solo v., pf.].

  6051 Hadow, W.H. MS pre-1937, L: Acott. Song: [v., pf.].

  6052 Liddle, Samuel. L: C, pre-1940. Song: solo v., pf.

  6053 O'Hara, Geoffrey. NY: Row, 1947. Song: ttbb, pf.

  6054 Oliver, Colin G.H. MS 1939, avail. University of
        Otago. Song: s or t solo, pf.

  6055 Peel, Graham. Two Songs, L: BH, 1903. Song: v., pf.

tevenson, Robert Louis continued

6056 Warlock, Peter. "To the Memory of a Great Singer",
L: A, 1923. Song: v., pf.

6057 Williams, Arnold. L: Curwen, pre-1940. Song: ttbb,
[a cap.?].

Country of the Camisards, The   "We travelled in the print of
olden wars"   Travels with a Donkey in the Cévennes (1879)

6058 Gurney, Ivor. "The Country Song of the Camisards",
MS 1909. Song: [solo v., pf.].

6059 Homer, Sidney. Six Songs from "Underwoods", NY: GS,
1904. Song: v., pf.

Cow, The   "Friendly cow all red and white, The"   Magazine
of Art (July 1884)

6060 Birge, Edward B. "The Friendly Cow", NY: Silver,
1929 in The Music Hour in the Kindergarten and
First Grade. Song: v., pf.

6061 Brook, Harry. L: OUP, 1930. Song: unison v., pf.

6062 Coleman, Henry. L: BW, 1962. Song: unison v. with
opt. 2nd treble and descant, pf.

6063 Conant, Grace W., arr. Springfield: Bradley, 1915 in
Children's Year. Song: v., pf. Text adapt. to a
16th century melody.

6064 Crowninshield, Ethel. Robert Louis Stevenson Songs,
Springfield: Bradley, 1910. Song: v., pf.

6065 Falk, Edward. A Child's Garden of Verses, NY: GS,
pre-1940. Song: [v., pf.].

6066 Hart, Fritz. Five Part Songs for Women's Unaccompanied Three-Part Choir, MS 1935. Song: 3 pt.
female choir, a cap.

6067 Jacobson, Maurice. L: Curwen, 1924. Song: sa, pf.

6068 Peel, Graham. Three Leaves from a Child's Garden,
MS pre-1937, L: JW. Song: [solo v., pf.].

Stevenson, Robert Louis continued

6069 Radnor, Marvin. Songs for Little Children, Book 1,
Buffalo: the composer, 1923. Song: v., pf.

6070* Rowley, Alec. "The Friendly Cow", L: Curwen, 1963.
Song: unison v., pf.

6071 Shaw, Geoffrey. L: Curwen, n.d. Song: unison v., pf.

6072 Wishart, Peter. A Book of Beasts, MS 1969. Cyc.:
med. v., pf.

Ditty "Cock shall crow, The" Songs of Travel and other
Verses (1896)

6073 Carpenter, John A. "The cock...", NY: GS, 1912.
Song: [med.] solo v., pf.

6074 Koch, John. Hastings-on-Hudson: GMP, 1965. Song: s
solo, pf.

Dumb Soldier, The "When the grass was closely mown" A
Child's Garden of Verses (1885)

6075 Hill, Edward B. Stevensonia Suite #2 for Orchestra,
NY: GS, 1925. Ste.: orch. only.

Envoy "Go, little book, and wish to all" Underwoods
(1887)

6076 Rieti, Vittorio. "Wishes", Three Choral Songs,
Hastings-on-Hudson: GMP, 1965. Song: satb, a cap.

Escape at Bedtime "Lights from the parlour and the kitchen
shone out, The" A Child's Garden of Verses (1885)

6077 Crowninshield, Ethel. Robert Louis Stevenson Songs,
Springfield: Bradley, 1910. Song: v., pf.

6078 Falk, Edward. A Child's Garden of Verses, NY: GS,
pre-1940. Song: [v., pf.].

6079 Jager, Robert. "Going to Sleep", A Child's Garden of
Verses, MS. Cyc.: s solo, pf. Also avail. for
s solo, wind ensemble or s solo, ch. orch.

698

tevenson, Robert Louis continued

Evensong "Embers of the day are red, The" Songs of Travel
and other Verses (1896)

6060 Homer, Sidney. Six Songs from "Underwoods", NY: GS,
1904. Song: v., pf.

Fairy Bread "Come up here, O dusty feet!" A Child's
Garden of Verses (1885)

6061 Gambogi, F. Elvira. Child-Land, L: BH, 1902. Cyc.:
solo v., pf.

6062 Radnor, Marvin. Songs for Little Children, Book 1,
Buffalo: the composer, 1923. Song: v., pf.

6063 Smith, Eleanor. Song Pictures, Chi.: Summy, pre-
1940. Song: [v., pf.].

Farewell to the Farm "Coach is at the door at last, The"
A Child's Garden of Verses (1885)

6084 Chadwick, George W. NY: Scribner's, 1892 in The
Stevenson Song-Book, 1897. Song: v., pf.

6085 Crawford, Thomas. Songs with Music from "A Child's
Garden of Verses", L: Jack, 1915. Song: v., pf.

6086 Crowninshield, Ethel. Robert Louis Stevenson Songs,
Springfield: Bradley, 1910. Song: v., pf.

6087 Curtis, Natalie. Songs from "A Child's Garden of
Verses", Newton Center: Wa-Wan, 1902. Song: med.
v., pf.

6088 Groocock, Joseph. "The coach...", A Child's Garden,
L: Elkin, 1957. Song: ssa, pf.

6089 Shepard, Thomas. A Cycle of Songs, B: Schmidt, 1901.
Cyc.: solo v., pf.

6090 Thomas, Muriel. Four Songs for Children, L: EA,
1957. Song: med. unison v., pf. Score contains
Welsh transl. by Wil Ifan.

6091 Williams, Patrick. L: BW, 1971. Song: sa, pf. or ss,
pf.

699

Stevenson, Robert Louis continued

Fine Pacific Island, The   "Jolly English Yellowboy, The"
Longman's Magazine (Jan. 1889)

6092 Whitfield, J.B.R. "Jolly English Yellowboy", L: BH,
1954. Song: chorus (opt. 2nd pt.), [pf.].

Flowers, The   "All the names I know from nurse"   A Child's
Garden of Verses (1885)

6093 Radnor, Marvin. Songs for Little Children, Book 1,
Buffalo: the composer, 1923. Song: v., pf.

6094 Rosenstein, Arthur. "Baby's Garden", NY: GS, pre-
1940. Song: [v., pf.].

6095 Williamson, Malcolm. From a Child's Garden, L: Weinberger, 1968. Song: high v., pf.

Foreign Children   "Little Indian, Sioux or Crow"   A Child's
Garden of Verses (1885)

6096 Andrews, Mark. Nine Songs from "A Child's Garden of
Verse", NY: HWG, 1911. Song: [v., pf.].

6097 Crawford, Thomas. Songs with Music from "A Child's
Garden of Verses", L: Jack, 1915. Song: v., pf.

6098 Falk, Edward. A Child's Garden of Verses, NY: GS,
pre-1940. Song: [v., pf.].

6099 Herbert, Victor. NY: Silver, 1920 in The Progressive
Music Series, Book 2. Song: v., unacc.

6100 Lehmann, Liza. The Daisy Chain, L: BH, 1893. Song:
vocal qrt. (s, a, t, bar or b), pf. Portions of
the collection require soli.

6101 Quilter, Roger. Four Child Songs, L: C, 1914. Song:
solo v., pf.

6102 Radnor, Marvin. Songs for Little Children, Book 1,
Buffalo: the composer, 1923. Song: v., pf.

6103 Rowley, Alec. L: Curwen, 1963. Song: equal voices
(ss), pf.

6104   Spencer, Ruth McConn. NY: HH&E, 1933 in New Univer-
        sal School Music Series: Rhythm Songs. Song: v.,
        unacc.

6105   Stanford, C.V. A Child's Garland of Songs, L: Long-
        mans, Green, 1892 (L: Curwen, 1914). Song: unison
        v., pf.

6106   Wardale, Joseph. L: Elkin, 1958. Song: ss, pf.

6107   Warner, Lorraine, arr. B: ECS, 1923 in A Kinder-
        garten Book of Folk-Songs. Song: v., pf. Text
        adapt. to a Russian folk air.

6108   Zaninelli, Luigi. The World Is So Full, DWG: SPI,
        1962. Song: ssa, fl., ob., cl., bsn., pf. or ssa,
        pf.

Foreign Lands   "Up into the cherry tree"   Magazine of Art
(Sept. 1884)

6109   Falk, Edward. A Child's Garden of Verses, NY: GS,
        pre-1940. Song: [v., pf.].

6110   Radnor, Marvin. Songs for Little Children, Book 1,
        Buffalo: the composer, 1923. Song: v., pf.

6111   Salter, Mary E.T. NY: HH&E, 1933 in New Universal
        School Music Series: Rhythm Songs. Song: v., un-
        acc.

6112   Shepard, Thomas. A Cycle of Songs, B: Schmidt, 1901.
        Cyc.: solo v., pf.

6113   Stanford, C.V. A Child's Garland of Songs, L: Long-
        mans, Green, 1892 (L: Curwen, 1914). Song: unison
        v., pf.

From a Railway Carriage   "Faster than fairies"   A Child's
Garden of Verses (1885)

6114   Bentley, Alys. "Song of the Train", Chi.: Laidlaw,
        1923 in The Song Series, Book 3. Song: v., unacc.

Stevenson, Robert Louis continued

6115 Butterworth, Arthur. Trains in the Distance, MS
       (Opus 41). Symph.: orator, chorus, semichorus,
       orch., tape.

6116 Gambogi, F. Elvira. Child-Land, L: BH, 1902. Cyc.:
       solo v., pf.

6117 Hadley, Henry. B: Birchard, 1906 in The Laurel
       Music-Reader. Song: voices (pts. unspecif.), un-
       acc.

6118 Jackson, Francis A. L: N, 1958. Song: unison v., pf.

6119 Jager, Robert. A Child's Garden of Verses, MS. Cyc.:
       s solo, pf. Also avail. for s solo, wind
       ensemble or s solo, ch. orch.

6120* Rowley, Alec. L: Curwen, 1963. Song: unison v., pf.

6121 Williamson, Malcolm. From a Child's Garden, L: Wein-
       berger, 1968. Song: high v., pf.

Good and Bad Children   "Children, you are very little"
Magazine of Art (Sept. 1884)

6122 Warner, Lorraine, arr. B: ECS, 1923 in A Kinder-
       garten Book of Folk-Songs. Song: v., pf. Text
       adapt. to a Russian folk air.

Good Boy, A   "I woke before the morning"   A Child's Garden
of Verses (1885)

6123 Bartlett, Homer. NY: Scribner's, 1897 in The Steven-
       son Song-Book. Song: v., pf.

6124 Crawford, Thomas. Songs with Music from "A Child's
       Garden of Verses", L: Jack, 1915. Song: v., pf.

6125 del Riego, Teresa. "Sleepsin-by", Children's
       Pictures, L: C, 1909. Song: solo v., pf

6126 Quilter, Roger. "A Good Child", Four Child Songs,
       L: C, 1914. Song: solo v., pf.

6127 Williamson, Malcolm. From a Child's Garden, L: Wein-
       berger, 1968. Song: high v., pf.

702

Happy Thought   "World is so full of a number of things, The"
A Child's Garden of Verses (1885)

6128   Baker, Clara B., arr. NY: AD, 1921 in Songs for
        Little Children. Song: v., pf. Text adapt. to an
        Engl. nursery air.

6129   Bright, Houston. From "A Child's Garden of Verses",
        DWG: SP, 1967. Cyc.: satb, a cap.

6130   Clark, Joan. NY: HH&E, 1933 in New Universal School
        Music Series: My First Song Book. Song: v., un-
        acc.

6131   Conant, Grace W., arr. Springfield: Bradley, 1915 in
        Children's Year. Song: v., pf. Text adapt. to a
        German air.

6132   Dann, Hollis E., arr. NY: ABC, 1914-17 in Hollis
        Dann Music Course, Book 3. Song: v., pf. Text
        adapt. to an anon. air.

6133   Falk, Edward. A Child's Garden of Verses, NY: GS,
        pre-1940. Song: [v., pf.].

6134   Jager, Robert. "A Happy Thought", A Child's Garden
        of Verses, MS. Cyc.: s solo, pf. Also avail. for
        s solo, wind ensemble or s solo, ch. orch.

6135*   Parker, Horatio, et al., arr. NY: Silver, 1920 in
        The Progressive Music Series. Song: v., unacc.
        Text adapt. to an Engl. air.

6136   Radnor, Marvin. Songs for Little Children, Book 1,
        Buffalo: the composer, 1923. Song: v., pf.

6137   Williamson, Malcolm. From a Child's Garden, L: Wein-
        berger, 1968. Song: high v., pf.

6138   Zaninelli, Luigi. "The world...", The World Is So
        Full, DWG: SPI, 1962. Song: ssa, fl., pf., cl.,
        bsn., pf. or ssa, pf.

Hayloft, The   "Through all the pleasant meadow-side"   A
Child's Garden of Verses (1885)

Stevenson, Robert Louis continued

6139 Bell, Florence E.E., arr. L: Longmans, Green, 1911
      in Singing Circle. Song: v., pf. Text adapt. to
      an anon. score.

6140 Milford, Robin. Rain, Wind and Sunshine, L: OUP,
      1930, Song (in children's cta.): unison v., pf.
      Publ. sep. L: OUP, 1931.

6141 Moule-Evans, David. L: EA, pre-1951. Song: unison
      v., pf.

6142 Rhodes, Harold. L: EA, pre-1951. Song: unison v.,
      pf.

"He hears with gladdened heart the thunder"   Songs of Travel
and other Verses (1896)

6143 Davies, H. Walford. Twenty-One Songs, MS ca. 1931.
      Song: v., pf.

"Home no more home to me, whither must I wander?"   Scots
Observer (Jan. 1889)

6144 Vaughan Williams, Ralph. "Whither must I wander",
      publ. 1902 in Vocalist; publ. sep. L: BH, 1912;
      subsequently incl. in complete edns. of Songs of
      Travel. Song: solo v., pf. Orchn. (1962) by Roy
      Douglas.

"I have trod the upward and the downward slope"   Songs of
Travel and other Verses (1896)

6145* Vaughan Williams, Ralph. L: BH, 1960. Song: solo v.,
      pf. Orchn. (1962) by Roy Douglas.

"I will make you brooches and toys for your delight"   Pall
Mall Gazette (Jan. 1895)

6146 Allen, Harold. The White River, MS 1971. Cyc.: as
      solo, gtr. and perc. ensemble.

6147 Bury, Winifred. "I Will Make You Brooches", Glasgow:
      PT, 1936. Song: med. v., pf.

Stevenson, Robert Louis continued

6148   Butterworth, George. "I Will Make You Brooches", L:
       A, 1920. Song: solo v., pf.

6149* Clarke, Robert C. L: Cary, 1903. Song: [solo v.,
       pf.].

6150   Collins, Anthony. "I Will Make You Brooches", L: A,
       pre-1940. Song: [solo v., pf.].

6151   Cory, George. "And this shall be for music...",
       Hastings-on-Hudson: GMP, 1955. Song: ms solo, pf.

6152   Diemer, Emma Lou. "Romance", NY: CF, 1974. Setting
       for satb, pf., opt. triangle.

6153   Farrar, Ernest. "The Roadside Fire", Vagabond Songs,
       MS (Opus 10), L: S&B. Song: v., pf.

6154   Fast, Willard. "I Will Make You Brooches", NY: AMP,
       1968. Song: satb, a cap.

6155   Ford, Donald. "Romance", L: MM, 1922, copyright as-
       signed L: C, 1943. Song: solo v., pf.

6156   Gurney, Ivor. "I will Make You Brooches", MS 1910.
       Song: [solo v., pf.].

6157   Helyer, Marjorie. "I Will Make You Brooches", L: N,
       1958. Song: unison v., pf.

6158   Hundley, Richard. "For Your Delight", Hastings-on-
       Hudson: GMP, 1962. Song: s solo, pf.

6159   Ide, Chester. "Lovers of the Wild", Newton Center:
       Wa-Wan, 1907. Song: v., pf.

6160   Korte, Karl. "I will Make You Brooches", Aspects of
       Love, B: ECS, 1971. Cyc.: satb, pf.

6161   Noble, Harold. "I Will Make You Brooches", L: N,
       1960. Song: unison v., pf.

6162   Pritchard, Arthur J. "The Roadside Fire", L: AH&C,
       1958. Song: ssa, pf.

6163   Sharman, Cecil. "The Roadside Fire", L: EA, ca.
       1956. Song: satb, a cap.

Stevenson, Robert Louis continued

6164 Vale, Charles. "The Roadside Fire", L: Elkin, 1956.
      Song: ttbb, a cap.

6165 Vaughan Williams, Ralph. "The Roadside Fire", Songs
      of Travel, 1st set, L: BH, 1905. Cyc.: solo v.,
      pf. Orchn. (1905) by the composer.

6166 Warlock, Peter. "Romance", L: Curwen, 1921. Song:
      solo v., pf.

"In dreams, unhappy, I behold you stand"   Songs of Travel
and other Verses (1896)

6167 Schenck, Elliott. The Unforgotten, L: B&H, 1902.
      Song: [v., pf.?].

6168 Vaughan Williams, Ralph. "In Dreams", Songs of
      Travel, 2nd set, L: BH, 1907. Cyc.: solo v., pf.
      Orchn. (1962) by Roy Douglas.

In Port   "Last, to the chamber where I lie"   Magazine of
Art (Mar. 1884) as one of "North-West Passage"

6169 Gambogi, F. Elvira. Child-Land, L: BH, 1902. Cyc.:
      solo v., pf.

"In the highlands, in the country places"   Pall Mall Gazette
(Dec. 1894)

6170 Butterworth, George. L: A, 1930. Song: ssa, pf.

6171 Clark, Harold. L: EA, pre-1951. Song: unison v., pf.

6172 Davies, H. Walford. Twenty-One Songs, L: N, 1931.
      Song: v., pf.

6173 Gibbs, C. Armstrong. L: Curwen, 1928. Song: solo v.,
      pf.

6174 Quilter, Roger. Two Songs, L: Elkin, 1922. Song:
      med. or low v., pf.

6175 Robbins, Reginald. P: MST, ca. 1922. Song: bar (or
      a) solo, pf. Also suitable for b solo.

706

Stevenson, Robert Louis continued

6176 Rodewald, Pernice. MS 1949, avail. University of
      Auckland. Song: ms solo, pf.

6177 Rootham, C.B. In_Highland_and_Meadow, L: S&B, 1910.
      Song: satb, orch. or satb, pf.

6178 Shapleigh, Bertram. Zwei_Lieder, Lz.: B&H, 1901.
      Song: med. v., pf. German title: "O mein Hoch-
      land", transl. by F.H. Scaneider.

6179 Stevenson, Ronald. MS 1967, Four_Robert_Louis
      Stevenson_Songs (MS 1961-67). Song: med. v., pf.

6180 Victory, Gerard. MS 1958. Song: t solo, satb, a cap.

"Infinite shining heavens, The" Songs_of_Travel_and_other
Verses (1896)

6181 Colburn, S.C. B: BMC, pre-1940. Song: [v., pf.].

6182 Vaughan Williams, Ralph. Songs_of_Travel, 2nd set,
      L: BH, 1907. Cyc.: solo v., pf. Orchn. (1962) by
      Roy Douglas.

Keepsake Mill   "Over the borders"   A_Child's_Garden_of
Verses (1885)

6183 Bell, Florence E.E., arr. L: Longmans, Green, 1911
      in Singing_Circle. Song: v., pf. Text adapt. to
      an anon. score.

6184 Crowninshield, Ethel. Robert_Louis_Stevenson_Songs,
      Springfield: Bradley, 1910. Song: v., pf.

6185 Lehmann, Liza. The_Daisy_Chain, L: BH, 1893. Song:
      bar solo, pf. Portions of the collection require
      various soli.

6186 Morawetz, Oskar. A_Child's_Garden_of_Verses, MS
      1972, avail. CMC. Cyc.: s solo, pf.

Lamplighter, The   "My tea is nearly ready"   A_Child's
Garden_of_Verses (1885)

Stevenson, Robert Louis continued

6187 Bell, Florence E.E., arr. L: Longmans, Green, 1911
in Singing Circle. Song: v., pf. Text adapt. to
an anon. score.

6188 Crowninshield, Ethel. Robert Louis Stevenson Songs,
Springfield: Bradley, 1910. Song: v., pf.

6189 Edwards, Henry J. L: Curwen, 1913. Song: unison v.,
pf.

6190 Lekberg, Sven. Park Ridge: Kj, 1959. Song: satb,
a cap.

6191 Mason, Daniel G. Five Children's Songs, B: BMC, pre-
1940. Song: [v., pf.].

6192 Quilter, Roger. Four Child Songs, L: C, 1914. Song:
solo v., pf.

6193* Rowley, Alec. L: AH&C, pre-1967. Song: unison v.,
pf.

6194 Shepard, Thomas. A Cycle of Songs, B: Schmidt, 1901.
Cyc.: solo v., pf.

6195 Smith, Eleanor. Song Pictures, Chi.: Summy, pre-
1940. Song: [v., pf.].

6196 Stevenson, Ronald. MS 1961, Four Robert Louis
Stevenson Songs (MS 1961-67). Song: med. v., pf.

6197 Whitfield, J.B.R. L: AH&C, 1958. Song: unison v.,
pf.

6198 Williamson, Malcolm. From a Child's Garden, L: Weinberger, 1968. Song: high v., pf.

Land of Counterpane, The "When I was sick and lay a-bed"
Magazine of Art (July 1884)

6199 Bell, Florence E.E., arr. L: Longmans, Green, 1911
in Singing Circle. Song: v., pf. Text adapt. to
an anon. score.

6200 Chadwick, George W. NY: Scribner's, 1897 in The
Stevenson Song-Book. Song: v., pf.

6201 Crowninshield, Ethel. Robert Louis Stevenson Songs, Springfield: Bradley, 1910. Song: v., pf.

6202 Jager, Robert. A Child's Garden of Verses, MS. Cyc.: s solo, pf. Also avail. for s solo, wind ensemble or s solo, ch. orch.

6203 Miessner, William. NY: Silver, 1929 in Music Hour in the Kindergarten and First Grade. Song: v., pf.

6204 Radnor, Marvin. Songs for Little Children, Book 1, Buffalo: the composer, 1923. Song: v., pf.

6205 Shepard, Thomas. A Cycle of Songs, B: Schmidt, 1901. Cyc.: solo v., pf.

Land of Nod, The   "From breakfast on through all the day" A Child's Garden of Verses (1885)

6206 Crowninshield, Ethel. Robert Louis Stevenson Songs, Springfield: Bradley, 1910. Song: v., pf.

6207 Falk, Edward. A Child's Garden of Verses, NY: GS, pre-1940. Song: [v., pf.].

6208 Gilchrist, William W. NY: Scribner's, 1897 in The Stevenson Song-Book. Song: v., pf.

6209 Norris, Homer. B: STV, 1903. Song: v., pf., vln. obbl.

6210 Radnor, Marvin. Songs for Little Children, Book 1, Buffalo: the composer, 1923. Song: v., pf.

6211 Zaninelli, Luigi. The World Is So Full, DWG: SPI, 1962. Song: ssa, fl., ob., cl., bsn., pf. or ssa, pf.

Land of Story-Books, The   "At evening, when the lamp is lit" A Child's Garden of Verses (1885)

6212 Bartlett, Homer. NY: Scribner's, 1897 in The Stevenson Song-Book. Song: v., pf.

709

Stevenson, Robert Louis continued

"Let Beauty awake in the morn from beautiful dreams"   Songs
of Travel and other Verses (1896)

6213 Vaughan Williams, Ralph. "Let Beauty Awake", Songs
of Travel, 2nd set, L: BH, 1907. Cyc.: solo v.,
pf. Orchn. (1962) by Roy Douglas.

Little Land, The   "When at home alone I sit"   A Child's
Garden of Verses (1885)

6214 Cheatham, Katharine S., arr. NY: GS, 1917 in Nursery
Garland. Song: v., pf. Text adapt. to a melody by
W.A. Mozart.

Looking Forward   "When I am grown to man's estate"   A
Child's Garden of Verses (1885)

6215 Falk, Edward. A Child's Garden of Verses, NY: GS,
pre-1940. Song: [v., pf.].

6216 Warner, Lorraine, arr. B: ECS, 1923 in A Kindergarten Book of Folk-Songs. Song: v., pf. Text
adapt. to a Lithuanian folk air.

6217 Williamson, Malcolm. From a Child's Garden, L: Weinberger, 1968. Song: high v., pf.

Looking-Glass River   "Smooth it slides upon its travel"
A Child's Garden of Verses (1885)

6218 Carpenter, John A. MS 1909, NY: GS. Song: v., pf.

6219 Gurney, Ivor. MS 1909. Song: [solo v., pf.].

6220 Warner, Lorraine, arr. B: ECS, 1923 in A Kindergarten Book of Folk-Songs. Song: v., pf. Text
adapt. to a Russian folk air.

Marching Song   "Bring the comb and play upon it!"   A
Child's Garden of Verses (1885)

6221 Andrews, Mark. Nine Songs from "A Child's Garden of
Verse", NY: HWG, 1911. Song: [v., pf.].

Stevenson, Robert Louis continued

6222 Bell, Florence E.E., arr. L: Longmans, Green, 1911
      in Singing Circle. Song: v., pf. Text adapt. to
      an anon. air.

6223 Crawford, Thomas. Songs with Music from "A Child's
      Garden of Verses", L: Jack, 1915. Song: v., pf.

6224 Crowninshield, Ethel. Robert Louis Stevenson Songs,
      Springfield: Bradley, 1910. Song: v., pf.

6225 de Koven, Reginald. NY: Silver, 1928-30 in The Music
      Hour, Book 3. Song: v., unacc.

6226 Drozdoff, Vladimir. Stevensonia, NY: Omega, 1951.
      Song: pf. solo or v., pf.

6227* Falk, Edward. A Child's Garden of Verses, NY: GS,
      pre-1940. Song: [v., pf.].

6228 Grosvenor, Mrs. Norman. Six Songs from "A Child's
      Garden of Verses", L: N, pre-1940. Song: [v.,
      pf.].

6229 Lehmann, Liza. More Daisies, L: BH, 1902. Cyc.: v.,
      pf.

6230 Lekberg, Sven. Evanston: Summy-B, 1958. Song: satbb,
      a cap.

6231 Naylor, Peter. L: N, 1964. Song: unison v., pf.

6232 Peel, Graham. Three Leaves from a Child's Garden, MS
      pre-1937. Song: [solo v., pf.].

6233* Rowley, Alec. L: Curwen, 1963. Song: unison v., pf.

6234 Spedding, Frank. L: OUP, 1959. Song: unison v., pf.

6235 Stanford, C.V. "Marching Songs", A Child's Garland
      of Songs, L: Longmans, Green, 1892 (L: Curwen,
      1914). Song: v., pf. This setting also publ. L:
      Curwen for sa.

6236 Thompson, E. Roy. L: EA, pre-1951. Song: unison v.,
      pf.

6237 Whitfield, J.B.R. L: AH&C, pre-1967. Song: unison
      v., pf.

Stevenson, Robert Louis continued

6238   Williams, Patrick. L: BW, 1968. Song: unison v., pf.

6239   Williamson, Malcolm. From a Child's Garden, L: Wein-
       berger, 1968. Song: high v., pf.

6240   Zaninelli, Luigi. The World Is So Full, DWG: SPI,
       1962. Song: ssa, fl., ob., cl., bsn., pf. or ssa,
       pf.

Markheim   (SS)   Broken Shaft (Christmas Number 1885)

6241   Floyd, Carlisle. NY: BH, 1968. Opera: s, 2 t, b-bar
       soli, 2 fl. (doubl. pic.), 2 ob. (doubl. eng.
       hn.), 2 cl. (doubl. b. cl.), 2 bsn., 4 hn., 2
       tpt., 2 trbn., tuba, timp., perc., hp. Text
       adapt. by the composer.

6242   Miles, Philip. MS pre-1924, L: Curwen. Opera.

Moon, The   "Moon has a face like the clock in the hall, The"
A Child's Garden of Verses (1885)

6243   Balendonck, Armand. NY: Pro Art, pre-1940. Song:
       [v., pf.?].

6244   Bell, Florence E.E., arr. L: Longmans, Green, 1911
       in Singing Circle. Song: v., pf. Text adapt. to
       an anon. score.

6245   Covert, Mary. Oakville: FH, 1954. Song: v., pf.

6246   Falk, Edward. A Child's Garden of Verses, NY: GS,
       pre-1940. Song: [v., pf.].

6247   Helyer, Marjorie. Tor.: Clarke, Irwin, 1959 in The
       Classroom Chorister. Song: unison v., pf.

6248   Hovhaness, Alan. "The Moon has a Face", NY: CFP,
       1968. Song: med. v., pf.

6249   Lehmann, Liza. The Daisy Chain, L: BH, 1893. Song:
       L: BH, 1893. Song: t solo, pf. Portions of the
       collection require various soli.

6250   Radnor, Marvin. Songs for Little Children, Book 1,
       Buffalo: the composer, 1923. Song: v., pf.

Stevenson, Robert Louis continued

6251 Shields, Arnold. L: OUP, 1937. Song: unison v., pf.

6252 Wilkinson, Philip G. L: N, 1955. Song: unison v., pf.

6253 Williams, Patrick. L: BW, 1961. Song: unison v., pf.

My Bed is a Boat   "My bed is like a little boat"   A_Child's Garden_of_Verses (1885)

6254 Bell, Florence E.E., arr. L: Longmans, Green, 1911 in Singing_Circle. Song: v., pf. Text adapt. to an anon. score.

6255 Brook, Harry. L: OUP, 1930. Song: unison v., pf.

6256 del Riego, Teresa. Children's_Pictures, L: C, 1909. Song: solo v., pf.

6257 Gilchrist, William W. NY: Scribner's, 1897 in The Stevenson_Song-Book. Song: v., pf.

6258 Loftus, Cissie. "My bed is like...", B: W-S, pre-1940. Song: [v., pf.].

6259 Peel, Graham. L: C, 1910. Song: solo v., pf.

6260 Radnor, Marvin. Songs_for_Little_Children, Book 1, Buffalo: the composer, 1923. Song: v., pf.

6261 Turnbull, Percy. L: BA, ca. 1925. Song: unison v., pf.

6262 Williamson, Malcolm. From_a_Child's_Garden, L: Weinberger, 1968. Song: high v., pf.

My Kingdom   "Down by a shining water well"   A_Child's Garden_of_Verses (1885)

6263 Crawford, Thomas. Songs_with_Music_from_"A_Child's Garden_of_Verses", L: Jack, 1915. Song: v., pf.

6264 Goldman, Richard. NY: M, 1952. Song: [med.] solo v., pf.

713

6265   Morawetz, Oskar. A Child's Garden of Verses, MS
       1972, avail. CMC. Cyc.: s solo, pf.

My Shadow   "I have a little shadow"   A Child's Garden of
Verses (1885)

6266   Andrews, Mark. Nine Songs from "A Child's Garden of
       Verse", NY: HWG, 1911. Song: [v., pf.].

6267   Blaney, Norah. L: C, 1918. Song: solo v., pf.

6268   Bradley, William. York: Banks, 1914. Song: unison
       v., pf.

6269   Crawford, Thomas. Songs with Music from "A Child's
       Garden of Verses", L: Jack, 1915. Song: v., pf.

6270   Crowninshield, Ethel. Robert Louis Stevenson Songs,
       Springfield: Bradley, 1910. Song: v., pf.

6271   Falk, Edward. A Child's Garden of Verses, NY: GS,
       pre-1940. Song: [v., pf.].

6272   Grosvenor, Mrs. Norman. Six Songs from "A Child's
       Garden of Verses", L: N, pre-1940. Song: [v.,
       pf.].

6273   Hadley, Henry. B: Schmidt, 1903. Song: v., pf.

6274   Lehmann, Liza. More Daisies, L: BH, 1902. Cyc.: v.,
       pf.

6275   Leoni, Franco. L: C, 1908. Song: solo v., pf.

6276   Morawetz, Oskar. A Child's Garden of Verses, MS
       1972, avail. CMC. Cyc.: s solo, pf.

6277   Radnor, Marvin. Songs for Little Children, Book 1,
       Buffalo: the composer, 1923. Song: v., pf.

6278   Samuels, Homer. NY: CF, 1919. Song: high v., pf.

6279   Shepard, Thomas. A Cycle of Songs, B: Schmidt, 1901.
       Cyc.: solo v., pf.

714

Stevenson, Robert Louis continued

6280 Smith, Eleanor. "The Shadow", Song Pictures, Chi.:
        Summy, pre-1940. Song: [v., pf.].

6281 Stanford, C.V. A Child's Garland of Songs, L: Long-
        mans, Green, 1892 (L: Curwen, 1914). Song: unison
        v., pf.

6282 Stephens, Ward. Bryn Mawr: TP, pre-1940. Song: [v.,
        pf.].

6283 Wardale, Joseph. L: LG&B, 1963. Song: unison v.
        (with canon),'pf.

6284 Whitfield, J.B.R. L: A, 1958. Song: unison v., pf.

My Ship and I   "O it's I that am the captain"   A Child's
Garden of Verses (1885)

6285 Andrews, Mark. Nine Songs from "A Child's Garden of
        Verse", NY: HWG, 1911. Song: [v., pf.].

6286 Clements, John H. York: Banks, 1937. Song: unison
        v., pf.

6287 Crawford, Thomas. Songs with Music from "A Child's
        Garden of Verses", L: Jack, 1915. Song: v., pf.

6288 Crowninshield, Ethel. Robert Louis Stevenson Songs,
        Springfield: Bradley, 1910. Song: v., pf.

6289 Grosvenor, Mrs. Norman. Six Songs from "A Child's
        Garden of Verses", L: N, pre-1940. Song: [v.,
        pf.].

6290 Mason, Daniel G. Five Children's Songs, B: BMC, pre-
        1940. Song: [v., pf.].

6291 O'Donoghue, Mary B. NY: Silver, 1928-30 in The Music
        Hour, Book 2. Song: v., unacc.

6292 Peel, Graham. Three Leaves from a Child's Garden, MS
        pre-1937, L: JW. Song: [solo v., pf.].

6293 Radnor, Marvin. Songs for Little Children, Book 1,
        Buffalo: the composer, 1923. Song: v., pf.

715

Stevenson, Robert Louis continued

6294   Shepard, Thomas. A Cycle of Songs, B: Schmidt, 1901.
        Cyc.: solo v., pf.

6295   Stanford, C.V. "My Ship and Me", A Child's Garland
        of Songs, L: Longmans, Green, 1892 (L: Curwen,
        1914). Song: v., pf. This setting was publ. L:
        Curwen for sa, pf.

My Treasures   "These nuts, that I keep"   A Child's Garden
of Verses (1885)

6296   Crowninshield, Ethel. Robert Louis Stevenson Songs,
        Springfield: Bradley, 1910. Song: v., pf.

My Wife   "Trusty, dusky, vivid, true"   Songs of Travel and
other Verses (1896)

6297   Shapleigh, Bertram. Zwei Lieder, Lz.: B&H, 1901.
        Song: med. v., pf. German title: "Mein Weib",
        transl. by F.H. Schneider.

Night and Day   "When the golden day is done"   A Child's
Garden of Verses (1885)

6298*   McConathy, Osbourne, et al., arr. NY: Silver, 1928-
        30 in The Music Hour, Book 4. Song: v., unacc.
        Text adapt. to a melody by F.J. Haydn.

6299   Radnor, Marvin. Songs for Little Children, Book 1,
        Buffalo: the composer, 1923. Song: v., pf.

Over the Sea to Skye   "Sing me a song of a lad that is gone"
Pall Mall Gazette (Dec. 1894), rev. 1896

6300   Burnham, Charles. "Sing me...", NY: GS, pre-1940.
        Song: [solo v., pf.?].

6301   Homer, Sidney. "Sing me...", Six Songs from "Under-
        woods", NY: GS, 1904. Song: v., pf.

6302*   Stevenson, Robert Louis. B: BMC, 1912. Song: v., pf.
        Pf. pt. arr. by H.J. Stewart.

Stevenson, Robert Louis continued

Picture-Books in Winter   "Summer fading, winter comes"   A
Child's Garden of Verses (1885)

6303 Bell, Florence E.E., arr. "Pictures in Winter", L:
      Longmans, Green, 1911 in Singing Circle. Song:
      v., pf. Text adapt. to an anon. score.

6304 Crawford, Thomas. Songs with Music from "A Child's
      Garden of Verses", L: Jack, 1915. Song: v., pf.

6305 Crowninshield, Ethel. Robert Louis Stevenson Songs,
      Springfield: Bradley, 1910. Song: v., pf.

6306 Mason, Daniel G. Five Children's Songs, B: BMC, pre-
      1940. Song: [v., pf.].

Pirate Story   "Three of us afloat in the meadow"   A Child's
Garden of Verses (1885)

6307 Falk, Edward. A Child's Garden of Verses, NY: GS,
      pre-1940. Song: [v., pf.].

6308 Groocock, Joseph. "Three...", A Child's Garden, L:
      Elkin, 1957. Song: ssa, pf.

6309 Hill, Edward B. Stevensonia Suite #2 for Orchestra,
      NY: GS, 1925. Ste.: orch. only.

6310 Homer, Sidney. Three Songs from "A Child's Garden of
      Verses", MS (Opus 16), NY: GS. Song: v., pf.

6311 Peel, Graham. L: C, 1910. Song: [v., pf.].

6312 Stanford, C.V. A Child's Garland of Songs, L: Long-
      mans, Green, 1892 (L: Curwen, 1914). Song: v.,
      pf. This setting also publ. L: Curwen for sa.

Rain   "Rain is raining all around, The"   A Child's Garden
of Verses (1885)

6313 Conant, Grace W. Springfield: Bradley, 1915 in
      Children's Year. Song: v., [pf.].

6314 Crowninshield, Ethel. Robert Louis Stevenson Songs,
      Springfield: Bradley, 1910. Song: v., pf.

717

6315 Curtis, Natalie. Songs from "A Child's Garden of Verses", Newton Center: Wa-Wan, 1902. Song: med. v., pf.

6316 Dann, Hollis E., arr. NY: ABC, 1914-17 in Hollis Dann Music Course, Book 1. Song: v., pf. Text adapt. to an anon. score.

6317 Drozdoff, Vladimir. Stevensonia, NY: Omega, 1951. Song: pf. solo or v., pf.

6318 Falk, Edward. A Child's Garden of Verses, NY: GS, pre-1940. Song: [v., pf.].

6319 Floyd, Carlisle. Two Stevenson Songs, NY: GH, 1967. Song: unison v., pf.

6320 Gartlan, George. NY: HH&E, 1934 in New Universal School Music Series: Introduction to Part Singing. Song: chorus, a cap.

6321 Gehrkens, Karl. NY: HH&E, 1933 in New Universal School Music Series: Unison Songs. Song: unison v., unacc.

6322 Radnor, Marvin. Songs for Little Children, Book 1, Buffalo: the composer, 1923. Song: v., pf.

6323 Rossman, Floy. "Raining", B: Birchard, 1928 in Pre-School Music. Song: v., pf.

6324 Williamson, Malcolm. From a Child's Garden, L: Weinberger, 1968. Song: high v., pf.

6325 Zaninelli, Luigi. The World Is So Full, DWG: SPI, 1962. Song: ssa, fl., ob., cl., bsn., pf. or ssa, pf.

Requiem   "Under the wide and starry sky"   Underwoods (1887)

6326 Bantock, Granville. L: Deanne (YBP), pre-1952. Song: ttbb, a cap.

6327 Billingham, Kathleen. Two Songs, L: S&B, pre-1940. Song: [v., pf.].

6328 Bissell, Keith. Waterloo: Waterloo, 1967. Song: ssa,
a cap. Publ. Waterloo: Waterloo, 1971 for ssa,
pf.

6329 Collingwood, Lawrance A. Glasgow: PT, 1928. Song:
satb, a cap. or ttbb, a cap.

6330 Craxton, Harold. "A Requiem", L: C, 1914. Song: solo
v., pf.

6331 Davies, H. Walford. Twenty-One Songs, L: N, 1931.
Song: v., pf.

6332 Edmonds, Paul. L: Curwen, 1920. Song: ssa, pf.

6333 Foote, Arthur. B: Schmidt, 1907. Song: [v., pf.].

6334 Fraser, Shena. L: Elkin, 1950. Song: ssa, a cap.

6335 Grinnell, Edmund. NY: CF, pre-1940. Song: [v., pf.].

6336 Homer, Sidney. Six Songs from "Underwoods", NY: GS,
1904. Song: v., pf. Also publ. sep. for 4 pt.
male chorus, pf. or 3-4 pt. female chorus (a II
ad lib.), pf., also for satb, pf. or ssaattbb,
a cap.

6337 Ives, Charles. Nineteen Songs, Bryn Mawr: NME,
Song: med. v., pf.

6338 Kalmanoff, Martin. "Under...", NY: Broude-B, 1960.
Song: ttbb, pf.

6339 Kountz, Richard. "Under...", NY: GX, 1949. Song:
solo v., unacc. or ttbb, a cap.

6340 Lander, Cyril. Flores de mi primavera, MS n.d.,
avail. National Library of N.Z. Song: high v.,
pf.

6341 Loftus, Cecilia. L: C, 1923. Song: solo v., pf.

6342 More, T. L: SB, pre-1940. Song: [v., pf.?].

6343 Naylor, Peter. MS. Song: t solo, pf.

6344 Osmond, Clara. L: A, pre-1940. Song: [v., pf.?].

Stevenson, Robert Louis continued

6345   Peel, Graham. Two Songs, L: BH, 1903. Song: v., pf.

6346   Rathaus, Karol. NY: BH, pre-1955. Song: satb, pf.

6347   Rogers, J.H. In Memoriam, NY: GS, pre-1940.
       Song: [v., pf.?].

6348   Rorem, Ned. NY: Peer, 1950. Song: med. v., pf.

6349   Scott, Cyril. L: Elkin, 1917. Song: high or med. v.,
       pf.

6350   Shanks, William. L: C, 1927. Song: solo v., pf.

6351   Speaks, Oley. NY: GS, pre-1940. Song: [v., pf.].

6352   Stevenson, Ronald. MS 1964, Four Robert Louis
       Stevenson Songs (MS 1961-67). Song: med. v., pf.

6353   Thompson, E. Roy. L: Curwen, 1920. Song: solo v.,
       pf.

6354   Woodman, Raymond H. NY: Silver, 1932 in Music of
       Many Lands and Peoples. Song: v., pf.

Shadow March   "All round the house is the jet-black night"
Magazine of Art (Mar. 1884) as one of "North-West Passage"

6355   Andrews, Mark. Nine Songs from "A Child's Garden of
       Verse", NY: HWG, 1911. Song: [v., pf.].

6356   del Riego, Teresa. Children's Pictures, L: C, 1909.
       Song: solo v., pf.

6357   Gilbert, Norman. L: N, 1953. Song: unison v., pf.

6358   Rathbone, George. L: Curwen, 1923. Song: unison
       children's v., pf. or unison female v., pf.

6359   Rowley, Alec. Monsieur de la plume, L: Curwen, 1963;
       re-issued L: ASH. Song (in play): unison child-
       ren's v., pf. or unison female v., pf.

6360   Stevenson, Ronald. MS 1961, Four Robert Louis
       Stevenson Songs (MS 1961-67). Song: med. v., pf.

6361 Thomas, Muriel. Four Songs for Children, L: EA,
       1957. Song: med. unison v., pf. Score contains
       Welsh transl. by Wil Ifan.

6362 Whitfield, J.B.R. L: AH&C, 1958. Song: unison v.,
       pf.

6363 Zaninelli, Luigi. The World Is So Full, DWG: SPI,
       1962. Song: ssa, fl., ob., cl., bsn., pf. or ssa,
       of.

"She rested by the Broken Brook"   Songs of Travel and other
Verses (1896)

6364 Coleridge-Taylor, Samuel. MS pre-1912, B: OD. Song:
       [v., pf.?].

6365 Homer, Sidney. "The Unforgotten", Six Songs from
       "Underwoods", NY: GS, 1904. Song: v., pf.

6366 Schenck, Flliott. The Unforgotten, L: B&H, 1902.
       Song: [v., pf.?].

Sick Child, The   "O Mother, lay your hand on my brow!"
Underwoods (1887)

6367 Homer, Sidney. MS (Opus 18), NY: GS. Song: [solo v.,
       pf.].

Sing me a song of a lad that is gone   See: Over the Sea to
Skye

Singing   "Of speckled eggs the birdie sings"   A Child's
Garden of Verses (1885)

6368 Baker, Clara B., arr. NY: AD, 1921 in Songs for
       Little Children. Song: v., pf. Text adapt. to a
       German air. Harmonis. by Caroline Kohlsaat.

6369 Bentley, Alys. Chi.: Laidlaw, 1923 in The Song
       Series, Book 3. Song: v., unacc. Setting of last
       stanza only.

Stevenson, Robert Louis continued

6370 Chadwick, George W. NY: Scribner's, 1897 in The
Stevenson_Song-Book. Song: v., pf.

6371 Crowninshield, Ethel. Robert_Louis_Stevenson_Songs,
Springfield: Bradley, 1910. Song: v., pf.

6372 Drozdoff, Vladimir. Stevensonia, NY: Omeja, 1951.
Song: pf. solo or v., pf.

6373 Falk, Edward. A_Child's_Garden_of_Verses, NY: GS,
pre-1940. Song: [v., pf.].

6374 Groocock, Joseph. "Of...", A_Child's_Garden, L:
Elkin, 1957. Song: ssa, pf.

6375 Hawley, Charles. NY: Scribner's, 1897 in The_Steven-
son_Song-Book. Song: v., pf.

6376 Homer, Sidney. Three_Songs_from_"A_Child's_Garden
of_Verses", MS (Opus 16), NY: GS. Song: v., pf.

6377 Nevin, Ethelbert. "Of...", Three_Songs, MS pre-1901,
B: BMC. Song: [v., pf.].

6378 Radnor, Marvin. Songs_for_Little_Children, Book 1,
Buffalo: the composer, 1923. Song: v., pf.

6379* Rowley, Alec. "Of...", L: Curwen, 1963. Song: unison v., pf.

6380 Warner, Lorraine, arr. B: ECS, 1923 in A_Kinder-
garten_Book_of_Folk-Songs. Song: v., pf. Text
adapt. to an Engl. folk air.

Song of Rahéro, The   "Ori, my brother in the island mode"
Ballads (1890)

6381 Stewart, D.M. "House of Mine", L: A, pre-1944. Song:
solo v., pf. Setting of lines beginning: "House
of mine (it went), house upon the sea".

Stormy evening closes now in vain, The"   Songs_of_Travel
and_other_Verses (1896)

6382 Homer, Sidney. "The Stormy Evening", Six_Songs_from
"Underwoods", NY: GS, 1904. Song: v., pf.

Stevenson, Robert Louis continued

<u>Strange Case of Dr. Jekyll and Mr. Hyde, The</u>   (NV)   (1886)

6383   Bart, Lionel. "Dr. Jekyll and Mr. Hyde", MS, perf.
       CBC, Mar. 1973. Musical play.

6384   Cannon, Philip. "Dr. Jekyll and Mr. Hyde", MS.
       Musical drama for TV: s, a, t bar, b soli, sps.,
       choir, orch. Lyrics adapt. from the novel by Jack
       Playfair and Jacqueline Laidlaw.

6385   De Pue, Wallace. "Dr. Jekyll and Mr. Hyde", MS,
       perf. Apr. 1974. Opera.

6386   Grossmith, George. "The Real Case of Hyde and
       Jekyll", MS, prod. London, Sept. 1888. Musical.
       Text adapt. by the composer.

Summer Sun   "Great is the sun"   <u>A Child's Garden of Verses</u>
(1885)

6387   Cheatham, Katharine S., arr. NY: GS, 1917 in <u>Nursery</u>
       <u>Garland</u>. Song: v., pf. Text adapt. to a melody by
       L. van Beethoven.

6388   Conant, Grace W. B: Pilgrim, 1925 in <u>Song and Play</u>
       <u>for Children</u>. Song: v., pf.

6389   Radnor, Marvin. <u>Songs for Little Children</u>, Book 1,
       Buffalo: the composer, 1923. Song: v., pf.

Sun's Travels, The   "Sun is not a-bed, when I, The"   <u>A</u>
<u>Child's Garden of Verses</u> (1885)

6390   Foote, Arthur. NY: Scribner's, 1897 in <u>The Stevenson</u>
       <u>Song-Book</u>. Song: v., pf.

6391   Rhodes, Harold. L: EA, pre-1951. Song: unison v.,
       pf.

6392   Shields, Arnold. L: 1937. Song: unison v., pf.

"Swallows travel to and fro"   <u>Poems by Robert Louis Steven-</u>
<u>son: Hitherto Unpublished</u>, Vol. I (1916)

723

Stevenson, Robert Louis continued

6393   Nixon, Roger. "Swallows", Bryn Mawr: TP, 1963. Song:
       satb, a cap.

Swing, The   "How do you like to go up in a swing"   A
Child's Garden of Verses (1885)

6394   Andrews, Mark. "Swing Song", Nine Songs from "A
       Child's Garden of Verse", NY: HWG, 1911. Song:
       [v., pf.].

6395   Bell, Florence E.E., arr. L: Longmans, Green, 1911
       in Singing Circle. Song: v., pf. Text adapt. to
       an anon. score.

6396   Chorbajian, John. MS copyright by composer 1966,
       avail. Julliard. Song: children's chorus of 2 pt.
       treble v., fl., pf.

6397   Crawford, Thomas. Songs with Music from "A Child's
       Garden of Verses", L: Jack, 1915. Song: v., pf.

6398   Curtis, Natalie. Songs from "A Child's Garden of
       Verses", Newton Center: Wa-Wan, 1902. Song: med.
       v., pf.

6399   de Koven, Reginald. NY: Scribner's, 1897 in The
       Stevenson Song-Book. Song: v., pf.

6400   Falk, Edward. A Child's Garden of Verses, NY: GS,
       pre-1940. Song: [v., pf.].

6401   Groocock, Joseph. "How...", A Child's Garden, L:
       Elkin, 1957. Song: ssa, pf.

6402   Grosvenor, Mrs. Norman. Six Songs from "A Child's
       Garden of Verses", L: N, pre-1940. Song: [v.,
       pf.].

6403   Hadley, Henry. B: Schmidt, 1903. Song: v., pf.

6404   Helyer, Marjorie. L: N, 1957. Song: unison v., pf.

6405   Judd, Percy. L: OUP, 1925. Song: unison v., pf.

6406   Lehmann, Liza. The Daisy Chain, L: BH, 1893. Song:
       s solo, pf. Portions of the collection require
       various soli.

Stevenson, Robert Louis continued

6407   Mason, Daniel G. Five Children's Songs, B: BMC, pre-
       1940. Song: [v., pf.].

6408   Moore, Francis. "Swing Song", [NY?]: HZ, pre-1940.
       Song: [v., pf.].

6409   Moule-Evans, David. L: EA, pre-1951. Song: unison
       v., pf.

6410   Radnor, Marvin. Songs for Little Children, Book 1,
       Buffalo: the composer, 1923. Song: v., pf.

6411   Rowley, Alec. L: Curwen, 1963. Song: ss, pf.

6412   Scott, Beatrice M. NY: HH&E, 1933 in New Universal
       School Music Series: Rhythm Songs. Song: v., un-
       acc. Also publ. NY: HH&E, 1934 in New Universal
       School Music Series: Introduction to Part Sing-
       ing. Song: voices, a cap.

6413   Shaw, Geoffrey. L: Curwen, 1915. Song: unison v.,
       pf.

6414   Smith, Eleanor. Song Pictures, Chi.: Summy, pre-
       1940. Song: [v., pf.].

6415   Thomas, Muriel. Four Songs for Children, L: EA,
       1957. Song: med. unison v., pf. Score contains
       Welsh transl. by Wil Ifan.

6416   Whitfield, J.B.R. L: AH&C, 1955. Song: unison v.,
       pf.

6417   Williams, Patrick. L: BW, 1961. Song: unison v., pf.

6418   Wood, William L. NY: ABC, 1915-17 in Hollis Dann
       Music Course, Vol. 5. Song: v., pf.

6419   Zaninelli, Luigi. The World Is So Full, DWG: SPI,
       1962. Song: ssa, fl., ob., cl., bsn., pf. or ssa,
       pf.

System   "Every night my prayers I say"   A Child's Garden of
Verses (1885)

725

6420 Curtis, Natalie. Songs from "A Child's Garden of Verses", Newton Center: Wa-Wan, 1902. Song: med. v., pf.

6421 Falk, Edward. A Child's Garden of Verses, NY: GS, pre-1940. Song: [v., pf.].

6422 Grosvenor, Mrs. Norman. Six Songs from "A Child's Garden of Verses", L: N, pre-1940. Song: [v., pf.].

6423 Lehmann, Liza. "Stars", The Daisy Chain, L: BH, 1893. Song: t solo, pf. Portions of the collection require various soli.

Thought, A   "It is very nice to think"   A Child's Garden of Verses (1885)

6424 Conant, Grace W. B: Pilgrim, 1915 in Songs for Little People. Song: v., pf.

6425 Falk, Edward. A Child's Garden of Verses, NY: GS, pre-1940. Song: [v., pf.].

6426 Radnor, Marvin. Songs for Little Children, Book 1, Buffalo: the composer, 1923. Song: v., pf.

Time to Rise   "Birdie with a yellow bill, A"   A Child's Garden of Verses (1885)

6427 Crowninshield, Ethel. Robert Louis Stevenson Songs, Springfield: Bradley, 1910. Song: v., pf.

6428 Curtis, Natalie. Songs from "A Child's Garden of Verses", Newton Center: Wa-Wan, 1902. Song: med. v., pf.

6429 del Riego, Teresa. Children's Pictures, L: C, 1909. Song: solo v., pf.

6430 Drozdoff, Vladimir. Stevensonia, NY: Omega, 1951. Song: pf. solo or v., pf.

6431 Falk, Edward. A Child's Garden of Verses, NY: GS, pre-1940. Song: [v., pf.].

6432 Gambogi, F. Elvira. Child-Land, L: BH, 1902. Cyc.:
solo v., pf.

6433 Radnor, Marvin. Songs for Little Children, Book 1,
Buffalo: the composer, 1923. Song: v., pf.

6434* Rowley, Alec. L: Curwen, 1963. Song: unison v., pf.

6435 Williamson, Malcolm. From a Child's Garden, L: Weinberger, 1968. Song: high v., pf.

To S.R. Crockett "Blows the wind to-day" Songs of Travel
and other Verses (1896)

6436 Brown, James. "Blows the Wind", MS. Song: ms or bar
solo, pf. Also suitable for s or t solo.

6437 Carey, Clive. "Blows...", Two "Songs of Travel", L:
S&B, pre-1940. Song: [v., pf.].

6438 Hopekirk, Helen. "Blows...", NY: GS, pre-1929. Song:
high or med. v., pf.

6439 Simpson, Donald. "Blows...", L: CR, 1957. Song: solo
v., pf.

6440 Voormolen, Alexander. "Grey Recumbent Tombs, Three
Songs on British Verse, Amst.: DM, 1948. Song:
b solo, pf.

"To you, let snow and roses" Songs of Travel and other
Verses (1896)

6441 Byars, Donald. "Song", Songs of Travel, MS 1948,
avail. University of Otago. Song: bar solo, pf.

6442 Peel, Graham. "Snow and Roses", L: C, 1913. Song:
solo v., pf.

Travel "I should like to rise and go" A Child's Garden of
Verses (1885)

6443 Protheroe, Daniel. NY: Silver, 1920 in The Progressive Music Series, Book 3. Song: v., unacc.

Stevenson, Robert Louis continued

Treasure Island (NV) Young Folks (Oct. 1881-Jan. 1882),
rev. & publ. sep. 1883

6444 Elkus, Jonathan. L: N, 1962. Musical play: 13 soli
treble v., 2 sp., 3 pt. treble chorus, pf. (or
orch. with opt. pts.). Text by Bruce M. Snyder.

6445 Gilbert, Henry F. "Pirate Song", Newton Center: Wa-
Wan, 1902 in Wa-Wan Series of American
Compositions, Vol. I. Song: v., pf. Setting of
lines beginning: "Fifteen men on the dead man's
chest". Additional lyrics by Alice C. Hyde.

6446 Meyer, Joseph. San Francisco: Paramount (Daniel &
Wilson), 1919. Film music. Text by Louis Weslyn.

6447 Ornadel, Cyril. L: SFM, 1973. Musical play: soli,
chorus, pf., acc. Lyrics by Hal Shaper, after
adapt. by Bernard Miles and Josephine Wilson.

6448 Tosatti, Vieri. MS pre-1962. Opera.

6449 Victory, Gerard. Wi.: Cranz, 1968. Overture: orch.

Unseen Playmate, The "When children are playing alone"
A Child's Garden of Verses (1885)

6450 Crowninshield, Ethel. Robert Louis Stevenson Songs,
Springfield: Bradley, 1910. Song: v., pf.

Vagabond, The "Give to me the life I love" Songs of
Travel and other Verses (1896)

6451 Byars, Donald. Songs of Travel, MS 1948, avail.
University of Otago. Song: bar solo, pf.

6452 Cain, Noble. NY: Silver, 1932 in Music of Many Lands
and Peoples. Song: v., pf.

6453 Davies, H. Walford. Twenty-One Songs, L: N, 1931.
Song: v., pf.

6454 Kalmanoff, Martin. "Give Me the Life I Love", Minn.:
SH&McC, 1958. Song: ttbb, pf. Also suitable for
solo v.

6455 Pease, Jessie L. NY: Maxwell, 1907. Song: [solo v.,
      pf.].

6456 Smith, Georgina. Songs of Travel, MS 1953, avail.
      University of Otago. Song: s or t solo, pf.

6457 Speaks, Oley. NY: GS, 1922. Song: [solo v., pf.].

6458 Thayer, William A. MS pre-1933, NY: GS. Song: [solo
      v., pf.].

6459 Vaughan Williams, Ralph. Songs of Travel, 1st set,
      L: BH, 1905. Cyc.: solo v., pf. Orchn. (1905) by
      the composer. This setting arr. by Harrison for
      ttbb, a cap.

6460 Wells, John B. MS pre-1935, B: BMC. Song: [solo v.,
      pf.].

6461 Young, Francis B. Songs for Voice & Pianoforte,
      MS pre-1913, L: WK, n.d. Song: v., pf.

Visit from the Sea, A   "Far from the loud sea beaches"
Magazine of Art (Nov. 1885)

6462 Gurney, Ivor. MS 1909. Song: [solo v., pf.].

6463 Smith, Eleanor. Songs Pictures, Chi.: Summy, pre-
      1940. Song: [v., pf.].

6464 Taylor, Colin. L: S&B, pre-1940. Song: [v., pf.].

"We uncommiserate pass into the night"   Songs of Travel and
Other Verses (1896)

6465 Jarrett, Brian C. "A Song of Travel", MS 1953,
      avail. University of Auckland. Song: bar solo,
      pf.

Weir of Hermiston   (NV)   Cosmopolis (Jan.-Apr. 1896), publ.
sep. 1896

6466 Orr, Robin. "Hermiston", MS, perf. Edinburgh, Aug.
      1975. Opera. Libr. by Bill Bryden.

Stevenson, Robert Louis continued

Where go the Boats? "Dark brown is the river" A Child's Garden of Verses (1885)

6467 Andrews, Mark. Nine Songs from "A Child's Garden of Verse", NY: HWG, 1911. Song: [v., pf.].

6468 Bacon, Ernst. Four Innocent Airs, NY: LG, 1958. Song: 2 pt. chorus, pf.

6469 Barnes, Marshall. Three Songs to Children, Cin.: Canyon, 1970, copyright reassigned Tor.: ECK, 1972. Song: sa, pf.

6470 Bell, Florence E.E., arr. L: Longmans, Green, 1911 in Singing Circle. Song: v., pf. Text adapt. to an "old air".

6471 Crawford, Thomas. Songs with Music from "A Child's Garden of Verses", L: Jack, 1915. Song: v., pf.

6472 del Riego, Teresa. Children's Pictures, L: C, 1909. Song: solo v., pf.

6473 Falk, Edward. A Child's Garden of Verses, NY: GS, pre-1940. Song: [v., pf.].

6474 Floyd, Carlisle. Two Stevenson Songs, NY: BH, 1967. Song: unison v., pf.

6475 Groocock, Joseph. "Dark brown...", A Child's Garden, L: Elkin, 1957. Song: ssa, pf.

6476 Hadley, Henry. B: Schmidt, 1903. Song: v., pf.

6477 Helyer, Marjorie. L: N, 1957. Song: unison v., pf.

6478 Kay, Ulysses. NY: Duchess, 1966. Song: solo v., pf. or unison v., pf.

6479 Macdonald, R. Houston. L: N, 1895 in Thirty Unison Songs. Song: unison v., pf.

6480 Miller, Anne S. "Boats of Mine", NY: HFL, 1919. Song: solo v., pf.

6481 Muschamp, Stanley. NY: [HWG?], pre-1940. Song: [v., pf.].

6482 Nevin, Ethelbert. "Dark brown...", Three Songs, MS
pre-1901, B: BMC. Song: [v., pf.].

6483 Peel, Graham. L: C, 1910. Song: [v., pf.].

6484 Quilter, Roger. Four Child Songs, L: C, 1914. Song:
solo v., pf.

6485 Radnor, Marvin. Songs for Little Children, Book 1,
Buffalo: the composer, 1923. Song: v., pf.

6486 Scott, Beatrice M. NY: HH&E, 1933 in New Universal
School Music Series: Rhythm Songs. Song: v.,
unacc.

6487 Smith, Eleanor. Song Pictures, Chi.: Summy, pre-
1940. Song: [v., pf.].

6488 Stanford, C.V. A Child's Garland of Songs, L: Longmans, Green, 1892 (L: Curwen, 1914). Song: unison
v., pf.

6489 Thiman, Eric. L: A, pre-1940. Song: [v., pf.].

6490 Thomas, Muriel. Four Songs for Children, L: EA,
1957. Song: med. unison v., pf. Score contains
Welsh transl. by Wil Ifan.

6491 Warner, Lorraine, arr. B: ECS, 1923 in A Kindergarten Book of Folk-Songs. Song: v., pf. Text
adapt. to a Fr. folk air.

6492 Weigl, Vally. MS, avail. ACA. Song: med. v., rec.,
pf.

6493 Williams, Patrick. L: BW, 1963. Song: unison v., pf.

6494 Williamson, Malcolm. From a Child's Garden, L: Weinberger, 1968. Song: high v., pf.

6495 Zaninelli, Luigi. The World Is So Full, DWG: SPI,
1962. Song: ssa, fl., ob., cl., bsn., pf. or ssa,
pf.

Whole Duty of Children   "Child should always say what's
true, A"   A Child's Garden of Verses (1885)

Stevenson, Robert Louis continued

6496   Bright, Houston. From "A Child's Garden of Verses",
       DWG: SPI, 1967. Cyc.: satb, a cap.

6497   Falk, Edward. A Child's Garden of Verses, NY: GS,
       pre-1940. Song: [v., pf.].

6498   Williamson, Malcolm. From a Child's Garden, L: Wein-
       berger, 1968. Song: high v., pf.

Wind, The   "I saw you toss the kites on high"   Magazine of
Art (July 1894)

6499   Bell, Florence E.E., arr. L: Longmans, Green, 1911
       in Singing Circle. Song: v., pf. Text adapt. to
       an "old air".

6500   Bullard, Frederic. B: Ginn, 1910 in Song Reader.
       Song: v., pf.

6501   Clark, Henry A. Vancouver: Western, 1966. Song: uni-
       son v., pf.

6502   Covert, Mary. Oakville: FH, 1954. Song: v., pf.

6503   Crawford, Thomas. Songs with Music from "A Child's
       Garden of Verses", L: Jack, 1915. Song: v., pf.

6504   Curtis, Natalie. Songs from "A Child's Garden of
       Verses", Newton Center: Wa-Wan, 1902. Song: med.
       v., pf.

6505   de Koven, Reginald. NY: Scribner's, 1897 in The
       Stevenson Song-Book. Song: v., pf.

6506   Fowler, Keith. L: Curwen, 1926. Song: unison v.,
       accompaniment unspecif.

6507   Gilchrist, William W. NY: Silver, 1928-30 in The
       Music Hour, Book 4. Song: v., unacc.

6508   Grosvenor, Mrs. Norman. Six Songs from "A Child's
       Garden of Verses", L: N, pre-1940. Song: [v.,
       pf.].

6509   Herbert, Victor. NY: Silver, 1920 in The Progressive
       Music Series, Book 3. Song: v., unacc.

6510 Jager, Robert. A Child's Garden of Verses, MS. Cyc.: s solo, pf. Also avail. for s solo, wind ensemble or s solo, ch. orch.

6511 Longmire, John. "A Windy Day", L: BW, 1970. Song: unison v., pf.

6512 Nixon, Roger. NY: LG, 1962. Song: satb, a cap.

6513 Radnor, Marvin. Songs for Little Children, Book 1, Buffalo: the composer, 1923. Song: v., pf.

Windy Nights   "Whenever the moon and stars are set"   A Child's Garden of Verses (1885)

6514 Andrews, Herbert K. "The Night Rider", L: EA, 195 . Canon: treble v., [a cap.].

6515 Andrews, Mark. Nine Songs from "A Child's Garden of Verse", NY: HWG, 1911. Song: [v., pf.].

6516 Balendonck, Armand. NY: Pro Art, pre-1940. Song: [v., pf.?].

6517 Bodde, Margaret. NY: Silver, 1916-19 in The Progressive Music Series: Teachers' Manual, Book 1. Song: v., pf.

6518 Bright, Houston. From "A Child's Garden of Verses", DWG: SPI, 1967. Cyc.: satb, a cap.

6519 Brook, Harry. L: OUP, 1939. Song: unison v., stgs.

6520 Crowninshield, Ethel. Robert Louis Stevenson Songs, Springfield: Bradley, 1910. Song: v., pf.

6521 del Riego, Teresa. Children's Pictures, L: C, 1909 Song: solo v., pf.

6522 Drozdoff, Vladimir. Stevensonia, NY: Omega, 1951. Song: pf. solo or v., pf.

6523 Falk, Edward. A Child's Garden of Verses, NY: GS, pre-1940. Song: [v., pf.

6524 Forst, Rudolf. NY: Musicus, 1942. Hp. solo.

6525 Foulds, John H. "Phantom Horseman (Windy Nights)", Chelmsford: MV, 1975. Song: bar solo, pf.

6526 Gambogi, F. Elvira. Child-Land, L: BH, 1902. Cyc.: solo v., pf.

6527 Gilbert, Norman. L: N, 1955. Canon: equal v., pf.

6528 Grant-Schaefer, G.A. B: Ginn, 1927 in Music Education Series: Two-Part Music. Song: 2 pt. chorus, a cap.

6529 Hand, Colin. L: BH, 1956. Song: unison v., pf.

6530 Holman, Derek. L: N, 1960. Song: unison v., pf.

6531 Mason, Daniel G. Five Children's Songs, B: BMC, pre-1940. Song: [v., pf.].

6532 Radnor, Marvin. Songs for Little Children, Book 1, Buffalo: the composer, 1923. Song: v., pf.

6533 Rhodes, Harold. L: EA, pre-1951. Song: unison v., pf.

6534 Rutter, John. Five Childhood Lyrics, L: OUP, 1974. Cyc.: satb, a cap.

6535 Scott, Beatrice M. NY: HH&E, 1935 in New Universal School Music Series: Art Songs and Part Songs. Song: v., unacc.

6536 Smith, Eleanor. Song Pictures, Chi.: Summy, pre-1940. Song: [v., pf.].

6537 Stanford, C.V. A Child's Garland of Songs, L: Longmans, Green, 1892 (L: Curwen, 1914). Song: unison v., pf.

Young Night Thought   "All night long and every night"   A Child's Garden of Verses (1885)

6538 Crowninshield, Ethel. Robert Louis Stevenson Songs, Springfield: Bradley, 910. Song: v., pf.

6539 Falk, Edward. A Child's Garden of Verses, NY: GS, pre-1940. Song: [v., pf.].

tevenson, Robert Louis continued

6540   Foote, Arthur. NY: Scribner's, 1897 in The Stevenson
       Song-Book. Song: v., pf.

6541   Groocock, Joseph. "All night...", A Child's Garden,
       L: Elkin, 1957. Song: ssa, pf.

6542   Hadley, Henry. B: Schmidt, 1903. Song: v., pf.

6543   Homer, Sidney. Three Songs from "A Child's Garden of
       Verses", MS (Opus 16), NY: GS. Song: v., pf.

6544   Peel, Graham. L: C, 1910. Song: [v., pf.].

6545   Radnor, Marvin. Songs for Little Children, Book 1,
       Buffalo: the composer, 1923. Song: v., pf.

Youth and Love: I   "Once only by the garden gate"   Songs of
Travel and other Verses (1896)

6546   Coleridge-Taylor, Samuel. "Once Only", MS pre-1912,
       B: OD. Song: [v., pf.?].

Youth and Love: II   "To the heart of youth the world is a
highwayside"   Pall Mall Gazette (Jan. 1895)

6547   Vaughan Williams, Ralph. Songs of Travel, 2nd set,
       L: BH, 1907. Cyc.: solo v., pf. Orchn. (1962) by
       Roy Douglas.

Miscellanea

6548   Baker, Clara B., arr. "Thanks to our Father", NY:
       AD, 1921 in Songs for Little Children. Song: v.,
       pf. Text (by Stevenson) adapt. to a melody by
       F.J. Haydn.

6549   Bantock, Granville. Grove's makes passing mention of
       Bantock's settings (for male chorus, a cap.) of
       Stevenson works.

6550   Bennett, R. Sterndale. Six Songs from "A Child's
       Garden of Verses", Glasgow: PT, 1908. Songs: solo
       v., pf.

735

6551   Betts, Lorne. <u>Six Songs</u>, MS 1956. Songs: a solo, orch. Texts by Stevenson.

6552   Blackburn, Marie. <u>Sixes and Sevens</u>, L: Feldman, 1968. 13 songs (texts by Stevenson) for voices, tuned perc., untuned perc.

6553   Blumenthal, Jacob. "A Dirge", L: N, pre-1940 in <u>Collection</u>, Vol. 1. Song: [v., pf.?].

6554   Bright, Houston. "The River", <u>From "A Child's Garden of Verses"</u>, DWG: SPI, 1967. Cyc.: satb, a cap. [Most likely a setting either of "Where Go the Boats" or of "Looking-Glass River".]

6555   Byars, Donald. "The Sea", <u>Songs of Travel</u>, MS 1948, avail. University of Otago. Song: bar solo, pf.

6556   Carew, Molly. "In the Quiet Eve", L: C. Song: solo v., pf.

6557   Carey, Clive. "The Far-Fares", L: OUP, pre-1940. Song: [v., pf.?].

6558   Carmichael, Mary. <u>A Child's Garden of Verses</u>, L: E, n.d. 12 songs.

6559   Charles, Ernest. "Over the Land is April", NY: HZ, pre-1940. Song: [v., pf.?].

6560   Eben, Petr. <u>I am with you children</u>, MS 1956, avail. SCSKU. Incidental music for radio (to accompany readings of Stevenson works): str. qrt., cl., pf.

6561   Elmore, David. An Aug. 1901 issue of <u>New York Sunday Press</u> incl. a song (by Elmore) entitled "O Golden Day". The score wrongly attributes the text to Stevenson.

6562   Gee, Norman. "The Exile's Song", NY: GS, pre-1940. Song: [v., pf.?].

6563   Gurney, Ivor. "County of Peebles", MS 1924. Song: [solo v., pf.].

6564   Hill, Edward B. <u>Stevensonia Suite #1 for Orchestra</u>, MS 1917. Orch. ste. Inspired by poems incl. in <u>A Child's Garden of Verses</u>.

Stevenson, Robert Louis continued

6565   Hughes, Gervase. The 1962 edn. (rev. by Sir Jack
        Westrup) of Eric Blom's Everyman's_Dictionary_of
        Music (L: Dent) indicates that Hughes' work incl.
        settings of texts by Stevenson.

6566   Lehmann, Liza. "A Moral", More_Daisies, L: BH, 1902.
        Cyc.: v., pf.

6567   Lutyens, Elisabeth. Islands, MS 1971, L: OP. Set-
        tings for s, t soli, narr., instr. ensemble.
        Incl. words by Stevenson.

6568   Marshall, M.E. A_Child's_Garden_of_Music, L: BW,
        ca. 1922. Pf. solo. The May 1922 issue of Musical
        Times notes that "Illustrations by I. Graeff
        appear at the head of each piece, to which is ap-
        pended an apt quotation from...A_Child's_Garden
        of_Verses".

6569   Oldroyd, George. "The Rivals", L: Elkin, pre-1940.
        Song: [v., pf.].

6570   Parker, Horatio. "Songs", Four_Songs, NY: GS, 1904.
        Song: med. v., pf. "Songs" employs a text by
        Stevenson.

6571   Quilter, Roger. "Over the Land is April", Two_Songs,
        L: Elkin, 1922. Song: [v., pf.].

6572   Radó, Aladár. Eight_English_Children's_Songs, MS ca.
        1911. Texts by Stevenson.

6573   Ramsay, Katharine M. Song_Flowers_from_"A_Child's
        Garden_of_Verses", L: Gardner Darton, 1897.

6574   Stothart, Herbert. "Treasure Island", MS ca. 1934,
        prod. M.G.M. Film music. Arrangements by Charles
        Maxwell. [Incidental music to film of ·Stevenson's
        Treasure_Island?]

6575   Swan, Alfred J. Robert_Louis_Stevenson_Songs, MS ca.
        1947. Songs: v., pf.

6576   Taylor, Colin. "Come, my little children", L: EA,
        pre-1951. Song: unison v., pf.

Stevenson, Robert Louis continued

6577 Weigl, Vally. "The Huntsmen", MS, avail. ACA. Song:
      med. v., rec., pf. The catalogue of the ACA at-
      tributes the text of this song to Stevenson.

6578 Westrup, Jack. Just prior to his death, Sir Jack
      provided the following information concerning his
      2 settings of texts by [Robert Louis?] Stevenson:
      1) "Prelude", L: YBP, 1927. Song: unison (s or t)
      v., pf. Text begins: "By sunny market-place and
      street", and 2) "Come, here is Adieu to the
      City", L: YBP, 1928. Song: unison (s or t) v.,
      pf.

6579 Whitaker, David. "Doctor Jekyll and Sister Hyde",
      MS ca. 1971. Film music.

6580 White, Felix. "Come my little children", L: C. Song:
      [v., pf.].

6581 White, Felix. "The Piper", L: C, 1921. Song: [v.,
      pf.]. The publisher has stated that, al-
      though the song is no longer in print, its copy-
      right agreement attributes the text to Stevenson.

6582 Wilson, Charles M. Six Songs, MS 1951. Songs: v.,
      pf. Texts by Stevenson.

STRACHEY, Lytton   1880-1932

Miscellanea

6583 Walton, William. "The Son of Heaven", MS, perf. Lon-
      don, July 1925. Incidental music to Strachey's
      unpubl. play.

738

Strong, L.A.G.

STRONG, Leonard Alfred George   1896-1958

Brewer's Man   "Have I a wife? Bedlam I have!"   In Dub-
    lin Days (1921)

    6584   Orr, C.W. Seven Sociable Songs from the Repertoire
           of John Goss, L: Curwen. Song: bar solo, male v.
           qrt., pf.

Buckland Monachorum   "Buckland bells, Buckland bells"   In
    The Lowery Road (1923) as one of "The Four Parishes"

    6585   Menges, Herbert. "Buckland Bells", Two Little Songs,
           L: OUP, pre-1940. Song: [v., pf.].

Highland Funeral   "Dead is with the dead, The"   In Call to
    the Swan (1936)

    6586* Swain, Freda. "Highland Burial", MS 1936, avail.
           Chinnor: Channel, NEMO. Setting for bar (or a)
           and pf. ensemble.

Love Entrapped Me   "When my gaze first was dazed"   In The
    Body's Imperfection (1957) as one of "Three Irish Airs"

    6587   Dalway, Ianthe. Three Irish Airs, L: OUP, 1952.
           Song: bar solo, pf.

Love Repaid   "Showers come and go, love"   In The Body's
    Imperfection (1957) as one of "Three Irish Airs"

    6588   Dalway, Ianthe. Three Irish Airs, L: OUP, 1952.
           Song: bar solo, pf.

Mad Woman of Punnet's Town, The   "Swell within her billowed
    skirts, A"   In Dublin Days (1921)

    6589* Bliss, Arthur. Four Songs, MS ca. 1927. Song: v.,
           vln., pf.

Strong, L.A.G. continued

Meavy   "Meavy is in the valley, sleepy and old"   In The
Lowery Road (1923) as one of "The Four Parishes"

6590* Swain, Freda. MS 1958, avail. Chinnor: Channel,
NEMO. Setting for s (or t) and pf. ensemble.

Mysteries, The   "When I was young I'd little sense"   In The
Body's Imperfection (1957)

6591* Swain, Freda. MS 1957, avail. Chinnor: Channel,
NEMO. Setting for bar and pf. ensemble.

Northern Light   "Here under Heaven ringed"   In Northern
Light (1930)

6592 Garlick, Antony. Twelve Madrigals, Cin.: WLP, 1967.
Madrigal: ssa, a cap.

6593* Swain, Freda. Cantata in Memoriam ("The Indwel-
ling"), MS, avail. Chinnor: Channel, NEMO. Cta.:
voices, stgs., pf. "Northern Lights" is also
avail. as a sep. song for t (or s) and pf. ensemble.

Old Man at the Crossing, The   "I sweep the street and lift
me hat"   In Dublin Days (1921)

6594 Pugh, Louis. L: H, pre-1962. Song: med. v., pf.

Rare Spirit, The   "Thoughts timorous as the swift deer's
shadow pass"   In Difficult Love (1927)

6595* Swain, Freda. Cantata in Memoriam ("The Indwel-
ling"), MS, avail. Chinnor: Channel, NEMO. Cta.:
voices, stgs., pf. "The Rare Spirit" is also
avail. as a sep. song for s and pf. ensemble.

Shadow and Shadower   "Night rolls on, the dark, The"   In
The Body's Imperfection (1957)

740

Strong, L.A.G. continued

6596* Swain, Freda. Cantata in Memoriam ("The Indwel-
ling"), MS, avail. Chinnor: Channel, NEMO. Cta.:
voices, stgs., pf. "Shadow and Shadower" is also
avail. as a sep. song for bar and pf. ensemble.

Spear of Gold, The   (DR)   (1923)

6597 Poston, Elizabeth. MS 1946. Incidental music for
radio.

Wings   "Heaven is pure and cold and full of wings, The"   In
Call to the Swan (1936)

6598* Swain, Freda. MS 1936, avail. Chinnor: Channel,
NEMO. Setting for t and pf. ensemble.

Miscellanea

6599 Dalway, Ianthe. "Killiney Strand", Three Irish Airs,
L: OUP, 1952. Song: bar solo, pf. [Possibly a
setting of "The Coloured World"?]

6600 Horrocks, Herbert. "Fisherman's Night Song", Six
Traditional Songs, Set II, L: OUP, 1958. Song:
2 pt. chorus, [pf.].

6601 Jacques, Reginald. "Fisherman's Night Song", L: OUP,
1954. Song: ssa, a cap.

6602 Menges, Herbert. "The Little Seamstress", Two Little
Songs, L: OUP, pre-1940. Song: [v., pf.].

SWINBURNE, Algernon Charles   1837-1909

Age and Song   See: Barry Cornwall

At Parting   "For a day and a night Love sang to us"
Athenaeum (Aug. 1875)

741

Swinburne, A.C. continued

6603   Farley, Roland. "For a Day and a Night", MS pre-
       1932, NY: GS. Song: [v., pf.].

6604   Harris, Victor. "A Day, A Night", NY: GS, pre-1940.
       Song: [v., pf.].

6605   O'Neill, Norman. "Before Dawn", MS 1917. Ballet
       music: female chorus, orch. Orch. interlude from
       the ballet (and pf. arr. of the interlude) publ.
       L: BH.

Atalanta in Calydon   (DR)   (1865)

6606   Bantock, Granville. L: B&H, 1911. Choral symph.:
       mixed chorus, a cap.

6607   Droste, Doreen. "When the Hounds of Spring are on
       Winter's Traces", NY: CF, 1966. Song: satb, pf.
       Setting of lines beginning: "When the hounds of
       spring are on winter's traces".

Ave Atque Vale   "Shall I strew on thee rose or rue or
laurel"   Fortnightly Review (Jan. 1868)

6608   Robbins, Reginald. P: MST, ca. 1922. Song: b solo,
       [pf.]. Also suitable for bar (or a) solo, [pf.].

"Baby, baby bright"   A Midsummer Holiday And Other Poems
(1884) as one of "Cradle Songs"

6609   Smith, Leo. "Cradle Song", Five Songs, priv. publ.
       1912. Song: v., pf.

"Baby, baby sweet"   A Midsummer Holiday And Other Poems
(1884) as one of "Cradle Songs"

6610   Diack, J. Michael. "Baby Sweet", NY: PT, 1939. Song:
       sa, pf. or unison v., pf.

Baby-Bird   "Baby-bird, baby-bird"   Poems and Ballads, Third
Series (1889)

Swinburne, A.C. continued

6611 Boughton, Rutland. Three Baby Songs, MS 1902. Song:
      v., orch., pf.

6612 Hyde, Lewis. MS 1949. Song: v., pf.

Baby's Death, A   "Little soul scarce fledged for earth, A"
A Century of Roundels (1883)

6613 Elgar, Edward. "Rondel", MS [1887?]. Song: v., pf.
      Setting of lines beginning: "Little eyes that
      never knew".

Baby's Epitaph, A   "April made me: winter laid me here away
asleep" Fortnightly Review (Jan. 1888)

6614 Densmore, John. B: BMC, pre-1940. Song: [v., pf.].

Ballad of Dreamland, A   "I hid my heart in a nest of roses"
Belgravia (Sept. 1876)

6615 Fitzgerald, Augustine. Three Songs, L: Curwen, pre-
      1940. Song: [v., pf.].

6616 Smith, Leo. "Ballad of Dreamland", MS, avail.
      National Library, Ottawa. Song: v., pf.

Barry Cornwall   "In vain men tell us time can alter"   Pall
Mall Gazette (Oct. 1874), rev. 1878

6617 Hyde, Lewis. "In vain...", MS 1950. Song: v., pf.

"Beloved and blest, lit warm with love and fame"   A Century
of Roundels (1883) as one of "In Guernsey"

6618 Smith, Leo. "Beloved and Blest", NY: GS, 1914. Song:
      ttbb, a cap.

Bride's Tragedy, The   "Wind wears roun', the day wears doun,
The"   (1889)

6619 Grainger, Percy. L: S, 1914. Setting for satb,
      chorus of t and high bar v. ad lib., orch.

743

Swinburne, A.C. continued

Change   "But now life's face beholden"   A Century of Roundels (1883)

    6620 Hyde, Lewis. MS 1950. Song: v., pf.

Dark Month, A   "Month without sight of sun, A"   Tristram of
Lyonesse and other Poems (1882)

    6621 Hyde, Lewis. MS 1950. Songs: v., pf. Settings en-
          titled: "Thirty-One Pale Maidens" (pt. V),
          "Child, were you kinless and lonely" (pt. XII),
          "The Incarnate Sun" (pt. XVII), "Out of Sight"
          (pt. XVIII), "Whiter and Whiter" (pt. XXV).

Death of Richard Wagner, The   "Mourning on earth, as when
dark hours descend" Musical Review (Feb. 1883)

    6622 Hyde, Lewis. "Mourning on Earth", MS 1952. Song: v.,
          pf.

East to West   "Sunset smiles on sunrise: east and west are
one" Daily Chronicle (Jan. 1893)

    6623 Stanford, C.V. "From East to West", L: N, 1893. Set-
          ting for mixed choir, orch.

England: An Ode   "Sea and strand, and a lordlier land"
United Service Magazine (May 1890)

    6624 MacMillan, Ernest. "England", MS 1918, avail. CMC.
          Song: s, bar soli, chorus, orch.

Envoi   "Fly, white butterflies, out to sea"   A Century of
Roundels (1883)

    6625 Bray, K.I. "White Butterflies", Tor.: GVT, 1968.
          Song: s solo, pf.

    6626 Cole, Rossetter G. "White Butterflies", NY: ABC,
          1914-17 in Hollis Dann Music Course, Vol. 4.
          Song: v., pf.

Swinburne, A.C. continued

6627 Corbett, Felix. "Butterflies", L: BH, 1892. Song:
solo v., pf.

6628 Hyde, Lewis. MS 1950. Song: v., pf.

6629 Lang, Margaret R. "White Butterflies", B: Birchard,
1906 in The Laurel Music-Reader, Special edn.
Song: chorus with b ad lib., a cap. Also publ.
B: Birchard for chorus, pf.

6630 Rogers, J.H. "Fly...", NY: GS, pre-1929. Song: med.
v., pf.

Eton: An Ode   "Four hundred summers and fifty have shone"
Athenaeum (May 1891)

6631 Parry, C.H.H. "Eton", L: N, 1891. Setting for
chorus, orch.

Étude Réaliste   "Baby's feet, like sea-shells pink, A"
A Century of Roundels (1883)

6632 Freer, Eleanor. Score [n.p.] dated 1921, avail.
NYPL. Song: solo v., pf.

Félise "What shall be said between us here"   Poems and
Ballads (1866)

6633 Crist, Bainbridge. "Like April's Kissing May", B:
BMC, pre-1940. Song: [v., pf.]. Setting of lines
beginning: "O lips that mine have grown into".

6634 Hadley, Henry. "Song from 'Felice'", B: BMC, 1894.
Song: high v., pf. Setting of lines beginning:
"O lips that mine have grown into".

Garden ct Proserpine   "Here, where the world is quiet"
Poems and Ballads (1866)

6635 Lesemann, Frederick. MS. Cta.: ms, bar soli, chorus,
ch. orch.

6636* Paston-Cooper, [?]. "We are not sure of sorrow", L:
C. Song: solo v., pf.

Swinburne, A.C. continued

   6637 Vaughan Williams, Ralph. MS 1897. Song: s solo,
         chorus, orch.

   6638 Walsworth, Ivor. "Here...", L: OUP, 1950. Song: a or
         bar solo, pf.

"Heavenly bay, ringed round with cliffs and moors, The"
   A_Century_of_Roundels (1883) as one of "In Guernsey"

   6639 Smith, Leo. "The Heavenly Bay", MS, avail. National
         Library, Ottawa. Song: v., pf.

Hymn of Man   "In the grey beginning of years"   Songs_Before
   Sunrise (1871)

   6640 Lutyens, Elisabeth. "The Hymn of Man", MS 1965, L:
         OP. Motet: male chorus, a cap. Rev. 1970 (and
         entitled "Hymn of Man") for mixed chorus, a cap.

In a Garden   "Baby, see the flowers!"   English_Illustrated
   Magazine (Dec. 1886)

   6641 Boughton, Rutland. Three_Baby_Songs, MS 1902. Song:
         v., orch., pf.

In Church   "Thou whose birth on earth"   Songs_Before_Sun-
   rise (1871) as one of "Christmas Antiphones"

   6642 Pasfield, W.R. "Thou...", L: ASH, 1972. Carol: satb,
         org. (or pf.) ad lib.

   6643 Roff, Joseph. "This Day Born Again", NY: Bourne,
         1958. Song: ssa, pf. Also avail. for sab, pf.

In Harbour   "Goodnight and goodbye to the life whose signs
   denote us"   A_Century_of_Roundels (1883)

   6644 Rogers, J.H. NY: GS, pre-1929. Song: high v., pf.

In the Orchard   "Leave go my hands"   Poems_and_Ballads
   (1886)

Swinburne, A.C. continued

6645 Fitzgerald, Augustine. Four Songs, L: G&T, pre-1940.
Song: [v., pf.].

Interlude, An "In the greenest growth of Maytime" Poems
and Ballads (1866)

6646 Foresman, Robert, arr. "Maytime", NY: ABC, 1932 in
Sixth Book of Songs. Song: v., pf. Arr. of a
melody by Giaochino Rossini.

6647 Ronald, Landon. MS pre-1938, L: E. Song: [v., pf.?].

Lyke-Wake Song, A "Fair of face, full of pride" Lesbia
Brandon (1917), rev. 1889

6648 Hyde, Lewis. MS 1949. Song: v., pf.

Madonna Mia "Under green apple-boughs" Poems and Ballads
(1866)

6649 Foresman, Robert, arr. "A Lady's Portrait", NY: ABC,
1932 in Sixth Book of Songs. Song: voices, pf.
Text adapt. to a melody by Giovanni L. Gregori.

Marching Song, A "We mix from many lands" Songs Before
Sunrise (1871)

6650 Webber, W.S. Lloyd. L: Elkin, ca. 1950. Song: "mas-
sed unison" voices, [a cap.].

Match, A "If love were what the rose is" Poems and
Ballads (1866)

6651 Ambrose, Paul. "If love...", B: Ginn, 1925 in Three-
Part Music. Song: 3 pt. chorus, pf.

6652 Billin, Reginald. "If love...", NY: Church, pre-
1940. Song: [v., pf.].

6653 Cowen, Frederic H. "If love...", L: C, 1883. Song:
solo v., pf.

747

Swinburne, A.C. continued

    6654 Hadley, Henry. "If love...", NY: Church, 1898. Song:
          solo v., pf.

    6655 Herbert, Victor. "If love...", NY: Witmark, 1907.
          Song: solo v., pf.

    6656 Mackenzie, Alexander. "If love...", Ten Songs, L: N,
          1885. Song: solo v., pf.

    6657 Moore, Francis. "Joy", NY: R, pre-1940. Song: [v.,
          pf.].

    6658 Olmstead, Clarence. "If Love were like the Tune",
          NY: GS, pre-1940. Song: [v., pf.].

    6659 Russell, Welford. "If love...", Sixteen Songs, MS,
          avail. CMC. Song: med. v., pf.

    6660 Stebbins, Charles A. "If love...", NY: B&H, 1900.
          Song: v., pf.

    6661 White, Maude V. "April's Lady", L: C, 1902. Song:
          [solo v., pf.].

Music: An Ode   "Was it light that spake from the darkness"
    (1892)

    6662* Duncan, William E. "Ode to Music", MS ca. 1893.

    6663 Wood, Charles. L: A, 1893. Setting for s solo,
          chorus, orch.

"My mother sea, my fostress, what new strand"   A Century of
Roundels (1883) as one of "In Guernsey"

    6664 Smith, Leo. "My Mother Sea", Four Songs, NY: GS,
          1914. Song: v., pf.

Neap-Tide   "Far off is the sea"   Poems and Ballads, Third
Series (1889)

    6665 Bailey, Judith M. MS. Cta.: bar solo, pf.

748

Swinburne, A.C. continued

Night   "Night, whom in shape so sweet thou here mayst see"
         Poems and Ballads, Third Series (1889)

    6666 Hyde, Lewis. MS 1949. Song: v., pf.

    6667 Stewart, D.M. L: A, 1944. Song: solo v., pf.

"Night, in utmost noon forlorn and strong, with heart athirst
and fasting"   A Century of Roundels (1883) as one of "In
Guernsey"

    6668 Smith, Leo. "Night", NY: GS, 1914. Song: ttbb, a
          cap.

Nympholet, A   "Summer, and noon, and a splendour of silence"
         Black and White (May 1891)

    6669 Bax, Arnold. "Nympholet", MS 1912-15, perf. London,
          May 1961. Orch. only.

Oblation, The   "Ask nothing more of me, sweet"   Songs
         Before Sunrise (1871)

    6670 Brown, Hubert. L: BH, pre-1940. Song: [solo v.,
          pf.].

    6671 Cowen, Frederic H. "Ask Nothing More", Cowen Album,
          Vol. 2, NY: GS, pre-1940. Song: [solo v., pf.].

    6672 Crist, Bainbridge. "Love's Offering", NY: GX, 1945.
          Song: solo v., pf.

    6673 Deis, Carl. "Ask Nothing More", NY: GS, 1943. Song:
          solo v., pf.

    6674 Marzials, Theodore. "Ask Nothing More", L: BH, ca.
          1935. Song: solo v., pf.

    6675 Rathaus, Karol. Three English Songs, NY: AMP, 1946.
          Song: high or med. v., pf.

    6676 Ware, Harriet. NY: Church, pre-1940. Song: [solo v.,
          pf.].

Swinburne, A.C. continued

"On Dante's track by some funereal spell"   A Century of
Roundels (1883) as one of "In Guernsey"

    6677 Smith, Leo. "On Dante's Track", NY: GS, 1914. Song:
        ttbb, a cap.

Reiver's Neck-Verse, A   "Some die singing"   Poems and Ballads, Third Series (1889) A portion was 1st publ. in
Lesbia Brandon (1877)

    6678 Grainger, Percy. L: S, 1911. Song: male v., pf.

Rondel   "Kissing her hair I sat against her feet"   Poems
and Ballads (1866)

    6679 Bergh, Arthur. "Kissing...", NY: S-C, 1939. Song:
        solo v., pf.

    6680 Vaughan Williams, Ralph. MS 1895-96. Song: a or bar
        solo, pf.

Roundel, The   "Roundel is wrought as a ring or a starbright
sphere, A"   A Century of Roundels (1883)

    6681 Smith, Leo. "A Roundel is Wrought", MS, avail.
        National Library, Ottawa. Song: ssaa, a cap.

Russia: An Ode   "Out of hell a word comes hissing"   Fortnightly Review (Aug. 1890), publ. sep. same year

    6682 Hyde, Lewis. "Russia", MS 1950. Song: v., pf.

Song   "Love laid his sleepless head"   Examiner (Dec. 1874)

    6683 Barbour, Florence N. "Joy Came With The Day", B:
        Schmidt, pre-1940. Song: [v., pf.].

    6684 Crossley, Hastings. L: N, pre-1919. Song: [v., pf.].

    6685 Herbert, Victor. "Love laid...", NY: Witmark, 1907.
        Song: v., pf.

Swinburne, A.C. continued

6686 Sullivan, Arthur. "Love laid...", MS (incl. as part
of Sullivan's incidental music to the Gaiety
Theatre's Dec. 1874 prod. of "The Merry Wives of
Windsor"), publ. sep. L: BH. Song: [v., pf.?].

To a Cat   "Stately, kindly, lordly friend"   Athenaeum (Dec.
1893)

  6687 Dickinson, Peter. "Elegy", MS 1966. Miniature cta.:
c-t solo, hpd., vcl.

  6688 Gipps, Ruth. The Cat, L: JW, 1960, avail. composer.
Oratorio: a, bar soli, ssaattbb, orch.

Wasted Love   "What shall be done for sorrow"   A Century of
Roundels (1883)

  6689 Hyde, Lewis. MS 1950. Song: v., pf.

What is Death?   "Looking on a page where stood"   Tristram
of Lyonesse and other Poems (1882)

  6690 Hyde, Lewis. MS 1950. Song: v., pf.

Winds, The   "O weary fa' the east wind"   Lesbia Brandon
(1877), rev. 1889

  6691 Hart, Fritz. MS 1917, avail. State Library of Victoria, Melbourne. Song: v., pf.

  6692 Hyde, Lewis. MS 1949. Song: v., pf.

  6693 Walton, William. L: Curwen, 1921. Song: high v.,
pf.

Miscellanea

  6694 Atherton, Percy. "Rondel", B: BMC, pre-1940. Song:
[v., pf.?].

  6695 Bainton, Edgar L. Before Sunrise, L: S&B, 1920.
Symph.: a solo, chorus, orch. Settings of 3 poems
from Swinburne's Songs Before Sunrise (1871).

Swinburne, A.C. continued

6696   Bartlett, Homer. "It's a' for the love of thee", MS
       pre-1920, NY: GS. Song: [solo v., pf.?].

6697   Bax, Arnold. "Spring Fire", MS 1913. Symph.: orch.
       only. Inspired by a work by Swinburne.

6698   Blumenthal, Jacob. "As I Loved Thee", L: C. Song:
       solo v., pf.

6699   Blumenthal, Jacob. "Saved", L: N, pre-1940. Song:
       [v., pf.].

6700   Boughton, Rutland. "A Cycle of Roundels", Three Baby
       Songs, MS 1902. Song: v., orch., pf.

6701   Deis, Carl. "Wake! For Night is Dead", NY: GS, pre-
       1940. Song: [v., pf.?].

6702   Fox, Oscar J. "Entreaty", NY: GS, pre-1940. Song:
       [v., pf.?].

6703   Herbert, Muriel. "Cradle Song", L: A, pre-1940.
       Song: [v., pf.?].

6704   Johns, Clayton. "Withered Roses", MS pre-1932, B:
       BMC. Song: [v., pf.?].

6705   Levy, Leon T. "Rondel", NY: GS, pre-1940. Song: [v.,
       pf.?].

6706   Miles, Philip. "Hymn before Sunrise", MS pre-1936,
       L: BH. Setting for chorus, orch.

6707* Pinsuti, Ciro. "If", L: C, 1877. Song: solo v., pf.
       Text attributed to Swinburne.

6708   Plumstead, Mary. "Questions", L: BH, 1960. Song:
       ssa, pf.

6709   Sauguet, Henri. Grove's lists a work entitled "Amour
       et Soleil" (dated 1929) employing a text by Swin-
       burne.

752

Swinburne, A.C. continued

6710 Whittaker, George. Seven Songs, MS pre-1939. The
       Oct. 1939 issue of Monthly Musical Record com-
       ments that "...the words...ranging from John
       Lydgate to the Japanese, via Dowson, Housman,
       Synge, Swinburne..., reveal wide literary
       interests".

6711 Williams, Gerrard. "Rondel", L: C. Song: solo v.,
       pf.

SYMONDS, John Addington   1840-1893

Adventante Deo   "Lift up your heads, gates of my heart,
  unfold"   Animi Figura (1882) as one of "Versöhnung"

    6712 Leighton, Kenneth. Sevenoaks: N, 1972. Anthem:
           satb, org.

Eyebright   "As a star from the sea new risen"   New and
  Old (1880)

    6713 Dello Joio, Norman. Six Love Songs, NY: CF, 1954.
           Song: [med.] solo v., pf.

Farewell   "Thou goest: to what distant place"   New and Old
  (1880)

    6714 Dello Joio, Norman. Three Songs of Adieu, NY: EBM,
           1962. Song: s or t solo, pf.

Invocation, An   "To God, the everlasting, who abides"
  Many Moods (1878)

    6715 Koutzen, Boris.   NY: Beekman, 1958. Setting for
           ssa, orch. or ssa, pf.

Prism of Life, The   "All that began with God, in God must
  end"   Animi Figura (1882) as one of "Versöhnung"

753

Symonds, John Addington continued

6716   Cruft, Adrian. "All that began with God", L: JW,
       1955 (hire). Motet: satb, orch. Avail. L: JW
       (sale) for satb, pf.

Singer, The   "He fills the world with his singing"   New and
Old (1880)

6717   Blower, Maurice. L: N, 1964. Song: ssa, pf.

"Sleep, baby, sleep! the Mother sings"   English Illustrated
Magazine (Dec. 1891)

6718   Lockwood, Normand. "A Lullaby for Christmas", Chi.:
       Kj, 1937. Song: ssaattb, [a cap.].

6719   Willan, Healey. "A Christmas Lullaby", Tor.: BMI,
       1950. Carol: t or bar solo, ssa, a cap.

To the Genius of Eternal Slumber   "Sleep, that are named
eternal!"   Sonnets of Three Centuries (1922); incl.
same year in Anima Figura as one of "L'Amour de L'
Impossible"

6720   Willan, Healey. MS 1902. Song: v., pf.

Vista, A*   "Sad heart, what will the future bring"   New and
Old (1880)

6721   Cable, Howard. "These Things Shall Be", NY: MCA,
       1968. Setting for satb, orch. and/or band.

6722   Clarke, Henry L. "These Things Shall Be", MS ca.
       1950. Setting for chorus, a cap.

6723   Davison, Archibald T., Thomas W. Surette, Augustus
       D. Zanzig, arr.   "These things shall be!", NY:
       ECS, 1924 in A Book of Songs. Hymn: unison
       children's v., pf. Also suitable for pt. singing.
       Arr. of a melody by J.S. Bach.

6724   Gordon, Edgar B., and Irene Curtis, arr.   "These
       Things Shall Be", Milwaukee: Hale, 1930 in Music
       for Youth. Song: v., unacc. Arr. of a tune by
       Charles Burney.

754

6725   Griffes, Charles T. "These Things Shall Be", NY, GS,
        1917. Song: unison chorus, pf. Text adapt. by the
        composer.

6726   Henderson, J. Raymond. "These Things Shall Be", NY:
        CF, 1959 (hire). Song: satb, band.

6727   Ireland, John. "These Things shall be", L: S&B,
        1919. Hymn: v., org. Employs the tune
        "Fraternity".

6728*   Ireland, John. "These Things shall be", L: BH, 1937
        (hire). Setting for t or bar solo, mixed chorus,
        orch., org., cel. Also avail. (hire) for t or
        bar solo, mixed chorus, reduced orch., org., cel.

6729   Sanders, Robert L. "A Hymn of the Future", NY: Beek-
        man, 1958. Hymn: satb, org.

6730   Shaw, Martin. "These Things Shall Be", L: Curwen,
        1922. [Hymn: v., org. or v., pf.?]

6731   Woodgate, Leslie. "Epilogue", A Song of Joys, L:
        S&B, pre-1967. Cta.: bar solo, chorus, orch.

Miscellanea

6732   Krones, [?], arr. "These Things Shall Be", Park
        Ridge: Kj, pre-1971. Arr. for sa and unison v.
        [Text by Symonds?]

6733   Nelson, Paul. "Death Takes All", Songs of Life, NY:
        CF, 1968. Song: mixed chorus, stgs., hp. Also
        avail. (in original version, MS 1957) for mixed
        chorus, pf. The text is Symonds' transl. of a
        medieval Norman song.

6734   Nelson, Paul. "My Love for Him", Three Songs for
        Soprano and Eight Horns, Far Hills: Horn Realm,
        1968. Song: s solo, 8 hn. The text is Symonds'
        transl. of a 13th century Latin MS.

6735   Ridout, Godfrey. "The Dance", L: N, 1964. Setting
        for satb, orch. The text is Symonds' transl. of
        Carmina Burana-137.

Symonds, John Addington continued

6736 Scott, Cyril. "A Spring Ditty", L: Elkin, 1910.
Song: v., pf.

SYMONS, Arthur   1865-1945

Adoration, The   "Why have you brought me myrrh"   Poems of
Arthur Symons, Vol. II (1914) as one of "The Loom of
Dreams"

6737 Ireland, John. Songs for a Medium Voice, L: JWC,
1919. Song: med. v. (best suited for a solo), pf.
Also publ. sep.

After Love   "O to part now, and, parting now"   In Silhouettes (1892)

6738 Dello Joio, Norman. Three Songs of Adieu, NY: EBM,
1962. Song: high v., pf.

6739 Lemont, Cedric. NY: GS, pre-1940. Song: [solo v.,
pf.?].

6740 Ronald, Landon. Four Silhouettes, L: E, 1919. Song:
high v., pf. Also avail. for med. v., pf. or low
v., pf.

After Sunset   "Sea lies quieted beneath, The"   In Silhouettes (1892) as one of "At Dieppe"

6741 Campbell-Tipton, Louis. Four Sea Lyrics, MS 1907,
NY: GS. Song: [v., pf.].

6742 Neuer, Berthold. NY: GS, pre-1940. Song: [v., pf.?].

6743 Smyth, Ethel. Three Moods of the Sea, Wien: UE,
1913. Song: ms, bar soli, orch.

Alla Passeretta Bruna   "If I bid you, you will come"   In
Silhouettes (1892)

6744 Ronald, Landon. "You are Mine", Four Silhouettes,
L: E, 1919. Song: high v., pf. Also avail. for
med. v., pf. or low v., pf.

At Dawn "She only knew the birth and death" In Silhouettes (1892)

6745 Leginska, Ethel. NY: GS, pre-1940. Song: [v., pf.].

Autumn Twilight "Long September evening dies, The" In
London Nights (1895) as one of "Intermezzo: Pastoral"

6746 Cockshott, Gerald. MS 1946. Song: v., pf.

6747 Warlock, Peter. L: OUP, 1923. Song: [ms or bar] solo
v., pf.

Before the Squall "Wind is rising on the sea, The" In
Silhouettes (1892) as one of "At Dieppe"

6748 Smyth, Ethel. Three Moods of the Sea, Wien: UE,
1913. Song: ms, bar soli, orch.

By the Pool at the Third Rosses "I heard the sighing of the
reeds" In Images of Good and Evil (1899) as one of "In
Ireland"

6749 Burleigh, Henry. NY: R, pre-1940. Song: [solo v.,
pf.?].

Crying of Water, The "O water, voice of my heart" Poems
of Arthur Symons, Vol. II (1914) as one of "The Loom of
Dreams"

6750 Campbell-Tipton, Louis. Four Sea Lyrics, MS 1907,
NY: GS. Song: [v., pf.].

6751 McIntyre, Paul. Three Poems of Arthur Symons [sic],
MS, avail. CMC. Song: [med.] solo v., pf.

During Music "Music had the heat of blood, The" In
Silhouettes (1892)

Symons, Arthur continued

6752 Watts, Wintter. <u>Two Poems by Arthur Symons</u>, MS (Opus
4), NY: GS, pre-1929. Song: high v., pf. Also
avail. for low v., pf.

Fisher's Widow, The   "Boats go out and the boats come in,
The"   In <u>Days and Nights</u> (1889)

6753 Coerne, Louis. MS pre-1922, B: BMC. Song: [v.,
pf.?].

6754 Edwards, Clara. NY: GS, pre-1940. Song: [v., pf.?].

6755 McIntyre, Paul. <u>Three Poems of Arthur Symons</u> [sic],
MS, avail. CMC. Song: [med.] solo v., pf.

6756 Tye, Henry. Cin.: Willis (L: C, 1966). Song: unison
v., accompaniment unspecif.

From "La Vida es Sueño" of Calderon   "We live, while we see
the sun"   In <u>Poems of Arthur Symons</u>, Vol. I (1914)

6757 Weinzweig, John. "Life is a Dream", <u>Wine of Peace</u>,
MS 1957, avail. CMC. Song: s solo, orch.

Grey Wolf, The   "Grey wolf comes again, The"   <u>Poems by
Arthur Symons</u>, Vol. II (1914) as one of "The Loom of
Dreams"

6758 Burleigh, Henry. NY: R, pre-1940. Song: [v., pf.?].

"If living sorrows any boon"   In <u>From Catullus: Chiefly
Concerning Lesbia</u> (1924)

6759 Tcimpidis, David. "Consolation", MS 1959, NY: CMP,
copyright by composer 1968. Song: satb, a cap.

"If, Lord, thy love for me is strong"   In <u>Poems of Arthur
Symons</u>, Vol. I (1914) as one of "From Santa Teresa"

6760 Berkeley, Lennox. <u>Four Poems of St. Teresa of Avila</u>,
L: JWC, 1949. Song: a solo, str. orch.

In Autumn   "Frail autumn lights upon the leaves"   In
Silhouettes (1892)

    6761   Cochran, Leslie. L: S&B, pre-1940. Song: [v., pf.?].

In Fountain Court   "Fountain murmuring of sleep, The"   In
Silhouettes (1892)

    6762   Besly, Maurice. L: BH, pre-1940. Song: [v., pf.].

    6763   Davidson, Malcolm. L: Curwen, pre-1940. Song: solo
            v., pf. Also avail. for solo v., stgs.

    6764   Forsyth, Cecil. "June", NY: GS, pre-1940. Song: [v.,
            pf.?].

    6765   Hunt, Wynn. MS. Song: ms solo, pf.

    6766   Ireland, John. "Tryst", Two Songs, L: OUP, 1929.
            Song: [ms or bar] solo v., pf.

    6767   Lemont, Cedric. NY: GS, pre-1940. Song: [v., pf.?].

    6768   McIntyre, Paul. Three Poems of Arthur Symonds [sic],
            MS, avail. CMC. Song: [med.] solo v., pf.

    6769   Russell, Alexander. MS 1916, NY: HZ. Song: [v.,
            pf.?].

In Kensington Gardens   "Under the almond tree"   In
Silhouettes (1892)

    6770   Hill, Edward B. B: BMC, pre-1940. Song: [v., pf.?].

In the Vale of Llangollen   "In the fields and the lanes
again!"   In London Nights (1895) as one of "Intermezzo:
Pastoral"

    6771   Normand-Smith, Gertrude. "Pastoral in the Vale of
            Llangollen", NY: GS, pre-1940. Song: [v., pf.?].

In the Wood of Finvara   "I have grown tired of sorrow"   In
Images of Good and Evil (1899) as one of "In Ireland"

6772 Burleigh, Henry. NY: R, pre-1940. Song: [solo v., pf.?].

6773 Sang, Henry. MS ca. 1937, NY: GX. Song: [solo v., pf.?].

Javanese Dancers "Twitched strings, the clang of metal" In Silhouettes (1892)

6774* Martinů, Bohuslav. "Dancers from Java", MS 1913. "Lyrical melodrama": vla., hp., pf.

"Let mine eyes see thee" In Poems of Arthur Symons, Vol. I (1914) as one of "From Santa Teresa"

6775 Berkeley, Lennox. Four Poems of St. Teresa of Avila, L: JWC, 1949. Song: a solo, str. orch.

Love and Sleep "I have laid sorrow to sleep" In Amoris Victima (1897) as one of "Amoris Exsul"

6776 Hart, Fritz. Melbourne: Allan, 1923. Song: solo v., pf.

Love in Dreams "I lie on my pallet bed" In Silhouettes (1892)

6777 Ronald, Landon. Four Silhouettes, L: E, 1919. Song: high v., pf. Also avail. for med. v., pf. or low v., pf.

Love's Paradox "Once I smiled when I saw you" In London Nights (1895) as one of "Céleste"

6778 MacCunn, Andrew. "Once I Smiled", L: C, 1908. Song: [solo v., pf.].

Magnificat "Praise God, who wrought for you and me" In London Nights (1895)

6779 Clough-Leighter, Henry. "Love's Magnificat", B: BMC, pre-1940. Song: [solo v., pf.?].

ymons, Arthur continued

Mater Liliorum   "In the remembering hours of night"   In
Images_of_Good_and_Evil (1899) as one of "Souls in the
Balance"

6780 Forsyth, Cecil. NY: GS, pre-1940. Song: [v., pf.?].

Mélinite, La: Moulin-Rouge   "Olivier Metra's Waltz of Roses"
In London_Nights (1895) as one of "Décor de Théâtre"

6781 Duke, Vernon. "Moulin-Rouge", NY: CF, 1944. Song:
s solo, ssaattbb, pf.

Memory   "As a perfume doth remain"   In London_Nights (1895)
as one of "Bianca"

6782 Campbell-Tipton, Louis. MS 1907, NY: GS. Song: [v.,
pf.].

6783 Dello Joio, Norman. "All Things Leave Me", Six_Love
Songs, NY: CF, 1955. Song: med. v., pf.

6784 Densmore, John. B: OD, pre-1940. Song: [v., pf.?].

6785 Hickey, Vivian. L: A, pre-1940. Song: [v., pf.?].

6786 Lemont, Cedric. NY: GS, pre-1940. Song: [v., pf.?].

6787 Lewis, Samuel R. B: Birchard, pre-1940. Song: [v.,
pf.?].

6788 Wald, Max. "As a Perfume", L: A, pre-1940. Song:
[v., pf.?].

Montserrat   "Peace waits among the hills"   In Images_of
Good_and_Evil (1899)

6789 Davies, H. Walford. "Peace...", Twenty-One_Songs, L:
N, 1931. Song: high v., pf.

6790 Treharne, Bryceson. NY: GS, pre-1940. Song: [v.,
pf.?].

On Craig Ddu   "Sky through the leaves of the bracken, The"
In London_Nights (1895) as one of "Intermezzo: Pastoral"

6791   Delius, Frederick. Berlin: Harmonie, 1910. Setting
       for sattbb, a cap.

On Judges' Walk   "That night on Judges' Walk"   In Silhouettes (1892)

6792   Ives, Charles. "Judges' Walk", MS 1893-1898. Song:
       v., pf.

Opium-Smoker, The   "I am engulfed, and drown deliciously"
In Days and Nights (1889)

6793   Campbell-Tipton, Louis. MS 1907, NY: GS. Song: [solo
       v., pf.].

Palm Sunday   "Because it is the day of Palms"   In Images of
Good and Evil (1899)

6794   Ireland, John. "Santa Chiara", L: A, 1925. Song:
       solo v., pf.

6795   Moeran, E.J. "The Day of Palms", L: CR, 1932. Song:
       med. v., pf.

6796   Noble, Harold. "Naples Bay", S. Croy.: L, 1956.
       Song: med. v., pf.

6797   Sheldon, Mary. L: Swan, pre-1940. Song: [v., pf.?].

Peace at Noon   "Here there is peace, cool peace"   In
Silhouettes (1892)

6798   Hill, Edward B. B: BMC, pre-1940. Song: [v., pf.?].

Prayer to Saint Anthony of Padua, A   "Saint Anthony of
Padua, whom I bear"   In London Nights (1895) as one of
"Céleste"

6799   Neuer, Berthold. NY: GS, pre-1940. Song: [solo v.,
       pf.?].

6800 Warlock, Peter. Two Songs, L: OUP, 1928. Song: bar
      solo, pf. Also suitable for t (or s) or high bar
      solo.

Rain on the Down   "Night, and the down on the sea"   In
Silhouettes (1892) as one of "At Dieppe"

6801 Normand-Smith, Gertrude. NY: GS, pre-1940. Song:
      [v., pf.?].

Rat, The   "Pain gnaws at my heart"   In Amoris Victima
(1897) as one of "Amoris Exsul"

6802 Ireland, John. Songs for a Medium Voice, L: JWC,
      1919. Song: med. v. (best suited for a solo), pf.
      Also publ. sep.

Requies   "O is it death or life"   In Silhouettes (1892) as
one of "At Dieppe"

6803 Campbell-Tipton, Louis. Four Sea Lyrics, MS 1907,
      NY: GS. Song: [v., pf.].

6804 Smyth, Ethel. Three Moods of the Sea, Wien: UE,
      1913. Song: ms, bar soli, orch.

Rest   "Peace of a wandering sky, The"   Poems of Arthur
Symons, Vol. II (1914) as one of "The Loom of Dreams"

6805 Howells, Herbert. "A Rondel of Rest", Three
      Rondeaux, MS (Opus 11), L: S&B. Song: [v., pf.].

6806 Ireland, John. Songs for a Medium Voice, L: JWC,
      1919. Song: med. v. (best suited for a solo),
      pf. Also publ. sep. Score contains Fr. transl.
      (under the title "Repos") by G. Jean-Aubrey.

6807* O'Neill, Norman. "A Rondel of Rest", Five Rondels,
      MS 1907, L: Avison. Song: med. v., pf.

6808 Scott, Cyril. "A Roundel of Rest", L: Elkin, 1906.
      Song: high v., pf. Also avail. for low v., pf.

Symons, Arthur continued

Return, The   "Little hand is knocking at my heart, A"   In
Amoris Victima (1897) as one of "Amor Triumphans"

    6809 Forsyth, Cecil. NY: GS, 1916. Song: solo v., pf.

Second Thoughts   "When you were here, ah foolish then!"   In
Silhouettes (1892)

    6810 Ronald, Landon. Four Silhouettes, L: E, 1919. Song:
          high v., pf. Also avail. for med. v., pf. or low
          v., pf.

"Shepherd, shepherd, hark that calling!"   In Poems of Arthur
Symons, Vol. I (1914) as one of "From Santa Teresa"

    6811 Berkeley, Lennox. Four Poems of St. Teresa of Avila,
          L: JWC, 1949. Song: a solo, str. orch.

Sick Heart, The   "O sick heart, be at rest!"   Poems of
Arthur Symons, Vol. II (1914) as one of "The Loom of
Dreams"

    6812* Warlock, Peter. Two Songs, L: OUP, 1928. Song: bar
          solo, pf. Also suitable for t (or s) or high bar
          solo.

Silence, The   "O voices of Love's silences"   In Amoris
Victima (1897) as one of "Amor Triumphans"

    6813 Hart, Fritz. MS 1909, avail. State Library of Vic-
          toria, Melbourne. Song: [med.] solo v., pf.

Spring Twilight   "Twilight droops across the day, The"   In
Silhouettes (1892)

    6814 Hill, Edward B. B: BMC, pre-1940. Song: [v., pf.?].

Tears   "O hands that I have held in mine"   In Silhouettes
(1892)

    6815 Kramer, A. Walter. MS 1917, B: OD. Song: [solo v.,
          pf.?].

Symons, Arthur continued

"To-day a shepherd and our kin"   In Poems_of_Arthur_Symons,
Vol. I (1914) as one of "From Santa Teresa"

  6816 Berkeley, Lennox. Four_Poems_of_St._Teresa_of_Avila,
        L: JWC, 1949. Song: a solo, str. orch.

Tune, A   "Foolish rhythm turns in my idle head, A"   In
Images_of_Good_and_Evil (1899)

  6817 Hold, Trevor. In_Praise_of_Music, MS 1971. Song: bar
        solo, cl., vln., vcl.

Wanderers, The   "Wandering, ever wandering"   In Amoris
Victima (1897) as one of "Amoris Exsul"

  6818 Hart, Fritz. MS 1907, avail. State Library of Vic-
        toria, Melbourne. Song: bar solo, pf. Originally
        composed for bar solo, orch. Orch. score no long-
        er extant.

Wanderer's Song   "I have had enough of women"   In Images_of
Good_and_Evil (1899)

  6819 Delius, Frederick. Berlin: Harmonie, 1910. Song:
        ttbb, a cap.

  6820 Farrar, Ernest. Vagabond_Songs, MS (Opus 10), L:
        S&B. Song: v., pf.

  6821 MacCunn, Andrew. L: C, 1908. Song: [solo v., pf.].

Miscellanea

  6822 Becker, John. "At Dieppe", MS, avail. ACA. Song:
        high v., pf.

  6823 Campbell-Tipton, Louis. "Darkness", Four_Sea_Lyrics,
        MS 1907, NY: GS. Song: [v., pf.].

  6824 Grinnell, Edward. "Through the Mist", NY: CF, pre-
        1940. Song: [v., pf.?].

765

Symons, Arthur continued

6825 Hart, Fritz. "New Year's Eve", MS 1924. Rhapsody: a
solo, chorus of female v., ch. orch. "Text by
Arthur Symonds" [sic?].

6826 McIntyre, Paul. "Amors Triumphans", MS 1958. Song:
v., pf.

6827 Watts, Wintter. "Dreams", Two Poems by Arthur
Symons, MS (Opus 4), NY: GS, pre-1929. Song: high
v., pf. Also avail. for low v., pf.

6828 Zandonai, Riccardo. "Francesca da Rimini", NY: R,
1914. Opera: 3 s, 2 ms, a, 4 t, 2 bar, 2 b soli,
satb, orch. (or pf.). Libr. by Tito Ricordi,
after Symons' transl.

SYNGE, John Millington   1871-1909

Beg-Innish   "Bring Kateen-beug and Maurya Jude"   Poems by
J.M. Synge (1909)

6829 Bax, Arnold. Five Irish Songs, L: MM, 1922, copyright assigned L: C, 1943. Song: solo v., pf.

Beside a Chapel   See: Dread

Danny   "One night a score of Erris men"   The Works of John
M. Synge, Vol. 2 (1910)

6830 Gardner, John L. Cambridge: CUP, 1966. Song: chorus
of equal v., a cap.

Deidre of the Sorrows   (DR)   (1910)

6831 Becker, John. "Deidre", MS 1945, avail. NYPL. Opera.
Libr. (completed ca. 1948) by the composer.

6832* Brian, Havergal. "Symphony No. 6: 'Sinfonia Tragica'", Chelmsford: MV, 1971. Symph.: orch. only.

6833 Hart, Fritz. MS 1915. Opera: voices, pf. Arr. 1916 for voices, orch.

6834 Orr, Robin. MS 1951. Incidental music: orch.

6835 Rankl, Karl. MS ca. 1950. Opera.

Dread "Beside a chapel I'd a room looked down" The Works of John M. Synge, Vol. 2 (1910)

6836 Dobson, Tom. Three Songs, NY: GS, 1916. Song: high or med. v., pf.

6837 Sirulnikoff, Jack. Three Songs, MS 1959, avail. CMC. Song: high or med. v., pf.

In Desolate Humour   See: Dread

In the Shadow of the Glen (DR) Samhain: An Occasional Review (Dec. 1904), publ. sep. same year, rev. 1905

6838 Anon. "The Shadow of the Glen", MS, perf. Swiss Opera, ca. 1933. German title: "Die Totenwache".

6839 Pedrollo, Arrigo. "The Shadow of the Glen", MS ca. 1919. Opera. Ital. title: "La veglia", adapt. from the play by Carlo Linati.

On an Island "You've plucked a curlew, drawn a hen" Poems by J.M. Synge (1909)

6840 Sirulnikoff, Jack. Three Songs, MS 1959, avail. CMC. Song: high or med. v., pf.

Playboy of the Western World, The (DR) (1907)

6841* Klebe, Giselher. "The True Hero", MS. Opera: Libr. by Heinrich Böll. German title: "Der Wahre Held".

6842　O'Farrell Sisters. "The Heart's a Wonder", MS ca.
　　　1957. Musical, based on Synge's play.

6843　Polovinkin, Leonid. "The Irish Hero", MS pre-1949.
　　　Opera.

Prelude　"Still south I went and west and south again"
Poems by J.M. Synge (1909)

6844　Sirulnikoff, Jack. Three Songs, MS 1959, avail. CMC.
　　　Song: high or med. v., pf.

6845　Brown, James. MS. Song: ms or bar solo, pf. Also
　　　arr. for s or t solo, pf.

6846　Roberts, Mervyn. MS. Song: v., pf.

Riders to the Sea　(DR)　Samhain: An Occasional Review
(Sept. 1903), rev. 1905, publ. sep. 1911

6847　Betts, Lorne. MS 1955, avail. CMC. Opera: s, ms, a
　　　soli, 3 male sp., sa, orch.

6848　Brecher, G. MS ca. 1927. Opera. Composition en-
　　　titled: "L'Appel de la Mer".

6849* Gilbert, Henry F. MS ca. 1904, rev. ca. 1914. Symph.
　　　prelude: orch. only. Music adapt. from trad.
　　　Irish melody.

6850　Hart, Fritz. MS 1915. Opera: voices, orch. Arr.
　　　same year for voices, 3 pf.

6851　Kosteck, George. "Maurya", MS, perf. East Carolina
　　　University, Apr. 1968. Opera. Libr. by the
　　　composer.

6852　Rabaud, Henri. P: Eschig, 1923. Opera. Fr. title:
　　　"L' Appel de la Mer". Libr. by the composer.

6853　Vaughan Williams, Ralph. L: OUP, 1936. Opera: 2 s,
　　　ms, a, bar soli, ssa, orch.

Shadow of the Glen, The　See: In the Shadow of the Glen

Synge, J.M. continued

Tinker's Wedding, The   (DR)   (1907)

6854   Brian, Havergal. "The Tinker's Wedding: Comedy
       Overture", Chelmsford: MV, 1971. Overture: orch.
       only.

6855   Smith, Robert. MS. Opera: s, a, t, b soli, satb,
       orch.

To the Oaks of Glencree   "My arms are round you, and I
lean"   Poems by J.M. Synge (1909)

6856   Burrows, Benjamin. L: A, pre-1940. Song: [v., pf.?].

Miscellanea

6857   Bécaud, Gilbert. "The Opera of Aran", MS, perf.
       Paris 1962. Opera.

6858   Whittaker, George. Seven Songs, MS pre-1939. The
       Oct. 1939 issue of Monthly Musical Record com-
       ments that "...the words..., ranging from John
       Lydgate to the Japanese, via Dowson, Housman,
       Synge..., reveal wide literary interests".

THOMAS, Dylan Marlais   1914-1953

After the funeral   See: In Memory of Ann Jones

Altarwise by owl-light   See: "Altarwise by owl-light in the
half-way house"

"Altarwise by owl-light in the half-way house"   Life and
Letters Today (Dec. 1935) as one of "Poems for a Poem",
rev. 1936, rev. 1952

6859   ApIvor, Denis. Cantata (Opus 32), MS 1960. Cta.:
       s, a, t, b soli, sp., satb, orch.

Thomas, Dylan continued

Among those Killed in the Dawn Raid was a Man Aged a Hundred
"When the morning was waking" Life and Letters Today
(Aug. 1941), rev. 1946

    6860 Short, Michael. Deaths and Music, MS. Cyc.: s, a
           soli, fl., ob., vla., vcl.

"And death shall have no dominion" See: "Death shall have
no dominion"

Birthday Poem "Twenty-four years remind the tears of my
eyes" Life and Letters Today (Dec. 1938), rev. 1939

    6861 Layton, Billy Jim. "Twenty-four years", Three Dylan
           Thomas Poems, NY: GS, 1964. Song: satb, 2 tpt.,
           2 hn., 2 trbn.

    6862 Roderick-Jones, Richard. "Twenty-four years...",
           Should Lanterns Shine, MS 1966. Cta.: ms solo,
           satb, fl., ob., bsn., vln., vla., vcl., db.

Ceremony After a Fire Raid "Myselves/The Grievers" Our
Time (May 1944), rev. 1945

    6863 Peterson, Wayne. MS. Song: s or t solo, pf.

    6864 Short, Michael. Deaths and Music, MS. Cyc.: s, a
           soli, fl., ob., vla., vcl.

    6865 Simons, Netty. "Trialogue No. 2: Myselves Grieve",
           MS, avail. ACA. Song: a, bar soli, vla.

"Death shall have no dominion" New English Weekly (May
1933), rev. 1936

    6866 Bliss, Arthur. "And death...", The Beatitudes, L:
           N, 1962. Cta.: s, t soli, chorus, orch., org.
           Text arr. by composer and Christopher Hassall.

    6867 Farquhar, David. "And death...", In Despite of
           Death, MS 1958, avail. New Zealand Broadcasting
           Corporation. Cyc.: bar solo, pf.

Thomas, Dylan continued

6868 Hearne, John. "And death...", Symphonic Cantata 3,
      MS 1959. Cta.: s, bar soli, satb, orch.

6869 Kasemets, Udo. "And death...", Two Symphonic Songs,
      MS 1956, avail. CMC. Song: a or bar solo, pf.

6870 Roberts, Trevor. "And death...", Three Songs for
      Baritone and Orchestra, MS. Song: bar solo, orch.

6871 Roderick-Jones, Richard. "And death...", Should
      Lanterns Shine, MS 1966. Cta.: ms solo, satb,
      fl., ob., bsn., vln., vla., vcl., db.

6872 Stein, Leon. "String Quartet No. 5", Five String
      Quartets, NY: CFE, 1967. Setting for s solo,
      str. qrt.

6873 Williams, Meirion. "And death...", MS. Song: bar
      solo, pf.

Deaths and Entrances   "On almost the incendiary eve"
Horizon (Jan. 1941), rev. 1946

    6874 Persichetti, Vincent. "The Incendiary Eve of Deaths
          and Entrances", Night Dances, Ph.: EV, 1972.
          Orch. only.

"Do not go gentle into that good night"   Botteghe Oscure
(Nov. 1951), rev. 1952

    6875 Hearne, John. Symphonic Cantata 3, MS 1959. Cta.:
          s, bar soli, satb, orch.

    6876* Lutyens, Elisabeth. Three Songs, L: OP, 1953. Song:
          ms solo, fl., vla. Complete work also requires
          pf. or acc.

    6877 McCabe, John. Five Elegies, L: OUP, 1963. Cyc.: s
          solo, ch. orch.

    6878 Orton, Richard. MS 1965. Song: s solo, 4 v. (t, bar,
          bar, b) wordless chorus, a cap.

    6879 Persichetti, Vincent. MS (Opus 132), Ph.: EV, in
          prep. for publ. Org. solo (pedals only).

771

6880 Reisberg, Horace. MS. Song: s, t soli (within chorus), satb, hn., vcl., pf.

6881 Riegger, Wallingford. "The Dying of the Light", NY: AMP, 1956. Song: high or med. v., pf. Also arr. for high or med. v., orch.

6882 Stravinsky, Igor. In Memoriam Dylan Thomas, L: BH, 1954. Dirge canons and song: t solo, str. qrt. Canons require str. qrt., 4 trbn. Also avail. for t solo, pf.

6883 Whettam, Graham. L: LD, 1968. Song: 5 v. (2 s, a, t, b), unacc. or ssatb, a cap.

Fern Hill   "Now as I was young and easy"   Horizon (Oct. 1945), rev. 1946

6884 ApIvor, Denis. MS 1973. Ch. cta.: t solo, ch. orch. (6 ww., pf., str. qrt.).

6885 Corigliano, John. NY: GS, 1963. Cta.: ms solo, satb, orch.

6886 Hanson, Raymond. MS 1969. Song: s solo, orch.

6887 Huse, Peter. MS 1960, avail. CMC. Madrigal: satb, a cap. Sets last three lines of the poem.

6888 Langley, Bernard P. MS 1968-69. Song: t solo, orch.

6889 McDermott, Vincent. "Time let me play and be golden in the mercy of his means", MS 1973. Sonata: gtr., hpd.

"Force that through the green fuse drives the flower, The"
See: Poem "Force..."

Foster the light   See: Poem "Foster the light..."

"Foster the light, nor veiled the manshaped moon"   See:
Poem "Foster the light..."

Thomas, Dylan continued

From love's first fever to her plague   See: Poem "From
love's first fever..."

I dreamed my genesis   See: "I dreamed my genesis in sweat
of sleep, breaking"

"I dreamed my genesis in sweat of sleep, breaking"   18 Poems
(1934), rev. 1952

    6890 Brindle, Reginald S. "Genesis Dream", L: P, 1961.
          Song: med. or low female v., fl. (doubl. pic.),
          cl., b. cl., tpt., 3 perc., pf.

"I have longed to move away"   New Verse (Dec. 1935) as one
of "Three Poems", rev. 1936

    6891 Diamond, David. NY: SMP, 1968. Song: solo v., pf.

In Memory of Ann Jones   "After the funeral, mule praises,
brays"   Life and Letters Today (Summer 1938), rev. 1939,
rev. 1952

    6892 Gerber, Edward. "After the Funeral", MS copyright
          by composer 1972, avail. ACA. Song: bar solo,
          vln., vla., vcl.

"In my craft or sullen art"   Life and Letters Today (Oct.
1945)

    6893 Dickinson, Peter. A Dylan Thomas Song Cycle, MS
          1959. Cyc.: bar solo, pf.

    6894 Hearne, John. Symphonic Cantata 3, MS 1959. Cta.: s,
          bar soli, satb, orch.

    6895 Layton, Billy Jim. Three Dylan Thomas Poems, NY:
          GS, 1964. Song: satb, 2 tpt., 2 hn., 2 trbn.

    6896 Lombardo, Robert M. Davis: CPE, 1967, avail. com-
          poser. Setting for narr., band.

773

Thomas, Dylan continued

6897* Lutyens, Elisabeth. Three Songs, L: OP, 1953. Song: ms solo, fl., vla. Complete work also requires pf. or acc.

In the beginning   See: "In the beginning was the three-pointed star"

"In the beginning was the three-pointed star"   18 Poems (1934), rev. 1952

6898 Kasemets, Udo. "In the Beginning", Two Symphonic Songs, MS 1956, avail. CMC. Song: a or bar solo, pf.

6899 Orrego-Salas, Juan. "In the Beginning", The Days of God, NY: P-S, 1974 (hire). Oratorio: s, t soli, satb, orch. Sets lines beginning: "In the beginning was the mounting fire".

6900 Raffman, Relly. "In the Beginning", NY: M, 1960. Song: solo v., satb, pf.

In the Direction of the Beginning   (PR)   New Directions in Prose and Poetry (1938)

6901 Lutyens, Elisabeth. L: OP, 1970. Song: b solo, pf.

Lie Still, Sleep Becalmed   "Lie still, sleep becalmed, sufferer with the wound"   Life and Letters Today (June 1945)

6902 Short, Michael. Deaths and Music, MS. Cyc.: s, a soli, fl., ob., vla., vcl.

Light   "Light breaks where no sun shines"   Listener (Mar. 1934), rev. same year, rev. 1952

6903 Chapple, Brian. "Light breaks...", MS, avail. L: JWC. Song: s solo, pf.

6904 Gilbert, Steven E. "Light breaks...", MS 1963. Song: satb, fl., cl., tpt., trbn., pf., vla., vcl.

6905 Roderick-Jones, Richard. "Light breaks...", Should Lanterns Shine, MS 1966. Cta.: ms solo, satb, fl., ob., bsn., vln., vcl., db.

6906 Stein, Leon. "String Quartet No. 4", Five String Quartets, NY: CFE, 1967. Str. qrt. only. Score bears the following motto: "Where no sea runs, the waters of the heart/Push in their tides".

"Light breaks where no sun shines"   See: Light

Me and My Bike*   (SP)   Esquire (Dec. 1964), publ. sep. 1965

6907 Roderick-Jones, Richard. MS 1974. Opera: 8 soli (ea. with a number of roles), fl., ob., tpt., hn., pf., perc., vla., vcl. Libr. by Michael Davies.

Now   See: "Now/Say nay"

"Now/Say nay"   Twenty-Five Poems (1936), rev. 1952

6908 Simons, Netty. "Trialogue III: Now, Say Nay", MS, avail. ACA. Song: ms, bar soli, vla.

O make me a mask   See: "O make me a mask and a wall to shut from your spies"

"O make me a mask and a wall to shut from your spies" Poetry, Chicago (Aug. 1938) as one of "Four Poems", rev. 1952

6909 Layton, Billy Jim. Three Dylan Thomas Poems, NY: GS, 1964. Song: satb, 2 tpt., 2 hn., 2 trbn.

On a Wedding Anniversary*   "Sky is torn across, The" Poetry, London (Jan. 1941), rev. 1946

6910 Dickinson, Peter. "The sky...", A Dylan Thomas Song Cycle, MS 1959. Cyc.: bar solo, pf.

Thomas, Dylan continued

6911 Short, Michael. Deaths and Music, MS. Cyc.: s, a
soli, fl., ob., vla., vcl.

On no work of words   See: Poem "On no work..."

"Once it was the colour of saying"   See: Poem "Once it
was..."

Our eunuch dreams   See: "Our eunuch dreams, all seedless
in the light"

"Our eunuch dreams, all seedless in the light"   New Verse
(Apr. 1934), rev. same year, rev. 1952

6912 Stein, Leon. "String Quartet No. 3", Five String
Quartets, NY: CFE, 1967. Str. qrt. only. Score
bears the following motto: "...show of
shadows...".

Paper and Sticks   "Paper and sticks and shovel and match"
Seven (Autumn 1939) as one of "Three Poems", rev. 1946

6913* Lutyens, Elisabeth. Three Songs, L: OP, 1953. Song:
ms solo, pf. or ms solo, acc. Complete work also
requires fl., vla.

Poem   "Force that through the green fuse drives the flower,
The"   Sunday Referee (Oct. 1933), rev. 1934

6914 Borden, David R. "The Force", MS 1962, NY: CMP,
copyright 1968 by composer. Song: s solo, ch.
orch.

6915 Brindle, Reginald S. "The force...", MS. Song:
satb, a cap.

6916 Farquhar, David. "The force...", In Despite of
Death, MS 1958, avail. New Zealand Broadcasting
Corporation. Cyc.: bar solo, pf.

776

Thomas, Dylan continued

Poem "Foster the light, nor veiled the manshaped moon"*
Sunday Referee (Oct. 1934), rev. 1936, rev. 1952

   6917 Stein, Leon. "String Quartet No. 1", Five String
        Quartets, NY: CFE, 1967. Str. qrt. only. Score
        bears the following motto: "And pluck a mandrake
        music from the marrowroot".

Poem "From love's first fever to her plague, from the soft
second" Criterion (Oct. 1934), rev. same year, rev. 1952

   6918 Stein, Leon. "String Quartet No. 3", Five String
        Quartets, NY: CFE, 1967. Str. qrt. only. Score
        bears the following motto: "...in my ears the
        light of sound,...in my eyes the sound of
        light".

Poem "On no work of words now for three lean months in the
bloody" Wales (Mar. 1939), rev. same year

   6919 Dickinson, Peter. "On no work...", A Dylan Thomas
        Song Cycle, MS 1959. Cyc.: bar solo, pf.

Poem "Once it was the colour of saying" Wales (Mar.
1939), rev. same year

   6920 Gilbert, Steven E. "Once it was...", Two Poems of
        Dylan Thomas, MS 1965. Song: s solo, cl., pf.

Poem "There was a saviour" Horizon (May 1940), rev. 1946

   6921 Douglas, James. "There was...", Light Shining Out
        of Darkness, MS 1966, avail. SMA. Song: med. v.,
        vcl.

   6922 Peterson, Wayne. "There was a Saviour", MS. Song:
        s (or high bar), t soli, org.

Poem "Tombstone told when she died, The" Seven (Winter
1938), rev. 1939

   6923 Simons, Netty. "Trialogue No. 1", MS 1964, avail.
        ACA. Song: a, bar soli, vla.

Thomas, Dylan continued

Poem   "Was there a time when dancers with their fiddles"
New English Weekly (Sept. 1936), rev. same year

    6924   Dickinson, Peter. "Was there...", A Dylan Thomas
        Song Cycle, MS 1959. Cyc.: bar solo, pf.

Poem in October   "It was my thirtieth year"   Horizon (Feb.
1945), rev. 1946

    6925   Corigliano, John. NY: GS, 1973 (copyright 1970).
        Cta.: t solo, fl., cl., ob., str. qrt., npd.
        Also avail. for t solo, pf.

    6926   Stein, Leon. "String Quartet No. 2", Five String
        Quartets, NY: CFE, 1967. Str. qrt. only. Score
        bears the following motto: "And I saw in the
        turning...his heart moved in mine".

Refusal to Mourn the Death, by Fire, of a Child in London, A
"Never until the mankind making"   New Republic (May 1945)

    6927   Mathias, William. L: N, 1969. Song: satb, a cap.

    6928   Short, Michael. Deaths and Music, MS. Cyc.: s, a
        soli, fl., ob., vla., vcl.

    6929   Westergaard, Peter. "Cantata II", MS 1958, Mz.: S
        (AVV), n.d. Cta.: b solo, pic., a fl., gl.,
        vibra., 2 tpt., 2 trbn., hp., pf.

Should lanterns shine   See: "Should lanterns shine, the
holy face"

"Should lanterns shine, the holy face"   New Verse (Dec.
1935) as one of "Three Poems", rev. 1936, rev. 1952

    6930   Roderick-Jones, Richard. Should Lanterns Shine, MS
        1966. Cta.: ms solo, satb, fl., ob., bsn., vln.,
        vla., vcl., db.

There was a saviour   See: Poem "There was..."

Thomas, Dylan continued

"Tombstone told when she died, The"   See: Poem "Tombstone
    told..."

"Twenty-four years mind the tears of my eyes"   See: Birthday
    Poem

"Was there a time when dancers with their fiddles"   See:
    Poem "Was there a time..."

Under Milk Wood   (DR)   (1954) Portions 1st publ. as
    "Llareggub (A Piece for Radio Perhaps)" in Bottegne
    Oscure (Apr. 1952)

    6931   Ellis, Osian. "A Sunset Poem", L: Mills, 1957.
            Song: solo v., pf. or solo v., hp. Sets lines
            beginning: "Every morning when I wake".

    6932   Jones, Daniel J. L: Dent, 1954. Songs: a, b soli,
            children's v., a cap. Settings accompanied 1st
            edn. of the play. Publ. sep. L: KP, 1957 for a,
            b soli, children's v., pf.

    6933   Křivinka, Gustav. MS 1964, avail. SČSKU. Incidental
            music for radio. Czech. title: "Pod Mléčným
            lesem", transl. by Eva Bromová and Antonín
            Přidal.

    6934   Nečas, Jaromír. MS 1964, avail. SČSKU. Incidental
            music for radio. Czech. title: "Pod Mléčným
            lesem", transl. by Eva Bromová and Antonín
            Přidal.

    6935   Steffens, Walter. Berlin: B&B, 1972. Opera: 6 s, a,
            5 t, 4 bar, 4 b soli, 7 actors, orch. German
            title: "Unter dem Milchwald". Libr. by composer,
            after transl. by Erich Fried.

Vision and Prayer   "Who/Are you/Who is born"   Horizon
    (Jan. 1945), rev. 1946

    6936   Babbitt, Milton. NY: AMP, 1961. Song: s solo, elec.
            synth. 4-track tape.

779

Thomas, Dylan continued

> 6937   Lutyens, Elisabeth. "Coda", _The Tears of Night_, L:
> OP, 1971. Setting for 6 s, c-t soli, fl., cl.,
> hn., vln., vcl. Sets lines beginning: "Under the
> night forever falling". Complete work requires
> various instr. ensembles.
>
> 6938   Malipiero, Riccardo. _Sei Posie di Dylan Thomas_, Mi.:
> SZ, 1959. Cyc.: s solo, 10 instr. All settings
> from "Vision and Prayer". Engl. text.
>
> 6939   Rainier, Priaulx. L: S, 1973. Song: t solo, pf.

We Lying By Seasand   "We lying by seasand, watching yellow"
Poetry, Chicago (Jan. 1937), rev. same year, rev. 1939

> 6940   Gilbert, Steven E. _Two Poems of Dylan Thomas_, MS
> 1965. Song: s solo, cl., pf.

"We lying by seasand, watching yellow"   See: We Lying By
Seasand

Miscellanea

> 6941   Jones, Daniel J. The MSS 1931-34 cited in _Grove's_
> have been withdrawn by the composer.
>
> 6942   Lutyens, Elisabeth. Incidental music for the Group
> Theatre's 'Homage to Dylan Thomas' perf. Globe
> Theatre, Jan. 1954.
>
> 6943   Lutyens, Elisabeth. "'Valediction' (Dylan Thomas
> 1953)", MS (Opus 28), Croy.: B-M. Composition for
> cl., pf.

Thomas, Edward

THOMAS, (Philip) Edward   1878-1917

Adlestrop   "Yes. I remember Adlestrop"   Poems (1917)

   6944 Gurney, Ivor. MS 1920. Song: [solo v., pf.].

And you, Helen   "And you, Helen, what should I give you?"
Poems (1917)

   6945 Lydiate, Frederick. An Edward Thomas Song Cycle, MS.
          Cyc.: t solo, pf.

As the clouds that are so light   "As the clouds that are so
light"   Poems (1917)

   6946 Harrison, Pamela. "The Clouds that are so light",
          The Dark Forest, MS. Cyc.: t solo, str. orch.

Bridge, The   "I have come a long way to-day"   Poems (1917)

   6947 Gurney, Ivor. MS 1920. Song: [solo v., pf.].

   6948 Rettich, Wilhelm. Eleven Songs for Voice and Piano,
          Berlin: Astoria, 1973. Song: t or bar solo, pf.

Bright clouds   "Bright clouds of may"   Poems (1917)

   6949 Garlick, Antony. Twelve Madrigals, Cin.: WLP, 1967.
          Madrigal: ssa, a cap.

   6950 Gurney, Ivor. Lights Out, L: S&B, 1926. Song: solo
          v., pf.

Cock-Crow, The   "Out of the wood of thoughts"   Six Poems
(1916) Publ. under the pseud. "Edward Eastaway"

   6951 Gurney, Ivor. "Cock-Crow", MS n.d. Song: [solo v.,
          pf.].

Thomas, Edward continued

Dark Forest, The   "Dark is this forest and deep"   Last
Poems (1918) & Twelve Poets: A Miscellany of New Verse
(1918)

   6952 Harrison, Pamela. The Dark Forest, MS. Cyc.: t solo,
     str. orch.

Digging   "Today I think"   Last Poems (1918)

   6953 Gurney, Ivor. "Scents", Lights Out, L: S&B, 1926.
     Song: solo v., pf.

Early One Morning   "Early one morning in May I set out"
Poems (1917)

   6954 Harrison, Pamela. The Dark Forest, MS. Cyc.: t solo,
     str. orch.

   6955 Hold, Trevor. Five Poems of Edward Thomas, MS 1966-
     73. Cyc.: t solo, gtr.

Gallows, The   "There was a weasel lived in the sun"   Poems
(1917)

   6956 Gurney, Ivor. MS 1920. Song: [solo v., pf.].

   6957 Hold, Trevor. Five Poems of Edward Thomas, MS 1966-
     73. Cyc.: t solo, gtr.

Huxter, The   "He has a hump like an ape"   Poems (1917)

   6958 Hold, Trevor. Five Poems of Edward Thomas, MS 1966-
     73. Cyc.: t solo, gtr.

   6959 Rafter, Leonard. L: Curwen, 1950. Song: bar solo,
     pf.

If I should ever by chance   "If I should ever by chance grow
rich"   Poems (1917)

   6960 Lydiate, Frederick. "If ever by chance I should grow
     rich", An Edward Thomas Song Cycle, MS. Cyc.: t
     solo, pf.

Thomas, Edward continued

It I were to own   "If I were to own this countryside"
    Poems (1917)

    6961 Lydiate, Frederick. An Edward Thomas Song Cycle, MS.
          Cyc.: t solo, pf.

In Memoriam (Easter 1915)   "Flowers left thick at nightfall,
    The"   Poems (1917)

    6962 Gurney, Ivor. "In Memoriam", MS n.d. Song: [solo
          v., pf.].

It Rains   "It rains, and nothing stirs within the fence"
    Poems (1917)

    6963 Gurney, Ivor. MS n.d. Song: [solo v., pf.].

Lights Out   "I have come to the borders of sleep"   Poems
    (1917)

    6964 Gurney, Ivor. Lights Out, L: S&B, 1926. Song: solo
          v., pf.

    6965 Harrison, Pamela. The Dark Forest, MS. Cyc.: t solo,
          str. orch.

    6966 Williams, Grace. MS 1965. Song: t solo, pf.

Mill-Pond, The   "Sun blazed while the thunder yet"   Poems
    (1917)

    6967 Gurney, Ivor. MS 1920. Song: [solo v., pf.].

Out in the dark   "Out in the dark over the snow"   Twelve
    Poets: A Miscellany of New Verse (1918)

    6968 Gurney, Ivor. MS 1925. Song: [solo v., pf.].

    6969 Rubbra, Edmund. Three Songs, L: OUP, 1925. Song:
          solo v., pf.

    6970 Wilson, Thomas. Night Songs, L: AH&C (copyright
          Glasgow: B&F, 1968). Song: satb, a cap.

Thomas, Edward continued

Owl, The   "Downhill I came, hungry"   Poems (1917)

    6971 Gurney, Ivor. MS 1919. Song: [solo v., pf.].

Penny Whistle, The   "New moon hangs like an ivory bugle,
The"   Poems (1917)

    6972 Gurney, Ivor. Lights Out, L: S&B, 1926. Song: solo
        v., pf.

Snow   "In the gloom of whiteness"   An Annual of New Poetry
(1917)

    6973 Hold, Trevor. Five Poems of Edward Thomas, MS 1966-
        73. Cyc.: t solo, gtr.

Song   "At poet's tears"   An Annual of New Poetry (1917)

    6974 Hold, Trevor. "A Song", Five Poems of Edward Thomas,
        MS 1966-73. Cyc.: t solo, gtr.

Source, The   "All day the air triumphs"   Annual of New
Poetry (1917)

    6975 Tippett, Michael. L: S, 1943. Madrigal: satb, a cap.

Sowing   "It was a perfect day"   Poems (1917)

    6976 Garlick, Antony. "It was...", Eleven Canzonets,
        Cin.: Westwood, 1967. Canzonet: 2 pt. chorus of
        equal v., a cap.

    6977 Gurney, Ivor. L: S&B, 1925. Song: solo v., pf.

Tall Nettles   "Tall nettles cover up, as they have done"
Poems (1917)

    6978 Garlick, Antony. Twelve Madrigals, Cin.: WLP, 1967.
        Madrigal: ssa, a cap.

Trumpet, The   "Rise up, rise up"   Poems (1917)

Thomas, Edward continued

6979 Gurney, Ivor. Lights Out, L: S&B, 1926. Song: solo
v., pf.

6980 Harrison, Pamela. The Dark Forest, MS. Cyc.: t solo,
str. orch.

6981 Jones, Kenneth V. Four Songs for High Voice, Oboe
and Pianoforte, MS 1954. Song: high v., ob., pf.

6982 Mase, Owen. L: Curwen, 1926. Song: high v., 4 tpt.

What shall I give?   "What shall I give my daughter the
younger?"   Poems (1917)

6983 Lydiate, Frederick. An Edward Thomas Song Cycle, MS.
Cyc.: t solo, pf.

Will you come?   "Will you come?"   Poems (1917)

6984 Gurney, Ivor. Lights Out, L: S&B, 1926. Song: solo
v., pf.

6985 Harrison, Pamela. The Dark Forest, MS. Cyc.: t solo,
str. orch.

6986 Kunz, Alfred. Will You Come?, Waterloo: Waterloo,
1966. Song: satb, pf.

6987 Lydiate, Frederick. MS. Song: t solo, pf.

Words   "Out of us all"   Poems (1917)

6988 Gurney, Ivor. MS 1925. Song: [solo v., pf.].

Miscellanea

6989 Mellers, Wilfrid H. A setting cited in the May 1950
issue of Monthly Musical Record has been withdrawn by the composer.

785

Thompson, Francis

THOMPSON, Francis Joseph   1859-1907

Arab Love-Song   "Hunchèd camels of the night, The"   Dome
   (Jan. 1899)

   6990   Dunkley, Ferdinand. NY: GS, pre-1940. Song: [v.,
          pf.?].

   6991   Jervis-Read, Harold. L: WR, pre-1940. Song: [v.,
          pf.?].

   6992   Terry, Robert E.H. NY: R, pre-1940. Song: [v.,
          pf.?].

Dream-Tryst   "Breath of kissing night and day, The"   Merry
   England (May 1888)

   6993* Holst, Gustav. L: N, 1902. Song: satb, a cap.

   6994   Jervis-Read, Harold. L: ASH, 1913. Song: satb, orch.

Envoy   "Go, songs, for ended is our brief, sweet play"
   New Poems (1897)

   6995   Hindemith, Paul. Nine English Songs, NY: AMP, 1945.
          Song: solo v., pf.

   6996   Lekberg, Sven. Glen Rock: JF, pre-1969. Song: satb,
          a cap.

   6997   Raynor, John. "Go, songs", Eleven Songs, Grt. Y.:
          G, 1971. Song: solo v., [pf.].

From the Night of Forebeing   "Cast wide the folding doorways
   of the East"   New Poems (1897)

   6998   Milner, Anthony. "Cast...", L: UE, 1958. Song: satb,
          a cap.

Hound of Heaven, The   "I fled Him, down the nights and down
   the days"   Merry England (July 1890), publ. sep. 1908

6999 Douglas, Clive. MS 1933-38. Setting for bar solo, chorus, orch.

7000 Gideon, Miriam. NY: CUMP, 1975. Setting for med. v., ob., str. trio. Sets lines beginning: "Across the margent of the world I fled".

7001 Harris, William H. L: S&B, 1921. Setting for bar solo, satb, orch.

7002 Jacobson, Maurice. L: Curwen, 1954. Setting for t solo, satb, orch.

7003 Langley, Bernard P. MS 1965-67. Setting for t solo, satb, orch.

7004 Stewart, Humphrey J. MS, perf. NY, Apr. 1924. Music drama: soli, mixed chorus, orch.

7005 Valen, Fartein. MS ca. 1941. Pf. sonata.

In no strange Land   "O world invisible, we view thee" Athenaeum (Aug. 1908), rev. 1913

7006 Boughton, Rutland. "The Kingdom of Heaven", Six Spiritual Songs, L: Reeves, 1908. Song: solo v., pf.

7007 Darke, Harold. "The Kingdom of God", L: S&B, 1921. Song: s solo, satb, orch.

7008 Woollen, Russell. "The Kingdom of God", Three Sacred Choruses for Women's Voices and Orchestra, Lacrosse, Wisc.: Viterbo College, 1969. Setting for ssaa (with occasional use of sssaaa), orch. or ssaa (with occasional use of sssaaa), pf.

7009 Wordsworth, William. S. Croy.: L, 1951. Song: satb, stgs., pf.

Kingdom of God, The   See: In no strange Land

Lilium Regis   "O Lily of the King!"   Dublin Review (Jan. 1910) as one of "Ecclesiastical Ballads"

Thompson, Francis continued

7010 Creston, Paul. NY: R, 1959 (reassigned NY: B-M).
Setting for satb, pf.

Lines for a Drawing of Our Lady of the Night   "This, could
I paint my inward sight"   Ushaw Magazine (Mar. 1891)

7011 Redman, Reginald. "Our Lady of the Night", L: L,
1960. Song: ssa, pf.

Love in Dian's Lap   "O beloved, O ye Two"   Poems (1893)
Portions 1st publ. in Merry England (Aug. & Sept. 1893)
Lines from the "Proæmion" publ. under the title "To Two
Friends" in Athenaeum (Nov. 1910)

7012 Whear, Paul W. "Proemion", Cl.: LW (hire). Orch.
only.

Making of the Viola, The   "Spin, daughter Mary, spin"
Merry England (May 1892)

7013 Bainton, Edgar L. L: JW, pre-1959. Cta.: 2 pt.
chorus of female v., [a cap.?].

May Burden, A   "Through meadow-ways as I tread"   New Poems
(1897)

7014 Tunnard, Thomas. L: OUP, 1958. Song: satb, a cap.

Messages   "What shall I your true-love tell"   Athenaeum
(Mar. 1913)

7015 Bridge, Frank. "What shall I...", L: WR, 1919. Song:
solo v., pf.

Sister Songs   "Shrewd winds and shrill"   (1895)

7016* Holst, Gustav. "O Spring's Little Children", MS
1897. Song: sssa, a cap. Rev. (MS 1899) as a glee
for satb, a cap. Rev. vers. publ. L: N, 1899
under the title "To Sylvia".

Thompson, Francis continued

To a Snowflake   "What heart could have thought you?"   New
Poems (1897) 1st publ. as part of "A Hymn to Snow" in
Merry England (Feb. 1891)

    7017 Gurney, Ivor. MS 1920. Song: [solo v., pf.].

    7018 Oldroyd, George. L: Curwen, 1924. Song: solo v., pf.

Veteran of Heaven, The   "O captain of the wars"   Dublin
Review (Jan. 1910) as one of "Ecclesiastical Ballads"

    7019 Baldwin, Ralph L. NY: Witmark, 1935. Setting for
          bar solo, ttbb, 2 pf., org.

Miscellanea

    7020 Lockwood, Normand. "The Hound of Heaven", MS 1937.
          Choral composition. [Text by Thompson?]

    7021 Milhaud, Darius. Poèmes de Francis Thompson, MS ca.
          1919. Fr. transl. by Paul Claudel.

TOLKIEN, John Ronald Renel   1892-1973

Hobbit, The   (NV)   (1937)

    7022 Blyton, Carey. L: F, 1971. Overture: orch. only.

Lord of the Rings, The   (NV)   (1954-55)

    7023 Swann, Donald. "Bilbo's Last Song", MS 1974. Song:
          [v., pf.].

789

Tolkien, J.R.R. continued

7024   Swann, Donald. The Road Goes Ever On, L: A&U, 1967.
       Cyc.: ms and/or bar solo, pf. (or hp.). Portions
       of the cyc. provide a gtr. pt. Songs entitled:
       "The Road Goes Ever On", "Upon the Hearth the
       Fire is Red", "In the Willow-mead of Tasarinan",
       "In Western Lands", "Namárië", "I Sit beside the
       Fire", "Errantry".

TREECE, Henry   1912-1966

Christ Child   "Warm as a little mouse he lay"   In The Black
    Seasons (1945)

    7025   Harries, David. L: OUP, 1967. Carol: satb, [a cap.].

Three Pleas   "Stand by me, Death, lest these dark days"   In
    The Black Seasons (1945)

    7026   Hold, Trevor. Requiescat, MS 1970. Setting (in cta.)
           for atb, a cap. The complete cta. also requires
           sp., satb, br. sextet, org. ad lib.

TRENCH, (Frederic) Herbert   1865-1923

Almond, wild Almond   "Almond, wild Almond"   In New Poems
    (1907)

    7027   Bax, Arnold. "Wild Almond (Scherzo)", Three Songs,
           MS 1924. Song: v., pf. Arr. 1934 for v., orch.

Apollo and the Seaman   "Apollo through the woods came down"
    In New Poems (1907)

    7028   Holbrooke, Joseph. MS ca. 1908. Symph.: orch. only.

Trench, Herbert continued

I Heard a Soldier   "I heard a soldier sing some trifle"   In
New Poems (1907)

    7029 Bax, Arnold. L: MM, 1926, copyright assigned L: C,
        1943. Song: ms or bar solo, pf.

Jean Richepin's Song   "Poor lad once and a lad so trim, A"
In New Poems (1907)

    7030 Clarke, Robert C. "The Mother's Heart", L: C, 1925.
        Song: [solo v., pf.].

O Dreamy, Gloomy, Friendly Trees   "O dreamy, gloomy, friendly Trees"   In New Poems (1907)

    7031 Gurney, Ivor. MS n.d. Song: [solo v., pf.].

Requiem of Archangels for the World   "Hearts, beat no more!"
In Lyrics and Narrative Poems (1911)

    7032 Harrison, Julius. MS pre-1954. [Song: v., pf.?]

Requital, The   "'What shall I give you, woman dear?...'"
In New Poems (1907)

    7033 Holbrooke, Joseph. L: N, 1910. Song: t solo, pf.

She comes not when Noon is on the Roses   "She comes not when
Noon is on the roses"   In Deirdre Wed and Other Poems
(1901)

    7034 George, Graham. MS 1939. Song: unison v., pf.

    7035 Harrison, Julius. L: Curwen, 1920. Song: solo v.,
        pf.

Turner, W.J.R.

TURNER, Walter James Redfern   1889-1946

Hymn to Her Unknown   "In despair at not being able"   In
    Songs and Incantations (1936)

    7036 Harvey, Jonathan. Iam dulcis amica, MS 1967. Setting
        for 2 s, a, t, bar, b soli, unacc. or ssatbb, a
        cap.

Men Fade Like Rocks   "Rock-like the souls of men"   In In
    Time Like Glass (1921)

    7037 Turner, W.J.R. Dublin: Cuala, 1937 in Broadside, No.
        6. Song: v., unacc.

Night Landscape   "Owl, the badger and the jar, The"   In
    Fossils of a Future Time? (1946)

    7038 Fricker, Peter Racine. Night Landscape, MS 1947.
        Cyc.: s solo, str. trio.

Romance   "When I was but thirteen or so"   In The Hunter and
    Other Poems (1916)

    7039 Coulthard, Jean. MS 1970, avail. CMC. Song: boys'
        v., tb, pf.

    7040 Mortensen, Otto. Four Songs, Copenhagen: WH, 1945.
        Song: v., pf.

Song   "Gently, sorrowfully sang the maid"   In The Dark Fire
    (1918)

    7041 Turner, W.J.R. Dublin: Cuala, 1937 in Broadside, No.
        8. Song: v., unacc.

Miscellanea

    7042 Turner, W.J.R. "Lovely Hill-Torrents Are", Dublin:
        Cuala, 1937 in Broadside, No. 1. Song: v., unacc.
        [1st publ. of the poem?]

Tynan, Katharine

TYNAN, Katharine   1861-1931

Desire, The   "Give me no mansions ivory white"   In In-
nocencies: A Book of Verse (1905)

   7043 Lohr, Hermann. "Four Years Old", L: C, 1908. Song:
        [solo v., pf.].

New Old Song, A   "Spring comes slowly up this way, The"   In
Ballads and Lyrics (1891) Incl. under the title "A Song of
Spring" in Herb o' Grace (1918)

   7044 Rubbra, Edmund. "Slow Spring", Two Songs, MS 1925.
        Song: v., pf.

Pink Almond   "So delicate, so airy"   In Collected Poems
(1930)

   7045 Howells, Herbert. L: EA, 1958. Song: 2 pt. chorus,
        pf.

Sheep and Lambs   "All in the April evening"   In Ballads and
Lyrics (1891)

   7046 Campbell-Watson, Frank. "All in...", NY: Witmark,
        1954. Song: satb, a cap.

   7047 Diack, J. Michael. "All in...", NY: BH. Song: sa,
        pf. Arr. by Cain for satb, pf. Arr. by Howorth
        for ssa, pf.

   7048 Homer, Sidney. MS (Opus 31). Song: [v., pf.?].

   7049 James, Phyllis M. L: C, 1921. Song: [v., pf.].

   7050 Roberton, Hugh. "All in...", L: Curwen (RP), 1911.
        Setting for satb, a cap. Score contains Welsh
        transl. by Islwyn Ffowc Elis. The following
        arrangements were also publ. L: Curwen (RP): male
        v. choir, a cap. (1929); solo v., pf. (1939);
        2 pt. female v., pf. (1939); 3 pt. female v., a
        cap. (1945); sab, a cap. (1950); unison v., pf.
        (1958).

7051   Taylor, Jean. NY: HB, 1928 in New Songs for New
        Voices. Song: v., pf. Text adapt.

Song of Spring, A   See: New Old Song, A

Miscellanea

7052   Gover, Gerald. Musical Times (Feb. 1956) reports
        a concert of 3 songs for a solo, incl. words by
        Tynan.

7053   Hart, Fritz. "Farewell", Book of Five Songs, MS
        1938, avail. State Library of Victoria, Mel-
        bourne. Song: v., pf.

7054   Harty, Hamilton. "An Irish Love Song", L: C, 1908.
        Song: [v., pf.].

7055   Klein, Ivy. "Chestnut in April", L: A, ca. 1958.
        Song: 2 pt. chorus of female v., pf. [Text pos-
        sibly adapt. from Tynan's poem entitled "Chestnut
        in May"?]

7056   May, Frederick. "Drought", MS pre-1968. Song: v.,
        pf. [Possibly a setting of Tynan's poem entitled
        "After Great Drought"?]

7057   Thomson, Bothwell. "The Grey Streets of London", L:
        C. Song: solo v., pf.

7058   Thomson, Bothwell. "The Irish Grass", L: C, 1909.
        Song: [v., pf.].

7059   Willan, Healey, arr. "Would God I Were the Tender
        Apple Blossom", Oakville: FH, 1928. Setting for
        v., pf. employing an old Irish air from County
        Derry.

Jstinov, Peter

JSTINOV, Peter Alexander   1921-

Love of Four Colonels, The   (DR)   (1951)

   7060 Hopkins, Antony. MS, perf. London, May 1951. In-
        cidental music: ch. orch.

Tragedy of Good Intentions, The   (DR)   In Plays about
     People (1950)

   7061 Darnton, Christian. MS, perf. Liverpool, Oct. 1945.
        Incidental music.

Unknown Soldier and His Wife, The   (DR)   (1967)

   7062 Shire, David. MS, per. London, Jan. 1973. In-
        cidental music.

WAIN, John Barrington   1925-

Wildtrack   "Engrave the snowflake"   (1965) Portions were
     1st publ. in Critical Quarterly & Carleton Miscellany

   7063 Rands, Bernard. "Metalepis 2", L: UE, 1974. Setting
        for ms solo, chorus of 6 v. (2 s, 2 a, t, b) ea.
        with individual microphone, 2 fl., hn., tpt.,
        trbn., 2 hp., pf., cel., elec. org., 3 perc.
        players. Setting of lines beginning: "Great cut-
        ting edge indifferent to tissue".

Warner, Rex

WARNER, Rex   1905-

Chough   "Desolate that cry as though the world were un-
    worthy"   In Poems_and_Contradictions, rev. edn. (1945)

    7064 Naylor, Peter. "The Chough", Bird_Songs, MS. Cyc.:
        t or bar solo, pf.

WARNER, Sylvia Townsend   1893-

Black Eyes   "Long Molly Samways"   In The_Espalier (1925)

    7065 Flothuis, Marius. Four_Trifles, Amst.: DM, 1949.
        Song: high v., pf.

Hymn for a Child   "Flocking to the Temple"   In The_Espalier
    (1925)

    7066 Ireland, John. Songs_Sacred_and_Profane, L: S, 1934.
        Cyc.: solo v., pf.

Mr._Fortune's_Maggot   (NV)   (1927)

    7067 Nordoff, Paul. "Mr. Fortune", MS 1936-1937. Opera.

Sailor, The   "I have a young love"   In The_Espalier (1925)

    7068 Bowman, Aubrey C. MS n.d., avail. NYPL. Song: v.,
        pf.

Scapegoat, The   "See the scapegoat, happy beast"   In The
    Espalier (1925)

    7069 Ireland, John. Songs_Sacred_and_Profane, L: S, 1934.
        Cyc.: solo v., pf.

796

Warner, Sylvia Townsend continued

Soldier's Return, The   "Jump through the hedge, lass!"   In
The Espalier (1925)

7070   Ireland, John. Songs Sacred and Profane, L: S, 1934.
        Cyc.: solo v., pf.

Miscellanea

7071   Buck, Percy. "A Carol of St. Brigit", L: EA, pre-
        1946. Song: sa, pf. Text begins: "When Brigit
        went out".

7072   Flothuis, Marius. "Falling Asleep in an Orchard",
        Four Trifles, Amst.: DM, 1949. Song: high v., pf.

7073   Kirbye, George. "O Jesu, look", L: OUP, 1964 (rev.
        edn.). Anthem for 5 voices.

WATKINS, Vernon Phillips   1906-1967

Discoveries   "Poles are flying where the two eyes set, The"
In Ballad of the Mari Lwyd (1941)

7074   Brindle, Reginald S. L: OUP, 1970. Song: mixed
        choir, a cap.

WATSON, William   1858-1935

Alpha and Omega   "He throned her in the gateways of the
world"   In For England (1903)

7075   Wood, Frederic H. Motherland, L: FD&H, ca. 1952.
        Cta.: female soli, female choirs (ssa), stgs.,
        pf.

Watson, William continued

Awakening, The   "Behold, she is risen who lay asleep so
   long"   In The Year of Shame (1897)

   7076 Wood, Frederic H. Motherland, L: FD&H, ca. 1952.
         Cta.: female soli, female choirs (ssa), stgs.,
         pf. The cta.'s 1st movement (entitled "The
         Awakening") sets the opening lines of the poem;
         its 2nd movement (entitled "The Northern Star")
         sets the poem's closing lines.

Ballad of Semmerwater, The   "Deep asleep, deep asleep"   In
   The Poems of William Watson (1905)

   7077 Gibbs, C. Armstrong. L: Curwen, 1930. Song: solo v.,
         pf.

   7078 Noble, Harold. S. Croy.: L, 1956. Song: med. v., pf.

   7079 Peel, Graham. L: BH, pre-1940. Song: [v., pf.].

England and Her Colonies   "She stands a thousand-wintered
   tree"   In Poems (1892)

   7080 Dyson, George. "Motherland", L: N, 1941. Song: uni-
         son v., opt. descant, a cap. Also arr. for satb,
         opt. descant with accompaniment of stgs., perc.
         (or stgs., ww. or stgs., br.). An arr. for satb,
         opt. descant, orch. is also avail.

   7081 Wood, Frederic H. "The Tree of Nations", Motherland,
         L: FD&H, ca. 1952. Cta.: female soli, female
         choirs (ssa), stgs., pf.

Frontier, The   "At the hushed brink of twilight"   In Odes
   and Other Poems (1894)

   7082 Persichetti, Vincent. Poems for Piano, Vol. I, Ph.:
         EV, 1947. Pf. solo. Incl. one composition after
         Watson's "Wake subtler dreams, and touch me nigh
         to tears".

Fugitive Ideal, The   "As some most pure and noble face"   In
   Lachrymæ Musarum and Other Poems (1892)

atson, William continued

7083 Dent, Edward. MS 1897. Song: [v., pf.].

Leavetaking "Pass, thou wild light" In The Poems of William Watson (1905)

7084 White, Maude V. L: S&B, pre-1940. Song: [v., pf.].

Lute-Player, The "She was a lady great and splendid" In Wordsworth's Grave and other Poems, 2nd edn. (1891)

7085 Allitsen, Frances. MS pre-1912, L: ASH. Song: [v., pf.?].

Mock Self, The "Few friends are mine" In Wordsworth's Grave and other Poems, 2nd edn. (1891)

7086 Persichetti, Vincent. Poems for Piano, Vol. I, Ph.: EV, 1947. Pf. solo. Incl. one composition after Watson's "...whose thin fraud I wink at privily".

Ode in May "Let me go forth, and share" In The Hope of the World And Other Poems (1897)

7087 Coppola, Piero. "Morn in May", L: [?], ca. 1924. Song: v., pf.

"Oh, like a queen's her happy tread" In The Father of the Forest And Other Poems (1895), rev. 1905

7088 Atherton, Percy. "Like a Queen", B: BMC, pre-1940. Song: [v., pf.].

7089 Colburn, S.C. "Like a Queen", B: BMC, pre-1940. Song: [v., pf.].

7090 Johns, Clayton. "Like a Queen", MS pre-1932, B: BMC. Song: [v., pf.].

7091 Liddle, Samuel. "O, like a Queen", MS pre-1951, L: C. Song: [v., pf.].

799

7092 Shepherd, Arthur. MS, avail. University of Utah.
      Song: v., pf. Setting of lines beginning: "'Neath
      oaks that mused and pines that dreamed".

Song "April, April" In The Hope of the World And Other
      Poems (1897)

7093 Fetler, Paul. "April", NY: LG, 1957. Song: satb, a
      cap.

7094 Freer, Eleanor. Five Songs to Spring, Berlin: Kaun,
      1905. Song: ms or bar solo, pf.

7095 Homer, Sidney. "April...", MS (Opus 23), NY: GS.
      Song: [v., pf.].

7096 Lloyd, Charles H. "April...", Two Songs, MS pre-
      1919, L: S&B. Song: [v., pf.?].

7097 Osgood, George L. "April, Laugh Thy Girlish Laugh-
      ter", MS 1904, B: BMC. Song: [v., pf.?].

7098 Peel, Graham. "April", The Country Lover, L: C,
      1910. Song: [solo v., pf.].

7099 Pyke, Helen. "April", L: Elkin, 1948. Song: med. v.,
      pf.

7100 Quilter, Roger. "April", Four Songs, L: BH, 1910.
      Song: v., pf.

Song "Oh, like a queen's..." See: "Oh, like a queen's her
      happy tread"

Tavern Song "When winterly weather doth pierce to the skin"
      In New Poems (1909)

7101 Fisher, Howard. L: BH, pre-1940. Song: [v., pf.].

Vita Nuova "Long hath she slept, forgetful of delight" In
      Odes and Other Poems (1894)

7102 Wickens, Dennis. MS. Song: ssattb, a cap.

Watson, William continued

"Well he slumbers, greatly slain"   In Poems (1892)

   7103   Mason, Daniel G. NY: Church, pre-1940. Song: [v.,
       pf.?].

When Birds were Songless   "When birds were songless on the
bough"   In Wordsworth's Grave and other Poems, 2nd edn.
(1891), rev. 1905

   7104   Atherton, Percy. "When...", B: BMC, pre-1940. Song:
       [v., pf.].

"When birds were songless on the bough"   See: When Birds
were Songless

World-Strangeness   "Strange the world about me lies"   In
Wordsworth's Grave and other Poems, 2nd edn. (1891)

   7105   Gurney, Ivor. MS 1925. Song: [solo v., pf.].

WEBB, Mary Gladys   1881-1927

Ancient Gods, The   "Certainly there were splashings in the
water"   In Poems and The Spring of Joy (1928)

   7106   Naylor, Bernard. Presences, MS 1947. Cyc.: high v.,
       pf.

'Be Still, You Little Leaves'   "Be still, you little leaves!
nor tell your sorrow"   In Poems and The Spring of Joy
(1928)

   7107   Chamberlain, Ronald. Three Songs, L: MM, 1932, as-
       signed L: C, 1943. Song: [solo v., pf.].

   7108   Glanville-Hicks, Peggy. P: OL, 1938. Song: solo v.,
       pf.

Webb, Mary continued

Beautiful House, The   "Large house, a fair house, fragrant,
   wide and high, A"   In Fifty-One Poems (1946)

   7109 Ford, Donald. L: C. Song: [v., pf.].

Dust   "On burning ploughlands, faintly blue with wheat"   In
   Poems and The Spring of Joy (1928)

   7110 Naylor, Bernard. Three Songs of Regret, MS 1947.
         Cyc.: low v., pf.

Eros   "Before his coming thunder breaks"   In Poems and The
   Spring of Joy (1928)

   7111 Boughton, Rutland. MS 1931. Song: solo v., pf.

Fairy-Led   "Fairy people flouted me, The"   In Poems and The
   Spring of Joy (1928)

   7112 Boughton, Rutland. "The Faery People", MS 1940.
         Song: solo v., pf.

   7113 Naylor, Bernard. Presences, MS 1947. Cyc.: high v.,
         pf.

Fallen Poplar, The   "Never any more shall the golden sun"
   In Poems and The Spring of Joy (1928)

   7114 Naylor, Bernard. Vancouver: Western, 1949. Song:
         med. v., pf.

Foxgloves   "Foxglove bells, with lolling tongue, The"   In
   Poems and The Spring of Joy (1928)

   7115 Head, Michael. More Songs of the Countryside, L: BH,
         1933. Song: high or low v., pf. Also avail. for
         high or low v., str. qrt.

Garden in Winter, The   "Winter sun that rises near the
   south, The"   In Poems and The Spring of Joy (1928)

Webb, Mary continued

7116 Chamberlain, Ronald. Three Songs, L: MM, 1932, as-
      signed L: C, 1943. Song: [solo v., pf.].

Gone to Earth (NV) (1917)

7117 Easdale, Brian. MS pre-1954. Film music.

Good-bye to Morning "I will say good-bye to morning"   In
Poems and The Spring of Joy (1928)

7118 Naylor, Bernard. Three Songs of Regret, MS 1947.
      Cyc.: low v., pf.

Green Rain "Into the scented wood we'll go" In Poems and
The Spring of Joy (1928)

7119 Boughton, Rutland. "By the Blackthorn", Five Songs,
      MS 1944. Song: solo v., pf., vln.

7120 Head, Michael. L: BH, 1938, Five Songs (ea. publ.
      sep.). Song: ms solo, pf. or ms solo, str. qrt.,
      hp. Other songs in the collection require various
      soli and accompaniment.

7121 Orr, Robin. Three Pastorals, MS 1951, L: H (hire).
      Song: ms solo, fl., vla., pf.

7122 Trimble, Joan. L: BH, 1938. Song: med. v., pf.

7123 Williams, Grace. MS pre-1954. Song: [v., pf.?].

Happy Life, The "No silks have I" In Poems and The Spring
of Joy (1928)

7124 Orr, Robin. Three Pastorals, MS 1951, L: H (hire).
      Song: ms solo, fl., vla., pf.

In Dark Weather "Against the gaunt, brown-purple hill" In
Poems and The Spring of Joy (1928)

7125 Rubbra, Edmund. L: A, 1933. Song: v., pf.

Little Hill, The   "This is the hill, ringed by the misty
   shire" In Poems and The Spring of Joy (1928)

   7126 Naylor, Bernard. Presences, MS 1947. Cyc.: high v.,
      pf.

Market Day "Who'll walk the fields with us to town" In
   Poems and The Spring of Joy (1928)

   7127 Brent-Smith, Alexander. L: S&B, pre-1938 Song: ss,
      [pf.?].

Presences "There is a presence on the lonely hill" In
   Poems and The Spring of Joy (1928)

   7128 Naylor, Bernard. Presences, MS 1947. Cyc.: high v.,
      pf.

Rose-Berries "Green pine-needles shiver glassily, The" In
   Poems and The Spring of Joy (1928)

   7129 Naylor, Bernard. Vancouver: Western, 1949. Song:
      high v., pf.

Secret Joy, The "Face to face with the sunflower" In
   Poems and The Spring of Joy (1928)

   7130 Chamberlain, Ronald. Three Songs, L: MM, 1932, as-
      signed L: C, 1943. Song: [solo v., pf.].

   7131 Naylor, Bernard. Presences, MS 1947. Cyc.: high v.,
      pf.

Spirit of Earth, The "Love me--and I will give into your
   hands" In Poems and The Spring of Joy (1928)

   7132 Dunlop, Isobel. MS pre-1954. Song: female chorus,
      stgs.

Summer Day, A "Long aisles of larches stretch away" In
   Poems and The Spring of Joy (1928)

Webb, Mary continued

7133 Orr, Robin. Three Pastorals, MS 1951, L: H (hire).
      Song: ms solo, fl., vla., pf.

Winter Sunrise   "All colours from the frozen earth have
    died" In Poems and The Spring of Joy (1928)

7134 Naylor, Bernard. Three Songs of Regret, MS 1947.
      Cyc.: low v., pf.

Miscellanea

7135 Dougherty, Celius. "Song for Autumn", NY: GS, 1962.
      Song: v., pf. Text by Webb. [Possibly a setting
      of "Autumn" or of "The Plain in Autumn"?]

WELCH, Denton   1917-1948

Babylon   "No branch, nor breath"   In A Last Sheaf (1951)

7136 Ferguson, Howard. Discovery, L: BH, 1952. Cyc.: high
      or med. v., pf.

Discovery   "Sound's deceit, The"   In A Last Sheaf (1951)

7137 Ferguson, Howard. Discovery, L: BH, 1952. Cyc.: high
      or med. v., pf.

Dreams Melting   "What are you in the morning"   In A Last
    Sheaf (1951)

7138 Ferguson, Howard. Discovery, L: BH, 1952. Cyc.: high
      or med. v., pf.

Freedom of the City, The   "'I am the fever in the head...'"
    In A Last Sheaf (1951)

Welch, Denton continued

7139   Ferguson, Howard. <u>Discovery</u>, L: BH, 1952. Cyc.: high
       or med. v., pf.

Jane Allen   "Our maid, Jane Allen"   In <u>A Last Sheaf</u> (1951)

7140   Ferguson, Howard. <u>Discovery</u>, L: BH, 1952. Cyc.: high
       or med. v., pf.

WELLS, Herbert George   1866-1924

<u>Ann Veronica</u>   (NV)   (1909)

7141   Ornadel, Cyril. L: Veronica, 1969. Musical. Text
       adapt. by Frank Wells and Ronald Gow; lyrics by
       David Croft.

<u>Kipps</u>   (NV)   <u>Pall Mall Magazine</u> (Jan.?-Dec.? 1905), publ.
sep. same year

7142   Heneker, David. "Half a Sixpence", L: C, 1967.
       Musical. Text adapt. by Beverly Cross; lyrics by
       Beverly Cross and the composer.

<u>Shape of Things to Come, The</u>   (NV)   (1933)

7143   Bliss, Arthur. "Things to Come", MS 1934-35,
       released 1936 by United Artists. Film music:
       orch. with chorus in the "Epilogue" (later
       renamed "Theme and Reconstruction"). Concert ste.
       publ. L: C, 1936; also publ. L: C for military
       band. Portions also publ. L: N, 1940 in full
       symph. edn. No. 7 of the ste. (entitled "March")
       publ. sep. L: N, 1939.

Miscellanea

7144   Alwyn, William. "The History of Mr. Polly", MS ca.
       1949. Film music [based on Wells' novel?].

7145 Brindle, Reginald S. "Homage to H.G. Wells", L: P,
      1962. Orch. only. The composer has indicated to
      the eds. that the work is divided into "futurist
      symphonias reflecting Wells' futurist writings"
      and "intermezzos in familiar musical idiom re-
      flecting Wells' more homely novels such as Mr.
      Polly".

7146 Oliver, Stephen. Sufficient Beauty, MS 1973, L: N.
      This work consists of 3 monodramas for bar solo,
      wind ensemble, vln. (doubl. bowed psaltery), db.,
      keyboard, perc. The monodramas, after texts by
      Kafka and Chekhov (the final text is by the com-
      poser), are entitled: "The Burrow", "The Kiss",
      "The Professor". They are linked together by a
      quotation from H.G. Wells that appears on the
      title page of the score: "Man comes to life to
      seek and find his sufficient beauty, to serve it,
      to win and increase it...".

WESKER, Arnold   1932-

Chicken Soup with Barley   (DR)   (1959) Incl. as one of
    The Wesker Trilogy (1960)

7147 Anon. "As Man is Only Human", NY: Random, 1961 in
      The Wesker Trilogy. Incidental music: v., unacc.
      The score accompanied the Random House edn. of
      the play.

7148 Anon. "England Arise", NY: Random, 1961 in The Wes-
      ker Trilogy. Incidental music: v., unacc. The
      score accompanied the Random House edn. of the
      play.

I'm Talking about Jerusalem   (DR)   (1960) Incl. as one of
    The Wesker Trilogy (1960)

Wesker, Arnold continued

7149   Anon., arr. "Come O my love and fare ye well", L:
       Penguin, 1960. Song: v., unacc. Arr. of an
       American folk song. The score accompanied the 1st
       edn. of the play.

7150   Anon. "Hoolyit Hoolyit", L: Penguin, 1960. Song: v.,
       unacc. The score accompanied the 1st edn. of the
       play.

Roots   (DR)   (1959) Incl. as one of The Wesker Trilogy
(1960)

7151   Anon. "I'll wait for you in the heavens blue", NY:
       Random, 1961 in The Wesker Trilogy. Incidental
       music: v., unacc. The score accompanied the Ran-
       dom House edn. of the play.

WHITING, John Robert   1917-1963

Devils, The   (DR)   (1962) Adapt. from Aldous Huxley's The
Devils of Loudun

7152   Davies, Peter Maxwell. MS, perf. London, Dec. 1971.
       Film music.

7153   Penderecki, Krzysztof. "The Devils of Loudun", MS
       1968-69, Mz.: S. Opera: 3 s, ms, 2 a, 3 t, 3 bar,
       b-bar, 3 b soli, 3 sp., actors, orch. Libr. by
       the composer. Transl. into German by Erich Fried.

Penny for a Song, A   (DR)   (1957), rev. 1964

7154* Bennett, Richard R. "Napoleon is Coming", L: UE,
       1967. Opera: 2 s, a, 2 t, 3 bar, 2 b-bar, b soli,
       2 sp., actor (non-speaking role), orch. Also
       publ. with pf. accompaniment. Libr. by Colin
       Graham. German title: "Napoleon Kommt", transl.
       by Kurt Hermann.

808

Wilde, Oscar

WILDE, Oscar Fingall O'Flahertie Wills   1854-1900

Ballad of Reading Gaol, The   "He did not wear his scarlet
coat"   (1898), rev. same year

7155   Ibert, Jacques. P: Leduc, 1924. Symph. poem: orch.
Fr. title: "Ballade de la geôle de Reading".

7156   Zagwijn, Henri. MS 1920. Setting for chorus,
[orch.?]. Dutch title: "Kerker-Ballade".

Ballons, Les   "Against these turbid turquoise skies"
Lady's Pictorial (Christmas Number 1887) as one of
"Fantaisies Décoratives"

7157   Gover, Gerald. Fantaisies Décoratives, MS pre-1956.
Song: s solo, 2 cl.

7158   Griffes, Charles T. MS 1915. Song: solo v., pf.

Birthday of the Infanta, The   See: Birthday of the Little
Princess, The

Birthday of the Little Princess, The   (SS)   Paris Illustré
(Mar. 1889), rev. 1891

7159   Carpenter, John A. "Birthday of the Infanta" (MS
1917), NY: GS, 1930. Ballet music: solo female
v., orch. Version for pf. duet (MS ca. 1938, rev.
1940) publ. NY: GS, 1938. Concert ste. (unpubl.)
composed 1949.

7160   Castelnuovo-Tedesco, Mario. "Birthday of the Infanta", MS 1944. Orch. ste.

7161   Fortner, Wolfgang. "The White Rose", Mz.: S, 1951.
Ballet music: orch.; pt. 7 requires a solo, uni-
son v., orch. Also arr. for pf. German title:
"Die weisse Rose".

7162   Lutyens, Elisabeth. "The Birthday of the Infanta",
MS ca. 1932. Ballet music.

Wilde, Oscar continued

7163   Radnai, Miklós. "Birthday of the Infanta", MS, prod.
Budapest, Apr. 1918. Ballet music. Hungarian
title: "Az infánsnő születesnapja".

7164   Schreker, Franz. "The Birthday of the Infanta",
Wien: UE, 1909. Ballet music. Arr. as orch. ste.
for cl., pf., 2 hp., vcl., str. orch.; arr. publ.
Wien: UE, 1923.

7165   Sekles, Bernhard. "The Dwarf and the Infanta", Lz.:
Brockhaus, 1913. Ballet music. German title: "Der
Zweg und die Infantin".

7166   Zemlinsky, Alexander. "The Dwarf and the Infanta",
Wien: UE, 1921. Opera. German title: "Der Zwerg
und die Infantin", after the transl. by Georg
C. Klaren.

7167   Zítek, Otakar, "On the Rose", MS 1941-42, avail.
SČSKU. Ballet music. Czech. title: "O růži".
Scenario by the composer. Employs music composed
1933 for the composer's revue entitled: "Cesta
kolem světa" ["The Journey around the World"].

Canterville Ghost, The   (SS)   Court and Society Review
(Feb.-Mar. 1887)

7168   Ducháč, Miloslav. MS 1969, avail. SČSKU. Incidental
music to "The Crazy Radio Musical" by Jiří Roll
and Jaroslav Pour. Czech. title: "Strašidlo
cantervillské".

7169   Kalmanoff, Martin. "Canterville Ghost", MS 1967.
Children's musical: 2 female roles, 3 male roles,
pf. Lyrics by Gerald Lebowitz, after the adapt.
by Abby Markson.

7170   Khaifel, Alexandre. MS, perf. Leningrad, Oct. 1974.
Opera. Text in Russian.

7171   Krička, Jaroslav. "The Gentleman in White", MS 1927-
29, avail. SČSKU. Opera. Czech. title: "Bílý
pán". Libr. by Jan Löwenbach-Budín.

810

Wilde, Oscar continued

7172 Křička, Jaroslav. "The Gentleman in White" [2nd ver-
sion], MS 1930, avail. SČSKU. Opera. Czech.
title: "Bílý pán". Libr. by Max Brod. Pf. arr.
(entitled "Spuk im Schloss") publ. Wien: UE,
1931. Orch. ste. from the opera, MS 1935, avail.
SČSKU.

7173 Sutermeister, Heinrich. MS 1962-63, Mz: S. Opera for
TV: 2 s, ms, t, bar soli, 4 sp., chorus, orch.

Canzonet   "I have no store"   Arts and Letters, Paris (Apr.
1888)

7174 Farley, Roland. NY: NME, pre-1940. Song: [solo v.,
pf.?].

Disciple, The   "When Narcissus died"   Spirit Lamp (June
1893), rev. 1894

7175 Capdevielle, Pierre. Deux Apologues d'Oscar Wilde,
MS 1930-32, P: EFM. Setting for ms, t soli, orch.
Fr. title: "Le disciple".

E Tenebris   "Come down, O Christ, and help me!"   Poems
(1881)

7176 Haubiel, Charles. L'Amore Spiritual, NY: CPI, 1937.
Song: ssaa, 2 pf. Also avail. for ssaa, orch. or
ssaa, org., hp. or ssaa, pf. Also publ. sep.

7177 Schulhoff, Erwin. Drei Lieder für eine Altstimme mit
Klavierbegleitung, MS 1914, avail. SČSKU. Song: a
solo, pf.

Endymion   "Apple trees are hung with gold, The"   Poems
(1881)

7178 McKenzie, Eric D. MS 1955, avail. Victoria University of Wellington. Song: s solo, str. qrt.

7179* Scott, Cyril. MS. Setting for sp., [pf.].

7180 Seeger, Charles. NY: GS, pre-1940. Song: [v., pf.?].

811

Wilde, Oscar continued

Fisherman and His Soul, The   (SS)   A House of Pomegranates
(1891)

    7181 Lange, Arthur. NY: B-M (hire). Symph. ste.: opt.
          narr., orch.

Florentine Tragedy, A   (DR)   Fragment 1st publ. in Collected Works, Vol. II (1908), rev. & completed by T. Sturge
Moore for inclusion in Collected Works, 2nd ed. (1909)

    7182 Floridia-Napolino, Pietro. MS 1916, avail. NYPL.
          Incidental music: str. qrt., hp. Also arr. for
          2 vln., vcl., hp. (or pf.).

    7183 Zemlinsky, Alexander. Wien: UE, 1916. Opera. German
          title: "Eine florentinische Tragödie", transl. by
          Max Meyerfeld.

From Spring Days to Winter   "In the glad spring time"
Dublin University Magazine (Jan. 1876)

    7184 Jervis-Read, Harold. L: AH&C, 1913. Song: [v., pf.].

    7185 McKenzie, Eric D. MS 1955, avail. Victoria Univer-
          sity of Wellington. Song: s solo, str. qrt.

Fuite de la Lune, La   "To outer senses there is peace"   Pan
(Apr. 1881) as one of "Impressions". 1st publ. as an untitled portion of "Lotus Leaves" in Irish Monthly (Feb.
1877)

    7186 Belchamber, Eileen. L: OUP, 1939. Song: ssa, [a
          cap.].

    7187 Deis, Carl. MS 1914, NY: GS. Song: [v., pf.?].

    7188 Griffes, Charles T. Tone-Images, NY: GS, 1915. Song:
          [ms] solo v., pf.

    7189 Slonimsky, Nicolas. B: W-S, pre-1940. Song: [v.,
          pf.?].

Happy Prince, The   (SS)   The Happy Prince and Other Tales
(1888)

Wilde, Oscar continued

7190   Bossi, Renzo. Mi.: SZ, 1953. Opera for radio: s, t
       soli, narr., orch. Ital. title: "Il Principe
       Felice", transl. by the composer.

7191   Fisher, William J. MS, perf. Iowa City 1962. Opera:
       3 s, ms (or 2 s, 2 ms), t, bar, 3 b-bar, b soli,
       dancer, orch. Libr. by John Gutman.

7192   Hadley, Henry. "The Golden Prince", NY: GS, 1914.
       Cta.: bar solo, 4 pt. female chorus, orch. Verse
       adapt. by David Stevens.

7193   Kovaříček, František. MS 1959, avail. SČSKU. In-
       cidental music to radio dramatisation by
       František Pavlíček. Czech. title: "Šťastný
       princ", transl. by Jiří Zdeněk Novák.

7194   Lehmann, Liza. L: C, 1908. Recitation: reciter, pf.
       solo.

7195   Raines, Vernon. MS, perf. Emporia 1955. Opera. Libr.
       by McCaffery.

7196   Williamson, Malcolm. L: Weinberger, 1965. Children's
       opera: 4 s, 2 ms, mc, a soli, ssa, ssmsa, ssss,
       pf. duet, perc., opt. str. qrt. Libr. by the
       composer.

Her Voice   "Wild bee reels from bough to bough, The"   Poems
(1881)

7197   Carpenter, John A. NY: GS, 1913. Song: med. v., pf.

Ideal Husband, An   (DR)   (1899)

7198   Hališka, Rostislav. MS 1968, avail. SČSKU. In-
       cidental music. Czech. title: "Ideální manžel",
       transl. by Václav Renč and Frank Tetauer.

7199   Kalach, Jiří. MS 1965, avail. SČSKU. Incidental
       music. Czech. title: "Ideální manžel", transl.
       by Frank Tetauer.

813

Wilde, Oscar continued

7200 Křivinka, Gustav. MS 1962, avail. SČSKU. In-
     cidental music for radio. Czech. title: "Ideální
     manžel". Radio script by Karel Gissübel, after
     transl. by Frank Tetauer.

7201 Mandel, Petr. MS 1968, avail. SČSKU. Incidental
     music. Czech. title: "Ideální manžel", transl.
     by Jiří Zdeněk Novák.

Importance of Being Earnest, The   (DR)   (1899)

7202 Blatný, Pavel. MS 1965, avail. SČSKU. Incidental
     music. Czech. title: "Jak je důležité mít Filipa",
     transl. by Jiří Zdeněk Novák.

7203 Bowers, Robert H. "Oh, Ernest!", MS, prod. NY, May
     1927. Opera. Libr. by Frances De Witt.

7204 Burkhardt, P. "Bunbury", MS, prod. Munich 1955.
     Opera.

7205 Castelnuovo-Tedesco, Mario. MS, perf. 1974. Opera.

7206 Doubravský, Petr. MS 1967, avail. SČSKU. Incidental
     music. Czech. title: "Jak je důležité mít
     Filipa", transl. by Jiří Zdeněk Novák.

7207 Frankel, Benjamin. MS pre-1954. Film music.

7208 Hrubý, K. in coll. with Arnošt Košťál. MS 1958,
     avail. SČSKU. Incidental music. Czech. title:
     "Jak je důležité mít Filipa", transl. by Jiří
     Zdeněk Novák.

7209 Kosina, Jiří in coll. with Miroslav Ponc. MS 1967,
     avail. SČSKU. Incidental music. Czech. title:
     "Jak je důležité mít Filipa", transl. by Jiří
     Zdeněk Novák.

7210 Košťál, Arnošt. MS 1951, avail. SČSKU. Incidental
     music. Czech. title: "Jak je důležité mít Filipa",
     transl. by Jiří Zdeněk Novák. Incl. song texts
     arr. by Ota Ornest.

7211 Košťál, Arnošt in coll. with K. Hrubý. MS 1958,
     avail. SČSKU. Czech. title: "Jak je důležité mít
     Filipa", transl. by Jiří Zdeněk Novák.

Wilde, Oscar continued

7212 Kučera, Antonín. MS 1950, avail. SCSKU. Incidental
      music. Czech. title: "Jak je důležité mít Filipa",
      transl. by Jiří Zdeněk Novák.

7213 Pockriss, Lee. "Ernest in Love", MS, prod. NY, May
      1960. Music drama. Text by Anne Croswell.

7214 Ponc, Miroslav in coll. with Jiří Kosina. MS 1967,
      avail. SCSKU. Czech. title: "Jak je důležité mít
      Filipa", transl. by Jiří Zdeněk Novák.

7215 Stancl, Ladislav. MS 1971, avail. SCSKU. Incidental
      music. Czech. title: "Jak je důležité mít Filipa",
      transl. by Jiří Zdeněk Novák.

Impression de Matin   "Thames nocturn[e] of blue and gold,
The"   World (Mar. 1881), rev. same year, rev. 1895

7216 Griffes, Charles T. "Impression du Matin", MS 1915,
      Four Impressions, ed. by Donna K. Anderson, NY:
      P, 1970. Song: s or t solo, of.

Impression du Matin   See: Impression de Matin

In the Forest   "Out of the mid-wood's twilight"   Lady's
Pictorial (Christmas Number 1889)

7217 Freed, Isadore. NY: GS, pre-1940. Song: [v., pf.].

7218 Scott, Francis G. "Idyll", MS 1913, avail. SMA.
      Song: high v., pf.

7219 Tilden, Edwin. B: M&T, 1891. Song: [v., pf.].

7220 Wyble, Melvin. NY: GS, pre-1940. Song: [v., pf.].

In the Gold Room   "Her ivory hands on the ivory keys"
Poems (1881)

7221 McKenzie, Eric D. MS 1955, avail. Victoria Univer-
      sity of Wellington. Song: s solo, str. qrt.

7222 Rogers, Bernard. NY: CPMC, pre-1940. Song: [v.,
      pf.].

Wilde, Oscar continued

Jardin, Le "Lily's withered chalice falls, The" Our
Continent (Feb. 1882) as one of "Impressions"

7223 Griffes, Charles T. MS 1915, Four Impressions, ed.
by Donna K. Anderson, NY: P, 1970. Song: s or t
solo, pf.

7224 Jervis-Read, Harold. "The Garden", Four Impressions,
L: AH&C, 1911. Song: [v., pf.?]. Score contains
German transl. by Maurice Fanshawe.

Lady Windermere's Fan (DR) (1892)

7225 Clayton, Don Allen. "A Delightful Season", MS copyright by composer 1960, avail. NYPL. Musical.
Lyrics by the composer.

7226 Coward, Noël. "After the Ball", L: EC, 1954.
Musical.

Lord Arthur Savile's Crime (SS) Court and Society Review
(May 1887)

7227 Bush, Geoffrey. L: N, 1972 (hire or priv. sale
only). Opera: 3 s, a, 2 t, 3 bar, 2 b-bar, opt.
satb, orch. Libr. by the composer, employing many
of Wilde's epigrams.

7228 Ferrari, [Gustave?]. "Lord Savile", MS, perf.
Catania, Italy, Mar. 1971. Opera.

Madonna Mia* "Lily-girl, not made for this world's pain, A"
Poems (1881)

7229 Haubiel, Charles. L'Amore Spirituale, NY: CPI, 1937.
Song: ssaa, 2 pf. Also avail. for ssaa, orch. or
ssaa, org., hp. or ssaa, pf. Also publ. sep.

7230 Schulhoff, Erwin. Drei Lieder für eine Altstimme mit
Klavierbegleitung, MS 1914, avail. SČSKU. Song: a
solo, pf. German title: "Madona mia".

Magdalen Walks "Little white clouds are racing over the
sky, The" Irish Monthly (Apr. 1878), rev. 1882

Wilde, Oscar continued

7231   Healey, Derek. Six Irish Songs, MS 1962, avail. CMC.
       Song: solo v., pf.

Master, The   "And when the darkness came over the earth"
Fortnightly Review (July 1894) as one of "Poems in Prose"

7232   Capdevielle, Pierre. Deux Apologues d'Oscar Wilde,
       MS 1930-32, P: EFM. Setting for ms, t soli, orch.
       Fr. title: "Le maître".

Mer, La   "White mist drifts across the shrouds, The"   Our
Continent (Feb. 1882) as one of "Impressions"

7233   Griffes, Charles T. MS 1914, Four Impressions, ed.
       by Donna K. Anderson, NY: P, 1970. Song: s or t
       solo, pf.

7234* Griffes, Charles T. MS 1916. Song: solo v., pf.

7235   Jervis-Read, Harold. "The Sea", Four Impressions, L:
       AH&C, 1911. Song: [v., pf.?]. Score contains
       German transl. by Maurice Fanshawe.

Nightingale and the Rose, The   (SS)   The Happy Prince and
Other Tales (1888)

7236   Bossi, Renzo. MS. Opera. Ital. title: "L'usignuolo e
       la rosa".

7237   Garwood, Margaret. MS, perf. Chester, Pennsylvania,
       Oct. 1973. Opera.

7238   Kalaš, Julius. Prague: Panton, 1963. Symph. poem:
       fl., orch. Czech. title: "Slavík a růže".

7239   Lessner, George. MS pre-1942, NY: Lance. Setting for
       11 soli, dancers, orch.

7240   Schaeffer, William. MS. Opera: 2 s, t, bar soli,
       narr., [orch.]. Libr. by the composer.

7241   Silberta, Rhea. "You shall have your red rose", NY:
       CF, 1950. Song: high v., pf. Setting of lines
       beginning: "'Be happy,' cried the Nightingale,
       'be happy; you shall have your red rose'".

Wilde, Oscar continued

7242 Steinert, Alexander. MS 1950. Setting for sp., orch.

Panneau, Le "Under the rose-tree's dancing shade" Lady's
Pictorial (Christmas Number 1887) as one of "Fantaisies
Décoratives"

7243 Gover, Gerald. Fantaisies Décoratives, MS pre-1956.
Song: s solo, 2 cl.

Picture of Darian Gray, The (NV) Lippincott's Monthly
Magazine (July 1890), rev. & publ. sep. 1891

7244 Kox, Hans. MS, perf. Amst. 1973 (London, Mar. 1974).
Opera. Dutch title: "Graenskibutzen".

7245 Marais, Jean in coll. with Ned Rorem. "Dorian Gray",
MS, perf. Barcelona 1952. Ballet music.

7246 Marttinen, Tauno. MS 1969. Ballet music: orch. Finnish title: "Dorian Grayn muotokuva".

7247 Orchard, William A. MS pre-1954. Opera.

7248 Rorem, Ned in coll. with Jean Marais. "Dorian Gray",
MS, perf. Barcelona 1952. Ballet music.

7249 Schaeuble, Hans. "Dorian Gray", MS 1947-48. Opera.

Requiescat "Tread lightly, she is near" Poems (1881)

7250 Butterworth, George. L: A, 1920. Song: solo v., pf.

7251 Clarke, Kathleen B. NY: GS, pre-1940. Song: [v.,
pf.].

7252 Clough-Leighter, Henry. B: BMC, pre-1940. Song: [v.,
pf.].

7253 Cory, George. NY: AMP, 1951 as one of Four Settings
of British Poets (publ. sep. NY: AMP). Song: med.
v., pf.

7254 Dallapiccola, Luigi. "Tread lightly...", Requiescant,
Mi.: SZ, 1960. Symph.-choral work for satb,
children's chorus, orch.

Wilde, Oscar continued

7255   Haubiel, Charles. L'Amore Spirituale, NY: CPI, 1937.
        Song: ssaa, 2 pf. Also avail. for ssaa, orch. or
        ssaa, org., hp. or ssaa, pf. Also publ. sep.

7256   Jervis-Read, Harold. "At Rest", MS (Opus 21), perf.
        London, June 1910. Song: male solo v., [pf.?].

7257   Jones, Robert W. MS. Song: high v. (preferably t
        solo), pf.

7258   Schulhoff, Erwin. "Rosa Mystica", Drei Lieder für
        eine Altstimme mit Klavierbegleitung, MS 1914,
        avail. SČSKU. Song: a solo, pf. German text only.

7259   Sharpe, Evelyn. L: CR, 1925. Song: solo v., pf.

7260   Young, Gordon. NY: GX, 1954. Song: med. v., pf.

7261   Van Vactor, David. Vocal Works, NY: NME, 1944. Song:
        solo v., pf.

Reveillon, Le   "Sky is laced with fitful red, The" Poems
(1881) as one of "Impressions". 1st publ. as an untitled
portion of "Lotus Leaves" in Irish Monthly (Feb. 1877)

7262   Griffes, Charles T. MS 1914, Four Impressions, ed.
        by Donna K. Anderson, NY: P, 1970. Song: s or t
        solo, pf.

Salomé (DR)   (1893) in Fr. The Engl. version (transl. by
Lord Alfred Douglas) was publ. 1894 under the title Salome

7263*   Alpaerts, Flor. MS pre-1954. Incidental music.

7264   Bantock, Granville. "Salomé (Dance of the Seven
        Veils)", MS (Opus 63), avail. Birmingham Univer-
        sity. Incidental music: pf.

7265   Glazunov, Alexander. "Salome (Introduction and
        Dance)", Lz.: Belaieff, 1912. Incidental music
        for ballet.

7266   Krein, Alexander. "Salomea", MS 1913. Symph. poem:
        orch.

819

Wilde, Oscar continued

   7267   Mariotte, Antoine. P: E, 1910. Opera. Ital. libr.
          by the composer.

   7268   Riadis, E. MS 1922. Ballet music.

   7269   Schmitt, Florent. "La Tragedie de Salomé", MS (Opus
          50); perf. Paris, Nov. 1907; publ. P: Durand.
          Ballet music.

   7270   Strauss, Richard. Berlin: Fürstner, 1905, assigned
          L: BH, 1943. Music drama: s, ms, a, 7 t, bar, 4
          b soli, orch. Transl. by Hedwig Lachmann. Adapt.
          for Engl. stage by Alfred Kalisch.

   7271   Tcherepnin, Alexander. MS pre-1927. Incidental
          music.

Selfish Giant, The   (SS)   The Happy Prince and Other Tales
   (1888)

   7272   Krane, Sherman. "The Giant's Garden", NY: CF, 1952.
          Opera: 5 s, bar, b soli, orch.

   7273   Perry, Julia. MS, avail. AMC. Opera. Libr. by the
          composer.

   7274   Shaw, Francis. L: JWC, 1974. Opera. Libr. by Michael
          Ffinch.

   7275   White, Raymond W. MS, perf. Cleveland 1965. Opera.

   7276   Wilson, Charles M. MS 1972, avail. CMC. Opera: bar
          solo, children's v. (s and a), perc. orch.
          (Orff), bells, xyl., vibra., pf.

Serenade   See: To Helen

Silhouettes, Les   "Sea is flecked with bars of grey, The"
   Pan (Apr. 1881) as one of "Impressions"

   7277   Carpenter, John A. NY: GS, 1913. Song: solo v., pf.
          Arr. 1943 for solo v., orch.

Wilde, Oscar continued

Sonnet On Hearing the Dies Irae Sung in the Sistine Chapel
"Nay, Lord, not thus!" Poems (1881), rev. 1882

7278 Williamson, Malcolm. "Sonnet", L: Weinberger, 1969.
Song: satb, a cap.

Sphinx, The   "In a dim corner of my room"   (1894)

7279 Bantock, Granville. MS 1941, avail. Birmingham
University. Cyc.: a or bar solo, orch. Settings
of lines beginning: "In a dim corner of my room",
"A thousand weary centuries are thine", "Sing to
me of the Jewish maid", "Sing to me of the Labyrinth", "How subtle-secret is your smile!", "With
Syrian oils his brows were bright", "On pearl and
porphyry pedestalled", "The god is scattered here
and there", "Away to Egypt! Have no fear", "Why
are you tarrying?", "What songless tongueless
ghost of sin", "False Sphinx! False Sphinx!".

7280 Castleman, Henry. "False Sphinx", Two Songs, L: WK,
1913. Song: [v., pf.?]. Setting of last two
stanzas only.

7281 Mossolov, Alexander. MS 1925. Cta.

Sonnet, Written During Holy Week   "I wandered in Scogliet-
to's green retreat"   Illustrated Monitor (July 1877),
rev. 1881, rev. 1882

7282 Sharpe, Evelyn. "Written in Holy Week at Genoa", L:
LG&B, 1929. Song: solo v., pf.

Sonnet Written in Holy Week at Genoa   See: Sonnet, Written
During Holy Week

Symphony in Yellow   "Omnibus across the bridge, An"
Centennial Magazine (Feb. 1889)

7283 Blyton, Carey. L: BH, 1973. Song: s solo, hp. or s
solo, pf. Also avail. (hire) for s solo, cl.,
hp. (or pf.).

7284   Griffes, Charles T. Tone-Images, NY: GS, 1915. Song:
        [ms] solo v., pf.

To Helen   "Western wind is blowing fair, The"   Pan (Musical
Supplement, Jan. 1881) as text to Cowen's music

    7285*   Cowen, Frederic H. In Pan (Musical Supplement, Jan.
            1881). Song: [v., pf.?].

    7286   Jervis-Read, Harold. "Ballad of the Greek Sea", L:
            AH&C, 1911. Song: [male] solo v., [pf.]. Score
            contains German transl. by Maurice Fanshawe.

    7287*   Wilde, Oscar. NY: Brentano, "copyright 1882". Song:
            [v., pf.?]. Setting of stanzas 1, 2 and 5.

To my friend Luther Munday   See: Impression de Matin

Under the Balcony   "O beautiful star with the crimson
mouth!"   Shaksperean Show Book (1884)

    7288   Baron, Maurice. "Beautiful Star", NY: R, pre-1940.
            Song: [v., pf.?].

    7289*   Kellie, Lawrence. "Oh! Beautiful Star", L: Cocks,
            ca. 1884. Song: [v., pf.?]. Setting of stanzas
            1, 3 and 4.

    7290*   Thomson, Bothwell. "Oh! Beautiful", MS ca. 1908.
            Song: [male] solo v., [pf.?].

Miscellanea

    7291   Blosdale, Don L. "O Beautiful Moon", NY: CPI, 1954.
            Song: ssatb, pf. Text (attributed to Wilde) be-
            gins: "Oh, oh beautiful moon with the ghostly
            face".

    7292   Lowther, Toupie. "Hazel Eyes", L: Curwen, 1922.
            Song: solo v., pf. The Dec. 1922 issue of Musical
            Times states that the song "is an apposite re-
            flection of an expressive little triolet by Oscar
            Wilde".

Wilde, Oscar continued

7293 McCabe, John. The composer has cancelled the project
for a ch. opera based on Wilde as cited in the
Aug. 1965 issue of Musical Times.

7294 Rogers, Bernard. "Dance of Salome", MS 1938, Phi.:
EV. Orch. only. [Inspired by Wilde's play?]

7295 Schaeffer, William. "Heavenly Ladders", NY: Blake,
1952. Song: v., pf.

7296 Schindler, Kurt. "Early Spring", NY: GS, pre-1940.
Song: [v., pf.?].

7297 Wassilenko, Sergey. "The Garden of Death", MS 1907-
08. Symph. poem.

WODEHOUSE, Pelham Greville*   1881-1975

WOLFE, Humbert   1885-1940

Alpine Chaces   "You called me, and I did not hear you"   In
Humoresque (1926)

7298 Hart, Fritz. Five Songs for Voice and Pianoforte,
MS 1930 (Opus 91), avail. State Library of Victoria, Melbourne. Song: v., pf.

Alpine Cross, The   "Christ, on Your Alpine Cross"   In This
Blind Rose (1928)

7299 Hart, Fritz. Five Songs for Voice and Pianoforte,
MS 1930 (Opus 93), avail. State Library of Victoria, Melbourne. Song: v., pf.

Wolfe, Humbert continued

Anacreon   "Bloom, four-fold ivy"   In Others_Abide (1928)
    Transl. from Antipater

    7300   van Someren-Godfery, Masters. MS pre-1947, L: A.
           Song: solo v., pf.

Betelgeuse   "On Betelgeuse/the gold leaves hang"   In The
    Unknown_Goddess (1925)

    7301   Holst, Gustav. L: A, 1930, Twelve_Humbert_Wolfe
           Songs, Grt. Y.: G, 1970. Song: v., pf.

Biton to His Gods   "To Bacchus, to the Nymphs and rural Pan"
    In Others_Abide (1928) Transl. from Leonidas of Tarentum
    or Gaetulicus

    7302   van Someren-Godfery, Masters. MS pre-1947, L: A.
           Song: solo v., pf.

Blackbird, The   "In the far corner"   In Kensington_Gardens
    (1924)

    7303   Taylor, H. Stanley. Six_Duets_in_Canon, L: Curwen,
           1964. Song: ss, pf.

Bright Hair Grow Dim   "Bright hair, grow dim"   In This
    Blind_Rose (1928)

    7304   Hart, Fritz. Five_Songs_for_Voice_and_Pianoforte,
           MS 1930 (Opus 94), avail. State Library of Vic-
           toria, Melbourne. Song: v., pf.

Candle Cool, A   "He has put by"   In This_Blind_Rose (1928)

    7305   Hart, Fritz. Five_Songs_for_Voice_and_Pianoforte,
           MS 1930 (Opus 94), avail. State Library of Vic-
           toria, Melbourne. Song: v., pf.

Cyclamen   "She rests"   In This_Blind_Rose (1928)

Wolfe, Humbert continued

   7306 Hart, Fritz. Five Songs for Voice and Pianoforte,
         MS 1930 (Opus 93), avail. State Library of Vic-
         toria, Melbourne. Song: v., pf.

Dream-City, The   "On a dream-hill we'll build our city"   In
The Unknown Goddess (1925)

   7307 Holst, Gustav. L: A, 1930, Twelve Humbert Wolfe
         Songs, Grt. Y.: G, 1970. Song: v., pf.

Eastern Court, An   "Here, quiet and long peace"   In This
Blind Rose (1928)

   7308 Hart, Fritz. Five Songs for Voice and Pianoforte,
         MS 1930 (Opus 93), avail. State Library of Vic-
         toria, Melbourne. Song: v., pf.

Envoi   "When the spark that glittered"   In The Unknown Goddess (1925)

   7309 Holst, Gustav. L: A, 1930, Twelve Humbert Wolfe
         Songs, Grt. Y.: G, 1970. Song: v., pf.

Epilogue   "I lay these lilies"   In This Blind Rose (1928)

   7310* Holst, Gustav. MS 1929. Song: v., pf.

Evening   "Now the first moth"   In Humoresque (1926)

   7311 Hart, Fritz. Five Songs for Voice and Pianoforte,
         MS 1930 (Opus 92), avail. State Library of Vic-
         toria, Melbourne. Song: v., pf.

Floral Bandit, The   "Beyond the town"   In The Unknown Goddess (1925)

   7312 Holst, Gustav. L: A, 1930, Twelve Humbert Wolfe
         Songs, Grt. Y.: G, 1970. Song: v., pf.

Forgiveness I   "If it should come to pass"   In Humoresque
(1926)

Wolfe, Humbert continued

7313   Hart, Fritz. "Forgiveness", Five Songs for Voice and
       Pianoforte, MS 1930 (Opus 92), avail. State
       Library of Victoria, Melbourne. Song: v., pf.

Green Candles   "'There's someone at the door,' said gold
   candlestick"   In The Unknown Goddess (1925)

       7314   van Someren-Godfery, Masters. Four Songs, MS pre-
              1947, L: A, ca. 1957. Song: solo v., pf.

Harebell   "Lie easy, harebell!"   In This Blind Rose (1928)

       7315   Hart, Fritz. Five Songs for Voice and Pianoforte,
              MS 1930 (Opus 93), avail. State Library of Vic-
              toria, Melbourne. Song: v., pf.

High Song, The   "High song is over, The"   In Requiem (1927)

       7316   Salter, Lionel. L: L, 1949. Song: s or t solo, pf.

In the Street of Lost Time   "Rest and have ease"   In The
   Unknown Goddess (1925)

       7317   Besly, Maurice. Four Poems, L: BH, pre-1940. Song:
              [v., pf.?].

       7318   Hart, Fritz. Five Songs for Voice and Pianoforte,
              MS 1930 (Opus 92), avail. State Library of Vic-
              toria, Melbourne. Song: v., pf.

       7319   Holst, Gustav. L: A, 1930, Twelve Humbert Wolfe
              Songs, Grt. Y.: G, 1970. Song: v., pf.

Journey's End   "What will they give me, when journey's
   done?"   In The Unknown Goddess (1925)

       7320   Bridge, Frank. L: A, 1925 (1926), Four Songs, L: G,
              1974. Song: solo v., pf.

       7321   Broones, Martin. NY: GS, pre-1940. Song: [solo v.,
              pf.?].

826

Wolfe, Humbert continued

7322 Hart, Fritz. Five Songs, MS 1930 (Opus 91), avail.
     State Library of Victoria, Melbourne. Song: v.,
     pf.

7323 Holst, Gustav. L: A, 1930, Twelve Humbert Wolfe
     Songs, Grt. Y.: G, 1970. Song: v., pf.

7324 van Someren-Godfery, Masters. Four Songs, MS pre-
     1947, L: A, ca. 1957. Song: solo v., pf.

Lamon, the Gardener, to Priapus   "This pomegranate in his
cloth of gold"   In Others Abide (1928) Transl. from
Phillipus

     7325 van Someren-Godfery, Masters. "Lamon to Priapus",
          Four Songs, MS pre-1947, L: A, ca. 1957. Song:
          solo v., pf.

Lamp in the Empty Room, The   "I looked back suddenly into
the empty room"   In Humoresque (1926)

     7326 Weisgall, Hugo. "I Looked Back Suddenly", MS 1943,
          Bryn Mawr: M (hire). Song: med. v., pf.

Lilac, The   "Who thought of the lilac?"   In Kensington Gardens (1924)

     7327 Adler, Samuel. In Nature's Ebb and Flow, NY: SMP,
          1968. Song: ssaa, pf.

Little Music, A   "Since it is evening"   In This Blind Rose
(1928)

     7328 Holst, Gustav. L: A, 1930, Twelve Humbert Wolfe
          Songs, Grt. Y.: G, 1970. Song: v., pf.

Love and Peter   "Love stood at the gates of heaven"   In
The Unknown Goddess (1925)

     7329 van Someren-Godfery, Masters. Four Songs, MS pre-
          1947, L: A, ca. 1957. Song: solo v., pf.

827

Wolfe, Humbert continued

Morning   "In the deep blue"   In Humoresque (1926)

    7330   Hart, Fritz. Five Songs for Voice and Pianoforte,
           MS 1930 (Opus 91), avail. State Library of Vic-
           toria, Melbourne. Song: v., pf.

Neither Moon nor Candle-Light   "If I looked out on any
    night" In Humoresque (1926)

    7331   Hart, Fritz. Five Songs for Voice and Pianoforte,
           MS 1930 (Opus 92), avail. State Library of Vic-
           toria, Melbourne. Song: v., pf.

Night   "Over the mountains"   In Humoresque (1926)

    7332   Hart, Fritz. Five Songs for Voice and Pianoforte,
           MS 1930 (Opus 91), avail. State Library of Vic-
           toria, Melbourne. Song: v., pf.

Noon   "Rose, shut your heart"   In Humoresque (1926)

    7333   Hart, Fritz. Five Songs for Voice and Pianoforte,
           MS 1930 (Opus 91), avail. State Library of Vic-
           toria, Melbourne. Song: v., pf.

Now in these Fairylands   "Now in these fairylands"   In
    This Blind Rose (1928)

    7334   Hart, Fritz. Five Songs for Voice and Pianoforte,
           MS 1930 (Opus 94). Song: v., pf.

    7335   Holst, Gustav. L: A, 1930, Twelve Humbert Wolfe
           Songs, Grt. Y.: G, 1970. Song: v., pf.

Nun, The   "There is a pool in the convent garden"   In
    Requiem (1927)

    7336   Archer, Violet. MS. Tone poem for orch.

Pale and Pilgrim Moon, The   "I stretched out my hands"   In
    This Blind Rose (1928)

Wolfe, Humbert continued

7337 Hart, Fritz. _Five Songs for Voice and Pianoforte_,
MS 1930 (Opus 93), avail. State Library of Victoria, Melbourne.

Persephone" "Come back Persephone!" In _The Unknown Goddess_
(1925)

7338 Holst, Gustav. L: A, 1930, _Twelve Humbert Wolfe
Songs_, Grt. Y.: G, 1970. Song: v., pf.

Queen Victoria "Queen Victoria's/statue is" In _Kensington
Gardens_ (1924)

7339 Adler, Samuel. _Three Encore Songs_, NY: LG, 1958.
Song: satb, a cap.

Rhyme "Rhyme/in your clear chime" In _The Unknown Goddess_
(1925)

7340 Holst, Gustav. L: A, 1930, _Twelve Humbert Wolfe
Songs_, Grt. Y.: G, 1970. Song: v., pf.

Rose, The "Why should a man" In _Kensington Gardens_ (1924)

7341 Adler, Samuel. _Three Encore Songs_, NY: LG, 19589
Song: satb, a cap.

Rue de Toutes Ames "Street of all souls, have in your moonless keeping" In _This Blind Rose_ (1928) as one of
"Geneva"

7342 Hart, Fritz. "Street of All Souls", _Five Songs for
Voice and Pianoforte_, MS 1930 (Opus 94), avail.
State Library of Victoria, Melbourne. Song: v.,
pf.

Summer--Renunciation "I have only asked you for a moment to
stay" In _Humoresque_ (1926)

7343 Hart, Fritz. "Renunciation", _Five Songs for Voice
and Pianoforte_, MS 1930 (Opus 92), avail. State
Library of Victoria, Melbourne. Song: v., pf.

Things Lovelier   "You cannot dream"   In The Unknown Goddess
(1925)

    7344 Adler, Samuel. Three Encore Songs, NY: LG, 19589
        Song: satb, a cap.

    7345 Head, Michael. "You cannot...", L: BH, 1936. Song:
        t solo, pf.

    7346 Holst, Gustav. L: A, 1930, Twelve Humbert Wolfe
        Songs, Grt. Y.: G, 1970. Song: v., pf.

Thought, The   "I will not write a poem for you"   In The
Unknown Goddess (1925)

    7347 Broones, Martin. NY: GS, pre-1940. Song: ⌐solo v.,
        pf.?].

    7348 Holst, Gustav. L: A, 1930, Twelve Humbert Wolfe
        Songs, Grt. Y.: G, 1970. Song: v., pf.

Two Sparrows   "Two sparrows, feeding"   In Kensington Gardens (1924)

    7349 Grant-Schaefer, G.A. NY: HB, 1928 in New Songs for
        New Voices. Song: v., pf.

    7350 Jacob, Gordon. L: EA, 1958. Song: 2 pt. chorus of
        s voices, pf.

Violins   "I have loved violins"   In This Blind Rose (1928)

    7351 Dunlop, Isobel. Two Tone Poems, MS pre-1954. Song:
        a solo, stgs.

Wadham Gardens   "Slides the dead"   In This Blind Rose
(1928)

    7352 Hart, Fritz. "Slide the Dead Cedar-Tree", Five Songs
        for Voice and Pianoforte, MS 1930 (Opus 94),
        avail. State Library of Victoria, Melbourne.
        Song: v., pf.

Wolfe, Humbert continued

White Dress, The   "Some evening when you are sitting alone"
In The Unknown Goddess (1925)

   7353 Duke, John. NY: GS, 1967. Song: med. v., pf.

   7354 van Someren-Godfery, Masters. L: A, 1953. Song: solo
      v., pf.

Miscellanea

   7355 de Menasce, Jacques. Two Poems, MS ca. 1944. Songs:
      v., pf. Texts by Wolfe.

   7356 Dougherty, Celius. "Listen! the wind", NY: BH, 1958.
      Song: high v., pf.

   7357 Dunlop, Isobel. "The Water Queen", Two Tone Poems,
      MS pre-1954. Song: a solo, stgs.

   7358 Weisgall, Hugo. Four Impressions, MS 1931. Song:
      high v., pf. Incl. words by Wolfe. Composition
      withdrawn by the composer.

YEATS, William Butler*   1865-1939

Aedh hears the Cry of the Sedge   "I wander by the edge"
Dome (May 1898) as one of "Aodh to Dectora. Three Songs",
rev. 1899, rev. 1906

   7359 Schwartz, Paul. "He hears the cry of the sedge", A
      Poet To His Beloved, MS 1945. Cyc.: high v., pf.
      or med. v., pf.

   7360* Warlock, Peter. "He hears the Cry of the Sedge",
      The Curlew, L: S&B, 1924 (1973). Cyc.: t solo,
      fl., eng. hn., str. qrt.

Aedh laments the Loss of Love   "Pale brows, still hands and
dim hair"   Dome (May 1898) as one of "Aodh to Dectora.
Three Songs", rev. 1899, rev. 1906

7361* Warlock, Peter. "The Lover mourns for the Loss of
Love", The Curlew, L: S&B, 1924 (1973). Cyc.:
t solo, fl., eng. hn., str. qrt.

7362 Warren, Raymond. "Elegy", Borough Green: N, 1964.
Song: satb, a cap.

7363 Warren, Raymond. "Elegy", Irish Madrigals, MS 1959.
Cta.: ssatb, a cap.

Aedh tells of a Valley full of Lovers   See: Valley of
Lovers, The

Aedh tells of the perfect Beauty   "O cloud-pale eyelids"
Senate (May 1896) as part of "O'Sullivan the Red to Mary
Lavell", rev. 1899, rev. 1906

7364 Schwartz, Paul. "He tells of the perfect beauty", A
Poet To His Beloved, MS 1945. Cyc.: high v., pf.
or med. v., pf.

Aedh tells of the Rose in his Heart   See: Rose in my Heart,
The

Aedh thinks of those who have spoken Evil of his Beloved
"Half close your eyelids"   Dome (May 1898) as one of
"Aodh to Dectora. Three Songs", rev. 1899, rev. 1906

7365* Dunhill, Thomas F. "Aodh to Dectora" in Dome (Jan.
1900); publ. sep. L: At the Sign of the Unicorn,
1901. Song: t solo, pf. Incl. under the title
"To Dectora" in The Wind Among the Reeds, L: S&B,
1905. Cyc.: solo v., pf.

7366 Schwartz, Paul. "He thinks of those who have spoken
evil of his beloved", A Poet To His Beloved, MS
1945. Cyc.: high v., pf. or med. v., pf.

Aedh wished for the Cloths of Heaven   "Had I the heavens'
embroidered cloths"   The Wind Among the Reeds (1899),
rev. 1906

Yeats, W.B. continued

7367* Austin, Frederic. Love's Pilgrimage, L: E, 1920.
      Song: med. v., pf.

7368 Bedford, Herbert. L: Curwen, 1922. Song: solo v.,
      unacc.

7369 Boydell, Brian. "The Cloths of Heaven", Three Yeats
      Songs, MS 1965, avail. RTE. Song: s solo, Irish
      hp. Arr. for s solo, orch. and incl. in Four
      Yeats Poems, MS 1966, avail. RTE.

7370 Brumby, Colin. "The Cloths of Heaven", L: BH, 1961.
      Song: ssa, accompaniment unspecified.

7371 Carter, John. "The Cloths of Heaven", B: FMC, 1968.
      Song: satb, a cap.

7372 Clarke, Rebecca. MS pre-1924, L: WR. Song: solo v.,
      pf.

7373 Dunhill, Thomas F. "The Cloths of Heaven", The Wind
      Among the Reeds, L: S&B, 1905. Cyc.: solo v., pf.

7374 Gurney, Ivor. "The Cloths of Heaven", MS 1920. Song:
      [solo v., pf.].

7375 Harvey, Jonathan. "He wishes for the Cloths of
      Heaven", Four Songs of Yeats, MS 1965. Song: b
      solo, pf.

7376 Heininen, Paavo. "The Cloths of Heaven", Love's
      Philosophy, MS 1968, avail. FMIC. Cyc.: s solo,
      pf.

7377 Marshall, Nicholas. "He wishes for the Cloths of
      Heaven", The Falling of the Leaves, MS. Song:
      high v., treble rec., vcl., hpd.

7378 Roberton, Hugh. "Cloths of Heaven", L: Curwen, 1944.
      Song: ttbb, a cap. Arr. by Maurice Jacobson for
      satb, a cap. Arr. publ. L: Curwen, 1966.

7379 Roderick-Jones, Richard. "He Wishes for the Cloths
      of Heaven", The Wind Among the Reeds, MS 1966.
      Cyc.: s solo, pf.

7380 Ronald, Landon. MS pre-1924. Song: solo v., pf.

833

Yeats, W.B. continued

7381 Stewart, D.M. "Had I...", L: A, pre-1940. Song:
[solo v., pf.].

7382 Van Nuys Fogel, Clyde. NY: GS, pre-1940. Song:
[solo v., pf.].

7383* Warlock, Peter. "The Cloths of Heaven", MS 1920-22.

Aedh wishes his Beloved were dead   See: Aodh to Dectora

After Long Silence   "Speech after long silence"   Words for
Music Perhaps and Other Poems (1932)

7384 Warren, Raymond. Songs of Old Age, Borough Green:
N, 1971. Cyc.: bar solo, pf.

"All the heavy days are over"   The Countess Kathleen and
Various Legends and Lyrics (1892) as part of the play
The Countess Kathleen, rev. 1895, rev. 1927

7385 Mallinson, Albert. "Dream of a Blessed Spirit",
Oakville: FH, 1907. Song: s or t solo, pf.

Anashuya and Vijaya   See: Jealousy

Anne Gregory   See: For Anne Gregory

Aodh to Dectora   "Were you but lying cold and dead"   Sketch
(Feb. 1898), rev. 1899, rev. subsequently

7386 Eichheim, Henry. "Aedh wishes his Beloved were
dead", B: BMC, pre-1940. Song: [v., pf.?].

7387 Van Nuys Fogel, Clyde. "Aedh wishes his Beloved
were dead", NY: GS, pre-1940. Song: [v., pf.?].

At the Hawk's Well   See: At the Hawk's Well or Waters of
Immortality

Yeats, W.B. continued

At the Hawk's Well or Waters of Immortality   (DR)   Harper's
Bazaar (Mar. 1917), rev. same year

    7388   Dulac, Edmund. L: MacM, 1921 in Four Plays for
           Dancers. Incidental music: 3 (singing) musicians
           playing bamboo fl., hp. (or z.), dr., gong. Score
           (attributed to Edmond [sic] Dulac) accompanied the
           1921 edn. of the play.

    7389   Warren, Raymond. MS 1968. Incidental music.

Ballad of the Foxhunter, The   See: Ballad of the Old Foxhunter, The

Ballad of the Old Foxhunter, The   "[Now] lay me in a
cushioned chair"   East and West (Nov. 1889), rev. 1895

    7390   Loeffler, Charles. "Ballad of the Foxhunter", Five
           Irish Fantasies, NY: GS, 1935. Song: solo v.,
           orch.

Before the World was Made   "If I made the lashes dark"   The
Winding Stair (1929) as one of "A Woman Young and Old"

    7391   Routh, Francis. A Woman Young and Old, MS 1962.
           Song sequence: s solo, pf.

    7392   Wilson, James. "If I made...", A Woman Young and
           Old, MS 1966. Cyc.: s solo, Irish hp. Also arr.
           for s solo, pf. or s solo, orch.

Brown Penny   See: Young Man's Song, The

Byzantium   "Unpurged images of day recede, The"   Words for
Music Perhaps and Other Poems (1932)

    7393   Ashforth, Alden. Byzantia: Two Journeys after Yeats,
           MS. Composition for quadraphonic tape. Also arr.
           for tape, org. Arr. in prep. for release on Orion
           recording.

Calvary   (DR)   Four Plays for Dancers (1921)

835

Yeats, W.B. continued

    7394   Pasatieri, Thomas. NY: B-M, 1972. Religious music
           drama: voices, pf.

    7395   Warren, Raymond. MS 1966. Incidental music.

    7396   Warren, Raymond. "The White Heron", MS 1962. Cta.:
           satb, a cap. Sets lines beginning: "Motionless
           under the moon-beam".

Cap and Bell   "Jester walked in the garden, The"   National
Observer (Mar. 1894), rev. same year

    7397   Ambros, Vladimír. "The Cap and Bells", MS 1949,
           avail. SČSKU. Song: a solo, pf. Czech title:
           "Čapka s rolničkami", transl. by Jaroslav
           Skalický.

Cap and Bells, The   See: Cap and Bell

Cat and the Moon, The   "Cat went here and there, The"   Nine
Poems (1918) Incl. as part of the play entitled "The Cat
and the Moon" in The Cat and the Moon and Certain Poems
(1924)

    7398   Marshall, Nicholas. Five Winter Songs, MS. Song:
           med. v., pf.

    7399   Rollin, Robert. Four Songs of Dreams and Love, MS.
           Song: ms solo, fl., ob., vcl., pf. Complete set
           of songs also requires bar solo, ms, bar duet,
           vln., vla.

    7400   Shifrin, Seymour. MS. Song: s solo, pf.

    7401   Wilson, James. Upon Silence, MS (Opus 54). Song: s
           solo, unacc.

    7402* Wilson, James. Yeats Songs, MS (Opus 39). Song: s
           solo, pf.

Cat and the Moon, The   (DR)   The Cat and the Moon and
Certain Poems (1924) A portion ("The cat went here and
there") was 1st publ. under the title "The Cat and the
Moon" in Nine Poems (1918)

Yeats, W.B. continued

7403 Clark, Rosemary. MS, avail. AMC. Opera.

7404 Putsche, Thomas. MS, perf. Hartford, Connecticut
      1960. Opera: s, t, b soli, orch.

7405 Warren, Raymond. MS 1965. Incidental music.

Cathleen ni Hoolihan (DR) Samhain (Oct. 1902), publ. sep.
same year, rev. 1906. Portions were 1st publ. in United
Irishman (May 1902)

7406* Anon. L: MacM, 1922 in Plays in Prose and Verse.
      Spoken song: v., unacc. Setting of lines
      beginning: "I will go cry with the woman". Score
      (trad. Irish air) accompanied the 1922 edn. of
      the play.

Cathleen ni Houlihan   See: Cathleen ni Hoolihan

Cathleen, the Daughter of Hoolihan   "Old brown thorn-trees,
The"   Broad Sheet (Apr. 1903), rev. same year, rev. 1906

7407 Boydell, Brian. "Red Hanrahan's Song", Three Yeats
      Songs, MS 1965, avail. RTE. Song: s solo, Irish
      hp. Arr. for s solo, orch. and incl. in Four
      Yeats Poems, MS 1966, avail. RTE.

7408 Boydell, Brian. "Red Hanrahan's Song about Ireland",
      A Terrible Beauty is Born, MS 1965. Cta.: s solo,
      satb, narr., orch.

7409 Gurney, Ivor. "Cathleen Ni Houlihan", A First Volume
      of Ten Songs, L: OUP, 1938. Song: solo v., pf.

Celtic Twilight, The   "Out-worn heart, in a time out-worn"
National Observer (July 1893), rev. same year

7410 Coerne, Louis. "Into the Twilight", MS pre-1922, NY:
      GS. Song: [v., pf.?].

7411 Crossley-Holland, Peter. "In the Twilight", Two
      Mystical Songs for Baritone and Orchestra, MS
      1945. Song: bar solo, orch.

837

Yeats, W.B. continued

Choice, The   "Lot of love is chosen, The"   The Winding
   Stair (1929) as one of "A Woman Young and Old", rev. 1933

   7412 Wilson, James. "The lot...", A Woman Young and Old,
         MS 1966. Cyc.: s solo, Irish hp. Also arr. for
         s solo, pf. or s solo, orch.

Chosen   See: Choice, The

Cloak, the Boat, and the Shoes, The   See: Voices

Coat, A   "I made my song a coat"   Poetry, Chicago (May
   1914)

   7413 Wilson, James. "The Coat", Upon Silence, MS (Opus
         54). Song: s solo, unacc.

Colonel Martin   "Colonel went out sailing, The"   Broadside
   (Dec. 1937)

   7414 O'Murnaghan, Art. Dublin: Cuala, 1937 in Broadside,
         No. 12. Song: v., unacc. Score accompanied the
         1st publ. of the poem.

Colonus' Praise   "Come praise Colonus' horses"   The Tower
   (1928)

   7415 Berkeley, Lennox. MS ca. 1949, avail. L: JWC. Set-
         ting for satb, orch.

Come Gather Round Me Parnellites   "Come gather round me,
   Parnellites", Broadside (Jan. 1937)

   7416 Anon. Dublin: Cuala, 1937 in Broadside, No. 1. Song:
         v., unacc. Score (trad. Irish tune) accompanied
         the 1st publ. of the poem.

Coming of Wisdom with Time, The   See: Youth and Age

838

Yeats, W.B. continued

Consolation   "O but there is wisdom"   The Winding Stair
(1929) as one of "A Woman Young and Old"

7417 Wilson, James. "O but...", A Woman Young and Old,
MS 1966. Cyc.: s solo, Irish hp. Also arr. for
s solo, pf. or s solo, orch.

Countess Cathleen, The   See: Countess Kathleen, The

Countess Cathleen in Paradise, The   See: "All the heavy days
are over"

Countess Kathleen, The   (DR)   The Countess Kathleen and
Various Legends and Lyrics (1892), rev. 1895. A portion
was 1st publ. under the title "Kathleen" in National
Observer (Oct. 1891). New version publ. sep. 1912

7418 Clarke, Douglas. "Countess Cathleen", MS pre-1952.
Incidental music.

7419 Egk, Werner. "Irische Legende", Mz.: S, 1955. Opera:
3 s, 2 a, 3 t, 4 bar, 3 b soli, female chorus,
mixed chorus, dancer, orch. German text transl.
and adapt. by the composer.

7420 Mallinson, Albert. See: "All the heavy days are
over".

7421 Nelson, Havelock. "Countess Cathleen", MS.
Incidental music for radio.

Cracked Mary and the Bishop   See: Crazy Jane and the Bishop

Cracked Mary and the Dancers   See: Crazy Jane and the
Dancers

Cracked Mary Reproved   See: Crazy Jane Reproved

Cradle Song, A*   "Angels are stooping, The"   Scots Observer
(Apr. 1890), rev. 1901

839

7422 Besly, Maurice. "The angels...", L: E, pre-1940.
Song: [v., pf.?].

7423 del Riego, Teresa. "How I Shall Miss You", L: C,
1914. Song: [solo v., pf.].

7424 Douty, Nicholas. NY: GS, pre-1940. Song: [v., pf.?].

7425 Duncan, Chester. Then and Now, Waterloo: Waterloo,
1974. Song: unison (s) v., pf. The other song in
the collection requires ssa.

7426 Ganz, Rudolph. "The angels...", NY: GS, pre-1940.
Song: [v., pf.?].

7427 Gurney, Ivor. A Fourth Volume of Ten Songs, L: OUP,
1959. Song: solo v., pf.

7428 Hart, Fritz. MS 1913, avail. State Library of Victoria, Melbourne. Song: v., pf.

7429 Healey, Derek. Six Irish Songs, MS 1962, avail. CMC.
Song: solo v., pf.

7430 Housman, Rosalie. "The angels...", MS 1935, avail.
NYPL. Song: solo v., pf.

7431 Ley, Henry G. Album of Songs, MS (Opus 8), L: Acott.
Song: solo v., pf.

7432 Weigel, Eugene. Four Songs for Women's Voices,
Northampton, Mass.: NVMP, 1950. Song: ssa, a cap.

7433 Whettam, Graham. Three Songs from "The Rose", MS,
perf. London 1967. Score rev. 1973 (title rev. to
read: Three Songs to Poems of W.B. Yeats). Song:
high v., pf.

7434 Worder, Magdalen. NY: GS, pre-1940. Song: [v.,
pf.?].

Crazy Jane and Jack the Journeyman   "I know, although when
looks meet"   Words for Music Perhaps and Other Poems
(1932)

7435 Lidov, David. Crazy Jane's Songs, MS 1967, rev.
1970, avail. CMC. Cyc.: solo v., pf.

7436 Paviour, Paul. "Jane with Jack the Journeyman",
Crazy Jane, MS copyright by composer 1969,
avail. St. Leonards: R. Cyc.: s solo, pf.

Crazy Jane and the Bishop   "Bring me to the blasted oak"
London Mercury (Nov. 1930), rev. same year

7437 Lidov, David. Crazy Jane's Songs, MS 1967, rev.
1970, avail. CMC. Cyc.: solo v., pf.

7438 Paviour, Paul. Crazy Jane, MS copyright by composer
1969, avail. St. Leonards: R. Cyc.: s solo, pf.

7439 Young, Douglas. Realities, MS 1970-73, L: F (hire).
Cyc.: s solo, fl. Complete cyc. also requires
t solo, cl., b. cl., vla., vcl., perc., hpd.

Crazy Jane and the Dancers   "I found that ivory image there"
London Mercury (Nov. 1930), rev. same year, rev. 1932

7440 Aston, Peter. "Crazy Jane grown old looks at the
dancers", Five Songs of Crazy Jane, L: N, 1964.
Cyc.: s solo, unacc.

7441 Lidov, David. "Crazy Jane Grown Old looks at the
Dancers", Crazy Jane's Songs, MS 1967, rev. 1970,
avail. CMC. Cyc.: solo v., pf.

7442 Paviour, Paul. "Crazy Jane Grown Old Looks at the
Dancers", Crazy Jane, MS copyright by composer
1969, avail. St. Leonards: R. Cyc.: s solo, pf.

7443 Young, Douglas. "Crazy Jane grown old looks at the
Dancers", Realities, MS 1970-73, L: F (hire).
Cyc.: s, t soli, b. cl., vla., vcl. Complete cyc.
also requires fl., cl., perc., hpd.

Crazy Jane grown old looks at the Dancers   See: Crazy Jane
and the Dancers

Crazy Jane on God   "That lover of a night"   Words for Music
Perhaps and Other Poems (1932)

841

Yeats, W.B. continued

7444   Beeson, Jack. Three Love Songs, MS. Song: low female
         v., pf.

7445   Lidov, David. Crazy Jane's Songs, MS 1967, rev.
         1970, avail. CMC. Cyc.: solo v., pf.

7446   Paviour, Paul. Crazy Jane, MS copyright by composer
         1969, avail. St. Leonards: R. Cyc.: s solo, pf.

Crazy Jane on the Day of Judgment   "Love is all/Unsatisfied"
Words for Music Perhaps and Other Poems (1932)

7447   Berger, Arthur. Three Poems of Yeats, NY: NME, 1950.
         Song: solo v., fl., cl., vcl.

7448   Lidov, David. Crazy Jane's Songs, MS 1967, rev.
         1970, avail. CMC. Cyc.: solo v., pf.

7449   Paviour, Paul. Crazy Jane, MS copyright by composer
         1969, avail. St. Leonards: R. Cyc.: s solo, pf.

Crazy Jane Reproved   "I care not what the sailors say"
London Mercury (Nov. 1930), rev. same year

7450   Beeson, Jack. Three Love Songs, MS. Song: low female
         v., pf.

7451   Lidov, David. Crazy Jane's Songs, MS 1967, rev.
         1970, avail. CMC. Cyc.: solo v., pf.

7452   Paviour, Paul. Crazy Jane, MS copyright by composer
         1969, avail. St. Leonards: R. Cyc.: s solo, pf.

Crazy Jane Talks with the Bishop   "I met the Bishop on the
Road"   The Winding Stair and Other Poems (1933)

7453   Aston, Peter. Five Songs of Crazy Jane, L: N, 1964.
         Cyc.: s solo, unacc.

7454   Lidov, David. Crazy Jane's Songs, MS 1967, rev.
         1970, avail. CMC. Cyc.: solo v., pf.

7455   Paviour, Paul. Crazy Jane, MS copyright by composer
         1969, avail. St. Leonards: R. Cyc.: s solo, pf.

Yeats, W.B. continued

7456   Young, Douglas. <u>Realities</u>, MS 1970-73, L: F (hire).
       Cyc.: s, t soli, b. cl., vla., vcl. Complete cyc.
       also requires fl., cl., perc., hpd.

Curse of Cromwell, The   "You ask what I have found"   <u>Broad-
side</u> (Aug. 1937)

7457   Anon. Dublin: Cuala, 1937 in <u>Broadside</u>, No. 8. Song:
       v., unacc. Score (trad. Irish tune) accompanied
       the 1st publ. of the poem.

Death of Cuchulain, The   (DR)   <u>Last Poems and Two Plays</u>
(1939)

7458   Brettingham Smith, Jolyon. "Cuchulains Tod", Berlin:
       B&B, 1975. Opera: s, a, t, bar soli, actor,
       dancer, "1 shape", orch. German transl. by Ursula
       Clemen.

7459   Warren, Raymond. MS 1968. Incidental music.

7460   Williamson, Malcolm. MS ca. 1971, L: Weinberger
       (hire). Setting for 5 v. (2 a, t, bar, b), perc.

<u>Deirdre</u>   (DR)   (1907), rev. 1908. Portions 1st publ. in
<u>Poems, 1899-1905</u> (1906)

7461* Allgood, Sarah. L: MacM, 1922 in <u>Plays in Prose
       and Verse</u>. Spoken song: v., unacc. Setting of
       passage beginning: "They are gone, they are
       gone". Score accompanied the 1922 edn. of the
       play.

7462   Boydell, Brian. "Musician's Song", MS 1965.
       Incidental music for TV prod.: s solo, Irish hp.
       Arr. for s solo, orch. and incl. in <u>Four Yeats
       Poems</u>, MS 1966, avail. RTE. Setting of lines
       beginning: "Love is an immoderate thing".

7463* Farr, Florence. L: MacM, 1922 in <u>Plays in Prose
       and Verse</u>. Spoken songs: v., unacc. Settings of
       lines beginning: "'Why is it,' Queen Edain said",
       "Love is an immoderate thing", "They are gone,
       they are gone". Scores accompanied the 1922 edn.
       of the play.

Yeats, W.B. continued

7464   Stein, Leon. NY: CFE, 1956, avail. ACA. Opera: s,
       2 ms, a, t, bar, b soli, pf.

7465   Warren, Raymond. MS 1966. Incidental music.

Diarmuid and Grania   (DR)   In coll. with George Moore
Dublin Magazine (Apr.-June 1951), publ. sep. same year
A portion was 1st publ. under the title "Spinning Song" in
Broad Sheet (Jan. 1902), although this song was not incl.
in the 1951 edn. of the play.

7466   Elgar, Edward. "Grania and Diarmid", MS 1901, L: N,
       1902. Incidental music, incl. a setting of "There
       are Seven that pull the Thread" ["Spinning
       Song"].

Do not love too long   "Sweetheart, do not love too long"
Acorn (Oct. 1905), rev. 1908

7467   Warren, Raymond. "O do not love too long", Songs of
       Old Age, Borough Green: N, 1971. Cyc.: bar solo,
       pf.

7468   Warren, Raymond. "O do not love too long", The Pity
       of Love, MS 1965. Cyc.: t solo, gtr.

Down by the Salley Gardens   See: Old Song re-sung, An

Dream of a Blessed Spirit, A   See: "All the heavy days are
   over"

Dream of Death, A   See: Epitaph, An

Dreaming of the Bones, The   (DR)   Little Review (Jan. 1919)

7469   Rummel, Walter. L: MacM, 1921 in Four Plays for
       Dancers. Incidental music for 4 players: med.
       (chanting) v. on hp. (or z.); sp. on fl., sp. on
       any bowed instr.; sp. on dr. Dr. part may be
       played by 2nd and 3rd players alternating. Score
       (dated 1917) accompanied the 1921 edn. of the
       play.

Yeats, W.B. continued

7470   Victory, Gerard. MS 1948. Incidental music: ned.
       v. trio (1 solo), fl., dr.

Drinking Song, A   "Wine comes in at the mouth"   The Green
Helmet and Other Poems (1910)

7471   Bodley, Seoirse. MS ca. 1953. Song: bar solo, pf.

7472   Boydell, Brian. "Drinking Song", Three Yeats Songs,
       MS 1965, avail. RTE. Song: s solo, Irish hp. Arr.
       for s solo, orch. and incl. in Four Yeats Poems,
       MS 1966, avail. RTE.

7473   Healey, Derek. Six Irish Songs, MS 1962, avail. CMC.
       Song: solo v., pf.

7474   Keats, Donald. NY: GS, 1965. Song: 4 pt. male
       chorus, a cap.

7475* Warlock, Peter. "Wine comes in...", MS 1920-22.

7476   Weigel, Eugene. Four Songs for Women's Voices,
       Northampton, Mass.: NVMP, 1950. Song: ssa, a cap.

Drunken Man's Praise of Sobriety, A   "Come swish around, my
pretty punk"   New Poems (1938)

7477   Harvey, Jonathan. Four Songs of Yeats, MS 1965.
       Song: b solo, pf.

Easter, 1916   "I have met them at close of day"   New
Statesman (Oct. 1920), publ. sep. (priv.) 1916

7478   Boydell, Brian. A Terrible Beauty is Born, MS 1965,
       avail. RTE. Cta.: s solo, satb, narr., orch.

Echtge of Streams   "I cried when the moon was murmuring"
Speaker (Aug. 1900), rev. 1903

7479* Warlock, Peter. "The Withering of the Boughs", The
       Curlew, L: S&B, 1924 (1973). Cyc.: t solo, fl.,
       eng. hn., str. qrt.

Yeats, W.B. continued

Ephemera   "'Your eyes that once were never weary of
    mine...'"   The Wanderings of Oisin and Other Poems (1889)

    7480 Hadley, Patrick. MS ca. 1924. Song: s or t solo, ch.
          orch.

Epitaph, An   "I dreamed that one had died"   National
    Observer (Dec. 1891), rev. 1895

    7481 Gilman, Lawrence. "A Dream of Death", Newton Center:
          Wa-Wan, 1903 in Wa-Wan Series of American
          Compositions, Vol. 2. Setting for reciter, pf.

    7482 Milford, Robin. "A Dream of Death", L: OUP, pre-
          1958. Song: b solo, pf.

    7483 Moeran, E.J. "A Dream of Death", L: OUP, 1925. Song:
          bar solo, pf.

    7484 Whettam, Graham. "A Dream of Death", Three Songs
          from "The Rose", MS, perf. London 1967. Score
          rev. 1973 (title rev. to read: Three Songs to
          Poems of W.B. Yeats). Song: high v., pf.

Everlasting Voices   "O sweet everlasting Voices, be still"
    New Review (Jan. 1896), rev. 1899

    7485 Kelly, Thomas. MS 1959, avail. RTE. Song: satb, a
          cap.

    7486 Roderick-Jones, Richard. "The Everlasting Voices",
          The Wind Among the Reeds, MS 1966. Cyc.: s solo,
          pf.

    7487 Warlock, Peter. "The Everlasting Voices", MS 1915.
          Song: [solo v., pf.].

    7488 Wickens, Dennis. "The Everlasting Voices", The Ever-
          lasting Voices, MS. Cyc.: high v., pf.

Everlasting Voices, The   See: Everlasting Voices

Faery Host, The   "Host is riding from Knocknarea, The"
    National Observer (Oct. 1893), rev. same year, rev. 1899

846

Yeats, W.B. continued

7489   Loeffler, Charles. "The Hosting of the Sidhe", The
        Wind Among the Reeds, NY: GS, 1908. Song: [high]
        solo v., pf. Incl. in Five Irish Fantasies, NY:
        GS, 1935. Song: solo v., orch.

Faery Song, A   "We who are old, old and gay"   National
Observer (Sept. 1891)

7490   Brian, Havergal. L: JWC, pre-1940. Song: [v., pf.?].

7491   Gurney, Ivor. "We Who Are Old", MS 1920. Song: [solo
        v., pf.].

7492   Warren, Raymond. Irish Madrigals, MS 1959. Cta.:
        ssatb, a cap.

Falling of the Leaves   "Autumn is over the long leaves"
The Wanderings of Oisin and Other Poems (1889), rev. 1895

7493   Blank, Allan. "The Falling of the Leaves", MS,
        avail. ACA. Song: med. v., pf.

7494   Marshall, Nicholas. "The Falling of the Leaves", The
        Falling of the Leaves, MS. Song: high v., treble
        rec., vcl., hpd.

7495   Parke, Dorothy. "The Falling of the Leaves", MS
        1963. Song: solo v., pf.

Falling of the Leaves, The   See: Falling of the Leaves

Father and Child   "She hears me strike the board"   The
Winding Stair (1929) as one of "A Woman Young and Old"

7496   Routh, Francis. A Woman Young and Old, MS 1962.
        Song sequence: s solo, pf.

Fiddler of Dooney, The   "When I play on my fiddle in Dooney"
Bookman (Dec. 1892)

7497   Andrews, Mark. MS pre-1939, NY: HWG. Song: [solo v.,
        pf.?].

Yeats, W.B. continued

7498   Bax, Arnold. MS 1907. Song: solo v., pf.

7499   Butler, Walter. Four Irish Lyrics, L: BH, pre-1940.
       Song: [v., pf.].

7500   Dunhill, Thomas F. The Wind Among the Reeds, L: S&B,
       1905. Cyc.: solo v., pf.

7501   Frank, Francis. L: N, pre-1940. Song: [solo v.,
       pf.?].

7502   Gurney, Ivor. A Fourth Volume of Ten Songs, L: OUP,
       1959. Song: solo v., pf.

7503   Hageman, Richard. NY: GS, pre-1940. Song: [solo v.,
       pf.?].

7504   Harty, Hamilton. Five Irish Songs, L: BH, pre-1938.
       Song: [v., pf.].

7505   Homer, Sidney. NY: GS, 1909. Song: solo v., pf.

7506   Loeffler, Charles. Five Irish Fantasies, NY: GS,
       1935. Song: solo v., orch.

7507   Marshall, Nicholas. The Falling of the Leaves, MS.
       Song: high v., treble rec., vcl., hpd.

7508   Milford, Robin. A Book of Songs, L: OUP, 1925. Song:
       b solo, pf. or unison v., pf.

7509   Rieti, Vittorio. Two Songs Between Two Waltzes,
       Hastings-on-Hudson: GMP, 1964. Song: ms solo,
       pf.

7510   Webber, W.S. Lloyd. L: AH&C, 1964. Song: 2 pt.
       chorus, [pf.?].

Fighting the Waves   (DR)   Wheels and Butterflies (1934)

7511   Antheil, George. L: MacM, 1934 in Wheels and
       Butterflies. Incidental music: v., pf. Score
       accompanied the 1st edn. of the play.

First Confession, A   "I admit the briar"   The Winding Stair
(1929) as one of "A Woman Young and Old"

Yeats, W.B. continued

7512 Wilson, James. "I admit...", A Woman Young and Old,
      MS 1966. Cyc.: s solo, Irish hp. Also arr. for
      s solo, pf. or s solo, orch.

Folk of the Air, The   See: Stolen Bride, The

Folly of Being Comforted, The   "One that is ever kind said
yesterday"   Speaker (Jan. 1902)

7513 Gurney, Ivor. A Second Volume of Ten Songs, L: OUP,
      1938. Song: solo v., pf.

Fool by the Roadside, The   "When all works that have"
Seven Poems and a Fragment (1922) as part of "Cuchulain
the Girl and the Fool", rev. 1925, rev. 1928

7514 Routh, Francis. A Woman Young and Old, MS 1962.
      Song sequence: s solo, pf.

For Anne Gregory   "Never shall a young man"   Spectator
(Dec. 1932), rev. same year

7515 Dalby, Martin. "Yellow Hair", MS. Song: s solo, pf.

7516 Duke, John. "Yellow Hair", NY: Row, 1953. Song: med.
      v., pf.

7517 Routh, Francis. A Woman Young and Old, MS 1962.
      Song sequence: s solo, pf.

7518 Warren, Raymond. The Pity of Love, MS 1965. Cyc.:
      t solo, gtr.

Four Ages of Man, The   "He with body waged a fight"   London
Mercury (Dec. 1934) & Poetry, Chicago (Dec. 1934)

7519 Harvey, Jonathan. Four Songs of Yeats, MS 1965.
      Song: b solo, pf.

From 'Oedipus at Colonus'   "Endure what life God gives"
October Blast (1927)

849

Yeats, W.B. continued

    7520 Bodley, Seoirse. "Never to have lived is best", MS
          1965, avail. RTE. Song: s solo, orch.

    7521 Warren, Raymond. Songs of Old Age, Borough Green: N,
          1971. Cyc.: bar solo, pf.

From the 'Antigone' "Overcome--O bitter sweetness" The
Winding Stair (1929) as one of "A Woman Young and Old"

    7522 Routh, Francis. A Woman Young and Old, MS 1962.
          Song sequence: s solo, pf.

Full Moon in March, A (DR) Poetry, Chicago (Mar. 1935),
publ. sep. same year

    7523 Harvey, Jonathan. MS 1966. Opera: 2 s, 2 bar soli,
          ch. orch.

    7524 Warren, Raymond. MS 1961. Incidental music.

Girl's Song "I went out alone" New Republic (Oct. 1930)

    7525 Berger, Arthur. Three Poems of Yeats, NY: NME, 1950.
          Song: solo v., fl., cl., vcl.

    7526 Duncan, Chester. MS 1966. Song: a solo, pf.

    7527 Eaton, John. Three Yeats Songs, MS, avail DWG: SPI.
          Song: s solo, pf.

Hanrahan laments because of his Wanderings See: Maid Quiet

Hanrahan reproves the Curlew See: O'Sullivan Rua to the
Curlew

Happy Townland, The "There's many a strong farmer" Weekly Critical Review (June 1903), rev. same year

    7528 Gurney, Ivor. MS 1920. Song: [solo v., pf.].

Harp of Aengus, The "Edain came out of Midhir's hill"

Yeats, W.B. continued

7529 Swain, Freda. MS 1922, avail. Chinnor: Channel,
      NEMO. Symph. poem: orch.

He bids his Beloved be at Peace   See: Shadowy Horses, The

He hears the Cry of the Sedge   See: Aedh hears the Cry of
the Sedge

He reproves the Curlew   See: O'Sullivan Rua to the Curlew

He tells of a Valley full of Lovers   See: Valley of Lovers,
The

He tells of the perfect Beauty   See: Aedh tells of the perfect Beauty

He thinks of those who have spoken Evil of his Beloved   See:
Aedh thinks of those who have spoken Evil of his Beloved

He wishes for the Cloths of Heaven   See: Aedh wishes for the
Cloths of Heaven

He wishes his Beloved were dead   See: Aodh to Dectora

Heart of the Woman, The   "O what to me the little room"
    Speaker (July 1894) as part of "Those Who Live in the
    Storm", rev. 1897

    7530 Eichheim, Henry. B: BMC, pre-1940. Song: [solo v.,
          pf.?].

    7531 Gilman, Lawrence. Newton Center: Wa-Wan, 1903 in
          the Wa-Wan Series of American Compositions, Vol.
          2. Song: [low] solo v., pf.

Her Anxiety   "Earth in beauty dressed"   New Republic (Oct.
1930)

851

7532 Beeson, Jack. Three Love Songs, MS. Song: low female v., pf.

Her Dream "I dreamed as in my bed I lay" New Republic (Oct. 1930)

7533 Young, Douglas. Realities, MS 1970-73, L: F (hire). Cyc.: s solo, fl., cl., vla. Complete cyc. also requires t solo, b. cl., vcl., perc., hpd.

Her Triumph "I did the dragon's will until you came" The Winding Stair (1929) as one of "A Woman Young and Old"

7534 Routh, Francis. A Woman Young and Old, MS 1962. Song sequence: s solo, pf.

7535 Wilson, James. "I did...", A Woman Young and Old, MS 1966. Cyc.: s solo, Irish hp. Also arr. for s solo, pf. or s solo, orch.

Her Vision in the Wood "Dry timber under that rich foliage" The Winding Stair (1929) as one of "A Woman Young and Old"

7536 Wilson, James. "Dry timber...", A Woman Young and Old, MS 1966. Cyc.: s solo, Irish hp. Also arr. for s solo, pf. or s solo, orch.

Hero, the Girl, and the Fool, The   See: Fool by the Road-side, The

His Confidence "Undying love to buy" New Republic (Oct. 1930)

7537 Berger, Arthur. Three Poems of Yeats, NY: NME, 1950. Song: solo v., fl., cl., vcl.

Host, The   See: Faery Host, The

Host of the Air, The   See: Stolen Bride, The

Yeats, W.B. continued

Hosting of the Sidhe, The   See: Faery Host, The

Hour-Glass, The   (DR)   North American Review (Sept. 1903),
     publ. sep. same year. New version 1st publ. in Mask (Apr.
     1913), publ. sep. 1914

     7538* Anon. L: MacM, 1922 in Plays in Prose and Verse.
           Spoken song: v., unacc. Setting of lines
           beginning: "I was going the road one day", Engl.
           transl. by the author of stanzas of a Gaelic
           ballad for use in the play. Score (trad. Aran
           air) accompanied the 1922 edn. of the play.

     7539 Warren, Raymond. MS 1962. Incidental music.

I am of Ireland   "I am of Ireland"   Words for Music Perhaps
     and Other Poems (1932)

     7540 Aston, Peter. Five Songs of Crazy Jane, L: N, 1964.
           Cyc.: s solo, unacc.

Indian Song, An   "Island dreams under the dawn, The"
     Dublin University Review (Dec. 1886), rev. 1895

     7541 Burtch, Mervyn. "The Island Dream", MS. Song: a
           solo, fl., pf.

Indian to his Love, The   See: Indian Song, An

Into the Twilight   See: Celtic Twilight, The

Jealousy   "Send peace on all the lands"   The Wanderings of
     Oisin and Other Poems (1889), rev. 1895

     7542 Burtch, Mervyn. "Anashuya and Vijaya", MS.
           Ch. opera: ms, t soli, fl., ob., cl., hn., str.
           qrt., pf.

King's Threshold, The   (DR)   (1904) New version 1st publ.
     in Poems, 1899-1905 (1906), publ. sep. 1911, rev. 1922

Yeats, W.B. continued

7543* Farr, Florence. L: MacM, 1922 in _Plays in Prose_
      and Verse. Spoken song: v., unacc. Setting of
      lines beginning: "The four rivers that run
      there". Score accompanied the 1922 edn. of the
      play.

7544 Nelson, Havelock. MS. Incidental music.

Lake Isle of Innisfree, The   "I will arise and go now"
      National Observer (Dec. 1890)

7545 Braun, Ruth. MS n.d., avail. NYPL. Song: solo v.,
      pf.

7546 Butler, Walter. _Four Irish Lyrics_, L: BH, pre-1940.
      Song: [v., pf.].

7547 Couch, Janette. MS 1955, avail. University of Auck-
      land. Song: low v., pf.

7548 Foote, Arthur. B: Schmidt, pre-1940. Song: s or t
      solo, pf.

7549 Gibbs, Geoffrey D. MS. Song: med.-low v., pf.

7550 Griffes, Charles T. "The Lake at Evening", _Three_
      Tone-Pictures, NY: GS, 1915. Pf. solo. Arr. for
      ch. ensemble, opt. ww., opt. hp.; also arr. for
      dbl. qnt., pf. Score contains the following
      quotation: "...for always...I hear lake water
      lapping with low sounds by the shore".

7551 Gurney, Ivor. MS 1918. Song: [solo v., pf.].

7552 Herbert, Muriel. L: Elkin, pre-1940. Song: solo v.,
      pf. Arr. by Basil Ramsey for sa, pf. Arr. publ.
      L: Elkin, 1963.

7553 Kelly, Thomas. "Innisfree", MS 1949. Song: solo v.,
      pf.

7554 Lehmann, Liza. MS pre-1918, L: BH. Song: [solo v.,
      pf.?].

7555 Ley, Henry G. _Album of Songs_, MS (Opus 8), L: Acott;
      publ. sep. L: OUP, 1950. Song: ms or t solo, pf.

Yeats, W.B. continued

7556 Morrison, A. L: BH, pre-1940. Song: [solo v., pf.?].

7557 Palmer, John. Chi.: Summy, pre-1940. Song: [solo v., pf.?].

7558 Peel, Graham. The Country Lover, L: C, 1910. Song: [solo v., pf.].

7559 Poston, Elizabeth. L: WR, pre-1940. Song: [solo v., pf.?].

7560 Ritchie, Tom. MS. Song: solo v., pf.

7561 Willan, Healey. Healey Willan Song Albums, No. 2, Oakville: FH, 1926. Song: med. v., pf.

7562 Willan, Healey. "Poem (or Celtic Sketch No. 1)", MS 1903-05, completed and rev. 1930. Str. qtr. only. Scored for str. orch. 1950, avail. For.: Berandol. Adagio movement contains the following quotation: "And evening full of the linnet's wings".

7563* Willan, Healey. "Sonata No. 3 in B minor", MS 1922, avail. CMC. Sonata: vln., pf. Score contains the following quotation: "An [sic] evening full of the linnet's wings".

7564 Zanders, Douglas. MS 1952, avail. University of Canterbury. Song: solo v., pf.

Land of Heart's Desire, The   (DR)   (1894), rev. 1903

7565 Boughton, Rutland. "Celtic Prelude", L: A, 1920. Rhapsody: vln., vcl., pf. Music is based on a song (not publ.) composed for the play.

7566 Hart, Fritz. MS 1914. Opera.

7567* Gilbert, Henry F. "Faery Song", Newton Center: Wa-Wan, 1905 in Wa-Wan Series of American Compositions Vol. 4. Song: [solo v., pf.].

7568 Gurney, Ivor. "The Wind blows out of the Gates of the Day", MS n.d. Song: [solo v., pf.]. Setting of lines beginning: "The wind blows out of the gates of the day".

Yeats, W.B. continued

    7569   Nelson, Havelock. "The Lonely of Heart", L: Curwen,
            1968. Song: ssa, pf. Setting of lines beginning:
            "The wind blows out of the gates of the day".

    7570   Shaw, Martin. L: Curwen, 1917. Song: solo v., pf.
            Also avail. for solo v., ob., stgs. Setting of
            lines beginning: "The wind blows out of the gates
            of the day".

Last Confession, A   "What lively lad most pleasured me"
The Winding Stair (1929) as one of "A Woman Young and
Old"

    7571   Wilson, James. "What lively...", A Woman Young and
            Old, MS 1966. Cyc.: s solo, Irish hp. Also arr.
            for s solo, pf. or s solo, orch.

Leda and the Swan   "Sudden blow: the great wings beating
    still, A"   Dial (June 1924), priv. publ. sep. 1935

    7572   Langert, Jules. MS. Song: bar solo, pf.

    7573   Tanenbaum, Elias. Cygnology (Three Songs on Leda and
            the Swan), MS copyright by composer 1958, avail.
            ACA. Song: s solo, orch.

    7574   Westergaard, Peter. "Cantata III (Leda and the
            Swan)", MS 1961, Mz.: S (AVV), n.d. Cta.: ms
            solo, cl., vla., vibra., mrmb.

Long-legged Fly   "That civilisation may not sink"   London
Mercury (Mar. 1939)

    7575   Wilson, James. Upon Silence, MS (Opus 54). Song: s
            solo, unacc.

Lover mourns for the Loss of Love, The   See: Aedh laments
the Loss of Love

Lover pleads with his Friend for old Friends, The   See:
Song "Though you are in..."

856

Yeats, W.B. continued

Lover tells of the Rose in his Heart, The   See: Rose in my
    Heart, The

Lullaby   "Beloved, may your sleep be sound"   The New
    Keepsake (1931)

    7576 Beeson, Jack. MS. Song: a solo, pf.

    7577 Eaton, John. Three Yeats Songs, MS, avail. DWG: SPI.
          Song: s solo, pf.

    7578 Tippett, Michael. L: S, 1960. Song: sextet (2 s, a,
          2 t, b), ssttb, a cap. or a (or c-t) solo,
          ssttb, a cap.

    7579 Wilson, James. Yeats Songs, MS (Opus 39). Song: s
          solo, pf.

Lyric from an Unpublished Play, A   "Put off that mask of
    burning gold"   The Green Helmet and Other Poems (1910),
    rev. 1913

    7580 Warren, Raymond. "The Mask", The Pity of Love, MS
          1965. Cyc.: t solo, gtr.

Mad Song, A   "I went out to the hazel wood"   Sketch (Aug.
    1897), rev. 1899

    7581 Bourgeois, Derek. "Song of Wandering Aengus", Six
          Songs of Wandering, MS 1962. Cyc.: bar solo, pf.

    7582 Brown, James. "The Song of Wandering Aengus", MS.
          Song: bar or b solo, pf.

    7583 Droste, Doreen. "The Song of Wandering Aengus", NY:
          GX, 1973. Song: satb, a cap.

    7584 Leitch, Donovan. "Song of Wandering Aengus", L:
          Donovan. Song: [v., pf.?].

Maid Quiet*   "Where has Maid Quiet gone to"   Poems Lyrical
    and Narrative (1908)

    7585 Gurney, Ivor. MS n.d. Song: [solo v., pf.].

857

Yeats, W.B. continued

7586 Rieti, Vittorio. <u>Two Songs Between Two Waltzes,</u>
      Hastings-on-Hudson: GMP, 1964. Song: ms solo, pf.

Mask, The   See: Lyric from an Unpublished Play, A

Meeting "Hidden by old age awhile" <u>The Winding Stair</u>
(1929) as one of "A Woman Young and Old"

      7587 Routh, Francis. <u>A Woman Young and Old,</u> MS 1962.
            Song sequence: s solo, pf.

Men Improve with the Years   "I am worn out with dreams"
<u>Little Review</u> (June 1917)

      7588 Warren, Raymond. <u>Songs of Old Age,</u> Borough Green: N,
            1971. Cyc.: bar solo, pf.

Michael Robartes bids his Beloved be at Peace   See: Shadowy
Horses, The

Moods, The   "Time drops in decay"   <u>Bookman</u> (Aug. 1893)

      7589 Warren, Raymond. <u>Irish Madrigals,</u> MS 1959. Cta.:
            ssatb, a cap.

Mother of God, The   "Threefold terror of love, The"   <u>Words</u>
<u>for Music Perhaps and Other Poems</u> (1932)

      7590 Harvey, Jonathan. <u>Cantata I,</u> L: N, 1968. Cta.: s,
            bar soli, satb, ch. orch.

Nativity   "What woman hugs her infant there?"   <u>London</u>
<u>Mercury</u> (Dec. 1938), rev. 1939

      7591 Duncan, Chester. "A Nativity", <u>Then and Now,</u> Water-
            loo: Waterloo, 1974. Song: ssa, pf. The other
            song in the collection requires unison (s) v.

Nativity, A   See: Nativity

858

Yeats, W.B. continued

No Second Troy   "Why should I blame her"   The Green Helmet
and Other Poems (1910)

7592   Shifrin, Seymour. MS. Song: s solo, pf.

O do not love too long   See: Do not love too long

Old Men admiring themselves in the Water, The   "I heard the
old, old men say"   Pall Mall Magazine (Jan. 1903)

7593   Bissell, Keith. MS 1973, avail. CMC. Song: satb, pf.

7594   Rollin, Robert. "The Old Men", Four Songs of Dreams
       and Love, MS. Song: bar solo, fl., vln., vla.,
       vcl. Complete set of songs also requires ms solo,
       ms, bar duet, ob., pf.

7595   Warren, Raymond. Songs of Old Age, Borough Green: N,
       1971. Cyc.: bar solo, pf.

Old Song re-sung, An   "Down by the salley gardens my love
and I did meet"   The Wanderings of Oisin and Other Poems
(1889), rev. 1895

7596   Blank, Allan. "Down by the Salley Gardens", MS,
       avail. ACA. Song: med. v., pf.

7597   Brash, James. "Down by the Salley Gardens", L: C,
       1945. Song: [solo v., pf.].

7598   Britten, Benjamin, arr. "The Salley Gardens", Folk
       Song Arrangements, Vol. I, L: BH, 1943. Song:
       trad. Irish tune arr. for high v., pf.

7599   Clarke, Rebecca. "Down by the Salley Gardens", L:
       WR, pre-1940. Song: [solo v., pf.].

7600   Collins, J.H. "Down by the Salley Gardens", Two
       Songs, L: OUP, 1929. Song: bar solo, pf. or
       a, bar duet, pf.

7601   Deale, Edgar M., arr. "Down by the Salley Gardens",
       L: Elkin, 1957. Song: trad. melody arr. for ssa,
       accompaniment unspecified.

859

7602   DeBeer, Allen. "Down by the Salley Gardens", L: JWC, pre-1940. Song: [solo v., pf.?].

7603   DeCevee, Alice. "Down by the Salley Gardens", NY: CF, pre-1940. Song: [solo v., pf.?].

7604   Gurney, Ivor. "Down by the Salley Gardens", A First Volume of Ten Songs, L: OUP, 1938. Song: solo v., pf.

7605   Hinchliffe, Irvin. "Down by the Salley Gardens", L: MM, 1931, copyright assigned L: C, 1943. Song: [solo v., pf.].

7606   Hughes, Herbert. "Down by the Salley Gardens", L: BH, 1909. Song: solo v., pf.

7607   Ireland, John. "The Salley Gardens", Songs Sacred and Profane, L: S, 1934. Cyc.: solo v., pf. Also publ. sep. (for low v., pf.).

7608   Methold, Diane. "Down by the Salley Gardens", L: CR, 1937. Song: solo v., pf.

7609   Plumstead, Mary. "Down by the Salley Gardens", L: Curwen, 1951. Song: solo v., pf.

7610   Rollin, Robert. "Down by the Salley Gardens", Four Songs of Dreams and Love, MS. Song: bar solo, fl., ob., pf. Complete set of songs also requires ms solo, ms, bar duet, vln., vla., vcl.

7611   Shaw, Martin. "Down by the Salley Gardens", L: Curwen, 1919. Song: bar voices, pf.

7612   Taylor, H. Stanley. "Down by the Salley Gardens", L: Curwen, 1963. Song: solo v., pf. (or hp.), rec. ad lib.

7613   Vine, John, arr. "Down by the Salley Gardens", L: OUP, 1937. Song: Irish air arr. for ssa, a cap. Also avail. for satb, a cap.

7614   Wieniawska, Irene. "Down by the Salley Gardens", L: C, 1900. Song: [solo v., pf.].

Yeats, W.B. continued

> 7615 Woodgate, Leslie, arr. "Down by the Salley Gardens",
>   L: OUP, 1950. Song: Irish air arr. for 2 pt.
>   chorus of equal v., [a cap.?].

On Baile's Strand (DR) In the Seven Woods (1903), publ.
sep. 1905. New version 1st publ. in Poems, 1899-1905
(1906), publ. sep. 1907

> 7616* Farr, Florence. L: MacM, 1922 in Plays in Prose
>   and Verse. Spoken songs: v., unacc. Settings of
>   lines beginning: "Cuchulain has killed kings",
>   "May this fire have driven out", "When you were
>   an acorn on the tree-top". Scores accompanied the
>   1922 edn. of the play.

> 7617 Warren, Raymond. MS 1968. Incidental music.

Only Jealousy of Emer, The (DR) Poetry, Chicago (1919)

> 7618 Harris, Russell G. MS, avail. ACA. Opera 2 s, a, t
>   soli, 5 speakers, vln., cl., eng. hn., bsn.,
>   trbn., db.

> 7619 Harrison, Lou. MS 1949. Incidental music: fl., vcl.,
>   cel., prepared pf., db. Issued on Esoteric re-
>   cording #ES-506.

> 7620 Hywel, John. MS. Incidental music: ms solo, fl.,
>   vln., perc.

> 7621 Rollin, Robert. MS. Incidental music: bar solo,
>   fl., vcl., mandolin.

> 7622 Warren, Raymond. MS 1968. Incidental music.

O'Sullivan Rua to the Curlew "O Curlew, cry no more in the
air" Savoy (Nov. 1896) as one of "Windlestraws", rev.
1899, rev. 1906

> 7623 Gilman, Lawrence. "The Curlew", Three Songs, Newton
>   Center: Wa-Wan, 1904 in Wa-Wan Series of American
>   Compositions, Vol. 3. Setting for reciter, pf.

Yeats, W.B. continued

7624 Roderick-Jones, Richard. "He Reproves the Curlew",
      The Wind Among the Reeds, MS 1966. Cyc.: s solo,
      pf.

7625* Warlock, Peter. "He Reproves the Curlew", The
      Curlew, L: S&B, 1924 (1973). Cyc.: t solo, fl.,
      eng. hn., str. qrt.

O'Sullivan the Red upon his Wanderings   See: Maid Quiet

Out of the Old Days   "Be you still, be you still"   Savoy
    (Nov. 1896) as one of "Windlestraws", rev. 1899, rev. 1922

7626 Roderick-Jones, Richard. "To his Heart, bidding it
      have no Fear", The Wind Among the Reeds, MS 1966.
      Cyc.: s solo, pf.

7627 Schwartz, Paul. "To his heart, bidding it have no
      fear", A Poet To His Beloved, MS 1945. Cyc.: high
      v., pf. or med. v., pf.

Pilgrim, The   "I fasted for some forty days"   Broadside
    (Oct. 1937)

7628 O'Murnaghan, Art, arr. Dublin: Cuala, 1937 in Broad-
      side, No. 10. Song: v., unacc. Trad. air (arr. by
      O'Murnaghan) accompanied the 1st publ. of the
      poem.

Pity of Love, The   "Pity beyond all telling, A"   The
    Countess Kathleen and Various Legends and Lyrics (1892)

7629 Warren, Raymond. The Pity of Love, MS 1965. Cyc.:
      t solo, gtr.

Player Queen, The   (DR)   Dial (Nov. 1922), publ. sep. same
    year

7630 Carpenter, John A. See: Song from an Unfinished
      Play.

7631* Hughes, Spike. MS 1927. Incidental music.

862

eats, W.B. continued

7632 Warren, Raymond. MS 1964. Incidental music.

Poet pleads with his Friend for old Friends, The   See:
Song "Though you are in..."

Poet to his Beloved, A   "I bring you with reverent hands"
Senate (May 1896) as part of "O'Sullivan the Red to Mary
Lavell", rev. 1899

  7633 Schwartz, Paul. A Poet To His Beloved, MS 1945.
        Cyc.: high v., pf. or med. v., pf.

Pot of Broth, The   (DR)   Gael (Sept. 1903), publ. sep. 1905

  7634* Anon. L: MacM, 1922 in Plays in Prose and Verse.
        Spoken song: v., unacc. Setting of lines
        beginning: "There's broth in the pot for you old
        man". Score (trad. air) accompanied the 1922 edn.
        of the play.

  7635 Haufrecht, Herbert. "A Pot of Broth", MS, prod.
        WNYC Radio, NY, 1964, avail. ACA. Opera: s, t,
        bar soli, orch.

Prayer for my Daughter, A   "Once more the storm is howling"
Irish Statesman (Nov. 1919) & Poetry, Chicago (Nov. 1919)

  7636 Crosse, Gordon. "Ceremony", L: OUP, 1962. Vcl. solo,
        orch. Score contains the following quotation:
        "How but in custom and in ceremony/Are innocence
        and beauty born?".

Purgatory   (DR)   Last Poems and Two Plays (1939)

  7637 Crosse, Gordon. L: OUP, 1968. Ch. opera: t, bar
        soli, ssa (or 2 s, a soli), fl., 2 cl., bsn.,
        tpt., hn., trbn., vln., vla., vcl., db., 2 perc.,
        hp., pf. Score contains German transl. by Ernst
        Roth.

  7638 Warren, Raymond. MS 1962. Incidental music.

Yeats, W.B. continued

7639 Weisgall, Hugo. Bryn Mawr: Merion, 1959. Opera:
      t (or high bar), b soli, orch.

Red Hanrahan's Song about Ireland   See: Cathleen, the
   Daughter of Hoolihan

Resurrection, The   (DR)   Adelphi (June 1927) New version
   publ. in Stories of Michael Robartes and his Friends
   (1931)

   7640 Joubert, John. "Incantation", L: N, 1957. Song: s
         solo, satb, a cap. Sets lines beginning: "I saw
         a staring virgin stand".

Rider from the North, The   See: Happy Townland, The

Rosa Mundi   "Who dreamed that beauty passes like a dream?"
   National Observer (Jan. 1892), rev. same year

   7641 Verrall, John. "The Rose of the World", MS n.d.,
         avail. ACA. Song: s solo, fl., pf.

Rose in my Heart, The   "All things uncomely and broken"
   National Observer (Nov. 1892), rev. 1899, rev. 1906

   7642 Marshall, Nicholas. "The Lover tells of the Rose in
         his Heart", The Falling of the Leaves, MS. Song:
         high v., treble rec., vcl., hpd.

Rose of the World, The   See: Rosa Mundi

Running to Paradise   "As I came over Windy Gap"   Poetry,
   Chicago (May 1914)

   7643 Stevens, Bernard. L: N, 1968. Song: satb, pf.

Sailing to Byzantium   "That is no country for old men"
   October Blast (1927)

Yeats, W.B. continued

7644 Ashforth, Alden. Byzantia: Two Journeys after Yeats,
MS. Composition for quadraphonic tape. Also arr.
for tape, org. Arr. in prep. for release on Orion
recording.

7645 Warren, Raymond. Songs of Old Age, Borough Green: N,
1971. Cyc.: bar solo, pf.

Second Coming, The "Turning and turning in the widening
gyre" Nation (Nov. 1920)

7646 Harvey, Jonathan. Cantata I, L: N, 1968. Cta.: s,
bar soli, satb, ch. orch.

Secrets of the Old, The "I have old women's secrets now"
London Mercury (May 1927) as one of "Two Songs from the
Old Countryman"; incl. as part of "The Old Countryman" in
October Blast (1927); incl. as part of "A Man Young and
Old" in The Tower (1928)

7647 Barber, Samuel. Four Songs, MS 1938, NY: GS. Song:
solo v., pf.

Shadowy Horses "I hear the Shadowy Horses" Savoy (Jan.
1896), rev. 1899, rev. 1906

7648 Homer, Sidney. "Michael Robartes bids his Beloved
be at Peace", MS (Opus 17), NY: GS. Song: [solo
v., pf.?].

Shadowy Waters, The (DR) North American Review (May
1900), publ. sep. same year. New version 1st publ. in
Poems, 1899-1905 (1906), publ. sep. 1907

7649* Kalomiris, Manolis. Athens: copyright by composer
1951. "Musical dramatic poem": s, t, bar, b soli,
chorus, orch. Greek paraphrase by Veta
Pezopoulos with Engl. adapt. to music by Denis
Georgilopoulos. Retransl. into Engl. by Geoffrey
Dunn; publ. in this form L: BBC, 1953.

7650 Swain, Freda. See: Harp of Aengus, The.

Yeats, W.B. continued

7651 Willan, Healey. MS 1960, avail. CMC. Incidental
       music for radio: hp. only.

Song "Though you are in your shining days" Saturday
Review (July 1897), rev. 1899, rev. 1906

7652 Schwartz, Paul. "The Lover pleads with his Friends
       for old Friends", A Poet To His Beloved, MS 1945.
       Cyc.: high v., pf. or med. v., pf.

Song, A "I thought no more was needed" Nine Poems (1918)

7653 Warren, Raymond. Songs of Old Age, Borough Green:
       N, 1971. Cyc.: bar solo, pf.

Song from an Unfinished Play "My mother dandled me and
sang" Poetry, Chicago (May 1914), rev. 1916

7654 Carpenter, John A. "The Player Queen", NY: GS, 1915.
       Song: solo v., pf.

Song from "The Player Queen", A   See: Song from an Unfinished Play

Song for Music, A   "Come, let me sing into your ear"
London Mercury (Nov. 1930), rev. 1932

7655 Aston, Peter. "Those Dancing Days are Gone", Five
       Songs of Crazy Jane, L: N, 1964. Cyc.: s solo,
       unacc.

7656 Huggler, John. "For Coloratura, Clarinet, Viola,
       Cello", MS 1958, avail. ACA. Setting for cs solo,
       cl., vla., vcl.

7657 Warren, Raymond. "Those dancing days are gone",
       Songs of Old Age, Borough Green: N, 1971. Cyc.:
       bar solo, pf.

7658 Young, Douglas. "Those Dancing Days are Gone",
       Realities, MS 1970-73, L: F (hire). Cyc.: t solo,
       vcl. Complete cyc. also requires s solo, fl.,
       b. cl., perc., hpd.

Yeats, W.B. continued

Song of Red Hanrahan, The   See: Cathleen, the Daughter of
    Hoolihan

Song of the Old Mother, The   "I rise in the dawn"   Bookman
    (Apr. 1894)

    7659 Housman, Rosalie. MS, avail. NYPL. Song: solo v.,
        pf.

Song of Wandering Aengus, A   See: Mad Song, A

Sophocles' King Oedipus   (DR)   (1928) Transl. from
    Sophocles

    7660* Robinson, Lennox. L: MacM, 1928 in Sophocles'
        King Oedipus. Incidental music: t, bar, b soli,
        chorus of b voices, a cap. Score accompanied the
        1st edn. of the play.

    7661 Shifrin, Seymour. NY: CFP (hire). Cta.: female
        chorus, str. qrt., pf. or female chorus, str.
        orch., pf. Setting of lines beginning: "What can
        the shadow-like generations of man attain".

Stolen Bride, The   "O'Driscoll drove with a song"   Bookman
    (Nov. 1893), rev. 1894, rev. 1899

    7662 Dunhill, Thomas F. "Host of the Air", The Wind Among
        the Reeds, L: S&B, 1905. Cyc.: solo v., pf.

    7663 Loeffler, Charles. "The Host of the Air", The Wind
        Among the Reeds, NY: GS, 1908. Song: [high] solo.
        v., pf. Incl. in Five Irish Fantasies, NY: GS,
        1935. Song: solo v., orch.

    7664 Marshall, Nicholas. "The Host of the Air", The
        Falling of the Leaves, MS. Song: high v., treble
        rec., vcl., hpd.

Stolen Child, The   "Where dips the rocky highland"   Irish
    Monthly (Dec. 1886)

Yeats, W.B. continued

7665 Manson, Gloria E. MS 1956, avail. University of
      Otago. Song: solo v., choir, pf.

7666 Rootham, C.B. L: S&B, 1911. Song: satb, pf. or satb,
      orch.

Sweet Dancer   "Girl goes dancing there, The"   London
Mercury (Mar. 1938)

   7667 Harvey, Jonathan. Four Songs of Yeats, MS 1965.
         Song: b solo, pf.

   7668 Wilson, James. Yeats Songs, MS (Opus 39). Song: s
         solo, pf.

Those Dancing Days are Gone   See: Song for Music, A

Three Bushes, The   "Said lady once to lover"   London
Mercury (Jan. 1937)

   7669 Dulac, Edmund. Dublin: Cuala, 1937 in Broadside, No.
         3. Song: v., unacc. Score (attributed to Edmond
         Dulac [sic]) accompanied the Cuala Press edn. of
         the poem.

Three Things   "'O cruel Death, give three things back'"
New Republic (Oct. 1929), publ. sep. same year

   7670 Young, Douglas. Realities, MS 1970-73, L: F (hire).
         Cyc.: s, t soli, fl., b. cl., vla., vcl., hpd.,
         perc. Complete cyc. also requires cl.

To a Child dancing in the Wind   See: To a Child dancing upon
the Shore

To a Child dancing upon the Shore   "Dance there upon the
shore"   Poetry, Chicago (Dec. 1912), rev. 1913

   7671* Wood, Hugh. "To a Child dancing in the Wind", L: N,
         1974. Song: satb, a cap.

868

Yeats, W.B. continued

To a Friend whose Work has come to Nothing   "Now all the
truth is out"   Poems Written in Discouragement (1913)

   7672* Wood, Hugh. MS 1973. Song: satb, a cap.

To a Squirrel at Kyle-na-no   "Come play with me"   New
Statesman (Sept. 1917)

   7673 Weigel, Eugene. Four Songs for Women's Voices,
        Northampton, Mass.: NVMP, 1950. Song: ssa, a cap.

To a Young Girl   "My dear, my dear, I know"   Nine Poems
(1918)

   7674 Rorem, Ned. NY: BH, 1972. Song: solo v., pf.

To an Isle in the Water   "Shy one, shy one"   The Wanderings
of Oisin and Other Poems (1889)

   7675 Blank, Allan. MS, avail. ACA. Song: med. v., pf.

   7676 Brian, Havergal. L: JWC, pre-1940. Song: [v., pf.?].

   7677 Clarke, Rebecca. "Shy One", L: WR, 1920. Song: solo
        v., [pf.].

   7678 Johnson, Phoebe. L: C, 1921. Song: [solo v., pf.].

   7679 Le Fleming, Christopher. L: JWC, 1931. Song: ms or
        bar solo, pf.

   7680 Mallinson, Albert. Oakville: FH, 1907. Song: s or t
        solo, pf.

   7681 Weigel, Eugene. Four Songs for Women's Voices,
        Northampton, Mass.: NVMP, 1950. Song: ssa, a cap.

   7682 Whithorne, Emerson. "Shy One", NY: GS, pre-1940.
        Song: [v., pf.?].

   7683 Willan, Healey. Healey Willan Song Albums, No. 2,
        Oakville: FH, 1926. Song: med. v., pf.

Yeats, W.B. continued

To his Heart, bidding it have no Fear   See: Out of the Old
   Days

To my Heart, bidding it have no Fear   See: Out of the Old
   Days

Under Ben Bulben   "Swear by what the sages spoke"   Irish
   Times (Feb. 1939) & Irish Independent (Feb. 1939)

   7684   Eaton, John. "Under Ben Bulben V", Three Yeats
          Songs, MS, avail. DWG: SPI. Song: s solo, pf.
          Sets lines beginning: "Irish poets, learn your
          trade".

Unicorn from the Stars, The   (DR)   In coll. with Lady
   Gregory   The Unicorn from the Stars and Other Plays
   (1908)

   7685* Anon. L: MacM, 1922 in Plays in Prose and Verse.
          Spoken song: v., unacc. Setting of
          lines beginning: "Oh come, all ye airy
          bachelors", "Oh, Johnny Gibbons, my five hundred
          healths to you", "When the lion will lose his
          strength". Scores (trad. Irish airs) accompanied
          the 1922 edn. of the play.

Valley of Lovers, The   "I dreamed that I stood in a valley"
   Saturday Review (Jan. 1897), rev. 1899, rev. 1906

   7686   Damon, Julia. NY: GS (Wa-Wan), pre-1940. Song: [solo
          v., pf.?].

Valley of the Black Pig, The   "Dews drop slowly and dreams
   gather, The"   Savoy (Apr. 1896) as one of "Two Poems
   Concerning Peasant Visionaries"

   7687   Roderick-Jones, Richard. The Wind Among the Reeds,
          MS 1966. Cyc.: s solo, pf.

Voices   "'What do you make so fair and bright?'"   Dublin
   University Review (Mar. 1885), rev. 1895

Yeats, W.B. continued

7688   Bryson, R. Ernest. "The Cloak, the Boat, and the
       Shoes", MS pre-1927. Song: chorus, orch.

7689   Butler, Walter. "The Cloak, the Boat, the Shoes",
       Four Irish Lyrics, L: BH, pre-1940. Song: [v.,
       pf.].

7690   Warren, Raymond. "The Cloak, the Boat, and the
       Shoes", Irish Madrigals, MS 1959. Cta.: ssatb,
       a cap.

When You are Old   "When you are old and grey and full of
sleep"   The Countess Kathleen and Various Legends and
Lyrics (1892)

7691   Bridge, Frank. L: C, 1920. Song: solo v., pf. Set-
       ting of stanzas 1 and 2.

7692   Droste, Doreen. NY: AMP, 1968. Song: satb, pf.

7693   Fearing, John. Vancouver: Western, 1968. Song: med.
       v., pf.

7694   Gurney, Ivor. "When You are Old and Gray", MS ca.
       1909. Song: [solo v., pf.].

7695   Mourant, Walter. MS, avail. ACA. Song: med. v., pf.

7696   Rieti, Vittorio. Two Songs Between Two Waltzes,
       Hastings-on-Hudson: GMP, 1964. Song: ms solo, pf.

7697   Ritchie, Tom. "When You are Old and Gray", MS. Song:
       high v., pf. or low v., pf.

7698   Warren, Raymond. The Pity of Love, MS 1965. Cyc.:
       t solo, gtr.

7699   Whettam, Graham. Three Songs from "The Rose", MS,
       perf. London 1967. Score rev. 1973 (title rev. to
       read: Three Songs to Poems of W.B. Yeats). Song:
       high v., pf.

Where my Books Go   "All the words that I gather"   Irish
Fairy Tales (1892)

7700 Campbell-Tipton, Louis. "All...", MS pre-1921, NY: GS. Song: [solo v., pf.?].

7701 Gurney, Ivor. "All the words that I utter ('Song in the Night')", MS 1925. Song: [solo v., pf.].

White Birds, The   "I would that we were, my beloved, white birds" National Observer (May 1892)

7702 Marshall, Nicholas. The Falling of the Leaves, MS. Song: high v., treble rec., vcl., hpd.

Wild Swans at Coole, The   "Trees are in their autumn beauty, The" Little Review (June 1917)

7703 Grant, Parks. MS (Opus 12). Song: ms or bar solo, pf.

Withering of the Boughs, The   See: Echtge of Streams

Young Man's Song, The   "I whispered, 'I am too young'" The Green Helmet and Other Poems (1910), subsequently rev.

7704 Blank, Allan. "Brown Penny", MS, avail. ACA. Song: med. v., pf.

7705 Rieti, Vittorio. "Brown Penny", Two Songs Between Two Waltzes, Hastings-on-Hudson: GMP, 1964. Song: ms solo, pf.

7706 Rollin, Robert. "Brown Penny", Four Songs of Dreams and Love, MS. Song: ms, bar duet, fl., ob., vln., vla., vcl., pf. Complete work also requires ms, bar soli.

7707 Warren, Raymond. "Brown Penny", The Pity of Love, MS 1965. Cyc.: t solo, gtr.

Youth and Age   "Though leaves are many, the root is one" McClure's Magazine (Dec. 1910), rev. same year

7708 Jones, Robert W. "The Coming of Wisdom with Time", Ph.: EV, 1973. Motet: satb, a cap.

Yeats, W.B. continued

7709   Schwartz, Francis. "Wisdom", NY: P-S, in prep. for
        publ. Song: low v., tape.

Miscellanea

7710   Anon. "The Cloths of Heaven", MS, avail. University
        of Canterbury. Song: satb, a cap. [Text by
        Yeats?]

7711   Bennett, Richard R. Crazy Jane, MS 1968-69, L: UE.
        Setting[s?] for s solo, ch. ensemble (cl., pf.,
        vcl.).

7712   Clarke, Rebecca. "A Dream", L: WR, 1928. Song: solo
        v., pf. Text by Yeats. [Possibly a setting of "A
        Dream of Death"?]

7713   Erickson, Elaine M. "Down by the Salley Gardens",
        NY: CMP. Song: s or t solo, str. orch. [Text by
        Yeats?]

7714   Forrest, Oswald. "The Wind Among the Reeds", L: C,
        1902. Song: solo v., pf.

7715   Hadley, Patrick. Crazy Jane, MS pre-1973. Cyc.: a
        solo, hp.

7716   Harvey, Jonathan. The July 1975 issue of Musical
        Times cites Four Images after Yeats (MS 1969),
        and "Its companion piece, 'Purgatory'".

7717   Hawkins, John. Three Cavatinas, Tor.: Berandol,
        1969. Cavatina: s solo, vln., vcl., cel., perc.
        Incl. fragments from The Winding Stair.

7718   Larchet, John F. Reference is made to Larchet's
        settings of poems by Yeats in Joseph Detheridge's
        A Chronology of Music Composers: 1810-1937
        (Birmingham: J. Detheridge, 1937).

7719   Maconchy, Elizabeth. Six Yeats Settings, MS 1951.
        Settings for s solo, ssa, cl., 2 hn., hp.

7720   Nelson, Havelock. "W.B. Yeats", MS. Incidental music
        to TV documentary.

Yeats, W.B. continued

   7721 O'Gallagher, Eamonn. "A Tribute to W.B. Yeats", MS
         1949. Film music.

   7722 Raxach, Enrique. The Looking-Glass, NY: P, 1972.
         Org. solo. A quotation from Yeats is appended
         to one leaf of the score.

   7723 Somers, Harry. Zen, Yeats and Emily Dickinson, MS,
         perf. CBC, Apr. 1975. Settings for s solo, 2 sp.,
         fl., pf., tape. Texts (selected and arr. by the
         composer) incl. single words, phrases and stanzas
         from Yeats' works.

   7724 Swain, Freda. The composer has discontinued an opera
         (cited in Grove's) which was to be based on a
         play by Yeats.

   7725 Tippett, Michael. Music for Words Perhaps, MS ca.
         1960. Incidental music: speaking voices, ch.
         ensemble. Text made up of a sequence of poems by
         Yeats.

YOUNG, Andrew John   1885-1971

   Last Snow   "Although the snow still lingers"   In The Collected Poems of Andrew Young (1960)

   7726 Rose, Michael. Winter Music, L: N, 1967. Cta.: satb,
         pf. duet, perc. ad lib.

   Stockdoves, The   "They rose up in a twinkling cloud"   In
   The Collected Poems of Andrew Young (1960)

   7727 Poston, Elizabeth. L: OUP, 1945. Song: v., pf.

   Miscellanea

   7728 Genzmer, Harald. "Entbietung", Irische Harfe, MS
         1965, L: P. Setting for 4-8 mixed v. Engl.
         transl.: "Summons". Text by [Andrew?] Young.

INDEX OF COMPOSERS

INDEX OF COMPOSERS

It should be noted that the spelling of certain names and,
in other instances, the dates of birth and death are in
dispute. Various sources provide various details. The editors
have attempted to verify their information as far as possible,
and have attempted to be accurate with respect to the spelling
of particular non-English language names (possible initial V
[as in Vassilenko] is here an initial W). Variant spellings
are not provided, as other sources often give this information.

ABADY, H. Temple   1903-1970

    Belloc, Hilaire   370

ABRAMSON, Robert   ?-

    Housman, A.E.   3272

ADAMS, A. Davies   ?-

    Kipling, Rudyard   4074 4101

ADAMS, Stephen   ?-

    Housman, A.E.   3424

ADDINSELL, Richard   1904-

    Beerbohm, Max   364
    Coward, Noël   1176 1177
    Dane, Clemence   1198 1199 1200 1202 1203 1204
                                 1205 1206 1207 1208 1209 1211
                                 1212 1213
    Priestley, J.B.   5490

ADDISON, John   1920-

    Graves, Robert   2378*
    Housman, A.E.   3195

ADENEY, Marcus   1900-

    Hardy, Thomas   2544

ADLER, Samuel Hans   1928-

    Binyon, Laurence   562

ADLER continued

de la Mare, Walter	1738
Dobson, Austin	1875
Graves, Robert	2431
Joyce, James	3852
Stephens, James	5875 5895 5954 5973
Wolfe, Humbert	7327 7339 7341 7344

AGASSIZ, Edward   ?-

Kipling, Rudyard   3981 4090

AGNEW, Roy E.   1893-1944

Masefield, John   4877

AINSWORTH, Robert   ?-

Housman, A.E.   3341 3358

AITKEN, G.   ?-

Kipling, Rudyard   4139

ALAIN, Jehan Ariste   1911-1940

Kipling, Rudyard   4339

ALISON-CROMPTON, C.   ?-
Nom de plume of Mrs. Constance Crompton

Masefield, John   4946 4961 4969

ALLAM, Edward   ?-

de la Mare, Walter   1409 1489 1618 1687 1778 1828

ALLEN, Creighton   1900-

Joyce, James   3604
Macleod, Fiona   4622

ALLEN, Elizabeth Youel   ?-

Henley, W.E.   2890

ALLEN, Harold   1917-

    Hopkins, Gerard Manley   3074
    Stevenson, Robert Louis   6146

ALLGOOD, Sarah   ?-

    Yeats, W.B.   7461*

ALLITSEN, Frances   1849-1912

    Bridges, Robert   783
    Dobson, Austin   1886
    Henley, W.E.   2829 2876
    Meredith, George   5066
    Watson, William   7085

ALPAERTS, Flor   1876-1954

    Wilde, Oscar   7263*

ALWYN, William   1905-

    Flecker, James Elroy   2190
    MacNeice, Louis   4815*
    Wells, H.G.   7144

AMBROS, Vladimír   1890-1956

    Yeats, W.B.   7397

AMBROSE, Paul   ?-

    Swinburne, A.C.   6651

AMES, Phillip   ?-

    Kipling, Rudyard   3982

AMRAM, David Werner   1930-

    Auden, W.H.   234

ANDERSON, A.   ?-

    Macleod, Fiona   4635

ANDERSON, Barry   ?-

   Joyce, James   3927

ANDERSON, Dwight   ?-

   Brooke, Rupert   815

ANDERSON, Ronald Kinloch   ?-

   Drinkwater, John   1986

ANDERSON, Rose   ?-

   Dobson, Austin   1887

ANDREWS, Herbert Kennedy   1904-1965

   Ford, Ford Madox   2218
   Housman, A.E.   3312
   Stephens, James   5959
   Stevenson, Robert Louis   6514

ANDREWS, Mark   1875-1939

   Aldington, Richard   73
   de la Mare, Walter   1688
   Masefield, John   4927
   Noyes, Alfred   5328
   Stevenson, Robert Louis   6024 6096 6221 6266 6285 6355
                                   6394 6467 6515
   Yeats, W.B.   7497

ANDRIESSEN, Jurriaan   1925-

   Shaw, George Bernard   5662

ANGEL, James   ?-

   Colum, Padraic   1074

ANHALT, Istvan   1919-

   de la Mare, Walter   1766
   Eliot, T.S.   2087

ANON.

Chesterton, G.K.	942
Dane, Clemence	1214
Gregory, Lady Augusta	2450*
Newbolt, Henry	5285
Synge, J.M.	6838
Wesker, Arnold	7147 7148 7150 7151
Yeats, W.B.	7406* 7416 7457 7538* 7634*
	7685* 7710

ANON., arr.

Wesker, Arnold	7149

ANSON, Hugo Vernon   1894-1958

Flecker, James Elroy	2207
Sackville-West, Victoria	5569

ANTHEIL, George   1900-1959

Joyce, James	3754 3886
Yeats, W.B.	7511

APIVOR, Denis   1916-

Aldington, Richard	78
Belloc, Hilaire	495
Dowson, Ernest	1919
Eliot, T.S.	2057 2077 2113 2129 2144 2153
	2160 2176
MacBeth, George	4517
Thomas, Dylan	6859 6884

ARAPOV, Boris Alexandrovitch   1905-

Maugham, Somerset	5014

ARCHER, Violet Balestreri   1913-

de la Mare, Walter	1689 1705 1739
Eliot, T.S.	2058 2114 2161
Wolfe, Humbert	7336

ARDAYNE, Paul   ?-

Ledwidge, Francis	4428

ARMITAGE, Irène   ?-

    de la Mare, Walter   1394

ARMITAGE, Marie T., arr.   ?-

    Kipling, Rudyard   3983

ARMSTRONG, Thomas H.W.   1898-

    Housman, A.E.   3220 3395 3514

ARNELL, Richard Anthony Sayer   1917-

    Doyle, Arthur Conan   1965

ARUNDELL, Dennis Drew   1898-

Conrad, Joseph	1140
Flecker, James Elroy	2191 2192
Ford, Ford Madox	2219
Graves, A.P.	2369
Herbert, A.P.	2938
Masefield, John	4909
Priestley, J.B.	5489
Shaw, George Bernard	5679

ASHBEE, C.R.   ?-

    Masefield, John   4889

ASHBEE, Janet E.   ?-

    Masefield, John   4890

ASHFORTH, Alden   1933-

    Yeats, W.B.   7393 7644

ASHTON, John H.   1938-

    Owen, Wilfred   5429

ASTON, Peter   1938-

Raine, Kathleen	5504 5510 5513 5515 5517
Yeats, W.B.	7440 7453 7540 7655

ATHERTON, Percy Lee   1871-1944

    Housman, A.E.   3484
    Swinburne, A.C.   6694
    Watson, William   7088 7104

ATKINS, Ivor Algernon   1869-1953

    Meynell, Alice   5096

ATKINS, Norton   ?-

    Kipling, Rudyard   4340

ATKINSON, Holway   ?-

    Kipling, Rudyard   4110

ATKINSON, Robert [Whitman]   [1868-1933?]

    Kipling, Rudyard   4167

AUERBACH, Norman   ?-

    de la Mare, Walter   1496 1736 1804

AURIC, Georges   1899-

    Shaw, George Bernard   5663

AUSTIN, Frederic   1872-1952

    Davies, W.H.   1295
    de la Mare, Walter   1758 1806
    Dowson, Ernest   1945
    Drinkwater, John   2010* 2013
    Hardy, Thomas   2536 2574 2729
    Herbert, A.P.   2940
    Yeats, W.B.   7367*

AUSTIN, Richard   ?-

    Herbert, A.P.   2946

AVERY, Stanley R.   1879-post-1910

    Meynell, Alice   5097

881

AVRIL, Edwin Frank   1920-

    Housman, A.E.   3221 3425

AVSHALOMOV, Jacob   1919-

    Housman, A.E.   3205
    Joyce, James   3634

AXT, William   1882-1959

    Shaw, George Bernard   5674

AYLWARD, Florence   ?-

    Doyle, Arthur Conan   1982
    Kipling, Rudyard   4306
    Newbolt, Henry   5276 5283

AYRES, Frederic   1876-1926
Also known as Frederick Ayres Johnson

    Kipling, Rudyard   4114 4341
    Masefield, John   4856

BAAS, Alexius   ?-

    Chesterton, G.K.   964
    Kipling, Rudyard   4180

BABBIT, Milton Byron   1916-

    Hopkins, Gerard Manley 3075 3106
    Thomas, Dylan   6936

BABER, Joseph W.   1937-

    de la Mare, Walter   1470
    Hardy, Thomas   2575
    Hodgson, Ralph   2954
    Housman, A.E.   3342

BABIN, Victor   1908-1972

    Housman, A.E.   3207

BACON, Ernst   1898-

    Housman, A.E.   3374
    Stevenson, Robert Louis   6468

BAILEY, Judith M.   1941-

    Grahame, Kenneth   2350
    Sitwell, Sacheverell   5778
    Swinburne, A.C.   6665

BAINTON, Edgar Leslie   1880-1956

    A E   21
    Bottomley, Gordon   586 594 596
    Bridges, Robert   601
    Davies, W.H.   1258
    Gibson, W.W.   2289 2291 2329 2330
    Graves, Robert   2405
    Macleod, Fiona   4704
    Monro, Harold   5199
    Swinburne, A.C.   6695
    Thompson, Francis   7013

BAIRD, Tadeusz   1928-

    Conrad, Joseph   1141

BAIRSTOW, Edward Cuthbert   1874-1946

    Meynell, Alice   5074

BAKER, Clara Belle, arr.   ?-

    Stevenson, Robert Louis   6128 6368 6548

BAKER, Michael   1942-

    Rodgers, W.R.   5560

BAKSA, Robert F.   1938-

    Housman, A.E.   3386 3426 3469

BALDWIN, Ralph Lyman   1872-1943

    Kipling, Rudyard   4062
    Thompson, Francis   7019

BALENDONCK, Armand   ?-

    Stevenson, Robert Louis   6243 6516

BALMIRES, B.   ?-

    Kipling, Rudyard   3984

BANTOCK, Granville   1868-1946

    AE   8
    Bennett, Arnold   534
    de la Mare, Walter   1779
    Dowson, Ernest   1935 1936
    Flecker, James Elroy   2195
    Kipling, Rudyard   4004 4274
    Macleod, Fiona   4575 4581 4649 4664 4693 4699
                                4708 4720 4743 4750 4770
    Meredith, George   5039
    Newbolt, Henry   5240 5246 5256* 5278
    Squire, J.C.   5866
    Stevenson, Robert Louis   6326 6549
    Swinburne, A.C.   6606
    Wilde, Oscar   7264 7279

BARBER, Samuel   1910-

    Auden, W.H.   154 183
    Graves, Robert   2393 2406 2410
    Hopkins, Gerard Manley   2988
    Housman, A.E.   3485
    Joyce, James   3657 3698 3796 3829 3887
    Logue, Christopher   4507
    Spender, Stephen   5859*
    Stephens, James   5877 5883* 5898 5903* 5938
    Yeats, W.B.   7647

BARBOUR, Florence Newell   1866-1946

    Swinburne, A.C.   6683

BARGIELSKI, Zbigniew   1937-

    Auden, W.H.   198
    Eliot, T.S.   2052

BARLOW, David   1927-1975

Belloc, Hilaire   450
Chesterton, G.K.   943
de la Mare, Walter   1456
Hopkins, Gerard Manley   2989

BARNES, Fairbairn   ?-

Campbell, (I.) Roy   854

BARNES, Marshall H.   1921-

Macleod, Fiona   4617 4618 4628 4686
Masefield, John   4894 4915 4928 4981
Stevenson, Robert Louis 6469

BARNETT, Alice   ?-

Le Gallienne, Richard   4452
Macleod, Fiona   4690

BARON, Maurice   1889-1964

Wilde, Oscar   7288

BARRATT, Edgar   1877-

Masefield, John   4825

BARRELL, Bernard   1919-

Chesterton, G.K.   990

BARRELL, Joyce   1917-

Housman, A.E.   3256 3387

BART, Lionel   1930-

Stevenson, Robert Louis   6383

BARTHOLOMEW, Marshall Moore   1885-

de la Mare, Walter   1524 1663
Noyes, Alfred   5360

885

BARTLETT, Homer Newton   1845-1920

    Stevenson, Robert Louis   6123 6212
    Swinburne, A.C.   6696

BARTLEY, Ewart Andrew   1909-

    Masefield, John   4826

BASSETT, Karolyn Wells   1892-1931

    Henley, W.E.   2886
    Le Gallienne, Richard   4472

BATE, Stanley Richard   1913-1959

    Housman, A.E.   3515
    Joyce, James   3629 3823 3877 3880 3897 3928
                                   3929

BATH, Hubert   1883-1945

    Buchanan, Robert   845 846
    Gregory, Lady Augusta   2447
    Hardy, Thomas   2679
    Macleod, Fiona   4582 4593 4607 4615 4636 4771
                                   4772 4773

BATTEN, Mrs. George   ?-

    Kipling, Rudyard   4102

BATTON, Joseph   ?-

    Chesterton, G.K.   1001

BAWDEN, Clarence K.   ?-

    Noyes, Alfred   5343

BAX, Arnold Edward Trevor   1883-1953
Occasionally wrote under the pseud. "Dermot O'Byrne"

    AE   32 43 49 70
    Barrie, J.M.   291
    Bax, Clifford   299 301 302 303 304 305 306
    Campbell, Joseph   858 873
    Colum, Padraic   1066 1075 1109 1120 1121 1124

BAX continued

Cousins, James	1175
Hardy, Thomas	2597 2662 2687
Housman, A.E.	3173 3211 3427
Joyce, James	3898
Macleod, Fiona	4572 4595 4612 4623 4629 4634
	4637 4651 4653 4661 4665 4676
	4706 4711 4730 4748 4762 4774
Masefield, John	4912 4986
Read, Herbert	5533
Stephens, James	5948
Swinburne, A.C.	6669 6697
Synge, J.M.	6829
Trench, Herbert	7027 7029
Yeats, W.B.	7498

BAYNON, Arthur   1889?-1954

Davidson, John	1224
Gould, Gerald	2345
Housman, A.E.	3516

BEACH, John Parsons   1877-1953

| Henley, W.E. | 2893 |

BEACH, Mrs. Henry Harris Aubrey   1867-1944

| Henley, W.E. | 2774 2830* 2855 |

BEARD, Vivian   ?-

| Auden, W.H. | 93* |

BEAUMONT, Adrian   1937-

| Sassoon, Siegfried | 5579 5580 5588 5606 5627 5633 |

BÉCAUD, Gilbert   1927-

| Synge, J.M. | 6857 |

BECKER, John Joseph   1886-1961

| Symons, Arthur | 6822 |
| Synge, J.M. | 6831 |

BECKETT, John   ?-

    Beckett, Samuel   318* 361*

BECKWITH, John   1927-

    Sitwell, Edith   5698 5730 5749 5768

BEDFORD, David   1937-

    Clarke, Arthur C.   1018
    Dowson, Ernest   1916

BEDFORD, Herbert   1867-1945

    Yeats, W.B.   7368

BEECROFT, Norma   1934-

    Eliot, T.S.   2078

BEELER, Walter, arr.   ?-

    Barrie, J.M.   274

BEESON, Jack Hamilton   1921-

    Betjeman, John   539* 546*
    Eliot, T.S.   2076
    Huxley, Aldous   3561
    Lawrence, D.H.   4380
    Yeats, W.B.   7444 7450 7532 7576

BEHREND, Arthur Henry   1853-?

    Kipling, Rudyard   4297

BELCHAMBER, Eileen   ?-

    de la Mare, Walter   1444 1486 1789 1829 1830
    Drinkwater, John   1995
    Wilde, Oscar   7186

BELL, Florence Eveleen Elenore Olliffe, arr.   ?-

    Stevenson, Robert Louis 6025 6139 6183 6187 6199 6222
                          6244 6254 6303 6395 6470 6499

BELL, Maurice   ?-

    Kipling, Rudyard   4037

BELLAMY, Peter   1944-

    Kipling, Rudyard   3950 3954 3960 3969 3977 3978
                              4007 4008 4012 4025 4042 4049
                              4056 4084 4087 4089 4097 4099
                              4136 4182 4191 4195 4196 4197
                              4246 4250 4252 4259 4261 4270
                              4279 4280 4282 4285 4299*
                              4303 4307 4309 4313 4314 4317
                              4327 4336

BELLOC, (Joseph) Hilaire Pierre   1870-1953

    Belloc, Hilaire   449 526

BĚLOHLÁVEK, Jiří   1946-

    Shaw, George Bernard   5685

BENJAMIN, Arthur   1893-1960

    de la Mare, Walter   1379
    Dunsany, Lord   2028
    Hodgson, Ralph   2957
    Macleod, Fiona   4602 4691 4751 4768
    Moore, T. Sturge   5219
    O'Sullivan, Seumas   5405

BENNETT, Charles   ?-

    Le Gallienne, Richard   4465

BENNETT, J.S.L.D.   ?-
    [Also wrote under the pseud. "L. Dampier"?]

    Kipling, Rudyard   4005 4028 4130 4199

BENNETT, Joan   ?-

    de la Mare, Walter   1747

BENNETT, Richard Rodney   1936-

    Auden, W.H.   204

BENNETT continued

Binyon, Laurence	561
Conrad, Joseph	1143
Mitchell, Adrian	5196
Shaw, George Bernard	5666
Sitwell, Edith	5692
Whiting, John	7154*
Yeats, W.B.	7711

BENNETT, Robert Russell   1894-

Coward, Noël	1179
Huxley, Aldous	3562

BENNETT, Robert Sterndale   ?-1963

Stevenson, Robert Louis	6550

BENNETT, William Douglas   ?-

Auden, W.H.	91

BENSON, Warren   1924-

Davies, W.H.	1246

BENTLEY, Alys Eliza   ?-

Stevenson, Robert Louis	6114 6369

BERG, Josef   1927-1971

Shaw, George Bernard	5684

BERGER, Arthur Victor   1912-

Yeats, W.B.	7447 7525 7537

BERGER, Jean   1909-

Belloc, Hilaire	413 423 434 488 493 523
Kipling, Rudyard	3975 4289 4294

BERGH, Arthur   1882-1962

Swinburne, A.C.	6679

BERGMANN, Walter   ?-

   Belloc, Hilaire   444

BERIO, Luciano   1925-

   Auden, W.H.   164*
   Joyce, James   3605 3789 3853 3888* 3889
                      3915

BERKELEY, Lennox Randal Francis   1903-

   Auden, W.H.   97 122 144 149 160 236
   Bridges, Robert   739
   Davies, W.H.   1285
   de la Mare, Walter   1352 1482 1490 1519 1592 1601
                      1657 1664 1706 1759
   Durrell, Lawrence   2041
   Graves, Robert   2385
   Hopkins, Gerard Manley   2999 3118
   Lee, Laurie   4443 4446 4447 4449
   Symons, Arthur   6760 6775 6811 6816
   Yeats, W.B.   7415

BERNERS, Gerald Hugh Tyrwhitt-Wilson   1883-1950

   Graves, Robert   2408
   Masefield, John   4960
   Sitwell, Sacheverell   5781

BERNSTEIN, Leonard   1918-

   Auden, W.H.   83
   Barrie, J.M.   275

BERRIDGE, A.   ?-

   Kipling, Rudyard   4200*

BESLY, Maurice   1888-1945
                      °
   Belloc, Hilaire   470
   Chesterton, G.K.   965 994
   de la Mare, Walter   1457 1598 1740
   Hardy, Thomas   2705
   Macleod, Fiona   4591
   Noyes, Alfred   5333
   Stephens, James   5992

BESLY continued

Symons, Arthur	6762
Wolfe, Humbert	7317
Yeats, W.B.	7422

BETTS, Lorne M.   1918-

Joyce, James	3606 3642 3670 3672 3699 3711
	3714 3734 3761 3777 3785 3797
	3810 3830 3844 3854 3881 3906
	3916
Stevenson, Robert Louis	6551
Synge, J.M.	6847

BEVAN, Clifford   1934-

Graves, Robert	2430

BEVERIDGE, Thomas   1938-

Joyce, James	3762

BEVERLEY, Bewicka   ?-

Kipling, Rudyard	4115*

BEVERSDORF, Thomas   1924-

Eliot, T.S.	2136

BIALOSKY, Marshall   1923-

Auden, W.H.	81*

BIELAWA, Herbert   1930-

Graves, Robert	2389

BILGER, H.L.   ?-

Housman, A.E.	3428

BILLIN, Reginald   ?-

Swinburne, A.C.	6652

BILLINGHAM, Kathleen   ?-

    Stevenson, Robert Louis   6327

BILLINGSLEY, William A.   1922-

    Joyce, James   3624 3692 3715 3845 3903 3917
                  3925

BINGHAM, Seth   1882-1972

    Kipling, Rudyard   4033

BINKERD, Gordon W.   1916-

    Hardy, Thomas   2490 2553 2572 2642 2657 2660
    Kipling, Rudyard   4332*
    Muir, Edwin   5230
    O'Casey, Sean   5377

BIRGE, Edward Bailey   ?-

    Stevenson, Robert Louis   6060

BIRTWISTLE, Harrison   1934-

    Logue, Christopher   4508

BISHOP, Franklin H.   ?-

    Bottomley, Gordon   595

BISSELL, Keith Warren   1912-

    Bridges, Robert   740
    Housman, A.E.   3273
    Monro, Harold   5201
    Stevenson, Robert Louis   6328
    Yeats, W.B.   7593

BLACK, Charles   1903-

    Chesterton, G.K.   944

BLACK, Jennie Prince   1868-1945

    Macleod, Fiona   4688

BLACKBURN, Marie   ?-

    Stevenson, Robert Louis   6552

BLAIR, William   ?-

    Noyes, Alfred   5327

BLAKE, Anita Mary   ?-

    Gibson, W.W.   2318

BLAKE, David   1936-

    Read, Herbert   5530

BLAKE, Donna   ?-

    Grahame, Kenneth   2351

BLAKE, Leonard   ?-

    Chesterton, G.K.   991

BLANCHARD, G.F.   ?-

    Kipling, Rudyard   4201

BLANEY, Norah   ?-

    Stevenson, Robert Louis   6026 6267

BLANK, Allan   ?-

    Graves, Robert   2412 2436
    Housman, A.E.   3429
    Lawrence, D.H.   4415
    Yeats, W.B.   7493 7596 7675 7704

BLATNÝ, Pavel   1931-

    Beckett, Samuel   356
    Greene, Graham   2440
    Priestley, J.B.   5488
    Wilde, Oscar   7202

BLEADON, Alice M.   ?-

    Meynell, Alice   5098

BLISS, Arthur Edward Drummond   1891-1975

    Auden, W.H.   128
    Belloc, Hilaire   371
    Churchill, Winston   1017
    Cornford, Frances   1166 1170
    Crossley-Holland, Kevin 1182 1187 1189 1191 1194 1195
                             1196
    Davies, W.H.   1259 1286 1299 1302
    Day Lewis, C.   1324 1338 1339 1340
    de la Mare, Walter   1391 1502 1525 1578
    Eliot, T.S.   2177
    Fry, Christopher   2233
    Hardy, Thomas   2504 2534
    Hopkins, Gerard Manley   2972 2990 3097
    Housman, A.E.   3430*
    Joyce, James   3824
    Nichols, Robert   5295 5296 5302 5303
    Owen, Wilfred   5449
    Priestley, J.B.   5495
    Raine, Kathleen   5503 5505 5509 5512 5518 5520
                             5524 5525
    Reed, Henry   5537
    Sassoon, Siegfried   5585
    Strong, L.A.G.   6589*
    Thomas, Dylan   6866
    Wells, H.G.   7143

BLITZSTEIN, Marc   1905-1964

    O'Casey, Sean   5375
    Shaw, George Bernard   5655

BLOSDALE, Don L.   ?-

    Henley, W.E.   2904
    Wilde, Oscar   7291

BLOWER, Maurice   ?-

    Bridges, Robert   614 642
    Henley, W.E.   2819
    Symonds, John Addington 6717

BLUMENFELD, Harold   1923-

    Sassoon, Siegfried   5581 5582 5587 5631

BLUMENTHAL, Jacob Jacques   1829-1908

    Stevenson, Robert Louis 6553
    Swinburne, A.C.   6698 6699

BLYTON, Carey   1932-

    Herbert, A.P.   2932 2939
    Tolkien, J.R.R.   7022
    Wilde, Oscar   7283

BOARDMAN, Herbert Russell   1892-1941

    Noyes, Alfred   5341

BODDE, Margaret Peddle   ?-

    Stevenson, Robert Louis 6517

BODLEY, Seoirse   1933-

    Yeats, W.B.   7471 7520

BOEHLE, William R.   1919-

    Brooke, Rupert   825

BONNER, Eugene MacDonald   1889-

    Joyce, James   3680

BONTOFT, Frederic   ?-

    de la Mare, Walter   1353

BORDEN, David R.   1938-

    Thomas, Dylan   6914

BORNSCHEIN, Franz Carl   1879-1948

    Kipling, Rudyard   4091

```
BOSSI, Renzo        1883-1965

  Wilde, Oscar            7190 7236

BOUGHTON, Rutland    1878-1960

  Buchanan, Robert        843
  Carpenter, Edward       914 915 921 922 923 924 925
                          926 927
  Chesterton, G.K.        962 966 979
  Davies, W.H.            1229 1237 1245
  Drinkwater, John        1985 1991 1992 1994 2008 2022
  Hardy, Thomas           2535* 2569* 2647 2651 2730*
  Henley, W.E.            2919
  Housman, A.E.           3377
  Housman, Laurence       3530
  Kipling, Rudyard        4006 4023 4032 4275 4281
  Macleod, Fiona          4588 4598 4609 4630 4646 4677
                          4716 4721 4725 4775 4776
  Masefield, John         4861 4884
  Meredith, George        5043
  Swinburne, A.C.         6611 6641 6700
  Thompson, Francis       7006
  Webb, Mary              7111 7112 7119
  Yeats, W.B.             7565

BOULT, Adrian Cedric    1889-

  Kipling, Rudyard        4262

BOURGEOIS, Derek    1941-

  Chesterton, G.K.        995
  Eliot, T.S.             2066
  Hardy, Thomas           2568
  Yeats, W.B.             7581

BOUVERIE, H.M.P.    ?-
Also known as Countess Radnor

  Kipling, Rudyard        4202

BOVE, J. Henry    ?-

  Dunsany, Lord           2036
```

BOWER, Neville   ?-

    Belloc, Hilaire   460 485
    Buchanan, Robert   847

BOWERS, Robert Hood   1877-1941

    Wilde, Oscar   7203

BOWLES, M.   ?-

    Stephens, James   5888 5904 5961 5986 5993

BOWLES, Paul Frederic   1910-

    Koestler, Arthur   4364

BOWMAN, Aubrey C.   ?-

    Warner, Sylvia Townsend   7068

BOYD, Jeanne Margaret   1890-

    Masefield, John   4837

BOYD, Malcolm   ?-

    Bridges, Robert   648

BOYDELL, Brian   1917-

    AE   37
    Joyce, James   3618 3635 3682 3700 3778 3798
                          3812 3831 3855 3899
    Ledwidge, Francis   4437
    Yeats, W.B.   7369 7407 7408 7462 7472 7478

BOYER, [?]   ?-

    Hardy, Thomas   2752

BOYLE, Ina   ?-1967

    de la Mare, Walter   1744 1748
    Meredith, George   5024

```
BRADFORD, Humphrey Noel    ?-

    Kipling, Rudyard           4184
    Le Gallienne, Richard      4464

BRADLEY, William    ?-

    Stevenson, Robert Louis    6268

BRAINARD, H.L.    ?-

    Henley, W.E.               2831

BRAINE, Robert    1896-1940

    Galsworthy, John           2248  2254
    Johnson, Lionel            3599

BRAND, Margaret    1913-1953

    Colum, Padraic             1076

BRANSCOMBE, Gena    1881-

    Housman, A.E.              3486

BRANSON, David    1909-

    de la Mare, Walter         1831
    Hardy, Thomas              2753
    Housman, A.E.              3265  3396  3517
    Masefield, John            4987

BRASH, James    ?-

    Yeats, W.B.                7597

BRATT, C. Griffith    1914-

    Masefield, John            4929

BRAUN, Ruth Fisher    ?-

    Yeats, W.B.                7545

BRAY, K.I.    ?-

    Swinburne, A.C.            6625
```

BRECHER, G.   ?-

    Synge, J.M.   6848

BRENT-SMITH, Alexander   1889-1950

    Jacobs, W.W.   3591
    Webb, Mary   7127

BRETTINGHAM SMITH, Jolyon   ?-

    Yeats, W.B.   7458

BRIAN, Havergal   1876-1972

    Douglas, Lord Alfred   1902
    Le Gallienne, Richard   4473*
    Synge, J.M.   6832* 6854
    Yeats, W.B.   7490 7676

BRICCETTI, Thomas B.   1936-

    Hopkins, Gerard Manley   3110

BRIDGE, (John) Frederick   1844-1924

    Kipling, Rudyard   3956 4026 4036

BRIDGE, Frank   1879-1941

    Bridges, Robert   670 759 763
    Brooke, Rupert   794
    Coleridge, Mary   1032 1035 1046
    Colum, Padraic   1077
    Gould, Gerald   2344
    Joyce, James   3716
    Stephens, James   5915*
    Thompson, Francis   7015
    Wolfe, Humbert   7320
    Yeats, W.B.   7691

BRIDGEWATER, Ernest Leslie   1893-

    Bax, Clifford   307

BRIER, James   ?-

    Drinkwater, John   2005 2012

BRIGHT, Dora Estella   1863-1951

Chesterton, G.K.   967
Kipling, Rudyard   4069* 4163 4168* 4243 4319
                              4334

BRIGHT, Houston   1916-1970
Nom de plume of Robert Houston Bright

Stevenson, Robert Louis   6017 6129 6496 6518 6554

BRINDLE, Reginald Smith   1917-

Hopkins, Gerard Manley   3119
Thomas, Dylan   6890 6915
Watkins, Vernon   7074
Wells, H.G.   7145

BRINGS, Allen   1934-

Hardy, Thomas   2686

BRINKWORTH, Francis   ?-

de la Mare, Walter   1600
Henley, W.E.   2799

BRISTOL, Esmond   ?-

Masefield, John   4840

BRITTEN, (Edward) Benjamin   1913-

Auden, W.H.   85 86 90 96 98 106 111 113
                          117 126 129* 138 139 142 162
                          165 166 167 169 170 175 180
                          182 186 190* 207 210 213 214
                          218 222 229 235
Belloc, Hilaire   381
de la Mare, Walter   1363 1668 1673 1690 1707 1745
                          1793 1803 1832
Eliot, T.S.   2088*
Ford, Ford Madox   2220
Forster, E.M.   2223
Graves, Robert   2432
Hardy, Thomas   2470 2475 2478 2495 2594 2606
                          2618 2638 2701
Hopkins, Gerard Manley   3131

901

BRITTEN continued

    Isherwood, Christopher   3572 3573 3577 3580 3581 3582
                                         3585 3586
    James, Henry   3594 3595
    Lawrence, D.H.   4406
    MacNeice, Louis   4787 4797 4810
    Middleton, Christopher   5120
    Owen, Wilfred   5425 5428 5430 5432 5437 5440
                                         5441 5446 5450 5451
    Priestley, J.B.   5491
    Sackville-West, Edward   5568
    Sitwell, Edith   5754
    Soutar, William   5810 5814 5815 5826 5827 5829
                                       5832 5837 5838 5839 5844 5845

BRITTEN, (Edward) Benjamin, arr.   1913-

    Yeats, W.B.   7598

BROOK, Harry   ?-

    Bridges, Robert   615 653
    Read, Herbert   5531
    Stevenson, Robert Louis   6027 6061 6255 6519

BROONES, Martin   1900-1971

    Wolfe, Humbert   7321 7347

BROWN, Gwyneth L.   ?-

    Meynell, Alice   5075
    O'Sullivan, Seumas   5406

BROWN, Harold   1913-

    Hopkins, Gerard Manley   3032

BROWN, Hubert Sidney   ?-1949

    Belloc, Hilaire   424
    Chesterton, G.K.   1002
    Swinburne, A.C.   6670

BROWN, James   ?-

    Blunt, W.S.   584

BROWN continued

Brooke, Rupert	826
Campbell, (I.) Roy	852
Coppard, A.E.	1151
Cornford, Frances	1165 1167 1168 1171
de la Mare, Walter	1430 1439 1447 1510 1526 1776
	1802 1809 1833 1834
Hardy, Thomas	2706
Housman, A.E.	3474
Joyce, James	3693 3743 3907
Masefield, John	4956
O'Connor, Frank	5387
Stevenson, Robert Louis	6436
Synge, J.M.	6845
Yeats, W.B.	7582

BROWN, Newel Kay   1932-

Hopkins, Gerard Manley	2973 3049 3120
Spender, Stephen	5850 5855 5856 5857 5858 5860
	5861

BROWNE, W. Denis   ?-

de la Mare, Walter	1361

BRUBECK, Howard   ?-

Shaw, George Bernard	5667

BRUCE, Margaret Campbell   ?-

de la Mare, Walter	1383 1734 1819
Meynell, Alice	5116
Monro, Harold	5202

BRUCE, Robert   1915-

Stephens, James	5994

BRUMBY, Colin   1933-

Yeats, W.B.	7370

BRYAN, Gordon   ?-

Galsworthy, John	2239 2243 2244 2249 2250 2252

903

BRYAN continued

    Sackville-West, Victoria   5572 5575

BRYDSON, John Callis   1900-

    Barrie, J.M.   276

BRYSON, (Robert) Ernest   1867-1942

    Yeats, W.B.   7688

BUCK, Percy Carter   1871-1947

    Eliot, T.S.   2097
    Warner, Sylvia Townsend   7071

BUCK, Vera   ?-

    Belloc, Hilaire   382
    Chesterton, G.K.   968 1009

BUCZYNSKI, Walter J.   1933-

    Belloc, Hilaire   383
    Chesterton, G.K.   969
    de la Mare, Walter   1441 1658 1708 1800

BUJARSKI, Zbigniew   1933-

    Eliot, T.S.   2178

BULLARD, Alan   ?-

    Belloc, Hilaire   404

BULLARD, Frederic Field   1864-1904

    Bridges, Robert   735
    Stevenson, Robert Louis   6500

BULLER, John   ?-

    Joyce, James   3658 3659

BULLOCK, Ernest   1890-

    Bridges, Robert   643 755

BULLOCK continued

de la Mare, Walter   1395

BULLOCK, Flora   ?-

Masefield, John   4930

BUNNING, Herbert   1863-1937

Hope, Anthony   2963
Kipling, Rudyard   4203

BURKHARDT, P.   ?-

Wilde, Oscar   7204

BURKINSHAW, Sydney   1911-

Eliot, T.S.   2079 2142 2170
Galsworthy, John   2240 2245 2251 2255
Masefield, John   4844

BURLEIGH, Henry Thacker   1866-1949

Kipling, Rudyard   4140
Symons, Arthur   6749 6758 6772

BURNETT, R.   ?-

Colum, Padraic   1117*

BURNEY, Angela   ?-

Sackville-West, Victoria   5576

BURNHAM, Charles   ?-

Stevenson, Robert Louis   6300

BURNS, Lorraine J.   ?-

Housman, A.E.   3431

BURRITT, Lloyd E.   1940-

Eliot, T.S.   2059 2080 2115 2130 2154 2162
Hardy, Thomas   2576

BURROWS, Benjamin   ?-

    de la Mare, Walter   1597 1662 1665
    Housman, A.E.   3417* 3507*
    Hyde, Douglas   3565
    Synge, J.M.   6856

BURT, George James   1929-

    Eliot, T.S.   2116

BURTCH, Mervyn   ?-

    Auden, W.H.   191
    Belloc, Hilaire   496
    de la Mare, Walter   1835
    Kipling, Rudyard   4057
    Lewis, Alun   4491 4492
    Owen, Wilfred   5452
    Yeats, W.B.   7541 7542

BURY, Winifred   ?-

    Stevenson, Robert Louis   6147

BUSCH, William   1901-1945

    AE   55
    Bridges, Robert   767
    Coleridge, Mary   1041
    Gibson, W.W.   2331
    Stephens, James   5892

BUSH, Alan Dudley   1900-

    Day Lewis, C.   1332
    Monro, Harold   5209
    O'Casey, Sean   5379

BUSH, Geoffrey   1920-

    Belloc, Hilaire   384
    Drinkwater, John   2021
    Raine, Kathleen   5499 5501 5506 5508
    Wilde, Oscar   7227

BUTLER, Walter   ?-1945

   Yeats, W.B.   7499 7546 7689

BUTT, James   1929-

   Dunsany, Lord   2034
   Hardy, Thomas   2707

BUTTERLEY, Nigel   1935-

   Chesterton, G.K.   1010

BUTTERWORTH, Arthur   1923-

   de la Mare, Walter   1516 1709 1771 1805
   Durrell, Lawrence   2046
   Hardy, Thomas   2615
   Noyes, Alfred   5339
   Sassoon, Siegfried   5612
   Stephens, James   5893
   Stevenson, Robert Louis   6115

BUTTERWORTH, George Sainton Kaye   1885-1916

   Henley, W.E.   2792* 2811 2824 2850
   Housman, A.E.   3147 3240* 3250* 3266* 3274*
                                    3275* 3320 3343 3388* 3432*
                                    3470 3487
   Stevenson, Robert Louis   6148 6170
   Wilde, Oscar   7250

BUTTERWORTH, Neil   ?-

   de la Mare, Walter   1527

BUZZI-PECCIA, Arturo   1858-1943

   Macleod, Fiona   4638 4666 4777

BYARS, Donald A.   ?-

   Stevenson, Robert Louis   6441 6451 6555

BYFIELD, J. Allen   ?-

   Hardy, Thomas   2754

CABLE, Howard   1920-

    Symonds, John Addington   6721

CADORET, Charlotte   ?-

    Colum, Padraic   1078

CAGE, John Milton   1912-

    Joyce, James   3660

CAIN, Noble   1896-

    Le Gallienne, Richard   4466
    Stevenson, Robert Louis   6452

CALABRO, Louis   ?-

    Joyce, James   3607 3763 3846

CALVIN, Susan   ?-

    Housman, A.E.   3197

CAMPBELL, Arthur M.   ?-

    Hopkins, Gerard Manley   2966 2974 3050 3076 3121

CAMPBELL, Colin MacLeod   ?-1953

    Belloc, Hilaire   471

CAMPBELL, E.M.   ?-

    Kipling, Rudyard   4063

CAMPBELL, Vance   ?-

    de la Mare, Walter   1691

CAMPBELL-TIPTON, Louis   1877-1921

    Symons, Arthur   6741 6750 6782 6793 6803 6823
    Yeats, W.B.   7700

909

CARR, Edwin James Nairn   1926-

    Sitwell, Edith   5728 5732 5748 5750

CARR, Howard   1880-

    Rattigan, Terence   5529

CARTER, John Wallace   1929-

    Yeats, W.B.   7371

CARTWRIGHT, Patricia   ?-

    de la Mare, Walter   1607

CARTY, Doreen G.   ?-

    de la Mare, Walter   1432

CARWITHEN, Doreen   1922-

    Masefield, John   4900

CARY, Tristram   ?-

    MacNeice, Louis   4800 4817

CASALS, Pablo   1876-1973

    Auden, W.H.   140

CASHMORE, Donald Joseph   1926-

    Chesterton, G.K.   945

CASTELNUOVO-TEDESCO, Mario   1895-1968

    Wilde, Oscar   7160 7205

CASTLEMAN, Henry [C.ff.?]   ?-

    Stephens, James   5995*
    Wilde, Oscar   7280

CAVIANI, Ronald   1931-

    Hardy, Thomas   2487

CHADWICK, George Whitefield   1854-1931

    Haggard, Rider   2457
    Newbolt, Henry   5247
    Stevenson, Robert Louis   6084 6200 6370

CHAGRIN, Francis   1905-1972

    Shaw, George Bernard   5672

CHAMBERLAIN, Ronald   ?-

    Webb, Mary   7107 7116 7130

CHAMPION, Constance Maclean   ?-

    Housman, A.E.   3257

CHANDLER, Mary   1911-

    Bridges, Robert   662
    Hopkins, Gerard Manley   3051
    Pitter, Ruth   5468 5470 5472 5479

CHANLER, Theodore Ward   1902-1961

    de la Mare, Walter   1372 1402 1505* 1506 1508
                             1509 1547 1623 1639 1680 1692
                             1772 1784 1786 1836
    Henley, W.E.   2894

CHANTER, R.J.C.   ?-

    Kipling, Rudyard   3985

CHANWAI, Mayme   ?-

    Housman, A.E.   3409 3488

CHAPMAN, Marion Conklin   ?-

    Chesterton, G.K.   946

CHAPPLE, Brian   1945-

    Thomas, Dylan   6903

CHARLAP, Mark   ?-

    Barrie, J.M.   277

CHARLES, Ernest   1895-

    Noyes, Alfred   5362
    Stevenson, Robert Louis   6559

CHARPENTIER, Gabriel   1925-

    Beckett, Samuel   319
    O'Casey, Sean   5381

CHASINS, Abram   1903-

    Belloc, Hilaire   519

CHAUN, František   1921-

    Joyce, James   3890

CHEATHAM, Katharine Smiley, arr.   ?-

    Stevenson, Robert Louis   6214 6387

CHESLOCK, Louis   1898-

    Soutar, William   5812

CHORBAJIAN, John   1936-

    Stevenson, Robert Louis   6396

CHRISTIANSEN, Henning   1932-

    Beckett, Samuel   324 328 332 338 345

CHRISTOPHER, Cyril Stanley   1897-

    Bridges, Robert   644

CHRISTOU, Jani   1926-

    Eliot, T.S.   2069 2095 2117 2163 2172 2174

CITKOWITZ, Israel   1909-1974

   Joyce, James   3639 3683 3779* 3847 3856
                                3904

CLAASSEN, Arthur   1859-1920

   Kipling, Rudyard   4141

CLAIR, Leonard   ?-

   Auden, W.H.   108

CLAMAN, Dolores Olga   1927-

   Joyce, James   3930

CLARK, Harold   ?-

   Keyes, Sidney   3947
   Meredith, George   5052
   Stevenson, Robert Louis   6171

CLARK, Henry A.   ?-

   Stevenson, Robert Louis   6501

CLARK, Joan   ?-

   Stevenson, Robert Louis   6130

CLARK, Joyce McGowan   ?-

   Stephens, James   5923

CLARK, Rosemary   ?-

   Yeats, W.B.   7403

CLARK, S.   ?-

   Kipling, Rudyard   4204

CLARKE, Douglas   1893-1962

   Yeats, W.B.   7418

CLARKE, Fred R.C.   1931-

    Chesterton, G.K.   1011
    Eliot, T.S.   2081

CLARKE, Garry E.   1943-

    Milne, A.A.   5133 5146 5152 5157 5164 5135

CLARKE, Henry Leland   1907-

    Symonds, John Addington   6722

CLARKE, Kathleen Blair   ?-

    Wilde, Oscar   7251

CLARKE, Laurence   ?-

    Joyce, James   3684 3735 3857 3908 3926

CLARKE, Rebecca   1886-

    Housman, A.E.   3167
    Masefield, John   4878 4943
    Yeats, W.B.   7372 7599 7677 7712

CLARKE, Reginald   ?-

    Dobson, Austin   1877

CLARKE, Robert Coningsby   1879-1934

    Henley, W.E.   2813 2851 2908
    Johnson, Lionel   3602
    Masefield, John   4845 4870 4891 4931 4979
    Stevenson, Robert Louis 6149*
    Trench, Herbert   7030

CLAYTON, Don Allen   ?-

    Wilde, Oscar   7225

CLEMENTS, John Harvey   1910-

    Bridges, Robert   663 741
    Reeves, James   5540
    Stevenson, Robert Louis 6286

CLEMENTS, Peter   1940-

    Eliot, T.S.   2179

CLOUGH-LEIGHTER, Henry   1874-1956

    Henley, W.E.   2920
    Kipling, Rudyard   4205
    Macleod, Fiona   4583 4667 4705
    Symons, Arthur   6779
    Wilde, Oscar   7252

COBB, Gerard F.   ?-

    Kipling, Rudyard   3952 3961 3979 4013 4041 4043
                             4050 4096 4113 4127 4181 4247
                             4251 4253 4268 4271 4300 4305
                             4310 4328 4337

COCHRAN, Leslie   ?-

    Hardy, Thomas   2619
    Symons, Arthur   6761

COCKSHOTT, Gerald Wilfred   1915-

    Bridges, Robert   772
    de la Mare, Walter   1458 1500
    Housman, A.E.   3276
    Ledwidge, Francis   4432
    Levi, Peter   4487
    Symons, Arthur   6746

COERNE, Louis Adolphe   1870-1922

    Symons, Arthur   6753
    Yeats, W.B.   7410

COHEN, David   1927-

    Auden, W.H.   233

COHEN, Dudley   ?-

    Chesterton, G.K.   996

COHN, Arthur   1910-

    Lawrence, D.H.   4422

COHN, James Myron   1928-

    Auden, W.H.   99 168 230

COLBURN, S.C.   ?-

    Stevenson, Robert Louis   6181
    Watson, William   7089

COLE, Hugo   1917-

    Hughes, Ted   3556
    Kirkup, James   4352 4353 4354 4355 4356 4359
    Sitwell, Edith   5697* 5713* 5731* 5737* 5755*
                      5757*

COLE, Rossetter Gleason   1866-1952

    Swinburne, A.C.   6626

COLEMAN, Ellen   ?-1973

    Nichols, Robert   5311

COLEMAN, Henry   1888-1965

    Stevenson, Robert Louis   6062

COLERIDGE-TAYLOR, Samuel   1875-1912

    Buchanan, Robert   844
    Newbolt, Henry   5248
    Noyes, Alfred   5342 5364
    Phillips, Stephen   5455 5456 5458 5461
    Stevenson, Robert Louis   6364 6546

COLLINGWOOD, Lawrance Arthur   1887-

    Dowson, Ernest   1940
    Stevenson, Robert Louis   6329

COLLINS, Anthony Vincent Benedictus   1892?-1963

    Baring, Maurice   248

COLLINS continued

    Stevenson, Robert Louis   6150

COLLINS, J.H. [June Harple?]   [1915?-   ]

    Yeats, W.B.   7600

COLSON, William   1945-

    Housman, A.E.   3277 3463 3489

CONANT, Grace Wilbur   ?-

    Stevenson, Robert Louis   6313 6388 6424

CONANT, Grace Wilbur, arr.   ?-

    Stevenson, Robert Louis   6063 6131

CONANT, J. Willis   ?-

    Chesterton, G.K.   947

CONE, Edward T.   1917-

    Bridges, Robert   704
    de la Mare, Walter   1471 1678 1816 1821 1824 1826
    Eliot, T.S.   2082 2089
    Housman, A.E.   3146 3168 3208 3212 3222 3278
        3354 3378 3490
    Stephens, James   5922 5927 5974

CONN, Dwight   ?-

    de la Mare, Walter   1415

CONVERSE, Frederick Shepherd   1871-1940

    Meredith, George   5048

COOK, Albert Melville   ?-

    Belloc, Hilaire   512

COOK, Greville   ?-

    Meynell, Alice   5099

COOK, Theodore   ?-

    Kipling, Rudyard   4085

COOKE, Arnold Atkinson   1906-

    Colum, Padraic   1079
    Hardy, Thomas   2466 2471 2537 2586 2589 2671
    Lawrence, D.H.   4405

COOLIDGE, Elizabeth Sprague   1864-1953

    Noyes, Alfred   5344

COOPER, Walter Gaze   1895-

    Binyon, Laurence   565
    Masefield, John   4962
    Owen, Wilfred   5426

COPE, Cecil   ?-

    Masefield, John   4827
    Reeves, James   5541

COPLAND, Aaron   1900-

    James, Henry   3596
    Meredith, George   5025

COPLEY, Ian Alfred   1926-

    Belloc, Hilaire   509
    Hardy, Thomas   2513
    Masefield, John   4871

COPPOLA, Piero   1888-1971

    Henley, W.E.   2881
    Watson, William   7087

CORBETT, Felix   ?-1940

    Swinburne, A.C.   6627

CORBETT, Horton   ?-

    Le Gallienne, Richard   4460

CORIGLIANO, John   1938-

    Spender, Stephen   5862
    Thomas, Dylan   6885 6925

CORK, Peter   ?-

    Belloc, Hilaire   513

CORY, George [C.?]   [1920?-   ]

    Stevenson, Robert Louis   6151
    Wilde, Oscar   7253

COUCH, Janette E.   1932-

    Yeats, W.B.   7547

COULTER, A.J. Humphrey   ?-

    Kipling, Rudyard   4206

COULTHARD, Jean   1908-

    AE   22
    Belloc, Hilaire   497
    Colum, Padraic   1080
    de la Mare, Walter   1485
    Gibbon, Monk   2270 2276
    Joyce, James   3608 3685 3717 3799 3858
    Ledwidge, Francis   4433
    Mansfield, Katherine   4821
    Monro, Harold   5200 5206
    Noyes, Alfred   5334
    Turner, W.J.R.   7039

COUPER, Mildred   ?-

    Belloc, Hilaire   489

COUSINS, John E.   ?-

    Owen, Wilfred   5427 5431 5433 5436 5447
    Smith, Stevie   5799

COVERT, Mary E.   ?-

    Stevenson, Robert Louis   6245 6502

COWARD, Noël Pierce   1899-1973

    Wilde, Oscar   7226

COWELL, Henry Dixon   1897-1965

    Chesterton, G.K.   970

COWEN, Frederic Hymen   1852-1935
Originally named Hymen Frederick Cowen

    Buchanan, Robert   842
    Swinburne, A.C.   6653 6671
    Wilde, Oscar   7285*

COX, Ralph   1884-1941

    Macleod, Fiona   4639

CRAFTON, Cyril   ?-

    Galsworthy, John   2253

CRAWFORD, Dawn C.   1919-

    Masefield, John   4932

CRAWFORD, John C.   1931-

    Eliot, T.S.   2051

CRAWFORD, Thomas   ?-

    Stevenson, Robert Louis   6028 6085 6097 6124 6223 6263
                                              6269 6287 6304 6397 6471 6503

CRAXTON, Harold   ?-

    Stevenson, Robert Louis   6330

CREIGHTON, J.   ?-

    Dobson, Austin   1888
    Le Gallienne, Richard   4459

CRERAR, Louis   ?-

    Housman, A.E.   3321 3379 3410 3433

CRESTON, Paul   1906-

   Thompson, Francis   7010

CRIMP, Herbert E.   ?-

   Kipling, Rudyard   4258

CRIPPS, A. Redgrave   ?-

   Brooke, Rupert   806 808
   Graves, A.P.   2370
   Housman, A.E.   3174 3223 3241 3248 3251 3258
                          3267 3327 3344 3380 3389 3434
                          3491 3512

CRIST, Bainbridge   1883-1969

   Brooke, Rupert   832
   de la Mare, Walter   1346 1478 1534 1540 1566 1571
                          1593 1641 1693 1741 1790 1817
   Henley, W.E.   2887
   Swinburne, A.C.   6633 6672

CROMPTON, G.   ?-

   Kipling, Rudyard   3986

CROOK, John   ?-1922

   Barrie, J.M.   278 288*

CROSSE, Gordon   1937-

   Eliot, T.S.   2180
   Graves, Robert   2376 2384 2438
   Heath-Stubbs, John   2767
   Hughes, Ted   3544 3547 3548 3549 3550 3551
                          3552 3557 3558
   Smith, Stevie   5793
   Yeats, W.B.   7636 7637

CROSSLEY, Hastings   1846-?

   Swinburne, A.C.   6684

CROSSLEY-HOLLAND, Peter Charles   1916-

 Hardy, Thomas   2708
 O'Sullivan, Seumas   5407
 Yeats, W.B.   7411

CROWDER, Henry   ?-

 Acton, Harold   4
 Aldington, Richard   77
 Beckett, Samuel   336

CROWNINSHIELD, Ethel   ?-

 Stevenson, Robert Louis   6029 6044 6064 6077 6086 6184
                            6188 6201 6206 6224 6270 6238
                            6296 6305 6314 6371 6427 6450
                            6520 6538

CRUFT, Adrian   1921-

 Hopkins, Gerard Manley   2991
 Symonds, John Addington   6716

CUMMING, Richard   1928-

 Durrell, Lawrence   2037
 Housman, A.E.   3202

CUNDICK, Robert Milton   1926-

 Masefield, John   4963

CURTIS, Natalie Burlin   1875-1921

 Stevenson, Robert Louis   6008 6087 6315 6398 6420 6428
                            6504

DALBY, Martin   1942-

 Eliot, T.S.   2171
 MacDiarmid, Hugh   4552
 MacNeice, Louis   4811 4812*
 Soutar, William   5809 5811 5818 5822 5828 5836
                                  5840 5846
 Yeats, W.B.   7515

922

DALE, Benjamin James   1885-1943

    Bridges, Robert   654

DALE, Frederic   ?-

    Kipling, Rudyard   4092

DALLAPICCOLA, Luigi   1904-1975

    Joyce, James   3673 3790
    Wilde, Oscar   7254

DALWAY, Ianthe   ?-

    Strong, L.A.G.   6587 6588 6599

DAMASE, Jean-Michel   1928-

    James, Henry   3597

DAMON, Julia   ?-

    Yeats, W.B.   7686

DAMPIER, L.   ?-
[Pseud. used by J.S.L.D. Bennett?]

    Kipling, Rudyard   3964* 4131* 4157* 4242*

DAMROSCH, Walter Johannes   1862-1950

    Kipling, Rudyard   4014 4098 4116

DANIELS, Mabel Wheeler   1879-1971

    Chesterton, G.K.   948
    Sitwell, Edith   5718

DANKWORTH, John Philip William   1927-

    Eliot, T.S.   2148

DANN, Hollis Ellsworth, arr.   ?-

    Stevenson, Robert Louis   6132 6316

DAREWSKI, Herman   1883-1947

    Barrie, J.M.   289

DARKE, Harold Edwin   1888-

    Thompson, Francis   7007

DARNTON, (Philip) Christian   1903-

    Nichols, Robert   5290 5301 5305 5306 5310
    Ustinov, Peter   7061

DAUBNEY, Brian   ?-

    de la Mare, Walter   1694

DAUNTON, Frank   ?-

    Chesterton, G.K.   1007

DAVIDSON, Malcolm Gordon   1891-1949

    Masefield, John   4828 4857 4947
    Symons, Arthur   6763

DAVIE, Cedric Thorpe   1913-

    Lindsay, Maurice   4496

DAVIES, Eiluned   ?-

    Gregory, Lady Augusta   2451

DAVIES, Henry Walford   1869-1941

    Barrie, J.M.   279
    Belloc, Hilaire   385
    Bridges, Robert   664
    Coleridge, Mary   1021
    de la Mare, Walter   1624
    Gould, Gerald   2346*
    Kipling, Rudyard   4064 4161 4169 4183
    Masefield, John   4988
    Meynell, Alice   5086
    Milne, A.A.   5123 5130 5135 5165
    Newbolt, Henry   5286
    Noyes, Alfred   5355 5367*

DAVIES continued

    Stevenson, Robert Louis   6143 6172 6331 6453
    Symons, Arthur   6789

DAVIES, Hubert   1893-1965

    Hopkins, Gerard Manley   3011

DAVIES, Peter Maxwell   1934-

    Huxley, Aldous   3559
    Whiting, John   7152

DAVIS, Carl   ?-

    Arden, John   80

DAVISON, Archibald T., arr.   ?-

    Kipling, Rudyard   3987
    Symonds, John Addington   6723

DAWNEY, Michael   1942-

    Sitwell, Edith   5700

DAY, Edgar F.   ?-

    Carpenter, Edward   917

DEALE, Edgar Martin   1902-

    AE   71
    Campbell, Joseph   899 900
    Colum, Padraic   1068 1081 1082 1083 1130 1133
    de la Mare, Walter   1459 1469 1574 1795
    Graves, A.P.   2364

DEALE, Edgar Martin, arr.   1902-

    Yeats, W.B.   7601

DEAR, James Richard   ?-

    Colum, Padraic   1084
    Newbolt, Henry   5266
    Noyes, Alfred   5346

DEBEER, Alan [Allen?]   ?-

   Housman, A.E.   3435

DEBEER, Allen [Alan?]   ?-

   Yeats, W.B.   7602

DECEVEE, Alice   1904-

   Yeats, W.B.   7603

DE FILIPPI, Amadeo   1900-

   Drinkwater, John   2011

DEGOLIER, Palph [?] J.   ?-

   Sassoon, Siegfried   5610

DE HARTMANN, Thomas   ?-

   Joyce, James   3891*

DEIS, Carl   1883-1960

   Noyes, Alfred   5314
   Swinburne, A.C.   6673 6701
   Wilde, Oscar   7187

DE KOVEN, (Henry Louis) Reginald   1859-1920

   Kipling, Rudyard   4207
   Macleod, Fiona   4778
   Stevenson, Robert Louis   6225 6399 6505

DELAGE, Maurice Charles   1879-

   Kipling, Rudyard   4164 4170 4320 4342

DELIUS, Frederick   1862-1934
Baptised Fritz Albert Theodor Delius

   Dowson, Ernest   1908 1914 1918 1921 1924
                                1925* 1930 1943 1952
   Flecker, James Elroy   2198
   Henley, W.E.   2820 2832
   Macleod, Fiona   4644

926

DELIUS continued

    Symons, Arthur   6791 6819

DELLO JOIO, Norman Joseph   1913-

    Chesterton, G.K.   949
    de la Mare, Walter   1560
    Dunsany, Lord   2035*
    Lawrence, D.H.   4373
    Symonds, John Addington 6713 6714
    Symons, Arthur   6738 6783

DEL RIEGO, Teresa Clotilde   1876-1968

    Dobson, Austin   1878
    Stevenson, Robert Louis 6125 6256 6356 6429 6472 6521
    Yeats, W.B.   7423

DEL TREDICI, David Walter   1937-

    Joyce, James   3609 3654* 3674 3701 3740
                        3744 3755* 3811 3825

DE MENASCE, Jacques   1905-1960

    Wolfe, Humbert   7355

DEMUTH, Norman   1898-1968

    Barker, George   261

DENNIS, Terrence P.   ?-

    Kipling, Rudyard   4301*

DENSMORE, John Hopkins   1880-1943

    Henley, W.E.   2833
    Masefield, John   4916 4933
    Swinburne, A.C.   6614
    Symons, Arthur   6784

DENT, Edward Joseph   1876-1957

    de la Mare, Walter   1385 1782
    Flecker, James Elroy   2202
    Hardy, Thomas   2620

DENT continued

    Watson, William   7083

DE PUE, Wallace Earl   1932-
Nom de plume of Wallace E. De Pue

    Stevenson, Robert Louis 6385

DE REGO, Iris   ?-

    Noyes, Alfred   5350

D'ERLANGER, Frederic   1868-1943

    Hardy, Thomas   2675

DE ZULUETA, Pedro   ?-

    Henley, W.E.   2815
    Noyes, Alfred   5347

DIACK, John Michael   ?-

    Kipling, Rudyard   3988
    Swinburne, A.C.   6610
    Tynan, Katharine   7047

DIAMOND, David Leo   1915-

    Eliot, T.S.   2175
    Hardy, Thomas   2608
    Joyce, James   3640 3675 3686 3695 3791
    Masefield, John   4896
    Thomas, Dylan   6891

DICKINSON, Peter   1934-

    Auden, W.H.   100 123 157 187 192 200 237
    Blackburn, Thomas   571 572 573 574
    Eliot, T.S.   2098
    Hardy, Thomas   2483 2560
    Heath-Stubbs, John   2765
    Hopkins, Gerard Manley 2975 2992 3052 3111
    Swinburne, A.C.   6687
    Thomas, Dylan   6893 6910 6919 6924

```
DIEMER, Emma Lou    1927-

    Stevenson, Robert Louis    6152

DILLON, Shaun    1944-

    AE                        26 67
    Campbell, Joseph          887
    Colum, Padraic            1071
    Hyde, Douglas             3566
    O'Sullivan, Seumas        5402 5403

DIXON, Harold    ?-

    Kipling, Rudyard          4015 4051 4117

DOBSON, Tom    ?-

    Flecker, James Elroy      2214
    Housman, A.E.             3436
    Masefield, John           4846 4901 4970
    Stephens, James           5881 5885 5920 5928 5970 5934
                              5996
    Synge, J.M.               6836

DODGSON, Stephen    1924-

    Belloc, Hilaire           421
    MacNeice, Louis           4788 4798 4808 4809 4819
    Sitwell, Osbert           5772

DORR, T.A.    ?-

    Stevenson, Robert Louis   6018

DORWARD, David Campbell    1933-

    Bridges, Robert           649 705 733
    Buchan, John              838 839
    de la Mare, Walter        1616

DOUBRAVSKÝ, Petr    1925-

    Wilde, Oscar              7206

DOUGHERTY, Celius    1902-

    Hopkins, Gerard Manley    2993
```

DOUGHERTY continued

Housman, A.E.	3279
Webb, Mary	7135
Wolfe, Humbert	7356

DOUGLAS, Clive   1903-

Thompson, Francis	6999

DOUGLAS, James   1932-

Beckett, Samuel	325 329 339 342 346 352 359
Crossley-Holland, Kevin	1181 1183 1184 1185 1186 1188 1190 1192 1193 1197
Gascoyne, David	2259 2265
Hardy, Thomas	2506 2508 2676
Heath-Stubbs, John	2764 2766
Hopkins, Gerard Manley	2976
Lawrence, D.H.	4369 4376 4383 4387 4401 4410 4411
Meynell, Alice	5087
Thomas, Dylan	6921

DOUGLAS, Keith   ?-

Housman, A.E.	3508

DOUTY, Nicholas   1870-1955

Yeats, W.B.	7424

DRAKEFORD, Richard   1936-

Auden, W.H.	141 158 178 231

DREVER, Rose   ?-

Bridges, Robert	773

DRINKWATER, George   1880-

Drinkwater, John	2000 2004

DROSTE, Doreen   ?-

Swinburne, A.C.	6607
Yeats, W.B.	7583 7692

DROZDOFF, Vladimir   ?-

    Stevenson, Robert Louis   6014 6226 6317 6372 6430 6522

DRUCKMAN, Jacob   1928-

    Hopkins, Gerard Manley   3003 3053 3066

DUARTE, John William   1919-

    Belloc, Hilaire   386
    Colum, Padraic   1085
    de la Mare, Walter   1460
    Meredith, George   5026

DUBLINERS, The, arr.

    Behan, Brendan   369*

DUCHÁČ, Miloslav   1924-

    Wilde, Oscar   7168

DUCKWORTH, Arthur Dyce   ?-

    Henley, W.E.   2844
    Stephens, James   5933

DUFF, Arthur   ?-

    Gogarty, Oliver St. John   2337
    Sitwell, Edith   5719
    Stephens, James   5936 5962

DUFF, Arthur, arr.   ?-

    O'Connor, Frank   5384

DUKE, John Woods   1899-

    de la Mare, Walter   1579 1669 1710
    Hardy, Thomas   2731
    Heath-Stubbs, John   2769
    Housman, A.E.   3148 3280 3437 3475
    O'Sullivan, Seumas   5408
    Stephens, James   5950
    Wolfe, Humbert   7353
    Yeats, W.B.   7516

931

DUKE, Vernon   1903-1969
   Pseud. of Vladimir Dukelsky

   Housman, A.E.   3224 3281 3319 3332 3459 3492
   Maugham, Somerset   5015
   Symons, Arthur   6781

DUKELSKY, Vladimir   1903-1969
   Also wrote under the pseud. "Vernon Duke"

   Dobson, Austin   1879

DULAC, Edmund   1882-

   Yeats, W.B.   7388 7669

DUNCAN, Chester   1913-

   Auden, W.H.   87* 95 109 130* 161 177 201
                              215
   Barker, George   262
   Belloc, Hilaire   411 419 467 472 475 476
   Bridges, Robert   760
   Dane, Clemence   1210
   Dowson, Ernest   1917
   Flecker, James Elroy   2199
   Housman, A.E.   3225 3333 3411 3493
   Isherwood, Christopher   3574* 3587
   MacNeice, Louis   4789
   Yeats, W.B.   7425 7526 7591

DUNCAN, William Edmondstoune   1866-1920

   Swinburne, A.C.   6662*

DUNHILL, Thomas Frederick   1877-1946

   Brooke, Rupert   787
   Hardy, Thomas   2514
   Herbert, A.P.   2944
   Housman, A.E.   3245*
   Stephens, James   5997
   Yeats, W.B.   7365* 7373 7500 7662

DUNKLEY, Ferdinand Luis   1869-1956

   Thompson, Francis   6990

```
DUNLOP, Isobel      1901-1975

    Soutar, William           5847 5848
    Webb, Mary                7132
    Wolfe, Humbert            7351 7357

DURKÓ, Zsolt    1934-

    Masefield, John           4887

DURRANT, F.T.    ?-

    de la Mare, Walter        1837 1838

DUSHKIN, Dorothy    ?-

    de la Mare, Walter        1535 1642 1695

DYSON, George    1883-1964

    Day Lewis, C.             1341
    de la Mare, Walter        1599
    Housman, A.E.             3361
    Masefield, John           4944
    Watson, William           7080

EAGLES, Moneta    1924-

    Bridges, Robert           616 665 686

EASDALE, Brian    1909-

    Lawrence, D.H.            4423
    Mitchison, Naomi          5197
    Webb, Mary                7117

EATON, John    1935-

    Yeats, W.B.               7527 7577 7684

EBEN, Petr    1929-

    Stevenson, Robert Louis   6560

EDESON, Donald    ?-

    Masefield, John           4917
```

EDGE, Dorothea   ?-

    Bridges, Robert   655

EDMONDS, Paul   ?-

    Bridges, Robert   599
    Campbell, Joseph   901*
    Colum, Padraic   1086
    Kipling, Rudyard   4029 4288 4323
    Stevenson, Robert Louis   6332

EDMUNDS, Christopher Montague   1899-

    Baring, Maurice   247 250 251
    Macleod, Fiona   4656
    Noyes, Alfred   5351

EDMUNDS, John   1913-

    AE   35
    Hardy, Thomas   2509
    Housman, A.E.   3246 3355 3518

EDWARDS, Clara   1887-1974

    Sassoon, Siegfried   5591
    Symons, Arthur   6754

EDWARDS, Henry J.   ?-

    Stevenson, Robert Louis   6189

EDWYN, Richard E.   ?-

    Macleod, Fiona   4779

EFFINGER, Cecil S.   1914-

    Day Lewis, C.   1318

EGK, Werner   1901-

    Yeats, W.B.   7419

EICHHEIM, Henry   1870-1942

    Macleod, Fiona   4624 4657 4738 4753

EICHHEIM continued

   Yeats, W.B.   7386 7530

EISLER, Hanns   1898-1962

   Shaw, George Bernard   5686

ELGAR, Edward William   1857-1934

   Belloc, Hilaire   498
   Binyon, Laurence   551 555 558 564 566*
   de la Mare, Walter   1536
   Gosse, Edmund   2340
   Kipling, Rudyard   3958 3962* 4020 4072 4254
   Lang, Andrew   4365 4366
   Masefield, John   4989
   Moore, George   5211
   Noyes, Alfred   5368
   Swinburne, A.C.   6613
   Yeats, W.B.   7466

ELKIN, Robert Stiebel   1896-1964

   Bridges, Robert   742

ELKIN, W.A.   ?-

   Kipling, Rudyard   4193

ELKUS, Albert   1884-1962

   Binyon, Laurence   554
   Henley, W.E.   2805*

ELKUS, Jonathan   1931-

   Eliot, T.S.   2099
   Hardy, Thomas   2621
   Stevenson, Robert Louis 6444

ELLIOTT, D. Morgan   ?-

   Kipling, Rudyard   4208

ELLIOTT, Michael   1926-

   Davies, W.H.   1311

ELLIOTT, Muriel   ?-

    Kipling, Rudyard   4185

ELLIOTT, Zo   1891-1964
Nom de plume of Alonzo Elliott

    Masefield, John   4990

ELLIS, Osian   ?-

    Thomas, Dylan   6931

ELLIS, Vivian   1904-

    Herbert, A.P.   2933 2934 2945

ELMORE, David   ?-

    Stevenson, Robert Louis   6561

ELSTON, Arnold   ?-

    Eliot, T.S.   2149

ELUCHEN, Alexander   ?-

    Doyle, Arthur Conan   1981*

ELWELL, Herbert   1898-ca. 1973

    Beerbohm, Max   365
    Meynell, Alice   5091 5117

ELWYN-EDWARDS, Dilys   ?-

    de la Mare, Walter   1354
    Meredith, George   5064

EMELEUS, John   ?-

    de la Mare, Walter   1347 1369 1511 1528 1586 1654
                               1711 1767

ENGEL, A. Lehman   1910-

    Barrie, J.M.   267
    Eliot, T.S.   2100

ENNA, August   1860-1939

    Bennett, Arnold   532
    Haggard, Rider   2455

ENOS, Joseph T.   1911-

    Masefield, John   4934

EPPERT, Carl   1882-1961

    Kipling, Rudyard   4244*

EPSTEIN, David M.   1930-

    Hopkins, Gerard Manley   3067 3083 3102

ERICKSON, Elaine M.   1941-

    Yeats, W.B.   7713

ERICKSON, Robert   ?-

    Joyce, James   3661

ESPOSITO, Michele   1855-1929

    Hyde, Douglas   3570

EVANS, T. Hopkins   ?-

    de la Mare, Walter   1608

EYRE, Laurence   ?-

    Le Gallienne, Richard   4474

FAGGE, Arthur   ?-

    Belloc, Hilaire   387

FALK [FALCK?], Edward   ?-

    Stevenson, Robert Louis   6009 6015 6030 6065 6078 6098
                                 6109 6133 6207 6215 6227*
                                 6246 6271 6307 6318 6373 6400
                                 6421 6425 6431 6473 6497 6523
                                 6539

FARJEON, Harry   1878-1948

    de la Mare, Walter   1568 1583 1712 1807

FARLEY, Roland   1892-1932

    Davies, W.H.   1270
    Stephens, James   5905 5998
    Stevenson, Robert Louis   6049
    Swinburne, A.C.   6603
    Wilde, Oscar   7174

FARQUHAR, David Andross   1928-

    Day Lewis, C.   1326 1334
    Hopkins, Gerard Manley   3015 3084
    MacNeice, Louis   4791 4813 4816
    Thomas, Dylan   6867 6916

FARR, Florence   ?-

    Yeats, W.B.   7463* 7543* 7616*

FARRAR, Ernest Bristow   1885-1918

    Stevenson, Robert Louis   6153
    Symons, Arthur   6820

FARWELL, Arthur   1872-1952

    Newbolt, Henry   5249

FAST, Willard Samuel   1922-

    Housman, A.E.   3438
    Stevenson, Robert Louis   6154

FAULKNER, David   ?-

    Belloc, Hilaire   416
    de la Mare, Walter   1791

FEARING, John   ?-

    Belloc, Hilaire   388
    Yeats, W.B.   7693

FELMAN, Hazel H.S.   ?-

    Joyce, James   3662
    Kipling, Rudyard   3965

FENTON, Howard   1917-

    Joyce, James   3931

FERGUSON, Howard   1908-

    Welch, Denton   7136 7137 7138 7139 7140

FERRARI, [Gustave   1872-1948?]

    Wilde, Oscar   7228

FERRARI, Gustave   1872-1948

    Macleod, Fiona   4668

FERRIS, Joan   ?-

    Joyce, James   3610 3643 3764 3859 3876 3918

FETLER, Paul   1920-

    Joyce, James   3611
    Watson, William   7093

FIELD, Robin   1935-

    Belloc, Hilaire   408
    de la Mare, Walter   1554
    Gascoyne, David   2266
    Hardy, Thomas   2496
    Housman, A.E.   3175* 3176 3226 3249 3282
                      3365 3439
    Joyce, James   3620 3630 3826 3900
    MacNeice, Louis   4814
    Powys, John Cowper 5486 5487

FINCH, Harold N.   ?-

    Masefield, John   4918

FINE, Vivian   1913-

    Joyce, James   3813 3878

FINLAYSON, Barbara   ?-

    Kipling, Rudyard   4009 4021

FINNEY, Ross Lee   1906-

    Joyce, James   3932
    Spender, Stephen   5849 5863

FINZI, Gerald   1901-1956

    Barker, George   258
    Blunden, Edmund   575 578* 581 582
    Bridges, Robert   620 627 632 650 671 702 706
                          731 734 761
    de la Mare, Walter   1382
    Flecker, James Elroy   2213
    Graves, Robert   2392
    Hardy, Thomas   2458 2462 2464 2465 2472 2477
                          2480 2482 2489 2491 2494 2497
                          2502 2511 2512 2515 2529 2530
                          2531 2532 2539 2540 2546 2548
                          2551 2552 2556 2561 2562 2564
                          2566 2567 2577 2585 2587 2590
                          2592 2598 2601 2604 2605 2607
                          2610 2612 2613 2614 2617 2622
                          2631 2633 2635 2639 2640 2649
                          2652 2659 2661 2664 2668 2670
                          2672 2674 2678 2685 2691 2692
                          2696 2697 2700 2702 2709 2732
                          2742 2743 2750 2751
    Shanks, Edward   5649

FISCHER, Irwin   1903-

    de la Mare, Walter   1520 1749
    Sassoon, Siegfried   5608 5625

FISCHER, Jan F.   1921-

    Shaw, George Bernard   5656 5668 5680

FIŠER, Luboš   1935-

   Priestley, J.B.   5494

FISHER, Howard   ?-

   Watson, William   7101

FISHER, William J.   ?-

   Wilde, Oscar   7191

FISKE, Roger   1910-

   de la Mare, Walter   1429 1588
   Hardy, Thomas   2710

FITZGERALD, Augustine   ?-

   Kipling, Rudyard   4260 4308
   Swinburne, A.C.   6615 6645

FLAGLER, Robert F.   ?-

   Kipling, Rudyard   3966 4052*

FLANAGAN, William   1923-1969

   Hopkins, Gerard Manley   2994
   Housman, A.E.   3519
   Sassoon, Siegfried   5589

FLAY, Alfred Leonard   ?-

   de la Mare, Walter   1636

FLEISCHMANN, Aloys   1910-

   Colum, Padraic   1072 1108 1122 1132
   O'Connor, Frank   5382 5386 5388 5389

FLEMING, Robert James Berkeley   1921-

   Belloc, Hilaire   372 443 451
   Colum, Padraic   1087
   Davies, W.H.   1265 1287 1292
   de la Mare, Walter   1367 1410 1659 1839
   Hardy, Thomas   2623

FLETCHER, H. Grant   1913-

    Henley, W.E.   2899
    Macleod, Fiona   4731
    O'Sullivan, Seumas   5396

FLETCHER, Percy E.   ?-

    Macleod, Fiona   4584 4722

FLORIDIA-NAPOLINO, Pietro   1860-1932
    Also known as Pietro Floridia and as
    Baron Napolino di San Silvestro

    Wilde, Oscar   7182

FLOSMAN, Oldřich   1925-

    Kipling, Rudyard   3971
    Shaw, George Bernard   5657

FLOTHUIS, Marius   1914-

    Raine, Kathleen   5516
    Warner, Sylvia Townsend   7065 7072

FLOYD, Carlisle   1926-

    Stevenson, Robert Louis   6241 6319 6474

FOGG, (Charles William) Eric   1903-1939

    Kipling, Rudyard   4060

FOGG, D. St. C.   ?-

    Kipling, Rudyard   4209

FONTRIER, Gabriel   1918-

    Belloc, Hilaire   418 425 499

FOOTE, Arthur William   1853-1937

    Brooke, Rupert   809
    Dobson, Austin   1871 1889
    Henley, W.E.   2853
    Kipling, Rudyard   4103* 4118 4210 4343

FOOTE continued

Noyes, Alfred   5315
Stevenson, Robert Louis   6333 6390 6540
Yeats, W.B.   7548

FORD, Donald   ?-

de la Mare, Walter   1625
Galsworthy, John   2246
Gibson, W.W.   2296
Stevenson, Robert Louis   6155
Webb, Mary   7109

FORD, Ernest A. Clair   1858-1919

Barrie, J.M.   266
Doyle, Arthur Conan   1979

FORDHAM, Corysande   ?-

Masefield, John   4991
Noyes, Alfred   5336

FORESMAN, Robert, arr.   ?-

Swinburne, A.C.   6646 6649

FORREST, Oswald   ?-

Yeats, W.B.   7714

FORST, Rudolf   1900-1973

Stevenson, Robert Louis   6524

FORSYTH, Cecil   1870-1941

de la Mare, Walter   1396
Dowson, Ernest   1920 1946 1953
Henley, W.E.   2775 2854
Macleod, Fiona   4625 4780
Masefield, John   4858 4881
Stephens, James   5982
Symons, Arthur   6764 6780 6809

FORTNER, Wolfgang   1907-

    Eliot, T.S.   2101 2150
    Wilde, Oscar   7161

FOSS, Hubert James   1899-1953

    Chesterton, G.K.   984
    Davidson, John   1225
    Flecker, James Elroy   2205
    Hardy, Thomas   2505 2543 2550 2611 2653 2663
                        2689
    Henley, W.E.   2867
    Housman, A.E.   3310

FOSS, Lukas   1922-

    Auden, W.H.   105
    Housman, A.E.   3468

FOSTER, G.   ?-

    Kipling, Rudyard   4211

FOSTER, Grant   ?-

    Barrie, J.M.   280

FOSTER, Ivor   ?-

    Hardy, Thomas   2591 2644 2699

FOTHERGILL, Helen   ?-

    Masefield, John   4862
    Moore, George   5215

FOULDS, John Herbert   1880-1939

    Macleod, Fiona   4616 4659 4695 4700 4709
    Shaw, George Bernard 5681
    Stevenson, Robert Louis 6525

FOWLER, Keith   ?-

    Stevenson, Robert Louis 6506

FOX, Fred   1931-
    Nom de plume of Frederick Alfred Fox

    Bennett, Arnold   536

FOX, George   ?-

    Davies, W.H.   1266

FOX, J. Bertram   1881-1946

    Baring, Maurice   252
    Joyce, James   3860

FOX, Oscar J.   1879-1961

    Housman, A.E.   3476
    Swinburne, A.C.   6702

FRACKENPOHL, Arthur R.   1924-

    Belloc, Hilaire   490 520 524

FRANCE, William Edward   1912-

    Housman, A.E.   3520

FRANCHI, Dorothy   ?-

    Hardy, Thomas   2755

FRANCILLON, Rosamond   ?-

    Dobson, Austin   1882
    Henley, W.E.   2845

FRANCO, Johan   1908-

    Housman, A.E.   3191

FRANK, Francis   ?-

    Yeats, W.B.   7501

FRANKE-HARDING, W.   ?-

    Dobson, Austin   1876
    Le Gallienne, Richard   4475

FRANKEL, Benjamin   1906-1973

    Gibson, W.W.   2298
    Nichols, Robert   5291 5293 5294 5297 5299 5307
    Wilde, Oscar   7207

FRASER, Shena   1910-

    Belloc, Hilaire   461
    Macleod, Fiona   4698
    Stevenson, Robert Louis   6334

FRASER-SIMSON, Harold   1879?-1944

    Grahame, Kenneth   2352
    Milne, A.A.   5121 5122 5124 5125 5126 5127
                                   5128 5129 5131 5132 5134 5136
                                   5137 5138 5139 5140 5141 5142
                                   5143 5144 5145 5147 5148 5149
                                   5151 5153 5154 5155 5156 5159
                                   5160 5161 5162 5163 5167 5168
                                   5169 5170 5171 5172 5173 5174
                                   5175 5178 5179 5180 5181 5182
                                   5183 5184 5186 5188 5189 5192
                                   5193

FREED, Arnold   1926-

    Joyce, James   3765

FREED, Arthur   1894-1973

    Hopkins, Gerard Manley   2995

FREED, Dorothy Whitson   ?-

    Mansfield, Katherine   4822

FREED, Isadore   1900-1960

    Housman, A.E.   3440
    Shaw, George Bernard   5687
    Wilde, Oscar   7217

FREER, Eleanor Everest   1864-1942

    Dobson, Austin   1869
    Swinburne, A.C.   6632

FREER continued

Watson, William   7094

FRICKER, Peter Racine   1920-

de la Mare, Walter   1703 1827
Turner, W.J.R.   7038

FULTON, (Robert) Norman   1909-

Auden, W.H.   131 132
Causley, Charles   933 934 937
Gibson, W.W.   2283
Hardy, Thomas   2694
Macleod, Fiona   4585 4599

FUSSELL, Charles Clement   1938-

Sitwell, Edith   5707

FÜSSL, Karl Heinz   1924-

Hopkins, Gerard Manley   3068

GACCON, J.A.   ?-

Kipling, Rudyard   3989

GALLAHER, Christopher S.   1940-

Raine, Kathleen   5511* 5522*

GALLOWAY, The Countess of   ?-

Meynell, Alice   5115

GALLOWAY, Tod B.   ?-

Dobson, Austin   1890* 1893*
Kipling, Rudyard   4047* 4104*

GALWAY, Victor Edward   ?-

Bridges, Robert   656
de la Mare, Walter   1442 1746
Meynell, Alice   5100

947

GAMBOGI, Frederica Elvira   ?-1940

    Stevenson, Robert Louis   6010 6081 6116 6169 6432 6526

GANZ, Rudolph   1877-1972

    Brooke, Rupert   833
    Colum, Padraic   1088
    Yeats, W.B.   7426

GARDINER, Henry Balfour   1877-1950

    Carpenter, Edward   913
    Hardy, Thomas   2680 2681*
    Housman, A.E.   3359 3441
    Masefield, John   4852 4898 4902

GARDINER, Julian   ?-

    Hardy, Thomas   2682

GARDNER, John Linton   1917-

    Auden, W.H.   120 133 156
    Chesterton, G.K.   941
    Maugham, Somerset   5010*
    Mitchell, Adrian   5195
    Reeves, James   5539
    Synge, J.M.   6830

GARLICK, Antony   1927-

    Abercrombie, Lascelles 3
    Belloc, Hilaire   414
    Bottomley, Gordon   588
    Coleridge, Mary   1040
    Davies, W.H.   1231 1240 1248 1255 1271
                            1272* 1283 1290
    Housman, A.E.   3313
    Ledwidge, Francis   4431
    Noyes, Alfred   5335
    Strong, L.A.G.   6592
    Thomas, Edward   6949 6976 6978

GARRETT, Gaynor D.   ?-

    de la Mare, Walter   1355 1443 1503

GARTLAN, George Hugh   1882-1963

    Kipling, Rudyard   3990
    Stevenson, Robert Louis   6320

GARWOOD, Margaret   ?-

    Wilde, Oscar   7237

GAUL, Harvey Bartlett   1881-1945

    Graves, A.P.   2360
    Henley, W.E.   2905

GAYFER, James McDonald   1916-

    Bridges, Robert   602
    Chesterton, G.K.   950

GEE, Norman   ?-

    Stevenson, Robert Louis   6562

GEHRKENS, Karl Wilson   1882-

    Belloc, Hilaire   417
    Stevenson, Robert Louis   6011 6321

GELLMAN, Steven   ?-

    Hopkins, Gerard Manley   3132

GENTRY, A.J.   ?-

    Kipling, Rudyard   4212

GENZMER, Harald   1909-

    Joyce, James   3702
    Kipling, Rudyard   4119
    Macleod, Fiona   4740
    Young, Andrew   7728

GEORGE, Graham   1912-

    Barrie, J.M.   281
    Hopkins, Gerard Manley   3054 3085
    Meynell, Alice   5113

GEORGE continued

    Trench, Herbert   7034

GERBER, Edward   ?-

    Thomas, Dylan   6892

GERMAN, Edward   1862-1936
Born Edward German Jones

    Hope, Anthony   2964
    Kipling, Rudyard   3959 3976 4002 4058 4066 4058
                         4070 4073 4133 4134 4198 4290
                         4295* 4296 4318 4326
    Masefield, John   4892

GERSTLE, Henry S.   ?-

    Dowson, Ernest   1949

GEST, Elizabeth   ?-

    Masefield, John   4935

GHEDINI, Giorgio Federico   1892-1965

    Beerbohm, Max   366

GIBB, Robert W.   1893-1964

    Kipling, Rudyard   4213

GIBBS, Cecil Armstrong   1889-1960

    Bax, Clifford   297
    Bottomley, Gordon   597
    de la Mare, Walter   1343 1344 1362 1371 1373 1380
                         1397 1406 1407 1412 1413 1425
                         1426 1431 1451 1468 1479 1487
                         1493 1501 1512 1517 1529 1541
                         1549 1555 1559 1561 1569 1575
                         1584 1589 1594 1603 1613 1621
                         1626 1634 1635 1637 1640 1643
                         1650 1670 1674 1682 1696 1713
                         1728 1732 1733 1750 1760 1758
                         1773 1774 1775 1781 1810
                         1812* 1814* 1818 1840 1841

GIBBS continued

```
    de la Mare continued      1842
    Hardy, Thomas             2516  2624  2733
    Housman, A.E.             3442
    Masefield, John           4992
    Noyes, Alfred             5329
    Shanks, Edward            5643  5650
    Stephens, James           5937
    Stevenson, Robert Louis   6173
    Watson, William           7077
```

GIBBS, Geoffrey David   1940-

```
    Auden, W.H.               101  205  223
    Housman, A.E.             3239
    Kipling, Rudyard          4095
    Masefield, John           4882
    Yeats, W.B.               7549
```

GIDEON, Miriam   1906-

```
    Thompson, Francis         7000
```

GILBERT, Anthony   1934-

```
    Hopkins, Gerard Manley    3133
    MacBeth, George           4518
```

GILBERT, Henry Franklin Belknap   1868-1928

```
    Stevenson, Robert Louis   6445
    Synge, J.M.               6849*
    Yeats, W.B.               7567*
```

GILBERT, Norman   1912-

```
    Bax, Clifford             294
    Belloc, Hilaire           389  432
    Chesterton, G.K.          997  1003
    Grahame, Kenneth          2353
    Hardy, Thomas             2711
    Masefield, John           4829
    Stevenson, Robert Louis   6357  6527
```

GILBERT, Steven E.   1943-

```
    Thomas, Dylan             6904  6920  6940
```

GILCHRIST, William Wallace   1846-1916

    Kipling, Rudyard   4214
    Stevenson, Robert Louis   6208 6257 6507

GILKYSON, Terry   ?-

    Kipling, Rudyard   4075

GILL, Harry   ?-

    Belloc, Hilaire   452
    Reeves, James   5542
    Sackville-West, Victoria 5573

GILLIS, Ivan M.   1918-1946

    Hardy, Thomas   2756

GILMAN, Lawrence   1878-1939

    Yeats, W.B.   7481 7531 7623

GIPPS, Ruth   1921-

    Brooke, Rupert   790 798 799 804 830
    Noyes, Alfred   5313
    Swinburne, A.C.   6688

GLANVILLE-HICKS, Peggy   1912-

    AE   23 56
    Dunsany, Lord   2025
    Graves, Robert   2401
    Housman, A.E.   3194 3200 3201 3206 3375
    Webb, Mary   7108

GLASS, Dudley   ?-

    Belloc, Hilaire   527
    O'Sullivan, Seumas   5420
    Potter, Beatrix   5481 5482

GLAZUNOV, Alexander Konstantinovich   1865-1936

    Wilde, Oscar   7265

GLEN, Katherine A.   ?-

    Le Gallienne, Richard   4457

GODFREY, Graham   ?-

    Flecker, James Elroy   2196

GODWIN, Joscelyn   1945-

    Housman, A.E.   3443
    Joyce, James   3892

GOLDMAN, Richard Franko   1910-

    Stevenson, Robert Louis   6264

GOLDSMITH, Jerry   ?-

    Durrell, Lawrence   2050

GOODE, Herbert   ?-

    Aldington, Richard   74*

GOODHART, A.M.   1905-1955
Also wrote under the nom de plume "Al Goodhart"

    Belloc, Hilaire   373 528

GOODWIN, Ron   ?-

    Maugham, Somerset   5011

GOOSSEN, Frederic   1927-

    Hardy, Thomas   2459 2460 2467 2541 2581 2599
                   2744

GOOSSENS, (Aynsley) Eugene   1893-1962

    Bennett, Arnold   533 535
    de la Mare, Walter   1704
    Joyce, James   3612 3651 3687 3703 3741 3756
             3766
    Maugham, Somerset   5009

GORDON, Edgar B., arr.   ?-

   Symonds, John Addington   6724

GORE, W.C.   ?-

   Kipling, Rudyard   3991

GORECKI, Thaddeus   ?-

   Housman, A.E.   3268* 3283* 3322* 3350* 3405*

GOVER, Gerald   1914-

   Belloc, Hilaire   486
   Brooke, Rupert   810
   de la Mare, Walter   1609
   Dunsany, Lord   2029
   Meynell, Alice   5118
   Tynan, Katharine   7052
   Wilde, Oscar   7157 7243

GOW, David   1924-

   Belloc, Hilaire   514
   Hopkins, Gerard Manley   2971 3041 3086

GOWER, E. Leveson   ?-

   Kipling, Rudyard   4111

GRAINGER, Percy Aldridge   1882-1961

   Doyle, Arthur Conan   1975
   Kipling, Rudyard   3953 3955 3957 3974 4016 4030
      4035 4040 4061 4067 4105 4112
      4132 4137 4142 4158 4165 4178
      4186* 4190 4194 4215 4239*
      4240 4272 4276 4277 4278 4287
      4291 4292* 4293 4302 4321
      4329 4333 4338
   Swinburne, A.C.   6619 6678

GRANT, William Parks   1910-

   Hardy, Thomas   2595 2683
   Housman, A.E.   3209 3284 3397 3444 3477
   Masefield, John   4847

GRANT continued

Yeats, W.B.   7703

GRANT-SCHAEFER, G. Alfred   ?-

    de la Mare, Walter   1660
    Stevenson, Robert Louis 6528
    Wolfe, Humbert   7349

GRAVES, William L.   1916-

    Auden, W.H.   224
    Hopkins, Gerard Manley 3134

GRAY, Alan   1855-1935

    Brooke, Rupert   795 797 805 807 811 828
    Housman, A.E.   3149
    Newbolt, Henry   5241

GREAVES, Ralph   1889-1966

    Masefield, John   4993 4994 4995 4996
    Sassoon, Siegfried   5619

GREAVES, Terence   ?-

    de la Mare, Walter   1348 1370 1408 1649 1655 1697

GREEN, Charles   ?-

    Kipling, Rudyard   4022 4160 4238

GREENBERG, David Lawrence   ?-

    Joyce, James   3933

GREENBERG, Noah, ed.   1919-1966

    Auden, W.H.   176 238

GREENE, R.G.H.   ?-

    de la Mare, Walter   1349 1374 1411 1446

GREENHILL, [Harold?]   [?-   ]

    Davies, W.H.   1312

GREENHILL, Harold   ?-

    Coleridge, Mary   1050
    de la Mare, Walter   1714
    Hardy, Thomas   2712
    O'Sullivan, Seumas   5409

GREVILLE, Ursula   ?-

    Sackville-West, Victoria   5570

GRIFFES, Charles Tomlinson   1884-1920

    Brooke, Rupert   831
    Henley, W.E.   2900
    Macleod, Fiona   4571 4596 4601* 4620 4658
                                4685 4697 4703 4732 4749 4754
    Masefield, John   4903 4948
    Symonds, John Addington   6725
    Wilde, Oscar   7158 7188 7216 7223 7233
                                7234* 7262 7284
    Yeats, W.B.   7550

GRIFFIS, Elliot   1893-1967

    Joyce, James   3718
    Le Gallienne, Richard   4453

GRIFFITHS, T. Vernon   ?-

    Chesterton, G.K.   982 998
    Masefield, John   4885

GRINNELL, Edmund   ?-

    Stevenson, Robert Louis   6335

GRINNELL, Edward   ?-

    Symons, Arthur   6824

GRISWOLD, Ruth Redington   ?-

    Noyes, Alfred   5322

GRO, Josephine   ?-

   Kipling, Rudyard   4128

GROOCOCK, Joseph   ?-

   Stevenson, Robert Louis   6088 6308 6374 6401 6475 6541

GROSSMITH, George   ?-

   Stevenson, Robert Louis   6386

GROSVENOR, (Hon.) Mrs. Norman
   [Caroline Susan Theodora Grosvenor   1858-1940?]

   Stevenson, Robert Louis   6228 6272 6289 6402 6422 6508

GRUBER, Albion   1931-

   Hopkins, Gerard Manley   3087

GRUEN, John   ?-

   Eliot, T.S.   2053 2070
   Joyce, James   3621 3631 3901

GRUENBERG, Louis   1884-1964

   Hudson, W.H.   3541

GURNEY, Ivor Bertie   1890-1937

   Belloc, Hilaire   390 426 453 482 500 515
   Blunden, Edmund   576
   Bridges, Robert   626 640 647 651 666 692 701
                     719 723 730 768 774 780
   Brooke, Rupert   788* 803* 816* 817 827* 829*
   Campbell, Joseph   876 894
   Davidson, John   1217
   Davies, W.H.   1228 1233 1238 1251 1273 1307
                     1308
   de la Mare, Walter   1351 1356 1381 1388 1461 1472
                     1684 1843
   Drinkwater, John   2015
   Flecker, James Elroy 2193 2209 2215
   Freeman, John   2227
   Gibson, W.W.   2279 2280 2285 2292 2306 2310
                     2311 2319 2321

GURNEY continued

Gould, Gerald	2342					
Graves, Robert	2382	2399*	2416	2419	2420*	
	2428					
Hardy, Thomas	2479	2517	2632	2634		
Henley, W.E.	2788	2800	2803	2864		
Hodgson, Ralph	2959					
Housman, A.E.	3139	3169	3177	3227	3242	3252
	3259	3285	3286	3307	3345	3348
	3351	3362	3398	3406	3445	3464
	3494					
Ledwidge, Francis	4427					
Masefield, John	4841	4876	4906	4997		
O'Sullivan, Seumas	5410					
Sassoon, Siegfried	5592					
Shanks, Edward	5641	5644	5646	5647	5651	5653
Squire, J.C.	5865	5870	5874			
Stevenson, Robert Louis	6050	6058	6156	6219	6462	6553
Thomas, Edward	6944	6947	6950	6951	6953	6956
	6962	6963	6964	6967	6968	6971
	6972	6977	6979	6984	6988	
Thompson, Francis	7017					
Trench, Herbert	7031					
Watson, William	7105					
Yeats, W.B.	7374	7409	7427	7491	7502	7513
	7528	7551	7568	7585	7604	7694
	7701					

GWYTHER, Geoffrey   ?-

Belloc, Hilaire	391				
de la Mare, Walter	1751				
Stephens, James	5916				

HADLEY, Henry Kimball   1871-1937

Henley, W.E.	2793				
Kipling, Rudyard	4216				
Stevenson, Robert Louis	6117	6273	6403	6476	6542
Swinburne, A.C.	6634	6654			
Wilde, Oscar	7192				

HADLEY, Patrick Arthur Sheldon   1899-1973

Hardy, Thomas	2749	
O'Sullivan, Seumas	5418	
Yeats, W.B.	7480	7715

HADOW, William Henry   1859-1937

    Bridges, Robert   628
    Stevenson, Robert Louis   6051

HAGEMAN, Richard   1882-1966

    Belloc, Hilaire   473 501
    Binyon, Laurence   559
    Chesterton, G.K.   971
    Dowson, Ernest   1904
    Dunsany, Lord   2030
    Masefield, John   4830
    Stephens, James   5957
    Yeats, W.B.   7503

HALE, Alfred M.   ?-1960

    Douglas, Lord Alfred   1900
    Hardy, Thomas   2461 2468 2510 2542 2547 2582
                                2600 2645 2667 2745

HALIŠKA, Rostislav   1937-

    Wilde, Oscar   7198

HALSKI, Czeslaw Raymund   1908-

    Chesterton, G.K.   1012
    Dobson, Austin   1897

HAMERTON, Ann   ?-

    Gould, Gerald   2343

HAMILTON, Janet   ?-

    Housman, A.E.   3150 3287 3399 3495

HAMMOND, Richard   ?-

    Le Gallienne, Richard   4467

HAND, Colin   1929-

    de la Mare, Walter   1567 1605 1675 1715
    Grahame, Kenneth   2354
    Masefield, John   4957

959

HAND continued

    Meynell, Alice   5081
    Monro, Harold   5198 5203
    Noyes, Alfred   5357
    O'Sullivan, Seumas   5411
    Sitwell, Osbert   5773
    Stevenson, Robert Louis 6529

HANSON, Raymond   1913-

    Thomas, Dylan   6886

HARMATI, Sandor   1892-1936

    de la Mare, Walter   1627

HARRIES, David   1933-

    Hopkins, Gerard Manley   3135
    Treece, Henry   7025

HARRIS, G. Percy   ?-

    Kipling, Rudyard   3992

HARRIS, George   ?-

    Aldington, Richard   79

HARRIS, Russell G.   ?-

    Yeats, W.B.   7618

HARRIS, Victor   1869-1943

    de la Mare, Walter   1416 1628 1716
    Henley, W.E.   2834
    Swinburne, A.C.   6604

HARRIS, William Henry   1883-1873

    Bridges, Robert   610
    Noyes, Alfred   5369
    Sassoon, Siegfried   5593
    Thompson, Francis   7001

HARRISON, Julius Allan Greenway   1885-1963

    Housman, A.E.   3151
    Trench, Herbert   7032 7035

HARRISON, Lou   1917-

    Yeats, W.B.   7619

HARRISON, Pamela   1915-

    de la Mare, Walter   1384* 1440* 1448 1452 1499*
                                     1522* 1619* 1622 1679 1681
                                     1777 1808 1811* 1813* 1815*
                                     1820 1844
    Dowson, Ernest   1909 1926 1934 1941 1954
    Thomas, Edward   6946 6952 6954 6965 6980 6985

HARRISON, Sidney   1903-

    Hardy, Thomas   2734
    Joyce, James   3704

HART, Fritz Bennicke   1874-1949

    AE   5 6 7 9 10 11 12 13 14 15 16
                                     17 18 19 20 24 25 27 29 30 31
                                     33 34 36 38 39 40 41 42 44 45
                                     46 47 48 50 51 53 54 57 58 59
                                     60 61 63 64 65 66 68 69
    Austin, Alfred   242 243 244
    Bottomley, Gordon   585 587 589 590 592
    Bridges, Robert   603 623 667 678 694 707 714
                                     720 737 743 765 775
    Campbell, Joseph   859 860 862 864 866 869 870
                                     871 872 882 888 892 895 898
    Chesterton, G.K.   1000
    Coleridge, Mary   1044
    Colum, Padraic   1089
    Davies, W.H.   1256
    Dobson, Austin   1874
    Gibbon, Monk   2271 2272 2273 2274 2275 2277
    Gibson, W.W.   2278 2294 2303 2312 2313 2316
                                     2320 2324 2326 2328
    Gregory, Lady Augusta   2449
    Hardy, Thomas   2735
    Henley, W.E.   2776 2806 2807* 2812 2817
                                     2825 2828 2835* 2848 2862

HART continued

Henley continued	2865 2866 2868 2874 2877 2880
	2882 2897 2912 2917 2921
Joyce, James	3719
Macleod, Fiona	4573 4576 4580 4590 4592 4597
	4600 4603 4604 4605 4608 4610
	4614 4619 4621 4631 4633 4647
	4648 4650 4552 4655 4662 4659
	4673 4680 4684 4687 4692 4696
	4702 4707 4710 4712 4715 4727
	4728 4729 4733 4735 4736 4739
	4741 4742 4744 4746 4747 4754
	4759 4760 4763 4765 4766 4767
	4769 4781
Meynell, Alice	5076 5082 5090
Phillips, Stephen	5457
Stevenson, Robert Louis	6066
Swinburne, A.C.	6691
Symons, Arthur	6776 6813 6818 6825
Synge, J.M.	6833 6850
Tynan, Katharine	7053
Wolfe, Humbert	7298 7299 7304 7305 7306 7308
	7311 7313 7315 7318 7322 7330
	7331 7332 7333 7334 7337 7342
	7343 7352
Yeats, W.B.	7428 7566

HARTY, (Herbert) Hamilton   1879-1941

Campbell, Joseph	861 902 903
Colum, Padraic	1090 1125
Tynan, Katharine	7054
Yeats, W.B.	7504

HARVEY, Alex   ?-

Auden, W.H.	188

HARVEY, Jonathan   1939-

Eliot, T.S.	2090
Muir, Edwin	5227
Turner, W.J.R.	7036
Yeats, W.B.	7375 7477 7519 7523 7590 7646
	7667 7716

HARVEY, Trevor   ?-

    Belloc, Hilaire   464

HASTINGS, Frank Seymour   ?-

    Henley, W.E.   2777

HATCH, Homer B.   ?-

    Kipling, Rudyard   3951 4322

HATHAWAY, Joseph William George   ?-1956

    Henley, W.E.   2778

HATTEY, Philip   ?-

    Graves, Robert   2398 2402 2407 2423 2424 2433
                                 2437

HAUBENSTOCK-RAMATI, Roman   1919-

    Beckett, Samuel   321 357

HAUBIEL, Charles   1892?-

    Wilde, Oscar   7176 7229 7255

HAUPRECHT, Herbert   1909-

    Campbell, Joseph   868 889
    Yeats, W.B.   7635

HAWES, Jack   1916-

    Macleod, Fiona   4574 4586 4606 4611 4674 4713
                                 4752

HAWKINS, John   1944-

    Yeats, W.B.   7717

HAWLEY, Charles Beach   1858-1915

    Le Gallienne, Richard   4476
    Stevenson, Robert Louis   6375

                                 963

HAYDON, Claude   1884-1960

    Kipling, Rudyard   4344

HAZLEHURST, Cecil   1880-

    Bridges, Robert   776

HEAD, Michael Dewar   1900-

    Abercrombie, Lascelles   1
    Davies, W.H.   1242 1264 1269 1278 1288 1297
    de la Mare, Walter   1428
    Drinkwater, John   1987 1998 2016
    Grahame, Kenneth   2355
    Hardy, Thomas   2545 2713
    Housman, A.E.   3187
    Joyce, James   3720
    Ledwidge, Francis   4429 4430 4434 4435 4436 4438
    Masefield, John   4958
    Noyes, Alfred   5352
    O'Sullivan, Seumas   5412
    Pitter, Ruth   5466 5467 5473 5476 5478 5480
    Sitwell, Edith   5720
    Webb, Mary   7115 7120
    Wolfe, Humbert   7345

HEALEY, Derek   1936-

    Eliot, T.S.   2096 2118
    Gogarty, Oliver St. John   2334
    Hardy, Thomas   2484 2578 2637 2714 2747
    Joyce, James   3705 3861
    Wilde, Oscar   7231
    Yeats, W.B.   7429 7473

HEARNE, John Michael   1937-

    Thomas, Dylan   6868 6875 6894

HEATH, John Rippiner   1887-

    Stephens, James   5987

HEDGCOCK, Walter William   1864-?

    Kipling, Rudyard   4120
    Newbolt, Henry   5250

HEDGES, Anthony   1931-

    Muir, Edwin   5226
    Reeves, James   5543 5544 5545 5546 5547
    Smith, Stevie   5784

HEILNER, Irwin   1908-

    Hardy, Thomas   2492 2558 2565 2669 2736
    Housman, A.E.   3163 3164 3317 3373

HEININEN, Paavo   1938-

    Yeats, W.B.   7376

HELLERMAN, William   1939-

    Owen, Wilfred   5444

HELYER, Marjorie   ?-

    Stevenson, Robert Louis   6157 6247 6404 6477

HELY-HUTCHINSON, (Christian) Victor   1901-1947

    Belloc, Hilaire   529
    Chesterton, G.K.   985 987 999
    de la Mare, Walter   1375 1417 1433 1530 1572 1644
                                        1717 1761 1796 1823
    Kipling, Rudyard   4003 4010 4315

HENDERSON, J. Raymond   1929-

    Symonds, John Addington   6726

HENEKER, David William   1906-

    Wells, H.G.   7142

HENRIQUES, Fini Valdemar [Valdemar Fini?]   1867-1940

    Barrie, J.M.   282

HENZE, Hans Werner   1926-

    Auden, W.H.   94 119 155

HERBERT, Ivy   ?-

    Bridges, Robert   657

HERBERT, Muriel E.   ?-

    Belloc, Hilaire   454
    Bridges, Robert   769
    de la Mare, Walter   1364
    Housman, A.E.   3288
    Meredith, George   5047 5060
    Meynell, Alice   5092
    Swinburne, A.C.   6703
    Yeats, W.B.   7552

HERBERT, Victor   1859-1924

    Carpenter, Edward   930
    Stevenson, Robert Louis   6099 6509
    Swinburne, A.C.   6655 6685

HERLINGER, Jan   ?-

    Joyce, James   3893

HERRESHOFF, Constance Mills   ?-

    Colum, Padraic   1067
    Housman, A.E.   3289

HEUSSENSTAMM, George   1926-

    Housman, A.E.   3334 3496
    Meredith, George   5027

HEWITT-JONES, Tony   1926-

    Davies, W.H.   1234
    Masefield, John   4914 4983

HEYS, Sidney   ?-

    Chesterton, G.K.   951

HICKEY, F.G.   ?-

    Noyes, Alfred   5370

```
HICKEY, Vivian    ?-

     Masefield, John          4853 4919 4968
     Meynell, Alice           5077
     Symons, Arthur           6785

HICKS, Mary    ?-

     Grahame, Kenneth         2356

HILL, Edward Burlingame    1872-1960

     Dowson, Ernest           1913 1955
     Henley, W.E.             2869
     Stevenson, Robert Louis  6006 6075 6309 6564
     Symons, Arthur           6770 6798 6814

HINCHLIFFE, Irvin    ?-

     Yeats, W.B.              7605

HIND, John    ?-

     Belloc, Hilaire          455
     Colum, Padraic           1091

HINDEMITH, Paul    1895-1963

     Moore, T. Sturge         5220
     Thompson, Francis        6995

HODDINOTT, Alun    1929-

     Sitwell, Edith           5769
     Stevenson, Robert Louis  6023

HODEIR, André    1921-

     Joyce, James             3663

HOGGETT, Alan    ?-

     de la Mare, Walter       1462

HOIBY, Lee    1926-

     Kipling, Rudyard         4046
```

HOLBROOKE, Joseph Charles   1878-1958
    Also known as Josef Holbrooke

    Masefield, John   4886
    Trench, Herbert   7028 7033

HOLD, Trevor   1939-

    Hopkins, Gerard Manley   2965 3042 3055 3112
    Reeves, James   5548
    Symons, Arthur   6817
    Thomas, Edward   6955 6957 6958 6973 6974
    Treece, Henry   7026

HOLFORD, Franz   ?-

    Drinkwater, John   1989 2007 2023

HOLLAND, Theodore Samuel   1878-1947

    Davies, W.H.   1282
    Flecker, James Elroy   2201* 2203* 2210*

HOLLANDER, Frederick   ?-

    Conrad, Joseph   1144

HOLLISTER, David M.   1929-

    Housman, A.E.   3314

HOLLOWAY, Robin   1943-

    Blunden, Edmund   580
    Cornford, Frances   1172
    de la Mare, Walter   1473 1475
    Eliot, T.S.   2151 2181 2182
    Hardy, Thomas   2757
    Housman, A.E.   3521 3522
    Joyce, James   3934
    Smith, Stevie   5805 5806 5807
    Stephens, James   5999

HOLMAN, Derek   ?-

    de la Mare, Walter   1762
    Stevenson, Robert Louis   6530

```
HOLMES, Horace Reuben, arr.      ?-

    Graves, A.P.                 2363

HOLMES, Rae      1940-

    Hardy, Thomas                2715

HOLOUBEK, Ladislav      1913-

    Haggard, Rider               2456

HOLST, Gustav Theodore      1874-1934

    Bax, Clifford                295 308 310 311
    Bridges, Robert              604 611* 631 633 645 676* 681
                                 695 715 721 738 762 764
    Hardy, Thomas                2481* 2559 2573* 2641 2654*
    Masefield, John              4859 4910 4920
    Meredith, George             5067
    Thompson, Francis            6993* 7016*
    Wolfe, Humbert               7301 7307 7309 7310* 7312
                                 7319 7323 7328 7335 7338 7340
                                 7346 7348

HOLST, Gustav Theodore, arr.      1874-1934

    Bax, Clifford                309
    Housman, Laurence            3535

HOLT, G.E.      ?-

    Kipling, Rudyard             4217

HOMER, Sidney      1864-1953

    Bridges, Robert              770
    Henley, W.E.                 2789 2796 2871
    Masefield, John              4866 4982
    Stephens, James              5930
    Stevenson, Robert Louis      6059 6080 6301 6310 6336 6365
                                 6367 6376 6382 6543
    Tynan, Katharine             7048
    Watson, William              7095
    Yeats, W.B.                  7505 7648
```

HONEGGER, Arthur   1892-1955

    Shaw, George Bernard   5675

HOPEKIRK, Helen   1856-1945

    Macleod, Fiona   4577 4589 4613 4626 4640 4663
                              4682 4689* 4726 4734 4755
    Stevenson, Robert Louis   6438

HOPKINS, Antony   1921-
Originally named Antony Reynolds

    Sayers, Dorothy L.   5637
    Shaw, George Bernard   5660
    Ustinov, Peter   7060

HOPKINS, Bill   1943-

    Beckett, Samuel   326 330 333 340 343 347 353
    Joyce, James   3786 3814

HOPKINS, E.G. [G.E.?]   ?-

    Kipling, Rudyard   4218*

HORDER, Mervyn   1910-

    Betjeman, John   540 541 542* 543 548 550

HORNE, Jonathan Thomas   ?-

    Henley, W.E.   2821

HORROCKS, Amy Elsie   1867-?

    Dobson, Austin   1881

HORROCKS, Herbert   ?-

    Sassoon, Siegfried   5594
    Strong, L.A.G.   6600

HORSMAN, Edward   ?-

    Meynell, Alice   5088 5101

```
HOSKINS, William R.      1917-

    Housman, A.E.              3228*

HOUSMAN, Rosalie      1888-1949

    Davies, W.H.              1284
    de la Mare, Walter        1450 1463 1629
    Gibson, W.W.              2304 2317
    Yeats, W.B.               7430 7659

HOVHANESS, Alan      1911-
    Originally named Chakmakjian

    Stevenson, Robert Louis   6248

HOWE, Mary      1882-1964

    de la Mare, Walter        1521

HOWELL, Dorothy      1898-

    Eliot, T.S.               2145

HOWELLS, Herbert Norman      1892-

    Bridges, Robert           700
    de la Mare, Walter        1350 1398 1445 1491 1550 1590
                              1606 1792 1845 1846 1847
    Dobson, Austin            1894
    Gibson, W.W.              2295 2307 2308
    Joyce, James              3671
    Newbolt, Henry            5258
    O'Sullivan, Seumas        5399 5421
    Stephens, James           5918
    Symons, Arthur            6805
    Tynan, Katharine          7045

HOYLAND, D. Victor      1945

    Beckett, Samuel           351*

HRUBÝ, K.      1913-
    Pseud. of Ota Ornest

    Wilde, Oscar              7208
```

HUBERS, Klaus   ?-

   Joyce, James   3935

HUGGLER, John   ?-

   Yeats, W.B.   7656

HUGHES, Gervase   1905-

   Brooke, Rupert   837
   Stevenson, Robert Louis   6565

HUGHES, Herbert   1882-1937

   Campbell, Joseph   904
   Colum, Padraic   1069 1073 1092 1110 1111 1116
                                 1123 1127 1134
   Joyce, James   3815
   O'Casey, Sean   5380*
   Yeats, W.B.   7606

HUGHES, Herbert, arr.   1882-1937

   Campbell, Joseph   886
   Colum, Padraic   1112 1126

HUGHES, Spike   1908-
Also known as Patrick Cairns Hughes

   Yeats, W.B.   7631*

HUGHES-JONES, Llifon   ?-

   de la Mare, Walter   1617

HUHN, Bruno Siegfried   1871-1950

   Henley, W.E.   2856

HUNDLEY, Richard   1931-

   Stevenson, Robert Louis   6158

HUNT, Raymond   ?-

   Kipling, Rudyard   4027 4255

HUNT, Thomas   ?-

    Kipling, Rudyard   4106*

HUNT, Wynn   1910-

    Davies, W.H.   1243 1252 1300 1301 1309
    Meynell, Alice   5102
    Symons, Arthur   6765

HURD, Michael   1928-

    Causley, Charles   932 935 936 938 939
    de la Mare, Walter   1386 1414 1427 1551 1604 1638
                         1653 1656 1729 1787

HUSE, Peter   1938-

    Thomas, Dylan   6887

HUSS, Henry Holden   1862-1953

    Kipling, Rudyard   4219

HYDE, Lewis   1899-
Nom de plume of John Reginald Lang-Hyde

    Auden, W.H.   102 107 114 116 124 127 143
                         150 172 179 181 189 196 219
                         220 225 227
    Isherwood, Christopher 3578 3583
    Swinburne, A.C.   6612 6617 6620 6621 6622 6628
                         6648 6666 6682 6689 6690 6692

HYWEL, John   1941-

    Yeats, W.B.   7620

IBERT, Jacques François Antoine   1890-1962

    Wilde, Oscar   7155

IDE, Chester Edward   1878-

    Stevenson, Robert Louis 6159

IHRKE, Walter   1908-

    Gould, Gerald   2349

IRELAND, John Nicholson   1879-1962

    Brooke, Rupert   796 812 818
    Coleridge, Mary   1043 1047
    Dowson, Ernest   1905 1944 1947
    Drinkwater, John   1993
    Hardy, Thomas   2501 2549 2554 2557 2596 2673
                          2677 2716 2748
    Housman, A.E.   3210 3260 3269 3270* 3308*
                          3381 3400 3401 3407 3412 3461
                          3513
    Huxley, Aldous   3563
    Joyce, James   3882
    Kirkup, James   4358
    Masefield, John   4936 4951 4980
    Meynell, Alice   5089 5110
    Monro, Harold   5210
    Newbolt, Henry   5263
    Stevenson, Robert Louis 6031
    Symonds, John Addington 6727 6728*
    Symons, Arthur   6737 6766 6794 6802 6806
    Warner, Sylvia Townsend 7066 7069 7070
    Yeats, W.B.   7607

ISHERWOOD, Cherry   ?-

    Sassoon, Siegfried   5624

ISSACS, Lewis M.   ?-

    Henley, W.E.   2870

ITO, Teiji   ?-

    Joyce, James   3664

IVES, Charles Edward   1874-1954

    Brooke, Rupert   802
    Kipling, Rudyard   4034* 4107 4179* 4286* 4345
    Meredith, George   5044
    Stevenson, Robert Louis 6337
    Symons, Arthur   6792

JACKSON, Francis Alan   ?-

    Masefield, John   4952
    Stevenson, Robert Louis   6118

JACKSON, Stanley   ?-

    Cornford, Frances   1173

JACOB, Archibald   ?-

    de la Mare, Walter   1698

JACOB, Gordon Percival Septimus   1895-

    Bridges, Robert   744
    Moore, George   5212
    Wolfe, Humbert   7350

JACOBSON, Maurice   1896-

    Bridges, Robert   641
    Drinkwater, John   1999
    Freeman, John   2228
    Masefield, John   4873
    Stevenson, Robert Louis   6067
    Thompson, Francis   7002

JACQUES, Reginald   ?-

    Strong, L.A.G.   6601

JAGER, Robert Edward   1939-

    Stevenson, Robert Louis   6079 6119 6134 6202 6510

JAMES, Philip Frederick Wright   1890-

    Auden, W.H.   134

JAMES, Phyllis M.   ?-

    Belloc, Hilaire   392 407
    Tynan, Katharine   7049

JARRE, Maurice   1925-

    Fowles, John   2225

JARRETT, Brian C.   1925-

    Stevenson, Robert Louis   6465

JARRETT, Jack M.   1934-

    Grahame, Kenneth   2357
    Joyce, James   3622 3644 3652 3665 3688 3694
                              3706 3721 3736 3739 3745 3757
                              3787 3800 3816 3832 3862 3883
                              3902

JARVIS, Joyce E.K.   ?-

    Freeman, John   2226

JERVIS-READ, Harold Vincent   1883-

    Johnson, Lionel   3600
    Moore, T. Sturge   5218
    Thompson, Francis   6991 6994
    Wilde, Oscar   7184 7224 7235 7256 7286

JEŽEK, Jaroslav   1906-1942

    Chesterton, G.K.   988

JÍRA, Milan   1935-

    Shaw, George Bernard   5682

JIRKO, Ivan   1926-

    Greene, Graham   2444

JOHNS, Clayton   1857-1932

    Henley, W.E.   2872 2888
    Kipling, Rudyard   4171
    Swinburne, A.C.   6704
    Watson, William   7090

JOHNS, E.W.   ?-

    Noyes, Alfred   5354 5358

JOHNSON, Horace   1893-1964

    de la Mare, Walter   1783*
    Dobson, Austin   1872

JOHNSON, Ora Agatha   ?-

    Housman, A.E.   3446

JOHNSON, Phoebe Wynn   ?-

    Yeats, W.B.   7678

JOHNSON, Reginald T.   1941-

    Housman, A.E.   3152

JOHNSON, W. Noel   1863-?

    Henley, W.E.   2779

JOHNSON, William Spencer   ?-

    Bottomley, Gordon   598
    Henley, W.E.   2883
    Macleod, Fiona   4756

JOHNSTON, Richard   1917-

    O'Sullivan, Seumas   5392 5400 5419

JOHNSTON, Tom   ?-

    Graves, A.P.   2368

JOHNSTONE, Margaret   ?-

    Chesterton, G.K.   952

JOHNSTONE, Maurice   ?-

    Meynell, Alice   5078

JONES, Daniel Jenkyn   1912-

    Thomas, Dylan   6932 6941

JONES, John Owen   1876-1962

    Newbolt, Henry   5261

JONES, Kenneth V.   1924-

    Bridges, Robert   708
    Eliot, T.S.   2137
    Thomas, Edward   6981

JONES, Robert William   1932-

    Dowson, Ernest   1927 1956
    Maugham, Somerset   5017
    Meredith, George   5028
    Munro, H.H.   5239
    Russell, Bertrand   5566
    Wilde, Oscar   7257
    Yeats, W.B.   7708

JORDAN, Jules   1850-1927

    Kipling, Rudyard   4346

JOSEPHS, Wilfred   1927-

    Belloc, Hilaire   448

JOUBERT, John   1927-

    Conrad, Joseph   1142
    Holbrook, David   2961
    Spender, Stephen   5852
    Yeats, W.B.   7640

JOYCE, Mary Ann   ?-

    Eliot, T.S.   2183
    Hopkins, Gerard Manley 3136

JUDD, Percy   ?-

    Coleridge, Mary   1056
    Stevenson, Robert Louis 6405

KADLEC, Jaroslav   1914-

    Shaw, George Bernard 5676

KAGEN, Sergius   1909-1964

de la Mare, Walter	1591
Housman, A.E.	3509
Joyce, James	3613 3767 3801 3817 3833 3863

KALACH, Jiří   1934-

| Wilde, Oscar | 7199 |

KALAŠ, Julius   1902-1967

| Wilde, Oscar | 7238 |

KALMANOFF, Martin   1920-

Housman, A.E.	3356 3447
Hudson, W.H.	3542
Kipling, Rudyard	4093
Sassoon, Siegfried	5578 5583
Stevenson, Robert Louis	6338 6454
Wilde, Oscar	7169

KALOMIRIS, Manolis   1883-

| Yeats, W.B. | 7649* |

KAPER, Bronislaw   1902-

| Conrad, Joseph | 1138 |

KAREL, Jaromír Otto   1920-

| Shaw, George Bernard | 5658 |

KARLINS, M. William   1932-

| Joyce, James | 3768 3864 |

KASEMETS, Udo   1919-

| Raine, Kathleen | 5502 5514 5523 |
| Thomas, Dylan | 6869 6898 |

KAUDER, Hugo   ?-

| Joyce, James | 3614 3625 3722 3746 3769 3802 |
| | 3834 3865 3909 3920 |

KAY, Ulysses Simpson   1917-

    Stevenson, Robert Louis   6478

KEATS, Donald   1929-

    Eliot, T.S.   2111
    Yeats, W.B.   7474

KEEL, (James) Frederick   1871-1954

    de la Mare, Walter   1399 1498 1542 1570 1671 1752
    Hardy, Thomas   2655
    Masefield, John   4838 4875 4883 4895 4913 4974
                               4975 4984
    Noyes, .Alfred   5371

KEENEY, Wendell   ?-

    Housman, A.E.   3140

KELLAM, Ian   ?-

    Eliot, T.S.   2102

KELLIE, Lawrence   ?-

    Wilde, Oscar   7289*

KELLOGG, Arthur   ?-

    Kipling, Rudyard   4143

KELLY, Bryan   1934-

    Auden, W.H.   199
    Graves, Robert   2390
    Sitwell, Edith   5704

KELLY, Thomas C.   1917-

    Yeats, W.B.   7485 7553

KENT, Ada Twohy   1888-

    de la Mare, Walter   1480

KERN, Jerome David   1885-1945

   Barrie, J.M.   290

KERN, Mary Root   ?-

   Noyes, Alfred   5318

KERNOCHAN, Marshall Rutgers   1880-1955

   Henley, W.E.   2857
   Kipling, Rudyard   4108 4187 4263
   Meredith, George   5036

KHAIFEL, Alexandre   ?-

   Wilde, Oscar   7170

KILBY, Muriel Laura   1929-

   Housman, A.E.   3229

KINSEY, Tony   ?-

   Logue, Christopher   4501 4509

KIRBYE, George   ?-

   Warner, Sylvia Townsend 7073

KIRCHNER, Leon   1919-

   Hopkins, Gerard Manley   3116

KITTLESON, Carl J.   1920-

   Belloc, Hilaire   516
   Hardy, Thomas   2533 2648 2717
   Joyce, James   3712 3770 3910 3919

KLEBE, Giselher   ?-

   Synge, J.M.   6841*

KLEIN, Ivy Frances   1895-

   Blunden, Edmund   579
   Church, Richard   1014

KLEIN continued

    Stephens, James   5991
    Tynan, Katharine   7055

KLIMKO, Ronald James   1936-

    Hopkins, Gerard Manley   3016

KLOTZMAN, Dorothy Hill   1937-
Nom de plume of Dorothy Klotzman

    Joyce, James   3645 3723 3921

KLUSÁK, Jan   1934-

    Rattigan, Terence   5528

KNIGHT, Gerald Hocken   1908-

    Sayers, Dorothy L.   5638

KNIGHT, Morris   1933-

    Lawrence, D.H.   4381 4386 4396 4397 4398 4400
                           4408 4416 4417

KOCH, John G.   1928-

    de la Mare, Walter   1464 1718
    Stevenson, Robert Louis 6074

KOCSÁR, Miklós   1933-

    Joyce, James   3936

KODÁLY, Zoltán   1882-1967

    Masefield, John   4998

KOECHLIN, Charles Louis Eugène   1867-1950

    Kipling, Rudyard   4076 4077 4088 4135 4166 4172
                           4245 4256 4284

KOEMMENICH, Louis   1866-1922

    Joyce, James   3771

KOPELENT, Marek   1932-

    Beckett, Samuel   322 334 349
    Greene, Graham   2441

KORBAY, Francis Alexander   1846-1913

    Henley, W.E.   2780 2801 2858 2884 2906

KORNGOLD, Erich Wolfgang   1897-1957

    Maugham, Somerset   5012

KORNGOLD, Erich Wolfgang, arr.   1897-1957

    Herbert, A.P.   2937

KORTE, Karl   1928-

    Stevenson, Robert Louis   6160

KOSINA, Jiří   1926-

    Wilde, Oscar   7209

KOSŤÁL, Arnošt   1920-

    Wilde, Oscar   7210 7211

KOSTECK, George   ?-

    Synge, J.M.   6851

KOSTELANETZ, Andre   1901-

    Meredith, George   5046

KOUNTZ, Richard   1896-1950

    Stevenson, Robert Louis   6339

KOUTZEN, Boris   1901-1966

    Symonds, John Addington   6715

KOVAŘÍČEK, František   1924-

    Wilde, Oscar   7193

KOX, Hans   1930-

    Wilde, Oscar   7244

KRAFT, William   1923-

    Belloc, Hilaire   377

KRAMER, Arthur Walter   1890-1969

    Kipling, Rudyard   4144
    Lawrence, D.H.   4388
    Masefield, John   4831
    Sitwell, Edith   5721*
    Symons, Arthur   6815

KRANE, Sherman M.   1927-

    Wilde, Oscar   7272

KREIN, Alexander Abramovich   1883-1951

    Wilde, Oscar   7266

KRENEK, Ernst   1900-

    Hopkins, Gerard Manley   2987 3026 3036 3039 3043

KREUGER, Randall B.   ?-

    Auden, W.H.   92

KŘIČKA, Jaroslav   1882-1969

    Hewlett, Maurice   2950
    Wilde, Oscar   7171 7172

KŘIVINKA, Gustav   1928-

    Thomas, Dylan   6933
    Wilde, Oscar   7200

KROEGER, Ernest Richard   1862-1934

    Hewlett, Maurice   2951

KRONES, [?], arr.   ?-

   Symonds, John Addington   6732

KUBIK, Gail T.   1914-

   Maugham, Somerset   5008

KUČERA, Antonín   1912-

   Wilde, Oscar   7212

KUČEROVÁ-HERBSTOVÁ, Marie   1896-1962

   Kipling, Rudyard   4078

KUNZ, Alfred   1929-

Davies, W.H.	1241 1253 1260
Hopkins, Gerard Manley	3004
Joyce, James	3707 3772
Thomas, Edward	6986

KUPKA, Karel   1927-

   Shaw, George Bernard   5683

LAJTHA, László   1892-1963

   Eliot, T.S.   2103

LAMBERT, Agnes H.   ?-

   Henley, W.E.   2836 2922

LAMBERT, Constant   1905-1951

   Sitwell, Sacheverell   5779

LAMBERT, Frank   ?-

Henley, W.E.	2787 2790 2826
Housman, A.E.	3382

LA MONTAINE, John   1920-

Graves, Robert	2434
Hopkins, Gerard Manley	3024

LANCHBERY, John   ?-

    Potter, Beatrix   5484

LANDER, Cyril Bertram   ?-

    de la Mare, Walter   1562
    Housman, Laurence   3534
    Le Gallienne, Richard   4468
    Stevenson, Robert Louis   6340

LANE, Edgar A.   ?-

    Hardy, Thomas   2518 2665

LANG, Craig Sellar   1891?-1971

    Sassoon, Siegfried   5595

LANG, Margaret Ruthven   1867-

    Housman, A.E.   3230
    Swinburne, A.C.   6629

LANGE, Arthur   1888-1956

    Wilde, Oscar   7181

LANGERT, Jules   1932-

    Yeats, W.B.   7572

LANGLEY, Bernard P.   ?-

    Hopkins, Gerard Manley   2967 3000 3005 3009 3029 3031
                                   3113 3126
    Owen, Wilfred   5439 5445 5448
    Thomas, Dylan   6888
    Thompson, Francis   7003

LANGLEY, James W.   1927-

    de la Mare, Walter   1365

LAPP, Horace   1904-

    Stephens, James   5889 5899 5943 5978

987

LE FLEMING continued

Brooke, Rupert	791
Coleridge, Mary	1027
de la Mare, Walter	1477 1504 1507 1537 1548 1731 1785
Gibbon, Monk	2269
Hardy, Thomas	2463 2498 2555 2570 2703 2718 2737
Joyce, James	3866
Kipling, Rudyard	4264
Potter, Beatrix	5483 5485
Yeats, W.B.	7679

LEGINSKA, Ethel   1886-1970
  Originally named Ethel Liggins

Symons, Arthur	6745

LEHMANN, Liza   1862-1918
  Born Elizabeth Nina Mary Frederika Lehmann

Belloc, Hilaire	405 433 441 445 491
Bridges, Robert	672
Dobson, Austin	1885
Graves, A.P.	2371
Housman, Laurence	3536
Kipling, Rudyard	4173 4335
Stevenson, Robert Louis	6100 6185 6229 6249 6274 6406 6423 6566
Wilde, Oscar	7194
Yeats, W.B.	7554

LEICH, Roland   ?-

Kipling, Rudyard	4174

LEICHTLING, Alan R.   1947-

Housman, A.E.	3145 3161 3231 3290 3335 3340 3353 3363 3448 3471 3497

LEIGH, Eric   ?-

Davies, W.H.	1261
de la Mare, Walter	1392 1418 1556 1580 1788

LEIGHTON, Kenneth   1929-

    de la Mare, Walter   1557
    Eliot, T.S.   2138
    Hardy, Thomas   2643
    Hopkins, Gerard Manley   2977
    Symonds, John Addington   6712

LEITCH, Donovan   ?-

    Yeats, W.B.   7584

LEKBERG, Sven   1899-

    de la Mare, Walter   1630
    Dowson, Ernest   1931 1950
    Dunsany, Lord   2031
    Stevenson, Robert Louis   6045 6190 6230
    Thompson, Francis   6996

LE LACHEUR, Rex   ?-

    Brooke, Rupert   819

LEMONT, Cedric Wilmot   1879-1954

    Macleod, Fiona   4717
    Symons, Arthur   6739 6767 6786

LEONARD, Lady Barrett   ?-

    Newbolt, Henry   5251

LEONI, Franco   1865-1949

    Stevenson, Robert Louis   6275

LEPPARD, Raymond   1927-

    Golding, William   2339

LERDAHL, Alfred   ?-

    Joyce, James   3666

LESEMANN, Frederick   1936-

    Swinburne, A.C.   6635

LESSNER, George   1904-

    Wilde, Oscar   7239

LEVY, Leon T.   ?-

    Swinburne, A.C.   6705

LEVY, Marvin David   1932-

    Auden, W.H.   135

LEWIS, Anthony Carey   1915-

    Day Lewis, C.   1319
    Muir, Edwin   5231

LEWIS, Samuel R.   ?-

    Masefield, John   4832 4839 4848 4854 4899 4921
                       4976
    Symons, Arthur   6787

LEY, Henry George   1887-1962

    Housman, A.E.   3178 3478
    Yeats, W.B.   7431 7555

LIDDLE, Samuel   ?-1951

    Bridges, Robert   724
    de la Mare, Walter   1376 1585 1753
    Henley, W.E.   2885
    Kipling, Rudyard   4145
    Stevenson, Robert Louis 6052
    Watson, William   7091

LIDGEY, Charles Albert   ?-1924

    Henley, W.E.   2771 2791 2795 2802 2859 2873
                       2909
    Herbert, A.P.   2947

LIDOV, David   ?-

    Yeats, W.B.   7435 7437 7441 7445 7448 7451
                       7454

LOEWE, Frederick   1904-

    Shaw, George Bernard   5677

LOFTUS, Cecilia   ?-
Also known as Cissie Loftus

    Stevenson, Robert Louis   6341

LOFTUS, Cissie   ?-

    Stevenson, Robert Louis   6258

LOHR, Hermann Frederic   1872-1943

    Gibson, W.W.   2332
    Le Gallienne, Richard   4456 4477
    Masefield, John   4824 4833 4922
    Meynell, Alice   5093 5111
    Newbolt, Henry   5267
    Tynan, Katharine   7043

LOMBARDO, Robert M.   1932-

    Joyce, James   3636 3637*
    Thomas, Dylan   6896

LONGMIRE, John   1902-

    Stevenson, Robert Louis   6511

LOOMIS, Harvey Worthington   1865-1931
Also wrote under the pseud. "Walter F. Scollard"

    Macleod, Fiona   4782

LOOTS, Joyce Mary Ann   1907-

    Bridges, Robert   745

LORA, Antonio   ?-

    AE   28

LORD, David   1944-

    Heath-Stubbs, John   2768

```
LOUD, John Adams      ?-1935?

    Masefield, John              4937

LOUGHBOROUGH, H. Raymond       ?-1967

    Colum, Padraic               1094

LOURIÉ, Arthur Vincent       1892-1966

    Eliot, T.S.                  2091

LOVELOCK, William      ?-

    Hardy, Thomas                2719

LOVERING, Mabel      ?-

    Meynell, Alice               5079

LOWTHER, Toupie      ?-

    Wilde, Oscar                 7292

LUCAS, Leighton       1903-

    Dickinson, Patric            1868
    Sitwell, Edith               5745
    Stephens, James              6000

LUCAS, Mary Anderson       1882-1952

    Stephens, James              5975

LUCKE, Katharine F.      ?-

    Macleod, Fiona               4670 4681

LUTYENS, (Agnes) Elisabeth      1906-

    Auden, W.H.                  174 185 206
    Conrad, Joseph               1145
    Dobson, Austin               1870
    Housman, A.E.                3165
    Joyce, James                 3667
    MacNeice, Louis              4801
    Rodgers, W.R.                5563 5564
    Sitwell, Edith               5733
```

LUTYENS continued

Sitwell, Osbert	5774
Smith, Stevie	5783 5786 5788 5792 5794 5798
	5800 5801 5802 5803
Stevenson, Robert Louis	6567
Swinburne, A.C.	6640
Thomas, Dylan	6876* 6897* 6901 6913* 6937
	6942 6943
Wilde, Oscar	7162

LYDIATE, Frederick   1906-

Davies, W.H.	1249
Housman, A.E.	3418
Joyce, James	3724
Thomas, Edward	6945 6960 6961 6983 6987

MACCUNN, Andrew   ?-

Symons, Arthur	6778 6821

MACCUNN, Hamish   1868-1916

Bridges, Robert	605 624 636 679 697

MACDONALD, R. Houston   ?-

Stevenson, Robert Louis	6479

MACFADYEN, Alexander   ?-

Le Gallienne, Richard	4478

MÁCHA, Otmar   1922-

Kipling, Rudyard	4048 4065 4071 4094

MACINNIS, Donald   ?-

Eliot, T.S.	2173

MACK, Albert A.   ?-

Meredith, George	5037

MACKENZIE, Alexander Campbell   1847-1935

    Barrie, J.M.   271
    Buchanan, Robert   848 849 850
    Graves, A.P.   2372
    Swinburne, A.C.   6656

MACMILLAN, Ernest Campbell   1893-1973

    Swinburne, A.C.   6624

MACMURROUGH, Dermot   ?-

    Meynell, Alice   5103

MACONCHY, Elizabeth   1907-

    Campbell, Joseph   905
    Hardy, Thomas   2684
    Hopkins, Gerard Manley   3017* 3044* 3098*
    Meredith, George   5049
    Ridler, Anne   5557 5558 5559
    Sackville-West, Victoria   5571
    Yeats, W.B.   7719

MADDISON, Adela   ?-

    Gregory, Lady Augusta   2452 2453

MAGANINI, Quinto   1897-1974

    Brooke, Rupert   800
    Dowson, Ernest   1928

MAINZER, Joseph   ?-

    Kipling, Rudyard   3994

MALIPIERO, Riccardo   2924-

    Thomas, Dylan   6938

MALLINSON, Albert   1870-1946

    Austin, Alfred   245
    Henley, W.E.   2781 2852 2889 2896
    Stevenson, Robert Louis   6032
    Yeats, W.B.   7385 7420 7680

MALOTTE, Albert Hay   1895-1964

    Squire, J.C.   5869

MANA-ZUCCA   1887-
Pseud. of Augusta Zuckerman

    Le Gallienne, Richard   4479

MANDEL, Petr   1938-

    Wilde, Oscar   7201

MANN, Adolph   1873?-1941

    Joyce, James   3780

MANN, Leslie   1924-

    Housman, A.E.   3291 3309 3421 3498
    Stephens, James   5906 5979 5989

MANNERS, Brian F.   ?-

    Drinkwater, John   2017

MANNES, Leopold Damrosch   1899-1964

    Belloc, Hilaire   378

MANNEY, Charles Fonteyn   1872-1951

    Housman, A.E.   3232 3292 3390 3449 3479 3499
    Kipling, Rudyard   4221

MANSFIELD, Purcell James   ?-

    Milne, A.A.   5194

MANSON, Gloria Edith   ?-

    Yeats, W.B.   7665

MANSON, Willie B.   ?-

    Housman, A.E.   3293 3391 3422

MARAIS, Jean   ?-

    Wilde, Oscar   7245

MARILLIER, Christabel   ?-

    Housman, A.E.   3294 3311
    Newbolt, Henry   5273

MARIOTTE, Antoine   1875-1944

    Wilde, Oscar   7267

MARPLES, Anne   ?-

    Masefield, John   4971

MARRIOTT, I.N.   ?-

    Le Gallienne, Richard   4463

MARSHALL, M.E.   ?-

    Stevenson, Robert Louis   6568

MARSHALL, Nicholas   1942-

    Drinkwater, John   1996
    Hardy, Thomas   2583 2658
    Yeats, W.B.   7377 7398 7494 7507 7642 7654
                                7702

MARSHALL, Patricia A.   ?-

    Bridges, Robert   683

MARTIN, Easthope   ?-1925

    Masefield, John   4834 4849 4879 4904 4953

MARTIN, George Clement   1844-1916

    Kipling, Rudyard   4222

MARTINO, Donald   1931-

    Joyce, James   3623 3742 3884

MARTINŮ, Bohuslav   1890-1959

    Kipling, Rudyard   3972
    Symons, Arthur   6774*

MARTTINEN, Tauno   1912-

    Wilde, Oscar   7246

MARZIALS, Theodore   1850-1920

    Swinburne, A.C.   6674

MASCAGNI, Pietro   1863-1945

    Caine, Hall   851

MASE, Owen   1892-1973

    de la Mare, Walter   1454 1801
    Thomas, Edward   6982

MASON, Daniel Gregory   1873-1953

    Housman, A.E.   3166 3170 3216 3419
    Milne, A.A.   5166
    Stevenson, Robert Louis   6191 6290 6306 6407 6531
    Watson, William   7103

MASSEY, Gwen W.   ?-

    Gould, Gerald   2341

MATHER, Bruce   1939-

    Graves, Robert   2381 2386 2395 2409 2414 2415
                              2421

MATHIAS, William   1934-

    Thomas, Dylan   6927

MATTHEWS, Harry Alexander   1879-

    Kipling, Rudyard   4223

MATTILA, Edward C.   1927-

   Bridges, Robert   709

MATUSZCZAK, Bernadetta   1931-

   Eliot, T.S.   2083

MAUDE, Mrs. Raymond   ?-

   Kipling, Rudyard   4146

MAVES, David W.   1937-

   Bridges, Robert   757
   Hopkins, Gerard Manley   2978

MAW, Nicholas   1935-

   Auden, W.H.   163
   Day Lewis, C.   1327*
   Graves, Robert   2387
   Hardy, Thomas   2473 2507 2563 2584 2609 2690
   Hyde, Douglas   3567 3569
   Lewis, Alun   4488
   Munro, H.H.   5238
   Read, Herbert   5534
   Spender, Stephen   5851

MAY, Frederick   1911-

   Bridges, Robert   608
   Campbell, Joseph   906
   Colum, Padraic   1113 1131
   Gregory, Lady Augusta   2448 2454
   Hardy, Thomas   2758
   Hyde, Douglas   3571
   Lawrence, D.H.   4424
   Masefield, John   4999
   O'Sullivan, Seumas   5397
   Stephens, James   5921
   Tynan, Katharine   7056

MAYER, Lutz L.   1934-

   Fry, Christopher   2230

MAYER, Max   1859-1931

   Meredith, George   5029 5068

MCBRIDE, Robert Guyn   1911-

   Doyle, Arthur Conan   1966

MCCABE, John   1939-

   Eliot, T.S.   2071*
   Henri, Adrian   2930 2931
   Johnson, Lionel   3601
   Lewis, C.S.   4494
   McGough, Roger   5018 5019 5020 5021
   Nicholson, Norman   5312
   Patten, Brian   5454
   Thomas, Dylan   6877
   Wilde, Oscar   7293

MCCALL, J.P.   1882-1961
Pseud. of Peter Dawson

   Kipling, Rudyard   3967 3980 4248

MCCONATHY, Osbourne, arr.   ?-

   Stevenson, Robert Louis   6298*

MCCOURT, Tom M.   ?-

   Hardy, Thomas   2738

MCCRACKEN, Colleen   1924-

   Sitwell, Osbert   5775

MCDERMOTT, Vincent   1933-

   Hopkins, Gerard Manley   3117
   Thomas, Dylan   6889

MCDONALD, Harl   1899-1955

   Henley, W.E.   2923

MCEWEN, John Blackwood   1868-1948

   Kipling, Rudyard   4086

MCGEAR, Mike   ?-

   McGough, Roger   5022

MCINTYRE, Paul ╲ ?-

   Colum, Padraic   1095
   de la Mare, Walter   1359 1602 1666 1763
   Symons, Arthur   6751 6755 6768 6826

MCKAY, George Frederick   1899-1970

   Macleod, Fiona   4783
   Meredith, George   5034

MCKENZIE, Eric Donald   ?-

   Wilde, Oscar   7178 7185 7221

MCKINLEY, Carl K.   1895-1966

   Henley, W.E.   2837

MCKINNEY, Howard D.   1890-

   de la Mare, Walter   1419 1513 1573 1587

MCLAUGHLIN, Marian   ?-

   Stevenson, Robert Louis   6019

MEACHEN, Margaret   ?-

   Drinkwater, John   2018
   Meynell, Alice   5083

MEALE, Richard   1932-

   Sitwell, Edith   5759
   Spender, Stephen   5864

MECHEM, Kirke Lewis   1925-

   Housman, A.E.   3295*

MELLERS, Wilfrid Howard   1914-

    Auden, W.H.   145
    Holbrook, David   2962
    Hopkins, Gerard Manley   3023 3107
    Lawrence, D.H.   4412
    Moore, George   5216
    Raine, Kathleen   5498 5500 5507 5521 5526
    Thomas, Edward   6989

MENGELBERG, (Kurt) Rudolf   1892-1959

    Joyce, James   3638 3708 3725 3747 3781 3803
                                      3835 3867 3922

MENGES, Herbert   1902-

    Strong, L.A.G.   6585 6602

MEREDITH, Evan   ?-

    Chesterton, G.K.   986 1006
    Graves, Robert   2439

MERRIMAN, Margarita L.   1927-

    Housman, A.E.   3204 3315

METHOLD, Diana   ?-

    Yeats, W.B.   7608

MEWS, Douglas   ?-

    Kirkup, James   4357

MEYER, Joseph   1894-

    Stevenson, Robert Louis   6446

MEYEROWITZ, Jan   1913-

    Housman, A.E.   3186 3376

MIESSNER, William Otto   1880-

    de la Mare, Walter   1420 1434 1848
    Stevenson, Robert Louis   6012 6203

MIHALOVICI, Marcel   1898-

    Beckett, Samuel   320* 323 350

MIHÁLY, András   1917-

    Joyce, James   3696 3784 3348 3868 3911

MILES, J.B.   ?-

    Kipling, Rudyard   3995

MILES, Philip Napier   1865-1935

    Benson, E.F.   537
    Freeman, John   2229
    Gibson, W.W.   2288 2297 2299 2301 2314 2315
    Masefield, John   4874 4949
    Monro, Harold   5204
    Moore, T. Sturge   5221
    Stevenson, Robert Louis 6242
    Swinburne, A.C.   6706

MILFORD, Robin Humphrey   1903-1959

    Bridges, Robert   609 613 617* 621 677 688 746
                             758
    Davies, W.H.   1262
    de la Mare, Walter   1366 1495* 1849 1850*
    Hardy, Thomas   2488 2499 2571 2636 2693 2695
                             2720 2759
    Hodgson, Ralph   2953 2956
    Stevenson, Robert Louis 6140
    Yeats, W.B.   7482 7508

MILHAUD, Darius   1892-1974

    Eliot, T.S.   2104
    Meynell, Alice   5095
    Thompson, Francis   7021

MILLER, Anne Stratton   ?-

    Stevenson, Robert Louis 6480

MILNER, Anthony Francis Dominic   1925-

    Belloc, Hilaire   375

MILNER continued

    de la Mare, Walter   1377 1403 1421 1435 1514 1576
                                   1646 1699 1719
    Hopkins, Gerard Manley   3022
    Thompson, Francis   6998

MILVAIN, Hilda   ?-

    Housman, A.E.   3261

MITCHELL, Cyril J.   ?-

    Newbolt, Henry   5274

MITCHELL, Raymond Earle   1895-1967

    Masefield, John   4938 4964

MOERAN, Ernest John   1894-1950

    Bridges, Robert   747 777
    Housman, A.F.   3179 3184 3253 3296 3323 3366
                               3402 3465
    Joyce, James   3646 3676 3758 3773 3782 3804
                               3818 3869 3879 3912
    Masefield, John   4972
    Nichols, Robert   5298 5304
    O'Sullivan, Seumas   5393 5394 5395 5398 5401 5416
                               5423
    Sayers, Dorothy L.   5639
    Symons, Arthur   6795
    Yeats, W.B.   7483

MOIR, F.L.   ?-

    Meredith, George   5069

MOLLOY, [?]   ?-

    Kipling, Rudyard   4024

MONICO, L.J.   ?-

    Kipling, Rudyard   4347

MONTGOMERY, Merle   1900-

    Davies, W.H.   1313

MOORAT, Joseph   ?-

    Housman, Laurence   3526 3527 3528* 3531 3533

MOORE, Douglas Stuart   1893-1969

    de la Mare, Walter   1422
    James, Henry   3598

MOORE, Francis   1886-1946

    Stevenson, Robert Louis   6005 6408
    Swinburne, A.C.   6657

MOORE, Timothy   1922-

    Moore, T. Sturge   5217

MOPPER, Irving   1914-

    Housman, A.E.   3143

MORAWETZ, Oskar   1917-

    Housman, A.E.   3196
    Stevenson, Robert Louis   6186 6265 6276

MORE, T.   ?-

    Stevenson, Robert Louis   6342

MORGAN, Diane   ?-

    Hopkins, Gerard Manley   2968 3045 3056 3077 3088 3127

MORGAN, Howard   1945-

    Sassoon, Siegfried   5577 5604 5617 5618 5620

MORRISON, A.   ?-

    Yeats, W.B.   7556

MORTENSEN, Otto   ?-

   Turner, W.J.R.   7040

MORTIMER, Charles G.   ?-

   Kipling, Rudyard   4265

MOSSOLOV, Alexander Vassilievich   1900-1973

   Wilde, Oscar   7281

MOULE-EVANS, David   1905-

   Belloc, Hilaire   431 436 511
   Macleod, Fiona   4645 4757
   Masefield, John   4973
   Stevenson, Robert Louis   6033 6141 6409

MOURANT, Walter   ?-

   Stephens, James   5878 5879 5880 5882 5884 5886
                                 5887 5894 5896 5900 5907 5913
                                 5914 5919 5929 5934 5939 5940
                                 5944 5945 5947 5949 5951 5963
                                 5967 5969 5971 5977 5980 5981
                                 5985 5988 5990 6001 6002
   Yeats, W.B.   7695

MOWREY, Dent   ?-

   Le Gallienne, Richard   4458

MUELLER, Carl F.   1892-

   Henley, W.E.   2860

MÜLLER, Max   ?-

   Kipling, Rudyard   4266

MULLINER, Michael   1896?-1973

   Campbell, Joseph   877 907
   Chesterton, G.K.   1004
   de la Mare, Walter   1465
   Drinkwater, John   2019
   Kipling, Rudyard   4267

MULLINER continued

    Masefield, John   4923
    Stephens, James   5908

MURRAY, Dom Gregory   ?-

    Belloc, Hilaire   393 487
    de la Mare, Walter   1610

MURRILL, Herbert Henry John   1909-1952

    Auden, W.H.   110 115 197
    Isherwood, Christopher   3579 3584
    Priestley, J.B.   5493

MUSCHAMP, Stanley   ?-

    Stevenson, Robert Louis   6481

MUSGRAVE, Thea   1928-

    Davies, W.H.   1314
    James, Henry   3593
    Lindsay, Maurice   4497 4498 4499

MYERS, H. Emerson   1910-

    Owen, Wilfred   5434

MYERS, Stanley   ?-

    Joyce, James   3894
    Logue, Christopher   4502 4510

NABAKOV, Nicolas   1903-
    Originally named Nikolay [Nicolai?] Nabakov

    Auden, W.H.   239

NÁPRAVNÍK, Edward F.   1839-1916

    Phillips, Stephen   5459

NAYLOR, Bernard James   1907-

    Bax, Clifford   312
    Bridges, Robert   725

NAYLOR continued

Davies, W.H.	1235 1279 1280 1281 1294
Day Lewis, C.	1316 1321 1329 1336 1337
Gascoyne, David	2256 2257 2258 2260 2261 2263 2267 2268
Hardy, Thomas	2476 2593
Joyce, James	3655
Pitter, Ruth	5471 5475 5477
Webb, Mary	7106 7110 7113 7114 7118 7126 7128 7129 7131 7134

NAYLOR, Edward Woodall   1867-1934

    Kipling, Rudyard   4224

NAYLOR, Peter   1933-

Davies, W.H.	1257
Day Lewis, C.	1322
de la Mare, Walter	1558
Stevenson, Robert Louis	6231 6343
Warner, Rex	7064

NEČAS, Jaromír   1922-

    Thomas, Dylan   6934

NELSON, Havelock   1917-

Dunsany, Lord	2032
Yeats, W.B.	7421 7544 7569 7720

NELSON, Herbert H.   ?-

Doyle, Arthur Conan	1977
Macleod, Fiona	4784

NELSON, Paul   1929-

    Symonds, John Addington   6733 6734

NEUER, Berthold   ?-

    Symons, Arthur   6742 6799

NEVIN, Arthur Finley   1871-1943

   Colum, Padraic   1135

NEVIN, Ethelbert Woodbridge   1862-1901

   Kipling, Rudyard   4017
   Stevenson, Robert Louis   6034 6377 6482

NEVIN, George Balch   1859-1933

   Kipling, Rudyard   4225

NEWMAN, Alfred   1901-1970

   Kipling, Rudyard   4348
   Maugham, Somerset   5016

NEWMAN, Roy   ?-

   Campbell, Joseph   884 908

NEWSOME, Eliot   1934-

   Gilbert, W.S.   2333
   Sassoon, Siegfried   5622

NICHOLS, Dr. [?]   ?-

   Housman, A.E.   3523

NISBET, Peter C.   1928-

   Day Lewis, C.   1330
   Hopkins, Gerard Manley   3089

NIXON, Roger   1921-

   Stevenson, Robert Louis   6393 6512

NOBLE, Harold   ?-

   Belloc, Hilaire   428 503
   Bridges, Robert   658
   Dobson, Austin   1873
   Flecker, James Elroy   2208
   Stevenson, Robert Louis   6161
   Symons, Arthur   6796

NOBLE continued

    Watson, William   7078

NOBLE, Thomas Tertius, arr.   1867-1953

    Chesterton, G.K.   953

NORDOFF, Paul   1909-

    Ford, Ford Madox   2221
    Warner, Sylvia Townsend 7067

NORÉN, Helmer   ?-

    Nichols, Robert   5292

NORMAND-SMITH, Gertrude   ?-

    Symons, Arthur   6771 6801

NORRIS, Homer Albert   1860-1920

    Kipling, Rudyard   4147*
    Stevenson, Robert Louis 6209

NOWAK, Lionel   1911-

    Hopkins, Gerard Manley 3018

NUNLIST, Juli   ?-

    Housman, A.E.   3336

O'BRIEN, Katharine E.   ?-

    Hardy, Thomas   2739

O'DONOGHUE, Mary Bolton   ?-

    Stevenson, Robert Louis 6291

O'FARRELL SISTERS, The

    Synge, J.M.   6842

O'GALLAGHER, Eamonn   1906-

   Yeats, W.B.   7721

OGDON, Wilbur L.   ?-

   Durrell, Lawrence   2047

O'HARA, Geoffrey   1882-1967

   Stevenson, Robert Louis   6053

OLDROYD, George   1886-1951

   Stevenson, Robert Louis   6569
   Thompson, Francis   7018

OLIVER, Colin George Henry   ?-

   Stevenson, Robert Louis   6054

OLIVER, Stephen   ?-

   Hopkins, Gerard Manley   3128
   Monro, Harold   5205
   Wells, H.G.   7146

OLMSTEAD, Clarence   1892-

   Dobson, Austin   1880
   Swinburne, A.C.   6658

O'MURNAGHAN, Art   ?-

   de la Mare, Walter   1531
   Yeats, W.B.   7414

O'MURNAGHAN, Art, arr.   ?-

   Colum, Padraic   1128
   O'Connor, Frank   5383
   Yeats, W.B.   7628

O'NEILL, Florence   ?-

   Kipling, Rudyard   4316

O'NEILL, Norman Houstoun   1875-1934

    Barrie, J.M.   268 272 287
    Belloc, Hilaire   462
    Dunsany, Lord   2026 2027
    Henley, W.E.   2913 2924
    Meredith, George   5070
    Milne, A.A.   5158 5176
    Moore, George   5213
    Phillips, Stephen   5462
    Swinburne, A.C.   6605
    Symons, Arthur   6807*

ORCHARD, William Arundel   1867-1961

    Wilde, Oscar   7247

ORLAND, Henry   ?-

    Day Lewis, C.   1328

ORNADEL, Cyril   ?-

    Stevenson, Robert Louis   6447
    Wells, H.G.   7141

ORNSTEIN, Leo   1895-

    Kipling, Rudyard   4148

ORR, Charles Wilfrid   1893-

    Bridges, Robert   726
    Housman, A.E.   3141 3162 3185 3203 3217 3233
                    3243 3247 3254 3262 3297 3324
                    3328 3337 3352 3372 3394 3403
                    3416 3450 3460 3466 3472 3500
    Joyce, James   3632
    Strong, L.A.G.   6584

ORR, Robin   1906-

    Muir, Edwin   5228 5229 5234 5236
    Stevenson, Robert Louis   6466
    Synge, J.M.   6834
    Webb, Mary   7121 7124 7133

ORREGO-SALAS, Juan A.   1919-

    Thomas, Dylan   6899

ORTON, Richard   1940-

    Abercrombie, Lascelles   2
    Auden, W.H.   151
    Hill, Geoffrey   2952
    Hopkins, Gerard Manley   2998 3069 3072 3103
    Middleton, Christopher   5119
    Smith, Stevie   5804
    Thomas, Dylan   6878

OSBORNE, Reginald   ?-

    Bridges, Robert   748 778
    de la Mare, Walter   1539
    Le Gallienne, Richard   4469

OSGOOD, George Laurie   1844-1922

    Watson, William   7097

OSMOND, Clara   ?-

    Bridges, Robert   680
    Stevenson, Robert Louis   6344

OWEN, Morfydd Llwyn   1891-1918

    Housman, A.E.   3423
    Kipling, Rudyard   3996
    Noyes, Alfred   5372

PAGE, Nathaniel Clifford   1866-1956

    Graves, A.P.   2361

PAGET, Michael   ?-

    Housman, Laurence   3537

PAGET, Richard Arthur Surtees   1869-1955

    Newbolt, Henry   5280

1013

PALM, Augustus O.   ?-

    Noyes, Alfred   5356

PALMER, Courtlandt   1872-?

    Henley, W.E.   2878

PALMER, Florence Margaret Spencer   ?-
    Also wrote under the name Peggy Spencer Palmer

    Noyes, Alfred   5337

PALMER, Geoffrey Molyneux   1882-

    Joyce, James   3939

PALMER, John   ?-

    Yeats, W.B.   7557

PARFREY, Raymond J.   1928-

    Church, Richard   1013
    Davies, W.H.   1232
    de la Mare, Walter   1735
    Noyes, Alfred   5319
    Reeves, James   5549
    Squire, J.C.   5871

PARISH, F. Wilson   ?-

    Hardy, Thomas   2666

PARKE, Dorothy   ?-

    Campbell, Joseph   890 909 910
    Colum, Padraic   1096
    de la Mare, Walter   1423
    Stephens, James   5876 5890 5897 5901 5909 5932
                                 5941 5952
    Yeats, W.B.   7495

PARKER, Alice   ?-

    Smith, Stevie   5785

PARKER, Horatio William   1863-1919

    Henley, W.E.   2782 2838
    Housman, A.E.   3360
    Kipling, Rudyard   3997
    Stevenson, Robert Louis   6570

PARKER, Horatio William, arr.   1863-1919

    Macleod, Fiona   4785*
    Stevenson, Robert Louis   6035* 6135*

PARKER, Kitty   ?-1948

    Meredith, George   5038 5071

PARKS, J.A.   ?-

    Kipling, Rudyard   4226

PARMOR, Arthur A.   ?-

    Kipling, Rudyard   4227

PARRIS, Robert   1924-

    Eliot, T.S.   2084
    Hopkins, Gerard Manley   3019

PARROTT, (Horace) Ian   1916-

    Bridges, Robert   659
    Flecker, James Elroy   2200

PARRY, Charles Hubert Hastings   1848-1918

    Bridges, Robert   619 635 646 682 684 698 727
                                  782
    Coleridge, Mary   1022 1038 1048 1051 1052 1058
                                  1061
    Dobson, Austin   1895*
    Graves, A.P.   2365 2373
    Kipling, Rudyard   4039
    Meredith, George   5030 5041
    Swinburne, A.C.   6631

1015

PARRY, W.H.   1916-

     Bridges, Robert   673
     Chesterton, G.K.   1005
     de la Mare, Walter   1474 1488
     Drinkwater, John   2020
     Hardy, Thomas   2721
     Stevenson, Robert Louis   6036*

PASATIERI, Thomas John   1943-

     Yeats, W.B.   7394

PASCAL, Florian   1847-1924
     Pseud. of Joseph Williams

     Newbolt, Henry   5242 5257

PASFIELD, William Reginald   1909-

     Belloc, Hilaire   394 429
     Douglas, Lord Alfred   1899
     Hardy, Thomas   2625
     Masefield, John   4924
     Swinburne, A.C.   6642

PASTON-COOPER, [?]   ?-

     Swinburne, A.C.   6636*

PATRICK, Laughton W.   ?-

     Joyce, James   3819 3827

PATTEN, James   1936-

     Beckett, Samuel   362 363

PATTERSON, Paul   ?-

     Belloc, Hilaire   492

PATTISON, Lee Marion   1890-1966

     de la Mare, Walter   1596
     Joyce, James   3836

                1016

PAVIOUR, Paul   1931-

    Yeats, W.B.   7436 7438 7442 7446 7449 7452
                                    7455

PAWLE, Ivan   ?-

    Joyce, James   3870

PAYNTER, John Frederick   1931-

    Eliot, T.S.   2060 2119 2131 2155 2164
    Hopkins, Gerard Manley 3122 3137

PEACH, Clare I.   ?-

    Bridges, Robert   689

PEARSON, T.E.   ?-

    Macleod, Fiona   4683

PEASE, Jessie L.   ?-

    Stevenson, Robert Louis 6455

PECH, Josef   1931-

    Coward, Noël   1180

PEDLEY, David   ?-

    de la Mare, Walter   1754
    Sitwell, Osbert   5776

PEDROLLO, Arrigo   1878-

    Synge, J.M.   6839

PEEL, (Gerald) Graham   1877-1937

    Belloc, Hilaire   379 409 415 439 525 530
    Gould, Gerald   2347
    Hardy, Thomas   2626
    Housman, A.E.   3153 3298 3364 3367 3383 3473
    Noyes, Alfred   5361
    Stevenson, Robert Louis 6055 6068 6232 6259 6292 6311
                                6345 6442 6483 6544

PEEL continued

    Watson, William   7079 7098
    Yeats, W.B.   7558

PELLEGRINI, Ernesto P.   1932-

    Hopkins, Gerard Manley   2979 3078 3129
    Joyce, James   3871

PENDERECKI, Krzysztof   1933-

    Fry, Christopher   2234
    Huxley, Aldous   3560
    Whiting, John   7153

PENDLETON, Edmund [Edmond?]   ?-

    Joyce, James   3641

PENN, Arthur A.   1875-1941

    Kipling, Rudyard   4228

PENNICUICK, Ramsay   ?-1968

    Masefield, John   4905

PENTLAND, Barbara   1912-

    Colum, Padraic   1097
    Davies, W.H.   1263 1268
    Dowson, Ernest   1957
    Gibson, W.W.   2300

PERKS, Robert Edward   ?-

    Shanks, Edward   5640

PERRY, Julia   1927-

    Wilde, Oscar   7273

PERRY, Malcolm   ?-

    Hopkins, Gerard Manley   2980

PERRY, Zenobia P.   ?-

   Hardy, Thomas   2474 2486 2616

PERSICHETTI, Vincent   1915-

   Auden, W.H.   136
   Belloc, Hilaire   395 446
   Campbell, Joseph   911
   Eliot, T.S.   2085 2143
   Flecker, James Elroy   2194
   Joyce, James   3615 3774 3792 3837 3838*
   Thomas, Dylan   6874 6879
   Watson, William   7082 7086

PETERKIN, (George) Norman   1886-

   Brooke, Rupert   820
   Campbell, Joseph   865 874 875 879 881 883
   de la Mare, Walter   1378 1390 1494 1538 1581 1615
                                1651 1700 1769
   Dowson, Ernest   1910
   Gibson, W.W.   2284
   Macleod, Fiona   4594 4723
   O'Sullivan, Seumas   5413

PETERSON, Wayne   1927-

   Eliot, T.S.   2126
   Hopkins, Gerard Manley   3010 3070
   Thomas, Dylan   6863 6922

PETRŽELKA, Vilém   1889-1967

   Kipling, Rudyard   4149

PFAUTSCH, Lloyd   1921-

   Hardy, Thomas   2760

PHILLIPS, Montague Fawcett   1885-1969

   Newbolt, Henry   5245

PIGGOT, Robert Stuart   ?-

   Kipling, Rudyard   4150

1019

PIGGOTT, David   ?-

    Bridges, Robert   732

PIGGOTT, H.E.   ?-

    de la Mare, Walter   1393

PIMSLEUR, Solomon   1900-1962

    Masefield, John   4888

PINKHAM, Daniel   1923-

    Auden, W.H.   103 193 208
    Hopkins, Gerard Manley   2996 3012 3025 3037 3057 3079
                             3090 3104
    Sassoon, Siegfried   5611

PINSUTI, Ciro
[PINSUTO, Circo?   1829-1888]

    Swinburne, A.C.   6707*

PISK, Paul Amadeus   1893-

    Joyce, James   3633 3726 3737 3748 3805

PITCHER, Doland   ?-

    de la Mare, Walter   1400

PITFIELD, Thomas Baron   1903-

    Chesterton, G.K.   954
    de la Mare, Walter   1523 1543
    Mansfield, Katherine   4823
    Pitter, Ruth   5469

PITT, Percy   1870-1932

    Austin, Alfred   241
    Phillips, Stephen   5460

PIZZETTI, Ildebrando   1880-1968

    Eliot, T.S.   2105

PLUMSTEAD, Mary   1905-

    Hopkins, Gerard Manley   3058
    Meredith, George   5053
    Reeves, James   5550
    Swinburne, A.C.   6708
    Yeats, W.B.   7609

POCKRISS, Lee J.   1924-

    Wilde, Oscar   7213

POLIN, Claire   1926-

    Eliot, T.S.   2054 2065 2067 2092

POLOVINKIN, Leonid   1894-1949

    Synge, J.M.   6843

PONC, Miroslav   1902-

    Fry, Christopher   2231
    Shaw, George Bernard   5661 5664
    Wilde, Oscar   7214

PORTER, Quincy C.   1897-1966

    Eliot, T.S.   2152

POSAMANICK, Beatrice   ?-

    Hopkins, Gerard Manley   3138
    Masefield, John   4835

POSPISIL, Milos   1923-

    Greene, Graham   2442

POSTON, Elizabeth   1905-

    Aldington, Richard   75
    Hopkins, Gerard Manley   3071
    Strong, L.A.G.   6597
    Yeats, W.B.   7559
    Young, Andrew   7727

POTTER, Archie James   1918-

    Belloc, Hilaire   374 420 456 468 469 474 477
                            478 480 481 483 484 508 531

POULENC, Francis   1899-1963

    Barrie, J.M.   293

POWELL, John   1882-1963

    Conrad, Joseph   1137

PREMRU, Raymond Eugene   1934-

    Davies, W.H.   1250
    Lee, Laurie   4439

PRICE, Beryl   ?-

    Eliot, T.S.   2146
    Pitter, Ruth   5474

PRIESTLEY-SMITH, Hugh   ?-

    Housman, A.E.   3192 3234 3299 3392 3480

PRINCE, Dyneley   ?-

    Kipling, Rudyard   4121

PRITCHARD, Arthur John   ?-

    Hardy, Thomas   2722
    Stevenson, Robert Louis 6162

PROCTOR, Charles   1906-

    de la Mare, Walter   1552

PROCTOR-GREGG, Humphrey   1895-

    Housman, A.E.   3235 3300

PROSSER, Edward   ?-

    Drinkwater, John   2001

PROTHEROE, Daniel   1866-1934

    Kipling, Rudyard   4151
    Noyes, Alfred   5323 5373
    Stevenson, Robert Louis   6443

PUGH, Louis   ?-

    Strong, L.A.G.   6594

PURDIE, Hunter   ?-

    Chesterton, G.K.   972

PURSER, John W.R.   1942-

    Eliot, T.S.   2061 2120 2132 2156 2165

PURVIS, Richard Irven   1915-

    Buchanan, Robert   841

PUTSCHE, Thomas   1929-

    Yeats, W.B.   7404

PYKE, Helen Lucas   ?-1954

    Watson, William   7099

QUILTER, Roger   1877-1953

    Binyon, Laurence   567 568
    Campbell, Joseph   863 878 880
    Coleridge, Mary   1023 1024
    Dowson, Ernest   1911 1915 1922 1958
    Henley, W.E.   2794 2797 2839
    Kipling, Rudyard   4162
    Stephens, James   5910
    Stevenson, Robert Louis   6101 6126 6174 6192 6484 6571
    Watson, William   7100

RABAUD, Henri Benjamin   1873-1949

    Synge, J.M.   6852

RADCLIFFE, Philip   ?-

    Meredith, George   5040

RADNAI, Miklós   1892-1935

    Wilde, Oscar   7163

RADNOR, Marvin   ?-

    Stevenson, Robert Louis   6020 6037 6046 6069 6082 6093
                               6102 6110 6136 6204 6210 6250
                               6260 6277 6293 6299 6322 6378
                               6389 6410 6426 6433 6485 6513
                               6532 6545

RADÓ, Aladár   1882-1914

    Stevenson, Robert Louis   6572

RAFFMAN, Relly   1921-

    Thomas, Dylan   6900

RAFTER, Leonard   1912-1964

    Gibson, W.W.   2309
    Lawrence, D.H.   4425
    Sassoon, Siegfried   5596
    Thomas, Edward   6959

RAINES, Vernon   ?-

    Wilde, Oscar   7195

RAINIER, Priaulx   1903-

    Gascoyne, David   2264*
    Sitwell, Edith   5691
    Thomas, Dylan   6939

RAKSIN, David   1912-

    Doyle, Arthur Conan   1967

RAMSAY, Katharine M.   ?-

    Stevenson, Robert Louis   6573

RANDS, Bernard   1935-

    Beckett, Samuel   327 331 341 344 348 354 355
                             360
    Joyce, James   3668
    Wain, John   7063

RANKL, Karl   1898-1968

    Synge, J.M.   6835

RAPHAEL, Mark   ?-

    Bridges, Robert   637 696
    Lawrence, D.H.   4371 4378 4414

RASBACH, Oscar   1888-1975

    Masefield, John   4985

RATCLIFFE, Desmond   1917-

    Bridges, Robert   652

RATHAUS, Karol   1895-1954

    Eliot, T.S.   2166
    Stevenson, Robert Louis 6346
    Swinburne, A.C.   6675

RATHBONE, George   ?-

    Belloc, Hilaire   396
    Chesterton, G.K.   955
    Stevenson, Robert Louis 6358

RAUTAVAARA, Einojuhani   1928-

    Eliot, T.S.   2127

RAWLING, Barbara   ?-

    Hardy, Thomas   2588

RAWLINSON, Bertha   ?-

    Belloc, Hilaire   504
    Macleod, Fiona   4718

RAWLINSON continued

    Meynell, Alice   5084

RAWSTHORNE, Alan   1905-1971

    Beerbohm, Max   367
    Day Lewis, C.   1342
    Eliot, T.S.   2056 2075 2112 2124 2125 2147
    Hardy, Thomas   2627
    MacNeice, Louis   4792
    Rodgers, W.R.   5561 5565

RAXACH, Enrique   ?-

    Yeats, W.B.   7722

RAYBOULD, Clarence   ?-

    Henley, W.E.   2809

RAYNOR, John   1909-

    Belloc, Hilaire   435 437 494 517
    Housman, A.E.   3154 3301
    Thompson, Francis   6997

READ, Gardner   1913-

    AE   62
    Barrie, J.M.   264
    Davies, W.H.   1274
    de la Mare, Walter   1611*
    Flecker, James Elroy 2197
    Joyce, James   3616 3709

READ, John   ?-

    Drinkwater, John   1984
    Macleod, Fiona   4678

REDMAN, Reginald   1892-1972

    de la Mare, Walter   1720
    Macleod, Fiona   4627
    Masefield, John   4907 4965
    Thompson, Francis   7011

REED, Alfred   1921-

    Joyce, James   3820

REIF, Paul   1910-

    Eliot, T.S.   2073*

REISBERG, Horace   1930-

    Thomas, Dylan   6880

REMICK, Bertha   ?-

    Kipling, Rudyard   4152
    Le Gallienne, Richard   4480

REPPER, Charles   ?-

    O'Sullivan, Seumas   5424

RETTICH, Wilhelm   1892-

    Flecker, James Elroy   2211
    Galsworthy, John   2241
    Joyce, James   3872
    Nichols, Robert   5309
    Noyes, Alfred   5338 5340
    Shanks, Edward   5642 5652
    Thomas, Edward   6948

REUTTER, Hermann   1900-

    Joyce, James   3728 3749 3339 3873

REYNOLDS, Alfred   1884-1969

    Bax, Clifford   313
    Herbert, A.P.   2935 2936 2941

REYNOLDS, W.B.   ?-

    Joyce, James   3940

RHODES, Harold   1889-

    Stevenson, Robert Louis   6142 6391 6533

RIADIS, E.   ?-

    Wilde, Oscar   7268

RICHARDS, Howard L.   1927-

    Joyce, James   3806 3913

RICHARDS, Kathleen   ?-

    de la Mare, Walter   1484 1518
    Stevenson, Robert Louis 6007

RICHARDS, Kathleen, arr.   ?-

    de la Mare, Walter   1851 1852

RICHARDSON, A.   ?-

    de la Mare, Walter   1853

RIDGE, Kirk   ?-

    Le Gallienne, Richard   4481

RIDOUT, Alan John   1934-

    Campbell, (I.) Roy   855 856
    Day Lewis, C.   1317*
    Hopkins, Gerard Manley   3108
    Read, Herbert   5532

RIDOUT, Godfrey   1918-

    Chesterton, G.K.   992
    Symonds, John Addington 6735

RIEGGER, Wallingford   1885-1961

    Thomas, Dylan   6881

RIESENFELD, Hugo   1879-1939

    Henley, W.E.   2891

RIETI, Vittorio   1898-

    Lawrence, D.H.   4368 4374 4391 4404

RIETI continued

    Stevenson, Robert Louis   6076
    Yeats, W.B.   7509 7586 7696 7705

RILEY, Dennis   1943-

    Lawrence, D.H.   4382 4407

RILEY, Leonard George Winter   ?-

    Kipling, Rudyard   3998

RIMMER, John Francis   1939-

    Auden, W.H.   112 137 202 221

RITCHIE, John   ?-

    Bridges, Robert   638 687 690 703 716 749

RITCHIE, Tom V.   1922-

    Joyce, James   3626 3727 3885 3905
    Masefield, John   4897 4939 4977
    Yeats, W.B.   7560 7697

ROBBINS, Reginald C.   1871-?

    Binyon, Laurence   569
    Bridges, Robert   710 717
    Davies, W.H.   1236
    Meynell, Alice   5104
    Stevenson, Robert Louis   6175
    Swinburne, A.C.   6608

ROBERTON, Hugh Stevenson   1874-1952

    Campbell, Joseph   891*
    Chesterton, G.K.   973
    de la Mare, Walter   1436 1481 1532 1647 1676 1770
            1797
    Housman, A.E.   3155 3302
    Masefield, John   4954
    Meynell, Alice   5105
    Tynan, Katharine   7050
    Yeats, W.B.   7378

ROBERTS, (William Herbert) Mervyn   1906-

    Meredith, George   5023 5031 5050 5059 5061 5063
    Synge, J.M.   6846

ROBERTS, Trevor   1940-

    Thomas, Dylan   6870

ROBERTSON, Donna N.   1935-

    Hopkins, Gerard Manley   2981 3001 3027 3099 3114

ROBINSON, Clarence   ?-

    Housman, A.E.   3451

ROBINSON, Lennox   ?-

    Yeats, W.B.   7660*

RODER, Milan   1878-1956

    Conrad, Joseph   1146
    Dowson, Ernest   1932

RODERICK-JONES, Richard   1947-

    Davies, W.H.   1226 1230 1239 1254 1293 1305
                              1306
    Thomas, Dylan   6862 6871 6905 6907 6930
    Yeats, W.B.   7379 7486 7624 7626 7687

RODEWALD, Bernice A.   1928-

    de la Mare, Walter   1455
    Stevenson, Robert Louis   6176

ROE, Betty   ?-

    Owen, Wilfred   5443

ROFF, Joseph   1910-

    Belloc, Hilaire   397
    Chesterton, G.K.   974
    Noyes, Alfred   5359
    Swinburne, A.C.   6643

ROGERS, Bernard   1893-1968

    Wilde, Oscar   7222 7294

ROGERS, James Hotchkiss   1857-1940

    de la Mare, Walter   1389
    Masefield, John   4940
    Noyes, Alfred   5348
    Stevenson, Robert Louis 6347
    Swinburne, A.C.   6630 6644

ROGERS, Milton A.   ?-

    Henley, W.E.   2804 2840
    Kipling, Rudyard   4189

ROLLIN, Robert Leon   1947-

    Yeats, W.B.   7399 7594 7610 7621 7706

ROMA, Caro   1866-1937

    Kipling, Rudyard   4153

ROMBERG, Sigmund   1887-1951

    Carpenter, Edward   931

RONALD, Landon   1873-1938
Originally named Landon Ronald Russell

    Dowson, Ernest   1907
    Gould, Gerald   2348
    Henley, W.E.   2783 2841 2879 2892 2898 2918
    Swinburne, A.C.   6647
    Symons, Arthur   6740 6744 6777 6810
    Yeats, W.B.   7380

RONSHEIM, John R.   1927-

    Lawrence, D.H.   4370* 4375* 4384* 4392* 4393
                        4403 4420* 4421*

ROOPER, Jasper   1898-

    Sassoon, Siegfried   5597

ROOTHAM, Cyril Bradley   1875-1938

    Binyon, Laurence   556
    Bridges, Robert   600 606 685 718 756 766
    Coleridge, Mary   1029 1033 1034 1045 1049 1054
    Masefield, John   4966
    Sassoon, Siegfried   5584 5586 5598 5607 5613 5621
                                5630
    Sitwell, Edith   5723
    Squire, J.C.   5873
    Stevenson, Robert Louis   6177
    Yeats, W.B.   7666

ROPER, Antony   ?-

    de la Mare, Walter   1357

ROREM, Ned   1923-

    Auden, W.H.   88 216*
    Beardsley, Aubrey   317
    Hopkins, Gerard Manley   3035 3038 3080 3091 3109
    Isherwood, Christopher   3575 3588*
    Stevenson, Robert Louis   6348
    Wilde, Oscar   7248
    Yeats, W.B.   7674

ROSE, Edith   1892-1972

    Masefield, John   4925*

ROSE, Edwin C.   ?-

    de la Mare, Walter   1515 1854
    Housman, A.E.   3236

ROSE, Michael   ?-

    Belloc, Hilaire   422 440
    Blunden, Edmund   577
    de la Mare, Walter   1701
    Reeves, James   5551
    Young, Andrew   7726

ROSENSTEIN, Arthur   ?-

    Stevenson, Robert Louis   6094

ROSS, Colin   ?-

    Housman, A.E.   3303

ROSSER, Mervyn S.   1926-

    Binyon, Laurence   560
    Bridges, Robert   750
    Noyes, Alfred   5366

ROSSITER, Aleta   ?-

    Stevenson, Robert Louis   6021

ROSSMAN, Floy Adele   ?-

    Stevenson, Robert Louis   6323

ROUSSEL, Albert Charles Paul Marie   1869-1937

    Joyce, James   3677

ROUTH, Francis   1927-

    Auden, W.H.   148 211 212
    Campbell, (I.) Roy   853
    Durrell, Lawrence   2038 2042 2044 2048 2049
    Keyes, Sidney   3946
    Raine, Kathleen   5519
    Yeats, W.B.   7391 7496 7514 7517 7522 7534
                                 7587

ROWLEY, Alec   1892-1958

    Brooke, Rupert   834
    Campbell, Joseph   896
    Dobson, Austin   1896
    Drinkwater, John   1988 1990 1997 2003 2014
    Reeves, James   5552
    Sassoon, Siegfried   5609 5615 5626 5628
    Stevenson, Robert Louis   6038* 6070* 6103 6120* 6193*
                                 6233* 6359 6379* 6411 6434*

ROWTON, S.J.   ?-

    Brooke, Rupert   792 801 821 835

ROY, William   1928-

    Barrie, J.M.   292

RÓZSA, Miklós Nicholas   1907-

    Doyle, Arthur Conan   1968
    Kipling, Rudyard   4079*

RUBBRA, (Charles) Edmund   1901-

    Belloc, Hilaire   457
    Campbell, (I.) Roy   857
    Colum, Padraic   1098
    Davies, W.H.   1289
    Hodgson, Ralph   2958
    Hopkins, Gerard Manley   2982 3014 3059 3081
    Moore, T. Sturge   5222
    Thomas, Edward   6969
    Tynan, Katharine   7044
    Webb, Mary   7125

RUMMEL, Walter Morse   1887-1953

    Le Gallienne, Richard   4462
    Macleod, Fiona   4641 4671 4737 4745
    Yeats, W.B.   7469

RUSSELL, Alexander   1880-

    Symons, Arthur   6769

RUSSELL, Leslie   ?-

    Bridges, Robert   669 751
    Housman, A.E.   3198 3218 3237 3263 3316 3318
                               3331 3420 3462 3467 3501 3510

RUSSELL, Lionel   ?-

    Masefield, John   4863

RUSSELL, Sydney King   1897-

    Sackville-West, Victoria 5574

                    1034

RUSSELL, Welford   1900-

    Swinburne, A.C.   6659

RUTTER, John   ?-

    Stevenson, Robert Louis   6534

R-W., A.C.   ?-

    Kipling, Rudyard   4192*

RYAN, Margaret   ?-

    Le Gallienne, Richard   4482

RYDER, Arthur Hilton   1875-1944

    Johnson, Lionel   3603

SAAR, Louis Victor Franz   1868-1937

    Bridges, Robert   711

SABIN, Wallace A.   ?-

    Masefield, John   4941

SACCO, P. Peter   1928-

    Bridges, Robert   712

SACHS, Henry   ?-

    Kipling, Rudyard   4349

SAFFLE, Michael B.   ?-

    Auden, W.H.   203

SALTER, Hans J.   1896-

    Doyle, Arthur Conan   1969 1970

SALTER, Lionel   1914-

    Meynell, Alice   5106
    Wolfe, Humbert   7316

SALTER, Mary Elizabeth (Turner)   ?-

   Stevenson, Robert Louis   6111

SAMUELS, Homer   ?-

   Stevenson, Robert Louis   6278

SANDERS, Robert L.   1906-

   Kipling, Rudyard   4350
   Symonds, John Addington   6729

SANG, Henry   ?-

   Squire, J.C.   5872
   Symons, Arthur   6773

SARGENT, (Harold) Malcolm Watts, arr.   1895-1967

   Herbert, A.P.   2948

SARSON, (Hilda) May   1901?-1958

   Hardy, Thomas   2519

SAUGUET, Henri   1901-
Pseud. of Jean Pierre Poupard

   Swinburne, A.C.   6709

SAUNDERS, Neil   1918-

   de la Mare, Walter   1721

SCHAEFER, Theodor   1904-1969

   Kipling, Rudyard   4080

SCHAEFFER, William A.   1918-

   Wilde, Oscar   7240 7295

SCHAEUBLE, Hans   1906-

   Wilde, Oscar   7249

SCHELLING, Ernest Henry   1876-1939

   Noyes, Alfred   5365

SCHENCK, Elliott   ?-

   Stevenson, Robert Louis   6167 6366

SCHERMAN, Thomas   1918?-

   Belloc, Hilaire   380 521
   Milne, A.A.   5150

SCHICKELE, Peter Johann   1935-

   Joyce, James   3656 3793

SCHINDLER, Kurt   1882-1935

   Meredith, George   5042
   Wilde, Oscar   7296

SCHLOTEL, Brian   1927-

   Bridges, Robert   618 639

SCHMIDT, Joye Zelda   1930-

   de la Mare, Walter   1822

SCHMITT, Florent   1870-1958

   Wilde, Oscar   7269

SCHNEIDER, Edwin   ?-

   Macleod, Fiona   4758

SCHOENBERG, Arnold   1874-1951

   Dowson, Ernest   1939

SCHOLL, Barbara   1931-

   Housman, A.E.   3524

SCHREKER, Franz   1878-1934

    Wilde, Oscar   7164

SCHULHOFF, Erwin   1894-1942

    Wilde, Oscar   7177 7230 7258

SCHUMAN, William Howard   1910-

    Conrad, Joseph   1147

SCHWARTZ, Francis   ?-

    Yeats, W.B.   7709

SCHWARTZ, Paul   1907-

    Yeats, W.B.   7359 7364 7366 7627 7633 7652

SCOLLARD, Walter F.   1865-1931
Pseud. of Harvey Worthington Loomis

    Henley, W.E.   2842

SCOTT, Annie D.   ?-

    Campbell, Joseph   867 885 893 912

SCOTT, Anthony L.W.   1911-

    Davidson, John   1218
    Kipling, Rudyard   4109 4159 4325

SCOTT, Beatrice Mcgowan   ?-

    Stevenson, Robert Louis   6412 6486 6535

SCOTT, Cyril Meir   1879-1970

    Dowson, Ernest   1906 1912 1933 1937 1938 1942
                                    1948 1951 1959 1961 1962 1963
    Hardy, Thomas   2520
    Hudson, W.H.   3543
    Kipling, Rudyard   4081 4138 4241
    Meredith, George   5072
    Stevenson, Robert Louis   6349
    Symonds, John Addington   6736

SCOTT continued

    Symons, Arthur   6808
    Wilde, Oscar   7179*

SCOTT, Francis George   1880-1958

    Day Lewis, C.   1325
    Gibson, W.W.   2293
    Henley, W.E.   2814
    Lindsay, Maurice   4500
    MacDiarmid, Hugh   4520 4529 4530 4531 4532 4534
                               4539 4540 4541 4543 4546 4547
                               4548 4549 4550 4551 4553 4556
                               4558 4559 4561 4562 4564 4565
                               4567
    Masefield, John   4864
    Muir, Edwin   5232
    O'Sullivan, Seumas   5404
    Soutar, William   5817 5823 5825 5835* 5842
    Wilde, Oscar   7218

SCOTT, Harold   ?-

    Herbert, A.P.   2942

SCULL, [?]   ?-

    Masefield, John   5000

SCULTHORPE, Peter   1929-

    Lawrence, D.H.   4377 4394 4399 4419

SEARLE, Humphrey   1915-

    Brooke, Jocelyn   784 785 786
    Chesterton, G.K.   975
    Eliot, T.S.   2074 2094
    Gascoyne, David   2262
    Graves, Robert   2388
    Housman, A.E.   3346 3506
    Joyce, James   3669
    Rodgers, W.R.   5562
    Sitwell, Edith   5695 5712 5744

SEEGER, Charles Louis   1886-

    Wilde, Oscar   7180

SEGERSTAM, Leif   1944-

    Auden, W.H.   171 173

SEIBER, Mátyás György   1905-1960

    Joyce, James   3794 3895
    MacNeice, Louis   4804 4805
    Orwell, George   5391

SEILER, C. Linn   ?-

    Noyes, Alfred   5332

SEKLES, Bernhard   1872-1934

    Wilde, Oscar   7165

SENATOR, Ronald   1926-

    Auden, W.H.   125 152 209

SERLY, Tibor   1901?-

    Joyce, James   3617 3689 3840 3850

SERRELL, Alys F.   ?-

    Hardy, Thomas   2485

SESSIONS, Roger Huntington   1896-

    Joyce, James   3788

SHACKFORD, Charles   1918-

    Reeves, James   5538

SHANKS, William   ?-

    Stevenson, Robert Louis   6350

SHAPLEIGH, Bertram   1871-1940

    Stevenson, Robert Louis   6178 6297

SHARMAN, Cecil   ?-

    Stevenson, Robert Louis   6163

SHARP, Cecil James   1859-1924

    Hardy, Thomas   2521

SHARPE, Evelyn   ?-

    Wilde, Oscar   7259 7282

SHAUER, Mel   ?-

    Barrie, J.M.   283

SHAW, Christopher   1924-

    Joyce, James   3941
    Muir, Edwin   5237

SHAW, Francis   ?-

    Wilde, Oscar   7274

SHAW, Geoffrey Turton   1879-1943

    Housman, Laurence   3538
    Stevenson, Robert Louis   6039 6071 6413

SHAW, Martin Fallas   1875-1958

    Bax, Clifford   298 300 314 315
    Binyon, Laurence   553 563
    Buchan, John   840
    Dane, Clemence   1201
    Eliot, T.S.   2139 2140 2141
    Fry, Christopher   2232
    Graves, A.P.   2374
    Hardy, Thomas   2522
    Henley, W.E.   2846 2861 2901
    Hopkins, Gerard Manley   2983
    Kipling, Rudyard   3949 3970 4011 4177 4331
    Masefield, John   4850 4860 4893 5001 5002 5003

SHAW continued

    Meredith, George   5056 5058
    O'Casey, Sean   5378
    Symonds, John Addington   6730
    Yeats, W.B.   7570 7611

SHAW, Martin Fallas, arr.   1875-1958

    Binyon, Laurence   570
    Chesterton, G.K.   956
    de la Mare, Walter   1368
    Graves, Robert   2391 2435

SHELDON, Mary   ?-

    Colum, Padraic   1099
    de la Mare, Walter   1466
    Hardy, Thomas   2500 2538 2646 2688
    Symons, Arthur   6797

SHELLEY, Harry Rowe   1858-1947

    Kipling, Rudyard   4229

SHEPARD, Thomas Griffin [Griffen?]   1848-1905

    Stevenson, Robert Louis   6089 6112 6194 6205 6279 6294

SHEPHERD, Arthur   1880-1958

    Brooke, Rupert   824
    Campbell, Joseph   897
    de la Mare, Walter   1476 1631 1672 1722 1799
    Gogarty, Oliver St. John 2335 2336 2338
    Henley, W.E.   2822
    Macleod, Fiona   4724
    Masefield, John   4868
    Monro, Harold   5207
    Noyes, Alfred   5331
    O'Sullivan, Seumas   5417
    Sassoon, Siegfried   5614 5629
    Sitwell, Edith   5752
    Sitwell, Sacheverell   5780
    Stephens, James   5911 5968
    Watson, William   7092

SHERMAN, Richard M.   1928-

   Kipling, Rudyard   4082
   Milne, A.A.   5190

SHERMAN, Robert B.   1925-

   Kipling, Rudyard   4083
   Milne, A.A.   5191

SHIELDS, Arnold McC.   ?-

   Stevenson, Robert Louis   6251 6392

SHIFRIN, Seymour J.   1926-

   Hardy, Thomas   2503 2704 2728
   Hopkins, Gerard Manley   3092
   Yeats, W.B.   7400 7592 7661

SHIRE, David   ?-

   Ustinov, Peter   7062

SHORT, Michael   ?-

   Dickinson, Patric   1862 1863 1864 1865 1866 1857
   Thomas, Dylan   6860 6864 6902 6911 6928

SHUKEN, Leo   1906-

   Conrad, Joseph   1148

SIBSON, Arthur R.   1906-

   Brooke, Rupert   793

SIEGMEISTER, Elie   1909-

   O'Casey, Sean   5376

SILBERTA, Rhea   1897-1959

   Wilde, Oscar   7241

SILVER, Alfred J.   ?-

   Noyes, Alfred   5326

SIMON, Ladislav   1929-

    Shaw, George Bernard   5678

SIMONS, Netty   ?-

    Thomas, Dylan   6865 6908 6923

SIMPSON, Donald   ?-

    Stevenson, Robert Louis   6439

SIMPSON, H. Haley   ?-

    Belloc, Hilaire   398

SINGTON, Louie   ?-

    Kipling, Rudyard   4154

SIRULNIKOFF, Jack   ?-

    Synge, J.M.   6837 6840 6344

SKINNER, Frank   1897-

    Doyle, Arthur Conan   1971 1972 1973

SKOLNIK, Walter   1934-

    Belloc, Hilaire   403 410 522

SLATER, Gordon Archbold   1896-

    Hardy, Thomas   2579
    Masefield, John   4945

SLONIMSKY, Nicolas   1894-

    Wilde, Oscar   7189

SMALL, Neville Charles Christopher   ?-

    Auden, W.H.   194

SMALLEY, Roger   1943-

    Lawrence, D.H.   4426

SMETANA, Josef   1915-

    Coward, Noël   1178

SMIT, Leo   1921-

      Auden, W.H.   82
      Chesterton, G.K.   976
      Hardy, Thomas   2493

SMITH, Boyton   ?-

    Hardy, Thomas   2523 2524 2525 2656 2698

SMITH, Boyton, arr.   ?-

    Hardy, Thomas   2761

SMITH, Breville   ?-

    Masefield, John   4865

SMITH, David Stanley   1877-1949

      de la Mare, Walter   1360 1632 1648 1667 1683
      Dobson, Austin   1891
      Meynell, Alice   5107

SMITH, Edwin M.   1938-

    de la Mare, Walter   1612 1702 1723

SMITH, Eleanor   ?-

    Stevenson, Robert Louis   6022 6083 6195 6280 6414 6453
                                      6487 6536

SMITH, Georgina Elsie   ?-

    Stevenson, Robert Louis   6456

SMITH, Gregg   1931-

    Eliot, T.S.   2062* 2121 2133 2157 2167

SMITH, Leland C.   1925-

    Owen, Wilfred   5453

SMITH continued

    Sassoon, Siegfried   5603

SMITH, Leo (Joseph Leopold)   1881-1952

    Swinburne, A.C.   6609 6616 6618 6639 6664 6658
                          6677 6681

SMITH, Robert   1922-

    Davies, W.H.   1303
    Owen, Wilfred   5438
    Synge, J.M.   6855

SMITH, Robert Vale   ?-

    Davies, W.H.   1275

SMITH, Russell   1927-

    Auden, W.H.   121
    Joyce, James   3783

SMITH, William Russell   1927-

    Joyce, James   3807*

SMOLDON, William Lawrence, ed.   1892-

    Auden, W.H.   240

SMYTH, Ethel Mary   1858-1944

    Baring, Maurice   249 253
    Jacobs, W.W.   3590 3592
    Shanks, Edward   5654
    Symons, Arthur   6743 6748 6304

SOMERS, Harry   1925-

    Yeats, W.B.   7723

SOMERS-COCKS, John P.   1907-

    Bottomley, Gordon   591

SOMERVELL, Arthur   1863-1937

    Housman, A.E.   3156 3238 3255 3304 3347 3334
                                3385 3393 3452 3481

SOUSA, John Philip   1854-1932

    Dobson, Austin   1883
    Kipling, Rudyard   3968

SOUSTER, Tim   ?-

    Eliot, T.S.   2184
    Hopkins, Gerard Manley   3006

SOUTHAM, T. Wallace   ?-

    Auden, W.H.   89 217 232
    Baldwin, Michael   246
    Causley, Charles   940
    Durrell, Lawrence   2039 2040 2043 2045
    Henri, Adrian   2929
    Isherwood, Christopher   3576 3589
    Logue, Christopher   4511
    Lucie-Smith, Edward   4513

SOUTHER, Louise   ?-

    Colum, Padraic   1118

SOWERBY, Leo   1895-1968

    Henley, W.E.   2914

SPALDING, Walter Raymond   1865-1962

    Henley, W.E.   2925 2926
    Kipling, Rudyard   4175

SPEAKS, Oley   1874-1948

    Kipling, Rudyard   4044 4122
    Macleod, Fiona   4587
    Stevenson, Robert Louis   6351 6457

SPECTOR, Irwin   1916-

    Hardy, Thomas   2746

SPECTOR continued

    Joyce, James   3627 3729 3750 3759 3874

SPEDDING, Frank   1929-

    MacNeice, Louis   4795 4807
    Stevenson, Robert Louis   6234

SPENCER, Ruth McConn   ?-

    Stevenson, Robert Louis   6104

SPENCER, Williametta   ?-

    Joyce, James   3647 3713 3730 3775 3808 3914
                              3923

SPEYER, Charles A.   ?-

    Hardy, Thomas   2526 2740

SPIER, Harry R.   1888-1952

    Stephens, James   5976

SPROOS, Charles Gilbert   1874-1962

    Kipling, Rudyard   4053

SQUIRE, Hope   ?-

    Newbolt, Henry   5268

SRNKA, Jiří   1907-

    Shaw, George Bernard   5671

ŠTANCL, Ladislav   1925-

    Wilde, Oscar   7215

STANFORD, Charles Villiers   1852-1924

    Binyon, Laurence   552
    Bridges, Robert   630 634 674 728 736
    Coleridge, Mary   1025 1030 1031 1036 1037 1039
                              1042 1053 1055 1057 1059 1060

STANFORD continued

Coleridge continued	1062 1063 1064 1065
Doyle, Arthur Conan	1974 1976
Graves, A.P.	2375
Henley, W.E.	2818
Lang, Andrew	4367
Newbolt, Henry	5252 5255 5262 5264 5265 5270
	5271 5272 5275 5279 5284 5288
Quiller-Couch, Arthur	5497
Stevenson, Robert Louis	6040 6105 6113 6235 6281 6295
	6312 6488 6537
Swinburne, A.C.	6623

STARER, Robert   1924-

Lawrence, D.H.   4413 4418

STARK, Fleurette   1932-

Day Lewis, C.   1323

STATHAM, F.R.   ?-

Kipling, Rudyard   3999*

STEBBINS, Charles Albert   ?-

Swinburne, A.C.   6660

STEEL, N. McLeod   ?-

Flecker, James Elroy   2204

STEERE, William C.   ?-

Noyes, Alfred   5316

STEFFENS, Walter   1934-

Thomas, Dylan   6935

STEIN, Leon   1910-

Thomas, Dylan   6872 6906 6912 6917 6918 6926
Yeats, W.B.   7464

STEINER, Gitta   1932-

    Joyce, James   3731 3841

STEINER, Maximilian Raoul   1888-1971

    Maugham, Somerset   5013

STEINERT, Alexander Lang   1900-

    Wilde, Oscar   7242

STEPHENS, Ward   1872-1940

    Macleod, Fiona   4654
    Stevenson, Robert Louis 6282

STEPHENSON, Robin   ?-

    de la Mare, Walter   1563

STERNE, Colin   ?-

    Joyce, James   3653 3690 3849

STERNS, G.C.   ?-

    Kipling, Rudyard   4230

STEVENS, Bernard   1916-

    Yeats, W.B.   7643

STEVENS, Halsey   1908-

    Belloc, Hilaire   479
    Dane, Clemence   1215
    de la Mare, Walter   1544 1780
    Housman, A.E.   3144
    Pudney, John   5496

STEVENS, James   1930-

    Auden, W.H.   195
    Eliot, T.S.   2072
    MacNeice, Louis   4793 4802 4818

STEVENSON, Robert Louis   1850-1894

    Stevenson, Robert Louis   6302*

STEVENSON, Ronald   1928-

Davidson, John	1219 1220 1221 1222 1223
Joyce, James	3678
MacDiarmid, Hugh	4519 4521 4522 4523 4524 4525
	4526 4527 4528 4533 4535 4536
	4537 4538 4542 4544 4545 4554
	4555 4557 4560 4563 4568 4559
	4570
Soutar, William	5813 5816 5819 5820 5821 5824
	5830 5831 5833 5834 5841 5843
Stevenson, Robert Louis	6179 6196 6352 6360

STEWART, Charles Hylton   1884-1932

    Bridges, Robert   675

STEWART, D.M.   ?-

de la Mare, Walter	1855
Hardy, Thomas	2650
Housman, A.E.	3188 3213 3369 3413
Masefield, John	4967
Stevenson, Robert Louis	6381
Swinburne, A.C.	6667
Yeats, W.B.	7381

STEWART, Humphrey John   1856-1935

    Thompson, Francis   7004

STICKLES, William C.   1883-1971

    Stephens, James   5955

STOCK, George Chadwick   ?-

    Kipling, Rudyard   4249

STOKER, Richard   1938-

de la Mare, Walter	1685
Hopkins, Gerard Manley	3082
Milne, A.A.	5187

STOLL, David   ?-

    de la Mare, Walter   1730 1856

STONE, David E.   1922-

    Bridges, Robert   660
    de la Mare, Walter   1467 1825
    Hardy, Thomas   2723

STOREY-SMITH, Warren   ?-

    Le Gallienne, Richard   4454

STOTHART, Herbert   1885-1949

    Stevenson, Robert Louis   6574

STOUT, Alan   1932-

    Colum, Padraic   1100

STRAKER, John A.   1908-

    Kipling, Rudyard   4231

STRAUS, Oscar   1870-1954

    Shaw, George Bernard   5659

STRAUSS, Richard Georg   1864-1949

    Wilde, Oscar   7270

STRAVINSKY, Igor Feodorovich   1882-1971

    Auden, W.H.   118 184
    Eliot, T.S.   2093 2185
    Huxley, Aldous   3564
    Thomas, Dylan   6882

STRICKLAND, Lily Teresa   1887-1958

    Kipling, Rudyard   4311

STRICKLAND, William   1914-

    Joyce, James   3679 3821

STRILKO, Anthony   1931-

    Auden, W.H.   153
    Grahame, Kenneth   2358
    Stephens, James   5891

STRINGHAM, Edwin John   1890-

    de la Mare, Walter   1437

STRONG, May A.   ?-

    de la Mare, Walter   1424

STYNE, Jule   1905-

    Barrie, J.M.   284

SULLIVAN, Arthur Seymour   1842-1900

    Kipling, Rudyard   3948
    Pinero, Arthur   5464
    Swinburne, A.C.   6686

SUMSION, Corbett C.   ?-

    Brooke, Rupert   813 836
    Housman, A.E.   3180 3271* 3325* 3453*

SUSA, Conrad   1935-

    Joyce, James   3697 3710 3738 3751 3776 3875

SUTERMEISTER, Heinrich   ?-

    Wilde, Oscar   7173

SUTHERLAND, Gordon   ?-

    Kipling, Rudyard   4283*

SWAIN, Freda Mary   1902-

    Bridges, Robert   622*
    Brooke, Rupert   822*
    Clarke, Austin   1019* 1020*
    Coppard, A.E.   1150* 1152* 1153* 1154* 1155*
                              1156* 1157* 1158* 1159* 1160

1053

SWAIN continued

Coppard continued   1161* 1162* 1163* 1164*
de la Mare, Walter   1404* 1553* 1645* 1764* 1794*
Douglas, Lord Alfred   1901*
Graves, A.P.   2366*
Graves, Robert   2377* 2411* 2426* 2427*
Housman, A.E.   3181* 3326* 3404* 3482* 3511*
Masefield, John   4869*
Stephens, James   5917* 5931* 5946* 5958*
Strong, L.A.G.   6586* 6590* 6591* 6593* 6595*
                        6596* 6598*
Yeats, W.B.   7529 7650 7724

SWAN, Alfred Julius   1890-

Stevenson, Robert Louis 6575

SWANN, Donald   1923-

Betjeman, John   544 545 547 549
Day Lewis, C.   1333*
Lewis, C.S.   4495
Tolkien, J.R.R.   7023 7024

SWANSON, Howard   1909-

Bridges, Robert   713
Eliot, T.S.   2128*

SWEETING, E.T.   ?-

Henley, W.E.   2823
Kipling, Rudyard   4232

SWEETMAN, Paul W.   ?-

Belloc, Hilaire   399
Colum, Padraic   1101

SWIFT, Newton   ?-

de la Mare, Walter   1742
Graves, Robert   2403
Newbolt, Henry   5289
Sitwell, Edith   5724

SWIFT, Richard   1927-

    Auden, W.H.   104

SYKES, Harold Hinchcliffe   ?-

    Coleridge, Mary   1026
    de la Mare, Walter   1387
    Masefield, John   4955
    Meynell, Alice   5085

SYLVESTER, S.W.   ?-

    Drinkwater, John   2006

SYMONDS, Norman   1920-

    Auden, W.H.   84

SYMONS, Dom Thomas   1887-

    de la Mare, Walter   1661 1857
    Housman, A.E.   3171 3189

SZYMANOWSKI, Karol Maciej   1882-1937

    Joyce, James   3691 3732 3752 3842

TAG, Ralph W.   ?-

    Kipling, Rudyard   4054

TALMA, Louise Juliette   1906-

    Auden, W.H.   146
    Hopkins, Gerard Manley 2969 3007 3020 3046 3060 3093
    Meredith, George   5054

TANENBAUM, Elias   ?-

    Yeats, W.B.   7573

TATE, Phyllis   1911-
    Pseud. of Margaret Duncan

    Davies, W.H.   1315
    Hardy, Thomas   2762
    Herbert, A.P.   2943

TATE continued

    Keyes, Sidney   3943

TATTON, J. Meredith   ?-

    Chesterton, G.K.   957
    Colum, Padraic   1070
    Flecker, James Elroy   2206

TAUBER, Patricia B.   ?-

    de la Mare, Walter   1497
    Housman, A.E.   3329

TAVENER, John   1944-

    Eliot, T.S.   2186
    Lucie-Smith, Edward   4514 4515* 4516

TAYLOR, Albert   ?-

    Meynell, Alice   5114

TAYLOR, Clifford   1923-

    Flint, F.S.   2216
    Hodgson, Ralph   2955
    Lawrence, D.H.   4372
    Sassoon, Siegfried   5590

TAYLOR, Colin   1881-1973

    Galsworthy, John   2242
    Gibson, W.W.   2302
    Macleod, Fiona   4578
    Noyes, Alfred   5321 5345 5353
    Stephens, James   6003
    Stevenson, Robert Louis 6464 6576

TAYLOR, E. Kendal   ?-

    Housman, A.E.   3483

TAYLOR, Gladys   ?-

    de la Mare, Walter   1858

```
TAYLOR, Henry Stanley      ?-

    Wolfe, Humbert              7303
    Yeats, W.B.                 7612

TAYLOR, James    1907-

    Sassoon, Siegfried          5616

TAYLOR, Jean     ?-

    Tynan, Katharine            7051

TAYLOR, (Joseph) Deems    1885-1966

    Masefield, John             4842
    Noyes, Alfred               5330
    Stephens, James             5942 5964 5972

TAYLOR, M.L.     ?-

    Belloc, Hilaire             376

TAYLOR, Phyllis    ?-

    Stephens, James             5956

TCHEREPNIN, Alexander Nikolayevich      1899-

    Wilde, Oscar                7271

TCIMIPIDIS, David     1938-

    Symons, Arthur              6759

TEED, Roy     1928-

    Belloc, Hilaire             406 412
    Chesterton, G.K.            958
    de la Mare, Walter          1533
    Drinkwater, John            2002
    Kirkup, James               4360 4361 4362 4363
    Lee, Laurie                 4440
    Stephens, James             5965

TEPPER, Albert     1921-

    Owen, Wilfred               5442
```

TEPPER continued

    Reed, Henry   5535 5536

TERRY, Robert E. Huntington   1867-1953

    Thompson, Francis   6992

THACKRAY, Rupert   ?-

    Graves, Robert   2417

THAYER, Arthur Wilder   1857-1934

    Doyle, Arthur Conan   1983
    Kipling, Rudyard   4123

THAYER, William Armour   1874-1933

    Stevenson, Robert Louis 6458

THIMAN, Eric Harding   1900-1975

    Belloc, Hilaire   400
    Bridges, Robert   752
    Carpenter, Edward   918
    Hardy, Thomas   2724
    Masefield, John   4959
    Stevenson, Robert Louis 6489

THOMAS, Alan   ?-

    Eliot, T.S.   2063 2122 2134 2158 2168

THOMAS, Christopher J.   ?-

    Colum, Padraic   1102

THOMAS, Harold Flower   ?-

    Housman, A.E.   3414

THOMAS, Mansel   1909-

    de la Mare, Walter   1859

THOMAS, Muriel   ?-

    Brooke, Rupert   823
    Stevenson, Robert Louis   6090 6361 6415 6490

THOMPSON, Alan Dales   1901-

    Hardy, Thomas   2725

THOMPSON, E. Roy   ?-

    Gibson, W.W.   2287 2322
    Macleod, Fiona   4672 4679 4719
    Stevenson, Robert Louis   6236 6353

THOMPSON, Randall   1899-

    Belloc, Hilaire   505
    de la Mare, Walter   1743
    Grahame, Kenneth   2359
    Kipling, Rudyard   3973

THOMSON, Bothwell   ?-

    Coleridge, Mary   1028
    Meredith, George   5073
    Tynan, Katharine   7057 7058
    Wilde, Oscar   7290*

THORNLEY, Barbara   ?-

    Macleod, Fiona   4642
    Noyes, Alfred   5374

THORP, L. Gordon   ?-

    Masefield, John   4926

TICCIATI, Francesco   ?-

    Davies, W.H.   1276

TILDEN, Edwin   ?-

    Wilde, Oscar   7219

TIPPETT, Michael Kemp   1905-

    Eliot, T.S.   2106*
    Fry, Christopher   2235 2236 2237 2238
    Hopkins, Gerard Manley   3123
    Hudson, W.H.   3540
    Keyes, Sidney   3944 3945
    Lewis, Alun   4489 4490 4493
    Sitwell, Edith   5764
    Thomas, Edward   6975
    Yeats, W.B.   7578 7725

TITHERINGTON, Frederick   ?-

    Macleod, Fiona   4714

TOBIN, John   1891-

    de la Mare, Walter   1633

TOCH, Ernst   1887-1964

    Barrie, J.M.   285

TOD, Kenneth   ?-

    Colum, Padraic   1103

TOGNI, Camillo   1922-

    Eliot, T.S.   2107

TOMBLINGS, Philip   ?-

    Masefield, John   4851

TOMLINS, Greta   1912-1972

    Bridges, Robert   625 629 753 779
    Chesterton, G.K.   977
    Sassoon, Siegfried   5599

TOSATTI, Vieri   1920-

    Stevenson, Robert Louis   6448

TOURS, Frank E.   ?-

    Kipling, Rudyard   4155

TOWSEY, Cyril Patrick   1918-

    Dowson, Ernest   1929

TOYE, (John) Francis   1883-1964

    Belloc, Hilaire   506
    Cornford, Frances   1169 1174
    Herbert, A.P.   2949

TRANCHELL, Peter Andrew   1922-

    Beerbohm, Max   368
    Hardy, Thomas   2602
    Kipling, Rudyard   4059
    Priestley, J.B.   5492
    Squire, J.C.   5867

TRAVANNION, H.   ?-

    Kipling, Rudyard   4124*

TREACHER, Graham Martin   1932-

    Joyce, James   3648 3753 3924

TREHARNE, Bryceson   1879-1948

    AE   52
    Belloc, Hilaire   458
    Chesterton, G.K.   978 980
    Colum, Padraic   1104 1129
    Dowson, Ernest   1903
    Gibson, W.W.   2282
    Masefield, John   4942
    Meynell, Alice   5080 5094 5108
    Stephens, James   5924 5983
    Symons, Arthur   6790

TREMAIN, Ronald   ?-

    Eliot, T.S.   2108

TREVALSA, Joan   ?-

    Barrie, J.M.   286

TRIGGS, Harold   ?-

    Joyce, James   3822

TRIMBLE, Joan   1915-

    Hyde, Douglas   3568
    Stephens, James   5902 5925 5926 5953
    Webb, Mary   7122

TROUBRIDGE, Amy   ?-

    Kipling, Rudyard   4324

TUNBRIDGE, Joseph Albert   ?-1961

    Barrie, J.M.   269

TUNNARD, Thomas   ?-

    Thompson, Francis   7014

TURNBULL, Percy   1902-

    Masefield, John   4855
    Stevenson, Robert Louis   6261

TURNER, Charles   1921-

    Housman, A.E.   3408

TURNER, James Oldfield   ?-

    Bridges, Robert   661
    de la Mare, Walter   1577

TURNER, Robert   1920-

    Chesterton, G.K.   981 983 989 1008

TURNER, Walter James Redfern   1889-1946

    Turner, W.J.R.   7037 7041 7042

TWARDOWSKI, Romauld   1930-

    Conrad, Joseph   1139

TWEEDY, Donald Nicholas   1890-1948

    Ford, Ford Madox   2222

TWIGG, Douglas J.   ?-

    Housman, A.E.   3157

TYE, Henry   ?-

    Symons, Arthur   6756

TYSON, Mildred Lund   ?-

    Moore, George   5214

UNSWORTH, Arthur   1935-

    Hopkins, Gerard Manley   2984

USZLER, Marienne Joan   1930-

    Hopkins, Gerard Manley   3094

UTERHART, Josephine   ?-

    Le Gallienne, Richard   4455

VALE, Charles   ?-

    Davies, W.H.   1304
    Stevenson, Robert Louis   6164

VALEN, (Olav) Fartein   1887-1952

    Thompson, Francis   7005

VAN BAAREN, Kees   1906-1970

    Eliot, T.S.   2086

VAN DIEREN, Bernard   1884-1936

    Joyce, James   3795 3942

VAN DIEREN continued

    Nichols, Robert   5308

VAN NUYS FOGEL, Clyde   ?-

    Le Gallienne, Richard   4483
    Yeats, W.B.   7382 7387

VAN SOMEREN-GODFERY, Masters   ?-1947

    Sitwell, Edith   5725 5735
    Wolfe, Humbert   7300 7302 7314 7324 7325 7329
                         7354

VAN VACTOR, David   1906-

    Housman, A.E.   3182 3368 3454 3502
    Wilde, Oscar   7261

VAUGHAN THOMAS, David   1873-1934

    Meredith, George   5032 5045 5051 5055 5057 5062
                         5065

VAUGHAN WILLIAMS, Ralph   1872-1958

    Carpenter, Edward   919
    Chesterton, G.K.   963
    Forster, E.M.   2224
    Graves, Robert   2429
    Hardy, Thomas   2527 2603* 2628*
    Henley, W.E.   2902
    Housman, A.E.   3142 3158 3172 3193 3214 3219
                         3244 3330 3338 3349 3370 3415
                         3503
    Kipling, Rudyard   4000
    Meredith, George   5035
    O'Sullivan, Seumas   5414 5422
    Shaw, George Bernard   5669
    Stevenson, Robert Louis 6144 6145* 6165 6168 6182
                         6213 6459 6547
    Swinburne, A.C.   6637 6680
    Synge, J.M.   6853

VEAL, Arthur   ?-

    Reeves, James   5553

WALD, Max   1889-1954

    Flecker, James Elroy   2189
    Henley, W.E.   2784
    Le Gallienne, Richard   4451 4484
    Symons, Arthur   6788

WALKER, A.F.   ?-

    Kipling, Rudyard   4233

WALKER, Ernest   1870-1949

    Henley, W.E.   2786 2910
    Meredith, George   5033

WALKER, George   ?-

    Housman, A.E.   3504

WALKER, May Sabeston   ?-

    Sassoon, Siegfried   5600

WALLBANK, Newell   1914-

    Davies, W.H.   1244

WALLER, H.   ?-

    Henley, W.E.   2875

WALLER, Jack   ?-

    Barrie, J.M.   270

WALSWORTH, Ivor   1909-

    Swinburne, A.C.   6638

WALTER, Arnold   1902-1973

    Binyon, Laurence   557

WALTERS, Leslie   1902-

    AE   72
    Belloc, Hilaire   401

WALTERS continued

```
    Colum, Padraic           1136
    Hardy, Thomas            2741
    Masefield, John          4867
```

WALTON, William Turner   1902-

```
    Auden, W.H.              228
    Barrie, J.M.             265
    Churchill, Winston       1015
    Greene, Graham           2443
    MacNeice, Louis          4794
    Masefield, John          5004
    Shaw, George Bernard     5673
    Sitwell, Edith           5688 5689 5690 5693 5694
                             5696* 5699 5701 5702 5703*
                             5705 5708* 5709 5710* 5711
                             5714 5715* 5716 5717 5727
                             5729 5734 5736 5738 5739 5740
                             5741 5742 5743 5746 5747 5751
                             5753 5756 5758 5760 5761*
                             5762 5763 5765 5766
    Sitwell, Osbert          5777
    Sitwell, Sacheverell     5782
    Strachey, Lytton         6583
    Swinburne, A.C.          6693
```

WARD, Robert E.   1917-

```
    Bax, Clifford            296
    Hopkins, Gerard Manley   2985 2997 3061
    Housman, A.E.            3505
    Joyce, James             3809
    Masefield, John          4950
    Stephens, James          5935
```

WARDALE, Joseph   ?-

```
    Stevenson, Robert Louis  6041 6106 6283
```

WARD-CASEY, S[amuel?]   ?-

```
    Housman, A.E.            3159*
```

WARD-HIGGS, W.   ?-

```
    Kipling, Rudyard         3963 4018 4038 4100 4129 4269
```

WARD-HIGGS continued

   Kipling continued   4312 4330

WARE, Harriet   1877-1962

   Swinburne, A.C.   6676

WARE, John Marley   1942-

   Eliot, T.S.   2109

WARFORD, Claude   1877-1950

   Macleod, Fiona   4786

WARLOCK, Peter   1894-1930
Pseud. of Philip Heseltine

   Aldington, Richard   76
   Belloc, Hilaire   402 430 438 459 463
   Dowson, Ernest   1923
   Ford, Ford Madox   2217
   Masefield, John   4843
   Nichols, Robert   5300
   Shanks, Edward   5645 5648
   Squire, J.C.   5868
   Stevenson, Robert Louis 6056 6166
   Symons, Arthur   6747 6800 6812*
   Yeats, W.B.   7360* 7361* 7383* 7475* 7479*
                         7487 7625*

WARNER, Lorraine d'Oremieulx, arr.   ?-

   Stevenson, Robert Louis 6013 6016 6107 6122 6216 6220
                         6380 6491

WARRELL, Arthur S.   1882?-1939

   Carpenter, Edward   920

WARREN, Elinor Remick   1903-

   Hardy, Thomas   2763
   Hodgson, Ralph   2960
   Lawrence, D.H.   4402
   Masefield, John   4836 5005
   Noyes, Alfred   5324

WARREN, George William   ?-

    Kipling, Rudyard   4234

WARREN, Raymond   1928-

    Auden, W.H.   226
    Betjeman, John   538
    MacNeice, Louis   4790
    Yeats, W.B.   7362 7363 7384 7389 7395 7396
                                 7405 7459 7465 7467 7468 7492
                                 7518 7521 7524 7539 7580 7583
                                 7589 7595 7617 7622 7629 7632
                                 7638 7645 7653 7657 7690 7698
                                 7707

WASSILENKO, Sergey Nikiforovich   1872-?

    Wilde, Oscar   7297

WATERS, Rosemary   1937-

    de la Mare, Walter   1680

WATTS, Harold E.   ?-

    Meynell, Alice   5109

WATTS, Wintter   1884-1962

    Henley, W.E.   2785 2798 2847 2907
    Le Gallienne, Richard   4485
    Macleod, Fiona   4632 4643
    Symons, Arthur   6752 6827

WAXMAN, Donald   1925-

    Hardy, Thomas   2469

WAXMAN, Franz   1906-1967

    Greene, Graham   2446

WEAVER, Mary Denny   ?-

    Drinkwater, John   2009

WEAVER, Mary Watson   1903-

   Colum, Padraic   1105

WEAVER, Powell   1890-1951

   Le Gallienne, Richard   4461

WEBBER, William Southcombe Lloyd   ?-

   Davies, W.H.   1227 1247 1267 1277 1291 1296
                                           1298 1310
   de la Mare, Walter   1765
   Dobson, Austin   1884
   Henley, W.E.   2863
   Noyes, Alfred   5349
   O'Sullivan, Seumas   5415
   Swinburne, A.C.   6650
   Yeats, W.B.   7510

WEDBERG, Conrad F.   ?-

   Housman, A.E.   3455

WEIGEL, Eugene   1910-

   Yeats, W.B.   7432 7476 7673 7681

WEIGL, Karl   1881-1949

   Colum, Padraic   1106
   Masefield, John   5006

WEIGL, Vally   ?-

   Chesterton, G.K.   959
   de la Mare, Walter   1725
   Stevenson, Robert Louis   6492 6577

WEILL, Kurt   1900-1950

   Kipling, Rudyard   4351

WEINZWEIG, John   1913-

   de la Mare, Walter   1453
   Symons, Arthur   6757

WEISGALL, Hugo   1912-

    de la Mare, Walter   1860
    Graves, Robert   2413
    Owen, Wilfred   5435
    Sassoon, Siegfried   5632
    Wolfe, Humbert   7326 7358
    Yeats, W.B.   7639

WELLESZ, Egon   1885-

    Hopkins, Gerard Manley   3021

WELLS, Howard   ?-

    Dowson, Ernest   1960
    Sassoon, Siegfried   5601

WELLS, John Barnes   1880-1935

    Stevenson, Robert Louis   6460

WERLÉ, Frederick   ?-

    Dunsany, Lord   2033

WESLEY-SMITH, Martin   1945-

    Orwell, George   5390

WEST, John Ebenezer William   1863-1929

    Noyes, Alfred   5320

WESTERGAARD, Peter   1931-

    Hopkins, Gerard Manley   3095
    Thomas, Dylan   6929
    Yeats, W.B.   7574

WESTERN, Joan   ?-

    Newbolt, Henry   5244

WESTRUP, Jack Allan   1904-1975

    Hardy, Thomas   2726
    Stevenson, Robert Louis   6578

WEYMAN, B. Maxwell   ?-

    Kipling, Rudyard   4156*

WHEAR, Paul William   1925-

    Eliot, T.S.   2055
    Hopkins, Gerard Manley   2986
    Housman, A.E.   3357
    Thompson, Francis   7012

WHEELER, J.R.   ?-

    Newbolt, Henry   5253

WHELPLY, Benjamin   ?-

    Henley, W.E.   2772 2843

WHETTAM, Graham   1927-

    Eliot, T.S.   2068*
    Russell, Bertrand   5567
    Thomas, Dylan   6883
    Yeats, W.B.   7433 7484 7599

WHITAKER, David   ?-

    Stevenson, Robert Louis   6579

WHITCOMB, Mervin   ?-

    Housman, A.E.   3339 3456

WHITE, Felix Harold   1884-1945

    Meynell, Alice   5112
    Stevenson, Robert Louis   6580 6581

WHITE, James Graham   ?-

    de la Mare, Walter   1358

WHITE, John D.   1931-

    Joyce, James   3628 3760 3328

WHITE, L.J.   ?-

    de la Mare, Walter   1564
    Stephens, James   5966

WHITE, Maude Valérie   1855-1937

    Doyle, Arthur Conan   1978 1980
    Henley, W.E.   2816 2895 2927
    Swinburne, A.C.   6661
    Watson, William   7084

WHITE, Raymond W.   ?-

    Wilde, Oscar   7275

WHITEHEAD, Percy   ?-

    Kipling, Rudyard   4257
    Macleod, Fiona   4675

WHITEHORNE, Annie   ?-

    Kipling, Rudyard   4031

WHITFIELD, John Brown Russell   ?-

    Bridges, Robert   691
    Stevenson, Robert Louis   6092 6197 6237 6284 6362 6416

WHITHORNE, Emerson   1884-1958
    Originally named Emerson Whittern

    Conrad, Joseph   1149
    Yeats, W.B.   7682

WHITING, Arthur Battelle   1861-1936

    Bridges, Robert   699
    Kipling, Rudyard   4019 4045 4125 4273

WHITTAKER, George   ?-

    Dowson, Ernest   1964
    Housman, A.E.   3525
    Swinburne, A.C.   6710
    Synge, J.M.   6858

WHITTAKER, William Gillies   1876-1944

    Bridges, Robert   754 781
    de la Mare, Walter   1405 1438 1755
    Gibson, W.W.   2281 2286 2290 2323 2325
    Kipling, Rudyard   4001
    Masefield, John   4978

WICKENS, Dennis   1926-

    de la Mare, Walter   1345 1449 1614
    Sassoon, Siegfried   5605 5634
    Watson, William   7102
    Yeats, W.B.   7488

WIDDOES, Lawrence L.   1932-

    Hopkins, Gerard Manley   3062

WIENIAWSKA, Irene   ?-

    Yeats, W.B.   7614

WIER, Lilias   ?-

    Newbolt, Henry   5269

WILDE, Oscar Fingall O'Flahertie Wills   1854-1900

    Wilde, Oscar   7287*

WILDING-WHITE, Raymond   ?-

    Housman, A.E.   3199 3215 3371

WILIAMS, William Sidney Gwynn   1896-

    Rhys, Ernest   5554 5555 5556

WILKINSON, Marc   1929-

    Beckett, Samuel   358
    Pinero, Arthur   5465

WILKINSON, Philip George   1929-

    Belloc, Hilaire   518
    Colum, Padraic   1107

WILKINSON continued

    de la Mare, Walter   1401
    Hardy, Thomas   2528
    Stevenson, Robert Louis   6042 6252

WILLAN, Healey   1880-1968
    Also wrote under the pseud. "Raymond Clare"

    Barrie, J.M.   273
    Belloc, Hilaire   465
    Bridges, Robert   607 729
    Eliot, T.S.   2110
    Henley, W.F.   2903 2911
    Housman, Laurence   3529 3532 3539
    Kipling, Rudyard   4235
    Noyes, Alfred   5363
    Symonds, John Addington   6719 6720
    Yeats, W.B.   7561 7562 7563* 7651 7683

WILLAN, Healey, arr.   1880-1968

    Graves, A.P.   2362 2367
    Tynan, Katharine   7059

WILLEBY, Charles   ?-1955

    Dobson, Austin   1892
    Henley, W.E.   2770 2773 2808 2810 2827 2849
                                2915 2916 2928
    Kipling, Rudyard   4126
    Noyes, Alfred   5317

WILLIAMS, (John) Gerrard   1888-1947

    Sitwell, Osbert   5771
    Swinburne, A.C.   6711

WILLIAMS, Arnold   ?-

    Stevenson, Robert Louis   6057

WILLIAMS, Bryn   1924-

    Eliot, T.S.   2187

WILLIAMS, Dorothy I.   ?-

    Sassoon, Siegfried   5602

WILLIAMS, Grace   1906-

    Belloc, Hilaire   507
    Hopkins, Gerard Manley   3002 3033 3047 3063 3096 3124
    Lawrence, D.H.   4409
    Raine, Kathleen   5527
    Thomas, Edward   6966
    Webb, Mary   7123

WILLIAMS, Meirion   ?-

    Thomas, Dylan   6873

WILLIAMS, Patrick   ?-

    Stevenson, Robert Louis   6091 6238 6253 6417 6493

WILLIAMS, Robert   ?-

    Hardy, Thomas   2629

WILLIAMSON, Malcolm   1931-

    Barker, George   254 255 256 257 259 260
    Chesterton, G.K.   960
    Churchill, Winston   1016
    Greene, Graham   2445
    Sitwell, Edith   5706 5767 5770
    Stevenson, Robert Louis   6095 6121 6127 6137 6198 6217
                               6239 6262 6324 6435 6494 6498
    Wilde, Oscar   7196 7278
    Yeats, W.B.   7460

WILLS, Arthur   ?-

    Chesterton, G.K.   961

WILSON, Charles Mills   1931-

    Stevenson, Robert Louis   6582
    Wilde, Oscar   7276

WILSON, James   1922-

    Hopkins, Gerard Manley   2970 3008 3030 3034 3040 3073
                                       3100 3115 3130
    Stephens, James   5960
    Yeats, W.B.   7392 7401 7402* 7412 7413
                                       7417 7512 7535 7536 7571 7575
                                     7579 7668

WILSON, Ray R.   1917-

    de la Mare, Walter   1861

WILSON, Stanley   ?-

    Housman, A.E.   3183 3190 3264 3305 3457
    Masefield, John   5007

WILSON, Thomas   1927-

    Belloc, Hilaire   447
    Thomas, Edward   6970

WINN, Cyril   1886-

    de la Mare, Walter   1546

WINSLOW, Richard K.   1918-

    Beckett, Samuel   335
    Hardy, Thomas   2630

WISHART, Peter   1921-

    Graves, Robert   2379 2380 2383 2396 2400 2404
                                       2418 2422 2425
    Masefield, John   4880
    Stevenson, Robert Louis 6004 6072

WOOD, Charles   1866-1926

    de la Mare, Walter   1798
    Kipling, Rudyard   4236
    Swinburne, A.C.   6663

WOOD, Erskine   ?-

    Kipling, Rudyard   4055 4176

WOOD, Frederic H.   ?-

    Watson, William   7075 7076 7081

WOOD, Hugh   1932-

    Graves, Robert   2394 2397
    Hughes, Ted   3545 3546 3553 3554
    Joyce, James   3896
    Lawrence, D.H.   4379 4385 4395
    Lee, Laurie   4441 4442 4444 4445 4448
    Logue, Christopher   4503 4504 4505 4506 4512
    Muir, Edwin   5223 5224 5225 5233 5235
    Spender, Stephen   5854
    Yeats, W.B.   7671* 7672*

WOOD, Nora F.   ?-

    Macleod, Fiona   4579

WOOD, Ralph Walter   1902-

    Joyce, James   3650
    Kipling, Rudyard   4298
    Monro, Harold   5208

WOOD, Thomas   1892-1950

    Flecker, James Elroy   2188
    Masefield, John   4872 4911
    Noyes, Alfred   5325

WOOD, William Luton   ?-

    Stevenson, Robert Louis 6418

WOODGATE, Leslie   1902-

    Galsworthy, John   2247
    Symonds, John Addington 6731

WOODGATE, Leslie, arr.   1902-

    Bax, Clifford   316
    Yeats, W.B.   7615

WOOD-HILL, Mabel   1870-1954

  Macleod, Fiona   4660 4694 4701 4761

WOODMAN, H.H.   ?-

  Kipling, Rudyard   4237*

WOODMAN, Raymond Huntington   1861-1943

  Stevenson, Robert Louis   6354

WOOLLEN, Russell   1923-

  Hopkins, Gerard Manley   3013 3028 3048 3064 3101 3125
  Thompson, Francis   7008

WOOLLEY, C.   ?-

  Housman, A.E.   3306 3458

WORDER, Magdalen S.   ?-

  Yeats, W.B.   7434

WORDSWORTH, William B.   1908-

  Bridges, Robert   612
  Brooke, Rupert   789
  Chesterton, G.K.   993
  de la Mare, Walter   1483 1492 1620 1737 1756
  Gibson, W.W.   2305 2327
  Hopkins, Gerard Manley   3105
  Lawrence, D.H.   4389
  Phillips, Stephen   5463
  Snow, P.C.   5808
  Thompson, Francis   7009

WORTH, Amy   1888-1967

  Le Gallienne, Richard   4450
  Milne, A.A.   5177

WRIGHTSON, Herbert J.   ?-

  Newbolt, Henry   5254

WYBLE, Melvin   ?-

   Wilde, Oscar   7220

WYMAN, Frances   ?-

   Le Gallienne, Richard   4471

WYNER, Yehudi   1929-

   Colum, Padraic   1114

WYRILL, Marion   ?-

   Stephens, James   5912

YANNAY, Yehuda   1937-

   Auden, W.H.   147

YOUNG, Dalhousie   1866-1921

   Housman, A.E.   3160

YOUNG, Douglas   1947-

Auden, W.H.	159					
Davidson, John	1216					
de la Mare, Walter	1565	1726				
Eliot, T.S.	2064	2123	2135	2159	2169	
Hughes, Ted	3555					
Lawrence, D.H.	4390					
Smith, Stevie	5787	5789	5790	5791	5795	5796
	5797					
Yeats, W.B.	7439	7443	7456	7533	7658	7670

YOUNG, Francis Brett   1884-1954

   Stevenson, Robert Louis   6461

YOUNG, Gordon   ?-

   Wilde, Oscar   7260

YOUNG, Monroe   ?-

   Bridges, Robert   771
   Le Gallienne, Richard   4486

YOUNG, Percy Marshall   1912-

    de la Mare, Walter   1652 1677 1757

YOUNG, Percy Marshall, arr.   1912-

    Blunden, Edmund   583

YOUNG, Victor   1900-1956

    Du Maurier, Daphne   2024

ZAGWIJN, Henri   1878-1954

    Wilde, Oscar   7156

ZANDERS, Douglas W.A.   ?-

    de la Mare, Walter   1727
    Yeats, W.B.   7564

ZANDONAI, Riccardo   1883-1944

    Symons, Arthur   6828

ZANINELLI, Luigi   1932-

    Stevenson, Robert Louis   6043 6108 6138 6211 6240 6325
                                  6363 6419 6495

ZEMLINSKY, Alexander   1872-1942

    Wilde, Oscar   7166 7183

ZÍTEK, Otakar   1892-1955

    Wilde, Oscar   7167

ZUPKO, Ramon   1932-

    Hardy, Thomas   2580 2727
    Hopkins, Gerard Manley   3065

FOOTNOTES

FOOTNOTES

74 Goode's setting may have been publ. originally under a
   title different from that listed.

81 The composer has set the following sections of the
   poem: Saint Thomas Aquinas, Johann Sebastian Bach,
   Lord Byron, Joseph Haydn, Christina Rossetti, Ludwig
   van Beethoven, and Charles Dickens.

87 Duncan's incidental music to the play is comprised of
   songs entitled: "Epigraph" ("Ghosts whom Honour never
   paid"), "I've got a Date with Love", "Dover would
   like Us, Margate would welcome us", "Michael, you
   shall be renowned", "Go, Ga, morum tonga tara",
   "Make us Kind", "Some love tennis-elbow", "Dance,
   John, Dance", "Him who comes to set us free", "Stop
   all the clocks", and "Free Now From Indignation".

93 The (et al.) arrangers are the following students of
   Wykeham School (Washington, Connecticut): Kate Blair,
   Melissa Ehrlich, Carleen Embovitz, Mary Harris, Susan
   Howe, Mary Jo Matel, Susan Riley, Susan Shelion,
   Janet Sprangler, and Brooke Thomson.

Entertainment
   The Redcliffe Concerts of British Music commissioned
   this antimasque as an interpolation for James
   Shirley's masque entitled Cupid_and_Death (1953).

129 This carol was originally set for a BBC programme in
    1944 entitled "Poet's Christmas".

130 The composer has indicated that this work is a complete
    setting of "all the settable material" of the
    oratorio.

Lauds
   "Lauds" (as it appeared in The_Shield_of_Achilles) is
   actually a revised version of the final part of
   "Delia" (or "A Masque of Night")--a one act opera by
   Auden and Chester Kallmann--which was 1st publ. in
   Botteghe_Oscure (Autumn 1953).

164 According to Musical_Quarterly (Jan. 1958), p. 97,
    this work was originally conceived as an oratorio
    inspired by Auden's poem. The publisher (Milan:
    SZ) states that the final composition (for orch.
    only) makes no reference to Auden.

190 It was after Auden had seen Britten's score for this
    poem--which Britten had entitled "Seascape" rather
    than "Seaside", Auden's title--that Auden himself
    publ. subsequent edns. of the poem under the title
    "Seascape".

216 Although this cycle contains two settings of the same
    text, each score is completely different. The cycle
    is comprised of "double" settings of each poem
    employed. Notes (Sept. 1966), p. 1321, states that
    it was Rorem's intention to set each poem twice in
    as contrasting a manner as possible.

288 Bibliographies of the works of J.M. Barrie have cited
    "Rosy Rapture" as a "revue". The term "burlesque" is
    employed in Brian A.L. Rust's London Musical Shows on
    Records, 1894-1954 (L: British Institute of Recorded
    Sound, 1958).

Bax
    The eds. were not able to consult Lovat Dickson's 1933
    Bedford edn. of Bax's works. It is possible that
    many of the works cited in the "Miscellanea" section
    were publ. in this volume.

Hymn
    This poem was written 1916 "to a Melody in the Genevan
    Psalter, 1551". It has been subsequently incl. in
    various hymnals as a text to the melody upon which
    it was founded.

Beckett
    Certain Beckett works were 1st publ. in Engl. and were
    then transl. by the author and publ. in Fr. Certain
    others were 1st publ. in Fr. and were subsequently
    transl. into and publ. in Engl. When a composer has
    used the Fr. rather than the Engl. publ. of a work,
    the reader will find the bibliographic details and
    the entry under the Fr. title. When a composer has
    used the Engl. rather than the Fr. publ. of a work,
    the reader will find the bibliographic details and
    the entry under the Engl. title.

318 The contract for performing rights to the play
    specifies that "Acte sans Paroles" cannot be perf.
    without Beckett's music.

320 Since Cascando was written as "a radio play for music
and voice", Mihalovici's score cannot properly be
described as "incidental music". The contract for
performing rights to the play specifies that Cascando
cannot be perf. without Mihalovici's music.

351 The form of this composition is specifically that given
by the composer.

361 The author's radio play was "written to a musical score
by John Beckett". Since the music is an integral part
of the play, Beckett's score cannot rightly be called
"incidental music".

369 Copyright arrangements prohibit the perf. of Behan's
play without the use of The Dubliners' music.

539 See note #546.

542 The composer has made use of the tune "St. Pancras"
for this setting.

546 Although this setting was composed as a "twin piece"
to the composer's setting of "Calvinistic Evensong",
the composer does not regard them as constituting a
collection.

566 "Carillon" was originally publ. L: Elkin 1914 as a set-
ting (for reciter and orch.) of a poem by Emile
Cammaerts; it was subsequently rev. as a setting of
Binyon's work.

578 Blunden's poem was written for the Festival Concert of
22 November 1947, at the Royal Albert Hall. The text
as publ. in A Hong Kong House (1962) is the original
version (as written by the poet). Several changes
were made when it was used as Finzi's text (in order
to meet the needs of the setting and the singers).

Bridges
    Bridges' contribution to music is important--consider
    his essays on musical subjects--and mention must be
    made of his editorship (with H. Ellis Wooldridge) of
    The Yattendon Hymnal, Pts. I-IV (L: H. Milford, OUP,
    1895-1899). Since all his words in Yattendon are
    translations (not given in the Complete Works of RB)
    from various sources (German, Latin, Greek, etc.) or
    were written by Bridges specifically for the hymn

1084

tunes in the volume, and since all the music for the
words was composed by persons who lived during years
not covered by this Catalogue (e.g., by Johann
Crüger, harmonisations of trad. hymn tunes by J.S.
Bach and Claude Goudimel), the eds. have not incl.
the Yattendon works in the main Bridges section of
the Catalogue. Many hymnals have reprinted works from
Yattendon (e.g., The Harvard University Hymn Book
(1964)), and many composers within the period covered
by this Catalogue have made use of Bridges'
translations, creating completely new settings for
the words (e.g., Robert Milano, Philip Miles, H.C.L.
Stock, W.G. Whittaker, A.D. Miller, Healey Willan,
Martin Shaw, John Ireland, Herbert Howells, and Ralph
Vaughan Williams).

611 This song was conceived as one of Opus 4 (1896-98).
This Opus is entitled Four Songs. Its constituent
parts have never been publ. together; certain songs
have been publ. sep. One song has never been publ.
"Awake..." was 1st publ. (as shown) by Schmidt--and
was also publ. sep. by L: S in 1914 and by L: E in
1927.

617 Some sources indicate that the composition is a cyc.
for children's v.; others state that it is a
children's cantata.

622 The composer prefers the term "ensemble" for v. and
pf.; she states that an accompanist of "concert
quality" is required.

676 This is one of Six Songs (Opus 15, 1902-03). Although
this particular song is unpubl., other songs in the
Opus have been publ. by various companies.

788 The MSS of Gurney's Five Songs are missing.

803 See note #788.

816 See note #788.

822 See note #622.

827 See note #788.

829 See note #788.

891 This setting is also avail. in many various arrange-
    ments.

901 The publisher was unable to provide the eds. with
    turther information.

O God
    This poem has been used in various hymnals, including
    The_English_Hymnal (1906), Songs_of_Praise (1925),
    The_Westminster_Hymnal (New and rev. edn., 1940),
    Congregational_Praise (1951), and The_Hymn_Book_of
    the_Anglican_Church_of_Canada_and_the_United_Church
    of_Canada (1971, rev. 1972).

1019 See note #622.

1020 See note #622.

1117 The publisher was unable to provide the eds. with
     turther information.

1150 See note #622.

1152 See note #622.

1153 See note #622.

1154 See note #622.

1155 See note #622.

1156 See note #622.

1157 See note #622.

1158 See note #622.

1159 See note #622.

1161 See note #622.

1162 See note #622.

1163 See note #622.

1164 See note #622.

Coward
    A large body of Coward's work consists of musical
    plays, revues, and operettas. He was responsible for
    the conception of words, music, and, in many cases,
    direction of their early performances. Certain of
    these works (e.g., Conversation Piece, This Year of
    Grace! and Bitter-Sweet) were subsequently publ.
    (some separate from, others together with their
    scores). Certain lyrics from these works were publ.
    together with separate songs written by the author in
    such vols. as The Noël Coward Song Book. Readers
    wishing details concerning the above-mentioned works
    are referred to Raymond Mander & Joe Mitchenson's
    extensive bibliography entitled Theatrical Companion
    to Coward (NY: Macmillan, 1957). The entries in the
    Coward section of this Catalogue can be regarded as
    "musical settings" in the strict sense of that term.

1272 This is an entirely different setting of the poem from
     that documented in the setting immediately preceding.

Ways
    The 1907 publ. of the poem consists of two additional
    opening stanzas that begin: "As far as my own heart's
    concerned". These are omitted in later publications
    of the poem.

1317 The form of this work is quoted from the 1961 issue of
     the British Catalogue of Music.

1327 The work was copyrighted 1973 and publ. 1974.

1333 The composer has indicated to the eds. that the cim-
     balon may be replaced by "some suitable 'exotic'
     instrument", and that, if necessary, the entire perc.
     pt. can be incl. "within" the pf. part.

Blindman's
    This work earlier appeared in Saturday Review of
    Literature (Nov. 1929) with a 1st line of "Twinklum,
    twirlum, twistum, twy". It was completely rev. for
    inclusion under the title "Blindman's In" in Bells
    and Grass: A Book of Rhymes.

1384 Although various OUP catalogues have indicated that
     this collection of songs requires ms, t and bar soli,
     the composer has told the eds. that it requires s or
     t solo.

1404 See note #622.

1440 See note #1384.

1495 Grove's cites this work (in terms of its form) as a
     children's cantata.

1499 See note #1384.

1505 A published piece from Three Epitaphs, MS 1940--other
     two unpublished.

1522 See note #1384.

1553 See note #622.

Last
     This poem originally appeared untitled in On the Edge
     with a 1st line which reads: "Last evening, as I sat
     alone".

1611 A song for ssa, pf. (entitled "Music") was originally
     composed in 1947 employing de la Mare's text. Permis-
     sions could not be secured (for its 1948 publication
     by Carl Fischer, New York). The music was, instead,
     used as a setting of a text by the composer's wife,
     Vail Read--the score remained entitled "Music" and
     was copyrighted NY: CF, 1948.

1619 See note #1384.

1645 See note #622.

1764 See note #622.

1783 The publisher has no record of having published this--
     however a copy is held by NYPL giving publication
     details as cited.

1794 See note #622.

1811 See note #1384.

1812 This song was publ. tog. with a setting of "Why?".

1813 See note #1384.

1814 This song was publ. tog. with a setting of "White".

1815 See note #1384.

1850 See note #1495.

1890 The title of Galloway's collection is often cited as
     Seven Memory Songs.

1893 See note #1890.

1895 This setting was Parry's contribution to the Album of
     Choral Songs collected in 1899 in honour of Queen
     Victoria.

1901 See note #622.

1925 It is noted in Musical Times (Mar. 1966), p. 274, that
     "'Cynara' was completed only with [Eric] Fenby's
     assistance in 1929".

1981 The composer's name has been transliterated by the eds.
     from the Russian. The score of this work held by NYPL
     reads "Berlin: Russian publishing House 'Culture';
     the present address of this firm is unknown to the
     editors.

2010 Copyright arrangements prohibit the perf. of this play
     without the use of Austin's music.

2035 Some sources indicate that this work is on hire only,
     and that, in addition to the vocal specifications
     shown, it requires 3 speakers.

2062 The score reads "Cape Anne", not "Cape Ann".

2068 The thematic substance of this anthem was the basis for
     the composer's "String Quartet No. 1". A note on the
     title page of the score (publ. L: LD, 1970) connects
     the two works.

2071 Although published in 1963, this work was on hire from
     OUP during the years 1958-63.

2073 Certain sources have indicated that this work was
     publ. as follows: NY: Leslie Productions, Inc.,
     1957. However, the score was certainly publ. as
     indicated (i.e., NY: GMP, 1957).

2088 This cta. is often cited under the title "Canticle IV".

2106 The score of this oratorio bears the following
     quotation from Eliot's play: "...the darkness
     declares the glory of light".

2128 The score reads "4 Preludes", not "Four Preludes".

2201 Several sources have listed ea. of the _Three_Songs_ sep.
     It is possible they were not publ. as a collection.

2203 See note #2201.

Tenebris
     This poem originally appeared in _The_Bridge_of_Fire_
     (1907) with a 1st line which read: "Once a poor song-
     bird that had lost her way"; the poem was rev. for
     inclusion in _Forty-Two_Poems_ (1911).

2210 See note #2201.

2264 The text of this work was written specifically for the
     composer; it was later incl. in _Collected_Poems_
     (1965).

Gilbert
     The coll. between Gilbert and Sir Arthur Sullivan has
     been fully documented in many bibliographies. Since
     Sullivan's scores cannot be termed "musical settings"
     in the strict sense, details have been omitted from
     this Catalogue. Information concerning Gilbert's
     work with Sullivan, and with Alfred Cellier and Os-
     mond Carr can be found in such vols. as _Plays_and_
     _Poems_of_W.S._Gilbert_ (NY: Random House, 1935); _The_
     _Complete_Plays_of_Gilbert_and_Sullivan_ (NY: Garden
     City Publishing Co., Inc., 1938); Townley Searle's
     _A_Bibliography_of_Sir_William_Schwenck_Gilbert_ (NY:
     B. Franklin, 1968); Herbert Sullivan and Newman
     Flower's _Sir_Arthur_Sullivan:_His_Life,_Letters_and_
     Diaries (L: Cassell, 1927). The reader is also refer-
     red to William Herbert Scott's _Sir_Edward_German:_An_
     _Intimate_Biography_ (L: Chappell, 1932) in which is
     cited the opera entitled "Fallen Fairies" (libr. by
     Gilbert); this work was prod. at the Savoy Theatre,
     Dec. 1909.

2346 This song was originally publ. in a vol. entitled _The_
     _Fellowship_Songbook_.

Graves
A.P. Graves states in the prefatory notes to his Irish
Songs and Ballads (1880) that "most of the Songs and
Ballads in this volume, if not actually composed to
the music of old Irish airs, owe to them their prime
impulse and complete character". The prefatory notes
to various other volumes of Graves' poetry document
his keen interest in the Gaelic language and its
music. Although his poems are not translations from
the Irish (and only occasionally are they adaptations
of Irish legends), a large body of Graves' writing
has been strongly influenced by specific melodies and
rhythms employed in traditional Irish folk songs.
Various composers worked in collaboration with Graves
to arrange and publish the tunes upon which these
poems were based. The eds. have not included these in
the main Graves section of the Catalogue since, in
the strict sense of the term "musical setting" (viz.,
the literary work is anterior to the musical composition), they are not "musical settings". Readers are
referred, however, to the following vols.: Esposito,
Michele, arr. Roseen Dhu, L: B&H, 1901; Esposito,
Michele, arr. "The Postbag" [operetta], prod. 1902,
publ. L: BH; Stanford, C.V., arr. Irish Songs and
Ballads, L: N, 1893; Stanford, C.V., arr. Songs of
Erin, L: BH, 1892; Stanford, C.V., arr. Songs of Old
Ireland, L: BH, 1882; and Wood, Charles, arr. Irish
Folk Songs, L: BH.

2366 See note #622.

2377 See note #622.

2378 This is an unpubl. item in the Contemporary Poetry
Set to Music series put out by L: Turret.

2399 Graves gave Gurney permission to publ. this setting
only if the text was attributed to Graves' pseud.
"John Doyle".

In the Wilderness
The 1st line of this poem was subsequently rev. to
read: "He, of his gentleness".

2411 See note #622.

2420 "Nine of the Clock" is a different score from the setting entitled "Goodnight to the Meadow" (preceding).

Graves gave Gurney permission to publ. this setting
only if the text was attributed to Graves' pseud.
"John Doyle". Note, however, that the preceding
entry--"Goodnight to the Meadow"--attributes the text
to Graves and not to Doyle.

2426 See note #622.

2427 See note #622.

2450 See note #7406.

2481 These three songs form part of Six Songs (Opus 15,
1902-1903). Certain songs in this Opus are unpubl.;
certain others have been publ. by various companies.

2535 Portions of this music drama were 1st publ. as Three
Hardy Songs (L: JW, 1924).

2569 This setting was composed 1923-24 as part of Boughton's
music drama entitled The Queen of Cornwall. It was
slightly changed in order to be performable sep. and
was then incl. in Three Hardy Songs publ. L: JW,
1924. Finally, it was publ. as originally intended
(i.e., as part of The Queen of Cornwall) when that
music drama appeared L: JW, 1926.

2573 See note #2481.

2603 Vaughan Williams' "Prelude on an Old Carol Tune" (L:
OUP, 1953) was based on this incidental music for
The Mayor of Casterbridge.

2628 This cta. is often cited as Hodie (This Day). Some
sources indicate that the work (particularly Part
VII which employs "The Oxen") requires bar solo. Some
sources also indicate that it requires boys' chorus
as well as satb.

2654 See note #2481.

2681 This setting was incl. under the title "The Hangman's
Song" in the programme of The Three Wayfarers prod.
London, Nov. 1911.

2730 See note #2569.

2792 This one song was not incl. in Butterworth's 1914
orchn. of the cycle.

2805 Although Grove's indicates that this song is set for
"Chorus and orch.", no such arr. exists either in
publ. form or in MS.

2807 Unlike the MSS of the other songs of Opus 16, the MS
of this work is not avail. State Library of Victoria,
Melbourne.

2830 The eds. feel, given their reading of Rupert Hughes,
American Composers (B: The Page Co., 1914), p. 431,
that Mrs. Beach's song entitled "The Blackbird" is
probably another of her Henley settings.

2835 The other songs of Opus 11 are still in MS.

Herbert
    The eds. have incl. in the Herbert section of the
    Catalogue details regarding those of the author's
    libretti which were publ. sep. by Herbert (e.g.,
    Derby Day, L: Methuen, 1931). Details concerning
    Herbert's coll. with such composers as Vivian Ellis
    and C. Armstrong Gibbs will be found in Brian A. L.
    Rust's London Musical Shows on Records, 1894-1954
    (L: British Institute of Recorded Sound, 1958), and
    in Herbert's autobiography entitled A.P.H.: Is Life
    and Times (L: Heinemann, 1970). Certain items incl.
    in the "Miscellanea" section will not be found in
    either of the vols. cited above.

3017 The May 1975 issue of Musical Times cites the recent
publication (L: C) of Maconchy's Three Settings of
Poems by G. Manley Hopkins for s or t solo, orch.

3044 See note #3017.

3098 See note #3017.

3159 The publisher has indicated that this score is out of
print and that no records exist providing the
composer's full name or dates; however, the publisher
has reason to believe that Ward-Casey's given name
was "Samuel".

3175 This diptych for orch. was inspired by phrases from
Housman's poem. The music itself has absolutely no

connection with the work noted in the entry
immediately following.

3181 See note #622.

3228 The composer has stipulated the number of the various
instruments required.

3240 Often cited as Cycle of Songs from "A Shropshire Lad".
The cover of the score reads "Six Songs..."; the
title page of the score reads "Cycle of Songs...".

3245 When the publishing house was contacted in order to
verify this entry, it indicated that there was no
trace of the work. However, such a composition is
cited in Sergius Kagen's Music for the Voice
(Bloomington: Indiana University Press, 1968).

3250 See note #3240.

3266 See note #3240.

3268 This American composer sent Housman photocopies of
MS settings for these five songs; they were received
by Housman ca. Dec. 1933. See Henry Maas, ed., The
Letters of A.E. Housman (L: Rupert Hart-Davis, 1971),
p. 350.

3270 The music for this setting was rewritten from a MS
ca. 1906.

3271 J. Merrill Knapp in Selected List of Music for Men's
Voices (Princeton: Princeton University Press,
1952) indicates that the song was arr. by H.J.
Timothy. It is probable that the original composition
was written for other than ttbb, a cap.

3274 Butterworth's prelude for orch. is based on his cyc.
entitled Six Songs from "A Shropshire Lad", L: A,
1911.

3275 See note #3240.

3283 See note #3268.

3295 Angelo Eagon in Catalog of Published Concert Music by
American Composers, 2nd edn. (Metuchen, N.J.:
Scarecrow Press, 1969), states that this work was

publ. by E.C. Schirmer (Boston). Schirmer states,
however, that the firm did not publish the piece.

3308 Various sources list different dates of publication--
from 1917 to 1919.

3322 See note #3268.

3325 See note #3271.

3326 See note #622.

3350 See note #3268.

3388 See note #3240.

3404 See note #622.

3405 See note #3268.

3417 No details could be obtained from the publisher.
Musical Times (Jan. 1952), p. 42, provides the title
"The Fair", yet references have been found to a
Burrows composition entitled "When first my way to
fair I took".

3430 It is possible that such a setting may have been
wrongly attributed to Arthur Bliss. There is no
reference to this work in the "Catalogue of Works"
compiled by Kenneth L. Thompson for inclusion in the
the Aug. 1966 (and supplemented in the Aug.1971)
issue of Musical Times.

3432 See note #3240.

3453 See note #3271.

3482 See note #622.

3507 No details could be obtained from the publisher.
Musical Times (Jan. 1952), p. 42, provides the title
"Yonder See", yet references have been found to a
Burrows composition entitled "Yonder See the Morning
Blink".

3511 See note #622.

3528 The 1902 publication of "Christmas Songs" incl. a note
     by the author to the effect that the work was written
     specifically for Moorat's use.

3574 See note #87.

3588 See note #216.

3637 This setting is different from the one immediately
     preceding.

3654 This work is cited according to details provided by the
     composer; it is listed, however, in the 1st interim
     issue of the 1975 British Catalogue of Music as a
     cta. for s solo, ch. orch., horn.

Finnegan's
     The eds. have used the Viking Press edn. pagination
     which is identical with that in all early edns.

3755 See note #3654.

3779 The score reads "O it was out by Donneycarney".

Portrait
     The Egoist Ltd. edn. (1916) pagination has been used.

3807 The publisher could not locate a copy of the score in
     order to verify whether or not an accompaniment is
     required.

3838 This setting is different from the one immediately
     preceding.

Ulysses
     The Random House edn. pagination has been used.

3888 The publ. score of this work does not incl. a passage
     from Ulysses; this was added for this particular
     RCA Victor recording only.

3891 The June 1947 issue of Musical Times indicates that
     these "commentaries" are set for s solo, piano.

Kipling
     The Kipling entries have been compiled with the help
     of the list of settings in James McGregor Stewart's
     Rudyard Kipling: A Bibliographical Catalogue (Tor.:

Dalhousie University Press & University of Toronto
Press, 1959). Stewart's list was compiled largely
from information in Kipling Journal (Dec. 1932-June
1933) and from corrections which appeared in Kipling
Journal (Sept. 1933). These items in the journals
have been compared with Stewart's list; there are
many discrepancies. In certain cases other sources
have provided what the eds. believe to be the correct
details; in other cases the eds. have had to decide
which piece of information is most likely to be
accurate--since most items are dated early in this
century, the process has not always been easy. The
reader will find that portions of Kipling's larger
works (e.g., individual poems which are part of The
Jungle Book or of Just So Stories) are given sep. and
do not appear under the collective heading of The
Jungle Book, etc., for most (although not all) poems
which appeared in the stories, etc., were gathered
together in Kipling's collected verses, and most are
known by readers as individual poems. An exception
to this practice occurs when a setting has been made
of an entire Kipling work or when a setting has been
inspired by one, e.g., Cyril Scott's Impressions of
"The Jungle Book". Various bibliographies of
Kipling's works differ with respect to punctuation,
etc. As far as possible, this Catalogue employs
the wording and punctuation of a work as 1st
publ. Some Kipling scholars believe that when he
wrote, for instance, "Night Song in the Jungle"
following the poem, he meant it as a title. The eds.
have adopted the practice of those who do not agree
and who, rather, index the poem by its 1st line.

3962 James McGregor Stewart in Rudyard Kipling: A
Bibliographical Catalogue (Tor.: Dalhousie University
Press & University of Toronto Press, 1959) indicates
that this setting was publ. in 1911. Bibliographies
of Elgar state that it was both composed and publ. in
1918.

3964 James McGregor Stewart in Rudyard Kipling: A
Bibliographical Catalogue (Tor.: Dalhousie University
Press & University of Toronto Press, 1959) has
indicated that the composer is "L. Dampier";
throughout Stewart's work and throughout the lists
provided in Kipling Journal a composer is cited as
J.S.L.D. Bennett, Rev. J.S.L.D. Bennett, and J.S.L.
Dampier Bennett. No one has yet been able to provide

details about him, about his name, and an indication as to whether or not "L. Dampier" was a name under which he composed.

Children's
   This poem has been a popular text for inclusion in various hymnals, e.g., Church & School Hymnal, Psalmodica Evangelica. Names of composers are unknown--in such cases, these have been omitted as settings.

3999 The publisher has no record of this work.

4034 The text of this setting is attributed to "a text quoted by Arthur Twining Hadley".

4047 This song was later used as the focal point for a film (dated 1918--released by Famous Players--Lasky Corp.). See also note #1890.

4052 As cited in the Kipling Journal, the composer's name is "R.S. Flagler", and the work was publ. in Milwaukee.

4069 Some sources indicate that this setting is entitled "The Song Tommai's Mother Sang to the Baby".

4079 Rozsa's incidental music to the 1942 film entitled The Jungle Book was issued in 1957 on RCA recording #LM 2118.

4103 It is possible--references are vague--that this song is one and the same as the following: "In the Story 'Beyond the Pale'", Selected Songs, B: Schmidt, pre-1940.

4104 See note #1890.

4106 One reference has "Thomasa Hunt".

4115 R.T. Hopkins in Rudyard Kipling: A Literary Appreciation (NY: F.A. Stokes Co., 1916) cites the composer as "Berwicke Beverly".

4124 As cited in the Kipling Journal, the composer's name is "H. Trevannion".

4131 See note #3964.

4147 As cited in the Kipling Journal, the composition was originally copyrighted by H. Stevens, 1900, and was subsequently publ. Ph.: TP, 1903.

4156 As cited in the Kipling Journal, the composition was publ. NY: Witmark, 1909.

4157 See note #3964.

4168 Some sources indicate that this setting is entitled "Sea Lullaby".

4179 This setting has not been cited in various Ives bibliographies which have been publ. It is, however, included--without any other details than those provided in this Catalogue--in the following: Newman, P.E. The Songs of Charles Ives (1874-1954), 2 vols. Ann Arbor: University Microfilms, 1967.

4186 "MS 1899?" includes the composer's own question mark.

4192 The composer's full name could not be established. The source is James McGregor Stewart, Rudyard Kipling: A Bibliographical Catalogue (Tor.: Dalhousie University Press and Toronto University Press, 1959).

Recessional
     This poem has been a popular text for inclusion in various hymnals. Names of composers are unknown--in such cases, these have been omitted as settings.

4200 No other information is avail. The reader is referred to R.T. Hopkins, Rudyard Kipling: A Literary Appreciation (NY: F.A. Stokes Co., 1916), p. 330.

4218 Musical Times of Oct. 1910 (p. 667) notes a setting entitled "Recessional" by G.E. Hopkins publ. L: N. It is uncertain whether this setting and the one noted in the entry are one and the same.

4237 Although the composer as cited in James McGregor Stewart's Rudyard Kipling: A Bibliographical Catalogue (Tor.: Dalhousie University Press & University of Toronto Press, 1959) is "H.H. Woodman", it is quite possible that the composer is, in fact, Raymond H. Woodman.

4239 Stewart R. Manville, archivist of the Percy Grainger

Library Society, has indicated that there exists a
sketch of an accompaniment to this setting, but one
which would be impossible to play on the keyboard;
he feels that Grainger obviously intended the setting
to have orch. accompaniment.

4242 See note #3964.

4244 The following source indicates that this setting was
publ. in 1930 but provides no further details: Claire
Reis, comp., American Composers (NY: The International Society for Contemporary Music, 1932), p.
46.

4283 R.T. Hopkins in Rudyard Kipling: A Literary
Appreciation (NY: F.A. Stokes Co., 1916) indicates
that the title of this setting is "The Widow of
Windsor".

4286 This song was composed in 1902. Since Ives did not
receive permission to use the text, it was publ. with
the 1st four words only. As publ. in Thirteen Songs
(the eds. have had access to the vol. publ. NY: Peer,
1958) the foot of the score reads: "Singers can refer
to the rest of the poem". The song was rev. in 1902
and employed as music to a song entitled "Slugging a
Vampire" (words by the composer). This rev. version
was publ. NY: NME, 1935.

4292 This setting for orch. is not musically related to the
setting noted in the entry immediately preceding.

4295 When Gordon Jacob arr. this song he added ten
introductory bars.

4299 The vocal specifications are those indicated by the
composer.

4301 This setting is cited by James McGregor Stewart in
Rudyard Kipling: A Bibliographical Catalogue (Tor.:
Dalhousie University Press & University of Toronto
Press, 1959), but he provides no further details.

To Wolcott
   This poem was originally publ. in National Observer
   (Dec. 1890) under the title "The Blind Bug"; it was,
   however, vastly rev. for incl. in Barrack-Room
   Ballads And Other Verses (1892).

Wind
The 1st line of this poem was later rev. to read: "The wind took off with the sunset."

4332 There are also references to this song as a setting for high v., piano.

4370 The composer has stated that this is a very early MS and permission will not be granted for its perf. during his lifetime.

4375 See note #4370.

4384 See note #4370.

4392 See note #4370.

4420 See note #4370.

4421 See note #4370.

4473 The original setting of "Little Sleeper" was composed in 1905. Brian was unable to gain permission for its publication. The score was publ. in 1913 as a setting of words by Gerald Cumberland. The composer restored the original (Le Gallienne) version in 1972, repudiating the 1913 publication.

4515 The composer's text begins: "How odd the World inside my Head my comb is bigger than my head".

4601 Although this composition was composed in 1915, Griffes did not refer to it by the title "De Profundis" until 1916.

Murias
This work was previously publ. under the title "Requiem".

4689 Some sources cite the title of this song as "Bonnie Birdeen".

4785 See note #6035.

4812 The work is designated by the composer as "chamber music" for clarinet and piano.

4815 This is one of the <u>Three Songs</u> mentioned in <u>Grove's</u>;
the composer says that the other two are in MS.

4869 See note #622.

4925 Reference to this setting is also made in the 1949
vocal catalogue put out by Remick Music Corp. of New
York.

Seal
"The Seal Man" was rev. and reprinted in the 1913 edn.
of <u>A Mainsail Haul</u> (unavail. for verification of
the 1st line of the poem).

5010 The music of a ballad incl. in the opera was later
employed by the composer for a song entitled "Jemima"
(one of <u>Two Tunes for Mixed Chorus</u>, L: OUP, 1963).

5256 The original setting for ttbb, a cap. was re-issued
Wendover: RP, 1975.

5281 The poem, with music by Lloyd, was incl. as part of
the <u>Cycle of Song</u> presented to Queen Victoria in
celebration of her second Jubilee. See Newbolt's
<u>Collected Poems 1897-1907</u> (1910), p. 1719.

5367 The present address of the Girls' Friendly Society is
unknown to the eds. At the time Davies' score was
publ., the Society's headquarters was located at
Townsend House, Greycoat Place, London, SW1.

5380 Certain of the songs are Hughes' arrangements of old
tunes, while others are original compositions.

Parable
All printings of this poem prior to the 1963 edn. of
<u>The Collected Poems of Wilfred Owen</u> gave the title
as "The Parable of the Old Men and the Young". The
MS held by the British Museum reads "The Parable of
the Old Man and the Young".

5511 The form of this composition is specifically that given
by the composer.

5522 The form of this composition is specifically that given
by the composer.

5696 An alternate title for this setting is "Swiss Jodelling Song".

5697 This cyc. originally consisted of seven songs; one was withdrawn by the composer before publication.

5703 This setting of "Daphne" is different from the one immediately preceding. See also note #5710.

5708 The score bears the footnote: "In collaboration with C.L.". Constant Lambert, in fact, composed the 1st eleven bars.

5710 Walton's Bucolic Comedies (MS 1924) originally consisted of five songs, three of which had orchestral accompaniment for six instruments. These three were publ. (L: OUP, 1932) as Three Songs. The titles of the other two songs are unknown.

5713 See note #5697.

5715 An alternate title for this setting is "Tango".

5721 Publ. sep. B: OD, [1930?].

5731 See note #5697.

5737 See note #5697.

Rose
        This poem has not been subsequently reprinted.

5755 See note #5697.

5757 See note #5697.

Tarantella
        This poem was 1st publ. in the programme notes of the Façade perf. given June 1926 and publ. in 1951 in Walton's Façade; this poem has never appeared in Edith Sitwell's collected editions.

5761 See note #5710.

5835 A 2nd poem by Soutar entitled "Samson" (beginning: "The hands that riv'd the lion's maw") is incl. in Collected Poems (1948). Although they have not had Scott's MS at their disposal, the eds. believe the composer's setting employs the text from In the Time of Tyrants (1939), for the McPherson Library of the University of Victoria holds Soutar's autographed copy of this vol., inscribed: "F.G. and Mrs. Scott, with every good wish. Christmas 1939".

To the Future
    The 1st line of this poem (as it appears in the posth. publ. vol. entitled The Expectant Silence, and in the collected edns. of Soutar's work) reads: "He, the unborn, shall bring".

5859 The poem as it appears in Spender's Collected Poems 1928-1953 (1955) bears the inscription "To Samuel Barber".

5883 The songs of Opus 2 were 1st publ. in different years.

Buds
    The 1st line of the 1915 publ. of the poem reads: "I can see".

5903 See note #5883.

5915 Contrary to the date of 1916 provided in Grove's, this song was both composed and publ. in 1918.

5917 See note #622.

Hesperus
    The 1st line of the 1915 publ. of the poem reads: "Upon the sober sky".

5931 See note #622.

Lesbia
    As publ. in 1924 this poem has an additional 1st stanza (excluded in later edns. of the poem) which begins: "If she be fair".

Midnight
    The 1st line of the 1915 publ. of the poem reads: "And then I wakened up in such a fright".

5946 See note #622.

Ora
The 1st line of the 1926 publ. of the poem (under the
title "A Bird sings now") reads: "A bird sings now".

5958 See note #622.

5995 Some sources indicate that the composer's name is
Henry C.ff. Castleman.

6035 The (et al.) arrangers are: Edward B. Birge, William
Miessner, and Osbourne McConathy.

6036 _Musical Times_ (Dec. 1952) lists this setting as a
unison song.

6038 This song was publ. tog. with Rowley's setting of
Stevenson's poem entitled "Singing".

6070 This song was publ. tog. with Rowley's setting entitled
"From a Railway Carriage".

6120 This song was publ. tog. with Rowley's setting entitled
"The Friendly Cow".

6135 See note #6035.

6145 This setting was found among the composer's MSS after
his death; it was 1st perf. and publ. in 1960. The
complete edn. of _Songs of Travel_ incl. this work as
an epilogue. A footnote to the score indicates that
this epilogue should be sung in public only when the
entire cyc. is performed.

6149 This setting--under the title "Romance"--has been
publ. by Woolhouse.

6193 Since the publisher has indicated that the score
cannot be located in the firm's records, further
details are not available.

6227 A setting of this poem is attributed to one "Edward
Falck" in Helen Grant Cushing's _Children's Song Index_
(NY: H.W. Wilson, 1936). It is possibly the same.

6233 This song was publ. tog. with Rowley's setting entitled
"Time to Rise".

6298 The (et al.) arrangers are: Edward B. Birge, Mabel E.

Bray, and William Miessner.

6302 Although this setting with "words and music by Robert
Louis Stevenson" is avail. NYPL, the publisher was
unable to give any details. It is not unreasonable
to surmise that Stevenson wrote the melody subsequently scored, perhaps at Stevenson's request,
by H.J. Stewart.

6379 This song was publ. tog. with Rowley's setting entitled
"Bed in Summer".

6434 This song was publ. tog. with Rowley's setting entitled
"Marching Song".

6586 See note #622.

6589 One of Four Songs (MS ca. 1927) was publ. L: N, 1968;
the other three remain unpublished.

6590 See note #622.

6591 See note #622.

6593 See note #622.

6595 See note #622.

6596 See note #622.

6598 See note #622.

6636 The publishers were unable to trace this work; the song
was, however, listed in early Chappell catalogues.

6662 The only reference to this setting appears to be the
listing in Grove's.

6707 Although the composer's name is cited as "Ciro Pinsuti"
in early Chappell catalogues, perhaps the correct
citing would be "Circo Pinsuto". See p. 806 of The
Oxford Companion to Music, 10th edn. (1974).

Vista
As indicated in Granger's Index to Poetry, "A Vista"
has appeared in various anthologies under such titles
as: "These things shall be--a loftier race", "The
Coming Day", "The Human Outlook", etc.

1106

6728 Except for the words, this setting has no connection with the hymn listed immediately above.

6774 The term "lyrical melodrama" is taken verbatim from the following source: Miloš Šafránek, Bohuslav Martinů: His Life and Works (L: Allan Wingate, 1961 [English transl. copyrighted 1962]), p. 335.

6807 This song is cited under the title "A Roundel of Rest" in various other sources.

6812 See note #7360.

6832 The May 1975 issue of Gramophone notes that this work "...was originally conceived as the Sinfonia (Prelude) to a projected opera, Deirdre of the Sorrows, which [Brian] never composed because he was refused copyright permission to set J.M. Synge's text".

6841 This opera, written for the Zurich Opera Co., was to be premiered in the 1974-75 season. (See Central Opera Service Bulletin (Spring 1973).)

6849 John T. Howard in Our Contemporary Composers (NY: Crowell, 1941), p. 126, states that this is "... a Symphonic Prelude to Synge's drama, Riders to the Sea, in which Gilbert made use of an old Irish melody. This was first written for small orchestra, to be played at some performances of the drama at the Twentieth Century Club in Boston, in 1904. Later Gilbert expanded the work, and it was performed at the music festival of the Macdowell Memorial Association at Petersborough, September, 1941".

6876 A catalogue of Lutyens' publ. works distr. by The Olivan Press cites the work as follows:

Three Songs (and Incidental Music) for Group Theatre's 'Homage to Dylan Thomas', perf. Globe Theatre, Jan. 1954.

The catalogue indicates that the songs are settings for s solo. The eds. have quoted information received from SUNYAB.

6897 See note #6876.

Me
> A note accompanying the 1st publication of Me and My Bike indicates that Thomas intended the work as a "film operetta".

On a Wedding
> As originally publ., the 1st line of this poem read: "At last, in a wrong rain".

6913 See note #6876.

Poem
> This poem was originally publ. with a 1st line which read: "Foster the light, nor veiled the feeling moon".

6993 This song is one of five incl. in Opus 12. Certain songs of this Opus are unpubl.; those that are publ. have been put out as sep. songs under their own titles, e.g., "Dream-Tryst" (L: N, 1902).

7016 This song is one of five incl. in Opus 9a. Certain songs of this Opus are unpubl.; certain others are publ. as sep. songs by various companies, e.g., "To Sylvia".

7154 Some sources cite Bennett's opera as "A Penny for a Song" rather than as "Napoleon is Coming".

7179 Stuart Mason in Bibliography of Oscar Wilde, new edn., introduced by T. d'Arch Smith (L: Bertram Rota, 1967), p. 304, states that "'Endymion' has been recited by Miss Ella Erskine to a musical setting by Cyril Scott". The eds. have no further details.

Madonna
> This poem was 1st publ. in Kottabos (Michaelmas Term 1877) under the title "Wasted Days" with a 1st line of "Fair slim boy not made for this world's pain". It was then revised and appeared in Poems (1881) under the title "Madonna Mia" with a 1st line of "A lily-girl not made for this world's pain". Wilde finally changed it back to its original form; it appeared as such in The Poems of Oscar Wilde (1908). Collected edns. now usually provide both versions.

7234 This setting is completely different from the one immediately preceding.

7263 Brussels' Bibliothèque du Conservatoire Royal de
     Musique was unable to provide any additional
     information.

7285 Further details concerning this work have not been
     found. Stuart Mason in Bibliography_of_Oscar_Wilde,
     new edn., introduced by T. d'Arch Smith (L: Bertram
     Rota, 1967), p. 171, states that "the only copy
     known was sold at Hodgson's 12 June 1913".

7287 Stuart Mason in Bibliography_of_Oscar_Wilde, new edn.,
     introduced by T. d'Arch Smith (L: Bertram Rota,
     1967), p. 173, states that although a lithographed
     wrapper was printed, it is unlikely that the setting
     itself ("with words and music by Oscar Wilde") ever
     saw publication. The publishers were unable to give
     Mason any details concerning the piece.

7289 Stuart Mason in Bibliography_of_Oscar_Wilde, new edn.,
     introduced by T. d'Arch Smith (L: Bertram Rota,
     1967), p. 198, states that the composer claimed
     that Wilde wrote "Under the Balcony" specifically
     as a text to his setting.

7290 This setting was announced to be sung at a London
     concert in Nov. 1908, but as a result of difficulties
     over copyright another song was substituted. See
     Stuart Mason, Bibliography_of_Oscar_Wilde, new edn.,
     introduced by T. d'Arch Smith (L: Bertram Rota,
     1967), p. 199.

Wodehouse
     Readers interested in P.G. Wodehouse's work as a
     lyricist in coll. with such writers as Guy Bolton
     (e.g., "Leave it to Jane"), Ira Gershwin (e.g.,
     "Rosalie"), George Grossmith ("The Cabaret Girl"),
     and Oscar Hammarstein II (e.g., "Show Boat") and in
     coll. with such composers as Ivan Caryll (e.g., "Kis-
     sing Time: The Girl Behind the Gun"), Max Dareswki
     (e.g., "Hearts and Diamonds"), Jerome Kern (e.g.,
     "Show Boat", "Sitting Pretty"), and Cole Porter
     (e.g., "Anything Goes") are referred to documentation
     provided, for example, in Brian A.L. Rust's compila-
     tion entitled London_Musical_Shows_on_Records,_1894-
     1954 (L: British Institute of Recorded Sound, 1958),
     and in Richard Usborne's Wodehouse_at_Work (L: Harold
     Jenkins, 1961).

7310 This setting was originally intended to form part of
Opus 48 (the songs of which were 1st publ. L: A,
1930).

Yeats
The eds. have relied on the Soho Bibliography of Yeats'
work; certain discrepancies exist between this vol.
and information cited in The Variorum Edition of the
Poems of W.B. Yeats (NY: Macmillan, 1957) (e.g., the
latter vol. cites the 1st publ. of "Sweet Dancer" as
being in the Apr. [rather than the Mar.] issue of London Mercury).

7360 The song cyc. originally consisted of: "He reproves
the curlew", "The lover mourns", "Wine comes in at
the mouth", "Cloths of heaven", and "He hears the
cry of the sedge". It was 1st perf. this way. A
revised version was perf. in 1923 which saw the
substitution of "The Withering of the Boughs" for
the 3rd and 4th items in the original. Yeats refused
permission for the work to be publ. until the
Carnegie Award was presented (see Musical Times
(Feb. 1922), p. 123). The score for "Wine comes in at
the mouth" was lost--presumed destroyed. The music
for "Cloths of Heaven" was eventually adapt. to
fit Arthur Symons' text "Sick Heart".

7361 See note #7360.

7365 The present address of "At the Sign of the Unicorn" is
unknown to the editors.

7367 Herbert Bedford's article in Music and Letters (Apr.
1924), pp. 116 ff., provides an excerpt from the
score stating that the work is for v., pf., and str.
qrt.

7383 See note #7360.

7402 Note that this setting is different from the one
immediately preceding.

7406 See Yeats' notes to the music in Plays in Prose and
Verse (L: Macmillan, 1922) for an explanation of
his term "spoken song".

1110

Cradle
   Early printings of this poem give the following 1st
   line: "The angels are bending".

7461 See note #7406.

7463 See note #7406.

7475 See note #7360.

7479 See note #7360.

7538 See note #7406.

7543 See note #7406.

7563 There is no thematic relationship between Sonata No.
   3 in B minor and Poem (or Celtic Sketch No. 1).

7567 This is very probably a setting of the faery's passage
   beginning: "The wind blows out of the gates of the
   day".

Maid
   This poem 1st appeared under the title "O'Sullivan
   the Red upon his Wanderings" in New Review (Aug.
   1897). Its 1st line read: "O where is our Mother of
   Peace". A revision under the title "Hanrahan laments
   because of his Wanderings" was publ. in 1899. A
   complete reworking of the poem followed and was
   publ. as "Maid Quiet" in 1908.

7616 See note #7406.

7625 See note #7360.

7631 Grove's gives 1927 as the date of this work; Die Musik
   gives 1921.

7634 See note #7406.

7649 The form of this work (i.e., "musical dramatic poem")
   is that given by the composer in the score.

7660 Robinson staged the 1st prod. of the play (Dublin,
   Dec. 1926) and was responsible for the musical
   direction. There are settings of five choruses from
   the play.

7671 This was composed as one of Two Choruses (Opus 16), the other of which is unpubl.

7672 This was composed as one of Two Choruses (Opus 16), the other of which is publ. (L: N, 1974).

7685 See note #7406.